ALSO BY RICHARD PIPES

The Formation of the Soviet Union: Communism and Nationalism,
   1917–23 (1964)
Struve: Liberal on the Left, 1870–1905 (1970)
Russia under the Old Regime (1974)
Struve: Liberal on the Right, 1905–1944 (1980)
Survival Is Not Enough (1984)
Russia Observed (1989)

The Russian Revolution

1. Lenin: 1919.

THE RUSSIAN
REVOLUTION

Richard Pipes

Alfred A. Knopf   New York   1990

THIS IS A BORZOI BOOK
PUBLISHED BY ALFRED A. KNOPF, INC.

Copyright © 1990 by Richard Pipes
Maps copyright © 1990 by Bernhard H. Wagner
All rights reserved under International and Pan-American
Copyright Conventions. Published in the United States by
Alfred A. Knopf, Inc., New York, and simultaneously in Canada
by Random House of Canada Limited, Toronto. Distributed by
Random House, Inc., New York.
Owing to limitations of space, acknowledgment of
permission to reprint previously published
material will be found on page 945.

Library of Congress Cataloging-in-Publication Data
Pipes, Richard.
The Russian Revolution / Richard Pipes.—1st ed.
p. cm.
Bibliography: p.
Includes index.
ISBN 0-394-50241-8
1. Soviet Union—History—Revolution, 1917–1921.
2. Soviet Union—History—Nicholas II, 1894–1917. I. Title.
DK265.P474 1990
947.084′1—dc20   89-35129
CIP

Manufactured in the United States of America

Жертвам

To the victims

CONTENTS

ILLUSTRATIONS

MAPS

ACKNOWLEDGMENTS

In the course of working on this book I have benefited from the generous support of the National Endowment for the Humanities and the Smith Richardson Foundation, to which I would like to express my warm appreciation. I am also grateful to the Hoover Institution at Stanford, California, for giving me access to its unrivaled collections.

ABBREVIATIONS

ARR	*Arkhiv russkoi revoliutsii*
BK	*Bor'ba klassov*
BM	*Berliner Monatshefte*
Brogkauz & Efron	*Entsiklopedicheskii Slovar' Ob-va Brogkauz i Efron,* 41 vols.
BSE	*Bol'shaia sovetskaia entsiklopediia,* 65 vols.
Dekrety	*Dekrety sovetskoi vlasti,* 11 vols. (Moscow, 1957–)
DN	*Delo naroda*
EV	*Ekonomicheskii vestnik*
EZh	*Ekonomicheskaia zhizn'*
Forschungen	*Forschungen zur Osteuropäischen Geschichte*
GM	*Golos minuvshego*
Granat	*Entsiklopedicheskii Slovar' Tov-va Granat,* 55 vols.
IA	*Istoricheskii arkhiv*
IM	*Istorik Marksist*
IR	*Illustrirovannaia Rossiia*
ISSSR	*Istoriia SSSR*
IV	*Istoricheskii vestnik*
IZ	*Istoricheskie zapiski*
Jahrbücher	*Jahrbücher für Geschichte Osteuropas*
KA	*Krasnyi arkhiv*
KL	*Krasnaia letopis'*
KN	*Krasnaia nov'*
Lenin, *Khronika*	V. I. Lenin: *Biograficheskaia Khronika, 1870–1924,* 13 vols. (Moscow, 1970–85)
Lenin, *PSS*	V. I. Lenin, *Polnoe sobranie sochinenii,* 5th ed. 55 vols. (Moscow, 1958–65)
Lenin, *Sochineniia*	V. I. Lenin, *Sochineniia,* 3rd ed., 30 vols. (Moscow-Leningrad, 1927–33)
LN	*Literaturnoe nasledstvo*
LS	*Leninskii sbornik*
MG	*Minuvshie gody*
NChS	*Na chuzhoi storone*
ND	*Novyi den'*

NKh	*Narodnoe khoziaistvo*
NoV	*Novoe vremia*
NS	*Nashe slovo*
NV	*Nash vek*
NVCh	*Novyi vechernyi chas*
NZ	*Die Neue Zeit*
NZh	*Novaia zhizn'*
OD	L. Martov *et al.*, eds., *Obshchestvennoe dvizhenie v Rossii v nachale XX veka,* 4 vols. (St. Petersburg, 1910–14)
Padenie	P. E. Shcheglovitov, ed., *Padenie tsarskogo rezhima,* 7 vols. (Leningrad, 1924–27)
PN	*Poslednie novosti*
PR	*Proletarskaia revoliutsiia*
PRiP	*Proletarskaia revoliutsiia i pravo*
Revoliutsiia	N. Avdeev *et al., Revoliutsiia 1917 goda: khronika sobytii,* 6 vols. (Moscow, 1923–30)
RL	*Russkaia letopis'*
RM	*Russkaia mysl'*
RR	*Russian Review*
RS	*Russkoe slovo*
RV	*Russkie vedomosti*
RZ	*Russkie zapiski*
SB	*Staryi Bol'shevik*
SD	*Sotsial-Demokrat*
SiM	*Strana i mir*
SR	*Slavic Review*
SS	*Soviet Studies*
SUiR	*Sobranie uzakonenii i rasporiazhenii*
SV	*Sotsialisticheskii vestnik*
SZ	*Sovremennye zapiski*
VCh	*Vechernyi chas*
VE	*Vestnik Evropy*
VI	*Voprosy istorii*
VIKPSS	*Voprosy istorii KPSS*
VO	*Vechernye ogni*
VS	*Vlast' sovetov*
VZ	*Vierteljahreshefte für Zeitgeschichte*
VZh	*Vestnik zhizni*
ZhS	*Zhivoe slovo*

INTRODUCTION

This book is the first attempt in any language to present a comprehensive view of the Russian Revolution, arguably the most important event of the century. There is no shortage of surveys of the subject, but they concentrate on the political and military struggles for power over Russia between 1917 and 1920. Seen from the perspective of time, however, the Russian Revolution was a great deal more than a contest for power in one country: what the victors in that contest had in mind was defined by one of its leading protagonists, Leon Trotsky, as no less than "overturning the world." By that was meant a complete redesign of state, society, economy, and culture all over the world for the ultimate purpose of creating a new human being.

These far-reaching implications of the Russian Revolution were not evident in 1917–18, in part because the West considered Russia to lie on the periphery of the civilized world and in part because the Revolution there occurred in the midst of a World War of unprecedented destructiveness. In 1917–18 it was believed by virtually all non-Russians that what had occurred in Russia was of exclusively local importance, irrelevant to them and in any event bound to settle down once peace had been restored. It turned out otherwise. The repercussions of the Russian Revolution would be felt in every corner of the globe for the rest of the century.

Events of such magnitude have neither a clear beginning nor a neat end. Historians have long argued over the terminal dates of the Middle Ages, the Renaissance, and the Enlightenment. Similarly, there is no indisputable way to determine the time span of the Russian Revolution. What can be said with certainty is that it did not begin with the collapse of tsarism in February–March 1917 and conclude with the Bolshevik victory in the Civil War three years later. The revolutionary movement became an intrinsic element of Russian history as early as the 1860s. The first phase of the Russian Revolution in the narrow sense of the word (corresponding to the constitutional phase of the French Revolution, 1789–92) began with the violence of 1905. This was brought under control by a combination of concessions and repression, but violence resumed on an even grander scale after a hiatus of twelve years, in February 1917, culminating in the Bolshevik coup d'etat of October. After three years of fighting against internal and external opponents, the Bolsheviks succeeded in establishing undisputed mastery over most of what had been the Russian Empire. But they were as yet too weak to realize their ambitious program of economic, social, and cultural transformation. This had to be postponed for several years to give the ravaged country time to recover. The Revolution was resumed in 1927–28 and consummated ten years later after frightful upheavals that claimed millions of lives. It may be said to have run its course only with the death of Stalin in 1953, when his successors initiated and carried out, by fits and starts, a kind of counterrevolution from above, which in 1990 appears to have led to a rejection of a good part of the Revolution's legacy.

Broadly defined, the Russian Revolution may thus be said to have lasted a century. A process of such duration in a country of Russia's size and population was bound to be exceedingly complex. An autocratic monarchy that had ruled Russia since the fourteenth century could no longer cope with the demands of modernity and gradually lost out to a radical intelligentsia in whom commitment to extreme utopian ideas combined with a boundless lust for power. Like all such drawn-out processes, however, it had its culminating period. In my estimation, that period was the quarter of a century extending from the outbreak of large-scale unrest at Russian universities in February 1899 to the death of Lenin in January 1924.

Because the aspirations of the intellectuals who assumed power in October 1917 were so extreme, I found it necessary to treat many topics besides the customary political-military power struggle. To the Russian revolutionaries, power was merely a means to an end, which was the remaking of the human species. In the first years of their rule they lacked the strength to attain an objective so contrary to what their people desired, but they did try and in so doing laid the foundations of the Stalinist regime, which would resume the attempt with far greater resources. I devote considerable attention to these social, economic, and cultural antecedents of Stalinism, which, even if only imperfectly realized under Lenin, from the outset lay at the very heart of the Russian Revolution.

This volume is divided into two parts.

Part I, "The Agony of the Old Regime," describes the decay of tsarism, culminating in the mutiny of the Petrograd military garrison in February 1917, which in surprisingly short time not only brought down the monarchy but tore apart the country's political and social fabric. It is a continuation of my *Russia under the Old Regime,* which traced the development of the Russian state and society from their origins to the end of the nineteenth century. Part II, "The Bolsheviks Conquer Russia," recounts how the Bolshevik Party seized power first in Petrograd and then in the provinces inhabited by Great Russians, imposing on this region a one-party regime with its terror apparatus and centralized economic system. Both these parts appear in the present volume. A sequel, *Russia under the New Regime,* will deal with the Civil War, the separation and reintegration of the non-Russian borderlands, Soviet Russia's international activities, Bolshevik cultural policies, and the Communist regime as it took shape in the final year of Lenin's dictatorship.

The difficulties confronting a historian of a subject of such complexity and magnitude are formidable. They are not, however, as is commonly believed, caused by a shortage of sources: although some of these are, indeed, inaccessible (especially documents bearing on Bolshevik decision-making), the source materials are quite sufficient, far beyond the capacity of any individual to absorb. The historian's problem, rather, is that the Russian Revolution, being part of our own time, is difficult to deal with dispassionately. The Soviet Government, which controls the bulk of the source materials and dominates the historiography, derives its legitimacy from the Revolution and wants it treated in a manner supportive of its claims. By single-mindedly shaping the image of the Revolution over decades it has succeeded in determining not only how the events are treated but which of them are treated. Among the many subjects that it has confined to historiographic limbo are the role of the liberals in the 1905 and 1917 revolutions; the conspiratorial manner in which the Bolsheviks seized power in October; the overwhelming rejection of Bolshevik rule half a year after it had come into being, by all classes, including the workers; Communist relations with Imperial Germany in 1917–1918; the military campaign of 1918 against the Russian village; and the famine of 1921, which claimed the lives of over five million people. Writing a scholarly history of the Russian Revolution, therefore, demands, in addition to absorbing an immense mass of facts, also breaking out of the mental straitjacket that seventy years of politically directed historiography have managed to impose on the profession. This situation is not unique to Russia. In France, too, the revolution was for a long time mainly grist for political polemics: the first academic chair devoted to its history was founded at the Sorbonne only in the 1880s, a century after the event, when the Third Republic was in place and 1789 could be treated with some degree of dispassion. And still the controversy has never abated.

But even approached in a scholarly manner, the history of modern revolutions cannot be value-free: I have yet to read an account of the French or the Russian revolution that does not reveal, despite most authors' intention to appear impartial, where the writer's sympathies lie. The reason is not far to seek. Post-1789 revolutions have raised the most fundamental ethical questions: whether it is proper to destroy institutions built over centuries by trial and error, for the sake of ideal systems; whether one has the right to sacrifice the well-being and even the lives of one's own generation for the sake of generations yet unborn; whether man can be refashioned into a perfectly virtuous being. To ignore these questions, raised already by Edmund Burke two centuries ago, is to turn a blind eye to the passions that had inspired those who made and those who resisted revolutions. For post-1789 revolutionary struggles, in the final analysis, are not over politics but over theology.

This being the case, scholarship requires the historian to treat critically his sources and to render honestly the information he obtains from them. It does not call for ethical nihilism, that is, accepting that whatever happened had to happen and hence is beyond good and evil: the sentiment of the Russian philosopher Nicholas Berdiaev, who claimed that one could no more judge the Russian Revolution than the coming of the Ice Age or the fall of the Roman

Empire. The Russian Revolution was made neither by the forces of nature nor by anonymous masses but by identifiable men pursuing their own advantages. Although it had spontaneous aspects, in the main it was the result of deliberate action. As such it is very properly subject to value judgment.

Recently, some French historians have called for an end to the discussion of the causes and meaning of the French Revolution, declaring it to be "terminated." But an occurrence that raises such fundamental philosophical and moral questions can never end. For the dispute is not only over what has happened in the past but also over what may happen in the future.

Richard Pipes

Chesham, New Hampshire
May 1989

The Russian Revolution

RUSSIAN EMPIRE CIRCA 1900

Franz-Josef-La

GERMAN EMPIRE

Berlin

SWEDEN

NORWAY

ARC

Gulf of Bothnia

BALTIC SEA

Vienna

AUSTRIA-HUNGARY
Budapest

Warsaw

Revel

Finland

Helsingfors
(Helsinki)

Murmansk

BARENTS SEA

Nova
Zem.

Poland

Vilno

Riga

SERBIA

Brest-Litovsk

Pskov

St. Petersburg
(Petrograd)

WHITE SEA

Minsk

Novgorod

Archangel

K.

Sofia

ROMANIA

Kiev

Smolensk

Vologda

Northern Dvina

Arctic Circle

BULGARIA

Bucharest

Briansk

Moscow

Odessa

Dnieper

Poltava

Riazan

Nizhnii Novgorod

Ob

Constantinople
(Istanbul)

Kharkov

Lipetsk

Volga

Kazan

Perm

West

M
o
u
n
t
a
i
n
s

Gallipoli

Sevastopol

Crimea

Donetsk

Penza

Simbirsk

Saratov

SEA OF AZOV

Don

Tsaritsyn
(Volgograd)

Samara

Ufa

Ekaterinburg
(Sverdlovsk)

Tobolsk

R U S S I A **N**

Stavropol

Ural

Orenburg

U
r
a
l

Irtysh

Si b e r i a

Astrakhan

Orsk

O
T
T
O
M
A
N

BLACK SEA

Tiflis (Tblisi)

Caucasus Mts.

Erivan

Ishim

Omsk

Transiberian Railroad

To

E
M
P
I
R
E

Baghdad

Baku

CASPIAN SEA

ARAL SEA

Novonikolaevsk
(Novosibirsk)

T u r k e s t a n

Barnaul

Tehran

Syr Daria

Lake Balkash

Semipal

P E R S I A

Askhabad

Amu Daria

Bukhara

Tashkent

Vernyi

Ili

Samarkand

Fergana

AFGHANISTAN

Kabul

BRITISH INDIA

0	200	400	600	800	1000 Miles

The Agony of the Old Regime

The paralytics in the government are struggling
feebly, indecisively, as if unwillingly, with the
epileptics of the revolution.
    —*Ivan Shcheglovitov, Minister of Justice, in 1915*

PART ONE

The Agony of
the Old Regime

1

1905: The Foreshock

In the preface to an autobiographical novel, Somerset Maugham explains why he prefers to write narratives in a literary rather than strictly factual manner:

> Fact is a poor story teller. It starts a story at haphazard, generally long before the beginning, rambles on inconsequently and tails off, leaving loose ends hanging about, without a conclusion . . . a story needs a supporting skeleton. The skeleton of a story is of course its plot. Now a plot has certain characteristics that you cannot get away from. It has a beginning, a middle and an end. . . . This means that story should begin at a certain point and end at a certain point.[1]

The historian does not have the luxury of reshaping events to fit the skeleton of a plot, which means that the story he tells can have neither a clear beginning nor a definite end. It must begin at haphazard and tail off, unfinished.

When did the Russian Revolution begin? Peter Struve, a leading liberal publicist at the turn of the century, surveying the wreckage of Imperial Russia, concluded that it had been preordained as early as 1730, when Empress Anne reneged on the promise to abide by a set of constitutional limitations that the aristocracy had forced upon her as a condition of giving her the throne. A case can also be made that the Revolution began in 1825 with the abortive Decembrist Revolt. Certainly in the 1870s Russia had a full-fledged revolutionary movement: the men who led the 1917 Revolution looked to the radicals of the 1870s as forerunners.

If, however, one wishes to identify events that not merely foreshadowed 1917 but led directly to it, then the choice has to fall on the disorders that broke out at Russian universities in February 1899. Although they were soon quelled by the usual combination of concessions and repression, these disorders set in motion a movement of protest against the autocracy that did not abate until the revolutionary upheaval of 1905–6. This First Revolution was also eventually crushed but at a price of major political concessions that fatally weakened the Russian monarchy. To the extent that historical events have a beginning, the beginning of the Russian Revolution may well have been the general university strike of February 1899.

And a haphazard beginning it was. Since the 1860s Russian institutions of higher learning had been the principal center of opposition to the tsarist regime: revolutionaries were, for the most part, either university students or university dropouts. At the turn of the century, Russia had ten universities as well as a number of specialized schools which taught religion, law, medicine, and engineering. They had a total enrollment of 35,000. The student body came overwhelmingly from the lower classes. In 1911, the largest contingent was made up of sons of priests, followed by sons of bureaucrats and peasants: hereditary nobles constituted less than 10 percent, equal to the number of Jews.[2] The Imperial Government needed an educated elite and promoted higher education, but it wished, unrealistically, to confine education strictly to professional and vocational training. Such a policy satisfied the majority of students, who, even if critical of the regime, did not want politics to interfere with their studies: this is known from surveys taken in the revolutionary year of 1905. But whenever the authorities overreacted to the radical minority, which they usually did, the students closed ranks.

In 1884, in the course of the "counterreforms," which followed the assassination of Alexander II, the government revised the liberal University Statute issued twenty-one years earlier. The new regulations deprived the universities of a great deal of autonomy and placed them under the direct supervision of the Ministry of Education. Their faculties could no longer elect rectors. Disciplinary authority over the students was entrusted to an outsider, a state inspector, who had police functions. Student organizations were declared illegal, even in the form of *zemliachestva,* associations formed by students from the same province to provide mutual assistance. Students were understandably unhappy with the new regulations. Their unhappiness was aggravated by the appointment in 1897 as Minister of Education of N. P. Bogolepov, a professor of Roman law, the first academic to hold the post but a dry and unsympathetic conservative whom they dubbed "Stone Guest." Still, the 1880s and 1890s were a period of relative calm at the institutions of higher learning.

The event which shattered this calm was trifling. St. Petersburg University traditionally celebrated on February 8 the anniversary of its founding.*

*Unless otherwise stated, dates for the period preceding February 1918 are given according to the Julian calendar in use until then ("Old Style," or OS), which in the nineteenth century was

2. Nicholas II and family shortly before outbreak of World
War I. By his side, Alexandra Fedorovna. The daughters,
from left to right: Marie, Tatiana, Olga, and Anastasia.
In front, Tsarevich Alexis.

On that day it was customary for the students, after taking part in formal
festivities organized by the faculty, to stage celebrations in the center of the
city. It was pure fun in which politics played no part. But in the Russia of that
time any public event not officially sanctioned was treated as insubordination
and, as such, as political and subversive. Determined to put a stop to such
disturbances, the authorities requested the Rector, the well-known and popular law professor V. I. Sergeevich, to warn the students that such celebrations
would no longer be tolerated. The warning, posted throughout the university
and published in the press, deserves full citation because it reflected so faithfully the regime's police mentality:

> On February 8, the anniversary of the founding of the Imperial St. Petersburg
> University, it has been not uncommon for students to disturb peace and order

12 days behind the Western calendar, and in the twentieth, 13 days. From February 1, 1918, dates
are given New Style (NS)—that is, according to the Western calendar, which the Soviet Government
adopted at that time.

on the streets as well as in public places of St. Petersburg. These disturbances begin immediately after the completion of university celebrations when students, singing and shouting "Hurrah!," march in a crowd to the Palace Bridge and thence to Nevsky Prospect. In the evening, noisy intrusions into restaurants, places of amusement, the circus, and the Little Theater take place. Deep into the night the streets adjoining these establishments are cut off by an excited crowd, causing regrettable clashes and annoyance to the public. St. Petersburg society has long taken note of these disorders: it is indignant and blames the university and the entire student body, even though only a small part is involved.

The law makes provisions for such disorders and subjects those guilty of violating public order to imprisonment for 7 days and fines of up to 25 rubles. If such disorders involve a large crowd which ignores police orders to disperse, the participants are subject to terms of imprisonment for up to one month and fines of up to 100 rubles. And if the disorder has to be quelled by force, then those guilty are subject to terms of imprisonment of up to three months and fines of up to 300 rubles.

On February 8, the police are obliged to preserve peace in the same manner as on any other day of the year. Should order be disturbed, they are obliged to stop the disturbance at any cost. In addition, the law provides for the use of force to end disorders. The results of such a clash with the police may be most unfortunate. Those guilty may be subject to arrest, the loss of privileges, dismissal and expulsion from the university, and exile from the capital. I feel obliged to warn the student body of this. Students must respect the law in order to uphold the honor and dignity of the university.[3]

The tactless admonition infuriated the students. When on February 8 Sergeevich mounted the speakers' rostrum, they booed and hissed him for twenty minutes. They then streamed outside singing "Gaudeamus Igitur" and the "Marseillaise." The crowd attempted to cross the Palace Bridge into the city but, finding it blocked by the police, proceeded instead to the Nikolaev Bridge. Here more police awaited them. The students claimed that in the ensuing melee they were beaten with whips, and the police that they were pelted with snowballs and chunks of ice.

Greatly excited, the students held during the following two days assemblies at which they voted to strike until the government assured them that the police would respect their rights.[4] Up to this point the grievance was specific and capable of being satisfied.

But the protest movement was promptly taken over by radicals in charge of an illegal Mutual Aid Fund (Kassa vzaimoposhchi) who saw in it an opportunity to politicize the student body. The Fund was dominated by socialists, some of whom would later play a leading role in the revolutionary movement, among them Boris Savinkov, a future terrorist, Ivan Kaliaev, who in 1905 would assassinate Grand Duke Sergei, the governor-general of Moscow, and George Nosar (Khrustalev), who in October 1905 would chair the Petrograd Soviet.[5] The leaders of the Fund at first dismissed the strike as a "puerile" exercise, but took charge once they realized that the movement enjoyed broad support. They formed an organizing committee to direct the strike and dispatched emissaries to the other schools with requests for support. On February 15, Moscow University joined the strike; on February 17, Kiev followed suit; and before long all the major institutions of higher learning in the Empire were shut down. An estimated 25,000 students boycotted classes. The strikers called for an end to arbitrary discipline and police brutality; they posed as yet no political demands.

The authorities responded by arresting the strike leaders. More liberal officials, however, managed to persuade them that the protests had no political purpose and were best contained by satisfying legitimate student grievances. Indeed, the striking students believed themselves to be acting in defense of the law rather than challenging the tsarist regime.[6] A commission was appointed under P. S. Vannovskii, a former Minister of War, a venerable general with impeccable conservative credentials. While the Commission pursued its inquiries, the students drifted back to classes, ignoring the protests of the organizing committee. St. Petersburg University voted to end the strike on March 1, and Moscow resumed work four days later.[7]

Displeased by this turn of events, the socialists on the organizing committee issued on March 4, in the name of the student body, a Manifesto that claimed the events of February 8, 1899, were merely

> one episode of the regime that prevails in Russia, [a regime] that rests on arbitrariness, secrecy [*bezglasnost'*], and complete lack of security, including even the absence of the most indispensable, indeed, the most sacred rights of the development of human individuality . . .

The Manifesto called on all the oppositional elements in Russia to "organize for the forthcoming struggle," which would end only "with the attainment of its main goal—the overthrow of autocracy."[8] In the judgment of the police official reporting on these events, this Manifesto was not so much the expression of student disorders as a "prelude to the Russian Revolution."[9]

The episode just described was a microcosm of the tragedy of late Imperial Russia: it illustrated to what extent the Revolution was the result not of insufferable conditions but of irreconcilable attitudes. The government chose to treat a harmless manifestation of youthful spirits as a seditious act. In response, radical intellectuals escalated student complaints of mistreatment at the hands of the police into a wholesale rejection of the "system." It was, of course, absurd to insinuate that student grievances which produced the university strike could not be satisfied without the overthrow of the country's political regime: restoring the 1863 University Statutes would have gone a long way toward meeting these grievances, as most students must have believed, since they returned to classes following the appointment of the Vannovskii Commission. The technique of translating specific complaints into general political demands would become a standard procedure for Russian liberals and radicals. It precluded compromises and partial reforms: nothing, it was alleged, could be improved as long as the existing system remained in place, which meant that revolution was a necessary precondition of any improvement whatsoever.

Contrary to expectations, the Vannovskii Commission sided with the students, placing the blame for the February events on the police. It concluded that the strikes were neither conspiratorial in origin nor political in spirit, but a spontaneous manifestation of student unhappiness over their treatment. Vannovskii proposed a return to the 1863 University Statutes, as well as a number of specific reforms including the legalization of student assemblies and *zemliachestva,* reducing the amount of time devoted to the study of Latin, and abolishing the Greek requirement. The authorities chose to reject these recommendations, preferring to resort to punitive measures.[10]

On July 29, 1899, the government issued "Temporary Rules" which provided that students guilty of political misconduct would lose their military deferments. At the time of publication, it was widely assumed that the measure was intended to frighten the students and would not be enforced. But enforced it was. In November 1900, after a year and a half of quiet, fresh university disturbances broke out, this time in Kiev, to protest the expulsion of two students. Several universities held protest meetings in support of Kiev. On January 11, 1901, invoking the July 1899 ordinance, Bogolepov ordered the induction into the army of 183 Kievan students. When St. Petersburg University struck in sympathy, 27 of its students were similarly punished. One month later, a student by the name of P. V. Karpovich shot and fatally wounded Bogolepov: the minister was the first victim of the new wave of terrorism which in the next few years would claim thousands. Contemporaries regarded Bogolepov's measures against the students and his assassination as marking the onset of a new revolutionary era.[11]

More university strikes followed at Kharkov, Moscow, and Warsaw. Hundreds of students were expelled by administrative procedures. In 1901, hoping to calm the situation, the government appointed Vannovskii, then seventy-eight years of age, to take Bogolepov's place. Vannovskii introduced modifications in the university rules, authorizing student gatherings and relaxing the ancient language requirements. The concessions failed to appease the students; indeed, student organizations rejected them on the grounds that they indicated weakness and should be exploited for political ends.[12] Having failed to calm the universities, Vannovskii was dismissed.

Henceforth, Russian institutions of higher learning became the fulcrum of political opposition. Viacheslav Plehve, the arch-conservative director of the Police Department, was of the opinion that "almost all the regicides and a very large number of those involved in political crimes" were students.[13] According to Prince E. N. Trubetskoi, a liberal academic, the universities now became thoroughly politicized: students increasingly lost interest in academic rights and freedoms, caring only for politics, which made normal academic life impossible. Writing in 1906, he described the university strikes of 1899 as the beginning of the "general crisis of the state."[14]

The unrest at institutions of higher learning occurred against a background of mounting oppositional sentiment in *zemstva,* organs of local self-
government created in 1864. In 1890, during the era of "counterreforms," the
rights of *zemstva* were restricted, which caused as much unhappiness among
its deputies as the 1884 University Statutes did among students. In the late
1890s, *zemtsy* began to hold semi-legal national conclaves with political overtones.[15]

The government at this point had two alternatives: it could seek to placate
the opposition, so far confined mainly to the educated elements, with concessions, or it could resort to still harsher repressive measures. Concessions would
have certainly been the wiser choice, because the opposition was a loose
alliance of diverse elements from which it should have been possible, at a
relatively small cost, to satisfy the more moderate elements and detach them
from the revolutionaries. Repression, on the other hand, drove these elements
into each other's arms and radicalized the moderates. The Tsar, Nicholas II,
was committed to absolutism in part because he believed himself duty-bound
by his coronation oath to uphold this system, and in part because he felt
convinced that the intellectuals were incapable of administering the Empire.
Not entirely averse to some concessions if they would restore order, he lacked
patience: whenever concessions did not immediately produce the desired results, he abandoned them and had recourse to police measures.

When in April 1902 a radical student killed the Minister of the Interior,
D. S. Sipiagin, it was decided to give the police virtually unlimited powers. The
appointment of Viacheslav Plehve as Sipiagin's successor signaled the beginning of a policy of unflinching confrontation with "society," a declaration of
war against all who challenged the principle of autocracy. During Plehve's
two-year tenure in office, Russia came close to becoming a police state in the
modern, "totalitarian" sense of the word.

To contemporaries, Plehve was a man of mystery: even his date and place
of birth were unknown. His past has come to light only recently as a result
of archival researches.[16] Of German origin, he had been raised in Warsaw. He
attended law school, following which he served for a time as procurator. His
bureaucratic career began in earnest in 1881 with the appointment to the post
of director of the newly formed Department of Police, established to fight
sedition. He is said to have feigned liberalism to qualify for this post under the
relatively enlightened ministry then in office.[17] Henceforth, he lived and
worked in the shadow world of political counterintelligence. Introducing the
technique of infiltration and provocation, he achieved brilliant successes in
penetrating and destroying revolutionary organizations. He had excellent
understanding of the issues touching on state security, an indomitable capacity
for work, and skill in adjusting to the shifting winds of Court politics. The
personification of bureaucratic conservatism, he was unwilling to grant the

3. Viacheslav Plehve.

population a voice in affairs of state. Such changes as were required—and he did not oppose them in principle—had to come from above, from the Crown: in the words of his biographer, he was "not so much opposed to change as to loss of control."[18] While intolerant of public initiatives, he was prepared to have the government take direct charge of everything that required reforms in the status quo. The police in his view had not merely a negative function— that is, preventing sedition *(kramola)*—but also the positive one of actively directing the forces that life brought to the surface and that left to themselves could undermine the government's political monopoly. In this extraordinary extension of police functions into the realm of positive management of society lay the seed of modern totalitarianism. Because Plehve refused to distinguish between the moderate (loyal) and radical opposition, he inadvertently forged a united front which, under the name Liberational Movement *(Osvoboditel'noe dvizhenie)* would in 1904–5 compel the government to give up its autocratic prerogatives.

On assuming office, Plehve tried to win over the more conservative wing of the *zemstvo* movement. But he persisted in treating *zemstvo* deputies as government functionaries and any sign of independence on their part as in- subordination. His effort to make the *zemstva* a branch of the Ministry of the Interior not only lost him the sympathy of the *zemstvo* conservatives but radicalized the *zemstvo* constitutionalists, with the result that by 1903 he had to give up his one effort at conciliation.

Plehve's standing with society suffered a further blow with the outbreak of a vicious anti-Jewish pogrom on Easter Sunday (April 4) of 1903 in the Bessarabian town of Kishinev. Some fifty Jews were killed, many more injured, and a great deal of Jewish property looted or destroyed. Plehve made no secret of his dislike of Jews, which he justified by blaming them for the revolutionary ferment (he claimed that fully 40 percent of the revolutionaries were Jews). Although no evidence has ever come to light that he had instigated the Kishinev pogrom, his well-known anti-Jewish sentiments, as well as his tolerance of anti-Semitic publications, encouraged the authorities in Bessarabia to believe that he would not object to a pogrom. Hence they did nothing to prevent one and nothing to stop it after it had broken out. This inactivity as well as the prompt release of the Christian hooligans strengthened the widely held conviction that he was responsible. Plehve further alienated public opinion with his Russificatory policies in Finland and Armenia.

The epitome of Plehve's regime was a unique experiment in police-operated trade unions, known as "Zubatovshchina," after S. V. Zubatov, the chief of the Moscow political police *(Okhrana)*. It was a bold attempt to remove Russian workers from the influence of revolutionaries by satisfying their economic demands. Russian workers had been stirring since the 1880s. The nascent labor movement was apolitical, confining its demands to improvements in working conditions, wages, and other typically trade-unionist issues. But because in Russia of that time any organized labor activity was illegal, the most innocuous actions (such as the formation of mutual aid or educational circles) automatically acquired a political and, therefore, seditious connotation. This fact was exploited by radical intellectuals who developed in the 1890s the "agitational" technique which called for inciting workers to economic strikes in the expectation that the inevitable police repression would drive them into politics.[19]

Zubatov was a onetime revolutionary who had turned into a staunch monarchist. Working under Plehve, he had mastered the technique of psychologically "working over" revolutionary youths to induce them to cooperate with the authorities. In the process he learned a great deal about worker grievances and concluded that they were politically harmless and acquired a political character only because existing laws treated them as illegal. He thought it absurd for the government to play into the hands of revolutionaries by transforming the workers' legitimate economic aspirations into political crimes. In 1898, he presented a memoir to the police chief of St. Petersburg, D. F. Trepov, in which he argued that in order to frustrate radical agitators, workers had to be given lawful opportunities to improve their lot. Radical intellectuals posed no serious threat to the system unless they gained access to the masses, and that could be prevented by legitimizing the workers' economic and cultural aspirations.[20] He won over Trepov and other influential officials, including Grand Duke Sergei Aleksandrovich, the ultrareactionary governor-general of Moscow, with whose help he began in 1900 to organize official trade unions.[21] This innovation ran into opposition from those who feared that police-sponsored labor organizations not only would annoy and confuse the business community but in the event of industrial conflicts place the government in a most awkward position of having to support workers against their employers. Plehve himself was skeptical, but Zubatov enjoyed

powerful backing of persons close to the Tsar. Great things were expected of
his experiment. In August 1902, Zubatov was promoted to head the "Special
Section" of the Police Department, which placed him in charge of all the
Okhrana offices. He expanded the Okhrana network beyond its original three
locations (St. Petersburg, Moscow, and Warsaw) to the provincial towns,
assigning it many functions previously exercised by other police groups. He
required officials involved in political counterintelligence to be thoroughly
familiar with the writings of the main socialist theoreticians as well as the
history of European socialist parties.[22]

Zubatov's scheme seemed vindicated by the eagerness with which workers joined the police-sponsored trade unions. In February 1903, Moscow witnessed the extraordinary spectacle of 50,000 workers marching in a procession
headed by Grand Duke Sergei to the monument of Alexander II. Jewish
workers in the Pale of Settlement, who suffered from a double handicap in
trying to organize, flocked to Zubatov's unions in considerable numbers.

The experiment nearly came to grief, however, in the summer of 1903,
following the outbreak in Odessa of a general strike. When Plehve ordered the
police to quell the strike, the local police-sponsored trade union collapsed: by
backing the employers, the authorities revealed the hollowness of the whole
endeavor. The following month Plehve dismissed Zubatov, although he allowed some of his unions to continue and even authorized some new ones.*

In January 1904, Russia became involved in a war with Japan. The origins
of the Russo-Japanese conflict have long been distorted by the self-serving
accounts of Sergei Witte, the relatively liberal Minister of Finance and Plehve's
bitter enemy, which assigned the responsibility partly to reactionaries anxious
to divert attention from internal difficulties ("We need a small, victorious war
to avert a revolution" was a sentiment he attributed to Plehve) and partly to
unscrupulous adventurers close to the Court. It has since become known that
Plehve did not want a war and that the adventurers played a much smaller
role than Witte would have had posterity believe. In fact, Witte himself bore
a great deal of the blame for the conflict.[23] As the main architect of Russia's
industrialization, he was eager to ensure foreign markets for her manufactured
goods. In his judgment, the most promising export outlets lay in the Far East,
notably China. Witte also believed that Russia could provide a major transit
route for cargo and passengers from Western Europe to the Pacific, a potential
role of which she had been deprived by the completion in 1869 of the Suez
Canal. With these objectives in mind, he persuaded Alexander III to authorize
a railway across the immense expanse of Siberia. The Trans-Siberian, begun

*Witte (*Vospominaniia*, II, Moscow, 1960, 218–19) says that in July 1903 Zubatov confided to
him that Russia was in a revolutionary situation which could not be resolved by police measures.
Zubatov also predicted Plehve's assassination. This was betrayed to Plehve, who fired Zubatov and
exiled him to the provinces. In March 1917, on learning of the Tsar's abdication, he committed
suicide.

in 1886, was to be the longest railroad in the world. Nicholas, who sympathized with the idea of Russia's Far Eastern mission, endorsed and continued the undertaking. Russia's ambitions in the Far East received warm encouragement from Kaiser Wilhelm II, who sought to divert her attention from the Balkans, where Austria, Germany's principal ally, had her own designs. (In 1897, as he was sailing in the Baltic, Wilhelm signaled Nicholas: "The Admiral of the Atlantic greets the Admiral of the Pacific.")

In the memoirs he wrote after retiring from public life, Witte claimed that while he had indeed supported a vigorous Russian policy in the Far East, he had in mind exclusively economic penetration, and that his plans were wrecked by irresponsible generals and politicians. This thesis, however, cannot be sustained in the light of the archival evidence that has surfaced since. Witte's plans for economic penetration of the Far East were conceived in the spirit of imperialism of the age: it called for a strong military presence, which was certain sooner or later to violate China's sovereignty and come in conflict with the imperial ambitions of Japan. This became apparent in 1895, when Witte had the idea of shortening the route of the Trans-Siberian Railroad by cutting across Chinese Manchuria. He obtained China's consent with bribes given the Chinese statesman Li Hung-chang and the promise of a defensive alliance. An agreement to this effect was signed in June 1896 during Li Hung-chang's visit to Moscow to attend the coronation of Nicholas II. The signatories pledged mutual help in the event of an attack on either of them or on Korea. China allowed Russia to construct a line to Vladivostok across Manchuria, on the understanding that her sovereignty in that province would be respected.

Russia immediately violated the terms of the treaty by introducing numerous police and military units into Manchuria and establishing in Kharbin a quasi-independent base of operations. More Russian troops were sent to Manchuria during the anti-Western Boxer Rebellion (1900). In 1898 Russia extracted from China the naval base at Port Arthur on a long-term lease.

With these steps, and despite Nicholas's desire for peaceful relations and the reservations of some ministers, Russia headed for a confrontation with Japan. In November 1902, high-ranking Russian officials held a secret conference in Yalta to discuss China's complaints about Russia's treaty violations and the problems caused by the reluctance of foreigners to invest in Russia's Far Eastern ventures. It was agreed that Russia could attain her economic objectives in Manchuria only by intense colonization; but for Russians to settle there, the regime needed to tighten its hold on the area. It was the unanimous opinion of the participants, Witte included, that Russia had to annex Manchuria, or, at the very least, bring it under closer control.[24] In the months that followed, the Minister of War, A. N. Kuropatkin, urged aggressive action to protect the Trans-Siberian Railroad: in his view, unless Russia was prepared to annex Manchuria she should withdraw from there. In February 1903, Nicholas agreed to annexation.[25]

The Japanese, who had their own ambitions in the region, tried to fore-

stall a conflict by agreement on spheres of influence: they would recognize
Russian interests in Manchuria in return for an acknowledgment of their
interests in Korea. An accord might have been reached along these lines were
it not that in August 1903 Nicholas dismissed Witte as Minister of Finance:
after that, Russia's Far Eastern diplomacy began to drift, with no one in
charge. It is then that socially prominent speculators, interested in exploiting
Korean lumber resources, aggravated relations with Japan.* Persuaded that
Russia would not negotiate, the Japanese in late 1903 decided to go to war.
Although aware of Japan's preparations, the Russians did nothing, willing to
let her bear the blame for initiating hostilities. They held the Japanese in utter
contempt: Alexander III had called them "monkeys who play Europeans,"
and the common people joked that they would smother the *makaki*
(macaques) with their caps.

On February 8, 1904, without declaring war, Japan attacked and laid siege
to the naval base at Port Arthur. Sinking some Russian warships and bottling
up the rest, they secured command of the sea which permitted them to land
troops on the Korean peninsula. The battles that followed were fought on
Manchurian soil, along the Korean border, far away from the centers of her
population and industry, which presented Russia with considerable logistic
difficulties. These were compounded by the fact that the Trans-Siberian was
not yet fully operational when the war broke out because of an unfinished
stretch around Lake Baikal. In every engagement, Japan displayed superior
quality of command as well as better intelligence.

The Socialist-Revolutionary Combat Organization, which directed the
party's terrorist operations, had Plehve at the top of its list of intended victims.
The minister took every conceivable precaution, but he felt confident of his
ability to outwit the terrorists because he had achieved the seemingly impossible feat of placing one of his agents, Evno Azef, in the combat organization.
Azef betrayed to the police an attempt on Plehve's life, which led to the
apprehension of G. A. Gershuni, the terrorist fanatic who had founded and
led the group. At Gershuni's request, Azef was named his successor. In 1903
and 1904 several more attempts were made on Plehve's life, each of them failing
for one reason or another. By then some SRs began to suspect Azef's loyalty,
and to salvage his reputation and very likely his life, Azef had to arrange for
the assassination of Plehve. The operation, directed by Boris Savinkov, was
successful: Plehve was blown to pieces on July 15, 1904, by a bomb thrown at
his carriage.†

*Witte's dismissal resulted from the Tsar's dislike of him and Plehve's intrigues. It occurred,
however, as a result of a sudden illumination. Nicholas told Plehve that during a church service
he heard the Lord instructing him "not to delay that which I was already persuaded to do": V. I.
Gurko, *Features and Figures of the Past* (Stanford, Calif., 1939), 225.

†On Azef, see Boris Nikolajewsky [Nikolaevskii], *Azeff the Spy* (New York, 1934). After
Plehve's murder, Azef's reputation among revolutionaries grew immensely, and he managed to
continue his double role until exposed by the director of the Police Department, A. A. Lopukhin,
in December 1908, following which he fled to Germany and went into business. He died in 1918.

4. Remains of Plehve's body after terrorist attack.

At the time of his death, Plehve was the object of universal hatred. Even liberals blamed his death not on the terrorists but on the government. Peter Struve, who at the time was editing in Germany the main liberal organ, spoke for a good deal of public opinion when he wrote immediately after the event:

> The corpses of Bogolepov, Sipiagin, Bogdanovich, Bobrikov, Andreev, and von Plehve are not melodramatic whims or romantic accidents of Russian history. These corpses mark the logical development of a moribund autocracy. Russian autocracy, in the person of its last two emperors and their ministers, has stubbornly cut off and continues to cut off the country from all avenues of legal and gradual political development. . . . The terrible thing for the government is not the physical liquidation of the Sipiagins and von Plehves, but the public atmosphere of resentment and indignation which these bearers of authority create and which breeds in the ranks of Russian society one avenger after another. . . . [Plehve] thought that it was possible to have an autocracy which introduced the police into everything—an autocracy which transformed legislation, administration, scholarship, church, school, and family into police [organs]—that such an autocracy could dictate to a great nation the laws of its historical development. And the police of von Plehve were not even able to avert a bomb. What a pitiful fool![26]

Struve and other liberals would come to rue these incautious words, for it would soon become apparent that for the terrorists terrorism was a way of life, directed not only against the autocracy but also against the very "avenues of legal and gradual political development." But in the excited atmosphere of the time, when politics turned into a spectator sport, the terrorists were widely admired as heroic champions of freedom.

Plehve's death deeply affected Nicholas: the emotional diary entry on this event contrasts strikingly with the cold indifference with which he would

5. Prince P. D. Sviatopolk-Mirskii.

record seven years later the murder of Stolypin, a statesman of incomparably greater caliber but one who happened to believe that Russia no longer could be run as an autocracy. He had lost to terrorist bombs two Ministers of the Interior in two years. Once again he stood between the alternatives of conciliation and repression. His personal inclinations always ran toward repression, and he might well have chosen another die-hard conservative were it not for the uninterrupted flow of bad news from the war front. On August 17, 1904, a numerically inferior Japanese force attacked the main Russian army near Liaoyang, forcing it to retreat to Mukden.

This happened on August 24, and the very next day Nicholas offered the Ministry of the Interior to Prince P. D. Sviatopolk-Mirskii. On the spectrum of bureaucratic politics, Mirskii stood at the opposite pole from Plehve: a man of utmost integrity and liberal temperament, he believed that Russia could be effectively governed only if state and society respected and trusted each other. The favorite word in his political vocabulary was *doverie*— "trust." An officer of the General Staff who had served as governor in several provinces and as Deputy Minister of the Interior—that is, head of the police—he represented a type of enlightened bureaucrat more prevalent in late Imperial Russia than commonly thought. He completely rejected the police methods of Sipiagin and Plehve, and rather than serve under them in the Ministry of the Interior, had himself posted as governor-general to Vilno.

Mirskii was not overjoyed by Nicholas's offer. Considerations of personal safety played a part in his hesitation: on his retirement half a year later, he would toast his good fortune in having survived so dangerous an assignment.[27] But he also did not think that someone holding his views could work with the

Court. To prevent misunderstandings, he laid out before Nicholas his political credo:

> You know little of me and perhaps think that I share the opinions of the two preceding ministers. But, on the contrary, I hold directly opposite views. After all, in spite of my friendship with Sipiagin, I had to quit as Deputy Minister because I disagreed with his politics. The situation has become so acute that one can consider the government to be at odds with Russia. It is imperative to make peace, or else Russia will soon be divided into those who carry out surveillance and those who are under surveillance, and then what?[28]

He advised Nicholas that it was necessary to introduce religious tolerance, to broaden the competence of self-government (he referred to himself as a *"zemstvo* man"), to confine the concept of political crime to acts of terror and incitement to terror, to improve the treatment of the minorities, to ease censorship, and to invite *zemstvo* representatives for consultations. Nicholas, whose upbringing precluded open disagreement, seemed to approve of everything Mirskii told him.[29]

Mirskii's appointment to the most important administrative post in Russia was very favorably received. As an experienced official with a broad base of popular support, he seemed the ideal man to resolve the political crisis. His main shortcomings were softness of character and lack of decisiveness which caused him to send signals that encouraged the opposition in the belief the government was prepared to make greater concessions than was the case.

Mirskii immediately went to work to win public support. He abolished corporal punishment, relaxed censorship, and restored to their posts a number of prominent *zemtsy* whom Plehve had exiled. He further expressed the intention of lifting the disabilities of the Old Believers and easing the lot of the Jews. He made a strong impression with an address to the officials of the Ministry of the Interior, published in the press, in which he said that experience had taught him that government had to have a "genuinely well-meaning and genuinely trustful attitude toward civic and estate institutions and the population at large."[30]

A new era seemed to be dawning. The *zemtsy* read in Mirskii's remarks an invitation to hold a national congress. They had held one such gathering in 1902, but surreptitiously because it was illegal. The idea of a public *zemstvo* congress emerged in late August 1904, immediately after Mirskii's appointment, and quickly gained the endorsement of both the liberal (constitutionalist) and conservative (Slavophile) wings of the movement. Initially, the planners intended to confine the agenda to *zemstvo* affairs. But having learned of Mirskii's remarks, they concluded that the government would welcome their views on national issues and expanded the agenda accordingly. The *zemtsy* felt it was essential to institutionalize the latest changes in government policy: Mirskii, after all, could prove merely a tool of the "dark forces"—the Court camarilla, above all—to be discarded as soon as he had served his purpose by pacifying the country. In the words of Dmitrii Shipov, the most prominent among the conservative *zemtsy,* many of his associates felt

> that so far, trust in society had been expressed only by the individual placed at the head of the Ministry of the Interior . . . it was necessary for that one official's sense of trust to be assimilated by the entire government and clothed in legal form, protected by safeguards, which would preclude shifts in the government's attitude to society being dependent on such happenstance as the change of personnel at the head of government offices. It was further said that it had become an urgent need to make proper arrangements for legislative activity and to grant a national representative body participation in it.[31]

These sentiments spelled constitution and a legislative parliament. Some conservative *zemtsy* thought this went too far, but persuaded that the government wanted to hear the whole range of opinions, they agreed to place constitutional proposals on the agenda of the forthcoming congress, scheduled for early November.

When he first learned that the *zemtsy* planned a national congress Mirskii not only approved but asked and received the Tsar's blessing for it. In so doing he was under the misapprehension that the gathering would confine itself, as, indeed, had originally been planned, to *zemstvo* matters; in this belief, he inadvertently misled the Tsar. When he learned of the revised agenda, he requested Shipov to have the congress postponed for several months. Shipov thought this impossible to arrange, whereupon the minister requested that it move to Moscow. This, too, was rejected, so Mirskii agreed to have the congress proceed as planned but in the guise of a "private consultation" *(chastnoe soveshchanie).* His approval conveyed the misleading impression that the government was prepared to contemplate a constitutional and parliamentary regime.

Expecting the Zemstvo Congress to come up with a constitutional project, Mirskii asked Sergei Kryzhanovskii, an official in his ministry, to draft a counterproposal. His intention was to formulate a program that would include the maximum of oppositional demands conceivably acceptable to the Tsar.[32]

In this atmosphere of great expectations, the oppositional groups felt the time had come to combine forces. On September 17, representatives of the constitutionalist Union of Liberation met secretly in Paris with Socialists-Revolutionaries as well as Polish and Finnish nationalists, to forge a united front against the autocracy.*

The Paris Conference was a prelude to the great Zemstvo Congress held in St. Petersburg on November 6–9, 1904, an event that in terms of historical importance may be compared with the French Estates-General of 1789. The analogy was not lost on some contemporaries.[33]

The congress met in private residences, one of them the apartment of

---

*Shmuel Galai, *The Liberation Movement in Russia, 1900–1905* (Cambridge, Mass., 1973), 214–19; Richard Pipes, *Struve: Liberal on the Left* (Cambridge, Mass., 1970), 363–66. The Social-Democrats, who wanted to lead the revolution on their own, stayed away, but Azef was present.

Vladimir Nabokov (the father of the future novelist) on Bolshaia Morskaia, within sight of the Winter Palace.[34] On arrival in the capital, the delegates were directed to their destination by the police.

A number of resolutions were put up for a vote, of which the most important as well as the most controversial called for an elected legislature with a voice in the shaping of the budget and control over the bureaucracy. The conservatives objected to this motion on the grounds that political democracy was alien to Russia's historic traditions: they wanted a strictly consultative body modeled on the Muscovite Land Assemblies that would convey to the throne the wishes of its subjects but not interfere with legislation. They suffered defeat: the resolution in favor of a legislative parliament carried by a vote of 60–38. There was near-unanimity, however, that the new body should have a voice in the preparation of the state budget and oversee the bureaucracy.[35] It was the first time in the history of modern Russia that a legally assembled body—even if assembled under the guise of a "private consultation"—passed resolutions calling for a constitution and a parliament—even if the resolutions did not use these taboo words.

In the weeks that followed, the platform adopted by the Zemstvo Congress provided the text for the many public and private bodies that met to take a stand on national questions, among them the Municipal Council of Moscow, various business associations, and the students of nearly all the institutions of higher learning.[36] To spread the message as widely as possible, the Union of Liberation organized a campaign of nationwide banquets—modeled on 1848 France—at which the guests toasted freedom and the constitution.[37] The first took place in St. Petersburg on November 20, the fortieth anniversary of the judiciary reform; 676 writers and representatives of the intelligentsia affixed their signatures to a petition calling for a democratic constitution and a Constituent Assembly. Similar banquets were held in other cities during November and December 1904. The socialist intelligentsia, which at first had poured scorn on these "bourgeois" affairs, eventually joined in and radicalized the resolutions. Of the forty-seven banquets on which there exists information, thirty-six are known to have followed the Zemstvo Congress, while eleven went further and demanded a Constituent Assembly.[38] The provincial authorities, confused by conflicting signals from the capital, did not interfere, even though Mirskii instructed them in secret circulars to prevent the banquets from taking place and to disperse them if they defied government prohibitions.[39]

After the Zemstvo Congress had adjourned, Shipov briefed Mirskii on its resolutions; the minister listened sympathetically. Later that month, Prince Sergei Trubetskoi, the rector of Moscow University, submitted at Mirskii's request a reform proposal, which Mirskii gave to Kryzhanovskii and Lopukhin, the director of the Police Department, to edit for submission to the Tsar.[40]

The Trubetskoi-Kryzhanovskii-Lopukhin reform proposal which Mirskii presented to Nicholas early in December 1904 was a cleverly worded appeal to the Tsar's conservative instincts.[41] The authors made the proposed constitutional and parliamentary concessions appear to be a restoration of old practices rather than the revolutionary innovation that they really were. The reforms of Alexander II, they wrote, had ended the "patrimonial" *(votchinnyi)* regime in Russia by introducing the notion of public interest. They

> marked the end of the old patrimonial order and, along with it, of the personalized notions of rulership. Russia ceased to be the personal property and fiefdom of its ruler. . . . [The concepts] of "public interest" and "public opinion" suggested the emergence of the impersonal state . . . with its own body politic, separate from the person of the ruler.[42]

Legality *(zakonnost')* was depicted as entirely compatible with autocracy because the Tsar would remain the exclusive source of laws, which he could repeal at will. The proposed representative body—envisaged as limited to consultative function—was depicted as a return to the days of "true autocracy" when tsars used to heed the voice of their people.

Mirskii's draft was discussed on December 7 by high officials under Nicholas's chairmanship. The most controversial clause called for the introduction into the State Council, at the time an exclusively appointed body, of deputies elected by the *zemstva*. It was an exceedingly modest measure, but it did inject the elective principle into a political system in which legislation and administration were the exclusive preserve of the monarch and officials designated by him. In advocating its adoption, Mirskii argued that it would "ensure domestic tranquility better than the most determined police measures."[43] According to Witte, the meeting was very emotional. The majority of the ministers sided with Mirskii. The chief adversary was Konstantin Pobedonostsev, the procurator of the Holy Synod and the regime's most influential conservative, who saw in the introduction of elected representatives into state institutions a fatal breach in Russia's traditional political system. Having heard out both sides, Nicholas agreed to all of Mirskii's proposals. Those present left the meeting with the sense of having been witnesses to a momentous event in Russia's history.[44]

At the Tsar's request, Witte prepared an appropriate document for his signature. But Nicholas had second thoughts: he needed reassurance. Before signing it into law, he consulted Grand Duke Sergei and Witte. Both advised against adding elected representatives to the State Council—Sergei out of conviction, Witte more likely out of opportunism. Nicholas did not require much convincing: relieved, he struck out this provision. "I shall never, under any circumstances," he told Witte, "agree to a representative form of government because I consider it harmful to the people whom God has entrusted to my care."[45]

When he learned of the Tsar's change of heart on the key provision in his draft, Mirskii fell into despondency. Convinced that all was lost he offered to resign, but Nicholas persuaded him to stay on.

On December 12, 1904, the government made public a law "Concerning the Improvement of the Political Order," which, its title notwithstanding, announced all kinds of reforms except in the realm of politics.[46] One set of measures addressed the condition of the peasantry, "so dear to OUR heart." Others dealt with the population's legal and civil rights. Government officials would be held accountable for misdemeanors. The sphere of activity of *zemstva* would be broadened and *zemstvo* institutions introduced into lower administrative units. There were pledges of state insurance for workers, equal justice for all, religious tolerance, and the easing of censorship. The emergency regulations of 1881 providing for the suspension of civil rights in areas placed under Safeguard would be modified.

All this was welcome. But the absence of any political concessions was widely seen as a rejection of the demands of the November 1904 Zemstvo Congress.[47] For this reason the Law of December 12 was given little chance to resolve the national crisis, which was first and foremost political in nature.

Commissions were named to draft laws implementing the December 12 edict, but they had no issue because neither Nicholas nor the Court desired changes, preferring to procrastinate. They may have been hoping for some miracle, perhaps a decisive victory over the Japanese now that the Minister of War, Kuropatkin, had taken personal command of the Russian armies in the Far East. On October 2, Russia's Baltic Fleet sailed to relieve Port Arthur.

But no miracle occurred. Instead, on December 20, 1904/January 2, 1905, Port Arthur surrendered. The Japanese captured 25,000 prisoners and what was left of Russia's Pacific Fleet.

Throughout 1904, Russia's masses were quiet: the revolutionary pressures on the government came exclusively from the social elite—university students and the rest of the intelligentsia, as well as the *zemstvo* gentry. The dominant trend was liberal, "bourgeois." In these events the socialists played a secondary role, as terrorists and agitators. The population at large—peasants and workers alike—watched the conflict from the sidelines. As Struve wrote on January 2, 1905: "In Russia, there is as yet no revolutionary people."[48] The passivity of the masses encouraged the government to wage a rearguard action against its opponents, confident that as long as the demands for political change were confined to "society" it could beat them off. All this changed dramatically on January 9 with the massacre of worker demonstrators in St. Petersburg. This so-called Bloody Sunday spread the revolutionary fever to all strata of the population and made the Revolution truly a mass phenomenon: if the 1904 Zemstvo Congress was Russia's Estates-General, then Bloody Sunday was her Bastille Day.

This said, it would be incorrect to date the beginning of the 1905 Revolution from January 9 because by then the government had been under siege for more than a year. Indeed, Bloody Sunday would not have occurred were it not for the atmosphere of political crisis generated by the Zemstvo Congress and the banquet campaign.

It will be recalled that in 1903 Plehve had dismissed Zubatov but continued the experiment of police-sponsored trade unions. One of the post-Zubatov unions which he authorized was led by a priest, Father George Gapon.[49] The son of a Ukrainian peasant, Gapon was a charismatic figure who genuinely identified with the workers and their grievances. He was inspired by Leo Tolstoy and agreed to cooperate with the authorities only after considerable hesitation. With the blessing of the governor-general of the capital, I. A. Fullon, he founded the Assembly of Russian Factory and Plant Workers to work for the moral and cultural uplifting of the working class. (He stressed religion rather than economic issues and admitted only Christians.) Plehve approved Gapon's union in February 1904. It enjoyed great popularity and opened branches in different quarters of city: toward the end of 1904, it was said to have 11,000 members and 8,000 associates,[50] which overshadowed the St. Petersburg Social-Democratic organization, numerically insignificant to begin with and composed almost entirely of students. The police watched Gapon's activities with mixed feelings, for as his organization prospered he displayed worrisome signs of independence, to the point of attempting, without authorization, to open branches in Moscow and Kiev. It is difficult to tell what was on Gapon's mind, but there is no reason to regard him as a "police agent" in the ordinary meaning of the term—that is, a man who betrayed associates for money—because he indubitably sympathized with his workers and identified with their aspirations. Unlike the ordinary agent provocateur, he also did not conceal his connections with the authorities: Governor Fullon openly participated in some of his functions.[51] Indeed, by late 1904 it was difficult to tell whether the police were using Gapon or Gapon the police, for by that time he had become the most outstanding labor leader in Russia.

At first, Gapon's only concern was for the spiritual welfare of his flock. But in late 1904, impressed by the Zemstvo Congress and the banquet campaign, and possibly afraid of isolation, he concluded that the Assembly had to enter politics, side by side with the other estates.[52] He tried to make contact with the Social-Democrats and Socialists-Revolutionaries, but they spurned him. In November 1904 he communicated with the St. Petersburg branch of the Union of Liberation, which was only too happy to involve him in its campaign. As Gapon recalled in his memoirs:

Meanwhile, the great conference of the Zemstvos took place in November, and was followed by the petition of Russian barristers for a grant of law and liberty. I could not but feel that the day when freedom would be wrested from the hands of our old oppressors would be near, and at the same time I was terribly afraid that, for lack of support on the side of the masses, the effort might fail. I had a meeting with several intellectual Liberals, and asked their opinion as to what the workmen could do to help the liberation movement. They advised me that we also should draft a petition and present it to the Government. But

6. Governor Fullon visits Father Gapon
and his Assembly of Russian Workers.

I did not think that such a petition would be of much value unless it were
accompanied by a large industrial strike.*

Gapon's testimony leaves no doubt that the worker petition that led to Bloody
Sunday was conceived by his advisers from the Liberation Movement as part
of the campaign of banquets and professional gatherings. At the end of November, Gapon agreed to introduce into his Assembly the resolutions of the
Zemstvo Congress and to distribute to its members publications of the Union
of Liberation.[53]

The opportunity for a major strike presented itself on December 20, 1904,

---

*George Gapon, *The Story of My Life* (New York, 1906), 144. The "intellectual Liberals"
whom Gapon consulted are known to have been Ekaterina Kuskova, her common-law husband
S. N. Prokopovich, and V. Ia. Bogucharskii (Iakovlev).

with the dismissal of four workers belonging to his Assembly by Putilov, the largest industrial enterprise in the capital. Because the Putilov management had recently founded a rival union, the workers viewed the dismissals as an assault on their Assembly and went on strike. Other factories struck in sympathy. On January 7, an estimated 82,000 workers were out; the following day, their number grew to 120,000. By then, St. Petersburg was without electricity and newspapers; all public places were closed.[54]

Imitating the banquet campaign, Gapon on January 6 scheduled for Sunday, January 9, a worker procession to the Winter Palace to present the Tsar with a petition. As was the case with all the documents drafted by or with the assistance of the Union of Liberation, the petition generalized and politicized specific and unpolitical grievances, claiming that there could be no improvement in the condition of the workers unless the political system was radically changed. Written in a stilted language meant to imitate worker speech, it called for a Constituent Assembly and made other demands taken from the program of the Union of Liberation.[55] Gapon sent copies of the petition to high officials. Preparations for the demonstration went ahead despite the opposition of the socialists.

Since Gapon's Assembly enjoyed official sanction, the workers had no reason to think that the planned demonstration would be anything but orderly and peaceful. But the government feared that a procession of tens of thousands of workers could get out of control and lead to a breakdown of public order. In the eyes of the authorities Gapon was not so much a police agent as a "fanatical socialist" who exploited police protection for his own revolutionary purposes. It was further feared that the socialists would take advantage of the unrest to press their own agenda.[56] On January 7, Fullon appealed to the workers to stay away, threatening to use force, if necessary. The next day, orders went out for the arrest of Gapon, but he managed to hide.

That evening, January 8, Mirskii convened an emergency meeting of ministers and such high officials as happened to be on hand: a haphazard gathering to deal with what threatened to become a major crisis. It was decided to allow the demonstration to proceed but to set physical boundaries beyond which it was not to go. The Winter Palace was to be off limits. If persuasion failed to deter the workers, the troops deployed at these boundary lines were to shoot. There was a general sense, however, that force would not be required. The Tsar dismissed the strike of 120,000 workers and the planned demonstration as a trivial incident: on the eve of the massacre, he noted in his diary: "At the head of the workers' union is some kind of a priest-socialist, Gapon." Assured that the situation was under control, he departed for Tsarskoe Selo, his country residence.

Fullon, who had responsibility for the city's security, although a professional Gendarme, was a gentle, cultivated person who, according to Witte, disliked police methods and would have been better employed running a girls' boarding school.[57] Implementing decisions taken the previous night, he placed armed troops at several key points in the city.

By the time Gapon's workers began to gather Sunday morning at the six

7. Bloody Sunday.

designated assembly points it was evident that a confrontation had become unavoidable. The demonstrators were in the grip of a religious exaltation and prepared for martyrdom: the night before, some had written farewell letters. The marching columns looked like religious processions, the participants carrying ikons and singing hymns. As the groups advanced toward the city's center, bystanders took off their hats and crossed themselves; some joined. Church bells tolled. The police did not interfere.

Eventually, the demonstrators ran into army pickets. In some places the troops fired warning shots into the air, but the masses, pushed from behind, pressed on. The soldiers, untrained in controlling crowds, reacted in the only way they knew, by firing point-blank at the advancing crowd. The worst altercation occurred at the Narva Gate, in the southwestern part of the city, where Gapon led the demonstrators. The troops fired and the crowd fell to the ground: there were 40 dead. Gapon rose to his feet and cried: "There is no God anymore, there is no Tsar." Massacres occurred also in other parts of the city. Although journalists spoke of 4,600 killed and wounded, the best estimate is 200 killed and 800 injured.* Immediately, disorders spread throughout St. Petersburg. In the evening, there was much looting, especially of shops carrying liquor and firearms.[58]

Bloody Sunday caused a wave of revulsion to sweep across the coun-

---

*KL, No. 2/3 (1922), 56, cited in Galai, *Liberation Movement*, 239. The official figure was 130 dead and 299 wounded: A. N. Pankratova *et al., Revoliutsiia 1905–1907 gg. v Rossii: Dokumenty i materialy,* IV, Pt. 1 (Moscow, 1961), 103, 811, note 12.

try: among the masses, it damaged irreparably the image of the "good Tsar."

Mirskii received his walking papers on January 18 without so much as a word of thanks: he was the first Minister of the Interior since the post had been created a century earlier to be let go without some honorific title or even a medal.[59] His replacement, a colorless bureaucrat named Alexander Bulygin, also resisted as long as he decently could the honor of being named minister. Real power now passed into the hands of D. F. Trepov, who took over from Fullon the post of governor-general in the capital. A dashing officer, he had the complete confidence of Nicholas, who appreciated his candor and lack of personal ambition: in the months that followed, Trepov would exert a rather beneficial influence on Nicholas, persuading him to make concessions that he would rather have avoided.*

In the wake of Bloody Sunday protest meetings took place throughout Russia: *zemstva,* municipal councils, and private organizations condemned in the sharpest terms the government's brutality. The workers responded with strikes. In January 1905 over 400,000 workers laid down their tools: it was the greatest strike action in Russian history until that time.[60] University students left their classrooms; in some localities the unrest spread to secondary schools. On March 18, 1905, the authorities ordered all institutions of higher learning closed for the rest of the academic year. The released students swelled radical ranks. Disturbances were especially violent in the borderlands. On January 13, in the course of a general strike in Riga, Russian troops killed 70 persons. The following day, during a strike in Warsaw, 93 people lost their lives; 31 more were killed there during May Day celebrations (April 18).[61] The worst massacres occurred in mid-June in Odessa, where striking workers were joined by the crew of the mutinous battleship *Potemkin.* Here 2,000 are said to have died and 3,000 to have been gravely injured.[62] In many localities, criminals took advantage of the breakdown of order to ply their trade. In Warsaw, for example, Jewish gangsters disguised as "anarcho-Communists" broke into affluent residences, "expropriating" money and whatever else struck their fancy.[63]

Russia stood on the edge of an abyss. It seemed as if the country was boiling over from anger, envy, and resentments of every imaginable kind which until then had been kept contained under a lid of awe and fear. Now that the population had lost respect for the government, there was nothing to hold society together: neither civic sense nor patriotism. For it was the state that made Russia a country, not vice versa. It was a horrifying spectacle to many Russians to see how tenuous the bonds holding the Empire together were and how powerful the divisive passions.

As was its custom in such cases, the government's first (and often last) reaction to a domestic crisis was to appoint a commission to investigate its

*Gapon fled abroad. He returned to Russia after the amnesty that followed the October Manifesto, and was killed by an SR on the orders of Azef. After January 9, all his unions were closed, despite worker protests.

causes, which in this instance were worker grievances. Chaired by Senator N. V. Shidlovskii, the commission took the unprecedented step of inviting factory workers to send representatives. In the second week of February 1905 elections were held in St. Petersburg factories, in which 145,000 workers cast ballots: the delegates they chose in turn picked representatives to the commission. Despite its dramatic beginning, the commission accomplished nothing because the workers posed conditions which were found unacceptable, whereupon it was dissolved. Even so, it was of considerable historic importance. Not only were these the "first free worker elections ever" held in Russia,[64] but "for the first time in Russian history there was an elected representation of a large body of workers . . . and not merely workers in separate factories."[65] By recognizing workers as a distinct social group, with its own interests, the government laid the foundations of what later in the year would emerge as the St. Petersburg Soviet of Workers' Deputies.

The turmoil, verging on civil war, confounded and paralyzed Nicholas. He could not for the life of him understand why people would not be content with the lot which destiny had assigned them, as he was: after all, he carried on even though he derived no enjoyment from his difficult and often tedious responsibilities. ("I maintain autocracy not for my own pleasure," he told Sviatopolk-Mirskii, "I act in its spirit only because I am convinced that it is necessary for Russia. If it were for myself, I would gladly be rid of it."[66]) In the first decade of his reign he had faithfully followed in the footsteps of his father: but Alexander had not had to contend with a country in rebellion. Nicholas's inclination was to quell the unrest by force. The police, however, were pitifully inadequate to the task, while the bulk of the army, over one million men, was thousands of miles away fighting the Japanese. According to Witte, the country was virtually depleted of military forces.[67] There was no alternative, therefore, to political concessions: but just how little one could get away with was unclear. Nicholas and his confidential advisers were torn between the realization that things could not go on as they were and the fear that any change would be for the worse.

Some officials now urged the Tsar to expand on the promises made in the December 12 edict. They were joined by industrialists who worried about a breakdown of production. Among the events that softened Nicholas's opposition to further concessions was the murder on February 4, 1905, at the hands of a terrorist, of his uncle, the Grand Duke Sergei Aleksandrovich, a friend and confidant.

On January 17, Nicholas met with A. S. Ermolov, the Minister of Agriculture and State Properties, an experienced and wise official. The advice which Ermolov proffered, first in person and then in a memorandum, made a strong impression on him and seems to have been the main inspiration behind the important legislative acts of February 18.[68] Ermolov depicted Russia as a country on the verge of revolution. To prevent collapse, two measures had to be taken without delay. A cabinet of ministers had to be formed to give the government the necessary unity and the ability to coordinate policy in face of the opposition, neither of which was possible under the existing system.* Concurrently, a Land Assembly (consultative in nature) had to be convened of representatives of all the Tsar's subjects without distinction of social rank, religion, or nationality. Only such a body would enable the Tsar to establish direct contact with the nation: after the November Zemstvo Congress, in which the gentry dominated, one could no longer hope to rely on that class, the monarchy's traditional support. Ermolov assured Nicholas that he could trust his people. "I know," he wrote,

> that Your Majesty also hears from his closest advisers different voices. I know the opinion exists that it is dangerous to convene the nation's representatives, especially at the present troubled time, when passions have been stirred. There is the fear that at a gathering of such representatives voices may resound calling for a fundamental change in the ancient foundations of our state system, for limiting tsarist authority, for a constitution; the fear that the Land Assembly may turn into a Constituent Assembly, the peasantry raise the question of a Black Repartition,† that the very unity of the Russian land may be challenged. That such voices may indeed be heard in such an Assembly cannot be denied. But, on the other hand, one cannot help but feel confident that in an Assembly where all the classes of the population will be represented, where the views and spirit of the people will find true reflection, these individual voices will be drowned out by the vast majority which remains faithful to national traditions, to the native foundations of the Russian state system. After all, such voices resound now, too, and now they are the more dangerous because the silence of the masses offers them no refutation. No, Your Majesty, there is nothing to fear from such phenomena, and they represent no real danger.[69]

In effect, Ermolov was proposing to isolate the intelligentsia by bringing into the political process the silent majority. The alternative, in his opinion, was a massive peasant uprising such as Russia had not seen since Pugachev's rebellion in the reign of Catherine the Great.

Impressed by these arguments, Nicholas told Bulygin the next day that he was prepared to consider a representative body to discuss drafts of legislative bills.

On February 18, Nicholas signed three documents. The first was a manifesto urging the population to help restore order. The second was an invitation to the Tsar's subjects to submit "suggestions" "on matters concerning the improvement of the state and the nation's well-being." The last was a "re-

*In pre-1905 Russia, there was no cabinet with a Prime Minister: the ministers reported to the Tsar separately and received from him personal instructions. On the reasons for this practice, see Chapter 2.
†"Black Repartition" was a peasant and Socialist-Revolutionary slogan that called for the abolition of the right of property to land and the distribution ("repartition") of all privately held land among peasant communes. See Chapter 3.

script" to Bulygin informing him that the Tsar had decided to "involve the worthiest men, endowed with the nation's confidence and elected by the people, in the preliminary working out and evaluation of legislative bills."[70]

While experts were drafting the proposal for an advisory *(zakonosoveshchatel'naia)* assembly or Duma, across the country hundreds of meetings took place to draw up petitions. The response to its invitation exceeded anything the government had anticipated:

> The newspaper carried accounts of the meetings and thus publicized the grievances and demands that were being voiced by a growing number of people. Instead of curbing unrest, the monarch's ukase proved to be [the] catalyst that mobilized masses of people who had not previously dared to express opinions on political issues. Dominated by liberals and liberal demands, the petition campaign really amounted to a revival, in more intense form, of the liberal offensive of the fall and winter of 1904–5.[71]

The liberals seized the opportunity offered by the February 18 edict to press their program, resuming the banquet campaign in the guise of a "petition campaign." It was now possible, not only at private gatherings but also at public assemblies, to demand a constitution and a legislative parliament. The *zemtsy* held their Second Congress in Moscow in April 1905: the majority of the delegates would be satisfied with nothing less than a Constituent Assembly. Various professional associations met and passed resolutions in the spirit of the Union of Liberation. The bureaucrats, fearful of the effect of the manifesto on the village, tried to keep it out of peasants' hands, but the liberals foiled them, using provincial and district *zemstva* to distribute it in hundreds of thousands of copies. As a consequence, in the spring of 1905, 60,000 peasant petitions flooded St. Petersburg.[72] (Except for a handful, they remain unpublished and unstudied.) The petition campaign inadvertently contributed to the politicization of the village, even though the peasants' *cahiers* seem to have dealt mainly with land and related economic matters.*

It was in the course of the petition campaign that the liberals created their third and most powerful national organization, the Union of Unions, which was to play a decisive role in the climactic stage of the 1905 Revolution. The Union of Unions (Soiuz Soiuzov) was the most radical of the liberal organizations, standing to the left of both the Zemstvo Congress and the Union of Liberation. The decision to create this body was taken at the October 1904 congress of the Union of Liberation: its mission was to broadcast the liberal message to the mass constituency of professional people as well as white- and blue-collar employees in order to involve them in the political struggle. The intention was for the professional and trade associations formed under the Union's auspices not to serve their members' special interests, but to involve

---

*The first to call attention to this important source was F.-X. Coquin in F.-X. Coquin and C. Gervais-Francelle, eds., *1905: La Première Révolution Russe* (Paris, 1986), 181–200. The invitation for the population to submit petitions was officially withdrawn on August 6, 1905, following the publication of the so-called Bulygin Constitution.

them in the campaign for political freedom. V. A. Maklakov, a prominent liberal, recalls that the Union of Lawyers, of which he was a member, did not promote the collective interests of its members or the cause of law, but used the prestige of the legal profession to add to the clamor for a parliament and a constitution.[73] The same held true of the other unions. The movement for the formation of such unions accelerated significantly after the publication of the February 18 manifesto. In addition to the Union of Lawyers, unions were formed of Medical Personnel, Engineers and Technicians, Professors, Agronomists and Statisticians, Pharmaceutical Assistants, Clerks and Bookkeepers, Journalists and Writers, Veterinarians, Government, Municipal, and Zemstvo Employees, Zemstvo Activists, and School Teachers. Separate organizations were set up to work for the equality of Jews and of women.[74] The Union also organized mass associations: its outstanding success was in setting up the All-Russian Union of Railroad Employees and Workers, the largest labor organization in the country. Later on, it was instrumental in forming the Peasant Union. All the member unions adhered to a minimum program calling for the replacement of autocracy with a constitutional regime and full civil rights for the population. On other issues, such as the Constituent Assembly, they showed considerable divergencies.[75] On May 8, 1905, a congress of fourteen unions organized by the Union of Liberation in Moscow federated into the Union of Unions under the chairmanship of Paul Miliukov. Miliukov, the leading figure in the liberal movement, by this time was a liberal only in name because he was prepared to use any means, including the general strike, to topple the autocracy. In the next five months, the Union of Unions virtually set the course of the Russian Revolution.

The news from the Far East went from bad to worse. In February 1905, the Russians fought the Japanese for Mukden, a Manchurian city that Kuropatkin had vowed never to surrender. It was a ferocious engagement in which 330,000 Russians battled 270,000 Japanese. After losing 89,000 men (to 71,000 of the enemy), Kuropatkin decided to abandon the city.

As if this humiliation were not enough, in May came news of the worst disaster in Russian naval history. The Baltic Fleet was sailing off the east coast of Africa when it learned of the surrender of Port Arthur. Since his mission was to relieve Port Arthur, the fleet's commander, Admiral Z. P. Rozhestvenskii, requested permission to return to his home base. The request was denied. Joined by the Black Sea Fleet, which had sailed through the Suez Canal, he reached the China Sea and headed for Vladivostok by way of the Strait of Tsushima between Korea and southern Japan. Here a Japanese fleet under Admiral Togo lay in wait. The Russian vessels were more heavily armed but slower and less maneuverable. Togo also had the benefit of superior intelligence. The engagement fought on May 14/27, 1905, was an unmitigated disaster for the Russians. All their battleships and many auxiliary vessels were sunk and most of the remainder captured; only a few managed to escape under the

8. Paul Miliukov, leader of the Constitutional-
Democratic Party.

cover of darkness. Rozhestvenskii himself was taken prisoner. Tsushima ended
any hope the Imperial Government may have had of staving off constitutional
reforms by a glorious military victory.

Nicholas's immediate reaction to Tsushima was to designate Trepov Deputy Minister of the Interior with extensive police powers, which, according to
Witte, made him "unofficial dictator."[76] He also resolved to seek peace. The
difficult mission was assigned to Witte, who in June left for Portsmouth, New
Hampshire, where the peace talks were to take place under the patronage of
the U.S. President Theodore Roosevelt.

Sergei Witte was late Imperial Russia's most outstanding politician. It
would strain the word to call him a statesman, because he was rather short
of political vision. But he did have the talent—rare in Russia where government and opposition were equally prone to lock themselves into doctrinaire
positions—of practicing politics as the art of the possible, content, when
making or recommending policies, to settle on the lesser of evils. Like many
successful politicians, he was an opportunist skilled at pursuing his private
interests in the guise of public service. No one was better suited to steer Russia
through the revolutionary storms: he had a remarkably acute political instinct
and energy to spare. Unfortunately for Witte, and possibly Russia, Nicholas disliked and mistrusted him. The diminutive, exquisitely mannered Tsar
could not abide the rough, overbearing minister who had married a divorcée of dubious reputation, chewed gum, and was rumored (wrongly) to be a
Freemason.

Witte descended from a Russified Swedish family. He began his career in
the Railroad Department of the Ministry of Commerce. His early politics were

nationalist and pro-autocratic: after the assassination of Alexander II he joined the right-wing "Holy Brotherhood," which planned to turn the weapon of terrorism against the terrorists. In his view, Russia had to have a strong and unlimited monarchy because over one-third of her population consisted of "aliens."[77] But he was willing to come to terms with the opposition and always preferred compromise to repression. He had uncommon managerial talents and advanced rapidly: in 1889 he was placed in charge of State Railways and in 1892 was appointed Minister of Finance. He formulated and implemented ambitious plans for the industrial development of Russia, and was instrumental in securing loans from abroad, a good part of which went into constructing railways and buying out private railroad companies. His policies of forced industrial growth aroused the enmity of diverse groups: the landed gentry and the officials of the Ministry of the Interior in particular, who thought that he was subverting the country's agrarian foundations.

Dismissed in 1903 and given the purely honorific post of Chairman of the Council of Ministers, Witte was now recalled and sent to the United States. His instructions were vague. He was under no circumstances to agree to an indemnity or to surrender one foot of "ancient Russian soil."[78] Otherwise he was on his own. Witte, who had a fine sense of the "correlation of forces," realized that Russia was not without strong cards, for the war had severely strained Japan's economy and made her no less eager to come to terms. While in the United States, he exploited American anti-Japanese feelings, and made himself popular with the public by such democratic gestures as shaking hands with railway engineers and posing for ladies with Kodak cameras, which he admitted came hard to him, unaccustomed as he was to acting.

In Russia, the news of Tsushima raised the political tension still higher. On May 23, the St. Petersburg Municipal Council voted for political reforms; the Municipal Council of Moscow followed suit the next day. These were significant developments because up to that time the institutions of urban self-government had been more restrained than the *zemstva* and stayed clear of the Liberation Movement. On May 24–25, the *zemtsy* held in Moscow a gathering of their own people along with representatives of the nobility and Municipal Councils.[79] Its resolution called for the convocation of a national representative body elected on a secret, equal, universal, and direct ballot: among the signatories were the chairmen of twenty Municipal Councils.[80] The meeting chose a deputation to see the Tsar, which he received on June 6. Speaking for the group, Prince Sergei Trubetskoi, the rector of Moscow University, urged Nicholas to allow public representatives to enter into a direct dialogue with him. He spoke of the military defeats raising among the people the specter of "treason" in high places. Without specifying whether the proposed body should be advisory or legislative, Trubetskoi asked that it be elected, not by estates, but on a democratic franchise. "You are Tsar of all Russia," he reminded him. In his response, Nicholas assured the deputation he was determined to convene representatives of the nation.[81] The encounter set a historic precedent in that it was the first time a Russian ruler had met

9. Sergei Witte at Portsmouth, N.H.: Summer 1905.

with representatives of the liberal opposition to hear pleas for constitutional change.

How widespread the demand for such change had become after Tsushima can be gathered from the fact that a Conference of the Marshals of the Nobility (June 12–15) concluded that Russia stood at the threshold of anarchy because she had only a "shadow" government. To restore state authority, the Tsar had to stop relying exclusively on the officialdom and avail himself of the assistance of "elected representatives of the entire land."[82]

The entire opposition movement at this point was driven by liberals and liberal-conservatives who saw in constitution and parliament a way of strengthening the state and averting revolution.[83] The revolutionaries continued to play a marginal role and followed the liberals. This would remain the case until October.

On June 23, a newspaper carried the first reports on the discussions underway in government concerning the Duma, as the new representative body was to be called. In July more information on this subject leaked from a secret meeting at Peterhof. (The leaks originated with the professor of Russian history at Moscow University, Vasilii Kliuchevskii, who participated in the drafting commission as a consultant.[84]) The provisions of what came to be popularly known as the Bulygin Constitution were officially released on August 6.[85] Because of the leaks, the public, even if disappointed, was not surprised. It was the usual story of too little, too late. A proposal that would have been welcomed six months earlier now satisfied no one: while the opposition was demanding a legislative parliament and even a Constituent Assembly, the government was offering a powerless consultative body. The new State Duma was to be limited to deliberating legislative proposals submitted for its consideration by the government and then forwarding them to the State Council for final editing. The government was not even obligated to consult the Duma: the document explicitly reaffirmed the "inviolability of autocratic power." As a concession to liberal demands, the franchise was based, not on estate, but on property qualifications, which were set high. Many of the non-Russian regions were deprived of the vote; industrial workers, too, were disenfranchised. In St. Petersburg and Moscow, only 5 to 10 percent of the residents qualified; in the provincial cities, 1 percent or even fewer.[86] The franchise was deliberately skewed in favor of Great Russian peasants. According to Witte, during the deliberations of the Bulygin Commission it was assumed

> that the only [group] on which one could rely in the present turbulent and revolutionary condition of Russia was the peasantry, that the peasants were the conservative bulwark of the state, for which reason the electoral law ought to rely primarily on the peasantry, i.e., that the Duma be primarily peasant and express peasant views.[87]

The assumption had never been put to a test and turned out to be entirely wrong: but it fitted with the Court's deeply held conviction that the pressures for political change emanated exclusively from the cities and the non-Russian ethnic groups.

Even though the so-called Bulygin Duma offered little, it represented a major concession, inadequately appreciated by contemporaries: "The autocrat and his government, who had always claimed to be the best and only judges of the people's true interests, now at least were willing to consult with the people on a permanent and comprehensive basis. . . ."[88] In so doing, the Tsar accepted the principle of representation, which a mere eight months earlier he had declared he would "never" do. Witte, who also knew the proposal fell far short of what was needed, nevertheless felt certain that the Duma would in no time develop from an advisory into a full-blooded legislative institution: only "bureaucratic eunuchs" could have deluded themselves that Russia would be content with a "consultative parliament."[89]

The liberals now faced the choice of accepting the Bulygin Duma as given, petitioning the Tsar to change it, or appealing to the nation to pressure the government. A joint Zemstvo and Municipal Councils Congress held in early July, by which time the substance of the government's proposal was already known, discussed these options. The more conservative participants feared that a direct appeal to the population would inflame the peasants, who were beginning to stir, but there was near-unanimity that it was pointless to petition the Tsar. The majority decided to call on the population to help achieve "peaceful progress"—a veiled way of exhorting it to civil disobedience.[90]

Notwithstanding these developments, in August and September 1905, the country seemed to be settling down: the announcement of August 6, promising a Duma, and the prospect of peace with Japan had a calming effect. Nicholas, convinced that the worst was over, resumed the routine of Court life. He ignored warnings of informed officials, including Trepov, that the calm was deceptive.

Witte returned to Russia in triumph, having managed to obtain far better terms than anyone had dared to hope. In the Treaty of Portsmouth, concluded on September 5 (NS), Russia surrendered the southern half of Sakhalin and consented to Japan's acquiring the Liaotung Peninsula with Port Arthur, as well as establishing hegemony over Korea, neither of which were Russian property. There was to be no indemnity. The price was small, considering Russia's responsibility for the war and her military humiliation.*

Witte was not deceived by appearances. Not only was the government unable to reassert authority, but Russian society was in the grip of a psychosis that had it convinced "things cannot go on like this." He thought all of Russia was on strike.[91]

And, indeed, a nationwide strike was in the making.

The idea of resorting to a general strike to force the government to its knees had been placed on the agenda of the Union of Unions shortly after the Tsushima debacle. At that time, the Union's Central Bureau took under advisement the resolutions of two of its more radical affiliates—the Union of Railroad Employees and Workers and the Union of Engineers—to organize a general political strike. A committee was formed to look into the matter,[92] but little was done until early October, when the center of political resistance once again shifted to the universities.

As the opening of the new academic year drew near, the government made unexpectedly generous concessions to the universities. On the advice of Trepov, rules were issued on August 27 allowing faculties to elect rectors and

---

*Russia's defeat at the hands of the Japanese was to have grave consequences for the whole of Europe by lowering the esteem in which whites had been held by non-Western peoples: for it was the first time in modern history that an Asiatic nation defeated a great Western power. One observer noted in 1909 that the war had "radically reshaped" the mood of the Orient: "There is no Asiatic country, from China to Persia, which has not felt the reaction of the Russo-Japanese war, and in which it has failed to wake new ambitions. These usually find expression in a desire to assert independence, to claim equality with the white races, and have had the general result of causing Western prestige to decline in the East" (Thomas F. Millard, *America and the Far Eastern Question,* New York, 1909, 1–2). In a sense, the war marked the beginning of the process of colonial resistance and decolonization that would be completed half a century later.

students to hold assemblies. To avoid confrontations with the students, Trepov ordered the police to keep out of university precincts: responsibility for maintaining discipline was given to faculty councils.[93] These liberalizing measures went far in meeting objections to the unpopular 1884 University Statutes. But they had the opposite of the anticipated effect: instead of mollifying the students, they provided the radical student minority with the opportunity to transform universities into arenas of worker agitation.

In August and early September 1905, the students were debating whether to resume studies. They overwhelmingly wanted the schools to reopen: a vote taken at St. Petersburg University showed that those favoring this course enjoyed a seven-to-one plurality.[94] But being young and therefore sensitive to charges of selfishness, they struck a compromise. A nationwide student conference in September representing twenty-three institutions of higher learning rejected motions calling for a boycott of classes. It did agree, however, as a concession to the radicals and proof of political awareness, to make university facilities available to non-students for political rallies.[95]

This tactic had been formulated the preceding summer by the Menshevik Theodore Dan in the pages of the Social-Democratic organ *Iskra.* Dan urged the students to return to school, not to study, but to make revolution:

> The systematic and overt violation of all the rules of the police-university "regulations" [*rasporiadok*], the expulsion of all kinds of disciplinarians, inspectors, supervisors, and spies, opening the doors of the lecture halls to all citizens who wish to enter, *the transformation of universities and institutions of higher learning into places of popular gatherings and political meetings*—such should be the students' objective when they return to the lecture halls which they have abandoned. *The transformation of universities and academies into the property of the revolutionary people:* this is how one can succinctly formulate the task of the student body . . . Such a transformation, of course, will make the universities into one of the centers for the concentration and organization of the national masses.[96]

Trepov's rules inadvertently made such revolutionary tactics possible.

The militant minority immediately took advantage of this opportunity to invite workers and other non-students to political gatherings on university grounds. Academic work became impossible as institutions of higher learning turned into "political clubs": non-conforming professors and students were subjected to intimidation and harassment.[97] The workers were slow to respond to the invitation of student militants but curiosity got the better of them. As word got around that the students treated them with respect, increasing numbers of workers turned up. They listened to speeches and soon began to speak up themselves.[98] Similar scenes took place in other university towns, including Moscow. It was an unprecedented spectacle to have radical students incite workers to strike and rebel without police interference. Trepov's hope that his relaxed rules would allow students to "blow off steam" had completely misfired. In Witte's view, the university regulations of August 27 were a disaster:

"it was the first breach through which the Revolution, which had ripened underground, emerged into the open."[99]

At the end of September a new wave of strikes broke out in central Russia. Although economic in origin, they became rapidly politicized thanks to the efforts of the Union of Unions and the radical students who followed its lead.

The strikes which were to culminate in the general strike of mid-October began with a walkout of Moscow printers on September 17. The dispute, which began peacefully, was over wages, but university students soon gave it a political coloration. The strikers clashed with the police and Cossacks. Other workers joined in the protests. On October 3, St. Petersburg printers struck in sympathy.[100] Until the formation of the St. Petersburg Soviet on October 13, the universities served as coordinating centers for the strike movement because they were then the only institutions in Russia where it was possible to hold political meetings without police interference.[101] Their lecture halls and other facilities were taken over for political rallies, attended by thousands. Trubetskoi, the rector of Moscow University, was determined not to allow his institution to be turned into a political battleground and ordered it closed on September 22. (It was his last act, for he died suddenly a week later: his funeral in Moscow was an occasion for a grandiose political demonstration.) But St. Petersburg University and the St. Petersburg Technological Institute stayed open and this allowed them to play a critical role in the events that led to the general strike.

Industrial unrest in Moscow and St. Petersburg assumed a national dimension when the railroad workers joined in. It was noted previously that the All-Russian Union of Railroad Employees and Workers, an affiliate of the Union of Unions, had been discussing since the summer of 1905 the possibility of a general political strike. The railroad action began with a minor incident. In late September the authorities convened a conference to discuss with railroad representatives questions connected with their pension rights. On October 4–5 false rumors spread that the workers attending this conference had been arrested. The Railroad Employees and Workers Union used this opportunity to execute its plan. On October 6, the Moscow railroads struck, isolating the city. The strike spread to other cities, soon joined by communication and factory workers and white-collar employees. In all instances, the Union of Unions and its affiliates made certain that the strikers posed political demands, calling for the convocation of a Constituent Assembly elected on a "four-tail" franchise (universal, direct, secret, and equal ballot). Partly spontaneous, partly directed, the movement headed toward a complete work stoppage. On October 8, the Union of Unions instructed its members to join in support of the railroad workers and set up strike committees throughout the country. The stage was set for a general strike.*

*Galai, *Liberation Movement*, 262–63. The Union of Railroad Employees and Workers, the largest labor organization in Russia, with 700,000 members, had only 130,000 workers: the majority of its members were local hands, mostly peasants: Oskar Anweiler, *The Soviets* (New York, 1974), 269, note 53.

On October 6, as the movement was gathering momentum, Witte requested an audience with the Tsar, which was granted three days later. Witte, who in the past was inclined to tell the Tsar what he wanted to hear, was now brutally frank. He told Nicholas that he had two choices: appoint a military dictator or make major political concessions. The rationale for the latter was outlined in a memorandum which he brought along.* Nicholas almost certainly told his wife what had transpired, for Witte was requested to return to Peterhof the following day, October 10, to repeat his arguments in her presence. Throughout the encounter, Alexandra never uttered a word.

Close reading of Witte's memorandum indicates that he was familiar with the program of the Union of Liberation and, in particular, the writings of Struve, its chief theorist. Without saying it in so many words, he proposed the adoption of the platform which Struve had been urging in the pages of the Union's organ, *Liberation:* "The slogan of 'freedom' must become the slogan of government activity. There is no other way of saving the state."† The situation was critical. The country had become dangerously radicalized, and the masses, having lost confidence in the government, were poised to destroy the country's very foundations:

> The advance of human progress is unstoppable. The idea of human freedom will triumph, if not by way of reform then by way of revolution. But in the latter event it will come to life on the ashes of a thousand years of destroyed history. The Russian *bunt* [rebellion], mindless and pitiless, will sweep everything, turn everything to dust. What kind of Russia will emerge from this unexampled trial surpasses human imagination: the horrors of the Russian *bunt* may exceed everything known to history. It is possible that foreign intervention will tear the country apart. Attempts to put into practice the ideals of theoretical socialism—they will fail but they will be made, no doubt about it—will destroy the family, the expression of religious faith, property, all the foundations of law.[102]

To prevent such a catastrophe, Witte proposed to satisfy the demands of the liberals and in this manner detach them from the revolutionaries. The

---

*Vitte, *Vospominaniia,* III, 11. See Andrew M. Verner, *Nicholas II and the Role of the Autocrat during the First Russian Revolution, 1904–1907,* Ph.D. dissertation, Columbia University, 1986, 370–76. Verner maintains that Witte misdated his first meeting with Nicholas and that it actually took place one day earlier (October 8), but this seems most unlikely, especially in view of the testimony of a third person, D. M. Solskii (Vitte, *Vospominaniia,* III, 25).

†Witte's memorandum of October 9, 1905, is in *KA,* No. 11–12 (1925), 51–61. The above passage appears on p. 55. This is what Struve had written four months earlier: "Russia needs a strong government which will not fear revolution because it will place itself at its head . . . The Revolution in Russia must become the government": Richard Pipes, *Struve: Liberal on the Left, 1870–1905* (Cambridge, Mass., 1970), 384. Struve's program, from which Witte generously borrowed: *Ibid.,* 376–85. The concept is an echo of the French Revolution: when, in February 1791, Louis XVI urged the National Assembly to pursue the work of reform, Brissot, the Girondist leader, declared: "The King is now the Head of the Revolution" (J. M. Thompson, *The French Revolution,* Oxford, 1947, 192).

united front of the opposition broken up, the liberals could be pacified and the radicals isolated. The only realistic course of action—it had to be taken at once, there was no time to lose—was for the government "boldly and openly to take charge of the Liberation Movement." The government should adopt the principle of constitutionalism and democratize the restricted franchise adopted for the consultative Duma. It should consider having ministers chosen by and responsible to the Duma, or at least enjoying its confidence. Neither a constitution nor a legislative parliament, Witte assured Nicholas, would weaken his authority: they would rather enhance it. Witte further proposed, as a means of calming social unrest, improvements in the condition of workers, peasants, and the ethnic minorities, as well as guarantees of the freedom of speech, press, and assembly.

It was a revolutionary program, born of desperation, for Witte realized that the government did not dispose of the military strength required to restore order by force.* Although on October 9–10 and the days that followed he would list military repression as an alternative, he did so *pro forma,* knowing full well that the only realistic option was surrender.

His proposals were subjected to intense discussions at the Court and in high bureaucratic circles. Because Nicholas could not decide on the drastic changes that Witte had suggested, he initially agreed only to a bureaucratic measure which had long been urged on him—namely, creating a cabinet of ministers. On October 13, Witte received a telegram appointing him Chairman of the Council of Ministers "for the purpose of unifying the activity of all the ministers."[103] Assuming that this meant his reform proposals had been turned down, he requested to see the Tsar. He told him he saw no possibility of serving as Prime Minister unless his entire program was adopted. But on October 14 he was invited to return to Peterhof the next morning with the draft of a manifesto.

While Nicholas was mulling over Witte's suggestions, the country was coming to a standstill. The week that followed Witte's first visit to Peterhof (October 10–17), critical in the history of Russia, is difficult to disentangle because of contrary claims of various oppositional groups which the sources presently available do not make it possible to sort out. In the eyes of the well-informed police authorities, the general strike and the St. Petersburg Soviet were the work of the Union of Unions. Trepov unqualifiedly credited the Union with creating the St. Petersburg Soviet and serving as its "central organization."[104] Such was also the opinion of the chief of the St. Petersburg Okhrana, General A. V. Gerasimov, for whom the Union exerted its impact in October 1905 by providing the scattered oppositional groups with a common

---

*The entire St. Petersburg garrison at this time consisted of 2,000 men: Abraham Ascher, *The Revolution of 1905* (Stanford, Calif., 1988), 225. Cf. Vitte, *Vospominaniia,* II, 9–10, 26–27.

program: "The principal initiative and organizational work in the aforementioned strikes belongs to the Union of Unions."[105] Nicholas wrote his mother on November 10 that "the famous Union of Unions . . . had led all the disorders."[106] Miliukov in his memoirs endorsed this view although he preferred to credit the parent organization, the Union of Liberation. He states that the initial meetings of the workers which led to the creation of the Soviet took place in the homes of members of the Union of Liberation and the first appeal to convoke the Soviet was printed on the Union's presses.[107] The Mensheviks hotly denied this claim, insisting it was they who had launched the Soviet; in this, they received support from some early Communist historians.[108] There is, indeed, evidence that on October 10 the Mensheviks, mostly students, appealed to the workers of St. Petersburg to elect a Workers' Committee to direct their strike.[109] But indications also exist that the workers, following the precedent established by the Shidlovskii Commission, independently chose their representatives, whom they called *starosty,* the name given elected village officials: some of these had served on the Shidlovskii Commission.[110] The most likely explanation is that the Union of Unions initiated the Soviet and that Menshevik youths helped rally factory workers in its support. This was the conclusion reached by General Gerasimov.[111]

On October 10 communication workers and service employees of public as well as private enterprises in St. Petersburg went on strike. The following evening, over 30,000 people, mostly workers and other non-students, filled the assembly halls and lecture rooms of the university. The crowd voted to join the railroad strike.[112] By October 13 virtually all rail traffic in Russia stopped; the telegraph lines were also dead. More and more industrial workers as well as white-collar employees joined the strike.

On October 13, the Soviet held its first session in the St. Petersburg Technological Institute. On hand were some forty intellectuals and workers' representatives. The meeting was called to create a center to direct the strike. Initially, the Soviet was no more than that, a fact reflected in the names which it used in the first four days of its existence: Strike Committee *(Stachennyi komitet),* United Workers' Soviet *(Obshchii rabochii sovet),* and Workers' Committee *(Rabochiii komitet).* The name Soviet of Workers' Deputies was adopted only on October 17.* Fifteen of the workers' representatives present were elected that day, the remainder having been chosen earlier in the year to serve on the Shidlovskii Commission.[113] The opening session dealt with the strike. An appeal was issued calling on workers to maintain the work stoppage in order to force the convocation of a Constituent Assembly and the adoption of the eight-hour working day.

At the second meeting of the Soviet, on October 14, the Menshevik George Nosar (Khrustalev) was elected permanent chairman. (In 1899, he had been one of the leaders of the student strike at St. Petersburg University.) By then,

---

*The earliest Soviet had emerged in May 1905 in the textile center of Ivanovo-Voznesensk to manage the workers' economic conflict with the employers. It had no political program. Oscar Anweiler, *The Soviets* (New York, 1974), 40–42.

public life in St. Petersburg had come to a standstill. Nevsky Prospect was illuminated by projectors mounted on the Admiralty spire.

At this point (October 14) Trepov issued a warning against further disorders, threatening to resort to firearms.[114] He had St. Petersburg University surrounded by troops and after October 15 allowed no more rallies there. A few days later, he shut down the university for the rest of the academic year. Right-wing elements began to beat up Jews, students, and anyone else who looked like an intellectual. It became dangerous to wear eyeglasses.* This was the beginning of mob violence, which after the proclamation of the October Manifesto would assume massive proportions, claiming hundreds if not thousands of lives and causing immense destruction of property.

At its third session on October 15, the Soviet acquired a formal organization. Present were 226 delegates from 96 industrial enterprises. Socialists came in force, too, among them the Bolsheviks, who had initially boycotted the Soviet because they opposed the formation "of organs of proletarian self-rule before power had been seized."†

At the October 15 session an organizational step was taken which, although hardly noticed at the time, would have the most weighty consequences in February 1917, when the St. Petersburg Soviet was resuscitated. An Executive Committee (Ispolnitenyi Komitet, or Ispolkom for short) of thirty-one persons was formed: fourteen from the city's boroughs, eight from the trade unions, and nine (29 percent) from the socialist parties. The latter allotted three seats each to the Menshevik and Bolshevik factions of the Social-Democratic Party and three to the Socialists-Revolutionaries. The socialist intellectuals were not elected by the Soviet but appointed by their respective parties. Although they had only a consultative vote, their experience and organizational skills assured them of a dominant role in the Ispolkom and, through it, the Soviet at large. In 1917, the Executive Committee of the Petrograd Soviet would consist exclusively of intellectuals nominated by the socialist parties.[115] The rising influence of the radical intelligentsia found expression in an appeal to the workers issued by the Soviet on October 15 with an explicit threat of physical coercion against strikebreakers. "Who is not with us is against us, and to them the Soviet of Deputies has decided to apply extreme methods—force." The appeal urged the strikers forcibly to shut down shops which ignored the strike and to prevent the distribution of government newspapers.[116]

At the meeting of October 17, the Soviet adopted the name Soviet of Workers' Deputies *(Sovet rabochikh deputatov)* and expanded the Executive

---

*In the revolutionary years 1905–6 as well as 1917, persons wearing glasses, called *ochkastye,* risked the fury of both monarchist and radical mobs: Albert Parry in the preface to A. Volskii [Machajski], *Umstvennyi rabochii* (New York-Baltimore, 1968), 15–16.

†L. Geller and N. Rovenskaia, eds., *Peterburgskii i Moskovskii Sovety Rabochikh Deputatov 1905 g. (v dokumentakh)* (Moscow-Leningrad, 1926), 17. This position was grounded in the conviction of Lenin, the Bolshevik leader, that left to follow their own inclinations, the workers would not make revolution but seek accommodation with capitalism. For this reason the revolution had to be done for them but not by them.

Committee to fifty, with the socialist parties being allotted seven seats each, for a total of twenty-one (42 percent). It was decided to issue *Izvestiia* as the Soviet's official organ.

Similar soviets sprang up in some fifty provincial cities, as well as certain rural areas and in a few military units, but the St. Petersburg Soviet enjoyed from the beginning a position of undisputed primacy.

In the evening of October 14, Witte was in receipt of a telegram from Peterhof asking him to appear the following morning with the draft of a manifesto. Witte claims that he was unable to write the manifesto because he was feeling unwell, and entrusted the task to Alexis Obolenskii, a member of the State Council who happened to be spending the night at his home.[117] Since it is unlikely that he failed to realize the importance of this document, and he appeared healthy enough both before and after the event, the more likely explanation for his missing this unique opportunity to make history was the fear of bearing the blame for a step which he knew the Tsar took with the utmost distaste. If one is to believe him, he first familiarized himself with the manifesto the following morning aboard a ship which was taking him and Obolenskii to Peterhof (the railroads being on strike).[118]*

For his basic text, Obolenskii drew on the resolutions of the Zemstvo Congress held in Moscow on September 12–15. The *zemtsy* had rejected the Bulygin Duma as entirely inadequate, and offered their own program:

1. Guarantees of personal rights, freedom of speech and publication, freedom of assembly and association;
2. Elections to the Duma on the basis of a universal franchise;
3. The Duma to be given a determining voice in legislation as well as control over the state budget and the administration.[119]

In drafting his text, Obolenskii borrowed not only the contents but also the format of the September Zemstvo Congress resolutions. As a result, the substantive part of the October Manifesto turned out to be little more than a paraphrase of the *zemstvo* demands.

The Tsar spent most of October 15 with Witte and other dignitaries discussing and editing the manifesto. Among those he consulted was Trepov, in whose judgment and good faith he retained unbounded confidence. He forwarded to him Witte's memorandum and the draft of the manifesto, requesting his frank opinion. Even while getting ready to sign the manifesto,

---

*Vitte, *Vospominaniia*, III, 26–27. Witte asserted that he opposed issuing the reform program in the form of a manifesto because such a document, written in succinct and solemn language, could not provide the rationale behind the reforms and might unsettle the population: *Ibid.*, 33. Imperial manifestos were read at church services.

Nicholas must still have contemplated resort to military force, for he also asked Trepov how many days he thought it possible to maintain order in St. Petersburg without bloodshed and whether it was altogether feasible to reassert authority without numerous victims.[120]

In his response the next day (October 16), Trepov agreed in general with Witte's proposals, even as he urged restraint in making concessions to the liberals. To the question whether he could restore order in the capital without risking a massacre, he answered that

> he could give no such guarantee either now or in the future: rebellion [*kramola*] has attained a level at which it was doubtful whether [bloodshed] could be avoided. All that remains is faith in the mercy of God.[121]

Still unconvinced, Nicholas asked Grand Duke Nikolai Nikolaevich to assume dictatorial powers. The Grand Duke is said to have responded that the forces for a military dictatorship were unavailable and that unless the Tsar signed the manifesto he would shoot himself.[122]

On October 17, Witte presented the Tsar with a report *(doklad)* summarizing the rationale for the manifesto which was to be issued jointly with it. Here he restated the conviction that the unrest afflicting Russia resulted neither from specific flaws in the country's political system nor from the excesses of the revolutionaries. The cause had to be sought deeper, "in the disturbed equilibrium between the intellectual strivings of Russia's thinking society and the external forms of its life." The restoration of order, therefore, required fundamental changes. In the margin, Nicholas wrote: "Adopt for guidance."[123]

That evening, having crossed himself, Nicholas signed the manifesto. Its operative part consisted of three articles paralleling the three-part resolution of the September 1905 Zemstvo Congress:

> We impose on the government the obligation to carry out our inflexible will:
> 1. To grant the population inviolable foundations of civil liberty [based] on the principles of genuine inviolability of person, the freedoms of conscience, speech, assembly, and association;
> 2. Without postponing the projected elections to the State Duma, insofar as possible, in view of the short time that remains before the convocation of that body, to include in its work those classes of the population which until now have been entirely deprived of the right to vote, and to extend in the future, through the new legislature, the principle of universal franchise; and,
> 3. To establish as inviolate the rule that no law shall acquire force without the approval of the State Duma and that the people's representatives shall have an effective opportunity to participate in supervising the legality of the actions of the authorities whom We have appointed.*

*G. G. Savich, ed., *Novyi gosudarstevennyi stroi Rossii* (St. Petersburg, 1907), 24–25. The only demand of the September 1905 Zemstvo Congress which the October Manifesto ignored concerned the Duma's control over the budget, but that power was granted to it later in the Fundamental Laws.

Before retiring, Nicholas wrote in his diary: "After such a day, the head has grown heavy and thoughts have become confused. May the Lord help us save and pacify Russia."

The proclamation of the October Manifesto, accompanied by Witte's report of October 17, set off tumultuous demonstrations in all the cities of the Empire: no one had expected such concessions. In Moscow, a crowd of 50,000 gathered in front of the Bolshoi Theater. Thousands also assembled spontaneously in the other cities, singing and cheering. On October 19, the St. Petersburg Soviet voted to end the general strike.[124] The strike also collapsed in Moscow and elsewhere.

Two aspects of the October Manifesto call for comment, for otherwise a great deal of the political history of the last decade of the Imperial regime will be incomprehensible.

The manifesto was extracted from Nicholas under duress, virtually at the point of a gun. For this reason he never felt morally obligated to respect it.

Second, it made no mention of the word "constitution." The omission was not an oversight. Although the claim has been made that Nicholas did not realize he had committed himself to a constitution,[125] contemporary sources leave no doubt that he knew better. Thus, he wrote his mother on October 19 that granting the Duma legislative authority meant "in essence, constitution."[126] Even so, he wanted at all costs to avoid the detested word in order to preserve the illusion that he remained an autocrat. He had been assured by the proponents of liberal reforms that under a constitutional regime he would continue as the exclusive source of laws and that he could always revoke what he had granted.* He believed this explanation because it helped assuage his conscience, which was troubled by the thought that he might have violated his coronation oath. This self-deception—the absurd concept of a constitutional autocrat—would cause no end of trouble in relations between the Crown and the Duma in the years to come.

But when the October Manifesto was proclaimed, these problems were not apparent to the liberals and liberal-conservatives who felt confident that a new era had dawned. Even high police officials were telling each other, only half in jest, that they would soon have nothing left to do.[127]

Witte agreed to assume the chairmanship of the Council of Ministers only on condition that he be permitted to act as a genuine Prime Minister and select his cabinet. Like Ermolov, Kryzhanovskii, and other experienced officials, he felt that a cohesive, disciplined ministry was an absolute necessity in view of the government's imminent confrontation with an elected legislature.[128] Although there was no reason why such a ministry could not consist exclu-

*This is what Witte told Nicholas during his audience of October 9: Verner, *Nicholas II,* 373–74.

sively of bureaucrats, Witte believed that the cabinet would be much more effective if it included some respected public figures.

On November 19, he initiated talks with Dmitrii Shipov, Alexander Guchkov, a prominent industrialist, Prince E. N. Trubetskoi, a professor of philosophy and the brother of the recently deceased rector of Moscow University, and several other public figures.[129] The persons he approached with offers of posts in the government were liberal-conservatives, on good terms alike with the opposition and the bureaucracy. The mere fact of a minister choosing a cabinet was without precedent (and, one may add, without sequel): "For the first time in tsarist history someone beside the tsar had single-handedly dictated the identity of most of the ministers."[130]

The negotiations collapsed within a week. Those whom Witte had approached turned down his offer on the ostensible ground that they could not work together with Peter Durnovo, whom Witte had offered the Ministry of the Interior. Durnovo had once been implicated in a sordid affair involving his mistress and the Spanish Ambassador. He was further mistrusted because of his long-standing connection with the police. But the country was in chaos, virtually in a condition of civil war, and it required an experienced administrator to restore order. Durnovo happened to have the experience and the practical intelligence needed for the job. Witte refused to yield to Durnovo's critics, for he realized that the fate of the reforms hinged on his ability to pacify the country as quickly as possible. But judging by the fate of subsequent attempts to bring public figures into the government, all of which would also fail, it is

10. Crowds celebrating the proclamation of the Manifesto of October 17, 1905.

questionable that Durnovo was anything more than a pretext. The leaders even of the moderate, liberal-conservative opposition feared being accused of betrayal by the liberals and the socialists, for whom the October Manifesto was only a stepping-stone toward a Russian Republic. By entering the government they risked isolating themselves from society without gaining effective influence on policy, for they had no guarantee that the bureaucracy would not use them for its own purposes. But concern over physical safety also played its part: "I would not be candid," Witte wrote in retrospect,

> if I did not voice the impression, perhaps an entirely groundless one, that at the time public figures were frightened of the bombs and the Brownings which were in common use against those in power, and that this was one of the inner motives which whispered to each, in the depths of his soul: "As far as possible from danger."[131]

Witte behaved like a Western Prime Minister not only in selecting his cabinet but in requiring the governors and the military authorities, who in Russia carried administrative responsibilities, to submit daily reports to him. He also established a press bureau to promote favorable news coverage for himself.[132] These practices were not appreciated at the Court, which suspected him of using the crisis to accumulate personal power and make himself into a "Grand Vizier." How insecure Witte's position was may be judged from the fact that in a letter to his mother Nicholas referred to his Prime Minister, who had to deal with Jewish bankers abroad to secure loans for Russia, as a "chameleon" trusted only by "foreign Yids."[133]

The October Manifesto, and the political amnesty act that followed, succeeded in good measure in calming strikes and other forms of radical unrest in the cities. At the same time it unleashed even more violent disorders by right-wing elements against those whom they held responsible for forcing the Tsar to concede something as un-Russian as a constitution, as well as by peasants against landed proprietors. It would be futile to seek any logic in these excesses which would rage for the next two years. They were outbursts of pent-up resentments set off by the breakdown of authority: irrational and even anti-rational, without a program, they represented the Russian *bunt* which Witte feared and hoped to prevent.

The day after the proclamation of the October Manifesto, anti-Jewish pogroms broke out throughout the Empire, accompanied by attacks on students and intellectuals. Panic spread among Jews in the Pale of Settlement and in cities like Moscow where many of them resided on temporary permits: Jews had not experienced such fear since the Middle Ages. There were beatings and killings, accompanied by the looting and burning of Jewish properties. Odessa, which had a record of extreme violence, witnessed the most savage pogrom, in which around five hundred Jews perished. It was common for thirty, forty, or more Jews to lose their lives in a medium-sized city.[134]

Although subjecting Jews to severe discriminations, the Russian Govern-

11. After an anti-Jewish pogrom in Rostov on Don—the burnt out shells of a prayer house and private residence: October 1905.

ment had in the past not encouraged pogroms; it had even repressed them, from fear that anti-Jewish violence would get out of control and victimize Russian landlords and officials. Indeed, the two kinds of violence had a common psychological basis: for although radical intellectuals considered anti-Jewish pogroms "reactionary" and assaults on landlords "progressive," their perpetrators made no such distinction. The spectacle of policemen and Cossacks standing by while mobs beat and robbed Jews the peasants interpreted to mean that the authorities condoned assaults on all non-communal properties and their owners. In 1905–6, in many localities, peasants attacked landed estates of Christian owners under the impression that the Tsar who tolerated anti-Jewish pogroms would not object to pogroms of landlords.* So that, in preventing anti-Jewish violence, the establishment acted in its own best interests.

But in their frustration with the course of events, the monarchists now lost sight of these realities: they not only tolerated anti-Jewish excesses but actively promoted them. After assuming the premiership Witte learned that the Department of Police, using equipment which it had seized from the revolutionaries, secretly printed and distributed appeals for anti-Jewish pogroms—a practice which he stopped but not before it had claimed many lives.[135] Unable to explain what had happened to their idealized Russia in any

---

*A survey of the rural disorders in 1905–6 carried a report from the Central Agricultural Region which stated that the "agrarian movement was caused by the fact that from all ends of Russia at a certain time the villages heard reports that in the cities people beat Yids [*zhidov*] and were allowed to steal their property without being punished": *Agrarnoe dvizhenie v Rossii v 1905–1906 gg.*, I (St. Petersburg, 1908), 48. Similar observations were made about agrarian violence in the Ukraine: *Ibid.*, II, 290.

other way than by blaming alleged villains, among whom Jews occupied the place of honor, the monarchists vented their fury in a manner that encouraged generalized violence. Nicholas shared in this self-destructive delusion when he wrote his mother on October 27 that "nine-tenths of the revolutionaries are Yids [*zhidy*]." This explained and presumably justified popular wrath against them and the other "bad people," among whom he included "Russian agitators, engineers, lawyers."[136]* In December 1905, Nicholas accepted the insignia of the Union of Russian People (Soiuz Russkogo Naroda), a newly formed monarchist organization which wanted the restoration of autocracy and persecution of Jews.

The main cause of the unrest now, however, was not Jews and intellectuals but peasants. The peasantry completely misunderstood the October Manifesto, interpreting it in its own manner as giving the communes license to take over the countryside. Some rural disorders occurred in the spring of 1905, more in the summer, but they exploded only after October 17.[137] Hearing of strikes and pogroms in the cities going unpunished, the peasants drew their own conclusions. Beginning on October 23, when large-scale disorders broke out in Chernigov province, the wave of rural disorders kept on swelling until the onset of winter, reemerging in the spring of 1906 on an even vaster scale. It would fully subside only in 1908 following the adoption of savage repressive measures by Prime Minister Stolypin.

The agrarian revolt of 1905–6 involved surprisingly little personal violence; there is only one authenticated instance of a landlord being killed, although there are reports of the murder of fifty non-communal peasants who were particularly detested.[138] In some localities attacks on estates were accompanied by anti-Jewish pogroms. The principal aim of the *jacquerie* was neither inflicting physical harm nor even appropriating land, but depriving landlords and other non-peasant landowners of the opportunity to earn a livelihood in the countryside—"smoking them out," as the saying went. In the words of one observer: "The [peasant] movement was directed almost exclusively against landed properties and not against the landlords: the peasants had no use whatever for landlords but they did need the land."[139] The notion was simple: force the landlords to abandon the countryside and to sell their land at bargain prices. To this end, the peasants cut down the landlord's forests, sent cattle to graze on his pasture, smashed his machinery, and refused to pay rent. In some places, manors were set on fire. The violence was greatest in the central Russian provinces and the Baltic areas; it was least in the western and southwestern regions, once part of Poland. The most prone to engage in it were village youths and soldiers returning from the Far East; everywhere, the city acted as a stimulant. In their assaults on landlord properties, the peasants did not discriminate between "good" and "bad" landlords—the estates of liberal and revolutionary intellectuals were not spared. Conservative owners who

---

*Two weeks after he had explained the anti-Jewish pogroms as justifiable punishment, he noted with dismay that these pogroms were followed by the destruction of estates of Russian landlords: *KA*, No. 3/22 (1927), 174.

defended themselves suffered less than liberals with a guilty conscience.[140] As we shall see, the peasants had considerable success with their campaign to evict non-peasant landowners from the countryside.

In an effort to stem the agrarian unrest, the government in early November reduced the due installments of the redemption payments (payments for the land given the emancipated serfs in 1861) and promised to abolish them altogether in January 1907, but these measures did little to calm the rural districts.

In 1905 and 1906 peasants by and large refrained from seizing the land they coveted from fear they would not be allowed to keep it. They still expected a grand national repartition of all the non-communal land, but whereas previously they had looked to the Tsar to order it, they now pinned their hopes on the Duma. The quicker they drove the landlords out, they reasoned, the sooner the repartition would take place.

To Nicholas's great disappointment, the October Manifesto failed to pacify Russia. He was impatient with Witte: on November 10 he complained that Witte had promised he would tolerate no violence after the Manifesto had been issued but in fact the disorders had gotten even worse.[141]

The government faced one more trial of strength, this time with the radical left. In this conflict, there was no room for compromises, for the socialists would be satisfied with nothing less than a political and social revolution.

The authorities tolerated the St. Petersburg Soviet, which continued to sit in session although it no longer had a clear purpose. On November 26, they ordered the arrest of Nosar, its chairman. A three-man Presidium (one of whose members was Leon Trotsky) which replaced Nosar resolved to respond with an armed uprising. The first act, which it was hoped would bring about a financial collapse, was an appeal to the people (the so-called Financial Manifesto), issued on December 2, urging them to withhold payments to the Treasury, to withdraw money from savings accounts, and to accept only bullion or foreign currency. The next day, Durnovo arrested the Soviet, putting some 260 deputies (about one-half of its membership) behind bars.[142] Following these arrests a surrogate Soviet assembled under the chairmanship of Alexander Helphand (Parvus), the theoretician of "permanent revolution."[143] On December 6, the St. Petersburg Soviet issued a call for a general strike to begin two days later. The call went unheeded, even though the Union of Unions gave it its blessing.[144]

The socialists were more successful in Moscow. The Moscow Soviet, formed only on November 21 by intellectuals of the three principal socialist parties, decided to press the revolution beyond its "bourgeois" phase. Their followers consisted of semi-skilled workers, many of them employed in the textile industry, professionally and culturally less mature than their counterparts in the capital. The principal force behind this effort was the Moscow Bolshevik Committee.[145] The Moscow rising was the first occasion in the 1905 Revolution when the socialists took the lead. On December 6, the Moscow Soviet voted to begin the following day an armed insurrection for the purpose

12. Members of St. Petersburg Soviet en route to Siberian
exile: 1905. On the left in front, wearing dark coat, Leon
Trotsky.

of overthrowing the tsarist government, convoking a Constituent Assembly,
and proclaiming a democratic republic.*

On December 7, Moscow was paralyzed: the strike was enforced by Soviet
agents who threatened with violence anyone who refused to cooperate. Two
days later, government forces launched an attack on the insurgents; the latter
responded with urban guerrilla tactics. The arrival of the Semenovskii Regiment, which used artillery to disperse the rioters, settled the issue. On December 18 the Executive Committee of the Moscow Soviet capitulated. Over 1,000
people lost their lives in the uprising and whole areas of the ancient capital
were gutted.

There followed an orgy of reprisals in which the police singled out students for beatings. An unknown number of persons involved or suspected of
involvement in the insurrection were summarily executed. Punitive expeditions were sent to the provinces.

In mid-April 1906, Witte resigned, mainly because he felt that the Tsar
no longer showed confidence in him. Before leaving, he managed to obtain for
Russia an international loan of 844 million rubles—the largest ever contracted
up to that time by any country—which had the effect of stabilizing Russia's
finances, damaged by the war and revolution. It further freed the Crown for
some time from dependence on the Duma, which was due to open shortly.[146]
He was replaced by Ivan Goremykin, a bureaucrat beloved by the Court for
his slavish devotion. Appointed to the State Council, the upper house of the
new parliament, Witte spent his remaining years (he died in 1915) dictating
memoirs and hating Goremykin's successor, Peter Stolypin.

*Pankratova *et al.,* eds., *Revoliutsiia 1905–1907 gg. v Rossii,* IV, Pt. 1, 650. The authors of this
program apparently decided on their own that the Assembly would replace the monarchy with a
republic.

The year 1905 marked the apogee of Russian liberalism—the triumph of its program, its strategy, its tactics. It was the Union of Liberation and its affiliates, the *zemstvo* movement and the Union of Unions, that had compelled the monarchy to concede a constitutional and parliamentary regime. Although they would later claim credit, the socialists in general and the Bolsheviks in particular played in this campaign only an auxiliary role: their one independent effort, the Moscow uprising, ended in disaster.

The liberals' triumph, nevertheless, was far from secure. As events would soon show, they were a minority caught in a cross fire of conservative and radical extremism. Concerned like the conservatives to prevent revolution, they were nevertheless beholden to the radicals, since the threat of revolution was the only lever they had to prod the Crown into making still more concessions. Ultimately, this contradiction would cause their demise.

The 1905 Revolution substantially altered Russia's political institutions, but it left political attitudes untouched. The monarchy continued to ignore the implications of the October Manifesto and to insist that nothing had really changed. Its supporters on the right and the mobs they inspired longed to punish those who had humiliated the Tsar. The socialist intelligentsia, for its part, was more determined than ever to exploit the demonstrated weakness of the government and press on with the next, socialist phase of the revolution. The experiences of 1905 had left it more, not less, radical. The terrible weakness of the bonds holding Russia together was revealed to all: but to the government it meant the need for firmer authority, whereas to the radicals it signaled opportunities to destroy the existing order. Not surprisingly, the government and the opposition alike viewed the Duma, not as a vehicle for reaching compromises, but as an arena of combat, and sensible voices, pleading for cooperation, were vilified by both sides.

It is fair to say, therefore, that the 1905 Revolution not only failed to resolve Russia's outstanding problem—estrangement between rulers and ruled—but aggravated it. And to the extent that attitudes rather than institutions or "objective" economic and social realities determine the course of politics, only unbounded optimists could look to the future with any confidence. In fact, Russia had gained only a breathing spell.

EUROPEAN RUSSIA

2

Official Russia

The events we have described occurred in a country that in many respects was unique. Ruled (until 1905) by an absolute monarchy, administered by an all-powerful bureaucracy, and composed of social castes, Russia resembled an Oriental despotism. Its international ambitions, however, and the economic and cultural policies which these ambitions necessitated, injected into Russia a dynamism that was Western in origin. The contradiction between the static quality of the political and social order and the dynamism of the economy and cultural life produced a condition of endemic tension. It lent the country a quality of impermanence, of expectation: as one contemporary French visitor put it, Russia seemed somehow "unfinished."[1]

Until the October Manifesto, Russia was an autocracy *(samoderzhavie).* The old Fundamental Laws defined her sovereign, formally designated Emperor *(Gosudar' Imperator),* as "unlimited" *(neogranichennyi)* and "autocratic" *(samoderzhavnyi).* The first adjective meant that he was subject to no constitutional restraints; the second, that he was not limited institutionally.[2] The Emperor's authority received its original definition in 1716 in the Military Regulation of Peter the Great (Chapter 3, Article 20), which was still in force in 1900:

> His Majesty is an absolute [*samovlastnyi*] monarch, who is not obliged to answer for his actions to anyone in the world but has the power and the

authority to govern his states and lands as a Christian sovereign, in accord with his desire and goodwill [*blagomnenie*].

The Emperor was the exclusive source of laws and ordinances. According to Article 51 of the old Fundamental Laws, "no post [*mesto*] or office [*pravitel'stvo*] of the realm may, on its own initiative, pass a new law, and no law can go into effect without the sanction of the autocratic authority." In practice it proved impossible to enforce such a rigid absolutism in a country with 125 million inhabitants and the world's fifth-largest economy, and in time, increasing discretionary authority was vested in the officialdom. Nevertheless, the autocratic principle was strictly insisted upon and any challenge to it, in word or deed, led to savage persecution.

On the face of it, the autocracy did not differ from the monarchies of *ancien régime* Europe, and it was thus widely regarded, in and out of Russia, as an anachronism. But viewed more closely, in the context of her own past, Russia's absolutism showed peculiar qualities that distinguished it from that of the Bourbons, Stuarts, or Hohenzollerns. European travelers to Muscovy in the sixteenth and seventeenth centuries, when *ancien régime* absolutism stood at its zenith, were impressed by the differences between what they were accustomed to at home and what they saw in Russia.[3] The peculiar features of Russian absolutism in its early form, which lasted from the fourteenth until the late eighteenth century, were marked by the virtual absence of the institution of private property, which in the West confronted royal power with effective limits to its authority. In Russia, the very concept of property (in the Roman sense of absolute dominion over objects) was unknown until introduced in the second half of the eighteenth century by the German-born Catherine II. Muscovite Russia had been run like a private estate, its inhabitants and territories, with everything they contained, being treated as the property of the Crown.

This type of regime has been known since the time of Hobbes as "patriarchal" or "patrimonial."* Its distinguishing feature is the fusion of sovereignty and ownership, the monarch viewing himself and being viewed by his subjects as both ruler of the realm and its proprietor. At its height patrimonial rule in Russia rested on four pillars:

1. Monopoly on political authority
2. Monopoly on economic resources and wholesale trade
3. The ruler's claims to unlimited services from his subjects; absence of individual as well as group (estate) rights
4. Monopoly on public information

Having in the early 1700s laid claim to the status of a European power, Russia had to be able to match her Western rivals in military might, economic

*The origins and evolution of Russian patrimonialism are the theme of my *Russia under the Old Regime* (London and New York, 1974).

productivity, and culture. This requirement forced the monarchy partially to dismantle the patrimonial institutions which had served it well as long as Russia had been essentially an Oriental power competing with other Oriental powers. In the middle of the eighteenth century, the monarchy recognized the right to property in land and in its other forms: the word "property" *(sobstvennost',* from the German *Eigentum)* entered the Russian vocabulary at this time. Concurrently, the Crown began to withdraw from manufacture and trade. Although by Western standards the Russian state of 1900 still loomed large in the national economy, the country by then had a flourishing free market and corresponding capitalist institutions. Even while violating human rights, tsarism respected private property. The government also gradually gave up the claim to unlimited services from its subjects, freeing from compulsory state service first the gentry *(dvorianstvo)* (1762) and a century later (1861) the serfs. It continued to insist on the right to censor publications, but since it did not exercise this right either strictly or consistently, the flow of ideas was not seriously affected, the more so that there were few restrictions on foreign travel.

Thus, by 1900, with one exception, the patrimonial regime was a thing of the past: the exception was the country's political system. While "manumitting" society economically, socially, and culturally, the Crown persisted in refusing to give it a voice in legislation and administration.* It continued to insist that it had the sole right to legislative and executive power, that the Tsar was "unlimited" as well as "autocratic," and that all laws had to emanate from him. The incompatibility of Russia's political constitution with her economic, social, cultural, and even administrative realities was widely recognized at the time as an anomaly by most educated Russians. For, indeed, how could one reconcile the advanced state of Russia's industrial economy and culture with a political system that treated her inhabitants as incapable of governing themselves? Why did a people that had produced a Tolstoy and a Chekhov, a Tchaikovsky and a Mendeleev, need to be ruled by a caste of professional bureaucrats, most of whom had no higher education and many of whom were notoriously corrupt? Why could the Serbians, Finns, and Turks have a constitution and parliament but not the Russians?

On the face of it, these questions seem unanswerable, and yet they did have answers which, in view of what happened after 1917, deserve a hearing.

The educated and economically advanced elements of Russia's population which clamored for political rights were a visible but small minority. The main concern of the Imperial administration was the fifty million Great Russian peasants concentrated in the central provinces, for it was on their tranquillity and loyalty that the internal security of the Empire ultimately depended.†

---

*The *zemstva* and Municipal Councils, organs of local self-government introduced in 1864–70, performed important cultural and economic functions (education, sanitation, etc.) but had no administrative authority.

†Russia was a multinational empire in which the dominant nation, the Great Russians, constituted at the turn of the century 44.4 percent of the population. The majority were other Orthodox Slavs (Ukrainians, 17.8 percent, and Belorussians, 4.7 percent); Poles (6.3 percent); Muslims, mostly Turkic speaking and Sunni (11.1 percent); Jews (4.2 percent); and various Baltic, Caucasian, and Siberian nationalities. The total population of the Empire, according to the first

The peasant had his grievances but they were not political: he could no more imagine a different system of government than a different climate. The existing regime suited him well because he could understand it from his personal experience in the peasant household, which was organized on the same model:

> The sovereign's authority is unlimited—like the father's. This autocracy is only a prolongation of paternal authority. . . . From base to summit, the immense Empire of the North appears, in all its parts, and on all its tiers, constructed on one plan and in one style; all the stones seem to have come out of the same quarry, and the entire building rests on one foundation: patriarchal authority. With this side of her Russia leans toward the old monarchies of the East and decidedly turns away from the modern states of the West, which are all based on feudalism and individualism.[4]

The Great Russian peasant, with centuries of serfdom in his bones, not only did not crave for civil and political rights, but, as will be indicated later on, held such notions in contempt. Government had to be willful and strong— that is, able to exact unquestioned obedience. A limited government, subject to external restraints and tolerant of criticism, seemed to him a contradiction in terms. To the officials charged with administering the country and familiar with these peasant attitudes, a Western-type constitutional order spelled one thing only: anarchy. The peasants would interpret it to mean the release from all obligations to the state which they fulfilled only because they had no choice: no more taxes, no more recruits, and, above all, no more tolerance of private property in land. Even relatively liberal officials regarded the Russian peasants as savages who could be kept in check only as long as they believed that their rulers were made of different "clay."[5] In many respects, the bureaucracy treated its population as the European powers treated their colonials: some observers actually drew parallels between the Russian administration and the British civil service in India.[6] Even the most conservative bureaucrats realized that one could not forever base internal security on coercion and that sooner or later a constitutional regime was bound to come: but they were content to leave this matter to future generations.

The other obstacle to liberalization was the intelligentsia, broadly defined as a category of citizens, mostly upper- and middle-class and educated, in permanent opposition to tsarism, who demanded, in the name of the nation, that the Crown and bureaucracy turn over to them the reins of power. The monarchy and its officialdom regarded this intelligentsia as unfit to govern. Indeed, as events would demonstrate, the intelligentsia vastly underestimated the difficulties of administering Russia: it regarded democracy, not as the product of a slow evolution of institutions and habits, but as man's natural condition, which only the existing despotism prevented from exerting its beneficial influence. Since they had no administrative experience, they tended

census taken in 1897, was 125.7 million (exclusive of Finland, which was a separate Grand Duchy under the Russian Tsar, and the Central Asian Muslim protectorates of Khiva and Bukhara). Of the 55.7 million Great Russians, some 85 percent were peasants.

to confuse governing with legislating. In the eyes of bureaucrats, these professors, lawyers, and publicists, if given access to the levers of power, would promptly let it slip from their hands and unleash anarchy, the only beneficiaries of which would be the radical extremists. Such was the conviction of the Court and its officials. There existed among the intelligentsia sensible, pragmatic individuals, aware of the difficulties of democratizing Russia and willing to cooperate with the establishment, but they were few and under constant assault from the liberals and socialists who dominated public opinion.

The Russian establishment of 1900 believed that the country simply could not afford "politics": it was too vast, ethnically too heterogeneous, and culturally too primitive to allow for the free play of interests and opinions. Politics had to be reduced to administration carried out under the aegis of an impartial arbiter personified in the absolute ruler.

An autocracy required an autocrat: an autocrat not only in terms of formal prerogatives but also by virtue of personality; barring that, at least a ceremonial monarch content to reign while the bureaucracy ruled. As genetic accident would have it, however, on the eve of the twentieth century Russia had the worst of both worlds: a tsar who lacked the intelligence and character to rule yet insisted on playing the autocrat.

In the nineteenth century, strong rulers succeeded weak and weak strong with unexceptional regularity: the vacillating Alexander I was followed by the martinet Nicholas I, whose successor, Alexander II, had a gentle disposition. His son, Alexander III, personified autocracy: a giant of a man who twisted pewter tankards with bare hands, amused company by crashing through locked doors, loved the circus, and played the tuba, he had no qualms about resorting to force. Growing up in his father's shadow, the future Nicholas II displayed early all the traits of a "soft" tsar. He had no lust for power and no love of ceremony: his greatest pleasures came from the hours spent in the company of his wife and children and from outdoor exercise. Though cast in the role of an autocrat, he was actually ideally suited for the role of a ceremonial monarch. He had exquisite manners and great charm: Witte thought Nicholas the best-bred person he had ever met.[7] Intellectually, however, he was something of a simpleton. He treated autocracy as a sacred trust, viewing himself as the trustee of the patrimony which he had inherited from his father and was duty-bound to pass on to his successor. He enjoyed none of its perquisites, confiding to a minister that if he did not think it would harm Russia, he would gladly be rid of his autocratic powers.[8] Indeed, he seemed never as happy as after being compelled in March 1917 to abdicate. He learned early to hide his feelings behind a frozen mask. Although suspicious and even vengeful, he was basically a decent man, simple in his tastes, quiet and shy, disgusted with the ambitions of politicians, the intrigues of officials, and the general morals of the age. He disliked powerful personalities, keeping at arm's

length and sooner or later dismissing his most capable ministers in favor of
amiable and deferential nonentities.

Brought up in a very circumscribed Court atmosphere he was given no
opportunities to mature either emotionally or intellectually. At the age of
twenty-two he impressed one high official as a

> rather attractive officer [*ofitserik*]. He looks well in the white, fur-lined uniform
> of a Guards Hussar, but in general his appearance is so common that it is
> difficult to distinguish him in a crowd. His face is expressionless. His manners
> are simple, but he lacks both elegance and refinement.[9]

Even when Nicholas was twenty-three, according to the same official, Alexander III bullied and treated him as if he were a child. When on one occasion
the Tsarevich dared to defy his father by siding with the bureaucratic opposition, Alexander made his displeasure known by pelting him at dinner with
bread balls.[10] He spoke of his son contemptuously as a "girlie," with a puerile
personality and ideas, entirely unfit for the duties that were awaiting him.[11]

In consequence of his upbringing, the future Nicholas II was unprepared
to ascend the throne. After his father had passed away, he told a minister he
had no idea what was expected of him: "I know nothing. The late sovereign
had not anticipated his death and had not initiated me into anything."*[12] His
instinct told him faithfully to follow his father in all matters, especially in
upholding the ideology and institutions of patrimonial absolutism, and he did
so long as the circumstances permitted.

To make matters worse, Nicholas was dogged by bad fortune from the
day of his birth, which happened to fall on the name day of Job. Everything
he tried turned to dust and he soon acquired the reputation of an "unlucky"
tsar. He came to share this popular belief. It greatly affected his self-
confidence, fostering in him a mood of resignation interrupted by periodic
bursts of stubbornness.

To assert his independence, Nicholas traveled in 1890–91 to the Middle
East and Far East, the latter of which some diplomats viewed as Russia's
proper sphere of influence—a view he shared. The journey almost ended in
tragedy when he was assaulted by a deranged Japanese terrorist.

On the day of his coronation in 1895, a terrible accident occurred when
a crowd estimated at 500,000, assembled at Khodynka Field outside Moscow
to receive souvenirs, panicked, trampling or choking to death nearly 1,400
people.[13] Ignoring the tragedy, the Imperial couple attended the Coronation
Ball that evening. Both events were considered an evil omen.

Perhaps because it was known how badly the high-handed Alexander III
had treated his son, on coming to the throne in 1894 Nicholas II enjoyed the

---

*Compare this with the strikingly similar remark of Louis XVI. On being informed of his
father's death, he exclaimed: "What a burden! And I have been taught nothing! It seems as though
the universe were about to fall upon me": Pierre Gaxotte, *The French Revolution* (London-New
York, 1932), 71.

13. The future Nicholas II as tsarevich (in front, wearing
white uniform) entertained by his uncle, the Grand Duke
Nikolai Nikolaevich (on his right).

reputation of a liberal. He quickly disabused these expectations. In an address
to a *zemstvo* delegation in January 1895, he dismissed talk of liberalization as
"senseless dreams" and pledged to "safeguard the principle of autocracy as
firmly and steadfastly" as his late father had done.[14] This ended his brief
political honeymoon. Although he rarely pronounced on political matters, he
made it no secret that he regarded Russia as the dynasty's "patrimony." One
example of this attitude was his decision to give three million rubles paid
Russia by Turkey as part of a peace settlement as a present to the Prince of
Montenegro, at the request of two Russian grand dukes married to the Prince's
daughters. It was with great difficulty that he was dissuaded from disposing
of money belonging to the Russian Treasury in such a cavalier manner.[15] It
was not the only instance of anachronistic patrimonialism in his reign.

Given his diffident personality and lack of appetite for power, Nicholas
might have proven willing to come to terms with the opposition were it not
for his spouse, who was destined to play a major and very negative role in the
final years of the old regime. A granddaughter, on her mother's side, of Queen
Victoria, Alexandra Fedorovna (Alix) was born in the German principality of
Hesse and in Russia was always looked upon, by society and the masses, as
"the German woman."* Haughty and cold, she managed in no time to alienate
St. Petersburg society: as her estrangement increased, her entourage became

---

*In fact, Nicholas himself had hardly any Russian blood in his veins: since the eighteenth
century, through intermarriage with German and Danish families, Russian monarchs were Russians
in name only. Their opponents liked to taunt them as the "Gottorp-Holstein" dynasty, which,
genealogically speaking, was not far from the truth.

limited to a confidante, Anna Vyrubova, and, later, Rasputin. She was rarely seen to smile and in photographs usually looks away from the camera. Suffering from headaches and what she believed to be a weak heart, she developed an addiction to pills. She had a strong inclination to mysticism. The French Ambassador, Maurice Paléologue, left a thumbnail sketch of Alexandra: "Moral disquiet, constant sadness, vague longing, alternation between excitement and exhaustion, constant thought given to the invisible and supernatural, credulousness, superstition."[16] Isolated at the Imperial residence in Tsarskoe Selo from everyone except courtiers, she developed a faith in a mythical Russian "people," who, it was her firm conviction, boundlessly loved the Imperial family. She mistrusted everyone else, including Nicholas's relatives, whom she suspected of scheming to remove him from the throne.

None of which would have mattered much were it not that the Empress saw herself obliged to compensate for her husband's vacillating character by keeping him from making political concessions and eventually taking a direct hand in appointments: she frequently exercised a wife's prerogative of turning her husband against people to whom, for one reason or another, she had taken a dislike. Treating Nicholas as a good-natured child (she liked to draw him as a baby in arms), she manipulated her husband by playing on his sense of duty and his suspicious nature. Although born and raised in Western Europe, she quickly assimilated the most extreme patrimonial attitudes of her adopted country. Time and again she reminded Nicholas of his heritage: "You and Russia are one and the same," she would exhort him.[17] After giving birth to a male heir, she made it her mission in life to safeguard unalloyed the institution of autocratic monarchy until the time when he would ascend the throne. By her actions she greatly contributed to widening the breach between the monarchy and society until it became unbridgeable: by 1916, even the staunchest monarchists, including many grand dukes, would turn against her and plot to have her removed. Her historic role in this respect was not dissimilar to Marie Antoinette's.

To humor her, Nicholas usually followed his wife's advice, but not slavishly; on rare occasion he could even oppose her wishes. They were a very loving couple, completely devoted to one another and usually of one mind. Both despised "public opinion," which they identified with St. Petersburg society and the intelligentsia and viewed as an artificial "wall [*sredostenie*] erected to separate from them the adoring people."* It has been said that when Nicholas used the word "intelligentsia" he made the same face as when pronouncing the word "syphilis." He thought it should be erased from the Russian dictionary.[18]

Given the misfortune that dogged Nicholas in all his endeavors, it caused no great surprise that it also afflicted his domestic life. His wife bore four daughters in succession but there was no male heir. In desperation, she turned

---

*A. A. Mossolov, *At the Court of the Last Tsar* (London, 1935), 127–31. Witte recalls that when he used the expression "public opinion" in the Tsar's presence, Nicholas responded with passion: "And what is public opinion to me?": S.Iu. Vitte, *Vospominaniia*, II (Moscow, 1960), 328.

to charlatans, one of whom, a French physician by the name of Dr. Philippe, assured her that she was pregnant with a boy. Alexandra expanded in bulk until a medical examination in the ninth month revealed she had had a sympathetic pregnancy.[19] When in 1904 a boy was finally born, he turned out to suffer from hemophilia, an incurable disease of which she had been the transmitter. The blow deepened Alexandra's mysticism, but also her determination to see the child, christened Alexis, resplendent on the throne as Tsar of All the Russias.

The courtiers surrounding Nicholas II reinforced these preferences for anachronistic political practices. At the Tsar's Court immense stress was laid on decorum and the observance of ritualistic forms:

The circle of intimates [of the Imperial family] consisted of dull-witted, igno-rant remnants of *dvoriane* clans, lackeys of the aristocracy, who had lost the freedom of opinion and conviction, as well as the traditional notions of estate honor and pride. All these Voeikovs, Nilovs, Mosolovs, Apraksins, Fedoseevs, Volkovs—colorless, untalented slaves—stood at the entrances and exits of the Imperial Palace and protected the integrity of autocratic power. This honorary duty they shared with the Fredericks, Benckendorffs, Korfs, Grotens, Grün-walds—pompous, smug [Baltic] Germans who had sunk firm roots at the Russian Court and wielded a peculiar kind of influence behind the stage. The highly placed lackeys were united by a profound contempt for the Russian people. Many of them did not know Russia's past, living in a kind of dumb ignorance of the needs of the present and indifference for the future. For the majority of them, conservative thought meant simply mental inertia and immo-bility. For people of this ilk, autocracy had lost sense as a political system, because their mental level was incapable of rising to general ideas. Their life flowed from one episode to another, from decorations to shifts on the ladder of ranks and honors. From time to time, the flow of events for them was interrupted by some shock—an uprising, a revolutionary upheaval, or a terror-ist attempt. These portentous symptoms spread among them fear, even alarm, but never aroused their deep interest or attracted their serious attention. In the final analysis, everything reduced itself to hopes placed on a new energetic administrator or skillful police chief.[20]

The monarchy governed Russia with the assistance of five institutions: the civil service, the security police, the gentry, the army, and the Orthodox Church.

The bureaucracy *(chinovnichestvo)* descended from the household staff of medieval princes, originally slaves, and it retained into the twentieth century strong traces of its origin. It continued to act, first and foremost, as the personal staff of the monarch rather than as the civil service of the nation. Its members had little sense of the state *(gosudarstvo)* as an entity separate from and superior to the monarch *(gosudar')* and his bureaucracy.[21]

On being admitted into the service, a Russian official swore loyalty, not to the state or the nation, but to the person of the ruler. He served entirely at the pleasure of the monarch and his own immediate superiors. Bureaucratic executives had the authority to dismiss subordinates without being required to furnish reasons and without giving the officials concerned the opportunity to defend themselves. The Service Regulations denied a discharged official all means of redress:

> Officials who, in the opinion of their superiors, are incapable of carrying out their obligations, or who, for whatever reason, are [deemed] unreliable [*neblagonadëzhnye*], or who have committed a misdemeanor their superior is aware of but which cannot be factually proven, may be discharged from the service by qualified superiors at the latters' discretion. . . . Officials who have been simply dismissed from the service at the discretion of their superiors without being informed of the reasons cannot lodge a complaint against such action. Their petitions for reinstatement in their previous posts or for a court trial not only must be left without action but must not even be accepted by the Governing Senate of His Imperial Majesty's Chancery. . . .*

As if to emphasize that civil servants were descended from bonded domestics, an official, no matter how prominent, could not resign from the service without permission. As late as 1916, ministers, most of whom by then were at odds with the Tsar's policies, had to request his permission to quit, which in a number of cases he refused to grant—a situation difficult for a European even to imagine.

Except for judges and certain categories of specialists, Russian officials were not required to furnish proof of educational qualifications. Unlike contemporary Western Europe, where appointment to the civil service called for either a school diploma or the passing of an examination, or both, in Russia admission requirements were perfunctory. To qualify for the post of Chancery Servitor *(Kantseliarskii sluzhitel'),* the stepping-stone to the lowest rung on the service career ladder, a candidate had only to demonstrate the ability to read and write grammatically and to have mastered the rudiments of mathematics. For advancement to the next higher rank, he had to pass an examination that tested for knowledge expected of a graduate of a grammar school. Once established in the lowest civil service rank, an official or *chinovnik* was not obliged to demonstrate any further competence, and moved up the career ladder in accord with the rules of seniority and the recommendations of his superior. Thus, Imperial officials were appointed and advanced on the basis of undefined criteria which in practice centered on complete loyalty to the dynasty, blind obedience in the execution of orders, and unquestioning acceptance of the status quo.

*The rules governing the Russian bureaucracy were formalized in Volume III of the Code of Laws: *Ustav o sluzhbe po opredeleniiu ot pravitel'stva: Izdanie 1896 goda, Svod Zakonov Rossiiskoi Imperii* (St. Petersburg, 1913). All further references are to this edition. In Imperial Russia the term *neblagonadëzhnyi* had legal standing and could lead to the dismissal from any state institution, including the universities. It was formally defined by Minister of the Interior N. P. Ignatev, in 1881: P. A. Zaionchkovskii, *Krizis samoderzhaviia na rubezhe 1870–1880kh godov* (Moscow, 1964), 395.

As personal servants of the Tsar, officials of the Imperial civil service stood above the law. A *chinovnik* could be indicted and put on trial only with the permission of his superior.[22] Lacking such authorization, the judiciary was powerless to indict officials. Permission to try officials was rarely forthcoming, and this for two reasons. Since all appointments were made, at any rate in theory, by the Tsar, the failure of a bureaucrat properly to perform his duties reflected adversely on the Tsar's judgment. Second, there was always the risk that if he were allowed to defend himself in court, the accused official could implicate his superiors. In practice, therefore, guilty officials were quietly transferred to another post or, if sufficiently distinguished, promoted to impressive but meaningless positions in the Senate or Council of State.[23] In such matters the Tsar himself had to bow to custom. Following a train accident in which he almost lost his life, Alexander III wanted to bring to trial the Minister of Transport. He was ultimately dissuaded on the grounds that a public trial of a minister who had held his post for fourteen years would mean that he had "undeservedly enjoyed the confidence of the monarch"[24]—that is, that the Tsar had shown poor judgment. In the eyes of some contemporaries, the unaccountability of the Russian officialdom to the law or any body external to itself represented the principal difference between the Russian and Western European civil services. In fact, it was only one of many manifestations of the patrimonial spirit still embedded in the Russian state.

The Russian bureaucracy, especially in the last years of the monarchy, had in its ranks many well-educated and dedicated officials. These were especially numerous in the ministries and the agencies located in St. Petersburg. Bernard Pares, the English historian of Russia, on his frequent visits there before 1917, observed that when out of uniform a *chinovnik* often turned out to be an intellectual, troubled by the same thoughts that agitated society at large. In uniform, however, while performing his duties, he was expected to act haughtily and insolently.* The conditions of service, especially the absence of security, did, in fact, encourage servility toward superiors and rudeness toward everyone else. To the outside world, a *chinovnik* was expected to act with complete self-assurance:

> Always the underlying intent was to present the "Government" as an all-wise, deliberate and ultimately infallible group of servants of the state, selflessly working in unison with the monarch for the best interests of Russia.[25]

An essential element of this self-image was secrecy, which helped maintain the illusion of an authority that knew neither discord nor failures. There was nothing that the bureaucracy dreaded more than *glasnost'*, or the open con-

---

*Bernard Pares, *Russia and Reform* (London, 1907), 328. According to one contemporary source, some Russian officials believed that treating their own population brutally enhanced the country's standing abroad. Western powers, which provided Russia with loans, were said to be impressed by strength: "the more cruelly affairs were conducted inside Russia, the more her respect grew in Europe": *Die Judenpogrome in Russland,* I (Köln-Leipzig, 1910), 230. There is, indeed, a relevant Russian proverb: "Beat your own people and others will fear you."

duct of public affairs, for which public opinion had been clamoring since the middle of the nineteenth century.

Beginning in 1722, when Peter the Great introduced the Table of Ranks, Russia's officialdom was divided into hierarchic grades called *chiny,* of which nominally there were fourteen but in fact only twelve, Ranks 11 and 13 having fallen into disuse. It had been Peter's intention that as officials qualified for higher responsibilities they would receive the rank appropriate to the office they occupied. But the system quickly became perverted, with the result that Russia acquired a civil service ranking system that was probably unique in the world. To gain the support of the bureaucracy for her dubious claim to the throne, Catherine II introduced in the 1760s the principle of automatic promotion: henceforth, the holder of a *chin* was advanced to the next higher grade on the basis of seniority, after he had held a given rank a specified length of time, regardless of whether or not he was assigned greater responsibilities. Unlike the usual practice in bureaucratic establishments where a person moves up in grade as he assumes higher duties, in Imperial Russia he rose in grade more or less automatically, without regard to his functions: promotion was not from post to post, but from rank to rank.[26] This made the Russian civil service a closed caste: with minor exceptions, to be eligible for a government position one had to hold *chin.* [27] Ordinary subjects, no matter how well qualified, were excluded from participating in the country's administration, except in the rare instances of direct appointment by the Tsar. Only those willing and able to make it a lifelong career were able to join the government. Others were barred from public service and therefore deprived of opportunities to acquire administrative experience.

Appointments to the top four ranks (of which in 1903 there were 3,765 holders)[28] could not be attained by regular advancement: since they entitled to hereditary nobility, they were made personally by the Tsar. Ranks 14 through 5 were open to regular career promotions, procedures for which were prescribed in minute detail. In most cases, a prospective functionary of non-noble origin began his career as a Chancery Servitor in some government bureau. This post carried no *chin.* He remained in it anywhere from one to twelve years, depending on his social status and education, before becoming eligible for promotion to Rank 14: hereditary nobles with completed secondary education served only one year, whereas boys discharged from the Imperial Choir because of a change in voice had to serve twelve. Once installed, a *chinovnik* worked his way up the career ladder one rung at a time. The Service Regulations determined how long an official remained in each rank (three years in the lower ones, four in the higher), but advancement could be speeded up for outstanding performance. In theory, it required twenty-four years from one's first appointment until the attainment of the highest career rank (*Chin* 5). Ranks 14 through 5 bestowed personal (non-hereditary) ennoblement.

One could qualify for direct entry into the civil service by virtue of either appropriate social status or education. Sons of nobles *(dvoriane)* and personal nobles *(lichnye dvoriane)* were the only ones eligible for admission to Rank 14 or higher regardless of education. Others qualified by virtue of educational attainments. In theory, civil service careers were open to all subjects without distinction of nationality or religion, but an exception was made for Jews, who were ineligible unless they had a higher education, which in practice meant a medical degree. Catholics were subject to quotas. Lutherans were very much in demand and a high proportion of the officials in St. Petersburg chanceries were Baltic Germans. Excluded, unless they met the educational criteria (university degree or completed secondary schooling with honors), were members of the urban estates, peasants, and all persons who had received their secondary education abroad.

While on duty, holders of rank (which included university professors) were required to wear uniforms, the cut and color of which was prescribed in fifty-two articles of the Service Regulations. They had to be addressed in a specified form appropriate to their rank, the titles being translated from German. Each rank had its perquisites, which included minutely regulated precedence rules.

Remuneration consisted of salary, expense accounts, and living quarters or a suitable housing allowance. Salary differentials were enormous, officials in Rank 1 receiving over thirty times the pay of those in Rank 14. Few officials held landed properties or had other sources of private income: in 1902, even of those in the four topmost ranks, only one in three owned land.[29] On leaving the service, like faithful domestics high officials usually were given monetary rewards by the Tsar; thus, Minister of Justice Nicholas Maklakov received on his retirement 20,000 rubles, Minister of the Interior Peter Durnovo, 50,000, and the Court's favorite, Prime Minister Ivan Goremykin, 100,000.[30] For distinguished service there were also other rewards, notably medals of various designations, strictly graded in order of importance and precedence: their description occupies no fewer than 869 paragraphs in the Service Regulations.

The civil service was thus a closed caste, separated from the rest of society, access to which and promotion within which were strictly regulated on the basis of social origin, education, and seniority. This caste—225,000 strong in 1900, including members of the police and the gendarmerie—was a personal staff of the monarch subject neither to the laws of the land nor to any external supervision. It served at the monarch's pleasure. The institution was a carryover from medieval times, before the emergence of a distinction between the person of the ruler and the institution of the state.

The legacy of patrimonialism was also apparent in the structure and operations of the principal executive agencies, the ministries.

In the medieval principalities of northern Russia, where political authority was exercised by virtue of ownership, administration had been divided into *puti* or "paths." Arranged geographically (territorially) rather than functionally, they served first and foremost the purposes of economic exploitation. The men in charge were stewards responsible for a given area. They had no corporate existence and they did not act as a body. Such practices survived in Russia's administrative structure after the introduction of ministries in 1802. The administration of Russia in the nineteenth century was organized in a vertical manner, with almost no lateral links, the lines of command converging at the top, in the person of the monarch. This arrangement hampered cooperation among the ministries and hence the formulation of a coherent national policy, but it had the advantage of preventing the officialdom from acting in concert and thereby impinging on the Tsar's autocratic prerogatives.

With one exception, the Ministry of the Interior, Russian ministries did not much differ in structure and operation from the corresponding institutions in the West. But in contrast to the West, Russia had no cabinet and no Prime Minister. There existed a so-called Committee of Ministers, which also included heads of other central agencies, with a casually appointed chairman, but it was a body with no authority. Attempts to give Russia a regular cabinet in the 1860s and again in the 1880s had no success because the Court feared such a body would weaken its authority. The very idea of a cabinet or even ministerial consultations was regarded as subversive. "Unlike other absolute monarchs," a French observer wrote in the 1880s,

> the Russian emperors have never had prime ministers. From instinct or system, in order to retain, in deed as well as in theory, their authority unimpaired, they all undertake to be their own prime ministers. . . . Russia, nevertheless, does feel the need of a homogeneous cabinet, as a means toward that unity of direction in which the government is so deficient . . . such a council, with or without official premiership, would of necessity modify all the relations between sovereign and ministers, as its members, collectively responsible, would be fatally led to assume toward the Emperor a more independent attitude. They would gradually feel responsible before society and public opinion no less than before the sovereign, who might thus slip into the part of a constitutional monarch, without the official restraint of either constitution or parliament. In fact, this reform, seemingly unassuming, would almost amount to a revolution . . .[31]

This, as we have seen, is precisely what happened in 1905, when, forced to present a united front against the newly created Duma, the monarchy consented to the creation of a Council of Ministers under a chairman who was Prime Minister in all but name. But even though it had to make this concession, it never reconciled itself to this arrangement and in a few years reverted to the old practices.

Until 1905, the ministers reported directly to the Tsar and received from him their instructions: they had no agreed-upon common policy. Such a practice inevitably gave rise to confusion, since the Tsar was bound to issue them incompatible or even contradictory orders. Under this arrangement, each minister sought the Tsar's ear for his own ends, without regard for the concerns of his colleagues. Foreign policy was made by at least three ministries

(Foreign Affairs, Finance, and War), while domestic matters were caught up in constant feuding between the ministries of the Interior and Finance. Essentially, each ministry acted as it saw fit, subject to the Tsar's personal approval. "Being responsible to the Emperor alone, and that only individually, [the ministers] really [were] mere secretaries, almost private clerks of the Tsar."[32]

Russian ministers and their associates had an even lower opinion of their status. Their diaries and private communications are filled with complaints about the medieval arrangement under which the country was treated as the Emperor's private domain and they as his stewards. They were bitter about the way they were treated, about the peremptory manner with which the Tsar gave them instructions, and angry over the absence of regular ministerial consultations. Peter Valuev, Minister of the Interior under Alexander II, referred to Russia's ministers as the "sovereign's servants"—*les grandes domestiques*—rather than *les grandes serviteurs de l'état,* whose relationship to him was "Asiatic, semi-slave or primitively patriarchal."[33] It is this situation that one official had in mind when he said that Russia had "departments" *(vedomstva)* but no government *(pravitel'stvo).* [34] Such was the price Russia had to pay for maintaining so late into the modern era the regime of patrimonial monarchy.

Within their bureaus, ministers enjoyed immense power: one Russian compared them to Ottoman pashas lording over their *pachalics.* [35] Each had in the provinces a network of functionaries responsible only to him and not to the provincial governors.[36] They could hire and fire employees at will. They also had great latitude in disposing of the moneys budgeted for their ministries.

Because Russia was so visibly run by a bureaucracy, it is possible to overestimate the extent to which the country was bureaucratized. The Russian civil service was unusually top-heavy, with a high proportion of the bureaucracy located in St. Petersburg. The Empire was relatively under-administered.[37]

Such neglect of the provincial administration was due to fiscal constraints: Russia simply could not afford the expenditures required to administer properly a country of such distances and poor communications. After Peter I had taken Livonia from Sweden he discovered that the Swedes had spent as much on running this small province as his government allowed for administering the whole Empire: this meant that any hope of adopting Swedish administrative models had to be given up.[38] In 1763, proportionate to her territory, Prussia had nearly one hundred times as many officials as Russia.[39] Around 1900, the proportion of administrators in relation to the population in Russia was almost one-third that of France and one-half that of Germany.[40] Because of inadequate resources, Russians adopted a very simple model of administration. They placed in each province a powerful governor, with broad discretionary powers, and deployed across the country military garrisons to help him preserve order. There were also small contingents of police and gendarmerie, and agents of such ministries as Finance, Justice, and War. But essentially the countryside was self-administering through the institution of the peasant commune, which was held collectively responsible for the payment of taxes and delivery of military recruits, and the canton or *volost'*, which performed simple judiciary and administrative functions. None of this cost the Treasury anything.

This meant, however, that the authority of the Imperial Government, for all practical purposes, stopped at the eighty-nine provincial capitals where the governors and their staff had offices: below that level yawned an administrative vacuum. Neither the district *(uezd)*, into which provinces were subdivided, nor the *volost'*, the principal unit of rural administration, had any regular agents of the central government: these showed up periodically, on forays as it were, to carry out specific missions, usually to collect tax arrears, and then disappeared from view. Indeed, the *volost'* itself was not a territorial but a social entity, since it included only peasants and not the members of the other estates living within its territory. Some intellectuals and officials, aware of the anomaly of such an arrangement, urged the government to introduce as the lowest administrative unit an all-estate *volost'*, but this advice was ignored because the authorities preferred that the peasants remain isolated and self-governing. In the words of one experienced bureaucrat, there was in Russia "no common unifying authority comparable to the German *Landrat* or French *souspréfet,* capable of coordinating policies in the interest of central authority":

> There was no apparatus of local administration but only officials of various [central] agencies: financial, judiciary, forestry, postal, etc., who were unconnected, or else the executive organs of various types of self-government, dependent more on the voters than on the government. There was no common binding authority.[41]

The absence of government agents in the small towns and the countryside would make itself painfully felt after 1905, when, attempting to win majorities in the new parliament, the monarchy found it had no mechanism to mobilize potential supporters against the ubiquitous liberal and radical intelligentsia.

In terms of its attitudes and programs, the Imperial bureaucracy can be divided into three groups.

The majority of *chinovniki,* especially those serving in the provinces, were careerists pure and simple, who joined to benefit from the prestige and privileges that went with government service. Monarchists in 1916, in 1917 most of them would place themselves at the disposal first of the Provisional Government and then of the Bolsheviks. They usually supplemented their meager salaries with bribes and tips.* It is difficult to speak of their having an ideology

---

*H.-J. Torke makes the interesting suggestion that the notorious venality of Russian officials was at least in part due to their self-identification with the state and the resulting difficulty of distinguishing private property from public: *Jahrbücher,* 227.

or mentality, save to say that they saw themselves as responsible for protecting the state from "society."*

There was a wide gulf separating the provincial officialdom from that ensconced in the ministries and chanceries of St. Petersburg. One historian notes that "men who started work in the provinces rarely moved to central agencies. In the provinces at mid-century, only at the highest levels do we find any significant group that had started work in the center."[42] This situation did not change in the final decades of the old regime.

It is in the higher ranks of St. Petersburg officialdom that one can discover something resembling an ideology. Before the Revolution this was not considered a subject worthy of investigation, since the intelligentsia considered it to be obvious that Russia's bureaucrats were a herd of self-seeking dunderheads. Events were to prove the intelligentsia a poor judge in such matters: for on coming to power in February 1917, it allowed the state and society to disintegrate in a matter of two or at most four months—the same state and society that the bureaucrats had somehow managed to keep intact for centuries. Clearly, they knew something that the intelligentsia did not. The Menshevik Theodore Dan had the honesty to admit in retrospect that "the extreme reactionaries of the tsarist bureaucracy much sooner and better grasped the driving forces and the social content of [the] coming revolution than all the Russian 'professional revolutionaries,' and, in particular, the Russian Marxist Social Democrats."[43]

Theodore Taranovsky distinguishes in the upper layers of the Russian bureaucracy toward the end of the nineteenth century two principal groups: one which espoused the ideal of a police state *(Polizeistaat),* the other which wanted a state based on the rule of law *(Rechtsstaat).*[44] They agreed that Russia required firm autocratic authority, but the former stressed repression, while the latter preferred to bring society into some kind of limited partnership. Their differing programs derived from different perceptions of the population: the right-wing conservatives saw it as a savage mob while the liberal-conservatives felt it could be nurtured and taught citizenship. By and large, the more liberal bureaucrats were better educated, many of them having completed legal and other professional training. The conservatives tended to be administrative "generalists," lacking in professional skills or higher education.

The advocates of the police state saw Russia as under permanent siege by her inhabitants, believed ready to pounce and tear the country apart at the slightest hint that government authority was weakening. To prevent this from happening, Russia had to be ruled with an iron hand. They were not troubled by charges of arbitrary behavior: that which their opponents labeled "arbitrariness" *(proizvol)* they saw as the correct technique for managing a country as spacious and undisciplined as Russia. Law to them was an instrument of

---

*It must be noted, however, that in the lower ranks of the bureaucracy it was not uncommon to find officials who resented the existing regime and sympathized with the opposition: Sergius A. Korff, *Autocracy and Revolution in Russia* (New York, 1923), 13–14.

administration rather than a higher principle binding both rulers and ruled, in the spirit of the police chief of Nicholas I who hearing complaints that his agents were acting unlawfully retorted, "Laws are written for subjects, not for the government!"[45] They treated all criticism of the bureaucracy by "society" as camouflage to disguise the critics' political ambitions.

The police state, as they conceived it, was an eighteenth-century mechanism, managed by professionals, which provided minimum opportunity for the free play of political, social, and economic forces. They objected to every institution and procedure that disturbed administrative unity and the smooth functioning of the bureaucratic chain of command, such as the independent judiciary and organs of local self-government. To the extent that such institutions had a right to exist, they had to be subordinated to the bureaucracy. They opposed *glasnost'* on the grounds that revelations of dissent within the government or admission of failure would undermine its most precious asset, namely prestige. Centralized bureaucratic administration was in their view unavoidable until such time as "the population's general level has risen, until there [are] in the provinces enough genuine public servants, until society [has developed] intelligent attitudes toward the nation's problems."[46] Officials of this school pleaded for time without indicating how, under their strict tutelage, the population could ever develop "intelligent attitudes toward the nation's problems." They wanted to preserve the existing social caste system, with the leading role assigned to the landed gentry and the peasantry kept isolated. Their headquarters were in the Ministry of the Interior.

The bureaucratic conservatives and their supporters on the extreme right wing of public opinion relied heavily on anti-Semitism as an instrument of politics. Although modern anti-Semitism originated in France and Germany, it is in Russia that it first entered official ideology. To the conservatives, Jews presented the single most dangerous threat to that political and social stability which they regarded as the main concern of state policy. Jews destabilized Russia in two capacities: as revolutionaries and as capitalists. The police authorities were convinced that they formed the principal element in the revolutionary parties: Nicholas II only echoed them when he claimed that nine-tenths of the revolutionaries and socialists in Russia were Jews.[47] But Jews also upset the socioeconomic equilibrium of Russia by introducing free market operations. The obvious contradiction in the claim that the members of the same religious group were both beneficiaries and mortal foes of capitalism was resolved in the *Protocols of the Elders of Zion,* a scurrilous forgery concocted at the end of the nineteenth century by the tsarist police, which claimed that in the pursuit of their alleged historic mission—the destruction of Christianity and world domination—Jews resorted to every conceivable means, even to the extent of organizing pogroms against themselves. The monarchists, "lacking a monarch who could have embodied the autocratic principle with vigor and infectious conviction, . . . had only anti-Semitism and the notion of universal evil, with the Jews as its carriers, to make sense of a world which was escaping their control and intellectual grasp."[48] The infamous Beilis case, prosecuted in the courts in 1913, in which an obscure Kievan Jew was charged with the "ritual murder" of a Ukrainian youth, was the culmination of this desperate search for a scapegoat.* Although (with some minor exceptions) the Imperial Government did not encourage, let alone instigate, anti-Jewish pogroms, its unconcealed policy of discrimination against Jews and tolerance of anti-Semitic propaganda conveyed to the population the impression that it approved of them.

Liberal-conservative bureaucrats rejected such a system as hopelessly out of date. In their judgment, a country as complex and dynamic as modern Russia could not be governed by bureaucratic whim, in disregard of the law and without popular involvement. The liberal-conservative trend in the bureaucracy first emerged, in the 1860s, at the time of the Great Reforms. It was reinforced by the emancipation of serfs in 1861, which deprived the monarchy of the services of 100,000 serf-owning landlords who had previously performed on its behalf, free of charge, a variety of administrative functions in the countryside. At that time P. A. Valuev was of the opinion that

> already now, in the conduct of administration, the Sovereign is Autocrat in name only; that is, autocracy manifests itself only in bursts, in flashes. But given the growing complexity of the administrative mechanism, the more important questions of government elude, and must of necessity elude, the Sovereign's immediate attention.[49]

Which was to say that the sheer mass of administrative business required authority to be more widely distributed.

The liberal-conservatives conceded that the Tsar had to remain the exclusive source of laws, but they insisted that laws, once promulgated, were binding on all the officials included. This was the distinguishing quality of the *Rechtsstaat*. They also had a higher opinion of Russia's capacity for self-government and wanted the educated part of the population to be brought into participation in a consultative capacity. They disliked the estate system as an anachronism, preferring that the country move toward common and egalitarian citizenship. They attached particular importance to the gradual elimination of the special status and isolation of the peasantry. The liberal-conservatives had their bastions in the Council of State (which framed laws), the Senate (the highest court of appeals), and the ministries of Justice and Finance.[50]

Historic developments favored the liberal bureaucracy. The rapid growth of the Russian economy in the second half of the nineteenth century alone raised doubts about the feasibility of running Russia in a patrimonial manner.

---

*On this, see Maurice Samuel, *Blood Accusation* (New York, 1966). It is testimony, however, of the independence of the Russian judiciary of the time that notwithstanding immense pressure brought on it by the bureaucracy and the Church, the court acquitted Beilis. The role of anti-Semitism in late Imperial politics is dealt with in Heinz-Dietrich Loewe's *Antisemitismus und Reaktionäre Utopie* (Hamburg, 1978), which lays stress on the identification of Jews with international capital, and Hans Rogger's *Jewish Policies and Right-wing Politics in Imperial Russia* (Berkeley, Calif., 1986).

It was very well for Konstantin Pobedonostsev, the main ideologue of patrimonial conservatism, to argue that in Russia "there cannot exist separate
authorities [*vlasti*], independent of the central state authority [*vlast'*]."[51] This
principle may have been enforceable in a static, agrarian society. But in a
capitalist economy such as developed in Russia in the late nineteenth century
with the government's active encouragement, every corporation, every business entrepreneur, every commercial bank made, on its own, decisions affecting the state and society: they acted as "independent authorities" even under
the autocratic regime. The conservatives instinctively understood this and
resisted economic development, but they fought a losing battle inasmuch as
Russia's international standing and fiscal stability had come increasingly to
depend on the growth of industry, transport, and banking.

Perhaps the monarchy would have moved decisively in the direction
favored by its more liberal servants were it not for the revolutionary movement. The wave of terror that struck Russia in 1879–81 and again after 1902
had no parallel in the world to that time or since. Each terrorist assault played
into the hands of those advocating repression. In August 1881, Alexander III
put in place a set of emergency rules that made it possible for the officials in
turbulent areas to impose martial law and govern as they would enemy territory. These laws, which remained on the statute books until the demise of
the monarchy, foreshadowed some of the salient features of the modern
police state.[52] They greatly enhanced the arbitrary power of the right-wing
bureaucrats, offsetting the gains of the liberals from economic and educational progress.

The contrary pulls to which the late Imperial Government was subjected
can be illustrated in the example of legal institutions. In 1864, Alexander II
gave Russia her first independent judiciary system, with juries and irremovable
judges. It was a reform that the conservatives found especially galling because
it created a formal enclave of decision-making independent of the monarch
and his officials. Pobedonostsev accused the new courts of violating the principle of unity of authority: in Russia, irremovable judges were an "anomaly."[53]
In terms of autocratic principles he was undeniably correct. The conservatives
succeeded in having political offenses removed from the jurisdiction of civilian
courts and transferred to administrative courts, but they could not undo the
court reform because it had become too embedded in Russian life, and, in any
event, they had no realistic alternative.

The squabbling between the two bureaucratic camps was typified by the
rivalry between the ministries of the Interior and of Finance.

The Ministry of the Interior was an institution *sui generis,* virtually a state
within a state, resembling less a branch of the executive than a self-contained
system within the machinery of government.[54] While the other ministries had
clearly defined and therefore limited functions, Interior had the general function of administering the country. In 1802, when it came into existence, it had
been responsible for promoting economic development and supervising transport and communications. Its sphere of competence was immensely broadened

in the 1860s, partly as a result of serf emancipation, which deprived landlords of administrative authority, and partly in response to the revolutionary unrest. By 1900, the Minister of the Interior was something of a Chief Imperial Steward. The ambitions of the holders of the post knew no bounds. In 1881, in the wake of a campaign of terror that culminated in the assassination of Alexander II, the Minister of the Interior, N. P. Ignatev, proposed that in order to extirpate dissent not only in society but also in the government, which he believed was filled with subversives, his ministry be authorized to engage, in effect, in what one historian has described as "administrative-police supervision . . . of all other government agencies."[55] A proposal in the same spirit was made twenty years later by Minister of the Interior Viacheslav Plehve on behalf of the governors.[56] Both proposals were rejected, but it is indicative of the authority of the ministry that they dared to make them. It was logical that after 1905, when the equivalent post of Prime Minister was created, its holder usually also held the portfolio of the Interior.

The Minister of the Interior headed the national administration by virtue of authority to appoint and supervise the country's principal administrative officials, the governors. These tended to be selected from among the less educated and more conservative bureaucrats: in 1900, half of them had no higher education. Governors chaired provincial boards *(gubernskie pravleniia)* and a variety of committees, of which the most important were the bureaus *(prisutstviia)* charged with overseeing the industrial, military, and agricultural affairs of their province. They also had responsibility for the peasants: they appointed, from among trustworthy local landed gentry, land commandants *(zemskie nachal'niki),* who acted as wardens of the *volost'* administration and enjoyed broad authority over the peasantry. The governors also supervised the *zemstva.* In case of unrest, they could request the Minister of the Interior to declare their province under either Reinforced or Extraordinary Safeguard, which resulted in the suspension of all civil rights and rule by decree. With the exception of the courts and agencies of fiscal control, the governors encountered few barriers to their will. Through them, the Minister of the Interior ran the Empire.*

Within the purview of the Interior Minister fell also the supervision of non-Orthodox subjects, including the Jews, as well as the dissenting branches of the Orthodox faith; censorship; and the management of prisons and forced labor camps.

But the greatest source of the Interior Minister's power derived from the fact that after 1880 he was in charge of the police: the Department of Police and the Corps of Gendarmes, as well as the regular constabulary force. In the words of Witte, "the Minister of the Interior is the Minister of Police of an

---

*Exempt from his authority were the governors-general placed in charge of selected areas and accountable directly to the Tsar. In 1900, there were seven of them: one in Moscow, three in the troublesome western provinces (Warsaw, Vilno, and Kiev), and three in remote Siberia (Irkutsk, the Steppe, and the Amur River region). Combining civil with military authority, they resembled viceroys.

Empire which is a police state par excellence."* The Department of Police was
unique to Russia: only Russia had two kinds of police, one to protect the
interests of the state, the other to maintain law and order among the citizens.
The Police Department was charged exclusively with responsibility for combating crimes against the state. It constituted, as it were, a private security
service of the patrimonial sovereign, whose interests were apparently perceived
as separate from those of his subjects.

The constabulary was to be seen mainly in the urban centers. "Outside
the cities the central authorities relied essentially upon a mere 1,582 constables
and 6,874 sergeants to control a village population of ninety million."[57] Each
district *(uezd)* had, as a representative of the Interior Ministry, a police chief
called *ispravnik.* These officials enjoyed broad powers, including that of issuing
internal passports, without which members of the lower classes could not
travel thirty kilometers beyond their place of residence. But as is clear from
their numbers, they would hardly have been said to police the countryside.

As constituted in 1880, the security police consisted of three elements, all
subject to the Minister of the Interior: the Department of Police in St. Petersburg, the Okhrana (security police) with branches in some cities, and the
Corps of Gendarmes, whose personnel was distributed in all the metropolitan
areas. A great deal of Russian administration was carried out by means of
secret circulars sent to the officials in charge of security from the minister's
office.

There was a certain amount of duplication among the three services in
that all had the mission of preventing anti-governmental activities, which
included industrial strikes and unauthorized assemblies. The Okhrana, at first
established only in St. Petersburg, Moscow, and Warsaw, and later installed
in other cities, engaged principally in counterintelligence, whereas the Gendarmes were more involved in formal investigation of individuals apprehended
in illegal activities. The Gendarmes had a paramilitary force to control railroads and to quell urban disorders. There were 10,000 to 15,000 gendarmes in
the Empire. Each city had a Gendarme official, clad in a familiar light blue
uniform, whose responsibility it was to gather information on all matters
affecting internal security. The force was very thinly distributed. Hence in time
of massive unrest the government had to call in the regular army, the force
of last resort: and when the army was engaged in war, as happened in 1904–5
and again in 1917, the regime was unable to cope.

The security services evolved over time into a highly effective political
counterintelligence using an array of techniques to combat revolutionaries,
including a network of informants, agents who shadowed suspects, and agents
provocateurs who infiltrated subversive organizations. The police intercepted
and read private mail. It employed as informers residential superintendents.
It had branches abroad (it maintained a permanent bureau in Paris) and

*S. Iu. Vitte, *Vospominaniia,* III (Moscow, 1960), 107. In 1905 Witte refused the post of
Minister of the Interior because he did not want to become a policeman.

collaborated with foreign police to keep track of Russian revolutionaries. In the years immediately preceding the outbreak of World War I, through arrests and penetration it succeeded in virtually eliminating the revolutionary parties as a threat to the regime: suffice it to say that both the head of the Socialist-Revolutionary terrorist organization and Lenin's chief deputy in Russia were on the police payroll. The security police was the best informed and politically the most sophisticated agency of the Imperial Government: in the years immediately preceding the Revolution it submitted remarkably prescient analyses of Russia's internal conditions and prospects.

Of all the services of the Russian bureaucracy, the police were the least constrained by law. All its operations, affecting the lives of millions, were carried out free of external controls, save those of the Minister of the Interior and the director of the Department of Police. Under regulations issued in 1881, the police organs had no judiciary powers. However, in areas subject to the August 1881 provisions for "Safeguard," high officials of the Corps of Gendarmes had the right to detain suspects for two weeks, and for two weeks longer with a governor's authorization. After one month, a detainee was either released or turned over to the Ministry of the Interior for further investigation. Once that was completed, if the evidence warranted, the suspect was brought to trial either before a court (sometimes the Senate) or before administrative boards of the Ministry of the Interior composed of two representatives each of that ministry and the Ministry of Justice: a bureaucratic body functioning in a judiciary capacity.[58] Under such procedures, Russians could be sentenced for up to five years of administrative exile. The population had no recourse against the security organs, least of all in areas placed under Safeguard, where the police could act with complete impunity.

The authority of the Minister of the Interior was enhanced by virtue of the fact that his police and gendarmerie were the only vehicles for enforcing directives of the other ministries. If Finance ran into a taxpayers' revolt, or War had trouble recruiting, they had to go to Interior for help. In the words of a contemporary source,

> the outstanding position of the Ministry of the Interior is determined not only by the number, variety, and importance of its functions but also and above all by the fact that it administers the police force, and that the enforcement of all government decrees, regardless of which ministry's competence they happen to fall under, is, as a rule, carried out by the police.[59]

In the closing decades of the century, Interior Ministers supported and implemented various "counterreforms" designed to emasculate the liberal reforms of the 1860s. Among them were restrictions on *zemstva,* the introduction of land commandants, expulsion of Jews from areas where law forbade them to reside, and repression of student unrest. Had they had their wish, Russia would have been frozen not only politically but also economically and socially.

The inability of the Interior Ministers to carry out their programs provides a telling commentary on the limitations that life imposed on the practices of patrimonial autocracy. From considerations of state security, its proponents opposed nearly every measure designed to modernize the Russian economy. They fought currency reform and the adoption of the gold standard. They disliked railroads. They opposed foreign borrowing. Above all, they resisted industrialization on the grounds that it hurt cottage industries, without which peasants could not make ends meet, led to dangerous concentrations of industrial labor, and enabled foreigners, especially Jews, to penetrate and corrupt Russia.

There were weighty reasons of state why this resistance was ignored. Russia had no choice but to industrialize. Witte, the Minister of Finance and chief advocate of industrialization, made his case largely in political and military terms, because he knew that they would appeal to Nicholas II. In February 1900, in a memorandum to the Tsar, he argued, consciously or unconsciously echoing the nineteenth-century German political economist Friedrich List, that

> without her own industry [Russia] cannot achieve genuine economic independence. And the experience of all nations indicates palpably that only countries which enjoy economic independence have also the capacity fully to unfold their political might.*

To prove his point, Witte pointed to China, India, Turkey, and Latin America.

Persuasive as this argument was, fiscal exigencies were even more so: Russia urgently needed capital to balance the budget, to broaden the revenue base of the Treasury, and to ease the tax burden of the peasant. The alternative was state bankruptcy and possibly widespread agrarian unrest. Thus fiscal considerations overrode the interests of internal security, pushing the Imperial Government to take the "capitalist" road with all its social and political consequences.

Russia has suffered chronic budgetary deficits ever since the middle of the nineteenth century. There were the immense costs of serf emancipation, the provisions of which committed the government to advance the landlords 80 percent of the value of the land given to their ex-serfs: this money the peasants were supposed to repay over forty-nine years, but they soon fell into arrears. Then there was the costly Balkan War of 1877–78, which caused the Russian ruble to lose 60 percent of its value on foreign exchanges. The govern-

---

*IM, No. 2–3 (1935), 133. Von Laue cites Witte to the effect that "a modern body politic cannot be great without a well-developed national industry": Theodore H. Von Laue, *Sergei Witte and the Industrialization of Russia* (New York-London, 1963), 262.

ment also incurred heavy expenses in connection with its involvement in railroad construction.*

Russia lacked the capital to meet such expenditures. Her revenues rested on a very narrow basis. Direct taxes in 1900 accounted for only 7.9 percent of state income, a fraction of what advanced industrial countries drew from this source. The bulk of the revenues derived from taxes on consumption: sales taxes and customs duties (27.2 percent), proceeds of the liquor monopoly (26 percent), and operations of railways (24 percent). This covered the ordinary expenses but not the military outlays and the costs of railroad construction. Russia partly made good the deficit with sales of grain abroad: in 1891–95 she exported on the average 7 million tons of cereals a year, and in 1902, as much as 9.3 million.[60] Most of the revenue, directly and indirectly, came from the peasant, who paid a land tax as well as taxes on articles of necessity (salt, matches, kerosene) and vodka. In the 1870s and 1880s, Russian Finance Ministers obtained the money with which to try to balance the budget mainly by increasing taxes on articles of consumption, which had the effect of forcing the peasant to sell grain that the government then exported. The famine of 1891–92 made clear the limits to such practices: the peasants' ability to pay, it was now acknowledged, had been exhausted. Fears arose that the continuation of the policy of squeezing the peasant could lead to chronic famines.

On taking over the Ministry of Finance in 1892, Witte adopted a different policy: rather than squeeze the countryside, he borrowed abroad and worked to increase the country's wealth through industrialization. The development of productive capacities would, he was convinced, improve living standards and, at the same time, enhance government revenues.[61] He had initially believed that Russia could raise the capital for her industrialization at home, but he soon realized that domestic financial resources were insufficient[62]—not only because capital was in short supply but because affluent Russians preferred to invest in mortgages and government bonds. The need for foreign loans became especially pronounced after the crop failures of 1891 and 1892, which forced a temporary curtailment of grain exports and resulted in a fiscal crisis.† Russia's foreign borrowing, which until 1891 had been on a modest scale, now began in earnest.

To create the impression of fiscal solvency, the Imperial Government occasionally falsified budgetary figures, but its main device to this end was a unique practice of dividing the state budget. The expenses comprised under the "ordinary" budget were more than covered by domestic revenues. Those incurred in maintaining the armed forces and waging war, as well as building railroads, were treated as "non-recurrent" and classified as "extraordinary." This part of the budget was met from foreign borrowing.

*Bertrand Gille, *Histoire Economique et Sociale de la Russie* (Paris, 1949), 163–65. According to Geoffrey Drage [*Russian Affairs* (New York-London, 1904) 287], in 1900, 60.5 percent of the Russian railroad network was state property.

†In September–November 1891, as the news of the crop failures spread abroad, the price of 4 percent Russian bonds dropped from 97.5 to 87, raising the return from 4.1 percent to 4.6 percent: René Girault, *Emprunts Russes et Investissements Français en Russie, 1887–1914* (Paris, 1973), 197.

To attract foreign credit, Russia required a convertible currency.

By maintaining in the 1880s a foreign trade surplus, largely with the help of grain exports, and by intensive gold mining, Russia managed to accumulate enough bullion to adopt in 1897 the gold standard. This measure, carried out by Witte in the teeth of strong opposition, made the paper ruble convertible on demand into gold. It attracted massive foreign investments in state obligations as well as securities. Stringent rules on bank-note emissions and an excellent record of debt servicing earned Russia a high credit rating, which enabled her to borrow at interest rates only slightly above those paid by Germany (usually 4 or 4.5 percent). The bulk of the foreign money—four-fifths of that invested in state bonds—came from France; the remainder was supplied by British, German, and Belgian investors. In 1914, the total debt of the Russian Government amounted to 8.8 billion rubles, of which 48 percent or 4.2 billion ($2.1 billion or the equivalent of 3,360 tons of gold) was owed to foreigners: at the time, it was the largest foreign indebtedness of any country in the world.[63] In addition, in 1914 foreigners held 870 million rubles of state-guaranteed securities and 422 million rubles of municipal bonds.

Fiscal needs also drove the government to encourage industrial expansion as a means of broadening its tax base. Here, too, foreign capital flowed readily, for European investors believed that Russia, with its huge population and inexhaustible resources, needed only capital and technical know-how to become another United States.[64] Between 1892 and 1914, foreigners placed in Russian enterprises an estimated 2.2 billion rubles ($1.1 billion), which represented approximately one-half of the capital invested in these enterprises during the period.[65] The largest share (about one-third) of these investments went into mining, mainly petroleum and coal; the metalworking, electrical, and chemical industries as well as real estate also benefited. French capital accounted for 32.6 percent of that money, English for 22.6 percent, German for 19.7 percent, and Belgian for 14.3 percent.[66] Witte estimated in 1900 that approximately one-half of all Russian industrial and commercial capital was of foreign origin.*

Such heavy foreign involvement in the economy led conservative and radical opponents of Witte alike to claim that he had transformed Russia into a "colony of Europe." The charge had little merit. As Witte liked to point out, foreign capital went exclusively for productive purposes†—that is, enhancing Russia's productive capacity and therefore her wealth. It was in large measure owing to the growth of the non-agrarian sectors of the economy, made possible by the infusion of foreign capital, that the revenues of the Treasury between

---

*IM, No. 2–3 (1935), 135. John P. McKay [Pioneers for Profit (Chicago, 1970), 37] believes that in 1914 "foreigners held at least two-fifths of the total of nominal capital of corporations operating in Russia."

†Vitte, Vospominaniia, II, 501. Although basically correct, this claim is an exaggeration, since the Extraordinary Budget, based on foreign borrowings, also paid a good part of the defense expenditures. It was also used for debt servicing.

1892 and 1903 more than doubled (from 970 million to 2 billion).[67] It has also been pointed out that foreign investors did not simply "milk" the Russian economy by repatriating their profits, but reinvested them, which had a cumulatively beneficial effect.* In this connection, it is often ignored that the economic development of the United States also benefited greatly from foreign investments. European investments in the United States in mid-1914 are estimated to have been $6.7 billion,† twice the capital invested by Europeans in Russia. "In considerable measure the funds for the national expansion and development [of the United States]," writes an economic historian, "had been obtained from abroad."[68] And yet the role of foreign capital is rarely mentioned in American histories and never led to charges that it had made the United States a "colony" of Europe.

The opening phase of the Industrial Revolution in Russia got underway around 1890 with a rapid spurt in industrial production. Some Western European economists have calculated that during the decade of the 1890s Russian industrial productivity increased by 126 percent, which was twice the rate of the German and triple that of the American growth.[69] Even allowing that Russia started from a much lower base, the rise was impressive, as the following figures indicate:

GROWTH OF RUSSIAN INDUSTRIAL PRODUCTION[70]

Industry	1890	1900	Growth
Pig iron (tons)	927,100	2,933,700	216%
Petroleum (tons) (1885)	1,883,700	10,335,800	449%
Railroads (km)	30,596	53,234	71%

Between 1890 and 1900, the value of Russian industrial output more than doubled (from 1.5 billion to 3.4 billion rubles).‡

In 1900, Imperial Russia was the world's largest producer of petroleum, her annual output exceeding that of all the other countries combined. It is generally agreed by economic historians that on the eve of World War I, by which time the value of her industrial production had risen to 5.7 billion rubles, Russia had the fifth-largest economy in the world, which was impres-

*McKay, *Pioneers*, 383–86. McKay stresses, in addition to capital investments, the great contribution made by foreigners in bringing to Russia advanced industrial technology: *Ibid.*, 382–83.

†Edward C. Kirkland, *A History of American Economic Life*, 3rd ed. (New York, 1951), 541. Other historians estimate that in 1914 Europeans held between $4.5 and $5.5 billion in U.S. bonds: William J. Shultz and M. R. Caine, *Financial Development of the United States* (New York, 1937), 502.

‡Leo Pasvolsky and Harold G. Moulton, *Russian Debts and Russian Reconstruction* (New York, 1924), 112. To these figures must be added the value of products turned out by cottage industries *(kustarnaia promyshlennost')*, which Pasvolsky estimates at approximately 50 percent of the above: *Ibid.*, 113.

sive even if, proportionate to her population, her industrial productivity and income remained low. Thus, in 1910, Russia's per capita consumption of coal was 4 percent of the American, and of iron, 6.25 percent.*

As the conservatives feared, Russia's reliance on foreign capital had political consequences, intensifying the pressures on the Imperial Government to come to terms with its own society—that is, to liberalize. Investors everywhere have little tolerance for political instability and civil unrest, and when threatened with them, either withhold capital or demand a risk premium. Every internal crisis, especially if attended by popular disturbances, led to the fall in the price of Russian state obligations, forcing the government to pay higher interest. In consequence of the Revolution of 1905, Russian bonds floated in Europe the next two years had to be heavily discounted. Foreign investors preferred that the Imperial Government operate in a lawful manner and with public support institutionalized in a parliament. Thus by reaching out to the parliamentary democracies for capital, Russia became susceptible to influences promoting parliamentary forms of government. Quite naturally, the Ministry of Finance, the main agent in these fiscal operations, became a spokesman for liberal ideals. It did not quite dare to raise the slogans of constitutionalism and parliamentarism, but it did press for curtailing bureaucratic and police arbitrariness, respect for law, and extending equality to the ethnic minorities, especially the Jews, who were a major force in international banking.

Thus the requirements of the Treasury drove the Russian Government in the opposite direction from that demanded by its ideology of autocratic patrimonialism and urged on it by conservative bureaucrats. A government whose philosophy and practices were under the spell of patrimonial absolutism had no alternative but to pursue economic policies that undermined such absolutism.

The Russian army was, first and foremost, the guarantor of the country's status as a great power. Witte had the following to say on the subject:

> In truth, what is it that has essentially upheld Russian statehood? Not only primarily but exclusively the army. Who has created the Russian Empire, transforming the semi-Asiatic Muscovite tsardom into the most influential, most dominant, grandest European power? Only the power of the army's bayonet. The world bowed not to our culture, not to our bureaucratized church, not to our wealth and prosperity. It bowed to our might . . .[71]

The military establishment was to an even greater extent than the bureaucracy the personal service of the autocrat, if only because the Tsars took a very personal interest in the armed forces and favored them over the bureaucracy, whose interference and pressures often annoyed the Court.[72] All the

---

*Based on statistics in Jürgen Nötzold, *Wirtschaftpolitische Alternativen der Entwicklung Russlands in der Ära Witte und Stolypin* (Berlin, 1966), 110.

trappings and symbols of the military, beginning with the oath sworn by officers and soldiers, were filled with the patrimonial spirit:

> In the military oath, which had to be renewed upon the death of every sovereign, inasmuch as it was sworn to the person [of the ruler], the Emperor appears solely as the Autocrat, without the Fatherland being mentioned. It was the mission of the military to safeguard "the interests of His Imperial Majesty" and "all the rights and privileges that belong to the Supreme Autocracy, Power and Authority of His Imperial Majesty." The swearer of the oath committed himself to defend these prerogatives whether they already existed or were still to be acquired or even claimed—i.e., "present and future." [In the oath] the state was treated simply as the Emperor's command [*Machtbereich*]: it was mentioned only once along with the Emperor, moreover in a context that assumed their identity of interests . . ."[73]

With a standing army of 2.6 million men, Russia had the largest military establishment in the world: it was nearly equal to the combined armies on active service of Germany and Austria-Hungary (1.9 and 1.1 million, respectively). Its size can be accounted for by two factors.

One was slowness of mobilization. Great distances aggravated by an inadequate railroad network meant that in the event of war Russia required much more time than her potential enemies, Germany and Austria-Hungary, to bring her forces to full combat strength: in the early years of the century, Russia's mobilization was expected to take seven times as long as Germany's.*

The other, no less weighty consideration had to do with internal security. Since the early eighteenth century, the Russian army was regularly employed in quelling popular disorders. Professional officers intensely disliked such work, considering it demeaning, but the regime had no choice in the matter since the police and gendarmes were inadequate to the task. During periods of widespread civil disturbances, the army was regularly employed for this purpose: in 1903, one-third of the infantry and two-thirds of the cavalry stationed in European Russia engaged in repressive action.† Furthermore, the government frequently appointed officers as governors-general in areas prone to violence. The government welcomed retired officers in the civil service, offering them equivalent *chin* and precedence over regular bureaucrats. While the security police concentrated on preventing sedition, the military was the monarchy's main instrument of repression.

To ensure the loyalty of the armed forces, the authorities distributed non-Slavic inductees in such a manner that at least 75 percent of the troops in every unit were "Russians"—i.e., Great Russians, Ukrainians, or Belorussians. In the officer corps, the proportion of the East Slavic component was maintained at 80–85 percent.[74]

The officer corps, 42,000 men strong in 1900, was a professional body in

*See below, Chapter 6.

†P. A. Zaionchkovskii, *Samoderzhavie i russkaia armiia na rubezhe XIX–XX stoletii* (Moscow, 1973), 34. Zaionchkovskii provides a table showing Russian army involvement in suppressing disorders between 1883 and 1903 (*Ibid.*, 35). The subject is treated at length in William C. Fuller's *Civil-Military Conflict in Imperial Russia, 1881–1914* (Princeton, N.J., 1985).

many ways isolated from society at large.[75] This is not to say that it was "feudal" or aristocratic, as it is often pictured. The military reforms carried out after the Crimean War had as one of their objectives opening the ranks of the officer corps to commoners; to this end, education was given as much weight in promotion as social origin. At the end of the century, only one-half of the officers on active duty were hereditary nobles,[76] a high proportion of them sons of officers and bureaucrats. Even so, there remained a certain distinction between officers of high social standing, often serving in elite Guard Regiments, and the rest—a distinction which was to play a not insignificant role in the Revolution and Civil War.

A commission required a course of training in a military school. These were of two kinds. The more prestigious Military Academies *(Voennye Uchilishcha)* enrolled graduates of secondary schools, usually Cadet Schools, who planned on becoming professional officers. They were taught by civilian instructors on the model of the so-called *Realgimnaziia,* which followed a liberal arts curriculum. Upon completion of their studies, graduates received commissions. The Iunker Academies *(Iunkerskie Uchilishcha)* had nothing in common with Prussian Junkers, enrolling mostly students of plebeian origin who, as a rule, had not completed secondary schooling, either for lack of money or because they could not cope with the classical-language requirements of Russian gymnasia. They admitted pupils of all social estates and religious affiliations except for Jews.* The program of study in these institutions was shorter (two years), and their graduates still had to undergo a stint as warrant officers before becoming eligible for a commission. The majority of the officers on active duty in 1900—two-thirds by one estimate, three-quarters by another—were products of the Iunker Academies; in October 1917 they would prove themselves the staunchest defenders of democracy. The upper grades of the service, however, were reserved for alumni of the Military Academies.

The military uniform carried little prestige in Russia. Salaries were too low to permit officers who had no independent means to aspire to a gentleman's life: with a monthly wage of 41.25 rubles, an infantry second lieutenant earned not much more than a skilled worker. Officers of field rank could barely make ends meet or even feed themselves properly.[77] Foreign observers were struck by the lack of a sense of "honor" among Russian officers and their willingness to tolerate abuse from superiors.

The most prestigious service was with the Guard Regiments, commissions in which required social standing as well as independent income.[78] Nearly all the officers serving in the Guards were hereditary nobles: their system of cooptation kept out undesirables. Guard officers billeted in comfortable quarters in St. Petersburg, Moscow, and Warsaw enjoyed certain privileges, among them accelerated promotion. These, however, were gradually whittled down, and abolished by the time World War I broke out.

*In 1886 the Russian army had at most twelve Jewish officers: Zaionchkovskii, *Samoderzhavie i russkaia armiia,* 201–2.

The uppermost elite of the late Imperial Army was made up of alumni of the Military Academies, especially the two-and-a-half-year course of studies at the Nicholas Academy of the General Staff, which prepared specialists for high command posts. Admission was open to officers with three years of active duty who passed with distinction an appropriate examination; only one in thirty applicants qualified. Social origin made no difference: here "the son of an emancipated serf served . . . together with members of the Imperial family."* The 1,232 graduates of the General Staff School—*Genshtabisty*—on active duty in 1904 developed a strong esprit de corps, helping each other and maintaining a solid front against outsiders. The brightest among them were assigned to the General Staff, which had responsibility for developing strategic policy. The rest took command posts. Their preponderance among officers of general rank was striking: although constituting between 5 and 10 percent of the officers on active duty, they commanded, in 1912, 62 percent of the army corps, 68 percent of the infantry divisions, 77 percent of the cavalry divisions, and 25 percent of the regiments. All seven of the last Ministers of War were alumni of the General Staff Academy.[79]

General Anton Denikin, the leader in 1918–19 of the anti-Bolshevik Volunteer Army, claimed that relations between officers and enlisted men in the Imperial Army were as good as if not better than similar relations in the German and Austro-Hungarian armies, and the treatment of the troops less brutal.[80] Contemporary evidence, however, does not support this claim. The Russian authorities insisted on observing very strict rank distinctions, subjecting soldiers to treatment that reminded some observers of serfdom. The men were addressed by officers in the second person singular, received an allowance of three or four rubles a year (one-hundredth of the pay of the most junior officer), and in some military districts were subjected to various indignities such as having to walk on the shady side of the street or to ride on streetcar platforms.[81] The resentments which these discriminatory rules bred were a major cause of the mutiny of the Petrograd garrison in February 1917.

For the historian of the Revolution, the most important aspect of the late Imperial Army was its politics. Students of the subject agree that the Russian officer class was largely apolitical: not only did it not involve itself in politics, it showed no interest in it.† In officers' clubs, political talk was considered in poor taste. Officers looked down on civilians, whom they nicknamed *shpaki*, most of all on politicians. Moreover they felt they could not uphold their oath to the Tsar if they became embroiled in partisan politics. Taught to regard loyalty to the powers that be as the supreme virtue, they were exceedingly ill

---

*Matitiahu Mayzel in *Cahiers du Monde Russe et Soviétique*, XVI, No. 3/4 (1975), 300–1. According to Zaionchkovskii (*Samoderzhavie i russkaia armiia*, 320n.–321n.), the number of nobles attending the Academy at the turn of the century was very small.

†This was in contrast to the Japanese army, which paid great attention to ideological indoctrination: Carol Gluck, *Japan's Modern Myths* (Princeton, N.J., 1985). Russian soldiers received no indoctrination: A. I. Denikin, *Staraia armiia* (Paris, 1929), 50–51.

14. Dancing class at Smolnyi Institute, c. 1910.

prepared to cope with the conflicts that erupted in 1917. As long as the struggle for power was undecided, they stood on the sidelines. Once the Bolsheviks took over, many went into their service, since they were now "the authority" *(vlast'),* which they had been trained to obey. The specter of Russian Bonapartism, which so frightened Russian revolutionaries, was a figment of the imagination of intellectuals raised on the history of the French Revolution.

After 1905 there emerged in the military a group of patriotic officers whose loyalty extended beyond the throne. Like the liberal bureaucrats, they saw themselves as serving the nation rather than the Crown. They were regarded with great suspicion.

The fourth instrument of tsarist authority, the gentry or *dvorianstvo,* was an eroding asset.*

Like the bureaucracy, the Russian gentry descended from a medieval service class which had performed for the princes a great variety of missions, principally military duty.[82] Their service was lifelong and compensated mainly by income from fiefs, worked by serfs, who technically remained the Crown's

---

*According to the 1897 Census there were in the Empire 1,220,000 hereditary *dvoriane* (of both sexes), of them 641,500 native speakers of "Russian" (i.e. Great Russian, Ukrainian, and Belorussian): N. A. Troinitskii, ed., *Pervaia Vseobshchaia Perepis' Naseleniia Rossiiskoi Imperii 1897 g.: Obshchii Svod,* II (St. Petersburg, 1905), 374. *Dvoriane* thus constituted nearly 1 percent of the population.

property. They were not a nobility in the true sense of the word because they had no corporate rights: such benefits as they enjoyed were perquisites of service. The *dvoriane* rose to a privileged position in the late eighteenth century when the monarchy, eager to divert their attention from politics, admitted them into partnership. In return for the gentry conceding the Tsars complete control over the sphere of high politics, they were given title to their estates as well as de facto ownership of the serfs (then about one-half of the population) and granted a corporate charter of rights, which included release from the obligation of bearing state service. The Golden Age of the *dvoriane* was between 1730 and 1825. Even then, the vast majority lived in poverty: only one-third had landed estates with serfs and of that number only a minority had enough land and serfs to live in any style.[83] Many rural gentry were hard to distinguish from their peasants.

The decline of the Russian gentry began in 1825, as a consequence of the Decembrist Revolt in which young members of the most distinguished noble families took up arms against the monarchy in the name of constitutional and republican ideals. Stung by this "betrayal," Nicholas I increasingly came to rely on the professional bureaucracy. The economic death knell of the *dvorianstvo* rang in 1861 when the monarchy, overruling gentry opposition, emancipated the serfs. For although the number of gentry who owned serfs was not very large and most of those who did had too few to live off their labor, the monopoly on serf ownership was the most important advantage which that class had enjoyed. After 1861 the gentry retained certain valuable benefits (e.g., assured admission into the civil and military service), but even so it began to lose status as a privileged social estate.

This was a highly deplorable trend to most Russian conservatives, for whom the survival of Russia depended on a strong monarchy and on the support of privileged and prosperous landed gentry. In the closing three decades of the nineteenth century, much was written on this subject: this literature represented the last gasp of gentry conservatism, a doomed effort to revive the age of Catherine the Great.[84] The argument held that the landed gentry were the principal bearers of culture in the countryside. They could not be replaced by the bureaucracy because the latter had no roots in the land and merely "bivouacked" there: indeed, the bureaucracy itself was becoming radicalized due to the government's preference for officials with higher education over those with proper social credentials. The decline of the gentry inevitably paved the way for the triumph of the radical intelligentsia who, working as rural teachers and professional staff of the *zemstva,* incited the peasantry instead of enlightening it. Such conservatives criticized the Great Reforms of Alexander II for diluting social distinctions. Their plea was for a return to the tradition of partnership between Crown and gentry.

This argumentation had an effect, the more so in that it received political backing from organized landowning groups close to the Court.[85] The latter managed to fend off social legislation injurious to their interests; but in this case, too, life was running in the opposite direction and it would be wrong to ascribe great influence to the conservative gentry on the regime of Nicholas

II. The conservatives fantasized about restoring the partnership between the Crown and the gentry, but Russia was moving, however haltingly, toward social egalitarianism and common citizenship.

For one, an increasing number of gentry turned their back on the conservative ideology, adopting constitutional and even democratic ideals. The *zemstvo* movement, which gave a major impetus to the 1905 Revolution, had in its ranks a high proportion of *dvoriane,* scions of Russia's oldest and most distinguished families. According to Witte, at the turn of the century at least one-half of the provincial *zemstva,* in which nobles played a leading role, demanded a voice in legislation.[86] Ignoring these realities, the monarchy continued to treat the gentry as a dependable pillar of absolutism. In 1904–5, when the necessity of granting the country a representative institution of some sort could no longer be ignored, some advisers urged giving the gentry a preponderant number of seats. It took an old grand duke to remind Nicholas that the nobles stood in the forefront of the current disturbances.[87]

No less important was the fact that the gentry were steadily losing ground in the civil service and in land ownership.

The need for technically proficient administrative personnel forced the government, in hiring civil servants, increasingly to favor education over ancestry. As a consequence, the share of *dvoriane* in the bureaucracy steadily declined.[88]

The gentry were pulling out of the countryside as well: in 1914, only 20 to 40 percent of Russian *dvoriane* still lived on the land, the rest having moved to the cities.[89] Under the 1861 Emancipation settlement the gentry had retained about one-half of their land; for the other half, which they were forced to cede to the liberated serfs, they received generous compensation. But the gentry did not know how to manage: some experts thought that in Great Russia it was impossible in any event to make a profit from agriculture using hired (rather than bonded) labor. Whatever the reason, the gentry disposed of their estates to peasants and others at a rate of approximately 1 percent a year. At the beginning of the century, they retained only 60 percent of the properties that had been theirs in 1861. Between 1875 and 1900, the proportion of the country's privately owned (i.e., non-communal) land held by the gentry declined from 73.6 percent to 53.1 percent.[90] In January 1915, the gentry (including officers and officials) owned in European Russia 39 million *desiatiny** of economically useful land (arable, woodland, and pasture), out of a total of 98 million—only slightly more than the peasants held in private ownership.[91] The landowning gentry were a vanishing breed, squeezed from the countryside by the twin forces of economic pressure and peasant hostility.

Of the several institutions serving the Russian monarchy, the Orthodox Church enjoyed the greatest measure of popular support: it provided the main

---

*One *desiatina* equals 2.7 acres or 1.1 hectares.

cultural link with the 80 million Great Russians, Ukrainians, and Belorussians professing the faith. The monarchy attached great importance to the Church by bestowing on it the status of the Established Church and granting it privileges not enjoyed by official Christian churches elsewhere.

The religiousness of Great Russians is a matter of dispute, some observers arguing that the peasant was deeply Christian, others viewing him as a superstitious agnostic who observed Christian rituals exclusively from concern for life after death. Others yet hold that the Great Russian population was "bi-religious," with Christian and pre-Christian elements of its faith intermingled. The matter need not detain us. There is no dispute that the masses of the Orthodox population—the great majority of Russians, Ukrainians, and Belorussians—faithfully observed the rituals of their church. Russia before the Revolution was visually and aurally filled with Christian symbols: churches, monasteries, ikons, and religious processions, the sound of liturgical music and the ringing of church bells.

The link between state and religion derived from the belief that Orthodoxy *(Pravoslavie)* was the national faith of Russia and that only its adherents were true Russians. A Pole or a Jew, no matter how assimilated and patriotic, remained in the eyes of the authorities as well as the Orthodox population an outsider. Membership in the Orthodox Church was a lifelong bond from which there was no escape:

> Everybody is free to remain true to the religion of their fathers, but forbidden to make new proselytes. That privilege is reserved for the Orthodox Church alone; it is explicitly so stated in the text of the law. Everybody may enter that church; nobody may leave it. Russian Orthodoxy has doors which open only one way. The confessional laws fill out several chapters of vols. x., xiv., and xv. of the voluminous collection known as "the Code." Every child born of Orthodox parents is perforce Orthodox; so is every child born of a mixed marriage. Indeed, such a marriage is possible only on this condition. . . . One article of the Code forbids Orthodox Russians to change their religion; another states the penalties incurred for such offences. The stray sheep is, in the first instance, paternally exhorted by his parish clergy, then made over to the consistory, then to the Synod. A term of penance in a convent can be inflicted. The apostate forfeits all civic rights; he cannot legally own or inherit anything. His kindred may seize on his property or step into his inheritance. . . . It is a crime to advise anybody to abandon the Orthodox religion; it is a crime to advise anybody against entering it.[92]

The Imperial Government did not interfere with the religious observances of the other faiths, but as if to underscore the indissoluble link between Orthodoxy and Russianness, it classified all the other religions as "foreign confessions."

The Russian regime was not "Caesaropapist," in the sense of combining secular and spiritual authority, for the Tsar had no say in matters of dogma or ritual: his power was confined to the administration of the Church. Nevertheless, it is true that since the time of Peter the Great, the Russian Orthodox

Church was to an extreme degree dependent on the state. By abolishing the Patriarchate and confiscating Church properties (a task completed by Catherine II) Peter made the Church beholden to the monarchy administratively as well as financially. The highest body regulating its affairs, the Holy Synod, was since Peter's day chaired by a secular person, often a retired general, who functioned as a de facto Minister of Religion. The administrative structure of the Church paralleled that of the civil administration, in that the boundaries of the dioceses coincided with those of the provinces *(gubernii)*. As was true of the bureaucracy, clergymen could be promoted, in this case from bishop to archbishop and then to metropolitan, without regard to the responsibilities entrusted to them, clerical title being treated like *chin*—that is, as a personal distinction rather than as an attribute of office.[93] The clergy were duty-bound to report to the police any information of conspiracies against the Emperor or the government, including that obtained during confession. They also had to denounce the appearance of suspicious strangers in their parishes.

The Orthodox Church was financially dependent on the government for salaries and subsidies, but derived most of its revenues independently.[94] All bishops and higher ecclesiastical dignitaries received generous salaries as well as living allowances, which they supplemented with incomes from Church and monastic properties. The parish clergy, too, was on state pay. In 1900, state appropriations to the Church amounted to 23 million rubles. This sum provided approximately one-fifth of the Church's income—a respectable amount but hardly an explanation why the clergy stood by the monarchy in the 1905 Revolution.[95]

The principal political responsibility of the Church was indoctrination. The Imperial Government eschewed in schools and the military establishment anything resembling national or ideological propaganda from fear that arguments used to justify the status quo would invite counterarguments. The fact that the country was a multinational empire also inhibited appeals to nationalism. The government preferred to act as if the existing political and social arrangement were a given. Only religious indoctrination was permitted, and that was the function the Orthodox clergy, especially in the classroom.

The Orthodox Church became first heavily engaged in popular education in the 1880s, after a decade of revolutionary turmoil. To counteract the influence of both radical propagandists and secular teachers on the rural population, the government charged the Church with operating a network of primary schools. At the turn of the century, slightly more than one-half of the grade schools in the Empire, with approximately one-third of the pupils, were under Church supervision.[96] Heavy stress was placed on ethics as well as language training (Church Slavonic and Russian). Their teachers, however, were so miserably paid compared with those employed by secular schools that they had difficulty competing and kept losing pupils to their rivals.

Students of the Orthodox faith in all primary and secondary schools were required to take courses in religion, usually taught by clergymen. (Pupils of other faiths had the option of having religion taught by their own teachers.) The instruction stressed, along with moral precepts, loyalty to and respect for the Tsar. These feeble efforts were the best that the Imperial Government had to offer in the realm of political indoctrination.

In times of internal unrest, the Church played its part in support of law and order through sermons and publications. The Church depicted the Tsar as the vicar of God and condemned disobedience to him as a sin. In this connection, the Orthodox Church frequently resorted to anti-Semitic appeals. The most anti-Semitic of all the Christian churches, it played a major part in excluding Jews from Russia prior to the partitions of Poland in the eighteenth century and keeping them confined to the provinces of what had been Poland (the "Pale of Settlement") afterward. The clergy blamed Jews for the crucifixion of Christ, and without endorsing pogroms, did not condemn them either. In 1914, the Synod authorized the construction of a church to commemorate the victim of Beilis's alleged "ritual murder."[97] In 1905 and after, Orthodox publications placed on Jews responsibility for the revolutionary ferment, accusing them of conspiring to destroy Christianity and take over the world.

The last decade of the Imperial regime saw developments within the Church that from the government's point of view augured ill for the future.

The formal monopoly of the Established Church on the dogmas and rituals of the Orthodox religion had long been challenged by two heresies, that of the Old Believers and those known collectively as Dissenters or Sectarians. The Old Believers (*staroobriadtsy* as they called themselves or *raskol'niki*— "splitters"—as they were labeled by the official Church) descended from those Russians who in the seventeenth century had rejected the ritualistic changes introduced by Patriarch Nikon. Although persecuted and discriminated against, they held their own and even managed, surreptitiously, to make converts. They developed a strong spirit of cohesion and, as is often the case with persecuted minorities, became successful at business. The Sectarians divided into numerous branches, some of which resembled Protestant sects, others of which reverted to pre-Christian practices, accompanied by all kinds of sexual excesses. Official censuses placed the number of Old Believers and Sectarians at 2 million (1897), approximately one-half of them Old Believers, but their actual number was certainly much higher, for the government, treating adherents of these groups as apostates, did not hesitate to falsify statistics. Some estimates place their memberships as high as 20 million. If correct, this would mean that at the turn of the century approximately one out of four Great Russians, Belorussians, and Ukrainians was outside the official Church. Not surprisingly, the Church was in the forefront of those urging the persecution of the Old Believers and Dissenters, who were making serious inroads on its membership.

There also developed within the Church, especially among the parish clergy, dangerous oppositional trends. Enlightened clergymen pressed for reforms in the status of the Church: worried about too close an identification with the monarchy, they demanded greater independence. After 1905, the government was disturbed to see some clergymen elected to the Duma take their seats alongside liberal and even radical deputies and join in criticizing the regime.

But the clerical hierarchy remained staunchly conservative, as became evident every time lay Christians wanted the Church to pay less attention to ritual and more to good works. In 1901, the Synod excommunicated Leo Tolstoy, the most influential religious writer in Russia, on the grounds that he incited the population against social distinctions and patriotism.

The close identification of the Orthodox Church with the state proved a mixed blessing. While it gave the clerical Establishment all kinds of benefits, it linked its destiny too closely to that of the monarchy. In 1916–17, when the Crown would come under assault, the Church could do very little to help: and when the monarchy sank, it went down with it.

In the eyes of foreign observers Russia of 1900 was a mixture of contradictions. A French commentator compared her to "one of those castles, constructed at different epochs, where the most discordant styles are seen side by side, or else those houses, built piecemeal and at intervals, which never have either the unity or convenience of dwellings erected on one plan and at one rush."[98] The Revolution of 1905 was an explosion of these contradictions. The fundamental question facing Russia after the October Manifesto was whether the settlement offered by the Crown would suffice to calm passions and resolve social and political conflicts. To understand why the prospect for such a compromise was poor, it is necessary to know the condition and mentality of the two main protagonists, the peasantry and the intelligentsia.

3

Rural Russia

In the early 1900s, Russia was overwhelmingly rural. The peasantry constituted four-fifths of her inhabitants by legal status and three-quarters by occupation: the same proportion as in France on the eve of her revolution. Agriculture was far and away the largest source of national wealth. Russia's exports consisted primarily of foodstuffs. The small industrial working class issued directly from the village and maintained close links with it. In terms of her social and economic structure, therefore, Imperial Russia resembled more an Asiatic country like China than Western Europe, though she considered herself a part of Europe, in whose politics she actively participated as one of the great powers.

To an extent inconceivable either in the West or in countries untouched by Westernization, Russia's rural population was a world unto itself. Its relationship to the officialdom and the educated class was in all respects but the racial like that of the natives of Africa or Asia to their colonial rulers. The peasantry was hardly affected by the Westernization which had transformed Russia's elite into Europeans, and in its culture remained loyal to Muscovite Russia. Russian peasants spoke their own dialect, followed their own logic, pursued their own interests, and viewed their betters as aliens to whom they had to pay taxes and deliver recruits but with whom they had nothing in common. The Russian peasant of 1900 owed loyalty only to his village and canton; at most he was conscious of some vague allegiance to his province. His sense of national identity was confined to respect for the Tsar and suspicion of foreigners.

Under assault from the Westernized intelligentsia, the monarchy came to regard the peasant as the bearer of "true" Russianness and it went to great lengths to protect him from the corrupting influence of the city. It institutionalized the cultural isolation of the peasantry by tying it to the village commune and subjecting it to special laws and taxes. It offered peasants few educational opportunities, and such little schooling as it provided it preferred to entrust to the clergy. It placed obstacles to the entry of outsiders into villages and forbade Jews to settle in them. At the turn of the century, the conservative establishment saw in the alliance of the Crown and the village the cornerstone of the country's stability. As events were to show, this was a profound misconception. As conservative as the *muzhik* indeed was, his world outlook, his values, and his interests made him exceedingly volatile. Unlikely to initiate a revolution, he was certain to respond to urban disorders with a revolution of his own.

The life of the Russian peasantry revolved around three institutions: the household *(dvor)*, the village *(derevnia* or *selo)*, and the commune *(mir* or *obshchina)*. All three were distinguished by a low degree of continuity, structural fluidity, poorly developed hierarchies, and the prevalence of personal rather than functional relations. In these respects, Russian rural conditions differed sharply from those found in Western societies and certain Oriental ones (notably Japan's), a fact which was to have profound consequences for Russia's political development.

The peasant household was the basic unit of rural Russia. In 1900, the Empire had 22 million such households, 12 million in European Russia. The typical Great Russian *dvor* was a joint family, with the parents living under the same roof with their sons, married and unmarried, and their respective families, as well as unmarried daughters. This kind of family structure was encouraged by Russia's climatic conditions, under which the brevity of the agricultural season (four to six months) called for coordinated seasonal work by many hands in brief bursts of intense effort. Statistical evidence indicates that the larger the household, the more efficiently it functioned and the richer it was likely to be: a large *dvor* cultivated more land, owned more livestock, and earned more money per head. Small households, with one or two adults, either merged with others or died.[1] At the turn of the century, the largest number of Russian rural households (40.2 percent) had between six and ten members.[2] Despite their proven economic advantages, the proportion of large households kept on declining: to escape quarrels common in joint families, many peasant couples preferred to leave and set up their own households. The disintegration of large joint family households would accelerate in the twentieth century for economic reasons which will be described in due course.

15. Russian peasants: late nineteenth century.

Although the typical household was based on kinship relations and its members were most commonly connected by blood or marriage, the determining criterion was economic—namely, work. The *dvor* owed its cohesion to the fact that it engaged in disciplined field work under the direction of a headman. A son who left the village to make his living elsewhere ceased to be a member of the household and forfeited his claim to its property. Conversely, strangers (e.g., sons-in-law, stepsons, and adopted children) admitted into the household as regular workers acquired the rights of family members.[3] Occasionally, households were formed entirely on such a voluntary basis by peasants who were not related either by blood or marriage.

The Russian peasant household was organized on a simple authoritarian model, under which full authority over the members and their belongings was entrusted to one person, known as *bol'shak* or *khoziain*. This family patriarch was usually the father, but the post could also be assigned, by common consent, to another adult male. The elder's functions were many: he assigned farm and household duties, he disposed of property, he adjudicated domestic disputes, and he represented the household in its dealings with the outside world. Customary peasant law endowed him with unquestioned authority over his *dvor*: in many ways, he was heir to the authority of the serf owner. Since the Emancipation Edict of 1861, the *bol'shak* was also authorized by the government to turn over members of his household to administrative organs for punishment. He was the paterfamilias in the most archaic sense of the word, a replica in miniature of the Tsar.

The political and economic attitudes of Russian peasants had been formed in the first five hundred years of the current millennium, when no government inhibited their movement across the Eurasian plain and land was available in unlimited quantities. The collective memory of this era lay at the root of the peasantry's primitive anarchism. It also determined the practices of inheritance followed by Russian peasants into modern times. It has been observed that in regions of the world where land is in short supply, landowners, both nobles and peasants, are likely to practice primogeniture, under which the bulk of the property is left to the eldest son. Where it is available in abundance, the tendency is to adopt "partible" inheritance, dividing the land and other belongings equally among the male heirs.* Even after agricultural land had become scarce, Russians continued to adhere to the old practices. Until 1917–18, when inheritance was outlawed, Russian landlords and peasants divided their properties in equal shares among male descendants. So entrenched was the custom that the monarchy's attempts, launched under Peter I, to have the upper class keep its estates intact by bequeathing them to a single heir proved unenforceable.

The *muzhik* held most of his land as a communal allotment *(nadel)* to which he held no title: when the household died out or moved away, it reverted to the commune. But any land held by the peasant in private property outside the commune, as well as all his movable wealth (money, implements, livestock, seed grain, etc.), customary law allowed his heirs to distribute among themselves.

The practice of partible inheritance had profound effects on Russian rural conditions and, indeed, on many other seemingly unrelated aspects of Russian life. For as has been pointed out, the

> transmission *mortis causa* [by reason of death] is not only the means by which the reproduction of the social system is carried out . . . it is also the way in which interpersonal relationships are structured.[4]

After the passing of its head, the household's belongings were divided, whereupon the household dissolved and the brothers parted to set up households of their own. As a result, the *dvor* did not outlast the life span of its head, which made this basic institution of the Russian countryside exceedingly transient. In every generation—that is, three or four times a century—households throughout Russia broke apart and subdivided, much as do amoebas or other rudimentary biological organisms. Russian rural life perpetuated itself by a ceaseless process of fission, which inhibited the development of higher, more complex forms of social and economic organization. One *dvor* begat other

*Jack Goody in Jack Goody *et al.,* eds., *Family and Inheritance* (Cambridge, 1976), 117. Another factor affecting inheritance practices is the proximity of cities: Wilhelm Abel, *Agrarpolitik,* 2nd ed. (Göttingen, 1958), 154.

dvory, which, in turn, multiplied in the same manner, like producing like and nothing new and different being given an opportunity to emerge.

The consequences of this custom become apparent when examined in the light of societies where the peasantry practiced indivisibility of property. Primogeniture makes possible a high degree of rural stability and gives the state a firm base of support in rural institutions. A Japanese sociologist thus compares the situation in Chinese and Indian villages, where primogeniture was unknown, with that in his own country, where it was prevalent:

> Because the principle of primogeniture succession held in Japan, the ruling stratum of a village tended to be comparatively stable over the generations. This stability was lacking in China and India. . . . The Chinese rule of equal sharing [of inheritance] prevents the maintenance of family status, and the status changes from generation to generation. As a result, the village power center shifts, the leaders' authority wanes, and no village-wide domination or status-subordination develops. . . . In Japan, lineally determined familism permeates the entire village structure; the main, or parent, house can easily perpetuate itself through the family inheritance system, and thereby acquire traditional authority. The family, clan, and village function together and promote unity. Thus, in Japanese rural society, the main-branch family, parent-child, or master-servant relationship influences to some degree all aspects of village social life.[5]

The observations here made about China apply to Russia: in both cases rural institutions were underdeveloped and ephemeral.

Several features of the peasant *dvor* call for emphasis. The household allowed no room for individuality: it was a collective which submerged the individual in the group. Second, given that the will of the *bol'shak* was absolute and his orders binding, life in the *dvor* accustomed the peasant to authoritarian government and the absence of norms (laws) to regulate personal relations. Third, the household made no allowance for private property: all belongings were held in common. Male members acquired outright ownership of the household's movable property only at its dissolution, at which time it once again turned into the collective property of the new household. Finally, there was no continuity between households, and consequently neither pride in ancestry nor family status in the village, such as characterized Western European and Japanese rural societies. In sum, the Great Russian peasant, living in his natural environment, had no opportunity to acquire a sense of individual identity, respect for law and property, or social status in the village—qualities indispensable for the evolution of more advanced forms of political and economic organization. Enlightened Russian statesmen became painfully aware of this reality in the early years of the twentieth century and tried to do something to integrate the peasant into society at large, but it was late.

Russian peasants lived in villages, called *derevni,* after *derevo,* meaning wood, of which they were constructed. Large villages were known as *sela.*

16. Village assembly.

Individual farmsteads *(khutora)* located on their land were practically unknown in central Russia: they existed mainly in the western and southern
provinces of the Empire which had been under Polish rule until the eighteenth
century. The number of households per village varied greatly from region to
region, depending on natural conditions, of which the availability of water was
the most important. In the north, where water was abundant, the villages
tended to be small; they increased in size as one proceeded southward. In the
central industrial regions of European Russia villages averaged 34.8 households, and in the central black-earth region, 103.5.[6] Whereas in the case of
individual households size meant prosperity, in the case of villages the opposite
held true: smaller villages were likely to be better off. The explanation lies in
the practice of strip farming. For reasons which will be spelled out below,
Russian communes divided the land into narrow strips, scattered at varying
distances from the village. In a large village, peasants had to waste a great deal
of time moving with their equipment from strip to strip, often many kilometers
apart, which presented special difficulties at harvest time. When villages grew
too large to cultivate the land efficiently, the inhabitants either "hived off"
to form new ones or else abandoned agriculture and turned to industrial
occupations.

At the turn of the century, central Russia consisted of tens of thousands
of such villages, usually five to ten kilometers apart.

Compared with rural settlements in other parts of the world, the Russian
village was loosely structured and fluid, with few institutions to provide continuity. It was the household rather than the village that served as the building
block of Russian rural society. The principal village official, the *starosta,* was
chosen, often against his will, at the insistence of the bureaucracy, which
wanted a village representative with whom to deal. Since he could be removed

by the same bureaucrats, he represented not so much the population as the government.[7]

The all-male village assembly, or *sel'skii skhod,* was connected with the commune rather than the village—institutions which, as will be pointed out below, were not identical. Composed of household elders, it met periodically to decide on matters of common concern and then dispersed: it had no other responsibilities and no standing organization. The absence in the village of institutional forms bears emphasis because it explains the extreme paucity of political experience in the life of Russian peasants. The Russian village could display great cohesion when threatened from the outside. But within its own confines, it never developed organs of self-government able to provide the peasants with political practice—that is, teach them to translate the habits of personal relations acquired within the walls of the household into more formal social relations.

The critical factor in the underdevelopment in Russia of a durable and functional village structure, the reason for the village's fluidity, was, as in the case of the *dvor,* the absence of traditions of primogeniture. Compared with an English or Japanese village, the Russian village resembled a nomadic encampment: the peasant's log cabin *(izba),* constructed in a few days and frequently destroyed by fire, was not much more durable than a tent.

The third peasant institution, the commune *(obshchina),* usually overlapped with the village but was not identical with it. Whereas the village was a physical entity—cottages in close proximity—the commune was a legal institution, a collective arrangement for the distribution among its members of land and taxes. Residence in a given village did not automatically confer membership: peasants without land allotments as well as non-peasants (e.g., the priest or schoolteacher) did not belong and could not take part in communal decisions. Furthermore, although the great majority of Russian communes were of the "single" type, which embraced one village, this was not universal practice. In the north, where villages were small, several of them sometimes combined to form one commune; in the central regions and even more often in the south, large villages would divide into two or more communes.

The commune was an association of peasants holding communal land allotments. This land, divided into strips, it periodically redistributed among members. Redistributions *(peredely),* which took place at regular intervals— ten, twelve, fifteen years or so, according to local custom—were carried out to allow for changes in the size of households brought about by deaths, births, and departures. They were a main function of the commune and its distinguishing characteristic. The commune divided its land into strips in order to assure each member of allotments of equal quality and distance from the village. By 1900, approximately one-third of the communes, mostly in the western and southern borderlands, had ceased the practice of repartitioning even though formally they were still treated as "repartitional communes." In the Great Russian provinces, the practice of repartition was virtually universal.

Through the village assembly, the commune resolved issues of concern to its members, including the calendar of field work, the distribution of taxes and other fiscal obligations (for which its members were held collectively responsible), and disputes among households. It could expel troublesome members and have them exiled to Siberia; it had the power to authorize passports, without which peasants could not leave the village, and even to compel an entire community to change its religious allegiance from the official church to one of the sects. The assembly reached its decisions by acclamation: it did not tolerate dissent from the will of the majority, viewing it as antisocial behavior.*

The commune was largely confined to central Russia. On the periphery of the Empire—in what had been the Polish-Lithuanian Commonwealth, the Ukraine, and the Cossack regions—most of the peasants tilled individually, by households, under a system known as *podvornoe zemlevladenie.* Here, each household held, either in ownership or under lease, a parcel of land which it cultivated as it pleased. By contrast, in northern and central Russia, the peasants held the bulk of their land in strips and cultivated it under communal discipline. They did not own the land, the title to which was held by the commune. At the beginning of the twentieth century, 77.2 percent of the rural households in the fifty provinces of European Russia tilled the land communally; in the thirty or so Great Russian provinces, communal ownership was virtually universal (97–100 percent).[8] Membership in a commune and access to a communal allotment did not preclude peasants from buying land for private use from landlords or other owners. In the more prosperous regions it was not uncommon for peasants to till both communal allotments and their private land. In 1910, the peasants of European Russia held communally 151 million hectares and 14 million hectares in outright ownership.†

The origins of the Russian commune are obscure and a subject of controversy. Some see in it the spontaneous expression of an alleged Russian sense of social justice, while others view it as the product of state pressures to ensure collective responsibility for the fulfillment of obligations to the Crown and landlord. Recent studies indicate that the repartitional commune first appeared toward the end of the fifteenth century, became common in the sixteenth, and prevalent in the seventeenth. It served a variety of functions, as useful to officials and landlords as to peasants. The former it guaranteed, through the institution of collective responsibility, the payment of taxes and delivery of recruits; the latter it enabled to present a united front in dealings with external authority.[9] The principle of periodic redistribution of land ensured (at any rate, in theory) that every peasant had enough to provide for his family and, at the same time, to meet his obligations to the landlord and state. Such considerations moved the Imperial Government at the time of Emancipation to retain the commune and extend it to some areas where it had been

---

*Aversion to dissent seems to be universal among peasants: Robert Redfield notes that "villages do not like factions" (*Little Community,* Uppsala-Stockholm, 1955, 44).

†Calculated on the basis of figures in *Ezhegodnik Rossii, 1910 g.* (St. Petersburg, 1911), 258–63. Most of that private land was owned by associations and villages rather than by individual households.

unknown. It was expected that once the villages had redeemed their land by repaying the state the moneys it had advanced the landlords on their behalf, the communes would dissolve and the peasants assume title to their allotments. However, during the conservative reign of Alexander III legislation was passed which made it virtually impossible for peasants to withdraw. This policy was inspired by the belief that the commune was a stabilizing force which strengthened the authority of the *bol'shak,* curbed peasant anarchism, and inhibited the formation of a volatile landless proletariat.

17. Peasants in winter clothing.

By 1900, many Russians had grown disenchanted with the commune. Government officials and liberals noted that while the commune did not prevent the emergence of a landless proletariat it did keep down the enterprising peasant. Social-Democrats saw it as doomed to disintegrate under the pressure of intensifying "class differentiation" among poor, middle, and rich peasants. A conference on rural problems convened in 1902, in the wake of recent peasant disturbances, concluded that the commune was the main cause of the backwardness of Russian peasant farming.*

But the peasantry itself held fast to communal forms of agriculture because it promised access to a fair and adequate share of arable land and helped maintain the cohesion of the household. If land allotments had shrunk considerably by 1900, the peasant could console himself with the hope that sooner or later all privately held land in the country would be confiscated and transferred to the communes for repartitioning.

The three rural institutions—the household, the village, and the commune—provided the environment which shaped the *muzhik*'s social habits. They were well adapted to the harsh geographic and climatic conditions in which Russian agriculture had to be carried out. But nearly everything the

*A. A. Kofod, *Russkoe zemleustroistvo,* 2nd. ed. (St. Petersburg, 1914), 23. As early as the 1880s, Leroy-Beaulieu says that he met with universal disenchantment with the commune: Anatole Leroy-Beaulieu, *The Empire of the Tsars and the Russians,* II (New York-London, 1898), 45–46.

peasant learned in his familiar environment proved to be useless and sometimes positively harmful when applied elsewhere. Living in a small community, the Russian peasant was unequipped for the transition to a complex society, composed of individuals rather than households and regulated by impersonal relations, into which he would be thrust by the upheavals of the twentieth century.

There exists a widespread impression that before 1917 Russia was a "feudal" country in which the Imperial Court, the Church, and a small minority of wealthy nobles owned the bulk of the land, while the peasants either cultivated minuscule plots or worked as tenant farmers. This condition is believed to have been a prime cause of the Revolution. In fact, nothing could be further from the truth: the image derives from conditions in pre-1789 France, where, indeed, the vast majority of peasants tilled the land of others. It was in such Western countries as England, Ireland, Spain, and Italy (all of which happened to avoid revolution) that ownership of agricultural land was concentrated in the hands of the wealthy, sometimes to an extreme degree. (In England in 1873, for example, four-fifths of the acreage was the property of fewer than 7,000 persons; in 1895, only 14 percent of Britain's cultivated land, exclusive of Ireland, was tilled by its owners, the rest being leased.) Russia, by contrast, was a classic land of small peasant cultivators. Latifundia here existed primarily in the borderlands, in regions taken from Poland and Sweden. At the time of their Emancipation, the ex-serfs received approximately one-half of the land which they had previously tilled. In the decades that followed, with the help of the Land Bank, which offered them credit on easy terms, they bought additional properties, mainly from landlords. By 1905, peasant cultivators owned, either communally or privately, 61.8 percent of the land in private possession in Russia.[10] As we shall see, after the Revolution of 1905 the exodus of non-peasant landowners from the countryside accelerated, and in 1916, on the eve of the Revolution, peasant cultivators in European Russia owned nine-tenths of the arable land.

Notwithstanding their intent, by 1900 Russia's communes could no longer assure their members of equitable allotments: over time, larger, stronger households had managed to accumulate more of them as well as to acquire most of the land bought by peasants for private use. In 1893, 7.3 percent of the communal households had no land.[11] These landless peasants, called *batraki,* were one of the four identifiable categories of peasants. The others consisted of peasants whose allotments were entirely communal (the great majority), those who had land both inside and outside the commune, and those (very few in number) who cultivated their own.* Peasants in the two last-named categories were sometimes labeled "kulaks" ("fists"). This term, beloved of radical

*Under a last-minute provision inserted into the Emancipation Edict, a peasant who did not want to pay could take a fraction of the allotment due to him free of charge. Such allotments were called *otrezki.*

intellectuals, had no precise economic meaning for the peasants themselves, being applied sometimes to the rich, those who employed hired labor, traded, and lent money, sometimes to the hardworking, thrifty, and sober.[12]

The physical distribution of land in the villages was exceedingly complicated, due partly to communal practices, partly to the legacy of serfdom. The pre-1861 Russian estate was not a plantation. The custom was for the landlord to divide his arable acreage in two parts, one of which the serf household cultivated for him, the other for itself. The halves were, as a rule, commingled. Under serfdom, the typical Russian village, especially in the northern and western provinces, consisted of a mosaic of long, narrow strips: the strips which the serfs cultivated for the landlord and those which they cultivated for themselves lay side by side. This arrangement, known as *cherespolositsa*, continued after Emancipation. Frequently, the land which the landlord retained as a result of the Emancipation settlement and now exploited with the help of hired labor remained wedged among the communal holdings. The land which the landlords subsequently sold to peasants, therefore, continued to be held and tilled alongside communal allotments, to the intense annoyance of communal peasants, who hated these private lots, which they called "babylons" *(vavilony)* and wanted for communal distribution.[13]

Serfdom bequeathed yet another painful legacy. While allotting the emancipated serf generous quantities of arable land (about five hectares per adult male), the Emancipation Edict left pasture and woodland in the landlord's possession. Under serfdom, the peasant had enjoyed the rights of grazing cattle and gathering firewood and lumber. These rights he lost once property lines had been drawn. Some landlords began to charge for the use of pasture; others collected tolls for letting peasants' cattle cross their properties. At the turn of the century, one of the loudest peasant complaints concerned the shortage of grazing land. The peasant had to have access to adequate pasture—ideally, at a ratio of one hectare of pasture to two of arable, but at a very minimum one to five, below which he could not feed his cattle and draft horses.[14] Much unhappiness was also caused by the lack of access to forest. In 1905 the most prevalent form of rural violence took the form of cutting lumber.

Russia was widely believed to suffer from an acute shortage of agricultural land. At first sight it may appear surprising that a country as large as Russia should have experienced land shortages (or rural overpopulation, which is the same). And, indeed, Russia had a long way to go to match the population densities of Western Europe. With 130 million inhabitants and 22 million square kilometers of territory, the Empire in 1900 had an overall population density of 6 persons per square kilometer. Even such a young country as the United States had at that time a higher population density (8 per square kilometer). And yet, while the United States suffered endemic labor shortages, which it met by opening its doors to millions of European immigrants, Russia suffocated from rural overcrowding.

The explanation of this seeming paradox lies in the fact that in agricultural countries population densities acquire meaning only by relating the number of inhabitants to that share of the territory which is suitable for farming. Viewed in these terms, Russia was hardly a country of boundless expanses. Of the 15 million square kilometers of European Russia and Siberia, only 2 million could be cultivated and another 1 million used for pasture. In other words, in the homeland of the Great Russians, only one square kilometer out of five was suitable for agriculture. Once allowance is made for this fact, the figures for Russian population densities change dramatically. In Siberia, the average density in 1900 was 0.5 per square kilometer, a negligible figure. In the fifty provinces of European Russia, it rose to 23.7 per square kilometer, which exceeded slightly the figure estimated by economic geographers to be optimal for the region.* But even this figure misleads because it includes the sparsely populated provinces of northern Russia. The regions which really mattered, because they held the great mass of Russian peasants, were the central provinces, and here the population density ranged from 50 to 80. This figure matches that of contemporary France and exceeds that of Ireland and Scotland. In other words, had St. Petersburg given up Siberia and the northern provinces, its population densities would have equaled those of Western Europe.

Densities of this magnitude might have proven tolerable were it not for pre-revolutionary Russia's extraordinary population growth. With an annual excess of births over deaths on the order of 15 per 1,000, Russia had the highest rate of natural increase in Europe.† The implications of such a rapid population growth for agriculture can be demonstrated statistically. In the Empire of 1900, three-quarters of the population was employed on the land. With an increase of 15 per 1,000 each year and a population of 130 million, 1,950,000 new inhabitants were added annually, 1,500,000 of them in the countryside. Allowing for the very high infant mortality rate, we are left with a million or so additional mouths which the countryside had to feed each year. Given that an average Great Russian household had five members and tilled ten hectares, these figures mean that Russia required annually an additional 2 million hectares of arable land.‡

In Western Europe, the pressures generated by a somewhat smaller but still rapid population growth from the middle of the eighteenth century onward was solved in part by overseas migration and in part by industrialization. During the nineteenth century and the early years of the twentieth, the agrar-

*Friedrich Ratzel, *Anthropogeographie,* II (Stuttgart, 1891), 257–65. If one recalculates Ratzel's figures, given in leagues, a country with Russia's climate should support 23 inhabitants per square kilometer.

†Recent researches indicate that the population growth in pre-revolutionary Russia may have been even higher than believed at the time. The current estimate places the excess of births over deaths in 1900 at 16.5 per 1,000 and rising. In European Russia it is estimated to have been 18.4 (1897–1916) and in the Lower Volga region was high as 20: S. I. Bruk and V. M. Kabuzan in *ISSSR,* No. 3 (1980), 81. H. J. Habbakuk believes that partible (or "equal division") inheritance promotes population growth in that it encourages marriage: *Journal of Economic History,* XV (1955), 5–6.

‡The government estimated that between 1861 and 1901 the rural population in the Empire grew from 52 to 86.6 million and that the annual accretion of rural inhabitants in the closing years of the nineteenth century came to 1.5 million: Alexander Kornilov in Josef Melnik, *Russen über Russland* (Frankfurt, 1906), 404. This was the figure used by Stolypin in 1907: see below, Chapter 5. The margin of error in all Russian statistics, however, is wide and these figures do not make allowance either for non-rural inhabitants or for infant mortality.

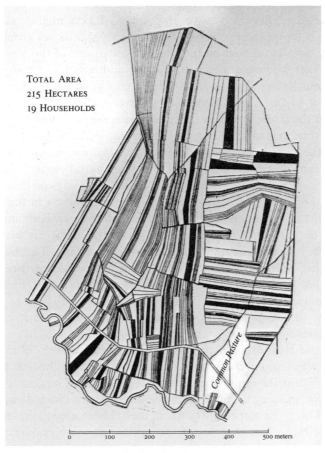

TOTAL AREA
215 HECTARES
19 HOUSEHOLDS

Common Pasture

| 0 | 100 | 200 | 300 | 400 | 500 meters |

18. Strip farming as practiced in Central Russia, c. 1900.
The strips in black are cultivated by one household.

ian countries of Europe (e.g., Italy, Ireland, Austria-Hungary) sent much of their excess rural population to the Americas. The net outflow of overseas migrants from Western Europe between 1870 and 1914 is estimated at 25 million, which took care of approximately one-half of the continent's excess rural population. Much of the remainder found employment in industry. Industrialization permits unprecedented levels of population density. For instance, Germany, which in the first half of the nineteenth century had been a major source of overseas migration, in the second half of the century, in consequence of industrial development, not only ceased to send people abroad but had to import labor. Some industrial countries attained staggering population densities: England and the Low Countries accommodated 250–270 inhabitants a square kilometer, or several times that of the most crowded areas of central Russia, without suffering from overpopulation. There can be little doubt that the ability of the Western countries, through emigration and industrialization, to relieve population pressures played a major role in enabling them to avoid social revolution.

Russia had neither safety valve. Her citizens did not migrate abroad: they preferred to colonize their own country. The only significant groups to leave Russia were non-Russians from the Western provinces: of the 3,026,000 subjects of the Tsar who emigrated between 1897 and 1916, more than 70 percent were Jews and Poles.[15] But as Jews did not engage in agriculture and Poles engaged in it in their own homeland, their departure did nothing to ease pressures on the Russian village. Why Russians did not emigrate is far from clear, but several explanations suggest themselves. Perhaps the most important cause was the practice of cultivating by joint families and in communes. Russian peasants were not accustomed to pulling up stakes and leaving for the unknown, except in groups. Although peasants were always on the lookout for fresh land, they never moved by families, as was common in the American West, but only with enough fellow peasants to set up a new commune, usually by villages or parts of villages.[16] Second, living in a largely self-sufficient economy, they lacked money to pay the shipping fare. Third, they were convinced that before long there would occur a general repartition of non-peasant land in Russia and did not want to be excluded from it. Finally, living in a self-contained universe of Orthodox Slavs, on land hallowed as Holy Rus, little exposed to foreign cultures, Russian peasants found life among infidels hard to conceive.

Nor could Russian industry absorb significant numbers of excess peasants. In the 1880s and even more so in the 1890s, rapid industrial growth led to a rise in industrial employment: in 1860, Russia had 565,000 industrially employed, and in 1900, 2.2 million (of the latter, about one-half were factory workers).[17] Using the same figures for households as above, this means that during the closing four decades of the nineteenth century, the number of Russians freed from dependence on agriculture grew from 3 to perhaps as much as 12 million. But with an annual accretion of 1 million rural inhabitants, it also meant that industry at best absorbed from the land one-third of the new population.*

Population growth without a commensurate expansion of arable land or emigration meant that the quantity of land available for distribution in the communes shrank steadily: the average allotment per male "soul," which in 1861 had been 5.24 hectares, decreased in 1880 to 3.83 and in 1900 to 2.84 hectares.† The peasants compensated for this by leasing land. Around 1900, more than one-third of landlord land was rented by peasants.[18] Even so, many peasants had access neither to land nor to regular employment.

---

*There were also 7 to 8 million persons occupied in household industries *(kustarnaia promysh-lennost'),* which operated largely to supply the peasants with consumer durables: P. A. Khromov, *Ekonomika Rossii perioda promyshlennogo kapitalizma* (Moscow, 1963), 105. The majority of the persons who worked in these industries did so at times free from field work and they continued to rely primarily on agricultural income.

†The reliability of these figures has been questioned, however, on the grounds that they make no allowance for peasants who had left the land for the cities and industrial centers although nominally still counted as members of the commune: A. S. Ermolov, *Nash zemel'nyi vopros* (St. Petersburg, 1906), 62.

Many of the landless or land-poor peasants found employment as farm-hands: they usually spent the winter in the village and at sowing and harvest time hired themselves out to richer peasants or landlords, often far away from home. These workers provided the bulk of the labor force on private estates and privately held peasant land. Others took occasional work in industry, while retaining their rural connections. In the villages, landless peasants had no status. Excluded from the commune, they took part in no organized life.

Many peasants whom the commune could not accommodate went to the cities on temporary permits in search of work. It is estimated that in the early twentieth century, each year some 300,000 peasants, most of them males, moved into Russia's cities, looking for casual jobs, peddling products of cottage industries, or simply milling around for lack of anything better to do. Their presence significantly altered the character of the cities. The 1897 census revealed that 38.8 percent of the Empire's urban inhabitants were peasants and that they represented the fastest-growing element in the urban population.[19] In the large cities, their proportion was still higher. Thus, at the turn of the century in St. Petersburg and Moscow, respectively, 63.3 and 67.2 percent of the residents (actual, not those legally registered) were peasants.[20] In the smaller cities, these unwelcome guests were known as *inogorodnye* or "out-of-towners." They were especially attracted to towns in the prosperous agrarian regions where agriculture was carried out by households rather than communally, such as the Cossack settlements on the Don and Terek rivers and southwestern Siberia.[21] Here gathered multitudes of *batraki,* who cast avaricious eyes on the large, prosperous farms, awaiting the signal announcing the onset of the grand repartition.

In striking contrast to Western Europe, Russian cities did not urbanize the rural newcomers: it has been said that the only discernible difference between the peasant in the village and his brethren in the city was that the former wore the shirt outside and the latter inside his trousers.[22] The peasants who flooded the cities, lacking in institutional attachments of any sort, without steady employment, their families usually left behind, represented an unassimilable and potentially disruptive element.

This was the essence of the "land problem" which greatly exercised Russians in and out of government: there was a widespread feeling that unless something drastic was done, and done soon, the countryside would explode. It was axiomatic among the peasants, as well as among socialist and liberal intellectuals, that the crux of the problem was land shortage, and that this difficulty could be resolved only by expropriating all privately held (non-communal) land. The liberals wanted large properties to be taken with compensation. The socialists preferred either the "socialization" of land which would place the arable at the disposal of the cultivators or its "nationalization" on behalf of the state.

But historians and agrarian specialists have cast doubts on the evidence of a severe agrarian crisis and the remedies proposed for it.

One of the principal arguments of those who held that the Russian village was in a state of deep and worsening crisis was the fact that it was constantly falling into arrears on the redemption payments (mortgage money owed the government for its help in procuring land for the peasants in the 1861 Emancipation settlement). The question has recently been raised whether these arrears really prove the impoverishment of the village.[23] Instead of making mortgage payments, the peasant steadily increased purchases of consumer goods, as shown by the rise in government revenues from sales taxes, which more than doubled in the decade 1890–1900. Citing this evidence, an American historian concludes:

> If the peasants were the primary source of indirect tax income, then they must have been the major consumer of the goods taxed, that is, sugar, matches, and so forth. Therefore, since they *could* purchase nonagricultural goods, one can hardly depict the rural sector as ravaged by a ruthless tax system . . . Peasant land redemption arrears grew not because of an inability to pay, but because of an unwillingness to pay.[24]

This argument is reinforced with evidence of a rise in peasant savings and an increase in farm work wages. It raises doubts whether the Russian village was indeed suffering from severe undernourishment as claimed by liberal and socialist politicians.*

Well-informed contemporaries, while conceding that the country faced serious agrarian problems, questioned whether these were caused by land shortages and whether the transfer of privately held, non-peasant land into peasant hands would significantly improve things. One such observer, A. S. Ermolov, a onetime Minister of Agriculture, formulated a cogent counterargument to conventional wisdom, the soundness of which subsequent events amply confirmed.[25] Ermolov held that one could not reduce all of Russia's agrarian difficulties to the inadequacy of peasant allotments: the problem was much more complex and had to do mainly with the way the peasant tilled his allotments. The peasants deluded themselves, and were encouraged in their delusion by intellectuals, that seizing landlord properties would greatly improve their economic situation. In fact, there was not enough private land to go around: even if all privately held arable land were distributed among peasants, the resulting increase, which Ermolov estimated at 0.8 hectare per male peasant, would not make much of a difference. Second, even if adequate land reserves could be found, their distribution would be counterproductive because it would only serve to perpetuate outmoded and inefficient modes of cultivation. The problem with Russian agriculture was not the shortage of land but the antiquated manner of cultivating it—a legacy of the times when it had

---

*Ivan Oserow (Ozerov) in Melnik, *Russen,* 211–12. From the statistics provided by A. S. Nifontov (*Zernovoe proizvodstvo Rossii vo vtoroi polovine XIX veka,* Moscow, 1974, 310), it transpires that even after rising grain exports are taken into account, the amount of grain domestically available per capita in the 1890s was larger than it had been twenty years earlier; in other words, food production outpaced population growth. Cf. James Y. Simms, Jr., in *SR,* XXXVI, No. 3 (1977), 310.

been available in unlimited quantities: "In the vast majority of cases, the problem lies not in the absolute land shortage, but in the inadequacy of land for the pursuit of the traditional forms of extensive agriculture." The peasant had to abandon the habits of superficial cultivation and adopt more intensive forms: if he could increase cereal yields by no more than one grain per grain sown, Russia would overflow with bread.* To prove his point, Ermolov noted the paradox that in Russia the prosperity of peasants stood in inverse ratio to the quality and size of their land allotments, a fact which he ascribed to the need of land-poor peasants to pursue more intensive forms of agriculture. In central Russia, at any rate, he saw no correlation between the size of communal allotments and the well-being of peasants. Furthermore, the elimination of landlord estates would deprive the peasantry of wages earned from farm work, an important source of additional income. Ermolov concluded that "nationalization" or "socialization" of land, by encouraging the peasant in his traditional ways of cultivation, would spell disaster and force Russia to import grain. The author suggested a variety of measures resembling those that would be introduced in 1906–11 by Peter Stolypin.

Such voices of experience, however, were ignored by intellectuals who preferred simplistic solutions that appealed to the *muzhik*'s preconceived ideas.

At the turn of the century, Russian industrial workers were, with minor exceptions, a branch of the peasantry rather than a distinct social group. Because of the long winters during which there was no field work, many Russian peasants engaged in non-agrarian pursuits known as *promysly*. Such cottage industries produced farm implements, kitchenware, hardware, and textiles. The custom of combining agriculture with manufacture blurred the distinction between the two occupations. Peasants engaged in *promysly* furnished a pool of semi-skilled labor for Russian industry. The availability of cheap labor in the countryside, which, if not needed, could fall back on farming, explains why the majority (70 percent) of Russian workers held jobs in industrial enterprises located in rural areas.[26] It also explains why Russian workers failed to develop until very late the professional mentality of their Western counterparts, many of whom were descendants of urban artisans.

Russia's first full-time industrial workers were serfs whom Peter I had bonded to state-owned manufactures and mines. To this group, known as "possessional peasants" *(possessionnye krest'iane),* were subsequently added all kinds of people who could not be fitted into the estate system, such as wives and children of army recruits, convicts, prisoners of war, and prostitutes.

The German economist Schulze-Gävernitz divided the 2.4 million full-

*A. S. Ermolov, *Nash zemel'nyi vopros* (St. Petersburg, 1906), 2, 5. Russia, in fact, lagged far behind all European countries in agricultural yields. "Intensive" agriculture also meant adoption of technical crops, for instance, hemp and flax, which brought in more income.

time industrial employees in Russia at the end of the nineteenth century into four subgroups:[27]

1. Peasants seasonally employed in local industries, usually in time free from agricultural work; they slept under the open sky in the summer and in the shops, near the machines, in the winter.

2. Workers banded in cooperatives *(arteli)* who hired themselves out and distributed among members the cooperative's earnings. Housed in barracks furnished by the employer, they usually left their families behind. Because they did not lead a normal family life, workers in this group regarded their status as transient and usually returned to the village to help out with the harvest. Russia's largest industry, textile manufacture, relied heavily on such labor.

These two groups constituted the majority of Russians classified by the 1897 census as industrial workers. They consisted mostly of peasants. The next two categories had severed ties with the village.

3. Workers who lived with their families. Because wages were low, their wives usually also sought full-time employment. They often resided in communal quarters provided by the employers, the living spaces of which were separated by curtains, with kitchens used communally. The employers also often provided them with factory shops and schools. This arrangement would be adopted by the Soviet Government during its industrialization drive in the 1930s.

4. Skilled workers who no longer depended on their employers for anything but wages. They found their own lodgings, bought provisions on the open market, and if laid off, no longer had a village to which to return. It is only in this category that the dependence of the worker on the employer, reminiscent of serf conditions, came to an end. Workers in this category were to be found mainly in the technically advanced industries, such as machine-building, centered in St. Petersburg.

As this classification indicates, industrial employment, in and of itself, did not lead to urbanization. The majority of industrially employed Russians continued to reside in the countryside, where most of the factories were located, and retained close connections with their villages. It comes as no surprise, therefore, that they also retained a rural outlook: Schulze-Gävernitz concluded that the principal differences between Russian and Western European industrial workers derived from the fact that the former had not yet broken ties to the land.[28] The only significant departure from this pattern could be found among skilled workers (Group Four) who as early as the 1880s began to display "proletarian" attitudes. They developed an interest in mutual aid associations and trade unions, about which they had learned from foreign sources, as well as in education. The illegal Central Labor Circle, formed by a group of skilled St. Petersburg workers in 1889, was Russia's first rudimentary trade union. The strikes of textile workers in St. Petersburg in 1896–97 to protest working conditions were the earliest overt manifestations of this new spirit.[29]

Despite the rural origins and outlook of the majority of industrial workers, the government eyed them with suspicion, fearing that their concentration and proximity to cities made them susceptible to corrupting influences. And, indeed, there was cause for concern. In the early 1900s, industrial workers in St. Petersburg and Moscow were 80 to 90 percent literate, which made them an inviting target for the propaganda and agitation of radicals, to which the rural population was quite immune.

T he most difficult aspect of rural Russia to understand is peasant mentality, a subject on which the scholarly literature is quite unhelpful. There exist many works on the economic conditions of the pre-revolutionary peasantry, on its folklore and customs, but virtually no scholarly studies that explain what the *muzhik* believed and how he reasoned.[30] It is as if Russian intellectuals regarded the peasant mind as an immature specimen of the progressive mind (their own) and hence undeserving of serious attention. To understand the peasant mentality, one must have recourse to other than scholarly sources, mainly belles lettres.[31] These can be supplemented with information gathered by students of peasant customary law, which provides an oblique insight into the peasant mind as revealed by the way he coped with problems of daily life, especially property disputes.[32] Familiarity with this material leaves little doubt that the culture of the Russian peasant, as that of the peasantry of other countries, was not a lower, less developed stage of civilization but a civilization in its own right.

As has been pointed out, the world of the Russian peasant was largely self-contained and self-sufficient. It is no accident that in the Russian language the same word—*mir*—is used for the peasant commune, the world, and peace. The peasant's experiences and concerns did not extend beyond his own and neighboring villages. A sociological inquiry into peasant attitudes carried out in the 1920s indicated that even after a decade of war, civil war, and revolution which had dragged the Russian peasantry into the vortex of national and international affairs, the *muzhik* had no interest in anything outside the confines of his canton. He was willing to let the world go its own way as long as it left him alone.[33] Pre-revolutionary literary sources similarly stress the absence among the peasantry of a sense of belonging to the state or nation. They depict it as insulated from influences external to the village and lacking in awareness of national identity. Tolstoy emphatically denied the peasant a sense of patriotism:

> I have never heard any expression of patriotic sentiments from the people, but I have, on the contrary, frequently heard the most serious and respectable men from among the masses giving utterance to the most absolute indifference or even contempt for all kinds of manifestations of patriotism.[34]

The truth of this observation was demonstrated during World War I, when the Russian peasant soldier, even while performing courageously under difficult conditions (shortages of weapons and ammunition), did not understand why he was fighting since the enemy did not threaten his home province. He fought from the habit of obeying: "They order, we go."[35] Inevitably, once the voice of authority grew faint, he stopped obeying and deserted. Equal to the Western soldier in physical courage, he lacked the latter's sense of citizenship, of belonging to a wider community. General Denikin, who observed this behavior at close quarters, blamed it on the total absence of nationalist indoctrination in the armed forces.[36] But it is questionable whether indoctrination by itself would have made much difference. Judging by Western experience, to bring the peasant out of his isolation it was necessary to develop institutions capable of involving him in the country's political, economic, and cultural life: in other words, making him a citizen.

The majority of French and German citizens in the early 1900s were also either peasants or urban dwellers a mere generation or two removed from the peasantry. Until quite recent times the Western European peasant had not been culturally superior to the Russian *muzhik*. Speaking of nineteenth-century France, Eugen Weber draws a picture familiar to the student of Russia: large parts of the country populated by "savages" living in hovels, isolated from the rest of the nation, brutalized and xenophobic.* The situation was not much better in other rural areas of Western Europe. If by 1900 the European peasant had become something different, the reason is that in the course of the nineteenth century institutions had been created that pulled him out of rural isolation.

Using Norway as a model, several such institutions can be identified: the church, the school, the political party, the market, and the manor.† To these we must add private property, which Western scholars take so much for granted that they ignore its immense socializing role. All were weakly developed in late Imperial Russia.

Observers of pre-revolutionary Russia concur that the Orthodox Church, represented in the village by the priest *(pop)*, exerted little cultural influence on the parishioners. The priest's primary function was ritualistic-magic, and his main duty to ensure the flock's safe passage into the next world. A. S. Ermolov, in discussing with Nicholas II the revolutionary unrest, disabused him of the notion that the government could rely on the priests to keep the villages in line: "the clergy in Russia has no influence on the population."[37] The cultural role of the Church in the rural districts was confined to elementary schooling, which taught children to read and write, with bits of religious didacticism thrown in. Higher values—theology, ethics, philosophy—were the preserve of the monastic or "black" clergy, which alone had access to Church careers but was not directly involved in parish life. Because, unlike his Western

---

*Peasants into Frenchmen (Stanford, Calif., 1982), 3, 5, 48, 155–56. "La patrie," the author quotes a French priest, "a fine word . . . that thrills everyone except the peasant": *Ibid.*, 100. On this subject, see further Theodore Zeldin, *France: 1848–1945* (Oxford, 1977), II, 3.

†Robert Redfield, *Peasant Society and Culture* (Chicago-London, 1956), 42–64. In his study of the acculturation of the French peasantry, Weber lists as "agencies of change" roads, participation in the political process ("politization"), migration, military service, schools, and the church.

counterpart, the village priest received little if any financial support from the Church and had no hope of making a career in the clerical hierarchy—this was reserved for unmarried, monastic priests—the vocation did not attract the best elements. The peasant is said to have treated priests "not as guides and advisers, but as a class of tradesmen, who have wholesale and retail dealings in sacraments."[38]

Before 1917, Russia had no system of compulsory education, even on the elementary level, such as France had introduced in 1833 and most of Western Europe adopted by the 1870s. The need for such a system was often discussed in government circles but it was never realized, partly for lack of money, partly from fear of the influence that secular teachers, mostly intellectuals with left-of-center political ideas, would have on peasant youths. (Conservatives complained that schools taught disrespect for parents and old people and made pupils dream of "far-off rivers flowing with milk and honey.")[39] In 1901, Russia had 84,544 elementary schools with an enrollment of 4.5 million pupils, the administration of which was divided between the Ministry of Education (47.5 percent) and the Holy Synod (42.5 percent). In terms of pupils enrolled, the ministry enjoyed a clear advantage (63 percent and 35.1 percent).[40] This was hardly adequate for a country with 23 million children of school age (seven to fourteen years). Literacy, promoted by the *zemstva* and volunteer organizations, did make rapid progress, especially among males, largely because recruits with a certificate attesting to the completion of primary school served shorter terms of military service (four years instead of six): in 1913, nearly 68 percent of the recruits were said to be literate, but it is doubtful whether many of them could do more than sign their name. Approximately only one in five of these recruits had a school certificate qualifying him for shorter service.[41] Neither the schools nor the private associations dedicated to the spread of literacy inculcated national values, because in the eyes of the government, nationalism, a doctrine that considers the "nation" or "people" to be the ultimate sovereign, was a threat to autocracy.[42]

Until 1905, Russia had no legal political institutions outside the bureaucratic chain of command. Political parties were forbidden. Peasants could vote in elections to *zemstva,* but even in this case their choice was narrowly circumscribed by bureaucrats and government-appointed officials. In any event, these organs of self-government dealt with local, not national issues. Peasants could not even aspire to a career in the Imperial civil service, since its ranks were for all practical purposes closed to them. In other words, peasants, even more than the members of the other non-noble estates, were excluded from the country's political life.

Peasants in Russia were not entirely insulated from the commercial marketplace, but the latter played a marginal role in their lives. For one, they did not care to eat food that they did not grow themselves.[43] They bought little, mainly household and farm implements, much of it from other peasants. Nor did they have much to sell: most of the grain that reached the market came from landlord estates or large properties owned by merchants. The ups and downs of the national and international commodity markets, which directly affected the well-being of American, Argentinian, or English farmers, had little bearing on the condition of the *muzhik.*

The manor was viewed by conservative Russians as the outpost of culture in the countryside, and some well-meaning agrarian specialists opposed the expropriation of landlord properties for distribution among peasants from fear of the cultural consequences. This fear may have been justified in the economic sense of the word "culture," in that landlord estates were indeed operated more efficiently and yielded consistently better crops: according to official statistics 12–18 percent more, but in fact possibly as much as 50 percent.* The cultural influence of the manor on the countryside in the spiritual and intellectual sense of the word, however, was insignificant. For one, there were not enough gentry in the countryside: as we have noted, seven out of ten *dvoriane* resided in the cities. Second, an unbridgeable psychological gulf separated the two classes: the peasant insisted on treating the landlord as an interloper and felt he had nothing to learn from him. Tolstoy's "A Landlord's Morning" ("Utro pomeshchika") and Chekhov's village tales show the manor and the hut talking at cross-purposes, without a common language of communication: and where such a language was absent, there could be no transmission of ideas or values. A Frenchman who visited Russia in the 1880s saw the Russian landlord "isolated in the midst of his quondam serfs, outside of the commune, outside even of the *volost'* in which he usually resides: the chain of serfdom broken, nothing else binds him to his former subjects."[44]

Private property is arguably the single most important institution of social and political integration. Ownership of property creates a commitment to the political and legal order since the latter guarantees property rights: it makes the citizen into a co-sovereign, as it were. As such, property is the principal vehicle for inculcating in the mass of the population respect for law and an interest in the preservation of the status quo. Historical evidence indicates that societies with a wide distribution of property, notably in land and residential housing, are more conservative and stabler, and for that reason more resilient to upheavals of all sorts. Thus the French peasant, who in the eighteenth century was a source of instability, became in the nineteenth, as a result of the gains of the French Revolution, a pillar of conservatism.

From this point of view, Russia's experience left a great deal to be desired. Under serfdom, the peasant had, legally speaking, no property rights: the land was the landlord's, and even his movable belongings, although safeguarded by custom, enjoyed no legal protection. The Emancipation Act entrusted his allotment to the commune. And although after 1861 the peasant avidly accumulated real estate, he failed clearly to distinguish it from his communal allotment, which he held only in temporary possession. In his mind, ownership of land, the principal form of wealth, was indissolubly bound up with personal

---

*Ermolov, *Zemel'nyi vopros,* 25. The discrepancy is due to the fact that official statistics counted as landlords' property the land which they leased to peasants.

cultivation and he had no respect for the property rights of non-peasants merely because they held a piece of paper granting them title. In contrast to the peasantry of Western Europe, the *muzhik* lacked a developed sense of property and law, which made him poor material for citizenship.

Thus, there were few bridges connecting the Russian village with the outside world. The officials, the gentry, the middle classes, the intelligentsia lived their lives and the peasants theirs: physical proximity did not make for the flow of ideas. The appearance (in 1910) of Ivan Bunin's novel *The Village,* with its devastating picture of the peasantry, struck the reading public as something from the darkest ages. The book, writes a contemporary critic, "had a shattering effect":

> Russian literature knows many unvarnished depictions of the Russian village, but the Russian reading public had never before confronted such a vast canvas, which with such pitiless truth revealed the very innards of peasant and peasant-like existence in all its *spiritual* ugliness and impotence. What stunned the Russian reader in this book was not the depiction of the material, cultural, legal poverty—to this he had been accustomed from the writings of talented Russian Populists—but the awareness of precisely the *spiritual* impoverishment of Russian peasant reality; and, more than that, the awareness that there was no escape from it. Instead of the image of the almost saintly peasant from which one should learn life's wisdom, on the pages of Bunin's *Village* the reader confronted a pitiful and savage creature, incapable of overcoming its savagery through either material prosperity . . . or education. . . . The maximum that the Russian peasant, as depicted by Bunin, was capable of achieving, even in the person of those who rose above the "normal" level of peasant savagery, was only the awareness of his hopeless savagery, of being doomed . . .[45]

The peasant, who knew how to survive under the most trying circumstances in his native countryside, was utterly disoriented when separated from it. The instant he left the village, his *mir* or world, ruled by custom and dominated by nature, for the city, run by men and their seemingly arbitrary laws, he was lost. The Populist writer Gleb Uspenskii, who rather idealized rural Russia, thus described the effects of the uprooting on the *muzhik:*

> the vast majority of the Russian people is patient and majestic in bearing misfortunes, youthful in spirit, manly in strength, and childishly simple . . . as long as it is subjected to the *power of the earth,* as long as at the root of its existence lies the *impossibility* of flaunting its *commands,* as long as these commands dominate its mind [and] conscience and fill its being . . . Our people *will* remain what it is for as long . . . as it is permeated with and illuminated . . . by the warmth and glow of the mother raw earth . . . Remove the peasant from the land, from the anxieties it brings him, the interests with which it agitates him, make him forget his "peasantness"—and you no longer have the same people, the same ethos, the same warmth which emanates from it. There remains nothing but the vacuous apparatus of the vacuous human organism. The result is a spiritual void—"unrestrained freedom," that is, boundless, empty distance, boundless, empty breadth, the dreadful sense of "go wherever your legs will carry" . . .[46]

The outstanding qualities of the peasant's mind, especially of one inhabiting an environment as harsh as Russia's, derived from the fact that he lived at the mercy of nature. To him nature was not the rational abstraction of philosophers and scientists, but a capricious force that assumed the shape of floods and droughts, of extremes of heat and cold, of destructive insects. Being willful, it was beyond comprehension and, of course, beyond mastery. This outlook bred in the peasant a mood of acquiescence and fatalism: his religion consisted of magic incantations designed to propitiate the elements. The notion of a supreme order permeating alike the realms of nature and law had for the peasant no meaning. He thought rather in the archaic terms of Homeric epics in which the whims of gods decide human destiny.

Although he had nothing resembling the concept of natural law, the *muzhik* had a sense of legality rooted in custom. Some students of the subject believed that the Russian village had a system of legal practices that fully equaled that embodied in formal jurisprudence.[47] Others denied that Russian peasant custom had the necessary characteristics of a genuine legal system, such as cohesion and uniform applicability.[48] The latter view seems the more convincing. Russian peasants knew law *(lex)* but not justice *(jus)*. This is hardly surprising. Self-contained and largely isolated communities have no need to distinguish between custom and law. The distinction first arose in the third century B.C.E. as a result of practical problems raised by Macedonian conquests which for the first time brought under one scepter scattered communities with the most diverse legal customs. It was in response to this situation that Stoic philosophers formulated the concept of the law of nature as a universal set of values binding mankind. To the extent that Russian rural communities continued to lead isolated existences they had no need for a comprehensive system of legal norms and were content with a mixture of common sense and precedent, settling their disagreements informally, much as do families.

This is seen in the fact that the rural courts run by peasants for peasants could show wild swings in their verdicts without revealing patterns. One student of the subject concluded that peasants viewed law "subjectively" rather than objectively, which really meant they knew no law.[49] Others conveyed the same idea by claiming that the *muzhik* acknowledged only "living law" *(zhivoe pravo),* judging each case on its own merits, with "conscience" as the decisive factor.[50] Whether or not one is justified in regarding such practice as falling within the definition of law, it is certain that the Russian peasant treated *ukazy* issued by the government not as laws but as one-time ordinances, which had the effect of forcing the authorities to issue repeatedly the same orders, or else the peasant paid no heed:

> Without a fresh ordinance, no [peasant] will carry out [a previous directive]: everyone thinks that this directive had been given "for that time only." An

order is issued forbidding the cutting of birch trees for the construction of May huts. Where the order had been received, that year no birches were cut. The following year no order came out and the people everywhere proceeded to build May huts. A "strict" instruction is issued to plant birches along the streets. It is done. The birches dry up. The next year there is no directive, and therefore no one replants them: the district officials themselves forget all about it. The district official . . . reasons like the peasants that the directive had been given for that one occasion only. . . . It is time to pay taxes. One might expect everyone to know from experience that they must be paid when due, that they will not be omitted. And still, without a special and, moreover, stern directive no one, no rich peasant, will pay. Perhaps [it is thought] they will manage without taxes . . .[51]

This attitude toward law, as directives issued for no discernible reason and, therefore, binding only insofar as they are imposed by force, prevented the peasant from developing one of the basic attributes of citizenship.

The notion advanced by Slavophile and Populist writers that the *muzhik* had a system of law and, moreover, one based on superior moral principles was challenged by jurists and practicing lawyers. There are interesting remarks on this subject by an attorney who had much professional experience before the Revolution with peasant legal practices.

Liberal minds in Russia were infected with Romanticism and saw in customary law some sort of peculiarity of Russian life which, allegedly, distinguished Russia favorably from other countries. . . . Many people collected materials on customary law; attempts were made to analyze it and efforts of a rather feeble kind were undertaken to ascertain its norms.

All these attempts came to naught for a simple reason: there was in Russia no customary law, as there was in general no law for the peasants. Here it must be stated that . . . every *volost'* and *volost'* court had its own customary law. . . . As proprietor of an estate, I had . . . occasion to establish close contact with the rural population, which turned to me, as a specialist, with requests to resolve all kinds of disputes and misunderstandings in the realm of land ownership and property rights in general. I was commonly appealed to in matters involving divisions of family property. I had in my hands many decisions of *volost'* courts, and notwithstanding the habit of making juridical generalizations, I was never able to detect the existence of some kind of general formula which even the given *volost'* court would apply to concrete, frequently recurring questions. Everything was based on arbitrariness, and, moreover, not the arbitrariness of the court's members, consisting of peasants, but that of the *volost'* clerk, who awarded verdicts at his whim, even though the members of the court affixed their signatures to it. The people had no faith in the court. The verdict of a *volost'* court was invariably seen as the result of pressures from one of the parties or of hospitality in the form of a bottle or two of vodka. . . . And when the case reached a higher instance, that is, the [*volost'*] assembly, and subsequently the *guberniia* office . . . then the scanty juridical knowledge which the members of the higher instances had at their command was powerless to cope with the arbitrariness, inasmuch as reference to customary law sanctified every lawless act. If this customary law could not be ascertained by specialists with professional training and determined to derive general norms

from the practice of customary law—i.e., the decisions of the *volost'* courts—
then one can imagine what ignorance of laws and obligations prevailed among
the population itself in all property matters and all those conflicts which had
to and did arise every hour of the day.

Our one hundred million peasants lived, in their everyday life, without
law.[52]

One of the consequences of a poorly developed legal sense was the absence
of the concept of human rights. There is no indication that the peasant regarded serfdom, which so appalled intellectuals, as an intolerable injustice:
indeed, his often quoted statement to the master—"We are yours but the land
is ours"—suggests the opposite. The peasant held "freedom" of no account.
Under serfdom, bonded peasants not only did not feel inferior to freemen but
identified with and were proud of their masters. The Slavophile Iurii Samarin
observed that serfs treated free peasants with contempt as footloose and un-
protected creatures. Some of them even viewed the Emancipation as a rejection
by their masters.[53]

Given a weakly developed sense of rights in general, the *muzhik* had no
notion of property rights in the Roman sense of absolute dominion over things.
According to one authority, Russian peasants did not even have a word for
landed property *(zemel'naia sobstvennost'):* they only spoke of possession
(vladenie), which in their mind was indissolubly bound up with physical labor.
Indeed, the *muzhik* was not even able clearly to distinguish the land to which
he held legal title by virtue of purchase from his communal allotment and from
the land which he leased, all of which he called "our land":

> The expression "our land" in the mouth of the peasant includes indiscrimi-
> nately the whole land he occupies for the time being, the land which is his
> private property . . . , the land held in common by the village (which is therefore
> only in temporary possession of each household), and also the land rented by
> the village from the neighboring landlords.[54]

The *muzhik*'s whole attitude toward landed property derived from a collective
memory of centuries of nomadic agriculture, when land was as abundant as
water in the sea and available to all. The "slash-and-burn" method of cultivating virgin forest had gone out of use in most of Russia in the late Middle Ages,
but the recollection of the time when peasants roamed the forest, felling trees
and cultivating the ash-covered clearings, remained very much alive. Labor
and labor alone transformed *res nullius* into possession: because virgin soil was
not touched by labor, it could not be owned. To the peasant's mind, appropriation of lumber was a crime, because it was the product of labor, whereas felling
trees was not. Similarly, peasants believed that "he who cuts down a tree with
a beehive in it is a thief, because he appropriates human labor; he who cuts
down a forest which no one has planted benefits from God's gift, which is as
free as water and air."[55] Such a viewpoint, of course, had nothing in common
with the rights of property as upheld in Russia's courts. No wonder that a high

proportion of the criminal offenses for which peasants were convicted had to do with illegal cutting of trees. This attitude was not motivated by class antagonism: it applied as much to land and forest owned by fellow peasants. The belief that the expenditure of *manual* labor alone justified wealth was a fundamental article of faith of the Russian peasantry, and for this reason it despised landlords, bureaucrats, industrial workers, priests, and intellectuals as "idlers."[56] Radical intellectuals exploited this attitude to denigrate business-men and officials.

Such thinking underlay the universal belief of the Russian peasantry after Emancipation in the inevitable advent of a nationwide repartition of private land. In 1861, the liberated serfs could not understand why approximately one-half of the land which they had previously tilled was given to the land-lords. At first, they refused to believe in the genuineness of such an absurd law. Later, after they had reconciled themselves to it, they decided that it was a temporary arrangement, soon to be annulled by a new law that would turn over to them, for communal distribution, all privately held land, including that of other peasants. Legends circulating in the villages had as one of their recurrent themes the prediction of the imminent appearance of a "Savior" who would make all of Russia into a land of communes.[57] "The peasants believe," according to A. N. Engelgardt, who spent many years living in their midst and wrote what is possibly the best book on their habits and mentality,

> that after the passage of some time, in the course of census-taking, there will take place a *general leveling of all the land* throughout Russia, just as presently, in every commune, at certain intervals, there takes place a repartitioning of the land among its members, each being allotted as much as he can manage. This completely idiosyncratic conception derives directly from the totality of peas-ant agrarian relations. In the communes, after a lapse of time, there takes place a redistribution of land, an *equalization* among its members. Under the [antici-pated] general repartition, all the land will be repartitioned, and the communes will be equalized. The issue here is not simply the seizure of landlord land, as the journalists would have it, but the equalization of *all the land,* including that which belongs to peasants. Peasants who have purchased land as property, or, as they put it, "for eternity," talk exactly as do all the other peasants, and have no doubt whatever that the "lands to which they hold legal title" can be taken away from their rightful owners and given to others.[58]

The soundness of this insight would be demonstrated in 1917–18.

Peasants expected the national repartition of land to occur any day and to bring them vast increments: five, ten, twenty, and even forty hectares per household. It was a faith that kept the central Russian village in a state of permanent tension:

> In 1879 [following the war with Turkey] all expected that a "new decree" would be issued concerning land. At the time, every small occurrence gave rise to rumors of a "new decree." Should a local village official . . . deliver the landlord

a paper requiring some sort of statistical information about land, cattle, structures, etc., the village would at once call a meeting, and there it would be said that a paper had come to the landlord about the land, that soon a "new decree" would be issued, that in the spring surveyors would come to divide the land. Should the police prohibit the landlord of a mortgaged estate to cut lumber for sale, it was said that the prohibition was due to the fact that the Treasury would soon take over the forest, and then it would be available to all: pay one ruble and cut all you want. Should anyone take out a loan on his estate, it was said that the landlords had gotten wind that the land would be equalized, and so they hurried to turn their properties over to the Treasury for cash.[59]

Such thinking meant that the Russian village was forever poised to attack private (non-communal) properties: it was kept in check only by fear. This produced a most unhealthy situation. The revolutionary potential was an ever-present reality, in spite of the peasant's anti-revolutionary, pro-monarchist sentiments. But then his radicalism was not inspired by political or even class animus. (When asked what should happen to the landlords who had been evicted from their lands in consequence of the "Black Repartition," some peasants would suggest they be placed on a government salary.[60]) Tolstoy put his finger on the crux of the problem when shortly after Emancipation he wrote: "The Russian revolution will be not against the Tsar and despotism but against landed property. It will say: from me, from the human being, take what you want, but leave us all the land."[61]

In the late nineteenth century, the peasant assumed that the nationwide repartition would be ordered by the Tsar: in peasant legends of the time, the "Savior," the "Great Leveler," was invariably the "true tsar." The belief fortified the peasantry's instinctive monarchism. Accustomed to the authority of the *bol'shak* in the household, by analogy it viewed the Tsar as the *bol'shak* or master *(khoziain)* of the country. The peasant "saw in the Tsar the actual owner and father of Russia, who directly managed his immense household"[62]—a primitive version of the patrimonial principle underlying Russian political culture. The reason why the peasant felt so confident that the Tsar would sooner or later order a general repartition of the land was that, as he saw it, it lay in the monarch's interest to have all the lands justly distributed and properly cultivated.[63]

Such attitudes provide the background to the peasant's political philosophy, which, for all its apparent contradictions, had a certain logic. To the peasant, government was a power that compelled obedience: its main attribute was the ability to coerce people to do things which, left to themselves, they would never do, such as pay taxes, serve in the army, and respect private property in land. By this definition, a weak government was no government. The epithet *Groznyi* applied to the mentally unbalanced and sadistic Ivan IV, usually rendered in English as "Terrible," actually meant "Awesome" and carried no pejorative meaning. Persons who possessed *vlast'* (authority) and did not exercise it in an "awe-inspiring" manner could be ignored. Observance of laws for the peasant invariably represented submission to a *force majeure,* to the will of someone stronger, not the recognition of some commonly shared principle or interest. "Today, as in the days of serfdom," wrote the Slavophile Iurii Samarin, "the peasant knows no other sure pledge of the genuineness of imperial commands than the display of armed force: a round of musketry still is to him the only authentic confirmation of the imperial commands."[64] In this conception, moral judgment of governments or their actions was as irrelevant as approval or condemnation of the vagaries of nature. There were no "good" or "bad" governments: there were only strong and weak ones, and strong ones were always preferable to weak ones. (Similarly, serfs used to prefer cruel but efficient masters to kindly but ineffective ones.[65]) Weak rulers made it possible to return to primitive freedom or *volia,* understood as license to do whatever one wanted, unrestrained by man-made law. Russian governments took account of these attitudes and went to great lengths to impress on the country the image of boundless power. Experienced bureaucrats opposed freedom of the press and parliamentary government in good part because they feared that the existence of an overt, legitimized opposition would be interpreted by the peasantry as a sign of weakness and a signal to rebel.

The overall effect of these peasant attitudes was very deleterious for Russia's political evolution. They encouraged the conservative proclivities of the monarchy, inhibiting the democratization which the country's economic and cultural development demanded. At the same time, they made it possible for demagogues to play on the peasantry's resentments and unrealistic expectations to incite a rural revolution.

At the turn of the century, observers noted subtle changes in the attitudes of the peasantry, particularly the younger generation. They were religiously less observant, less respectful of tradition and authority, restless, and somehow disaffected not only over land but over life in general.

The authorities were especially perturbed by the behavior of those who moved into the cities and industrial centers. Such peasants were no longer intimidated by uniformed representatives of authority and were said to act "insolently." When they returned to the village, permanently or to help out with the field work, they spread the virus of discontent. The Ministry of the Interior, observing this development, objected, on security grounds, to further industrialization and excessive rural mobility, but, for reasons previously stated, it had little success.

One of the causes of changes in the mood of the peasantry seems to have been the spread of literacy, actively promoted by the authorities. The 1897 census revealed a very low level of literacy for the Russian Empire as a whole: only one in five (21 percent) of the inhabitants could read and write. But disaggregated the statistics looked considerably better. As a result of the combined efforts of rural schools and private associations, literacy showed a dramatic spurt among the young, especially males: in 1897, 45 percent of the

Empire's male inhabitants aged ten to twenty-nine were recorded as literate.*
At this rate, the population of the Empire could have been expected to attain
universal literacy by 1925.

Literate peasants and workers read most of all religious books (the gospels
and lives of saints), followed by cheap escapist literature, the Russian equivalent of "penny dreadfuls"[66]—a situation not unlike that observed in England
half a century earlier. Yellow journalism emerged to meet the demand for the
printed word. Access to publications, however, did not bring the mass reader
into closer contact with the urban culture: "the vast majority of the lower-class
readers in the countryside and in the cities . . . remained estranged, in their
cultural sensibilities and in their daily lives, from the milieu of the intelligentsia
and the intellectual world of modernist creativity."[67]

Growing literacy, unaccompanied by proportionately expanding opportunities to apply the knowledge acquired from reading, probably contributed
to the restlessness of the lower classes. It has been noted in other regions of
the world that schooling and the spread of literacy often produce unsettling
effects. African natives educated in missionary schools, as compared with
untutored ones, have been observed to develop a different mentality, expressed
in an unwillingness to perform monotonous work and in lower levels of
honesty and truthfulness.[68] Similar trends were noted among young Russian
peasants exposed to urban culture, who also seemed less ready to acquiesce to
the routine of rural work and lived in a state of powerful, if unfocused expectations aroused by reading about unfamiliar worlds.[69]

All of which gave more thoughtful Russians cause for anxiety. Sergei
Witte, having familiarized himself with rural conditions as chairman of a
special commission to study peasant needs, felt deeply apprehensive about the
future. Russia, he wrote in 1905,

> in one respect represents an exception to all the countries in the world. . . . The
> exception consists in this, that the people have been systematically, over two
> generations, brought up without a sense of property and legality. . . . What
> historical consequences will result from this, I hesitate now to say, but I feel
> they will be very serious. . . . Scholarship says that communal land belongs to
> the village commune, as a juridical person, but in the eyes of the peasants
> . . . it belongs to the state which gives it to them for temporary use. . . . [Legal
> relations among the peasants] are regulated not by precise, written laws, but
> by custom, which often "no one knows." . . . Under these conditions, I see one
> gigantic question mark: what is an empire with one hundred million peasants
> who have been educated neither in the concept of landed property nor that of
> the firmness of law in general?[70]

---

*Pervaia Vseobshchaia Perepis' Naseleniia Rossiiskoi Imperii 1897 g., Obshchii Svod, I
(St. Petersburg, 1905), 56. Among females in the same age group, the proportion of literates was
not quite 21 percent.

The Intelligentsia

Nothing presents less of an obstacle than the
perfecting of the imaginary.

— *Hippolyte Taine*

Whether the conflicts and resentments that exist in every society are
peacefully resolved or explode in revolution is largely determined by two
factors: the existence of democratic institutions able to redress grievances
through legislation and the ability of intellectuals to fan the flames of social
discontent for the purpose of gaining power. For it is intellectuals who trans-
mute specific, and therefore remediable, grievances into a wholesale rejection
of the status quo. Rebellions happen; revolutions are made:

> Initially, a rebellion is without thought: it is visceral, immediate. A revolution
> implies a doctrine, a project, a program. . . . A revolution under one aspect or
> another has intellectual lines of force which rebellions lack. Moreover, a revolu-
> tion seeks to institutionalize itself. . . . That which characterizes the transforma-
> tion of a rebellion into a revolution is the effort to initiate a new organization
> (in the absence of society!) and this . . . implies the existence . . . of "managers"
> of the revolution.[1]

In the words of Joseph Schumpeter, social discontent is not enough to produce
a revolution:

> Neither the opportunity to attack nor real or fancied grievances are in them-
> selves sufficient to produce, however strongly they may favor, the emergence

of active hostility against a social order. For such an atmosphere to develop it is necessary that there be groups to whose interest it is to work up and organize resentment, to nurse it, to voice it and to lead it.[2]

These groups, these "managers," are the intelligentsia, who may be defined as intellectuals craving for political power.

Nothing in early-twentieth-century Russia inexorably pushed the country toward revolution, except the presence of an unusually large and fanatical body of professional revolutionaries. It is they who with their well-organized agitational campaigns in 1917 transformed a local fire, the mutiny of Petrograd's military garrison, into a nationwide conflagration. A class in permanent opposition, hostile to all reforms and compromises, convinced that for anything to change everything had to change, it was the catalytic agent that precipitated the Russian Revolution.

For an intelligentsia to emerge two conditions are required:

1. An ideology based on the conviction that man is not a unique creature endowed with an immortal soul, but a material compound shaped entirely by his environment: from which premise it follows that by reordering man's social, economic, and political environment in accord with "rational" precepts, it is possible to turn out a new race of perfectly rational human beings. This belief elevates intellectuals, as bearers of rationality, to the status of social engineers and justifies their ambition to displace the ruling elite.

2. Opportunities for intellectuals to gain social and occupational status to advance their group interests—that is, the dissolution of estates and castes and the emergence of free professions which make them independent of the Establishment: law, journalism, secular institutions of higher learning, an industrial economy in need of experts, an educated reading public. These opportunities, accompanied by freedom of speech and of association, make it possible for intellectuals to secure a hold on public opinion.

The word "intelligentsia" entered the English vocabulary in the 1920s from the Russian. The Russians, in turn, adopted it from France and Germany, where *"intelligence"* and *"Intelligenz"* had gained currency in the 1830s and 1840s to designate educated and "progressive" citizens.* It soon went out of fashion in the West, but in Russia it acquired great popularity in the second half of the nineteenth century to describe not so much the educated elite as those who spoke and acted on behalf of the country's silent majority—a counterpart of the patrimonial establishment (bureaucracy, police, the military, the gentry, and the clergy). In a country in which "society" was given

---

*The history of this term in Western Europe and Russia is recounted by Otto Wilhelm Müller in *Intelligencija: Untersuchungen zur Geschichte eines politischen Schlagwortes* (Frankfurt, 1971). According to the author (p. 98n.), the word *"intelligent"* was applied in France to experts as early as the fifteenth century.

no political outlets, the emergence of such a group was inevitable. The term was never precisely defined, and pre-revolutionary literature is filled with disputes over what it meant and to whom it applied. Although in fact most of those regarded as *intelligenty* had a superior education, education in itself was not a criterion: thus, a businessman or a bureaucrat with a university degree did not qualify as a member of the *intelligentsia,* the former because he worked for his own profit, the latter because he worked for the profit of the Tsar. Only those qualified who committed themselves to the public good, even if they were semi-literate workers or peasants. In practice, this meant men of letters—journalists, academics, writers—and professional revolutionaries. To belong, one also had to subscribe to certain philosophical assumptions about man and society derived from the doctrines of materialism, utilitarianism, and positivism. The popularity of the word derived from the fact that it made it possible to distinguish social "activists" from passive "intellectuals." However, we shall use the two terms interchangeably since in Western languages the distinction has not been established.

As a self-appointed spokesman for all those not members of the establishment—that is, more than nine-tenths of the population—the Russian intelligentsia saw itself and was seen by its rivals as the principal threat to the status quo. The battle lines in the last decades of Imperial Russia were drawn between official Russia and the intelligentsia, and it was eminently clear that the victory of the latter would result in the destruction of the former. The conflict grew so bitter that anyone advocating conciliation and compromise was liable to find himself caught in a deadly cross fire. While the establishment counted mainly on its repressive apparatus to keep the intelligentsia at bay, the latter used, as a lever, popular discontent, which it aggravated with all the means at its disposal, mostly by persistent discrediting of tsarism and its supporters.

Although circumstances caused the intelligentsia to be especially important in Russia, it was, of course, not unique to that country. Tönnies, in his seminal distinction between "communities" and "societies," allowed that in addition to communities linked by territorial proximity and ties of blood there existed "communities of mind" whose bond was ideas.[3] Pareto identified a "non-governing elite" which closely resembles the Russian intelligentsia.[4] Because these groups are international, it is necessary at this point to engage in a digression from Russian history: neither the emergence of the Russian intelligentsia nor the impact of the Russian Revolution on the rest of the world can be properly appreciated without an understanding of the intellectual underpinnings of modern radicalism.

Intellectuals first appeared in Europe as a distinct group in the sixteenth century in connection with the emergence of secular society and the concurrent advances of science. They were lay thinkers, often men of independent means, who approached the traditional questions of philosophy outside the framework of theology and the clerical establishment, which had previously enjoyed a monopoly on such speculation. Montaigne was a classic representative of the type which at the beginning of the seventeenth century came to be referred to as "intellectualist." He reflected on life and human nature without giving any thought to the possibility that either could be changed. To humanists like him, man and the world in which he lived were givens. The task of philosophy was to help man acquire wisdom by coming to terms with that changeless reality. The supreme wisdom was to be true to one's nature and so restrain one's desires as to gain immunity to adversity, especially the inevitable prospect of death: in the words of Seneca, "to have the weaknesses of a man and the serenity of a god" *("habere imbecillitatem hominis, securitatem dei").* The task of philosophy, as stated in the title of the book by the sixth-century writer Boethius, was "consolation." In its more extreme forms, such as Chinese Taoism, philosophy counseled complete inactivity: "Do nothing and everything will be done." Until the seventeenth century, the immutability of man's "being" was an unquestioned postulate of all philosophic thought, both in the West and in the East. It was considered a mark of folly to believe otherwise.

It was in the early seventeenth century that a contrary trend emerged in European thought. Its stimulus came from the dramatic findings of astronomy and the other sciences. The discovery that it was possible to uncover nature's secrets, and to use this knowledge to harness nature in the service of man, inevitably affected the way man came to view himself. The Copernican revolution displaced him and his world from the center of the universe. In one respect, this was a blow to man's self-esteem; in another, it greatly enhanced it. By laying bare the laws governing the motions of celestial bodies, science elevated man to the status of a creature capable of penetrating the deepest mysteries of nature: the very same scientific knowledge which toppled him from the center of the universe gave him the power to become nature's master. Francis Bacon was the earliest intellectual to grasp these implications of the scientific method and to treat knowledge—knowledge acquired through scientific observation and induction—as a means not only of gaining an understanding of the world but also of acting upon it. In his *Novum Organum* he asserted that the principles of physical science were applicable to human affairs. By establishing the methods through which true knowledge was acquired—that is, by rejecting classical and scholastic models in favor of the empirical and inductive methodology employed in the natural sciences—Bacon believed himself to be laying the foundations of man's mastery over both nature and himself: he is said to have "epitomize[d] the boundless ambition to dominate and to exploit the material resources of nature placed by God at the disposal of man."[5] That he was aware of the implications of the theory he advanced is indicated by the subtitle of his treatise on scientific methodology: *De Regno Hominis (Of Man's Dominion).*

Although scientific methodology progressively came to dominate Western thought, it took some time for man to view himself as an object of scientific inquiry. Seventeenth-century thought continued to adhere to the view inherited from antiquity and the Middle Ages, that man was composed of two discrete parts, body *(soma)* and soul *(psyche),* the one material and perishable, the other metaphysical and immortal and hence beyond the reach of empirical investigation. This conception, expressed by Socrates in Plato's *Phaedo* to explain his equanimity in the face of impending death, entered the mainstream of Western thought through the writings of St. Augustine. Related was a theory of knowledge based on the concept of "innate ideas," that is, ideas believed to have been implanted in the soul at birth, including the notions of God, good and evil, the sense of time and space, and the principles of logic. The theory of innate ideas dominated European thought in the sixteenth and seventeenth centuries.[6] The political implications of this theory were distinctly conservative: the immutability of human nature posited the immutability of man's behavior and the permanence of his political and social institutions.

Bacon already had expressed doubts about innate ideas, since they did not fit his empirical methodology, and hinted that knowledge derived from the senses. But the principal assault on the theory of innate ideas was undertaken by John Locke in 1690 in his *Essay on Human Understanding.* Locke dismissed the whole concept and argued that all ideas without exception derived from sensory experience. The human mind was like a "dark room" into which the sensations of sight, smell, touch, and hearing threw the only shafts of light. By reflecting on these sensations, the mind formed ideas. According to Locke, thinking was an entirely involuntary process: man could no more reject or change the ideas which the senses generated in his mind than a mirror can "refuse, alter, or obliterate the images or ideas which objects set before it do therein produce." The denial of free will, which followed from Locke's theory of cognition, was to be a major factor in its popularity, since it is only by eliminating free will that man could be made the subject of scientific inquiry.

For several decades after its appearance, the influence of Locke's *Essay* was confined to academic circles. It was the French *philosophe* Claude Helvétius who, in his anonymously published *De l'Esprit* (1758), first drew political consequences from Locke's theory of knowledge, with results that have never been adequately recognized.

It is known that Helvétius studied intensely the philosophical writings of Locke and was deeply affected by them.[7] He accepted as proven Locke's contention that all ideas were the product of sensations and all knowledge the result of man's ability, through reflection on sensory data, to grasp the differences and similarities that are the basis of thought. He denied as categorically as did Locke man's ability to direct thinking or the actions resulting from it: for Helvétius, his biographer says, "a philosophical treatise on liberty [was] a treatise on effects without a cause."[8] Moral notions derived exclusively from man's experience with the sensations of pain and pleasure. People thus were neither "good" nor "bad": they merely acted, involuntarily and mechanically, in their self-interest, which dictated the avoidance of pain and the enhancement of pleasure.

Up to this point Helvétius said nothing that had not been said previously by Locke and his French followers. But then he made a startling leap from philosophy into politics. From the premise that all knowledge and all values were by-products of sensory experience he drew the inference that by controlling the data that the senses fed to the mind—that is, by appropriately shaping man's environment—it was possible to determine what he thought and how he behaved. Since, according to Locke, the formulation of ideas was wholly involuntary and entirely shaped by physical sensations, it followed that if man were subjected to impressions that made for virtue, he could be made virtuous through no act of his own will.[9]

This idea provides the key to the creation of perfectly virtuous human beings—required are only appropriate external influences. Helvétius called the process of molding men "education," by which he meant much more than formal schooling. When he wrote *"l'éducation peut tout"*—"education can do anything"—he meant by education everything that surrounds man and affects his thinking, everything which furnishes his mind with sensations and generates ideas. First and foremost, it meant legislation: "It is . . . only by good laws that we can form virtuous men."[10] From which it followed that morality and legislation were "one and the same science."[11] In the concluding chapter of *L'Esprit,* Helvétius spoke of the desirability of reforming society through legislation for the purpose of making men "virtuous."*

This is one of the most revolutionary ideas in the history of political thought: by extrapolation from an esoteric theory of knowledge, a new political theory is born with the most momentous practical implications. Its central thesis holds that the task of politics is to make man "virtuous," and that the means to that end is the manipulation of man's social and political environment, to be accomplished mainly by means of legislation, that is, by the state. Helvétius elevates the legislator to the status of the supreme moralist. He must have been aware of the implications of his theory for he spoke of the "art of forming man" as intimately connected with the "form of government." Man no longer is God's creation: he is his own product. Society, too, is a "product" rather than a given or "datum."[12] Good government not only ensures "the greatest happiness of the greatest number" (a formula which Helvétius seems to have devised), but it literally refashions man. The logic of Helvétius's ideas inexorably leads to the conclusion that in the course of learning about human nature man "acquires an unlimited power of transforming and reshaping man."[13] This unprecedented proposition constitutes the premise of both liberal and radical ideologies of modern times. It provides the theoretical justification for using politics to create a "new order."

Such ideas, whether in their pure or diluted version, hold an irresistible attraction for intellectuals. If, indeed, human existence in all its manifestations obeys mechanical laws that reason can lay bare and direct into desirable channels, then it follows that intellectuals, as the custodians of rational knowl-

---

*The notion that the task of politics is to inculcate virtue and that virtue is attained by laws and education is as old as political theory, since it goes back to Plato. But the innovation of Helvétius is that to him politics, by creating a propitious environment, not only enables man to act virtuously but compels him to do so by remaking his personality.

edge, are man's natural leaders. Progress consists of either the instantaneous or the gradual subordination of life to "reason," or, as it used to be said in Russia, the replacement of "spontaneity" by "consciousness." "Spontaneous" existence, as shaped by millennia of experience and embodied in tradition, custom, and historic institutions, is, in this conception, "irrational."

A life ruled by "reason" is a life ruled by intellectuals: it is not surprising, therefore, that intellectuals want to change the world in accord with the requirements of "rationality."* A market economy, with its wasteful competition and swings between overproduction and shortages, is not "rational" and hence it does not find favor with intellectuals. They prefer socialism, which is another word for the rationalization of economic activity. Democracy is, of course, mandatory, but preferably interpreted to mean the "rational" rather than the actual will of the people: Rousseau's "general will" instead of the will made manifest through elections or referenda.

The theories of Locke and Helvétius permit intellectuals to claim status as mankind's "educators" in the broadest sense of that word. They are the repository of reason, which they believe to be always superior to experience. While mankind gropes in darkness, they, the "illuminati," know the path to virtue and, through virtue, to happiness. This whole conception puts intellectuals at odds with the rest of humanity. Ordinary people, in pursuit of their livelihood, acquire specific knowledge relevant to their particular occupation under the specific conditions in which they have to practice it. Their intelligence (reasoning) expresses itself in the ability to cope with such problems as they happen personally to confront: in the words of William James, in attaining "some particular conclusion or . . . gratify[ing] some special curiosity . . . which it is the reasoner's temporary interest to attain." The farmer understands the climatic and other requirements for his crops: knowledge that may be of little use in another place and useless in another occupation. The real estate agent knows the value of properties in his area. The politician has a sense of the aspirations and worries of his constituents. Societies function thanks to the immense variety of the concrete kinds of knowledge accumulated from experience by the individuals and groups that constitute them.

Intellectuals and intellectuals alone claim to know things "in general." By creating "sciences" of human affairs—economic science, political science, sociology—they establish principles said to be validated by the very "nature" of things. This claim entitles them to demand that existing practices be abandoned and existing institutions destroyed. It was the genius of Burke to grasp the premises and consequences of this kind of thinking, as expressed in the slogans and actions of the French Revolution, and to insist, in response to this experience, that where human affairs are concerned, things never exist in "general" but only in particular ("Nothing is good, but in proportion, and with Reference"[14]), and abstract thinking is the worst possible guide to conduct.

---

*Francis G. Wilson has noted that even in early modern times, before the influence of science had made itself fully felt, intellectuals favored centralized authority and a powerful state: *American Political Science Review*, XLVIII, No. 2 (1954), 325, 335–38.

Helvétius's theory can be applied in two ways. One may interpret it to mean that the change in man's social and political environment ought to be accomplished peacefully and gradually, through the reform of institutions and enlightenment. One can also conclude from it that this end is best attained by a violent destruction of the existing order.

Which approach—the evolutionary or revolutionary—prevails seems to be in large measure determined by a country's political system and the opportunities it provides for intellectuals to participate in public life.

In societies which make it possible through democratic institutions and freedom of speech to influence policy, intellectuals are likely to follow the more moderate alternative. In eighteenth- and nineteenth-century England and the United States, intellectuals were deeply involved in political life. The men who shaped the American republic and those who led Victorian England along the path of reform were men of affairs with deep intellectual interests: of some of them it would be difficult to say whether they were philosophers engaged in statesmanship or statesmen whose true vocation was philosophy. Even the pragmatists among them kept their minds open to the ideas of the age. This interplay of ideas and politics lent political life in Anglo-Saxon countries their well-known spirit of compromise. Here the intellectuals had no need to withdraw and form an isolated caste. They acted on public opinion, which, through democratic institutions, sooner or later affected legislation.

In England and, through England, in the United States, the ideas of Helvétius gained popularity mainly from the writings of Jeremy Bentham and the utilitarians. It was to Helvétius that Bentham owed the ideas that morality and legislation were "one and the same science," that man could attain virtue only through "good laws," and that, consequently, legislation had a "pedagogic" function.[15] On these foundations, Bentham constructed his theory of philosophical radicalism, which greatly affected the movement for parliamentary reform and liberal economics. The preoccupation of modern Anglo-Saxon countries with legislation as a device for human betterment is directly traceable to Bentham and, through him, to Helvétius. In the speculations of Bentham and the English liberals, there was no place for violence: the transformation of man and society was to be accomplished entirely by laws and enlightenment. But even under this reform-minded theory lay the tacit premise that man could and ought to be remade. This premise links liberalism and radicalism and helps explain why, for all their rejection of the violent methods employed by revolutionaries, when forced to choose between them and their conservative opponents, liberals can be counted on to throw their lot in with the revolutionaries. For what separates liberals from the extreme left is disagreement over the means employed, whereas they differ from the right in the fundamental perception of what man is and what society ought to be.

In countries which excluded intellectuals from participation in public life—of which old regime France and Russia were prime examples—intellectuals were prone to form castes committed to extreme ideologies. The fact was noted by Tocqueville:

> In England, writers on the theory of government and those who actually governed cooperated with each other, the former setting forth their theories, the latter amending or circumscribing these in the light of practical experience. In France, however, precept and practice were kept quite distinct and remained in the hands of two quite distinct groups. One of these carried on the actual administration while the other set forth the abstract principles on which good government should, they said, be based; one took the routine measures appropriate to the needs of the moment, the other propounded general laws without a thought for their practical application; one group shaped the course of public affairs, the other that of public opinion. Thus, alongside the traditional and confused, not to say chaotic, social system of the day there was gradually built up in man's minds an imaginary ideal society in which all was simple, uniform, coherent, equitable, and rational in the full sense of the term.[16]

It is always dangerous to seek in historical analogies explanations for historical events: the model of the French Revolution employed by Russian radicals brought no end of grief to them and many others. However, in at least one respect the example of eighteenth-century France is applicable to twentieth-century Russia—namely, in the realm of ideas, which are less affected by concrete historic circumstances than are political and social conditions. The intellectual atmosphere of late Imperial Russia closely resembled that of *ancien régime* France on the eve of the Revolution, and the circles of *philosophes* anticipated those of the Russian intelligentsia. The analogy emphasizes to what extent intellectual trends can be self-generated: it reinforces the impression that the behavior of the Russian intelligentsia was influenced less by Russian reality than by preconceived ideas.

A brilliant if little-known French historian, Augustin Cochin, first showed the peculiarly destructive intellectual atmosphere that had prevailed in France in the decades immediately preceding the Revolution. He began his inquiries with a study of Jacobinism.* Seeking its antecedents, he was led to the social and cultural circles formed in France in the 1760s and 1770s to promote "advanced" ideas. These circles, which he called *sociétés de pensée,* were made up of literary associations, Masonic lodges, academies, as well as various "patriotic" and cultural clubs. According to Cochin, the *sociétés de pensée* insinuated themselves into a society in which the traditional estates

---

*Cochin fell in battle in 1916. His principal works are *La Crise de l'Histoire Révolutionnaire* (Paris, 1909) and the posthumously published *Les Sociétés de pensée et la Démocratie* (Paris, 1921). His ideas are summarized in François Furet's *Penser la Révolution Française* (Paris, 1983).

were in the process of disintegration. To join them required severing connections with one's social group and dissolving one's class (estate) identity in a community bound exclusively by a commitment to common ideas. Jacobinism was a natural product of this phenomenon: in France, unlike England, the movement for change emanated not from parliamentary institutions but from literary and philosophical clubs.

These circles, in which the historian of Russia recognizes many of the features of the Russian intelligentsia of a century later, had as their main mission the forging of a consensus: they achieved cohesion not through shared interests but through shared ideas, ruthlessly imposed on their members and accompanied by vicious attacks on all who thought differently:

> Prior to the bloody terror of '93, there existed, between 1765 and 1780, a dry terror in the republic of letters, of which the Encyclopedia was the Committee of Public Safety and d'Alembert was Robespierre. It mowed down reputations as the other did heads: its guillotine was defamation . . .[17]

For intellectuals of this kind, the criterion of truth was not life: they created their own reality, or rather, sur-reality, subject to verification only with reference to opinions of which they approved. Contradictory evidence was ignored: anyone inclined to heed such evidence was ruthlessly cast out.

This kind of thinking led to a progressive estrangement from life. Cochin's description of the atmosphere in the French *sociétés de pensée* of the late eighteenth century perfectly fits that prevailing in intelligentsia circles in Russia a century later:

> Whereas in the real world the arbiter of all thought is proof and its issue is the effect, in this world the arbiter is the opinion of others, and the aim their approbation. . . . All thought, all intellectual effort here exists only by way of concurrence. It is opinion that makes for existence. That is real which others see, that true which they say, that good of which they approve. Thus the natural order is reversed: opinion here is the cause, and not, as in real life, the effect. Appearance takes the place of being, speaking, doing. . . . And the goal . . . of that passive work is destruction. It consists, in sum, of eliminating, of reducing. Thought which submits to this initially loses the concern for the real, and then, little by little, the sense of the real. And it is precisely to this deprivation that it owes its freedom. It does not gain in freedom, orderliness, clarity except to the extent that it sheds its real content, its hold on that which exists.[18]

It is only with the help of this insight that we can understand the seeming paradoxes in the mentality of the genus intelligentsia, and especially its more extreme species, the Russian intelligentsia. Theories and programs, on which Russian intellectuals spent their waking hours, were indeed evaluated in relation not to life but to other theories and programs: the criterion of their validity was consistency and conformity. Live reality was treated as a perversion or caricature of "genuine" reality, believed to lurk invisible behind appearances and waiting to be set free by the Revolution. This attitude would enable the intelligentsia to accept as true propositions at total variance with demonstrable fact as well as common sense—for example, that the living standards of European workers in the nineteenth century were steadily declining, that the Russian peasant in 1900 was on the verge of starvation, that it was legitimate, in the name of democracy, to disperse in January 1918 the democratically elected Constituent Assembly, or that, more generally, freedom meant bowing to necessity. To understand the behavior of the intelligentsia it is imperative to keep in mind at all times its deliberate detachment from reality: for while the revolutionaries can be ruthlessly pragmatic in exploiting, for tactical pur- poses, the people's grievances, their notion of what the people desire is the product of sheer abstraction. Not surprisingly, when they come to power, revolutionary intellectuals immediately seize control of the means of informa- tion and institute a tight censorship: for it is only by suppressing free speech that they can impose their "sur-reality" on ordinary people bogged down in the quagmire of facts.*

The habit calls for the creation of a special language by means of which initiates of the movement can communicate with one another and, when in power, impose their fantasy on the population at large. This language, with its own vocabulary, phraseology, and even syntax, which reached its apogee in the stultified jargon of the Stalinist era, "describes not reality but an ideal conception of it." It is severely ritualized and surrounded by lexical taboos.[19] Long before 1917, Russian revolutionary polemics were carried out in this medium.

Nowhere is this penchant for creating one's own reality more apparent— and pernicious—than in the intelligentsia's conception of the "people." Radi- cals insist on speaking for and on acting on behalf of the "people" (sometimes described as "the popular masses") against the allegedly self-seeking elite in control of the state and the nation's wealth. In their view, the establishment of a just and free society requires the destruction of the status quo. But contact with the people of flesh and blood quickly reveals that few if any of them want their familiar world to be destroyed: what they desire is satisfaction of specific grievances—that is, partial reform, with everything else remaining in place. It has been observed that spontaneous rebellions are conservative rather than revolutionary, in that those involved usually clamor for the restitution of rights of which they feel they have been unjustly deprived: they look backward.[20] In order to promote its ideal of comprehensive change, the intelligentsia must, therefore, create an abstraction called "the people" to whom it can attribute its own wishes. According to Cochin, the essence of Jacobinism lay not in terror but in the striving of the intellectual elite to establish dictatorial power

---

*Eric Hoffer sees in imperviousness to reality an essential feature of all fanaticism: "the effectiveness of a doctrine should not be judged by its profundity, sublimity or the validity of the truths it embodies, but by how thoroughly it insulates the individual from his self and the world as it is" (*The True Believer*, New York, 1951, 79).

over the people in the name of the people. The justification for such procedure was found in Rousseau's concept of "general will," which defined the will of the people as what enlightened "opinion" declared it to be:

> For the doctrinaires of the [French revolutionary] regime, the *philosophes* and politicians, from Rousseau and Mably to Brissot and Robespierre, the true people is an ideal being. The general will, the will of the citizenry, transcends the actual will, such as it is, of the greatest number, as in Christian life grace dominates and transcends nature. Rousseau has said it: the general will is not the will of numbers and it has reason against it; the liberty of the citizen is not the independence of the individual, and suppresses it. In 1789, the true people did not exist except potentially, in the consciousness or imagination of "free people," of "patriots," as they used to be called . . . that is to say, a small number of initiates, recruited in their youth, trained without respite, shaped all their lives in societies of *philosophes* . . . in the discipline of liberty.[21]

It is only by reducing people of flesh and blood to a mere idea that one can ignore the will of the majority in the name of democracy and institute a dictatorship in the name of freedom.

This whole ideology and the behavior to which it gave rise—a mélange of ideas formulated by Helvétius and Rousseau—was historically new, the creation of the French Revolution. It legitimized the most savage social experiments. Although for personal reasons Robespierre despised Helvétius (he believed him to have persecuted his idol, Rousseau), his entire thinking was deeply influenced by him. For Robespierre, the mission of politics was the "reign of virtue." Society was divided into "good" and "bad" citizens, from which premise he concluded that "all those who do not think as we do must be eliminated from the city."[22]

Tocqueville was perplexed by this whole phenomenon when late in life he turned his attention to the history of the French Revolution. A year before his death, he confided to a friend:

> There is something special about the sickness of the French Revolution which I sense without being able to describe it or analyze its causes. It is a *virus* of a new and unfamiliar kind. The world has known violent revolution: but the boundless, violent, radical, perplexed, bold, almost insane but still strong and successful personality of these revolutionaries appears to me to have no parallel in the great social upheavals of the past. From whence comes this new race? Who created it? Who made it so successful? Who kept it alive? Because we still have the same men confronting us, although the circumstances differ, and they have left progeny in the whole civilized world. My spirit flags from the effort to gain a clear picture of this object and to find the means of describing it fairly. Independently of everything that is comprehensible in the French Revolution, in its spirit and in its deeds, there is something that remains inexplicable. I sense where the unknown is to be found but no matter how hard I try, I cannot lift the veil that conceals it. I feel it through a strange body which prevents me from really touching or seeing it.[23]

Had he lived into the twentieth century, Toqueville might have found it easier to identify the "virus," because its peculiar blend of ideas and group interests has become commonplace since his day.

Intellectuals can acquire influence only in an egalitarian and open society, in which estate barriers have broken down and politics are shaped by opinion. In such a society they assume the role of opinion-makers, to which end they employ the printed word and other media as well as educational institutions. Although the intelligentsia likes to see itself as selflessly dedicated to the public good, and hence a moral force rather than a social group, the fact of its members sharing common values and goals inevitably means that they also share common interests—interests which may well clash with their professed ideals. The intelligentsia has difficulty admitting this. Its profound aversion for sociological self-analysis—in such contrast to its penchant for analyzing all other social groups and classes, especially its main obstacle to power, the "bourgeoisie"—has resulted in a striking paucity of works on the subject. The sparse literature on the intelligentsia as a social and historic phenomenon is entirely disproportionate to that group's importance.[24]

Although they can flourish only in societies free of estate privileges, with egalitarian citizenship, such as have arisen in the West in modern times, such societies place intellectuals in an ambivalent position. While they enjoy immense influence on public opinion, they constitute socially a marginal element, since they control neither wealth nor political power. A good part of them make up an intellectual proletariat which barely manages to eke out a living: even the more fortunate representatives of this group are economically and politically insignificant, often forced to serve as paid spokesmen of the nation's elite. This is a painful position to be in, especially for those who regard themselves as far more deserving of the prerogatives of power than those who actually wield it by virtue of accident of birth or economic exploitation.

Capitalism benefits the intelligentsia by increasing the demand for its services and giving its members opportunity to practice the profession of opinion-molding:

> The cheaper book, the cheap newspaper or pamphlet, together with the widening of the public that was in part their product but partly an independent phenomenon due to the access of wealth and weight which came to the industrial bourgeoisie and to the incident increase in the political importance of an anonymous public opinion—all these boons, as well as increasing freedom from restraint, are by-products of the capitalist engine.[25]

"Every society of the past," writes Raymond Aron,

> has had its scribes . . . its artists or men of letters . . . and its experts. . . . None of these three species belongs strictly to our modern civilisation, but the latter

has nonetheless its own special characteristics which affect the numbers and status of the intellectuals. The distribution of manpower among the different professions alters with the progress of economic development: the percentage of manpower employed in industry grows, the proportion employed in agriculture decreases, while the size of the so-called tertiary sector, which includes a multitude of professions of varying degrees of prestige—from the quill-driver in his office to the research worker in his laboratory—is enormously inflated. Modern industrial societies comprise a greater number of non-manual workers, absolutely and relatively, than any society of the past. . . . The three categories of non-manual workers—scribes, experts, and men of letters—develop simultaneously, if not at the same rate. Bureaucracies offer outlets to scribes with inferior qualifications; the management of labor and the organization of industry require more and more specialized experts; schools, universities, and various mediums of entertainment or communication employ men of letters, artists, or mere technicians of speech and writing, hacks and popularizers. . . . Though its significance is not always fully recognized, the growth in the number of jobs remains a crucial fact . . .[26]

By filling the ranks of the "tertiary sector" of the modern economy, intellectuals turn into a social group with its own interests, the most important of which calls for the increase in the number and prestige of white-collar jobs—an objective best promoted by centralization and bureaucratization. Their interests further require untrammeled freedom of speech, and intellectuals, even while helping put in power regimes which suppress liberties, have always and everywhere opposed restraints on free expression: they often are the first victims of their own triumphs.

Paradoxically, therefore, capitalism and democracy, while enhancing the role of intellectuals, also increase their discontent. Their status in a capitalist society is far beneath that of politicians and businessmen, whom they scorn as amateurs in the art of social management. They envy their wealth, authority, and prestige. In some respects it was easier for intellectuals to accommodate to pre-modern society, in which status was fixed by tradition and law, than to the fluctuating world of capitalism and democracy, in which they feel humiliated by lack of money and status: Ludwig von Mises thought that intellectuals gravitate to anti-capitalist philosophies "in order to render inaudible the inner voice that tells them that their failure is entirely their own fault."[27]

As previously pointed out, intellectuals can avoid these humiliations and rise to the top only under one condition: if society becomes "rationalized"— that is, intellectualized—and "reason" replaces the free play of economic and political forces. This means socialism. The main enemy of the socialists, in their peaceful ("utopian") as well as violent (revolutionary) guise, has always been "spontaneity," by which is meant laissez-faire in its economic as well as political manifestations. The call for the abolition of private property in the means of production on behalf of "society," common to all socialist programs, makes it theoretically possible to rationalize the production of goods and to equalize their distribution. It also happens to place those who claim to know what is "rational"—intellectuals—in a commanding position. As in the case of other class movements, interest and ideology coincide: just as the bourgeoisie's demands for the abolition of restraints on manufacture and trade in the name of public welfare served its own interests, so the radical intellectuals' call for the nationalization of manufacture and trade, advanced for the sake of the masses, happens to work to its own advantage.

The anarchist leader, and Marx's contemporary, Michael Bakunin, was the first to note this coincidence and insist that behind the intellectuals' yearning for socialism lay ordinary class interests. He opposed Marx's vision of the socialist state on the grounds that it would result in Communist domination of the masses:

> According to Mr. Marx, the people should not only not abolish [the state], but, on the contrary, fortify and strengthen it, and in this form turn it over to the full disposal of their benefactors, guardians, and teachers, the chiefs of the Communist Party—in other words, to Mr. Marx and his friends, who will then proceed to liberate [them] in their own fashion. They will concentrate the reins of government in a strong hand, because the ignorant people are in need of strong guardianship. They will create a central state bank, which will concentrate in its hands all commercial-industrial, agricultural, and even scientific production. They will divide the mass of the people into two armies, the industrial and the agricultural, under the direct command of state engineers, who will form the new privileged political-scientific class.[28]

Another anarchist, the Pole Jan Machajski, depicted socialism as an ideology formulated in the interest of the intelligentsia, "an emergent privileged class," whose capital consisted of higher education. In a socialist state they would achieve dominance by replacing the old class of capitalists as administrators and experts. "Scientific socialism" promises the "slaves of bourgeois society happiness after they are dead: it guarantees the socialist paradise to their descendants."*

This was not a message likely to appeal to intellectuals. And so it was no accident that Marx defeated Bakunin and had him expelled from the First International, and that in the modern world anarchism is but a faint shadow of socialism. Historical experience indicates that any movement that questions the ideology and interests of intellectuals dooms itself to defeat, and that any intellectual who challenges his class condemns himself to obscurity.

Socialism is commonly thought of as a theory which aims at a fairer distribution of wealth for the ultimate purpose of creating a free and just

---

*A. Volskii (Machajski), *Umstvennyi rabochii* (New York-Baltimore, 1968), 328. (Originally published in 1904–5.) In the preface (p. 14), Albert Parry notes that this work aroused the "fierce opposition" of virtually all revolutionary intellectuals of the time: "They at once mobilized the entire corps of their theoretical publicists, orators, and agitators. The whole propaganda apparatus of the Socialist movement, be it Bolshevik, Menshevik, or Socialist-Revolutionary, went into action against this new common enemy. The virulence of their attack was unprecedented." Machajski's writings have been placed on the Soviet Index Librorum Prohibitorum.

society. Indisputably this is the stated program of socialists. But behind this
program lurks an even more ambitious goal, which is creating a new type of
human being. The underlying premise is the idea of Helvétius that by establishing an environment which makes social behavior a natural instinct, socialism
will enable man to realize his potential to the fullest. This, in turn, will make
it possible, ultimately, to dispense with the state and the compulsion which is
said to be its principal attribute. All socialist doctrines, from the most moderate to the most extreme, assume that human beings are infinitely malleable
because their personality is the product of the economic environment: a change
in that environment must, therefore, alter them as well as their behavior.

Marx pursued philosophical studies mainly in his youth. When, as a
twenty-six-year-old émigré in Paris, he immersed himself in philosophy, he at
once grasped the political implications of the ideas of Helvétius and his French
contemporaries. In *The Holy Family* (1844–45), the book which marked his
and Engels's break with idealistic radicalism, he took his philosophical and
psychological premises directly from Locke and Helvétius: "The whole development of man . . . ," he wrote, "depends on *education* and *environment.*"

> If man draws all his knowledge, sensations, etc., from the world of the senses
> and the experience gained in it, the empirical world must be arranged so that
> in it man experiences and gets used to what is really human. . . . If man is
> shaped by his surroundings, his surroundings must be made human.[29]

This, the *locus classicus* of Marxist philosophy, justifies a total change in
the way society is organized—that is, revolution. According to this way of
thinking, which indeed inexorably flows from the philosophical premises formulated by Locke and Helvétius, man and society do not come into existence
by a natural process but are "made." This "radical behaviorism," as it has been
called, inspired Marx in 1845 to coin what is probably his most celebrated
aphorism: "The philosophers have only interpreted the world in various ways:
the point, however, is to change it."[30] Of course, the moment a thinker begins
to conceive his mission to be not "only" observing the world and adapting to
it, but changing it, he ceases to be a philosopher and turns into a politician
with his own political agenda and interests.

Now, the world can conceivably be "changed" gradually, by means of
education and legislation. And such a gradual change is, indeed, what all
intellectuals would advocate if their exclusive concern were with improving
the human condition, since evolution allows for trial and error, the only
proven road to progress. But many of those who want to change the world
regard human discontent as something not to be remedied but exploited.
Exploitation of resentment, not its satisfaction, has been at the center of
socialist politics since the 1840s: it is what distinguished the self-styled "scientific" socialists from their "utopian" forerunners. This attitude has led to the
emergence of what Anatole Leroy-Beaulieu called in 1902, in a remarkably
prescient book, the "politics of hatred." Socialism, he noted, elevates "hatred

to the heights of principle," sharing with its mortal enemies, nationalism and anti-Semitism, the need "chirurgically" to isolate and destroy the alleged enemy.[31] Committed radicals fear reform because it deprives them of leverage and establishes the ruling elite more solidly in power: they prefer the most savage repression. The slogan of Russian revolutionaries—*"chem khuzhe, tem luchshe"* ("the worse, the better")—spelled out this kind of thinking.

There are, of course, many varieties of socialists, from the most democratic and humane to the most despotic and cruel, but they differ over means, not ends. In tracing the attitude of Russian and foreign socialists toward the brutal experiments of the Bolsheviks, we will have occasion to see their inconsistencies: revulsion at Bolshevik atrocities combined with admiration for their undeviating commitment to the common cause and support for them whenever they were threatened. As we will show, the Bolsheviks could neither have seized power nor have kept it were it not for the support, active and passive, given them by the democratic, nonviolent socialists.

We have it on the authority of Leon Trotsky that the architects of the October 1917 coup d'état looked far beyond correcting the inequities of capitalism. Describing the future in the early 1920s, he predicted:

> Communist life will not be formed blindly, like coral reefs, but it will be built consciously, it will be tested by thought, it will be directed and corrected. Having ceased to be spontaneous, life will cease to be stagnant.

Having dismissed all of human history until October 1917 as an era of "stagnancy," Trotsky proceeded to depict the human being whom the new regime would create:

> Man will, at last, begin to harmonize himself in earnest. . . . He will want to master first the semi-conscious and then also the unconscious processes of his own organism: breathing, the circulation of blood, digestion, reproduction, and, within the necessary limits, will subordinate them to the control of reason and will. Even purely physiological life will become collectively experimental. The human species, the sluggish *Homo sapiens,* will once again enter the state of radical reconstruction and will become in its own hands the object of the most complex methods of artificial selection and psychophysical training. . . . Man will make it his goal to master his own emotions, to elevate his instincts to the heights of consciousness, to make them transparent . . . to create a higher sociobiological type, a superman, if you will. . . . Man will become incomparably stronger, wiser, subtler. His body will become more harmonious, his movements more rhythmic, his voice more melodious. The forms of life will acquire a dynamic theatricality. The average human type will rise to the heights of an Aristotle, Goethe, Marx. And beyond this ridge, other peaks will emerge.[32]

These reflections, not of an adolescent daydreamer but of the organizer of Bolshevik victories in October 1917 and in the Civil War, provide an insight into the psyche of those who made the greatest revolution of modern times.

They and those who emulated them aimed at nothing less than reenacting the Sixth Day of Creation and perfecting its flawed product: man was to remake himself "with his own hands." We can now understand what Nicholas Chernyshevskii, a prominent Russian radical of the 1860s and a major influence on Lenin, had in mind when he defined his "anthropomorphic principle" to mean *"Homo homini deus"* ("Man is god to man").

The Russian intelligentsia made its appearance in the 1860s in connection with the Great Reforms of Alexander II. After its humiliating defeat in the Crimean War, the tsarist government decided it had to activate Russian society and involve it more in public life. But society proved difficult to stir: "The country, patiently trained to inertia, lost all power of initiative and when . . . informed that it was expected to act for itself, to settle its own local affairs, scarcely knew how to respond to the invitation, having lost the habit of action, lost interest in public life, especially in the provinces."[33] This inertia gave Russian intellectuals the opportunity to step forward as spokesmen for society, which in any event had no opportunities to express itself through elections.

Several policies which the government initiated at this time created favorable conditions for the growth of the intelligentsia. Censorship was eased. During the preceding reign of Nicholas I, it had attained a level of mindless severity which made it increasingly difficult to communicate by means of the printed word. Under the new reign, preliminary censorship was abolished and the rules governing publication sufficiently relaxed to permit the spread of the most radical ideas by means of a coded ("Aesopian") language. The periodical press became the principal vehicle through which opinion-makers in Moscow and St. Petersburg influenced thinking in the provinces. The Russian press in the second half of the nineteenth century had surprising latitude to criticize the authorities: by 1900, most dailies and monthlies upheld oppositional views.

In 1863, universities received autonomy, which made their faculties self-governing. Admission to the institutions of higher learning was opened to commoners, who under Nicholas I had been virtually excluded. They quickly turned into centers of political ferment. A high proportion of the Russian intelligentsia became radicalized during their student years.

The introduction in 1864–1870 of organs of self-government—the *zemstva* and Municipal Councils—offered intellectuals opportunities for professional public employment. Together with rural schoolteachers, agronomists, physicians, statisticians, and other experts hired by the *zemstva,* known collectively as the "Third Element," they formed an active body with a radical, if nonrevolutionary, bent which gave the tsarist bureaucracy cause for much anxiety.[34] Professional revolutionaries scorned this kind of work on the grounds that it helped to solidify the existing regime. The elected *zemstvo* deputies, on the other hand, held liberal or liberal-conservative views.

Lastly, the growth of the Russian economy created a demand for professional specialists of all sorts: lawyers, engineers, scientists, managers. Independent of the government, these experts formed professional associations or "unions" *(soiuzy)*, which were in varying degrees permeated with an anti-autocratic, pro-Western spirit. As we have seen, in 1900–5 these associations played a major role in unleashing revolutionary unrest.

Thus, between 1860 and 1900, one precondition for the emergence of an intelligentsia was met: opportunities emerged for economic independence from the government along with the instruments for the spread of unconventional ideas. Under these favorable conditions, an ideology binding the intelligentsia into a cohesive group was not slow to emerge.

The Russian intelligentsia was prone to the wildest excesses of thought, to bickering and theoretical hair-splitting, but these quarrels should not obscure the fact that its members held a body of philosophical ideas in common. These ideas were in no wise original: in nearly all cases they were adopted from the Enlightenment and brought up to date in the light of modern science. From the eighteenth-century French materialists and their nineteenth-century German followers, Russian intellectuals adopted the "monistic" conception of man as a creature made up exclusively of material substances in which there was no room for a "soul." Ideas which failed to meet materialist criteria, beginning with God, were treated as figments of the imagination. Applying the utilitarian principle, the usual corollary of materialism, they rejected customs and institutions that did not satisfy the criterion of bringing the "greatest happiness to the greatest number." The early exponents of this ideology in Russia were called "nihilists," a term often misunderstood to mean that they believed in nothing; in fact, they had very strong beliefs but held nothing sacred and insisted on the universal validity of materialism and utilitarianism.

Positivism, the doctrine of August Comte, influenced Russian intellectuals in two ways. As a methodology for the study of human society (for which Comte coined the word "sociology"), it reinforced materialism and utilitarianism in that it taught that human behavior follows laws, which, if studied scientifically, make it fully predictable. Mankind can be scientifically managed with the help of the science of society, or sociology, which is to society what physics is to inert matter and energy and biology to living organisms. This proposition gained the status of an axiom in Russian intelligentsia circles from the 1860s onward. Positivism also exerted a more short-lived influence with its theory of progress as the advance of enlightenment, revealed in the gradual displacement of "theological" and "metaphysical" modes of thought by the scientific or "positivistic" one.

Materialism, utilitarianism, and positivism became the ideology of the Russian intelligentsia and the test which determined qualifications for membership. No one who believed in God and the immortality of the soul, no matter how otherwise "enlightened" and "progressive," could lay claim to being an *intelligent*. Nor was there place in the intelligentsia for those who allowed accident a role in human affairs or believed either in the immutability of "human nature" or in transcendental moral values. Russian intellectual history is replete with examples of *intelligenty* who, having developed doubts about one or more aspects of this ideology, suffered expulsion from its ranks. The "dry terror" which Cochin found in pre-revolutionary France was much in evidence in pre-revolutionary Russia: here, too, defamation of deviants and outsiders served to preserve group cohesion. Inasmuch as the survival of the intelligentsia depended on its members adhering to an ideological consensus, the consensus was ruthlessly enforced. This made the intelligentsia incapable of adjusting to changing reality, causing Peter Struve to describe it as "perhaps the most conservative breed of human beings in the world."[35]

The intelligentsia had tenuous relations with the creators of Russian culture—the novelists, poets, and artists. The latter intensely disliked attempts of political activists to impose restraints on their work. These restraints were much more onerous in their way than the government's official censorship: for while the government exercised negative censorship, forbidding certain themes, the intelligentsia practiced it in a positive form by demanding that art and literature serve the cause of social progress, as they defined it. Relations between the two groups worsened further in the 1890s when Russia came under the influence of Modernist art and literature with their commitment to "art for art's sake." The control that radical intellectuals sought to exercise over culture, to have it serve utilitarian rather than aesthetic goals, had little effect on genuine talent: no Russian writer or artist of distinction submitted to this kind of tyranny. Its main effect was to cut off the intelligentsia from the most vital sources of contemporary culture. Once in a while the simmering conflict became explicit, as when Chekhov confessed to a friend in what for him was an unusual outburst of anger:

> I do not believe in our intelligentsia—hypocritical, false, hysterical, uneducated, lazy. I do not believe in it even when it suffers and complains, because its oppressors come from its own inner depths.*

Dissent in Russia first became open and endemic at the universities. Although the 1863 statutes gave them considerable autonomy, its main beneficiaries were the faculty: the students continued to be treated as minors, subject to strict discipline. They chafed under it and from time to time gave vent to their frustration by staging protests. The pretexts were often minor and usually not political. Under a more tolerant regime they would have been allowed to dissipate. But the Russian authorities knew only one way of dealing with "insubordination" and that was by repression. Students guilty of nothing worse than rowdyism or breaches of regulations were arrested and expelled,

*Letter to Aleksei Suvorin, in Anton Chekhov, *Pis'ma*, V (Moscow, 1915), 352. Bernard De Voto in *The Literary Fallacy* (Boston, 1944) voices similar complaints about American writers of the interwar period, which indicates to what extent the problem that afflicted Imperial Russia had become international.

sometimes permanently. Such severity radicalized student bodies and helped transform institutions of higher learning into centers of opposition.

In the latter part of the 1860s, students formed circles to discuss public questions and their role in society. These circles initially showed no political, let alone revolutionary, inclinations. Influenced by French positivism, they identified progress with science and enlightenment, and saw their mission as spreading the gospels of materialism and utilitarianism. At this time, thousands of Russian youths who had neither interest in nor talent for science enrolled at the scientific faculties in the belief that by peering into microscopes or dissecting frogs they were advancing the cause of human happiness.

This naïve scientism soon ran its course: it was only the first of the enthusiasms a French visitor found characteristic of Russian intellectuals, who were quickly captivated by new ideas and just as quickly grew bored with them.[36] The fresh ideas that penetrated the universities in the early 1870s already had activist and, in the Russian context of the time, revolutionary implications. The emancipation of the serfs, the centerpiece of the Great Reforms, had transformed twenty million Russians from chattel into subjects. This gave the students a mission: to carry the message of positivism and materialism to the rural masses. In the spring of 1874, hundreds of students left the lecture rooms and dispersed in the countryside. The majority were "propagandists," followers of Peter Lavrov, who took it upon themselves to enlighten the peasants about the injustices of the regime, in the expectation that this knowledge would stir them into action. The smaller body of "agitators," followers of Bakunin, believed the peasants were instinctive rebels and would turn to violence once they were told they had large company. For the major part, the young "socialists-revolutionaries" who participated in this first "going to the people" crusade were still committed to the idea of change through enlightenment. But the persecution to which the authorities, frightened of peasant unrest, subjected them turned many into full-time revolutionaries. By 1877, when the second "going to the people" movement took place, Russia had several hundred experienced radical activists. Supporting them were thousands of sympathizers at the universities and in society at large.

Face-to-face contact with the "people" proved to be a bewildering experience for the radical youths. The *muzhik* turned out to be a very different creature from the one they had imagined: a "noble savage" steeped in communal life, an egalitarian, and a born anarchist who required only encouragement to rise against the Tsar, landlords, and capitalists. The following excerpt from the recollections of a "propagandist" of the 1870s reflects this bewilderment. A peasant is speaking:

> As far as land goes, we've got little. No place to put a chicken. But the Tsar will give. Absolutely. There is nothing doing without land. Who will pay taxes? How fill the treasury? And without the treasury, how can one rule? We will get the land! Ab-so-lute-ly! You will see.

The author noted with dismay the effects of radical propaganda on the peasants:

> How curiously our speeches, our concepts were interpreted by the peasant mind! . . . their conclusions and comparisons utterly astonished me. "We have it better under the Tsar." Something struck me in the head, as if a nail had been driven into it. . . . There, I said, are the fruits of propaganda! We do not destroy illusions but reinforce them. We reinforce the old faith of the people in the Tsar.[37]

The disillusionment with the people pushed the most determined radicals to terrorism. While many of the disappointed Socialists-Revolutionaries abandoned the movement and a handful adopted the doctrines of German Social-Democracy, a dedicated minority decided to carry on by different means. In the fall of 1879 this minority formed a secret organization called the People's Will (Narodnaia Volia). The mission of its thirty full-time members, banded in an Executive Committee, was to fight the tsarist regime by means of systematic terror: on its founding, it passed a "sentence" of death on Alexander II. It was the first political terrorist organization in history and the model for all subsequent organizations of this kind in Russia and elsewhere. Resort to terror was an admission of isolation: as one of the leaders of the People's Will would later concede, terror

> requires neither the support nor the sympathy of the country. It is enough to have one's convictions, to feel one's despair, to be determined to perish. The less a country wants revolution, the more naturally will they turn to terror who want, no matter what, to remain revolutionaries, to cling to their cult of revolutionary destruction.[38]

The stated mission of the People's Will was to assassinate government officials, for the twin goal of demoralizing the government and breaking down the awe in which the masses held the Tsar. In the words of the Executive Committee:

> Terrorist activity . . . has as its objective undermining the fascination with the government's might, providing an uninterrupted demonstration of the possibility of struggling against the government, in this manner lifting the revolutionary spirit of the people and its faith in the success of the cause, and, finally, organizing the forces capable of combat.[39]

The ultimate political goal of the People's Will was the convocation of a National Assembly through which the nation would express its wishes. The People's Will was a highly centralized organization, the decisions of the Executive Committee being binding on all followers, known as "vassals." Members were expected to dedicate themselves totally to the revolutionary cause, and if called upon, to sacrifice to it their properties and even their lives.

The emergence of the People's Will marked a watershed in the history of the Russian Revolution. For one, it established violence as a legitimate instrument of politics: enlightenment and persuasion were rejected as futile and even counterproductive. But even more important was the arrogation by the revolutionary intelligentsia of the right to decide what was good for the people: the name People's Will was a deceptive misnomer, since the "people" not only did not authorize an organization of thirty intellectuals to act on their behalf but had made it unmistakably clear that they would have no truck with anti-tsarist ideology. When the terrorists defined as one of their tasks "lifting the revolutionary spirit of the people," they were well aware that the real people, those tilling the fields and working in the factories, had no revolutionary spirit to lift. This attitude had decisive implications for the future. Henceforth all Russian revolutionaries, whether favoring terrorism or opposed to it, whether belonging to the Socialist-Revolutionary or the Social-Democratic Party, assumed the authority to speak in the name of the "people"—an abstraction without equivalent in the real world.

The terrorist campaign launched by the People's Will against a government entirely unprepared for it—the Third Department, in charge of state security, had about as many personnel as the Executive Committee—succeeded in its immediate objective: on March 1, 1881, Alexander II fell victim to a terrorist bomb. The political benefits of this outrage were nil. The public reacted with horror and the radical cause lost a great deal of popular support. The government responded with a variety of repressive measures and counter-intelligence operations which made it increasingly difficult for the revolutionaries to function. And the "people" did not stir, unshaken in the belief that the land which they desired would be given them by the next Tsar.

There followed a decade of revolutionary quiescence. Russians who wanted to work for the common good now adopted the doctrine of "small deeds"—that is, pragmatic, unspectacular activities to raise the cultural and material level of the population through the *zemstva* and private philanthropic organizations.

Radicalism began to stir again in the early 1890s in connection with the spurt of Russian industrialization and a severe famine. The Socialists-Revolutionaries of the 1870s had believed that Russia would follow a path of economic development different from the Western because she had neither the domestic nor the foreign markets that capitalism required. The Russian peasantry, being poor and heavily dependent on income from cottage industries (estimated at one-third of the peasant total income), would be ruined by competition from the mechanized factories and lose that little purchasing power it still possessed. As for foreign markets, these had been preempted by the advanced countries of the West.* Russia had to combine communal agriculture with rural (cot-

---

*This theory has recently received fresh support from a German scholar who argues that because of the poverty of her rural population, pre-revolutionary Russia lacked the conditions for the development of a market-based industrial economy: Jürgen Nötzold, *Wirtschaftspolitische Alternativen der Entwicklung Russlands in der Ära Witte und Stolypin* (Berlin, 1966), 193, 204.

tage) industry. From these premises Socialist-Revolutionary theoreticians developed a "separate path" doctrine according to which Russia would proceed directly from "feudalism" to "socialism," without passing through a capitalist phase.

This thesis was advanced with the help of arguments drawn from the writings of Marx and Engels. Marx and Engels initially disowned such an interpretation of their doctrine, but they eventually changed their minds, conceding that there might be more than one model of economic development. In 1877, in an exchange with a Russian, Marx rejected the notion that every country had to repeat the economic experience of Western Europe. Should Russia enter the path of capitalist development, he wrote, then, indeed, nothing could save her from its "iron laws," but this did not mean that Russia could not avoid this path and the misfortunes it brought.[40] A few years later Marx stated that the "historical inevitability" of capitalism was confined to Western Europe, and that because Russia had managed to preserve the peasant commune into the era of capitalism, the commune could well become the "fulcrum of Russia's social rejuvenation."* Marx and Engels admired the terrorists of the People's Will, and, as an exception to their general theory, Engels allowed that in Russia a revolution could be made by a "handful of people."[41]

Thus, before a formal "Marxist" or Social-Democratic movement had emerged in Russia, the theories of its founders were interpreted, with their sanction, when applied to an autocratic regime in an agrarian country, to mean a revolution brought about, not by the inevitable social consequences of matured capitalism, but by terror and coup d'état.

A few Russians, led by George Plekhanov, dissented from this version of Marxism. They broke with the People's Will, moved to Switzerland, and there immersed themselves in German Social-Democratic literature. From it they concluded that Russia had no alternative but to go through full-blown capitalism. They rejected terrorism and a coup d'état on the grounds that even in the unlikely event that such violence succeeded in bringing down the tsarist regime, the outcome would be not socialism, for which backward Russia lacked both the economic and cultural preconditions, but a "revived tsarism on a Communist base."

From the premises adopted by the Russian Social-Democrats there followed certain political consequences. Capitalist development meant the rise of a bourgeoisie committed, from economic self-interest, to liberalization. It further meant the growth of the industrial "proletariat," which would be driven by its deteriorating economic situation to socialism, furnishing the socialist movement with revolutionary cadres. The fact that Russian capitalism developed in a country with a pre-capitalist political system, however, called for a particular revolutionary strategy. Socialism could not flourish in

---

*K. Marks, F. Engels' i revoliutsionnaia Rossiia (Moscow, 1967), 443–44. According to N. Valentinov, The Early Years of Lenin (Ann Arbor, Mich., 1969), 183, this letter was kept secret for many years, presumably because it ran contrary to the views of the Russian Social-Democratic establishment.

19. L. Martov (on the left) and T. Dan, two
leading Mensheviks.

a country held in the iron grip of a police-bureaucratic regime: it required
freedom of speech to propagate its ideas and freedom of association to organize
its followers. In other words, unlike the German Social-Democrats, who, since
1890, were able to function in the open and run in national elections, Russian
Social-Democrats confronted the prior task of overthrowing autocracy.

The theory of a two-stage revolution, as formulated by Plekhanov's associate, Paul Akselrod, provided for the "proletariat" (read: socialist intellectuals) collaborating with the bourgeoisie for the common objective of bringing
to Russia "bourgeois democracy." As soon as that objective had been attained,
the socialists would rally the working class for the second, socialist phase of
the revolution. From the point of view of this strategy, everything that promoted in Russia the growth of capitalism and the interests of the bourgeoisie
was—up to a point—progressive and favorable to the cause of socialism.

The decade of the 1890s witnessed intense debates between the two radical
camps about the economic and, implicitly, the political future of Russia. One
group, which in 1902 would form the Party of Socialists-Revolutionaries (SRs
for short), adhered to the traditions of "separate path" and "direct" struggle—
that is, terrorism.* Their Social-Democratic rivals believed in the inevitability
of capitalism and the political liberalization of Russia. The two groups had
many strategic and tactical disagreements, which we will describe below, but
they shared an equal commitment to revolution. In the early 1900s, each had
several thousand adherents, virtually all intellectuals, most of them university
students and dropouts, a minority of whom formed a cadre of professional
revolutionaries: persons whose sole occupation in life was promoting revolution. They diligently studied social and economic conditions favoring or hin-
dering their objective, and engaged in continuous polemics from their foreign

---

*In English, the adherents of this group are usually called either Social-Revolutionaries
or Socialist-Revolutionaries. Both renditions are inaccurate. They called themselves Sotsialisty-
Revoliutsionery—that is, Socialists-Revolutionaries.

residences and even from prison and exile. The description of the professional revolutionary by the French political writer Jacques Ellul well fits the Russian representative of the genre. According to him, people of this type

> spend their life on study, on formulating the theory of revolution, and, accidentally, on agitation. They live off the revolution—intellectually, but also materially . . . Marx was a typical example of such professional revolutionaries, perfect idlers, veritable rentiers of the revolution. They spend most of their lives in libraries and clubs. They do not directly prepare the revolution. They analyze the disintegration of society, they classify the conditions favorable to it. But when the revolution breaks out, then their preparation enables them to play a decisive role in it: they turn into its managers, organizers. They are not men who cause trouble, but men of order: once the disturbance is over, they reorganize the structures, they are intellectually prepared for this, and, above all, their names are known to the public as specialists in revolution. They thus naturally come to power.*

Russia's political parties began to take shape at the turn of the century. The Socialist-Revolutionary Party, formed in 1902, was, in word and deed, the most radical, with a penchant for anarchism and syndicalism and an abiding commitment to terrorism.[42] The Social-Democrats founded their party at a clandestine congress in Minsk in 1898. The police, however, got wind of the meeting and arrested the participants. The Russian Social-Democratic Labor Party (Rossiiskaia Sotsial-Demokraticheskaia Rabochaia Partiia, or RSDRP) came into existence five years later at its Second Congress, held in Belgium and England.

The liberals formed their own Constitutional-Democratic Party (also known as the Party of National Freedom) in October 1905.

All these parties were led by *intelligenty,* and although the socialists referred to the liberals as "bourgeois" and the Bolsheviks labeled their socialist opponents "petty bourgeois," there was no discernible difference in the social background of the leaders of the three principal opposition parties. They competed for much the same constituency, and even though the liberals wanted to avoid the revolution which the socialists promoted, in their strategy and tactics they were not averse to employing revolutionary methods and benefiting from terrorism.

Russian liberalism was dominated by intellectuals with a pronounced left-wing orientation: its complexion was radical-liberal. The Constitutional-Democrats, or Kadets as they were popularly known, espoused the traditional liberal values: democratic franchise, parliamentary rule, liberty and equality of all citizens, respect for law. But operating in a country in which the overwhelming majority of the population had little understanding of these im-

---

*Jacques Ellul, *Autopsie de la Révolution* (Paris, 1969), 69. Ellul concedes that Lenin represented a new type of revolutionary activist.

ported ideas and the socialists were busy inciting revolution, they felt it necessary to adopt a more radical stance.

The Socialist-Revolutionary Party was the elder of the two leading socialist parties, since it could trace its origins to the People's Will. Its platform had three main planks: anti-capitalism, terrorism, and socialization of land. Following the Socialists-Revolutionaries of the 1870s and 1880s, the SRs espoused the theory of "separate path." They could not entirely ignore the spectacular growth in Russia after 1890 of capitalism in its industrial and financial forms, but they argued that this was an artificial and transient phenomenon, that by its very success undermined itself, laying waste the rural economy, its principal market. They allowed the "bourgeoisie" some role in the revolutionary process; on the whole, however, they considered it loyal to the autocracy. Russia would be liberated by armed action of the masses in the cities and villages.

Since they did not believe that the Russian bourgeoisie would lead or even join in the political struggle, the task devolved on the intelligentsia. This mission it could fulfill best by acts of political terrorism which had the same objective as that formulated by the People's Will—that is, undermining the prestige of the government in the eyes of the population and encouraging it to rebellion. Terror occupied the central plank in the SR program. To the SRs it was not only a political tactic but a spiritual act, a quasi-religious ritual, in which the terrorist took life but paid for it with his own. SR literature contains curiously barbaric paeans to the "holy cause," the "creative ecstasy," and the "highest peak of human spirit," which found expression, it was said, in the spilling of blood.[43] Terrorist operations were directed by the conspiratorial SR Combat Organization (Boevaia Organizatsiia), which "sentenced" government officials to "execution." But local SR cells and individual members also engaged in assassinations on their own initiative. The first act of political terror directed by the SRs was the murder in 1902 of the Minister of the Interior, D. S. Sipiagin. Subsequently, until crushed in 1908–9, the SR Combat Organization perpetrated hundreds of political murders.

Its daring terrorist undertakings, which often ended with the death of the terrorist, won the SRs much admiration in oppositional circles, including those formally opposed to terrorism. The Social-Democrats, who rejected this tactic, suffered serious defections to their rivals, reputed to be "real" revolutionaries.[44]

The social program of the SRs centered on the "socialization" of land, which called for the abolition of private property in land and the transfer of its management to local organs of self-government: these were to ensure that any citizen able and willing to cultivate the land received an adequate allotment. The SRs adopted the peasant slogan of "Black Repartition"—that is, the expropriation and distribution to the communes of all privately held land. This program, which reflected the desires of the rural population of Orthodox Russia, gained the SRs the support of nearly the entire peasantry. The much more modest demands on behalf of the peasants in the SD program, and the general contempt in which the SDs held the *muzhik,* kept that party from gaining any following in the countryside.

Although their main base of support lay in the village, the SRs did not ignore industrial workers: in their program, they described the proletariat as an essential element in the revolution and allowed for a transitional period of "proletarian revolutionary dictatorship."[45] Unlike the SDs, the SRs did not treat the peasants and industrial workers as distinct and hostile classes. Their theoreticians, of whom Victor Chernov was the most prominent, defined classes not by the relationship to the means of production but by the source of income. By this standard, societies had only two classes: the exploited or "toilers" and the exploiters—those who earned their livelihood and those who lived off the labor of others. In the latter category they placed landlords, capitalists, officials, and clergy; in the former, peasants, workers, and themselves, the intelligentsia. A self-employed peasant was to them a "toiler" and a natural ally of the industrial worker. They were vague, however, on what to do about industrial enterprises in a post-revolutionary society and had difficulty attracting workers.

The SR Party, extremist as it was, had a still more extreme wing known as Maximalists. This minority wanted to supplement political terror with "economic terror," by which they meant assassinations of landlords and factory owners. In practice, their strategy reduced itself to indiscriminate bombings, as illustrated by the attack on Prime Minister Stolypin's villa in 1911 in which dozens of bystanders lost their lives. To finance their operations, the Maximalists carried out bank holdups, euphemistically called "expropriations," which brought them hundreds of thousands of rubles. (In these operations, as we shall see, they sometimes collaborated with the Bolsheviks.) The movement had a maniacal quality, as is evident from the ideas of the Maximalist I. Pavlov. In a pamphlet published legally in Moscow in 1907, *The Purification of Mankind (Ochistka chelovechestva),* Pavlov argued that "exploiters" were not only a social class but a "degenerate race," which inherited and developed beyond anything known in the animal world the vilest characteristics of the gorilla and the orangutan. Since they bequeathed these vicious traits to their own offspring, all representatives of that "race," including women and children, had to be exterminated.[46] The SR Party formally disowned the Maximalists and the Union of Socialists-Revolutionaries Maximalists, formed in October 1906, but in practice it managed to accommodate itself to their outrages.

The SRs were loosely organized in good measure because the police, for whom prevention of terrorist acts had the highest priority, kept on infiltrating and decimating SR ranks. (According to G. A. Gershuni, the founder of the SR terrorist apparatus, for the denunciation of a member of the SR Combat Organization, the Okhrana paid a reward of 1,000 rubles, for an SR intellectual, 100, and for an SR worker, 25, but for a Social-Democrat, at most 3.[47]) The party's cells were filled with students: in Moscow they were said to constitute at least 75 percent of SR activists.[48] In the countryside, the most loyal supporters of the SRs were schoolteachers. Propaganda and agitation among the peasantry, consisting mainly of a scattering of pamphlets and leaflets, seems to have had little direct success in stimulating anti-governmental disorders, since at least until 1905 the peasants remained loyal to the notion that the land they craved would be provided by the Tsar.

We shall deal with the Social-Democratic Party at length elsewhere. Here it will be sufficient to point out certain features of that party that were to have political consequences in the early years of the century. Unlike the SRs, who divided society into "exploiters" and "exploited," the SDs defined classes in relation to the means of production, and regarded the industrial working class ("proletariat") as the only truly revolutionary class. The peasants, with the possible exception of those without access to communal land, they considered "petty bourgeois" and, as such, reactionary. On the other hand, to the SDs the "bourgeoisie" was a temporary ally in the common struggle against the autocracy, and capitalism was both inevitable and progressive. The SDs disparaged terror on the grounds that it diverted attention from the main immediate task of the socialists, that of organizing workers, although they benefited considerably from it.

The social background of the leaders as well as the rank and file of the two socialist parties showed no significant differences.[49] Their leadership was drawn from the gentry and the middle class—that is, from the same social milieu as that of the liberal party. The SRs had in their top ranks a surprising number of sons of millionaires, among them V. M. Zenzinov, Abraham Gots, and I. I. Fundaminskii.[50] For all their dedication to the peasantry, the SRs admitted no peasants into their directing organs, and the SDs, the self-proclaimed party of the working class, allowed very few manual workers into their top ranks.[51] In times of unrest (1905–6 and 1917), both parties relied heavily on rural immigrants to the cities, uprooted peasants who had acquired only the most superficial qualities of city dwellers. Psychologically and economically insecure, some of these peasants flocked to the socialists, while others joined the "Black Hundred" gangs that terrorized students and Jews. According to the Social-Democrat P. P. Maslov:

> Essentially the activity of local SR groups differed little from that of the SDs. The organizations of both parties usually consisted of small groups of *intelligenty,* formed into committees, who had little connection with the masses and viewed them mainly as material for political agitation.[52]

Russian liberals belonged only partly to the ranks of the intelligentsia. They did not share the basic philosophical premise of the radicals—that is, the belief in the perfectibility of man and society. Their stated objectives were not different from those of Western liberals. In their strategy and tactics, however, the Russian liberals drew very close to the radicals: as Paul Miliukov, their leader, liked to boast, their political program "was the most leftist of all those advanced by analogous groups in Western Europe."[53] Ivan Petrunkevich, another leading Kadet, thought that Russian "liberals, radicals, and revolutionaries" were distinguished not by political objectives but by temperament.[54]

This left-wing tendency was dictated by two considerations. The liberals, appealing to the mass electorate, had to compete with radical parties, which also stood to the left of their Western European counterparts, making the most extreme and utopian promises to the electorate. It was a challenge they had to meet. To steal the thunder from the socialists, the liberals adopted a radical social program, which included a demand for the expropriation of large landed estates (with compensation at "fair" rather than market prices), as well as Church and state properties, for distribution to the peasants.* Their platform also called for a comprehensive program of social welfare. They would turn a deaf ear to counsels of moderation, afraid of "compromising" themselves in the eyes of the masses and losing out to the socialists.

Even more compelling were tactical reasons. To wrest from the autocracy first a constitution and a legislative parliament and then parliamentary democracy, the liberals required leverage. This they found in the threat of revolution. In 1905–7 and then again in 1915–17, they urged the monarchy to make political concessions to them as a way of avoiding a much worse fate. The party maintained discreet silence in regard to SR terror, which its liberal principles should have caused it to condemn outright.

The political practice of the Kadets thus displayed a troublesome ambivalence—dread of revolution and exploitation of the revolution—and proved a gross miscalculation: playing with the revolutionary threat contributed not a little to promoting the very thing the liberals most wished to avoid. But this they would realize only after the event, when it was too late.

Although more moderate than the socialists, the liberals gave the Imperial regime greater trouble, because they had in their ranks socially prominent individuals who could engage in politics under the disguise of legitimate professional activity. Socialist students were fair game for the police. But who would dare to lay hands on a Prince Shakhovskoi or a Prince Dolgorukov, even as they were busy organizing a subversive liberal party? And how could one interfere with gatherings of physicians or jurists, although it was common knowledge that the participants discussed forbidden subjects? This difference in social status explains why the directing organizations of the liberals could function inside Russia, virtually free of police interference, while the SRs and SDs had to operate from abroad. It also explains why in both 1905 and 1917 the liberals were the first on the scene and in charge, weeks before their socialist rivals made an appearance.

The Russian liberal movement had two main bases of support: the *zemstva* and the intelligentsia.

---

*Ingeborg Fleischhauer (*Cahiers du Monde Russe et Soviétique,* XX, No. 2, 1979, 173–201) draws attention to the close similarities between the agrarian programs of the Kadets and the German Social-Democrats.

The *zemstva* were elected on a franchise that ensured solid representation of the landed gentry, then considered by the monarchy to be a staunch supporter. They functioned on the district and provincial level, but the government did not allow them to form a national organization, fearing that it would arrogate to itself quasi-parliamentary functions. The elected deputies tended to be either liberal-constitutionalists or Slavophile conservatives, both hostile to the autocracy and bureaucratic rule, but opposed to revolution. The salaried personnel hired by the *zemstva* (agronomists, physicians, teachers, etc.), known as the Third Element, was more radical but also non-revolutionary.

Properly treated, the *zemstva* might have helped stabilize the monarchy. But for the conservatives in the bureaucracy, and especially those in the Ministry of the Interior, the *zemtsy* were an intolerable irritant: busybodies who meddled in affairs that were none of their business and hindered the efficient administration of the provinces. Under their influence, Alexander III in 1890 restricted the authority of the *zemstva,* giving the governors wide latitude to interfere with their personnel and activities.

Harassed by the authorities, *zemstvo* leaders in the 1890s held informal national consultations, often disguised as professional and scientific meetings. In 1899, they went further, organizing in Moscow a discussion group called Beseda (Symposium). Its membership was sufficiently prominent socially and professionally for the police to look at its meetings through their fingers: these took place in the Moscow mansion of Princes Peter and Paul Dolgorukov.[55]

In June 1900, the government once again restricted the competence of the *zemstva,* this time in the realm of taxation. It further ordered the dismissal of *zemstvo* deputies who were especially active in promoting constitutional causes. In response, Symposium, which until then had confined its deliberations to *zemstvo* affairs, turned attention to political questions. To many *zemtsy,* the government's persecution raised the fundamental question whether it made sense to pursue "constructive," apolitical work under a regime dominated by bureaucracy and police bent on stifling every manifestation of public initiative. These doubts were heightened by the publication in 1901 in Germany of a confidential memorandum by Witte which urged the total abolition of *zemstva* as institutions incompatible with autocracy.

The ranks of *zemstvo* constitutionalists were augmented in 1901 by a small but influential group of intellectuals, defectors from Social-Democracy who had found intolerable its partisanship and dogmatism. The most prominent among them was Peter Struve, the author of the founding manifesto of the Social-Democratic Party and one of its outstanding theoreticians. Struve and his friends proposed to forge a national front, encompassing parties and groupings from the extreme left to the moderate right, under the slogan "Down with the Autocracy." Struve emigrated to Germany and with money provided by *zemstvo* friends founded there in 1902 the journal *Osvobozhdenie (Liberation).* The periodical carried information not permitted in censored publications, including secret government documents supplied by sympathizers within the bureaucracy. Issues smuggled into Russia helped forge a community of "Liberationists" (Osvobozhdentsy) from which, in time, would emerge the Constitutional-Democratic Party. In January 1904, its supporters founded in St. Petersburg the Union of Liberation (Soiuz Osvobozhdeniia) to promote constitutionalism and civil rights. Its branches in many towns attracted moderate elements as well as socialists, especially Socialists-Revolutionaries. (The Social-Democrats, insisting on their "hegemony" in the struggle against the regime, refused to collaborate.) These circles, operating semi-legally, did much to stimulate discontent with existing conditions.[56]

The rank and file of the liberal movement was highly diversified. The Constitutional-Democratic Party, which in 1906 had 100,000 members—several times the combined membership of the socialist parties—rested on a broader social base than its rivals on the left, attracting many artisans, junior officials, salesmen, and tradesmen. The liberal intelligentsia consisted mainly of professionals, such as professors, lawyers, physicians, and editors, rather than the students who filled socialist ranks.[57]

At the beginning of the twentieth century, there were in Russia thousands of men and women committed to fundamental change. A good part of them were "professional revolutionaries," a novel breed who dedicated their lives to plotting political violence. They and their supporters might quarrel among themselves about strategy and tactics—whether to engage in terror, whether to "socialize" or "nationalize" the land, whether to treat the peasant as an ally or as an enemy of the worker. But they were at one on the central issue: that there was to be no accommodation, no compromise with the existing social, economic and political regime, that it had to be destroyed, root and branch, not only in Russia but throughout the world. So strong was the influence of these extremists that even Russia's liberals came under their spell. Clearly, the limited political concessions spelled out in the October Manifesto satisfied none of them.

The existence of such an intelligentsia created, in and of itself, a high risk of permanent revolution. For just as lawyers make for litigation and bureaucrats for paperwork, so revolutionaries make for revolution. In each case, a profession emerges with an interest in promoting situations that demand its particular expertise. The fact that the intelligentsia rejected any accommodation with official Russia, that it exacerbated discontent and opposed reform, made it unlikely that Russia's problems could be peacefully resolved.

5

The Constitutional Experiment

The October Manifesto provided a framework within which the Russian state and Russian society should have found it possible to reduce the tension dividing them. This it failed to accomplish. A constitutional regime can function properly only if government and opposition accept the rules of the game: in Russia, neither the monarchy nor the intelligentsia was prepared to do so. Each regarded the new order as an obstacle, a deviation from the country's true system, which for the monarchy was autocracy and for the intelligentsia, a democratic republic. As a result, the constitutional interlude, while not without achievements, was largely wasted—a missed opportunity that would not recur.

In affixing his signature to the manifesto, Nicholas vaguely realized that it meant "constitution," but neither he nor his advisers were intellectually or psychologically ready to acknowledge that a constitution spelled an end to the autocracy. Although the manifesto pledged that henceforth no law would go into effect without the approval of a popularly elected legislature, the Court seemed unaware that this pledge entailed a constitutional charter. According to Witte, it was only two months later that Trepov broached the need for such a document.[1] And when a constitutional charter was issued in April 1906, its drafters studiously avoided the word "constitution," designating it as "Fundamental Laws" *(Osnovnye zakony),* the name traditionally used for the first volume of the Code of Laws.

Nicholas did not regard either the October Manifesto or the new Fundamental Laws as affecting his autocratic prerogatives. In his mind, the Duma was a consultative, not a legislative body ("I created the Duma, not to be directed by it, but to be advised," he told the Minister of War).[2] He further felt that in having "granted" the Duma and the Fundamental Laws of his own free will he was not bound by them: and since he had not sworn an oath to uphold the new order, he could also revoke it at will.[3] The obvious contradiction between the reality of a constitutional regime and the Court's insistence that nothing had changed had bewildering consequences. Thus, even Peter Stolypin, the closest Russia had to a genuine parliamentary Prime Minister, in private conversation insisted that Russia had no constitution because such a document had to be the product of agreement between rulers and subjects whereas the Fundamental Laws of 1906 had been granted by the Tsar. In his view Russia's government was not "constitutional" but "representative" and the only limitations on imperial authority were such as the Tsar saw fit to impose on himself.[4] And what is one to make of Vladimir Kokovtsov, Stolypin's successor, who while addressing the parliament exclaimed, "Thank God, we have as yet no parliament!"[5] Maurice Baring, an English student of Russia, concluded from personal observation in 1905–6 that ideally Russia's bureaucracy wanted "parliamentary institutions and autocratic government." Russians similarly joked that "the Tsar was ready to give a constitution as long as autocracy remained intact."[6] To the extent that such contradictory attitudes lend themselves to rational explanation, this is best sought in the tradition of Muscovite consultative bodies called Land Assemblies *(Zemskie sobory),* convened from time to time to give tsars non-binding advice. But, of course, by the terms of the October Manifesto and the Fundamental Laws of 1906 the Duma was a legislative, not a consultative body, so that the analogy with the past had no relevance except perhaps on the psychological level.

The behavior of the Crown under the constitutional regime cannot be understood without reference to the various monarchist groups which treated the October Manifesto as a trick played on the Tsar by the wily Witte and his alleged Jewish backers. In their view, too, neither the manifesto nor the Fundamental Laws were inviolate: what the Tsar had given, he could take back. These groups, composed largely of landowners (many from the western provinces), right-wing publicists, and Orthodox clergy, backed by lower-middle-class groups, espoused a very simple ideology: autocracy and Russia for the Russians. Increasingly, their outlook reduced itself to a rabid anti-Semitism, which saw in Jews the source of all of Russia's woes—enemies of Christianity and a race bent on attaining world domination. The most influential of these bodies was the Union of the Russian People, which organized patriotic demonstrations, published virulently anti-Semitic literature, and from time to time arranged for Jewish pogroms, using gangs of urban thugs called "Black Hundreds" *(Chërnye sotni)*. These extreme right-wing groupings, which in many ways anticipated the German National Socialists of the 1920s, in democratic elections would have been unlikely to gain a single seat in the Duma. They owed their disproportionate influence to the identity of their views and interests with those of the Crown and its more reactionary officialdom. It was they who encouraged Nicholas and his wife in the belief that the country remained staunchly loyal to the Romanov dynasty and the ideals of autocracy.[7]

The more liberal bureaucrats were not averse to conceding limited power to a representative body: according to a high official, the idea of a representative institution with which to divide responsibility (if not authority) for governing Russia "grew like grass" in governmental circles.[8] The rationale behind such sympathies was spelled out by Kaiser Wilhelm II in a letter to the Tsar in August 1905 in connection with the announcement of the so-called Bulygin Duma:

> Your manifest directing the formation of the "Duma" made an excellent impression in Europe . . . you get an excellent insight into the mind of your People and make them carry a part of the responsibility for the future, which it would have probably liked to saddle solely upon you, thereby making a wholesale "critique" and dissatisfaction with deeds done by *you alone* impossible.[9]

But in the eyes of the bureaucracy these benefits could accrue only if parliament confined itself to largely ceremonial functions. Vasilii Maklakov thus describes the attitude on the eve of the First Duma of Ivan Goremykin, the Tsar's favorite minister:

> As concerned the Duma, it was for him exclusively a factor complicating legislative procedures. This complication seemed to him, at bottom, unnecessary: but once it had been regrettably made, then it had to be reduced to a minimum. This was not difficult. The government's plan for the Duma was simple. To begin with, it would be sufficient for the deputies to have the honor of being received in audience by the Emperor: then their mandates would be verified and the rules worked out. This would be followed by a recess, brought about as quickly as possible: in this manner, the session would be prorogued until autumn. Next would come the discussion of the budget. The practical exigencies of life would assert themselves, turmoil calmed, order restored, and everything would be as before.[10]

Not all Crown ministers thought in these terms: Stolypin, in particular, would try to bring the Duma into a genuine partnership. But Goremykin reflected more accurately the attitudes prevalent at the Court and among its conservative supporters—attitudes which precluded effective parliamentary government at a time when autocratic government had ceased to be feasible. As if to demonstrate his feelings toward the Duma, Nicholas refused to cross its threshold, preferring to receive the deputies in the Winter Palace.*

Later, after the Revolution, some officials of the tsarist regime justified the

---

*V. S. Diakin, *Russkaia burzhuaziia i tsarizm v gody pervoi mirovoi voiny, 1914–17* (Leningrad, 1967), 169. Nicholas first made a personal appearance in the Duma in February 1916, ten years after the parliament had been established, in the midst of a grave political crisis brought about by Russia's defeats in World War I.

20. Ivan Goremykin.

monarchy's unwillingness to share power with the Duma with the argument that Russian "society," as represented by the intelligentsia, would have been incapable of administering the country: introducing parliamentary government in 1906 would merely have served to unleash the anarchy of 1917 that much sooner.[11] But these arguments, voiced in emigration, had the benefit of hindsight: a conservative-liberal parliamentary coalition cooperating with the monarchy and its officialdom would certainly have proven more effective than the same coalition turned out to be in March 1917, after the monarchy had abdicated, when it had no alternative but to seek support from the revolutionary intelligentsia.

Had the Russian intelligentsia been politically more mature—more patient, that is, and more understanding of the mentality of the monarchic establishment—Russia might perhaps have succeeded in making an orderly transition from a semi-constitutional to a genuinely constitutional regime. But these qualities the educated classes sorely lacked. From the day the constitution went into force, they exploited every opportunity to wage war against the monarchy. The radical intellectuals rejected the very principles of constitutional monarchy and parliamentary government. Initially they boycotted the Duma elections; later, after concluding that the boycott was a mistake, they ran in the elections but only to disrupt parliamentary proceedings and incite the population to rebellion. The Constitutional-Democratic Party was in this respect only marginally more constructive. While the liberals accepted the principle of constitutional monarchy, they regarded the Fundamental Laws of 1906 as a travesty and did all in their power to deprive the monarchy of effective authority.*

---

*There is a striking difference between the deputies to the first two Russian Dumas and those who in 1789–91 ran the French National Assembly. The Russians were overwhelmingly intellectuals without practical experience. The Third Estate, which dominated the Estates-General and the National Assembly, by contrast, consisted of practical lawyers and businessmen, "men of action and men of affairs." J. M. Thompson, *The French Revolution* (Oxford, 1947), 26–27.

As a result, the traditional conflict between the authorities and the intelligentsia grew more intense rather than less, since it now had a formal arena where to play itself out. Struve, who observed this struggle with a sense of alarm because he believed it was bound to end in catastrophe, wrote that "the Russian Revolution and the Russian reaction somehow hopelessly claw at each other, and from every fresh wound, every drop of blood which they draw, grows the vengeful hatred and untruth of Russian life."[12]

The experts whom the government charged with drafting the new Fundamental Laws were told to produce a document that would fulfill the promises of the October Manifesto and still preserve most of the traditional prerogatives of the Russian monarchy.[13] Between December 1905 and April 1906, when the work was completed, they came up with several drafts, which were discussed and revised at cabinet meetings, sometimes chaired by the Tsar. The final product was a conservative constitution—conservative in terms of both the franchise and the powers reserved for the Crown.

The electoral law was worked out at meetings of officials and public representatives. The principal question was whether to provide for an equal and direct vote or a vote organized by estates and cast indirectly, through electoral chambers.[14] Following the recommendation of the bureaucracy, it was decided to adopt a system of indirect voting by estates in order to reduce the weight of constituencies regarded as more likely to elect radical deputies. There were to be four electoral curiae: for the gentry *(dvoriane),* for burghers *(meshchane),* for peasants, and for workers, the last-named group now given the vote which the Bulygin project had denied it. The franchise was so contrived that one gentry vote carried the weight of three burgher, fifteen peasant, and forty-five worker votes.[15] Except in the large cities, the voters cast their ballots for electors who, in turn, selected either other electors or the deputies themselves. These electoral provisions rejected the democratic franchise advocated by Russian liberal and socialist parties which called for the "four-tail" vote—universal, direct, equal, and secret. It was the government's hope that by reducing the urban vote it would ensure a tractable Duma.

While the experts worked on the constitution, the government published laws implementing the pledges of civil rights in the October Manifesto.[16] On November 24, 1905, preliminary censorship of periodical publications was abolished: henceforth newspapers and journals which published what the authorities considered seditious or libelous material could be prosecuted only in court. Although during World War I some preliminary censorship was restored, after 1905 Russia enjoyed full press freedom, which made it possible to criticize the authorities without restrictions. Laws issued on March 4, 1906, guaranteed the rights of assembly and association. Citizens were allowed to hold lawful assemblies, provided they notified the local chief of police seventy-two hours in advance and observed certain provisions when meeting in the open. Forming associations also required prior notification to the authorities:

if no objections were raised within two weeks, the organizers were free to proceed. This law made possible the formation of trade unions as well as political parties, although, in practice, in both cases governmental permission would frequently be withheld under one pretext or another.*

These rights and freedoms had no precedent in Russian history. Nevertheless, the bureaucracy found ways of circumventing them by recourse to the provisions of the law of August 14, 1881, authorizing governors to place provinces under "Safeguard," which remained on the statute books until 1917. Throughout the constitutional period, vast expanses of the Russian Empire would be declared subject to this status, which resulted in the suspension for their inhabitants of civil rights, including those of assembly and association.[17]

The new Fundamental Laws, made public on April 26, while the elections to the Duma were in progress, was a curious document. It had been composed in such a way as to depart minimally from the traditional Fundamental Laws, with the main emphasis placed, as before 1905, on the powers and prerogatives of the Crown. The powers and prerogatives of the legislative branch were inserted almost like an embarrassing afterthought. To compound the confusion between the new and old orders, the monarch was still defined as an "autocrat," using a formula that dated to the reign of Peter the Great:

> Article 4: To the Emperor of All the Russias belongs the Supreme Autocratic power. God Himself commands that he be obeyed, not only from fear of God's wrath, but also for the sake of one's conscience.[18]

Traditionally, the corresponding article had described the Tsar's powers as both "unlimited" and "autocratic." The former term was now omitted, but the omission was of little consequence because in modern Russian usage "autocratic," which in Peter's time had meant "sovereign"—that is, independent of other powers—had also acquired the sense of authority subject to no limitations.

Russia was given a two-chamber parliament. The lower, the State Duma (Gosudarstvennaia Duma), was composed entirely of popularly elected representatives, chosen according to the franchise outlined above. The upper chamber, the State Council (Gosudarstvennyi Sovet), was the institution by the same name which had been functioning since 1802 to translate imperial commands into laws. It consisted of appointed officials augmented with representatives of public bodies (the Church, *zemstva*, Noble Assemblies, and universities). Its purpose was to serve as a brake on the Duma. Because it had not been mentioned in the October Manifesto, liberals saw in its creation a breach of promise.

All bills, in addition to requiring the approval of the Crown, needed the consent of both chambers: the State Council, along with the Tsar, could veto legislative proposals emanating from the lower chamber. In addition, the two

---

*According to M. Szeftel, the tsarist government authorized no oppositional political parties prior to its collapse in 1917 (*The Russian Constitution of April 23, 1906*, Brussels, 1976, 247). They existed and functioned in a legal limbo.

chambers had to pass annually on the state budget—a powerful prerogative which in the Western democracies served to control the executive branch. However, in Russia's case the budgetary powers of the parliament were diluted by a provision which exempted from its scrutiny payments on state debts, expenses of the Imperial household, and "extraordinary credits."

The parliament enjoyed the right of "interpellation" or formal questioning of ministers. If deputies raised questions about the legality of government actions—and only then—the appropriate minister or ministers had to appear in the Duma to answer questions. Although the legislature had no authority to interrogate ministers on the general conduct of policy, since such a right would have allowed it to pass a no-confidence vote, interpellation served as an important device to keep the Crown and its officials in line.

In some respects, perhaps the single most important prerogative of the new parliament was its members' right to free speech and parliamentary immunity. From April 1906 until February 1917, the Duma provided a forum for unrestrained and often intemperate criticism of the regime. This probably contributed more to undermining the prestige of the Russian Government in the eyes of the population than all the revolutionary outrages, because it stripped the establishment of the aura of omniscience and omnipotence which it strove so hard to maintain.

To the disappointment of the opposition, the Crown retained the power to appoint ministers. This provision intensely annoyed the liberals, who wanted a parliamentary cabinet made up of their own people: it would prove the most contentious issue in relations between the government and the opposition during the final decade of the monarchy. The liberals refused to compromise on this issue: the government's willingness in 1915–16 quietly to adopt the American system of nominating ministers acceptable to the parliament met with no response from them. Nicholas, for his part, adamantly refused to grant the Duma the power to appoint ministers because he was certain that they would make a mess of things and then wash their hands of it by resigning.

The Crown retained the right to declare war and make peace.

Last, but not least, the Crown did not fulfill the promise of the October Manifesto to assure those elected by the nation of "an effective opportunity to supervise the legality of the actions" of the administration. Apart from the right of interpellation, which could be used to embarrass the administration but not to influence its policies, parliament had no control over the bureaucracy. Members of the bureaucratic establishment, the police included, remained for all practical purposes immune to legal prosecution. The administrative corps of Imperial Russia remained, as before, a body outside parliamentary supervision and above the law—a "meta-juridical" body, as it were.

Two further provisions of the Fundamental Laws of 1906 call for comment: for although they were also to be found in other European constitutions, in Russia they would be particularly abused. As in Britain, the Duma had a normal term of five years, but it could be dissolved earlier at the monarch's pleasure. The English Crown in modern times would not have dreamt of dissolving Parliament and calling for elections except on the advice of the leader of the parliamentary majority. In Russia, it was different: the First Duma lasted only 72 days and the Second 105 days, both sent home because the Crown was unhappy with their conduct. Only after June 1907, when it unilaterally and unconstitutionally altered the electoral law to ensure a more tractable Duma, did the Crown allow the lower chamber its normal five-year span.

Even more pernicious was the government's recourse to Article 87 of the Fundamental Laws, which authorized it to issue emergency laws when parliament was not in session. Under the terms of this article, such laws lapsed unless approved by parliament within sixty days of reconvening. The authorities made free use of this clause, not so much to deal with emergency situations as to bypass normal legislative procedures, either because they were considered too cumbersome or because parliament was unlikely to act favorably: occasionally, the Duma was deliberately prorogued to enable the government to legislate by decree. Such practices made a mockery of the legislative powers of parliament and undermined respect for the constitution.

The existence of a legislature made it impractical to continue conducting ministerial business in the traditional manner. The Council of Ministers (Sovet Ministrov), previously a body without authority, was now made into a cabinet under a Chairman who was in fact, if not in name, a Prime Minister. In its new guise, it marked a departure from the patrimonial custom of having ministers report individually to the Tsar. Under the new arrangement, decisions taken by the Council were binding on all the ministers.*

Whether one regards the Fundamental Laws of 1906 as a major advance in Russia's political development or as a deceptive half measure, a "pseudo-constitution" *(Scheinkonstitution)* as Max Weber called it, depends on one's criteria. Judged by standards of the advanced industrial democracies, the Russian constitution certainly left a great deal to be desired. But in terms of Russia's own past, of five hundred years of autocracy, the 1906 charter marked a giant step toward a democratic order. For the first time the government allowed elected representatives of the nation to initiate and veto legislative measures, to scrutinize the budget, to criticize the monarchy and to interrogate its ministers. If the constitutional experiment ultimately failed to bring state and society into partnership, the fault lay not so much in the shortcomings of the constitution as in the unwillingness of Crown and parliament to accept the new arrangement and function responsibly within its provisions.

Once the country had been given a parliament, it was virtually certain that its leadership would fall to the liberals. The 1905 Revolution, of which the

---

*According to Witte (*Vospominaniia,* II, Moscow, 1960, 545), this body was deliberately called "Council of Ministers" rather than "cabinet" further to distinguish Russia from Western constitutional states.

October Manifesto had been the main fruit, had two distinct phases, the first successful, the second not. The first phase had been initiated and managed by the Union of Liberation, and reached its climax in the October Manifesto. The second phase, which began the day after the Manifesto had been issued, dissipated itself in brutal pogroms instigated by both the revolutionary and reactionary parties. It was ultimately crushed by the forces of order. As the organizers of the first, successful phase of the Revolution, the liberals were its main beneficiaries. They intended to exploit this advantage to push Russia into a full-fledged parliamentary democracy. The decision of the two principal socialist parties, the Social-Democrats and Socialists-Revolutionaries, to boycott the Duma elections ensured their victory.

The Constitutional-Democrats adopted an extremely aggressive parliamentary strategy for they saw in the socialists' boycott a unique opportunity to capture the socialists' constituency. They insisted on treating the new Fundamental Laws as illegitimate: only the sovereign nation, through its democratically elected representatives, had the right to draw up a constitution. The conservative liberal Vasilii Maklakov thought that the leadership of his party, spellbound by the vision of 1789, would settle for nothing less than a Constituent Assembly:

> I recall the indignation of the Congress [of the Kadet Party] over the promulgation of a constitution on the eve of the Duma's convocation. What made it especially dangerous was the absence of pretense in this indignation. The liberals should have understood that if the Emperor had convened a national representative body without setting for it legal limits, he would have opened the gates to a *revolution*. They did understand this now and were not frightened by the prospect. On the contrary: they rebelled against the idea that the Duma must work within the *framework* of rights set forth by the *Constitution*. Which goes to prove that they did not take this Constitution seriously. According to them, the "national representation" was sovereign and had the right to demolish all the walls which the Constitution had erected around it. One saw the source of their mentality. Their spirits were fired by memories of the Great Revolution. The Duma appeared to them as the Estates-General. Like it, it had to turn into a National Assembly and give the country a true Constitution in place of one which the vigilant Monarchy had surreptitiously granted.[19]

To the Kadets, the Duma was a battleground: with appeals to the "masses," they meant to force the Crown to give up all power. Such doubts as sober-minded liberals may have entertained over the wisdom of a confrontational strategy were stilled by the spectacular victory which the Kadets won in the Duma elections. As the most radical party on the ballot, they attracted much of the vote that would have otherwise gone to the SRs and SDs: this created the illusion that they had become the principal national opposition party. With 179 out of 478 deputies, they emerged as the strongest group in the lower house: owing to the worker votes, they captured all the seats in Moscow and St. Petersburg. Even so, they controlled only 37.4 percent of the seats; lacking an absolute majority, they needed allies. They could have sought them on the right, among conservative liberals. But determined to maintain a hold on the peasant and worker electorate, they turned leftward, to the agrarian socialists who had been elected as individual candidates and came to be collectively known as Laborites (Trudoviki).

Drunk with success, believing themselves to be on the eve of a second, decisive Revolution, the Kadets went on the offensive. Under the leadership of Miliukov, they expressed a willingness to join the cabinet but on one condition: that the Tsar agree to convoke a Constituent Assembly. As has been noted, Witte's negotiations with liberal conservatives (Shipov, Guchkov, and others) also had had no issue.[20] The Crown would make several more attempts to bring liberals and liberal-conservatives into the cabinet, to be rebuffed each time. The stage was thus set for a parliamentary confrontation not over policies but over the very nature of Russia's constitutional regime.

The Crown approached the opening of the Duma with trepidation but without a program. What actually transpired when the Duma convened exceeded its worst fears.

Nicholas had been assured by liberal bureaucrats that elections presented no threat to him because the provisions ensuring the preponderance of peasants would produce a cooperative Duma: it was the same mistake the French monarchy had committed in 1789 when it doubled the representation of the Third Estate in the Estates-General. Not all shared this optimism: Durnovo, the ex-Minister of the Interior and one of the most astute politicians in Russia, had cautioned that the majority of the deputies would be drawn from the radical rural "semi-intelligentsia," who were eager to solidify their hold on the peasantry.[21] Indeed, nearly one-half of the deputies to the First Duma were peasants, many of them of this type. And they turned out to be very different from the deferential *muzhiki* with whom the imagination of Slavophile conservatives populated Russia. Kryzhanovskii thus describes the revulsion that seized official circles at the sight of the hordes of peasant representatives who descended on St. Petersburg in the spring of 1906:

> It was enough to take a look at the motley mob of "deputies"—and it was my lot to spend among them entire days in the corridors and the garden of Taurida Palace—to experience horror at the sight of Russia's first representative body. It was a gathering of savages. It seemed as if the Russian land had sent to St. Petersburg everything that was barbarian in it, everything filled with envy and malice. If one were to assume that these individuals really represented the people and its "innermost aspirations," then one would have been forced to concede that Russia could survive for at least one more century only by the force of external constraint, not by that of inner cohesion, and that enlightened absolutism was for her the sole salutary form of government. The attempt to found the political system on the will of the people was obviously doomed to

failure because in this mass any consciousness of statehood, let alone of shared statehood, was totally submerged in social hostility and class envy: more correctly, such consciousness was entirely lacking. It was equally futile to place one's hope in the intelligentsia and its cultural influence. In the Duma the intelligentsia was relatively weakly represented and it clearly yielded to the seething energy of the dark masses. It believed in the power of good words, it upheld ideals that were entirely alien and unnecessary for the masses, and its only role was to serve as a springboard for the Revolution. It could not act creatively. . . .

The attitude of the peasant Duma delegates toward their responsibilities was curious in the extreme. They brought with them petitioners on various matters: these they placed in the [deputies'] seats, from which Duma personnel had no little trouble evicting them. On one occasion, the police detained on a street adjacent to Taurida Palace two peasants who were selling entrance tickets to it: both turned out to be Duma deputies, of which fact the Chairman was duly apprised.

Some deputies immediately began to carry on revolutionary propaganda in the factories, to organize street demonstrations, to incite the mobs against the police, and so on. During one such demonstration on Ligovka, the leader of a brawling mob, one Mikhailenenko, a deputy representing the miners of the Urals, was beaten up. He showed up the next day in the Duma and participated in the discussion of this incident with a face so heavily bandaged that only his nose and eyes were visible. Peasant deputies got drunk in taverns and engaged in brawls: when attempts were made to have them arrested, they claimed personal immunity. The police were at first very confused, uncertain what they could and could not do in such cases. In one such incident, the doubts were resolved by an old woman, the tavern owner, who, in response to a drunken deputy's claim of inviolability, gave him a thrashing, shouting: "For me, you are quite violable, you SOB," following which she threw him out. . . . There were grand ceremonies at the burial of one Duma deputy, whose name escapes me, who had died of delirium tremens: in one funeral speech he was referred to as a "fighter fallen on the field of honor."

Following their arrival [in St. Petersburg], some deputies were sentenced by *volost'* and other courts for petty theft and other swindles: one for having stolen a pig, another for purse snatching, etc. Altogether, according to information gathered by the Ministry of the Interior, the number of deputies in the First Duma, mainly peasants, who, owing to the careless makeup of the lists of voters and electors, turned out to have been convicted of pecuniary crimes that disqualified them from participating in the elections, either before they had entered the Duma or within one year after its dissolution, exceeded forty persons—that is, about 8 percent of the Duma's membership.[22]

On the opening day of the Duma, the Tsar received the deputies in a solemn session at the Winter Palace and delivered an address in which he promised to respect the new order. The Duma, on a Kadet motion, responded with a revolutionary challenge, approved by all but five deputies. It demanded the abolition of the upper chamber, the power to appoint and dismiss ministers, compulsory expropriations of certain landed properties, and amnesty for political prisoners, including those sentenced for terrorist crimes. When the Court, having gotten wind of the Duma's response, refused to receive the

Duma deputation sent to present it, the Duma passed with virtual unanimity a vote of no confidence in the cabinet coupled with a demand that it yield to a ministry chosen by itself.[23]

This behavior threw the government, accustomed to conducting its affairs with utmost decorum, into disarray. The security services were especially alarmed, fearing the inflammatory effect of Duma rhetoric on the countryside. According to one police official, the very existence of a constitutional regime confused the peasants. Unable to figure out why the authorities allowed Duma deputies to demand changes in the system of government while punishing private persons for making similar demands, they concluded that the Duma's "revolutionary propaganda was carried out with the approval and even encouragement of the government."[24] Given that the prestige of the government among the peasants had declined anyway from the loss of the war with Japan and its inability to suppress the Socialist-Revolutionary terror, the police had reason to fear losing control of the villages.

In these circumstances, the Court decided on dissolution. As soon as they learned of this decision, the Kadets and other left-of-center deputies wanted to stage a sit-in, but they had to give up this plan because the government had the Duma surrounded by troops. The dissolution order may have violated the spirit of the Fundamental Laws but it was certainly legitimate. Nevertheless, the Kadets and some of their associates saw it as an opportunity to throw down the revolutionary gauntlet. Adjourning to nearby Vyborg, a Finnish city outside the reach of the Russian police, they issued an appeal to the citizens of Russia to refuse paying taxes and providing recruits. The protest was both unconstitutional and futile. The country ignored the Vyborg Manifesto, and its only consequence was to bar the signatories, among whom were many leading liberals, from running in future elections.

Thus, the overconfident liberals lost the opening skirmish in the war they had declared on the constitutional monarchy.

The October Manifesto had mollified the moderate, liberal-conservative opposition, but neither the liberal-radical nor the socialist politicians. The latter regarded it as merely a preliminary concession: the Revolution had to continue until total victory. Under the incitement of left-of-center intellectuals, the violence in the country went on unabated, evoking from the right a counterterror in the form of pogroms against students and Jews.

The agrarian unrest of 1905–6 had two consequences. It ended, once and for all, the peasantry's traditional pro-monarchic sentiments. Henceforth, the *muzhik* no longer looked to the Tsar to give him the land he coveted, but to the Duma and the liberal and radical parties. Second, the peasants of central Russia succeeded in "smoking out" many landlords, who, frightened of the assaults on their properties, disposed of their estates and cleared out. These developments accelerated the liquidation of landlord agriculture which had begun with the Emancipation Edict and would be completed in 1917. After 1905, the peasantry was the largest purchaser (37–40 percent) of land that appeared on the market. Landlords, who in 1863–72 had bought 51.6 percent of the land, in 1906–9 accounted for only 15.2 percent of the purchasers.

The peasant *jacquerie* was exacerbated by the Socialist-Revolutionary campaign of political terror.[25] The world had never known anything like it: a wave of murder which soon gripped hundreds if not thousands of young men and women in a collective psychosis—murder as an end in itself, its ostensible objective having long been lost sight of. Although the declared targets were government officials, notably policemen, in practice the terror could be quite indiscriminate. As is usual, it shaded into ordinary criminality, some of its perpetrators extorting money and intimidating court witnesses. The majority of the terrorists were youths—two-thirds of them twenty-two or younger—for whom the daring, often suicidal operations turned into a kind of rite of passage into manhood. The most rabid element among the terrorists, the Maximalists, killed for the sake of killing, in order to speed the collapse of the social order. The effects of SR terror extended beyond the lives it extinguished and the repressive countermeasures it provoked. It lowered still further the already low level of political life in Russia, demoralizing those actively engaged in politics and making resort to violence a normal way of dealing with difficult problems.

The Socialists-Revolutionaries decided on a massive terror campaign in January 1906—that is, after the country had been promised a constitution. The scope of the campaign was staggering. Stolypin told the Duma in June 1906 that in the preceding eight months there had occurred 827 assaults with the intent to kill against officials of the Ministry of the Interior (which included the police and the gendarmerie), as a consequence of which 288 persons lost their lives and 383 suffered injuries.[26] The director of the Police Department informed the Duma a year later that in the two Baltic provinces of Livonia and Courland there had taken place 1,148 terrorist acts, which resulted in the loss of 324 lives, the majority of the victims being policemen and soldiers.[27] It has been estimated that in the course of 1906 and 1907 terrorists killed or maimed in the Russian Empire 4,500 officials.[28] If private persons are added, the total number of the victims of left-wing terror in the years 1905–7 rises to over 9,000.[29]

The government's hope that the Duma would help it deal with these outrages were not realized. Even the Constitutional-Democrats refused to condemn them on the grounds that the revolutionary terror was a natural reaction to governmental terror. When a Duma deputy ventured to declare that in a constitutional regime there was no place for terror, he was attacked by his colleagues as a "provocateur" and the resolution which he moved received only thirty votes.[30]

In these difficult circumstances—a rebellious parliament, rural violence, and nationwide terror—the monarchy turned to a "strong man," the governor of Saratov, Peter Arkadevich Stolypin.

Stolypin, who would serve as Prime Minister from July 1906 until his death in September 1911, was arguably the most outstanding statesman of Imperial Russia. For all their remarkable gifts, his only possible rivals—Speranskii and Witte—lacked his combination of the statesman's vision and the politician's skills. Not an original thinker—most of his measures had been anticipated by others—he impressed Russians and foreigners alike with his strength of character and integrity: Sir Arthur Nicolson, the British Ambassador to Russia, thought him simply the "most remarkable figure in Europe."[31] In his actions he was guided by the ideas of the liberal bureaucracy, believing that Russia required firm authority but that under modern conditions such authority could not be exercised without popular support. The *dvorianstvo,* in his view, was a vanishing class: the monarchy should rely on an independent yeomanry, the creation of which was one of his principal objectives. Parliament was indispensable. He was virtually the only Russian Premier to address representatives of the nation as equals and partners. At the same time he did not believe that parliament could run the country. Like Bismarck, whom he in many ways emulated, he envisioned it as an auxiliary institution.* That he failed in his endeavors demonstrates how irreconcilable were the divisions in Russia and how unlikely it was that the country would escape violent collapse.

Born in 1862 in Germany, Stolypin descended from a *dvorianstvo* family which had served the tsars since the sixteenth century: Struve described him as a typical "servitor in the medieval sense, instinctively loyal to the Imperial sovereign."[32] His father was an artillery general who had distinguished himself in the Crimean War; his mother was related to Alexander Gorchakov, the Russian Minister of Foreign Affairs under Alexander II. Stolypin would probably also have followed a military career were it not for a physical disability incurred in childhood. After attending secondary school in Vilno, he enrolled at the Physical-Mathematical Faculty of St. Petersburg University, from which he graduated in 1885 with the Highest Honors and a Candidate's Degree (the Russian equivalent of an American Ph.D.) for a dissertation on agriculture. A highly cultivated man (he is said to have spoken three foreign languages), he liked to think of himself as an intellectual rather than a bureaucrat, a feeling the St. Petersburg officialdom reciprocated by treating him as an outsider even after he had reached the topmost rung of the bureaucratic ladder.[33]

After completing his studies, Stolypin joined the Ministry of the Interior. In 1889 he was sent to Kovno, in what used to be Polish-Lithuanian territory, where his wife, the socially prominent O. B. Neidgardt, owned property. Here

---

*"I am in no sense in favor of absolutist government," Bismarck told the Reichstag in 1884. "I consider parliamentary cooperation, if properly practiced, necessary and useful, as I consider parliamentary rule harmful and impossible": Max Klemm, ed., *Was sagt Bismarck dazu?,* II (Berlin, 1924), 126.

21. P. A. Stolypin: 1909.

he spent thirteen years (1889–1902), serving as Marshal of the Nobility (an appointed office in this area), devoting his spare time to the improvement of his wife's estate and studies of agriculture.

The years which he spent in Kovno were to exert a decisive influence on Stolypin's thinking. In the western provinces of Russia communal landholding was unknown: here peasant households held their land as outright property. Comparing the superior condition of the rural population in this region with that of central Russia, Stolypin came to agree with those who saw in the peasant commune the main impediment to rural progress; and because he considered rural prosperity a precondition of national stability, he concluded that the preservation in Russia of law and order demanded the gradual elimination of the commune. The commune inhibited improvement in the peasant's economic condition in several ways. The periodic redistribution of land deprived the peasant of incentives to improve the soil since it was not his property; at the same time, it ensured him of the minimum needed to survive. It also encouraged the enterprising and industrious peasant to engage in usury. Stolypin believed that Russia needed a large class of independent, landowning peasants to replace the decaying *dvorianstvo* and provide a model for the rest of the rural population.[34]

In May 1902, impressed with his performance as Marshal of the Nobility, the Ministry of the Interior appointed Stolypin governor of Grodno: at forty, he was the youngest holder of that office in the Empire. After serving less than one year, he was transferred to Saratov, one of the Empire's most troublesome provinces, with a record of agrarian unrest and a strong SR presence. He is said to have owed this appointment to Plehve, who sought to appease public opinion by selecting officials with a liberal reputation.[35] His experience in Saratov strengthened Stolypin's hostility to the commune, but it also made him aware of the strong hold it exerted on the *muzhik,* who liked its "leveling" effect. As Stolypin saw it, however, the commune allowed only for "leveling down." To allow the peasants' energies to "level up," he came on the idea of having the government distribute Crown and State lands to independent farmers in order for a significant private peasant sector to emerge alongside the communal.[36]

Saratov was very turbulent in 1905. Stolypin displayed intelligence and courage in coping with rural unrest. Unlike many governors who reacted to peasant violence by closeting themselves in their offices and leaving the task of pacification to gendarmes and soldiers, he visited the areas of disturbance, spoke with the rebellious peasants, and debated radical agitators. He persisted in this policy despite several attempts on his life, in one of which he was wounded. Such initiatives enabled him to quell the agrarian disorders in Saratov with minimal resort to force. In right-wing circles this earned him a reputation for "softness" and "liberalism" which was not helpful in his subsequent career.

St. Petersburg, however, took notice. His proven administrative abilities, his courage, and his known devotion to the dynasty made him an ideal candidate for ministerial office. On April 26, 1906, following Witte's resignation, he was offered the portfolio of the Interior in Goremykin's cabinet. After some hesitation, he accepted the post and moved to the capital. Although favored by the Court for his slavish devotion, the sixty-seven-year-old Goremykin proved entirely unable either to handle the Duma or to quell public disorders. The archetypal bureaucrat-steward, dubbed "His Illustrious Indifference" *(Ego Vysokoe Bezrazlichie),* he was let go on the day of the First Duma's dissolution (July 8, 1906). Stolypin now assumed the chairmanship of the Council of Ministers while retaining the portfolio of the Interior.

In approaching his new responsibilities, Stolypin acted on the premise that the October Manifesto had marked a watershed in Russian history: as he told Struve, "there was no possibility of restoring absolutism."[37] This outlook placed him at odds with the Court and its conservative supporters. Stolypin found himself from the outset pursuing a policy that did not enjoy the sympathy of either the Crown or many of his subordinates in the Ministry of the Interior. The latter preferred the traditional repressive measures. Stolypin, albeit with a heavy heart, agreed to repression, to quell disorders, but he thought it futile unless accompanied by reform. He had an ambitious program in mind which centered on administrative decentralization as a device for raising the cultural level of the population.[38]

In March 1907, he outlined a sweeping program of reforms which called for the expansion of civil liberties (freedom of religion, personal inviolability, civic equality), improvements in agriculture, state insurance for industrial workers, extension of the powers of organs of local self-government, reform of the police, and the introduction of a graduated income tax.[39]

Determined to carry out his duties with the cooperation of society, he established contact with the leaders of all political parties save those committed to revolution. He also sought to build up in parliament a coalition of supporters, on the example of George III's "King's Friends" and Bismarck's *Reichsfreunde.* He was prepared to go to great lengths to achieve this end, agreeing to legislative compromises and resorting to bribery. His Duma addresses were outstanding examples of parliamentary oratory, by virtue of not only the force of arguments but also their tone: he spoke as a Russian patriot to fellow patriots rather than as a royal steward communicating the master's wishes. In actions as well as public pronouncements, he took it for granted that the interests of Russia had precedence over all private and partisan interests.

This endeavor met with little response in a country in which the sense of nationhood and statehood was as yet poorly developed. To the opposition Stolypin was a lackey of the despised monarchy; to the monarchy he was an ambitious, self-seeking politician. The bureaucratic establishment never accepted him, because he had not risen through the ranks of the St. Petersburg ministries.

The most urgent task confronting Stolypin was the restoration of public order. This he accomplished by harsh measures which earned him odium among the intelligentsia.

The immediate justification for launching a campaign of counterterror was a nearly successful attempt on his life.

After moving to St. Petersburg, Stolypin maintained the gubernatorial custom of keeping on Sundays open house for petitioners. He insisted on this practice despite warnings from the police. In the afternoon of August 12, 1906, three Maximalists, two disguised as gendarmes, sought admission to his villa on Aptekarskii Island. When a suspicious guard tried to detain them, they threw briefcases, loaded with explosives, into the building.[40] A frightful carnage ensued: twenty-seven petitioners and guards, as well as the terrorists themselves, were torn to pieces by the explosion and thirty-two people suffered wounds. Stolypin miraculously escaped harm but both his children were injured. Reacting with characteristic coolness, he directed the removal of the victims.

The assault on Stolypin was only the most sensational manifestation of terrorism which continued to hold the country in its bloody grip. The commander of the Black Sea Fleet and the governors of Warsaw and Saratov fell victim to it. Hardly a day passed without a police official losing his life. To make matters worse, monarchists, emulating revolutionary tactics, resorted to counterterror, and on July 18 murdered the Jewish deputy, Michael Gertsenshtein, who had presented to the Duma the Kadet land program with a demand for compulsory expropriations.* No government in the world could have remained passive in the face of such violence. Since a new Duma had not yet been elected, Stolypin had recourse to Article 87. He subsequently made frequent use of this clause: during the half year that elapsed between the dissolution of the First Duma and the convocation of the Second, Russia was in effect administered by decree. Because he believed in the rule of law, he regretted having to do so, but he saw no alternative: such procedures were "a deplorable necessity," justified on the grounds that at times the interests of the state took precedence.[41]

Since 1905, a good part of Russia had been placed under martial law: in August 1906, eighty-two of the Empire's eighty-seven provinces were under "Reinforced Safeguard."[42] These measures proved insufficient, and under strong pressure from the Court, Stolypin resorted to summary justice. On August 19—one week after the failed attempt on his life—he introduced, under Article 87, field courts for civilians.[43] The law provided that in areas placed under either martial law or Extraordinary Safeguard, the governors and commandants of the military districts could turn over to military courts persons whose guilt was so obvious as to require no further investigation. The personnel of these courts were to be appointed by local commanders and to consist of five officers. Hearings were to take place behind closed doors: defendants were allowed no lawyer but could call on witnesses. The field courts had to convene within twenty-four hours of the crime and reach a verdict in forty-eight hours. There was no appeal from their sentences, which were to be carried out within twenty-four hours.

This law remained in force for eight months, expiring in April 1907. It is estimated that Stolypin's field courts meted out up to 1,000 death sentences.[44] Subsequently, terrorists and other persons accused of violent political crimes were tried by ordinary courts. A contemporary source estimates that in 1908 and 1909 the courts convicted for political crimes and armed assault 16,440 persons, 3,682 of them to death and 4,517 to hard labor.[45]

Stolypin's repressive measures evoked cries of outrage from public circles which displayed considerable tolerance for revolutionary terror. The Kadets, who ignored SR murders, spared no words of condemnation for the quasi-juridical procedures employed by Stolypin to prevent them: one of their spokesmen, Fedor Rodichev, referred to the gallows used by the field courts

---

*In March 1907, a worker incited by a right-wing politician named Kazantsev killed Grigorii Iollos, another Kadet Duma deputy, also Jewish. When he realized that Kazantsev had misled him into believing that Iollos was a police agent, the worker lured Kazantsev into a forest and murdered him.

as "Stolypin's neckties" and the name stuck. In July 1908, Tolstoy wrote *Ne mogu molchat'!—I Cannot Keep Silent!*—in which he argued that government violence was a hundredfold worse than criminal and terrorist violence because it was perpetrated in cold blood. His recipe for ending revolutionary terrorism was abolishing private property in land. The issue was so divisive that Guchkov's defense of Stolypin's field courts as a "cruel necessity"[46] split the Octobrist Party and led to the resignation of Shipov, one of its most respected figures.

But public order was eventually restored, enabling Stolypin to launch his program of economic and political reforms.

Without awaiting the convocation of the second Duma, Stolypin enacted, again with resort to Article 87, a series of agrarian reforms which he viewed as the key to Russia's long-term stability.

An initial step in this direction was a law of October 5, 1906, which accorded the Russian peasant, for the first time in history, civil equality with the other estates.[47] It removed all restrictions on peasant movement, depriving the communes of the power to refuse members permission to leave. The land commandants could no longer punish peasants. Thus disappeared the last vestiges of serfdom.

Stolypin addressed himself concurrently to the issue of land shortage, increasing the reserve of agricultural land available for purchase by peasants and facilitating access to mortgage money. The Peasant Land Bank, founded in the 1880s, had already in 1905 received broad powers to provide easy credit to help peasants acquire land. Stolypin now made much more land available for this purpose by persuading the Court to offer for peasant purchase Crown and State lands. This was formalized in laws of August 12 and 27, 1906.[48] The Crown *(udel'nye)* lands used for this purpose amounted to 1.8 million *desiatiny* (2 million hectares) of arable land, and the State lands to 3.6 million (4 million hectares). Approximately the same acreage of woodland was put on the market, for a total of 11 million *desiatiny* (12 million hectares).[49] These properties, augmented with land which the landlords sold after the 1905–6 rural disturbances, considerably increased peasant holdings.

To provide access to these lands it was necessary to organize and finance a large-scale resettlement program to move peasants out of the overcrowded provinces of central Russia. This the government initiated as early as March 1906, before Stolypin had assumed office, in a reversal of previous policy discouraging peasant movement. Under Stolypin, the state-sponsored resettlement program assumed massive proportions, with the peak years being 1908 and 1909. Between 1906 and 1916, 3 million peasants moved to Siberia and the steppes of Central Asia, settling on lands which the government had made available (547,000 of them later returned).[50]

Russian liberals and socialists considered it axiomatic that the country's "agrarian question" could be solved only by expropriations of properties belonging to the State, the Crown, the Church, and private landlords. Like Ermolov, Stolypin felt this belief rested on an illusion: there simply was not enough non-peasant land in the Empire to satisfy those who needed it as well as those who were added each year to the rural population from natural growth. In a masterfully reasoned speech to the Duma on May 10, 1907, he argued that the Social-Democratic program of nationalizing land was without merit:

> Let us assume for the sake of argument that the government accepts [the nationalization of land] as a desirable thing, that it sidesteps the issue of driving to ruin a whole . . . numerous educated class of landowners, that it reconciles itself to the destruction of the sparse centers of culture in the countryside. What would result? Would this at least solve the material aspect of the agrarian question? Would it or would it not make it possible to satisfy the peasants in the localities where they reside?
>
> These questions can be answered with figures, and the figures, gentlemen, tell the following: If one were to transfer to the peasantry all the privately owned land, without exception, even that located in the neighborhood of cities, then in the province of Vologda the communal land as now constituted, together with that added to it, would provide 147 *desiatiny* per household, in Olonetsk 185 *desiatiny,* and in Archangel as much as 1,309 *desiatiny.* At the same time, in fourteen other provinces there would not be enough land to give each household 15 *desiatiny,* while in Poltava there would be only 9 and in Podolia less than 8. This is due to the extremely uneven distribution in the various provinces not only of State and Crown lands but also of lands held in private ownership. One-fourth of the privately held land happens to be located in those twelve provinces which have communal allotments in excess of 15 *desiatiny* per household, whereas only one-seventh of it lies in the ten provinces with the smallest allotments of 7 *desiatiny* per household. It must be noted that these figures include all the land of all the owners—that is, not only that of the 107,000 *dvoriane* but also that of 490,000 peasants who have purchased land on their own account, as well as that belonging to 85,000 burghers—the latter two categories accounting for up to 17 million *desiatiny.* From this it follows that the division of all the land on a per capita basis can hardly remedy local land shortages. It will be necessary to have recourse to the measure proposed by the government—namely, resettlement. One will have to give up the idea of ensuring land for the entire toiling population and [instead] divert from that group a certain proportion to other occupations.
>
> This is also confirmed by other figures which indicate the population growth over a ten-year period in the fifty provinces of European Russia. Russia, gentlemen, is not dying out. Her population increase exceeds that of all the other countries in the world, attaining an annual rate of 15.1 per 1,000. Thus, in the fifty provinces of European Russia, the natural population growth adds each year 1,625,000 people: assuming five persons per family, this represents 341,000 families. If we allow 10 *desiatiny* per household, we will require annually 3.5 million *desiatiny* to provide with land only that population which is added each year.
>
> Clearly, gentlemen, the land question cannot be solved by the device of

expropriating and distributing private lands. This [method] is tantamount to putting a plaster on an infected wound.*

Stolypin next turned to his favorite subject, the need to privatize agriculture in order to improve productivity:

But apart from the aforementioned material results, what will this method do to the country, what will it accomplish from the moral point of view? The picture which we now observe in our rural communities—the need of all to subordinate themselves to a single method of pursuing agriculture, the requirement of constant repartitions, the impossibility for a farmer with initiative to apply to the land temporarily at his disposal his inclination toward a particular branch of economy—all that will spread throughout Russia. All and each will be equal, and land will become as common as water and air. But neither water nor air benefit from the application of human hands, neither is improved by labor, or else the improved air and water undoubtedly would fetch a price, they would become subject to the right of property. I suggest that the land which would be distributed among citizens, alienated from some and offered to local Social-Democratic bureaus, would soon acquire the same qualities as water and air. It would be exploited, but no one would improve it, no one would apply to it his labor in order to have someone else benefit from it. . . . As a result, the cultural level of the country will decline. A good farmer, an inventive farmer, will be deprived by the very force of things of the opportunity to apply his knowledge to the land. One is driven to the conclusion that such conditions would lead to a new upheaval, and that the talented, strong, forceful man would restore his right to property, to the fruit of his labor. After all, gentlemen, property has always had as its basis force, behind which stood also moral law.[51]

Stolypin well realized the hold which the commune had on the Great Russian peasant and had no illusion that he could dissolve it by government fiat. He rather wanted to achieve this end by example, setting up alongside the communes a parallel system of privately held farms. All the land turned over by the Crown and the State to the Peasant Land Bank was to be used for this purpose; to augment this reserve, he was not averse to a limited expropriation of large private estates. The critical issue to him was that the land turned over to the peasants be kept out of the hands of the communes in order to create enclaves of prosperous, independent farmsteads which in time, he hoped, would exert an irresistible attraction on peasants and encourage them to give up communal landholding. To the same end he also favored legislation that would make it easy for peasants to withdraw from the commune and claim title to their allotments.

Such a program was for Stolypin a precondition of economic improvement, which, in turn, would provide the foundations of national stability and grandeur. ("They," he concluded his May 1907 speech, referring to the revolutionary parties, "need great upheavals. We need a Great Russia!") But the

---

*Gosudarstvennaia Duma, *Stenograficheskie Otchëty, 1907 god*, II, Vtoroi Sozyv, Sessiia Vtoraia, Zasedanie 36 (St. Petersburg, 1907), 435–36. Stolypin's statistics were somewhat strained: not all the natural population increase (which was actually higher than he estimated—namely, 18.1 per 1,000) occurred in the rural areas of central Russia. Still, his conclusion was correct, as the results of the agrarian expropriations of 1917 would demonstrate.

dissolution of the commune was to him also an essential means for raising the level of citizenship in Russia. He fully shared Witte's dismay over the peasantry's low cultural level.[52] In his view, Russia's greatest need was for civic education, which meant, first and foremost, inculcating in the rural population a sense of law and respect for private property. His agrarian reforms were meant, therefore, ultimately to serve a political purpose—namely, to provide a school of citizenship.

The principles of Stolypin's agrarian reform were by no means original, having been the subject of frequent discussions in government circles since the end of the nineteenth century.[53] In February 1906, the Imperial Government discussed proposals to enable peasants to leave the commune and consolidate their holdings. A few days before he left office in April 1906, Witte had submitted a similar plan.[54] The idea of dissolving the commune and promoting resettlement in Siberia now found favor even with some of the most conservative landlords, who saw in such measures a way of avoiding expropriations. The All-Russian Union of Landowners as well as the United Nobility had favored such a policy before Stolypin appeared on the scene. Stolypin's deputy, Kryzhanovskii, says these reforms had become so urgent that if not Stolypin then some other minister would have carried them out, even the archconservative Durnovo.[55] Nevertheless, as it was Stolypin who put these ideas into practice, they are indissolubly bound up with his name.

The keystone of Stolypin's agrarian reforms was the law of November 9, 1906: its importance becomes apparent when one considers that the communes to which it applied comprised 77.2 percent of European Russia's rural households.[56] The law freed communal peasants from the obligation of remaining in the commune. The law's critical clause provided that "any head of a household who holds a land allotment by virtue of communal right may at any time demand to have it deeded to him as private property"—insofar as practicable, in a single, enclosed parcel. To leave the commune, peasants no longer required the concurrence of the majority of members; the decision was theirs. Having gone through the required formalities, a peasant household had the choice of claiming property title to its allotment and remaining in the village or selling out and moving away. In communes which had not practiced repartition since 1861, the allotments automatically became the property of the cultivators. Since the government concurrently annulled all remaining arrears on redemption payments (as of January 1, 1907), and one *desiatina* of arable land at the time fetched well over 100 rubles, the typical household of ten *desiatiny* could lay claim to an allotment worth over 1,000 rubles. On November 15, 1906, the Peasant Land Bank was instructed to make loans available to help peasants desiring to leave the commune.[57]

The law made possible, for the first time in modern history, the emergence in central Russia of an independent peasantry of a Western type.* But it also

---

*One of the misleading commonplaces in Russian historiography, promoted by Communist historians, is that Stolypin's agrarian measures were meant to promote a class of kulaks, defined as rural usurers and exploiters. In fact, they had the very opposite purpose: to give enterprising peasants an opportunity to enrich themselves by productive work rather than by usury and exploitation.

had a deeper and more revolutionary significance in that it challenged the peasants' deeply held conviction that the land belonged to no one: it introduced the idea of the "supremacy of the fact of ownership over the juridical fact of use."[58] It is typical of late Imperial Russia that such a radical transformation of Russian agrarian conditions was promulgated under Article 87— that is, as an emergency measure: the Duma approved it only on June 14, 1910, three and a half years after it had gone into effect.

How successful were Stolypin's agrarian reforms? The matter is the subject of considerable controversy. One school of historians claims that they led to rapid changes in the village which would have prevented revolution were it not for Stolypin's death and the disruptions of World War I. Another school dismisses them as a reform foisted upon unwilling peasants and undone by them immediately after the collapse of the Imperial regime.[59]

The facts of the case are as follows.[60] In 1905, the fifty provinces of European Russia had 12.3 million peasant households cultivating 125 million *desiatiny;* 77.2 percent of these households and 83.4 percent of this land were under a communal regime. In the Great Russian provinces, communal landholding embraced 97–100 percent of the households and land. Notwithstanding claims of the opponents of the commune that repartition was falling into disuse, in central Russia it was universally practiced.

Between 1906 and 1916, 2.5 million (or 22 percent) of the communal households, with 14.5 percent of the acreage, filed petitions to take title to their allotments. As these figures indicate, those who availed themselves of the new legislation were the poorer peasants, usually with small families, who had difficulty making ends meet: whereas the average household allotment in European Russia was around ten *desiatiny,* the households that withdrew from the commune averaged only three *desiatiny.*[61]

In sum, slightly more than one communal household in five took advantage of the law of November 9. But this statistic ignores one important fact and, by doing so, makes the reform appear still more successful than it actually was. The economic drawback of the commune lay not only in the practice of repartition but also in that of strip farming, or *cherespolositsa,* which was an essential corollary of communal organization. Economists criticized this practice on the grounds that it forced the peasant to waste much time moving with his equipment from strip to strip and precluded intensive cultivation. Stolypin, well aware of the disadvantages of *cherespolositsa,* was eager to do away with it, and to this end inserted in the law a clause authorizing peasants wishing to withdraw from the commune to demand that their holdings be consolidated (enclosed). The communes, however, ignored this provision: the evidence indicates that three-quarters of the households which took title to their allotments under the Stolypin law had to accept them in scattered strips.[62] Such properties were known as *otruba; khutora,* independent farmsteads with enclosed land, which Stolypin wanted to encourage, existed mainly in the borderlands. Thus, the pernicious practice of strip farming was little affected by the Stolypin legislation. On the eve of the 1917 Revolution, a decade after Stolypin's reforms had gone into effect, only 10 percent of Russian peasant households operated as *khutora;* the remaining 90 percent continued as before to pursue strip farming.[63]

On balance, therefore, the results of Stolypin's agrarian reforms must be judged as exceedingly modest. No "agrarian revolution" occurred and no Russian yeomanry emerged. When asked why they claimed title to their allotments, one-half of the respondents said that they did so in order to sell and get out of the village: only 18.7 percent took title in order to farm more efficiently. In effect, the reform encouraged the exodus of the poorer communal elements: the better-off peasants remained in the commune, often with enlarged allotments, and nearly every peasant, communal or not, continued to practice strip farming.

Overwhelmingly, Russian peasants rejected the very premise of Stolypin's agrarian reforms. Surveys conducted after the reforms had been introduced show that they resented those of their neighbors who pulled out of the commune to set up private farms. Communal peasants were unshakable in the belief that the only solution to their economic difficulties lay in communal appropriation of all privately held lands. They opposed the Stolypin legislation from fear that withdrawals would worsen communal land shortages and in some cases refused to allow them, in contravention of the law.[64] In the eyes of their neighbors, those who availed themselves of the Stolypin reform ceased to be peasants: indeed, under the terms of the electoral law of June 3, 1907, peasants owning 2.5 or more *desiatiny* qualified as "landlords." They lived, therefore, on borrowed time. In 1917, once the old regime broke down, the *otruba* and *khutora* would be the very first objects of peasant assault: they were in no time swept away and dissolved in the communal sea like sand castles.

Even so, significant changes did occur in Russian agriculture during and after Stolypin's ministry, although not in consequence of his legislation.

The gentry, having lost "taste for the land," continued to abandon the countryside. Between 1905 and 1914, gentry landholding in European Russia declined by 12.6 percent, from 47.9 to 41.8 million *desiatiny.* Most of the land which the landlords sold was acquired by peasants either communally or privately. As a result, on the eve of the Revolution Russia was more than ever a country of small, self-sufficient cultivators.

During this time, agricultural yields improved:

CEREAL YIELDS IN 47 PROVINCES OF
EUROPEAN RUSSIA[65] (kilograms per *desiatina*)

	Rye	*Wheat*
1891–1895	701	662
1896–1900	760	596
1901–1905	794	727
1906–1910	733	672
1911–1915	868	726

Russian yields were still the lowest in Europe, bringing in one-third or less of the crops harvested in the Low Countries, Britain, and Germany—the result of unfavorable natural conditions, the virtual absence of chemical fertilizers, and the communal system. Improved yields made possible increased exports of foodstuffs: in 1911, Russia sold abroad a record 13.5 million tons of cereals.[66]

Stolypin's vision of "Great Russia" required, in addition to the restoration of public order and changes in agricultural practices, political and social reforms. As with agrarian measures, his political reforms grew out of projects formulated by the Ministry of the Interior before his arrival on the scene: a good part had been anticipated in Witte's proposals to Nicholas II.[67] Stolypin adopted and expanded these ideas, whose purpose was to modernize and Westernize Russia. Very little of this program was realized: Stolypin declared that he required twenty years to change Russia and he was given a mere five. Even so, its provisions are of interest because they indicate what the liberal bureaucracy, which was far better informed than either the Court or the intelligentsia, saw as the country's most pressing needs. As formulated in public addresses, notably his Duma speech of March 6, 1907, and the program which he dictated privately in May 1911,* Stolypin intended the following:

Civil rights: Protection of citizens from arbitrary arrest; abolition of administrative exile; bringing to trial officials guilty of criminal abuse of authority.

Police: Abolition of the Corps of Gendarmes as a separate entity and its merger with the regular police; gendarmes to be deprived of the authority to conduct political investigations; an end to the practice of employing agents provocateurs to infiltrate revolutionary movements.

Administration: Creation of a Ministry of Self-government; replacing the peasant *volost'* with an all-estate, self-governing unit whose officials would combine administrative and police functions; major reform of *zemstva* which would endow them with powers comparable to those enjoyed by state governments in the United States; elections to *zemstva* to be based on a democratic franchise; the bureaucracy's authority over *zemstva* to be confined to ensuring the legality of their actions; the introduction of *zemstva* into the western provinces of the empire.

Ethnic minorities: Creating a Ministry of Nationalities; full equality for all citizens regardless of nationality and religion; administrative decentralization in the areas populated largely by non-Russians to allow the latter a greater voice in running their affairs; elimination of the Pale of Settlement and other discriminatory laws against the Jews.

Social legislation: Formation of ministries of Social Security, of Health,

---

*The program, which disappeared after his death and was presumed lost, was made public forty-five years later by Stolypin's secretary, A. V. Zenkovskii, in his *Pravda o Stolypine* (New York, 1956), 73–113. See further Kryzhanovskii, *Vospominaniia*, 130–32, 137–38, 218.

and of Labor; compulsory elementary schooling; state insurance for the aged and disabled; a national health program; full legalization of trade unions.

To carry out this program Stolypin required the powers of a Peter the Great, or, barring that, at least the unstinting support of the Crown. He enjoyed neither, and hence only a small part of his reform agenda saw the light of day.

The difficulties he faced are illustrated by his unsuccessful effort to improve the status of Russia's Jews. High bureaucratic circles had recognized for years that something had to be done about the medieval legislation regulating Jewish subjects. This sense was inspired less by humanitarian than by political considerations. The security police had been aware for some time of the disproportionate number of Jewish youths in the revolutionary movement, and although many of its members believed that Jews were a sinister race bent on subverting and destroying Christian society, more intelligent police officials attributed the young Jews' radicalism to the obstacles which Russian laws placed in the way of their career opportunities. There were also powerful financial reasons for abolishing Jewish disabilities. The director of the Banc de Paris et Pays Bas expressed a view prevalent among foreign financiers when he advised Kokovtsov, the Finance Minister, that it would benefit Russia's international standing if she granted her Jewish subjects civil equality.[68] Russia's treatment of Jews poisoned relations with the United States, which objected repeatedly to the refusal of the Russian authorities to grant entry visas to American citizens of Jewish faith. In December 1911, the U.S. Senate, on the recommendation of President Taft, would unanimously renounce the U.S.-Russian treaty of 1832 on these grounds.*

Stolypin raised the Jewish issue before the Council of Ministers, and secured a solid majority in favor of doing away with many restrictions on Jewish residential and occupational rights. He forwarded a proposal to this effect to the Tsar. Nicholas rejected it on the grounds of "conscience."[69] The refusal ended the possibility of Imperial Russia ridding herself of her anachronistic Jewish legislation and ensured the animosity of Jews at home and abroad.

Stolypin was determined not to repeat the mistake of his predecessor, Goremykin, who had no government program with which to attract voters. Having announced his reform program, he involved the government in the electoral campaign by paying subsidies to friendly newspapers and staging spectacles for potential supporters of pro-government candidates. For this purpose he allocated modest sums, such as 10,000 rubles to be spent in Kiev on electoral propaganda, "allowances" for needy voters, and the staging for peasant voters of Glinka's *A Life for the Tsar*. He soon became painfully aware of the paucity of means at the government's disposal to rally public support. Later he resorted to bribing deputies to vote for government bills.[70]

The New York Times, December 14, 1911, p. 1. This action was denounced in some Russian circles as intolerable interference in Russia's internal affairs, and by a German conservative newspaper as reflective of the "parvenu spirit that rules not only American society but American politics": *Ibid.,* p. 2.

Stolypin tried, without success, to bring representatives of society into the cabinet.

On assuming office, he engaged in negotiations with Alexander Guchkov and Nicholas Lvov, offering the former the portfolio of Trade and Industry and the latter that of Agriculture. The two made their acceptance conditional on other representatives of society being included in the cabinet. Stolypin next contacted Dmitrii Shipov and Prince George Lvov, the future head of the Provisional Government. They posed stiff demands: a government commitment to expropriating some landed property, the abolition of capital punishment, and an end to martial law. These terms may have been acceptable, but the government could not possibly agree to a further demand that a majority of the ministerial portfolios, including that of the Interior, be turned over to non-bureaucrats.[71] Using Kryzhanovskii as intermediary, Stolypin also made approaches to the Kadets with the view of having them join the cabinet, but nothing came of this effort either.[72] In January 1907, he attempted once more to come to terms with the Kadets, hoping to wean them away from the radical parties. At this time the Kadets had not yet secured status as a legally recognized association. Stolypin offered to grant them such status if they would denounce terrorism. Ivan Petrunkevich, one of the patriarchs of the liberal movement and a member of the Kadet Central Committee, responded that he would rather the party perish than suffer "moral destruction" by acquiescing to this demand. This terminated the discussions.[73]

To the government's dismay, the Second Duma, which opened on February 20, 1907, was even more radical than the First, for the SRs and the SDs had now abandoned the boycott. The socialists had 222 deputies (of them, 65 SDs, 37 SRs, 16 Popular Socialists, and 104 Trudoviki, affiliated with the SRs): they outweighed right-wing deputies by a ratio of two to one. The Kadets, tempered by the failure of their previous tactics, were prepared to behave more responsibly, but their representation was cut by nearly one-half (from 179 to 98) and the opposition was dominated by the socialists, who had no intention of pursuing legislative work. The SRs had resolved in November 1906 to participate in the elections in order to "utilize the State Duma for organizing and revolutionizing the masses."[74] The Social-Democrats at the Fourth (Stockholm) Congress, held in April 1907, agreed to commit themselves "to exploiting systematically all conflicts between the government and the Duma as well as within the Duma itself for the purpose of broadening and deepening the revolutionary movement." The congress instructed the Social-Democratic faction to create a mass movement that would topple the existing order by "exposing all the bourgeois parties," making the masses aware of the futility of the Duma, and insisting on the convocation of a Constituent Assembly.[75] The socialists thus entered the Duma for the explicit purpose of sabotaging legislative work and disseminating revolutionary propaganda under the protection of parliamentary immunity.

To make matters still worse from the government's point of view, Orthodox priests elected to the Duma, usually by peasants, shunned the conservative parties, preferring to sit in the center; several joined the socialists.

The Second Duma had barely begun its deliberations when in high circles it was whispered that the Duma was incapable of constructive work and should be abolished or at least thoroughly revamped. Fedor Golovin, the chairman of the Second Duma, remembered Nicholas speaking to him in this vein in March or April 1907.[76] The outright abolition of the Duma, however, proved impractical for political as well as economic reasons.

The political argument in favor of retaining a parliamentary body has been mentioned earlier: it was the need of the bureaucracy for a representative body with which to share the blame for the country's ills.

The economic argument had to do with international banking. A prominent French financier informed Kokovtsov that the dissolution of the First Duma had struck French financial markets like a "bolt of lightning."[77] Later, in 1917, Kokovtsov explained the close relationship which had existed under tsarism between parliamentary government and Russia's standing in international credit markets. The market price of the Russian state loan of 1906 sunk rapidly after the dissolution of the First Duma. When rumors spread that the Second Duma was to suffer a similar fate, Russian obligations with a face value of 100 dropped from 88 to 69, or by 21 percent.[78] Experience thus strongly suggested that the liquidation of the Duma would have had a disastrous effect on Russia's ability to raise foreign loans at acceptable interest rates.

Stolypin was prepared to keep on dissolving Dumas and calling for new elections as long as necessary: he confided to a friend that he would emulate the Prussian Crown which had once dissolved parliament seven times in succession to gain its ends.[79] But this procedure was unacceptable to the Court. Reluctantly giving up its preference for outright abolition of the lower chamber, the Court ordered a revision of the electoral law to ensure a more conservative Duma.

It is known from the recollections of Kryzhanovskii that while the First Duma was still in session, Goremykin had submitted to the Tsar a memorandum complaining of the "failure" of the elections and criticizing the revisions in the franchise originally devised for the Bulygin Duma which had the result of giving the vote to workers and greatly increasing peasant representation. Nicholas shared Goremykin's view. Early in May 1906, certainly with the Tsar's authorization, Goremykin requested Kryzhanovskii to draft a new electoral law which, without disenfranchising any one group or altering the basic constitutional functions of the Duma, would make it more cooperative. Kryzhanovskii's hastily drawn-up proposal was submitted to the Tsar later that month but it had no issue, possibly because the prospect of having Stolypin take over as Prime Minister aroused hopes that he would know how to cope with the second Duma.[80]

Now that these hopes were dashed, Stolypin asked Kryzhanovskii to devise a change in the electoral law which would enhance the representation of "wealthier" and "more cultured" elements.

Although in the eyes of many contemporaries and historians the unilateral change in the franchise announced on June 3, 1907, amounted to nothing less than a coup d'état, in the eyes of the government it represented a compromise, an alternative to the abolition of the Duma. Using the draft which he had prepared for Goremykin, Kryzhanovskii wrote three proposals that substantially altered the franchise as well as certain provisions of the Fundamental Laws for the purpose of ensuring greater legislative authority for the Crown.

The formal pretext for dissolving the Second Duma was the charge that some of its Social-Democratic deputies had plotted to incite mutiny in the St. Petersburg garrison. Stolypin has been accused then and since of provoking the incident, but in fact the conspiracy had been uncovered by police agents who had caught the SDs meeting secretly in the home of one of their deputies with representatives of military and naval units belonging to revolutionary circles.[81] With this evidence in hand, Stolypin appeared before the Duma and requested that the parliamentary immunity of all the SD deputies be lifted so that the accused could be turned over to a court. The Duma agreed to suspend the immunity only of those deputies against whom there existed concrete evidence of sedition. Stolypin would have preferred to dissolve the Duma and order new elections, but he came under irresistible pressure from the Court to revise the Duma's electoral procedures.* The Second Duma was dissolved on June 2, 1907.

The new electoral law, made public the next day, unquestionably violated the constitution, which forbade using Article 87 to "introduce changes . . . in the provisions for elections to the [State] Council or Duma." That much even Kryzhanovskii conceded.[82] To get around this limitation, the change in the franchise was decreed by Imperial Manifesto, a law issued on matters of urgent state importance. This procedure was justified on the grounds that since the Tsar had not sworn an oath to observe the new Fundamental Laws, he was free to revise them at will.[83] The new law favored the propertied classes by using assets rather than legal status as the criterion of franchise. The representation of industrial workers and national minorities was sharply reduced. Disappointed with the behavior of communal peasants in the first two Dumas, the government also cut down their share of the seats. As a result of these changes, the representation of landowners (a category which included many peasant proprietors) increased by one-half while that of communal peasants and workers fell by one-half. The result was a more conservative and ethnically more Great Russian body.

The term "coup d'état," often applied in the polemical and historical literature to the change of the electoral law on June 3, 1907, is hardly justified. After all, the Duma continued to function, retaining the legislative and budgetary powers granted it in the Fundamental Laws: the Manifesto of June 3 explicitly reconfirmed the Duma's prerogatives. In the years that followed the Duma would give the government a great deal of trouble. Only the outright abolition of the lower house or the abrogation of its legislative powers would

---

*The SD deputies, tried after the dissolution of the Duma, when their parliamentary immunity had expired, were convicted and sentenced to hard labor: P. G. Kurlov, *Gibel' Imperatorskoi Rossii* (Berlin, 1923), 94.

have qualified as a coup. June 3 is more properly viewed as a violation of the constitution. It was in the Russian tradition of integrating every independent political institution into the state system.

The Third Duma, convened on November 1, 1907, was the only one to be permitted the normal five-year span. As intended, the new body was much more conservative than its predecessors: of the 422 deputies, 154 belonged to the Party of the 17th of October, and 147 to right-wing and nationalist groupings. This representation assured the conservatives of a two-thirds majority. The Kadets were whittled down to 54 seats; associated with them were 28 Progressives. The socialists had 32 deputies (19 Social-Democrats and 13 Trudoviki). Although the government could feel much more comfortable with a legislature in which conservatives had such preponderance, it did not enjoy automatic majorities: Stolypin had to engage in a great deal of political maneuvering to secure passage for some of his bills. Ministers were frequently called to account and on occasion the government failed to have its way.

The Octobrists, who dominated the Third Duma as the Kadets had dominated the First and the socialists the Second, were committed to the existing constitutional arrangement. They defined their task as follows:

> to create in the Duma a constitutional center, not aiming to seize governmental power, but at the same time, determined to defend the rights of the people's representative assembly within the limits laid down for it in the Fundamental Laws.[84]

Its guiding philosophy was a state based on law—law equally binding on the administration and society. Alexander Guchkov, the party's leader, was descended from a prominent Moscow merchant family founded by a serf and had received his education in Western Europe. According to Alexander Kerensky, who described him as "something of a dour loner with an air of mystery," he had opposed the Liberation Movement.[85] He had a low opinion of the Russian masses and did not feel comfortable with politicians. A devoted patriot, in temperament and outlook he resembled Stolypin, whom he helped to split the right-wing in the Third Duma, separating from it the more moderate elements; these, organized as the Nationalist faction, together with the Octobrists, formed an absolute majority and helped Stolypin push through many of his legislative bills.[86] Much of the rank and file of the Octobrist Party had its roots in the *zemstvo* movement and maintained close links with it.

To gain support for his legislative programs, Stolypin annually assigned 650,000 rubles from secret funds for subsidizing newspapers and bribing influential right-wing deputies.[87]

The Third Duma was an active body: it voted on 2,571 bills introduced by the government, initiated 205 of its own, and questioned or "interpellated" ministers 157 times.[88] Its commissions dealt with agrarian problems, social legislation, and many other issues. The year 1908 and even more so 1909 were periods of bountiful harvests, declining violence, and renewed industrial development. Stolypin stood at the pinnacle of his career.

Yet at this very time the first clouds appeared on the horizon. As noted, the constitution had been granted under extreme duress as the only alternative to collapse. The Court and its right-wing supporters viewed it, not as a fundamental and permanent change in Russia's system of government, but as an emergency measure to tide it over a period of civil unrest. The refusal to admit that Russia even had a constitution and the insistence that the Tsar's not swearing an oath to the new Fundamental Laws absolved him from having to observe their provisions were not lame excuses, but deeply held convictions. Thus, as the situation in the country improved, and the emergency attenuated, the Court had second thoughts: with public order and rural prosperity restored, did one really need a parliamentary regime and a Prime Minister who played parliamentary politics? Stolypin, who had said of himself that he was "first and foremost a loyal subject of the sovereign and the executor of his designs and commands," now appeared "a most dangerous revolutionary."[89] The main objection to him was that instead of acting in parliament exclusively as an agent of the Crown he forged there his own political constituency. Stolypin believed that he was putting together a party of "King's Friends," not for his own, but for the King's benefit. The monarchists, however, saw only that his political practices led to a diminution of Imperial authority, or at least such authority as Nicholas and his entourage believed him to be entitled to:

> Stolypin would have been the last to admit that his policy tended to weaken the Emperor's independent power—indeed, he considered the source of his own authority to lie in the fact that it had been entrusted to him by the autocratic monarch. Yet, inevitably, that was the effect of his policy, since he realised that in modern conditions that state could only be strengthened against revolution by increasing in it, through parliament, the influence of the land-owning, professional and educated classes. And this could only happen at the expense of the Emperor's own independent power. It was this undeniable fact which gave the reactionaries' arguments such force in the mind of the Emperor.[90]

This was the crux of Stolypin's difficulties with the Court, the cause of his waning support and ultimate disgrace. After his death, the Tsarina would admonish his successor, Vladimir Kokovtsov, with reference to Stolypin, "not to seek support in political parties."[91] In general, the more successful Stolypin's policies were, the less were his services required and the greater grew the Court's antagonism to him. Such was the paradox of Russian politics.

His reforms and reform projects also alienated powerful interests. The agrarian reforms, designed to give Russia a class of peasant landlords, threatened that segment of the rural gentry which saw itself as irreplaceable *Kulturträger*. His efforts to decentralize the administration and make bureaucrats legally accountable aroused the hostility of the officialdom, while his plans to curb the police gained him no friends in those quarters. His unsuccessful efforts on behalf of Jews infuriated the extreme right.

Nor did he gain in public support what he lost at the Court. The liberals never forgave him for "Stolypin's neckties" and for the manner in which he abused Article 87 to circumvent the Duma's legislative power. To the extreme right he was an outsider brought in to extinguish a revolutionary conflagration who abused his position to accumulate independent power. Those who, in Struve's words, regarded the constitution as "camouflaged rebellion" *(zamaskirovannyi bunt)* [92] despised him for taking it seriously instead of working to restore autocracy. In the militant atmosphere of Russian politics, with one set of "purist" principles confronting others, equally uncompromising, there was no room for Stolypin's pragmatic idealism. Assailed from all sides, he began to falter and commit political blunders.

Stolypin's first conflict with the Third Duma arose over the naval budget of 1909. [93] At the beginning of 1908, the government proposed to construct four battleships of the Dreadnought class to protect Russia's Baltic shores. In the Duma, the Kadets and the Octobrists joined forces to oppose this bill. Guchkov argued that Russia could not afford a large and expensive navy. Miliukov supported him: Russia, he said, already was spending proportionately more on her navy than Germany although she had little sea commerce and no overseas colonies. The two parties preferred the funds designated for the Dreadnoughts to be spent on the army. [94] In 1908 and again in 1909 the Duma turned down requests for naval appropriations. Although the passage of the budget by the State Council sufficed to get the naval program underway, the Duma's rebuff forced Stolypin to seek support from parties to the right of the Octobrists—a shift which led him to pursue a more nationalistic policy.

His most fateful parliamentary crisis came about indirectly because of this shift over the bill to introduce *zemstva* into the western provinces of the Empire. The bill encountered strong opposition in the upper chamber, where *zemstva* did not enjoy popularity. Determined to make this issue a test of his ability to administer, Stolypin decided to force it regardless of the cost.

On their creation in 1864, *zemstva* had not been introduced into nine of the provinces taken from Poland in the Partitions. The elections to the *zemstva* were heavily skewed in favor of the landowning nobility, and in the western provinces, a high proportion of this nobility were Catholic Poles, who the government feared would exploit the *zemstva* for their nationalistic ends. (The Polish Rebellion of 1863 had just been crushed.) Intelligent bureaucrats, however, came eventually to realize that given the low cultural level of the Russian element in the borderlands, it was necessary to give non-Russians there a voice in local government. [95] Stolypin had spoken of introducing *zemstva* into the western provinces as early as August 1906, but he first formulated a legislative

22. Right-wing Duma deputies. Sitting in front on extreme
left, V. Purishkevich, the assassin of Rasputin.

bill to this effect in 1909. Although it had a liberal aspect in that it gave, for
the first time, the ethnic minorities of that area a voice in self-government, the
bill was primarily designed to please the right wing, on which Stolypin had
now come increasingly to depend: according to Kryzhanovskii, the landed
gentry deputies from the western provinces were insistently pressing such a
demand on him.[96]

In his bill, Stolypin sought to ensure a preponderant voice in the western
zemstva for the Russian landed gentry and peasant proprietors. Because there
were virtually no Russian landlords or landowning peasants in Vilno, Kovno,
and Grodno, these provinces were excluded from the bill, which applied only
to six western provinces (Vitebsk, Volhynia, Kiev, Minsk, Mogilev, and
Podolia). In the latter provinces, Russian preponderance was to be guaranteed
by a complicated voting procedure employing electoral chambers. Jewish
citizens were to be entirely disenfranchised.[97]

The Duma opened discussion on the western *zemstvo* bill on May 7, 1910.
In a speech urging passage, Stolypin asserted that its main purpose was to
ensure that the western provinces remained "forever Russian": this required
protecting the Russian minority from the Polish Catholic majority. The bill,
supported by the Nationalists and other deputies of the right, passed on May
29, after heated debate and with amendments, on a close vote.

In January 1911 the revised bill went before the upper chamber. Given its
nationalistic tenor, passage seemed a foregone conclusion. Stolypin felt so
confident that he did not even bother to attend the discussions in the State
Council, since a commission of that body had approved the bill.[98]

Unbeknownst to him, however, a backstage intrigue was set in motion.

Several members of the State Council, led by Vladimir Trepov, organized, with the help of Durnovo, opposition to Stolypin. The bill's opponents charged that by offering the Poles a separate electoral chamber Stolypin institutionalized ethnic particularism, thus violating the traditional "Imperial" character of Russian legislation. Witte, one of the bill's most vociferous opponents, argued that "under the flag of patriotism they are striving to create in the western land a local oligarchy in place of tsarist authority."[99] But the true purpose of the camarilla was to bring down Stolypin.

Trepov and Durnovo asked for private audiences with the Tsar. After they had laid before him their objections, Nicholas agreed to release the right-wing deputies in the State Council from having to follow the government's recommendation: they could vote as their conscience dictated.[100] In giving them this freedom, Nicholas neither sought the advice of his Prime Minister nor informed him of it. Stolypin, therefore, had no cause for apprehension when he appeared in the State Council on March 4 to witness the final vote on his bill. Many of the deputies who would have voted for it if the Tsar had instructed them to do so now felt free to cast negative ballots. As a consequence, the bill's key clause, with the controversial proposal for two electoral chambers, one for Russians, the other for Poles and the other ethnic groups, went down in defeat, 92–68. Stunned, Stolypin stalked out of the Council chamber.

He could be under no illusion: the incident was a vote of no confidence in him, ostensibly cast by the upper chamber but in fact engineered by the Imperial Court. Furious, he decided to force the Tsar to reveal his hand. The next day, he submitted his resignation. Nicholas rejected it and urged Stolypin to reconsider. Why not resubmit the bill to the Duma and the State Council, he suggested, implying that on the next round he would ask that it be supported. Stolypin refused. When the Tsar asked what he would like him to do, he requested that both houses be prorogued long enough to allow the bill to be enacted under Article 87.* He further asked that Trepov and Durnovo be exiled from St. Petersburg.

Nicholas pondered Stolypin's request for four days, and then granted it. On March 12, both chambers were prorogued until March 15. Having learned of this decision, the State Council quickly took a vote on the entire bill, which resulted in its being rejected by the overwhelming majority of 134–23.[101] On March 14 the western *zemstvo* bill was promulgated under Article 87. Durnovo and Trepov had to to leave the capital until the end of the year.†

Stolypin's precipitate action had disastrous consequences, alienating from him all political parties.[102] When he appeared before the Duma to justify his

---

*When told by Kokovtsov that this was an unwise move and that he would do better to accept the Tsar's suggestions, Stolypin replied that he had no time to fight intrigues against him and was politically finished in any event: V. N. Kokovtsov, *Iz moego proshlogo,* I (Paris, 1933), 458; A. Ia. Avrekh, *Stolypin i Tret'ia Duma* (Moscow, 1968), 338.

†Trepov was taken prisoner by the Bolsheviks and executed along with many other hostages at Kronshtadt on July 22, 1918: Kokovtsov, *Iz moego proshlogo,* I, 462. Durnovo died in 1915.

actions, he had virtually no supporters. The press condemned him; so did high society. Guchkov resigned in protest as head of the Octobrist Party: the cooperation between Stolypin and the Octobrists, which had proved so constructive in the first two years of the Third Duma, now came to an end. Last, but not least, Stolypin incurred the enmity of the Tsar, who never forgave anyone for humiliating him: and that Stolypin had done so was clear to public opinion, which realized full well that in proroguing the Duma and exiling Durnovo and Trepov the Tsar had acted under duress.[103] In official circles it was said at this time that Nicholas had made up his mind to be rid of Stolypin, and that his days as Prime Minister were numbered.[104] Isolated and spurned, he became, in the words of Kokovtsov, "a completely changed man"[105]—brooding and irritable where he had been supremely self-confident and magnanimous.

The Empress Dowager Marie, the mother of Nicholas II, who had always urged him to come to terms with society and favored liberal officials, shared with Kokovtsov her sense of despair at these developments:

> My poor son, how little luck he has with people. Someone turns up whom no one here knew, but who proves to be intelligent and energetic, and manages to restore order after the horrors which we had gone through nearly six years ago. And now this man is being pushed into the abyss. And by whom? By those who claim to love the Tsar and Russia, and in reality are destroying him and the Fatherland. . . . How dreadful![106]

Stolypin was in virtual disgrace when he departed in late August 1911 for Kiev for celebrations attending the unveiling of a monument to Alexander II. He had long had premonitions of violent death: in his last will, drawn up in 1906, he had requested to be buried near the site of his murder.[107] Before leaving, he told Kryzhanovskii that he feared he might not return, and entrusted to him a strongbox with secret papers, which he asked to be destroyed if anything happened to him.* He took no precautions to protect himself, however, leaving behind his bodyguards as well as his bulletproof vest.

In Kiev, he was ignored by the Imperial couple and high dignitaries: the humiliation was unmistakable.

In the evening of September 1, the Kiev Municipal Theater scheduled a performance of Rimskii-Korsakov's *The Story of Tsar Saltan*. Nicholas, accompanied by his daughters, occupied the governor's loge on the orchestra level. Stolypin sat nearby, in the front row. During the second intermission, around 10 p.m., as he stood chatting in front of the orchestra pit with Counts Potocki and Fredericks, a young man in coattails drew near. He pulled a

---

*Kryzhanovskii Archive, Columbia University, Box 2, File 5. Kryzhanovskii carried out Stolypin's request, saving only his letters to the Tsar: *Ibid.* Stolypin's fear of being assassinated in Kiev may have been occasioned by the disinformation which his future killer supplied to the Okhrana, as described below.

Browning from under the program with which he had concealed it and fired twice at the Prime Minister. Both bullets struck, one in the hand, the other in the chest: the first ricocheted and wounded a musician; the other hit Stolypin's chest but was deflected by a medal and lodged in the liver. According to an eyewitness, Stolypin at first seemed not to realize what had happened:

> He lowered his head and stared at his white tunic, which on the right side, under the chest, was beginning to stain with blood. With slow and sure motions he put his service hat and gloves on the barrier, unbuttoned the tunic, and seeing the waistcoat thick with blood, made a motion as if to say, "It's all over." He then sank into a chair and clearly, distinctly, in a voice audible to all who were nearby, said, "I am happy to die for the Tsar." On seeing the Tsar enter the loge and stand in front, he lifted his hands motioning him to withdraw. But the Tsar did not move, remaining in place, whereupon Peter Arkadevich, in full view of all, blessed him with a broad sign of the cross.[108]

Stolypin was rushed to a hospital. He seemed to be making a good recovery when an infection set in; he died in the evening of September 5.* The next day, the central Kiev railroad terminal teemed with panic-stricken Jews. Thanks to the firm action by the authorities, however, no anti-Jewish violence occurred.

The assassin, who had been caught and pummeled while attempting to flee the scene of the crime, turned out to be a twenty-four-year-old lawyer, Dmitrii Grigorevich Bogrov, the son of a wealthy Jewish Kievan family.[109] At home and on his frequent trips abroad he had flitted in and out of SR and anarchist circles. Although well provided for by doting parents, he often ran out of money because of his passion for gambling and it is fairly certain that it was financial need that drove him to become a police agent. According to his testimony, from the middle of 1907 until late 1910 he had served as an informer for the Kiev Okhrana, supplying information that enabled it to apprehend SR and anarchist terrorists.

The revolutionaries grew suspicious of Bogrov. At first they accused him of embezzling party funds, but eventually concluded that he had to be a police agent. On August 16, 1911, Bogrov was visited by a revolutionary who told him that his role as a police informer had been established beyond doubt and that he faced "execution": he could save himself only by committing a terrorist act, preferably against Colonel N. N. Kuliabko, the chief of the Kiev Okhrana. This had to be done by September 5. Bogrov visited Kuliabko, but he received from him such a warm welcome that he could not go through with his mission. He next considered assassinating the Tsar, due in Kiev in a few days, but gave up this plan for fear of precipitating anti-Jewish pogroms. He finally settled on Stolypin as the "man mainly responsible for the reaction which had established itself in Russia."†

---

*A postmortem revealed that Stolypin's heart and liver were so diseased that he would probably have died of natural causes before long: G. Tokmakoff, *P. A. Stolypin and the Third Duma* (Washington, D.C., 1981), 207–8.

†B. Strumillo in *KL*, No. 1/10 (1924), 230. In his fictional account of these events, Aleksandr Solzhenitsyn attributes Bogrov's action to the desire to protect Jewish interests allegedly threatened

To divert attention from himself and his plans, Bogrov concocted an imaginary plot against Stolypin and L. A. Kasso, the Minister of Education, by two fictitious terrorists. On August 26, he told Colonel Kuliabko that the pair would come to Kiev during the celebrations and use his apartment as a base of operations. Kuliabko, who is said to have been of a "soft" and "trusting" disposition,[110] had no reason to disbelieve Bogrov, since he had proven a reliable informant in the past. He had Bogrov's apartment house surrounded with agents, giving Bogrov the run of the city. On August 29, Bogrov stalked Stolypin in a park, and on September 1 daytime approached him as he was being photographed in the Hippodrome, but on neither occasion could he get close enough to shoot.

The Okhrana, in possession of information supplied by Bogrov, recommended to the Prime Minister that he not appear in public unattended, but he disregarded this warning. He behaved like a man reconciled to his fate, a man who had nothing left to live for, who may have even courted martyrdom.

For Bogrov, time was running out: his last opportunity might very well be the evening of September 1 during the performance at the Municipal Theater. Tickets were hard to come by because of tight security precautions and public demand. Bogrov told the police that he feared for his safety if the terrorists whom he had identified were apprehended and he could not produce a satisfactory alibi. He had to have a ticket to the theater. This was delivered to him only one hour before the beginning of the performance.

On September 9, after a week of questioning, Bogrov was turned over to the Kiev Military Court, which sentenced him to death. He was hanged during the night of September 10–11, in the presence of witnesses who wanted to make sure that an ordinary convict was not substituted for Bogrov, whose police connections had become public knowledge by then.

As soon as it became known that Bogrov had entered the theater on a police pass, rumors spread that he had acted on behalf of the government.

---

by Stolypin's ideal of a "Great Russia." Solzhenitsyn thus "reconstructs" Bogrov's thinking: "Stolypin had done nothing directly against the Jews; he has even succeeded in easing their lot somewhat. But this was not sincere. One must know how to identify an enemy of the Jews more deeply than from appearances. Stolypin promotes too insistently, too openly, too provocatively *Russian* national interests, *Russian* representation in the Duma, the *Russian* state. He is building, not a country free to all, but a national monarchy. Thus, the future of Jews in Russia depends on the will of someone who is not their friend. Stolypin's development does not promise prosperity to Jews." (A. Solzhenitsyn, *Krasnoe koleso*, Uzel I: *Avgust Chetyrnadtsogo,* Part 2, Paris, 1983, 126). There is no evidence to support this interpretation. Quite the contrary. Bogrov, who came from a thoroughly assimilated family (his grandfather had converted to Orthodox Christianity and his father belonged to the Kievan Nobles' Club), was a Jew only in the biological ("racial") sense. Even his given name, which Solzhenitsyn chooses to be the Yiddish "Mordko," was the very Russian Dmitrii. In his depositions to the police, Bogrov stated that he had shot Stolypin because his reactionary policies had brought great harm to Russia. In a farewell letter to his parents written on the day of the murder, he explained that he was unable to lead the normal life which they had expected of him (A. Serebrennikov, *Ubiistvo Stolypina: Svidetel'stva i dokumenty* (New York, 1986), 161–62). The most likely source of the claim that Bogrov acted as a Jew and on behalf of Jewish interests is a false report in the right-wing daily, *Novoe vremia,* of September 13, 1911, that prior to his execution Bogrov told a rabbi he had "struggled for the welfare and happiness of the Jewish people" (Serebrennikov, *loc.cit.,* 22). In reality, he had refused to see a rabbi before his execution (*Rech',* September 13, 1911, in Serebrennikov, *loc.cit.,* 23–24.)

These rumors have not died to this day. The leading suspect was and remains General P. G. Kurlov, the chief of the Corps of Gendarmes, who took charge of Kievan security during the Imperial visit and was known to have had bureaucratic differences with the Prime Minister.[111] This theory, however, rests on very slender evidence. The inability of the police to prevent the murder of the Prime Minister appears rather the result of a not uncommon failure of the technique of using double agents: after all, the greatest double agent of all, Evno Azef, also occasionally had had to betray his employers in order to maintain credibility with the terrorists—to the point of arranging for the murder of his chief, Plehve. As for the fact that the police gave Bogrov an admission ticket to the theater, that, too, makes good sense in view of the scenario which he had managed to foist on them. In his memoirs, Kurlov recalled that five years earlier, under similar circumstances, the Kiev Okhrana had allowed a double agent into the Municipal Theater to forestall a terrorist attack on the governor-general.[112] On closer scrutiny, the conspiratorial theories of Stolypin's death do not hold up. Since it was widely believed that he would soon be dismissed, his enemies had no need to resort to murder to be rid of him, the more so in view of the fact that the prime suspect of the crime, the gendarmerie, had no assurance that Bogrov, acting in self-defense, would not betray its involvement. That the tsarist authorities could have been suspected of instigating the murder of the Prime Minister tells more about the poisoned political atmosphere of late Imperial Russia than about the facts of the case.

An assessment of Stolypin has to distinguish the man from his achievement.

He towered over the Russian statesmen of his era: to appreciate his stature, one only needs to compare him with his successors, mostly nonentities, sometimes incompetents, selected on the criterion of personal loyalty to the Crown and dedicated to serving its interests, not those of the nation. He gave Russia, traumatized by the Revolution of 1905, a sense of national purpose and hope. He elevated politics above both partisanship and utopianism.

To admit his personal greatness, however, is not to concede that had he lived Stolypin would have prevented a revolution. To steer the country toward stability, he required unfailing backing from the Crown and at least some measure of support from liberal and conservative parties. He had neither. His grand project of political and social reform remained largely on paper and his main accomplishment, the agrarian reform, was wiped out in 1917 by the spontaneous action of communal peasants. By the time he died, he was politically finished: as Guchkov put it, Stolypin "had died politically long before his physical death."[113]

Nothing illustrates better the hopelessness of Stolypin's endeavors than the indifference with which the Imperial couple reacted to his murder. Ten days after the Prime Minister had been shot, Nicholas wrote his mother an account of the visit to Kiev. In it, he treated Stolypin's death as a mere episode in the round of receptions, parades, and other diversions. When he communicated the news of Stolypin's death to his wife, he wrote, "she took the news rather calmly."[114] Indeed, when not long afterward Alexandra discussed the event with Kokovtsov, Stolypin's successor, she chided him for being too much affected by Stolypin's death:

> It seems that you hold in too high esteem [Stolypin's] memory and attach too much importance to his activity and person. . . . One must not feel such sorrow for those who have departed. . . . Everyone fulfills his role and mission, and when someone no longer is with us it is because he has carried out his task and had to be effaced since he no longer had anything left to do. . . . I am convinced that Stolypin died to yield his post to you, and that this is for Russia's good.[115]

Although he lost his life to a revolutionary, Stolypin was politically destroyed by the very people whom he had tried to save.

The three years that separated the death of Stolypin from the outbreak of World War I are difficult to characterize because they were filled with contradictory trends, some of which pointed to stabilization, others to breakdown.

On the surface, Russia's situation looked promising: an impression confirmed by the renewed flow of foreign investments. Stolypin's repression, accompanied by economic prosperity, had succeeded in restoring order. Conservatives and radicals agreed, with different emotions, that Russia had weathered the Revolution of 1905. In liberal and revolutionary circles the prevailing mood was one of gloom: the monarchy had once again managed to outwit its opponents by making concessions when in trouble and withdrawing them as soon as its position solidified. Although terrorism did not entirely die out, it never recovered from revelations made in 1908 that the leader of the SR Combat Organization, Azef, was a police agent.

The economy was booming. Agricultural yields in central Russia increased measurably. In 1913 iron production, compared with 1900, grew by 57.8 percent, while coal production more than doubled. In the same period, Russian exports and imports more than doubled as well.[116] Thanks to strict controls on the emission of bank notes, the ruble was among the stablest currencies in the world. A French economist forecast in 1912 that if Russia maintained until 1950 the pace of economic growth that she had had since 1900, by the middle of the twentieth century she would dominate Europe politically, economically, and financially.[117] Economic growth allowed the Treasury to rely less than before on foreign loans and even to retire some debt: by 1914, after decades of continuous growth, Russia's state indebtedness finally showed a downward trend.[118] The budget also showed a positive course: between 1910 and 1913 it had a surplus three years out of four, with the "extraordinary" part of the budget taken into account.[119]

Stolypin had learned from experience that a prosperous village was a tranquil village. And, indeed, in the years immediately preceding the outbreak of World War I, the countryside, benefiting from improved yields, gave the authorities little trouble. But prosperity had a different effect on industrial centers located in the countryside. The massive hiring of new workers, most of them landless or land-poor peasants, injected into the labor force a volatile element. Between January 1910 and July 1914, the number of workers in Russia grew by one-third (from 1.8 to 2.4 million); in mid-1914, more than one-half of the workers of St. Petersburg were newcomers. These employees found even the Mensheviks and SRs too moderate, preferring the simpler, more emotional slogans of the anarchists and Bolsheviks.[120] Their restlessness and sense of estrangement contributed to the increase in industrial strife on the eve of the war, notably in the first half of 1914.

This said, grounds are lacking for maintaining that Russia in 1914 was less "stable" than at any time since 1900, except for 1905–6, and heading for revolution.[121] This argument, mandatory in Communist histories, rests primarily on evidence of increased strike activity after 1910. It is unconvincing for several reasons:

Industrial strikes do not necessarily signify social instability: more often than not, they accompany the progression of labor to a more advanced economic and social status. Poorly paid, unskilled, and unorganized workers rarely strike. There exists a demonstrated correlation between the formation of trade unions and strike activity.* By legitimizing trade unions, the Imperial Government also legitimized strikes, previously unlawful. Seen in this light, the increase in work stoppages (more than half of them one- or two-day affairs, in any event) may be more correctly interpreted as symptomatic of the maturation of Russian labor, which, judging by the Western experience, was likely in time to lead to greater social stability.

In many Western industrial countries, the period immediately preceding the outbreak of World War I also saw a rise in labor unrest. In the United States, for example, twice as many workers struck in 1910–14 as in the preceding five years: in 1912 and 1913 there were more workers out on strike than at any time in the preceding thirty years.[122] In Great Britain, too, strike activity showed a dramatic spurt in 1912, in terms of both workers involved and working days lost.[123] Yet neither country was destabilized and neither experienced a revolution.

In the final analysis, Russia's social stability depended on the peasant: radical intellectuals acknowledged that no revolution in Russia was possible

---

*"Most strikes . . . arise in organized trades and industries. As trade unionism spreads to previously unorganized industries, it is often accompanied by strike waves": J. A. Fitch in *Encyclopedia of the Social Sciences,* XIV (New York, 1934), 420. A similar conclusion is drawn, on the basis of U.S. experience, by J. I. Griffin in *Strikes* (New York, 1939), 98.

as long as the village remained quiet. And it is a demonstrable fact that the Russian village did not stir either immediately before the war or in the first two years after its outbreak. The half a million workers who were on strike in 1912 represented an insignificant minority compared with 100 million peasants who went peacefully about their business.

Nor can much be inferred from instances of political restlessness in the liberal movement, as symbolized by the eccentric offer of A. I. Konovalov, the millionaire textile manufacturer, to provide financial subsidies to Lenin.[124] This not untypical tactic of Russian liberals to pressure the authorities for political concessions by invoking the specter of revolution cannot be interpreted as signifying a radicalization of liberal opinion. Indeed, the very opposite trend was noticeable in Russia on the eve of the war—namely, a shift to conservatism. There is much evidence to indicate a growth of patriotic sentiment among educated Russians, including university youths.

A similar shift to the right was noticeable in Russian thought and culture. The preoccupation with civic issues and the politicization of Russian life which had set in in the middle of the nineteenth century showed signs of waning even before it drew to a close. With the rise of the Symbolist school in poetry and the triumph of aesthetic standards in criticism, literature and art turned to different means and subjects: poetry replaced the novel as the principal vehicle of creative literature, while painting turned away from realism toward fantasy and abstraction. The challenge issued to artists and composers by Serge Diaghilev, Russia's foremost impresario—"Astonish me!"—flew in the face of the didactic precepts upheld by the arbiters of Russian taste in the preceding generation. Other manifestations of this change were the preoccupation of novelists with sex and violence and the popularity among socialites of spiritualism and theosophy. Idealism, metaphysics, religion replaced positivism and materialism. Nietzsche was in high fashion.[125]

The intelligentsia was reeling from the assault on it by the symposium *Landmarks (Vekhi),* brought out in 1909 by a group of liberals and ex-Marxists. A unique *succès de scandale* in Russian intellectual history, the book was a broadside attack on the Russian intelligentsia, whom it charged with narrow-mindedness, bigotry, lack of true culture, and a multitude of other sins. The book called on it to begin the arduous task of self-cultivation. The traditional intelligentsia, grouped around the socialist and liberal parties, rejected this appeal, as it did the dominant trends in modernist culture. It persisted in its old ways, the custodian of the stultified culture of the mid-nineteenth century. Maxim Gorky was one of the few prominent creative writers to associate himself with this outmoded trend. Other talented writers adopted "Modernism" and in their politics turned increasingly patriotic.

And yet, notwithstanding social peace, economic progress, and the exuberance of her culture, on the eve of World War I Russia was a troubled and anxious country. Neither the violence of 1905 nor the reforms of Stolypin had solved anything: for the socialists the Revolution of 1905 might as well not have occurred, so meager were its results; for the liberals it was unfinished business;

for the conservatives its only legacy was confusion. Since there seemed to be no way of peacefully reconciling the divergent interests of Russia's 150 million inhabitants, another revolution was a distinct possibility. And the fresh memory of the "masses" on the march, sweeping everything before them in their destructive fury, was enough to sow terror in the hearts of all but a small minority.

To the historian of this period, the most striking—and most ominous—impression is the prevalence and intensity of hatred: ideological, ethnic, social. The monarchists despised the liberals and socialists. The radicals hated the "bourgeoisie." The peasants loathed those who had left the commune to set up private farms. Ukrainians hated Jews, Muslims hated Armenians, the Kazakh nomads hated and wanted to expel the Russians who had settled in their midst under Stolypin. Latvians were ready to pounce on their German landlords. All these passions were held in check only by the forces of order—the army, the gendarmerie, the police—who themselves were under constant assault from the left. Since political institutions and processes capable of peacefully resolving these conflicts had failed to emerge, the chances were that sooner or later resort would again be had to violence, to the physical extermination of those who happened to stand in the way of each of the contending groups.

It was common in those days to speak of Russia living on a "volcano." In 1908, the poet Alexander Blok used another metaphor when he spoke of a "bomb" ticking in the heart of Russia. Some tried to ignore it, some to run away from it, others yet to disarm it. To no avail:

whether we remember or forget, in all of us sit sensations of malaise, fear, catastrophe, explosion. . . . We do not know yet precisely what events await us, *but in our hearts the needle of the seismograph has already stirred.* [126]

6

Russia at War

Judging by the result of the war with Japan, which was defeat followed by revolution, it can hardly be disputed that for the men who in 1914 ruled Russia prudence dictated neutrality. The immediate cause of the Revolution of 1917 would be the collapse of Russia's fragile political and economic structure under the strains of war. It can be argued, of course, that the deteriorating ability of tsarism to govern and the presence of a militant intelligentsia made revolution likely, war or no war. But even if this point is conceded, a revolution under peacetime conditions, without the mutiny of millions of conscripts, would likely have been less violent and would have offered moderate elements a better chance to pick up the reins of power. As will be shown below, some of Russia's most perceptive statesmen realized this and desperately tried to keep their country out of the war.

Why, then, did Russia intervene? Russian opinion then and later has been prone to seek the answer in external influences—namely, Russia's economic and moral commitments to her allies. Socialist writers attribute tsarism's involvement to the pressures of Western democracies whom Russia owed vast amounts of money. For Russian conservatives, Russia acted out of a selfless devotion to the alliance: to fulfill her pledges to France and England and save them from defeat, she risked her own destruction. This sacrifice, however, is said to have earned her no gratitude, for when Russia subsequently found herself hard pressed by the Germans and fell prey to extremists supported and financed by them, the Allies failed to come to her assistance.

Such explanations are unconvincing. Imperial Russia entered into defensive alliances and honored her commitments neither in response to Allied pressures nor from altruistic motives, but from soundly perceived self-interest. Long before 1914 Russian statesmen had a good notion of the designs Germany had on her. These called for the dismemberment of the Empire and German economic mastery over Russia and her borderlands. Post-World War II archival research has confirmed that German political, military, and business circles regarded the breakup of Russia and control of her resources as essential to Germany's global aspirations. Berlin assigned high priority to neutralizing the Russian military threat and the related prospect of a two-front war as well as to gaining access to Russia's human and material wealth with which to match that of France and Britain.[1]

Given Germany's *Russlandpolitik* after the dismissal of Bismarck, the choice before the rulers of Russia was not whether to withdraw into isolation or to join in great-power politics, with all the risks that this entailed: that had been decided for her by Germany. Her choice lay between facing Germany alone or acting in partnership with France and possibly England. Posed in this manner, the question answered itself. Unless Russia was prepared to give up her empire, shrink to the territory of seventeenth-century Muscovy, and acquiesce to the status of a German colony, she had to coordinate her military plans with the Western democracies. The alternative was to stand by while Germany smashed France, as she was certain to do if her eastern flank was secure, and then transferred her armies east to dispose of Russia. This was well understood in Russia long before the outbreak of the war. In 1892, as the two countries were moving toward an alliance, Alexander III had observed:

> We must, indeed, come to terms with the French, and, in the event of a war between France and Germany, at once attack the Germans so as not to give them the time first to beat France and then turn against us.[2]

A Russian historian summarizes his country's position before 1914 as follows:

> One must not forget that tsarist Russia prepared for the war against Germany and Austria-Hungary in alliance with France, which, it was expected, would in the initial period of the war bear the more difficult task of repelling the pressure of nearly the entire German army. France experienced a certain degree of dependence on the conduct of Russia, on the level of her effort in the fight against Germany [and] the distribution of her forces. The tsarist government, for its part, was no less interested than France in her armies surviving the first trial. This is the reason why the Russian command paid so much attention to the operations on the German front. One must also not leave out of account Russia's striving to take advantage of the diversion of the main forces of the German army to the West to deal Germany a decisive defeat in the very first months of the war. . . . For this reason, characterizing the relations between Russia and France at the beginning of the war, it is more correct to speak of the mutual dependence of the Allies.[3]

After the crushing defeat which its forces had inflicted on France in 1870, Berlin had every reason to expect that France would sooner or later attempt to regain her traditional hegemony on the Continent. In itself, this prospect posed no fatal threat, since the war potential of France at the end of the nineteenth century was only one-half of Germany's. But the matter looked differently if France had on her side Russia, which by virtue of her geographic location and large standing army was ideally suited to counterbalance German might. Immediately after the conclusion of the Franco-Prussian War, when Russia and Germany were still on friendly terms, Helmuth von Moltke, the German chief of staff, warned his government of the prospect of a two-front war.[4] This danger became near-certainty in 1894, when France and Russia signed an accord of mutual defense committing them to come to each other's aid if attacked by Germany or one of her allies. After 1894, the General Staffs of Germany, France, and Russia concentrated on devising strategies that would turn the prospect of a two-front war to their best advantage.

Germany faced the more serious problem by far, since a general continental war would compel her to fight simultaneously in the west and east. To win such a contest Germany had to desynchronize, as it were, the expected enemy offensives and dispose of them one at a time. Should France and Russia (and, after 1907, England) succeed in coordinating their strategies, Germany faced a bleak prospect, for even her superb army could not cope with the combined forces of the other two great land armies and the world's leading naval power. This consideration lay behind the Schlieffen Plan, on which the German military set to work in 1895 and which it kept on perfecting down to the smallest detail until the outbreak of World War I. The Schlieffen Plan required that Germany crush France before Russia fully mobilized, and then rapidly shift the bulk of her armies to the east. Its essential feature, its very precondition, was speed: speed of mobilization, speed of offensive operations, and speed of troop transfers. The plan posited a slow pace of Russian mobilization, expected to require 105–110 days, compared with the 15 days estimated for the mobilization of German and Austrian armies.[5] This disparity—on paper, as much as three months—offered the opportunity to defeat the French before the Russians were able to come to their assistance.

The Schlieffen Plan provided for up to nine-tenths of the German effectives being allocated to the Western Front. Outflanking the short, heavily fortified, and topographically difficult Franco-German border, the right wing was to execute a wheeling movement across Belgium, encircle and capture Paris, and trap the main French forces. While this decisive campaign was in progress, the Russians were to be held at bay by the main mass of the Austro-Hungarians, reinforced with one-eighth or one-ninth of the German army, deployed along the northeastern frontier and in East Prussia. The Schlieffen Plan called for the French campaign to be completed within forty days of mobilization, by which time the Russian army would have less than half of its manpower under arms. Mobilization was the critical factor: the instant the Russians began to mobilize, the Germans had to follow suit or risk the collapse of their entire war plan.

The Allied staffs knew, in broad outline, what the Germans had in mind.[6] After many false starts, the French General Staff adopted what came to be known as Plan XVII. This provided for a defensive posture against the anticipated German thrust through Belgium accompanied by a vigorous assault on the linchpin of the German wheeling operation in the center. This attack was to penetrate German territory and, by threatening to cut off the enemy's right wing, bring the German offensive to a halt.

The success of Plan XVII depended on Russian assistance. It posited that the Russians would threaten Berlin as soon as the German mobilization was completed—that is, by the fifteenth day of the war. The Russian assault was to compel the Germans to withdraw troops from the Western Front before the issue there had been decided and bring about Germany's collapse.

The Franco-Russian defensive treaty of 1894 did not spell out in detail the operational plans for the eventuality of war. These were worked out in talks between the General Staffs of the two countries which began in 1911. Immediately sharp differences of opinion emerged. The Russian strategic plan, first formulated in the 1880s, called for deploying major forces in central Poland, from where, protected by fortresses, they were to launch simultaneous offensives against Vienna and Berlin. This plan was substantially revised in 1909–10. The new version called for Russia to assume a defensive stance against the Germans and to throw her main forces against the Austro-Hungarians, who were judged inferior and from whose ranks she expected massive desertions of Slavic recruits.* General M. V. Alekseev, widely regarded as Russia's ablest strategic thinker, believed that after beating the Austrians and advancing into Silesia, the Russians would be able to threaten the very heart of Germany.

The French thought that the Russians paid too much attention to the Austrians; they could contribute more to the common Allied cause by committing the bulk of their forces against the Germans, for once the Germans had been defeated, their allies would sue for peace. The French wanted the Russians to concentrate on the Germans and to attack them even before they had fully mobilized.

A compromise plan was agreed upon at inter-Allied conferences in 1912 and 1913. The Russians promised that by the fifteenth day of the mobilization order, with only one-third of their forces under arms, they would strike at the German armies either in East Prussia or on the approaches to Berlin, depending on where they were more heavily concentrated. To this mission they would assign two armies totaling 800,000 men. The French calculated that by the thirty-fifth day of the war such a strike would penetrate so deeply into German territory that the Germans would have no alternative but to transfer east sizable troop contingents to stop the Russian "steamroller," and thus abort the Schlieffen Plan. Once this occurred, the outcome could no longer be in doubt

---

*The Russians gained additional confidence in their ability to crush the Austrians from access to Austrian operational plans provided by their agent, Colonel Alfred Redl, who worked for them between 1905 and 1913. See William C. Fuller, Jr., in E. R. May, ed., *Knowing One's Enemies* (Princeton, N.J., 1984), 115–16.

because the vastly superior human and material resources of the Allies were bound to bring them victory.

Although the Russians, under French pressure (sweetened with promises of assistance in modernizing Russian armies and military transport), agreed to modify their strategic plan, they did not entirely abandon it. While assigning two armies to fight the Germans, they deployed four against the Austrians. Some military historians believe that this was a fatally flawed compromise, since the Russians lacked the forces to carry out offensive operations on so broad a front. As a result, they would fail to achieve their objectives against either enemy.[7] There is reason to believe that adherence to their plan of 1909–10 would have enabled them to maul the Austrians so severely that the Germans would have had to rush to their assistance with massive reinforcements drawn from the west, as they, in fact, did, albeit on a more modest scale, first in the fall of 1914 and then again in the summer of 1916. The decision to stretch the Russian forces along an overextended front, backed by inadequate reserves, and to push them into a premature, poorly planned attack on East Prussia, may well have been one of the costliest Allied blunders of the war.

In order to improve the chances of Russian success, the French agreed to finance improvements in the country's military infrastructure. They provided money to modernize the railway lines leading to the front as well as strategic roads and bridges, which gave the German High Command cause for apprehension.

Berlin was even more alarmed by the announcement made in 1912 in St. Petersburg of the so-called Great Military Program *(Bol'shaia Voennaia Programma)*. Scheduled for completion in 1917, it called for major improvements in artillery, transport, and mobilization procedures. Although this undertaking, initiated in 1914, remained largely on paper, it threatened to enable the Russians to complete their mobilization in 18 days, with the result that the "Russians would be in Berlin before the Germans were in Paris."[8] So disturbed were some German generals and civilian leaders by this prospect that they contemplated a preventive war.[9] During the diplomatic crisis which followed the assassination of Archduke Ferdinand in July 1914, they were heard to argue that this gave them as good a pretext as any to fight. Colonel Alfred Knox, the British military attaché in Russia, believed that Russian military modernization plans might have been the decisive consideration that pushed the Germans to declare war on Russia and France in August 1914.[10]

Given the immense literature on the subject, the diplomatic antecedents of World War I need not detain us.[11] Speaking in the most general terms, the immediate cause of the war was Germany's decision to support Austria in her struggle with Russia in the Balkans. This conflict was of long standing, but it became aggravated by the emergence in 1871 of the German Empire, which deprived Austria of northern outlets for her political ambitions, deflecting them southward, toward the Ottoman Empire. Russia, with her own designs on the Balkans, claimed the role of protector of the Orthodox Christians under Turkish rule. The two powers clashed over Serbia, which stood in Austria's way in her drive on Turkey. In several previous confrontations in the Balkans, Russia had yielded, to the outrage of her conservative nationalists. To have done so again in the crisis that developed in July 1914 following the Austrian ultimatum to Serbia, worded with deliberate insolence and backed by Germany, could have spelled the end of Russia's influence in the Balkan Peninsula and possibly domestic difficulties. St. Petersburg, therefore, decided, with French concurrence, to support Serbia.

The critical Russian moves followed Austria's declaration of war on Serbia on July 15/28, 1914. The exact course of events leading to the issuance of orders for general mobilization of the Russian armed forces—events which the Germans subsequently blamed for the outbreak of World War I—remains confused to this day. The Russian Minister of Foreign Affairs, Sergei Sazonov, felt that his country had to make some kind of military gesture to give credibility to her diplomatic efforts in support of Serbia. Under his influence, and against the advice of the military, who feared that it would cause disarray in the general mobilization plans, Nicholas II initially ordered on July 15/28 a partial mobilization in four of the thirteen military districts.* The step was meant as a warning, but it inevitably led to full-scale mobilization. If one is to believe the Minister of War, Vladimir Sukhomlinov, the Tsar hesitated, being in receipt of warnings from the Kaiser urging him not to act precipitously. His decision to proceed with full mobilization, taken on July 17/30 without the concurrence or even the knowledge of the Minister of War, seems to have been taken on the advice of Grand Duke Nikolai Nikolaevich (soon to be named Commander in Chief) and his protégé, the chief of staff, General N. N. Ianushkevich.[12] On July 18/31, the Germans sent Russia an ultimatum demanding that she stop massing forces on their frontier. They received no answer. The same day, France and Germany began to mobilize and on July 19/August 1 Germany declared war on Russia. Russia responded in kind the day after, and the fatal chain of events was set in motion.

How well prepared was Russia for war? The answer depends on the kind of war one has in mind: a short one, measured in months, or a long one, measured in years.

The General Staffs of all the major belligerents prepared for the kind of quick war that Germany had waged with such impressive success in 1866 against the Austrians and in 1870–71 against the French. The 1866 campaign lasted seven weeks; and while the war with France dragged on for half a year due to the resistance of beleaguered Paris, it was decided in six weeks. Each conflict culminated in a major battle. The expectation before 1914 was that a general war would also be settled in a matter of months, if not weeks, if only because the highly interdependent economies of the industrial powers were believed to be unable to withstand a conflict of longer duration. In the coming war, the decisive factor was expected to be the size and quality of the armed

---

*This procedure followed the one adopted in the war with Japan, when Russia had also carried out a partial mobilization: L. G. Beskrovnyi, *Armiia i flot Rossii v nachale XX veka* (Moscow, 1986), 11.

forces, both those on active service and those held in reserve. In fact, however, to everyone's surprise, World War I came to resemble the American Civil War, turning into a protracted war of attrition in the course of which the determining factors proved to be the ability of the rear to supply the front with the human and material resources needed to replace staggering losses, as well as to maintain morale in the face of casualties and deprivations. By blurring the lines between the front and the rear, such a war called for the mobilization of national life and intimate cooperation among the belligerent countries' military, political, and economic sectors. In that sense, it provided the supreme test of a nation's vitality and cohesion. World War I lasted so long and proved so destructive precisely because the great industrial nations passed this test with flying colors.

Russia was reasonably well prepared for the short war that everyone expected. Her standing army of 1,400,000 men was the largest in the world, exceeding the combined peacetime forces of Germany and Austria-Hungary. Fully mobilized, she could field over 5 million soldiers; and behind these stood many more millions of able-bodied men who, if necessary, could be quickly trained and thrown into battle. Russian soldiers enjoyed a good reputation for courage and endurance, which made them formidable fighters when well led. The war with Japan had humiliated the Russian army, but it also benefited it in that alone of the European powers it had cadres of officers and noncommissioned officers with recent combat experience. Matters looked less promising in regard to weapons and other equipment. The Russians were very short of artillery, especially in comparison with the Germans. Transport was poor. The Russian navy, rebuilt after the debacle of Tsushima, in terms of tonnage the third largest in the world, was mediocre in quality and hopelessly deployed, with the bulk of the ships assigned to the Baltic to defend the capital, where they were certain to be bottled up by the Germans. Even so, for all its deficiencies, some of which the French sought to correct, judged in battle-ready terms Imperial Russia was a power to be reckoned with, and the French General Staff had good reason to rely on its support.

Russia's military power, however, appeared in a very different light when assessed in terms of a protracted conflict. From this standpoint her prospects looked unpromising, owing to the weaknesses of her political system as well as her economy. The longer the war lasted, the more these weaknesses were bound to make themselves felt.

Russia's single greatest asset, her seemingly inexhaustible manpower, loomed large in the eyes of her allies, who fantasized about hordes of barefoot *muzhiki* driving in a dense, unstoppable "steamroller" on Berlin. Russia, indeed, had the largest population of any European country and the highest rate of natural increase. But the implications of these demographic facts were misconstrued. It was precisely because Russia had such a high birthrate that an exceptionally large proportion of her population was below draft age: the 1897 census showed 47 percent of the male inhabitants to be twenty or younger.[13] Second, a number of ethnic groups were exempt from military service: the inhabitants of Finland, the Muslims of Central Asia and the Caucasus, and, for all practical purposes, subjects of the Jewish faith.*

Even so, Russia had an impressive pool of manpower. If, nevertheless, during the war she would experience manpower shortages the cause lay in shortcomings of her military reserve system. These affected adversely not only the army's combat performance but also the political situation, because the peasants hurriedly pressed into service in 1915–16 were the mutinous element that would spark the February Revolution.

Like the other continental powers, Russia adopted in the 1870s the German reserve system, under which young males, after active service, were placed in the reserve, subject to recall in the event of war. The Russian reserve system, however, left much to be desired. Professional officers, contemptuous of civilians, assigned low priority to reserve training. Even more compelling were fiscal considerations. Training eligible men for combat duty and then recalling them for periodic retraining was a costly operation that siphoned off funds from the regular army. As a result, the government favored the professional cadres and granted generous exemptions from military service: among those exempted were only sons and university students. This practice explains why such a large proportion of Russian manpower was not available when required during the war: the number of trained reserves was low compared with the potential manpower.

The procedures adopted by the infantry called for three years of active duty beginning at the age of twenty-one, followed by seven years of reserve status in the so-called First Levy and eight more in the Second Levy. After this, the reservist, now in his late thirties, spent five years in the National Militia (Opolchenie), following which all his military obligations ceased. But because refresher courses were given to reservists in a desultory manner, if at all, for all practical purposes the only reservists on whom the army could count were those in the First Levy: the remainder, men in their thirties and early forties, many years out of uniform, were of no more use than civilians without any military training. In the first six months of the war, Russia would field 6.5 million men: 1.4 million on active duty, 4.4 million trained reservists of the First Levy, and 700,000 fresh recruits. Between January and September 1915, the army would induct another 1.4 million reservists of the First Levy.[14] Once this pool of trained manpower was exhausted—and this would happen one year after the outbreak of the war—Russia had at her disposal (apart from 350,000 reservists of the First Levy) only the Second Levy, the Militia, and newly inducted, untrained recruits: an impressive mass of millions, but neither in motivation nor in skill a match for the Germans.

Thus, subjected to closer scrutiny, the Russian "steamroller" appeared quite unimpressive. In the course of the war, Russia managed to mobilize a

---

*Russian Jews were, in theory, liable to military service. But because there were more men available for the annual draft than the services required, Jews had little difficulty buying their way out of conscription by bribing the examining doctors or the clerks in charge of birth certificates. In 1914–17, however, they were drafted en masse: it is estimated that some half a million Jews served in the Russian army during World War I.

considerably smaller proportion of her population for active military duty than either France or Germany: 5 percent compared with Germany's 12 and France's 16 percent.[15] To everyone's surprise, in 1916 Russia ran out of manpower for her armed forces.[16]

The army that went into combat in August 1914 was a highly professional body, in some respects not unlike the British Expeditionary Force, with great emphasis on regimental esprit de corps. Its outlook, however, was pre-industrial and even militantly anti-industrial. The command staff, dominated by the Minister of War, Vladimir Sukhomlinov, and his appointees, modeled itself on Russia's most successful general, the eighteenth-century marshal Alexander Suvorov, emphasizing offensive operations and hand-to-hand combat. It had little use for the whole technological and scientific dimension of modern warfare. Its preferred weapon was the bayonet; its favorite tactic, storming enemy positions without regard to casualties.[17] Greatest value was attached to courage under fire—a quality for which the mechanized, depersonalized combat of World War I, after the initial battles, would provide few opportunities. The Russian High Command believed that too much reliance on technology and too scientific a calculation of the balance of forces adversely affected troop morale. Russian generals disliked war games: a game scheduled in 1910 was peremptorily called off an hour before it was to have started on orders of Grand Duke Nikolai Nikolaevich.[18]

The Russian soldier on whom, in the ultimate reckoning, everything depended was an uncertain quantity. For the most part, he was a peasant. Village experience, reinforced by army discipline, had taught him to obey orders: as long as these were given in a manner that brooked no opposition and carried the threat of punishment, he cheerfully obeyed. He faced death with fatalism. But he lacked inner motivation. As noted previously, he was a virtual stranger to the sentiment of patriotism. The failure of the Imperial Government to develop mass education meant that much of the citizenry lacked awareness of a common heritage and common destiny, which is its principal ingredient. The *muzhik* had little sense of "Russianness." He thought of himself, not as a "Russkii," but as a "Viatskii" or "Tulskii"—that is, a native of Viatka or Tula province—and as long as the enemy did not threaten his home territory, he had no quarrel with him.[19] Some Russian peasants, on reading the Imperial Manifesto declaring war on the Central Powers, were uncertain whether it applied to their village. This lack of commitment accounts for the extraordinary number of Russians who during the war would either surrender or desert. The absence of a sense of national identity was, of course, aggravated in the case of non-Russian soldiers, such as the Ukrainians. If one considers further that the *muzhik* had his ears keenly attuned for the approach of the "Great Leveler" who would distribute land, it is clear that he made a good soldier only for as long as the Imperial regime held firmly together and enforced discipline. Any weakening of military discipline, any sign that the village was stirring, was likely to transform the men in uniform into rabble.

The British military attaché, Colonel Knox, who spent the war at the

Eastern Front and got to know Russian soldiers probably better than any other foreigner, formed a low opinion of them:

> The men had the faults of their race. They were lazy and happy-go-lucky, doing nothing thoroughly unless driven to it. The bulk of them went willingly to the war in the first instance, chiefly because they had little idea what war meant. They lacked the intelligent knowledge of the objects they were fighting for and the thinking patriotism to make their *morale* proof against the effects of heavy loss; and heavy loss resulted from unintelligent leading and lack of proper equipment.[20]

"Unintelligent leading" and "lack of proper equipment" were, indeed, the Achilles' heel of the Russian military effort.

The Ministry of War was entrusted in 1909 to General Sukhomlinov, whose only combat experience had been in the Turkish war of 1877–78, in which he is said to have displayed impressive courage. By the time he reached the pinnacle of his career he had turned into a courtier, a servitor of the old patrimonial kind, whose loyalty was not to the country but the dynasty. Good at amusing the Tsar with anecdotes, he enjoyed popularity at the Court for his devotion and bonhomie. As Minister of War, he was nowhere as incompetent as later charged, when he became a scapegoat for Russia's defeats; and he was certainly not guilty of treason. But he did live far above his means and is known to have supplemented his modest income with bribes: after his arrest in 1916 it was discovered that he had in his bank account hundreds of thousands of rubles in excess of his salary.[21] Perhaps his worst sin, however, was the refusal to grasp the requirements of modern warfare. For one, he rejected the "interference" of private citizens in the war effort and disdained the politicians and industrialists who wished to help prepare Russia for the coming war. For another, he carried out in 1912 a destructive purge of officers, popularly known as "Young Turks," versed in modern warfare, among them his deputy, Alexis Polivanov, who in 1915 would replace him. By favoring officers of the Suvorov school and demoting more talented rivals, he bore heavy responsibility for Russia's poor performance in the first year of the war.

The higher a Russian's rank, the less likely was he to possess the requisite military qualities. Many of the generals were careerists more adept at politicking than fighting. After the 1905 Revolution, officers were advanced mainly on the basis of personal loyalty to the Imperial dynasty. Promotion to the post of commander of a division or higher had to be confirmed by a Supreme Examination Board *(Vysshaia Attestatsionnaia Kommissiia),* chaired by Grand Duke Nikolai Nikolaevich, which used dynastic loyalty as its main criterion. Photographs of Russian generals of the period show amiable, portly gentlemen, usually bearded, who must have made better dinner companions than combat leaders. According to Knox,

> the bulk of the regimental officers of the Russian army suffered from the national faults. If not actually lazy, they were inclined to neglect their duties

23. General V. A. Sukhomlinov.

unless constantly supervised. They hated the irksome duty of everyday training. Unlike our officers, they had no taste for outdoor amusements, and they
were too prone to spend a holiday in eating rather more and in sleeping much
more.[22]

Some of the highest commanders of Russian troops in World War I, including
chiefs of staff and heads of armies, had made their entire careers in administration and lacked any combat experience.

Field-grade officers were better, but in short supply. Because of the low
pay and low prestige of officers (except in the elite Guard Regiments, open only
to persons with the proper social background and wealth), the army had
difficulty recruiting able young men into the service. There was a persistent
shortage of junior-grade officers. The situation with noncommissioned officers
was plainly disastrous. Inasmuch as few NCOs reenlisted, a high proportion
of those on active service were privates given stripes after cursory training.
They enjoyed little respect from the troops.

Russia's capacity for waging a protracted war did not look much more
promising from the economic point of view.

The one sector of the economy that was adequate to the demands of a war
of attrition was agriculture. Throughout the war years, Russia would produce
ample food surpluses, which allowed her to avoid food rationing. The suspension of grain exports and two successive bumper harvests (1915 and 1916)
provided an abundant reserve of food. This was one of the reasons for the
smugness with which many Russians contemplated the prospect of war. But,

as will be noted later, this advantage was in good measure vitiated by the government's difficulties in extracting grain from the cash-rich peasants who withheld it in anticipation of higher prices, and by the inadequacies of transport.

Russia's industries and transport fell in nearly every respect short of the task that lay ahead of them.

Russia traditionally depended for the production of military equipment on government factories, a practice motivated by an unwillingness to entrust national security to civilians.* How poorly Russian state industries were prepared to cope with the demands of modern warfare may be illustrated by the following figures. At the end of 1914, with the initial mobilization completed, Russia had under arms 6.5 million men, but only 4.6 million rifles. To meet these shortages and compensate for combat losses, the army required each month a minimum of 100,000 to 150,000 new rifles, but Russian industry could at best provide only 27,000.[23] In the first months of the war, therefore, some Russian soldiers had to wait for their comrades to fall in order to arm themselves. Serious proposals were then advanced to equip the troops with hatchets mounted on poles.[24] Even after energetic measures had been adopted in 1915 and 1916 to involve civilian industry in war production, Russia lacked the capacity to manufacture all the needed rifles and had to import from the United States and Japan; even so, there were never enough of them.[25]

Another serious shortcoming occurred in artillery ammunition, especially 76mm shells, the standard caliber of Russian field artillery, which the armed forces would expend at a much higher rate than the General Staff had anticipated. At the beginning of the war, Russian artillery was allotted 1,000 shells per gun. The actual consumption proved many times higher, with the result that after four months of combat the ordnance depots were depleted.[26] The most that existing manufacturers could provide in 1914 was some 9,000 shells a month.[27] The result was an acute shortage, which had the most adverse effect on Russian performance in the campaigns of 1915.

Transport was arguably the weakest link in Russia's war preparedness: Alexander Guchkov, who would serve as Minister of War in the First Provisional Government, told Knox in early 1917 that the disorganization of transport had dealt the Russian cause a worse blow than any military defeats.[28] It was also the most difficult one to rectify under war conditions because of the time required to lay down railroad beds, especially in the cold northern regions. In relation to her territory, Russia fell far behind the other major belligerents: whereas for each 100 square kilometers, Germany had 10.6 kilometers of railways, France 8.8, and Austria-Hungary 6.4, Russia had a mere 1.1.[29] This was one of the major reasons for the slowness of her mobilization. According to a German expert, in Western countries a mobilized soldier had to travel 200–300 kilometers from his home to the induction point; in Russia

---

*Beskrovnyi, *Armiia i flot,* 70. After the Japanese war, Russia also adopted the policy of not ordering abroad any military equipment that could be produced at home: A. A. Manikovskii, *Boevoe snabzhenie russkoi armii v mirovuiu voinu,* I, 2nd ed. (Moscow-Leningrad, 1930), 363.

the distance was 900–1,000 kilometers.* But even these dismal comparisons do not tell the whole story, because three-quarters of Russian railways had only one track. As soon as the war broke out, the army requisitioned one-third of the rolling stock, which left too little for industrial and consumer needs, eventually causing shortages of food and raw materials in areas remote from their sources of production.

Nothing better reveals the lack of foresight on the part of Russia's leaders than their failure during peacetime to prepare transportation outlets to the West. It should have been evident for some time before hostilities that the Germans would seal off the Baltic and the Turks the Black Sea, leaving Russia effectively blockaded. Wartime Russia has been compared to a house to which entry could be gained only by way of the chimney.[30] Alas, even that chimney was clogged. Aside from Vladivostok, thousands of miles away and linked to central Russia by the single-track Trans-Siberian Railroad, Russia had only two naval outlets to the external world. One, Archangel, frozen six months of the year, was linked to the center by a one-track narrow-gauge railroad. Murmansk, far and away the most important port under wartime conditions because it was permanently ice-free, had no railway in 1914: a line to connect it with Petrograd was begun only in 1915 with the help of English engineers and completed in January 1917, on the eve of the Revolution.† This incredible situation is explainable in part by the unwillingness of the tsarist government to rely on foreign suppliers of military equipment and in part the incompetence of the Minister of Transport from 1909 to 1915, S. V. Rukhlov, a dyed-in-the-wool, anti-Semitic reactionary. In consequence, the Russian Empire, a great Eurasian power, found itself as effectively blockaded during the war as Germany and Austria. Much of the raw materials and equipment sent to Russia by the Allies in 1915–17 ended up stockpiled at Archangel, Murmansk, and Vladivostok for lack of transport.‡ Inadequacies of railroad transport also bore heavy responsibility for the food shortages which afflicted the cities of Russia's north in 1916 and 1917. Here, as in so many other respects, the mistaken expectation that the war would be short accounted for the initial shortcomings; but it was political and managerial failures that prevented Russia from overcoming these deficiencies once they had become apparent.

The Russian performance in a protracted war would also be hampered by flaws in the military command as well as in the relationship between the military and civilian authorities.

---

*N. N. Golovin, *Voennye usiliia Rossii v mirovoi voine*, I (Paris, 1939), 56–57. A. L. Sidorov in *Ekonomicheskoe polozhenie Rossii v gody pervoi mirovoi voiny* (Moscow, 1973), 567, calculates that in terms of territorial coverage, Russia's railroad network was one-eleventh of Germany's and one-seventh of Austria-Hungary's.

†St. Petersburg, which sounded Germanic, was renamed Petrograd on the outbreak of the war.

‡In early 1915, the British attempted, without success, at Gallipoli to break through this blockade. See W. S. Churchill, *The Unknown War: The Eastern Front* (New York, 1931), 304, and John Buchan, *A History of the Great War*, II, (Boston, 1922), 12. Had the Gallipoli campaign met the expectations of Churchill, its main protagonist, the course of Russian history may have been very different.

Although Russia had, in theory, a Commander in Chief of all armed forces, in practice the conduct of military operations was decentralized. The combat zone was divided into several "fronts," each with its own commander and its own strategic plan. Such an arrangement precluded a comprehensive strategy. According to one authority, the function of headquarters was in large measure limited to registering the plans of operations of the commanders of the separate fronts.[31]

A statute of field administration, adopted at the outbreak of the war, vested the army command with full authority over territories in the zone of combat as well as military installations in the rear. In these areas, the command administered both the civilian population and the military personnel without even being required to communicate with the civilian authorities. The Commander in Chief was empowered here to dismiss any and all officials, including governors, mayors, and chairmen of *zemstvo* boards. In consequence of this procedure, designed for a brief war, vast regions of the Empire— Finland, Poland, the Caucasus, the Baltic provinces, Archangel, Vladivostok, and even Petrograd itself—were withdrawn from civilian control.[32] Russia found herself administratively bifurcated. Grand Duke Nikolai Nikolaevich, the Commander in Chief, said that Prime Minister Goremykin felt quite comfortable with this arrangement, believing it was none of his business to interfere with the areas in or near the theater of operations.[33]

Paradoxically, some of Russia's leading figures saw her economic backwardness as a source of strength. It was said that the advanced industrial countries had become so dependent on the supply from abroad of raw materials and foodstuffs, on the cooperation of the various sectors of their economies, and on the availability of skilled labor that they could not withstand the rigors of war. With her more primitive economy, Russia was less vulnerable to disruption: abundant foodstuffs and inexhaustible manpower enabled her to fight indefinitely.* The optimism did not go unchallenged. In 1909 Struve warned:

> Let us say frankly: compared to Germany and Austria, which, realistically viewed, are our potential enemies, Russia's weakness lies in her insufficient economic power, her economic immaturity, and the resulting financial dependence on other countries. Under modern conditions of military conflict, all the imaginary advantages of Russia's natural or semi-natural economy will turn into a source of military weakness. . . . Theoretically, no idea is more perverse and none more dangerous in practice than the one which holds that the economic backwardness of Russia can bring some sort of military advantages.[34]

Such "defeatist" arguments were ignored. When the Duma Defense Committee expressed concern over Russia's industrial unpreparedness for war, the Court expressed displeasure and the matter had to be dropped.[35] Sukhomlinov

---

*A leading proponent of this theory was I. S. Bliokh, whose six-volume study appeared in an English condensation as *The Future of War* (New York, 1899).

got rid of Polivanov and the other Young Turks precisely because they wanted to establish working relations with the leaders of the nation's economy, whom the Court suspected of political ambitions.

The Court and its bureaucracy, both civilian and military, were determined not to allow "society" to profit from the war to enhance its political influence. This attitude explains a great deal that would otherwise be inexplicable in the behavior of the tsarist regime in preparing for and conducting the war. The patrimonial spirit remained very much alive despite the introduction of a constitutional regime. Deep in their hearts, Nicholas, Alexandra, and their entourage continued to regard Russia as the dynasty's private domain and to treat every manifestation of patriotic concern on the part of the population as intolerable "meddling." A general recalled an incident illustrative of this attitude. During one of their conversations at Army Headquarters, the Tsar let drop the phrase "I and Russia." The general had the temerity to correct: "Russia and you." The Tsar looked at him and replied in a low voice, "You are right."[36] But the patrimonial mentality would not die and there were times when the government found itself waging war on two fronts: a military one against the Germans and Austrians and a political one against domestic opponents. It was only under the pressure of military disasters that the Court finally and grudgingly made concessions to society and agreed to involve it in the management of the war.

Unfortunately for Russia, the attitude of society, as articulated in the Duma, was even more uncompromising. The liberal and socialist deputies undoubtedly wanted to do everything possible to bring victory, but they were also not averse to taking advantage of the war to promote their political interests. In 1915 and 1916, the opposition would prove unwilling to meet the Crown halfway, aware that the discomfiture of the government offered unique opportunities to strengthen parliament at the expense of the monarchy and bureaucracy—opportunities unlikely to recur once the war was over. In a sense, therefore, the liberals and socialists entered into an unwritten alliance with the Germans, exploiting German victories at the front to gain political advantages at home.

Thus, in the final analysis, Russia's collapse in 1917 and withdrawal from the war was due, first and foremost to political causes—namely, the unwillingness of government and opposition to bury their differences in face of a foreign enemy. The absence in Russia of an overriding sense of national unity was never more painfully in evidence.

The tsarist government entered the war confident of its ability to keep society at bay. It counted on a quick triumph and a surge of patriotism to silence the opposition: its formula was "no politics until victory." These expectations were initially fulfilled. Swept by an outburst of xenophobia not seen since 1812 when foreigners had last set foot on Great Russian soil, the country rallied behind the government. But the mood proved ephemeral. With the first major reverses, in the spring of 1915, as the Germans swept into Poland, Russia exploded with fury—not so much against the invader as against her own government—with a vehemence experienced by no other belligerent power in the face of defeat. This was the price tsarism had to pay for the semi-patrimonial system of government under which the bureaucracy, appointed by and responsible to the Tsar, had to bear the brunt of responsibility for whatever went wrong. This allowed the Duma to accuse the Crown of hopeless incompetence and even worse, treason. Military defeats, instead of drawing government and citizenry closer, drove them further apart than ever.

Such wartime rivalry between the establishment and society was unique to Russia. It had a disastrous effect on the mobilization of the home front. The unconquerable aversion with which the country's political and business leaders and the bureaucracy viewed one another precluded effective cooperation. The bureaucrats felt certain—and they were not entirely mistaken—that the politicians meant to take advantage of the war to capture the entire political apparatus. Opposition politicians, for their part, believed—also with some justification—that in their eagerness to keep power the bureaucrats would risk military defeat, and in the event of victory liquidate the constitutional regime and restore unalloyed autocracy.

This rivalry is illustrated by an incident which occurred in the summer of 1915, at the height of the crisis caused by the debacle in Poland. As will be detailed below, in response to these reverses, believed caused by shortages of artillery ammunition and other matériel, the business community launched, with the government's approval, an effort to organize private industry for war production. The leader of this effort was Guchkov. Though no stranger to political ambitions, Guchkov proved more than once that he was a devoted patriot. In August 1915 he received an invitation—as it turned out, the first and only one—to join the cabinet in a discussion of the role of private enterprise in the war. A participant described the scene that ensued as follows:

> Everyone felt tense and uneasy. Guchkov looked as if he had wandered into the den of a band of robbers, and stood in danger of some frightful punishment. . . . As a result, the discussion was short, everyone seeming to be in a hurry to finish this not very agreeable encounter.[37]

In the forefront of the forces determined to resist the attempts of the Duma and the business community to become involved in the war effort stood the Court, dominated by the Empress, and its most devoted servitors, led by Prime Minister Goremykin and General Sukhomlinov. When, in April 1915, at the start of the German offensive, Guchkov, accompanied by some Duma deputies, went to Army Headquarters at Mogilev to familiarize himself with the situation at the front, Sukhomlinov noted in his diary:

> A. I. Guchkov is really sticking his paws into the army. At headquarters they cannot be unaware of this and yet they do nothing, apparently attaching no importance to the visit of Guchkov and some members of the State Duma. In my opinion, this may produce a very difficult situation for our existing state system.[38]

Some bureaucratic diehards went so far as to regard the "enemy on the home front"—that is, opposition politicians—as more of a threat than the enemy on the battlefield. This "war on two fronts" proved more than the country could bear.

Few intellectuals realized Russia's political unfitness for a war which most of them enthusiastically endorsed. At its outbreak, Russia's literary establishment was seized with patriotic frenzy: virtually to a man they supported the war effort and exhorted the nation to victory.[39] Only some of the more experienced bureaucrats seem to have been aware of the immense dangers which war posed because of the fragility of the country's political structure, its vulnerability to external humiliations, and the need for a strong army to preserve domestic order. One of them was Sergei Witte, who argued that Russia could not afford to risk defeat in battle because the army was the mainstay of the regime. He so eagerly pursued a Russo-German accord even after leaving office that his loyalties came under suspicion.[40] Stolypin, too, had urged an isolationist course to give Russia time to carry out his reform program; so did Kokovstov.[41]

No one articulated more eloquently the forebodings of the high officialdom than the onetime Minister of the Interior and director of the Police Department, Peter Durnovo. In February 1914, Durnovo submitted a memorandum to Nicholas II on the dangers of war for Russia. This document, discovered and published after the Revolution, so accurately foretold the course of events that if its credentials were not impeccable one might well suspect it to be a post-1917 forgery. In Durnovo's estimate, if the war went badly "a social revolution in its most extreme form will be unavoidable in Russia." It will begin, he predicted, with all strata of society blaming the government for the reverses. Duma politicians will take advantage of the government's predicament to incite the masses. The army's loyalty will weaken after the loss in combat of professional officers: their replacements, freshly commissioned civilians, will have neither the authority nor the will to restrain the yearning of the peasants in uniform to head for home to take part in land seizures. In the ensuing turmoil, the opposition parties, which, according to Durnovo, enjoyed no mass support, will be unable to assert power, and Russia "will be thrown into total anarchy, the consequences of which cannot even be foreseen."[42]

From the first day of hostilities, the French bombarded the Russians with appeals to move against the Germans. The German assault on Belgium turned out to be conducted on a broader front and with larger forces than they had anticipated. France now found herself in great jeopardy, the more so because the assault on the German center, the key to Plan XVII, made little headway.

Russian mobilization, as planned, was completed by early November.[43]

Nicholas wanted to lead the army into battle personally, but allowed himself
to be dissuaded (for the time being) by the Council of Ministers on the grounds
that reverses at the front would damage his prestige.[44] Since it was custom for
the army's supreme command to be entrusted to a member of the Imperial
family, given the nearly autocratic powers accorded the Commander in Chief
in the zone of combat, the post went to the Tsar's uncle, Grand Duke Nikolai
Nikolaevich. This appointment was received with some surprise, because even
though the Grand Duke had graduated from the General Staff Academy and
was popular with the military, he had not been involved in the preparation of
strategic plans. Nevertheless, it was indubitably the best choice under the
circumstances.[45] Nikolai was one of the few members of the ruling dynasty to
be favorably viewed by public opinion, which credited him with persuading
the Tsar to sign the October Manifesto. His very popularity, however, made
him enemies at the Court: the Empress, in particular, suspected him of designs
on the throne.

As agreed with France, Russia deployed two armies in the northwest. The
First Army, commanded by General Paul-Georg Karlovich von Rennen-
kampf, a Baltic German, was stationed in the Vilno Military District. The
Second, under General Alexander Samsonov, was deployed near Warsaw.
Rennenkampf had participated in the Japanese war as division commander but
had never led larger units. Samsonov had no combat experience.

The sources differ on Russian strategic intentions in July 1914, but the
conduct of the operations suggests that they had initially planned to attack the
Germans and the Austrians simultaneously in drives on Berlin and Vienna.
According to one historian with access to the archives, the Russians changed
their plans at the last minute under French pressure in favor of immediate
operations against German forces in East Prussia. The hastily mounted East
Prussian campaign was meant to eliminate the threat of a flanking movement
against Russian armies advancing westwards in Poland and Galicia.[46] The
strategic plan now put into effect called for the First Army to invade East
Prussia from the east to pin down the bulk of the German forces deployed
there, while the Second Army struck north, in the direction of Allenstein, to
cut them off from Germany proper. Having accomplished these missions,
Rennenkampf and Samsonov were to join forces and advance on Berlin. The
two Russian armies enjoyed considerable preponderance in numbers (one and
a half to one), an advantage somewhat offset by the fact that the terrain in
which they were to operate, a region of lakes and forests, favored the defense.
They attacked on the fourteenth day of mobilization, one day earlier than they
had promised the French. It was a bravado performance, in the best
Suvorovian tradition, which Samsonov's chief of staff privately described as an
"adventure."[47]

The Russians at first made good progress. Indeed, they advanced so
rapidly that the forward units outran their logistic support. For lack of time
to string telephone wires, they sent reports and received their orders by wireless, usually in the clear. The Germans intercepted these messages, obtaining
from them a picture of Russian dispositions and movements which they were

to use to deadly effect. The two Russian armies acted independently, without coordination, each eager for the laurels of victory.

The invasion confounded the Germans. Their commander in East Prussia, General Friedrich von Prittwitz, panicked and urged a withdrawal to the western banks of the Vistula, which would have meant abandoning East Prussia. Berlin, fearing the effect such a surrender would have on German morale and already troubled by the spectacle of refugees streaming from the east, ignored von Prittwitz's advice. It relieved him in favor of the sixty-seven-year-old Paul von Hindenburg, whom it recalled from retirement. Hindenburg arrived at the Eastern Front on August 23 in the company of his chief of staff, Erich von Ludendorff. The two breathed new life into the shaken Eighth Army and drew up plans to trap Samsonov's forces. The latter were heedlessly pushing toward Allenstein, dispersing in the maze of Masurian lakes and losing contact with Rennenkampf's units operating near Königsberg. Counting on Russian carelessness, Ludendorff decided on a gamble. He secretly withdrew most of the forces facing Rennenkampf, leaving the approaches to Königsberg virtually undefended, and sent them into the breach which had formed between the two Russian armies. This had the effect of isolating Samsonov. Had Rennenkampf realized what was happening and attacked, he would have stood a good chance of rolling up the German left and inflicting a disastrous defeat on the enemy. But Ludendorff gambled that he would not and he was proven right. On August 28, the Germans counterattacked against Samsonov's army, trapping it in an area of marshes and lakes. The operation, in some respects the most decisive of World War I, was completed in four days: on August 31 the Russian Second Army, or what was left of it, surrendered. The Germans had killed or put out of commission 70,000 Russians and captured nearly 100,000 prisoners, at a loss to themselves of 15,000 casualties. Unable to bear the humiliation, Samsonov shot himself. Next came Rennenkampf's turn. On September 9, reinforced with freshly arrived units from the Western Front, Hindenburg took on the First Russian Army, forcing it to abandon East Prussia. In this operation, the Russians lost a further 60,000 men.*

One of the striking features of the East Prussian debacle was the casual reaction of the Russian elite—a nonchalance that passed for *bon ton* in the highest strata of the aristocracy. Grand Duke Nikolai Nikolaevich was unperturbed by the loss in two weeks of one army and almost a quarter of a million men. When the French military representative at headquarters expressed sympathy over the Russian losses, he replied, "We are happy to make such sacrifices for our allies." But Knox, who recounts this incident, thought the Russians had acted less out of concern for the Allies than plain irresponsibility: they were "just great big-hearted children who had thought out nothing and had stumbled half-asleep into a wasp's nest."[48]

Many Russian participants and historians have claimed that their coun-

*Rennenkampf was captured in early 1918 by the Bolsheviks near Taganrog while helping General Lavr Kornilov. According to a contemporary newspaper, he was frightfully tortured and then shot: *NZh*, No. 83/298, May 4, 1918, p. 3.

try's disastrous invasion of East Prussia was a supreme self-sacrifice which, by compelling the Germans to withdraw troops from the Western Front at a critical juncture, aborted the Schlieffen Plan and made it possible for Marshal Joffre to launch the counteroffensive of the Marne that saved France. This claim does receive some support in both German and French sources. Erich von Falkenhayn, the German chief of staff, believed that the withdrawal of troops from the Western Front had an "evil influence . . . [that] can scarcely be exaggerated."* Moltke, Falkenhayn's predecessor as chief of staff, and Joffre, who headed the French General Staff, also attached importance to the Russian August offensive as contributing to the failure of the Schlieffen Plan.[49] But it has also been argued, possibly with better justification, that the failure of the plan was due less to the transfer of divisions to the east than to such factors as the exhaustion of the German troops advancing across Belgium, the overburdening of transport facilities, and the unexpected appearance of the British Expeditionary Force. The Schlieffen Plan has been denounced as unrealistic because it had ignored such possibilities. General Alexander von Kluck, the commander of the German First Army on the extreme right flank of the Belgian campaign, whose mission it was to envelop Paris, had no alternative but to swing his forces on a shorter axis that took them north instead of south of the French capital. This maneuver, which had nothing to do with the battles that were being waged at the time in East Prussia, saved Paris and made possible the Marne counteroffensive.†

The East Prussian victory greatly bolstered the morale of the Germans: for they had not only inflicted heavy losses on the Russians and saved their homeland from invasion but succeeded, with inferior forces and relatively small casualties, in stopping dead the Russian hordes. In a symbolic gesture, intended to avenge the defeat of the Teutonic Knights at the hands of the Poles and Lithuanians near the village of Tannenberg five centuries earlier, they designated their victory the "Battle of Tannenberg."

These disasters did not have a correspondingly debilitating effect on the morale of the Russians because they were in some measure offset by their victories over the Austrians. In mid-August, Russian armies broke the enemy front in Galicia, forcing the Austrians into disorganized retreat. At the end of the month, at the very time when Samsonov's troops were in headlong flight, the Russians approached the capital of Galicia, Lemberg (Lwow), which they captured on September 3. One hundred thousand prisoners of war and 400 artillery guns fell into their hands: they had put out of commission one-third of the Austro-Hungarian army. Before long, advance units of Russian cavalry,

---

*E. von Falkenhayn, *Die Oberste Heeresleitung, 1914–1916* (Berlin, 1920), 17. In evaluating Falkenhayn's assessment, however, it must be borne in mind that, convinced that Germany could gain victory only in the west, he had strenuously opposed offensive operations against the Russians. In his memoirs he could have hardly been expected to show impartiality toward Hindenburg, who in August 1916 replaced him as chief of staff.

†It must also be remembered that Hindenburg and Ludendorff destroyed the Russian Second Army without the help of reinforcements from the west. The latter arrived in time to help expel the Russian First Army from East Prussia.

24. Nicholas II at army headquarters: September 1914.
Sitting by him, Grand Duke Nikolai Nikolaevich, the
Commander in Chief. In rear on left, Generals Danilov
and Ianushkevich.

having crossed the Carpathian Mountains, reconnoitered the Hungarian plain,
while the main Russian force approached Cracow and menaced Silesia.

Russian successes against the Austrians cast a shadow on German jubilation because of the danger they posed to Germany's rear. In early September,
responding to Austrian pleas, the German High Command hastily assembled
a fresh army, the Ninth, which under Hindenburg was to attack Warsaw and
threaten from the north Russian forces in Galicia.

The next seven months on the Eastern Front were spent on intense but
inconclusive fighting, none of the principals enjoying enough power to gain a
decision. Hindenburg's advance on Warsaw was checked by Russian bravery
and Austrian vacillation. The Russians, for their part, proved unable to penetrate into Silesia because of the threat to their flanks from the north, while the
Germans lacked the forces to compel them to withdraw from Galicia. As the
winter of 1914–15 drew to a close, the Eastern Front fairly stabilized.

It was then that the Russians began first to experience shortages in
military matériel. As early as the end of 1914, one-half of the replacements
reaching the front had no rifles.[50] In a major engagement fought near the Polish
town of Przasnysz in February 1915, Russian troops charged the Germans
virtually with bare hands:

> The battle was fought under conditions which are scarcely to be paralleled from
> the history of modern war. Russia, hard put to it for munitions and arms, was
> unable to equip masses of the trained men that she had ready, and it was the
> custom to have unarmed troops in the rear of any action, who could be used
> to fill gaps and take up the weapons of the dead. At Przasnysz men were flung
> into the firing line without rifles, armed only with a sword-bayonet in one hand

and a bomb in the other. That meant fighting, desperate fighting, at the closest quarters. The Russians had to get at all costs within range to throw their bombs, and then they charged with cold steel. This was berserker warfare, a defiance of all modern rules, a return to conditions of primitive combat.[51]

The Russians won this particular engagement, which helped to stem the German drive on Warsaw. But their casualties in the first five months of war were staggering: by December 1914 they had lost in killed, wounded, missing, and prisoners of war (mostly the latter) 1.2 million men, among them a high proportion of junior and noncommissioned officers for whom there were no ready replacements. In October 1914 and again in February 1915, the army called up 700,000 fresh recruits, men in their early twenties, who were given four weeks' training and sent to the front. As yet the older reservists were spared.[52]

The Russian army kept on massing reserves in the rear. To this end it adopted a policy that was convenient and cheap, but destined to have the most calamitous political consequences. While some of the inducted reservists were billeted and trained near the front, the majority—fully three-quarters—were housed in major cities in barracks occupied in peacetime by regiments, then in combat, to which they were assigned as replacements. This caused no problem as long as the regime held together, but later on, in early 1917, these urban reserve garrisons, filled with sullen conscripts from the National Militia, would become the principal breeding ground of revolutionary discontent.

After months of savage fighting, Russia wanted to make sure she would receive compensation for her sacrifices: she wanted, above all, Constantinople and the Straits, major objectives of her foreign policy since the eighteenth century. She was stimulated to demand this prize by the British action against the Turks in Gallipoli, which was designed to open a naval passage to Russia. Rather than welcoming this operation, which might free her of the blockade, and joining in it, as she had promised, Russia grew anxious about British designs on the area. On March 4, 1915 (NS), the Foreign Minister Sazonov dispatched a note to the French and British governments claiming for his country Constantinople and the Straits as a prize of war. The Allies reluctantly acceded to this demand from fear that Russia might sign a separate peace with Germany and limit her military operations to the Turks. A year later, in the secret Sykes-Picot Agreement between France and England, which provided for the division of the Ottoman Empire, Russia was allotted, in addition, generous territories in eastern and northeastern Anatolia.

Surveying the situation after three months of combat, the German High Command faced a bleak prospect. Schlieffen's grand strategic design had failed: the Western Front had solidified, with neither side able to make significant advances. No quick victory was in sight here. Germany now confronted the prospect of a protracted two-front war, which her generals had worked so assiduously to avoid. Von Moltke the Younger, the chief of the General Staff at the outbreak of the war, concluded as early as the beginning of September 1914 that the war may well have been lost.[53]

The only remaining hope of victory lay in knocking Russia out of the war. Moltke expressed a view that gained ascendancy toward the end of 1914: that the decision had to be reached on the Eastern Front because the French would not sue for peace as long as the Russians held on, but would do so once their ally had gone down in defeat. "Our general military situation is now so critical," he advised the Kaiser in January 1915, "that only a complete and full success in the east can save it."[54] An additional argument in favor of launching a major offensive in the east was to keep the demoralized Austrians from dropping out of the war and leaving Germany's southeastern frontier exposed to Russian invasion. From these considerations, late in 1914, at the urging of Hindenburg and Ludendorff, but against the advice of Falkenhayn, the German High Command decided to launch early in the spring an all-out offensive against the Russians for the purpose of annihilating their forces and compelling them to sue for peace. German troops in the west were ordered to dig themselves in: thus began the static trench warfare that was to dominate operations there for the next three years. Concurrently, in utmost secrecy, the Germans began to transfer established and newly formed divisions to the east. By the time spring arrived they had assembled, south of Cracow, unbeknownst to the enemy, an Eleventh Army under General August von Mackensen, of ten infantry divisions and one division of cavalry. This army was reinforced in the months that followed, until by September 1915 over two-thirds of German combat divisions (sixty-five out of ninety) were deployed on the Eastern Front. In April, the Germans enjoyed a considerable advantage in manpower over the Russians and an overwhelming superiority in heavy artillery, forty German guns facing one Russian. The strategic plan called for a giant pincer movement: Mackensen, assisted by the Austrian Fourth Army, was to drive the Russians in a northeasterly direction, whereupon the German Twelfth Army would strike southeast from Pomerania. When the two met, they would have trapped up to four Russian armies, as well as cut off Warsaw.[55]

The Russians were in poor shape to meet this threat. Their troops were exhausted. They lacked heavy artillery and had only two rounds of ammunition left for each field gun. Rifles and shoes were in short supply. Unprepared for what was to come, their troops took shelter in shallow dugouts that offered little protection against German heavy guns.

The German offensive opened in complete surprise on April 15/28 with a withering artillery barrage of several days' duration: it was the first saturation shelling of the war, which would be repeated the next year on an even greater scale at Verdun and the Somme. In the words of Bernard Pares, the Russian troops were "overwhelmed by metal" that blasted them out of their improvised trenches. When the guns fell silent, German infantry, with Austrian support, struck at the Russians and sent them reeling eastward. Then and throughout the 1915 campaign, the Russians continued to communicate in the clear using wireless, which, in Falkenhayn's understated verdict, gave the war in the east a "much simpler character than in the west."[56] On June 9/22, the enemy recaptured Lemberg and approached Warsaw. There was no end to the tales of disaster pouring out of Poland and Galicia on the stunned Russian public, which had expected 1915 to bring decisive offensive operations on the part of the Allied armies.

25. Russian prisoners of war taken by the Germans in Poland: Spring 1915.

Still worse loomed ahead. Intelligence indicated that German forces in Pomerania and East Prussia were massing for an attack. Indeed, on June 30/July 12, the Twelfth German Army went into action, heading toward Mackensen's advancing troops. A pincer movement was in the making: if allowed to close, the First, Second, and Fourth Russian armies would have been trapped. Although aware of this danger, Nikolai Nikolaevich and his staff hesitated. From the strategic point of view there was no alternative to evacuating central Poland. Politically, however, this was a most unpalatable and even dangerous course, given the effect it was bound to have on Russian opinion. In the end, strategic considerations prevailed. On July 9/22, the Russians began a general retreat, abandoning central Poland but escaping the trap that had been set for them. The fortresses in Poland, which had cost so much to construct and held a high proportion of the Russian heavy artillery, surrendered, some without putting up a fight. The Germans kept on pressing eastward, running into diminished resistance. They suspended offensive operations only at the end of September, by which time they had established a nearly straight north-south front running from the Gulf of Riga to the Romanian border. All of Poland as well as Lithuania and much of Latvia were in their possession. The Russian threat to the German homeland had been eliminated for the duration of the war.

To the Russians, 1915 brought unmitigated disaster, as painful politically and psychologically as militarily. They had lost rich lands that had been under their rule for a century or more, as well as Galicia, which they had conquered recently. Twenty-three million of the Tsar's subjects—13 percent of the Empire's population—came under enemy occupation. The defeats dealt a hard blow to the morale of Russian troops. Soldiers who had fought smartly against the Germans the preceding fall and winter now came to regard the enemy as invincible: the mere sight of a German helmet sowed panic in Russian ranks. The Germans, it was said, "could do anything."[57] One effect of this sense of hopeless inferiority that spread in the Russian armies in 1915 was a readiness to surrender. In 1915 the Germans and Austrians captured over one million Russians, whom they sent to work in the fields. Russian troops began to show signs of demoralization. To appease them, General Ianushkevich unsuccessfully urged the government to issue a pledge that after victory every war veteran would receive twenty-five acres of land. Officers were heard to grumble about the failure of France and Britain to help Russia with diversionary attacks as Russia had done for their benefit the year before.

The old Russian army was no more. By the fall of 1915, the frontline forces were reduced to one-third of what they had been at the start of hostilities, 870,000 men at most. Nearly all the cadres of the Russian army of 1914, including most of its field officers, were gone; so was a good part of the trained reserves. It was now necessary to induct reserves of the Second Levy and the National Militia, made up of older men, many of them without previous training.

And yet it can be argued that the splendid German victory of 1915 led to the German defeat of 1918. The 1915 offensive on the Eastern Front had had a double objective: to destroy the enemy's armies in Poland and force Russia to make peace. It attained neither goal. The Russians managed to extricate their forces from Poland and they did not sue for peace. The German High Command, summing up the lessons of the 1915 campaign, concluded that given the willingness of the Russians to sacrifice lives and territory without limit, they could not be decisively defeated.[58] This conclusion led Germany to put out peace feelers to Petrograd.[59] Second, the 1915 campaigns gave the British the breathing spell they needed to assemble a citizen army and place their industrial establishment on a war footing. When, in early 1916, the Germans resumed operations in the west, they found their opponents well prepared. For all its brilliant battlefield successes, therefore, the German campaign of 1915 must ultimately be classified as a strategic defeat, both because it failed to attain its military purpose and because it lost precious time. The debacle of 1915 may well have been Russia's greatest, if unintended, contribution to Allied victory.

Civilians, however, rarely think in strategic terms. The Russian population knew only that its armies had suffered a humiliating defeat, one of the worst, if not the very worst, in their modern history. They were fed by the press an unremitting diet of disaster stories. From the moment the Germans launched their April offensive until they suspended operations half a year later, the country was in a state of mounting outrage. This at first found outlets in a quest for scapegoats; but as the extent of the debacle became known, clamor arose for a change in the country's political leadership. By June 1915, the spirit of common purpose that had united the government and opposition in the early months of the war vanished, yielding to recriminations and hostility even more intense than the mood of 1904–5 when the Russians were reeling from Japanese blows.

Military historians have observed that in war demoralization and panic usually begin, not at the front, but in the rear, among civilians who are prone to exaggerate both defeats and victories.[60] So it was in Russia. Measures were taken to evacuate Riga and Kiev, and the government discussed the possible evacuation of Petrograd itself.[61] In May 1915, a Moscow mob carried out a vicious anti-German pogrom, demolishing stores and business firms bearing German names. Anyone overheard speaking German risked lynching.

The public clamored for heads. The prime target of popular wrath and the obvious scapegoat was Sukhomlinov, who was blamed for the shortages of weapons and ammunition with which the military explained their reverses. Recent historical studies indicate that he was not to blame for these shortages[62] and that the lack of artillery shells had been blown out of proportion to cover up more deep-seated shortcomings of Russia's military establishment.[63] The Imperial couple were very fond of the War Minister, but demands for his dismissal became irresistible and on June 11 he was let go with a warm letter of thanks.[64] He was imprisoned a year later on charges of treason and peculation. Freed in October 1916, he was rearrested by the Provisional Government and sentenced to lifelong hard labor. He managed to escape to Paris, where he died in 1926.[65]

The man who replaced him, General Alexis Polivanov, was cut from different cloth, a leading member of the Young Turks, who before the war had urged a more modern approach to warfare, with greater emphasis on military technology and the mobilization of domestic resources.[66] Sukhomlinov, whose deputy he had been, had kept him at arm's length, suspecting him of conspiring with Grand Duke Nikolai Nikolaevich and Guchkov against the Court and himself. Polivanov's appointment suggested that the government had at last come to embrace the concept of a "nation in arms" and that Russia, like the other belligerent powers, was ready to proceed in earnest with the mobilization of the home front. But this prospect, of course, automatically incurred the enmity of the Empress, who could not bear Imperial officials "politicking" and viewed efforts to rally the nation as directed against the Crown. Rasputin also did not approve of him and busied himself looking for his successor.[67] On June 24, after she had met the new minister, Alexandra wrote:

> saw *Polivanov* yesterday—don't honestly ever care for the man—something aggravating about the man, cant explain what—preferred *Sukhomlinov* tho' this one is cleverer, but doubt whether as devoted.[68]

26. General A. Polivanov.

To further appease public opinion, Nicholas let go of other unpopular ministers. In June, he dismissed Nicholas Maklakov, the Minister of the Interior, then Vladimir Sabler, the Procurator of the Holy Synod, and Ivan Shcheglovitov, the Minister of Justice, all of whom public opinion regarded as incorrigible reactionaries. Their replacements were, for the most part, more acceptable. In this manner, the Court, without yielding to demands that it turn over ministerial appointments to the Duma, appointed officials likely to find favor with it. To further placate the opposition, Rasputin was persuaded to retire to his village in Siberia, until relations with the Duma, scheduled to reconvene in July, had been "settled."[69]

These measures failed to appease public opinion. Many Russians now concluded that their defeats were due not so much to personalities as to fundamental flaws in the "system." This system, then, had to be thoroughly restructured if Russia were to survive.

Once World War I exceeded its expected duration and no quick decision seemed in sight, all the major belligerents took steps to mobilize the rear. Germany led the way, followed by Britain. A kind of symbiotic relationship developed between the public and private sectors to supply the military with all its needs. Something of the sort occurred in Russia as well, beginning in the summer of 1915, but here the relationship between the two sectors was hampered as nowhere else by mutual suspicion. As a consequence, the mobilization of the rear in Russia was only partially and imperfectly realized. This conceded, it must be emphasized that it is generally unappreciated to what extent the Imperial Government during the war allowed society a voice in the affairs of state and how much its concessions altered Russia's political system.

By the early summer, the liberals and liberal-conservatives concluded that the bureaucracy was incompetent to manage the war effort. They wanted fundamentally to improve Russia's military performance but, like the government, they never lost sight of the postwar consequences of wartime actions. The debacle of 1915 offered an opportunity to complete the 1905 Revolution, that is, to transform Russia into a genuine parliamentary democracy. The Duma opposition wanted the concessions wrung from the monarchy for the sake of victory to become so embedded in the country's institutions that they would remain in place after victory had been won and peace restored. Its principal objective was to secure for the Duma the authority to appoint ministers, which would have the effect of subordinating to it the entire Russian bureaucracy.

The result was a tug-of-war. The government wanted society's assistance, but it did not want to surrender to it the prerogatives it had managed to salvage from the 1905 Revolution, while the leaders of society wanted to take advantage of the war to realize the unfulfilled promise of that revolution. In the conflict that ensued, it was the government that showed the greater willingness to make concessions. It met with no response, however, each concession being interpreted as weakness and encouraging still greater demands.

The Duma sat in session until January 9, 1915, when it was prorogued, partly to forestall "inflammatory" criticism of the conduct of the war, partly to enable the government to legislate by means of Article 87. At the time, the Duma was told it would be promptly reconvened if the military situation required it. Such a situation had now arisen. Opposition leaders demanded a recall. The Empress opposed them and urged her husband to stand fast. "Deary," she wrote him on June 25,

> I heard that that horrid *Rodzianko* & others went to *Goremykin* to beg the *Duma* to be at once called together—oh please dont, its not their business, they want to discuss things not concerning them & bring more discontent—they must be kept away—I assure you only harm will arise—they speak too much.
>
> Russia, thank God, is not a constitutional country [!], tho' those creatures try to play a part & meddle in affairs they dare not. Do not allow them to press upon you—its fright if one gives in & their heads will go up.[70]

But the pressures became too strong to resist, and Nicholas authorized Michael Rodzianko, chairman of the Duma, to reconvene the legislature for a six-week session.[71] It was to open on July 19, the first anniversary of the outbreak of the war according to the Russian calendar.

The month and a half that lay ahead gave Duma deputies an opportunity to caucus. The initiative for these informal meetings came from the small Progressive Party, representing the wealthy and liberal industrial bourgeoisie. Its leaders hoped to repeat the achievement of the Union of Liberation and forge a broad patriotic front of all the parties save those of the extreme right and left. The military reverses had now driven into the opposition conservative elements that in peacetime would never have joined a cabal against the Crown. Participating, in addition to the Progressives, were the Kadets, Left Octobrists, and Left Nationalists. Such was the origin of the Progressive Bloc, which would soon gain a majority in the Duma and in 1916 decisively influence the events leading up to the Revolution.*

The main theme running through these discussions, known to historians largely from the reports of police informers, was that in her tragic hour Russia required firm authority, but that such authority could no longer be provided by the discredited bureaucracy: it could only come from a popular mandate, as represented by the Duma. This principle agreed upon, the participants nevertheless had difficulty formulating a concrete program. The more radical wing, led by P. P. Riabushinskii, Russia's leading entrepreneur and spokesman for the Moscow business community, wanted to force the issue and compel the góvernment to capitulate. A more moderate group, led by the Kadet M. V. Chelnokov, the head of the Union of Cities, preferred some sort of compromise.[72]

The explosive atmosphere in which the Duma held its meetings in July and August 1915 cannot be appreciated without reference to the military disasters which accompanied them. By the time the Duma reconvened, the Russian armies had abandoned Poland and the enemy was in sight of Riga. The mood at headquarters in Mogilev was one of unrelieved gloom. General G. N. Danilov, the Quartermaster General and one of Russia's most influential strategists, told a friend a few weeks earlier that one might as well give up all thought of strategy because the Russians had no capability to undertake active operations: their only hope lay in the "exhaustion of the German forces, good luck, and the protection of St. Nicholas the Miracle Worker."[73] At the cabinet meeting of July 16, Polivanov prefaced his remarks with the terse statement: "The country is in danger."[74] Alexander Krivoshein, in charge of agriculture, told friends that the government resembled an "asylum."[75]

The Duma opened as Russian troops were evacuating Warsaw. The senile, universally despised Goremykin addressed the assembly in an uncharacteristically conciliatory tone, conceding that the government had a "moral obligation" to cooperate with it. When he finished, deputy after deputy, representing the entire spectrum of opinion save for the extreme right, assailed the government for its incompetence.[76]

Notably virulent was the leader of the Trudovik group, Alexander Fedorovich Kerensky, who was destined to play a major role in the revolution. Kerensky, who was only thirty-three when the war broke out, was an ambitious lawyer and a rising star in Russian socialist politics.[77] He first acquired

---

*Sources on the Progressive Bloc have been published in *KA,* No. 1–2/50–51 (1932), 117–60, No. 3/52 (1932), 143–96, and No. 1/56 (1933), 80–135, as well as in B. B. Grave, ed., *Burzhuaziia nakanune fevral'skoi revoliutsii* (Moscow-Leningrad, 1927), 19–32. See further V. S. Diakin, *Russkaia burzhuaziia i tsarizm v gody pervoi mirovoi voiny, 1914–17* (Leningrad, 1967), *passim.*

fame as a defense attorney in well-publicized political trials. A skilled orator,
he had a hypnotic influence on crowds, but was without either strategic sense
or analytic powers. In the Fourth Duma, he promptly rose to the fore as the
most inflammatory speaker on the left. After the arrest in November 1914 of
the Bolshevik deputies (whom he defended in court), he became the chief
spokesman of the socialist factions, easily outshining the leader of the Menshevik deputation, the Georgian Nicholas Chkheidze. In 1917, with the publication of police dossiers on Kerensky, it became known that from the instant
the war had broken out he rallied socialist intellectuals against the government
and attempted to organize a workers' soviet.[78] After the defeat of the Russian
armies in Poland, Kerensky worked for the overthrow of the tsarist regime and
the sabotaging of the war effort. In the fall of that year, he agitated against
worker participation in the joint committees established to improve defense
production (see below) and identified himself with the Zimmerwald resolution
of anti-war socialists, in the drafting of which Lenin had played a major role.
Indeed, by then there was little to distinguish him from Lenin, and in the eyes
of the police he was the "chief ringleader of the present revolutionary movement."[79] His biographer believes that in the summer of 1915, Kerensky, in
association with his friend and fellow Mason N. V. Nekrasov, and Chkheidze,
"came close to precipitating a revolution of the masses around 'bourgeois'
leadership."[80]

In August 1915, Nicholas took two decisions which many contemporaries
regarded as a death sentence on the dynasty. One was to dismiss Nikolai
Nikolaevich and assume personal command of Russia's armed forces. The
other was to prorogue the Duma.

It is difficult to ascertain what moved Nicholas to take over the military
command, for he made the decision in private and persisted in it, without
explanation, in the face of solid opposition from most of his family and
virtually the entire cabinet. A year earlier he had let himself be dissuaded from
such a course; now he grew intransigent. One indubitable factor was concern
for his beloved army. He may also have wished to inspire the country in the
hour of its severe trials, and set an example by sharing the simple life of a
soldier. Perhaps he also thought that his action would calm the political
turmoil and put an end to rumors of a separate peace. He received vigorous
support from his wife, behind whom loomed the sinister figure of Rasputin.
Alexandra, for all her love and devotion to Nicholas, thought him a weakling,
too soft to stand up to the politicians: with him away at the front, she could
look forward to enhanced political influence with which to defend the monarchy's prerogatives.

In this endeavor she was seconded by Rasputin. Rasputin, who is sometimes called a "mad monk," was neither mad nor a monk. A peasant from
western Siberia who probably belonged to the outlawed Khlysty sect, he was
introduced to the Imperial family in 1905 by Nikolai Nikolaevich. He quickly
gained their confidence with his ability, which probably involved hypnosis, to
stop the bleeding of the hemophiliac Tsarevich. He also posed, with some

success, as a "man of the people," an unlettered but genuine voice of the Russian masses, who the Imperial couple liked to believe were staunchly royalist. Although his connections at the Court enabled him to behave with growing brazenness, until the fall of 1915 he had no political influence. Rumors of his boasting, drinking, and sexual escapades reached the Court, but both Nicholas and his wife dismissed them as the malicious gossip of their enemies.

It was very much in Rasputin's interest to have Nicholas out of the way. In encouraging Nicholas to leave for the front, he thought of the influence and the money which would then lie within his reach. He knew that Nicholas tolerated him for familial reasons, but neither liked nor trusted him. With Nicholas out of sight, he could manipulate the Empress and become the regime's *éminence grise*. To encourage the Tsar to leave, he spread rumors that Nikolai Nikolaevich, whom he came to count among his enemies, aspired to the throne.[81] Later on, he would boast that he had "sunk" the Grand Duke.[82] Having returned to Petrograd from his exile, he saw the Tsar on July 31 and August 4 and urged him to assume the supreme command. He followed this advice with telegrams.[83] Thus, a combination of patriotism and political intrigue seem the most likely reasons behind Nicholas's fateful step.

If we cannot be entirely certain what caused Nicholas to assume command of the army, we know well why his advisers opposed his doing so. The Council of Ministers feared that the Tsar would jeopardize his prestige by taking charge of the army when its fortunes were at their lowest ebb. If, as was likely, further misfortunes befell the troops, the Tsar would bear personal blame.[84] Second, Nicholas had a reputation for being "unlucky": born on Job's name day, his coronation marred by the Khodynka tragedy, father to a single male heir who suffered from an incurable malady, he had lost the Japanese war and was the first Russian Tsar to surrender autocratic authority. What inspired confidence that a man with such a record could lead Russia to victory? Last, but not least, apprehensions arose that with Nicholas at the front, power would pass into the hands of the "German" Empress and her disreputable confidant.

Such considerations moved all those who had his interests at heart, except for Alexandra and Goremykin, to implore Nicholas to reconsider. Among them were the Empress Dowager, Polivanov, and Rodzianko, the latter of whom called this "the worst mistake" of Nicholas's reign.[85] On August 21, the Council of Ministers sent Nicholas a collective letter begging him not to go through with his decision. Signed by most of the ministers, Goremykin excepted, it warned that the move "threaten[ed] . . . with serious consequences Russia, your person, and your dynasty." The eight signatories concluded that they were unable to continue working with Goremykin and "were losing faith in the possibility of serving [the Tsar] and the Fatherland in a useful manner."[86]

Two days before his scheduled departure for the front, Nicholas met with the cabinet. Once again the ministers pleaded with him to change his mind. Nicholas, clutching an ikon and perspiring profusely, listened, then rose to his feet and said: "I have heard what you have to say, but I adhere to my decision."[87] For the time being, he kept the rebellious ministers at their posts, despite their desire to be relieved, only to purge later those who had waxed especially eloquent on this occasion.

On August 22, Nicholas departed for Mogilev, where he was to remain, except for brief visits to the family, until late December of the following year. Here, he led a quiet, modest life which suited him better than the formality of the Court. He attended daily briefings, but did not interfere with military decisions, which he left to the chief of staff, General Alekseev, the actual Commander in Chief.*

By departing, Nicholas escaped the political storm raging in the capital. Throughout August, the metropolitan press waged a relentless campaign against Goremykin, demanding his replacement by a Prime Minister chosen by the Duma. Some newspapers carried lists of a putative "national" cabinet, similar to the one that would actually assume power in February 1917.[88]

The political crisis came to a head on August 25, when the Progressive Bloc, now numbering 300 out of the Duma's 420 deputies, made public a nine-point program.[89] Out of deference to the Nationalists, it was more moderate than many signatories would have liked, but it was an audacious document nevertheless. Its first and foremost demand was for a ministry that would enjoy "the confidence of the nation" and promptly agree with the legislature on a "definite program"—a demand that fell short of calling for a ministry chosen by the Duma and accountable to it. Next came a list of proposed measures subjecting the bureaucracy to legal restraints, eliminating the division of authority between the military and civilian administrations in matters not directly related to military operations, setting free political and religious prisoners, abolishing disabilities on religious minorities, including the Jews, granting autonomy to Poland and political concessions to the Finns and Ukrainians, restoring trade unions, and reviewing many existing laws.[90] It was to a large extent the platform that the Provisional Government would adopt on coming to power in March 1917. Thus, in terms of both personnel and program, the first revolutionary government may be said to have been conceived as early as August 1915, when tsarism was still in charge and revolution seemed a remote prospect.

The program of the Progressive Bloc had strong reverberations.[91] The Council of Ministers came out in favor of negotiations with the bloc to determine the feasibility of a compromise. Most of the ministers were prepared to step down and give way to a new cabinet.[92] The Council acted in defiance of Goremykin, who consulted regularly with the Empress and agreed with her that it would be best to request the Tsar to prorogue the Duma.

An extraordinary situation thus emerged in the last days of August 1915: liberal and conservative legislators, representing nearly three-quarters of a

_____

*Nikolai Nikolaevich went to the Caucasus as viceroy. He would play a minor role in the events leading up to the February Revolution.

Duma elected on a very conservative franchise, made common cause with the highest officials appointed by the Tsar to call for the introduction of parliamentary democracy. Little wonder that the educated classes were seized with euphoria.[93]

Nicholas, however, refused to surrender the power to appoint ministers, and this for two reasons, one practical, the other theoretical or moral. He did not believe that the intellectuals likely to fill ministerial posts in a parliamentary cabinet would know how to administer the country. He also convinced himself (or perhaps was convinced by his wife) that on the day of his coronation in 1896 he had sworn to uphold autocracy. In fact, he did nothing of the kind. The coronation ceremony demanded of him only a prayer in which no reference was made to the mode of government and the word "autocracy" *(samoderzhavie)* did not even appear.[94] But Nicholas believed otherwise and said on many occasions that giving up the authority to name the cabinet would have violated his oath of office.

He was furious with the politicians for plying their trade while the troops were being bled white. Determined not to repeat the mistake he believed he had committed in October 1905, he stood his ground. On August 28, Goremykin came to Mogilev. He was virtually the last holdout in the cabinet to refuse to join in the demands for political reform. When Rodzianko had complained to him that the cabinet was not acting decisively enough to dissuade the Tsar from going to the front, Goremykin had brushed him off, saying that the chairman of the Duma was taking upon himself an "improper" role.[95] He was alarmed by the anti-government speeches heard in the Duma, which the press broadcast nationwide. To deprive the opposition of a platform and to calm the situation in the country, he proposed to Nicholas to prorogue the Duma as soon as its six-week session was up. Nicholas assented and instructed Goremykin to adjourn the Duma no later than September 3: all the ministers, himself included, were in the meanwhile to remain at their posts.[96] This decision, taken by the two men without consulting the Duma and against the wishes of nearly the entire cabinet, was viewed as a slap in the face of Russian society. Foreign Minister Sazonov expressed a widespread feeling when he said that Goremykin must have taken leave of his senses to make such a recommendation to the Tsar.[97] The decision resulted in the isolation of Nicholas from virtually all the political and social circles in the country, except for sycophantic courtiers and politicians of the most extreme right.

Nevertheless, as the days went by the crisis subsided because in September the German offensive ground to a halt, lifting the threat to the Russian homeland. Newspapers favorable to the Progressive Bloc now began to argue that everything possible had been done and there was no point in pressing the government further. At the end of September, the Central Committee of the Constitutional-Democratic Party, the core of the Progressive Bloc, decided to postpone further demands for political reform until the conclusion of the war.[98] The conservative Kadet Vasilii Maklakov wrote a widely quoted article which provided the rationale for this course. He compared Russia to an automobile driven along a narrow and steep road by a thoroughly incompetent chauffeur. In it sits one's mother (read: Russia). The driver's slightest mistake will send the vehicle plunging down a precipice, killing all passengers. Among the passengers are capable drivers, but the chauffeur refuses to yield the wheel to them, confident that they will not seize it by force for fear of a fatal accident. In these circumstances, Maklakov assured his readers, you will "postpone settling accounts with the driver . . . until you have reached level ground."[99]

As was his habit, once the crisis was over Nicholas punished those who had dared to oppose him. In late September he dismissed the ministers who had been especially vocal in their opposition to his assuming military command: Alexander Samarin, the Procurator of the Holy Synod, who had drafted the Council of Ministers' letter of August 21; Nicholas Shcherbatov, the Minister of the Interior; and Krivoshein. Shcherbatov's successor, Alexander N. Khvostov, appointed in November, was widely regarded as a nominee of Rasputin—the first of several.[100] So once again—and now for the last time—Nicholas had managed to weather the storm and beat back a challenge to his prerogatives. But it was a Pyrrhic victory that isolated him and his appointees from nearly all of society. At a meeting of the cabinet that followed these events, Sazonov (who would soon lose his post as well) said that the government hung suspended in midair "without support either from above or from below," while Rodzianko thought the country was a "powder keg." Nicholas, Alexandra, and Goremykin succeeded in uniting against themselves nearly all of Russia's political circles, achieving the seemingly impossible feat of forging a consensus between the revolutionary Kerensky and the monarchist Rodzianko.

The decisions which Nicholas took in August 1915 made a revolution virtually unavoidable. Russia could have averted a revolutionary upheaval only on one condition: if the unpopular but experienced bureaucracy, with its administrative and police apparatus, made common cause with the popular but inexperienced liberal and liberal-conservative intelligentsia. In late 1915 neither of these groups was capable of governing Russia on its own. By preventing such an alliance when it was still possible, Nicholas ensured that sooner or later both would be swept away and he along with them, plunging Russia into anarchy.

To compensate for its refusal to grant parliamentary democracy, the monarchy took steps to give representatives of society a greater voice in the administration. Such moves were inspired mainly by the realization that the shortages of war matériel could not be rectified without the help of the private sector. But there was also the hope that such concessions would deflect demands for political reform.

At a conference at headquarters in July 1915, General Alekseev listed in order of descending importance the shortages responsible for the Russian reverses: (1) artillery shells, (2) troop replacements, (3) heavy artillery, (4) rifles and rifle ammunition, and (5) officers. Deficiencies in manpower were the responsibility of the military. But the shortages of weapons and ammunition required expanding the base of war production to involve private industry; and this, in turn, called for the cooperation of the business community. Involving representatives of the legislature in defense production, while not essential, was considered politically prudent.

The idea of establishing joint boards of government officials, private entrepreneurs, and Duma deputies to deal with military shortages emerged at informal meetings of businessmen and political figures in Moscow and Petrograd in early May. Rodzianko, one of its most enthusiastic advocates, traveled to Army Headquarters to discuss it with Grand Duke Nikolai Nikolaevich. The latter readily agreed and recommended it to the Tsar, who went along as well.[101] Such was the origin of the Special Council for the Coordination of Measures to Ensure the Supply of Artillery to the Active Army. Sukhomlinov, then still Minister of War, viewed with misgivings the intrusion of non-official persons into affairs that, in his opinion, were none of their business, but he was given no choice and assumed the council's chairmanship. This organization made it possible dramatically to increase the production of artillery shells in 1915. Its success led to the creation later in the year of other Special Councils.

In July, the cabinet agreed to introduce a mixed government-private board, modeled on the recently established British Ministry of Munitions, to mobilize the nation's industrial economy for war, to be called the Special Council of Defense of the Country (Osoboe Soveshchanie po Oborone Strany). Nicholas approved this resolution and in August it was submitted to the two chambers of the legislature. The Duma majority enthusiastically welcomed it, even if the socialist spokesmen, Kerensky and Chkheidze, argued against the proposal for not going far enough.[102] The Special Council promised to improve war production, but it also, and no less importantly, gave the Duma an opportunity to involve itself in the political process. To enhance its role further, the Duma recommended that three more Special Councils be established to deal with transport, food, and fuel.[103] Since each council was to have representation from the two legislative chambers, more councils meant that more deputies would participate in the war effort. The four Special Councils came into being at the end of August.

Of these, far and away the most important was the Defense Council. As with the other Special Councils, it was chaired by a minister, in this case the Minister of War, Polivanov. It consisted of 36–40 members, the majority private persons, including ten deputies each from the Duma and the State Council, four representatives of the Central Military-Industrial Committee (see below), and two from *zemstva* and Municipal Councils.[104] Rodzianko received virtual carte blanche to select the non-governmental representatives.[105] The Defense Council enjoyed broad authority. It lay in its power to confiscate private enterprises that were not performing satisfactorily, to hire and dismiss managers, and to determine wages. It held its first meeting on

August 26, 1915, in the presence of Nicholas and Alexandra, and subsequently met twice a week.

To help implement the decisions of the Defense Council, the government authorized the creation of a Central Military-Industrial Committee (Tsentral'-nyi Voenno-Promyshlennyi Komitet). Based in Moscow and chaired by Guchkov, it had the mission of bringing medium and small plants into war production. The committee opened some 250 branch offices throughout the country and through them placed orders for the production of artillery shells, hand grenades, cartridges, and other hardware. As a result of its efforts, around 1,300 small and medium-sized industrial establishments went over to war production.[106] Just as the government felt it necessary to invite the participation of private enterprise, so private enterprise found it desirable to secure the cooperation of industrial labor. To this end, the Military-Industrial Committee took the unusual step of inviting factories working for the military and employing 500 or more people to send worker representatives. Bolshevik agitators opposed this proposal and for a while discouraged worker participation,[107] but the Mensheviks, who enjoyed greater labor following, managed to overcome the boycott. In November 1915 there came into being the Central Workers' Group (Tsentral'naia Rabochaia Gruppa), chaired by the Menshevik worker K. A. Gvozdev, which helped the Central Military-Industrial Committee maintain labor discipline, prevent strikes, and resolve worker grievances.[108] The participation of workers in industrial management and, indirectly, in the management of the war economy was without precedent in Russia, serving as yet another indicator of the social and political changes that the pressures of war had helped to bring about.

The leaders of the Military-Industrial Committees tended to exaggerate their contribution to the war effort: recent studies indicate that they accounted for only 2 to 3 percent of the defense procurements.[109] Even so, they played an important part in helping to break bottlenecks in certain sectors of the war economy, and it is unfair to describe them as "unnecessary," let alone a "nuisance."[110]

The achievement of the Defense Council and the Military-Industrial Committee can be demonstrated on the example of artillery ammunition. Whereas in 1914 Russian industries were capable of turning out only 100,000–150,000 shells a year, in 1915 they produced 950,000 and in 1916, 1,850,000. By then, shell shortages were a thing of the past. On the eve of the February Revolution, the Russian army had more than enough artillery ammunition for its needs, estimated at 3,000 shells for each light gun and 3,500 for each heavy gun.* To speed production, the Defense Council in early 1916 nationalized two of the largest defense manufacturers, the Putilov and Obukhov plants in Petrograd, which had been plagued by poor management and strikes.

Of the three other Special Councils—Transport, Food Supply, and Fuel

*Sidorov, *Ekonomicheskoe polozhenie,* 117–19. As will be noted in the next chapter, a significant portion of the shells available in 1916–17 came from foreign suppliers.

Supply—the first ranked as the most important. Its accomplishments included improving the railroad line from Archangel to Vologda by converting it from a narrow to a normal gauge, which tripled the freight it could carry from this port of entry for Allied supplies.[111] The council also initiated the construction of the railroad line to Murmansk.

While the immediate importance of the Special Councils lay in their contribution to the war effort, they also had a major political significance. In the words of the historian Maxim Kovalevskii, they were a "complete innovation"[112]—the first institutions in Russia in which private persons sat side by side on terms of equality with government functionaries. This went a long way toward the dissolution of one of the last vestiges of patrimonialism still embedded in the Russian state structure, which held that the administration of the realm was the exclusive domain of officials appointed by the Tsar and in possession of "rank." It was a development perhaps less dramatic than granting the parliament the right to choose ministers would have been, but one scarcely less important in the country's constitutional evolution.

A third organization created at this time to assist the government in running the war effort was the All-Russian Union of Zemstvo and Municipal Councils, known as Zemgor. The government, which in the past had forbidden national associations of self-government organs, now finally relented, and in August 1915 permitted the *zemstva* and Municipal Councils to form their own national unions to help take care of invalids and refugees. As if to emphasize its humanitarian mission, the Zemstvo Union (Zemskii Soiuz) adopted the Red Cross as its emblem. The chairmanship of this organization was assumed by Prince George Evgenevich Lvov, a prominent *zemstvo* figure who had directed a like effort during the war with Japan. Similar authorization was given concurrently to the Municipal Councils. In November 1915, the two groups combined into the Zemgor, which, with the help of many thousands of volunteers as well as salaried employees, assisted the civilian population to cope with the hardships of war. When masses of refugees fled into the interior of Russia from the combat zone (among them Jews forcefully evicted on suspicion of pro-German sympathies), it was Zemgor that took care of them. Bureaucrats and army officers dismissed these civilian busybodies as *"zemstvo* hussars." Nevertheless, as in so many other areas of activity, the authorities had no choice but to rely on private bodies for lack of adequate resources of their own.[113]

In addition to these quasi-public private bodies, volunteer organizations of all kinds sprang up in Russia at the time, notably producer and consumer cooperatives.[114]

Thus, in the midst of the war, a new Russia was quietly taking shape within the formal structure of what on the war's eve had been a semi-patrimonial, semi-constitutional state: its development resembled the vigorous growth of saplings in the shade of an old and decaying forest. The participation of citizens without rank alongside rank holders in governmental institutions and the introduction of worker representatives into industrial management were symptoms of a silent revolution, the more effective in that it was accomplished to meet actual needs rather than to realize utopian visions. Conservative bureaucrats were dismayed by the rise of this "second" or shadow government.[115] For the very same reason, the opposition brimmed with confidence. Kadet leaders boasted that the mixed and civic organizations created during the war would demonstrate so convincingly their superiority over the bureaucracy that once peace was restored nothing would be able to prevent them from taking charge of the country.[116]

7

Toward the Catastrophe

The whole purpose of the Progressive Bloc was to
prevent revolution so as to enable the government to
finish the war.

—*V. V. Shulgin*[1]

In the second year of the war, Russia succeeded in solving her most
pressing military problems. The shortages of artillery shells and rifles were
largely made good by the efforts of the Defense Council and imports. The front
which in the late summer of 1915 had seemed close to collapse, stabilized once
the German High Command decided to suspend offensive operations in the
east. By the summer of 1916, the Russian army had recovered sufficiently to
launch a major offensive. But just as the front stiffened, the rear displayed
alarming symptoms of malaise. In contrast to 1915, when disaffection had been
largely confined to the educated elite, it now spread to the mass of the urban
population. Its causes were primarily economic—namely, growing shortages
of consumer goods, especially foodstuffs, and inflation. The government, treating these problems as transitory and self-correcting, did next to nothing to
correct them.

The urban inhabitants of Russia, having had no previous experience with
shortages and rising prices, had difficulty grasping their causes. Their instinct
was to blame the government, an attitude in which they were encouraged by
the liberal and radical intelligentsia. By October 1916 the discontent in the
cities reached such intensity that the Department of Police in confidential
reports compared the situation to 1905 and warned that another revolution
could be in the offing.

In the hope of averting an explosion, the Duma resumed pressures on the government to concede it the power to make ministerial appointments, something that had become an *idée fixe* with a good part of its membership. This demand, which Nicholas and Alexandra stubbornly resisted, added fuel to popular passions, with the result that economic discontent acquired a political dimension. The sudden contact between the restless urban masses, with the mutinous military garrisons, and the frustrated politicians which occurred in the winter of 1916–17 produced the short circuit that sent the Imperial regime up in flames.

Although compared with the major industrial powers, Russia was poor, before the war her currency was regarded as one of the soundest in the world. The Russian Treasury followed stringent rules for the issuance of paper money. The first 600 million rubles of notes had to be backed 50 percent with gold reserves: all bank-note emissions above that sum required 100 percent gold backing. In February 1905, the Treasury had in its vaults 1,067 million rubles' worth of bullion; with 1,250 million paper rubles in circulation, the ruble was 85 percent gold-backed.[2] On the eve of World War I, Russian bank notes were 98 percent backed by gold. At the time, Russia had the largest gold reserve in Europe.[3]

The outbreak of World War I threw Russia's finances into disarray from which they never recovered.

The steep inflation in the latter stages of the war can be traced partly to national poverty and partly to fiscal mismanagement. Unlike the richer belligerents, Russia could not extract much of the money needed to pay for the war either from current revenues or from internal loans. It has been estimated that whereas the national per capita income of England in 1913 was $243, of France $185, and of Germany $146, Russia's was a mere $44. And yet Russia's war costs would be equal to England's and inferior only to Germany's.[4] Even so, the government could have done more to pay for the war from revenues had it imposed direct taxes, made a greater effort to sell war bonds, and maintained state income at the prewar level. As it was, a good part of the war deficit had to be covered by emissions of paper money and foreign borrowing.

One cause of the decline of state revenues was the introduction at the outbreak of the war of prohibition on the manufacture and sale of alcoholic beverages. Russia took this measure—the first major country in the world to do so—in an effort to reduce alcoholism, which was believed responsible for the physical and moral degeneration of her inhabitants. Prohibition, however, had little effect on alcohol consumption since the closing of state-owned outlets immediately led to a rise in the output of moonshine. During the war, in addition to homemade vodka, a popular beverage was *khanzha,* made of fermented bread reinforced with commercial cleaning fluids. But while alcoholism did not decline, the Treasury's income from alcohol taxes did, and these had formerly accounted for one-fourth of its revenues. These and other losses of income, such as declines in customs duties, caused a sharp drop in revenues.

During the war, the "ordinary" income of the Russian Treasury more than covered the "ordinary" part of the budget; but this part did not include the costs of the war. In 1915, "ordinary" revenues were 3 billion rubles and "ordinary" expenditures 2.2 billion; in 1916, they were 4.3 billion and 2.8 billion, respectively.[5] But, of course, the bulk of expenses went for the war, and here "ordinary" revenues were of little help. Russia's total wartime deficit is estimated at 30 billion rubles, half of which was covered by domestic and foreign loans and the rest by emissions of paper currency.

On July 27, 1914, the government suspended for the duration of the war (but, as it turned out, permanently) the convertibility of paper rubles into gold as well as the gold-reserve requirements for the issuance of bank notes. The Treasury was empowered to print notes upon receipt of authorization without regard to the amount of gold in its vaults. The immediate effect of this ruling was the disappearance from circulation of specie. On the outbreak of the war, the Treasury issued 1.5 billion rubles in bank notes, which had the effect of doubling the quantity of paper money. This procedure would be repeated several times in the course of the war. By January 1917, the quantity of paper in circulation had increased fourfold, according to some sources, and fivefold or even sixfold according to others.* The gold backing of paper currency declined proportionately, from 98 percent (July 1914) to 51.4 percent (January 1915), 28.7 percent (January 1916), and 16.2 percent (January 1917).[6] This development contributed to the drop in the exchange rate of Russian currency abroad: in Stockholm, between July 1914 and January 1916, the ruble declined by 44 percent; it stayed at this level until the summer of 1917.†

Thus, in two and a half years, the amount of paper notes in Russia increased by as much as 600 percent. This compares with a 100 percent increase in France, a 200 percent increase in Germany, and no increase at all in Great Britain during the four years these countries were at war.[7] Russia printed more money than any other belligerent power and, as a consequence, suffered more severely from inflation.

In theory, the sale of domestic bonds covered slightly more than one-quarter of the Russian wartime deficit. This sum, estimated (through October 1916) at 8 billion rubles,[8] was, however, in some measure fictitious, for neither the population nor the banks showed much enthusiasm for Russian war bonds. The government cajoled banks to make purchases, but even so, the bonds were difficult to move. A German expert estimates that the 3 billion bond issue of October 1916 brought in only 150 million rubles.[9] Thus, the deficit had to have been larger than the official statistics indicated.

---

*Rudolf Claus, *Die Kriegswirtschaft Russlands* (Bonn-Leipzig, 1922), 15. A. L. Sidorov, *Finansovoe polozhenie Rossii v gody pervoi mirovoi voiny, 1914–1917 gg.* (Moscow, 1960), 147, gives the higher figure.

†Claus, *Die Kriegswirtschaft,* 156–57. The London currency market registered a similar decline: Emil Diesen, *Exchange Rates of the World,* I (Christiania, n.d.), 144.

The overwhelming bulk of foreign loans incurred during the war, totaling between 6 and 8 billion rubles, came from England, which helped finance Russia's purchases of war matériel from herself as well as the United States and Japan.

Russia was not immediately afflicted by inflation because the suspension of exports at the beginning of the war meant that for a while the quantity of goods on the market matched and even exceeded demand. Inflation made itself felt only toward the end of 1915, rising dramatically the following year. It fed on itself as owners of commodities, especially foodstuffs, withheld them from the market in anticipation of still higher prices. The following table depicts the relationship between the emissions of paper money and the movement of prices in wartime Russia:*

Period	Total Money in Circulation (in Millions of Rubles)	Growth of Money Supply June 1914 = 100	Rise in Prices	Relationship of Prices to Money
1914: first half	2,370	100	100	0.00
1914: second half	2,520	106	101	−1.05
1915: first half	3,472	146	115	−1.27
1915: second half	4,725	199	141	−1.41
1916: first half	6,157	259	238	−1.08
1916: second half	7,972	336	398	+1.18

Inflation not only did not hurt but positively benefited the rural population, for the peasants commanded the most valuable commodity of all, food. Descriptions of the countryside in 1915–16 concur that the village basked in unaccustomed prosperity. The military draft had claimed millions of men, easing pressures on the land and, at the same time, raising wages for farm laborers. The conscripted millions were now on the governmental payroll. True, the same draft caused seasonal labor shortages, which the employment of prisoners of war and refugees from the combat zone only partly alleviated. But the *muzhik* managed to cope with these difficulties, in part by curtailing the area under cultivation. He was swimming in money. It came from a variety of sources: higher prices fetched by farm produce, payments made by the government for requisitioned livestock and horses, and allowances sent to the families of soldiers. The closing of taverns also left large sums at the peasants' disposal. The peasant saved some of this "mad money," as it came to be known, by depositing it in government savings accounts or hoarding it at home. The rest he spent on such luxuries as "cocofee" *(kakava),* "shchocolate" *(shchokolat),* and phonographs. The more industrious used excess cash

*Sidorov, *Finansovoe polozhenie,* 147. Of the sum for the first half of 1914, 1,633 million rubles was in paper currency, the remainder in coinage.

to buy land and livestock: statistics compiled in 1916 indicate that peasants owned 89.2 percent of the cultivated (arable) land in European Russia.[10] Contemporary observers were struck by the prosperity of the Russian village in the second year of the war: the war was said to have put an end to its "Chinese-like" immobility.[11] Perhaps the best authority of all, the Department of Police, while growing increasingly alarmed over the situation in the cities, reported in the fall of 1916 that the village was "contented and calm."[12] Such sporadic violence as occasionally erupted in the countryside was directed against neither the government nor landlords, but against the owners of the detested *otruba* and *khutora,* fellow peasants who had taken advantage of the Stolypin legislation to withdraw from the commune.[13]

Inflation and shortages bore exclusively on the urban population, which had expanded considerably from the influx of industrial workers and war refugees and the billeting of troops. The urban population is estimated to have grown from 22 to 28 million between 1914 and 1916.[14] The 6 million newcomers from the rural areas swelled the ranks of peasants who had moved into the cities before the war. Like them, they were not urban inhabitants in any meaningful sense, but rather peasants who happened to live in the cities: peasants in uniform waiting to be shipped to the front, peasants employed in war industries to replace workers inducted into the armed forces, peasant peddlers. Their roots remained in the village, to which they were prepared to return at a moment's notice, and to which, indeed, most of them would return after the Bolshevik coup.

Russia's urban inhabitants first suffered the effects of inflation and food shortages in the fall of 1915. These shortages grew worse in 1916 and came to a head in the fall of that year. Everyone was affected: the industrial and white-collar workers and, in time, the lower ranks of the bureaucracy and even police employees. Although it is impossible to determine the matter with mathematical precision, contemporary sources agree that during 1916 the rise in prices exceeded wages by a wide margin. The workers themselves believed that while their earnings had doubled, prices had quadrupled. In October 1916, the Police Department estimated that in the preceding two years wages had risen on the average 100 percent while prices of essential goods had gone up 300 percent.[15] Inflation meant that many town residents could not afford to buy even those commodities that were available. And they became less and less available as the war went on, largely because of the deterioration of transport. Russia's principal food-growing areas as well as deposits of fossil fuels (coal and petroleum) were in the southern, southeastern, and eastern regions, at some distance from the urban and industrial areas of the north. Before the war it had been more economical to bring coal to St. Petersburg from England than from the Donets Basin. When the sea lanes to England through the Baltic were closed to Allied shipping on the outbreak of the war, the Russian capital immediately experienced fuel shortages. The supply of food was affected by two additional factors: the unwillingness of peasants to sell and the shortage of farmhands to cultivate the private estates, in peacetime a major supplier of grain to the market. By 1916, while the grain-growing regions drowned in food, the northern cities suffered shortages: here as early as February 1916 it was common to see "long queues of poor people waiting for hours in the cold for their turn at the bread-shops."[16]

Alexander Khvostov, who would soon be appointed Minister of the Interior, warned already in October 1915 of looming shortages of fuel and food in the central and northwestern regions. Petrograd, in his judgment, was especially vulnerable: instead of the 405 railway cars needed daily to meet the capital city's needs, that month it received on the average only 116.[17] During 1916, the transport situation grew worse still from breakdowns of equipment caused by overuse and inadequate maintenance. Rolling stock ordered in the United States piled up at Archangel and Vladivostok for lack of facilities to move it inland.

People grumbled, but they did not, as yet, revolt: Russians patiently bore deprivations. The government's threat to induct troublemakers into the armed forces also had a sobering effect.

The recovery of the army in 1916 surprised everyone, including Russia's allies, who had more or less written it off. This was in good measure due to the ability of Polivanov and his associates to secure the cooperation of the Duma and the business community. The military command was now staffed with able officers who had profited from the lessons of the 1914 and 1915 campaigns. The flow of war supplies from the West which had gotten underway in mid-1915 made a great difference: in the winter of 1915–16, Russia's allies sent her over 1 million rifles, a quantity equal to the annual output of the home industries.[18] Adequate supplies of artillery shells were also assured. After Polivanov had taken over the Ministry of War, Russia began to place orders for artillery shells abroad: in 1915–16, she obtained from the West over 9 million 76mm shells as well as 1.7 million medium-caliber shells: this compared with 28.5 million and 5.1 million such shells produced at home. Of the 26,000 machine guns delivered to the armed forces in 1915–16, nearly 11,000 came from abroad, mainly the United States.[19]

In early 1916, the Allies prepared for the Somme offensive, scheduled to begin on June 25. It was agreed with the Russian General Staff that ten days prior to its opening—that is, on June 2/15—the Russians would attack Galicia: this operation, it was hoped, would finish off the Austrians. The command of the four armies assigned to the operation was entrusted to General Aleksei Brusilov:

> The preparations ordered by Brusilov's staff were thorough beyond anything hitherto seen on the Eastern Front. The front-trenches were sapped forward, in places to within fifty paces of the enemy lines—at that, on more or less the entire front. Huge dug-outs for reserve-troops were constructed, often with

earth ramparts high enough to prevent enemy gunners from seeing what was going on in the Russian rear. Accurate models of the Austrian trenches were made, and troops trained with them; aerial photography came into its own, and the position of each Austrian battery noted . . .[20]

In response to pleas from the Italians, who came under heavy Austrian pressure in the Trentino, the Russian operation was advanced to May 22/June 4. It began with an intense one-day bombardment, following which the Russians charged Austrian trenches north of Lemberg. As it unfolded, the offensive extended along a front 300 kilometers wide, from Pinsk to the Romanian border. The Austrians were caught napping: believing the Russians incapable of further offensive operations, they had drained the front to support their operation against the Italians. The Russians took 300,000 prisoners and killed and wounded possibly double that number. Austria-Hungary stood on the verge of collapse, from which she was saved, once again, by the Germans, who transferred fifteen divisions from the west to help her.

The Russian advance continued for ten weeks, after which it ran out of steam. It neither conquered much territory nor altered significantly the strategic position on the Eastern Front, but it did shatter the morale of the Austro-Hungarian army beyond repair: for the rest of the war, the Austrian armies had to be meshed with and reinforced by German units. The 1916 offensive marked the emergence of a fresh spirit in the Russian army, as officers with strategic insight and technical knowledge began to replace commanders who owed their posts to seniority and political patronage.

By departing for the front, Nicholas lost direct contact with the political situation in the capital. Much of his information on conditions there came from Alexandra, who did not understand much of politics to begin with and had a personal interest in persuading him that everything was under control. He was unaware of the grumbling in the cities and the mounting economic problems. He was, nevertheless, nervous and ill at ease. The outward composure which never left him was deceiving: the French Ambassador learned in November 1916 that the Tsar was suffering from insomnia, depression, and anxiety, for which Alexandra supplied sedatives prepared by a friend of Rasputin's, the Tibetan healer P. A. Badmaev, believed to contain hashish.[21]

The Tsar's absence left a great deal of power in the hands of Alexandra, who thought herself much more capable of handling the obstreperous opposition. She sent him reassuring letters:

Do not fear for what remains behind—one must be severe & stop all at once. Lovy, I am here, dont laugh at silly old wify, but she has "trousers" on unseen, & I can get the old man to come & keep him up to be energetic—whenever I can be of the smallest use, tell me what to do—use me—at such a time God will give me the strength to help you—because our souls are fighting for the right against the evil. It is all much deeper than appears to the eye—we, who have been taught to look at all from another side, see what the struggle here really is & means—you showing your mastery, proving yourself the Autocrat without wh[om] Russia cannot exist. Had you given in now in these different questions, they would have dragged out yet more of you. Being firm is the only saving—I know what it costs you, & have & do suffer hideously for you, forgive me, I beseech you, my Angel, for having left you no peace & worried you so much—but I too well know y[ou]r marvelously gentle character—& you had to shake it off this time, had to win your fight alone against all. It will be a glorious page in y[ou]r reign & Russian history the story of these weeks & days—& God, who is just & near you—will save your country & throne through your firmness.*

In the final year and a half of the monarchy, Alexandra had much to say about who would and would not be a minister and how domestic policies would be conducted. She was heard to boast of being the first woman in Russia since Catherine II to receive ministers—an idea which could have been planted in her mind by Rasputin, who liked to compare her with Catherine.[22] It is only now that Rasputin began to influence policies. He communicated with the Empress daily by telephone, visited her occasionally, and maintained indirect contact through her only intimate friend, Anna Vyrubova. Rasputin and Alexandra led Russia toward disaster by their refusal to acknowledge political and economic realities and blind insistence on the principle of autocracy.

With her lack of knowledge of politics and economics, Alexandra concentrated on personalities. In her view, placing in authority individuals of proven loyalty to the dynasty was the surest way of preserving the country and the Crown, between which she drew no clear distinction. With her encouragement, Nicholas carried out purges of high officials, usually replacing them with incompetents whose principal qualification was devotion to him and his wife. This "ministerial leapfrog," as it came to be known, not only removed able and patriotic functionaries but disorganized the entire bureaucracy by making it impossible for ministers to remain in office long enough to master their responsibilities.

The dismissal in September 1915 of three ministers who had opposed Nicholas's decision to go to the front has already been mentioned. In January 1916, Goremykin was let go. This step was taken, not in response to the almost universal clamor from both bureaucracy and parliament, but from a fear that he would be unable to cope with the Duma, which was scheduled to reconvene for a brief session in February. He was not only seventy-seven years old but, judging from his testimony the following year to a commission of inquiry, also in an advanced stage of senility. Worried about the Duma, Nicholas wanted as chief of cabinet a more competent and forceful personality. Goremykin wished to limit Duma debates to purely budgetary matters,

---

*Bernard Pares, ed., *Letters of the Tsaritsa to the Tsar, 1914–16* (London, 1923), 114. "The old man" refers to Goremykin.

27. Alexandra Fedorovna and her confidante,
Anna Vyrubova.

which the Tsar thought unrealistic.[23] He was replaced by Boris Stürmer
(Shtiurmer), a sixty-eight-year-old bureaucrat with a background of service
as governor and member of the State Council. Although Nicholas believed
that Stürmer would get along with the Duma, this was not to be. He was a
dyed-in-the-wool monarchist who had once been close to Plehve and was
chiefly remembered for manhandling the Tver *zemstvo*. He also had a reputation for servility and corruption. The appointment to the highest administrative post of a man with a German surname at a time when anti-German
feelings ran high testified to the insensitivity of the Court. But Stürmer was
loyal and close to Rasputin.

Few regretted Goremykin's departure, but the dismissals which followed
were badly received. On March 13, 1916, Polivanov was let go. His splendid
work in restoring the fighting capacity of the Russian armies did not save him:
he was politically quite unacceptable. In the letter in which he informed
Polivanov of his dismissal, Nicholas gave as the reason the minister's insufficient "control" of the Military-Industrial Committees.[24] This was a polite way
of expressing displeasure with Polivanov's closeness to Guchkov, the chairman
of these committees, and through him to the business community. The authorities were especially chagrined that Guchkov had invited worker representatives to the Central Military-Industrial Committee: Alexander Protopopov,
the Minister of the Interior, told Knox that the committee was a "dangerous
syndicalist society."[25] Such was the reward given a man whom no less an

authority than Hindenburg credited with having saved the Russian army.*
Polivanov was replaced, again on Rasputin's recommendation, by the decent
but unqualified General Dmitrii Shuvaev. A specialist in military logistics,
with particular expertise in footwear, he had neither combat nor command
experience. ("They said about him," according to one contemporary, "that in
every question which he discussed he invariably turned to that of boots."[26]) He
had the advantage of being untainted by any political connections. He was also
mindlessly devoted to the Imperial couple and was their "Friend": he once told
Colonel Knox, with tears in his eyes, that if the Tsar ordered him to jump from
the window he would gladly do so.[27] Since jumping out of windows was not
part of his duties, the poor man found himself swamped by responsibilities
beyond his capacity to manage. He had no illusions about his merits. When
the public began to complain of "treason in high places," he is said to have
exclaimed indignantly: "I may be a fool, but I am no traitor!" *("Ia byt' mozhet
durak, no ia ne izmennik")*—a bon mot that was to provide the rhetorical
theme for Miliukov's Duma address of November 1, 1916.

The next to go was the Minister of Foreign Affairs. The ostensible reason
for Sazonov's dismissal was advocacy of Polish autonomy; the real one was
contact with oppositional circles. His departure was badly received in London
and Paris, where he was known as a reliable friend of the alliance. Stürmer
took over Sazonov's post, adding the Foreign Ministry portfolio to that of
Prime Minister and Minister of the Interior—a heavy load indeed.

The Council of Ministers, considerably weakened after the death of Stolypin by the absence of strong chairmen, now reverted to its pre-1905 prototype—that is, an assemblage of individuals who no longer acted as a body. It
met less and less frequently since it had less and less to do.[28]

The disorganization of the administrative machinery was not confined to
the ministries. It now became practice also to shuffle governors, the main
representatives of state authority in the provinces. In 1914, twelve new governors had been appointed. In 1915, the number of new appointees rose to
thirty-three. In the first nine months of 1916 alone, forty-three gubernatorial
appointments were made, which meant that in less than one year most of
Russia's provinces received a new head.[29]

The situation brought to mind the witticism of the Minister of Justice,
Ivan Shcheglovitov, who in 1915 had spoken of "the paralytics in the government . . . struggling feebly, indecisively, as if unwillingly, with the epileptics
of the revolution."[30]

The scent of revolution, indeed, hung in the air. It took two forms:
resentment of the government for its failure to deal with economic difficulties,
and something new, animosity of the urban population toward the peasantry.
The war produced tension between town and country which Russia had not
experienced before. The city accused the village of hoarding and profiteering:

*Pares, *Letters,* xxxiii. After his dismissal, Polivanov was appointed to the State Council. In
1918–19, he helped Trotsky organize the Red Army. He died in 1920 while serving as adviser to the
Soviet delegation at the Polish peace talks in Riga.

Knox warned as early as June 1916 that the "town population may give trouble in the winter."[31]

During the summer and fall of 1916, the Police Department was in receipt from its provincial branches of a steady flow of disturbing reports. They stated with near-unanimity that in the cities of the Empire inflation and shortages gave rise to dissatisfaction and wild rumors. Industrial workers, after long hours in the factory, went shopping only to find the shelves bare. The strikes which occurred with growing frequency at this time were mostly one-day stoppages to enable workers to buy provisions. The department denied any political motives behind the economic unrest: it felt confident that it was spontaneous in origin and that the professional revolutionaries, most of whom were in prison, Siberian exile, or abroad, had no influence on the masses. But it warned that the economic unrest could easily assume political forms. A police report to the Ministry of the Interior in October 1916 summarized the situation as follows:

> It is essential to concede as an unqualified and incontrovertible fact that at present the internal structure of Russia's political life confronts the very strong threat of the relentless approach of great turbulence brought about and explainable exclusively by economic factors: hunger, the unequal distribution of food and articles of prime necessity, and the monstrous rise in prices. For the broadest strata of the population of the vast empire, the problem of food is the one dreadful inspiring impulse that drives the masses toward gradual affiliation with the growing movement of discontent and hostility. There exist in this case concrete and precise data that make it possible to assert categorically that until now this entire movement has had a purely economic basis, virtually free of any affiliation with strictly political programs. But this movement needs only to take a concrete form and find expression in some specific act (a pogrom, a large-scale strike, a major clash between the lower strata of the population and the police, etc.) to assume at once, absolutely, a purely political aspect.[32]

In the fall of 1916, the chief of the Petrograd Corps of Gendarmes reported:

> The exceptional seriousness of the period which the country is living through and the countless catastrophic disasters with which the possible imminent rebellious actions of the lower classes of the Empire, angered by the difficulties of daily existence, can threaten the entire vital structures of the state, urgently demand, in the opinion of loyal elements, the extreme necessity of speedy and comprehensive measures to remove the existing disorder and to relieve the excessively laden atmosphere of social dissaffection. As recent experience has shown, under existing conditions, halfway decisions and some palliative, accidental measures are entirely inappropriate . . .[33]

Especially disturbing to the security organs were indications that popular discontent was beginning to focus on the monarchy. The police chief of Petrograd reported toward the end of September 1916 that in the capital opposition sentiment among the masses had attained a level of intensity not seen since 1905–6. Another high-ranking police official noted that for the first time in his experience, popular anger directed itself not only against the ministers but against the Tsar himself.[34]

In sum, in the view of the best-informed as well as most loyal observers, Russia in October 1916 found herself in a situation which the radical lexicon classified as "revolutionary." These assessments should be borne in mind in evaluating allegations of pro-monarchist politicians and historians that the February Revolution, which broke out a few months later, was instigated by liberal politicians and foreign powers. Contemporary evidence indicates that it was mainly self-generated.

While the rear was beginning to seethe, the morale of the front-line troops remained reasonably satisfactory, at least on the surface. The army held together. Such is the verdict of two foreign observers most familiar with the subject from personal observation. Knox says that as late as January–February 1917 the "army was sound at heart," and Bernard Pares concurs: "the front was clean; the rear was putrid."[35] But even among the troops destructive forces were quietly at work. Desertions assumed massive proportions: Grand Duke Sergei, the Inspector General of Artillery, estimated early in January 1917 that one million or more soldiers had shed their uniforms and returned home.[36] There were problems with military discipline. By 1916, most of the professional officers had fallen in battle or retired because of wounds: the casualties were especially heavy among junior staff who lived in closest contact with the troops. These had been replaced with freshly commissioned personnel, many of them of lower-middle-class background, who had the reputation of "throwing their weight around" and on whom the troops, especially combat veterans, looked with disdain. Instances occurred of officers refusing to lead troops into combat for fear of being shot by them.[37] The inductees taken into service in 1916 were largely drawn from the older categories of reservists in the National Militia who had believed themselves exempt from conscription and served very grudgingly.

Another troubling factor involved rumors current in the trenches and rear garrisons. In the letters which the soldiers sent home and received from home at the end of 1916, military censors found a great deal of malicious gossip about the Tsar and his wife. The police reported the wildest rumors circulating at the front: that soldiers' wives were evicted and thrown out on the streets, that the Germans gave the ministers a billion-ruble bribe, and so on.[38]

These disturbing trends affected the 8 million troops deployed at the front, but they were especially troublesome among the 2 to 3 million reservists and recruits stationed in the rear. Living in overcrowded barracks and in contact with the increasingly disaffected civilian population, they constituted a highly volatile element. In Petrograd and environs alone there were 340,000 of them: disgruntled, excitable, and armed.

The authorities realized the social dangers of scarcities and inflation, but had no solutions: there was a great deal of talk and hand-wringing but no action.

As noted, the landlords, for lack of farm labor, were unable to fulfill their traditional role as suppliers of food to the cities. The peasants had a surplus, but did not want to part with it since they already had more money than they knew what to do with, manufactured goods having become virtually unobtainable. Rumors circulated in 1916 that grain prices would soon rise sky-high: from the two and a half rubles per pud (16.38 kilograms) which grain was then fetching to twenty-five rubles and more. Naturally, they preferred to hoard.

The government discussed imposing fixed prices for grain, forceful requisitions, and even nationalizing grain and the related branches of agriculture and transport.[39] In September, the new Acting Minister of the Interior, Alexander Protopopov, took steps to transfer the management of food supply to his ministry on the grounds that it was acquiring a political dimension and affecting internal security. It was also planned to ensure industrial workers, especially those engaged in war production, of adequate food. But nothing came of these good intentions. Protopopov, a businessman and believer in laissez-faire, who disliked requisitions and other forms of regimentation, preferred to let things take their course. Instead of organizing the supply of foodstuffs to the cities, he persuaded the Minister of Agriculture, A. A. Bobrinskii, to restrain his provincial agents from showing excessive zeal in extracting grain from the peasants.

The possibility existed of allowing private bodies to collect and distribute food. On a number of occasions, the Municipal Councils offered to assume responsibility for this matter, but they were always turned down. Even though it lacked the ability to do the job, the government was afraid to entrust it to elected bodies.[40]

As a consequence, in late 1916 the food and fuel situation in the major cities became critical. By then, Petrograd and Moscow were getting only one-third of their food requirements and faced hunger: the reserves covered at best a few days' consumption.[41] Fuel shortages compounded the difficulties: Petrograd could obtain only half of the fuel it needed, which meant that even when bakeries got flour they could not bake. The Petrograd Municipal Council petitioned the government for authority to organize the distribution of foodstuffs, only to be once again turned down.[42] To prevent an explosion of popular fury, Stürmer drafted plans to evacuate from Petrograd 60,000–80,000 soldiers, as well as 20,000 refugees, but as with all the other good intentions of the Imperial Government in its last days, this proposal came to naught.

Petrograd, which by virtue of its remoteness from the food-producing areas suffered the most, entered the winter of 1916–17 in desperate straits. Factories had to be repeatedly shut either for lack of fuel or in order to enable their workers to scour the countryside for food.

These developments alarmed also liberal and conservative circles, because they threatened revolution, which they were desperately anxious to prevent. They blamed Nicholas and Alexandra, especially the latter. For the first time ever, liberals and monarchists made common cause in opposition to the Crown. In late 1916, the oppositional mood spread to the generals, the upper bureaucracy, and even some Grand Dukes who went over in order, as it was said, "to save the monarchy from the monarch." Russia had never known such unity and the Crown such isolation. The 1917 Revolution became inevitable once the uppermost layers of Russian society, which had the most to lose, began to act in a revolutionary manner.

They were inspired by diverse motives. The conservatives, including right-wing politicians, Grand Dukes, bureaucrats, and generals, rallied against the Crown from fear that it was dragging Russia either to defeat or to a disgraceful separate peace. The liberals worried about riots, which would enable the socialists to stir the masses. The Progressive Bloc, which revived in the fall of 1916, kept on expanding to the right and left, until it came to embrace virtually the entire political spectrum, including much of the official establishment. In early February 1917, in a memorandum prepared for a visiting English delegation, Struve wrote: "The old cry 'struggle with the bureaucracy' has lost meaning. In the present conflict, all the best elements of the bureaucracy are on the side of the people."[43]

Persistent rumors that the monarchy was secretly negotiating a separate peace added to the unhappiness of upper society. They were not entirely groundless, for the Germans and Austrians did, indeed, put out feelers to Petrograd. One such approach was made through Alexandra's brother, Prince Ernst Ludwig of Hesse.[44] Protopopov, while traveling in Sweden, was contacted by a German businessman. These and similar approaches met with no response from the Russian side. Researches in Russian and Western archives after the Revolution have failed to reveal any evidence that the Imperial Government desired or even contemplated a separate peace.[45] Nicholas and Alexandra were determined to wage war to the bitter end regardless of the domestic consequences. But the rumors caused the monarchy untold harm, alienating its natural supporters among the conservatives and nationalists who were ferociously anti-German.

Even more harmful was gossip about the alleged treasonous activities of the Empress and Rasputin. This also lacked any substance. Whatever sins Alexandra had on her conscience, she deeply cared for her adopted homeland, as she would prove later, after the Revolution, when her life was at stake. But she was a German and hence regarded as an enemy alien. Her reputation was further sullied by Rasputin's contacts with suspicious individuals from the Petrograd demimonde, some of whom were rumored to have German connections. The root of the problem was that even if Alexandra and Rasputin did not actually engage in demonstrable treason, in the eyes of many patriotic

Russians they could not have worked more effectively for the enemy if they were full-fledged enemy agents.

The liberal opposition faced a problem with which it did not quite know how to cope. The Kadets knew as well as the police of the popular discontent; they feared that unless they acted promptly and decisively to take charge, things would get out of control. They also were aware of the fact, reported on by the police, that the masses were losing faith in the Duma because it was not acting energetically enough.[46] From this assessment they concluded that unless they challenged the government, they would dissipate their prestige and lose out to the radicals. Some Kadets worried that even if Russia somehow muddled through the war without a revolution, she would certainly have one when it was over because peace would bring with it massive unemployment and peasant land seizures.[47] So it appeared essential to act in a bold, even revolutionary manner. And yet, pressing the government too hard would disorganize still further what was left of the administrative apparatus and fuel the very anarchy the liberals wished to prevent. One had to push the authorities hard enough to win over the masses and compel the government to yield power, but not so hard as to bring the state structure crashing down—a most delicate undertaking.

Unexpectedly, the monarchy seemed to make this task easier with the appointment in mid-September of Alexander Protopopov as Minister of the Interior.* This move aroused the most exaggerated hopes. The extraordinary aspect of Protopopov's appointment was that he was entrusted with the second most important post in the Imperial administration although he had neither bureaucratic experience nor rank. He was not the first private citizen to be given a ministerial post—he had been preceded in July 1916 by the Minister of Agriculture, Bobrinskii—but it was entirely without precedent for an individual without *chin* to be put in charge of the country's administrative machinery. This was the Crown's supreme effort at compromise, a step to meet the demand of the Duma for control of the cabinet, for Protopopov, a well-to-do landlord and textile manufacturer, an Octobrist and member of the Progressive Bloc, was not only a member of the Duma but also its deputy chairman. Rodzianko and Guchkov had a good opinion of him, as did other parliamentarians.[48] Given this background, Protopopov's appointment could have been reasonably interpreted as a surrender to the Progressive Bloc—the first of a succession of ministerial appointments which would result in a cabinet enjoying the Duma's confidence. This is how A. I. Konovalov, a leading Kadet and member of the Progressive Bloc, viewed the Tsar's move. At a private gathering of Kadets and associates early in October, he characterized Protopopov's appointment as a complete "capitulation" of the regime:

> By capitulating to society, the authorities have taken a giant, unexpected leap.
> The best that one might have expected was the appointment of some liberal-

*Protopopov was initially made acting minister; he was promoted to minister in mid-December, following the assassination of Rasputin: V. S. Diakin, *Russkaia burzhuaziia i tsarizm v gody pervoi mirovoi voiny (1914–1917)* (Leningrad, 1967), 265.

28. Alexander Protopopov.

minded bureaucrat. And all of a sudden it is the Octobrist Protopopov, a man essentially alien to the bureaucratic world. For the authorities, this capitulation is almost tantamount to the act of October 17. After an Octobrist minister, a Kadet minister will no longer be such a fright. Perhaps in a few months we will have a ministry of Miliukov and Shingarev.* It all depends on us. It is all in our hands.[49]

This assessment was shared by much of the press. The unofficial Petrograd stock exchange rose sharply when Protopopov took office.

Such sanguine expectations were soon shattered. The appointment of Protopopov was not a capitulation by the monarchy but a clever political maneuver. The Court had called on the Duma to convene on November 1 because the constitution required it to approve the budget. It was expected that the opposition would use this opportunity to renew the assault on the government. Protopopov seemed to the Court the ideal man to handle the legislature. His membership in the October Party and the Progressive Bloc gave him credibility in the eyes of the opposition; at the same time, the Court knew Protopopov for what he really was—a devoted monarchist. The strong endorsement which Rasputin gave Protopopov served as a guarantee of his loyalty. He was an exceedingly vain man, overwhelmed by the honor which the Imperial couple had bestowed on him, and unlikely to make common cause with the opposition. Alexandra understood well why and how Protopopov would serve the dynasty's interests: "Please, take *Protopopov* as Minister of the

---

*A. I. Shingarev was a prominent Kadet and expert on agrarian problems. He served as Minister of Finance in the Provisional Government and was murdered in early 1918 by pro-Bolshevik sailors.

Interior," she urged Nicholas on September 9, "as he is one of the *Duma* it will make a great effect amongst them & shut their mouths."[50] In the words of Pares, she wanted to use "a Duma man to curb the Duma."[51] Here was an ideal minister—endorsed by Rasputin and yet acceptable to Rodzianko and Guchkov. He had also made an excellent impression on King George V and the French the preceding summer while heading a diplomatic mission in the West. Nicholas gave Protopopov carte blanche to run the country: "Do what is necessary, save the situation," he asked.[52] Backed by the Tsar, who appreciated his polite manner and charm, and Alexandra, who is said to have wanted to run Russia as if it were "their farm,"[53] exuding boundless optimism in an atmosphere of widespread gloom, Protopopov became a virtual dictator.

He proved a disastrous choice. The only qualification Protopopov had for high office was a "talent for adapting himself to people of different political views," a relative rarity in Russia.[54] It gained him many supporters. But his driving force was vanity. Flattered by his appointment, he enjoyed to the limit its perquisites: access to the Court, the opportunity to treat condescendingly his onetime Duma colleagues, the power to conceive ambitious reform projects. It was the psychic gratifications of power that he held dear. Later, when things turned sour, to a friend who urged him to resign, he said indignantly: "How can you ask me to resign? All my life it was my dream to be a Deputy Governor, and here I am a Minister!"[55]

He had no administrative talents: he had even managed to drive his textile business to the brink of bankruptcy.[56] He spent little time at his desk, and ignored the remarkably prescient analyses of the country's internal situation prepared by the Department of Police. His achievement as the most important civil servant of the Empire at a critical juncture in its history was all image-building and public relations: his testimony given after the Revolution revealed a thoroughly confused man.[57] His erratic behavior spawned suspicions that he was mentally ill from the effects of venereal disease.

On assuming office, Protopopov drew up a liberal reform program, centered on the abolition of the Pale of Settlement and the other Jewish disabilities[58]—a long overdue move, but hardly at the heart of Russia's concerns, the more so that the mass expulsions of Jews from the front zone had the effect of lifting the Pale.* This proposal, meant to meet one of the demands of the Progressive Bloc, was inspired by Rasputin, who favored equality for Jews. Protopopov also toyed with the idea of a responsible ministry—responsible, however, for illegal as well as "inexpedient" *(netselesoobraznye)* actions, not to the Duma but to the Senate, a wholly appointed judiciary body.[59] He neither thought out nor pursued any of these plans. A few weeks after taking over the ministry, he met with the opposition in the hope of agreeing on a joint course of action, but this endeavor, too, had no result.

Disillusionment with the new Minister of the Interior set in very quickly:

---

*Because they were suspected of German sympathies, numerous Jews living near the combat zone—estimates run as high as 250,000—were forced in 1915 to move into the interior of the country.

hope gave way to hatred. His obsequiousness to Nicholas and Alexandra revolted Duma politicians. So did his tactless actions, such as releasing General Sukhomlinov from prison and placing him under house arrest (done at the request of Rasputin) and appearing in the Duma in a gendarme's uniform.[60] On the eve of the convocation of the Duma, he was widely perceived as a renegade. Instead of serving as a bridge between administration and parliament, he caused a virtual break between the two, because no respectable political figure would so much as talk to him.

Time was running out. Information reaching political leaders in Moscow and Petrograd (and corroborated confidentially, as we now know, by the police) indicated that the economic hardships of the urban population could any day explode in mass unrest. If such unrest was to be prevented, the Duma had to seize power and do so soon. There was not a moment to lose: if riots broke out before it took charge, the Duma, too, could be swept aside. This imperative—the perceived need to act before the outburst of popular fury—lay behind the irresponsible and, indeed, dishonorable conduct of the opposition leaders in late 1916. They felt they were racing against the clock: the question was no longer whether a revolution would occur, but when and in what form—from above, as a coup d'état directed by themselves, or from below, as a spontaneous and uncontrollable mass revolt.[61]

In September and October the main opposition parties, meeting at first separately and then jointly, as the Progressive Bloc, held secret conferences to devise a strategy for the forthcoming Duma session. Their mood was unyielding: the government had to surrender power. This time there would be no temporizing and no compromises.

The driving force behind this revolutionary challenge was the Constitutional-Democratic Party. At the meeting of its Central Committee on September 30–October 1, complaints were heard that the party had lost contact with the country because it no longer behaved like an opposition. The Left Kadets wanted to launch a "merciless war" against the government, even at the risk of provoking the Duma's dissolution.[62] The Kadet Party formally adopted the strategy of confrontation at a conference on October 22–24. Thanks to the information supplied by police agents,[63] we are well informed of the proceedings of this meeting, perhaps the most consequential in the party's history. Miliukov came under attack for being too cautious and too eager to maintain the legitimacy of the party in the eyes of the authorities. The country was lurching to the left and unless the Kadets followed suit they would lose influence. Some of the provincial delegates, who were more radical than the party's Duma deputies, thought it a mistake even to waste time on parliamentary debates: they preferred that the party appeal directly to the "masses"— that is, engage in revolutionary agitation as the Union of Liberation and the Union of Unions had done in 1904–5. Prince P. D. Dolgorukov thought that the moderate Miliukov retained his position as the party's leader only because there was still hope that the government would dismiss Stürmer: should it refuse to do so and send the Duma packing, Miliukov would be finished. It was the last chance to confront the government in parliament.[64] Colonel A. P. Martynov, the outstanding chief of the Moscow Okhrana, passed to his superiors the information gathered by agents at the Kadet conference, along with personal comments. In his opinion, the thrust of the Kadets' strategy lay in the resolution which spoke of the necessity of "maintaining contact with the broad masses of the population and organizing the country's democratic elements for the purpose of neutralizing the common danger." He added that the Kadets were terrified of a revolution breaking out either now or after the war, when the country would face problems beyond the government's ability to solve.[65]

To force the government to capitulate, the Kadets adopted the riskiest course imaginable: it was so out of character for a party which prided itself on respect for law and due process that it can only be explained by a mood of panic. The party resolved publicly to charge the Prime Minister with high treason. There was not a shred of evidence to support this accusation, and the Kadets well knew this to be the case. Stürmer was a reactionary bureaucrat, ill qualified to head the Russian government, but he had committed nothing remotely resembling treason. Rumors of treason, however, were so rife in the rear and at the front that they decided to exploit them for their own ends, playing on the Prime Minister's German surname.*

The Kadets coordinated their plan with the other parties in the Progressive Bloc. On October 25, the bloc agreed on a common platform: to demand the dismissal of Stürmer, to call for the repeal of laws issued under Article 87, and "to emphasize rumors that the right was striving for a separate peace."[66]

The opposition leaders thus set out on a collision course from which there was no retreat: they would confront the Crown with a revolutionary challenge.

Stürmer, whom the police kept informed of these developments, was understandably outraged. He informed Nicholas that when the Duma reconvened the opposition would launch an all-out attack charging the ministers with high treason.[67] Such behavior in time of war was nothing short of criminal, inconceivable in any other belligerent country. He recommended, as a first step, withholding the deputies' pay and threatening those of military age with conscription. He further requested the authority, if the situation required it, to dissolve both chambers of parliament and order new elections. Nicholas equivocated. He wanted to avoid, if at all possible, a confrontation. Stürmer could dissolve the Duma, he said, only in an "extreme case."[68] He was letting power slip from his hands. He was tired from lack of sleep and thoroughly discouraged. He could not even bear the sight of the daily press: the only

*E. D. Chermenskii, *IV Gosudarstvennaia Duma i sverzhenie tsarizma v Rossii* (Moscow, 1976), 204–6; Diakin, *Russkaia burzhuaziia,* 241. On the unpopularity of Stürmer due to his German name: *IA,* No. 1 (1960), 207. If not for that they would have targeted Protopopov, making an issue of his talks with a German representative in Stockholm.

newspaper he read was *Russkii invalid,* a patriotic daily put out by the Ministry of War.[69]

Although he had failed to obtain a carte blanche, Stürmer felt he had the authority privately to inform the Duma leaders that if they dared to accuse the government of treason, the Duma would be at once prorogued and possibly dissolved.[70]

These warnings threw confusion into the ranks of the Progressive Bloc, dividing its radical wing, represented by the Left Kadets and Progressives, from the more conciliatory wing of mainstream Kadets, Octobrists, and individual conservatives. The Kadets, bound by resolutions of the party conference, warned their conservatives that if they did not support them, the Kadets would introduce a still more sharply worded resolution.[71] V. V. Shulgin and other nationalists expressed unhappiness over the Kadet proposal, arguing that public accusations of treason could have disastrous consequences. Eager to retain conservative support, the Kadets agreed to a bloc resolution from which the word "treason" was removed.[72] The Progressive Party, unhappy over this compromise, withdrew from the bloc. The Left Kadets also threatened to defect, but Miliukov managed to dissuade them with the promise to deliver a "sharp" address in the Duma.[73]

The Duma opened at 2:30 p.m. on November 1 in an atmosphere laden with unprecedented tension.

Rodzianko, the chairman, began the proceedings with a brief patriotic address. As soon as he had finished, all the ministers, led by Stürmer and Protopopov, rose to their feet and left the chamber, followed by the foreign ambassadors.* The socialist deputies responded with hoots and catcalls.

S. I. Shidlovskii, the leader of the Octobrists and spokesman for the Progressive Bloc, delivered the first major address. He criticized the government for having prorogued the Duma in order to rule by Article 87, neglecting the food supply, and using military censorship to safeguard its "nonexistent prestige." He warned that Russia faced serious dangers. The country had to have a government of public confidence: the Progressive Bloc would strive for this objective "employing all the means permitted by law."[74]

Kerensky made a hysterical speech that in vituperation exceeded anything previously heard in the halls of the Duma.[75] He accused Europe's "ruling classes" of having pushed "democracy" into an intolerable war. He charged the Russian Government with conducting a "White Terror" and filling its prisons with working people. Behind all these acts stood "Grisha Rasputin." Excited by the sound of his own words, he demanded rhetorically:

---

*According to the French Ambassador, this was done at Stürmer's request: Maurice Paléologue, *La Russie des Tsars pendant la Grande Guerre,* III (Paris, 1922), 86–87.

Gentlemen! Will everything that we are living through not move us to declare with one voice: the main and worst enemy of our country is not at the front, but here, in our midst. There is no salvation for our country until, with a unanimous and concerted effort, we force the removal of those who ruin, humiliate, and insult it.

Comparing the ministers to "hired killers" and pointing at their empty seats, he demanded to know where they had gone, "these men suspected of treason, these fratricides and cowards."

Although reprimanded by the chair, Kerensky continued his diatribe, warning that Russia stood on the brink of her "greatest trials, unprecedented in Russian history," which threatened anarchy and destruction. Russia's real enemies were those who placed their private interests above those of the country:

You must annihilate the authority of those who do not acknowledge their duty: they [pointing again at the empty ministerial seats] must go. They are the betrayers of the country's interests.

At this point, the chairman asked Kerensky to step down.

Although cheered by the left, Kerensky did not enjoy much respect from the majority of the Duma since his rhetorical excesses were familiar. It was a different matter when Miliukov mounted the rostrum, for he was widely known as a responsible and levelheaded statesman. His speech, only slightly less vituperative than Kerensky's, carried, therefore, much greater weight. It must be borne in mind that his address was the result of a compromise struck between the left and right factions of the Progressive Bloc: in deference to the former, which included a sizable segment of his own party, Miliukov accused the government of treason; to placate the latter, he muted the charge, posing it in the form of a question.

Miliukov began by recalling the changes which had taken place in Russia in 1915 in consequence of military defeats and the hopes which these changes had aroused. But now, with the war in its twenty-seventh month, the mood of the country was different: "We have lost faith that the government can lead us to victory." All the Allied states had formed governments of national unity, involving in the management of the war effort the most qualified citizens, without regard to party. And in Russia? Here all the ministers capable of gaining parliamentary support had been forced from office. Why? To answer his question, Miliukov resorted to insinuation of treason based on information which he claimed to have secured on a recent trip to Western Europe:

The French Yellow Book has published a German document outlining the principles of how to disorganize an enemy country, to instigate in it unrest and disorders. Gentlemen, if our government wanted deliberately to carry out this mission, or if the Germans wanted to use for this purpose their own means, such as influence and bribery, they could not have done it better than the

Russian Government. [The Kadet deputy F. I. Rodichev from his seat: "Alas,
it is so!"][76]

The government's behavior caused rumors of treason in high places to sweep
the country. Then Miliukov produced his bombshell. Citing from the *Berliner
Tagwacht* of October 16, he reported that the private secretary of Stürmer,
Ivan Manasevich-Manuilov, a journalist with a shady past, had been employed
before the war by the German Embassy to bribe the conservative daily *Novoe
vremia*. Why was this individual first arrested and then released? Because,
Miliukov explained, as Manasevich-Manuilov himself had admitted to the
prosecutor, he had passed on some of that German money to Prime Minister
Stürmer. Miliukov went on to read from German and Austrian newspapers
expressions of satisfaction over the dismissal of Sazonov as Foreign Minister
and his replacement by Stürmer. The impression which these citations conveyed was that Stürmer had secret communications with the enemy and
worked for the conclusion of a separate peace.

At this point, the right disrupted Miliukov with shouts of slander. When
order was restored, Miliukov made some murky but ominous hints of pro-
German ladies active abroad and in Petrogad. What did all these bits and
pieces of information add up to? That something was seriously amiss:

> We need a judiciary inquiry of the kind given to Sukhomlinov. When we
> accused Sukhomlinov, after all, we did not have in our possession the facts that
> the inquiry would uncover. We had what we have now: the instinctive voice
> of the entire country and its subjective certainty.

On his visit to Paris and London, Miliukov went on, he had been told that the
Central Powers had access to Russia's most sensitive state secrets. This was
not the case when Sazonov ran foreign policy. Miliukov next mentioned a
meeting between Protopopov and a German businessman in Stockholm the
preceding spring (which was no secret and on which Protopopov had reported
to the Tsar), once again planting in the minds of his audience the ideas of
treason and separate peace. Referring to Stürmer's quitting the Duma earlier
that day, Miliukov exclaimed: "He heard the shouts with which you welcomed
his departure. Let us trust that he will never set foot here again!"

Reverting to the subject of his opening remarks, Miliukov said that once
there had been a possibility of cooperation between the Duma and government
but this was no longer the case. Citing Shuvaev's "I may be a fool, but I am
no traitor," Miliukov concluded his speech with a rhetorical flourish, repeated
several times. "Is it stupidity or is it treason" that Russia was unprepared to
conduct operations in the Balkans after Romania had entered the war on her
side? That she had delayed granting Poland autonomy until the Germans had
beaten her to it? That the government treated as sedition the Duma's efforts
to organize the home front? That the Police Department instigated factory
strikes and engaged in other "provocations" to provide an excuse for peace

negotiations? To each of these questions, the audience lustily responded: "Stupidity!" "Treason!" "Both!" But, Miliukov answered himself, it really did not matter, since the effect was the same. His parting words demanded the dismissal of the cabinet.

The "subjective certainty" which Miliukov claimed to possess of high officials' acts of collusion with the enemy had no basis in fact: to put it bluntly, it was a tissue of lies. Miliukov knew, even as he spoke, that neither Stürmer nor any other minister had committed treason, and that whatever his shortcomings, the Prime Minister was a loyal Russian. Later on, in his memoirs, he admitted as much.[77] Nevertheless, he felt morally justified slandering an innocent man and sowing the most damaging suspicions about the government because he thought it essential for the Kadets to take charge of the country before it fell apart.[78]

In reality, he contributed as much as anything the government did or failed to do to inflaming revolutionary passions. The effect of his speech, which attracted immense attention since he spoke for Russia's most important political party, was enhanced by his reputation as a prominent scholar: it seemed inconceivable that a man of his stature would make such grave accusations unless he had incontrovertible proof. Some Russians even believed that Miliukov received from Allied sources additional incriminating evidence which he withheld for security reasons. The government forbade the press to publish Miliukov's speech or to comment on it. The prohibition only served to heighten interest. Reproduced by typewriter, mimeographed, and printed on broadsheets, Miliukov's address is said to have spread in the rear and at the front in millions of copies.[79] It had an immense impact: "The people and the troops, simplifying the speech, concluded: Duma deputy Miliukov had proven that the Empress and Stürmer were selling out Russia to Kaiser Wilhelm."[80] The passions unleashed by Miliukov's speech played a major role in promoting the February Revolution,[81] in which anger over alleged government treason was initially the single most important motive.

The Duma sessions which followed brought the authorities little comfort. Shulgin, the leader of the Progressive Nationalists, said that the country which for two years had bravely fought the enemy "had come to be mortally afraid of its own government . . . the men who had fearlessly looked Hindenburg in the eye lost courage confronting Stürmer."[82] And the left applauded this monarchist and anti-Semite. The only speaker to defend the authorities was N. E. Markov (known as Markov II), a notorious reactionary and pathological Judeophobe, who later, in emigration, would back the Nazis: in this period he happened to receive regular subsidies from Protopopov.

The November 1–5, 1916, sessions of the Duma marked the onset of a revolutionary psychosis: an intensely felt, irrational desire to pull down the entire edifice of monarchic Russia. This psychosis, long prevalent among radical intellectuals, now seized the liberal center and even spilled into conservative ranks. General V. N. Voeikov, who observed this phenomenon from headquarters at Mogilev, speaks of a "widespread conviction that something

had to be broken and annihilated—a conviction that tormented people and
gave them no peace."[83] Another contemporary wrote in December 1916 of a
"siege of authority that has turned into sport."[84]

How pervasive this attitude had become may be demonstrated on the
behavior of the Tsar's immediate family, the grand dukes, who now lined up
with the Progressive Bloc. In late October, before the Duma had met, Nicholas
spent some days in Kiev with his mother and several relatives, who warned
him against the influence of his wife and Rasputin.[85] On November 1, he
received at headquarters Grand Duke Nikolai Mikhailovich, who, besides
being a well-known amateur historian, took pride in his reputation as the most
radical of the Romanovs, the Russian Philippe-Egalité. He brought a letter
addressed to the Tsar in which he implored him to be rid of Rasputin. But he
went further, alluding to the evil influence of the Empress, an issue obviously
of the greatest delicacy:

> You trust Alexandra Fedorovna, this is quite natural. Still, what she tells you
> is not the truth; she is only repeating what has been cleverly insinuated to her.
> If you are not able to remove this influence from her, at least protect yourself
> from constant systematic maneuvers attempted through the intermediacy of
> the wife you love. . . . When the hour comes—and it is already near—from the
> height of the throne you could make the ministers responsible to yourself and
> to the legislative institutions, and to do that simply, naturally, without pressure
> from the outside, and differently from the memorable act of October 17, 1905.
> . . . You stand on the eve of an era of new troubles, on the eve of an era of
> outrages [*attentats.*] Believe me, if I insist so much of your freeing yourself from
> the chains that have been forged, I do so . . . only in the hope of saving you
> and saving the throne of our dear country from the irreparable.[86]

Without bothering to read it, Nicholas forwarded the letter to Alexandra,
whom it sent into a paroxysm of rage: she asked that Nikolai Mikhailovich
be exiled from Petrograd.[87]

On November 7, the Tsar received Grand Duke Nikolai Nikolaevich,
now in command of the Caucasian Front, who urged him to let the Duma
choose the cabinet.[88] Incredibly, even the United Nobility, the staunchest pillar
of the monarchy, passed in Moscow and in Petrograd resolutions supporting
the program of the Progressive Bloc.[89] Indeed, it would be difficult to find any
prominent individual or group, including those on the most conservative,
nationalist end of the political spectrum, who did not join in the clamor for
fundamental changes in the structure and personnel of the government.

Stürmer felt justified, not only on personal grounds but also those of state
security, to request that the Duma be dissolved and Miliukov placed under
arrest.[90] But he did not find the support he had expected: the Tsar and the
cabinet were paralyzed with fear. In the Council of Ministers only Protopopov
sided with him. The others wanted to avoid anything rash. Nicholas did not
want a break with the Duma and sought to appease it without giving in on
the critical issue of a responsible ministry. On November 4 he sent the Minis-

ters of War and of the Navy to the Duma to deliver conciliatory speeches.[91] Alexandra was urging him to stand firm, but Nicholas no longer had the will. So instead of defending his Prime Minister against slanderous accusations— whose real target was the Crown—he decided to sacrifice him and put in his place someone more acceptable to the Duma. On November 8, Stürmer was dismissed. He never understood what had happened to him, why he was accused of treason which he had not committed, and why the Tsar did not defend him against these false charges. Shortly afterward, the French Ambassador saw him on the street, shuffling along, lost in thought.[92] He died the following year, a broken man.

The Duma rejoiced over Stürmer's dismissal, which it took as proof that no minister whom it did not want could stay in office.[93] This feeling received encouragement from the appointment, as Stürmer's successor, of the Minister of Transport, A. F. Trepov. The new Prime Minister, relatively young (fifty-two) by the standards of the late Imperial government—which saw in dotage assurance of loyalty—descended of an old servitor family. He wanted to emulate Stolypin, being similarly convinced that Russia could no longer be properly governed without the parliament's cooperation. To secure it, he was prepared to make far-reaching concessions: forming a cabinet acceptable to the Duma, putting a stop to legislating through Article 87, and improving the status of workers, Jews, and Finns.[94] In private meetings with Duma leaders during the recess (November 6–17), he obtained promises of support, on condition that he get rid of Protopopov.

In the first half of November 1916, Nicholas, for all practical purposes, capitulated to revolutionary demands; to his entourage he appeared apathetic and indifferent.[95] If Russia's liberal politicians had been able to view the situation rationally, they would have realized that they had achieved, in substance if not in form, their principal demands. By firing Stürmer for no good cause and replacing him with a Prime Minister amenable to the program of the Progressive Bloc, by keeping the revolutionary Duma in session instead of dissolving it, the Tsar had surrendered to the opposition. But the opposition, smelling blood, wanted more.

For all his good intentions, therefore, Trepov had little success. On November 19, when the Duma reconvened, he delivered to it a programmatic speech. The left, led by Kerensky and Chkheidze, received him with abusive screams that went on for forty minutes during which he could not utter a word.* When order was finally restored, he gave a conciliatory address very reminiscent, in tone and content, of Stolypin's Duma speeches. He promised to put an end to illegality. He asked for help:

> Let us forget our quarrels, let us postpone our feuds. . . . In the name of the government, I declare directly and openly that it wishes to commit its energies to constructive, pragmatic work in cooperation with the legislature.[96]

*Diakin, *Russkaia burzhuaziia,* 251. The most vociferous of the hecklers, Kerensky and Chkheidze among them, were suspended by Rodzianko for fifteen days.

The duty of patriots was not to destroy the government but to strengthen it. Trepov used the occasion to reveal that the Allies had promised Russia Constantinople and the Straits.

It was to no avail. Heckled and disrupted, Trepov faced an audience that spurned conciliation: now that Stürmer had been sacrificed, it wanted Protopopov's head. When he had finished, Vladimir Purishkevich asked for the floor. Cheered on by the socialists, this extreme monarchist demanded that the government cease "selling Russia out to the Germans" and rid itself of Rasputin and "Rasputinism."

The sessions that followed gave no sign that passions were cooling. The radical deputies now shed such few inhibitions as had constrained them in the past and openly incited the country to rebellion. The Mensheviks and the other socialists walked out of parliament on December 2, after the Progressive Bloc had unanimously supported the government's rejection of German proposals for a separate peace. Two weeks later, Kerensky exhorted the population to disobey the government.[97]

Nor did Trepov obtain countervailing support from the Court. Alexandra intrigued against him out of fear of losing influence. In letters to Nicholas she branded him a liar who deserved to be hanged.[98] Nicholas for once ignored his wife's advice and agreed with Trepov that Protopopov had to go. On November 11, he informed Alexandra that Protopopov was unwell and would be replaced: he asked her not to involve Rasputin in this matter because the responsibility for the decision was entirely his. Alarmed, Alexandra requested Nicholas by telegram not to act until they had had a chance to talk, and the next day departed with the children for Mogilev. Face to face, she promptly turned her husband around. When Trepov arrived in Mogilev to have the Tsar approve Protopopov's successor, Nicholas curtly informed him that Protopopov would stay, after all. Not even Trepov's threat of resignation would make him relent. A. I. Spiridovich cites this incident as the most glaring example of Rasputin's influence.[99]

As 1916 drew to a close, all the political parties and groupings united in opposition to the monarchy. They agreed on little else. The extreme left would be satisfied with nothing short of a radical transformation of Russia's political, social, and economic system. Liberals and liberal-conservatives would have been content with parliamentary democracy. Both, for all their differences, thought in terms of institutions. The extreme right, which by now had also joined the opposition, by contrast, dwelled on personalities. In its view, Russia's crisis was the fault, not of the system, but of the individuals in charge, notably the "German" Empress and Rasputin. Once these two were out of the way, all would be well. It was not possible to get at the Empress directly, since this would have required a palace coup, but some monarchists believed they could attain the same end by isolating her from Rasputin. Alexandra's well-known emotional attachment to the *starets* suggested that separation from him would induce in her a psychic breakdown. Freed from his wife's baneful influence, Nicholas would come to his senses and yield power to the Duma. Should he fail to do so, he could be replaced with a regent chosen from among the grand dukes, most likely Nikolai Nikolaevich. Such talk was common in November and December of 1916 in the capital's highest social circles: at the Yacht Club, frequented by the grand dukes, in the halls of the Duma and the State Council among monarchist deputies, in aristocratic salons, even at Army Headquarters in Mogilev. It was a repetition of February 1801 when the plot against Paul I, which ended in his murder, was the talk of St. Petersburg society.

Rasputin was a natural target of right-wing critics because of his influence on the Imperial couple and through them, on ministerial appointments. Stürmer, Protopopov, and Shuvaev, holders of the most important posts in the administration, owed their positions to him. True, his protege Stürmer was replaced by an enemy, Trepov, but even so it was widely believed that crossing Rasputin's path meant a broken career. Rasputin was even suspected of meddling in military operations. Indeed, in November 1915 he had given, through the Empress, strategic advice to headquarters. "Before I forget," Alexandra wrote Nicholas on November 15, 1915,

> I must give you a message from our Friend, prompted by what he saw last night. He begs you to *order* that one should *advance near Riga,* says it is necessary otherwise the Germans will settle down so firmly through all the winter, that it will cost endless bloodshed and trouble to make them move.[100]

Neither Nicholas nor his generals paid attention to such counsel. Rasputin was strictly forbidden to come near headquarters. Still, the fact that this semiliterate peasant felt free to give advice on military matters incensed the conservatives.

At Tsarskoe Selo, his word was law. Rasputin frequently prophesied that should any harm befall him, Russia would go through another Time of Troubles. He had visions of rivers of blood, of fire and smoke, an uncanny and rationally inexplicable foreboding of what would soon, in fact, occur.[101] His predictions alarmed the Empress and made her more than ever anxious to protect him from his enemies, who, in her eyes, were also the enemies of the dynasty and of Russia.

Rasputin basked in his power. His drinking bouts, his boasting and insolence, grew more scandalous with each day. Ladies of high society were fascinated by the brute with the hypnotic eyes and gift of prophesy. Rasputin belonged to the sect of Khlysty, who preached that sinning reduced the quantity of sin in the world. At his private villa, with the ever-present gypsies, liquor flowed freely. Whether Rasputin really possessed the sexual prowess with which he was credited is more than questionable. A physician named R. R. Vreden, who examined him in 1914 after he had been knifed by a jealous mistress, found Rasputin's genitals shriveled, like those of a very old man, which led him to wonder whether he was even capable of the sexual act: he ascribed this to the effects of alcohol and syphilis.*

Rasputin could behave so scandalously because he felt above the law. In March 1915, the chief of the Corps of Gendarmes, V. F. Dzhunkovskii, had the courage to inform the Tsar that his agents had overheard Rasputin boast at a dinner party in Moscow's Praga Restaurant that he "could do anything he wanted" with the Empress. His reward was to be sacked and sent to the front. After this incident, the police thought it prudent to keep to itself adverse information on Rasputin. Sycophants and aspirants to office fawned on him; honest patriots risked disgrace if they dared to incur his displeasure. Guchkov and Polivanov, who had done the most to revitalize Russia's war effort after the debacle of 1915, were kept at arm's length and, in the case of Polivanov, fired because of Rasputin's enmity. That such a charlatan had a hold on the monarchy offended the monarchists most of all.

Nicholas's attitude toward Rasputin was ambivalent. He told Protopopov that while he had not cared for Rasputin at first, in time he had grown "accustomed to him."[102] He rarely saw the *starets,* however, leaving him to Alexandra, who always received Rasputin in company, usually that of Vyrubova. Nicholas told Kokovtsov in 1912 that "personally he hardly knew 'this peasant' [*muzhichek*], having met him, in passing, no more than two or three times, and, moreover, at considerable intervals."[103] Even so, the Tsar would not listen to any criticism of Rasputin, treating him strictly as "une affaire de famille," as he told Stolypin, requesting him never again to allude to this matter.[104] Rasputin was a "family affair" in the sense that he had the unique ability to stop the bleeding of the tsarevich, whose illness never left the family's thoughts. The imperial children adored the old man. But Nicholas insisted Rasputin stay out of politics.[105]

By the end of 1916, the Imperial couple had concluded that the opposition, determined to unseat them, attacked their appointees and friends as a matter of principle: every choice of the monarchy, whatever his merits, was bound to come under fire. The true target of these attacks was the dynasty. That this was so Nicholas and Alexandra concluded from the example of Protopopov, who had been named to placate the opposition but upon assuming office became the target of its abuse. Alexandra wrote Nicholas:

> Remember that the question is not Protop[opov] or X, Y, Z. The question is *the monarchy and your prestige.* . . . Don't think that it will end with this. They will remove one after another all who are *devoted to you,* and then, ourselves.[106]

When Rodzianko assured Nicholas that Protopopov was mad, the Tsar responded, smiling: "Probably from the time I appointed him minister."[107] The

---

*Archive of S. E. Kryzhanovskii, Box 5, File "Rasputin," Bakhmeteff Archive, Columbia University, New York, N.Y. Vyrubova dismisses gossip of his alleged sexual excesses, saying that he was entirely unlovable and that she knew of no woman who had had an affair with him: Anna Viroubova, *Souvenirs de ma vie* (Paris, 1927), 115.

29. Rasputin with children in his Siberian village.

same held true for Rasputin. Alexandra, and to some extent her husband, came to believe that enemies abused their "Friend" only to get at them.

Rasputin's influence reached its apogee late in 1916 following an unsuccessful attempt to bribe him. Trepov was told by the Duma leaders that the price for their cooperation was the removal of Protopopov. He accordingly informed Protopopov that he wished him to give up the Ministry of the Interior and take over that of Commerce. As soon as he learned of this development, Rasputin concluded that a Trepov-Rodzianko intrigue was in the making and intervened with the Empress on Protopopov's behalf.[108] Protopopov stayed on the job. The incident persuaded Trepov that unless Rasputin was removed he would not be able to carry out his duties. Rasputin was known to take bribes left and right: Protopopov alone paid him a monthly subsidy of 1,000 rubles from the funds of the Department of Police.[109] Aware of these facts, Trepov decided to tempt Rasputin with a bribe to end all bribes. Using as intermediary his brother-in-law, General A. A. Mosolov, who happened to be one of Rasputin's drinking companions, he offered Rasputin up to 200,000 rubles in cash as well as a monthly allowance, if he would return to Siberia and stay out of politics. Rasputin promised to consider the offer, but

sensing an opportunity to bring down Trepov and enhance his own reputation
with the Court, he informed the Empress. This marked the beginning of the
end for Trepov.[110] Rasputin's prestige at the Court rose commensurately, for
he now had proven that he was, indeed, an "incorruptible man of the people."

The failure of Trepov's maneuver persuaded right-wing enemies of Rasputin that they had no choice but to kill him. A conspiracy was hatched in
Petrograd in early November, before Trepov's ill-fated venture, and got underway the following month. Implicated were persons from the very highest strata
of St. Petersburg society, including a grand duke and the husband of a grand
duchess. The central figure was twenty-nine-year-old Prince Felix Iusupov.
Educated in Oxford, handsome in an effeminate way, an admirer of Oscar
Wilde, he was known as a superstitious coward. Iusupov initially hoped to
influence Rasputin to change his ways and to this end befriended him, but
when this effort failed, he decided on drastic action, having become convinced
that Rasputin was drugging the Tsar as well as maintaining contact with
enemy agents. His mother, Zinaida Iusupov-Elston, the richest woman in
Russia (her family income for 1914 was estimated at 1.3 million rubles, equivalent to nearly one ton of gold), had once been friendly with the Empress, but
the two had fallen out over Rasputin. Suggestions have been made that it was
she who persuaded her apolitical son to organize the plot.[111] But it is more
likely that the main influence on Iusupov was twenty-five-year-old Grand
Duke Dmitrii Pavlovich, a favorite nephew of the Tsar and a leading contender for the hand of Grand Duchess Olga, who filled Iusupov's head with
stories of Rasputin's alleged treachery.

Once he had made up his mind to kill Rasputin, Iusupov looked for
accomplices.* Having heard Vasilii Maklakov attack Rasputin in the Duma,
Iusupov invited him to join the conspiracy. He assured Maklakov that no later
than two weeks after Rasputin's death, the Empress would be confined to a
mental institution:

> Her spiritual balance depends entirely on Rasputin: the instant he is gone, it
> will disintegrate. And once the Emperor has been freed of Rasputin's and his
> wife's influence, everything will change: he will turn into a good constitutional
> monarch.[112]

Iusupov told Maklakov that he intended to hire either revolutionary terrorists
or professional assassins, but Maklakov dissuaded him: if the deed must be
done—and he did not dispute that—then Iusupov and his accomplices had to
do it. Maklakov offered to provide advice and legal help, but regretted being
unable personally to take part in Rasputin's murder, because on the night

---

*There exist two eyewitness accounts of Rasputin's murder. Purishkevich wrote down his
recollections in diary form two days after the event, which he published in southern Russia in 1918;
this version was reprinted in Moscow in 1923 as *Ubiistvo Rasputina.* Iusupov's memoirs, *Konets
Rasputina,* came out in Paris four years later. Of secondary accounts, the most informative is that
by A. S. Spiridovich (*Raspoutine,* Paris, 1935): the author, a general in the Corps of Gendarmes,
was Commandant of the Guard at the Imperial residence in Tsarskoe Selo.

when it was to occur (December 16) he had a speaking engagement in Moscow. "Just in case," he gave Iusupov a rubber truncheon with a lead tip.

Iusupov next contacted Purishkevich, who had become persuaded from conversations with the military that the government was leading the country to disaster. Early in November, he used his private Red Cross trains to distribute Miliukov's speech among frontline troops. On November 3 he dined with Nicholas at headquarters and pleaded with him to be rid of the new False Pretender, as he called Rasputin.[113] The Duma speech which Purishkevich delivered against Rasputin on November 19 was second only to Miliukov's in the attention it received nationwide. Iusupov listened to it from the gallery and two days later contacted him. Purishkevich unhesitatingly agreed to join.[114] Two additional persons were brought in: a young lieutenant and a physician named Lazavert, who served on Purishkevich's train. Grand Duke Dmitrii, the fifth member of the group, was of invaluable assistance because his status as member of the Imperial family gave the conspirators immunity from police searches. The plotters were anything but tight-lipped. A number of outsiders, among them a visiting British diplomat, Samuel Hoare, knew well in advance what was about to happen.[115] Purishkevich boasted to more than one acquaintance that on December 16 he would assassinate Rasputin.[116]

The plan was to commit the murder in such a way as to give the impression that Rasputin was not dead but had disappeared. Iusupov, who had the victim's confidence, was to lure him to his palatial residence on the Moika, poison him, and with the help of associates tracelessly dispose of the corpse. Detailed preparations were made in late November. The conspirators pledged never to divulge what they had done—a pledge that both Purishkevich and Iusupov would break.

The date for the murder was set for the night of December 16–17, the eve of the closing session of the Duma.

Rasputin had received many warnings of a plot on his life and was not easily enticed from his apartment at Gorokhovaia 64, where he lived under the protection of the police and his own bodyguards. Nevertheless, on December 13 he agreed to visit Iusupov to make the acquaintance of his wife, Irina, a niece of the Tsar. On the fatal day, Rasputin received explicit warnings from Protopopov, Vyrubova, and anonymous callers. He seems to have had premonitions, for he was said during these days to have destroyed his correspondence, made deposits in his daughters' bank accounts, and spent much time in prayer.[117]

It was arranged that Iusupov would arrive at Rasputin's house by car at midnight, after the police guards had been withdrawn, and come up through the back stair. Rasputin attired himself for the occasion in his most seductive clothing: wide trousers of black velvet, new leather boots, a white silk shirt with blue embroidery, and a satin waistband decorated in gold, a gift from the Empress.[118] Iusupov recalled that he exuded a powerful odor of cheap soap and looked cleaner than he had ever seen him.

Iusupov pulled up at Gorokhovaia 64 shortly past midnight in Purish-

kevich's car, driven by Dr. Lazavert disguised as a chauffeur. Rasputin put on
a beaver hat and rubber boots. They then drove to Iusupov's residence. The
conspirators had carefully prepared the scene of the crime. Iusupov led his
guest to a room on the ground floor which normally stood empty but which
had now been furnished to look like a salon: scattered teacups and wineglasses
gave the impression that a party had recently taken place there. Iusupov said
that his wife was upstairs but would soon come down to join them (in reality,
she was in the Crimea, a thousand miles away). Iusupov's fellow conspirators
were gathered in the room directly above, which served as a study and was
linked to the ground floor by a narrow staircase. From there came the sounds
of "Yankee Doodle" played over and over on a gramophone. While pretending
to await his wife, Iusupov offered Rasputin refreshments from a nearby table,
on which stood a tray with almond and chocolate pastries: Dr. Lazavert had
inserted into the chocolate cakes powerful doses of powdered potassium cya-
nide. A bottle of Rasputin's favorite Madeira was also available, and next to
it glasses with the same poison in liquid form. Annoyed at being kept waiting,
Rasputin refused to drink or eat, but Iusupov eventually cajoled him into
partaking of the pastries and wine. He waited anxiously for the poison to take
effect (according to the physician, this should have happened within fifteen
minutes) and at Rasputin's request sang to the accompaniment of a guitar.
Rasputin seemed a bit unwell but he did not collapse. The alarmed Iusupov
excused himself and went upstairs. By now, two hours had passed since
Rasputin's arrival.

A consultation took place in the second-floor dining room. Grand Duke
Dmitrii thought it best to let Rasputin go and try again some other time. But
the others would not hear of it: Rasputin was not to be allowed to leave alive.
Iusupov offered to shoot Rasputin. He borrowed Dmitrii's revolver and returned to the ground floor, the weapon concealed behind his back. Rasputin
looked thoroughly sick and was breathing heavily, but a sip of Madeira revived
him and he suggested a visit to the gypsies—"with God in mind but mankind
in the flesh."[119] Like many murderers, Iusupov had a dread of his victim's eyes:
being superstitious, he also feared that Rasputin could be as impervious to
bullets as to poison. To ward off evil spirits, he invited Rasputin to inspect an
elaborate seventeenth-century Italian crucifix made of rock crystal and silver
which stood on a commode. As Rasputin bent over it and crossed himself,
Iusupov fired into his side. With a wild scream, Rasputin fell to the floor.

The instant they heard the shot, the conspirators rushed down. They saw
Iusupov bending over the body. In Iusupov's recollection, Rasputin was dead,
but Purishkevich recalled him writhing in agony and still breathing. Dmitrii,
Dr. Lazavert, and the lieutenant departed in Purishkevich's car to the Warsaw
Railroad Terminal to dispose of Rasputin's overcoat and rubber boots in the
stove of his Red Cross train. Purishkevich and Iusupov, awaiting their return,
relaxed in the study.

According to his memoirs, Iusupov was suddenly seized with an urge to
see Rasputin's body. Rasputin lay motionless, to all appearances dead. But on

scrutinizing the victim's face more closely, Iusupov noticed the left eye twitch and open, followed by the right: Rasputin stared at him with boundless hatred. As Iusupov watched in disbelief, frozen with fear, Rasputin struggled to his feet and seized him by the throat, screaming through foaming lips, "Felix, Felix!" Iusupov managed to tear himself away and run upstairs, where Purishkevich was enjoying a cigar. As Purishkevich recalled the scene:

> Iusupov was literally faceless: his lovely large blue eyes were still larger and bulging. Half conscious, virtually oblivious of me, seemingly out of mind, he flung himself at the door leading to the main hall and ran to his parents' apartment . . .[120]

Purishkevich seized his gun and rushed downstairs. Rasputin was gone. He found him in the garden, staggering through the snow toward the gate, bellowing, "Felix, Felix, I will tell everything to the Empress!" He fired at him but missed. He fired again and missed again. Rasputin was nearing the gate leading to the street. Steadying his arm, Purishkevich fired a third shot, which felled Rasputin. He shot him one more time and, bending over the lifeless body, kicked it in the temple.

A short time later a policeman who had been patrolling the neighborhood appeared and said that he had heard shots. Iusupov explained that a party had just broken up and some revelers had fired in the air. But as bad luck would have it, police officers at a nearby station at Moika 61 had also heard the sounds of shooting and soon more policemen appeared. Purishkevich, who never could control his tongue, blurted out: "We have killed Rasputin."

The sight of Rasputin's lifeless corpse in the snow drove Iusupov into a frenzy. He ran up to his study and brought out of the desk drawer the truncheon which Maklakov had given him. With it he beat the body like a man possessed, screaming, "Felix, Felix!" He then collapsed in a faint. On regaining consciousness, he ordered a servant to shoot one of the dogs to provide an alibi.

With the help of domestics, Rasputin's body was tied and weighed down with iron chains. Loaded into Dmitrii's car, it was driven to a remote and sparsely populated spot, the bridge linking Krestinskii and Petrovskii islands, and dumped into the Malaia Moika canal, along with his coat, which had not been destroyed because it was too large to fit into Purishkevich's train stove. Dr. Lazavert, noting the victim's rubber boots in the car, threw them into the canal, but he missed and one of them fell on the bridge, where its subsequent discovery led the police to Rasputin's body.

The news of Rasputin's death spread rapidly: the French Ambassador claims to have heard it before the day was out. The Empress received from Protopopov a fairly accurate account of what had happened, but as long as the corpse had not been found she continued to believe that Rasputin was hiding. On December 17, she wrote Nicholas: "I cannot & *won't* believe He has been killed. God have mercy." She drew some encouragement from Iusupov's letter in which he flatly denied any knowledge of Rasputin's whereabouts and indignantly rejected accusations of complicity in his murder.[121] In the city, however, Rasputin's death was taken for granted and joyously celebrated. Dmitrii, who attended the theater on the evening of December 17, had to leave because the public was about to give him an ovation.[122] One contemporary says that the atmosphere in Petrograd resembled Easter, as the rich toasted with champagne and the poor with such drink as they could lay their hands on.[123] *"Sobake sobachaia smert' "* ("For a dog, a dog's death"), the French envoy heard the people say.*

Rasputin's battered corpse, encased in ice, was dragged out on December 19. The autopsy revealed the victim had been dead from three bullet wounds by the time he struck water, which did not stop the spread of legends that the lungs were filled with water. No traces of poison were found.† At Alexandra's wish, Rasputin was buried in Tsarskoe Selo, outside the palace grounds, on land belonging to Vyrubova, and a chapel constructed over it, although officially he was reported to have been taken for burial to Siberia. Immediately after the outbreak of the February Revolution the body was disinterred, burned, and the ashes scattered.[124]

It fell to General Voeikov, the Tsar's aide, to communicate to him the news of Rasputin's death. In his recollections, he described Nicholas's reaction as follows:

> From the very first report, about Rasputin's mysterious disappearance, to the last, about the placement of his body in the chapel . . . I did not once observe signs of sorrow in His Majesty, but rather gathered the impression that he experienced a sense of relief.[125]

Iusupov claims having heard from people who traveled with Nicholas to Tsarskoe on December 18–19 that the Tsar was "in a happy mood such as he had not shown since the outbreak of the war."[126] In fact, in his diary for December 17–19 Nicholas made no reference to Rasputin, and noted that on the night of December 18–19 he had "slept soundly."[127]

It so happened that Nicholas had planned, before Rasputin's murder, to return home to be with the family for Christmas. The Okhrana now encouraged him to do so from fear that Rasputin could be the first victim of a terrorist campaign.[128] Indeed, as will be discussed later, several conspiracies against Nicholas were in progress.

---

*According to Miliukov and Maklakov, however, tales of popular rejoicing at Rasputin's death are "an aristocratic legend"; in reality, ordinary people were troubled by the murder: Spiridovich, *Raspoutine,* 413–15.

†The absence of poison in Rasputin's remains must mean that, in fact, it had not been inserted into the wine and pastries. The records of the judiciary inquiry into the Rasputin murder were offered for sale in Germany sometime in the interwar period by the firm of Karl W. Hiersemann (*Originalakten zum Mord an Rasputin,* Leipzig, n.d., Library of Congress, DK 254.R3H5), but their present whereabouts are unknown. The advertisement (pp. 8–9) confirms that the autopsy revealed no traces of poison.

Rasputin's death had the contrary result from the one the assassins had expected. They had intended to separate Nicholas from Alexandra and make him more amenable to Duma pressures. Instead, Rasputin's murder drew him closer to his wife and confirmed the correctness of her belief that there could be no compromises with the opposition. He was revolted by the involvement of his nephew Dmitrii in a murder plot and disgusted by the cowardly lies of Iusupov. "I am ashamed before Russia," he said, "that the hands of my relations should be smeared with the blood of this peasant."[129] After Dmitrii's involvement became known, he ordered him to Persia to join the Russian armies there. He was appalled by the reaction of high society to this punishment. When sixteen grand dukes and duchesses pleaded with him to allow Dmitrii to remain in Russia, he responded: "No one is entitled to engage in murder."[130] The petition compromised in his eyes many of the grand dukes and led him to cut off relations with them. Some, among them Nikolai Mikhailovich, were asked to leave Petrograd. To ingratiate himself with the Imperial couple, Protopopov would show Nicholas and Alexandra congratulatory messages sent by prominent public figures to Purishkevich and Iusupov intercepted by the police: among them was one from Rodzianko's wife.[131] This evidence embittered Nicholas and reinforced his sense of isolation.*

Trepov was dismissed in late December and replaced by Prince N. D. Golitsyn, who would be the last Prime Minister of the old regime. Aware that he was utterly unsuited for the job, Golitsyn begged to be spared on the grounds of ill health, old age, and inexperience, but the Tsar would not hear of it. By then, the cabinet, for all practical purposes, had ceased to function anyway, so that the office of Prime Minister had become largely ceremonial.

The Imperial family, having taken up residence in the more intimate Alexander Palace at Tsarskoe Selo, led a quiet life after the return of Nicholas. They broke off contact with most of the family: at Christmas of 1916, there were no exchanges of gifts. Protopopov came once or twice a week with his reports, which were subtly attuned to the Imperial couple's mood, as conveyed to him by Vyrubova.[132] He was invariably reassuring: rumors of plots against the Imperial family were groundless, the country was quiet, and the government disposed of ample force to quell any disorders. To make these assurances more convincing, Protopopov organized letter-writing campaigns from ordinary people who told the Court of their love and loyalty and opposition to political changes: these Alexandra proudly displayed to visitors.[133] They helped reinforce Nicholas and his wife in the conviction that all the troublemakers lived in the capital. The fact that an unusually severe winter had brought railway traffic in some parts of the country to a virtual standstill, further depleting food and fuel supplies in the cities, went unreported. So did the fact that workers

---

*The assassins of Rasputin were never tried, apparently owing to the intercession of the Dowager Empress. After spending some time with the Russian forces in Persia, Dmitrii went to England, where he led a carefree life among the British aristocracy. He later married an American heiress. His diaries, deposited at the Houghton Library, Harvard, show no concern for his native country. Iusupov, who was exiled to one of his estates, eventually made his way to the West. Purishkevich was arrested by the Bolsheviks and then released. He later joined the White armies and died in France in 1920.

in Petrograd, driven to desperation by shortages and high prices and locked out of their factories, were roaming the streets. So, too, did information obtained by the Police Department that conspiracies were being hatched to arrest Nicholas and force him to abdicate. Everything was under control, the genial Minister of the Interior assured the Imperial couple.

Life at Tsarskoe Selo followed a quiet, dull routine. The Empress spent much time in bed, attended by Vyrubova, who, for her own protection, had moved into the Alexander Palace. Nicholas sank into a depression, of which his furrowed face and expressionless eyes bore testimony. In the morning and afternoon he went through the motions of receiving officials and foreign diplomats: on such occasions, Alexandra eavesdropped from a back room reached by a secret passage.[134] In the late afternoon, he took walks and sometimes rode with the children in a motorized sled built by one of the chauffeurs. In the evening, he read aloud from the Russian classics, played dominoes, worked on puzzles, and from time to time viewed moving pictures: the last film shown, early in February, was *Madame Du Barry*.[135] Some visitors tried to warn the Imperial couple of an impending explosion. Alexandra reacted with anger, sometimes ordering the bearers of such unwelcome news to leave. Nicholas listened politely, fidgeting with a cigarette or studying his fingernails, without displaying great interest. He was deaf to the appeals of Grand Duke Aleksander Mikhailovich, his brother-in-law and father of Irina Iusupova, one of the few grand dukes with whom he remained on speaking terms.[136] When foreigners offered him advice, he cut them short. The British Ambassador, Sir George Buchanan, on a New Year's Eve call urged Nicholas to appoint as Prime Minister someone enjoying the nation's confidence, to which the Tsar responded: "Do you mean that *I* am to regain the confidence of my people or that they are to regain *my* confidence?"*

Power in his instance did not so much corrupt as isolate.

A frequent visitor to Tsarskoe Selo during those last weeks says that the atmosphere there resembled a household in mourning.[137] The Tsar's diaries, which he kept up regularly, give no hint of the state of his mind or psyche: only on December 31, the day when he saw the British Ambassador and dismissed rumors of danger, he noted that he and Alexandra had prayed fervently to the Lord "to have mercy on Russia."[138] On January 5, 1917, Golitsyn reported to him that Moscow talked openly of the "next tsar," to which Nicholas responded: "The Empress and I know that all is in God's hands—His will be done."[139]

Nicholas, who was always perfectly composed, only once lost self-control

---

*G. Buchanan, *My Mission to Russia*, II (Boston, 1923), 45–46; cf. A. I. Spiridovich, *Velikaia voina i fevral'skaia revoliutsiia, 1914–1917 gg.*, III (New York, 1962), 14. Buchanan, however, is not an entirely reliable witness. According to his Buchanan's daughter, Nicholas further said that rumors of impending unrest were exaggerated and that the army would save him: Meriel Buchanan, *Petrograd, the City of Trouble* (London, 1918), 81. Nicholas received from the police information that the British Embassy was in contact with anti-government groups in the Duma and even providing them with financial assistance: V. N. Voeikov, *S tsarem i bez tsaria* (Helsingfors, 1936), 175.

to reveal under his habitually frozen mask a deeply troubled human being. This occurred on January 7, 1917, during a visit by Rodzianko. He listened politely to the familiar warnings, asked some questions, but when Rodzianko pleaded with him "not [to] compel the people to choose between you and the good of the country," Nicholas "pressed his head between his hands," and said: "Is it possible that for twenty-two years I tried to work for the best, and that for twenty-two years it was all a mistake?"[140]

Having failed in their attempt to alter policy by disposing of Rasputin, the conservatives concluded that "the only way to save the monarchy was to remove the monarch."[141] Two conspiracies to this end have been identified, but there must have been more. One was organized by Guchkov. According to his memoirs, Guchkov concluded that the incipient Russian Revolution would not follow the French model of 1848, in which the workers toppled the monarchy and let the "better people" take charge. In Russia he expected power to pass into the hands of revolutionaries who would in no time drive her to ruin. Hence, arrangements had to be made for a legitimate transfer of Imperial authority from Nicholas to his minor son, Alexis, with the Tsar's brother, Grand Duke Michael, serving as Regent. Guchkov involved in his plot Nicholas Nekrasov, the deputy chairman of the Duma and member of the Progressive Bloc, M. I. Tereshchenko, a wealthy businessman, and Prince D. L. Viazemskii. The conspirators planned to seize the Imperial train while it was en route from headquarters to Tsarskoe Selo and force Nicholas to abdicate in favor of his son.[142] The plot did not make much headway because it failed to secure a broad base of support, especially among the senior officers.

More advanced was a second plot directed by Prince George Lvov, the chairman of Zemgor and the future Prime Minister of the First Provisional Government, with the assistance of the chief of staff, General Alekseev.[143] This group planned to compel Alexandra to retire to the Crimea and to have Nicholas turn over effective authority to Grand Duke Nikolai Nikolaevich. The plotters contacted the Grand Duke, then serving as commander on the Caucasian Front, through A. I. Khatisov, the mayor of Tiflis. Nikolai Nikolaevich requested a day to consider the proposal, then turned it down on the grounds that neither the peasants nor the soldiers would understand such a change. Khatisov sent Lvov a cable with the agreed code for a negative response: "The hospital cannot be opened." It is indicative of the mood of the time that Nikolai Nikolaevich did not see fit to inform his sovereign of the plot against him.

There were all kinds of rumors of "Decembrist" conspiracies among Guard officers and of a terrorist plot on the Imperial couple,[144] but none of these ever seems to have gone beyond the talking stage.

Protopopov, basking in his moment of glory as de facto Prime Minister of the Russian Empire, exuded confidence—a fact that caused many contemporaries to question his sanity. He did not worry about the plots against the Imperial family reported by the police: he dismissed the plotters, with good reason, as idle talkers. The village was quiet. It was another threat that troubled him, although he felt confident he could handle it. The Duma was scheduled to reconvene on February 14 for a twelve-day session. The police informed him that "society" talked of nothing else and that convening the Duma could provide an occasion for massive anti-government demonstrations; proroguing it, however, could produce a wave of popular protests. The police felt it essential to prevent street demonstrations, lest they provoke clashes with the police and trigger a revolt. K. I. Globachev, the highest police official in Petrograd, advised Protopopov on January 26 that the leaders of the opposition, among whom he listed Guchkov, Konovalov, and Lvov, already regarded themselves as the legitimate government and were distributing ministerial portfolios.[145] Protopopov wanted authority to arrest Guchkov, Konovalov, and the other political oppositionists, along with the Central Workers' Group, which they intended to use for mass demonstrations.[146] He would dearly have liked to take into custody Guchkov and three hundred "troublemakers" whom he viewed as the soul of the incipient rebellion, but he did not dare. So he did the next-best thing and ordered the arrest of the Workers' Group, which by this time (the end of January) had turned into an openly revolutionary body. Under the leadership of Gvozdev, the Workers' Group pursued a double policy, typical of the Mensheviks and, later, of the revived Petrograd Soviet, of which it was in some respects the immediate forerunner. On the one hand, it supported the war effort and helped the Central Military-Industrial Committee to maintain labor discipline in defense industries. On the other hand, it issued inflammatory appeals calling for the immediate abolition of the monarchy and its replacement by a democratic provisional government—that is, for a political revolution in the midst of the very war they wanted to pursue.[147] One of their proclamations, released on January 26, claimed that the government was exploiting the war to enslave the working class. Ending the war, however, would not improve the latter's situation "if carried out not by the people themselves but by the autocratic authority." Peace achieved by the monarchy will bring "yet more terrible chains":

> The working class and democracy can wait no longer. Every day that is allowed to pass brings danger: the decisive removal of the autocratic regime and the complete democratization of the country are tasks that must be solved without delay.

The proclamation concluded with a call for factory workers to prepare themselves for a "general organized" demonstration in front of Taurida Palace, the seat of the Duma, to demand the creation of a provisional government.[148]

This appeal stopped just short of calling for a violent overthrow of the government: but it was by any standard seditious. It is known that the Workers' Group indeed planned, almost certainly with the encouragement of Guchkov and other members of the Progressive Bloc, on the day of the opening session of the Duma to bring out hundreds of thousands of workers on the streets of Petrograd with calls for a radical change in government, the demonstration to be accompanied by massive work stoppages.[149] Protopopov was determined to prevent this.

On January 27, one day after the Workers' Group had issued its proclamation, its entire leadership was arrested and incarcerated in the Peter and Paul Fortress. Protopopov ignored the expressions of outrage from the business community, convinced that he had nipped in the bud a revolutionary coup planned for February 14. One month later, when the mobs freed the Workers' Group leaders from their prison, they would proceed directly to Taurida Palace and there help found the Petrograd Soviet.

After the arrest of the Workers' Group, Nicholas asked the onetime Minister of Justice Nicholas Maklakov to draft a manifesto dissolving the Duma. Elections to the new Duma—the Fifth—were to take place in December 1917, nearly a year later.[150] News of this proposed move reached the Duma, causing a great deal of excitement.[151]

To insure Petrograd against disturbances in connection with the opening of the Duma, Protopopov withdrew military control of the capital city from the Northern Front, whose commander, General N. V. Ruzskii, was regarded as sympathetic to the opposition. It was placed under a separate command headed by General S. S. Khabalov, an ataman of the Ural Cossacks.[152]

The measures produced the desired effect. The arrest of the Workers' Group and the stern warnings of Khabalov caused the February 14 pro-Duma demonstration to be called off. Even so, 90,000 workers in Petrograd struck that day and marched peacefully through the center of the city.[153]

In the meantime, the administration of the country was grinding to a halt. The Council of Ministers virtually ceased to function, as members absented themselves under one pretext or another, and even Protopopov failed to attend.[154] At this, the monarchy's most dangerous moment, the Department of Police was decapitated: General P. G. Kurlov, a personal friend of Protopopov's, whom the minister had invited to assume the post of director, met with strenuous opposition from the Duma, and after serving as acting director for a short time, retired without being replaced.[155] The chief of the Special Department (Osobyi Otdel) of the Police Department, charged with counterintelligence, I. P. Vasilev, later wrote that under Protopopov his office received no specific assignment.[156] The opposition was flouting government prohibitions on meetings and assemblies. Military censorship broke down in January 1917, as editors of newspapers and periodicals no longer bothered to submit advance copy to the Censor's office.[157]

None of this much troubled Protopopov, who was in regular communication with the spirit of Rasputin.[158]

8

The February Revolution

ollowing two mild winters, the winter of 1916–17 turned unseasonably cold: in Petrograd, the temperature in the first three months of 1917 averaged 12.1 degrees below zero centigrade (10 Fahrenheit) compared with 4.4 (40 F) degrees above zero the same time the previous year. In February 1917 it dropped to an average of minus 14.5 degrees (6 F). In Moscow it sank even lower, to 16.7 below zero (2 F).[1] The cold grew so severe that peasant women refused to cart food to towns. Blizzards piled mountains of snow on the railway tracks, where they lay untouched for lack of hands to clear them. Locomotives would not move in the freezing weather and sometimes had to stand in place for hours to build up steam. These climatic conditions aggravated further the serious transport difficulties. In the thirty months of war, the rolling stock had declined from wear and inadequate maintenance. By mid-February 1917, Russia had in operation only three-quarters of its peacetime railway equipment, and much of it stood immobilized by the weather: during the winter of 1916–17, 60,000 railroad cars loaded with food, fodder, and fuel could not move because of the snow—they represented about one-eighth of all the freight cars available.[2]

The breakdown of supply had a devastating effect on the food and fuel situation in the northern cities, especially Petrograd. The capital seems to have had sufficient stocks of flour: according to General S. S. Khabalov, the city's military commander, on February 25 the warehouses held 9,000 tons of flour, more than enough for several days.[3] But fuel shortages had idled many baker-

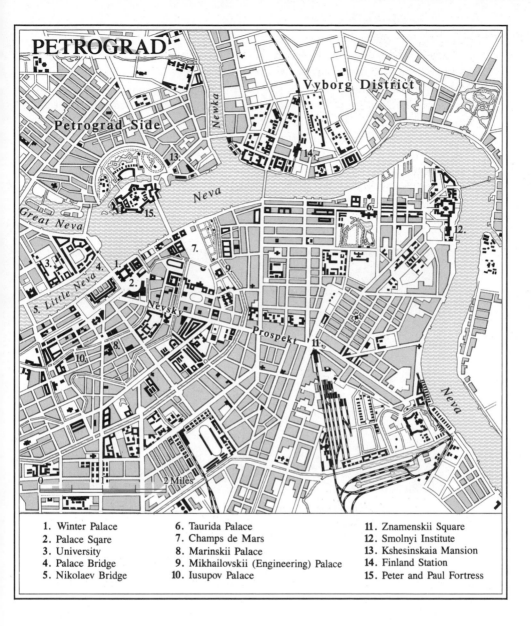

PETROGRAD

Vyborg District

Petrograd Side

Newka

Neva

Great Neva

15.

Little Neva

5.

3.

4.

1.

2.

8.

10.

Nevsky

7.

9.

Prospekt

11.

6.

12.

13.

14.

Neva

0   1   2 Miles

1. Winter Palace
2. Palace Sqare
3. University
4. Palace Bridge
5. Nikolaev Bridge

6. Taurida Palace
7. Champs de Mars
8. Marinskii Palace
9. Mikhailovskii (Engineering) Palace
10. Iusupov Palace

11. Znamenskii Square
12. Smolnyi Institute
13. Kshesinskaia Mansion
14. Finland Station
15. Peter and Paul Fortress

ies. Around February 20, rumors spread that the government was about to introduce bread rationing and limit purchases to one pound per adult. In the panic buying that ensued, the bakery shelves were stripped bare.[4] Long queues formed: some people braved the freezing weather all night to be first when the bakeries opened. The crowds were irritable and scuffles were not uncommon. Even police agents complained that they could not feed their families.[5] Fuel shortages also forced factories to close: the Putilov Works shut down on February 21. Tens of thousands of laid-off workers milled on the streets.

Nothing better illustrates the extent to which the government had lost touch with reality than the Tsar's decision, at this tense and difficult moment,

to leave for Mogilev. He intended to stay there one week consulting with
Alekseev, who had just returned from a period of convalescence in the Crimea.
Protopopov raised no objections. On the evening of February 21, he assured
the Tsar he had nothing to worry about and could leave confident that the rear
was in good hands.[6] Nicholas left the following afternoon. He would return
two weeks later as "Nicholas Romanov," a private citizen under house arrest.
The security of the capital city was entrusted to very unqualified personnel:
the Minister of War, General M. A. Beliaev, who had made his entire career
in the military bureaucracy and was known to his colleagues as "dead head"
(mertvaia golova); and the city's military commander, General Khabalov, who
had spent his professional life in chanceries and military academies.

30. International Women's Day in Petrograd, February 23,
1917. The sign reads: "If woman is a *slave* there will be no
freedom. Long live equal rights for women."

Suddenly, the temperature in Petrograd rose to 8 degrees centigrade
(46 F), where it would remain until the end of the month.[7] People whom the
freezing weather had for months kept at home streamed outdoors to bask in
the sun. Photographs of the February Revolution show gay crowds under a
brilliant sky. The climatic accident played no small role in the historic events
of the time.

The day after Nicholas's departure, disorders broke out in Petrograd:
they would not subside until the monarchy was overthrown.

Thursday, February 23/March 8 was International Women's Day. A
procession, organized by the socialists, marched on Nevsky, toward the Municipal Council, demanding equality for women and occasionally clamoring
for bread. All around rode Cossacks; here and there, the police dispersed
crowds of onlookers. At the same time, a group of workers, variously estimated at between 78,000 and 128,000, went on strike to protest food shortages.[8] But the day passed reasonably quietly, and by 10 P.M. the streets were

back to normal. The authorities, although unprepared for a demonstration of this size, succeeded in containing it without resorting to force. The governor of Petrograd, A. P. Balk, and Khabalov did all they could to avoid clashes with the population out of fear of politicizing what was still a strictly economic protest. The Okhrana, however, reporting on the events of February 23 and the following day, remarked that the Cossacks were reluctant to confront the crowds. Balk made a similar observation.[9]

The atmosphere was exacerbated by the attacks on the government from the halls of Taurida, where the Duma had sat in session since February 14. The February Revolution took place against the steady drumbeat of anti-government rhetoric. The familiar cast was on hand—Miliukov, Kerensky, Chkheidze, Purishkevich—accusing, demanding, threatening. In their own way they behaved as irresponsibly as Protopopov and those officials who treated the riots as a provocation instigated by a handful of agitators.

On February 24, the situation in Petrograd deteriorated. By now between 160,000 and 200,000 workers filled the streets, some striking, others locked out. Having gotten wind of the mood in the industrial quarters across the Neva, the authorities set up barriers on the bridges connecting them with the city's residential and business centers, but the workers got around them by walking across the frozen river. The catalytic agents were radical intellectuals, mainly the so-called Mezhraiontsy, Social-Democrats who favored the reunification of Bolsheviks and Mensheviks and whose program called for an immediate end to the war and revolution.[10] Their leader, Leon Trotsky, was at the time in New York. All day long skirmishes occurred between rioters and police. The crowds sacked some food stores and inflicted other damage.[11] The air was thick with that peculiar Russian air of generalized, unfocused violence—the urge to beat and destroy—for which the Russian language has coined the words *pogrom* and *razgrom*. On Nevsky, crowds formed themselves into a procession, shouting "Down with the autocracy!" and "Down with the war!" The Cossacks again displayed a reluctance to obey orders.

Aware of the gravity of the food situation, the authorities held a high-level meeting on the subject in the afternoon of February 24. Present were most members of the Municipal Duma and the ministers, save for Golitsyn, who had not been notified, and Protopopov, who was said to be attending a spiritualist séance.[12] The Petrograd Municipal Council was at long last granted its request to take charge of food distribution.

The following day, the crowds, emboldened by the lack of vigorous repressive measures, grew still more aggressive. The demonstrations on that day were evidently organized, for they assumed a pronounced political coloration. Red banners appeared, with revolutionary slogans, some of which read "Down with the German Woman!" By now, virtually all the industrial plants in the city were closed, and between 200,000 and 300,000 idled workers filled the streets. A crowd of students and workers gathered at Kazan Square, in the middle of Nevsky, shouting slogans and chanting the "Marseillaise." Not far from there, at the shopping center known as Gostinyi Dvor, three civilians were killed. Elsewhere a grenade was thrown at gendarmes. A crowd separated a police officer from his men and beat him to death. Attacks on policemen occurred especially frequently in the Vyborg District, sections of which the radicals declared "liberated."[13]

Alexandra recounted the day's events as follows:

> This is a *hooligan* movement, young people run & shout that there is no bread, simply to create excitement, along with workers who prevent others from working. If the weather were very cold they would probably all stay home. But all this will pass and become calm if only the Duma will behave itself.[14]

The socialist intellectuals sensed a revolution in the making. On February 25, the Menshevik Duma deputies discussed convoking a "workers' soviet."[15] And still it could be argued that the early disorders in Petrograd—and they had yet to occur in another city—were essentially a *golodnyi bunt,* a hunger riot, and that the political significance which the Menshevik and Mezhraiontsy intellectuals tried to give it reflected mainly their own aspirations. Such, at any rate, was the opinion of the leading Bolshevik in Petrograd, Alexander Shliapnikov. Told that a revolution was underway, he scoffed: "What revolution? Give the workers a pound of bread and the movement will peter out."[16]

Whatever chance there was of containing the riots was destroyed by the arrival in the evening of February 25 of a telegram from Nicholas to Khabalov demanding that the disorders be suppressed by military force. To understand Nicholas's action it must be borne in mind that neither he nor the generals in Mogilev realized the gravity of the situation in the capital because Protopopov had instructed the police to "soften" the reports sent to headquarters.[17] The dispatches from Khabalov to Mogilev of February 25 and 26 depicted the turbulence as manageable.[18] As a result, as late as February 26 no one in Mogilev knew how serious the situation really was.[19]

On the basis of such information as headquarters had at its disposal, it was not unreasonable to assume that a show of force would restore order. In his telegram, Nicholas wrote that at a time of war, with soldiers freezing in the trenches and about to risk their lives in the spring offensive, unrest in the rear could not be tolerated: "I order you to stop tomorrow the disorders in the capital, which are unacceptable at the difficult time of war with Germany and Austria."[20] Khabalov said later that he was dismayed by the Tsar's instructions, which called for a military confrontation with the rioters[21]—something he had so far managed to avoid. Obeying orders, he posted two proclamations. One outlawed street gatherings and warned that the troops would fire at crowds. The other ordered striking workers to return to work by February 28: those who failed to obey would have their deferments canceled and be liable to immediate induction for front-line duty.[22] Many of these posters were torn down the instant they went up.[23] In one of three communications to her husband on February 25, Alexandra advised against shooting demonstrators. She expressed surprise that rationing was not introduced and that the factories

31. Crowds on Znamenskii Square, Petrograd, the scene
of the first violence of the February Revolution.

had not been militarized: "This supply question is enough to drive one out of
one's mind."[24]

During the night of February 25–26, the authorities lost control of the
workers' quarters, especially in the Vyborg District, where mobs sacked and
set fire to police stations.

On Sunday morning, February 26, Petrograd was occupied by military
units in combat gear. A total curfew was imposed. The bridges over the Neva
were raised. In the morning all was quiet, but at midday thousands of workers
crossed the river into the center of the city, milling around and waiting for
something to happen. That afternoon, in several districts troops fired at
crowds. The bloodiest incident occurred at Znamenskii Square, in the center
of which stood Trubetskoi's famous equestrian statue of Alexander III, a
favorite gathering place of political agitators. When the crowd refused to
disperse, a company of the Volynskii Guard Regiment opened fire, killing forty
and wounding as many.*

Resort to force produced the desired result: by nightfall the capital was
calm. Nicholas Sukhanov, the author of the best eyewitness account of 1917
in Petrograd, thought that the government had succeeded in regaining control
of the center of the city.[25] That evening Princess Radziwill held her soiree,
which had had Petrograd society talking for weeks. To the French Ambassador the sight of her brilliantly illuminated palace on Fontanka brought to mind
similar scenes in the Paris of 1789.[26]

To remove the main source of political opposition, Nicholas ordered the

---

*According to E. I. Martynov, *Tsarskaia armiia v fevral'skom perevorote* (Leningrad, 1927),
85, the troops used machine guns, but this is almost certainly wrong. A noncommissioned officer
who took part in the incident claimed that the troops fired into the air and that the killing was done
by a drunken officer: *Byloe,* No. 5–6/27–28 (1917), 8–9.

Duma to adjourn until April. Golitsyn communicated this news to Rodzianko late at night on February 26.

As night fell, on the surface everything seemed in order. But then a succession of events occurred which to this day astonish with their suddenness and scope: a mutiny of the Petrograd garrison which in twenty-four hours transformed half the troops into rioters and by March 1 had the entire contingent of 160,000 uniformed men in open rebellion.

To understand this development, one must bear in mind the composition as well as living conditions of the Petrograd garrison. It consisted of freshly drafted recruits and superannuated reserves assigned to the reserve battalions of the Guard Regiments normally stationed in Petrograd but now away at the front. They were meant to stay in Petrograd for several weeks of basic training and then leave for the front. Organized into training units, they were heavily overmanned: some reserve companies had more than 1,000 soldiers, and there were battalions with 12,000–15,000 men; 160,000 soldiers were packed into barracks designed to hold 20,000.[27] The reservists drawn from the National Militia, many in their thirties and early forties, felt unfairly inducted. In Petrograd, they were subjected to the usual indignities inflicted on Russian soldiers, such as being addressed by officers in the second-person singular and being forbidden to ride inside streetcars.[28] Although dressed in uniform, they did not differ in any significant way from the workers and peasants crowding the streets of Petrograd, whom they were now ordered to shoot. Rodzianko, who observed them at close range, said one week after the events:

> Unexpectedly for all, there erupted a soldier mutiny such as I have never seen. These, of course, were not soldiers but *muzhiki* taken directly from the plow who have found it useful now to make known their *muzhik* demands. In the crowd, all one could hear was "Land and Freedom," "Down with the Dynasty," "Down with the Romanovs," "Down with the Officers." In many units officers were beaten. This was joined by the workers and anarchy reached its apogee.[29]

In view of the fact that the February Revolution is often depicted as a worker revolt, it is important to emphasize that it was, first and foremost, a mutiny of peasant soldiers whom, to save money, the authorities had billeted in overcrowded facilities in the Empire's capital city—in the words of one eyewitness, like "kindling wood near a powder keg."

The survival of the tsarist regime ultimately depended on the loyalty of the army since the usual forces of order—the police and the Cossacks—did not have the numbers to cope with thousands of rebels. In February 1917, these forces consisted of 3,500 policemen, armed with antiquated Japanese rifles, and Cossack detachments which, for an unaccountable reason, had been divested of *nagaiki,* their dreaded whips.[30] Nicholas showed that he was aware of his dependence on the troops when he assured the British Ambassador the army would save him. But the troops' loyalty wavered when ordered to fire on unarmed crowds. The Russian army never liked being used against civilians; it liked this role less than ever now because its green recruits shared the grievances of the crowds. Observing the Cossacks and troops during these critical days, Sukhanov felt they were merely looking for a pretext to join the demonstrators.[31] One of the very last reports filed by the Okhrana on February 26, just before it was shut down by the rioters, shared this assessment:

> The movement broke out spontaneously, without preparation and exclusively on the basis of the supply crisis. Inasmuch as the military units did not hinder the crowd and in individual cases even took steps to paralyze the actions of the police, the masses gained confidence that they could act with impunity. Now, after two days of unimpeded movement on the streets, when revolutionary circles have raised the slogans "Down with the war" and "Down with the government," the people have become convinced that the revolution has begun, that the masses are winning, that the authorities are powerless to suppress the movement by virtue of the fact that the military units are not on their side, that the decisive victory is near because the military either today or tomorrow will come out openly on the side of the revolutionary forces, that the movement which has begun will not subside but grow ceaselessly until ultimate victory and the overthrow of the government.[32]

E. I. Martynov, a tsarist general who after October went over to the Bolsheviks, in his excellent account of the role of the army in the February Revolution commented critically on the passivity of the Imperial authorities in the face of fraternization of the Petrograd garrison with the rioters. He contrasted this behavior with the energetic measures of the French President, Adolphe Thiers, in March 1871. As soon as the troops were observed fraternizing with the Parisian mobs, Thiers ordered them to Versailles, from where they later counterattacked and recaptured the capital.[33] Beliaev and Khabalov, by contrast, helplessly watched the rising storm.

The first break in the garrison's discipline occurred in the afternoon of February 26 in reaction to the shooting on Znamenskii Square. Immediately after the event, a group of angry workers went to the Champs de Mars, where the Pavlovskii Regiment had its billets. They told the men of the 4th Company of the Reserve Battalion that their comrades in the Volynskii Regiment had fired on an unarmed crowd. Incensed, the Pavlovtsy broke into the company arsenal, removed thirty rifles, and took to the streets. One hundred strong, they marched toward Nevsky intending to persuade or compel the Volyntsy on Znamenskii Square to stop the shooting. En route, they ran into a detachment of mounted policemen, with whom they exchanged fire. The leader of the mutineers, a young lieutenant, received a disabling wound. The loss of the commander threw them into confusion. No support came from other garrison units. By nightfall, when the Pavlovtsy returned to their barracks, nineteen of their ringleaders were placed under guard.[34] In cables sent to Mogilev that evening, Khabalov and Beliaev alluded to the mutiny of some units, but assured the Tsar they would be suppressed.[35]

If the February Revolution is to have a date when it began, that date

32. Mutinous soldiers in Petrograd: February 1917.

has to be February 27/March 12, 1917, when "worker demonstrations turned
into a soldier mutiny"[36] and the tsarist authorities lost control of the capital.
The most stupendous military revolt in recorded history, it started with the
Pavlovskii Regiment. The regiment's troops held meetings through the night
to protest the Znamenskii Square massacre and finally voted to disobey further orders to fire at civilians. Messengers were sent to the Preobrazhenskii
and Litovskii Guard Regiments, billeted nearby, which agreed to follow suit.
The next morning the three regiments went into the streets. The Pavlovtsy
killed one of their officers. Gendarme barracks were attacked and demol-
ished. Pushing aside pro-government pickets, soldiers made their way to the
Vyborg District, where they were joined by rebellious workers. The mutinous troops drove around the snow-covered streets in commandeered armored cars, waving their weapons and shouting. Anyone who stood in their
way risked being lynched. Other soldiers broke into the Peter and Paul Fortress, releasing prisoners. A mob sacked the Ministry of the Interior. The red
flag went over the Winter Palace. Policemen caught in uniform were beaten
and killed. In the late afternoon, crowds stormed the Okhrana headquarters,
scattering and burning files—Okhrana informers were observed to display
particular zeal on this occasion. Arsenals were broken into and thousands of
guns removed. There was widespread looting of shops, restaurants, and private residences.

By nighttime, Petrograd was in the hands of peasants in uniform. Of the 160,000-man garrison, half was in full mutiny, while the remainder adopted a "neutral" stance. Khabalov could count on a mere 1,000–2,000 loyal troops, mostly from the Izmailovskii Regiment.[37] Only half a dozen public buildings scattered throughout Petrograd still remained in government hands.

The rapidity with which the mutiny spread through the Petrograd garrison on February 27 cannot be explained by specific grievances, although these clearly existed. The progress of the mutiny suggests that nothing could have been done to stop it. It was not really a military mutiny of the kind that broke out during the war in other armies, including the French and German, but a typical Russian *bunt,* with powerful anarchist overtones.* The rebellious soldiers were, for the major part, peasants born in the 1880s. They carried in their bones three hundred years of serfdom. They obeyed only as long as disobedience carried mandatory punishment: the instant they sensed that they could do what they wished with impunity, they ceased to obey. The chronology of the mutiny indicates that it originated with the Pavlovskii Regiment, which rose during the night of February 26–27 following the aborted rebellion of one company. Beliaev wanted the participants in this rebellion to be court-martialed and those found guilty to be executed, but Khabalov overruled him and ordered instead the arrest of the ringleaders.[38] It was a fatal loss of nerve. Trotsky, who in such situations would act with unhesitating brutality, describes as follows the psychology of the Russian on the brink of military rebellion:

> The critical hour of contact between the pushing crowd and the soldiers who bar their way has its critical minute. That is when the gray barrier has not yet given way, still holds together shoulder to shoulder, but already wavers, and the officer, gathering his last strength of will, gives the command: "Fire!" The cry of the crowd, the yell of terror and threat, drowns the command, but not wholly. The rifles waver. The crowd pushes. Then the officer points the barrel of his revolver at the most suspicious soldier. From the decisive moment now stands out the decisive second. The death of the boldest soldier, to whom the others have involuntarily looked for guidance, a shot into the crowd by a corporal from the dead man's rifle, and the barrier closes, the guns go off of themselves, scattering the crowd into the alleys and backyards.[39]

On February 26, the hand of Imperial authority wavered: once it refused to shoot "the most suspicious soldiers" discipline collapsed and the mutiny spread like fire.

*In April–June 1917, mutinies broke out among French troops on the Western Front. They were fueled by soldier resentment of the heavy casualties suffered in the Nivelle offensive, but the news of the Russian Revolution, which led to a rebellion of Russian units in France, also played a part. Eventually, fifty-four divisions were affected: in May 1917 the French army was incapable of offensive operations. And yet the mutiny, which the French government managed to keep secret for decades, was eventually contained and at no time threatened to bring down the state—a telling commentary on the national and political cohesion of France as compared with that of Russia. See John Williams, *Mutiny 1917* (London, 1962), and Richard M. Watt, *Dare Call It Treason* (New York, 1963).

Nicholas still had no idea of the gravity of the situation. He was, therefore, understandably annoyed in the evening of February 26 when shown a cable from Rodzianko, so much at odds with the reassuring messages sent by Khabalov and Beliaev:

> Situation serious. In the capital anarchy. Government paralyzed. Transport of food and fuel completely disorganized. Public disaffection growing. On the streets chaotic shooting. Army units fire at each other. It is essential at once to entrust a person enjoying country's confidence with the formation of new government. There should be no delay. All delay is death. I pray to God that in this hour responsibility not fall on the sovereign.[40]

Nicholas chose to ignore this warning, convinced that Rodzianko spread alarm to extract political concessions for the Duma. The following morning another cable came from the Duma chairman: "Situation deteriorating. Imperative to take immediate steps for tomorrow will be late. The last hour has struck, decisive as the fate of the Fatherland and dynasty."[41] Nicholas glanced at the message and turned to his aide, Count Fredericks, saying: "That fat fellow Rodzianko has again written me all kinds of nonsense which I shan't even bother to answer."[42]

But as the day went on Nicholas's equanimity was severely tested, for Rodzianko's alarmist assessments received confirmation from sources in which he had greater confidence. A cable came from Khabalov to the effect that he could not prevent unauthorized assemblies because the troops were in mutiny and refused to fire on crowds.[43] There were several messages from the Empress, in one of which she tersely urged: "Concessions necessary."[44] Grand Duke Michael counseled the dismissal of the cabinet and its replacement by one responsible to the Duma under Prince G. Lvov. He offered himself as

33. Petrograd crowds burning emblems of the Imperial regime: February 1917.

34. Arrest of a police informer; informers were popularly known as "Pharaons."

Regent.* Golitsyn informed the Tsar at 2 p.m. in the name of the cabinet that the raging mobs were out of control and that the cabinet wished to resign in favor of a Duma ministry, preferably chaired by either Lvov or Rodzianko. He further recommended the imposition of martial law and the appointment of a popular general, with combat experience, to take charge of the capital's security.[45] Nicholas requested Voeikov to contact the Minister of War, Beliaev, for an assessment. Beliaev confirmed that Petrograd had become unmanageable.[46] The decisive communication came from Count Paul Benckendorff, the Grand Marshal of the Court, who inquired whether the Tsar wished his wife and children to join him. The children happened to be ill with measles, and since he did not want them to travel, Nicholas decided to return to Tsarskoe: he gave orders to have his train ready for departure that night (February 27–28).[47]

At this juncture Nicholas knew there was serious trouble in the capital city, but he did not yet realize its depth and intensity: like Louis XVI on July 14, 1789, he thought he was facing a rebellion, not a revolution. He believed that the disorder could be quelled by force. This is attested to by two decisions. Rejecting the Prime Minister's request that he and his colleagues be allowed to turn over the reins of administration to a Duma cabinet, he ordered the cabinet to remain at its post.[48] He accepted, however, Golitsyn's recommendation to appoint a military dictator in charge of Petrograd security. He chose for this role sixty-six-year-old N. I. Ivanov, a general who had distinguished himself in the Galician campaign of 1914 and had long experience in the Corps of Gendarmes. During dinner that night, looking pale, sad, and worried,[49] Nicholas drew Ivanov aside for a long talk. Ivanov was to proceed to Tsarskoe

*Martynov, *Tsarskaia armiia*, 105; *KA*, No. 2/21 (1927), 11–12. Michael alone signed the message, but it was the result of the joint efforts of himself, Prime Minister Golitsyn, Rodzianko, Beliaev, and Kryzhanovskii: *Revoliutsiia*, I, 40.

35. Workers toppling the statue of Alexander III
in the center of Moscow.

Selo at the head of loyal troops to ensure the safety of the Imperial family, and
then, as newly-appointed head of the Petrograd Military District, assume
command of the regiments ordered from the front to help him. All cabinet
ministers were to be subordinated to him.[50] At 9 p.m. Alekseev wired General
Danilov, the chief of staff of the Northern Front in Pskov, to arrange for the
dispatch of two cavalry and two infantry regiments composed of "the most
stable [and] reliable" troops led by "bold" officers to join Ivanov.[51] Similar
orders went out to the headquarters of the Western Front.[52] The size of the
contingent—eight combat regiments augmented by machine-gun units—indicated that Nicholas and his generals envisaged a major operation to put down
the mutiny.

Ivanov alerted the battalion of the Knights of St. George, composed of
wounded veterans awarded the Cross of St. George for bravery in combat and
assigned in Mogilev to guard headquarters. In conversation with friends, he

seemed far from confident of the reliability of his men and the success of his mission.[53] His contingent of eight hundred troops left Mogilev by train around 11 a.m., heading for Tsarskoe by the most direct route through Vitebsk and Dno. Ivanov himself followed two hours later.

One will never know whether, had Nicholas acted decisively in the days that followed, Ivanov would have succeeded, because his mission was aborted. But his prospects do not seem to have been as hopeless as the politicians and generals, under the politicians' influence, seemed to believe. On February 27, only Petrograd was in rebellion: save for some sympathy strikes in Moscow, the rest of the country was quiet. Determined action by disciplined frontline troops might have suppressed a revolt that was still primarily a garrison mutiny. But the plan was given up because the politicians had persuaded themselves—mistakenly, as events were to show—that only the Duma was capable of restoring order. They, in turn, convinced the generals, who brought irresistible pressure to bear on Nicholas to give up power. In fact, when they were finally made, political concessions had the opposite effect of the one intended, transforming the Petrograd garrison mutiny into a national revolution.

That the Petrograd garrison had turned into rabble incapable of offering resistance is illustrated by an incident that occurred at the opening session of the newly formed Soviet on February 28. As recalled by Shliapnikov, after Chkheidze had opened the meeting and the Executive Committee given an account of its activity,

> comments were heard on the report, a good many of them irrelevant. Soldiers spoke, representatives of regiments, bringing greetings and congratulations on the "people's victory." Owing to these speeches, the session of the Soviet quickly transformed itself from a businesslike meeting into a rally. . . . Near Taurida Palace resounded machine-gun fire. Sounds of the shooting penetrated the hall where the session was underway, reaching the keen ears of the soldiers. Instantly panic broke out. People rushed in a mob to the doors, filling Catherine's Hall like a wave. Soldiers in that vast space also attempted to reach exits in various directions. Some broke windows to the garden to jump through the broken glass.[54]

The Imperial train—blue with gold trim—left Mogilev at 5 a.m. on February 28, ahead of Ivanov and his troops, preceded by an escort train with staff and military guards. It did not take the most direct line to Tsarskoe, in order not to interfere with Ivanov's mission.[55] Instead, it followed a longer, circuitous route, heading initially east, in the direction of Moscow, then at Viazma changing directions northwest, toward Bologoe. This detour was to have grave consequences. Ivanov reached Tsarskoe on schedule, on March 1. Had the Imperial train followed the same route, Nicholas would have been with his wife on March 2, when he came under pressure to abdicate. The Empress was convinced that had she been at his side he would have resisted demands to give up the throne.

The Imperial entourage traveled all of February 28 without incident. But around 1 a.m., as the escort train pulled into Malaia Vishera, 170 kilometers southeast of the capital, an officer came aboard to say that the tracks ahead were under the control of "unfriendly" troops. When the Imperial car reached Malaia Vishera somewhat later, the Tsar was awakened. After a brief consultation, it was decided to return to Bologoe and from there proceed to Pskov, headquarters of the Northern Front, commanded by General N. V. Ruzskii, and the nearest point with a Hughes telegraph. Voeikov, who witnessed this episode, says that Nicholas maintained perfect composure throughout.[56] The Imperial train pulled into Pskov at 7:05 p.m. on March 1.

On arrival, Nicholas was welcomed by the governor, but to everyone's surprise and consternation, Ruzskii was missing. He appeared a few minutes later, "stooping, gray, and old, in rubber galoshes . . . his face pale and sickly, an unfriendly gleam from under his eyeglasses."[57] Ruzskii, who was to play a critical role in the events that unfolded, second only to that of Alekseev, was probably the most politicized of the commanding generals. He had often crossed swords with Protopopov over the latter's handling of food supplies as well as his decision to withdraw the Petrograd Military District from Ruzskii's command. His sympathies lay wholly with the Duma opposition. He disliked Nicholas and thought the institution of tsarism anachronistic. "Nicholas thus [would spend] the most crucial two days of his life under the influence of the military commander who was most decisively against [him]."[58] From the moment of the Tsar's arrival he sought to influence him first to grant concessions to the Duma and then to abdicate.*

Rodzianko was expected in Pskov that evening with a detailed report on the situation in the capital, but the Soviet prevented him from leaving. At 8:41 p.m. Pskov was informed of the fact.[59]

Nicholas had no inkling that he had become irrelevant, as events in the capital were moving under their own momentum. His civil and military officials there had lost all control over the situation. On March 1, the political conflict no longer pitted the Tsar against the Duma, but the Duma against a new contender for power, the Petrograd Soviet.

After the rioters had done their work, the center of attention shifted to Taurida. The Duma leaders had learned the previous night that the Tsar had ordered them to adjourn. Under the pressure of radical deputies, Rodzianko reluctantly scheduled for the following morning a session of the Progressive Bloc and the Council of Elders (Sen'oren Konvent), composed of representa-

---

*Ruzskii was arrested by the Bolsheviks in September 1918 while living in retirement in the North Caucasian city of Piatigorsk, and murdered, along with 136 other victims of terror, the following month. He was very anxious to clear his name of charges that he had pressured Nicholas to abdicate. (Alexandra called him "Judas" in a letter to Nicholas of March 3, 1917: *KA*, No. 4, 1923, 219.) His story, as recounted by S. N. Vilchkovskii, is in *RL*, No. 3 (1922), 161–86.

tives of the Duma parties.[60] Now was the chance for the Duma to show its mettle by defying the Tsar's order and reconvening as a revolutionary assembly. The Duma had so long stood in the forefront of the opposition to tsarism that as chaos spread in the city people's eyes intuitively turned to it for leadership. The expectation was that it would proceed at once to form a cabinet and take charge of the country's administration.

But now that it had, at long last, the opportunity to do so, the Duma took refuge in legalities. Nicholas was still sovereign: after he had ordered the Duma adjourned, it no longer had legal existence. Some deputies, from the left and right, urged that the Tsar's wishes be ignored, but Rodzianko refused: instead, he cabled Nicholas asking authorization for the Duma to form a cabinet. In the early afternoon Rodzianko consented to the Council of Elders deciding on the course of action. The senior statesmen of the Duma were very nervous. They did not want to inflame popular passions and contribute to anarchy by defying the Tsar. At the same time, they thought it impossible to do nothing because mobs were converging on the Duma building, demanding action. On February 27, a crowd of 25,000 filled the space in front of Taurida; some of the demonstrators penetrated the building.

Faced with this predicament, the Elders settled on a weak compromise. Deferring to the Tsar's wishes, they asked the deputies to assemble at 2:30 p.m. in another chamber of Taurida—the so-called Semicircular Hall—as a "private body." Present were most members of the Progressive Bloc, with the addition of socialists, but without the conservatives. This is how Shulgin describes the scene:

> The room barely accommodated us: the entire Duma was on hand. Rodzianko and the Elders sat behind a table. Around them sat and stood, crowding, the others in a dense mob. Frightened, excited, somehow spiritually clinging to one another. Even enemies of long standing suddenly sensed that there was something which was equally dangerous, threatening, repulsive to them all. That something was the street, the street mob. . . . One could feel its hot breath. . . . With the street approached She to whom very few then gave any thought, but whom, certainly, very many unconsciously sensed. That is why they were pale, their hearts secretly constricted. Surrounded by a crowd of many thousands, on the street stalked Death . . .[61]

After a chaotic discussion, in the course of which proponents of immediate assumption of power by the Elders clashed with the more cautious adherents of legitimacy, it was decided to form an executive of twelve Duma members, still of a "private" nature, to be known as the "Provisional Committee of Duma Members for the Restoration of Order in the Capital and the Establishment of Relations with Individuals and Institutions." Chaired by Rodzianko, it initially consisted of representatives of the Progressive Bloc with the addition of two socialists (Kerensky and Chkheidze)—a coalition that extended from the moderate Nationalists to the Mensheviks. The ludicrously cumbersome name given the organization reflected the timidity of its organiz-

36. Provisional Committee of the Duma. Sitting on
extreme left, V. N. Lvov, and on extreme right, M.
Rodzianko. Standing on extreme left, V. V. Shulgin,
and second from right, A. F. Kerensky.

ers. The revolutionary upheaval which they had so long anticipated had
caught them unprepared: experienced at dueling with ministers they had no
idea how to handle raging mobs. They did not even know how to claim power.
The writer Zinaida Gippius, observing the timidity of the Duma leaders and
contrasting it with the resolute behavior of the radical intelligentsia in the
Soviet, remarked in her diary on the psychological inhibition that held them·
back:

> They could only ask "legitimate authority." The Revolution has abolished this
> authority without their participation. They did not overthrow it: they have only
> mechanically remained on the surface, on top—passively, without a prior
> arrangement. But they are *naturally* powerless because they cannot *take*
> power—it must be given to them and given from above. Until they feel *invested*
> with power, they cannot exercise it.[62]

It has been argued[63] that the failure of the Duma to proclaim at once, in
an unequivocal manner, the assumption of power had disastrous consequences
because it deprived the Provisional Government which issued from it of legitimacy. However, such importance as one can attach to this fact derives less
from the legal aspects of sovereignty, which the population at large did not
care about, than from the mentality which it revealed—namely, a dread of
responsibility. An eyewitness says that the Duma group decided to constitute

its Provisional Committee in an atmosphere not unlike that in which, in normal times, the Duma might have appointed a Fisheries Committee.[64] The onetime head of the Petrograd Okhrana, A. V. Gerasimov, thought that in adhering to the fiction that it was not taking power, but forming a private body to deal with the disorders, the Duma leaders wanted also to protect themselves against criminal prosecution in the event that the crown succeeded in suppressing the rebellion—for in the course of the day they were apprised of the approach of General Ivanov's punitive expedition.[65]

A Polish proverb has it that where there are no fish crayfish will do. In the eyes of the Petrograd mob, the Duma was the government, and from February 27 to March 1 numerous deputations made their way to Taurida to pledge support and loyalty. Among them were not only workers, soldiers, and intellectuals but also thousands of officers, the military units guarding the Imperial palaces, and, strangest sight of all, a detachment of the Corps of Gendarmes, which marched to Taurida to the strains of the "Marseillaise" bearing red flags.[66] On March 1, Grand Duke Cyril Vladimirovich, the commandant of the Palace Guard at Tsarskoe Selo and a cousin of Nicholas, announced that he and his men acknowledged the authority of the Provisional Government.*[67]

The sudden shift of sentiment on the part of the most illiberal elements of Petrograd society—right-wing officers, gendarmes, policemen—who only a few days before were pillars of the monarchy, can only be explained by one factor: fear. Shulgin, who was in the thick of events, had no doubt that the officers in particular were paralyzed with it and sought the protection of the Duma to save their lives from the mutinous troops.[68]

The Provisional Committee sent cables to the commanders of the armed forces informing them that to put an end to the crisis of authority it had assumed power from the old cabinet. Order would soon be restored.[69]

In the evening, Rodzianko visited Prime Minister Golitsyn to inquire whether the Tsar would consent to the formation of a Duma ministry. Golitsyn told him of Nicholas's negative answer. When Rodzianko returned with this information to Taurida at 10 p.m. there followed lengthy discussions in the Provisional Committee which led to the inexorable conclusion that there was no choice but to assume de facto governmental authority. The alternative was either the complete collapse of order or the assumption of power by a rival and radical body, the Petrograd Soviet, which had come into existence the very same day.[70]

The revival of the Petrograd Soviet was first discussed by the Mensheviks on February 25, but the initiative came from two members of the Central

*After the Revolution, in emigration, he would proclaim himself successor to the Russian throne.

37. Troops of the Petrograd garrison assembling in front of
the Winter Palace to swear loyalty to the Provisional
Government.

38. A sailor removing an officer's epaulettes.

Workers' Group, who, having been jailed in January on orders of Protopopov, were freed by the insurgent mob on the morning of February 27: K. A. Gvozdev, its chairman, and B. O. Bogdanov, its secretary, both Mensheviks. An appeal was issued to the soldiers, workers, and other inhabitants of Petrograd to elect representatives to an organizing meeting of the Soviet that evening at Taurida. It was signed: "The Provisional Executive Committee of the Soviet of Worker Deputies."[71] This allowed almost no time for elections, and when the meeting opened that night few elected representatives were on hand. Although according to some accounts as many as 250 people showed up, most were onlookers; only forty to fifty were considered eligible to vote.[72] The meeting chose a Provisional Executive Committee, or Ispolkom, of eight or nine persons, mostly Mensheviks: Chkheidze took over as chairman, with Kerensky and M. I. Skobelev as deputies. Since no protocols were kept, it cannot be established exactly what transpired. Some soldiers spoke and it was decided to admit soldiers into the Soviet in a separate section. There followed discussions of the food problem, of the need to create a militia to maintain order. It was resolved to publish *Izvestiia* as the official organ of the Soviet and to ask the Provisional Committee to withhold funds from the Imperial authorities by taking charge of the State Bank and other fiscal institutions.[73]

On February 28 the factories and military units elected representatives to the Soviet. They chose overwhelmingly moderate socialists: the extremist parties (Bolsheviks, SR Maximalists, and Mezhraiontsy) received between them less than 10 percent of the votes.[74] Voting procedures were chaotic: they followed the traditional practices of Russian popular assemblies, which strove to secure not a mathematically accurate representation of individual opinions but a sense of the collective will. Small shops sent as many representatives as large factories, army units from regiments down to companies did likewise, with the result that the Soviet was overwhelmed by delegates from small enterprises and the garrison. In the second week of its existence, of the Soviet's 3,000 deputies more than 2,000 were soldiers[75]—this in a city in which industrial workers outnumbered soldiers two or three times. In photographs of the Soviet, military uniforms dominate.

The plenary sessions of the Soviet, the first of which took place on February 28, resembled a giant village assembly: it was as if the factories and barracks had sent their *bol'shaki.* They lacked agendas as well as procedures for arriving at decisions: the practice was through open discussion at which everyone who wished to speak had his say to reach a unanimous verdict. Like a village assembly, the Soviet at this stage resembled a school of fish capable of instantly reversing direction in response to an invisible command. Sukhanov thus describes these early gatherings:

"And what's going on in the Soviet?" I remember asking someone who had come in from beyond the curtain. He waved his hand in a hopeless gesture: "A palaver! Anyone who wants gets up and says whatever he likes . . ."

I had several occasions to pass through the meeting hall. At first it looked

39. K. A. Gvozdev: Menshevik labor leader
and one of the founders of the Petrograd Soviet.

as it had the night before: deputies were sitting on chairs and benches, at the
table inside the room, and along the walls; among those in the seats and the
aisles, and at each end of the hall, stood people of every description, creating
confusion and disrupting the meeting. Then the crowds of standing people
became so dense that it was difficult to get through, and they filled up the room
to such an extent that those who had chairs also abandoned them, and the
entire hall, except for the first rows, became one confused mass of standing
people craning their necks. . . . A few hours later the chairs had completely
vanished from the hall, so as not to take up space, and people, dripping with
sweat, stood tightly squeezed together. The "Presidium" itself stood on the
table, while a whole crowd of enterprising people who had climbed on the table
hovered over the chairman's shoulders, preventing him from running the meeting. The next day or the day after, the tables too had vanished, except for the
chairman's, and the assembly finally acquired the look of a mass meeting in a
riding school.*[76]

Because such a mob could serve no other purpose than to provide a forum
for speechmaking, and because, in addition, the intellectuals believed they
knew what was best for the "masses," the decision-making authority of the
Soviet quickly shifted to the Ispolkom. This body, however, was not representative of the workers and soldiers, for its members were not elected by the
Soviet but, as in 1905, nominated by the socialist parties. Members of the
Ispolkom represented not the workers and soldiers but their respective party
organizations, and could be replaced at any time by others from these parties.
This was a deliberate policy of the radical intellectuals, as the following

---

*"Riding school" apparently refers to the royal manège in Paris, the seat of the National
Assembly during the Revolution, notorious for its unruly proceedings.

40. Soldier section of the Petrograd Soviet meeting
in the State Duma.

incident illustrates. On March 19, the Soldiers' Section voted to enlarge the
Ispolkom by adding nine soldiers and nine workers. The Ispolkom rejected this
proposal on the grounds that its enlargement would take place at the All-
Russian Consultation of Soviets scheduled to meet at the end of the month.[77]
The intellectuals who ran the Ispolkom even sought to keep its composition
secret. They released the names of its members only at the end of March, after
leaflets appeared on the streets of Petrograd demanding that its composition
be made public.*

Rather than serving as the executive organ of the Soviet, therefore, the
Ispolkom was a coordinating body of socialist parties, superimposed on the
Soviet and speaking in its name. The Ispolkom's earliest cooptation occurred
on March 6, when it invited the Party of Popular Socialists to send a spokesman. Two days later a Socialist-Revolutionary was added to represent a group
calling itself "Republican Officers." On March 11, the Social-Democratic Party
of Poland and Lithuania and that of Latvia were accorded one place each. On
March 15, a Bolshevik delegate was added. This manner of staffing the Ispolkom became formalized on March 18 with the adoption of the principle that
every socialist party had a right to three seats: two from its Central Committee
and one from its local organizations.†

*A. Shliapnikov, *Semnadtsatyi god,* III (Moscow-Leningrad, 1927), 173. The secrecy may
have been due to embarrassment that so many Ispolkom members were non-Russians (Georgians,
Jews, Latvians, Poles, Lithuanians, etc.): V. B. Stankevich, *Vospominaniia, 1914–1919 g.* (Berlin,
1920), 86.

†B. Ia. Nalivaiskii, ed., *Petrogradskii Sovet Rabochikh i Soldatskikh Deputatov: Protokoly
Zasedanii Ispolnitel'nogo Komiteta i Biuro Ispolnitel'nogo Komiteta* (Moscow-Leningrad, 1925), 59.
According to Marc Ferro, *Des Soviets au Communisme Bureaucratique* (Paris, 1980), 36, the

41. Executive Committee (Ispolkom) of the Petrograd
Soviet. In front, holding briefcase, N. D. Sokolov. On his
left, leaning forward, N. S. Chkheidze.

The principle had three consequences. It expanded artificially the representation of the Bolshevik Party, which had a small following among the
workers and virtually none among the soldiers. It strengthened as well that
of the moderate socialists, which had the effect of giving the Ispolkom a
political complexion that in time would put it at odds with the country's
increasingly radical mood. And, most importantly, it bureaucratized the Ispolkom: this self-appointed executive organ of the "worker and soldier masses"
became in effect a committee of radical intellectuals, with hardly a worker
or soldier in its midst—intellectuals who pursued their own visions and
ambitions:

> The bureaucratic divestiture for the benefit of organizations proceeded irrevers-
> ibly. Representation was set by virtue of adherence to an organization, not by
> virtue of elections, which existed only for show. Yet nothing indicates that
> these democrats meant consciously to violate or parody democratic procedures.
> No protest or discussion disturbed the atmosphere of unanimity, except over
> the number of representatives who were to be admitted and the choice of
> organizations defined as "representative." Over this, there developed a verita-
> ble political struggle. The Bolshevik proposal was intended to double the
> number of their representatives, to assure them of a surplus of votes through
> the addition of Latvian Bolsheviks. The representatives of the other organiza-
> tions did not object: all in all, this procedure assured the non-Bolsheviks in
> equal measure of an even more consistent surplus of those elected. In that
> manner, every tendency and every subtendency of Social Democracy or of the

resolution was moved by Shliapnikov. It was by this procedure that in May, on his return from the
United States, Leon Trotsky would receive a seat on the Ispolkom.

SRs had a right to two representatives in the bureau, even if behind it stood no more than a handful of activists. Conversely, the thousands of soldiers and workers who had really made February, disappear[ed] forever from the scene. Henceforth, the "representatives" [spoke] in their name.[78]

Surprisingly, the gatherings of the Ispolkom, although involving small numbers of politically literate persons, were not much more orderly than those of the Soviet at large—at any rate, in the first weeks of its existence. As described by the representative of the Trudoviki, V. B. Stankevich, they also were a madhouse:

> At this time, the Ispolkom carried extraordinary weight and importance. Formally it represented only Petrograd, but in fact it was the revolutionary organ of all Russia, the highest authoritative institution which was everywhere listened to with intense attention as the guide and leader of the insurgent people. But this was complete illusion. There was no leadership and there could not have been any. . . .
> The meetings took place daily beginning at 1 p.m., sometimes earlier, and ran late into the night, except when the Soviet was in session and the Ispolkom, usually in a body, went over to join it. The agenda was usually set by the "commune" [*mir*], but it was very rare not only for all items on it but even for a single issue to be resolved, insofar as during the sessions there always emerged extraneous questions, which had to be dealt with outside the agenda. . . . Issues had to be resolved under the pressure of an extraordinary mass of delegates and petition-bearers from the Petrograd garrison, from the front, from the backwaters of Russia. All these delegates demanded, no matter what, to be heard at the plenary session of the Ispolkom, for they were unwilling to deal with individual members or commissions. When the Soviet met as an entity or in its Soldiers' Section, affairs disintegrated catastrophically. . . .
> The most important decisions were often reached by completely accidental majorities. There was no time to think matters over, because everything was done in haste, after many sleepless nights, in confusion. Everyone was physically exhausted. Sleepless nights. Endless meetings. The lack of proper food: people lived on bread and tea, and only occasionally got a soldier's meal, served without forks or knives.[79]

In this initial period, according to Stankevich, "one could always have one's way with the Ispolkom if one insisted stubbornly enough." Under these conditions, rhetoric substituted for analysis and good intentions for reality. Later, toward the end of March, when Irakli Tsereteli, a leading Georgian Menshevik, returned from Siberian exile and took over the chairmanship, the sessions of the Ispolkom acquired a somewhat more orderly appearance, in good measure because its decisions were predetermined at caucuses of the socialist parties.

Thus, in no time, the Petrograd Soviet acquired a split personality: on top, speaking on behalf of the Soviet, a body of socialist intellectuals organized as the Executive Committee; below, an unruly village assembly. Except for its intelligentsia spokesmen, the Soviet was a rural body wedged into the most cosmopolitan city of the Empire. And no wonder: Petrograd had been a predominantly peasant city even before the war, when peasants had formed 70 percent of its population. This rural mass was augmented during the war with 200,000 workers brought in from the countryside to staff the defense industries and 160,000 recruits and reservists, mostly of the same origin.

Consistent with the traditional Menshevik and SR view of the Soviets as organs of "democratic" control over the "bourgeoisie," the Ispolkom decided on March 1, with a majority of 13–8, not to join the government which the Duma was in the process of forming.* By this decision, the socialist intelligentsia reserved for itself the right to steer and criticize the government without having to bear governmental responsibility: a position very much like the one which the parliamentary opposition had enjoyed vis-à-vis tsarism. As in the case of the Duma leadership's hesitancy to claim political power, the radical intelligentsia was inspired not only by theoretical but also by personal considerations. The events of February 26–27, 1917, may appear in the eyes of posterity as marking an irreversible break with the past, but this is not how they appeared to contemporaries. At this time, only Petrograd had risen in rebellion—no one else followed its lead. Punitive expeditions from the front could arrive at any moment. A contemporary of these events, and their historian, Serge Melgunov, observes that at this point several thousand well led and armed men could easily have retaken control of Petrograd, after which the lives of the intellectuals would have been at great risk.[80] It seemed, therefore, more prudent to let the "bourgeois" Duma take charge and manipulate it from behind the scenes.

In this fashion, on February 27, 1917, there emerged in Russia a peculiar system of government called *dvoevlastie*, or dyarchy: it lasted until October 25–26, when it yielded to the Bolshevik dictatorship. In theory, the Provisional Committee of the Duma—soon renamed the Provisional Government—bore full administrative responsibility, and the Soviet confined itself to functions of control, much as a legislature might in relation to an executive. The reality, however, was very different. The Soviet, or more precisely its Ispolkom, administered and legislated on its own often without so much as informing the government. Second, the partners in this arrangement were unable to cooperate effectively because they had very different objectives in mind. The Duma leaders wanted to contain the Revolution; the Soviet leaders wanted to deepen it. The former would have been happy to stop the flow of events at the point reached by nightfall on February 27. For the latter, February 27 was a mere stepping-stone to the "true"—that is, socialist—revolution.

Having decided they had no alternative but to form a cabinet in defiance of the Tsar's wishes, the Duma leaders were still inhibited by two considera-

---

*N. Sukhanov, *Zapiski o revoliutsii,* I (Berlin-Petersburg-Moscow, 1922), 255–56. *Revoliutsiia,* I, 49; T. Hasegawa, *The February Revolution: Petrograd 1917* (Seattle-London, 1981) 410–12. The minority consisted of members of the Jewish Bund augmented by some Mensheviks and Mezhraiontsy.

tions: lack of legitimacy and lack of means to control the unruly mobs. The more conservative members of the Provisional Committee, among them Shulgin and Guchkov, were of the opinion that one more attempt should be made to persuade Nicholas to let the Duma name the cabinet. But the majority thought this futile, preferring to seek legitimacy from the Petrograd Soviet, or, more precisely, from the socialist intelligentsia in the Ispolkom.

The decision was curious in the extreme. The Soviet, after all, was a private body, irregularly constituted and directed by representatives of socialist parties whom no one had elected. The best that could be said for it was that it represented the workers and soldiers of the city of Petrograd and environs, at most 1 million citizens in a nation of 170 million. From the point of view of legitimacy, the Fourth Duma—even allowing for the restricted franchise on which it had been chosen—had a better claim to speak for the country at large. But its leaders believed that in numbers lay safety: cooperation with the socialist parties would enable them better to restrain the mobs as well as to cope with a potential counterrevolution. At this point, the Ispolkom was solidly in the hands of Mensheviks, who acquiesced to the Duma's assuming formal governmental authority. The decision to seek legitimacy from the Soviet, as represented by the Ispolkom, was therefore psychologically understandable. But it hardly provided the new government with the legitimacy it needed. When on March 2 Miliukov, the new Minister of Foreign Affairs, was challenged from the audience which he was addressing, "Who elected you?" he could only answer, "We have been elected by the Russian Revolution"[81]—a claim that any other aspirant to power could make with equal right.*

The socialist intellectuals in the Ispolkom had no intention of giving the new government carte blanche. They were prepared to support it only on condition that it accept and implement a program of action to its liking: the Russian formula was *postol'ku-poskol'ku* ("to the extent that"). To this end, it worked out on March 1 a nine-point program[82] to serve as a basis of cooperation with the new government. Representatives of the two bodies met at midnight of March 1–2. Miliukov negotiated on behalf of the Duma committee; the Ispolkom was represented by a multiparty delegation headed by Chkheidze. Rather unexpectedly, the Duma committee raised no objection to most of the terms posed by the Ispolkom, in good measure because they sidestepped the two most controversial issues dividing the liberals from the socialists—namely, the conduct of the war and agrarian reform. In the course of negotiations which lasted well into the night, Miliukov persuaded the socialists to drop the demand to have officers elected by the troops. He also succeeded in altering the demand for the immediate introduction of a "democratic republic," leaving open the possibility of retaining the monarchy, something he ardently desired.[83] The two parties reached agreement on what now

*When on March 18 General Ruzskii asked Rodzianko to explain the chain of authority in the new government, Rodzianko answered that the Provisional Government had been appointed by the Provisional Committee of the Duma, which retained control over its actions and ministerial appointments (*RL*, No. 3, 1922, 158–59). Since the Provisional Committee had ceased to function by then, this explanation was either delusion or deception.

became an eight-point program, to be issued in the name of the newly formed "Provisional Council of Ministers" with the approval of the Ispolkom, but without its countersignature. The program was meant to serve as the basis of the government's activity during the brief period that lay ahead until the convocation of the Constituent Assembly. It called for:

1. Immediate amnesty for all political prisoners, including terrorists;
2. Immediate granting of the freedom of speech, association, and assembly, and the right to strike, as promised by the tsarist government in 1906 but never fully implemented;
3. Immediate abolition of disabilities and privileges due to nationality, religion, or social origin;
4. Immediate preparations for the convocation of a Constituent Assembly, to be elected on a universal, secret, direct, and equal ballot;
5. All police organs to be dissolved and replaced by a militia with elected officers, to be supervised by local government;
6. New elections to organs of local self-government on the basis of universal, direct, equal, and secret vote;
7. Military units that had participated in the Revolution to keep their weapons and to receive assurances they would not be sent to the front;
8. Military discipline in the armed forces to be maintained, but when off duty soldiers were to enjoy the same rights as civilians.[84]

This document, drawn up by exhausted politicians in the middle of the night, was to have the direst consequences. The most pernicious were Points 5 and 6, which in one fell swoop abolished the provincial bureaucracy and police that had traditionally kept the Russian state intact. The organs of self-rule—that is, the *zemstva* and Municipal Councils—which were to replace them had never borne administrative responsibilities and were not equipped to do so. The result was instant nationwide anarchy: anarchy that the new government liked to blame on the old regime but that was, in fact, largely of its own doing. No revolution anywhere, before or after 1917, wreaked such administrative havoc.

Points 1 and 7 were only slightly less calamitous. It was, of course, impossible for a democratic government to keep in prison or exile political activists confined for their opinions. But the blanket amnesty, which covered terrorists, resulted in Petrograd's being flooded with the most extreme radicals returned from Siberia and abroad. They traveled at the government's expense, impatient to subvert it. When the British detained Leon Trotsky in Canada as he was making his way home from New York, Miliukov interceded and secured his release. The Provisional Government would issue entry visas to Lenin and his associates returning from Switzerland, who made no secret of the intention to work for its overthrow. The government thus let loose foes of democracy, some of them in contact with the enemy and financed by him—actions difficult to conceive of a more experienced government. And, finally, by allowing the Petrograd garrison to retain weapons and by pledging not to send it to the front, the new government not only surrendered much authority over 160,000 uniformed men but ensconced in the capital city a disgruntled and armed peasantry whom its enemies could turn against it.

Later on March 2, Iurii Steklov, a Mezhraionets, presented on behalf of the Ispolkom the eight-point accord to the Soviet for approval. It was agreed that the Soviet would appoint a "supervisory committee" *(nabliudatel'nyi komitet)* to keep an eye on the government. After the changes had been renegotiated, the Provisional Committee announced its assumption of power.* At Miliukov's request, the Ispolkom appealed to the nation to support the new government. The statement was lukewarm in tone and hedged with conditions: democracy should support the new authority "to the extent" that it carried out its obligations and decisively fought the old regime.[85]

Thus, from the moment of its creation, Russia's democratic government owed its legitimacy to and functioned at the sufferance of a body of radical intellectuals who, by seizing control of the Soviet executive, had arrogated to themselves the right to speak on behalf of "democracy." Although this dependence was in some measure conditioned by the need to gain the Soviet's help in calming the insurgent mobs, the liberals and conservatives who formed the first Provisional Government saw nothing wrong with the arrangement. It is they, after all, who requested from the Ispolkom a declaration in support of the government. They also had few objections to the terms on the basis of which the Ispolkom had consented to back them. According to Miliukov, apart from the two points that had been dropped or revised and Point 7, everything in the declaration drafted by the Ispolkom was not only fully acceptable to the Duma committee or allowed an acceptable interpretation but "flowed directly from the newly formed government's personal views of its tasks."[86] Indeed, the demands that the Ispolkom draft formulated under Points 1, 5, and 6 the Kadets had presented to Stolypin as early as 1906.[87]

The new cabinet was hand-picked by Miliukov. Its composition, agreed upon in the evening of March 2, was as follows:

Chairman of the Council of Ministers
and Minister of the Interior: Prince G. E. Lvov
Minister of Foreign Affairs: P. N. Miliukov
Minister of Justice: A. F. Kerensky
Minister of Transport: N. V. Nekrasov

*According to S. P. Melgunov, *Martovskie dni* (Paris, 1961), 107, the term "Provisional Government" was not officially used until March 10.

Minister of Trade:	A. I. Konovalov
Minister of Public Instruction:	A. A. Manuilov
Minister of War:	A. I. Guchkov
Minister of Agriculture:	A. I. Shingarov
Minister of Finance:	M. I. Tereshchenko
Controller of State Accounts:	I. V. Godnev
Procurator of the Holy Synod:	V. N. Lvov

All these roles had long been rehearsed, and the names had appeared in the press in 1915 and 1916. The Duma representatives showed the roster of the proposed cabinet to the Ispolkom and asked for approval, but the latter preferred to leave this matter to the discretion of the "bourgeoisie."[88]

The fifty-six-year-old Lvov was a well-to-do landlord with long experience in the *zemstvo* movement. During the war, he had chaired the Union of Zemstva and Municipal Councils (Zemgor). According to Miliukov, he had been chosen to head the cabinet because as chairman of Zemgor he came closest to fulfilling the role of society's "leader," but suspicions have been voiced that Miliukov chose him because, aspiring to leadership in the government, he saw in Lvov a convenient figurehead.[89] A less suitable individual to direct Russia's affairs in this turbulent era would be hard to conceive. Lvov not only had no experience in public administration, but he professed an extreme form of Populism rooted in an unbounded faith in the sagacity and goodwill of the "people." He considered central government an unmitigated evil. On assuming office, he declared: "The process of the Great Revolution is not yet completed, yet each day that we live through strengthens our faith in the inexhaustible creative powers of the Russian people, its political wisdom, the greatness of its soul."[90] Lvov carried democratic and Populist convictions to the point of anarchism. When during the weeks and months that followed, provincial delegations would come to Petrograd for instruction, he received them with invariable attention and respect, but flatly refused to give them directives. When asked to appoint new governors in place of those whom the government had dismissed, he responded: "This is a question of the old psychology. The Provisional Government has removed the old governors and will appoint no one. Let them be elected locally. Such questions must be solved not in the center but by the population itself."[91] He carried this principle to extremes, believing that in a genuine democracy all decisions were made by the people concerned,[92] the function of government presumably being confined to record-keeping. Vladimir Nabokov, the cabinet secretary, writes: "I do not recall a single occasion when [Lvov] used a tone of authority or spoke out decisively and definitively . . . he was the very embodiment of passivity."[93] Devoid of imagination, he was unaware of the magnitude of the events in the midst of which he found himself. But then what could one expect of a man who on a visit to Niagara Falls could think of nothing better to say than: "Really, now, what of it? A river flows and drops. That's all."[94] He trailed this solemn ennui wherever he went.

42. Prince G. Lvov.

Lvov was an utter disaster as Prime Minister, his failure aggravated by the fact that he also took over the Ministry of the Interior. After resigning his post in July, he faded from the picture and in 1926 died in Paris a forgotten man.

Because he was so ineffectual and bland, he was overshadowed by the two most powerful personalities in the cabinet, Paul Miliukov and Alexander Kerensky, Russia's best known politicians and bitter rivals.

Born in 1859, Miliukov belonged to an older generation than Kerensky. His major strength lay in inexhaustible energy: he could work round the clock, chairing political meetings and negotiating, and still find the time to write books, edit newspapers, and give lectures. He had a vast store of knowledge— his scholarly studies earned him a secure position as one of Russia's premier historians. He was also an experienced parliamentarian, neither vain nor emotional. What he totally lacked, and what would wreck his career, was political intuition. Struve said of him that he practiced politics as if it were chess, and if it were, Miliukov would have been a grand master. He would time and again arrive at a political position by the process of deduction and persist in it long after it was obvious to everyone else that it was doomed. As Foreign Minister, his insistence first on retaining the monarchy and then on claiming for Russia Constantinople and the Straits reflected this shortcoming.

Kerensky was Miliukov's opposite: if his rival was all theory and logic, he was all impulse and emotion. Thanks to his feel for the popular mood, he emerged early as an idol of the Revolution; thanks to his emotionalism, he proved incapable of coping with the responsibilities which he had assumed.

Only thirty-six in February 1917, he had long groomed himself to lead the coming revolution. In youth he had displayed no definite ideology: his biography reveals a man of immense ambition in search of a cause. Eventually, he joined the Socialists-Revolutionaries. He first attracted national attention as a defense lawyer in celebrated political trials (e.g., the Beilis case and that of the Lena workers). In the Fourth Duma, he assumed leadership of the amorphous Trudovik faction and thanks to his rhetorical gifts became the spokesman for the entire left. Police reports made public after the February Revolution revealed that in 1915 and 1916 he had led a double life. Taking advantage of parliamentary immunity, Kerensky had traveled throughout Russia to confer with revolutionaries, whom he sought to organize for subversive purposes.[95] Long before the Revolution he had been regarded—and regarded himself—as a rising star. Aware of a physical resemblance to the French Emperor, he liked to strike Napoleonic poses. He had great theatrical gifts and resorted to gestures and other devices which cooler heads dismissed as melodrama but which the crowds loved. He could arouse and sway the masses as no one else, but the effect of his rhetoric was short-lived. Contemporaries thought he lacked talent for judging people, a defect which, combined with an impetuous personality, in the end destroyed him politically.

Kerensky wanted to build his career in revolutionary Russia by providing a unique link between the two elements of the dyarchy, the "bourgeoisie" and "democracy," and in this ambition he to some extent succeeded. In drawing up the Duma cabinet, Miliukov set aside two portfolios for socialist deputies in the Ispolkom: his hope was that they would provide a bridge between the cabinet and the Soviet. Chkheidze was offered a specially created post of Minister of Labor. Faithful to the resolution of the Ispolkom to stay out of the "bourgeois" cabinet, he declined. Kerensky, on the other hand, was desperately eager to take over the Ministry of Justice: a cabinet post combined with membership on the Ispolkom would put him (after Chkheidze's refusal) in an unrivaled position as intermediary between the two central institutions of the new regime. He asked the Ispolkom for authorization to join the cabinet. When his request was denied, Kerensky went over the head of the Ispolkom to the "masses." In an impassioned speech to the Soviet he pledged that as minister he would never betray democratic ideals. "I cannot live without the people," he shouted in his pathetic manner, "and the moment you come to doubt me, kill me!" Having uttered these words, he made ready to faint. It was pure melodrama, but it worked. The workers and soldiers gave him a rousing ovation and carried him to the room where the Duma Provisional Committee was in session. Unable to stand up to this display of mass approval, the Ispolkom consented to Kerensky's accepting the Justice portfolio, but it never forgave him for the blackmail.[96] Kerensky now resigned as deputy chairman of the Soviet, but kept his seat on the Ispolkom. In the months ahead, as the authority of the Provisional Government waned, he inexorably rose to the top by virtue of his dual position.

An urgent responsibility of the Provisional Government was dealing with ex-tsarist officials, both those who had been taken into custody by vigilante

43. Alexander Kerensky.

groups and those who had turned themselves in to the Duma seeking protection. On February 28 and March 1, hundreds of such individuals crowded the halls and chambers of Taurida. Here, Kerensky, as Minister of Justice, came into his own. He would allow no violence: "The Duma sheds no blood" was the slogan he launched and managed to make good on in the face of ugly mobs ready to lynch those whom he himself only weeks before had denounced as traitors. He rescued high tsarist officials from certain death by having them taken into custody. Sometimes he personally snatched them from the hands of mobs bent on murder, including Protopopov and Sukhomlinov. He ordered the officials transferred to the Ministerial Pavilion, located next to Taurida and linked to it by a protected passageway. They sat here, under heavy guard, with strict orders not to converse. During the night of March 1–2, with a show of force to impress the crowds, they were transferred to the Peter and Paul Fortress: the diminutive Protopopov seemed shrunk still smaller from terror as he was driven with a guard's gun pressed to his head. When space in the fortress ran out, the overflow was put into Mikhailovskii Manege. It is estimated that in the first days of the Revolution, 4,000 persons were arrested or placed in protective custody. Many of them would perish in the Bolshevik "Red Terror."

The February Revolution was relatively bloodless. The total number of killed and wounded has been estimated at between 1,300 and 1,450, of whom 169 were fatalities. Most of the deaths occurred at the naval bases in Kronshtadt and Helsinki, where anarchist sailors lynched officers, often on suspicion of "espionage" because of their German-sounding surnames.*

The position of the government was unenviable. It had to share power with the Soviet, controlled by radicals determined to advance the revolution and prepared, in the name of social ideals, to sabotage the very war they wanted to pursue. Nor did it have a clear notion of its function. Ostensibly, it was a mere caretaker government, put in place to keep the country together until the convocation of the Constituent Assembly. "They believe that authority has fallen from the hands of the legal government," Zinaida Gippius noted in her diary on March 2, "they have picked it up, will safeguard it, and will turn it over to the new legal authority which will bear no resemblance whatever to the old."[97] But this attitude proved entirely impractical because the government was at once beset by a multitude of problems that would not wait. In other words, it suffered not only from having to share power with another body but also from confusion as to how to use the power that it was allowed to claim.

Although the Provisional Government had cleared its personnel and program with the Ispolkom, the latter felt no obligation to reciprocate and from the outset legislated on its own. The most striking example of such independence is the notorious Order No. 1, which it issued on March 1 without consulting the Duma, although it concerned the most vital institution of the country in time of war, its armed forces.

One of the myths of the Russian Revolution is that Order No. 1 was dictated by a crowd of grubby soldiers. Sukhanov has left a vivid picture of the Social-Democratic lawyer N. D. Sokolov seated at a table in Taurida and writing down the demands of the troops. There even exists a photograph which seems to lend visual credibility to this version of the order's origins.† Closer scrutiny, however, reveals that the document had a less spontaneous origin. It was initially formulated, not by rank-and-file soldiers, but by civilians and garrison delegates picked by the Ispolkom, some of them officers and most of them affiliated with the socialist parties. Shliapnikov leaves no doubt that the principal clauses of Order No. 1 were formulated by socialist intellectuals, eager to secure a dominant influence over the garrison.[98] Although the order reflected some genuine soldier grievances, it was first and foremost a political manifesto. Its authors were well versed in the history of revolutions and aware that traditionally the principal counterrevolutionary threat came from the armed forces. Determined not to allow this to happen in Russia, they wanted

---

*Martynov, *Tsarskaia armiia*, 148, gives the total casualties as 1,315. Avdeev's figures, which seem more accurate, are 1,443 victims, of which 168 or 169 were killed or died from wounds: 11 policemen, 70 military personnel, 22 workers, 5 students, and 60 others, 5 of them children (*Revoliutsiia*, I, 111).

†In this picture (Plate 44) most of the military appear to wear officer's uniforms.

44. N. D. Sokolov drafting Order No.1: March 1, 1917.

to reduce the authority of the officers over the troops and to keep weapons out of their hands. Martynov notes that from the first day of the Revolution the Provisional Government and the Ispolkom engaged in a tug-of-war over the army:

> The Provisional Government leaned on the commanding staff and officers, whereas the Soviet of Workers' and Soldiers' Deputies leaned on the rank-and-file. The celebrated Order No. 1 was, as it were, a wedge inserted into the body of the army, after which it split and began rapidly to fall apart.[99]

The Ispolkom exploited soldiers' complaints over their ill treatment by officers as a means of subverting the authority of the officer staff, which was not something the troops asked for. Suffice it to say that of the seven articles in Order No. 1 only the last two addressed themselves to the status of the men in uniform; the remainder dealt with the role of the armed forces under the new regime and had as their purpose depriving the "bourgeois" government of the opportunity to use them as Cavaignac had done in 1848 and Thiers in 1871. Some rank-and-file soldiers and sailors had no difficulty understanding this. A sailor, appropriately named Pugachev, who dropped in at the Merezhkovskiis' after having taken part in the vote on Order No. 1, told them: "Educated folk will read it differently. But we understood it straight: disarm the officers."[100]

The order was addressed to the "Garrison of the Petrograd Military District," but it was immediately interpreted as applicable to all the armed forces, at the front as well as in the rear.[101] Article 1 called for the election in every military unit, from company to regiment, as well as in the navy, of "committees" modeled on the soviets. Article 2 provided for every company

45. Political meeting at the front: Summer 1917.

to elect one representative to the Petrograd Soviet. Article 3 stated that in respect to all political actions, members of the armed forces were subordinated to the Petrograd Soviet and their committees. Article 4 gave the Petrograd Soviet the authority to countermand orders of the Provisional Government bearing on military matters. Article 5 stipulated that control over all military equipment (rifles, machine guns, armored vehicles, etc.) was to be assumed by company and battalion committees; they were not to be turned over to officers under any conditions. Article 6 accorded off-duty soldiers the same rights as civilians, relieving them of the obligation of saluting and standing at attention. Article 7 abolished the practice of addressing officers by honorary titles and forbade officers to speak to soldiers in a rude or familiar manner.

It is difficult to believe that when the Ispolkom approved Order No. 1 and distributed it to the armed forces, it did not realize the consequences. It is equally difficult to believe that in approving this extraordinary document it thought it was merely responding to soldier complaints. The order's inevitable effect was to subvert the authority of the government and the officer corps over the armed forces. As soon as it came to be known to the troops, they formed everywhere, at the front and in the rear, military "committees": army committees, corps committees, divisional committees, as well as regimental, battalion, and company committees, a bewildering array of overlapping groups. Those functioning at the lower levels (company, battalion, and regiment) were ordinarily staffed by rank-and-file soldiers and resembled, in their structure and procedures, urban soviets. But those operating at the higher echelons immediately fell under the control of Menshevik, Bolshevik, and SR intellectuals, often recently commissioned university students, who used them to advance their political agenda—a military equivalent of the Executive Committee of the Petrograd Soviet. At every military level there now took place endless meetings with interminable discussions, followed by a flood of mandatory "resolutions." Senior officers came to be treated as class enemies: as their authority waned, the chain of command broke down.

No less damaging was Article 4, which read: "The orders of the Military Commission of the State Duma are to be carried out only in those instances when they do not contradict the orders and resolutions of the Soviet of Workers' and Soldiers' Deputies." This clause struck at the very heart of the government's responsibility for the conduct of the war. The Ispolkom viewed itself as in charge of the armed forces and the Minister of War as its employee: on one occasion (March 6) it even complained that the Minister of War was "disinclined to subordinate himself" to the decisions of the Soviet.[102]

Guchkov, who learned of Order No. 1 only after its publication, sought in vain to have the Soviet retract it. The best he could get was to have the Ispolkom issue Order No. 2, which only compounded the damage. Guchkov wanted the Soviet to state unequivocally that Order No. 1 applied only to the troops in the rear. But Order No. 2, issued on March 5, did not say that. It dealt mainly with the question whether officers should be elected by their men and conveyed the impression that the Ispolkom approved of such a procedure. Nowhere did it state that Order No. 1 did not apply to front-line troops.[103]

On March 9, less than two weeks after the new government had been formed, Guchkov cabled General Alekseev:

> The Provisional Government has no real power of any kind and its orders are carried out only to the extent that this is permitted by the Soviet of Workers' and Soldiers' Deputies, which controls the most essential strands of actual power, insofar as the troops, railroads, [and] postal and telegraph services are in its hands. One can assert bluntly that the Provisional Government exists only as long as it is permitted to do so by the Soviet of Workers' and Soldiers' Deputies. In particular, in the military department, it is possible at present to issue only such orders as basically do not contradict the decisions of the above-mentioned Soviet.[104]

The monarchy played no part in these critical events. Nicholas's last order of any consequence was his February 25 instruction demanding the suppression of street disorders. Once this order proved unenforceable, the monarchy ceased to matter. After that date, it not only lost control over events but receded into the background as the political conflict began to revolve around the relationship between the Duma and the Soviet.

However, after the Provisional Government had come into being, the question of the monarchy's future acquired great urgency. Some ministers wanted to retain the monarchy on a strictly limited, constitutional basis. Proponents of this position, mainly Miliukov and Guchkov, felt that some sort of monarchical presence was essential, in part because to the Russian masses the Crown symbolized the "state" and in part because in a multinational empire it was the main supranational, unifying institution. Their opponents argued that the anti-monarchist passions of the crowds had made it unrealistic to expect the monarchy to survive in any form.

The monarchy's prestige in Russia had reached a nadir in the winter of 1916–17 when even committed monarchists turned against it. Guchkov, for all his royalist sentiments, had to admit that in the first days of the Revolution, "around the throne, there was an utter vacuum." And Shulgin noted on February 27: "in this whole immense city one could not find a few hundred men sympathetic to the government."[105] The significance of this fact can scarcely be overestimated: it exerted a critical influence not only on the outbreak of the Revolution but on its whole subsequent course. Centuries of historical experience had inculcated in Russians—that is, the mass of peasants, workers, and soldiers—the habit of viewing the tsar as the *khoziain* or proprietor of the country. This notion prevented them from conceiving of sovereignty as something distinct from the person of the sovereign. Russia without a true—that is, "terrible" or "awesome"—tsar, let alone without any tsar, in the people's minds was a contradiction in terms: for them it was the person of the tsar that defined and gave reality to the state, not the other way around. The decline in the prestige of tsardom which had occurred after the turn of the century, as a result of the monarchy's inability to suppress the opposition and its ultimate surrender of autocratic authority, lowered in their eyes the prestige of the state and its government as well. Without its *khoziain*, the country, as the people understood it, fell apart and ceased to exist, just as a peasant household fell apart and ceased to exist upon the death of its *bol'shak*. When this happened, Russia reverted to its original "Cossack" constitution of universal *volia*, or liberty, understood in the sense of unbridled license, in which the will of the commune was the only acknowledged authority.

In view of this tradition, one might have expected the mass of the population to favor the retention of the monarchy. But at this particular historic juncture two factors militated against such a stand.

The peasantry remained monarchist. Nevertheless, in early 1917 it was not averse to an interlude of anarchy, sensing that it would provide a chance finally to carry out a nationwide "Black Repartition." Indeed, between the spring of 1917 and the spring of 1918, the communal peasantry would seize and distribute among themselves virtually all the land in private possession. Once this process was completed, its traditional monarchist sentiments would reassert themselves, but then it would be too late.

The other consideration had to do with the fear of punishment on the part of the Petrograd populace, especially the troops. The February events could be seen in different ways: as a glorious revolution or as a sordid military mutiny. If the monarchy survived, even though constitutionally circumscribed, it was likely to view the actions of the Petrograd garrison as mutiny:

The half-conscious revulsion against the monarchy among the [Petrograd] masses seems to have been motivated by a sense of apprehension over what had

been done . . . a revolution that ended with the reestablishment of the old
dynasty would essentially turn into a rebellion, participation in which . . .
carried the risk of retribution.[106]

When he arrived in Pskov on March 1, Nicholas had no thought of
abdicating. On the contrary, he was determined to reassert his authority by
force; in his diary the preceding day he noted that he had sent General Ivanov
to Petrograd "to introduce [*vodvorit'*] order." But in Pskov he fell under the
influence of opinions which touched him where he was the most sensitive: his
patriotism and love of the army. From a conversation with General Ruzskii
shortly after arrival and throughout the twenty-four hours that followed,
Nicholas heard from everyone that as long as he remained tsar Russia could
not win the war. Nicholas discounted the opinion of politicians as self-serving,
but he paid heed to the generals. As the Hughes telegraph at the Northern
Front headquarters registered telegram after telegram from the military commanders urging him, for the sake of the country and its armed forces, first to
allow the Duma to form the cabinet and then to abdicate, his resolve weakened. Alexandra anticipated the effects of such pressures on him and on March
2 urged him not to sign a "constitution" or some such "horror" *(uzhas)*. She
added:

> If you are compelled to make concessions, then you are *under no conditions*
> obliged to fulfill them, because they have been extracted in an unworthy
> manner.[107]

General Alekseev, who in the Tsar's absence from Mogilev assumed the
duties of Commander in Chief, had sound practical reasons to be worried by
the news from Petrograd: the continuation of strikes and mutinies in the
capital city threatened to disrupt the railway service and halt the flow of
supplies to the front.[108] In the longer run there was the danger of the mutiny
spreading to front-line troops. In the morning of February 28 he concluded
that there was no hope of suppressing the Petrograd mutiny by force because
Khabalov had wired that he had only 1,100 loyal troops left and even they were
running out of ammunition.[109] In these circumstances he saw no way of saving
the front from collapse other than by granting the political concessions urged
by Rodzianko. Having learned of the spread of disorders to Moscow, on
March 1 he cabled the Tsar:

> A revolution in Russia—and this is inevitable once disorders occur in the
> rear—will mean a disgraceful termination of the war, with all its inevitable
> consequences, so dire for Russia. The army is most intimately connected with
> the life of the rear. It may be confidently stated that disorders in the rear will
> produce the same result among the armed forces. It is impossible to ask the
> army calmly to wage war while a revolution is in progress in the rear. The
> youthful makeup of the present army and its officer staff, among whom a very
> high percentage consist of reservists and commissioned university students,
> gives no grounds for assuming that the army will not react to events occurring
> in Russia.

Insofar as the Duma was trying to restore order in the rear, Alekseev continued, it should be given the opportunity to form a cabinet of national confidence.[110] He followed this cable with the draft of a manifesto prepared, at his request, by N. A. Basily, the chief of the diplomatic chancellery at headquarters,[111] in which Nicholas empowered the Duma to form a cabinet. Alekseev's recommendation was endorsed by Grand Duke Sergei Mikhailovich, the Inspector of Artillery and the Tsar's cousin once removed.

Around 10 p.m., while these messages were en route, Nicholas received General Ruzskii. In response to the Tsar's request that he give free expression to his opinions, Ruzskii came out in support of a Duma cabinet. Having heard him out, Nicholas explained why he disagreed. As Ruzskii later recounted:

> The sovereign's basic thought was that he wished nothing for himself, in his own interest, that he held on to nothing, but that he did not feel he had the right to transfer the entire task of administering Russia into the hands of people who, being in power today, could inflict grievous harm on the fatherland and tomorrow wash their hands, "handing in their resignation." "I am accountable to God and Russia for all that has happened and will happen," the sovereign said. "It is a matter of no consequence that the ministers will be responsible to the Duma and State Council. If I see that they are not acting for Russia's good, I will never be able to agree with them, consoling myself with the thought that this is not the work of my hands, not my responsibility."

When Ruzskii urged the Tsar to adopt the formula "The sovereign reigns and the government rules," Nicholas said that

> this formula was incomprehensible to him, that he would have had to be differently brought up, to be reborn. . . . The Tsar, with remarkable lucidity, ran through the opinions of all those who could, in the near future, administer Russia in the capacity of ministers responsible to the [legislative] chambers, and expressed the conviction that the civic activists who would undoubtedly form the first cabinet had no administrative experience and, having been entrusted with the burden of authority, would prove unable to cope with their task.[112]

The conversation with Ruzskii ended around 11:30 p.m., at which time Nicholas was handed Alekseev's cable with Basily's draft manifesto. The documents from the highest officer in the armed forces made on him a deep impression. After retiring for a few minutes, Nicholas recalled Ruzskii and told him he had made two decisions. Ruzskii was to inform Rodzianko and Alekseev that he would yield and allow the Duma to form a cabinet. The second order concerned Ivanov. He was to be sent a message reading: "Until my arrival and receipt of your report, please undertake no action."*

With these instructions, Nicholas gave up the idea of suppressing the Petrograd disorders and took the path of political conciliation. He hoped that

---

*Martynov, *Tsarskaia armiia*, 145. The message to Ivanov was sent at Alekseev's request: *KA*, No. 2/21 (1927), 31.

his concessions would, in time, have the same calming effect on the country as the Manifesto of October 17, 1905.*

The date was March 2, the time 1 a.m. Nicholas retired to his sleeping car, but he stayed awake through the night, tormented by doubts whether his concessions would work and by worries about his family: "My thoughts and feelings are all the time there," he wrote in the diary, "how hard it must be on poor Alix to go through all this by herself." He was still awake at 5:15 a.m.[113] Ruzskii contacted Rodzianko at 3:30 a.m. Their conversation, which lasted four hours, was to have a decisive influence on Nicholas's decision to abdicate, because from it Ruzskii and, through him, the other commanding generals learned how desperate the situation in Petrograd had grown and realized that the manifesto granting the Duma the power to form a ministry had come too late.[114] They, in turn, exerted on Nicholas pressures to abdicate.

Ruzskii advised Rodzianko that the Tsar had consented to the formation of a cabinet appointed by and responsible to the legislature. Rodzianko responded:

> It is obvious that His Majesty and you do not realize what is going on here. One of the most terrible revolutions has broken out, which it will not be so easy to quell. . . . The troops are completely demoralized, they not only disobey but kill their officers. Hatred of Her Majesty has reached extreme limits. . . . I must inform you that what you propose is no longer adequate, and the dynastic question has been raised point-blank.

In response to Ruzskii's request for clarification, Rodzianko answered that

> troops everywhere are joining the Duma and the people and there is a definite, terrible demand for abdication in favor of the [Tsar's] son under a regency of Michael Aleksandrovich.†

He recommended that the dispatch of front-line troops to Petrograd be halted "since they will not move against the people."

As Ruzskii conversed with Rodzianko, the tapes of their exchange were passed on to telegraphists to be forwarded to Alekseev. Alekseev was stunned by what he read. At 9 a.m. (March 2), he wired to Pskov a request that the Tsar be awakened at once ("All etiquette must be set aside") and shown the Ruzskii-Rodzianko tapes—at stake was the fate not only of the Tsar but of the dynasty and Russia herself.[115] A general on the other end of the Hughes telegraph responded that the Tsar had just fallen asleep and that Ruzskii was scheduled to report to him in an hour.

Alekseev and the other generals at headquarters now decided that there

---

*Ivanov made his way to Tsarskoe Selo, where he met with the Empress (Martynov, *Tsarskaia armiia*, 148), but his men were stopped at the approaches to Petrograd at Luga by mutinous troops and dissuaded from proceeding with their mission: *RL,* No. 3 (1922), 126.

†In fact, the "people" were nowhere clamoring for the Tsarevich to assume the throne under a regency: this was wishful thinking on the part of Duma politicians.

was no alternative. Nicholas would have to follow Rodzianko's advice and abdicate.[116] But Alekseev knew the Tsar well enough to realize that he would do so only under the pressure of the military command. So he took it upon himself to communicate the text of the Ruzskii-Rodzianko conversation to the commanders of the fronts and fleets. He accompanied it with a personal recommendation that Nicholas step down in favor of Alexis and Michael, in order to save the armed forces, make it possible to pursue the war, and safeguard Russia's national integrity as well as the dynasty. He requested the recipients to communicate their views directly to Pskov, with copies to himself.[117]

Ruzskii reported to Nicholas at 10:45 a.m. bearing the tapes of his conversation with Rodzianko. Nicholas read them in silence. Having finished, he went to the window of his railway car and stood motionless, looking out. When he turned around, he said that he would consider Rodzianko's recommendation. He added that he thought the people would not understand such a move, that the Old Believers would not forgive him for betraying the coronation oath and the Cossacks for abandoning the front.[118] He affirmed

> his strong conviction that he had been born for misfortune, that he brought Russia great misfortune. He said that he had realized clearly the night before that no manifesto [about the Duma ministry] would be of help. . . . "If it is necessary, for Russia's welfare, that I step aside, I am prepared to do so."[119]

At this point, Ruzskii was handed the cable from Alekseev requesting his opinion of Alekseev's recommendation that Nicholas abdicate. Ruzskii read the message aloud to the Tsar.[120]

Around 2 p.m., Pskov was in receipt of the army commanders' responses to Alekseev's cable. All agreed with Alekseev. Grand Duke Nikolai Nikolaevich begged the Tsar "on his knees" to give up the crown to save Russia and the dynasty. General A. E. Evert, who commanded the Western Front, and General A. A. Brusilov, in charge of the Southwestern Front, concurred. General V. V. Sakharov of the Romanian Front thought the Provisional Government "a gang of bandits" but he, too, saw no way of avoiding abdication.*

Ruzskii called on Nicholas again, between 2 and 3:00 p.m., accompanied by Generals Iu. N. Danilov and S. S. Savvich and bearing the cables from Nikolai Nikolaevich and the other front commanders.[121] After perusing them, Nicholas requested the three generals to state their frank opinion. They responded, with much emotion, that in their view, too, the Tsar had no choice but to step down. After a moment of silence, Nicholas crossed himself and said that he was prepared to do so. The generals also made the sign of the cross.

---

*P. E. Shchegolev, ed., *Otrechenie Nikolaia II* (Leningrad, 1927), 203–5. Admiral A. I. Nepenin, commander of the Baltic Fleet, concurred as well. His telegram came late: he himself was murdered two days later by sailors: N. de Basily, *Diplomat of Imperial Russia, 1903–1917: Memoirs* (Stanford, Calif., 1973), 121, and *RL*, No. 3 (1922), 143–44. There was no response from Admiral Alexander Kolchak, who commanded the Black Sea Fleet.

Nicholas then retired, reappearing a quarter of an hour later (at 3:05 p.m.) with two messages that he had written by hand on telegraphic blanks, one addressed to Rodzianko, the other to Alekseev. The first read:

> There is no sacrifice that I would not make for the sake of the true well-being and salvation of our Mother Russia. For that reason, I am prepared to renounce the throne in favor of My Son, with the understanding that He will remain with Me until attaining maturity, and that My Brother, Michael Aleksandrovich, will serve as Regent.[122]

The cable to Alekseev was essentially the same except that it made no mention of the regency.[123]

Nicholas requested headquarters to draft an abdication manifesto. Alekseev entrusted the task to Basily. Drawing on the Code of Laws, Basily drafted the text, which at 7:40 p.m. was wired to Pskov for the Tsar's signature.[124]

All the evidence indicates that Nicholas abdicated from patriotic motives: the wish to spare Russia a humiliating defeat and to save her armed forces from disintegration. The argument which swayed him was the unanimous opinion of the commanders of the disparate fronts, especially the cable from Nikolai Nikolaevich.* No less significant is the fact that Nicholas carried on talks about his abdication, not with the Duma and its Provisional Government, but with General Alekseev, as if to emphasize that he was abdicating to the armed forces and at their request. If Nicholas's foremost concern had been with preserving his throne he would have quickly made peace with Germany and used front-line troops to crush the rebellion in Petrograd and Moscow. He chose instead, to give up the crown to save the front.

Although Nicholas showed no emotion throughout this ordeal, abdication was for him an immense sacrifice: not because he craved either the substance of power or its trappings—the one he thought a heavy burden, the other a tedious imposition—but because he felt that by this action he was betraying his oath to God and country.[125]

His trials were not yet over. At the very instant when he was signing the pledge to abdicate, in Petrograd two delegates from the Provisional Committee, Shulgin and Guchkov, were boarding a special train bound for Pskov. They carried their own draft of an abdication manifesto, hoping to extract from Nicholas what, unknown to them, he had already conceded. They were sent by the Provisional Committee, which had decided the preceding night that it required the Tsar's abdication to begin functioning. The hope of the government was that by acting swiftly it could present the country with a new tsar, the child Alexis, before the Soviet proclaimed Russia a republic.

As he was leaving the Imperial train, Ruzskii was told that Shulgin and Guchkov were on their way. He informed Nicholas and was requested to

---

*Martynov, *Tsarskaia armiia*, 159. Later, when he returned to Tsarskoe, Nicholas showed Count Benckendorff the cables from the front commanders to explain his decision to abdicate: P. K. Benckendorff, *Last Days at Tsarskoe Selo* (London, 1927), 44–45.

return the cables to Rodzianko and Alekseev. Ruzskii thought that the two deputies, both known monarchists, could be carrying a message from the Duma that would enable Nicholas to retain the throne.[126]

While awaiting their arrival, Nicholas sent for Professor S. P. Fedorov, the Court physician, to inquire about the prospects of Alexis's recovery. He told Fedorov of Rasputin's prediction that upon reaching the age of thirteen—that is, in 1917—Alexis would be completely cured. Was that correct? The physician responded that such a recovery would be a miracle, for medicine knew of no cure for hemophilia. Even so, Alexis could live for many years. He further expressed the personal opinion that it would be inconceivable that after abdicating Nicholas would be permitted to keep his son, now installed as tsar, with him, because he would almost certainly be required to go into exile abroad.[127] On hearing this, Nicholas changed his mind. He would not part with the boy: therefore, instead of abdicating in favor of Alexis he would hand the crown to Michael.

This impulsive decision was the last gasp of the patrimonial spirit, a reflex that showed how deeply this mentality was still embedded in the Russian monarchy. The order of succession was clearly established: according to Russian constitutional law, the crown automatically descended to the reigning tsar's eldest son, even if he was a minor and unable to rule.[128] Nicholas had no authority to abdicate on his son's behalf and appoint Michael successor: "The Russian throne [was] not the emperor's private property nor his patrimony [*votchina*] to dispose of according to his own free will."[129] The choice of Michael was doubly irregular in that Michael, having taken for his wife a commoner who was twice married and once divorced, had disqualified himself from the succession in any event.

Shulgin and Guchkov arrived in Pskov at 9:45 p.m. and were immediately taken to the Imperial train. Both were unshaven and dressed in rumpled clothes: Shulgin is said to have looked like a convict.[130] In the presence of Ruzskii, Count Fredericks, and General Naryshkin, who kept notes, Guchkov presented a somber account of the situation in the capital. Avoiding Nicholas's eyes, his own fixed on the table before him, he stressed the danger of unrest spilling to the frontline troops and the futility of dispatching punitive expeditions. He insisted that the mutiny was spontaneous: Khabalov's assistant told him that the troops joined the rebels immediately. According to Ruzskii, Nicholas was shattered when told that his own Guard unit participated in the mutiny: after that, he barely listened to Guchkov.[131] Guchkov went on to say that the Petrograd crowds were passionately anti-monarchist, blaming the Crown for Russia's recent misfortunes. This called for a drastic change in the manner in which the government was run. The Provisional Committee had been constituted to restore order, especially in the armed forces, but this move had to be accompanied by further changes. The difficulty of having Nicholas keep the throne lay not only in the animosity of the populace toward him and his wife but also in its fear of retribution: "All the workers and soldiers who had taken part in the disorders," Guchkov said, "are convinced that the retention [*vodvorenie*] of the old dynasty means punishment, for which reason a complete change is necessary."[132] Guchkov concluded that the best solution would be for Nicholas to abdicate in favor of his son and appoint Michael Regent: such was the opinion of the Provisional Committee. This step, if promptly taken, could save Russia and the dynasty.

Shulgin, who kept his eyes on Nicholas as his colleague was speaking, says that the Tsar displayed no emotion. When Guchkov finished, he responded, "calmly, as if it were an everyday matter," that he had made up his mind earlier in the day to lay down the crown in favor of his son, "but now, having thought the situation over, I have decided that in view of [my son's illness] I must abdicate simultaneously for him also, since I cannot be separated from him."[133] The crown would pass to Michael. This news left Guchkov and Shulgin speechless. When they recovered from the shock, the legal question was raised: was such procedure legitimate? Since no lawyers were present, it was held in abeyance. Shulgin and Guchkov expressed the opinion that quite apart from the legality of the matter, the assumption of the throne by the young Alexis would have a much better effect on the public: "A beautiful myth could have been created around this innocent and pure child," Guchkov thought to himself, "his charm would have helped to calm the anger of the masses."[134]

But Nicholas would not yield. He retired to his private car, where he remained for twenty minutes, in the course of which he revised the abdication manifesto so as to designate Michael his successor. At Guchkov and Shulgin's request he inserted a phrase asking his brother to take an oath to work in "union" with the legislature. The time was 11:50 p.m., but Nicholas had the document read 3:05 p.m., when he had made the original decision, to avoid giving the impression he had surrendered the throne under the Duma's pressure.

HEADQUARTERS   Copies to all Commanders
To the Chief of Staff

In the days of the great struggle against the external enemy, who has striven for nearly three years to enslave our homeland, the Lord God has willed to subject Russia to yet another heavy trial. The popular disturbances which have broken out threaten to have a calamitous effect on the further conduct of the hard-fought war. The fate of Russia, the honor of our heroic army, the welfare of the people, the whole future of our beloved Fatherland demand that the war be brought at all costs to a victorious conclusion. The cruel foe exerts his last efforts and the time is near when our valiant army, together with our glorious allies, will decisively overcome him. In these decisive days in Russia's life, WE have deemed it our duty in conscience to OUR nation to draw closer together and to unite all the national forces for the speediest attainment of victory. In agreement with the State Duma, WE have acknowledged it as beneficial to renounce the throne of the Russian state and lay down Supreme authority. Not wishing to separate OURSELVES from OUR beloved SON, WE hand over OUR succession to OUR Brother, the Grand Duke MICHAEL ALEK-

SANDROVICH, and give Him OUR BLESSING to ascend the throne of the Russian State. We command OUR Brother to conduct the affairs of state in complete and inviolate union with the representatives of the nation in the legislative institutions on such principles as they will establish, and to swear to this an inviolate oath. In the name of OUR deeply beloved homeland, WE call on all true sons of the Fatherland to fulfill their sacred duty to It by obeying the Tsar in the difficult moment of national trials and to help HIM, together with the representatives of the people, lead the Russian State to victory, prosperity, and glory. May the Lord God help Russia.

Pskov, 2 March 1917
15 hours 5 minutes   Nicholas

[Correct]
The Minister of the Imperial Household,
Vladimir Borisovich, Count Fredericks[135]

Two features of this historic document, which ended the three-hundred-year-old reign of the Romanovs, call for comment. One is that the abdication instrument was addressed, not to the Duma and its Provisional Committee, the de facto government of Russia, but to the chief of staff of the armed forces, General Alekseev. Apparently, in Nicholas's eyes the army command was the one remaining bearer of sovereignty. The second feature, which would be repeated in Nicholas's farewell address to the armed forces on March 7, was his acknowledgment that Russia was now a constitutional monarchy in the full sense of the word: the abdication instrument provided for the Duma to determine the new constitutional order and the role of the Crown in it.

While a copy of the abdication manifesto was being drawn up for the Duma deputies to take to Petrograd, Nicholas at their request wrote by hand two instructions to the Senate. In one, he appointed Prince Lvov Chairman of the Council of Ministers: this had the effect of legitimizing the Provisional Committee. According to Guchkov, after agreeing to Lvov's appointment, Nicholas asked what service rank he held. When Guchkov responded that he did not know, Nicholas smiled;[136] he found it difficult to conceive that a private person, without status on the Table of Ranks, could chair the cabinet. In the other instruction, he appointed Grand Duke Nikolai Nikolaevich his successor as Commander in Chief.[137] Although the actual time was midnight, both documents were dated 2 p.m., in order to precede the abdication.

This done, Nicholas told Shulgin that he intended to spend several days at headquarters, then visit his mother in Kiev, following which he would rejoin the family at Tsarskoe Selo, staying there until the children had recovered from measles.* The three documents were dispatched to Mogilev by courier for immediate release. Then the Imperial train departed for the same destination. In his diary, Nicholas wrote: "Left Pskov at 1 a.m. with oppressive feelings about events. All around treason and cowardice and deception." The

---

*Martynov, *Tsarskaia armiia*, 171. According to Voeikov (*Padenie*, III, 79), Nicholas chose to go to Mogilev rather than proceed directly to Tsarskoe because the road to there was still barred.

next day, en route to headquarters, he read "a great deal about Julius Caesar."

The news of Nicholas's abdication spread quickly, reaching Tsarskoe Selo in the afternoon of the following day. Alexandra at first refused to believe it: she said that she could not imagine her husband acting in such a hurry. When, in the evening, the rumors were confirmed, she explained that "the Emperor had preferred to abdicate the crown rather than to break the oath which he had made at his coronation to maintain and transfer to his heir the autocracy such as he had inherited from his father." Then she cried.[138]

In the context of the political situation of the time, Nicholas's abdication was anticlimactic, since he had been effectively deposed a few days earlier by Petrograd mobs. But in the broader context of Russian political life, it was an act of the utmost significance. For one, Russia's political and military officials swore the oath of loyalty to the person of the Tsar. By abdicating, Nicholas absolved them from their oath and their duties. Until and unless Michael assumed the throne, therefore, Russian bureaucrats and officers were left to shift for themselves, without a sovereign authority to obey. Second, since the masses of the Russian population were accustomed to identify the person of the monarch with the state and the government, the withdrawal of the monarch spelled to them the dissolution of the Empire.

Shulgin and Guchkov left for Petrograd, at 3:00 a.m. Before departing, they cabled the contents of the three Imperial documents to the government. The abdication manifesto threw the cabinet into disarray: no one had expected Nicholas to abdicate in favor of his brother. The Provisional Committee, fearing that the release of the manifesto as signed by Nicholas would set off even more violent riots, decided, for the time being, to withhold publication.

The committee spent what was left of the night heatedly debating what to do next. The chief protagonists were Miliukov and Kerensky. Miliukov argued on grounds he had often spelled out, that it was essential to retain the monarchy in some form. Kerensky dissented: whatever the merits of Miliukov's historic and constitutional argument, in view of the mood of the populace such a course was unfeasible. The cabinet sided with Kerensky. It was agreed as soon as possible to arrange a meeting with Michael to persuade him to renounce the crown. Rodzianko conveyed the news to Alekseev and Ruzskii, requesting them for the time being to keep Nicholas's abdication manifesto confidential.[139]

Under different circumstances, Michael might have made a suitable candidate for the role of a constitutional tsar. Born in 1878, from 1899 to 1904 he was the heir apparent. He disqualified himself in 1912 from any future role in this capacity by marrying in Vienna a divorcée without the Tsar's permission. For this action, his person and property were placed under guardianship; he was prohibited from returning to Russia and dismissed from the army. Nicholas later relented, readmitted him to the country, and allowed his wife, N. S.

46. Grand Duke Michael.

Vulfert, to assume the title of Countess Brasova. During the war, Michael served in the Caucasus as commander of the Savage Division and the Second Caucasian Corps. He was a gentle, modest person, not much interested in politics, as weak and irresolute as his elder brother. Though he was in Petrograd during the February Revolution, he proved quite useless to the Duma leaders, who sought his help in restoring order.

At 6 a.m. the Provisional Committee telephoned Michael at the residence of his friend Prince Putianin, where he happened to be staying. He was told of Nicholas's decision to pass to him the throne and requested to meet with the cabinet. Michael was both surprised and annoyed with his brother for having placed such responsibilities on him without prior consultation. The encounter between Michael and the cabinet was delayed until later in the morning, apparently because the ministers wanted to hear Shulgin and Guchkov's report on their mission to Pskov. The two, however, were delayed and reached the Putianin residence just as the meeting was about to begin.[140]

Speaking for the majority of the cabinet, Rodzianko told Michael that if he accepted the crown a violent rising would erupt in a matter of hours and, following it, a civil war. The government, without reliable troops at its disposal, could promise nothing. The question of the monarchy was, therefore, best left to the Constituent Assembly to determine. Kerensky spoke in the same vein. Miliukov presented the dissenting opinion, which only Guchkov supported. Refusal to accept the crown would spell the ruin of Russia, he said in a voice hoarse from days of incessant speaking, and continued:

> The strong authority required to reestablish order calls for support from a symbol of authority to which the masses are accustomed. Without a monarch,

the Provisional Government alone becomes an unseaworthy vessel [*utlaia ladia*] liable to sink in the ocean of mass unrest. Under these conditions, the country is threatened with the complete loss of the sense of statehood.[141]

Kerensky broke in:

P. N. Miliukov is wrong. By accepting the throne you will not save Russia! Quite the contrary. I know the mood of the masses . . . the monarchy now is powerfully resented . . . The question will cause bloody discord. I beg of you, in the name of Russia, to make this sacrifice.[142]

In an attempt to reconcile the opposing parties and save something of the monarchic principle, Guchkov proposed that Michael assume the title of Regent.[143]

Around 1:00 p.m., Michael, who had listened to these disagreements with growing impatience, expressed a wish to retire for a private talk with Rodzianko. Everyone assented, but Kerensky wanted assurances that the Grand Duke would not communicate with his wife, who had a reputation as a political intriguer. Smiling, Michael assured Kerensky that his wife was at their residence at Gatchina. According to Rodzianko, the main question which Michael posed to him when they were alone was whether the Duma could guarantee his personal safety: Rodzianko's negative answer decided the issue.[144]

When he returned Michael told the ministers that he had made the unalterable decision to abide by the will of the government majority and refuse the crown unless and until the Constituent Assembly were to offer it to him. Then he burst into tears. Kerensky exclaimed: "Your Highness! You are a most noble person. From now on, I shall say this everywhere!"[145]

Two jurists, Vladimir Nabokov and Boris Nolde, were sent for to draft Michael's manifesto renouncing the crown. They spent the afternoon on the task, with occasional assistance from the Grand Duke, who insisted that they stress his desire to abide by the will of the Constituent Assembly. At 6 p.m. the handwritten document was submitted for his signature:

A heavy burden has been placed on Me by the will of My Brother, who has handed Me the Imperial Throne at a time of unprecedented war and popular disturbances.

Inspired by the same thought that permeates the nation, that the well-being of our Fatherland is the supreme good, I have taken the firm decision to accept Sovereign Authority only in the event that such will be the desire of our great nation, which, by means of a national referendum, through its representatives in the Constituent Assembly, is to determine the form of government and the new constitution of the Russian State.

For this reason, calling on the Lord to give us His blessing, I request all Russian citizens to submit to the Provisional Government, created on the initiative of the State Duma and endowed with full authority until such time as the Constituent Assembly, convened with the greatest possible speed on the basis of universal, direct, equal, and secret vote, shall, with its decision concerning the form of government, give expression to the people's will.[146]

Michael signed the document and handed it to Rodzianko, who embraced him and called him the "noblest of men."

The following day, March 4, the two abdication manifestos—the one from Nicholas in his and his son's name, the other from Michael—were published on the same broadsheet. According to eyewitnesses, their appearance was joyfully welcomed by the population.[147]

Was Miliukov right? Could Michael have saved the country from bloodshed and anarchy had he followed his counsel rather than that of the majority? This is doubtful. The argument that the Russian masses understood statehood only in association with the person of the Tsar was indubitably valid. But this theoretical consideration had been temporarily eclipsed by the mood of the masses, their sense of having been betrayed by the monarchy, to which no one had contributed more than Miliukov himself with his November 1, 1916, Duma speech. Russia would be again ready for the monarchy only after a year of anarchy and Bolshevik terror.

Like the rest of the Imperial family, Michael now withdrew into private life.

The intellectuals who formed Russia's government had been preparing themselves for this task for many years. It is quite incorrect to say, therefore, as does Kerensky in one version of his memoirs, that the Provisional Government found itself "unexpectedly" at the helm;[148] its members had been clamoring for, indeed demanding, the power to form a cabinet since 1905. Nearly all of them belonged to the Progressive Bloc, and their names had appeared on various unofficial cabinet lists published in Russian newspapers for years. They were familiar to the educated public as the leading opponents of the tsarist regime, and they assumed power almost as if by natural right.

But as Nicholas had noted, none had any administrative experience. Such political expertise as they possessed they had gained in the Duma: politics to them meant battling the Imperial bureaucracy in and out of the halls of Taurida, debating legislative proposals, and in a crisis appealing to the masses. Academics, lawyers, and businessmen, they were qualified to grapple with broad issues of public policy, and in a stable parliamentary democracy they might have acquitted themselves well. But a government, of course, does not merely legislate—first and foremost, it administers: *"Administrer, c'est gouverner,"* Mirabeau is quoted as having said, *"gouverner, c'est régner; tout se réduit là."* Of this principle, they understood nothing, having been accustomed all their lives to leaving the ordinary, day-to-day running of the country to the despised bureaucracy. Indeed, in their zeal to do everything differently, they purposefully did the opposite: just as tsarism sought to reduce politics to administration, they wanted to eliminate administration from politics. The attention of the First Provisional Government centered on rectifying the abuses of the old regime, mainly by means of legislative acts, unhampered by the veto of the Tsar and the upper chamber. Throughout its existence, it showed far more zeal in destroying the legacy of the past than in building something to replace it. It never created a set of new institutions to supplant those which had collapsed either of their own weight or under its assault.

This lack of interest in administering and implementing the laws which poured out of their chanceries, the new leaders rationalized with professions of faith in the wisdom of the "people." Knowledge of politics derived largely from literary sources habituated the Russian intelligentsia to think of democracy, not as an ideal, attained by patient effort, but as a reality inhibited from asserting itself only by the legacy of tsarism. They were convinced—or perhaps needed to convince themselves—that in order to give democracy a chance, it was essential *not* to govern. In a country that throughout its history had been accustomed to centralized government and obedience to directives from above, the revolutionary government adopted an extreme form of political laissez-faire—and this in the midst of an unprecedented war, inflation, agrarian stirrings, and a host of other pressing problems.

But even under these circumstances it might have been possible to give the country some sort of rudimentary order had the Provisional Government not promoted anarchy by dissolving the provincial bureaucracy and the police. It is quite misleading of Kerensky to say, in self-justification, that it was the Imperial regime that had destroyed the administrative apparatus of Russia.[149] In fact, this was mainly accomplished by Points 5 and 6 of the eight-point program which the Provisional Committee had adopted on March 1–2 in its agreement with the Ispolkom.[150] On March 5, all governors and deputy governors were dismissed, their authority being transferred to the chairmen of the provincial *zemstvo* boards *(gubernskie zemskie upravy)*. This action was most perplexing. Although some of the officials had resigned on their own upon learning of the Tsar's abdication, and others were arrested by local citizens, in many provinces the governors welcomed the new government and took part in ceremonies honoring it.[151] The government acted as it did in the belief that the men of the old regime could not be trusted to be loyal to the new order and would sabotage it at the first opportunity.[152] This assumption was of dubious validity because the Provisional Government quickly acquired an aura of legitimacy in the eyes of the tsarist bureaucrats, accustomed to obeying central authority. If the government wanted to make certain of their loyalty, it only had to release Nicholas's farewell address to the armed forces, in which, as we shall note, he urged Russians to obey the Provisional Government—a document the government chose to withhold from the public. The removal of the governors, the traditional mainstays of Russia's administration, left a vacuum in the provinces. One can understand why the revolutionary government would have wanted to place its own men in these positions, but it is difficult to see why the old governors could not have been retained at their posts for the short time needed to find their replacements. This action resembled the abolition by the French National Assembly in 1789 of the office of *intendant*, the principal agent of royal absolutism, which had the immediate effect of depriving Paris of nearly all control over the countryside.[153] It may even have been modeled on it. But France had much stronger social institutions than Russia as well as a sense of national cohesion that Russia lacked. The effect of these measures in France was, therefore, much less drastic: unlike revolutionary Russia, France never fell apart.

The dissolution of the old provincial bureaucracy proved immensely popular with the intelligentsia, whose rhetoric about the "masses" and "democracy" camouflaged strong careerist impulses. In city after city, usually under the auspices of the local soviet, they set up their offices, complete with staffs of assistants and secretaries, telephones, stationery, and rubber stamps. However, lacking the experience of those whom they replaced, they merely mimicked them.

More understandable, although in the long run no less destabilizing, was the dissolution of the police and gendarmerie, symbols of state authority for the mass of the country's population. This decision implemented Point 5 of the eight-point accord. The Department of Police was abolished on March 4: the act was a mere formality, since it had ceased to operate on February 27, when a mob sacked its headquarters. On the same day, the government ordered the dissolution of the Okhrana and Corps of Gendarmes. The day after, it sent instructions to the local authorities to form citizens' militias commanded by elected officers and operating under the authority of *zemstva* and Municipal Councils. Such militias, to the extent that they were constituted, enjoyed no authority: Nabokov notes that in a number of areas they were even taken over by criminal elements.[154] Two weeks after the Revolution, Russia was without a police force of either a political or a civil kind. When, in April 1917, the government found itself challenged by Bolshevik-led mobs, it had no force on which to rely.

Thus, a task immensely difficult to begin with—to govern a country at war and in the grip of revolutionary euphoria—was rendered impossible by rash actions dictated by a doctrinaire vision of democracy, belief in the wisdom of the people, and distaste for the professional bureaucracy and police. Russia in the spring of 1917 may well represent a unique instance of a government born of a revolution dissolving the machinery of administration before it had a chance to replace it with one of its own creation.

Initially, however, this was not apparent. In the first weeks after its assumption of power, the Provisional Government enjoyed overwhelming support. The entire country swore allegiance to it, including the grand dukes, the generals, and thousands of junior officers. Even the ultras of the United Gentry, headed by the archreactionary Alexander Samarin, voted in its favor.[155] Foreign powers promptly accorded it diplomatic recognition, beginning with the United States (March 9), followed by Britain, France, Italy, and the other Allies. But this display of support from the population and foreign powers was deceptive, encouraging the new cabinet in the illusion that it was firmly in control, whereas it was floating on thin air. Vladimir Nabokov wrote in his memoirs of the Provisional Government: "I primarily remember an atmosphere in which everything experienced seemed unreal."[156]

One of the difficulties in understanding the course of the February Revolution lies in the ambivalent nature of *dvoevlastie,* or dual power (dyarchy).

In theory, under *dvoevlastie* the cabinet functioned as the combined executive and legislative, being in both capacities subject to the veto power of the Soviet as represented by the Ispolkom. But in practice, the Soviet not only controlled the Provisional Government but legislated on its own. With Order No. 1, it assumed effective control over the armed forces. As we shall see, it also dictated Russia's war aims. Thus the government was not even allowed authority in the realm of military and foreign policy. In more mundane matters, such as food supply and labor relations, transport and communications, the Ispolkom acted as the ultimate authority without bothering to coordinate with the government.

The leaders of the Soviet made no secret of the fact that the Provisional Government existed only at their sufferance. At the All-Russian Consultation of Soviets on March 29, Tsereteli, the Menshevik chairman of the Ispolkom, said that the Provisional Government owed its existence to an agreement which the Petrograd Soviet concluded with "the bourgeois privileged [*tsenzovye*] elements of society."[157] Another member of the Ispolkom, the Trudovik V. B. Stankevich, boasted that the Soviet had the power to dismiss the Provisional Government in fifteen minutes by giving it appropriate orders over the phone.[158] The apologists for the system of "dual power" later claimed that the leaders of the Soviet did all they could to bolster the government: far from subverting it, they are said to have provided it with its principal source of support.[159] The historical record does not bear out this claim. It indicates that even as it intervened to help it suppress disorders, the Ispolkom ceaselessly undermined the government's authority and prestige.

Its leaders delivered speeches which humiliated the government and lowered its standing in the eyes of a population accustomed to seeing authority treated with respect. A good example is the speech of Chkheidze on March 24 to a delegation of students who came to the Soviet with a banner hailing the Provisional Government. Chkheidze addressed them as follows:

> I see on your banner the slogan "Greetings to the Provisional Government," but for you it can be no secret that many of its members, on the eve of the Revolution, were trembling and lacked faith in the Revolution. You extend greetings to it. You seem to believe that it will carry high the new standard. If this is so, remain in your belief. As for us, we will support it for as long as

it realizes democratic principles. We know, however, that our government is not democratic, but bourgeois. Follow carefully its activity. We shall support all of its measures which tend toward the common good, but all else we shall unmask because at stake is the fate of Russia.[160]

Such remarks by the second most influential political figure in the Soviet and a leading candidate for President of the Russian Republic give lie to the claims of the apologists for the Soviet that they loyally supported the government. By treating it as an inherently counterrevolutionary institution, kept honest only by the Soviet, they played directly into the hands of their enemies on the left who would argue that if that was the case, then the government should be removed and the Soviet assume full authority.

If the Ispolkom shied away from this logical conclusion of its premise, it was because it lacked the courage of its convictions. The socialists who controlled it wanted the Provisional Government to serve as a lightning rod for popular discontent, while they manipulated affairs from behind the scenes: they wanted to rule without reigning. As Trotsky was later to boast, this gave the Bolsheviks the opportunity to seize power by demanding that the Soviet become de jure what it was de facto.

The relationship between the two organs of authority was symbolized by their respective locales. The Soviet and its Executive elbowed their way into Taurida Palace, the seat of the Duma and the center of opposition under tsarism. The Provisional Government installed itself first in Mariinskii Palace, the seat of the Imperial Council of Ministers, and in July moved to the Winter Palace, a tsarist residence.*

The Ispolkom legislated in every field of activity. Yielding to the pressure of workers, it decreed an eight-hour working day in all enterprises, including those working for defense. On March 3 it ordered the arrest of members of the Imperial dynasty, not excepting Nikolai Nikolaevich, the designated Commander in Chief.[161] The logic of its self-assigned role as the organ of "democratic control" over the "bourgeoisie" quickly led the Ispolkom to adopt repressive measures reminiscent of the worst days of tsarism. Thus, on March 3, it "authorized" the postal and telegraphic services to function, but subject to "surveillance" by Soviet organs.[162] Press censorship followed. On March 5, the Ispolkom ordered the closing of all publications of a "Black Hundred" orientation, including the right-wing daily *Novoe vremia,* which had the temerity to come out without securing its permission.[163] Two days later, the Ispolkom advised newspapers and journals they were not to publish without express authorization from the Soviet—that is, itself.[164] This attempt to restore pre-1905 censorship provoked such an outcry it had to be rescinded.[165] But it is indicative of the rapidity with which the socialist intelligentsia, while professing the most lofty democratic ideals, violated a cardinal principle of democracy—namely, freedom of opinion.

*At that time, the Soviet transferred to the Smolnyi Institute, which had housed a finishing school for aristocratic girls.

The Ispolkom continued to bureaucratize. As early as March 3, it created a network of "commissions" to deal with pressing problems, such as food supply, railroads, post and telegraphs, and finances—a regular shadow government that duplicated and, through duplication, controlled the operations of the government. The principal institution serving this purpose was the "Contact Commission" of five socialist intellectuals (N. S. Chkheidze, M. I. Skobelev, Iu. M. Steklov, N. N. Sukhanov, and V. N. Filippovskii) created on March 7. Its task was to "inform the Soviet of the intentions and actions of the Provisional Government and the latter about the demands of the revolutionary people, to exert pressure on the government to satisfy all these demands, and to exercise uninterrupted control over their implementation."[166] Thus, by a verbal sleight of hand, the wishes of a body of intellectuals appointed by the socialist parties became the wishes of the "revolutionary people." According to Miliukov, initially the government satisfied all the demands of the Contact Commission. Tsereteli concurred, declaring in late March that "there were no instances when, on matters of importance, the Provisional Government did not seek agreement" with the Contact Commission.[167] To make certain this practice continued, on April 21 the Ispolkom asked the Provisional Government to make no "major" political moves without informing it beforehand.[168]

For reasons stated, the Ispolkom paid particular attention to the armed forces. "To facilitate contact," on March 19 it appointed commissars to the Ministry of War, the Army headquarters, and the headquarters of the diverse fronts and fleets. These commissars were to follow instructions sent them by the Ispolkom. In the front-line zone, no orders issued by the military were to go into effect without prior approval of the Ispolkom and its commissars. The latter helped to resolve disputes that arose within the armed forces and between the military command and the civilian population in or near the combat zone. The Minister of War directed the military commanders to assist the Soviet commissars in executing their duties.[169]

The Ispolkom kept on expanding. On April 8 nine representatives (all SRs and Mensheviks) from the Soldiers' Section were added to the ten already in the Ispolkom: they were the first elected members of that body. The ten previously appointed members were reelected: no Bolshevik won a seat. The representatives of the Workers' Section were handpicked by the Menshevik, Bolshevik, and SR parties.[170]

During the first month of its existence, the Petrograd Soviet served only the capital city, but then it expanded its authority over the entire country. The All-Russian Consultation of Soviets, convened in Petrograd in late March, voted to have the Ispolkom admit into its membership representatives of the provincial city soviets and frontline army units, which transformed the Petrograd Soviet into the All-Russian Soviet of Workers' and Soldiers' Deputies.[171] Sixteen delegates from other parts of Russia were added to what now became the All-Russian Central Executive Committee (VTsIK or CEC). By now its membership had grown to seventy-two, among whom were twenty-three Mensheviks, twenty-two SRs, and twelve Bolsheviks.

To direct and systematize its work, the Ispolkom created on March 14 another bureaucratic body, a Bureau. In mid-April, the Bureau had twenty-four members (eleven Mensheviks, six SRs, three Trudoviki, and four "non-faction" Social-Democrats). The Bolsheviks initially refused to join on the grounds that they had been offered insufficient places.[172]

The Ispolkom and its Bureau supplanted the incorrigibly undisciplined Soviet Plenum, which convened less and less frequently; when it did, it was to approve by acclamation the decisions of the Executive. In the first four days of its existence (February 28–March 3), the Plenum met daily. In the rest of March it met four times, in April six. No one paid much attention to its noisy proceedings. The separate Workers' Section and Soldiers' Section met somewhat more frequently.

Although the Ispolkom, with its Bureau, and the Soviet, which followed their bidding, posed as the authentic voice of the country's masses, they had among their members no representatives of peasant organizations. The peasants, 80 percent of the population, had their Peasants' Union, which kept aloof from the Soviet. The All-Russian Soviet thus spoke for only a fraction of the country's inhabitants, 10 to 15 percent at best, if allowance is made for the peasantry and the "bourgeoisie," neither of which was represented.

O perating under such difficult conditions, the Provisional Government concentrated on "democratic" legislation, which was easy to turn out and certain to secure the approval of the Soviet. Cabinet meetings took place in the evening and sometimes late at night. The ministers arrived exhausted and were observed to doze off.

In the weeks that followed its assumption of power, the government passed numerous laws, some designed to rectify the abuses of the old regime, others to implement the eight-point program. Soldiers received full civil rights, and those serving in the rear were no longer subject to courts-martial. All civil disabilities due to religious or ethnic affiliation were lifted. The death penalty was abolished. The right of association and assembly was assured. Poland was promised full independence after the war (although qualified to the extent that it would remain "united with Russia in a free military union") and Finland was guaranteed the restoration of her constitutional rights. This legislative industry was the most productive sector of the Russian economy.[173] The trouble was that whereas laws that enhanced freedom were promptly acted upon, no one paid attention to those that imposed new obligations.

On the three issues that mattered most—land reform, the Constituent Assembly, and peace—the government acted in a dilatory manner.

Except for the areas adjacent to the large cities, the news of the Tsar's abdication traveled at a snail's pace to the rural districts, held in the grip of a savage winter. Most villages first learned of the Revolution four to six weeks after it had broken out, i.e., in the first half of April, with the onset of the spring thaw.[174] The peasants interpreted the news to mean they were free to resume assaults on private landed property halted ten years earlier by Stolypin. The Black Repartition got underway once again, as the communal peasants, at first cautiously and then with increasing boldness, raided landed property, first and foremost that belonging to fellow peasants who had withdrawn from the commune and taken title to private land. The earliest reports of agrarian disturbances reached Petrograd in the middle of March,[175] but they assumed mass proportions in April. The instigators were often army deserters and criminals released from prison in February; sometimes whole communes fell under their influence. In this initial phase of the agrarian revolution, the peasants attacked mainly isolated households and estates, cutting down trees, stealing seed grain, and chasing away prisoners of war employed as farm-hands.[176] As in 1905, physical violence was rare. The government appealed on April 8 to the peasants to desist from illegal seizures. It also appointed a commission under A. I. Shingarev, the Minister of Agriculture, to draft a program of agrarian reform for submission to the Constituent Assembly.[177]

The SRs were busy organizing the peasantry. They reconstituted the Peasants' Union, destroyed after 1905. The Union was favorable to the Provisional Government and its messages to the peasants urged patience and restraint.[178] The appeals from the government and the Peasants' Union had a calming effect: many peasants concluded that their claim to the land would be more secure if obtained legally rather than by force. But the agrarian disorders subsided only in June, after the socialists had entered the Provisional Government and the SR leader, Victor Chernov, took over the Ministry of Agriculture. Even so, the peasants could not be expected to wait forever: by failing to enact a land reform, the government soon dissipated its popularity with the communal peasantry.

To ensure the cities' food supply, Petrograd introduced on March 25 a state monopoly on trade in cereals. Under its provisions, peasants were required to turn over to government agents surplus grain at fixed prices. But there were no means of enforcing this law and the peasants ignored it, continuing to dispose of their surplus on the open market.

The early agrarian disturbances had a pernicious effect on the armed forces. News at the front of an imminent Black Repartition stimulated the first mass desertions of soldiers who hurried home from fear of being left out.[179]

To stabilize the situation nothing was more urgently required than a speedy convocation of the Constituent Assembly. Only a body elected on a democratic franchise would have enjoyed incontestable legitimacy and, as such, been able to beat back challenges both from the extreme right and from the extreme left. The electoral complexities admittedly were daunting. Still, the matter was of such urgency that practiced politicians would have realized it was better to convene an imperfect Assembly immediately than a perfect one later. When the July Monarchy in France collapsed in 1848, a Constituent Assembly met in two months to choose the new government. In Germany in late 1918 after defeat in the war, in the midst of social upheavals, the authorities who took over would manage to convene a National Assembly in less than four months. The Russian Provisional Government could not do it in the eight months that it stayed in office.

On March 25, the government appointed a commission of seventy jurists to work out the electoral procedures. They immediately got bogged down in technicalities; weeks passed by without anything being accomplished. Nabokov says, probably correctly, there were always more urgent matters to attend to.[180] By postponing the elections, the government not only violated a provision of the eight-point program but laid itself open to charges that it was playing for time until revolutionary passions subsided.[181] Its dilatoriness contributed heavily to the government's eventual overthrow: as we will note, one of the main pretexts the Bolsheviks would use when seizing power in the name of the Soviets was that only a Soviet government could ensure the convocation of a Constituent Assembly.

Then there was the issue of war and peace. In theory, all the leading parties represented in the government and the Soviet, the Bolsheviks excepted, favored continuation of the war until victory. This stand reflected the mood of the population. Contrary to a widespread belief that the February Revolution was brought about by war weariness, anti-German sentiment ran high. The overthrow of the tsarist regime had been in the first place inspired by the beliefs that it was too incompetent to lead the country to victory, it sought a separate peace, and it even betrayed secrets to the enemy. "In the first weeks [of the February Revolution]," observes Sukhanov, "the soldier mass in Petrograd not only would not listen to talk of peace, but would not allow it to be uttered, ready to bayonet any uncautious 'traitor' and anyone who 'opened the front to the enemy.' "[182] In March and April, it was common to see soldiers carry placards calling for "War to the End!"[183] A French historian who had the opportunity to read the messages sent to the Provisional Government and the Soviet in the first two months of the new regime, confirms Sukhanov's impression. Worker petitions placed at the head of demands the eight-hour working day; only 3 percent called for peace without annexations and contributions. Twenty-three percent of the peasants' petitions wanted a "quick and just peace," but even among them this was a secondary issue. As for the soldiers, their petitions indicated they "were likely to treat proponents of immediate peace as supporters of the Kaiser."[184] The issue was so sensitive that the Bolsheviks, who alone favored such a peace, exercised great caution in public pronouncements. It is indicative of the Petrograd garrison's animosity toward them because of their war stand that in the elections to the Ispolkom in the Soviet Soldiers' Section on April 8 no Bolshevik won a seat.[185] Much of the violence perpetrated in February and March was directed against individuals who bore German names and for this reason were suspected of treason. Admiral Kolchak, commander of the Black Sea Fleet, reported that the main disturbances under his command were against officers with German names.[186] The same held true for the naval base of Kronshtadt. When on February 27 a mob set fire to the Petrograd residence of Count Fredericks, the Tsar's aide

47. Officer candidates *(iunkers)* parading in Petrograd: March 1917. The sign reads: "War for Freedom until Victory."

(who happened to be of Swedish ancestry), it did so because his name aroused suspicions of pro-German sympathies.[187]

Despite the hatred of Germans and the general support of the war against them, the question of war aims acquired great importance in the popular mind due to socialist agitation. It was characteristic of the socialist intellectuals to advocate contradictory policies linked by pious intentions. They wanted war to victory, yet labeled the war "imperialist" and passed legislation (e.g., Order No. 1 and the eight-hour working day) that made the pursuit of the war all but impossible. They wanted national victory, yet in their declarations spoke of the masses of all the belligerent countries sharing a common interest in bringing down the "ruling classes." In an "Appeal to the Peoples of the World" on March 15, the Ispolkom called on the world's peoples to rise in revolution:

Turning to all nations, bled white and ruined by the monstrous war, we declare that the time has come to launch the decisive struggle against the rapacious strivings of the governments of all countries. The time has come to take the decision on war and peace into one's own hands.

Conscious of its revolutionary might, Russian democracy declares that it will resist with all means the rapacious policy of its ruling classes, and calls on the nations of Europe to undertake jointly decisive actions on behalf of peace. . . .

We shall staunchly defend our own freedom against all reactionary infringements from within and from without. The Russian Revolution will not yield to the bayonets of conquerors and will not allow itself to be crushed by foreign military might.[188]

Such rhetoric must have appeared reasonable to the intellectuals who drafted the "Appeal," but, like the concept of "dual power," it left the man in the street perplexed. If Russia's "ruling classes" indeed pursued a "rapacious policy," why keep them in power and why be "bled white" in their "monstrous war"?

Miliukov, who was in charge of foreign policy, went his own way. He did not share the socialists' optimism about the peace movement in Germany, and believed that their appeal would evoke no response. From Trepov's revelations the preceding December, it was known that the Allies had promised Russia Constantinople and the Straits. Miliukov did not wish to renounce these claims for two reasons: such renunciation would raise doubts in the West about Russia's commitment to stay in the war, and it would open the floodgates to German peace propaganda. His insistence on Russia's adhering to its territorial claims led to the first clash between the government and the Soviet.

At a press conference on March 22, Miliukov outlined the Government's war aims. These included "liberation" of the Slavic peoples of Austria-Hungary, the "fusion" of the Ukrainian territories of Austria-Hungary (i.e., Galicia) with Russia, and acquisition of Constantinople and the Straits.[189] Socialist intellectuals interpreted Miliukov's views as a challenge to their "Appeal," which demanded the renunciation of "rapacious" acquisitions. Under pressure from the Soviet, and at the insistence of several cabinet members, especially Kerensky, the government agreed to issue an official statement of war aims more in line with the position of the Ispolkom. Approved by the latter with some revisions, it was released on March 27.[190] The statement asserted that Russia had no desire to "lord it over other nations, to deprive them of their national property, to seize by force territories belonging to others": her objective was a "lasting peace on the basis of national self-determination." This formula represented a capitulation to the socialists, although Miliukov would later argue that it could have been interpreted to mean Russia's right to claim enemy territories.[191] One month later the controversy over war aims would flare up again, this time causing a major political crisis.

From February 23 until February 28, the Revolution was confined to Petrograd. The country went about its business, as if unaware that anything unusual had occurred. The chronicle of these days[192] indicates that the first city to react was Moscow, which had strikes and demonstrations on February 28 and the following day elected a workers' soviet. On March 1, meetings took place in several provincial towns, including Tver, Nizhnii Novgorod, Samara, and Saratov. On March 2, other cities followed suit. There was no violence: when the Communist chronicler says that the inhabitants of various cities "joined the Revolution," he means that crowds held peaceful celebrations in support of the Provisional Government. The slow pace at which the Revolution spread indicates the extent to which its origins were connected with the specific conditions in the capital city—namely, exceptionally severe shortages of food and fuel and grievances of the military garrison. It helps explain why as late as March 2 the generals and politicians could still believe that the Tsar's abdication would keep the Revolution confined to Petrograd. As it turned out, however, it was the news of Nicholas's abdication, published on March 3, that made the nation realize it had had a revolution: the result was a rapid breakdown of authority.

In the course of March there emerged in all the cities soviets modeled on that of Petrograd, the executives of which were taken over by socialist intellectuals. In early April, the provincial soviets sent representatives to Petrograd where they entered the Petrograd Ispolkom to form an All-Russian Ispolkom (VTsIK, or CEC).

The Revolution spread across the country peacefully: in the phrase of W. H. Chamberlin, it was "made by telegraph."[193] The change of regimes was everywhere accepted as an accomplished fact: no resistance was encountered and therefore no force used. As yet, neither class nor ethnic hostilities emerged to disturb the nearly unanimous relief at the end of the old regime. In some localities, celebrations in honor of the Provisional Government were joined by army officers and ex-tsarist officials.

One of the unanticipated effects of the Revolution and the ideal of democracy which it promoted was the emergence of nationalist movements in areas where the population was predominantly non-Russian. They were led by the indigenous intelligentsia which, in addition to the usual socialist or liberal demands, claimed for their regions some degree of autonomy. The first to be heard from were the Ukrainians, who on March 2 formed in Kiev a soviet called Rada: its initial demands on the government were cultural, but it soon also asked for political powers. Other nationalities followed suit, among them Russia's scattered Muslims, who in May held an All-Russian Congress.[194]

Vasilii Rozanov said of Nicholas's abdication that the Tsar let it be known he "disowned such a base people."[195]

According to his diary, Nicholas slept soundly the night that followed the signing of the abdication manifesto. He arrived in Mogilev on March 3 in the evening to learn from Alekseev that his brother had renounced the crown and left the fate of the monarchy up to the Constituent Assembly. "God knows who talked him into signing such rot," he noted. He now drafted yet another abdication manifesto in which he transferred the crown to his son. Alekseev decided not to inform the government of Nicholas's latest change of mind. He subsequently entrusted the document to General Denikin for safekeeping.[196]

The following day, Nicholas sent Prime Minister Lvov a list of requests. He asked to be allowed to proceed to Tsarskoe with his suite and to remain there until the children recovered, following which he wished to take up residence in Port Romanov on the Murmansk coast. Once the war was over, he wanted to retire to the Crimean resort of Livadia. In a coded message to headquarters, the Provisional Government approved these requests.[197]

Because the ex-Tsar threatened to become a major issue of contention between the government and the Soviet, the cabinet soon decided that it would be politically more expedient to have Nicholas and family out of the country. In the first week of March, it sounded out the British, Danish, and Swiss governments about the possibility of asylum for the Imperial family. On March 8/21, Miliukov told the British Ambassador that he was "most anxious that the Emperor should leave Russia at once" and would be grateful if Britain offered him asylum, with the proviso that Nicholas "would not be allowed to leave England during the war."[198] Britain hesitated at first but on March 9/22 the Foreign Secretary, Arthur Balfour, cabled to the British Embassy in Petrograd:

> After further consideration it has been decided that it would be better for the Emperor to come to England during the war rather than to a country contiguous to Germany. Apprehension is felt lest, through the influence of the Empress, the residence of the Emperor in Denmark or Switzerland might become a focus of intrigue, and that in the hands of disaffected Russian Generals the Emperor might become the possible head of a counter-revolution. This would be to play into the hands of Germany, and a risk that must be avoided at all costs.[199]

This offer, formally conveyed to the Provisional Government on March 13, was reinforced by a personal message from King George V to Nicholas in which he assured him of his undying friendship and extended the invitation to settle in England.*

The government's plans regarding the Imperial family failed to take into account the feelings of the socialist intellectuals, who feared that once abroad the ex-Tsar would become the center of counterrevolutionary plots. For this reason, they preferred to keep him at home and under their control. As noted, on March 3 the Ispolkom voted to arrest Nicholas and his family. The government promptly capitulated to this demand. On March 7 it announced that the Imperial family would be placed under detention at Tsarskoe, and dispatched to Mogilev four deputies to escort Nicholas home. On March 8, having learned of the negotiations with Britain, the Ispolkom voted again to arrest Nicholas and his family, confiscate their property, and deprive them of citizenship. To prevent Nicholas's departure for England, it resolved to send its own people to Tsarskoe to ensure that the Imperial family was securely guarded.[200]

While these developments were taking place, Nicholas was in Mogilev taking leave of the army. On March 8, he wrote a farewell letter to the armed forces in which he urged them to fight until victory and "obey the Provisional Government."[201] Alekseev forwarded this document to Petrograd, but Guch-

---

*Martynov, *Tsarskaia armiia,* 191; G. Buchanan, *My Mission to Russia,* II (Boston, 1923), 104–5. Miliukov withheld the King's message from Nicholas.

kov, acting on instructions from the cabinet, which probably feared antagonizing the Ispolkom, ordered it withheld.[202] Later that morning, Nicholas bade goodbye to the officers. He walked up to each and embraced him. Nearly everyone was in tears. When the strain became too great Nicholas bowed and withdrew. "My heart nearly burst," he wrote in the diary.[203] At 4:45 p.m. he boarded his train, without the two inseparable companions, Voeikov and Fredericks, whom he had to dismiss at the request of Alekseev. Before departure, Alekseev informed him he was under arrest.[204]

On that same day, March 8, General Lavr Kornilov, the new commandant of the Petrograd Military District (he had been appointed by Nicholas on Rodzianko's urging shortly before abdication) visited Tsarskoe. He informed the Empress that she was in custody and posted guards in the palace and on its grounds. This measure was taken in response to the demands of the Ispolkom, but it also had the effect of ensuring the safety of the Imperial family, for the Tsarskoe Selo garrison had begun to act in an insolent and threatening manner. According to Benckendorff, Kornilov also advised Alexandra that as soon as practicable the family would be taken to Murmansk to board a British cruiser bound for England.[205]

Nicholas's train arrived at Tsarskoe in the morning of March 9. Announced to the guards as "Colonel Romanov," he was surprised to see guards and patrols posted everywhere and to learn that his and his family's movements, even within the confines of the palace grounds, were severely restricted. He was not to leave his apartments unless accompanied by an armed soldier.

When it learned that Nicholas had left Mogilev, the socialist intelligentsia grew anxious that he meant to escape abroad: they remembered well the flight of Louis XVI to Varennes. On March 9 the Ispolkom met in a state of great agitation. Chkheidze issued a general alarm that the ex-Tsar, who actually had just arrived at Tsarskoe, was in flight and had to be stopped.[206] The Soviet resolved to prohibit Nicholas from leaving Russia "even if this should threaten a break with the Provisional Government": he was to be incarcerated in the Peter and Paul Fortress.[207] An Ispolkom delegation, headed by Chkheidze, met with the government that day and received assurances that Nicholas would not be allowed to leave the country without the Ispolkom's permission.[208]

To make certain that Nicholas was in fact at Tsarskoe, as it was now informed, the Ispolkom dispatched later that day (March 9) a detachment of three hundred infantry and one machine gun company to Tsarskoe under the command of S. D. Mstislavskii, an SR officer. On arrival, Mstislavskii demanded that the ex-Tsar be at once "presented to him." He thought to himself: "Let him stand before me—me, a simple emissary of the revolutionary workers and soldiers, he, the Emperor of All the Russias, Great, Little, and White, the autocrat, like an inmate at an inspection in what used to be his prisons."

Mstislavskii wore an old sheepskin coat, with the epaulettes of a military official, a fur cap on his head, a saber by his side and a Browning, the handle of which protruded from his pocket. Soon the ex-Tsar appeared in the corridor.

He approached the group, apparently wishing to speak with them. But Mstislavskii stood without saluting, without removing his cap, and even without uttering a greeting. The Emperor stopped for a second, looked him straight in the eye, then turned around and went back.*

By virtue of the rules set by General Kornilov[209] the Imperial family was cut off from the outside world: no one could enter Tsarskoe without permission, and all letters, telegrams, and phone calls were subject to oversight.

On March 21, Kerensky appeared unexpectedly at Tsarskoe. It was his first opportunity to meet face to face the object of some of his most virulent Duma speeches. His description of the encounter, and the impression which Nicholas made on him, is of considerable interest:

> The whole family was standing huddled in confusion around a small table near a window in the adjoining room. A small man in uniform detached himself from the group and moved forward to meet me, hesitating and smiling weakly. It was the Emperor. On the threshold of the room in which I awaited him he stopped, as if uncertain what to do next. He did not know what my attitude would be. Was he to receive me as a host or should he wait until I spoke to him? Should he hold out his hand, or should he wait for my salutation? I sensed his embarrassment at once as well as the confusion of the whole family left alone with a terrible revolutionary. I quickly went up to Nicholas II, held out my hand with a smile, and said abruptly "Kerensky," as I usually introduce myself. He shook my hand firmly, smiled, seemingly encouraged, and led me at once to his family. His son and daughters were obviously consumed with curiosity and gazed fixedly at me. Alexandra Feodorovna, stiff, proud and haughty, extended her hand reluctantly, as if under compulsion. Nor was I particularly eager to shake hands with her, our palms barely touching. This was typical of the difference in character and temperament between the husband and wife. I felt at once that Alexandra Feodorovna, though broken and angry, was a clever woman with a strong will. In those few seconds I understood the psychology of the whole tragedy that had been going on for many years behind the palace walls. My subsequent interviews with the Emperor, which were very few, only confirmed by first impression. . . .
>
> I for one do not think he was the outcast, the inhuman monster, the deliberate murderer I used to imagine. I began to realize that there was a human side to him. It became clear to me that he had acquiesced in the whole ruthless system without being moved by any personal ill will and without even realizing that it was bad. His mentality and his circumstances kept him wholly out of touch with the people. He heard of the blood and tears of thousands upon thousands only through official documents, in which they were represented as "measures" taken by the authorities "in the interest of the peace and safety of the State." Such reports did not convey to him the pain and suffering of the victims, but only the "heroism" of the soldiers "faithful in the fulfillment of their duty to the Czar and the Fatherland." From his youth he had been trained to believe that his welfare and the welfare of Russia were one and the same

---

*As described in Martynov, *Tsarskaia armiia,* 198, from the words of Mstislavskii. Benckendorff, who witnessed the scene, says that Mstislavskii was content to see the ex-Tsar pass in the corridor: Benckendorff, *Last Days,* 49–50.

48. Ex-Tsar Nicholas at Tsarskoe Selo, March 1917, under house arrest.

thing, so that the "disloyal" workmen, peasants and students who were shot down, executed or exiled seemed to him mere monsters and outcasts of humanity who must be destroyed for the sake of the country and the "faithful subjects" themselves. . . .

In the course of my occasional short interviews with Nicholas II at Tsarskoe Selo, I tried to fathom his character and, I think, on the whole I succeeded. He was an extremely reserved man, who distrusted and utterly despised mankind. He was not well educated, but he had some knowledge of human nature. He did not care for anything or anyone except his son, and perhaps his daughters. This terrible indifference to all external things made him seem like some unnatural automaton. As I studied his face, I seemed to see behind his smile and charming eyes a stiff, frozen mask of utter loneliness and desolation. I think he may have been a mystic, seeking communion with Heaven patiently and passionately, and weary of all earthly things. Perhaps everything on earth had become insignificant and distasteful to him because all his desires had been so easily gratified. When I began to know this living mask I understood why it had been so easy to overthrow his power. He did not wish to fight for it and it simply fell from his hands. Authority, like everything else, he held too cheap. He was altogether weary of it. He threw off authority as formerly he might have thrown off a dress uniform and put on a simpler one. It was a new experience for him to find himself a plain citizen without the duties or robes of state. To retire into private life was not a tragedy for him. Old Madame Naryshkina, the lady-in-waiting, told me that he had said to her: "How glad I am that I need no longer attend to these tiresome interviews and sign those everlasting documents! I shall read, walk and spend my time with the children." And, she added, this was no pose on his part. Indeed, all those who watched him in his captivity were unanimous in saying that Nicholas II seemed generally to be very good-tempered and appeared to enjoy his new manner of life. He chopped wood and piled up the logs in stacks in the park. He did a little gardening and rowed and played with the children. It seemed as if a heavy burden had fallen from his shoulders and that he was greatly relieved.[210].

Given the sentiments of the Ispolkom, it was unlikely ever to have approved the government's plans to allow Nicholas to leave for England. Nevertheless, it came as something of a shock when at the end of March (OS) Britain informed the Provisional Government that she was withdrawing her invitation to the ex-Tsar. It was believed then and for a long time afterward that it was Prime Minister David Lloyd George who had dissuaded George V from following his generous impulses. Lloyd George himself liked to perpetuate this impression.[211] But it has since become known that he did so to protect the King, who had vetoed the earlier decision for fear that it would embarrass the Crown and irritate Labor MPs who were "expressing adverse opinions to the proposal."[212] The King's role in this dishonorable action was kept in strict secrecy: instructions went out "to keep an eye on anything that may be put into the War Cabinet minutes likely to hurt the King's feelings."[213] It subsequently became Britain's stated policy not to allow any member of the Russian royal family on her soil while the war was on, with the exception of the Empress Dowager Marie, the Danish-born sister of Edward VII's widow, Alexandra.*

According to Kerensky, Nicholas was shattered to learn of the British refusal[214]—not because he wanted to leave Russia, but because it was further proof of the "treason and cowardice and deception" with which he felt surrounded. He spent the next four months in forced idleness—reading, playing games, taking walks, and working in the garden.

The February Revolution had many striking features that distinguish it from other revolutionary upheavals. But the most striking of all was the remarkable rapidity with which the Russian state fell apart. It was as if the greatest empire in the world, covering one-sixth of the earth's surface, were an artificial construction, without organic unity, held together by wires all of which converged in the person of the monarch. The instant the monarch withdrew, the wires snapped and the whole structure collapsed in a heap. Kerensky says that there were moments when it seemed to him that

the word "revolution" [was] quite inapplicable to what happened in Russia [between February 27 and March 3]. A whole world of national and political

*Although the daughter of the British Ambassador has gone to great lengths to depict her father as highly upset by his government's action (Meriel Buchanan, *The Dissolution of an Empire,* London, 1932, 196–98), English archives show that he endorsed it: Kenneth Rose, *King George V* (London, 1983), 214.

relationships sank to the bottom, and at once all existing political and tactical programs, however bold and well conceived, appeared hanging aimlessly and uselessly in space.[215]

Rozanov described the phenomenon in his own pungent style:

> Russia wilted in two days. At the very most, three. Even *Novoe vremia* could not have been shut down as quickly as Russia shut down. It is amazing how she suddenly fell apart, all of her, down to particles, to pieces. Indeed, such an upheaval had never occurred before, not excluding "the Great Migrations of Peoples" . . . There was no Empire, no Church, no army, no working class. And what remained? Strange to say, literally nothing. A base people remained.[216]

By late April, eight weeks after the Revolution had broken out, Russia was foundering. On April 26 the Provisional Government issued a pathetic appeal in which it conceded it was unable to run the country. Kerensky now voiced regrets that he did not die when the Revolution was still young and filled with hope that the nation could manage to govern itself "without whips and cudgels."[217]

Russians, having gotten rid of tsarism, on which they used to blame all their ills, stood bewildered in the midst of their newly gained freedom. They were not unlike the lady in a Balzac story who had been sick for so long that when finally cured thought herself struck by a new disease.

PART TWO

The Bolsheviks
Conquer Russia

Russia has been conquered by the Bolsheviks. . . .
                    —*Lenin, March 1918*

[The Bolshevik Party] set itself the task of overthrowing the world.
                    —*Trotsky,* The Revolution Betrayed

Lenin and the Origins
of Bolshevism

He will go far, for he believes all he says.
—Mirabeau of Robespierre

Ｏne need not believe that history is made by "great men" to appreciate the immense importance of Lenin for the Russian Revolution and the
regime that issued from it. It is not only that the power which he accumulated
allowed Lenin to exert a decisive influence on the course of events but also that
the regime which he established in October 1917 institutionalized, as it were,
his personality. The Bolshevik Party was Lenin's creation: as its founder, he
conceived it in his own image and, overcoming all opposition from within and
without, kept it on the course he had charted. The same party, on seizing
power in October 1917, promptly eliminated all rival parties and organizations
to become Russia's exclusive source of political authority. Communist Russia,
therefore, has been from the beginning to an unusual extent a reflection of the
mind and psyche of one man: his biography and its history are uniquely fused.

Although few historical figures have been so much written about, authentic information on Lenin is sparse. Lenin was so unwilling to distinguish
himself from his cause or even to concede that he had an existence separate
from it that he left almost no autobiographical data: his life, as he conceived
it, was at one with the party's. In his own eyes and in the eyes of his associates
he had only a public personality. Such individual traits as are attributed to him
in the Communist literature are the standard virtues of hagiography: self-
denying devotion to the cause, modesty, self-discipline, generosity.

Least known is Lenin's formative period. The entire corpus of writings for the first twenty-three years of his life consists of a mere twenty items, nearly all of them petitions, certificates, and other official documents.[1] There are no letters, diaries, or essays such as one would expect from a young intellectual. Either such materials do not exist or, as is more likely, they are secreted in Soviet archives because their release would reveal a young Lenin very different from the one portrayed in the official literature.* In either event, the biographer has very little to go on in attempting to reconstruct Lenin's intellectual and psychic development during the period (roughly 1887–93) when he evolved from an ordinary youth without political commitments or even interests into a fanatical revolutionary. Such evidence as we possess is largely circumstantial; much of it rests on negative knowledge—that is, what Lenin failed to do given his opportunities. Reconstructing the young Lenin requires a conscientious effort to peel off layers of distorting varnish deposited on his image by years of institutionalized cult.†

Lenin was born Vladimir Ilich Ulianov in April 1870 in Simbirsk into a conventional, comfortably well-off bureaucratic family. His father, a school inspector, had attained by the time of his death in 1886 the rank of a state councillor, which gave him status equal to a general and hereditary nobility. He was a man of conservative-liberal views who sympathized with the reforms of Alexander II and believed that education held the key to Russia's progress. He worked extremely hard and is said in his sixteen years as inspector to have founded several hundred schools. Lenin's mother, born Blank, was the daughter of a physician of German ancestry: in her photographs she looks as if she had stepped out of Whistler's portrait. It was a happy, close-knit family which faithfully observed the rituals and holidays of the Orthodox Church.

Tragedy struck the Ulianovs in 1887 when Lenin's elder brother, Alexander, was arrested in St. Petersburg carrying a bomb with which, in a plot with friends, he intended to assassinate the Tsar. A passionate scientist, Alexander had shown no interest in politics until after he had been three years at St. Petersburg University. There he familiarized himself with the writings of Plekhanov and Marx and adopted an eclectic political ideology calling for the grafting on the program of the People's Will (Narodnaia Volia) certain elements of Social-Democracy. According industrial labor a predominant role in the revolution, he accepted political terror as the means and the immediate transition to socialism as the objective. This peculiar amalgam of Marxism and Narodnaia Volia anticipated the program which Lenin would develop independently a few years later. Arrested on March 1, 1887, the sixth anniversary

---

*On the primary and secondary materials concerning the young Lenin which are kept concealed in Soviet depositories, see Richard Pipes, ed., *Revolutionary Russia* (Cambridge, Mass., 1968), 27, note 2.

†I have attempted to draw a picture of Lenin's early intellectual and spiritual evolution on the basis of the available documentary evidence in *Revolutionary Russia,* which I edited. Most of the information on the pages which follow comes from this work as supplemented by two other of my writings: *Struve: Liberal on the Left, 1870–1905* (Cambridge, Mass., 1970) and *Social Democracy and the St. Petersburg Labor Movement, 1885–1897* (Cambridge, Mass., 1963). Of the secondary sources, the most valuable is Nikolai Valentinov's *The Early Years of Lenin* (Ann Arbor, Mich., 1969).

of the assassination of Alexander II, Alexander Ulianov was given a public trial and executed along with his co-conspirators. He conducted himself throughout with exemplary dignity.

Alexander's execution, which occurred soon after the death of the elder Ulianov, had a profound effect on the family, which had known nothing of his revolutionary activity. But there is no evidence that it altered Vladimir's behavior in any way. Many years later Lenin's younger sister Maria claimed that on learning of his brother's fate, Lenin exclaimed: "No, we will not go this way. We must not go this way."[2] Apart from the fact that Maria Ulianova was a mere nine years old when this alleged remark was made, it cannot be true, because when his brother was executed Lenin was entirely innocent of politics. The purpose of this invention is to suggest that already as a seventeen-year-old gymnasium student Lenin inclined to Marxism, which is at odds with the available evidence. Moreover, from family recollections it can be determined that the two brothers had not been close and that Alexander took strong objection to Vladimir's rude manners and habitual sneer.

The striking fact about Lenin's youth is that, unlike most of his contemporaries, he showed no interest in public affairs.[3] The portrait which emerges from the pen of one of his sisters, published before the iron grip of censorship dehumanized Lenin, is that of an exceedingly diligent boy, tidy and punctilious—a type that modern psychology would classify as compulsive.[4] He was a model student, earning excellent grades in nearly all subjects, behavior included, for which he was awarded gold medals year after year. He graduated at the top of his class. The scanty evidence at our disposal shows no trace of rebelliousness toward either his family or the regime. Fedor Kerensky, the father of Lenin's future rival, Alexander, who happened to have been principal of the school which Lenin attended in Simbirsk, recommended him to the University of Kazan as a "reticent" and "unsociable" youth who "neither in school nor out of it gave his superiors or teachers by a single word or deed any cause to form of him an unfavorable opinion."[5] By the time he graduated from gymnasium in 1887, he held no "definite" political opinions.[6] Nothing in his early biography hinted at a future revolutionary; rather, the indications were that Lenin would follow in his father's footsteps and make a distinguished bureaucratic career. It is because of these traits that he was admitted to study law at Kazan University, from which his family's police record would otherwise have barred him.

On entering the university, Lenin was recognized by fellow students as the brother of a celebrated terrorist and drawn into a clandestine People's Will group. This organization, headed by Lazar Bogoraz, had made contact with like-minded students in other cities, including St. Petersburg, apparently with the intention of carrying out the deed for which Alexander Ulianov and his associates had been executed. How far its plans progressed and how much Lenin was involved is not possible to ascertain. The group was arrested in December 1887 following a demonstration to protest university regulations. Lenin, who was observed running, shouting, and waving his arms, was briefly detained. On returning home, he wrote a letter to the university announcing his withdrawal, but the attempt to forestall expulsion failed. He was arrested and expelled along with thirty-nine other students. Such savage punishment, typical of the methods which the regime of Alexander III used to stifle signs of independence or "insubordination," kept the revolutionary movement supplied with ever fresh recruits.

Lenin might perhaps have been forgiven in time and allowed to reenroll were it not that in the course of the investigation which followed the police uncovered his connections with the Bogoraz circle and learned of his brother's involvement in terrorism. Once these facts became known, he was placed on the list of "unreliables" and put under police surveillance. His and his mother's petitions for readmission were routinely rejected. Lenin saw before him no future. He spent the next four years in forced idleness, living off his mother's pension. His mood was desperate and, according to one of his mother's petitions, verging on the suicidal. Such accounts as we have of Lenin during this period depict him as an insolent, sarcastic, and friendless young man. In the Ulianov family, however, which idolized him, he was regarded as a budding genius and his opinions were gospel.[7]

During this period Lenin did a great deal of reading. He plowed through the "progressive" journals and books of the 1860s and 1870s, especially the writings of Nicholas Chernyshevskii, which, according to his own testimony, had on him a decisive influence.[8]* During this trying time, the Ulianovs were ostracized by Simbirsk society: people shunned association with relatives of an executed terrorist from fear of attracting the attention of the police. This was a bitter experience which seems to have played no small part in Lenin's radicalization. By the fall of 1888, when he moved with his mother to Kazan, Lenin was a full-fledged radical, filled with boundless hatred for those who had cut short his promising career and rejected his family—the tsarist establishment and the "bourgeoisie." In contrast to typical Russian revolutionaries, such as his late brother, who were driven by idealism, Lenin's dominant political impulse was and remained hatred. Rooted in this emotional soil, his socialism was from the outset primarily a doctrine of destruction. He gave little thought to the world of the future, so preoccupied was he, emotionally as well as intellectually, with smashing the world of the present. It was this obsessive destructiveness that both fascinated and repelled, inspired and terrified Russian intellectuals, themselves prone to alternate between Hamletic indecision and Quixotic folly. Struve, who had frequent dealings with Lenin in the 1890s, says that his

> principal *Einstellung*—to use the new popular German psychological term—was *hatred*. Lenin took to Marx's doctrine primarily because it found response

*Chernyshevskii was the leading radical publicist of the 1860s, the author of *What is to be done?*, a novel that urged young people to abandon their families and join communities committed to new positivistic and utilitarian ways of thinking. He regarded the existing world as rotten and doomed. The hero of the novel, Rakhmetov, is portrayed as a "new man" of iron will, totally dedicated to radical change. Lenin borrowed the title of Chernyshevskii's novel for his first political tract.

in that principal *Einstellung* of his mind. The doctrine of the class war, relentless and thoroughgoing, aiming at the final destruction and extermination of the enemy, proved congenial to Lenin's emotional attitude to surrounding reality. He hated not only the existing autocracy (the Tsar) and the bureaucracy, not only lawlessness and arbitrary rule of the police, but also their antipodes—the "liberals" and the "bourgeoisie." That hatred had something repulsive and terrible in it; for being rooted in the concrete, I should say even animal, emotions and repulsions, it was at the same time abstract and cold like Lenin's whole being.[9]

Lenin's official *vita,* as formalized in the 1920s, is in its essential features modeled on the life of Christ. Like Christology it depicts the protagonist as unaltered and unalterable, his destiny being predetermined on the day of birth. Lenin's official biographers refuse to allow that he had ever changed his ideas. He is said to have been a committed orthodox Marxist from the moment he became politically involved. This claim can easily be shown to be wrong.

To begin with, the term "Marxist" had in Lenin's youth not one but at least two distinct meanings. Classical Marxist doctrine applied to countries with mature capitalist economies. For these Marx purported to provide a scientific theory of development, the inevitable outcome of which was collapse and revolution. This doctrine had an immense appeal to Russian radical intellectuals both because of its claim to scientific objectivity and because of the inevitability of its prediction. Marx was popular in Russia before there was a Russian Social-Democratic movement: in 1880, he boasted that *Das Kapital* had more readers and admirers there than in any other country.[10] But since Russia at the time had hardly any capitalism, however liberally the term is defined, early Russian followers of Marx reinterpreted his theories to suit local conditions. In the 1870s they formulated the doctrine of "separate path," according to which Russia, developing her own form of socialism based on the rural commune, would make a direct leap to socialism, bypassing the capitalist phase.[11] Lenin's brother adopted this kind of ideology in the program for his People's Will organization and it was common in Russian radical circles in the 1880s.

Knowledge of the intellectual environment in which Lenin grew up sheds light on the evolution of his ideology. In 1887–91, Lenin was not and could not have been a Marxist in the Social-Democratic sense, because this variant of Marxism was still unknown in Russia. The evidence suggests that from 1887 until approximately 1891 he was a typical follower of the People's Will. He maintained close association with members of this organization, first in Kazan and then in Samara. He actively sought out its veterans, many of whom settled in the Volga region after being released from prison and exile, to learn the history of that movement and especially its organizational practices. This knowledge he deeply assimilated: even after becoming a leading figure in the Russian Social-Democratic Party, Lenin stood apart from his colleagues by virtue of his belief in a tightly disciplined, conspiratorial, and professional revolutionary party and his impatience with programs calling for a lengthy interlude of capitalism. Like the Narodnaia Volia he scorned capitalism and the "bourgeoisie," in which he saw not allies of socialism but its sworn enemies. It is noteworthy that in the late 1880s he failed to join the circles active in his region which were beginning to approach Marx and Engels in a "German"—that is, Social-Democratic—spirit.[12]

In June 1890, the authorities at long last relented and allowed Lenin to take the examinations for the bar as an external student. He passed them in November 1891, following which he devoted himself, not to the practice of law, but to the study of economic literature, especially statistical surveys of agriculture issued by the *zemstva*. His purpose, in the words of his sister Anna, was to determine the "feasibility of Social-Democracy in Russia."[13]

The time was propitious. In Germany, the Social-Democratic Party, legalized in 1890, won stunning successes at the polls. Its superb organization and ability to combine appeals to workers with a broad liberal program won it more parliamentary seats in each successive election. It suddenly appeared conceivable that socialism could triumph in the most industrialized country in Europe through democratic procedures rather than violence. Engels was so impressed by these developments that in 1895, shortly before his death, he conceded that the revolutionary upheavals which he and Marx had predicted in 1848 might never occur and that socialism could well triumph at the ballot box rather than the barricade.[14] The example of the German Social-Democratic Party exerted a strong influence on Russian socialists, discrediting the older theories of "separate path" and the revolutionary coup d'état.

Concurrently with the spread of these ideas, Russia experienced a dramatic spurt of industrial development which in the decade 1890–1900 doubled the number of industrial workers and gave Russia a rate of economic growth unmatched by any other country. The indications, therefore, were that Russia had missed the opportunity to bypass capitalism, which even Marx had conceded to be possible, and was destined to repeat the Western experience.

In this changed atmosphere, the theories of Social-Democracy gained a following in Russia. As formulated in Geneva by George Plekhanov and Paul Akselrod and in St. Petersburg by Peter Struve, Russia was to reach socialism in two stages. First she had to go through full-blown capitalism, which would vastly expand the ranks of the proletariat and, at the same time, bring the benefits of "bourgeois" freedoms, including a parliamentary system under which Russian socialists, like the Germans, could gain political influence. Once the "bourgeoisie" had swept autocracy and its "feudal" economic foundations out the way, the stage would be set for the next phase of historic development, the advance to socialism. In the mid-1890s these ideas captured the imagination of much of the intelligentsia and all but submerged the older ideology of "separate path," for which Struve now coined the derogatory term "Populism."[15]

Lenin was slow to make this transition, in part because, living in the provinces, he had no access to Social-Democratic literature and in part because its pro-capitalist, pro-bourgeois philosophy clashed with what Struve called "the principal *Einstellung*" or attitude of his mind. In 1892–93, having read Plekhanov, he seems to have arrived at a halfway position between the ideology of the People's Will and that of Social-Democracy, not unlike that which his brother had reached five years earlier. He abandoned the notion of a "separate path" and acknowledged the reality which stared everyone in the eye: Russia was destined to tread the path charted in *Das Kapital,* which he had read in 1889. But he was unwilling to concede that before being ready for revolution Russia had to undergo, for an indeterminate period, a stage of capitalist development during which the "bourgeoisie" lorded it over the country.

His solution to the problem was to declare that Russia already was capitalist. This eccentric view, which no other student of the Russian economy is known to have shared, rested on an idiosyncratic interpretation of statistical data on agriculture. Lenin convinced himself that the Russian village was in the throes of "class differentiation" which transformed a minority of peasants into a "petty bourgeoisie" and the majority into a landless rural proletariat. Such calculations, derived from those which Engels had made in regard to the German peasantry, had little to do with the facts of the case: but to Lenin they served as a guarantee that Russia did not have to postpone the revolution ad infinitum, until her capitalism was fully matured. Arguing that fully 20 percent of Russia's rural population in some provinces qualified as "bourgeois," and given the industrial boom then underway, Lenin felt emboldened to declare in 1893–94 that "at the present time capitalism already constitutes the basic background of Russia's economic life" and "essentially our order does not differ from the Western European."[16]

By declaring "capitalist" a country four-fifths of whose population consisted of peasants, most of them self-sufficient, small-scale communal farmers, Lenin could proclaim it ripe for revolution. Furthermore, since the "bourgeoisie" was already in power, it represented not an ally but a class enemy. In the summer of 1894, Lenin wrote a sentence that summarized the political philosophy to which, except for a brief interlude (1895–1900), he would remain faithful for the rest of his life:

> The Russian *worker,* leading all the democratic elements, will bring down absolutism and lead the *Russian proletariat* (along with the proletariat of *all the countries*) by the direct road of open political struggle to the triumphant *Communist Revolution.* [17]

Although the vocabulary was Marxist, the underlying sentiment of this passage was People's Will: indeed, as Lenin would many years later confide to Karl Radek, he had sought to reconcile Marx with the Narodnaia Volia.[18] The Russian worker, to whom the People's Will had also attributed the role of a revolutionary vanguard, was to launch a "direct" assault on the autocracy, topple it, and on its ruins erect a Communist society. Nothing is said about the mission of capitalism and the bourgeoisie in destroying the economic and political foundations of the old regime. It was an anachronistic ideology, for at the time when Lenin formulated it, Russia had a burgeoning Social-Democratic movement which rejected such an old-fashioned adaptation of Marx's theories.

On his arrival in St. Petersburg—the city that one day would bear his name—the twenty-three-year-old Lenin was a fully formed personality. The first impression which he made on new acquaintances, then and later, was unfavorable. His short, stocky figure, his premature baldness (he had lost nearly all hair before he was thirty), his slanted eyes and high cheekbones, his brusque manner of speaking, often accompanied by a sarcastic laugh, repelled most people. Contemporaries are virtually at one in speaking of his unprepossessing, "provincial" appearance. On meeting him, A. N. Potresov saw a "typical middle-aged tradesman from some northern Iaroslavl province." The British diplomat Bruce Lockhart thought Lenin looked like a "provincial grocer." For Angelica Balabanoff, an admirer, he resembled a "provincial schoolteacher."[19]

But this unattractive man glowed with an inner force that made people quickly forget their first impressions. His strength of will, indomitable discipline, energy, asceticism, and unshakable faith in the cause had an effect that can only be conveyed by the overused term "charisma." According to Potresov, this "unprepossessing and coarse" individual, devoid of charm, had a "hypnotic impact":

> Plekhanov was respected, Martov loved, but they only followed unquestioningly Lenin, the one indisputable leader. Because Lenin alone embodied the phenomenon, rare everywhere but especially in Russia, of a man of iron will, inexhaustible energy, combining a fanatical faith in the movement, in the cause, with an equal faith in himself.[20]

A fundamental source of Lenin's strength and personal magnetism was the quality alluded to by Potresov—namely, the identification of his person with the cause: in him, the two became indistinguishable. This phenomenon was not unknown in socialist circles. In his study of political parties, Robert Michels has a chapter called "Le Parti c'est moi," in which he describes similar attitudes among German Social-Democratic and trade-union leaders, including Bebel, Marx, and Lassalle. He quotes an admirer of Bebel's who said that Bebel "always regards himself as the guardian of party interests and his personal adversaries as enemies of the party."[21] Potresov made a similar observation about the future leader of Bolshevism:

> Within the framework of Social-Democracy or outside it, in the ranks of the general public movement directed against the autocracy, Lenin knew only two

categories of people and phenomena, his own and not his own. His own, those which in one way or another came within the sphere of influence of his organization, and the others, which did not, and which by virtue of this fact alone he regarded as enemies. Between these polar opposites—comrade-friend and dissenter-enemy—for Lenin there existed no intermediate spectrum of social and personal human relations . . .[22]

Trotsky left an interesting example of this mentality. Recounting his visit with Lenin in London, he says that when showing him the sights Lenin invariably referred to them as "theirs," by which he meant, according to Trotsky, not England's, but "the enemy's": "This note was always present when Lenin spoke of any kind of cultural values or new achievements . . . *they* understand or *they* have, *they* have accomplished or succeeded—but as enemies!"[23]

The normal "I/we—you/they" dichotomy, translated into the stark dualism "friend-enemy," which in Lenin's case went to uncompromising extremes, had two important historic consequences.

By thinking in this manner, Lenin was inevitably led to treat politics as warfare. He did not need Marx's sociology to militarize politics and treat all disagreements as susceptible of resolution in one way only: by the dissenter's physical annihilation. Lenin read Clausewitz late in life, but he was a Clausewitzian long before, intuitively, by virtue of his entire psychic makeup. Like the German strategist, he conceived war not as the antithesis of peace but as its dialectical corollary; like him, he was exclusively concerned with gaining victory, not with the uses to which to put it. His outlook on life was a mixture of Clausewitz and Social Darwinism: when, in a rare moment of candor, Lenin defined peace as a "breathing spell for war," he inadvertently allowed an insight into the innermost recesses of his mind.[24] This manner of thinking made him constitutionally incapable of compromise, except for tactical purposes. Once Lenin and his followers came to power in Russia, this attitude automatically permeated the new regime.

The other consequence of his psychological makeup was an inability to tolerate any dissent, whether in the form of organized opposition or even mere criticism. Given that he perceived any group or individuals not members of his party and not under his personal influence as ipso facto enemies, it followed that they had to be suppressed and silenced. That such actions were implicit in Lenin's mentality, Trotsky noted as early as 1904. Comparing Lenin to Robespierre, he attributed to him the Jacobin's dictum: "I know only two parties—that of good citizens and that of bad citizens." "This political aphorism," Trotsky concluded, "is engraved in the heart of Maximilian Lenin."[25] Here lay the germs of government by terror, of the totalitarian aspiration to complete control of public life and public opinion.

An attractive aspect of this quality was Lenin's loyalty and generosity toward "good citizens," a concept limited to his acolytes: it was the obverse side of hostility toward all outsiders. Much as he personalized disagreements with the latter, within his own ranks he displayed surprising tolerance of dissent. He did not purge dissenters but tried to persuade them; as the ultimate weapon he would use the threat of resignation.

Another attractive aspect of Lenin's total identification with the revolutionary cause as represented by his party was a peculiar form of personal modesty. Although his successors built a quasi-religious cult around his person, they did this for their private ends: for without him, there was nothing to hold the movement together. Lenin never encouraged such a cult, because he found unacceptable the implication that he had an existence separate from that of the "proletariat": like Robespierre, he thought that, in the literal sense, he was the "people."* His "aversion to being singled out as a personality apart from the movement"[26] was a modesty rooted in a sense of self-importance far in excess of ordinary vanity. Hence his aversion to memoirs: no leader of the Russian Revolution has left less autobiographical material.†

A stranger to moral qualms, he resembled a pope of whom Ranke wrote that he was endowed with such "complete self-reliance that doubt or fear as to the consequences of his own actions was a pain unknown to his experience." This quality made Lenin very attractive to a certain type of Russian pseudo-intellectual who would later flock into the Bolshevik Party because it offered certainty in a perplexing world. It appealed especially to the young, semi-literate peasants who left the village to seek industrial work and found themselves adrift in a strange, cold world where the personal relations to which they had been accustomed were replaced by impersonal economic and social ties. Lenin's party gave them a sense of belonging: they liked its cohesion and simple slogans.

Lenin had a strong streak of cruelty. It is a demonstrable fact that he advocated terror on principle, issued decrees which condemned to death countless people innocent of any wrongdoing, and showed no remorse at the loss of life for which he was responsible. At the same time, it is important to stress that his cruelty was not sadism which derives pleasure from the suffering of others. It rather stemmed from complete indifference to such suffering. Maxim Gorky gained the impression from conversations with Lenin that for him individual human beings held "almost no interest, that he thought only of parties, masses, states. . . ." On another occasion, Gorky said that for Lenin the working class was what "ore is for a metalworker"[27]—in other words, raw material for social experiments. This trait manifested itself as early as 1891–92, when the Volga region where Lenin lived was struck by famine. Committees were formed to feed the hungry peasants. According to a friend of the Ulianovs, Lenin alone (echoed, as always, by his family) opposed such aid on the grounds that by forcing peasants off the land and into the cities, where they

---

*In 1792, in a transport of exuberance, Robespierre exclaimed: "I am neither the courtier of the people, nor its moderator, nor its tribune, nor its defender—I am the people itself!" (Alfred Cobban, *Aspects of the French Revolution,* London, 1968, 188.)

†He eventually came to tolerate his personal cult because, as he explained to Angelica Balabanoff, it was "useful, even necessary": "Our peasants are suspicious; they don't read, they must see in order to believe. If they see my likeness, they are persuaded that Lenin exists." *Impressions of Lenin* (Ann Arbor, Mich., 1964, 5–6).

formed a "proletarian" reserve, the famine was a "progressive" phenomenon.[28] Treating human beings as "ore" to build a new society, he sent people to their death before execution squads with the same lack of emotion with which a general orders troops to advance into enemy fire. Gorky quotes a Frenchman that Lenin was a "thinking guillotine." Without denying the charge, he concedes that he was a misanthrope: "In general, he loved people: he loved them with abnegation. His love looked far ahead, through the mists of hatred."[29] When after 1917 Gorky pleaded with him to spare the life of this or that person condemned to death, Lenin seemed genuinely puzzled why he would bother him with such trivia.

As is usually the case (this held true of Robespierre as well), the obverse side of Lenin's cruelty was cowardice. This aspect of Lenin's personality is rarely touched upon in the literature, although there exists a great deal of evidence for it. Lenin showed a characteristic lack of courage while still in his teens when he tried to evade punishment for participating in student disturbances by attempting to withdraw from the university. As we shall note later, he will fail to admit authorship of a manuscript which cost an associate of his two additional years of exile. His invariable reaction to physical danger was flight: he had an uncanny ability to make himself scarce whenever there was the threat of arrest or shooting, even if it meant abandoning his troops. Tatiana Aleksinskii, the wife of the head of the Bolshevik faction in the Second Duma, saw Lenin run from danger:

> I first met Lenin in the summer of 1906. I would rather not recall that encounter. Lenin, admired by all Left Social-Democrats, had seemed to me a legendary hero. . . . Not having seen him up close, because he had lived abroad until the Revolution of 1905, we had imagined him as a revolutionary without fear or blemish. . . . How keen, therefore, was my disappointment on seeing him [in 1906] at a meeting in the suburbs of Petersburg. It was not only his appearance that made a disagreeable impression on me: he was bald, with a reddish beard, Mongol cheekbones, and an unpleasant expression. It was his behavior during the demonstration that followed. When someone, spotting the cavalry charging the crowd, shouted "Cossacks!" Lenin was the first to flee. He jumped over a barrier. His bowler hat fell off, revealing his bare skull, perspiring and glistening under the sunlight. He fell, got up, and continued to run. . . . I had a peculiar sensation. I realized there was nothing to do but save oneself. And still . . .[30]

These unattractive personal traits were well known to his associates, who consciously ignored them because of Lenin's unique assets: an extraordinary capacity for disciplined work and total commitment to the revolutionary cause. In the words of Bertram Wolfe, Lenin "was the only man of high theoretical capacity which the Russian Marxist movement produced who possessed at the same time the ability and the will to concern himself with detailed organization work."[31] Plekhanov, who on meeting him in 1895 dismissed Lenin as a second-rate intellect, nevertheless valued him and overlooked his shortcomings because, in the words of Potresov, "he saw the importance of this new man not at all in his ideas but in his initiative and talents as party organizer."[32] Struve, who was repelled by Lenin's "coldness, contempt, and cruelty," admits to having "driven away" such negative feelings for the sake of relations which he regarded as "both morally obligatory for myself and politically indispensable for our cause."[33]

Lenin was first and foremost an internationalist, a world revolutionary, for whom state boundaries were relics of another era and nationalism a distraction from the class struggle. He would have been prepared to lead the revolution in any country where the opportunity presented itself, and certainly in Germany rather than in his native Russia. He spent nearly one-half of his adult life abroad (from 1900 to 1917, except for two years in 1905–7) and never had a chance to learn much about his homeland: "I know Russia poorly, Simbirsk, Kazan, Petersburg, the exile—that's all."[34] He held Russians in low esteem, considering them lazy, soft, and not terribly bright. "An intelligent Russian," he told Gorky, "is almost always a Jew or someone with Jewish blood in his veins."[35] Although he was no stranger to the sentiment of nostalgia for his homeland, Russia was to him an accidental center of the first revolutionary upheaval, a springboard for the real revolution, whose vortex had to be Western Europe. In May 1918, defending the territorial concession he had made to the Germans at Brest-Litovsk, he asserted: "We insist that it is not national interests [but] the interests of socialism, of world socialism that are superior to national interests, to interests of the state."[36]

Lenin's cultural equipment was exceedingly modest for a Russian intellectual of his generation. His writings show only a superficial familiarity with Russia's literary classics (Turgenev excepted), most of it apparently acquired in secondary school. Tatiana Aleksinskii, who worked closely with Lenin and his wife, noted that they never went to concerts or the theater.[37] Lenin's knowledge of history, other than that of revolutions, was also perfunctory. He had a love for music, but he preferred to suppress it in accord with that asceticism that so impressed and alarmed contemporaries. He told Gorky:

> I cannot listen much to music, it excites my nerves. I feel like talking nonsense and caressing people who, living in such a filthy hell, can create such beauty. Because today one must not caress anyone: they will bite off your hand. One must break heads, pitilessly break heads, even if, ideally, we are opposed to all violence.[38]

Potresov found that with the twenty-five-year-old Lenin one could discuss only one subject: the "movement." He was interested in nothing else and had nothing interesting to say about anything else.* In sum, not what used to be called a man of many parts.

This cultural poverty was yet another source of Lenin's strength as a

---

*A. N. Potresov, *Posmertnyi sbornik proizvedenii* (Paris, 1937), 297. Tatiana Aleksinskii concurs: "For Lenin, politics superseded everything and left room for nothing else": *La Grande Revue,* XXVII, No. 9 (September 1923), 459.

revolutionary leader, for unlike better-educated intellectuals, he carried in his head no excess baggage of facts and ideas to act as a brake on his resolve. Like his mentor, Chernyshevskii, he dismissed differing opinions as "twaddle" and refused even to consider them except as objects of ridicule. Inconvenient facts he ignored or reinterpreted to suit his purposes. If his opponent was wrong in anything, he was wrong in everything: he never conceded the opposing party any merit. His manner of debating was combative in the extreme: he thoroughly assimilated Marx's dictum that criticism "is not a scalpel but a weapon. Its object is the enemy, [whom] it wishes not to refute but to destroy."[39] In this spirit, he used words like ammunition, to annihilate opponents, often by means of the crudest ad hominem assaults on their integrity and motives. On one occasion, he conceded that he saw nothing wrong with using calumny and confounding workers when this served his political purposes. When in 1907, having charged the Mensheviks with betrayal of the working class, he was made to appear before a socialist tribunal, he admitted with brazen effrontery the charge of slander:

> This formulation is calculated, as it were, to arouse in the reader hatred, revulsion, contempt for the people who act in this manner. This formulation is calculated not to persuade but to smash [their] ranks—not to correct the opponent's error, but to destroy, to rub his organization off the face of the earth. This formulation, indeed, arouses the worst thoughts, the very worst suspicions of the opponent, and, indeed, in contrast to the formulation which convinces and corrects, it "sows confusion in the ranks of the proletariat." . . . That which is not permissible among the members of a single party is permitted and obligatory for the parts of a party that has fallen apart.[40]

He thus constantly engaged in what one historian of the French Revolution, Auguste Cochin, called "dry terror": and from "dry terror" to "bloody terror" was, of course, only a short step. When a fellow socialist once warned Lenin that his intemperate attacks on an opponent (Struve) could inspire some worker to kill the object of his wrath, Lenin calmly responded: "He ought to be killed."[41]

The mature Lenin was made of one piece and his personality stood out in strong relief. After he had formulated the doctrine and practice of Bolshevism, which happened in his early thirties, he surrounded himself with an invisible protective wall which alien ideas could not penetrate. Henceforth, nothing could change his mind. He belonged to that category of men of whom the Marquis de Custine had said that they know everything except what one tells them. One either agreed with him or fought him: and disagreement with Lenin always awakened on his part destructive hatred, the urge to "rub" his opponents "off the face of the earth." This was his strength as revolutionary and weakness as statesman: invincible in combat, he lacked the human qualities necessary to understand and guide mankind. In the end, this flaw would defeat his effort to create a new society, for he simply could not comprehend how people could live side by side in peace.

In the fall of 1893 Lenin moved to St. Petersburg, ostensibly to practice law, but in fact to make connections with radical circles and launch his revolutionary career.[42] To the Social-Democrats whom he contacted on arrival he appeared "too red"—that is, still too much of a People's Will adherent. He soon broadened his circle of acquaintances, joining a group of brilliant Social-Democratic intellectuals, whose leading spirit was the twenty-three-year-old Peter Struve—like Lenin, the son of a high official, but unlike him, a cosmopolitan who had been in the West and acquired an extraordinarily broad range of knowledge. The two had many discussions. Their disagreements centered mainly on Lenin's simplistic notion of capitalism and his attitude toward the "bourgeoisie." Struve explained to Lenin that far from having acquired a Western-type capitalist economy, Russia had barely taken the first step on the path to capitalist development, as he would convince himself once he saw the West with his own eyes. He also explained to him that Social-Democracy could flourish in Russia only if the middle class, prodded by industrial labor, introduced such liberties as freedom of the press and the right to form political parties. Lenin remained unconvinced.

In the summer of 1895 he traveled abroad and met with Plekhanov and the other veterans of the Social-Democratic movement. He was told it was a profound mistake to reject the "bourgeoisie": "We turn our faces to the liberals," Plekhanov said, "whereas you turn your back."[43] Akselrod argued that in any joint action with the "liberal bourgeoisie" the Social-Democrats would not lose control because they would retain "hegemony" in the joint struggle, guiding and manipulating their temporary allies in a direction that best served their own interests.

Lenin, who worshipped Plekhanov, was impressed. How deeply he was convinced cannot be determined: but it is a demonstrable fact that upon his return to St. Petersburg in the autumn of 1895 he made the debut as an orthodox Social-Democrat, committed to organizing workers for the struggle against the autocracy in a common front with the "liberal bourgeoisie." The change was striking: in the summer of 1894, he had written that socialism and democracy were incompatible; now he argued that they were inseparable.[44] Russia in his eyes was no longer a capitalist but a semi-feudal country, and the main enemy of the proletariat was not the bourgeoisie allied with the autocracy but the autocracy itself. The bourgeoisie—at any rate, its progressive element—was an ally of the working class:

> The Social-Democratic Party declares that it will support all the strata of the bourgeoisie engaged in the struggle against the autocratic government.... The democratic struggle is inseparable from the socialist one; [it is] impossible to wage a successful fight for the cause of labor without the attainment of full liberty and the democratization of Russia's political and social regime.[45]

Conspiracy and coup d'état he now dismissed as impracticable. It is important to bear in mind, however, that Lenin's change of heart on the role of the "liberal bourgeoisie" was firmly anchored in the premise, stated by Akselrod, that in the campaign against the autocracy the revolutionary socialists would lead and the bourgeoisie follow.

After his return from abroad, Lenin established desultory contact with labor circles that were leading a precarious existence in the capital. He did some tutoring in Marxist theory, but he did not much care for educational work and he gave it up after a worker whom he was initiating into *Das Kapital* walked off with his overcoat.[46] He preferred to organize workers for action. At the time, there operated in St. Petersburg a circle of Social-Democratic intellectuals which maintained contact with individual workers as well as the Central Workers' Circle, formed by the workers themselves for purposes of mutual aid and self-improvement. Lenin joined the Social-Democratic circle, but involved himself in its work only late in 1895 when it adopted the technique of "agitation" formulated by Jewish socialists in Lithuania. To overcome the workers' aversion to politics, the "agitational" technique called for inciting industrial strikes based on the workers' economic (i.e., non-political) grievances. It was believed that once the workers saw how the government and the forces of order invariably sided with the proprietors of the affected enterprises, they would realize it was impossible to satisfy their economic grievances without a change in the political regime. This realization would politicize labor. Lenin, who learned of the "agitational" technique from Martov, joined in the distribution among St. Petersburg workers of agitational material which explained to the workers their rights under the law and showed how these rights were being violated by the employers. The output was meager, and the effect on the workers doubtful: but when in May 1896, 30,000 textile workers in the capital went on a spontaneous strike, the Social-Democrats had cause for jubilation.

By then Lenin and his comrades were in jail, having been arrested in the winter of 1895–96 for incitement to strikes. Nevertheless, Lenin felt that the "agitational" method of struggle had vindicated itself: "The struggle of workers with factory owners for their daily needs," he wrote in the wake of the textile strike, *"of itself and inevitably* suggests to the workers *problems of state and politics.* "[47] The task of the party Lenin defined as follows:

> The Russian Social-Democratic Party declares its task to be helping the struggle of the Russian working class by developing labor's class consciousness, assisting its organization, and showing it the real goals of the struggle. . . . The task of the party is not to invent in its head some fashionable methods of helping the workers, but to *join* the labor movement, to illuminate it, to *help* the workers in the struggle *which they have already begun to wage themselves.*[48]

During the investigation that followed his arrest, Lenin disclaimed authorship of a manuscript of his which the police had mistakenly attributed to an associate by the name of P. K. Zaporozhets. As a consequence, the latter drew two additional years of prison and exile. Lenin spent his three years of Siberian exile (1897–1900) in relative comfort and in constant communication with his comrades. He read, wrote, translated, and engaged in vigorous physical activity.*

As his term of exile drew to a close, Lenin was in receipt of disturbing news from home: the movement, which at the time of his imprisonment was going from success to success, was in the throes of a crisis not unlike that experienced by the revolutionaries of the 1870s. The agitational technique, which Lenin had expected to radicalize workers, turned into something very different: the economic grievances which had been intended to serve as a means of stimulating their political awareness had become an end in themselves. The workers struggled for economic benefits without getting politically involved, and the intellectuals who engaged in "agitation" found that they had become adjuncts of an incipient trade union movement. In the summer of 1899, Lenin received from Russia a document written by Ekaterina Kuskova and called "Credo" which urged socialists to leave the struggle against the autocracy to the bourgeoisie and concentrate instead on helping Russian labor improve its economic and social condition. Kuskova was not a full-fledged Social-Democrat, but her essay reflected a trend that was emerging within Social-Democracy. This incipient heresy Lenin labeled Economism. Nothing was further from his mind than to have the socialist movement turn into a hand-maiden of trade unions, which by their very nature pursued accommodation with "capitalism." The information which reached him from Russia indicated that the labor movement was maturing independently of the Social-Democratic intelligentsia and distancing itself from the political struggle—that is, revolution.

His anxiety was compounded by the emergence of yet another heresy in the movement: Revisionism. In early 1899, some leading Russian Social-Democrats, following Eduard Bernstein, called for a revision of Marx's social theory in the light of recent evidence. That year Struve published an analysis of Marx's social theory in which he charged it with inconsistency: Marx's own premises indicated that socialism could come about only as a result of evolution, not revolution.[49] Struve then proceeded to a systematic critique of the central concept of Marx's economic and social doctrine, the theory of value, which led him to the conclusion that "value" was not a scientific but a metaphysical concept.[50] Revisionism did not trouble Lenin as much as Economism for it did not have the same practical implications, but it heightened his fear that something was seriously amiss. According to Krupskaia, in the summer of 1899 Lenin grew distraught, lost weight, and suffered from insom-

*In order for his common-law wife, Nadezhda Krupskaia, to accompany him to Siberia, Lenin had to marry her. Since the Russian government did not recognize civil marriages, the wedding (July 10, 1898) had to take place in church: Robert H. McNeal, *Bride of the Revolution: Krupskaya and Lenin* (Ann Arbor, Mich., 1972), 65. Neither Lenin nor his bride ever referred in their writings to this embarrassing episode.

nia. He now devoted his energies to analyzing the causes of the crisis in Russian Social-Democracy and devising the means to overcome it.

His immediate practical solution was to launch with those associates who had remained faithful to orthodox Marxism a publication, modeled on the German *Sozialdemokrat,* to combat deviations in the movement, especially Economism. Such was the origin of *Iskra.* But Lenin's thoughts ran deeper and he began to wonder whether Social-Democracy should not reorganize as a tight, conspiratorial elite on the model of the People's Will.[51] These speculations marked the onset of a spiritual crisis which would be resolved only a year later with the decision to form a party of his own.

After his release from exile in early 1900, Lenin spent a short time in St. Petersburg negotiating with colleagues as well as Struve, who, although nominally still a Social-Democrat, was shifting into the liberal camp. Struve was to collaborate with *Iskra* and provide a good part of its financing. Later that year, Lenin moved to Munich where jointly with Potresov and Julius Martov he founded *Iskra* as an organ of "orthodox"—that is, anti-Economist and anti-Revisionist—Marxism.

The longer he observed the behavior of workers in and out of Russia, the more compelling was the conclusion, entirely contrary to the fundamental premise of Marxism, that labor (the "proletariat") was not a revolutionary class at all: left to itself, it would rather settle for a larger share of the capitalists' profits than overthrow capitalism. It was the same premise that moved Zubatov at this very time to conceive the idea of police trade unionism.* In a seminal article published at the end of 1900, Lenin uttered the unthinkable: "the labor movement, separated from Social-Democracy . . . inevitably turns bourgeois."[52] The implication of this startling statement was that unless the workers were led by a socialist party external to it and independent of it, they would betray their class interests. Only non-workers—that is, the intelligentsia—knew what these interests were. In the spirit of Mosca and Pareto, whose theories of political elites were then in vogue, Lenin asserted that the proletariat, for its own sake, had to be led by a minority of the elect:

> No single class in history has ever attained mastery unless it has produced political leaders, its leading representatives, capable of organizing the movement and leading it. . . . It is necessary to prepare men who devote to the revolution not only their free evenings, but their entire lives.†

Now, inasmuch as workers have to earn a living, they cannot devote "their entire lives" to the revolutionary movement, which means that it follows from

---

*See above, Chapter 1.

†Lenin, *PSS,* IV, 375–76. A decade later, Benito Mussolini, ten years Lenin's junior and a leading Italian socialist, arrived independently at the same conclusion. In 1912 he wrote that "a worker who is merely organized has become a petty bourgeois who obeys only the voice of interest. Every appeal to ideals finds him deaf": B. Mussolini, *Opera omnia,* IV (Florence, 1952), 156. On another occasion Mussolini said that workers were, by their very nature, "pacifistic": A. Rossi, *The Rise of Italian Fascism, 1918–1922* (London, 1938), 134.

Lenin's premise that the leadership of the worker's cause has to fall on the shoulders of the socialist intelligentsia. This notion subverts the very principle of democracy: the will of the people is not what the living people want but what their "true" interests, as defined by their betters, are said to be.

Having deviated from Social-Democracy on the issue of labor, Lenin required little effort to break with it over the issue of the "bourgeoisie." Observing the emergence of a vigorous and independent liberal movement, soon to coalesce in the Union of Liberation, Lenin lost faith in the ability of the poorer and less influential socialists to exercise "hegemony" over their "bourgeois" allies. In December 1900, following stormy meetings with Struve over the terms of liberal collaboration with *Iskra,* Lenin concluded that it was futile to expect the liberals to concede to the socialists leadership in the struggle against the autocracy: they would fight on their own and for their own non-revolutionary objectives, exploiting the revolutionaries to this end.[53] The "liberal bourgeoisie" was waging a spurious struggle against the monarchy and, therefore, constituted a "counterrevolutionary" class.[54] His rejection of the progressive role of the "bourgeoisie" signified a reversion to his previous People's Will position and completed his break with Social-Democracy.

Having concluded that industrial labor was inherently non-revolutionary, indeed "bourgeois," and the bourgeoisie "counterrevolutionary," Lenin had two choices open to him. One was to give up the idea of revolution. This, however, he could not do, for the psychological reasons spelled out earlier: revolution to him was not the means to an end but the end itself. The other choice was to carry out a revolution from above, by conspiracy and coup d'état, without regard for the wishes of the masses. Lenin chose the latter course. In July 1917 he would write:

> . . . in times of revolution it is not enough to ascertain the "will of the majority"—no, one must *be stronger* at the decisive moment in the decisive place and *win.* Beginning with the medieval "peasant war" in Germany . . . until 1905, we see countless instances of how the better-organized, more conscious, better-armed minority imposed its will on the majority and conquered it.[55]

The model of the party organization which was to accomplish this task Lenin adopted directly from the People's Will. The Narodovol'tsy had been very secretive about the structure and operations of their party, and to this day much about this subject remains obscure.[56] Lenin, however, had managed to acquire much firsthand knowledge from conversations with ex-Narodovol'tsy while living in Kazan and Samara. The People's Will was structured hierarchically and operated in a quasi-military manner. Unlike Land and Freedom, its parent organization, it rejected the principle of equality of members, replacing it with a command structure, at the head of which stood the all-powerful Executive Committee. To qualify for membership in the Executive Committee, one had not only to subscribe unquestioningly to its program but also devote oneself body and soul to its cause: "Every member," the committee's statutes read, "must unconditionally place all his talents, resources, connections, sympathies and antipathies, and even his life at the disposal of the organization."[57] The decisions of the Executive Committee, reached by majority vote, were binding on all members. These were chosen by co-optation. Serving under the committee were specialized organs, including a Military Organization, and regional or "vassal" branches: the latter had to carry out its instructions without demurrer. Because the members of the Executive Committee were full-time revolutionaries, most of them had to live on money that the party obtained from well-wishers.

Lenin took over these organizational principles and practices in toto. Discipline, professionalism, and hierarchical organization were all a legacy from the People's Will which he sought to inject into the Social-Democratic Party and, when the effort failed, imposed on his own Bolshevik faction. In 1904 he asserted that "the organizational principle of revolutionary Social-Democracy strives to proceed from the top downward" and requires the parts or branches to subordinate themselves to the party's central organ[58]—language which could have come from the statutes of the People's Will.

Lenin, however, departed from the practices of the People's Will in two important respects. The Narodnaia Volia, although hierarchically organized, did not allow for personal leadership: its Executive Committee functioned collegially. This was also the theoretical basis of the Bolshevik Central Committee (which had no formal chairman), but in practice Lenin completely dominated proceedings and it rarely took major decisions without his approval. Second, the People's Will did not intend to become the government of a Russia liberated from tsarism: its mission was to end with the convocation of a Constituent Assembly.[59] For Lenin, by contrast, the overthrow of autocracy was only a prelude to the "dictatorship of the proletariat," managed by his party.

Lenin popularized his views in *What Is to Be Done?*, published in March 1902. The book brought up to date and garbed in Social-Democratic vocabulary the ideas of the People's Will. Here Lenin called for the creation of a disciplined, centralized party composed of full-time, professional revolutionaries dedicated to the overthrow of the tsarist regime. He dismissed the notion of party "democracy" as well as the belief that the labor movement would, in the course of its natural development, carry out a popular revolution: the labor movement on its own was capable only of trade unionism. Socialism and revolutionary zeal had to be injected into labor from the outside: "consciousness" had to prevail over "spontaneity." Because the working class was a minority in Russia, Russian Social-Democrats had to involve the other classes in the struggle as temporary allies. *What Is to Be Done?* overturned, in the name of orthodox Marxism, the basic tenets of Marxist doctrine and rejected the democratic element of Social-Democracy. Nevertheless, it made an immense impression on Russian socialist intellectuals among whom the older traditions of the People's Will remained alive and who were growing impatient with the dilatory tactics advocated by Plekhanov, Akselrod, and Martov. Then, as later, in 1917, much of Lenin's appeal derived from the fact that he spelled out in plain language and translated into programs of action the ideas which his socialist rivals, lacking the courage of their convictions, hedged with countless qualifications.

Lenin's unorthodox theses became the subject of intense controversy in 1902–3, as the Social-Democrats were making preparations for the forthcoming Second Congress of the party—a congress which, its name notwithstanding, was to be the party's founding gathering. Quarrels broke out in which ideological differences fused with and often masked personal struggles over leadership. Lenin, supported by Plekhanov, called for a more centralized organization in which the rank and file would be subservient to the center, while Martov, the future leader of the Mensheviks, wanted a looser structure, offering admission to anyone who gave "the party regular personal cooperation, under the direction of one of the party organizations."[60]

The Second Congress convened in Brussels in July 1903; it was attended by forty-three voting delegates, authorized to cast fifty-one votes.* All but four of the participants, said to have been workers, belonged to the intelligentsia. Martov, leading the opposition to Lenin, regularly won majorities, but when he joined with his rival to deny the Jewish Bund autonomous status in the party and the five Bundists walked out, followed by the two Economist delegates, he temporarily lost his majority. Lenin promptly exploited the opportunity to seize control of the Central Committee and secure a dominant voice in its organ, *Iskra.* His ruthless methods and intrigues on this occasion caused a great deal of bad blood between him and the other leaders of the party. Although every effort was made then and subsequently to preserve a façade of unity, the split in fact became irreparable, not so much because of ideological differences, which could have been reconciled, but from personal animosities. Lenin seized the moment to claim for his faction the name Bolshevik, meaning "majority." This name he retained even after he found himself in a minority, which occurred soon after the Second Congress. It gave him the advantage of appearing as the leader of the more popular branch of the party. Throughout he maintained the pose of being the only "orthodox" Marxist, which had considerable appeal in a country whose religious tradition viewed orthodoxy as the supreme virtue and dissent as apostasy.

The next two years of the party's history (1903–5) were filled with vicious intrigues that are of small interest except for the light they cast on the personalities involved. Lenin was determined to subordinate the party to his will; failing that, he was prepared to create, under the party's cover, a parallel

---

*At the end of the month, to elude surveillance by the Russian and Belgian police, the congress moved to London.

organization under his personal control. By the end of 1904, he had, in effect, his own party with its own rump "Central Committee" called "Bureau of the Committees of the Party Majority." For this action, he was expelled from the legitimate Central Committee.[61] The technique of subverting legitimate institutions in which he was in a minority, by forming unauthorized, parallel, identically named organizations packed with his adherents, Lenin would apply in 1917–18 to other centers of power, notably the soviets.

By the time the 1905 Revolution broke out, the Bolshevik organization was in place:

> a disciplined order of professional committee men, grouped around a band of conspirators who were all linked by personal allegiance to their chieftain, Lenin, and ready to follow him in any adventure, as long as his leadership appeared sufficiently radical and extreme.[62]

Lenin's opponents accused him of Jacobinism: Trotsky noted that, like the Jacobins, the Leninists feared mass "spontaneity."[63] Unperturbed by such accusations, Lenin proudly claimed the title of Jacobin for himself.[64] Akselrod thought Leninism was not even Jacobinism but "a very simple copy or caricature of the bureaucratic-autocratic system of our Minister of the Interior."[65]

Neither the Bolsheviks nor the Mensheviks exerted much influence on the course of the 1905 Revolution, at any rate, until its concluding phase. The violence of 1905 caught the Social-Democrats by surprise and most of that year they had to confine themselves to issuing proclamations and fomenting the unrest which raged beyond their control. It was only in October 1905, with the formation of the Petrograd Soviet of Workers' Deputies, that the Mensheviks could assume a more active role in a revolution until then dominated by liberal personalities and liberal programs.

Lenin was not directly involved in these events, for unlike Trotsky and Parvus, he preferred to observe them from the safety of Switzerland; he judged it prudent to return to Russia only in early November, following the proclamation of political amnesty. He thought that January 1905 marked the onset of a general revolution in Russia. While the initial impetus came from the liberal "bourgeoisie," this class was certain to capitulate somewhere along the way and strike a deal with tsarism. It was imperative, therefore, for the Social-Democrats to take charge and lead the workers to full victory.

Although Lenin always had a predilection for what Martov called "anarcho-blanquism,"[66] he had to have a theoretical justification for his program of action. This he found in a seminal essay by Parvus, written in January 1905 under the immediate impact of Bloody Sunday. Parvus's theory of "uninterrupted" (or "permanent") revolution provided a happy compromise between the orthodox Russian Social-Democratic doctrine of a two-phase revolution in which a distinct phase of "bourgeois" rule preceded socialism, and the anarchist theory of "direct assault," which Lenin preferred temperamentally but was unable to reconcile with Marxism. Parvus allowed for a "bourgeois" phase, but insisted on no interval separating it from the socialist phase, which would get underway concurrently.* Under this scheme, once the anti-autocratic revolution broke out, the "proletariat" (meaning the Social-Democratic Party) would immediately proceed to take power. The justification for this theory was that Russia lacked a radicalized lower middle class which in Western Europe had supported and encouraged the bourgeoisie. In its exposed position, the Russian bourgeoisie would never allow the revolution to come to fruition but would stop it "halfway." The socialists had to prepare and organize the masses for the civil war that would follow the fall of tsarism. One of the prerequisites of success was for the party to keep an identity distinct from its allies: "fight together, but march apart." Parvus's conception had great influence on Russian Social-Democrats, notably Lenin and Trotsky: "For the first time in the history of the Russian movement, the thesis was advanced that the proletariat should at once grasp for political power and . . . form a provisional government."[67]

Lenin initially rejected Parvus's theory, as he was in the habit of doing whenever anyone challenged, with a new idea or tactic, his primacy in the movement. But he soon came around. In September 1905 he echoed Parvus:

> . . . immediately after the democratic revolution we will begin to proceed, to the extent that our strength allows it . . . to the socialist revolution. We favor an uninterrupted [*nepreryvnaia*] revolution. We will not stop halfway.†

The socialist revolution, in Lenin's view, could take only one form: armed insurrection. To learn the strategy and tactics of urban guerrilla warfare, he assiduously studied its history: among his authorities were the memoirs of Gustave Cluseret, the military commander of the Paris Commune. What he learned, he passed on to his followers in Russia. In October 1905, he advised them to form "Detachments of the Revolutionary Army," whose members should equip themselves with a

> gun, revolver, bomb, knife, brass knuckles, stick, rag soaked in kerosene to start fires, rope or rope ladder, shovel to build barricades, slab of guncotton, barbed

---

*Parvus first formulated the theory of "uninterrupted" or "permanent" revolution (without, however, using either name) in the introduction to Trotsky's pamphlet *Do deviatogo Ianvaria* (Geneva, 1905), pp. iii–xiv, dated Munich, January 18/31, 1905. On this subject, see Isaac Deutscher, *The Prophet Armed: Trotsky, 1879–1921* (New York-London, 1954), 112–14, 118–19, 149–62, and Z. A. B. Zeman and W. B. Scharlau, *The Merchant of the Revolution: The Life of Alexander Israel Helphand (Parvus)* (London, 1965), 76–79. The concept of "Revolution in Permanence" had been briefly promoted by Marx in 1848: Leonard Schapiro, *The Communist Party of the Soviet Union* (New York, 1960), 77.

†Lenin, *PSS*, XI, 222. Both Wolfe (*Three*, 291–94) and Schapiro (*Communist Party*, 77–78) believe this statement to be an aberration on Lenin's part, because he subsequently said on many occasions that Russia could not bypass the "capitalist" and "democratic" phase. But as his behavior in 1917 would reveal, he only paid lip service to the idea of a "democratic" revolution: his true strategy called for an immediate transition from "bourgeois" democracy to the "dictatorship of the proletariat."

wire, nails (against cavalry), and so forth. . . . Even without weapons the detachments can play a serious role by (1) leading the crowd; (2) attacking an ordinary Cossack who has gotten separated from his unit (as has happened in Moscow) and disarming him; (3) rescuing those who have been arrested or wounded, if the police force is very weak; (4) mounting to the rooftops and upper stories of houses, etc., and throwing stones at the troops, pouring boiling water on them, etc. . . . The killing of spies, policemen, gendarmes, the blowing up of police stations . . .[68]

One aspect of the armed struggle was terrorism. Although the Bolsheviks nominally adhered to the Social-Democratic platform, which rejected terrorism, in practice they engaged in terrorist acts both on their own and in collaboration with the SRs, including the Maximalists. These operations were, as a rule, organized in secret, but on occasion they openly exhorted their followers to terrorism. Thus, in August 1906, citing the example of the Polish Socialist Party, which had gunned down policemen in Warsaw, they urged attacks on "spies, active supporters of the Black Hundreds, police, army and navy officers, and the like."*

Lenin viewed with skepticism the emergence of the soviets, because they were conceived as "non-partisan" workers' organizations and, as such, outside the control of the political parties: given his belief in the accommodationist drift of the working class, the soviets did not strike him and his followers as dependable.[69] At the time of its formation, some Petrograd Bolsheviks urged the workers to boycott the Soviet on the grounds that granting a workers' organization primacy over the Social-Democratic Party would mean "subordinating consciousness to spontaneity"[70]—in other words, elevating the workers above the intelligentsia. Lenin himself was more flexible, although he could never quite make up his mind about the soviets' function and utility. In the end, after 1906, he decided that they could be of use but only as helpmates of the "revolutionary army." They were essential to the revolution ("insurrection") but had no utility in and of themselves.[71] He also rejected the soviets as organs of self-rule—their function was to serve as "instruments" of an insurrection carried out by disciplined armed detachments.

With the outbreak of the 1905 Revolution, Lenin decided that the time had come to distance himself from the main body of the party and openly form his own organization. In April 1905, he convened in London an unauthorized "Third Congress" of the Social-Democratic Party; all the delegates (thirty-eight in number) were members of his faction. According to Krupskaia:

At the Third Congress, there were no workers—at any rate, there was not one remotely noticeable worker. But there were at the congress many "committee

*Proletarii, August 21, 1906, No. 1, in A. I. Spiridovich, Istoriia Bol'shevizma v Rossii (Paris, 1922), 138. The Okhrana, whose agents kept it well informed on Bolshevik affairs, reported shortly before the February Revolution that Lenin was not opposed to terror but thought that the SRs attached too much importance to it: Report dated December 24, 1916/January 6, 1917, Hoover Institution, Okhrana Archives, Index No. XVIIa–XVIId, Folder 5, No. R. As we shall note, his organization supplied the SRs with explosives for their terrorist operations.

men." Whoever ignores this structure of the Third Congress will not understand much in its minutes.[72]

In such a friendly gathering, Lenin had no difficulty gaining approval of all his resolutions, which the legitimate Social-Democratic Labor Party—as evidenced by its actions the following year in Stockholm—would have rejected. The "Third Congress" marked the beginning of the formal split in the SD Party, which would be consummated in 1912.

Having returned to Russia in early November 1905, Lenin encouraged the Moscow uprising of the next month, but as soon as the shooting began he made himself scarce. The day after the barricades had gone up in Moscow (December 10, 1905), he and Krupskaia sought refuge in Finland. They returned only on December 17, after the uprising had been crushed.

In April 1906, the two branches of Russian Social-Democracy made a halfhearted attempt at reunification at a congress held in Stockholm. Here Lenin tried and failed to gain a majority on the Central Committee. He also suffered defeat on a number of practical issues: the congress condemned the creation of armed detachments and the idea of an armed insurrection, and rejected his agrarian program. Undaunted, Lenin formed, in secret from the Mensheviks, an illegal and clandestine "Central Committee" (a successor to the "Bureau") under his personal direction. Apparently composed at first of three members, it expanded in 1907 to fifteen.[73]

During and immediately after the revolutionary year of 1905, the ranks of Social-Democracy increased manifold, with tens of thousands of new adherents signing up, a high proportion of them intellectuals. By this time, the two factions acquired a distinct complexion.[74] The Bolsheviks in 1905 are estimated to have had 8,400 followers, roughly the same number as the Mensheviks and the Bundists. The Stockholm congress of the SD Party, held in April 1906, is said to have represented 31,000 members, 18,000 of them Mensheviks and 13,000 Bolsheviks. In 1907, the party had grown to 84,300 members—approximately equal to the membership of the Constitutional-Democratic Party—of whom 46,100 were Bolsheviks and 38,200 Mensheviks; affiliated were 25,700 Polish Social-Democrats, 25,500 Bundists, and 13,000 Latvian SDs. This marked the crest of the wave: in 1908 desertions began and in 1910 by Trotsky's estimate, the membership of the Russian Social-Democratic Party dwindled to 10,000 or fewer.[75]

The Menshevik and Bolshevik factions had different social and ethnic compositions. Both attracted a disproportionate number of *dvoriane,* or gentry—20 percent compared to a 1.7 percent share of *dvoriane* in the population at large (the Bolsheviks rather more, with 22 percent; the Mensheviks fewer, with 19 percent). The Bolsheviks had in their ranks a considerably higher proportion of peasants: 38 percent of their membership came from this group, compared with 26 percent in Menshevik ranks.[76] These were not farming peasants, who followed the Socialists-Revolutionaries, but uprooted, déclassé peasants who had moved to the city in search of work. This socially transitional element was to supply numerous cadres to the Bolshevik Party and exert much influence on its mentality. The Mensheviks attracted more lower-class urban inhabitants *(meshchane),* skilled workers (e.g., printers and railroad employees), as well as intellectuals and professional people.

As concerns the ethnic composition of the two factions, the Bolsheviks were predominantly Great Russian, whereas the Mensheviks attracted mostly non-Russians, especially Georgians and Jews. At the SD Second Congress, Lenin's support came principally from delegates sent by the central—that is, Great Russian—provinces. At the Fifth Congress (1907), nearly four-fifths (78.3 percent) of the Bolsheviks were Great Russian, compared with one-third (34 percent) of the Mensheviks. Approximately 10 percent of the Bolsheviks were Jewish; their proportion in Menshevik ranks was twice as high.*[77]

The Bolshevik Party, in its formative years, may thus be characterized as follows: (1) heavily rural in composition, its rank and file having been drawn "to a considerable extent from men born in and still having connections with the countryside," and (2) "overwhelmingly Great Russian" and based on regions inhabited by Great Russians.[78] Its social and cultural roots, in other words, were among groups and in areas with the oldest traditions of serfdom.

But the two factions also shared certain features, of which the most important was their tenuous relationship with industrial labor, the social group that they claimed to represent. Since the emergence of Social-Democracy in Russia in the 1880s, the workers treated the socialist intelligentsia with ambivalence. The unskilled and semi-skilled workers shunned them altogether, because they viewed intellectuals as gentlemen ("white hands") who used them to settle private scores with the Tsar. They remained immune to the influence of the Social-Democratic Party. The better-educated, more skilled and politically conscious workers often regarded the Social-Democrats as friends and supporters, without being prepared to be led by them: as a rule, they preferred trade unionism to party politics.[79] As a consequence, the number of workers in Social-Democratic organizations remained minuscule. Martov estimates that in the first half of 1905, when the Revolution was already well underway, the Mensheviks had in Petrograd some 1,200 to 1,500 active worker supporters and the Bolsheviks "several hundred"—and this in the Empire's most industrialized city with over 200,000 industrial workers.[80] At the end of 1905, the two factions had between them in St. Petersburg a total of 3,000 members.[81] In effect, therefore, both the Menshevik and Bolshevik factions were organizations of intellectuals. Martov's observations on this subject, published in 1914, anticipate the situation which would emerge after the February Revolution:

*These facts did not escape Stalin. Referring to the Fifth Congress, which he had attended, he wrote: "Statistics showed that the majority of the Menshevik faction consists of Jews. . . . On the other hand, the overwhelming majority of the Bolshevik faction consists of Russians. . . . In this connection, one of the Bolsheviks observed in jest (it seems it was Comrade Aleksinskii) that the Mensheviks are a Jewish faction, the Bolsheviks a genuine Russian faction, hence it would not be a bad idea for us Bolsheviks to organize a pogrom in the party": I. V. Stalin, *Sochineniia,* II (Moscow, 1946) 50–51.

> In such cities as Petersburg, where in the course of 1905 it had become actually possible to engage in active work on a broad arena, . . . in the party organization there remained only worker "professionals," who carried out central organizational functions, and labor youths, who enrolled in party circles for the purpose of self-development. The politically more mature worker element remained formally outside the organization or was only counted as belonging to it, which had the most deleterious effect on the relations of the organization and its centers with the masses. At the same time, the mass influx of the intelligentsia into the party, given the greater suitability of its organizational forms to the intelligentsia's conditions of life (more leisure and the possibility of devoting much time to "conspiracy," residence in the central quarters of the city, more favorable to eluding surveillance), resulted in all the higher cells of the [Social-Democratic] organization . . . being filled by the intelligentsia, which, in turn, led to their psychological isolation from the mass movement. Hence, the unending conflicts and friction between the "centers" and the "periphery" and the mounting antagonism between workers and the intelligentsia . . .[82]

In fact, even though the Mensheviks liked to identify themselves with the labor movement, both factions preferred to run the movement without worker interference: the Bolsheviks on principle, the Mensheviks in response to the facts of life.[83] Martov correctly noted this phenomenon, but did not draw from it the obvious conclusion that in Russia a democratic socialist movement, run not only for the workers but also by them, was not feasible.

Given these similarities, one might have expected the Mensheviks and Bolsheviks to join forces. But this did not happen: notwithstanding spells of amity, the two drifted apart, fighting each other with all the passion of sectarians of the same faith. Lenin missed no opportunity to distance himself from the Mensheviks, castigating them as traitors to the cause of socialism and the interests of the working class.

This bitter animosity was due less to ideological than to personal reasons. By 1906, in the wake of the Revolution's collapse, the Mensheviks agreed to adopt Lenin's program calling for a centralized, disciplined, and conspirational party. Even their tactical views were not dissimilar. Both factions, for example, supported the abortive Moscow uprising of December 1905. In 1906, they were at one in condemning as a breach of party discipline the notion of a Workers' Congress, advocated by Akselrod.[84] Given the minute, often scholastic differences separating the two factions, the principal obstacle to reunification was Lenin's overweening lust for power, which made it impossible to work with him in any capacity other than as a subordinate.

During the interval between 1905 and 1914, Lenin developed a revolutionary program that differed from that adopted by the other Social-Democrats in respect to two important issues: the peasantry and the ethnic minorities. The differences derived from the fact that whereas the Mensheviks thought in terms of solutions, Lenin's concern was exclusively with tactics: he wished to identify and exploit sources of discontent for the purpose of promoting revolution. As we have noted, he had concluded even before 1905 that in view of the numerical insignificance in Russia of industrial workers, the Social-Democrats had to attract and lead into battle every group opposed to the autocracy, except for the "bourgeoisie," which he considered "counterrevolutionary": after the battle had been won, there would be time for settling accounts with these temporary allies.

The traditional view of the Social-Democrats concerning the peasantry, following that of Marx and Engels, held that with the possible exception of the landless proletariat, it was a reactionary ("petty bourgeois") class.[85] However, observing the behavior of Russian peasants during the agrarian disturbances of 1902 and even more in 1905 and noting the contribution which their assaults on landlord property had made to the capitulation of tsarism, Lenin concluded that the *muzhik* was a natural, if transitory, ally of the industrial worker. To attract him, the party had to go beyond its official agrarian program, which promised the peasants only supplementing the so-called *otrezki,* land which the 1861 Emancipation Edict had given them an option of taking free of charge but which constituted only a portion of what they needed. He learned much about the mentality of the Russian peasant from lengthy conversations with Gapon after his flight to Europe following Bloody Sunday: according to Krupskaia, Gapon was familiar with the needs of the peasantry and Lenin was so taken with him that he tried to convert him to socialism.[86]

From observations and talks, Lenin was led to the unorthodox opinion that the Social-Democrats had to promise the peasant all the landlord property, even if this meant reinforcing his "petty bourgeois," "counterrevolutionary" proclivities: the SDs, in effect, had to adopt the agrarian program of the SRs. In his program the peasant now replaced the liberal "bourgeoisie" as the principal ally of the "proletariat."[87] At the "Third Congress" of his followers, he moved and passed a clause calling for peasant seizure of landlord property. After he had worked out the details, the Bolshevik program came out in favor of nationalizing all the land, private as well as communal, and transferring it for cultivation to the peasants. Lenin adhered to this program in the face of Plekhanov's objections that the nationalization of land encouraged the "Chinese" traditions of Russian history which led the peasant to view land as state property. The agrarian platform, however, would prove of great value to the Bolsheviks in neutralizing the peasantry in late 1917 and early 1918, during the critical phase in the struggle for power.

Lenin's agrarian program was endangered by Stolypin's reforms, which promised (or threatened, depending on one's viewpoint) to create a class of independent and conservative peasants. Ever the realist, Lenin wrote in April 1908 that if Stolypin's agrarian reforms succeeded, the Bolsheviks might have to give up their agrarian platform:

It would be empty and stupid democratic phrase-mongering if we said that the success of such a policy is "impossible." It is possible! . . . What if, despite the struggle of the masses, Stolypin's policy survived long enough for the "Prussian" model to triumph? The agrarian order in Russia would turn completely bourgeois, the stronger peasants would seize nearly all the allotments of communal land, agriculture would become capitalist, and under *capitalism* no "solution" of the agrarian problem—radical or non-radical—would be possible.[88]

The statement suffers from a curious contradiction: since, according to Marx, capitalism is supposed to carry the seeds of its own destruction, the capitalization of Russian agriculture, with its swelling masses of landless proletarians, should have made a "solution" of the "agrarian problem" easier for the revolutionaries rather than impossible. But as we know, Lenin's fears proved groundless in any event, for the Stolypin reforms hardly altered the nature of landownership in Russia and not at all the mentality of the *muzhik,* which remained solidly anti-capitalist.

Lenin also took an exploitative approach to the nationality question. It was axiomatic in Social-Democratic circles that nationalism was a reactionary ideology which diverted the worker from the class struggle and promoted the breakup of large states. But Lenin also realized that one-half of the population of the Russian Empire consisted of non-Russians, some of whom had a strongly developed national consciousness and nearly all of whom wanted a greater measure of territorial or cultural self-government. On this issue, as on the peasant question, the official party program of 1903 was very niggardly: it offered the minorities civic equality, education in their native languages, and local self-rule, accompanied by the vague formula of "the right of all nations to self-determination" but nothing more specific.[89]

In 1912–13, Lenin concluded that this was not enough: although admittedly nationalism was a reactionary force and probably anachronistic in the era of mounting class conflicts, one still had to allow for the possibility of its temporary appearance. The Social-Democrats, therefore, had to be prepared to exploit it on a conditional and transitory basis, exactly as in the case of peasant claims to private land:

> It is the support of an ally against a *given* enemy, and the Social-Democrats provide this support in order to speed the fall of the common enemy, but they expect *nothing for themselves* from these temporary allies and concede nothing to them.[90]

Searching for a programmatic formula, he rejected the two solutions popular among Eastern European socialists, federalism and cultural autonomy, the one because it promoted the disintegration of large states, the other because it institutionalized ethnic differences. After long hesitations, in 1913 he finally formulated a Bolshevik program for the nationality question. It rested on an idiosyncratic interpretation of the formula "national self-determination" of the Social-Democratic program to mean one thing and one only: the right of every ethnic group to secede and form a sovereign state. When his followers protested that this formula fostered particularism, Lenin reassured them. For one, the forces of capitalist development, which progressively fused the diverse regions of the Russian Empire into an economic whole, would inhibit separatism and ultimately render it impossible. Second, the "proletarian" right to self-determination always took precedence over the rights of nations, which meant that if, contrary to expectations, the non-Russian peoples separated themselves, they would be reintegrated by force. By offering the minorities a choice between all or nothing, Lenin was ignoring the fact that nearly all of them (the Poles and Finns excepted) wanted something in between. He fully expected the ethnic minorities not to separate but to assimilate with the Russians.[91] Lenin used this demagogic formula to good effect in 1917.

One of the most secretive and yet critical aspects of Bolshevik history before the 1917 Revolution concerns party finances. All political organizations require money, but the Bolsheviks' insistence that every member work full-time for the party made on them exceptionally heavy financial demands, for it meant that their cadres, unlike the Mensheviks, who were self-supporting, relied on subsidies from the party's treasury. Lenin also needed money to outmaneuver his Menshevik rivals, who usually had a larger following. The Bolsheviks secured this money in various ways, some conventional, others highly unconventional.

One source was wealthy sympathizers, such as the eccentric millionaire industrialist Savva Morozov, who contributed 2,000 rubles a month to the Bolshevik treasury. After he committed suicide on the French Riviera, another 60,000 rubles from his estate was transferred to the Bolsheviks by Maxim Gorky's wife, who served as trustee of Morozov's life insurance policy.[92] There were other donors, among them Gorky, an agronomist named A. I. Eramasov, Alexander Tsiurupa, who managed landed estates in Ufa province (in 1918 he would become Lenin's Commissar of Supply), Alexandra Kalmykova, the widow of a senator and an intimate friend of Struve's, the actress V. F. Komissarzhevskaia, and still others, whose identities remain unknown to this day.[93] Such patrons out of snobbery subsidized a cause that was fundamentally inimical to their interests: at this time, writes Leonid Krasin, Lenin's close associate, "it was regarded a sign of *bon ton* in more or less radical or liberal circles to contribute money to revolutionary parties, and among those who quite regularly paid dues of from 5 to 25 rubles were not only prominent attorneys, engineers, and physicians but also directors of banks and officials of government institutions."[94] The management of the Bolshevik treasury, operated independently of the common Social-Democratic one, was in the hands of a three-man Bolshevik "Center," formed in 1905, consisting of Lenin, Krasin, and A. A. Bogdanov. Its very existence was kept secret from the Bolshevik rank and file.

But contributions from repentant "bourgeois" proved insufficient and in early 1906 the Bolsheviks resorted to less savory means, the idea of which seems to have been inspired by the People's Will and the SR Maximalists. A great deal of Bolshevik funding henceforth derived from criminal activity, notably holdups, euphemistically known as "expropriations." In daring raids, they robbed post offices, railroad stations, trains, and banks. In a notorious robbery of the State Bank in Tiflis (June 1907), they stole 250,000 rubles, a good part of it in 500-ruble notes whose serial numbers had been registered. The proceeds of this loot were transferred to the Bolshevik treasury. Subsequently, several individuals who attempted to exchange the stolen 500-ruble notes in Europe were arrested—all (among them the future Soviet Minister of Foreign Affairs, Maxim Litvinov) proved to be Bolsheviks.[95] Stalin, who supervised this operation, and other participants were expelled from the Social-Democratic Party.[96] Ignoring the resolution of the 1907 party congresses condemning such activities, the Bolsheviks continued to commit robberies, sometimes in cooperation with the SRs. In this manner they acquired large sums, which gave them considerable advantages over the perennially cash-poor Mensheviks.[97] According to Martov, the proceeds of such crimes enabled the Bolsheviks to send their St. Petersburg and Moscow organizations, respectively, 1,000 and 500 rubles a month, at a time when the legitimate SD treasury's monthly earnings from membership dues did not exceed 100 rubles. As soon as the flow of these funds dried up, which happened in 1910 when the Bolsheviks had to give up their moneys to three German Social-Democrats acting as trustees, their Russian "committees" vanished into thin air.[98]

The overall direction of these secret operations was in the hands of Lenin, but the principal field commander and treasurer was Krasin, the head of the so-called Technical Group.[99] An engineer by profession, Krasin led a a double life: outwardly a respectable businessman (he worked for Morozov as well as the German firms AEG and Siemens-Schuckert), in his free time he ran the Bolshevik underground.* He operated a secret laboratory to assemble bombs, one of which was used in the Tiflis robbery.[100] In Berlin he also ran a counterfeit operation which turned out three-ruble notes. He engaged in gunrunning—sometimes from purely commercial motives, to make money for the Bolshevik treasury. On occasion, the Technical Group made deals with ordinary criminals—for instance, the notorious Lbov gang operating in the Urals, to whom it sold weapons worth hundreds of thousands of dollars.[101] Inevitably, such activities attracted into Bolshevik ranks shady elements for whom the "cause" served as a pretext for a life of crime.

The lengths to which Lenin was prepared to go to acquire money for his organization is illustrated by the so-called Schmit affair.[102] N. P. Schmit (Shmit), a wealthy furniture manufacturer related to Morozov, died in 1906, an apparent suicide, while awaiting trial on charges of having financed the

---

*Krasin's employment by this German electronics firm may not have been fortuitous. According to the head of Russian counterintelligence in 1917, Siemens had used its agencies for purposes of espionage, which led to the shutting down of its office in southern Russia: B. Nikitin, *Rokovye gody* (Paris, 1937), 118.

49. Leonid Krasin.

purchase of weapons used in the December Moscow uprising. He left no last will, but told Gorky and other friends that he wanted his fortune, amounting to some 500,000 rubles, to go to the Social-Democrats. This disposition had no validity in the eyes of the law because the party, being illegal, could not be the beneficiary of a legacy. The money went, therefore, to his next of kin, a minor brother. Determined to prevent Schmit's estate from being squandered by his heirs or transferred to the SD treasury, the Bolsheviks decided, at meetings chaired by Lenin, to get hold of it by any available means. The teenage brother was quickly talked into renouncing his share of the inheritance in favor of his two sisters. Arrangements then were made for two Bolsheviks to court and marry the heiresses. The younger girl, also a minor, was wed to a Bolshevik roughneck named Victor Taratuta; but to mislead the police, it was arranged for her to be married a second time, fictitiously, to a solid citizen. The 190,000 rubles which she subsequently received was forwarded to the Bolshevik treasury in Paris.[103]

The second installment of the Schmit legacy, owned by the elder sister, was in the hands of her husband, also a Social-Democrat with Bolshevik leanings. He, however, preferred to keep the money. The dispute was submitted to a socialist court of arbitration, which awarded the Bolsheviks only one-half or one-third of the inheritance. Under threats of physical violence, the husband was eventually persuaded to turn his wife's inheritance over to Lenin. In this manner, Lenin eventually acquired between 235,000 and 315,000 rubles from the Schmit estate.[104]

This sordid financial affair and others like it greatly embarrassed the Bolsheviks in socialist circles in Russia and abroad when they were revealed by Martov, compelling Lenin to agree to have the funds of the SD Party deposited with German Social-Democrats as trustees. Quarrels over money were one of the main bones of contention between the two factions during the decade preceding the 1917 Revolution. Working as Lenin's secretary, Krupskaia maintained a steady correspondence with Bolshevik agents in Russia using invisible ink, codes, and other devices to keep the police in the dark. According to Tatiana Aleksinskii, who helped her with this work, most of Lenin's letters contained demands for money.*[105]

In 1908, the Social-Democratic movement in Russia went into decline, in part because the intelligentsia's revolutionary ardor cooled and in part because police infiltration had made it all but impossible to conduct underground activity. The security services had penetrated the Social-Democratic organizations from top to bottom: before they could move, their members were exposed and arrested. The Mensheviks responded to this situation with a new strategy which called for emphasis on legal activity: publishing, organizing trade unions, working in the Duma. Some Mensheviks wanted to replace the Social-Democratic Party with a Workers' Party. They did not intend to give up illegal activity altogether, but the drift of their program was toward democratic trade unionism in which the party did not so much lead the workers as serve them. To Lenin this was anathema and he labeled the Mensheviks who supported this strategy "liquidators," on the grounds that their alleged aim was to liquidate the party and give up revolution. In his usage, "liquidators" became synonymous with counterrevolutionaries.

Nevertheless Lenin, too, had to accommodate himself to the difficult conditions created by police repression. This he did by exploiting for his own ends police agents who had infiltrated his organization. Although there cannot be any certainty about this, it seems the most convincing explanation of the otherwise puzzling case of the agent provocateur Roman Malinovskii, who for a while (1912–14) served as Lenin's deputy in Russia and chairman of the Bolshevik Duma faction. It was a case of police provocation which in the opinion of Vladimir Burtsev exceeded in importance even the more celebrated case of Evno Azef.[106]

Lenin ordered his followers to boycott the elections to the First Duma, while the Mensheviks left the matter to their local organizations, most of which, with the exception of the Georgian branch, also opted for a boycott. Lenin subsequently changed his mind and in 1907, disregarding the wishes of most of his associates, instructed the Bolsheviks to run. He intended to use the Duma as a forum from which to spread his message. It was here that Malinovskii proved of inestimable value.

*The importance of such subsidies was stressed by Lenin in a letter of December 1904 to a potential donor: "Our undertaking is faced with bankruptcy if we do not hold out with *the help of extraordinary resources* for at least half a year. And in order to hold out without cutting back, we need a minimum of two thousand rubles a month": Lenin, *PSS,* XLVI, 433.

A Pole by nationality, a metalworker by profession, and a thief by avocation, Malinovskii had served three jail sentences for theft and burglary. Driven, according to his own testimony, by political ambitions but unable to satisfy them because of his criminal record, and always in need of money, he offered his services to the Department of Police. On its instructions, he switched from the Mensheviks and in January 1912 attended the Prague Conference of the Bolsheviks. Lenin was most favorably impressed by him, praising Malinovskii as an "excellent fellow" and an "outstanding worker-leader."[107] He appointed the new recruit to the Russian Bureau of the Bolshevik Central Committee, with authority to add members at his discretion. On his return to Russia, Malinovskii used this authority to co-opt Stalin.[108]

On orders of the Minister of the Interior, Malinovskii's criminal record was suppressed to allow him to run for the Duma. Elected with the help of the police, he used his parliamentary immunity to deliver fiery speeches against the "bourgeoisie" and socialist "opportunists," some of which were prepared and all of which were cleared by the security services. Despite doubts voiced in socialist circles about his loyalty, Lenin unreservedly backed Malinovskii. One of the greatest services that Malinovskii rendered Lenin was to help found—with the permission of the police and very likely with its financial support—the Bolshevik daily *Pravda.* Malinovskii served as the newspaper's treasurer; the editorship went to another police agent, M. E. Chernomazov. The party organ, protected by the police, enabled the Bolsheviks to popularize their views inside Russia much better than the Mensheviks. For the sake of appearances, the authorities occasionally fined *Pravda,* but the paper kept on appearing, printing the text of the speeches that Malinovskii and other Bolsheviks delivered in the Duma as well as Bolshevik writings: Lenin alone, between 1912 and 1914, published 265 articles in the paper. With the help of Malinovskii, the police also founded in Moscow the Bolshevik daily *Nash put'.*[109]

While engaged in these capacities, Malinovskii regularly betrayed the party's secrets to the police. As we shall see, Lenin believed that he gained more than he lost from this arrangement.

Malinovskii's career as double agent was suddenly terminated in May 1914 by the new Deputy Minister of the Interior, V. F. Dzhunkovskii. A professional military man without experience in counterintelligence, Dzhunkovskii was determined to "clean up" the Corps of Gendarmes and put an end to its political activities: he was an uncompromising opponent of police provocation in any form.* When, on assuming his duties, he learned that Malinovskii was

---

Padenie, V, 69, and I, 315. He abolished police cells in the armed forces and in secondary schools, on the grounds that it was improper for men in uniform and students to inform on each other. S. P. Beletskii, the director of the Police Department and Malinovskii's immediate supervisor, believed that these measures disorganized the work of political counterintelligence: *Ibid.,* V, 70–71, 75. Both Dzhunkovskii and Beletskii were shot in September 1918 by the Cheka in the first wave of the Red Terror.

a police agent and that through him the police had penetrated the Duma, fearing a major political scandal, he confidentially apprised Rodzianko, the Duma's chairman, of this fact.* Malinovskii was forced to resign, given 6,000 rubles, his yearly salary, and sent abroad.

The sudden and unexplained disappearance of the Bolshevik leader from the Duma should have put an end to Malinovskii's career, but Lenin stood by him, defending him from Menshevik accusers and charging the "liquidators" with slander.† It is possible that in this case Lenin's personal loyalty to a valued associate outweighed his better judgment, but this seems unlikely. At his trial in 1918, Malinovskii said that he had informed Lenin of his criminal record: since such a record precluded a Russian from running in Duma elections, the mere fact that the Ministry of the Interior did not use the information at its disposal to bar Malinovskii from the Duma should have alerted Lenin to his police connections. Burtsev, Russia's leading specialist in matters of police provocation, concluded in 1918, from conversations with onetime officials of the tsarist police who testified at Malinovskii's trial, that "according to Malinovskii, Lenin understood and could not help understanding that his [Malinovskii's] past concealed not merely ordinary criminality but that he was in the hands of the gendarmerie—a provocateur."[110] The reason why Lenin might have wanted to keep a police agent in his organization is suggested by General Alexander Spiridovich, a high tsarist security officer:

> The history of the Russian revolutionary movement knows several major instances of leaders of revolutionary organizations allowing some of their members to enter into relations with the political police as secret informers, in the hope that in return for giving the police some insignificant information, these party spies could extract from it much more useful information for the party.[111]

When he testified before a commission of the Provisional Government in June 1917, Lenin hinted that, indeed, he may have used Malinovskii in this manner:

> I did not believe in provocateurship in this case and for the following reason: if Malinovskii were a provocateur, the Okhranka [sic] would not gain from that as much as our party gained from *Pravda* and the whole legal apparatus. It is clear that by putting a provocateur into the Duma, removing for him the rivals of the Bolsheviks, etc., the Okhranka was guided by a crude image of Bolshevism—I would say a comic book caricature: the Bolsheviks will not organize an armed uprising. To have in hand all the threads, from the point of view of the Okhranka, it was worth anything to get Malinovskii into the Duma and

*The possibility has been raised that Dzhunkovskii fired Malinovskii because he was alarmed by the effect his inflammatory Duma speeches were having on workers at a time when Russia was in the grip of a new wave of industrial strikes: Ralph Carter Elwood, *Roman Malinovsky* (Newtonville, Mass., 1977), 41–43.

†Lenin, *PSS*, XXV, 394. In 1915, Malinovskii volunteered for the Russian armies in France. Wounded and captured by the Germans, he conducted pro-German propaganda among Russian prisoners of war. During this time, he maintained a regular correspondence with Lenin: *Padenie*, VII, 374; Elwood, *Malinovsky*, 59; Grigorii Aronson, *Rossiia nakanune Revoliutsii* (New York, 1962), 53–54.

the [Bolshevik] Central Committee. But when the Okhranka achieved both these objectives, it turned out that Malinovskii had become one of those links in the long and solid chain connecting our illegal base with *Pravda.* *

Although Lenin denied knowledge of Malinovskii's police connections, this reasoning sounds like a convincing apology for employing a police agent to further the party's objectives—that is, exploiting to the maximum the opportunities for legal work to win mass support when no other means were available.† When Malinovskii went on trial in 1918, the Bolshevik prosecutor indeed pressured tsarist police witnesses to testify that Malinovskii had done more harm to the tsarist authorities than to the Bolsheviks.[112] The fact that Malinovskii returned of his own free will to Soviet Russia in November 1918, when the Red Terror was at its height, and demanded to see Lenin strongly suggests that he expected to be exonerated. But Lenin had no more use for him: he attended his trial but did not testify. Malinovskii was executed.

In fact, Malinovskii had performed for Lenin many valuable services. His help in the founding of *Pravda* and *Nash put'* has been mentioned. In addition, in his Duma speeches he read texts written by Lenin, Zinoviev, and other Bolshevik leaders: prior to delivery, he submitted these to Sergei Vissarionov, the deputy director of the Police Department, for editing.[113] By this means, the Bolshevik message was spread nationwide. But above all he worked assiduously to prevent the reunification of Lenin's followers in Russia with the Mensheviks. When the Fourth Duma convened, it transpired that the seven Menshevik and six Bolshevik deputies acted in a more cooperative spirit than either Lenin or the police desired: they behaved, in fact, like a single Social-Democratic delegation, as was usually the case when Lenin was not personally present to sow discord. Keeping them apart and thus weakening them was a mission to which the police assigned high priority: according to Beletskii, "Malinovskii was ordered to do everything possible to deepen the split in the parties."[114] It was a case of the interests of Lenin and the police coinciding.‡

Lenin's dictatorial methods and his complete lack of scruples alienated some of his staunchest supporters. Tired of intrigues and squabbles, caught in the prevailing mood of spiritualism, some of the brightest Bolsheviks began to seek solace in religion and idealistic philosophy: in 1909, the dominant tendency in Bolshevik ranks came to be known as *Bogostroitel'stvo,* or "God-

---

Vestnik Vremennogo Pravitel'stva, No. 81/127 (June 16, 1917), 3. Lenin's testimony on Malinovskii is published neither in the multivolume edition of the commission's records *(Padenie)* nor in his *Collected Works.*

†Tatiana Aleksinskii recalls that when questions were raised about the possible presence on the Central Committee of a police informer, Zinoviev quoted from Gogol's *Inspector General:* "A good household makes use even of garbage." *La Grande Revue,* XXVII, No. 9 (September 1923), 459.

‡The likelihood that Lenin was aware of Malinovskii's police connections is accepted, in addition to Burtsev, by Stefan Possony *(Lenin: The Compulsive Revolutionary,* Chicago, 1964, 142–43). Malinovskii's biographer rejects this hypothesis on the grounds that the Bolsheviks learned far less from Malinovskii about the police than the police learned about the Bolsheviks (Elwood, *Malinovsky,* 65–66). But he ignores Lenin's own argument as well as Spiridovich's statement about the use of double agents, cited above.

building." Led by Bogdanov, the future head of "Proletarian Culture," and A. V. Lunacharskii, the future Commissar of Enlightenment, the movement was a socialist response to *Bogoiskatel'stvo*, or "God-seeking," popular among non-radical intellectuals. In *Religion and Socialism*, Lunacharskii depicted socialism as a type of religious experience, a "religion of labor." In 1909, the proponents of this ideology established a school in Capri. Lenin, who found the whole development utterly distasteful, organized two counterschools, one in Bologna, the other in Longjumeau, near Paris. The latter, established in 1911, was a kind of Workers' University, in which workers sent from Russia underwent systematic indoctrination in social science and politics: the faculty included Lenin and his two most loyal followers, Zinoviev and Kamenev. The inevitable police informer, this time disguised as a student, reported that the instruction at Longjumeau consisted of

> mindless memorization by the pupils of snatches of lessons, which in their presentation bore the character of indisputable dogmas and which in no way encouraged critical analysis and a rationally conscious absorption.[115]

By 1912, after Martov's public revelations of Lenin's unscrupulous financial dealings and his use of money, much of it illicitly obtained, to achieve domination, the two factions gave up the pretense of being one party. The Mensheviks felt that the Bolshevik actions compromised the Social-Democratic movement. At the meeting of the International Socialist Bureau in 1912, Plekhanov openly accused Lenin of theft. But although the Mensheviks professed to be appalled by Lenin's resort to crime and slander and by his admission that he deliberately misled workers about them, and although they castigated him as a "political charlatan" (Martov), they refrained from expelling him, whereas Struve, whose only sin was to sympathize with Eduard Bernstein's "Revisionism," they got rid of in no time. Little wonder Lenin would not take them seriously.

The final break between the two factions occurred in January 1912 at Lenin's Prague Conference, following which they never again held joint meetings. Lenin appropriated the name "Central Committee" and appointed one consisting exclusively of hard-line Bolsheviks. Although the breach at the top was complete, rank and file Mensheviks and Bolsheviks inside Russia more often than not worked together and continued to view each other as comrades.

Lenin spent the two years preceding the outbreak of World War I in Cracow, from where he was able to maintain contact with his Russian followers. Either just before or immediately after the start of the war, he entered into a relationship with an agency of the Austrian Government, the Union for the Liberation of the Ukraine, which in return for his support of Ukrainian national aspirations paid him subsidies and assisted his revolutionary activi-

50. Lenin: Paris 1910.

ties.[116] The Union received funds from both Vienna and Berlin and operated under the supervision of the Austrian Ministry of Foreign Affairs. One of the people involved in its activities was Parvus, who in 1917 would play a critical part in securing Lenin passage through Germany to revolutionary Russia. An accounting statement submitted by the Union, dated Vienna, December 16, 1914, contains the following entry:

> The Union has given support to the Majority faction of Russian Social-Democracy in the form of money and help in the establishment of communications with Russia. The leader of that faction, Lenin, is not hostile to Ukrainian demands, as demonstrated by his lecture, reported on in *Ukrainische Nachrichten.* [117]

This connection proved very useful to Lenin when the Austrian police arrested him and Grigori Zinoviev (July 26/August 8, 1914) as enemy aliens and suspected spies. Influential persons in the Austrian and Polish socialist movements, among them Jacob Ganetskii (Haniecki, also known as Fürstenberg), an employee of Parvus's and a close associate of Lenin, intervened on their behalf. Five days later, the viceroy of Galicia in Lwow received a cable from Vienna advising him that it was not desirable to detain Lenin, who was identified as "an enemy of tsarism."[118] On August 6/19, the Cracow Military Procurator telegraphed the district court in Nowy Targ, where Lenin was incarcerated, ordering his immediate release.[119] On August 19/September 1, Lenin, Krupskaia, and Krupskaia's mother, on a pass from the Austrian police, left Vienna for Switzerland in an Austrian military mail train—a means of transport unlikely to be made available to ordinary enemy aliens.[120] Zinoviev and his wife followed two weeks later. The circumstances of Lenin and Zinoviev's release from an Austrian prison and the manner of Lenin's departure from Austria indicate that Vienna regarded them as valuable assets.

In Switzerland, Lenin immediately set to work to deal with the failure of the Socialist International to honor its anti-war platform.

It had been a fundamental maxim of the international socialist movement that the interests of the working class cut across national borders and that the "proletariat" would under no circumstances spill blood in the capitalist struggle for markets. The Stuttgart Congress of the Socialist International, convened in August 1907, in the midst of an international crisis, devoted a great deal of attention to militarism and the threat of war. Two tendencies developed, one led by Bebel, which favored opposing war and, if war did break out, struggling for its "early termination." The other trend was represented by three Russian delegates—Lenin, Martov, and Rosa Luxemburg, who, drawing on the Russian experience of 1905, wanted the socialists to take advantage of the fighting to unleash an international civil war.[121] At the latter's urging, the congress resolved that in the event of hostilities, it would be the duty of the workers and their parliamentary deputies

> to intervene in favor of its speedy termination and to do all in their power to utilize the economic and political crisis caused by the war to rouse the peoples and thereby to hasten the abolition of capitalist class rule.[122]

This clause represented a rhetorical concession by the right-wing majority to the left-wing minority to paper over their differences. But Lenin was not satisfied with the compromise. Pursuing the same divisive tactic which he had employed in the Russian Social-Democratic movement, he set out to split off from the more moderate majority of the Socialist International an intransigent left, committed to exploiting a future war for revolutionary purposes. He opposed a pacifist policy aimed at stopping hostilities endorsed by most European socialists: indeed, he wanted war very badly because war presented unique opportunities to make revolution. Since such a stance was unpopular and inadmissible for a socialist, Lenin refrained from expressing it publicly. But once in a while, as in a letter to Maxim Gorky written in January 1913, during yet another international crisis he wrote: "A war between Austria and Russia would be a most useful thing for the revolution (in all of Eastern

Europe) but it is not very likely that Franz Joseph and Nicky will give us this pleasure."[123]

Once the war broke out, socialist parliamentarians of both the Allied and Central powers reneged on their pledges. In the summer of 1914 they had spoken passionately for peace and brought masses of demonstrators into the streets to protest the drift to war. But when hostilities began, they fell in line and voted in favor of war budgets. Especially painful was the betrayal of the German Social-Democrats, who had the strongest party organization in Europe and formed the backbone of the Second International: the unanimous vote of their parliamentary delegation for war credits was a stunning and, as it turned out, near-fatal blow to the Socialist International.

Russian socialists took the pledges of the International much more seriously than their comrades in the West, in part because they had shallower roots in their native country and took little patriotic pride in it and in part because they knew they had no chance of coming to power except by exploiting "the economic and political crisis caused by the war" posited by the Stuttgart resolution. Apart from the patriarchs of the Social-Democratic movement, such as Plekhanov and L. G. Deich, and a number of Socialists-Revolutionaries in whom the clash of arms awakened patriotic sentiments (Savinkov, Burtsev), most luminaries of Russian socialism remained faithful to the anti-war resolutions of the International. This the Social-Democratic and Trudovik (SR) deputies in the Fourth Duma demonstrated with their unanimous refusal to vote for war credits—the only European parliamentarians, save for the Serbians, to do so.

On arrival in Switzerland, Lenin drafted a programmatic statement, called "The Tasks of Revolutionary Social Democracy in the European War."[124] After accusing the leaders of German, French, and Belgian Social-Democracy of betrayal, he outlined an uncompromisingly radical platform. Article 6 of "The Tasks" contained the following proposition:

> From the point of view of the working class and the toiling masses of all the peoples of Russia, the least evil [*naimenshee zlo*] would be the defeat of the tsarist monarchy and its armies, which are oppressing Poland, the Ukraine, and a number of peoples of Russia . . .*

No other prominent European socialist expressed himself publicly in favor of his country losing the war. Lenin's startling call for the defeat of Russia inevitably brought charges that he was an agent of the German Government.†

The practical conclusion of Lenin's statement on the war was spelled out

---

*Lenin, *PSS*, XXVI, 6. Lenin's puzzling emphasis on Russia's "oppression" of the Ukraine must be explained at least in part by his financial arrangements with the Austrian Government. He did not demand that the Ukrainians also be liberated from Austrian rule.

†An accusation to this effect is made by General Spiridovich, the usually well-informed official of the gendarmerie. He claims, without furnishing proof, that in June and July 1914 Lenin traveled twice to Berlin to work out with the Germans a plan of seditious activity in the rear of the Russian armies, for which he was to be paid 70 million marks: Spiridovich, *Istoriia Bol'shevizma*, 263–65.

in the seventh and final article of his theses, which called for energetic agitation and propaganda among the civilian and military personnel of the belligerent nations for the purpose of unleashing a civil war against the "reactionary and bourgeois governments and parties of all the countries." Copies of this document were smuggled into Russia and in November furnished the Imperial Government with grounds for closing down *Pravda* and arresting the Bolshevik Duma delegation. One of the lawyers who defended the Bolsheviks on this occasion was Alexander Kerensky. Tried on lesser charges than treason, which could have cost them their lives, the Bolsheviks were sentenced to exile, which all but put the party out of the picture until the February revolution.

The thrust of Lenin's program was that the socialists were to strive not to end the fighting but to exploit it for their own purposes: "The slogan of 'peace' is incorrect at this moment," he wrote in October 1914. "This is a slogan of philistines and priests. The proletarian slogan must be: civil war."[125] Lenin would remain faithful to this formulation throughout the war. It was much safer for him to uphold it in neutral Switzerland, of course, than it was for his followers in belligerent Russia.

Aware of Lenin's war program, the Germans were eager to use him for their own purposes: after all, Lenin's call for the defeat of the tsarist armies was tantamount to an endorsement of a German victory. Their main intermediary was Parvus, one of the leaders of the St. Petersburg Soviet in 1905, the originator of the theory of "uninterrupted revolution," and more recently a collaborator with the Union for the Liberation of the Ukraine. Parvus had one of the most impressive intellects in the Russian revolutionary movement as well as one of the most corrupt personalities. After the failure of the 1905 Revolution, he concluded that a successful revolution in Russia required the assistance of German armies: they alone were capable of destroying tsarism.* He placed himself at the disposal of the German Government, using his political connections to amass a sizable fortune. At the outbreak of the war he resided in Constantinople. He contacted the German Ambassador there and outlined to him the case for using Russian revolutionaries to promote German interests. His argument was that the Russian radicals could achieve their objective only if tsarism were destroyed and the Russian Empire broken up: since this objective happened also to suit Germany, "the interests of the German Government were . . . identical with those of the Russian revolutionaries." He asked for money and authorization to communicate with Russian left-wing émigrés.[126] With the encouragement of Berlin, in May 1915 he contacted Lenin in Zurich: familiar with Russian émigré politics, he knew that Lenin was the key figure on the left and that if he won him over the rest of the Russian anti-war left would fall in line.[127] For the time being, the plan failed. It was not that Lenin objected to dealing with the Germans or felt

---

*He felt vindicated by the events. In 1918, referring to the 1917 Revolution, he wrote that "Prussian guns played a larger role in it than Bolshevik leaflets. In particular, I believe that the Russian émigrés would still be wandering in emigration and stewing in their own juice if German regiments had not reached the Vistula": *Izvne* (Stockholm), No. 1 (January 22, 1918), 2.

qualms about taking money from them—he just would not negotiate with a traitor to the socialist cause, a renegade and "socialist chauvinist." Parvus's biographers suggest that in addition to personal dislike of Parvus, Lenin may also have feared that if he struck a deal with him, Parvus "would eventually acquire control of Russian socialist organizations, and, with his financial resources and his intellectual ability, be able to outmaneuver all the other party leaders."[128] Lenin never publicly referred to this encounter.

Although he rejected Parvus's overtures, Lenin did maintain political and financial contacts with the German Government through an Estonian, Alexander Keskküla.* In 1905–07 Keskküla had been a leading Bolshevik in Estonia. Later, he turned into an ardent Estonian nationalist, determined to gain independence for his homeland. Convinced, like Parvus, that the destruction of tsarist Russia could be accomplished only by the German army, at the outbreak of the war he placed himself at the disposal of the German Government, joining its intelligence services. With German subsidies, he operated out of Switzerland and Sweden to secure from Russian émigrés information on internal conditions in Russia and to smuggle Bolshevik anti-war literature into that country. In October 1914, he met with Lenin,† in whom he was interested as an enemy of the tsarist regime and a potential liberator of Estonia. Many years later, Keskküla claimed that he did not finance the Bolsheviks directly, contributing instead, indirectly, to their treasury and subsidizing their publications. These were important sources of support for the impoverished Bolshevik Party in any event, but he may have paid Lenin direct subsidies as well.

In September 1915, apparently in response to Keskküla's request, Lenin provided him with a curious seven-point program outlining the conditions on which revolutionary Russia would be prepared to make peace with Germany. The document was found after World War II in the archives of the German Foreign Office.‡ Its existence suggests that Lenin saw in Keskküla not only an Estonian patriot but also an agent of the German Government. Apart from several points affecting internal Russian affairs (proclamation of a republic, confiscation of large estates, introduction of an eight-hour workday, and autonomy for the ethnic minorities), Lenin affirmed the possibility of a separate peace, provided Germany renounced all annexations and contributions (although exceptions could be made for "buffer states"). He further proposed a Russian withdrawal from Turkish territory and an offensive against India. The Germans certainly had these proposals in mind when a year and a half later they allowed Lenin to travel across their territory to Russia.

Using funds placed at his disposal by Berlin, Keskküla arranged for the

---

*On him, see Michael Futrell in St. Antony's Papers, No. 12, *Soviet Affairs*, No. 3 (London, 1962), 23–52. The author had a unique opportunity to interview this Estonian but, unfortunately, chose to accept his testimony rather uncritically.

†Futrell in *Soviet Affairs*, 47, states that this was his only encounter with the Bolshevik leader, but this seems most unlikely.

‡It is reproduced in a cable from the German Minister in Berne, Count Romberg, to Chancellor Bethmann-Hollweg in Berlin, dated September 30, 1915: Werner Hahlweg, *Lenins Rückkehr nach Russland, 1917* (Leiden, 1957), 40–43 (English translation in Zeman, *Germany,* 6–7).

publication in Sweden of Lenin's and Bukharin's writings, which Bolshevik
runners smuggled into Russia. One such subsidy was stolen by a Bolshevik
agent.[129] Lenin reciprocated the favor by forwarding to Kesküla reports sent
by his agents in Russia on the internal situation there, in which the Germans,
for obvious reasons, were keenly interested. In a dispatch dated May 8, 1916,
an official of the German General Staff reported to the Foreign Office functionary in charge of subversive operations in the east:

> In the last few months, Kesküla has opened up numerous new connections with
> Russia. . . . . He has also maintained his extremely useful contact with Lenin,
> and has transmitted to us the contents of the situation reports sent to Lenin
> by Lenin's confidential agents in Russia. Kesküla must therefore continue to
> be provided with the necessary means in the future. Taking into account the
> exceptionally unfavorable exchange conditions, 20,000 marks per month
> should just be sufficient.*

As in the case of Parvus, Lenin maintained lifelong silence about his
relations with Kesküla, and understandably so, since they were nothing short
of high treason.

In September 1915, there convened, on the initiative of Italian socialists,
a secret conference of the International in the Swiss village of Zimmerwald,
near Berne. The Russians were strongly represented, with the leaders of both
Social-Democratic factions and the SR Party in attendance. The group quickly
broke up into two factions, a more moderate one, which wanted to preserve
links with those socialists who supported the war, and a left one, which
demanded a clean break. The latter, comprising eight of the thirty-eight delegates, was headed by Lenin. The majority rejected Lenin's draft proposal for
the transformation of the "imperialist" war into a civil war because it was
unfeasible as well as dangerous: as one delegate pointed out, the signatories
of such a proclamation would face death after returning home while Lenin
enjoyed the safety of Switzerland. It also turned down Lenin's demand for a
split from the Committee of the International, controlled by patriotic socialists. Even so, Lenin did not go down in defeat at Zimmerwald,[130] for the official
manifesto of the conference did make some verbal concessions to him, condemning those socialists who backed their government's war efforts and calling on workers of all countries to join in the "class struggle."[131] The Zimmerwald left issued its own statement, which was stronger but stopped short of
calling on the European masses to rise in rebellion, as Lenin wanted.[132] Under-
pinning the disagreements between the two wings were differing attitudes
toward patriotism, which most of the European socialists felt intensely and
most of the Russian ones did not.

In April 1916, a sequel to the Zimmerwald Conference met at Kiental in

---

*Hans Steinwachs of the Political Section, German General Staff, to Minister Diego von
Bergen of the Foreign Office, in Zeman, *Germany,* 17. The language of this document indicates that
Kesküla misinformed Futrell when he intimated that he had obtained such reports by infiltrating
Lenin's organization in Sweden: Futrell in *Soviet Affairs,* 24.

the Bernese Oberland. The gathering was called by the International Socialist Committee to deal with the war, about to enter its third year. The participants, representing the pacifist wing of the International, again refused to yield to the Zimmerwald left but went considerably further in accommodating it than the year before. In the resolution on "The Attitude of the Proletariat toward the Question of Peace," the conference, blaming the war on capitalism, asserted that neither "bourgeois nor socialist pacifism" could solve the tragedy facing mankind:

> If a capitalist society cannot provide the conditions for a lasting peace, then the conditions will be provided by socialism. . . . *The struggle for lasting peace can, therefore, be only a struggle for the realization of socialism.* [133]

The practical conclusion was for the "proletariat to raise the call for an immediate truce and an opening of peace negotiations." Again, no call for rebellion and turning the guns against the bourgeoisie, but such action was not precluded by the premise of the resolution and may even be said to have been implicit in it.

As he had done at Zimmerwald, Lenin drafted the minority report for the left, which concluded with this appeal to the proletariat: *"Lay down your weapons. Turn them against the common foe!*—the capitalist governments."* Among the twelve signatories under Lenin's statement (of the forty-four present) Zinoviev took it upon himself to represent Latvia and Karl Radek, Holland.

The key Kiental resolution on the "International Socialist Bureau," based on a draft by Zinoviev, came close to meeting the demands of the left by condemning this organization for turning into "an accomplice in the policy of the so-called 'defense of the fatherland' and of civil peace" and contending that the

> International can recover from its collapse as a definite political power only to the extent to which *the proletariat is able to liberate itself from all imperialist and chauvinist influences and reenter the road of class struggle and of mass action.* [134]

Even though Lenin's demand for a split in the International once again went down in defeat, after the conference adjourned a member of the right, S. Grumbach, declared that "Lenin and his friends have played an important role at Zimmerwald and a *decisive* role at Kiental."[135] Indeed, the Kiental resolutions laid the groundwork for the Third International, which Lenin was to found in 1919.

*Lenin, *Sochineniia,* XIX, 437. "And objectively who profits by the slogan of peace?" Lenin wrote at this time. "Certainly not the revolutionary proletariat. Not the idea of *using* the war to *speed up* the collapse of capitalism." Citing these words, Adam Ulam comments: "He overlooked the fact that the lives of millions of human beings also could have 'profited' by the 'slogan of peace' ": *The Bolsheviks* (New York, 1965), 306.

Lenin owed his relative success at Zimmerwald and Kiental in 1915–16, as he did later in the Russia of 1917, to the fact that he took the socialists at their word and demanded that they make good on their rhetoric. This earned him a small but devoted following in foreign socialist circles. More importantly, it paralyzed his opponents and prevented them from giving him battle because with this stand he seized the moral high ground of the socialist movement. The leaders of the International despised Lenin for his intrigues and slander, but they could not disown him without disowning themselves. His tactics enabled him to push the international socialist movement steadily leftward and eventually to split off from it his own faction, exactly as he had done in Russian Social-Democracy.

This said, it must be noted that the war years were for Lenin and Krupskaia a time of severe hardship, a time of poverty and isolation from Russia. They lived in quarters that bordered on slums, took their meals in the company of criminals and prostitutes, and found themselves abandoned by many one-time friends. Even some former followers came now to view Lenin as a crackpot and "political Jesuit," a spent man.[136] When Krasin, once one of Lenin's closest associates, now living in comfort as an official working for war industries, was approached for a contribution for Lenin, he pulled out two five-ruble notes, saying: "Lenin does not deserve support. He is a harmful type, and you never know what crazy ideas will sprout in his Tatar head. To hell with him!"[137]

The only shaft of light in Lenin's exile was an affair with Inessa Armand, the French-born daughter of two music-hall artists and the wife of a wealthy Russian. Influenced by Chernyshevskii, she broke with her husband and joined the Bolsheviks. She met Lenin and his wife in Paris in 1910. She soon became Lenin's mistress, tolerated by Krupskaia, as well as a faithful follower. Although Bertram Wolfe speaks of her as a "dedicated, romantic heroine," Angelica Balabanoff, who had many occasions to meet Inessa, describes her as "the perfect—almost passive—executrix of [Lenin's] orders," "the prototype of the perfect Bolshevik of rigid, unconditional obedience."[138] She seems to have been the only human being with whom Lenin ever established intimate personal relations.

Lenin did not lose faith in the ultimate outbreak of a European revolution, but the prospect seemed remote. The Imperial Government had sufficiently weathered the military and political crisis of 1915 to be able to launch a major offensive in 1916. From sporadic communications sent him by his Petrograd agent, Alexander Shliapnikov, he knew of the deteriorating economic situation in Russia and the popular discontent in its cities,[139] but he disregarded the information, apparently convinced of the ability of the Imperial regime to overcome such difficulties. Addressing a gathering of socialist youths in Zurich on January 9/22, 1917, he predicted that while a revolution in Europe was unavoidable, "we old-timers perhaps shall not live [to see] the decisive battles of the looming revolution."[140] These words he spoke eight weeks before the collapse of tsarism.

The Bolshevik Bid for Power

> In terms of modern opinion, the way to turn people
> into followers is to persuade them that in following
> your scheme, they are being active, critical, rebellious
> and free-spirited; behaving otherwise is passive and
> servile. The sheep were those who got hopelessly
> entangled in this set of confusions.
>
> —*Kenneth Minogue*

Although it is common to speak of two Russian revolutions in 1917—
one in February, the other in October—only the first merits the name. In
February 1917, Russia experienced a genuine revolution in that the disorders
that brought down the tsarist regime, although not unprovoked or unexpected,
erupted spontaneously and the Provisional Government which succeeded
gained immediate nationwide acceptance. Neither was true of October 1917.
The events that led to the overthrow of the Provisional Government were not
spontaneous but plotted and executed by a tightly organized conspiracy. It
took these plotters three years of civil war and indiscriminate terror to subdue
the majority of the population. October was a classic coup d'état, the capture
of governmental power by a small minority, carried out, in deference to the
democratic conventions of the age, with a show of mass participation, but
without mass engagement. It introduced into revolutionary action methods
more appropriate to warfare than to politics.

The Bolshevik coup went through two phases. In the first, which lasted
from April to July, Lenin attempted to take power in Petrograd by means of
street demonstrations backed by armed force. It was his intention to escalate
these demonstrations, on the pattern of the riots of February, into a full-scale
revolt that would transfer power initially to the soviets and immediately
afterward to his party. This strategy failed: the third attempt, in July, nearly
resulted in the destruction of the Bolshevik Party. By August, the Bolsheviks

recovered sufficiently to resume their drive for power, but this time they used
a different strategy. Trotsky, who took charge while Lenin was hiding from
the police in Finland, avoided street demonstrations. Instead, he disguised
preparation for a Bolshevik coup behind the façade of a spurious and illegitimate Congress of Soviets, while relying on special shock troops to seize the
nerve centers of the government. In name, the power seizure was carried out
provisionally and on behalf of the soviets, but, in fact, permanently and for
the benefit of the Bolshevik Party.

The outbreak of the February Revolution found Lenin in Zurich. Cut
off from his homeland since the outbreak of the war, he had thrown himself
into Swiss socialist politics, injecting into them an alien spirit of intolerance
and contentiousness.[1] His log for the winter of 1916–17 reveals a pattern of
frenetic but unfocused activity, now given to pamphleteering, now to intrigues
against deviant Swiss Social-Democrats, now to the study of Marx and Engels.

News from Russia reached Switzerland after a delay of several days.
Lenin first learned of the disorders in Petrograd nearly a week late from a
report in the *Neue Zürcher Zeitung* of March 2/15. The report, datelined
Berlin, inserted on page two between bulletins from the theater of war, said
that a revolution had broken out in the Russian capital and that the Duma
had arrested the tsarist ministers and assumed power.[2]

Lenin decided he had to get back to Russia at once: he now reproached
himself for not having "risked" a move to Scandinavia in 1915 when it had been
possible.*[3] But how? The only point of entry into Russia was through Sweden.
To reach Sweden, one had either to transit Allied territory, by way of France
or England and Holland, or to cross Germany. Lenin requested Inessa Armand to explore, with utmost discretion, the chances of obtaining a British
visa, but he placed little hope in this prospect because the British, aware of
his defeatist program, were almost certain to refuse. He next conceived a
fantastic scheme of traveling to Stockholm on a forged passport: he requested
his agent there, Fürstenberg-Ganetskii, to find a Swede whose papers he could
use, with the proviso that the man not only resemble him physically but also,
since he knew no Swedish, be both deaf and dumb.[4] None of these plans had
any realistic chance of success. Lenin, therefore, seized on a scheme proposed
by Martov in Paris on March 6/19 to a group of socialist émigrés: the Russians
would ask the German Government, through a Swiss intermediary, for transit
rights across its territory to Sweden in exchange for German and Austrian
internees.[5]

While raging in Zurich, in the words of Trotsky, like a caged animal,
Lenin did not lose sight of the political situation at home. He was concerned
that his followers in Russia adopt a correct political course until he appeared

---

*This apparently refers to an offer made to Lenin by Parvus at their 1915 meeting.

on the scene. He was particularly anxious that they not emulate the "opportunistic" tactics of the Mensheviks and SRs of supporting the "bourgeois" Duma government. He outlined his policy in a telegram dispatched on March 6/19 to Petrograd by way of Stockholm:

> Our tactics: complete mistrust, no support for the new government. We especially suspect Kerensky. The arming of the proletariat provides the only guarantee. Immediate elections to the Petrograd [Municipal] Duma. *No rapprochement with the other parties.* [6]

When Lenin cabled these instructions to his followers the Provisional Government had been in office only one week and had hardly had the opportunity to reveal its political physiognomy. In any event, far away from the scene and dependent on second- and third-hand accounts from Western news agencies, Lenin could not have known the intentions and actions of the new government. His insistence that it be treated with "complete mistrust" and denied support, therefore, could not have been due to disapproval of its policies: rather it reflected an a priori determination to remove it from power. His demand that the Bolsheviks not cooperate with the other parties indicated that he was bent on filling the ensuing power vacuum exclusively with the Bolshevik Party. This laconic document indicates that barely four days after he had learned of the February Revolution, Lenin was contemplating a Bolshevik coup d'état. His order to "arm the proletariat" suggests that he envisaged the coup as a military insurrection.

The Bolshevik Party in March 1917 was hardly in a condition to carry out such an ambitious plan. Police arrests during the war, culminating in those of February 26, 1917, when the party's most important entity, the Petrograd Committee, was taken into custody[7] had decapitated its apparatus: its leading figures were either in jail or in exile. In a report to Lenin in early December 1916, Shliapnikov described Bolshevik activities in some factories and garrison units during the preceding months under the slogans "Down with the War" and "Down with the Government," but he also had to admit that the Bolsheviks were so infiltrated by police informers that illegal party activity had become virtually impossible.[8] Subsequent Bolshevik claims of having inspired and even organized the February Revolution are, therefore, entirely spurious. The Bolsheviks rode the coattails first of the spontaneous demonstrators and then those of the Mensheviks and their soviets. Their following among the mutinous military units was close to nil and among the industrial workers at this time they had far fewer adherents than either the Mensheviks or the SRs. During the February days their role was limited to issuing appeals and manifestos: at most, they may have had a hand in preparing the revolutionary banners carried by workers and soldiers in the demonstrations of February 25–28.

The Bolsheviks, however, made up for what they lacked in numbers with organizational skills. On March 2, the Petrograd Committee of the party, freshly released from prison, set up a three-man Bureau consisting of Shliap-nikov, V. M. Molotov, and P. A. Zalutskii.[9] Three days later this Bureau brought out, under Molotov's editorship, the first issue of the revived party organ, *Pravda*. On March 10 it established a Military Committee (later re-named Military Organization) under N. I. Podvoiskii and V. I. Nevskii, to conduct propaganda and agitation among the troops of the Petrograd garrison. For their headquarters, the Bolsheviks chose the luxurious Art Nouveau villa of the ballerina M. F. Kshesinskaia, rumored to have been a mistress of the young Nicholas II. This building they "requisitioned" with the help of friendly troops, ignoring the protests of its owner. Here, until July 1917, officiated the Central Committee of the Bolshevik Party, as well as its Petrograd Committee and Military Organization.

During March 1917, the Bolsheviks in Russia, cut off from their leader, pursued a course that hardly differed from that of the Mensheviks and SRs. A resolution of the Central Committee passed that month described the Pro-visional Government as an agent of the "large bourgeoisie" and of "land-owners," but did not advocate that it be opposed. On March 3 the Petro-grad Committee, the most powerful of the Bolshevik organizations, adopted the Menshevik-SR position calling for support of the government *postol'ku-poskol'ku*—that is, "to the extent that" it advanced the interests of the "masses."[10] Both in theory and in practice the leading Bolsheviks in Petrograd followed a line diametrically opposed to that of Lenin. They could not have been pleased, therefore, with Lenin's advice contained in the telegram of March 6, which reached them after a delay of one week: the published minutes of the Petrograd Committee meetings do not record the discussion that fol-lowed its receipt.

This pro-Menshevik orientation was strengthened with the arrival in Petrograd from exile of three members of the Central Committee, L. B. Kamenev, Stalin, and M. K. Muranov, who, by virtue of seniority, assumed direction of the party and the editorship of *Pravda*. In their articles and speeches, the three rejected the position Lenin had taken at Zimmerwald and Kiental: instead of turning the war between nations into a civil war, they wanted the socialists to agitate for the immediate opening of peace negotia-tions.[11] On March 15 or 16, the Petrograd Bolsheviks held a party confer-ence; the fact that neither its minutes nor its resolutions have been published strongly suggests that many participants adopted an anti-Leninist position on the critical issues of the attitude toward the government and the war.[12] It is known, however, that on March 18, at a closed meeting of the Petrograd Committee, Kamenev argued that although the Provisional Government was unmistakably "counterrevolutionary" and destined to be overthrown, the time for that lay in the future: "the important thing is not to take power: it is to hold on to it."[13] Kamenev spoke in the same vein at the All-Russian Consultation of Soviets at the end of March.[14] At this time the Bolsheviks gave serious thought to reunification with the Mensheviks: on March 21, the Petrograd Committee declared that it was both "possible and desirable" to merge with those Mensheviks who accepted the Zimmerwald and Kiental platforms.*

Given these attitudes, it is understandable that the Petrograd Bolsheviks reacted with shock and disbelief when Alexandra Kollontai appeared before them bearing the first and second of Lenin's "Letters from Afar." Here, Lenin elaborated on his telegram of March 6/19: no support for the Provisional Government, arming the workers.[15] The program struck them as utterly fantastic, thought up by someone out of touch with the situation in Russia. After hesitating for several days, they printed in *Pravda* the first "Letter from Afar" but without the passages in which Lenin attacked the Provisional Government.[16] They refused to publish the second installment and those that followed.

At the All-Russian Conference of Bolsheviks held in Petrograd between March 28 and April 4, Stalin introduced and the delegates approved a motion calling for "control" over the Provisional Government and cooperation with the other "progressive forces" for the purpose of combating the "counterrevolution" and "broadening" the revolutionary movement.† The "un-Bolshevik" behavior of the Bolsheviks when on their own and their rapid shift after Lenin's arrival demonstrates that their conduct was based, not on principles that the members could assimilate and apply, but on their leader's will: that the Bolsheviks were bound together, not by what they believed, but in whom they believed.

The Germans had their own designs on the Russian radicals. The war was going nowhere and they had come to realize that their one remaining chance of winning was to break up the enemy alliance, preferably by forcing Russia out of the war. In the fall of 1916 the Kaiser mused along these lines:

> From the strictly military point of view, it is important to detach one or another of the Entente belligerents by means of a separate peace, in order to hurl our full might against the rest. . . . We can organize our war effort, accordingly, only insofar as the internal struggle in Russia exerts influence on the conclusion of peace with us.[17]

Having failed in 1915 to eliminate Russia from the war by military means, the Germans now resorted to political steps, exploiting the internal divisions inside revolutionary Russia. The Provisional Government was totally committed to

*N. F. Kudelli, *Pervyi legal'nyi Peterburgskii Komitet Bol'shevikov v 1917 g.* (Moscow-Leningrad, 1927), 66; A. G. Shliapnikov, *Semnadtsatyi god,* II (Moscow-Leningrad, 1925), 179–88. Shliapnikov claims that the Petrograd Bolsheviks were dismayed by the policies allegedly forced on them by Kamenev, Stalin, and Muranov, but in view of the policies which they themselves had pursued before the three senior Bolsheviks appeared in Petrograd, the more likely cause of the dismay seems to have been resentment at having to play second fiddle.

†The records of this conference, which have not been published in Russia, can be found in Leon Trotskii, *Stalinskaia shkola falsifikatsii* (Berlin, 1932), 225–90. The above resolutions appear on pp. 289–90.

the Allied cause: so much so that some Germans believed the February Revolution to have been engineered by the British.[18] The pronouncements of Foreign Minister Miliukov on Russia's war aims gave the Central Powers little grounds for optimism. The only hope of breaking Russia away from the alliance, therefore, lay in supporting radical extremists who were opposed to the "imperialist" war and wanted it transformed into a civil war: in other words, the Zimmerwald-Kiental left, of which Lenin was the undisputed leader. Back in Russia, Lenin could give the Provisional Government no end of trouble by inciting class antagonisms, playing on the people's war-weariness, and perhaps even grasping for power.

The strongest advocate of the "Lenin card" was Parvus. He had made one approach to Lenin in 1915: on that occasion, Lenin had refused to cooperate, but the situation was different now. In 1917 Parvus lived in Copenhagen where, as a cover for his intelligence activities, he operated an import company. He also had a spurious scientific institute from which to conduct espionage.[19] His business agent in Stockholm was Jacob Ganetskii, Lenin's trusted associate. Familiar with Russian émigré politics, Parvus placed high hopes on extremists like Lenin. He assured the German Ambassador to Denmark, Count V. Brockdorff-Rantzau, that if let loose, the anti-war left would spread such anarchy that after two or three months Russia would find it impossible to remain in the war.[20] He singled out Lenin for particular attention as "much more raving mad" than either Kerensky or Chkheidze. With uncanny foresight he predicted that once Lenin returned to Russia he would topple the Provisional Government, take over, and promptly conclude a separate peace.[21] He understood well Lenin's lust for power and believed he would strike a deal in order to be able to cross German territory to Sweden. Under Parvus's influence, Brockdorff-Rantzau cabled to Berlin:

> We must now unconditionally seek to create in Russia the greatest possible chaos. . . . We should do all we can . . . to exacerbate the differences between the moderate and extremist parties, because we have the greatest interest in the latter gaining the upper hand, since the Revolution will then become unavoidable and assume forms that must shatter the stability of the Russian state.[22]

The German envoy in Switzerland, G. von Romberg, gave similar advice on the basis of information obtained from local experts on Russian affairs. He called Berlin's attention to the fact that the followers of "Lehnin" caused discord in the Petrograd Soviet with calls for immediate peace negotiations and the refusal to cooperate with both the Provisional Government and the other socialist parties.[23]

Won over, the German Chancellor, Theobald von Bethmann-Hollweg, instructed Romberg to initiate talks with the Russian émigrés about transit to Sweden. These talks were carried out in late March and early April (NS) with the assistance of Swiss socialists, initially Robert Grimm and then Fritz Platten. Lenin acted on behalf of the Russians. It is symptomatic of the myopia of the Germans that in venturing on these dangerous political waters they did not bother to inform themselves about either Lenin or his program: all that mattered to them was that the Bolsheviks and other adherents of the Zimmerwald-Kiental position wanted Russia out of the war. A historian who has inspected the German archives found in them no document to indicate interest in the Bolsheviks: two issues of Lenin's journal, *Sbornik Sotsial-Demokrata,* forwarded to Berlin by the Berne embassy, lay in the archive forty years later, their pages uncut.[24]

In negotiating transit across Germany, Lenin took great pains to ensure that the émigrés would not lay themselves open to charges of collaborating with the enemy. He insisted that the train enjoy the status of an extraterritorial entity: no one was to enter it without the permission of Platten and there would be no passport controls.[25] The fact that a penurious refugee felt in a position to pose terms to the German Government indicates that he had a good appreciation of the services which he could render to it.

On the German side, the negotiations were carried out by the civilian authorities, with the active support of the Foreign Office, especially its chief, Richard von Kühlmann. Although subsequently it came to be believed that the driving force behind Lenin's return to Russia was Ludendorff, in fact the general played a marginal role, his contribution being confined to providing transport.[26]

On April 1 (NS), Platten transmitted Lenin's terms to the German Embassy. Two days later, he was advised they were acceptable. At this time the German Treasury approved a request from the Foreign Ministry to allocate five million marks for "Russian work."[27] What the Germans were doing in regard to Russia was part of a pattern:

> For each of their enemies, France, Britain, Italy, and Russia, the Germans had long since worked out a scheme for treason from within. The plans all bore a rough similarity: first, discord by means of the parties of the far left; next pacifist articles published by defeatists either paid or directly inspired by Germany; and, finally, the establishment of an understanding with a prominent political personality who would ultimately take over the weakened enemy government and sue for peace.[28]

For Britain, they used the Irishman Sir Roger Casement, for France, Joseph Caillaux, and for Russia, Lenin. Casement was shot, Caillaux imprisoned, and only Lenin justified the moneys spent on him.

At 3:20 P.M. on March 27/April 9, thirty-two Russian émigrés left Zurich for the German frontier. While a full list of passengers is not available—the agreement stipulated that the Germans would not inquire into who traveled in the train—it is known that among them were nineteen Bolsheviks, including Lenin, Krupskaia, Zinoviev with his wife and child, Inessa Armand, and Radek, as well as six members of the Bund and three followers of Trotsky.[29] Having crossed the border at Gottmadingen, they transferred to a German train, made up of two cars, one for the Russians, the other for their German escort. Contrary to legend, the train was not sealed.[30] Traveling through Stuttgart and Frankfurt, they arrived in Berlin in the early afternoon of March 29/April 11. There the train was held up for twenty hours, surrounded by German guards. On March 30/April 12 they departed for the Baltic port at Sassnitz, where they boarded a Swedish steamer bound for Trälleborg. On arrival, they were welcomed by the mayor of Stockholm. They then proceeded to the Swedish capital.[31]

Parvus was among those who awaited them there. He asked to meet with Lenin, but the cautious Bolshevik leader refused and passed him on to Radek, who, by virtue of being an Austrian subject, was not at risk of being accused of treason. Radek spent a good part of March 31/April 13 with Parvus. What transpired between them is not known. When they parted, Parvus dashed off to Berlin. On April 20 (NS), he met in private with the German State Secretary, Arthur Zimmermann. This encounter also left no record. He then returned to Stockholm.[32] Although documentary evidence is lacking—as is usual in matters involving high-level covert operations—in the light of subsequent events it seems virtually certain that Parvus worked out with Radek, on behalf of the German Government, the terms and procedures for financing Bolshevik activities in Russia.*

The Russian Consulate in Stockholm had entry visas ready for the arrivals. The Provisional Government seems to have hesitated over whether to allow entry to the anti-war activists, but changed its mind in the hope that Lenin would compromise himself politically by having traveled across enemy territory.[33] The party left Stockholm for Finland on March 31/April 13, reaching Petrograd three days later (April 3/16) at 11:10 p.m.†

Lenin arrived in Petrograd on the final day of the All-Russian Bolshevik Conference. Many Bolsheviks from the provinces were on hand and they prepared a welcome for their leader that in theatricality surpassed anything ever seen in socialist circles. The Petrograd Committee rallied workers to the Finland Station; along the tracks it deployed a guard of soldiers and a military band. When Lenin emerged from the train, the band struck up the "Marseillaise" and the guard sprang to attention. Chkheidze welcomed the arrivals on behalf of the Ispolkom, voicing the hope that socialists would close ranks to defend "revolutionary freedom" from both the domestic counterrevolution and foreign aggression. Outside the Finland Station, Lenin mounted an armored car and, illuminated by a projector, delivered some brief remarks, after which he rode to Kshesinskaia's followed by a crowd.[34]

Sukhanov has left us an eyewitness account of the proceedings at the Bolshevik headquarters that night:

> Below, in a fairly large hall, were assembled many people: workers, "professional revolutionaries," and ladies. Chairs were in short supply, and half of

---

*As an Austrian subject, Radek was considered an enemy alien by the Provisional Government. Refused an entry visa to Russia, he remained in Stockholm until October 1917 working for Lenin.

†Subsequently, several more parties of Russian émigrés crossed Germany en route to Russia.

those present had to stand uncomfortably or spread themselves out on tables. Someone was chosen chairman, and greetings in the form of reports from the localities got underway. This was, on the whole, monotonous and long-winded. But now and then there crept in what I thought were curious and characteristic features of the Bolshevik "style," the specific mode of Bolshevik Party work. And it became obvious with absolute clarity that all Bolshevik work was held in the iron frames of its foreign spiritual center, without which the party's members would have felt themselves utterly helpless, of which, at the same time, they were proud, of which the better ones among them felt themselves to be devoted servants, like the Knights of the Holy Grail. Kamenev, too, said something nondescript. Finally, they remembered Zinoviev, who was faintly applauded but said nothing. Finally, the greetings in the form of reports came to an end. . . .

And then, the grand master of the order rose to his feet with his "response." I cannot forget that speech, like lightning, which shook up and astonished not only me, a heretic accidentally thrown into delirium, but also the true believers. I aver that no one had expected anything like it. It seemed as if all the elemental forces had risen from their lairs and the spirit of universal destruction, which knew no obstacles, no doubts, neither human difficulties nor human calculations, circled in Kshesinskaia's hall above the heads of the enchanted disciples.[35]

The thrust of Lenin's ninety-minute speech was that the transition from the "bourgeois-democratic" to the "socialist" revolution had to be accomplished in a matter of months.* This meant that barely four weeks after tsarism had been overthrown, Lenin was publicly sentencing its successor to death. This proposition ran so contrary to the sentiments of the majority of his followers, it seemed so irresponsible and "adventurist," that the remainder of the night, until the meeting broke up at 4 a.m., was spent in tempestuous debate.

Later that day Lenin read to a group of Bolsheviks and then separately to a joint meeting of Bolsheviks and Mensheviks a paper which, anticipating resistance, he presented as reflecting his personal opinions. Subsequently known as the "April Theses," it outlined a program of action that must have appeared to his audiences as totally out of touch with reality if not positively mad.[36] He proposed no backing for the ongoing war; immediate transition to the "second" phase of the revolution; refusal to support the Provisional Government; transfer of all power to the Soviets; abolition of the army in favor of a popular militia; confiscation of all landlord property and nationalization of all land; the fusion of all banks into a single National Bank under Soviet supervision; Soviet control of production and distribution; creation of a new Socialist International.

Pravda's editorial board refused to print Lenin's "Theses" on the pretext of a mechanical breakdown at its printing plant.[37] A meeting of the Bolshevik Central Committee on April 6 passed a negative resolution on them. Kamenev

---

*There is no stenographic record of this speech, but the notes which Lenin used have been published: *LS,* XXI (1933), 33; see also *LS,* II (1924), 453–54, and F. F. Raskolnikov, *Na boevykh postakh* (Moscow, 1964), 67.

insisted that Lenin's analogy between the situation in contemporary Russia and the Paris Commune was faulty, while Stalin found the "Theses" "schematic" and short on facts.[38] But Lenin and Zinoviev, who had in the meantime joined the editorial board of *Pravda,* forced the issue, and the "Theses" appeared on April 7. Lenin's article was accompanied by an editorial comment by Kamenev which disassociated the party's organ from it. Lenin, Kamenev wrote,

> proceeds from the premise that the bourgeois-democratic revolution has been completed and counts on the immediate transformation of that revolution into a socialist one.

But, he went on, the Central Committee thought otherwise and the Bolshevik Party would be guided by its resolutions.* The Petrograd Committee met on April 8 to discuss Lenin's paper. Its verdict was also overwhelmingly negative, two voting in favor, thirteen against, with one abstention.[39] The reaction in the provincial cities was similar: the Bolshevik organizations in Kiev and Saratov, for instance, rejected Lenin's program, the latter on the grounds that the author was out of touch with the situation in Russia.[40]

Whatever the Bolsheviks' opinion of their leader's pronouncements, the Germans were delighted. On April 4/17, their agent in Stockholm cabled to Berlin: "Lenin's entry into Russia successful. He is working exactly as we wish."[41]

Lenin was a very secretive man: although he spoke and wrote voluminously, enough to fill fifty-five volumes of collected works, his speeches and writings are overwhelmingly propaganda and agitation, meant to persuade potential followers and destroy known opponents rather than reveal his thoughts. He rarely disclosed what was on his mind, even to close associates. As supreme commander in the global war between classes, he kept his plans private. To reconstruct his thinking, it is necessary, therefore, to proceed retroactively, from known deeds to concealed intentions.

On general issues—who the enemy was and what was to be done to him—Lenin was frank enough. The objective—the "program"—broadly defined, he made public; it was the tactics that he kept hidden. And herein lies the difficulty of divining Lenin's intentions. For as Mussolini, himself no mean expert in the art of the coup d'état, confided to Giovanni Giolitti, "a State has to be defended not against a program of the revolution but against its tactics."[42]

Lenin rejected the Menshevik-SR doctrine of a two-stage revolution and its corollary, *dvoevlastie* or dyarchy; he meant to topple the Provisional Government as soon as practicable and seize power. His remarkably keen political

---

*Iu. Kamenev in *Pravda,* No. 27 (April 8, 1917), 2. Kamenev refers to the resolutions of the Bolshevik Conference of March 28.

instinct—the flair possessed by every successful general—told him this could be done. He knew the liberal and socialist intelligentsia for what they were: "vegetarian tigers," to borrow a phrase from Clemenceau, who for all their revolutionary cant were deathly afraid of political responsibility and incapable of exercising it even if handed to them. In this respect, he judged them like Nicholas II. He further realized that underneath the appearance of national unity and universal support of the Provisional Government there seethed powerful destructive forces which, fanned and properly directed, could bring down the ineffective democracy and carry him to power: shortages of goods in the cities, agrarian unrest, ethnic aspirations. To accomplish their objective, the Bolsheviks had to set themselves clearly apart from both the Provisional Government and the other socialist parties as the sole alternative to the status quo. In line with this reasoning, after returning to Russia, Lenin compelled his followers to abandon the conciliatory attitude toward the Provisional Government and any thought of merging with the Mensheviks.

In view of the immense popularity of democratic slogans, Lenin could not openly claim power on behalf of the Bolshevik Party: no one outside Bolshevik ranks, and very few within them, would have found this prospect acceptable. For this reason, with one brief interlude, throughout 1917 he called for power to be transferred to the soviets. This tactic may appear puzzling in view of the fact that until the fall of 1917 the Bolsheviks were a minority in the soviets, so that, on the face of it, the implementation of this program would have transferred power to the Mensheviks and SRs. But the Bolsheviks felt confident the latter would not stand in their way. Tsereteli, who of all the Menshevik leaders had the fewest illusions about their rivals, wrote that the Bolsheviks believed they would have little trouble wresting national power from the soviet majority.[43] From Lenin's point of view the Provisional Government, for all its incompetence, was a more dangerous enemy than the democratic socialists because it had at its disposal a large armed force and because it enjoyed a certain measure of support from the peasantry and the middle class: by appealing to nationalism it could rally powerful forces against him. As long as the Provisional Government stayed in power, however nominally, the danger always existed of the country veering to the right. With the soviet as the locus of authority, it was a relatively simple matter to keep on radicalizing the political atmosphere and pulling the irresolute socialists along by frightening them with the specter of a "counterrevolution."

Lenin pursued his objective—seizure of power—in a manner that was rooted in the study of military history and military science. Genuine politics, even in its authoritarian form, entails some sort of accommodation both with other contenders for power and with the population at large, which leaves the governed scope for free initiative. But Lenin, for whom politics was always class war, thought in Clausewitzian terms: its purpose, as that of military strategy, was not accommodation with the opponent but his destruction. This meant, first and foremost, disarming him, in two senses: (1) depriving him of an armed force and (2) smashing his institutions. But it could also mean his physical annihilation, as on the field of battle. European socialists routinely talked of "class war," but they meant by it a struggle waged mainly with non-violent means, such as industrial strikes and the ballot box, which might, at a certain point, culminate in barricades. Lenin and he alone understood "class war" in the literal sense to mean civil war—warfare with every available weapon for the purpose of strategic destruction and, if need be, extermination of rivals that left the victor with unchallenged mastery of the political battle-field. Revolution in this view was war waged by other means, the difference being that the combatants were not states and nations but social classes: its battle lines ran vertically rather than horizontally. In this militarization of politics lay a critical source of Lenin's success, for those whom he designated as enemies could not conceive of anyone seriously treating politics as combat in which quarter was neither given nor expected.

This outlook on politics Lenin drew from the inner depths of his personality, in which the lust for domination combined with a patrimonial political culture shaped in the Russia of Alexander III in which he had grown up. But the theoretical justification for these psychological impulses and this cultural legacy he found in Marx's comments on the Paris Commune. Marx's writings on this subject made an overwhelming impression on him and became his guide to action. Observing the rise and fall of the Commune, Marx concluded that until then all revolutionaries had committed a cardinal mistake in that they took over existing institutions instead of destroying them. By leaving intact the political, social, and military structures of the class state and merely replacing their personnel, they provided a breeding ground for the counter-revolution. Future revolutionaries would have to proceed differently: "not transfer from one set of hands to another the bureaucratic-military machine, as has been done until now, but *smash* it."[44] These words etched themselves deeply in Lenin's mind: he repeated them at every opportunity and placed them at the heart of his principal political treatise, *State and Revolution.* They served to justify his destructive instincts and provided a rationale for his desire to erect a new order: an order all-encompassing in its "totalitarian" aspiration.

Lenin always viewed revolution in international terms; the Russian Revolution was for him a mere accident, a fortuitous snapping of "imperialism's" weakest link. He was never interested in reforming Russia, but only in subjugating it so as to have a springboard for a revolution in the industrial countries and their colonies. Even as dictator of Russia he never ceased to view 1917 and its sequel from an international viewpoint: for him it was never the "Russian Revolution," but the worldwide revolution that happened to have had its start in Russia. In his farewell address to the Swiss socialists, delivered the day before he left for home, he made this point with great emphasis:

> It has fallen to the Russian proletariat to have the great honor of *beginning* a series of revolutions. . . . It is not its special qualities but the special historical conditions that have made the Russian proletariat, for *a specific, perhaps very brief time,* the vanguard of the revolutionary proletariat of the whole world.
> Russia is a peasant country, one of the most backward in Europe. It is

not possible for socialism to triumph there *directly, presently.* But the peasant character of the country . . . *can* lend a vast sweep to the bourgeois-democratic revolution in Russia and make our revolution a *prologue* to the worldwide socialist revolution, a *step* toward it.[45]

Lenin's secretiveness about a worldwide socialist revolution was due in part to the desire to keep his opponents in the dark about his intentions and in part to the advantage that secrecy gave him of being able to avoid the stigma of failure if things did not work out as planned: whenever this happened, he always could (and in fact did) deny having had a plan. Even so, from the directives he issued in the spring and early summer of 1917, when he personally led the Bolshevik forces, one can form a general picture of his battle plan.

The experience of February seems to have persuaded Lenin that the Provisional Government could be brought down by massive street demonstrations. To begin with, the soil had to be prepared, as had been done in 1915–16, by a relentless campaign to discredit the government in the eyes of the population. To this end it had to be blamed for everything that went wrong: political disorders, shortages, inflation, military setbacks. It had to be charged with conspiring with the Germans to surrender Petrograd while pretending to defend it and of collaborating with General Kornilov while charging him with treason. The more preposterous the accusations, the more the politically inexperienced workers and soldiers were likely to believe them: why should an incredible reality not have incredible causes?

Unlike February, however, the militant street demonstrations had to be tightly supervised; Lenin had no faith in spontaneity even if he fully appreciated the need for giving his highly calculated endeavors the appearance of spontaneity. He learned from Napoleon and applied to civil war the principle of *tiraillerie,* or skirmishing, which some military historians regard as Napoleon's major contribution to warfare.[46] For purposes of combat, Napoleon used to divide his forces in two: the professional Guard and the mass of recruits. It was his practice at the beginning of a battle to send in the recruits to draw enemy fire: this provided a picture of enemy dispositions. At the critical moment, he sent the Guard into action to break the enemy's lines at the weakest point and put him to flight. Lenin applied this tactic to urban warfare. The masses were brought out into the streets under seditious slogans to provoke a government reaction that would reveal its strengths and weaknesses. Were the crowds to succeed in overwhelming the government's forces, then the Bolshevik equivalent of Napoleon's Guard—the armed workers and soldiers organized by the Bolshevik Military Organization—would take over. Were they to fail, the point would still be made that the masses wanted change and that by resisting them the government proved to be "anti-democratic." One would then await the next opportunity. The basic principle was Napoleon's *"on s'engage et puis on voit"*—"one commits oneself and then one sees."[47] In his three attempts at a putsch (April, June, and July 1917), Lenin called out the mobs into the streets, but kept himself well in the background, always pretending to follow the "people" rather than lead them. After each such attempt failed, he would deny having had any revolutionary intentions, and even pretend that his party did all in its power to restrain the impetuous masses.*

Lenin's technique of revolution required the manipulation of crowds. He followed, whether by instinct or from knowledge it is hard to tell, the theories of crowd behavior first formulated in 1895 by the French sociologist Gustave Le Bon in *La Psychologie des Foules (Crowd Psychology)*. Le Bon held that on joining a crowd men lose their individuality, dissolving it in a collective personality with its own distinct psychology. Its main characteristic is a lowered capacity for logical reasoning and a corresponding rise in the sense of "invincible power." Feeling invincible, crowds demand action, a craving that leaves them open to manipulation: "crowds are in a state of expectant attention which renders suggestion easy." They are especially responsive to exhortation to violence by associations of words and ideas that evoke "grandiose and vague images" accompanied by an air of "mystery," such as "liberty," "democracy," and "socialism." Crowds respond to fanatics who incite them with constantly reiterated, violent images. Since, according to Le Bon, in the ultimate analysis the force that motivates crowds is religious faith, it "demands a god before everything else," a leader whom it endows with supernatural qualities. The crowd's religious sentiment is simple:

> [the] worship of a being supposed superior, fear of the power with which the being is credited, blind submission to its commands, inability to discuss its dogmas, the desire to spread them, and a tendency to consider as enemies all by whom they are not accepted.[48]

A more recent observer of crowd behavior has called attention to the dynamism of crowds:

> The crowd, once formed, wants to grow rapidly. It is difficult to exaggerate the power and determination with which it spreads. As long as it feels that it is growing—in revolutionary states, for example, which start with small but highly-charged crowds—it regards anything which opposes its growth as constricting. . . . The crowd here is like a besieged city and, as in many sieges, it has enemies before its walls and enemies within them. During the fighting it attracts more and more partisans from the country around.[49]

In a rare moment of candor, Lenin revealed to an associate, P. N. Lepeshinskii, that he well understood the principles of mass psychology:

*This tactic has succeeded in confusing even some historians: since the Bolsheviks did not openly declare that they wanted power, it is argued, they did not want it. But in October 1917 they would also pretend to act under pressure from below although no such pressure existed. The duality of instruments used by the Bolsheviks and their emulators was first noted by Curzio Malaparte in his *Coup d'Etat.* A participant in Mussolini's power seizure, Malaparte realized what most contemporaries and many historians have missed—namely, that the Bolshevik revolution and its successors operated on two distinct levels, the observable and the concealed, the latter of which delivered the death blow to the existing regime's vital organs.

At the end of the summer of 1906, [Lenin] in an intimate conversation predicted with considerable assurance the defeat of the Revolution and hinted at the need to prepare for a retreat. If despite such a pessimistic mood, he nevertheless worked for the intensification of the proletariat's revolutionary forces, then this was, apparently, from the idea that the revolutionary spirit [*revoliutsionnaia aktual'nost'*] of the masses never does harm. If there should occur another chance for victory or even semi-victory, then it will be in large measure owing to this spirit.[50]

In other words, mass action, even if unsuccessful, was a valuable device to keep crowds at a high level of tension and combat readiness.*

In the three months that followed his return to Russia, Lenin acted with reckless impetuosity to bring down the Provisional Government by mob action. He subjected the government and its socialist supporters to ceaseless verbal assaults as traitors to the Revolution, and concurrently incited the population to civil disobedience—the army to ignore government orders, the workers to take control of their factories, the communal peasants to seize private land, the ethnic minorities to claim their national rights. He had no timetable, but felt confident of imminent success because each skirmish revealed the indecision as well as the impotence of his adversaries. Had he not lost nerve in the decisive moment during the July putsch he might well have taken power then rather than in October.

Paradoxically, although militarized, Lenin's (and, later, Trotsky's) tactics did not entail much physical violence. That was to come later, after power had been secured. The purpose of the propaganda campaigns and mass demonstrations, the barrage of words and the street disorders, was to implant in the minds of opponents as well as of the public at large a sense of inevitability: change was coming and nothing could stop it. Like his pupils and emulators Mussolini and Hitler, Lenin won power by first breaking the spirit of those who stood in his way, persuading them that they were doomed. The Bolshevik triumph in October was accomplished nine-tenths psychologically: the forces involved were negligible, a few thousand men at most in a nation of one hundred and fifty million, and victory came almost without a shot being fired. The whole operation served to confirm Napoleon's dictum that the battle is won or lost in the minds of men before it even begins.

The Bolsheviks made the first bid for power on April 21, taking advantage of a political crisis over Russia's war aims.

It will be recalled that at the end of March 1917, the Ispolkom compelled the Provisional Government to repudiate Miliukov's claim to Austrian and

*Cf. Eric Hoffer: "Action is a unifier. . . . All mass movements avail themselves of mass action as a means of unification. The conflicts a mass movement seeks and incites serve not only to down its enemies but also to strip its followers of their distinct individuality and render them more soluble in the collective medium": *The True Believer* (New York, 1951), 117, 118–19.

Turkish territories. To placate the socialists, the government issued on March 27 a declaration, cleared by the Ispolkom, in which, without in so many words renouncing annexationist ambitions, it declared Russia's objective to be "lasting peace" based on the "self-determination of nations."

This concession put the matter to rest, but only temporarily. It became once again a bone of contention in April with the return to Russia of Victor Chernov. The leader of the SR Party had spent the war years in the West, mainly in Switzerland, where he participated in the Zimmerwald and Kiental conferences, and published, allegedly with German funds, revolutionary literature for Russian prisoners of war in Germany and Austria.[51] Back in Petrograd, he immediately launched a campaign against Miliukov, calling for his resignation and asking the government to transmit its March 27 declaration to Allied governments as a formal statement of Russia's war aims. Miliukov objected to this demand on the grounds that the Allies could misinterpret Russia's formal renunciation of the territories promised to her to mean that she intended to leave the war. But the cabinet overruled him: Kerensky displayed particular zeal in this affair, which promised to undermine Miliukov, his principal rival, and to strengthen his own position in the Soviet.[52] Eventually, a compromise was reached. The government agreed to hand the Allies its declaration of March 27 but accompany it with an explanatory note which would remove any doubts about Russia's intention to stay in the war. In the words of Kerensky, the note drafted by Miliukov and approved by the cabinet "should have satisfied the most violent critic of Miliukov's 'imperialism.' "[53] It reaffirmed Russia's determination to fight for the alliance's common "high ideals" and "fully to carry out the obligations" toward it.[54] On April 18 (May 1 in the West), the two documents were cabled to Russian embassies abroad for transmittal to Allied governments.

When the government's note appeared in Russian newspapers on the morning of April 20 it enraged the socialist intelligentsia. Its displeasure was due not to the pledge to fight until victory, which was the stated objective of all the socialist parties save for a fringe minority, but to the ambivalent language about "annexations and contributions." The Ispolkom voted that day that "revolutionary democracy will not permit the spilling of blood for . . . aggressive objectives." Russia had to fight on, but only until the time when all the belligerents were prepared to make peace without annexations.[55]

This dispute could have been readily resolved by consultation between the government and the Ispolkom, which almost certainly would have led to the government's capitulating. But before a compromise could be reached, the anger spilled to the barracks and workers' quarters, which were linked to the Ispolkom with invisible threads.

The street disorders on April 20–21 began spontaneously, but they were quickly taken in hand by the Bolsheviks. A young Social Democratic officer, Lieutenant Theodore Linde, who had participated in the drafting of Order No. 1, interpreted the government's note as a betrayal of the revolution's democratic ideals. He summoned representatives of his regiment, the Finnish

Reserve Guards, and called on them to bring their men into the streets to demonstrate against Miliukov. He made the rounds of the other garrison units bearing a similar message.[56] Linde was an ardent patriot who wanted Russia to stay in the war: he lost his life soon afterward, lynched by front-line troops whom he exhorted to combat but who decided, from his German-sounding name, that he was an enemy agent.[57] Like most Russian socialists, however, he wanted the war to be waged for "democratic" ideals. He seems not to have realized that urging troops to take part in an unauthorized political manifestation was tantamount to inciting mutiny. From 3 p.m. onward, several military units, headed by the Finnish Guards, marched, fully armed, to Mariinskii Palace, the seat of the government, where they shouted for Miliukov's resignation.[58]

Because of the indisposition of Guchkov, the cabinet at this moment was meeting not in Mariinskii Palace but in Guchkov's office at the Ministry of War. Before it now appeared General Kornilov, who, as commander of the Petrograd Military District, bore responsibility for the capital's security. He requested permission to have troops disperse the mutineers. According to Kerensky, the cabinet unanimously denied this request: "We were all confident of the wisdom of our course and felt certain that the population would not permit any acts of violence against the Government."[59] It was the first, but not the last time that the Provisional Government, faced with an open challenge to its authority, flinched from using force—a fact that escaped neither Kornilov nor Lenin.

Up to this point, the Bolsheviks had nothing to do with the disturbance: indeed, it seems to have caught them by surprise. But they lost no time in exploiting it.

The activities of the Bolshevik high command at this time are far from clear, because most of the relevant documents remain unpublished. The official Communist version of the events holds that the party's Central Committee did not authorize the anti-government demonstrations which took place in Petrograd in the evening of April 20 and throughout April 21: the Bolsheviks who took to the streets carrying banners reading "Down with the Provisional Government" and "All Power to the Soviets" are said to have acted on instructions of second-rank Bolsheviks, including one S. Ia. Bagdaev.* But it is quite unthinkable that in a centralized party like the Bolsheviks, a minor functionary would have taken it upon himself to authorize revolutionary slogans in defiance of the Central Committee—a charge rendered the more preposterous by Bagdaev's documented opposition to Lenin's confrontational stance against the Provisional Government.[60] This misleading account of the events of April 20–21, 1917, has been made up in order to conceal the fact that the first Bolshevik attempt at a putsch ended in ignominious failure. To

---

*Ocherki istorii Leningradskoi organizatsii KPSS, I (Leningrad, 1962), 481. Bagdaev had in fact been charged by the Petrograd Committee of the Bolshevik Party with organizing the May 1 demonstration, which fell on April 18, the day the government's declaration and note on war aims were delivered to Allied governments: Kudelli, *Pervyi*, 82.

confuse the picture further, Communist historians have gone to the lengths of citing resolutions adopted by the party after the event as indicative of its intentions before it had taken place, and attributing directives written by Lenin to "unidentified sources."

In the afternoon of April 20, as the troops called out by Linde were converging on Mariinskii Square, the Bolshevik Central Committee convened an emergency session. It passed a resolution, which Lenin had drafted earlier in the day upon reading Miliukov's note, which provided the rationale for the Bolshevik-sponsored demonstrations that followed. Early editions of Lenin's writings denied his authorship; it has been finally acknowledged as his in the fifth edition of Lenin's works, published in 1962.[61] Lenin described the Provisional Government as "thoroughly imperialist" and dominated by domestic as well as Anglo-French capital. A regime of this kind was by its very nature incapable of renouncing annexations. Lenin criticized the Soviet for supporting the government and called on it to assume full power. This was not, as yet, an overt appeal for the overthrow of the government, but it required no deep reflection to draw such a conclusion from Lenin's words. It certainly entitled Bolshevik demonstrators to carry banners reading "Down with the Provisional Government" and "All Power to the Soviets," from which Lenin would later disassociate himself.

What tactical decisions the Central Committee adopted at this meeting are not known: the published version of the minutes of the Petrograd Committee, which often joined in the meetings of the Central Committee, records only organizational trivia. It omits all subsequent sessions until May 3.[62] Two things, however, are reasonably certain. Lenin seems to have been the main advocate of aggressive action and to have run into strong opposition: this much is known from the aftermath, when he came under criticism from his associates, notably Kamenev. Second, the demonstrations were intended as a full-scale putsch, a reenactment of February 26–27 when rioting workers and mutinous soldiers brought down the tsarist government.

Already in the evening of April 20, after the troops that took part in the afternoon demonstration had returned to their barracks, fresh groups of soldiers and workers appeared on the streets with anti-government banners: they were the advance troop of the Bolshevik-led rioters. Before long, a counter-demonstration took place carrying banners reading "Down with Lenin!" On Nevsky, the demonstrators clashed. Following the intervention of the Ispolkom, the crowds were pacified.

The Bolshevik Central Committee reconvened in the morning of April 21 to adopt directives for the day's operations.[63] One directive ordered the dispatch of agitators to factories and barracks to inform workers and soldiers about the demonstration planned for that day and urge them to join in.[64] Such agitators appeared during the noontime lunch break in many factories of the Vyborg District, whose workers were the most radicalized in Petrograd. Appeals to the workers to take the afternoon off and participate in an anti-government protest met with a disappointing response, most likely because SR and Menshevik agents from the Ispolkom were on hand to neutralize them. Workers in only three small plants passed Bolshevik resolutions: they numbered a mere one thousand,[65] less than .05 of 1 percent of Petrograd's labor force. Putilov, Obukhov, and the other large enterprises ignored the Bolsheviks. That the Bolsheviks planned armed action is indicated by the fact that on April 21, N. I. Podvoiskii, the head of their Military Organization, called on the Kronshtadt naval base to dispatch to Petrograd a detachment of reliable sailors.[66] The Kronshtadt sailors were the roughest, most violence-prone element in the city: heavily influenced by anarchists, they needed little encouragement to beat up and rob the *burzhui*. Bringing them into the city was almost certain to result in pogroms. To have invited them gives lie to Lenin's claim that on April 21 the Bolsheviks had intended a "peaceful reconnaissance."

In the early afternoon, a column bearing anti-government banners, preceded by units of the Bolshevik "Factory Militia" armed with guns, advanced along Nevsky toward the city center. Although a sorry performance, in which neither soldiers nor sailors took part, it was the first armed challenge to the democratic government. As the demonstrators approached the Kazan Cathedral, they ran into a counterprocession that shouted "Long Live the Provisional Government." A melee ensued and some random shooting, in which three persons died. It was the first street violence in Petrograd since February.

While his followers were on the streets, Lenin thought it prudent to stay at home.[67]

Kornilov, seeking again to restore order, instructed artillery units and troops to be brought out. This time he ran into the defiance of the Ispolkom, which insisted it could calm the crowds by persuasion. It phoned the Military Staff to countermand Kornilov's instructions. Kornilov then met with Ispolkom's representatives. They assumed responsibility for stopping the disorders, whereupon he revoked his instructions and ordered the troops to stay in the barracks. To make certain that neither the government nor the Bolsheviks resorted to arms, the Ispolkom issued a proclamation to the Petrograd garrison:

> Comrade Soldiers! During these troubled days do not come out with weapons unless called by the Executive Committee [Ispolkom]. The Executive Committee alone has the right to dispose of you. Every order concerning the appearance of military units on the street (except for routine detail duty) must be issued on the blank of the Executive Committee, bear its seal and the signatures of at least two of the following: Chkheidze, Skobelev, Binasik, Sokolov, Goldman, Filippovskii, Bogdanov. Every order must be confirmed by telephoning 104–06.[68]

This instruction subverted the authority of the military commander of Petrograd. Unable to carry out his duties, Kornilov asked to be relieved and assigned to the front. At the beginning of May he assumed command of the Eighth Army.

Later in the day, the Ispolkom voted to prohibit all demonstrations for the next forty-eight hours. It denounced anyone who led armed men into the streets as a "traitor to the Revolution."[69]

On April 21, analogous Bolshevik demonstrations under identical slogans took place in Moscow.

The disorders in Petrograd subsided toward the evening of April 21 from lack of mass support: demonstrators loyal to the government proved to be at least as militant as and considerably more numerous than those who followed the Bolshevik lead. In Moscow, Bolshevik riots went on for yet another day, terminating when angry mobs surrounded the rioters and tore anti-government banners from their hands.

The instant it became apparent that the putsch had failed, the Bolsheviks disclaimed all responsibility. On April 22, the Central Committee passed a resolution which conceded that the "petty bourgeois" mass, after some initial hesitation, had come out in support of the "pro-capitalist" forces, and condemned anti-government slogans as premature. The task of the party was defined as enlightening the workers about the true nature of the government. There were to be no more demonstrations and the instructions of the Soviet had to be obeyed. The resolution, most likely moved by Kamenev, represented a defeat for Lenin, whom Kamenev charged with "adventurism." Lenin lamely defended himself by blaming the anti-government character of the demonstration on hotheads from the Petrograd Committee.

But even while defending himself, he inadvertently revealed what had been on his mind:

> This was an attempt to resort to violent means. We did not know whether at that anxious moment the mass had strongly shifted to our side. . . . We merely wanted to carry out a peaceful reconnaissance of the enemy's strength, not to give battle . . .[70]

How to reconcile his admission that the April riots were "an attempt to resort to violent means" with the claim that they were meant as a "peaceful reconnaissance" Lenin did not explain.*

For the time being, the crowds followed the Ispolkom and, through its agency, the government. In this context, it is understandable why the socialist intellectuals opposed the use of force. But crowds are fickle, and the main lesson of April was not how weak the Bolshevik Party was but how unprepared the government and the leaders of the Soviet were to meet force with force. Analyzing the lessons of the April days a few months later, Lenin concluded that the Bolsheviks had been "insufficiently revolutionary" in their tactics, by which he could only have meant that they were wrong in not making a grab

---

*The American historian Alexander Rabinowitch, who adopts the Bolshevik thesis that the April demonstrations were a peaceful demonstration, avoids the problem by omitting in his citation of the above passage Lenin's reference to "violent means": *Prelude to Revolution* (Bloomington, Ind., 1968), 45.

for power.[71] Still, he drew much encouragement from this opening skirmish: according to Sukhanov, in April his hopes "sprouted wings."[72]

The April riots provoked the first serious government crisis. Barely two months after tsarism had collapsed, the intelligentsia saw the country disintegrating before their very eyes—and now they no longer had the tsar and the bureaucracy to blame. On April 26, the government issued an emotional appeal to the nation that it could no longer administer and wished to bring in "representatives of those creative forces of the country which until then had not taken a direct and immediate part" in administration, that is, the socialist intelligentsia.[73] The Ispolkom, still afraid of being compromised in the eyes of the "masses," on April 28 rejected the government's feeler.[74]

The event that caused the Ispolkom to change its mind was Guchkov's resignation, on April 30, as Minister of War. As he explains in his memoirs, Guchkov had concluded that Russia had become ungovernable: the only salvation lay in inviting into the government "healthy" forces as represented by General Kornilov and leaders of the business community.[75] Since this was not possible, given the attitude of the socialist intellectuals, he stepped down. According to Tsereteli, Guchkov's resignation, accompanied as it was by Miliukov's request to be relieved of his responsibilities, was symptomatic of a crisis of such dimensions that it could no longer be dealt with by palliative measures.[76] The "bourgeoisie" was abandoning the government. On May 1, the Ispolkom reversed itself and without consulting the plenum of the Soviet, voted 44–19, with two abstentions, to permit its members to accept cabinet posts.[77] The negative votes were cast by the Bolsheviks and Mensheviks-Internationalists (followers of Martov), who wanted the Soviet to assume full power. Tsereteli provided an explanation of the majority's reasoning. The government, he said, had admitted its inability to save the country from the impending catastrophe. In these circumstances, the "democratic" forces had the duty to step in and help save the Revolution. The Soviet could not take power on its own behalf and in its own name, as Martov and Lenin wanted, because by so doing it would push into the arms of reactionaries those numerous elements in the country which, although not committed to democracy, were willing to cooperate with the democratic forces. What he meant another Menshevik, V. Voitinskii, spelled out in arguing for a coalition with the "bourgeoisie" and in obliquely opposing the slogan "All Power to the Soviets" on the grounds that the peasants stood "to the right" of the soviet,[78] and presumably would refuse to recognize as government a body in which they were not represented.

In agreeing to join a coalition government, the Ispolkom posed a number of conditions: a review of inter-Allied accords, an effort to end the war, further "democratization" of the armed forces, an agrarian policy that would set the stage for the distribution of land to the peasants, and the prompt convocation of the Constituent Assembly. The government, for its part, demanded that the Ispolkom acknowledge it as the exclusive bearer of state authority, empowered to resort to force if the situation required it, as well as the sole source of commands to the armed forces. Representatives of the government and the Ispolkom spent the opening days of May negotiating the terms of the coalition. Agreement was reached during the night of May 4–5, following which a new cabinet was installed in office. The placid and inoffensive Prince Lvov stayed on as Prime Minister; Guchkov and Miliukov formally resigned. The Foreign Ministry portfolio was given to the Kadet M. I. Tereshchenko—a strange choice, for Tereshchenko, a young businessman, had little experience and was unfamiliar to the public. But it was common knowledge that, like Kerensky, he belonged to the Freemasons: suspicions were voiced that he owed his appointment to Masonic connections. Kerensky took over the Ministry of War. He, too, had no background for the post, but his prominence in the Soviet and his rhetorical gifts were expected to inspire the troops as they were preparing for the summer offensive. Six socialists entered the coalition government, among them Chernov, who took the portfolio of Agriculture, and Tsereteli, who became Minister of Post and Telegraphs. The cabinet would have a life of two months.

The May accords somewhat eased the anomalies of *dvoevlastie,* which had confused the population as to the ultimate source of authority. They were indicative not only of a growing sense of desperation but also of the growing maturity of the socialist intelligentsia, and, as such, were a positive development. On the face of it, a government that united the "bourgeoisie" and "democracy" promised to be more effective than one in which the two groups confronted each other as antagonists. But the agreement also raised fresh problems. The instant the socialist leaders of the Soviet joined the government, they forfeited the role of an opposition. By entering the cabinet, they automatically came to share blame for everything that went wrong. This allowed the Bolsheviks, who refused to join, to pose as the sole alternative to the status quo and the custodians of the Russian Revolution. And since under the hopelessly incompetent administration of liberal and socialist intellectuals events were bound to go from bad to worse, they emerged as the only conceivable saviors of Russia.

The Provisional Government now faced the classic predicament of moderate revolutionaries who take the reins of power from the fallen authority. "Little by little," writes Crane Brinton in his comparative study of revolutions,

> the moderates find themselves losing the credit they had gained as opponents of the old regime, and taking on more and more of the discredit associated by the hopeful with the status of heir of the old regime. Forced on the defensive, they make mistake after mistake, partly because they are so little used to being on the defensive.

Emotionally unable to bear thinking of themselves as "falling behind in the revolutionary process" and to break with rivals on the left, they satisfy no one and are ready to give way to better-organized, better-staffed, more determined rivals.[79]

In May and June 1917, the Bolshevik Party still ran a poor third to the other socialist parties: at the First All-Russian Congress of Soviets in early June, it had only 105 delegates as against 285 for the SRs and 248 for the Mensheviks.* But the tide was running in its favor.

The Bolsheviks enjoyed many advantages. In addition to their unique position as the sole alternative to the new Provisional Government and their determined and power-hungry leadership, there were at least two others.

The Mensheviks and SRs spouted socialist slogans, but they would not push them to their logical conclusions. This confused their constituency and helped the Bolsheviks. They insisted that since February 1917 Russia had a "bourgeois" regime which they controlled through the soviets: but if this was so, why not be rid of the "bourgeoisie" and vest full power in the soviets? The socialists called the war "imperialist": if it was so, why not lay down arms and go home? "All Power to the Soviets" and "Down with the War," though still unpopular slogans in the spring and summer of 1917, had about them a certain inexorable logic—they made "sense" in the context of ideas which the socialists planted in the mind of the population. Because the Bolsheviks had the courage to draw from the common socialist premises the obvious conclusions, the socialists could never really stand up to them: to have done so would have been tantamount to denying themselves. Time and again, whenever the followers of Lenin brazenly challenged democratic procedures and struck for power, the socialists would try to talk them out of it, yet, at the same time, they would prevent the government from reacting. It was difficult to stand up to the Bolsheviks if their only sin was seeking to reach the same goal by bolder means: in many ways, Lenin and his followers were the true "conscience of the Revolution." Their intellectual irresponsibility combined with the moral cowardice of the socialist majority created a psychological and ideological environment in which the Bolshevik minority battened and grew.

But perhaps the single greatest advantage the Bolsheviks enjoyed over their rivals lay in their total unconcern for Russia. The conservatives, the liberals, and the socialists, each in their own way, sought to preserve Russia as a national entity, in defiance of the particular social and regional interests that the Revolution had unleashed and that were pulling the country apart. They appealed to the soldiers to maintain discipline, to the peasants to wait for the land reform, to the workers to keep up production, to the ethnic minorities to hold in abeyance demands for self-rule. These were unpopular appeals because the absence in the country of a strong sense of statehood and

---

*W. H. Chamberlin, *The Russian Revolution,* I (New York, 1935), 159. The First Peasants' Congress, attended by over a thousand delegates, had in it twenty Bolsheviks: *VI,* No. 4 (1957), 26.

nationhood encouraged centrifugal tendencies and favored the advancement of special interests at the expense of the whole. The Bolsheviks, for whom Russia was no more than a springboard for a world revolution, had no such concerns. It suited them very well if spontaneous forces "smashed" existing institutions and destroyed Russia. For this reason, they encouraged to the fullest every destructive trend. And since these trends, once unleashed in February, were difficult to restrain in any event, they rode the crest of a swelling wave; by identifying themselves with the inevitable, they gained the appearance of being in control. Later on, when in power, they would in no time renege on all their promises and reconstruct the state in a more centralized, autocratic form than the country had ever known: but until then, their indifference to the fate of Russia proved for the Bolsheviks an immense, perhaps decisive asset.

The rapid disintegration of Russia from lack of firm leadership resulted in the weakening of all national institutions, including those run by the socialists, a process which gave the Bolsheviks an opportunity to outflank the Menshevik and SR leadership in the All-Russian Soviet and the major trade unions. Marc Ferro has noted that after the formation of the coalition government, the authority of the All-Russian Soviet in Petrograd declined while that of the regional soviets rose. A similar process occurred in the labor movement, where the national trade unions lost authority to local "Factory Committees."[80] The regional soviets and Factory Committees were managed by politically inexperienced individuals amenable to Bolshevik manipulation.

The Bolsheviks enjoyed little influence in the major national trade unions, which were dominated by the Mensheviks. But as transport and communications deteriorated, the large national unions, centered in Petrograd or Moscow, lost touch with their members, scattered over the vast country. The workers now tended to shift loyalties from the professional unions to the factories. This process occurred despite the immense growth of the national trade union membership in 1917. The worker organizations which enjoyed the most rapid rise in power and influence were the Factory Committees, or Fabzavkomy. These had come into existence at the beginning of the February Revolution in the state-owned defense plants, after the disappearance of their government-appointed managers. From there, they spread to privately owned enterprises. On March 10, the association of Petrograd industrialists agreed with the Ispolkom to introduce Factory Committees in all the plants in the capital.[81] The following month, the Provisional Government gave them official recognition, authorizing Factory Committees to act as representatives of workers.[82]

Initially, the Fabzavkomy adopted a moderate stance, concentrating on increasing production and arbitrating industrial disputes. Then they radicalized. Unhappy over worsening inflation and shortages of fuel and raw materials which led to plant closures, they charged the employers with speculation, false bookkeeping, and resort to lockouts. Here and there, they chased away the proprietors and managers and attempted to run the factories on their own.

Elsewhere, they demanded a stronger voice in the management. The Mensheviks viewed with disfavor these anarcho-syndicalist institutions and sought to integrate the Factory Committees into the national trade unions. But the trend ran in the opposite direction as the immediate, day-to-day concerns of the workers became increasingly more linked with fellow workers employed under the same roof than with their occupational counterparts elsewhere. The Bolsheviks found the Fabzavkomy an ideal device with which to neutralize Menshevik influence in the trade unions.[83] Although they disapproved of the syndicalist idea of "workers' control" and after seizing power would liquidate this institution, in the spring of 1917 it was in their interest to promote it. They helped form Factory Committees and organized them nationally. At the First Conference of Petrograd Factory Committees, which they convened on May 30, the Bolsheviks controlled at least two-thirds of the delegates. Their motion calling for workers to be given a decisive vote in factory management as well as access to the firms' accounting books passed with an overwhelming majority.[84] The Fabzavkomy were the first institution to fall under Bolshevik control.*

Because he envisaged the power seizure as a violent act, Lenin needed his own military detachments, independent of both the government and the Soviet and accountable only to his Central Committee. "Arming the workers" was central to his program for the coup d'état. During the February Revolution, crowds had looted arsenals: tens of thousands of guns had disappeared, some of them concealed in factories. The Petrograd Soviet organized a "People's Militia" to replace the dissolved tsarist police, but Lenin refused to have the Bolsheviks join it: he wanted a force of his own.[85] So as not to be accused of building up an instrument of subversion, he disguised his private army, initially called "Workers' Militia," as an innocuous guard to protect factories from looters. On April 28, this militia was incorporated into a Bolshevik Red Guard (Krasnaia Gvardiia), which had the additional mission of "defending the Revolution" and "resisting reactionary forces." The Bolsheviks ignored objections of the Soviet to this, their own army.[86] In the end, the Red Guards proved something of a disappointment because they turned either into an ordinary civil police or else merged with the People's Militia, in either case failing to develop that spirit of class militancy that Lenin had expected of them.[87] In October, when needed, they would be conspicuous by their absence.

In preparation for their coup, the Bolsheviks also engaged in propaganda and agitation among the garrison and frontline troops. Responsibility for this work was assigned to the Military Organization which, according to one Communist source, had agents and cells in three-fourths of the garrison units.[88] From them, it obtained information on the mood of the troops, and through them it carried out anti-government and anti-war propaganda. The Bolsheviks won very few adherents among the men in uniform, but they were

---

*The rivalry between trade unions and Factory Committees would recur twenty years later in the United States when plant-based unions, affiliated with the CIO, challenged the craft-oriented unions of the AFL. Here, as in Russia, the Communists favored the former.

successful in fanning the troops' discontent, which had the effect of making the soldiers less likely to obey calls of the government or the Soviet to move against them. According to Sukhanov, although even the most disgruntled garrison soldiers did not favor the Bolsheviks, their mood was one of "neutrality" and "indifference," which made them receptive to anti-government appeals. In this category was the garrison's largest unit, the First Machine Gun Regiment.[89]

The Bolsheviks influenced minds mainly by means of the printed word. By June, *Pravda* had a run of 85,000 copies. They also put out provincial papers, papers addressed to special groups (e.g., female workers and ethnic minorities), and a multitude of pamphlets. They paid particular attention to the men in uniform. On April 15, they brought out a soldiers' newspaper, *Soldatskaia Pravda,* which attained a printing of 50,000–75,000 copies. They followed it with a paper for sailors, *Golos Pravdy,* and another one for frontline troops, *Okopnaia Pravda,* printed in Kronshtadt and Riga, respectively. In the spring of 1917, they distributed to the troops about 100,000 papers a day, which, given that Russia had 12 million men under arms, was enough to supply one Bolshevik daily per company. In early July, the combined printing of the Bolshevik press was 320,000 copies. In addition, *Soldatskaia Pravda* printed 350,000 pamphlets and broadsheets.[90] This was a most remarkable achievement, considering that in February 1917 the Bolsheviks had had no press.

These publications spread Lenin's message, but in a veiled form. The method employed was "propaganda" which did not tell readers what to do (that was the task of "agitation") but planted in their minds ideas from which they would themselves draw the desired political conclusions. In appeals to the troops, for example, Bolshevik publications did not incite to desertion, since this would have made them liable to prosecution. In the first issue of *Soldatskaia Pravda,* Zinoviev wrote that the paper's objective was forging an indestructible bond between workers and soldiers so that the troops would come to understand their "true" interests and not allow themselves to be used for "pogroms" against the workers. On the issue of the war, he was equally circumspect:

> We *do not* favor *dropping guns* now. This is no way to end the war. Now the main task is to understand and explain to all soldiers for what purpose this war was begun, *who* began the war, who needs the war.[91]

The "who," of course, was the "bourgeoisie" against whom the soldiers were to turn their guns.

Such organizational and publishing activities required a great deal of money. Much, if not most, of it came from Germany.

German subversive activities in Russia in the spring and summer of 1917 have left few traces in the documents.* Reliable people in Berlin, using reliable

*A set of documents, purporting to demonstrate direct German involvement in Russian events, 1914–1917, and known as the "Sisson Papers," had surfaced in early 1918. They were published

intermediaries, delivered cash to Bolshevik agents by way of neutral Sweden, without written requests or receipts passing hands. Although the opening of the German Foreign Office archives after World War II has made it possible to establish with certainty the fact of German subsidies to the Bolsheviks and with some approximation the sums involved, the exact uses to which the Bolsheviks put the German money remains obscure. According to Minister of Foreign Affairs Richard von Kühlmann, the chief architect of Germany's pro-Bolshevik policy in 1917–18, the Bolsheviks used the German subsidies mainly for purposes of party organization and propaganda. On December 3, 1917 (NS), in a confidential report, Kühlmann thus summarized Germany's contribution to the Bolshevik cause:

> The disruption of the Entente and the subsequent creation of political combinations agreeable to us constitute the most important war aim of our diplomacy. Russia appeared to be the weakest link in the enemy chain. The task therefore was gradually to loosen it, and, when possible, to remove it. This was the purpose of the subversive activity we caused to be carried out in Russia behind the front—in the first place promotion of separatist tendencies and support of the Bolsheviks. It was not until the Bolsheviks had received from us a steady flow of funds through various channels and under different labels that they were able to build up their main organ, *Pravda*, to conduct energetic propaganda and appreciably to extend the originally narrow basis of their party.[92]

The total money assigned by the Germans to the Bolsheviks in 1917–18—to help them first take power and then to keep it—has been estimated by Eduard Bernstein, who had good connections in the German Government, at "more than 50 million deutsche marks in gold" ($6 to $10 million, which at that time would have bought nine or more tons of gold).[93]*

Some of these funds the Germans channeled to Bolshevik agents in Stockholm, the principal of whom was Jacob Fürstenberg-Ganetskii. Responsibility for maintaining contact with the Bolsheviks was assigned to the Russian expert at the German Embassy in Stockholm, Kurt Riezler. According to the counterintelligence service of the Provisional Government, directed by Colonel B. Nikitin, the Germans deposited the money for Lenin at the Diskontogesellschaft in Berlin, which forwarded it to the Nye Bank in Stockholm. Ganetskii

---

in the United States by the Committee on Public Information, War Information Series, No. 20 (October 1918), *The German-Bolshevik Conspiracy*. The German Government had at once proclaimed them a complete forgery (Z. A. B. Zeman, *Germany and the Revolution in Russia, 1915–1918*, London, 1958, p. X.) See further George Kennan in *The Journal of Modern History*, XXVIII, No. 2, June 1956, 130–54. Their effect has been to discredit for many years the very notion of German financial and political support of Lenin's party.

*Bernstein's figure was confirmed by postwar researches in German Foreign Ministry Archives. Documents found there indicate that until January 31, 1918, the German government had allocated for "propaganda" in Russia 40 million deutsche marks. This sum was exhausted by June 1918, following which (July 1918) an additional 40 million marks were assigned for this purpose, although apparently only 10 million were spent, not all of them on the Bolsheviks. A German mark at the time bought four-fifths of a tsarist ruble and approximately two post-1917 rubles (so-called "Kerenki"). Winfried Baumgart, *Deutsche Ostpolitik, 1918* (Vienna-Munich, 1966) 213–14, Note 19.

would make withdrawals from the Nye Bank, ostensibly for business purposes, but in fact for deposit at the Siberian Bank in Petrograd on the account of a relative of his, one Eugenia Sumenson, a lady of the Petrograd demimonde. Sumenson and one of Lenin's lieutenants, the Pole M. Iu. Kozlovskii, operated in Petrograd a spurious pharmaceutical business as cover for financial dealings with Ganetskii. The transfer of German funds to Lenin could thus be disguised as legitimate business.[94] After her arrest in July 1917, Sumenson confessed to having turned over the moneys which she withdrew from the Siberian Bank to Kozlovskii, a member of the Bolshevik Central Committee.[95] She admitted to having taken out of her bank account for this purpose 750,000 rubles.[96] Sumenson and Kozlovskii maintained with Stockholm a coded business correspondence, some of which the government intercepted with the help of French intelligence. The following telegram is an example:

> Stockholm from Petrograd Fürstenberg Grand Hotel Stockholm. Nestles sends no flour. Request. Sumenson. Nadezhdinskaia 36.[97]

The Germans also used other means of subsidizing the Bolsheviks, one of which consisted of smuggling into Russia counterfeit ten-ruble bank notes. Quantities of such forged money were found on pro-Bolshevik soldiers and sailors arrested in the aftermath of the July putsch.[98]

Lenin kept very much in the background in these transactions, entrusting financial dealings with the Germans to his lieutenants. Still, in a letter to Ganetskii and Radek of April 12, he complained he was receiving no money. On April 21 he acknowledged to Ganetskii that Kozlovskii had given him 2,000 rubles.[99] According to Nikitin, Lenin corresponded directly with Parvus badgering him for "more materials."* Three of these communications were intercepted on the Finnish border.[100]

Kerensky tackled his responsibilities as Minister of War with admirable energy, for he was convinced that the survival of democracy in Russia depended on a strong and disciplined army and that the army's flagging spirits would be best uplifted by a successful offensive. The generals thought that if the army remained inactive much longer it would fall apart.[101] He hoped to repeat the miracle of the French army in 1792, which stopped and then threw back the invading Prussians, rallying the nation to the revolutionary government. A major offensive was projected for June 12, in fulfillment of obligations to the Allies undertaken before the February Revolution. It had been origi-

---

*B. Nikitin, *Rokovye gody* (Paris, 1937), 109–10. According to the author (107–8), Kollontai also served as an intermediary delivering German money to Lenin. Despite overwhelming evidence of German subsidies to Lenin from German sources, some scholars still find the notion unacceptable. Among them is as well-informed a specialist as Boris Souvarine: see his article in *Est & Ouest*, No. 641 (June 1980), 1–5.

nally designed as a purely military operation, but it now acquired an added political dimension. A successful offensive was expected to enhance the government's prestige and reinfuse the population with patriotism, which would make it easier to deal with challengers from the right and the left. Tereshchenko told the French that if the offensive went well, measures would be taken to suppress mutinous elements in the Petrograd garrison.[102]

In preparation for the offensive Kerensky carried out reforms in the army. Alekseev, probably the best strategist in Russia, impressed him as a defeatist, and he replaced him with Brusilov, the hero of the 1916 campaign.* He tightened military discipline, giving officers wide discretion to deal with insubordinate troops. Emulating the *commissaires aux armées* which the French army introduced in 1792, he sent commissars to the front to raise the soldiers' morale and to arbitrate between them and the officers: it was an innovation of which the Bolsheviks would make extensive use in the Red Army. Kerensky spent most of May and early June at the front, delivering stirring patriotic speeches. His appearances had a galvanizing effect:

> "Triumphal progress" seems a weak term to describe Kerensky's tour of the front. In the violence of the agitation by which it was accompanied it resembled the passage of a cyclone. Crowds gathered for hours to catch a glimpse of him. His path was everywhere strewn with flowers. Soldiers ran for miles after his motor car, trying to shake his hand or kiss the hem of his garment. At his meetings in the great halls of Moscow the audiences worked themselves up into paroxysms of enthusiasm and adoration. The platforms from which he had spoken were littered with watches, rings, bracelets, military medals, and bank notes, sacrificed by admirers for the common cause.[103]

An eyewitness who compared Kerensky to "a volcano hurling forth sheaves of all-consuming fire," wrote that for Kerensky

> all impediments between himself and the audience are intolerable. . . . He wants to be all before you, from head to foot, so that the only thing between you and him is the air, completely impregnated by his and your mutual radiations of invisible but mighty currents. For that reason he will hear nothing of rostra, pulpits, tables. He leaves the rostrum, jumps on the table; and when he stretches out his hands to you—nervous, supple, fiery, all quivering with the enthusiasm of prayer which seizes him—you feel that he touches you, grasps you with those hands, and irresistibly draws you to himself.[104]

The impact of these speeches, however, evaporated as soon as Kerensky left the scene: professional officers dubbed him "Persuader in Chief." As he afterward recalled, he found the mood of the frontline troops on the eve of the June offensive ambivalent. German and Bolshevik propaganda had as yet had

---

*In his memoirs Brusilov claims to have known even as he assumed supreme command that Russian troops had no fighting spirit left in them and that the offensive would fail: A. B. Brusilov, *Moi vospominaniia* (Moscow-Leningrad, 1929), 216.

51. Kerensky addressing frontline troops: Summer 1917.

little influence: its effect was confined to garrison units and the so-called Third Divisions, which were reserve units made up of fresh inductees. But he encountered a widespread sense that the Revolution had made it pointless to fight. "After three years of bitter suffering," he writes, "millions of war-weary soldiers were asking themselves: 'Why should I die now when at home a new, freer life is only beginning?' "[105] They received no answer from the Soviet, the institution they trusted the most, because its socialist majority adopted a characteristically ambivalent attitude:

> If one looks through any typical resolution passed by the [Soviet's] Menshevik and Socialist-Revolutionary majority one finds an utterly negative characterization of the war as imperialistic, a demand that it be stopped as quickly as possible and an unobtrusive phrase or two, inserted at Kerensky's urgent demand, suggesting, with dubious logic and no emotional appeal whatever, that, pending a general peace, it would be a good thing if the Russian soldiers would continue to fight.[106]

The Bolsheviks, as aware as the government of the disaffection and demoralization of the garrison units, decided early in June to exploit this mood. On June 1, the Military Organization voted to hold an armed demonstration. Since this unit took orders from the Central Committee, it can be taken for granted that the decision was adopted with the latter's approval and probably on its initiative. On June 6, the Central Committee discussed bringing into the streets 40,000 armed soldiers and Red Guards to march under banners condemning Kerensky and the coalition government and then, at the appropriate moment, "go on the offensive."[107] What this meant we know from Sukhanov, who learned of the Bolshevik plans from Nevskii, the chairman of the Military Organization:

The target of the "manifestation," set for June 10, was to be the Mariinskii Palace, the seat of the Provisional Government. This was to be the destination of the worker detachments and regiments loyal to the Bolsheviks. Specially designated persons were to demand that members of the cabinet come out of the palace and answer questions. As the ministers spoke, specially designated groups were to voice "popular dissatisfaction" and excite the mood of the masses. Once the temperature had reached the appropriate level, the Provisional Government was to have been arrested on the spot. Of course, the capital was expected to react immediately. And depending on the nature of this reaction, the Bolshevik Central Committee, under one name or another, was to proclaim itself the government. If, in the course of the "manifestation," the atmosphere for all this would prove sufficiently favorable, and the resistance shown by Lvov and Tsereteli weak, resistance was to have been overcome by the force of Bolshevik regiments and weapons.*

One slogan of the demonstrators was to have been "All Power to the Soviets," but inasmuch as the Soviet refused to proclaim itself a government and indeed prohibited armed demonstrations, this slogan, as Sukhanov reasonably concludes, could have only meant that power was meant to pass into the hands of the Bolshevik Central Committee.[108] Since the demonstration was timed to coincide with the First All-Russian Congress of Soviets (scheduled to open on June 3), the Bolsheviks may have planned to confront the congress with a fait accompli and either compel it, against its will, to take power or claim power in its name. Lenin actually made no secret of his intentions. When, at the congress, Tsereteli stated that there was no party in Russia willing to assume power, Lenin shouted from his seat: "There is!" The episode became legend in Communist hagiography.

On June 6, four days before the projected Bolshevik demonstration, the Bolshevik high command met to make final preparations. The proceedings of this conference are known to us only from truncated minutes, in which the most important entry, Lenin's remarks, have been severely cut.[109] The idea of a putsch ran into stiff resistance. Kamenev, who had criticized Lenin's "adventurism" in April, again took the lead. The operation, he said, was certain to fail: the issue of the soviets assuming power was best left to the Congress. V. P. Nogin, from the Moscow branch of the Central Committee, was still more outspoken: "Lenin proposes a revolution," he said. "Can we do it? We are a minority in the country. One cannot prepare an offensive in two days." Zinoviev also joined the opposition, arguing that the projected action placed the party at great risk. Stalin, E. D. Stasova, the secretary of the Central Committee, and Nevskii vigorously supported Lenin's proposal. Lenin's arguments are not known, but judging from Nogin's remarks it is obvious what he wanted.

*N. Sukhanov, *Zapiski o revoliutsii*, IV (Berlin, 1922), 319. Sukhanov did not provide the source of this information, but Boris Nikolaevskii, the Menshevik historian, deduced that it had to come from Nevskii: *SV*, No. 9–10 (1962), 135n. Tsereteli notes that although in 1922, when Sukhanov published his memoirs, all the principals were still alive and could have denied his account, none of them did so: I. G. Tsereteli, *Vospominaniia o Fevral'skoi Revoliutsii*, II (Paris-The Hague, 1963), 185.

The Petrograd Soviet and the Congress of Soviets, on behalf of which the demonstration was to take place, were kept completely in the dark.

On June 9, Bolshevik agitators appeared in the barracks and factories and informed the soldiers and workers of the demonstration scheduled for next day. The organ of the Military Organization, *Soldatskaia Pravda,* issued detailed instructions to the demonstrators. Its editorial ended with the words: "War to a victorious conclusion against the capitalists!"[110]

The congress, which was in session at this time, was so spellbound by its rhetoric that it did not even know of the Bolsheviks' preparations until almost too late. It first learned what the Bolsheviks were up to in the afternoon of June 9 from Bolshevik posters. All the parties present—the Bolsheviks, of course, excepted—voted immediately to order a cancellation of the demonstration, and sent out agitators to workers' quarters and barracks to spread the message. The Bolsheviks met later that day to deal with new developments. Following discussions, of which no published record exists, they decided to bow to the will of the congress and cancel their demonstration. They further agreed to participate in a peaceful (i.e., unarmed) manifestation scheduled by the Soviet for June 18. Apparently the Bolshevik high command felt it inopportune as yet to challenge the soviets head on.

A Bolshevik coup had been averted, but the Soviet gained a victory of dubious value because it lacked the moral courage to draw from this incident the proper conclusions. On June 11, some 100 socialist intellectuals representing all the parties in the Soviet, the Bolsheviks included, met to discuss the events of the preceding two days. The Menshevik spokesman, Theodore Dan, criticized the Bolsheviks and moved that no party be allowed to hold demonstrations without the Soviet's approval and that armed units be brought out only in demonstrations sponsored by the Soviet. The penalty for violating these rules would be expulsion. Lenin chose to absent himself, and the Bolshevik case was defended by Trotsky, who had recently arrived in Russia and though not, as yet, formally a member, had drawn very close to the Bolshevik party. In the midst of the discussion, Tsereteli asked for the floor to oppose Dan's motion which he thought too timid. Pale, his voice quivering from excitement, he shouted:

> That which has happened . . . was nothing but *a conspiracy—a conspiracy to overthrow the government* and have the Bolsheviks *take power,* power which they know they will never obtain in any other way. The conspiracy was rendered harmless as soon as we discovered it. But it can recur tomorrow. It is said that the counterrevolution has raised its head. This is untrue. The counterrevolution has not raised its head; it has lowered its head. The counterrevolution can penetrate only by one door: the Bolsheviks. What the Bolsheviks are doing now is not propaganda of ideas but conspiracy. The weapon of criticism is replaced by the criticism of weapons. May the Bolsheviks forgive us, but we shall now adopt different methods of struggle. Revolutionaries unworthy of holding weapons must be deprived of them. The Bolsheviks must be disarmed. One must not leave in their hands those excessive technical means which they

have had at their disposal until now. We must not leave them machine guns and weapons. We shall not tolerate conspiracies . . .*

Tsereteli received some support but the majority was against him. What proof had he of a Bolshevik conspiracy? Why disarm the Bolsheviks who represented a genuine mass movement? Did he really want to render the "proletariat" defenseless?[111] Martov denounced Tsereteli with particular vehemence. The next day, the socialists voted in favor of Dan's milder motion, which meant that they refused to disarm the Bolsheviks and dismantle their subversive apparatus. It was a critical failure of nerve. Lenin had directly challenged the Soviet, and the Soviet averted its eyes. The majority preferred to make believe that the Bolsheviks were a genuine socialist party using questionable tactics rather than, as Tsereteli argued, a counterrevolutionary party bent on seizing power. The socialists thus lost the opportunity to delegitimize the Bolsheviks, to deprive them of a powerful political weapon, the claim that they acted on behalf and in the interest of the soviets against alleged enemies.

This cravenness was not lost on the Bolsheviks. The day after the defeat of Tsereteli's motion, *Pravda* put the Soviet on notice that the Bolsheviks had no intention, now or in the future, of submitting to its orders:

> We find it imperative to declare that, in having joined the Soviet and struggling to have it assume full power, we did not renounce for an instant for the benefit of the Soviet, which is in principle hostile to us, the right, separately and independently, to take advantage of all the freedoms to mobilize the working masses under the banner of our proletarian class party. We also categorically refuse henceforth to submit to such anti-democratic restrictions. *Even if state authority were to pass entirely into the hands of the Soviet*—and this we favor—and the Soviet would try to place fetters on our agitation, *we would not submit passively,* but risk prison and other punishments in the name of the idea of international socialism . . .[112]

This was a declaration of war on the Soviet, an assertion of the right to act in defiance of it if and when the Soviet became the government.

On June 16, the Russian army, generously supplied with guns and shells by the Allies, opened a two-day artillery barrage, following which it charged. The brunt of the Russian assault fell on the Southern Front and aimed at Lwow, the capital of Galicia. The Eighth Army, commanded by Kornilov, distinguished itself. Secondary offensive operations were launched on the Central and Northern Fronts. As the government had hoped, the offensive inspired

---

*Pravda, No. 80 (June 13, 1917), 2. This was a closed meeting and no other accounts exist. Tsereteli, however, affirms that the above citation from *Pravda* correctly renders his speech, with some minor, though not insignificant omissions: Tsereteli, *Vospominaniia*, II, 229–30.

52. Russian soldiers fleeing Germans: July 1917.

patriotic manifestations. In this atmosphere, the Bolsheviks did not dare to oppose the campaign: at the Congress of Soviets in June, neither Lenin nor Trotsky opposed motions in its support.[113]

The Russian operation against the Austrians made good progress for two days, and then it ground to a halt as the troops, feeling they had done their duty, refused to obey orders to attack. They were soon in headlong flight. On July 6, the Germans, having once again come to the assistance of their hard-pressed Austrian allies, counterattacked. At the sight of German uniforms, the Russians took to their heels, looting and spreading panic. The June offensive was the dying gasp of the old Russian army.

Since the old Russian army engaged in no significant operations after July 1917, this may be an appropriate place to tally the human casualties Russia suffered in World War I. It is difficult to determine these losses with reasonable accuracy because of the poor quality of Russian war statistics. In standard sources, Russian casualties are given as the highest of any belligerent power: Cruttwell, for instance, estimates 1.7 million Russian dead and 4.95 million wounded, which would slightly exceed the losses suffered by Germany and considerably those suffered by Britain and France, which had stayed in the war sixteen months longer than Russia. Other foreign estimates go as high as 2.5 million dead.[114] These figures have been shown to be highly inflated. Official Russian sources speak of 775,400 battlefield fatalities. More recent Russian estimates indicate somewhat higher losses: 900,000 battlefield deaths and 400,000 from combat wounds, for a total of 1.3 million, which is equal to the fatalities suffered by the French and the Austrians but one-third less than the Germans.[115]

The Russians had far and away the largest number of war prisoners in enemy hands. The 3.9 million Russian captives in German and Austrian POW camps exceeded threefold the total number of prisoners of war (1.3 million) lost by the armies of Britain, France, and Germany combined.[116] Only the Austro-Hungarian army, with 2.2 million prisoners, came close. For every 100 Russians who fell in battle, 300 surrendered. In the British army, the comparable figure was 20, in the French, 24, and in the German, 26.[117] In other words, Russians surrendered at a rate twelve to fifteen times that of Western soldiers.

The failure of the June offensive was a personal calamity for Kerensky, who had counted on it to rally the divided country around him and the government. Having gambled and lost, he grew distraught, irascible, and excedingly suspicious. In this mood he committed cardinal mistakes that turned him from an adored leader into a scapegoat, despised by the left and right alike.

In the atmosphere of demoralization and despair brought about by the failure of the June offensive, Lenin and his lieutenants ventured on yet another putsch.

No event in the Russian Revolution has been more willfully lied about than the July 1917 insurrection, the reason being that it was Lenin's worst blunder, a misjudgment that nearly caused the destruction of the Bolshevik Party: the equivalent of Hitler's 1923 beer-hall putsch. To absolve themselves of responsibility, the Bolsheviks have gone to unusual lengths to misrepresent the July putsch as a spontaneous demonstration which they sought to direct into peaceful channels.

The July 3–5 action was precipitated by the government's decision to dispatch units of the Petrograd garrision to the front for the anticipated enemy counteroffensive. Inspired primarily by military considerations, this decision was also meant to rid the capital of the units most contaminated by Bolshevik propaganda. To the Bolsheviks this move spelled disaster since it threatened to deprive them of the forces which they intended to use in their next bid for power.[118] They responded with a furious propaganda campaign among the garrison troops, attacking the "bourgeois" government, protesting the "imperialist" war, and urging them to refuse to go to the front. No country with a tradition of democracy would have tolerated such incitement to mutiny in time of war.

The Bolsheviks had their main base of support in the 1st Machine Gun Regiment, the largest unit of the garrison, with 11,340 men and nearly 300 officers, among the latter numerous left-wing intellectuals. Many of the men were misfits expelled from their original units for incompetence or insubordination.[119] Billeted in the Vyborg District, close to the radicalized factories, it was a seething mass. The Bolshevik Military Organization had here a cell of some thirty members, including junior officers, whom it provided with regular training in agitational techniques.[120] Bolsheviks as well as anarchists frequently addressed the regiment.

On June 20, the regiment received orders to dispatch to the front 500 machine guns with crews. The next day the troops held a meeting, at which they adopted a resolution—judging by its content, of Bolshevik origin—that they would go to the front only to fight a "revolutionary war"—that is, in defense of a government from which the "capitalists" had been removed and the Soviet had all the power. If, the resolution went on, the Provisional Government attempted to disband it, the regiment would resist.[121] Emissaries were dispatched to other units of the garrison in quest of support.

The Bolsheviks, who played a major role in this mutiny, feared precipitous action likely to provoke a patriotic backlash. They had many enemies, ready to pounce on them at the slightest provocation: according to Shliapnikov, "our supporters could not appear alone on Nevsky without putting their lives at risk."[122] Their tactics, therefore, had to combine boldness with prudence: they agitated vigorously among the troops and workers to maintain a high level of tension, but opposed impulsive actions which could get out of hand and end in an anti-Bolshevik pogrom. On June 22, *Soldatskaia Pravda* appealed to soldiers and workers to refrain from demonstrating without explicit instructions from the party:

> The Military Organization is not calling for public appearances. Should the need arise, the Military Organization will call for a public appearance in agreement with the leading institutions of the party—the Central Committee and the Petrograd Committee.[123]

The Soviet went unmentioned. Such calls for restraint, subsequently cited by Communist historians as evidence that the Bolshevik Party bore no responsibility for the July riots, prove nothing of the kind: they merely show that the party wanted to keep tight control of events.

The first wave of discontent in the regiment was contained when the Bolsheviks dissuaded it from demonstrating and the Soviet refused to endorse its resolution. Resigned, the regiment dispatched 500 machine guns to the front.[124]

At this time, the government, jointly with the Soviet, also quelled incipient violence at Kronshtadt. The garrison at this naval base near Petrograd was under strong anarchist influence but its political organization was in the hands of the Bolsheviks headed by F. F. Raskolnikov and S. G. Roshal.[125] The sailors had their grievance, namely the government's forceful ejection of anarchists from the villa of ex-Minister Peter Durnovo, which they had seized after the February Revolution and made into headquarters. The anarchists at the villa behaved in so disorderly a fashion that on June 19 troops were sent to retake it and arrest the squatters.[126] Incited by the anarchists, the sailors threatened on June 23 to march on Petrograd to free the prisoners. They, too, were restrained by the joint efforts of the Soviet and the Bolsheviks.

But even as they were restrained, the Machine Gunners were subjected to a steady barrage of inflammatory propaganda. The Bolsheviks called for the transfer of all power to the Soviet, to be followed by reelections to the Soviet which would leave it exclusively in Bolshevik hands; this, they promised, would immediately bring peace. They also demanded the "annihilation" of the "bourgeoisie." The anarchists incited the troops to "pogroms on the Miliukov streets—Nevsky and Liteinyi."[127]

According to V. D. Bonch-Bruevich, in the evening of June 29 an unexpected visitor appeared at his dacha in Neivola near the Finnish city of Vyborg, a short ride by commuter train from Petrograd. It was Lenin. Having traveled in a roundabout way—"from conspiratorial habit"—he explained that he was extremely exhausted and needed rest.[128] It was most unusual behavior, quite out of character for Lenin. He was not in the habit of taking vacations in the midst of important political events even when he had better cause to feel exhausted, as in the winter of 1917–18. In this case, the explanation is doubly suspect because in two days the Bolsheviks were to open a conference of their Petrograd organizations which it is hard to conceive Lenin would have wanted to miss. His "conspiratorial" behavior is also puzzling, since he had no ostensible need to conceal his movements. The reason for his sudden disappearance from Petrograd, therefore, must be sought elsewhere: it is virtually certain that he had gotten wind that the government, having obtained enough evidence of his financial dealings with the Germans, was about to arrest him.

On June 21, Captain Pierre Laurent of French intelligence turned over to Russian counterintelligence fourteen intercepted communications between the Bolsheviks in Petrograd and their people in Stockholm indicative of dealings with the enemy; soon he produced fifteen more.[129] The government claimed later that it had delayed arresting the Bolsheviks because it wanted to catch Lenin's principal Stockholm agent, Ganetskii, on his next trip to Russia with incriminating documents.[130] But in view of Kerensky's behavior after the putsch, there are grounds for suspicion that behind the government's procrastination lay fear of antagonizing the Soviet.

At the end of June, however, the authorities had enough evidence to proceed and on July 1 ordered the arrest of twenty-eight leading Bolsheviks within the week.[131]

Someone in the government alerted Lenin to this danger. The most likely suspect is the same Procurator of the Petrograd Judiciary Chamber (Sudebnaia Palata), N. S. Karinskii, who, according to Bonch-Bruevich, on July 4 would leak to the Bolsheviks that the ministry was about to make public information incriminating Lenin as a German agent.[132] Lenin may also have been alerted by indications that on June 29 intelligence agents began shadowing Sumenson.[133] Nothing else explains Lenin's sudden disappearance from Petrograd and his furtive escape to Finland, where he was out of reach of the Russian police.*

---

*Lenin was aware as early as mid-May that the government intercepted his communications with Stockholm. On May 16 in the pages of *Pravda* he taunted the "servants of the Kadets" who, although "lording it over the Russo-Swedish frontier," failed to catch all the letters and telegrams: Lenin, *PSS*, XXXII, 103–4. Cf. Zinoviev in *PR*, No. 8–9 (1927), 57.

Lenin hid in Finland from June 29 until the early-morning hours of July 4, when the Bolshevik putsch got underway. His role in the preparations for the July escapade cannot be established. But physical absence from the scene of action need not mean he was uninvolved: in the fall of 1917, Lenin would also hide out in Finland and still take an active part in the decisions leading to the October coup.

The July operation began in the Machine Gun Regiment when it learned that the government was about to disband it and disperse its men to the front.* On June 30, the Soviet invited regimental representatives to discuss their problems with the military authorities. The following day, regimental "activists" held their own meetings. The mood of the men, tense for some time, reached a feverish pitch.

On July 2, the Bolsheviks organized for the regiment a concert meeting at the People's House (Narodnyi Dom).[134] All outside speakers were Bolsheviks, among them Trotsky and Lunacharskii: Zinoviev and Kamenev were also scheduled to appear, but failed to show up, possibly because, like Lenin, they feared arrest.[135] Addressing an audience of over 5,000 men, Trotsky berated the government for the June offensive and demanded the transfer of power to the Soviet. He did not tell the troops in so many words to refuse to obey the government, but the Military Organization had the meeting pass a resolution in this spirit: it accused Kerensky of following in the footsteps of "Nicholas the Bloody" and demanded all power to the soviets.[136]

The troops returned to the barracks too excited to sleep. They held an all-night discussion in the course of which voices were raised demanding violent action: one of the slogans proposed was "Beat the *burzhui.*"[137]

A pogrom was in the making. The Bolsheviks, gathered at Kshesinskaia's, were uncertain how to react: join or try to abort it. Some argued that since the troops could not be held back, the Bolsheviks should take charge; others thought it was too soon to move.[138] Then, as later, the Bolsheviks were torn between the desire to ride to power on the wave of popular fury and the fear that spontaneous violence would provoke a nationalist reaction of which they would be the principal victims.

The company and regimental committees of the Machine Gun Regiment held further meetings on July 3: the atmosphere was that of a village assembly on the eve of a peasant rebellion. The main speakers were anarchists, the most prominent among them I. S. Bleikhman, "his shirt open on his breast and curly hair flying on all sides,"[139] who called on the troops to take to the streets, weapons in hand, and stage an armed uprising. The anarchists did not spell out the objective of such action: that "the street itself will show."[140] The Bolshevik agitators who followed the anarchists did not take issue with them; they only urged that before acting the regiment seek instructions from the Bolshevik Military Organization.

*The best account of the role of the regiment in July, based on archival documents, is by P. M. Stulov in *KL,* No. 3/36 (1930), 64–125. Cf. Leon Trotsky, *The History of the Russian Revolution,* II (New York, 1937), 17.

But the troops, determined to avoid front-line duty and whipped into frenzy by the anarchists, would not wait: by a unanimous vote they decided to take to the streets, fully armed. A Provisional Revolutionary Committee was elected to organize the demonstration, under the chairmanship of a Bolshevik, Lieutenant A. Ia. Semashko. This happened between 2:00 and 3:00 p.m.

Semashko and his associates, several of whom belonged to the Military Organization, sent out patrols to learn whether the government was taking countermeasures and to confiscate automobiles. They also dispatched emissaries to factories and barracks and to Kronshtadt.

The emissaries met with a mixed reception. A few units of the garrison agreed to join: mainly elements of the 1st, 3rd, 176th, and 180th Infantry Regiments.[141] The others refused. The Preobrazhenskii, Semenovskii, and Izmailovskii Guard Regiments declared "neutrality."[142] In the Machine Gun Regiment itself, despite threats of physical violence, many companies voted to stay on the sidelines: in the end only one-half of the regiment, some 5,000 men, participated in the putsch. Many factory workers also refused to take part.

For lack of adequate documentation, it is difficult to determine the attitude of the Bolsheviks toward these developments. In his report to the Sixth Congress of the Bolshevik Party later that month, Stalin claimed that at 4:00 p.m. on July 3 the Central Committee took a stand against an armed demonstration.[143] Trotsky confirms Stalin's claim.[144] It is not inconceivable that the Bolshevik leaders, without Lenin to encourage them and afraid that a mutiny under their slogans but without their guidance could end in disaster, initially opposed it, but one would feel more confident of this judgment if the protocols of the Central Committee for that day were made available.

As soon as it learned of the proposed demonstration the Ispolkom appealed to the troops to desist:[145] it had no desire to bring down the government and to assume the power that the Bolsheviks were so insistently thrusting into its hands.

That afternoon there appeared before the Executive Committee of the Kronshtadt Soviet two anarchist deputies from the Machine Gun Regiment, wild in appearance and seemingly illiterate.[146] They let it be known that their regiment, along with other military units and factory workers, was taking to the streets to demand the transfer of power to the Soviet. They needed armed support. The chairman of the Executive Committee responded that the sailors would take part in no demonstration which the Petrograd Ispolkom had not authorized. In that event, the emissaries said, they would appeal directly to the sailors. Word went out and 8,000 to 10,000 sailors assembled to hear a hysterical speech about the government's persecution of anarchists.[147] The sailors prepared to embark for Petrograd: it was unclear to what purpose, but beating up the *burzhui,* with some looting on the side, could not have been far from their minds. Roshal and Raskolnikov managed to restrain them long enough to call Bolshevik headquarters for instructions. After communicating with headquarters, Raskolnikov told the sailors the Bolshevik Party had decided to take part in the armed demonstration, whereupon the assembled sailors voted unanimously to join in.*

Delegates from the Machine Gunners appeared also before the workers of Putilov, many of whom they won over to their cause.[148]

Around 7 p.m. those units of the Machine Gun Regiment that had voted in favor of a demonstration assembled in their barracks. Advance elements, riding in confiscated automobiles with mounted machine guns, were already dispersed in the central parts of Petrograd. At 8 p.m. the soldiers marched to Troitskii Bridge, where mutinous troops from other regiments joined them. At 10 p.m. the mutineers crossed the bridge. Nabokov observed them at this instant: "They had the same dull, vacant, brutal faces that we all remembered from the February days."[149] Having made their way across the river, the troops divided into two columns, one of which went to Taurida, the other to Mariinskii, the seats of the Soviet and the government, respectively. There was some desultory shooting, mostly in the air, and a bit of looting.

The Bolshevik high command—Zinoviev, Kamenev, and Trotsky—appears to have decided on involving the party in these riots around midday on July 3—that is, as the troops of the Machine Gun Regiment were adopting resolutions to demonstrate. At the time, the three were in Taurida. Their plan was to take control of the Workers' Section of the Soviet, proclaim in its name the passage of power to the Soviet, and present the Ispolkom as well as the Soldiers' Section and the Plenum with an accomplished fact. The pretext was to have been the irresistible pressure of the masses.[150]

To this end, the Bolsheviks engineered later in the day a mini-putsch in the Workers' Section. Here, as in the Soldiers' Section, they were in a minority. The Bolshevik faction requested the Ispolkom on very short notice to convene an extraordinary session of the Workers' Section for 3 p.m. This allowed no time to contact all the SR and Menshevik members of the section: the Bolsheviks, however, made certain that their members turned up in a body, which assured them of a momentary majority. Zinoviev opened the meeting with a demand that the Soviet assume full governmental power. The Menshevik and SR deputies on hand opposed him and asked the Bolsheviks instead to help stop the Machine Gun Regiment. When the Bolsheviks refused, the Mensheviks and SRs walked out, leaving their rivals in full control. They elected a Bureau of the Workers' Section, which duly passed a resolution presented by Kamenev, the opening sentence of which read:

> In view of the crisis of authority, the Workers' Section deems it necessary to insist that the All-Russian Congress of Soviets of Workers', Soldiers', and Peasants' Deputies take power in its hands.[151]

---

*Raskolnikov in *PR*, No. 5/17 (1923), 60. Roshal was shot in December 1917 by anti-Communists. Raskolnikov, a party member since 1910 and in 1917 deputy chairman of the Kronshtadt Soviet, in the 1920s and 1930s held various Soviet diplomatic posts abroad. Recalled to Moscow in 1939, he refused to return and assailed Stalin in an open letter, following which he was declared "an enemy of the people." He died later that year in southern France under highly suspicious circumstances.

Of course, no such "All-Russian Congress" existed, even on paper. The message was clear: the Provisional Government was to be overthrown.

This accomplished, the Bolsheviks departed for Kshesinskaia's for a meeting of the Central Committee. At 10 p.m., as the meeting was about to start, a column of the mutinous troops drew near. According to Communist sources, Nevskii and Podvoiskii, speaking from the balcony, urged them to return to their barracks, for which they were booed.* The Bolsheviks were still wavering. They were itching to move, but they worried about the reaction to a coup of front-line troops, among whom, despite vigorous propaganda, they had managed to win over only a few regiments, most notably the Latvian Rifles. The bulk of the combat forces remained loyal to the Provisional Government. Even the mood of the Petrograd garrison was far from certain.[152] Still, the intensity of the disorders and the news that thousands of Putilov workers, accompanied by wives and children, were gathering in front of Taurida overcame their hesitations. At 11:40 p.m., by which time the rioting troops had returned to their barracks and calm had been restored to the city, the Central Committee adopted a resolution calling for the overthrow of the Provisional Government by armed force:

> Having considered the events currently taking place in Petrograd, the meeting concludes: the present crisis of authority will not be resolved in the interests of the people if the revolutionary proletariat and garrison do not, at once, firmly and unequivocally, declare that they favor the transfer of power to the Soviet of Workers', Soldiers', and Peasants' Deputies.
> To this end, it is recommended that the workers and soldiers at once take to the streets to demonstrate the expression of their will.[153]

The Bolshevik objective was unequivocal, but their tactics, as always, were cautious and left room for a face-saving retreat. Mikhail Kalinin, a participant in these events, thus describes the party's position.

> Responsible party workers faced a delicate question: "What is this—a demonstration or something more? Perhaps the beginning of a proletarian revolution, the beginning of a power seizure?" This appeared important at the time, and they especially badgered [Lenin]. He would answer: "We will see what happens; now one can't tell anything!" . . . This was, indeed, a review of the revolutionary forces, their numbers, quality, and activism. . . . This review could turn into a decisive encounter: everything depended on the correlation of forces and any number of chance occurrences. In any event, as if for purposes of insurance against unpleasant surprises, the commander's order was: "We will see." This in no way precluded the possibility of throwing the regiments into battle if the correlation of forces proved favorable or, on the other hand,

---

*Vladimirova in *PR*, No. 5/17 (1923), 11–13; Ia. M. Sverdlov in *ISSSR*, No. 2 (1957), 126. The report of the government commission appointed to investigate the July riots, reprinted in D. A. Chugaev, ed., *Revoliutsionnoe dvizhenie v Rossii v iiule 1917 g.* (Moscow, 1959), 95–96, describes the Bolshevik speeches as much more militant.

of retreating with the least possible losses, which is what actually happened on July 4.*

The Central Committee entrusted the management of its operation scheduled for the next day, July 4, to the Military Organization, with Podvoiskii in charge.[154] Podvoiskii and his associates spent the night communicating with pro-Bolshevik military units and factories, advising them of the pending action and giving them marching orders. Kronshtadt received a call from Bolshevik headquarters at Kshesinskaia's requesting troops.[155] The armed manifestation was to begin at 10 a.m.[156]

On July 4, *Pravda* appeared with a large empty space on its front page: visible evidence of the removal the preceding night of an article by Kamenev and Zinoviev urging restraint.[157] The role of Lenin in these decisions, if any, cannot be determined. Bolshevik historians insist that he was enjoying the peace and quiet of the Finnish countryside, oblivious of what his colleagues were doing. He is said to have first learned of the Bolshevik action at 6 a.m. on July 4 from a courier, following which he immediately left for the capital in the company of Krupskaia and Bonch-Bruevich. This version seems unconvincing in view of the fact that Lenin's followers never undertook any action which he did not personally approve: certainly not action which carried such immense risks. It is also known from Sukhanov (see below) that during the night preceding the riots, Lenin wrote an article for *Pravda* on the subject: this was almost certainly "All Power to the Soviets," which the paper printed on July 5.[158]

The Provisional Government had known as early as July 2 what the Bolsheviks were up to. On July 3 it contacted the headquarters of the Fifth Army in Dvinsk to request troops. None were forthcoming, at least in part because the socialists in the Soviet, whose approval was essential, hesitated to authorize resort to force.[159] In the early hours of July 4, General P. A. Polovtsev, the new commander of the Petrograd Military District, posted announcements forbidding armed demonstrations and "suggesting" to the garrison troops that they help preserve order.[160] The Military Staff surveyed the forces available to suppress street disorders and found them to be all but nonexistent:

---

*M. Kalinin in *Krasnaia gazeta,* July 16, 1920, 2. Since Lenin was not on the scene, Kalinin presumably refers to what he said the next day. Cf. a similar assessment by Raskolnikov in *PR,* No. 5/17 (1923), 59. The Bolshevik tactic was not lost on the Mensheviks. Tsereteli describes an incident that occurred in the afternoon of July 3 after Stalin had appeared before the Ispolkom to inform it that the Bolsheviks were doing all they could to stop the workers and soldiers from taking to the streets. Smiling, Chkheidze turned to Tsereteli, "Now the situation is clear." "I asked him," Tsereteli continues, "in what sense he considered the situation clear." "In the sense," Chkheidze responded, "that peaceful people have no need to enter into a protocol a statement of their peaceful intentions. It appears that we will have to deal with a so-called spontaneous demonstration which the Bolsheviks will join, saying that the masses cannot be left without leadership." Tsereteli, *Vospominaniia,* I, 267.

100 men of the Preobrazhenskii Guard Regiment, one company from the Vladimir Military Academy, 2,000 Cossacks, and 50 war invalids. The rest of the garrison had no desire to become involved in a conflict with the mutinous troops.[161]

July 4 began peacefully: only the eerie silence of the deserted streets suggested something was brewing. At 11 a.m., soldiers of the Machine Gun Regiment, accompanied by Red Guards in automobiles, occupied key points in the city. At the same time, 5,000 to 6,000 armed sailors from Kronshtadt disembarked in Petrograd. Their commander, Raskolnikov, later expressed surprise that the government did not stop his force by sinking one or two of the boats from shore batteries.[162] The sailors were under instructions to proceed from the landing pier near Nikolaevskii Bridge directly to Taurida. But as they lined up, a Bolshevik emissary told them that orders had been changed and they were to go instead to Kshesinskaia's. The protests of the SRs present were ignored, and the SR Maria Spiridonova, who had come to address the sailors, was left without an audience. Preceded by a military band and carrying banners reading "All Power to the Soviets," the sailors, drawn out in a long column, crossed Vasilevskii Island and the Stock Exchange Bridge to the Alexander Park, from where they continued to Bolshevik headquarters. There they were addressed from the balcony by Iakov Sverdlov, Lunarcharskii, Podvoiskii, and M. Lashevich. Lenin, who had arrived at Kshesinskaia's a short time before, displayed an uncharacteristic reluctance to speak. At first, he refused to address the sailors on the grounds that he was not well, but he finally yielded and delivered a few brief remarks. Hailing the sailors, he told them that

> he was happy to see what was happening, how the theoretical slogan, launched two months earlier, calling for the passage of all power to the Soviet of Workers' and Soldiers' Deputies was now being translated into reality.[163]

Even these cautious words could leave no doubt in anyone's mind that the Bolsheviks were engaged in a coup d'état. It was to be Lenin's last public appearance until October 26.

The sailors marched off to Taurida. What transpired inside Bolshevik headquarters after their departure is known from Sukhanov, who was told by Lunacharskii:

> . . . during the night of July 3–4, while sending to *Pravda* a declaration calling for a "peaceful demonstration," Lenin had in mind a concrete plan for a coup d'état. Political power—in reality assumed by the Bolshevik Central Committee—was to have been formally embodied in a "Soviet" ministry composed of outstanding and popular Bolsheviks. At this point, three ministers were appointed: Lenin, Trotsky, and Lunacharskii. This government was to have issued at once decrees on peace and land, gaining in this manner the sympathy of millions in the capital and the provinces, thereby solidifying its authority. Lenin, Trotsky, and Lunacharskii reached such an agreement after the Kron-

shtadt [sailors] had left Kshesinskaia's for Taurida Palace. . . . The revolution was to have been accomplished as follows: The 176th Regiment from Krasnoe Selo—the very same regiment to which Dan had entrusted the protection of Taurida—would arrest the Central Executive Committee, whereupon Lenin would arrive at the scene of action and proclaim the new government.*

The sailors, led by Raskolnikov, marched down Nevsky. Interspersed in their ranks were small army contingents and Red Guards. In front, on the side, and in the rear drove armored cars. The men carried banners with slogans prepared by the Bolshevik Central Committee.[164] As they turned into Liteinyi, in the heart of "bourgeois" Petrograd, shots rang out. The column broke up in panic, firing wildly and scattering in all directions: an eyewitness photographed the scene from a window, producing one of the few pictorial records of violence in the Russian Revolution (plate 53). When the shooting stopped, the demonstrators regrouped and resumed the march to Taurida, but they no longer kept an orderly formation and carried their guns at the ready. They arrived at the Soviet around 4 p.m., greeted with loud cheers from soldiers of the Machine Gun Regiment.

The Bolsheviks also brought to Taurida a large contingent of Putilov workers—estimates vary from 11,000 to 25,000.† Other factories and military units swelled the crowd, which came to number in the tens of thousands.‡ Miliukov thus describes the scene that unfolded in front of Taurida—a scene which despite the appearance of spontaneity was closely orchestrated by Bolshevik agents dispersed in the crowd:

> Taurida Palace became the focus of the struggle in the full sense of the word. Throughout the day armed military units gathered around it, demanding that the Soviet, at last, take power. . . . [Around 4 p.m.] the sailors of Kronstadt arrived and tried to penetrate the building. They called for the Minister of Justice, Pereverzev, to explain why the sailor Zhelezniakov and the anarchists

---

*Sukhanov, *Zapiski,* IV, 511–12. After Sukhanov had published these recollections in 1920, Trotsky vehemently repudiated them and so did, at Trotsky's prodding, Lunacharskii. Lunacharskii wrote Sukhanov a letter denouncing his statement as utterly baseless and warning that its publication could have for Sukhanov, "as a historian, an unpleasant consequence" (*ibid.,* 514n.–515n.). Sukhanov, however, refused to recant, insisting that he accurately recalled what Lunacharskii had told him. Yet that same year Trotsky himself admitted in a French Communist publication that the July affair had been intended as a power seizure—that is, the establishment of a Bolshevik government: "We never doubted for a moment that those July days were a prelude to victory": *Bulletin Communiste* (Paris) No. 10 (May 20, 1920), 6, cited in Milorad M. Drachkovitch and Branko Lazitch, *Lenin and the Comintern,* I (Stanford, Calif., 1972), 95.

†Nikitin, *Rokovye gody,* 133, gives the lower figure, *Istoriia Putilovskogo Zavoda, 1801–1917* (Moscow, 1961), 626, the higher. Trotsky's estimate of 80,000 (*History,* II, 29) is sheer fantasy.

‡The Bolshevik estimates of 500,000 or more demonstrators (V. Vladimirova in *PR,* No. 5/17, 1923, 40) are vastly inflated: the crowd which took part in the demonstration probably did not exceed one-tenth that number. An analysis of the garrison units known to have participated indicates that at most 15–20 percent of the troops were involved, and very likely considerably fewer: see B. I. Kochakov in *Uchënye Zapiski Leningradskogo Gosudarstvennogo Universiteta,* No. 205 (1956), 65–66, and G. L. Sobolev in *IZ,* No. 88 (1971), 77. It was Bolshevik policy then and later greatly to exaggerate the number of demonstrators in order to justify the claim that they were not leading the "masses" but responding to their pressures: see the account by an eyewitness, A. Sobolev, in *Rech',* No. 155/3,897 (July 5, 1917), 1.

53. July events.

had been arrested at Durnovo's villa. Tsereteli came out and told the hostile crowd that Pereverzev was not in the building, that he had already handed in his resignation and was no longer a minister: the first was true, the second not. Deprived of a direct excuse, the crowd for a while was at a loss what to do. But then shouts resounded that the ministers were responsible for each other: an attempt was made to arrest Tsereteli but he managed to escape inside the palace. Chernov emerged from the palace to calm the crowd. The crowd immediately threw itself on him and searched him for weapons. Chernov declared that under such circumstances he would not talk. The crowd fell silent. Chernov began a long speech about the activities of the socialist ministers in general and his own, as Minister of Agriculture, in particular. As for the Kadet ministers, bon voyage to them. The crowd shouted in response: "Why didn't you say so before? Declare at once that the land is being turned over to the toilers and power to the soviets!" A tall worker, raising his fist to the minister's face, shouted in a rage: "Take power, you s.o.b., when they give it to you!" Several men from the crowd seized Chernov and dragged him toward a car, while others pulled him toward the palace. Having torn the minister's coat, the Kronshtadt sailors shoved him into the car and declared that they would not let him go until the Soviet took power. Some workers broke into the hall where the Soviet was in session, shouting: "Comrades, they are beating up Chernov!" In the midst of the turmoil, Chkheidze appointed Kamenev, Steklov, and Martov to liberate Chernov. But Chernov was liberated by Trotsky, who had just arrived on the scene. The Kronshtadt sailors obeyed him and Trotsky accompanied Chernov back into the hall.*

*Miliukov, *Istoriia Vtoroi Russkoi Revoliutsii*, I, Pt. 1 (Sofia, 1921), 243–44. Other versions of the Chernov incident are in Vladimirova, *PR*, No. 5/17 (1923), 34–35, and Raskolnikov, *ibid.*, 69–71.

In the meantime, Lenin had unobtrusively made his way to Taurida, where he stayed out of sight, prepared, depending on how events unfolded, either to assume power or to declare the demonstration a spontaneous outburst of popular indignation and then disappear from sight. Raskolnikov thought he looked pleased.[165]

Not all the action occurred at Taurida. While the mobs were converging on the seat of the Soviet, small armed detachments directed by the Military Organization occupied strategic points. Bolshevik prospects improved considerably when the garrison of the Peter and Paul Fortress, 8,000 strong, went over to them. Motorized Bolshevik units took over the plants of several anti-Bolshevik newspapers; anarchists seized the most outspoken of them, *Novoe vremia*. Other detachments took up guard duty at the Finland and Nicholas railroad stations, and set up machine gun emplacements on Nevsky and its side streets, which had the effect of cutting off the staff of the Petrograd Military District from Taurida Palace. One armed unit attacked the seat of the counter-intelligence service where materials on Lenin's dealings with the Germans were stored.[166] No resistance was encountered. In the judgment of a liberal newspaper, in the course of the day Petrograd passed into Bolshevik hands.[167]

The stage was thus set for a formal takeover: nominally in the name of the Soviet, in reality on behalf of the Bolsheviks. In preparation for this crowning event the Bolsheviks had arranged for a delegation of handpicked "representatives" of fifty-four factories to call on Taurida with a petition demanding the Soviet assume power. These men forced their way into the room occupied by the Ispolkom. Several of them were allowed to speak. Martov and Spiridonova supported their demand: Martov declared that such was the will of history.[168] At this point it seemed that the rioters would physically inundate and take over the seat of the Soviet. The Soviet had no defense against this threat: its total protection consisted of six guards.[169]

And yet the Bolsheviks failed to deliver the coup de grace. It is impossible to tell whether this was due to poor organization, indecisiveness, or both. Nikitin blamed the Bolshevik failure to take power on poor planning.

> The uprising was improvised: all the actions of the enemy indicated that it had not been prepared. The regiments and large units did not know their immediate missions even in the main area. They were told from the balcony of Kshesinskaia's: "Go to Taurida Palace, take power." They went and while awaiting the promised further orders commingled with one another. By contrast, units of ten to fifteen men in trucks and armored cars and small detachments in automobiles enjoyed complete freedom of action, lorded it over the city, but they, too, received no concrete orders to take over the strongpoints such as railroad stations, telephone centers, supply depots, arsenals, the doors to all of which stood wide open. The streets flowed with blood, but there was no leadership . . .*

*Nikitin, *Rokovye gody,* 148. Nevskii says that the Military Organization, in anticipation of possible defeat, deliberately kept half its forces in reserve: *Krasnoarmeets,* No. 10/15 (October 1919), 40.

But in the ultimate analysis the Bolshevik failure seems to have been caused by factors other than inadequate forces or bad planning: contemporaries agree that the city was theirs for the asking. Rather, it was due to a last-minute failure of nerve on the part of the commander in chief. Lenin simply could not make up his mind: according to Zinoviev, who spent these hours by his side, he kept wondering aloud whether this was or was not the time to "try," and in the end decided it was not.[170] For some reason he could not summon the courage to make the leap: possibly the dark cloud which hung over him of government revelations about dealings with the Germans held him back. Later, when both of them sat in jail, Trotsky told Raskolnikov, in what Raskolnikov took to be veiled criticism of Lenin: "Perhaps we made a mistake. We should have tried to take power."[171]

When these events were taking place, Kerensky was at the front. The frightened ministers did nothing. The roar of thousands of armed men in front of Taurida, the sight of vehicles with soldiers and sailors racing to unknown destinations, the knowledge of being abandoned by the garrison filled them with a sense of hopelessness. According to Pereverzev, the government was effectively captive:

> I did not arrest the leaders of the uprising on July 4, prior to the publication of documents, only because at that moment they already in effect had under arrest a part of the Provisional Government in Taurida Palace, and could have arrested Prince Lvov, myself, and Kerensky's deputy without any risk to themselves, if their determination matched even one-tenth their criminal energy.[172]

In this desperate situation, Pereverzev decided to release part of the information at his disposal on Lenin's German connections, hoping that it would unleash a violent anti-Bolshevik reaction among the troops. He had urged two weeks earlier that this information be made public, but the cabinet overruled him, on the grounds (according to a Menshevik newspaper) that "it was necessary to display caution in a matter concerning the leader of the Bolsh[evik] Party."[173] Although Kerensky was later to accuse Pereverzev of an "unpardonable" mistake in having released the facts on Lenin, he himself, having learned on July 4 of the disturbances, urged Lvov to "speed up the publication of information in the possession of the Minister of Foreign Affairs."[174] After checking with Colonel Nikitin and General Polovtsev, Pereverzev invited to his office over eighty representatives of military units stationed in and around Petrograd as well as journalists. This occurred around 5 p.m., as the disturbance at Taurida was coming to a head and a Bolshevik coup seemed but minutes away.* In order to save the most damning material for

---

*NZh, No. 68 (July 7, 1917), 3. Pereverzev's account of these events can be found in a letter to the editor, NoV, No. 14,822 (July 9, 1917), 4. He is said also to have published recollections in PN, October 31, 1930, but this issue of the paper was unavailable to me.

54. P. N. Pereverzev.

the prospective trial of the Bolshevik leaders, Pereverzev released only fragments of the evidence at his disposal, and the least credible part at that. It
consisted of a shaky account by Lieutenant D. Ermolenko, who reported that
while a prisoner of war of the Germans he had been told that Lenin was
working for them. This hearsay evidence did a great deal of harm to the
government's case, especially with the socialists. Pereverzev also released some
of the information on Bolshevik financial dealings with Berlin by way of
Stockholm. He unwisely asked G. A. Aleksinskii, a discredited onetime Bolshevik Duma deputy, to attest to the veracity of Ermolenko's account.[175]

Karinskii, a friend in the Ministry of Justice, instantly warned the Bolsheviks what Pereverzev was about to do,[176] whereupon Stalin asked the Ispolkom to stop the spread of "slanderous" information about Lenin. Chkheidze
and Tsereteli obliged, telephoning the editorial offices of the Petrograd dailies
to request, in the name of the Ispolkom, that they not publish the government's
release. Prince Lvov did likewise; so did Tereshchenko and Nekrasov.* All
newspapers but one honored the request. The exception was the mass-circulation *Zhivoe slovo,* which appeared the next morning with banner headlines—
LENIN, GANETSKII & CO. SPIES—followed by the account of Ermolenko and
details concerning the moneys sent by the Germans to Kozlovskii and Sumenson through Ganetskii.[177] The report was endorsed by Aleksinskii. Broadsheets
containing this information were posted throughout the city.

The revelations about Lenin and the Germans, spread by the regimental
emissaries whom Pereverzev had briefed, had an electrifying effect on the
troops: little as most of them cared whether Russia was ruled by the Provisional Government in partnership with the Soviet or by the Soviet alone, they
felt passionately about collaboration with the enemy. The suspicions which

---

Zhivoe slovo, No. 54/407 (July 8, 1917), 1. Cf. Lenin, *PSS,* XXXII, 413. Lvov told the editors
that premature revelation would allow the guilty to escape.

lingered around Lenin because of his journey across enemy territory made him highly unpopular with the troops: according to Tsereteli, Lenin was so hated by the men in uniform that he had to ask the Ispolkom for protection.[178] The first to reach Taurida were units of the Izmailovskii Guards; they were followed by elements of the Preobrazhenskii and Semenovskii, the latter marching to a military band. Cossack units also turned up. At the sight and sound of approaching troops, the mob in front of Taurida fled pell-mell in all directions, some seeking safety in the palace.

At this moment, inside Taurida a discussion was underway between the Ispolkom and the Bolshevik factory "representatives." The Mensheviks and SRs were playing for time, hoping that the government would come to their rescue. The instant loyal troops made their way into Taurida, they threw out the Bolshevik motion.[179]

There was little violence because the rioters dispersed on their own. Raskolnikov ordered his sailors to return to Kronshtadt, keeping 400 men to defend Kshesinskaia's. The sailors at first refused to leave, but gave in when they were surrounded by a superior and unfriendly force of loyal troops. By midnight Taurida was cleared of the mob.

The unexpected turn of events threw the Bolsheviks into complete disarray. Lenin fled Taurida as soon as he had learned from Karinskii of Pereverzev's action, which must have been just before the soldiers arrived on the scene. After his departure, the Bolsheviks held a consultation, which ended with the decision to abort the putsch.[180] At noon they had been distributing ministerial portfolios among themselves; six hours later they were hunted quarry. Lenin thought all was lost. "Now they are going to shoot us," he told Trotsky, "it is the most advantageous time for them."[181] He spent the following night at Kshesinskaia's under the protection of Raskolnikov's sailors. In the morning of July 5, as street vendors were hawking copies of *Zhivoe slovo,* he and Sverdlov slipped out and hid in a friend's apartment. For the next five days he led an underground existence, changing quarters as often as twice daily. The other Bolshevik leaders, with the exception of Zinoviev, stayed in the open, risking arrest and in some cases demanding to be arrested.

On July 6, the government ordered the detention of Lenin and his accomplices, eleven in all, charging them with "high treason and organizing an armed uprising."* Sumenson and Kozlovskii were promptly apprehended. Soldiers came to Steklov's residence during the night of July 6–7; when they threatened to smash his rooms and beat him up, Steklov telephoned for help. The Ispolkom rushed two armored cars to protect him; Kerensky also intervened on his behalf.[182] The same night, soldiers appeared at the apartment of Anna Elizarova, Lenin's sister. As they searched the room, Krupskaia screamed at them: "Gendarmes! Just like under the old regime!"[183] The hunt for Bolshevik leaders went on for several days. On July 9, troops inspecting

---

*A. Kerensky, *The Crucifixion of Liberty* (New York, 1934), 324. They were: Lenin, Zinoviev, Kollontai, Kozlovskii, Sumenson, Parvus, Ganetskii, Raskolnikov, Roshal, Semashko, and Lunacharskii. Trotsky was not on the list, presumably because he was not yet a member of the Bolshevik Party, which he joined only at the end of July. He was taken into custody later.

55. The Palace Square in Petrograd occupied by loyal
troops after the suppression of the Bolshevik putsch:
July 1917.

private automobiles caught Kamenev: in this case a lynching was prevented
by Polovtsev, the commander of the Petrograd Military District, who not only
freed Kamenev but provided a car to take him home.[184] In all, some 800
participants in the insurrection were taken into custody.* As far as can be
determined, not one Bolshevik was physically harmed. Considerable damage,
however, was done to Bolshevik properties. The editorial office and printing
plant of *Pravda* were destroyed on July 5. After the sailors guarding Kshesinskaia's had been disarmed without offering resistance, the Bolshevik headquarters were occupied as well. The Peter and Paul Fortress surrendered.

On July 6, Petrograd was taken over by garrison troops and soldiers
freshly arrived from the front.

The Bolshevik Central Committee issued on July 6 a flat denial of the
accusations of treason leveled at Lenin and demanded an investigation.[185] The
Ispolkom obliged by appointing a five-man jury. It so happened that all five

---

*Zarudnyi in *NZh*, No. 101 (August 15, 1917), 2. Nikitin, *Rokovye gody*, 158, says more
than 2,000.

were Jews: since this might have laid the committee open to suspicion by the "counterrevolutionaries" that it was loaded in Lenin's favor, it was dissolved and none appointed to replace it.

The Soviet, in fact, never looked into the accusations against Lenin, which did not deter it, however, from deciding firmly in favor of the accused. Although Lenin's putsch was directed as much against the Soviet as against the government, with which, since May, it had been closely linked, the Ispolkom would not face reality. In the words of a Kadet newspaper, although the socialist intellectuals called the Bolsheviks "traitors," "at the same time, as if nothing had happened, they remained for them comrades. They continued to work with them. They flattered and reasoned with them."[186] The Mensheviks and SRs now, as before and later, viewed the Bolsheviks as errant friends and their opponents as counterrevolutionaries. They feared that the charges leveled at the Bolsheviks were merely a pretext for an assault on the Soviet and the entire socialist movement. The Menshevik *Novaia zhizn'* cited *Den'* as follows:

> Today it is the Bolshevik Committee that is being convicted; tomorrow they will cast suspicions on the Soviet of Workers' Deputies, and then they will declare a Holy War against the Revolution.[187]

The paper rejected out of hand the government's charges against Lenin, accusing the "bourgeois press" of "deplorable slander" and "wild howls." It urged the condemnation of those—presumably the Provisional Government—who engaged in "consciously slanderous defamation of prominent leaders of the working class."[188] Among the socialists who sprang to Lenin's defense, calling the charges against him "slander," was Martov.* These claims had nothing to do with the facts of the case: the Ispolkom neither asked the government for its evidence nor undertook its own investigation.

Even so, it went to great pains to protect the Bolsheviks from government retribution. As early as July 5, a delegation of the Ispolkom went to Kshesinskaia's to discuss with the Bolsheviks terms for a peaceful resolution of the affair. They all agreed that there would be no repressions against the party and that all those arrested in connection with the events of the preceding two days would be released.[189] The Ispolkom then requested Polovstev not to assault the Bolsheviks' headquarters, as he had been expected to do momentarily.[190] It also passed a resolution forbidding the publication of government documents implicating Lenin.[191]

Lenin defended himself in several brief articles. In a joint letter with Zinoviev and Kamenev to *Novaia zhizn'* he claimed never to have received "one kopeck" from Ganetskii and Kozlovskii, either for himself or for the party. The whole thing was a new Dreyfus or a new Beilis affair, engineered by Aleksinskii at the behest of the counterrevolution.[192] On July 7, he declared

*On August 4, Tsereteli presented and the Ispolkom adopted a motion protesting the persecution of persons involved in the July events on the grounds that such persecution marked the beginning of the "counterrevolution": *NZh*, No. 94 (August 6, 1917), 3.

that he would not stand trial because, under the circumstances, neither he nor Zinoviev could expect justice to be done.[193]

Lenin always tended to overestimate the determination of his opponents. He was convinced that he and his party were finished, and like the Paris Commune, destined merely to serve as an inspiration for future generations. He considered moving the party center abroad once again, to Finland and even Sweden.[194] He entrusted to Kamenev his theoretical last will and testament, the manuscript of "Marxism on the State" (later used as the basis for *State and Revolution*), with instructions for publication in the event he was killed.[195] After Kamenev had been caught and nearly lynched, Lenin decided to take no more chances. During the night of July 9–10, accompanied by Zinoviev, he boarded a train at a small suburban railroad station to escape and hide in the countryside.

Lenin's flight when his party faced the prospect of destruction was seen by most socialists as desertion. In the words of Sukhanov:

> The disappearance of Lenin when threatened with arrest and trial [was], in itself, a fact worthy of note. In the Ispolkom no one had expected Lenin to "extricate himself from the situation" in just this way. His flight produced in our circles an immense sensation and led to passionate discussions in every conceivable way. Among the Bolsheviks, some approved of Lenin's action. But the majority of the members of the Soviet reacted with a sharp condemnation. The Mameluks and the Soviet leaders shouted their righteous resentment. The opposition kept its opinion to itself: but this opinion reduced itself to an unqualified condemnation of Lenin from the political and moral points of view . . . the flight of the shepherd could not but deliver a heavy blow to the sheep. After all, the masses, mobilized by Lenin, bore the whole burden of responsibility for the July days. . . . And the "real culprit" abandons the army, his comrades, and seeks personal safety in flight![196]

Sukhanov adds that Lenin's escape was seen as all the more reprehensible in that neither his life nor his personal freedom was at risk.

Kerensky, who returned to Petrograd in the evening of July 6, was furious with Pereverzev and fired him. Pereverzev, in his view, had "lost forever the possibility of establishing Lenin's treason in final form, supported by documentary evidence."[197] This seems a spurious rationale for Kerensky's failure, in the days that followed, to take decisive action against Lenin and his followers. If no effort was made to "establish Lenin's treason in final form" it was from the desire to placate the socialists who had sprung to Lenin's defense: it was a "concession to the Soviets by a Government which had already lost Kadet support and could not afford to antagonize the Soviets as well."* This consideration, indeed, was decisive in Kerensky's behavior in July and the months ahead.

*Richard Abraham, *Alexander Kerensky* (New York, 1987), 223–24. Pereverzev was fired in the early hours of July 5 on the initiative of Nekrasov and Tereshchenko, but stayed in his post two days longer.

56. Mutinous soldiers of the 1st Machine Gun Regiment
disarmed: July 5, 1917.

Kerensky now replaced Lvov as Prime Minister, while retaining the
portfolios of War and Navy. He began to act as a dictator and, to give visible
expression to his new status, moved into the Winter Palace, where he slept in
the bed of Alexander III and worked at his desk.[198] On July 10 he asked
Kornilov to assume command of the armed forces. He ordered the disarming
and dissolution of units which participated in the July events; the garrison was
to be reduced to 100,000 men, the rest to be sent to the front. *Pravda* and other
Bolshevik publications were barred from the trenches.

Yet for all this display of determination, the Provisional Government did
not dare take the one step that would have destroyed the Bolshevik Party: a
public trial at which all the evidence in its possession of treasonous activity
would have been laid out. A commission was appointed under the new Minister of Justice, A. S. Zarudnyi, to prepare the case against the Bolsheviks. It
assiduously collected materials—by early October, eighty thick volumes—
yet no legal proceedings were ever instituted. The reason for this failure
was twofold: fear of "counterrevolution" and the wish not to antagonize the
Ispolkom.

The July putsch imbued Kerensky with an obsessive fear that the right
would exploit the Bolshevik threat to stage a monarchist coup. Addressing the
Ispolkom on July 13, he urged it to distance itself from the elements which
"with their actions inspire the forces of the counterrevolution" and pledged
that "any attempt to restore the Russian monarchic regime will be suppressed
in the most decisive, pitiless manner."[199] Like many socialists, he is said to have
been alarmed rather than gratified by the zeal with which loyal troops had

crushed the July riots.[200] In his eyes, the Bolsheviks were a threat only to the extent that their slogans and behavior encouraged the monarchists. It is almost certainly from the same consideration that he decided on July 7 to ship the Imperial family to Siberia. The departure was carried out in utmost secrecy during the night of July 31. Accompanied by an entourage of fifty attendants and servants, the Romanovs left for Tobolsk, a town which had no railroad and therefore offered fewer opportunities for escape.[201] The timing of the decision—three days after the Bolshevik putsch and the day after Kerensky's return to Petrograd—indicates that Kerensky's motive was to prevent right-wing elements from exploiting the situation to restore Nicholas to the throne. Such was the opinion of the British envoy.[202]

A related consideration was the desire to curry favor with the Ispolkom, which continued to regard the Bolsheviks as members in good standing and to treat all attacks against them as machinations of the "counterrevolution." The Mensheviks and SRs in the Soviet repeatedly assailed the government for its "campaign of vilification" against Lenin, demanding that the charges be dropped and the detained Bolsheviks released.

Kerensky's tolerant treatment of the Bolsheviks, who had almost over-thrown him and his government, contrasted sharply with the impetuous manner he would reveal in dealing with General Kornilov the following month.

As a result of the inaction of both the government and the Ispolkom the fury against the Bolsheviks, which Pereverzev's initiative had unleashed, dissipated. The two lost a unique opportunity to liquidate the genuine "counterrevolution" from the left out of fear of an imaginary "counterrevolution" from the right. The Bolsheviks soon recovered and resumed their bid for power. Trotsky later wrote that when, at the Third Congress of the Comintern in 1921, Lenin admitted the party had committed mistakes in its dealings with the enemy, "he had in mind our hasty uprising" in July 1917. "Fortunately," Trotsky added, "our enemies had neither sufficient logical consistency nor determination."[203]

11

The October Coup

It is the law of nature that predators must be more
intelligent than the animals on which they prey.
—Manual of Natural History

It was only from that quarter [the right] that we
faced any real danger at that time.
—Alexander Kerensky[1]

In September 1917, with Lenin in his hideaway, the command of Bolshevik forces passed to Trotsky, who had joined the party two months earlier. Defying Lenin's pressures for an immediate power seizure, Trotsky adopted a more circumspect strategy, disguising Bolshevik designs as an effort to transfer power to the soviets. With supreme mastery of the technique of the modern coup d'état, of which he was arguably the inventor, he led the Bolsheviks to victory.

Trotsky was an ideal complement to Lenin. Brighter and more flamboyant, a much better speaker and writer, he could galvanize crowds: Lenin's charisma was limited to his followers. But Trotsky was unpopular with the Bolshevik cadres, in part because he had joined their party late, after years of acerbic attacks on it, and in part because he was unbearably arrogant. In any event, being Jewish, Trotsky could hardly aspire to national leadership in a country in which, Revolution or no, Jews were regarded as outsiders. During the Revolution and Civil War he was Lenin's alter ego, an indispensable companion in arms: after victory had been won, he became an embarrassment.

The event which made it possible for the Bolsheviks to recover from the July debacle was one of the more bizarre episodes in the Russian Revolution, known as the Kornilov Affair.*

*Few subjects have aroused such interest among historians of the Russian Revolution, and the literature on it is correspondingly voluminous. The principal source materials have been pub-

57. Leon Trotsky.

General Lavr Kornilov was born in 1870 into a family of Siberian Cossacks. His father was a peasant and soldier; his mother, a housekeeper. Kornilov's plebeian background contrasted with that of Kerensky and Lenin,
whose fathers belonged to the uppermost strata of the service nobility. He had
spent his early years among the Kazakh-Kirghiz and retained a lifelong affec-
tion for Asia and Asians. Upon graduating from military school, he enrolled
in the General Staff Academy, which he completed with honors. He began
active service in Turkestan, leading expeditions into Afghanistan and Persia.
Kornilov, who mastered the Turkic dialects of Central Asia and became an
expert on Russia's Asiatic frontier, liked to surround himself with a bodyguard
of Tekke Turkomans, dressed in red robes, with whom he spoke in their native
language and to whom he was known as "Ulu Boiar," or "Great Boyar." He
took part in the war with Japan, following which he was posted to China as
military attaché. In April 1915, while in command of a division, he suffered
serious wounds and was taken prisoner by the Austrians, but escaped and

lished in D. A. Chugaev, ed., *Revoliutsionnoe dvizhenie v Rossii v avguste 1917 g.: Razgrom Kornilovskogo miatezha* (Moscow, 1959), esp. 419–72, and *Revoliutsiia,* IV, *passim.* Kerensky's account is
in *Delo Kornilova* (Ekaterinoslav, 1918) (in English: *The Prelude to Bolshevism,* New York, 1919);
Boris Savinkov's, in *K delu Kornilova* (Paris, 1919). Of the secondary literature, especially informative are: E. I. Martynov's partisan but richly documented *Kornilov* (Leningrad, 1927), P. N. Miliukov's *Istoriia Vtoroi Russkoi Revoliutsii,* I, Pt. 2 (Sofia, 1921), and George Katkov's *The Kornilov
Affair* (London-New York, 1980).

made his way back to Russia. In March 1917, the Provisional Committee of the Duma asked Nicholas II to appoint Kornilov commander of the Petrograd Military District. This post he held until the Bolshevik riots in April, when he resigned and left for the front.

Unlike most Russian generals, who were first and foremost politicians, Kornilov was a fighting man, a field officer of legendary courage. He had a reputation for obtuseness: Alekseev is reputed to have said that he had "a lion's heart and a sheep's brain," but this is not a fair assessment. Kornilov had a great deal of practical intelligence and common sense, although like other soldiers of this type he was scornful of politics or politicians. He was said to hold "progressive" opinions, and there is no reason to doubt him that he despised the tsarist regime.[2]

Early in his military career Kornilov displayed a tendency to insubordination, which became more pronounced after February 1917 as he observed the disintegration of Russia's armed forces and the impotence of the Provisional Government. His opponents later would accuse him of dictatorial ambitions. The charge can be made only with qualifications. Kornilov was a patriot, ready to serve any government that advanced Russia's national interests, especially in time of war, by maintaining internal order and doing whatever was necessary to win victory. In the late summer of 1917 he concluded that the Provisional Government was no longer a free agent but a captive of socialist internationalists and enemy agents ensconced in the Soviet. It is this belief that made him receptive to suggestions that he assume dictatorial powers.

Kerensky turned to Kornilov after the July putsch in the hope that he would restore discipline in the armed forces and stop the German counter-offensive. On the night of July 7–8 he put him in charge of the Southwestern Front, which bore the brunt of the fighting, and three days later, on the advice of his aide, Boris Savinkov, offered him the post of Commander in Chief. Kornilov was in no hurry to accept. He thought it pointless to assume responsibility for the conduct of military operations until and unless the government tackled in earnest the problems hampering Russia's entire war effort. These were of two kinds: narrowly military and more broadly political and economic. Having consulted other generals, he found wide agreement on what needed to be done to restore the fighting capacity of the armed forces: the army committees, authorized by Order No. 1, had to be disbanded or at least greatly reduced in power; military commanders had to regain disciplinary authority; measures had to be taken to restore order to the rear garrisons. Kornilov demanded the reintroduction of the death penalty for military personnel guilty of desertion and mutiny at the front as well as in the rear. But he did not stop there. He knew of the war mobilization plans of other belligerent countries and wanted something similar for Russia. It seemed to him essential that employees of defense industries and transport—the sectors of the economy most critical to the war effort—be subjected to military discipline. To the extent that he wanted greater authority than his predecessors, it was in emulation of General Ludendorff, who in December 1916 had received virtually dictatorial powers over the German economy: it was to enable the country to wage total war. This program, which Kornilov worked out jointly with the chief of staff, General A. S. Lukomskii, became the main source of conflict between himself, representing the officer corps and non-socialist opinion, and Kerensky, who had to act under the watchful eye of the Soviet. The conflict was irreconcilable because it pitted irreconcilables: the interests of Russia against those of international socialism. As Savinkov, who knew both men well, put it: Kornilov "loves freedom. . . . But Russia for him comes first, and freedom second, while for Kerensky . . . freedom and revolution come first, and Russia second."[3]

On July 19, Kornilov communicated to Kerensky the terms on which he was prepared to accept command: (1) he would owe responsibility only to his conscience and the nation; (2) no one would interfere with either his operational orders or command appointments; (3) the disciplinary measures which he was discussing with the government, including the death penalty, would apply to the troops in the rear; and (4) the government would accept his previous suggestions.[4] Kerensky was so angered by these demands that he considered withdrawing his offer to Kornilov, but on reflection decided to treat them as expressions of the general's political "naïveté."[5] In fact, he was heavily dependent on Kornilov's help because without the army he was powerless. To be sure, the first of Kornilov's four conditions verged on the impertinent: it can be explained, however, by the general's desire to be rid of interference by the Soviet, which in its Order No. 1 had claimed the authority to countermand military instructions. When Kerensky's commissar at headquarters, the SR M. M. Filonenko, told Kornilov that this demand could arouse the "most serious apprehensions" unless he meant by it "responsibility" to the Provisional Government, Kornilov replied that this was exactly what he had in mind.[6] Then, as later, until his final break with Kerensky, Kornilov's "insubordination" was directed against the Soviet and not against the government.

The terms under which Kornilov was willing to assume command of the armed forces were leaked to the press, probably by V. S. Zavoiko, Kornilov's public relations official. Their publication in *Russkoe slovo* on July 21 caused a sensation, earning Kornilov instant popularity in non-socialist circles and commensurate hostility on the left.[7]

The negotiations between the Prime Minister and the general dragged on for two weeks. Kornilov assumed his new duties only on July 24, after receiving assurances that his conditions would be met.

In fact, however, Kerensky neither could nor would keep his promises. He could not because he was not a free agent but the executor of the will of the Ispolkom, which viewed all measures to restore military discipline, especially in the rear, as "counterrevolutionary" and vetoed them. To have carried out the reforms, therefore, would have compelled Kerensky to break with the socialists, his main political supporters. And he would not honor his promises because he soon came to see in Kornilov a dangerous rival. It is always perilous for a historian to try to penetrate an individual's mind, but observing Kerensky's actions in July and August it is difficult to escape the conclusion

58. General Lavr Kornilov.

that he deliberately provoked a conflict with his military chief, rejecting every opportunity at reconciliation, because he wanted to bring down the one man who threatened his status as leader of Russia and custodian of the Revolution.*

Boris Savinkov, the acting director of the Ministry of War, a man ideally suited for the role of an intermediary because he enjoyed the confidence of both Kerensky and Kornilov, drafted early in August a four-point program calling for the extension of the death penalty to troops in the rear, the militarization of railroad transport, the application of martial law to war industries, and the restoration to officers of disciplinary authority with a corresponding reduction in the power of army committees.[8] According to him, Kerensky promised to sign the document, but kept on procrastinating and on August 8 said that he would "never, under any circumstances, sign a bill about the death penalty in the rear."[9] Feeling deceived, Kornilov kept on bombarding the Prime Minister with "ultimata" which so irritated Kerensky that he came close to dismissing him.[10] Since Kornilov knew of Kerensky's deep interest in the revitalization of the armed forces, his failure to act confirmed him in the suspicion that the

*This is also the opinion of General Martynov, who observed these events at close range and studied the archival evidence: *Kornilov,* 100. Cf. N. N. Golovin, *Rossiiskaia kontr-revoliutsiia v 1917–1918 gg.,* I, pt. 2 (Tallinn, 1937), 37.

THE RUSSIAN REVOLUTION

Prime Minister was not a free man but a tool of the socialists, some of them known since the July putsch to be consorting with the enemy.

Kornilov's badgering placed Kerensky in a difficult situation. He had managed since May to straddle the gulf between the government and the Ispolkom by conceding to the latter veto powers over legislation and going out of his way not to antagonize it, while, at the same time, vigorously pursuing the war, which won him the support of the liberals and even moderate conservatives. Kornilov compelled him to do something he wished at all costs to avoid—namely, to choose between the left and the right, between the interests of international socialism and those of the Russian state. He could be under no illusion: giving in to Kornilov's demands, most of which he thought reasonable, would mean a break with the Soviet. On August 18, the Plenum of the Soviet debated, on a Bolshevik motion, the proposal to restore the death penalty in the armed forces. It passed with a virtually unanimous vote of some 850 delegates against 4 (Tsereteli, Dan, M.I. Liber, and Chkheidze) a resolution rejecting the application of capital punishment to front-line troops as a "measure intended to frighten the soldier masses for the purpose of enslaving them to the commanding staff."[11] Clearly, there was no chance of the Soviet's approving the extension of the death penalty to troops not in the combat zone, let alone the subjection of defense and transport workers to military discipline.

In theory, Kerensky could have stood up to the Soviet and cast his lot with the liberals and conservatives. But that alternative was foreclosed for him by the very low esteem in which he was held by these circles, especially after the failure of the June offensive and his indecisive reaction to the July putsch. When he made an appearance at the Moscow State Conference on August 14, he was acclaimed by the left only: the right received him in stony silence, reserving its ovation for Kornilov.[12] The liberal and conservative press referred to him with unconcealed contempt. He had no choice, therefore, but to opt for the left, accommodating the socialist intellectuals of the Ispolkom while trying, with diminishing conviction and success, to advance Russia's national interests.

His desire to placate the left was evident not only in the failure to carry out the promised military reforms but also in the refusal to take resolute measures against the Bolsheviks. Although he had in hand a great deal of damning evidence, he failed to prosecute the leaders of the July putsch in deference to the Ispolkom and the Soviet, which regarded the charges against the Bolsheviks as "counterrevolutionary." He showed a similar bias in reacting to a proposal from the Ministry of War to take into custody both right-wing and left-wing "saboteurs" of Russia's war effort. He approved the list of right-wingers to be arrested, but hesitated when coming to the other list, from which he eventually struck more than half the names. When the document reached the Minister of the Interior, the SR N. D. Avksentev, whose countersignature it required, the latter reconfirmed the first list, but crossed out from the second all but two of the remaining names (Trotsky's and Kollontai's).[13]

Kerensky was a very ambitious man who saw himself destined to lead democratic Russia. His only opportunity to realize this ambition was to take charge of the democratic left—that is, the Mensheviks and SRs—and to do so he had to pander to its obsessive fear of the "counterrevolution." He not only saw but needed to see Kornilov as the focus of all the anti-democratic forces. Although he well knew what the Bolsheviks had intended with their armed "demonstrations" of April, June, and July, and could have easily determined what Lenin and Trotsky planned for the future, he persuaded himself that Russian democracy faced danger not from the left but from the right. Since he was neither uninformed nor unintelligent, this absurd assessment makes sense only if one assumes that it suited him politically. Having cast Kornilov in the role of the Russian Bonaparte, he reacted uncritically— indeed, eagerly—to rumors of a vast counterrevolutionary conspiracy allegedly being hatched by Kornilov's friends and supporters.[14]

Precious days went by without the military reforms being enacted. Knowing that the Germans intended soon to resume offensive operations and hoping to stir things up, Kornilov requested permission to meet with the cabinet. He arrived in the capital on August 3. Addressing the ministers, he began with a survey of the status of the armed forces. He wanted to discuss military reforms, but Savinkov interrupted him, saying that the War Ministry was working on this matter. Kornilov then turned to the situation at the front and reported on the operations he was preparing against the Germans and Austrians. At this point, Kerensky leaned over and asked him in a whisper to be careful;[15] moments later a similar warning came from Savinkov. This incident had a shattering effect on Kornilov and on his attitude toward the Provisional Government: he referred to it time and again as justification for his subsequent actions. As he correctly interpreted Kerensky's and Savinkov's warnings, one or more ministers were under suspicion of leaking military secrets. When he returned to Mogilev, Kornilov, still in a state of shock, told Lukomskii what had happened and asked what kind of government he thought was running Russia.[16] He concluded that the minister about whom he had been warned was Chernov, who was believed to convey confidential information to colleagues in the Soviet, the Bolsheviks included.[17] From that day on, Kornilov regarded the Provisional Government as unworthy to lead the nation.*

Not long after these events (on August 6 or 7), Kornilov ordered General A. M. Krymov, the commander of the Third Cavalry Corps, to move his troops from the Romanian sector northward, and, reinforced with other units, take up positions at Velikie Luki, a city in western Russia roughly equidistant from Moscow and Petrograd. The Third Corps consisted of two Cossack divisions and the so-called Native (or Savage) Division from the Caucasus, all undermanned (the Native Division had a mere 1,350 men) but regarded as dependable. Puzzled by these instructions, Lukomskii pointed out that Velikie

---

*His conviction that the government was riddled with disloyal elements and possibly enemy agents was reinforced by the leak to the press of a confidential memorandum which he had submitted to the government at this time. The left-wing press published excerpts from it and launched against Kornilov a campaign of vilification: Martynov, *Kornilov,* 48.

Luki was too far from the front for these forces to be used against the Germans. Kornilov replied that he wanted the corps to be in position to suppress a potential Bolshevik putsch in either Moscow or Petrograd. He assured Lukomskii they were not intended against the Provisional Government, adding that if it proved necessary, Krymov's troops would disperse the Soviet, hang its leaders, and make short shrift of the Bolsheviks—with or without the government's consent.[18] He also told Lukomskii that Russia desperately needed "firm authority" capable of saving the country and its armed forces:

> I am not a counterrevolutionary . . . I despise the old regime, which badly mistreated my family. There is no return to the past and there cannot be any. But we need an authority that could truly save Russia, which would make it possible honorably to end the war and lead her to the Constituent Assembly. . . . Our current government has solid individuals but also those who ruin things, who ruin Russia. The main thing is that Russia has no authority and that such authority must be created. Perhaps I shall have to exert such pressure on the government. It is possible that if disorders break out in Petrograd, after they have been suppressed I will have to enter the government and participate in the formation of a new, strong authority.[19]

Having heard Kerensky tell Kornilov more than once that he, too, favored "strong authority," Lukomskii concluded that Kornilov and the Prime Minister should have no difficulty cooperating.[20]

Kornilov returned to Petrograd on August 10 at the urging of Savinkov, but against the wishes of the Prime Minister. Having heard rumors of attempts on his life, he arrived with his Tekke guards, who mounted machine guns outside Kerensky's office. Kerensky refused to grant Kornilov's request to meet with the full cabinet and received him instead in the presence of Nekrasov and Tereshchenko, his kitchen cabinet. The general's sense of urgency stemmed from the knowledge that the Germans were about to initiate offensive operations near Riga, threatening the capital. He reverted to the subject of the reforms: restoration of discipline at the front and in the rear, including the death penalty for Russians who worked for foreign powers, and militarization of defense industries as well as transport.[21] Kerensky found much of what Kornilov requested, especially in regard to defense industries and transport, "absurd," but he did not refuse to tighten discipline in the armed forces. Kornilov told the Prime Minister he understood he was about to be dismissed and "advised" against such action as likely to provoke disorders in the army.[22]

Four days later Kornilov made a sensational appearance at the State Conference which Kerensky had convened in Moscow to rally public support. At first Kerensky refused Kornilov's request that he be allowed to address the conference, but then relented on condition that he confine himself to military matters. When Kornilov arrived at the Bolshoi Theater, he was cheered and carried aloft by crowds; the delegates on the right gave him a tumultuous welcome. Although in his rather dry speech Kornilov said nothing that could be construed as politically damaging to the government, for Kerensky this event was a watershed: he interpreted the outpouring of sympathy for the general as a personal affront. According to his subsequent testimony, "after the Moscow conference, it was clear to me that the next attempt at a blow would come from the right, and not from the left."[23] Once this conviction lodged in his mind, it became an *idée fixe;* everything that happened subsequently only served to reinforce it. His certainty that a right-wing coup was underway received encouragement from cables sent by officers and private citizens demanding that he keep Kornilov at his post and confidential warnings from army headquarters of conspiracies by staff officers.[24] The conservative press now opened up a barrage against Kerensky and his cabinet. Typical was an editorial in the right-wing *Novoe vremia* which argued that Russia's salvation lay in the unquestioned acceptance of the authority of the Commander in Chief.[25] No evidence exists that Kornilov inspired this political campaign: but as its beneficiary, he came under suspicion.

59. Kornilov feted on his arrival at the Moscow State Conference: August 14, 1917.

Viewed dispassionately, the outpouring of sympathy for the commanding general was an expression of unhappiness with Kerensky's leadership, not a symptom of the "counterrevolution." The country yearned for firm authority. But the socialists were insensitive to this mood. Better versed in history than in practical politics, they firmly believed that a conservative ("Bonapartist") reaction was inevitable.* As early as August 24–25, before anything had happened to justify it, the socialist press spoke of counterrevolution: on August

*In private conversation with the author, Kerensky conceded that his actions in 1917 had been strongly influenced by the lessons of the French Revolution.

25, the Menshevik *Novaia zhizn'* announced, under the heading "Conspiracy," that one was in full swing and expressed the hope that the government would prosecute it with at least as much zeal as it had displayed against the Bolsheviks.[26]

Thus, the plot was written: it only remained to find the protagonist.

In the middle of August the Germans launched the expected assault on Riga. The undisciplined and politicized Russian troops fell back and on August 20–21 abandoned the city. To Kornilov this was ultimate proof that Russia's war effort had to be urgently reorganized, or else Petrograd itself would soon share Riga's fate. To understand the atmosphere in which the Kornilov affair unfolded, the military backdrop must never be left out of sight: for although contemporaries as well as historians have treated the Kornilov-Kerensky conflict exclusively as a struggle for power, for Kornilov it was first and foremost a critical, possibly final effort to save Russia from defeat in the war.

In the middle of August, Savinkov received from reliable French intelligence sources information that the Bolsheviks planned another putsch for the beginning of September: the information was published on August 19 in the daily *Russkoe slovo.* * The date coincided with what headquarters believed to be the next phase of German operations, an advance from Riga on Petrograd.[27] The origin of this intelligence is not known: it appears to have been faulty for there is nothing in Bolshevik sources to indicate preparations for a coup at this time. Savinkov conveyed this intelligence to Kerensky. Kerensky seemed unfazed: then, as later, he thought a Bolshevik coup a figment of his opponents' imagination.[28] But he quickly realized the utility of information on an alleged Bolshevik putsch as an excuse to disarm Kornilov. He requested Savinkov to proceed immediately to Mogilev to carry out the following missions: (1) liquidate the officer conspiracy at headquarters reported on by Filonenko; (2) abolish the Political Department at Army Headquarters; (3) obtain Kornilov's consent to have Petrograd and its environs transferred from his command to that of the government and placed under martial law; and

> (4) request from General Kornilov a cavalry corps for the purpose of imposing martial law in Petrograd and defending the Provisional Government from any and all assaults, and, in particular, from an assault of the Bolsheviks, who had already rebelled on July 3–5 and who, according to information of foreign intelligence, are once again preparing to rise in connection with German landings and an uprising in Finland.[29]

This fourth task particularly deserves being kept in mind because Kerensky's subsequent claim that Kornilov had sent the cavalry against Petrograd to

*According to the paper (No. 189, p. 3), the government believed this would be an all-out Bolshevik effort.

overthrow his government would provide grounds for charging the general with treason.

The purpose of Savinkov's mission to Mogilev was to abort a counterrevolutionary conspiracy allegedly being hatched there and to do so under the pretext of preparations against a Bolshevik putsch. Kerensky later obliquely admitted that he had asked for military units—that is, the Third Cavalry Corps—to be placed under his command because he wanted to be "militarily independent of headquarters."[30] Withdrawing the Petrograd Military District from Kornilov's command served the same end.

Savinkov arrived in Mogilev on August 22 and stayed there until August 24.[31] He began his first meeting with Kornilov saying that it was essential for the general and the Prime Minister, for all their differences, to cooperate. Kornilov agreed: while he considered Kerensky weak and unfit for his responsibilities, he was needed. He added that Kerensky would be well advised to broaden the political base of the government by bringing in General Alekseev and patriotic socialists like Plekhanov and A. A. Argunov. Turning to Kornilov's reform proposals, and assuring him that the government was prepared to act on them, Savinkov produced a draft of the latest reform project. Kornilov found it not entirely satisfactory because it retained the army committees and commissars. Would these reforms be acted on soon? Savinkov responded that the government did not want as yet to make them public for fear of provoking a violent reaction from the Soviet. He now informed Kornilov that the government had information that the Bolsheviks were planning fresh disturbances in Petrograd at the end of August or the beginning of September: the premature release of the military reform program could spark an immediate uprising of the Bolsheviks, in which the Soviet, which also opposed military reforms, could make common cause with them.

Savinkov next turned to the subject of measures to deal with the anticipated Bolshevik coup. The Prime Minister wished to withdraw Petrograd and its suburbs from the Petrograd Military District and place it under his direct command. Kornilov was displeased by this request, but yielded. Since one could not predict the reaction of the Soviet to the proposed military reforms and in view of the anticipated Bolshevik putsch, Savinkov went on, it was desirable to reinforce the Petrograd garrison with reliable combat troops. He requested Kornilov in two days to move the Third Cavalry Corps from Velikie Luki to the vicinity of Petrograd, where it would come under the government's command; as soon as this was done, he was to notify Petrograd by telegraph. If necessary, he said, the government was prepared to carry out "merciless" action against the Bolsheviks and, should it side with them, the Petrograd Soviet as well. To this request Kornilov readily assented.

Kornilov also agreed to ask the Union of Officers at headquarters to move to Moscow, but he refused to do away with the Political Department. He further promised to liquidate any anti-government plots at headquarters that might come to his attention.[32]

In the morning of August 24, as he was about to depart for Petrograd,

Savinkov made two additional requests. Although Kerensky would later make much of Kornilov's failure to carry them out, it is known from Savinkov's recollections that they were made on his own initiative.³³ One was that General Krymov be replaced as commander of the Third Corps before its dispatch to Petrograd: Krymov's "reputation," in Savinkov's opinion, could create "undesirable complications." The other was that the Native Division be detached from the Third Corps on the grounds that it would be embarrassing to have Caucasian natives "liberate" the capital of Russia.

Did Kornilov see through Kerensky's deception? From his words and deeds one would have to conclude that he took the Prime Minister's instructions at face value, unaware that the true object of Kerensky's apprehension was not the Bolsheviks but he himself. As they were saying goodbye, Kornilov assured Savinkov that he intended to support Kerensky because the country needed him.³⁴ For all his faults, Kerensky was a true patriot, and to Kornilov patriotic socialists were a valuable asset.

Following Savinkov's departure, Kornilov issued orders to General Krymov, whom he retained in his post:

> 1. In the event you receive from me or directly on the spot information that the Bolshevik uprising has begun, you are to move without delay with the corps to Petrograd, occupy the city, disarm the units of the Petrograd garrison which have joined the Bolshevik movement, disarm the population of Petrograd, and disperse the Soviet.
>
> 2. Having carried out this mission, General Krymov is to detach one brigade with artillery to Oranienbaum; following the arrival there, he is to demand of the Kronshtadt garrison to disarm the fortress and relocate to the mainland.³⁵

The two assignments implemented Kerensky's instructions. The first—to dispatch the Cavalry Corps to Petrograd—followed the request delivered orally by Savinkov. The second—to disarm Kronshtadt—was in line with Kerensky's orders issued on August 8 but never carried out.³⁶ Both missions were to protect the Provisional Government from the Bolsheviks. Kornilov may be said to have shown insubordination in retaining Krymov as commander of the Third Cavalry Corps: in justification, he explained to Lukomskii that the government feared Krymov would be too harsh in dealing with the rebels, but it would be grateful to him when it was all over.³⁷ Lukomskii wondered whether the instructions brought by Savinkov were not some kind of trap: Kornilov dismissed these doubts, saying that Lukomskii was "too suspicious."³⁸

At this time, Kornilov was approached by officers who said they had in Petrograd 2,000 men willing to help suppress the Bolsheviks. They requested from Kornilov 100 officers to lead them: Kornilov promised to provide these men. He said that all should be in readiness by August 26, the earliest of the dates for the anticipated Bolshevik coup, so that when the Bolsheviks rose, at

60. Vladimir Lvov.

the approach of Krymov's cavalry the volunteers could seize Smolnyi, the seat
of the Soviet.[39]

Savinkov reported to Kerensky on August 25 that all his instructions
would be carried out.

At this point, an incident occurred which transformed the discord between the Prime Minister and the Commander in Chief into an open rift. The
catalyst was a self-appointed "savior" of the country, a kind of stormy petrel,
named Vladimir Nikolaevich Lvov. Forty-five years old, from a wealthy landowning family, a man of burning ambitions but no commensurate talents,
Lvov had led a restless life. Having studied philosophy at St. Petersburg
University, he enrolled at the Moscow Theological Seminary, then pursued
desultory studies and for a while contemplated becoming a monk. He eventually chose politics. He joined the Octobrists, and served in the Third and
Fourth Dumas. During the war, he belonged to the Progressive Bloc. Owing
to wide social connections, he got himself appointed Procurator of the Holy
Synod in the First Provisional Government, a post he held until July 1917,
when he was dismissed. He took the dismissal badly and harbored a grudge
against Kerensky. He is said to have had considerable personal charm, but was
regarded as naïve and "incredibly frivolous"; George Katkov questions his
sanity.[40]

In August, Lvov joined a group of conservative intellectuals in Moscow
who wanted to save Russia from looming collapse. The country had had no
real cabinet since early July, when Kerensky assumed dictatorial powers. Like
Kornilov, Lvov and his friends felt that the Provisional Government needed

to be strengthened with representatives of business and the armed forces. It was suggested to him that he convey these views to Kerensky. The initiator of the move seems to have been A. F. Aladin, one of those mysterious figures in the Russian Revolution (such as N. V. Nekrasov and V. S. Zavoiko) who exerted great influence without ever emerging from the shadows. A Social-Democratic revolutionary in his youth, Aladin led the Trudovik faction in the First Duma. After its dissolution, he moved to England, where he remained until February 1917. He was close to Kornilov. Affiliated with the group was I. A. Dobrynskii, a Red Cross official, and Lvov's elder brother, Nicholas, a prominent Duma deputy and leading figure in the Progressive Bloc.

According to Lvov's recollections (which, however, have been characterized as entirely unreliable), during the week of August 17–22, following the State Conference, he heard rumors of conspiracies at headquarters to proclaim Kornilov dictator and him Minister of the Interior.* He claimed he felt it a duty to inform Kerensky. The two met on the morning of August 22. Kerensky says that he had many visits from would-be saviors of the country and paid little heed to them, but Lvov's "message" carried a threat which gained his attention.† According to Kerensky, Lvov told him that the base of public support for the government had eroded to the point where it had become necessary to bolster it by inviting into it public figures who enjoyed good relations with the military. He claimed to speak on behalf of these figures, but who they were, he refused to say. Kerensky subsequently denied having given Lvov authority to negotiate in his name with anyone, saying that before he could "express an opinion" on Lvov's remarks he had to know the names of his associates. He specifically denied discussing the possibility of Lvov's going to Mogilev to consult Kornilov.[41] According to Kerensky, after Lvov left his office he gave the conversation no more thought. There is no reason to doubt Kerensky, but it is not improbable that, consciously or not, he gave Lvov the impression that he wished to know more, using him, if not as a proxy, then as an intelligence agent to learn whether there was any substance to persistent rumors of anti-government plots in Mogilev.‡

Lvov returned at once to Moscow to report to his friends on the talk with

---

*The original deposition of Lvov, drawn up on September 14, 1917, is reproduced in Chugaev, ed., *Revoliutsionnoe dvizhenie v avguste*, 425–28. His recollections, published in *PN* in November and December 1920, are reprinted in A. Kerensky and R. Browder, eds., *The Russian Provisional Government 1917*, III (Stanford, Calif., 1961), 1558–68. After Vladimir Nabokov *père* wrote a letter to *Poslednie novosti* dismissing Lvov's account of a conversation with him as "nonsense" (*PN*, No. 199, December 15, 1920, 3), their publication was terminated. It is said that Lvov ended his days as a derelict on the streets of Paris.

†Kerensky gave an account of his exchanges with Lvov to the commission investigating the Kornilov Affair on October 8, 1917. He later published it, with commentaries, in *Delo Kornilova*, 83–86.

‡This is the opinion of Golovin: *Kontr-revoliutsiia*, I, Pt. 2, 25. Lvov later claimed that he had requested and received from Kerensky authority to negotiate with his associates provided he acted with great discretion and in utmost secrecy: *PN*, No. 190 (December 4, 1920), 2. Given Kerensky's subsequent activities, such behavior would not have been out of character. Even more likely is the connivance of Nekrasov, Kerensky's closest adviser, who played a major role in exacerbating the conflict between the two men.

the Prime Minister: the interview had been successful, he told them, and Kerensky was prepared to discuss a reorganization of the cabinet. On the basis of Lvov's account, Aladin drafted a memorandum:

1. Kerensky is willing to negotiate with headquarters;
2. the negotiations should be conducted through Lvov;
3. Kerensky agrees to form a cabinet enjoying the confidence of the country and the entire military;
4. in view of these facts, specific demands must be formulated;
5. a specific program has to be worked out;
6. the negotiations must be conducted in secrecy.*

This document suggests that in reporting the conversation with Kerensky, Lvov exaggerated the Prime Minister's interest in his proposal.

Accompanied by Dobrynskii, Lvov went to Mogilev. He arrived on August 24, just as Savinkov was departing. Since Kornilov was too busy carrying out Kerensky's instructions to receive him, he checked in at a hotel, where he claimed to have heard rumors of Kornilov's plot to kill Kerensky. Horrified, he decided to protect the Prime Minister by pretending to act on his behalf and negotiate a reconstitution of the cabinet. "Although Kerensky had not given me specific authority to conduct negotiations with Kornilov," he recounted, "I felt that I could negotiate in his name inasmuch as, in general, he was agreeable to the reorganization of the government."[42] He saw Kornilov late that night and again the following morning (August 25). According to Kornilov's deposition and the recollections of Lukomskii, who was present, Lvov identified himself as a representative of the Prime Minister on an "important mission."[43] With reckless lack of caution, Kornilov neither requested to see Lvov's credentials nor asked Petrograd to confirm his authority to speak for the Prime Minister, but immediately entered with him into the most sensitive and potentially incriminating political discussions. His mission, Lvov said, was to learn Kornilov's views on how to assure firm government in Russia. In his own opinion, this could be accomplished in one of three ways: (1) if Kerensky assumed dictatorial powers; (2) if a Directory was formed with Kornilov as a member; (3) if Kornilov became dictator, with Kerensky and Savinkov holding ministerial portfolios.[44] Kornilov took this information at face value because he had been officially told some time earlier that the government was contemplating a Directory modeled on the English Small War Cabinet to improve the management of the war effort.[45]

Interpreting Lvov to mean that Kerensky was offering him dictatorial powers, Kornilov responded that he preferred the third option. He did not crave power, he said, and would subordinate himself to every head of state; but if asked to take on the main responsibility, as Lvov (and, presumably, the

*Martynov, *Kornilov,* 84–85. In his deposition, Lvov said that Aladin's memorandum represented "not my positions but Aladin's conclusions from my words": Chugaev, *Revoliutsionnoe dvizhenie v avguste,* 426.

Prime Minister) suggested he might, he would not refuse.[46] He went on to say that in view of the danger of an imminent Bolshevik coup in Petrograd, it might be wise for the Prime Minister and Savinkov to seek safety in Mogilev and there join him in discussions on the composition of the new cabinet.

The interview over, Lvov at once departed for Petrograd.

Lukomskii, who was politically more astute, expressed suspicions about Lvov's mission. Had Kornilov asked for his credentials? No, Kornilov replied, because he knew Lvov to be an honorable man. Why had Savinkov not asked his opinions of cabinet changes? Kornilov shrugged off this question.[47]

On the evening of August 25, Kornilov invited Rodzianko by telegraph to come to Mogilev, along with other public leaders, in three days' time. Lvov wired a similar message to his brother. The meeting was to deal with the composition of the new cabinet.[48]

At 6 p.m. the following day (August 26), Lvov met with Kerensky in the Winter Palace.* Just as in his interview with Kornilov he had posed as a representative of the Prime Minister, so he now assumed the role of an agent of the Commander in Chief. Without telling Kerensky that he had asked Kornilov's opinion of three options for restructuring the government, which he had formulated with his friends but presented as coming from the Prime Minister, he said that Kornilov demanded dictatorial authority. Kerensky recalls that on hearing this he burst out laughing. But amusement soon yielded to alarm. He asked Lvov to put Kornilov's demands in writing. Lvov jotted down the following:

> General Kornilov proposes:
>
> 1. That martial law be proclaimed in Petrograd.
> 2. That all military and civil authority be placed in the hands of the Commander in Chief.
> 3. That all ministers, not excluding the Prime Minister, resign and that provisional executive authority be transferred to deputy ministers until the formation of a cabinet by the Commander in Chief.
>
> V. Lvov[49]

Kerensky says that as soon as he read these words everything became clear:[50] a military coup was in the making. He might have asked himself why Kornilov had to employ as intermediary the former Procurator of the Holy Synod rather than Savinkov, or better yet, he might have rushed to the nearest telegraph to ask Kornilov or Filonenko whether the Commander in Chief had indeed commissioned Lvov to negotiate on his behalf. He did neither. His certainty that Kornilov was about to seize power was strengthened by Lvov's insistence that Kornilov wanted Kerensky and Savinkov to depart that very night for Mogilev. Kerensky concluded that Kornilov wanted to take them prisoner.

---

*Accounts of this meeting: Kerensky, *Delo Kornilova,* 132–36, and Miliukov, *Istoriia* I, Pt. 2, 204–5. Miliukov talked to Lvov immediately before and after his meeting with the Prime Minister.

There can be little doubt that the three "conditions" attributed by Lvov to Kornilov had been concocted by him and his friends in order to force the issue: they did not reflect Kornilov's answer to what he had been told were questions posed to him by the Prime Minister. But they were just what Kerensky needed to break Kornilov. In order to obtain incontrovertible proof of Kornilov's conspiracy, Kerensky decided for the time being to play along. He invited Lvov to meet him at 8 p.m. in the office of the Minister of War to communicate with the general by telegraph.

Lvov, who spent the interval with Miliukov, was late. At 8:30, having kept Kornilov waiting for half an hour, Kerensky initiated a telegraphic conversation, in the course of which he impersonated the absent Lvov. He hoped, he said later, with this deception to obtain either a confirmation of Lvov's ultimatum or else a "bewildered" denial.

What follows is the complete text of this celebrated exchange as recorded on telegraphic tapes:

Kerensky: Prime Minister on the line. We are waiting for General Kornilov.

Kornilov: General Kornilov on the line.

Kerensky: How do you do, General. V. N. Lvov and Kerensky are on the line. We ask you to confirm that Kerensky can act in accordance with the information conveyed to him by Vladimir Nikolaevich.

Kornilov: How do you do, Aleksandr Fedorovich. How do you do, Vladimir Nikolaevich. To confirm once again the outline of the situation I believe the country and the army are in, an outline which I sketched out to Vladimir Nikolaevich with the request that he should report it to you, let me declare once more that the events of the last few days and those already in the offing make it imperative to reach a completely definite decision in the shortest possible time.

Kerensky [impersonating Lvov]: I, Vladimir Nikolaevich, am enquiring *about this definite decision which has to be taken, of which you asked me to inform Aleksandr Fedorovich* strictly in private. Without such confirmation from you personally, Aleksandr Fedorovich hesitates to trust me completely.

Kornilov: Yes, I confirm that I asked you to transmit my urgent request to Aleksandr Fedorovich to *come to Mogilev.*

Kerensky: I, Aleksandr Fedorovich, take your reply to confirm the words reported to me by Vladimir Nikolaevich. It is impossible for me to do that and leave here today, but I hope to leave tomorrow. Will Savinkov be needed?

Kornilov: I urgently request that Boris Viktorovich come along with you. What I said to Vladimir Nikolaevich applies equally to Boris Viktorovich. I would beg you most sincerely not to postpone your departure beyond tomorrow . . .

Kerensky: Are we to come only if there are demonstrations, rumors of which are going around, or in any case?

Kornilov: In any case.

Kerensky: Goodbye. We shall meet soon.

Kornilov: Goodbye.[51]

This brief dialogue was a comedy of errors with the most tragic consequences. Kerensky later maintained—and he persisted in this version to the
end of his life—that Kornilov had "affirmed not only Lvov's authority to speak
in Kornilov's name, but confirmed also the accuracy of the words which Lvov
had attributed to him"—namely, that he demanded dictatorial powers.[52] But
we know from eyewitnesses at the other end of the Hughes apparatus that
when the conversation was over, Kornilov heaved a sigh of relief: Kerensky's
agreement to come to Mogilev meant to him that the Prime Minister was
willing to work jointly on the formation of a new, "strong" government. Later
that evening, Kornilov discussed with Lukomskii the composition of such a
cabinet, in which both Kerensky and Savinkov would hold ministerial posts.
He also sent telegrams to leading statesmen inviting them to join him and the
Prime Minister in Mogilev.[53]

Thanks to the availability of the tapes, it can be established that the two
men talked at cross-purposes. As concerned Kornilov, all that he had confirmed to Kerensky posing as Lvov was that he had, indeed, invited Kerensky
and Savinkov to Mogilev. Kerensky interpreted Kornilov's confirmation to
mean—without any warrant except such as provided by his fevered imagination—that Kornilov intended to take him prisoner and proclaim himself dictator. It was an omission of monumental proportions on Kerensky's part not to
inquire directly or even obliquely whether Kornilov had in fact given Lvov for
transmittal a three-point ultimatum. In the conversation with Kerensky, Kornilov said nothing about the cabinet resigning and full military and civilian
power being placed in his hands. From Kornilov's words—"Yes, I confirm
that I asked you [i.e., Lvov] to transmit my urgent request to Aleksandr
Fedorovich to come to Mogilev"—Kerensky chose to infer that the three
political conditions presented to him by Lvov were authentic as well. When
Filonenko saw the tapes, he observed that "Kerensky never stated what he was
asking and Kornilov never knew to what he was responding."* Kerensky
believed that by impersonating Lvov he was communicating with Kornilov in
an understandable code, whereas he was speaking in riddles. The best that can
be said in defense of the Prime Minister's behavior is that he was overwrought.
But the suspicion lurks that he heard exactly what he wanted to hear.

On the basis of such flimsy evidence, Kerensky decided on an open break
with Kornilov. When Lvov belatedly turned up, he had him placed under
arrest.† Ignoring Savinkov's pleas that before doing anything precipitous he

*Miliukov, *Istoriia*, I, Pt. 2, 213. Unlike Kerensky, Kornilov later admitted that he had acted
thoughtlessly in not asking Kerensky to spell out what Lvov had conveyed to him on his behalf:
A. S. Lukomskii, *Vospominaniia*, I (Berlin, 1922), 240.

†He spent the night in a room adjoining the Alexander III suite occupied by the Prime
Minister, who kept him awake bellowing operatic arias. He was later placed under house arrest and
treated by a psychiatrist: *Izvestiia*, No. 201 (October 19, 1917), 5.

communicate once again with Kornilov to clear up what in Savinkov's mind was an obvious misunderstanding, Kerensky called a cabinet meeting for midnight. He told the ministers what had transpired and requested "full authority"—that is, dictatorial powers—to enable him to deal with the military coup d'état. The ministers agreed that one had to stand up to the "general-conspirator" and that Kerensky should enjoy full powers to deal with the emergency. Accordingly, they tendered their resignations, which Nekrasov interpreted to mean that the Provisional Government had, in effect, ceased to exist.[54] Kerensky emerged from the meeting as nominal dictator. After the cabinet adjourned at 4 a.m. on August 27, no more regular cabinet meetings were held, decisions from now until October 26 being taken by Kerensky acting alone or in consultation with Nekrasov and Tereshchenko. In the early hours of the morning, either with or without the approval of the ministers—most likely on his personal authority—Kerensky sent Kornilov a telegram dismissing him and ordering him to report at once to Petrograd. Until his replacement had been named, General Lukomskii was to serve as Commander in Chief.* By breaking with Kornilov, Kerensky could pose as champion of the Revolution: according to Nekrasov, during the night meeting of the cabinet, Kerensky said, "I will not give them the Revolution"[55]—as if it were his to give or keep.

While these events were taking place, Kornilov, ignorant of Kerensky's interpretation of their brief exchange, proceeded with preparations to help the government suppress the anticipated Bolshevik rising. At 2:40 a.m. he cabled Savinkov:

> The corps is assembling in the environs of Petrograd toward evening August 28. Request that Petrograd be placed under martial law August 29.[56]

If any more proof is needed that Kornilov did not engage in a military putsch, this cable should furnish it: for surely if he were ordering the Third Corps to Petrograd to unseat the government, he would hardly have forewarned the government by telegraph. It is even less credible that he would have entrusted his alleged coup to a subordinate. Zinaida Gippius, pondering the mystery of the Kornilov Affair a few days after its occurrence, asked herself the obvious question: "How was it that Kornilov *sent* his troops while he himself sat quietly at headquarters?"[57] Indeed, had Kornilov really planned to topple the government and take over as dictator, a man of his temperament and military presence would certainly have commanded the operation in person.

The receipt at 7:00 a.m. on August 27, at headquarters of Kerensky's cable dismissing Kornilov threw the generals into complete confusion. Their initial reaction was that the cable had to be a forgery, not only because its

---

Revoliutsiia, IV, 99. According to Savinkov, between 9 and 10 p.m.—that is, before the cabinet had met—Kerensky told him it was too late to reach an understanding with Kornilov because the telegram dismissing him had already gone out: *Mercure de France*, No. 503 (June 1, 1919), 439.

contents made no sense in view of the Kerensky-Kornilov talk ten hours earlier but also because it was improperly formatted, lacking the customary serial number and bearing only the signature "Kerensky," without the title. It also had no legal force, since by law only the cabinet had the authority to dismiss the Commander in Chief. (Headquarters, of course, did not know that the previous night the cabinet had resigned and Kerensky assumed dictatorial powers.) On further thought the generals concluded that the message perhaps was genuine, but that Kerensky had sent it under duress, possibly while a prisoner of the Bolsheviks. From such considerations, Kornilov refused to resign and Lukomskii to assume his duties "until the circumstances had been fully clarified."[58] Convinced that the Bolsheviks were already in control of Petrograd, Kornilov, ignoring Kerensky's instructions to the contrary, ordered Krymov to speed up the advance of his troops.[59]

To clarify any confusion that may have arisen in Petrograd in connection with Kornilov's answer to Lvov's questions, whom no one in Mogilev as yet suspected of being an impostor, Lukomskii sent the government a telegram in his own name, reaffirming the need for strong authority to prevent the collapse of the armed forces.[60]

That afternoon Savinkov, as yet ignorant of Lvov's machinations but suspecting some monumental mistake, contacted Kornilov. Vasilii Maklakov stood by and toward the end joined in the conversation.[61] Referring to Lukomskii's latest telegram, Savinkov protested that on his visit to Mogilev he had never raised political matters. In response, Kornilov for the first time mentioned Vladimir Lvov and referred to the three options which Lvov had laid out before him. He went on to say that the Third Cavalry Corps was being moved toward Petrograd on instructions of the government, as conveyed by Savinkov. He was acting entirely loyally, carrying out the government's orders. "Deeply convinced that the [dismissal] decision, entirely unexpected to me, had been taken under pressure of the Soviet of Workers' and Soldiers' Deputies . . . I firmly declare . . . that I will not leave my post." Kornilov added that he would be happy to meet with the Prime Minister and Savinkov at his headquarters, confident that "the misunderstanding could be cleared up through personal explanations."

At this point, the breach was still mendable. Had Kerensky displayed the same circumspection in dealing with charges against Kornilov and held out for "documentary evidence" that would prove his "treason in final form," as he had done the month before in the case of Lenin, all that happened would have been avoided. But while Kerensky feared to repress Lenin, he had no interest in conciliation with the general. When Miliukov, upon being informed of the course of events, offered his services as mediator, Kerensky responded that there could be no conciliation with Kornilov.[62] Kerensky rejected a similar offer from the Allied ambassadors.[63] People who saw Kerensky at the time thought he was in a state of complete hysteria.[64]

All that was needed to prevent a complete break between the Provisional Government and the generals was for Kerensky or his proxy to ask Kornilov point-blank whether he had authorized Lvov to demand dictatorial powers. Savinkov urged him to do so, but Kerensky refused.[65] Kerensky's failure to take this obvious step can be explained only in one of two ways: that he was in a mental condition in which all judgment had deserted him or else that he chose deliberately to break with Kornilov in order to assume the mantle of the Revolution's savior and in this manner neutralize the challenge from the left.

Having learned from Kornilov of Lvov's actions, Savinkov rushed back to the Prime Minister's office. He ran into Nekrasov, who told him that it was too late to seek a rapprochement with Kornilov because he had already sent to the evening papers the Prime Minister's statement charging the Commander in Chief with treason.[66] This was done despite Kerensky's promise to Savinkov that he would delay release of this document until after he had had a chance to communicate with Kornilov.[67] A few hours later, the press published in special editions a sensational communiqué bearing Kerensky's signature, said to have been drafted by Nekrasov.[68] Golovin believes that Nekrasov released it deliberately before Savinkov had had a chance to report on his conversation with Kornilov.* It read:

> On August 26, General Kornilov sent to me Duma Deputy Vladimir Nikolaevich Lvov, to demand that the Provisional Government transfer to General Kornilov full civil and military authority with the proviso that he himself, at his own discretion, would appoint a new government to administer the country. The authority of Duma Deputy Lvov to make such a proposal was subsequently confirmed to me by General Kornilov in a direct wire conversation.[69]

To defend the country from the attempts of "certain circles of Russian society" to exploit its difficulties for the purpose of "establishing . . . a political system inimical to the conquests of the Revolution," the statement went on, the cabinet had authorized the Prime Minister to dismiss General Kornilov and place Petrograd under martial law.

Kerensky's accusation threw Kornilov into an uncontrollable rage because it touched his most sensitive nerve, his patriotism. After reading it, he no longer thought of Kerensky as a Bolshevik captive, but as the author of despicable provocation designed to discredit him and the armed forces. He responded by sending to all front commanders a counterappeal drafted by Zavoiko:†

> The telegram of the Prime Minister . . . in its first part is an out-and-out lie. I did not send Duma Deputy Vladimir Lvov to the Provisional Government—

---

*Golovin, *Kontr-revoliutsiia,* I, Pt. 2, 35. Nekrasov, the *éminence grise* of Kerensky's regime and a thoroughly sinister figure, throughout 1917 pushed the Prime Minister leftward. A professor of engineering at the Tomsk Polytechnic and a leading figure on the left wing of the Kadet Party, he was involved on January 1, 1918, in an unsuccessful attempt on Lenin's life. The would-be assassins were pardoned, following which Nekrasov went into Bolshevik service under an assumed name. His identity was eventually discovered and he seems to have been imprisoned (N. Iakovlev, *1 Avgusta 1914,* Moscow, 1974, 226–32).

†A businessman with political ambitions, Zavoiko was the counterpart of Nekrasov, pushing Kornilov toward the right: on him, see Martynov, *Kornilov,* 20–22.

61. N. V. Nekrasov.

he came to me as a messenger from the Prime Minister. . . . Thus, there occurred a grand provocation which gambles with the destiny of the Fatherland.

Russian people: our great homeland is dying!

The moment of death is near!

Forced to speak out publicly, I, General Kornilov, declare that the Provisional Government, under pressure from the Bolshevik majority in the Soviet, acts in full accord with the plans of the German General Staff and, concurrently with the imminent landings of enemy forces on the coast of Riga, destroys the army and convulses the country from within . . .

I, General Kornilov, the son of a Cossack peasant, declare to each and all that I personally desire nothing but to save Great Russia. I swear to lead the people through victory over the enemy to the Constituent Assembly, where it will decide its own destiny and choose its new political system.[70]

This, at last, was mutiny: Kornilov later admitted that he had decided on an open break with the government because he had been accused by it of open rebellion—that is, treason. Golovin believes that by his actions Kerensky provoked Kornilov to rebel:[71] the assessment is correct in the sense that Kornilov rebelled only after having been charged with rebelling.

That Kerensky wanted to exacerbate rather than heal the breach became apparent from the several communiqués he released on August 28. In one he instructed all military commanders to ignore orders from Kornilov, whom he accused of having "betrayed the Fatherland."[72] In another, he lied to the public about the reasons for the advance of Krymov's corps on Petrograd:

The ex-Commander in Chief, General Kornilov, having rebelled against the authority of the Provisional Government, while professing in his telegrams patriotism and loyalty to the people, has now by his deeds demonstrated his treachery. He has withdrawn regiments from the front, weakening its resistance to the pitiless enemy, the German, and has sent all these regiments against Petrograd. He has spoken of saving the Fatherland and consciously instigates a fratricidal war. He says that he stands for freedom, and sends against Petrograd Native Divisions.[73]

Had Kerensky forgotten, as he was later to claim, that only a week earlier he himself had ordered the Third Cavalry Corps to Petrograd to come under his command?[74] It would strain credulity to the utmost to find such an explanation plausible.

During the three days that followed, Kornilov tried without success to rally the nation "to pull our Fatherland out of the hands of the mercenary Bolsheviks, who lord it over Petrograd."[75] He appealed to the regular armed forces as well as the Cossacks and ordered Krymov to occupy Petrograd. Many generals gave him moral support and sent wires to Kerensky protesting his treatment of the Commander in Chief.[76] But neither they nor the conservative politicians joined him, being confused by the disinformation spread by Kerensky, which, by blatantly distorting the background of events, made Kornilov into a mutineer and counterrevolutionary. The refusal of all the top generals to follow Kornilov furnishes additional proof that they had not been involved in any conspiracy with him.

On August 29, Kerensky wired Krymov as follows:

In Petrograd complete calm. No disturbances [*vystupleniia*] expected. There is no need for your corps. The Provisional Government commands you, on your personal responsibility, to stop the advance on Petrograd, ordered by the removed Commander in Chief, and direct the corps not to Petrograd but to its operational destination in Narva.[77]

The message makes sense only if Kerensky assumed that Krymov was advancing to Petrograd to quell Bolshevik disturbances. Although confused, Krymov obeyed. The Ussuri Cossack Division stopped at Krasnoe Selo, near Petrograd, and on August 30 swore loyalty to the Provisional Government. The Native Division, apparently on orders of Krymov, also halted its advance. The actions of the Don Cossack Division cannot be determined. In any event, the available sources indicate that the role usually attributed to agitators sent by the Soviet to dissuade the Third Corps from advancing on Petrograd has been considerably exaggerated. The principal reason why Krymov's forces did not occupy Petrograd was the realization of its commanding officers that the city was not, as he and they had been told, in the hands of the Bolsheviks and that their services were not required.*

*Zinaida Gippius thus depicts the encounter between Kornilov's cavalry and the units sent from Petrograd to intercept them: "There was no 'bloodshed.' Near Luga and in some other places, the divisions dispatched by Kornilov and the 'Petrograders' ran into each other. They confronted each other, uncomprehending. The 'Kornilovites' were especially amazed. They had gone to 'defend

62. Soldiers of the "Savage Division" meet with the Luga Soviet.

Krymov arrived in Petrograd on August 31 on the invitation of Kerensky and with a promise of personal safety. He saw the Prime Minister later that day. He explained that he had moved his corps to Petrograd to assist him and the government. As soon as he had learned of a misunderstanding between the government and headquarters, he ordered his men to halt. He never intended to rebel. Without going into explanations and refusing even to shake hands with him, Kerensky dismissed Krymov and instructed him to report to the Military-Naval Court Administration. Krymov went instead to a friend's apartment and put a bullet through his heart.*

Because the two generals whom he had asked to assume Kornilov's duties—Lukomskii followed by V.N. Klembovskii—had turned him down, Kerensky found himself in the awkward position of having to leave the military command in the hands of a man whom he had publicly charged with treason. Having previously instructed the military commanders to ignore Kornilov's orders, he now reversed himself and allowed Kornilov's strictly military orders to be obeyed for the time being. Kornilov thought the situation extraordinary: "An episode has occurred which is unique in world history," he wrote, "the Commander in Chief, accused of treason, . . . has been ordered to continue commanding his armies because there is no one else to appoint."[78]

Following the breach with Kerensky, Kornilov fell into despondency: he

the Provisional Government' and encountered an 'enemy' who had also gone to 'defend the Provisional Government.' . . . So they stood and pondered. They couldn't understand a thing. But recalling the teaching of frontline agitators that 'one should fraternize with the enemy,' they fervently fraternized": *Siniaia kniga* (Belgrade, 1929), 181; diary entry of August 31, 1917.

*Kerenskii, *Delo Kornilova,* 75–76, *Revoliutsiia,* IV, 143; Martynov, *Kornilov,* 149–51. Krymov left a suicide note for Kornilov, which Kornilov destroyed: Martynov, *Kornilov,* 151. No reactionary monarchist, Krymov had participated in 1916 in plots against Nicholas II.

was convinced that the Prime Minister and Savinkov had deliberately trapped him. Afraid that he would commit suicide, his wife requested him to surrender his revolver.[79] Alekseev arrived in Mogilev on September 1 to assume command: it had taken Kerensky three days to enlist him for this mission. Kornilov yielded without resistance, asking only that the government establish firm authority and cease abusing him.[80] He was first placed under house arrest at a Mogilev hotel and then transferred to the Bykhov Fortress, where Kerensky incarcerated thirty other officers suspected of involvement in the "conspiracy." In both places he was guarded by the faithful Tekke Turkomans. He escaped from Bykhov shortly after the Bolshevik coup and made his way to the Don, where with Alekseev he would found the Volunteer Army.

Was there a "Kornilov plot"? Almost certainly not. All the available evidence, rather, points to a "Kerensky plot" engineered to discredit the general as the ringleader of an imaginary but widely anticipated counterrevolution, the suppression of which would elevate the Prime Minister to a position of unrivaled popularity and power, enabling him to meet the growing threat from the Bolsheviks. It cannot be a coincidence that none of the elements present in a genuine coup d'état ever came to light: lists of conspirators, organizational charts, code signals, programs. Such suspicious facts as communication with officers in Petrograd and orders to military units are in all instances perfectly explicable in the context of the anticipated Bolshevik putsch. Had an officer plot been hatched then surely some generals would have followed Kornilov's appeals to join in his mutiny. None did. Neither Kerensky nor the Bolsheviks have ever been able to identify a single person who would admit to or of whom it could be demonstrated that he was in collusion with Kornilov: and a conspiracy of one is an obvious absurdity. A commission appointed in October 1917 completed in June 1918 (that is, already under Bolshevik rule) an investigation into the Kornilov Affair. It concluded that the accusations leveled at Kornilov were baseless: Kornilov's military moves had been intended not to overthrow the Provisional Government but to defend it from the Bolsheviks. The Commission completely exonerated Kornilov, accusing Kerensky of "deliberately distor[ting] the truth in the matter of Kornilov from lack of courage to admit guilt for the grandiose mistake" he had committed.*[81]

Kornilov was not a particularly complicated person and his behavior in July–August 1917 can be explained without resort to conspiracy theories. His first and foremost concern was with Russia and the war. He was alarmed by the vacillating policies of the Provisional Government and its dependence on the Soviet, which with its meddling in military matters had made the conduct

---

*Suspicions that the whole Kornilov Affair was a provocation are buttressed by Nekrasov's uncautious remarks to the press. In a newspaper interview given two weeks after the event he praised Lvov for exposing Kornilov's alleged plot. Distorting Kornilov's answer to Kerensky to make it sound as if it confirmed Lvov's ultimatum, he added: "V. N. Lvov helped save the Revolution: he exploded a prepared mine two days before it was to go off. There undoubtedly was a conspiracy and Lvov only discovered it prematurely": *NZh,* No. 55 (September 13, 1917), 3. These words suggest that Nekrasov, possibly with Kerensky's connivance, used Lvov to destroy Kornilov.

of military operations all but impossible. He had reason to believe that the government was penetrated by enemy agents. But even though he considered Kerensky unfit for his post, he felt for him no personal animosity and regarded him as indispensable in the government. Kerensky's behavior in August caused him to doubt whether the Prime Minister was his own man. His inability to carry out the military reforms which Kornilov knew Kerensky wanted convinced Kornilov that the Prime Minister was a captive of the Soviet and the German agents in it. When Savinkov told him of the impending Bolshevik putsch and asked for military assistance to suppress it, Kornilov saw a chance to help the government liberate itself from the Soviet. He had every reason to expect that after the putsch had been liquidated an end would be put to the "duality of power" and Russia would receive a new and effective regime. Of this he wanted to be a part. General Lukomskii, who was at his side throughout these critical days, provides what sounds like a reasonable explanation of Kornilov's thinking during the brief interval between Savinkov's visit to Mogilev and his break with Kerensky:

> I presume that General Kornilov, being convinced of Bolshevik action in Petrograd and of the necessity of suppressing it in the most ruthless manner, assumed that this will naturally lead to a governmental crisis and the creation of a new government, new authority. He decided to participate in the formation of that authority along with some members of the current Provisional Government and major public and political figures on whose full support he had apparently reasons to rely. From his words I know that General Kornilov had discussed the formation of the new government, which he would join in the capacity of Commander in Chief, with A. F. Kerensky, Savinkov, and Filonenko.[82]

It is hardly justified to define as "treasonous" efforts by the Commander in Chief to revitalize the armed forces and help restore effective government. As we have seen, Kornilov rebelled only after having been accused, without cause, of being a traitor. He was the victim of Kerensky's boundless ambition, sacrificed to the Prime Minister's futile quest to shore up his eroding political base. A fair summary of what Kornilov wanted and failed to achieve is provided by an English journalist who observed the events at first hand:

> He wanted to strengthen the Government, not to weaken it. He did not want to encroach upon its authority, but to prevent others from doing so. He wanted to compel it to be what it had always professed to be but [had] never really been—the single and unchallenged depository of administrative power. He wanted to emancipate it from the illicit and paralyzing influence of the soviets. In the end, that influence destroyed Russia, and Kornilov's defiance of the Government was a last desperate effort to arrest the process of destruction.[83]

If it is correct that Kerensky provoked the break with Kornilov to enhance his authority, he not only failed but achieved the very opposite. The clash fatally compromised his relations with conservative and liberal circles without solidifying his socialist base. The main beneficiaries of the Kornilov Affair were the Bolsheviks: after August 27, the SR and Menshevik following on which Kerensky depended melted away. The Provisional Government now ceased to function even in that limited sense in which it may be said to have done so until then. In September and October, Russia drifted rudderless. The stage was set for a counterrevolution from the left. Thus, when Kerensky later wrote that "it was only the 27th of August that made [the Bolshevik coup of] the 27th of October possible," he was correct, but not in the sense in which he intended.[84]

As noted, Kerensky never carried out any serious punitive actions against the Bolsheviks for the July putsch. According to the chief of his counterintelligence, Colonel Nikitin, on July 10–11 he even deprived the Military Staff of the authority to arrest Bolsheviks and forbade it to confiscate weapons found in their possession.[85] At the end of July, he looked the other way as the Bolsheviks held their Sixth Party Congress in Petrograd.

This passivity derived in large measure from Kerensky's desire to appease the Ispolkom, which rallied to the Bolsheviks. As we have seen, on August 4 it adopted a resolution, moved by Tsereteli, to stop further "persecution" of those involved in what was delicately called the "events of July 3–5." At the August 18 session, the Soviet voted to "protest decisively the illegal arrests and excesses" committed against the representatives of the "extreme currents of the socialist parties."[86] In response, the government began to release one by one prominent Bolsheviks, sometimes on bail, sometimes on the guarantee of friends. The first to be freed (and cleared of all charges) was Kamenev, who regained freedom on August 4. Lunacharskii, Vladimir Antonov-Ovseenko, and Alexandra Kollontai were set free shortly afterward. Others followed.

In the meantime, the Bolsheviks were reasserting themselves as a political force. They benefited from the political polarization which occurred during the summer when the liberals and conservatives gravitated toward Kornilov and the radicals shifted toward the extreme left. Workers, soldiers, and sailors, disgusted with the vacillations of the Mensheviks and SRs, abandoned them in droves in favor of the only alternative, the Bolsheviks. But there was also political fatigue: Russians who had gone in droves to the polling stations in the spring grew tired of elections which did nothing to improve their condition. This held especially true for conservative elements who felt they stood no chance against the radicals, but it also applied to the liberal and moderate socialist constituencies. This trend can be demonstrated by the results of the municipal elections in Petrograd and Moscow. In the voting for the Petrograd Municipal Council on August 20, one week before the Kornilov incident, the Bolsheviks increased the share of the votes they had gained in May 1917 from 20.4 percent to 33.3 percent, or by more than one-half. In absolute numbers, however, their votes increased only by 17 percent due to the drop in the number of those casting ballots. Whereas in the Spring elections, 70 percent of those elegible had gone to the polls, in August the proportion dropped to 50 percent; in some districts of the capital city, half of those who had previously voted abstained.*[87] In Moscow, in the September municipal elections the decline in voter participation was even more dramatic. Here, 380,000 ballots were cast compared to 640,000 the previous June. More than half of them went to the Bolsheviks, who picked up 120,000 votes while the socialists (SRs, Mensheviks, and their affiliates) lost 375,000 voters; most of the latter presumably had chosen to stay home.

MUNICIPAL ELECTIONS IN MOSCOW
(in percentage of seats)[88]

Party	June 1917	September 1917	Change
SRs	58.9	14.7	−44.2
Mensheviks	12.2	4.2	−8.0
Bolsheviks	11.7	49.5	+37.8
Kadets	17.2	31.5	+14.3

One effect of this polarization was the erosion of the political base on which Kerensky had counted in his bid for unchallenged power. The poor showing by the socialist parties in the Petrograd municipal elections in mid-August may have been an important factor in Kerensky's behavior later that month. For with his political base melting away, what better way of enhancing his popularity and influence with the left than as the vanquisher of the "counter-revolution," even if only an imaginary one?

The Kornilov Affair raised Bolshevik fortunes to unprecedented heights. To neutralize Kornilov's phantom putsch and stop Krymov's troops from occupying Petrograd, Kerensky asked for help from the Ispolkom. At a night session of August 27–28 the Ispolkom approved, on a Menshevik motion, the creation of a "Committee to Fight the Counterrevolution." But since the Bolshevik Military Organization was the only force which the Ispolkom could invoke, this action had the effect of placing the Bolsheviks in charge of the Soviet's military contingent:[89] in this manner, yesterday's arsonists became today's firefighters. Kerensky also appealed directly to the Bolsheviks to help him against Kornilov by using their influence with the soldiers, which had grown appreciably at this time.[90] An agent of his requested the sailors of the cruiser *Aurora,* known for their Anarchist and Bolshevik sympathies, to assume responsibility for the protection of the Winter Palace, Kerensky's residence and the seat of the Provisional Government.[91] M. S. Uritskii would later claim that these actions of Kerensky's "rehabilitated" the Bolsheviks. Kerensky also made it possible for the Bolsheviks to arm themselves by distribut-

*Crane Brinton in his *Anatomy of Revolution* (New York, 1938, 185–86) observes that it is common in revolutionary situations for ordinary citizens to grow bored with politicking and to leave the field to extremists. The influence of the latter increases in proportion to the public's disenchantment and loss of interest in politics.

ing 40,000 guns to the workers, a good share of which fell into Bolshevik hands; these weapons the Bolsheviks kept after the crisis had passed.[92] How far matters had progressed with the rehabilitation of the Bolshevik Party may be judged by the decision of the government on August 30 to release all the Bolsheviks still in detention except those few against whom it had initiated legal proceedings.[93] Trotsky was one of the beneficiaries of this amnesty: freed from the Kresty prison on September 3 on 3,000 rubles' bail, he took charge of the Bolshevik faction in the Soviet. By October 10 all but twenty-seven Bolsheviks were at liberty[94] and preparing for the next coup, while Kornilov and other generals languished in the Bykhov Fortress. On September 12, the Ispolkom requested the government to offer guarantees of personal security and a fair trial to Lenin and Zinoviev.[95]

A no less important consequence of the Kornilov Affair was a break between Kerensky and the military. For although the officer corps, confused about the issues and unwilling to defy the government openly, refused to join in Kornilov's mutiny, it despised Kerensky for his treatment of their commander, the arrest of many prominent generals, and his pandering to the left. When, in late October, Kerensky would call on the military to help save his government from the Bolsheviks, his pleas would fall on deaf ears.

On September 1, Kerensky proclaimed Russia a "republic." One week later (September 8) he abolished the Department of Political Counterintelligence, depriving himself of the principal source of information on Bolshevik plans.[96]

It was only a question of time before Kerensky would be overthrown by someone able to provide firm leadership. Such a person had to come from the left. Whatever the differences dividing them, the parties of the left closed ranks when confronted with the specter of "counterrevolution," a term which in their definition included any initiative to restore to Russia effective government and a viable military force. But since the country had to have both, the initiative to restore order had to emerge from within their own ranks: the "counterrevolution" would come disguised as the "true" revolution.

In the meantime, Lenin, in his rural hideaway, was busy redesigning the world.

Accompanied by Zinoviev and a worker named N. A. Emelianov, he arrived in the evening of July 9 at Razliv, a railroad junction in a region of country dachas. Lenin had his beard shaved off, following which, disguised as farm laborers, the two Bolsheviks were led to a field hut nearby, which would serve as their home for the next month.

Lenin, who had an aversion to memoirs, left no reminiscences of this period in his life, but there exists a brief account by Zinoviev.[97] The two lived in concealment, but maintained contact with the capital by means of couriers. Lenin was so irritated by attacks on him and his party that for a while he refused to read newspapers. The events of July 4 preyed on his mind: he often wondered aloud whether the Bolsheviks could not have taken power and every time reached a negative conclusion. With the late summer rains flooding their hut, it was time to move. Zinoviev returned to Petrograd while Lenin went on to Helsinki. To cross into Finland, he used false papers identifying him as a worker: judging by the passport photograph, which shows him cleanly shaven and wearing a wig, the disguise gave him something of a rakish appearance.

Removed from the day-to-day direction of his party and probably resigned to the probability that he would never have another opportunity to seize power, Lenin devoted his attention to the long-term objectives of the Communist movement. He resumed work on the essay on Marx and the State, which he would publish the next year under the title *State and Revolution.* It was to be his legacy to future generations, a blueprint for revolutionary strategy after the capitalist order had been overthrown.

State and Revolution is a nihilistic work which argues that the Revolution must destroy root and branch all "bourgeois" institutions. Lenin begins with citations from Engels to the effect that the state, everywhere and at all times, has represented the interests of the exploiting class and reflected class conflicts. He accepts this proposition as proven and elaborates on it exclusively with reference to Marx and Engels, without referring to the history of either political institutions or political practices.

The central message of the work derives from the lessons which Marx had drawn from the Paris Commune and formulated in *Eighteenth Brumaire of Louis Napoleon:*

> The parliamentary republic, in its struggle against the revolution, found itself compelled to strengthen, along with the means of repression, the means of centralization of state power. All revolutions have perfected this machine instead of smashing it.*

Marx rephrased the argument in a letter to a friend:

> If you look into the concluding chapter of my *Eighteenth Brumaire,* you will find that I declare the next attempt of the French Revolution: not to transfer from one set of hands to another the bureaucratic-military machine, as was done until now, but to *smash* it.[98]

Nothing that Marx wrote on the strategy and tactics of revolution etched itself more deeply on Lenin's mind. He often quoted this passage: it was his guide to action after taking power. The destructive fury which he directed against the Russian state and Russian society and all their institutions found theoretical justification in this dictum of Marx's. Marx provided Lenin with a solution to the most troublesome problem confronting modern revolutionaries: how to prevent the successful revolution from being undone by a counter-

---

*Cited in Lenin, *PSS,* XXXIII, 28. Lenin underscored the concluding sentence.

revolutionary reaction. The solution was to liquidate the "bureaucratic-military machine" of the old regime in order to deprive the counterrevolution of a ground in which to breed.

What would replace the old order? Again referring to Marx's writings on the Paris Commune, Lenin pointed to such mass-participatory institutions as communes and people's militias that offered no haven to cadres of reactionary civil servants and officers. In this connection, he predicted the ultimate disappearance of the professional bureaucracy: "Under socialism, *all* will govern in turn and quickly become accustomed to no one governing."[99] Later, when the Communist bureaucracy grew to unheard-of proportions, this passage would be flung in Lenin's face. There is no question that Lenin was unpleasantly surprised and greatly worried by the emergence in Soviet Russia of a mammoth bureaucracy: it was probably his main concern in the final year of life. But he was never under the illusion that the bureaucracy would vanish with the fall of "capitalism." He realized that for a long time after the Revolution the "proletarian dictatorship" would have to assume the shape of a state, with all that this implied:

> In the *"transition"* from capitalism to communism, repression is *still* necessary, but it is already the repression of the minority of the exploiters by the majority of the exploited. A special apparatus, a special machine of repression, the "state," is *still* necessary.[100]

While working on *State and Revolution,* Lenin also addressed the economic policies of a future Communist regime. This he did in two essays written in September, after the Kornilov Affair, when Bolshevik prospects unexpectedly improved.[101] The thesis of these essays is very different from that of his political writings. While determined to "smash" the old state and its armed forces, Lenin favored preserving the "capitalist" economy and harnessing it in the service of the revolutionary state. We shall discuss this subject in the chapter devoted to "War Communism." Here suffice it to say that Lenin derived his economic ideas from reading certain contemporary German writers, notably Rudolf Hilferding, who held that advanced or "finance" capitalism had attained a level of concentration at which it became relatively easy to introduce socialism by the simple device of nationalizing banks and syndicates.

Thus, while intending to uproot the entire political and military apparatus of the old, "capitalist" regime, Lenin wanted to retain and use its economic apparatus. In the end, he would destroy all three.

But this lay in the future. The immediate problems involved revolutionary tactics, and here Lenin found himself at odds with his associates.

In spite of the willingness of the socialists in the Soviet to forgive and forget the July putsch and despite their defense of the Bolsheviks against the government's harassment, Lenin decided that the time for masking his bid for power under Soviet slogans had passed: henceforth, the Bolsheviks would have to strive for power directly, openly, by means of armed insurrection. In "The Political Situation," written on July 10, one day after reaching his rural hideaway, he argued:

> All hopes for the peaceful evolution of the Russian Revolution have disappeared without trace. The objective situation: either the ultimate triumph of the military dictatorship or the triumph of the *decisive struggle of the workers* . . .
> The slogan of the passage of all power to the soviets was the slogan of the peaceful evolution of the Revolution, which was possible in April, May, June, until July 5–9—that is, until the passage of actual power into the hands of the military dictatorship. Now this slogan is no longer correct, because it does not take into account the completed passage [of power] and the complete betrayal, in deed, of the Revolution by the SRs and Mensheviks.[102]

In the original version of the manuscript Lenin had written "armed uprising," which he later changed to "decisive struggle of the workers."[103] The novelty of these remarks was not that power had to be taken by force—the Bolshevik-led armed workers, soldiers, and sailors who had taken over the streets of Petrograd in April and July hardly staged a festival of song and dance—but that the Bolsheviks now had to strike for themselves, without pretending to act on behalf of the soviets.

The Sixth Bolshevik Congress held at the end of July approved this program. Its resolution stated that Russia was now ruled by a "dictatorship of the counterrevolutionary imperialist bourgeoisie" under which the slogan "All Power to the Soviets" had lost its validity. The new slogan called for the "liquidation" of Kerensky's "dictatorship." This was the task of the Bolshevik Party, which would rally behind itself all anti-counterrevolutionary groups, headed by the proletariat and supported by the poor peasantry.[104] Dispassionately analyzed, the premises of this resolution were absurd and its conclusions deceptive, but its practical meaning was unmistakable: henceforth the Bolsheviks would wage war against the Soviet as well as against the Provisional Government.

Many Bolsheviks were unhappy over the new tactic and the abandonment of pro-Soviet slogans. On another occasion that month, Stalin tried to put their minds at ease by assuring them that "the party is indubitably in favor of those soviets where we have a majority."[105]

But it was not long before the Bolsheviks, noting a general cooling of interest in the soviets, changed their minds once again: for this growing apathy gave them an opportunity to penetrate and manipulate the soviets for their own ends. *Izvestiia,* the official soviet organ, wrote at the beginning of September that

> in recent times one can observe indifference toward work in soviets. . . . Indeed, of the more than 1,000 delegates [of the Petrograd Soviet] only 400 to 500 attend its meetings, and those who fail to turn up are precisely representatives of parties which until now had formed a soviet majority[106]

—that is, Mensheviks and SRs. The same complaint could be read in *Izvestiia* one month later in an editorial called "Crisis of the Soviet Organization." Its author recalled that when the soviets had been at the peak of popularity the "interurban" *(inogorodnyi)* department of the Ispolkom listed up to 800 soviets in the country. By October, many of these soviets no longer existed or existed only on paper. Reports from the provinces indicated that the soviets were losing prestige and influence. The editorial complained of the inability of the Soviets of Workers' and Soldiers' Deputies to get together with peasant organizations, which resulted in the peasantry remaining "entirely outside" the soviet structure. But even in localities where the soviets continued to function, as in Petrograd and Moscow, they no longer represented all "democracy" because many intellectuals and workers stayed away:

> The soviets were a marvelous organization to fight the old regime, but they are entirely incapable of taking upon themselves the creation of a new one. . . . When autocracy fell, and the bureaucratic order along with it, we erected the soviets of deputies as temporary barracks to shelter all democracy.

Now, *Izvestiia* concluded, the soviets were being abandoned for permanent "stone structures," such as the Municipal Councils, chosen on a more representative franchise.[107]

The growing disenchantment with the soviets and the absenteeism of their socialist rivals enabled the Bolsheviks to gain in them an influence out of proportion to their national following. As their role in the soviets grew, they reverted to the old slogan: "All Power to the Soviets."

The Bolsheviks passed an important milestone on their march to power on September 25 when they won a majority in the Workers' Section of the Petrograd Soviet. (They had gained such a majority in Moscow on September 19.) Trotsky, who assumed the chairmanship of the Petrograd Soviet, immediately proceeded to turn it into an instrument with which to secure control of the urban soviets in the rest of the country. In the words of *Izvestiia,* the instant the Bolsheviks acquired a majority in the Workers' Section of the Petrograd Soviet, they "transformed it into their party organization and, leaning on it, engaged in a partisan struggle to seize all the soviets nationwide."[108] They largely ignored the Ispolkom chosen by the All-Russian Congress of Soviets, which remained under SR and Menshevik control, and proceeded to create a parallel pseudo-national soviet organization of their own, representing only those soviets in which they enjoyed pluralities.

In the more favorable political environment created by the Kornilov Affair and their successes in the soviets, the Bolsheviks revived the question of a coup d'état. Opinion was divided. The July debacle fresh in mind, Kamenev and Zinoviev opposed further "adventurism." Notwithstanding their growing strength in the soviets, they argued, the Bolsheviks remained a minority party, so that even if they managed to take power, they would soon lose it to the combined forces of the "bourgeois counterrevolution" and the peas-

antry. On the other extreme stood Lenin, the principal proponent of immediate and resolute action. The Kornilov incident convinced him that the chances
of a successful coup were better than ever and perhaps unrepeatable. On
September 12 and 14 he wrote from Finland two letters to the Central Committee, called "The Bolsheviks Must Take Power" and "Marxism and Insurrection."[109] "With a majority in the soviets of workers' and soldiers' deputies in
both capital cities," he wrote in the first, "the Bolsheviks can and *must* seize
power." Contrary to Kamenev and Zinoviev, the Bolsheviks not only could
seize power but hold on to it: by proposing an immediate peace and giving land
to the peasants, "the Bolsheviks can establish a government that *no one* will
overthrow." It was essential, however, to move swiftly because the Provisional
Government might turn Petrograd over to the Germans or else the war could
end. The "order of the day" was

> *armed insurrection* in Petrograd and Moscow (plus their regions), the conquest
> of power, the overthrow of the government. We must consider *how* to agitate
> for this, without so expressing ourselves in print.

Once power had been taken in Petrograd and Moscow, the issue would be
settled. Lenin dismissed as "naïve" the advice of Kamenev and Zinoviev that
the party should await the convocation of the Second Congress of Soviets in
the hope of obtaining a majority: "no revolution waits for *that.*"

In the second letter, Lenin dealt with the accusation that taking power
by armed force was not "Marxism" but "Blanquism" and disposed of analogies with July: the "objective" situation in September was entirely different.
He felt certain (possibly from information supplied by his German contacts)
that Berlin would offer the Bolshevik government an armistice. "And to secure
an armistice means to conquer *the whole* world."[110]

The Central Committee took up Lenin's letters on September 15. The
laconic and almost certainly heavily censored protocols of this meeting* indicate that while Lenin's associates hesitated to reject formally his advice (as
Kamenev urged them to do), neither were they prepared to follow it: according
to Trotsky, in September no one agreed with Lenin on the desirability of an
immediate insurrection.[111] On Stalin's motion, Lenin's letters were circulated
to the party's major regional organizations, which was a way of avoiding
action. Here the matter rested: at none of the six sessions that followed
(September 20–October 5) was Lenin's proposal referred to.†

---

*Protokoly Tsentral'nogo Komiteta RSDRP (b) (Moscow, 1958), 55–62. This, the only pres-
ently available record of the meetings of the Bolshevik Central Committee from August 4, 1917, until
February 24, 1918, first came out in 1929. It was meant to discredit Trotsky, Kamenev, and Zinoviev,
whom Stalin had defeated for party control, and for this reason must be used with extreme caution.
According to the editors of the second edition: "The texts of the protocols are published in full,
without omissions, except for matters of conflict [konfliktnye dela] removed, as in the first edition,
for reasons of inadequate explanation of these questions in the text of the protocols" (p. vii),
whatever that may mean.
†It cannot be excluded, of course, that Lenin's advice was turned down and the fact censored
from the published version of the minutes.

Such passivity infuriated Lenin: he feared that the favorable moment for an insurrection would pass. On September 24 or 25, he moved from Helsinki to Vyborg (still in Finnish territory) to be nearer the scene of action. From there, on September 29, he dispatched a third letter to the Central Committee, under the title "The Crisis Has Ripened." His principal operative recommendations were contained in the sixth part of the letter, first made public in 1925. It had to be frankly conceded, Lenin wrote, that some party members wanted to postpone the power seizure until the next Congress of Soviets. He totally rejected this approach: "To pass up such a moment and 'await' the Congress of Soviets is *complete idiocy* or *complete treason*":

> The Bolsheviks are now *guaranteed* the success of the uprising: (1) we can (if we do not 'await' the Congress of Soviets) strike *suddenly* from three points: Petersburg, Moscow, and the Baltic Fleet ... (5) we have the technical capability to take power in Moscow (which could even begin so as to paralyze the enemy with its suddenness); (6) we have *thousands* of armed workers and soldiers who can *at once* seize the Winter Palace and the General Staff, the telephone station and all the major printing plants. ... If we were to strike at once, suddenly, from three points—Petersburg, Moscow, the Baltic Fleet— then the chances are 99 percent that we will win with fewer losses than we suffered on July 3–5, because the *troops will not move* against a government of peace.*

In view of the fact that the Central Committee did not answer his "entreaties" and even censored his articles, Lenin submitted his resignation. This, of course, was bluff. To discuss their differences, the Central Committee requested Lenin to return to Petrograd.[112]

Lenin's associates to a man rejected his demand for an immediate armed uprising, preferring a slower, safer course. Their tactics were formulated by Trotsky, who thought Lenin's proposals too "impetuous." Trotsky wanted the armed uprising disguised as the assumption of power by an All-Russian Congress of Soviets—not, however, one properly convened, which would certainly refuse to do so, but one which the Bolsheviks would convene on their own initiative in defiance of established procedures, and pack with followers: a congress of pro-Bolshevik soviets camouflaged as a national congress. Seen in retrospect, this undoubtedly was the correct course to follow because the country would not have tolerated the overt assumption of power by a single party, as Lenin advocated. To succeed beyond the initial days, the coup had to be given some sort of "soviet" legitimacy, even if a spurious one.

Lenin's sense of urgency was in good measure inspired by the fear of being preempted by the Constituent Assembly. On August 9, the Provisional

*Lenin, *PSS*, XXXIV, 281–82. Lenin here inadvertently concedes that on July 3–5 the Bolsheviks had, indeed, attempted a power seizure.

Government finally announced a schedule for that body: elections on November 12 and the opening session on November 28. Although on some days the Bolsheviks deluded themselves that they could win a majority of the seats in the Assembly, in their hearts they knew they had no chance given that the peasants were certain to vote solidly for the Socialists-Revolutionaries. Since Bolshevik strength lay in the cities and in the army, and they alone had soviet organizations, the Bolsheviks' only hope of claiming a national mandate was through the soviets. Otherwise, all was lost. Once the country made known its will through a democratic election, they could no longer claim that they spoke for the "people" and that the new government was "capitalist." If they were to take power, therefore, they had to do so before the elections to the Assembly. Once they were in control, the adverse results of the elections could be neutralized: as a Bolshevik publication put it, the composition of the Assembly "will strongly depend on who convenes it."[113] Lenin concurred: the "success" of the elections to the Assembly would be best assured *after* the coup.[114] As events were to show, this meant that the Bolsheviks would either tamper with the electoral results or else disperse the Assembly. This was for Lenin a weighty reason to hurry his colleagues, to the point of threatening resignation.

The Bolsheviks had no hope of manipulating the Constituent Assembly into conceding them power, but they could conceivably use for this purpose the soviets, institutions that were irregularly elected, loosely structured, and without peasant representation. With this in mind, they began to agitate for the prompt convocation of a Second Congress of Soviets. They had a case. Since the First Congress in June, the situation in Russia had changed and so had the membership of the urban soviets. The SRs and Mensheviks were none too enthusiastic about another Congress, in part because they feared it would have a sizable Bolshevik contingent, and in part because it would interfere with the Constituent Assembly. The regional soviets and the armed forces were negative as well. At the end of September, the Ispolkom sent out questionnaires to 169 soviets and army committees, requesting their opinion on whether to convene a Second Congress of Soviets: of the sixty-three soviets that responded, only eight favored the idea.[115] The sentiment among the troops was even more negative: on October 1, the Soldiers' Section of the Petrograd Soviet voted against holding a national Congress of Soviets, and a report presented to it in mid-October indicated that the representatives of army committees had agreed unanimously that such a congress would be "premature" and would subvert the Constituent Assembly.[116]

But the Bolsheviks, enjoying preponderance in the Petrograd Soviet, kept up the pressure, and on September 26 the Bureau of the Ispolkom agreed to the convocation of a Second Congress of Soviets on October 20.[117] The agenda of this congress was to be strictly limited to drafting legislative proposals for submission to the Constituent Assembly. Instructions were issued to the interurban department of the Soviet to invite the regional soviets to send representatives.

The Bolsheviks thus won a victory, but it was only a first step. Although their position in the country's soviets was much stronger than it had been in June, it was unlikely that they would gain at the Second Congress an absolute majority.[118] This they could secure only by taking the convocation of the Second Congress into their own hands and inviting to it only those soviets, located mostly in central and northern Russia, and those army committees in which they had assured majorities. This they now proceeded to do.

On September 10, there opened in Helsinki the Third Regional Congress of Workers' and Soldiers' Soviets of Finland. Here the Bolsheviks enjoyed a solid majority.[119] The congress set up a Regional Committee which instructed civilian and military personnel in Finland to obey only those laws of the Provisional Government to which it gave assent.[120] The move was intended to delegitimize the Provisional Government through the agency of a pseudo-governmental center, run by the Bolsheviks.

Their success in Finland persuaded the Bolsheviks that they could use the same device to convene an equally compliant All-Russian Congress of Soviets. On September 29, the Bolshevik Central Committee discussed and on October 5 resolved to hold in Petrograd a Northern Regional Congress of Soviets.[121] Invitations were sent out in the name of an ephemeral Bolshevik front calling itself the Regional Committee of the Army, Navy, and Workers of Finland. The Bureau of the Ispolkom protested that the meeting was convened in an irregular manner.[122] Ignoring it, the Regional Committee proceeded to invite some thirty soviets in which the Bolsheviks had majorities to send representatives; among them were soviets of the Moscow province, which did not even belong to the Northern Region.[123] There exist strong indications that some Bolshevik leaders, Lenin among them, considered having this Regional Congress proclaim the passage of power to the soviets,[124] but the plan was given up.

The Congress of Soviets of the Northern Region opened in Petrograd on October 11. It was completely dominated by the Bolsheviks and their allies, the Left SRs, a splinter group of the Socialist-Revolutionary Party. This rump "congress" heard all kinds of inflammatory speeches, including one by Trotsky, who declared that the "time for words" had passed.[125]

The Bolshevik Party, of course, had no more authority than any other group to convene congresses of soviets, whether regional or national, and the Ispolkom declared the meeting a "private gathering" of individual soviets, devoid of official standing.[126] The Bolsheviks ignored this declaration. They regarded their body as the immediate forerunner of the Second Congress of Soviets, which they were determined to convene on October 20—according to Trotsky, by legal means if possible and by "revolutionary" ones if not.[127] The most important result of the Regional Congress was the formation of a "Northern Regional Committee," composed of eleven Bolsheviks and six Left SRs, whose task it was to "ensure" the convocation of a Second All-Russian Congress of Soviets.[128] On October 16 this body sent telegrams to the soviets, as well as to military committees at the regimental, divisional, and corps level, informing them that the Second Congress would meet in Petrograd on October 20 and requesting them to send delegates. The congress was to obtain an armistice, distribute land to peasants, and ensure that the Constituent Assembly met as scheduled. The telegrams instructed all soviets and army committees opposed to the convocation of the Second Congress—and these, as is known from the Ispolkom's survey, were the large majority—to be at once "reelected," which was a Bolshevik code word for dissolved.[129]

This Bolshevik move constituted a veritable coup d'état against the national organization of the soviets: it was the opening phase of the power seizure. With these measures, the Bolshevik Central Committee arrogated to itself the authority which the First Congress of Soviets had entrusted to the Ispolkom. It also preempted the Provisional Government, for the agenda which the Bolsheviks set for the so-called Second Congress was to be at the center of the government's activities until the convocation of the Constituent Assembly.[130]

The Mensheviks and SRs, well aware what the Bolsheviks were up to, refused to recognize the legitimacy of the Second Congress. On October 19, *Izvestiia* carried a statement by the Ispolkom which reasserted that only its Bureau had the authority to convene a national Congress of Soviets:

> No other committee has the authority or the right to take upon itself the initiative in convening this congress. The less does this right belong to the Northern Regional Congress, brought together in violation of all the rules established for the regional soviets and representing soviets chosen arbitrarily and at random.

The Bureau went on to say that the Bolshevik invitation to regimental, divisional, and corps committees violated established procedures for military representation, which called for delegates to be chosen by army assemblies and, when these could not be convened, by army committees on the basis of one delegate for 25,000 soldiers.[131] The Bolshevik organizers obviously bypassed the army committees because of their known opposition to the Second Congress.[132] Three days later *Izvestiia* pointed out that the Bolsheviks not only convened an illegal Congress, but flagrantly violated accepted norms of representation. While the electoral rules called for soviets representing fewer than 25,000 persons to send no delegates to the All-Russian Congress, and those representing between 25,000 and 50,000 to send two, the Bolsheviks invited one soviet with 500 members to send two delegates and another with 1,500 to send five, which was more than was allocated to Kiev.[133]

All of which was true enough. But even though the SRs and Mensheviks had declared the forthcoming Second Congress illegal as well as unrepresentative, they allowed it to proceed. On October 17, the Bureau of the Ispolkom approved the convocation of the Second Congress on two conditions: that it be postponed by five days, to October 25, to give provincial delegates time to get to Petrograd, and that it confine its agenda to the discussion of the internal situation in the country, preparations for the Constituent Assembly, and re-election of the Ispolkom.[134] It was an astonishing and inexplicable capitulation.

Although aware of what the Bolsheviks had in mind, the Ispolkom gave them what they wanted: a handpicked body, filled with their adherents and allies, which was certain to legitimize a Bolshevik power seizure.

The gathering of pro-Bolshevik soviets, disguised as the Second Congress of Soviets, was to legitimize the Bolshevik coup. On Lenin's insistence, however, the coup was to be carried out *before* the congress met, by shock troops under the command of the Military Organization. These troops were to seize strategic points in the capital city and declare the government overthrown, which would present the congress with an accomplished and irreversible fact. This action could not be carried out in the name of the Bolshevik Party. The instrument which the Bolsheviks used for this purpose was the Military-Revolutionary Committee, formed by the Petrograd Soviet in a moment of panic early in October to defend the city from an expected German assault.

The event was precipitated by German military operations in the Gulf of Riga. After Russian troops had evacuated Riga, the Germans sent reconnaissance units in the direction of Revel (Tallinn). These operations gave the Russian General Staff much concern because they posed a threat to Petrograd, only 300 kilometers away and unreliably defended.

The German threat to the capital grew more ominous in the middle of October. On September 6/19, the German High Command ordered the capture of the islands of Moon, Ösel, and Dagö in the Gulf of Riga. A flotilla which sailed on September 28/October 11 soon cleared Russian minefields and after overcoming unexpectedly stiff resistance, on October 8/21 completed the occupation of the three islands.[135] The enemy now was in a position to land behind Russian forces.

The Russian General Staff viewed this naval operation as preparatory to an assault on Petrograd. On October 3/16, it ordered the evacuation of Revel, the last major stronghold standing between the Germans and the capital. The next day Kerensky participated in discussions on ways to deal with the danger. The suggestion was made that since Petrograd could soon find itself in the combat zone, the government and the Constituent Assembly transfer to Moscow. The idea found general favor, the only disagreement being over the timing of the move, which Kerensky wanted to be done immediately while others argued for a delay. It was decided to evacuate after securing approval from the Pre-Parliament, a gathering of political leaders which the government scheduled on October 7 as a forum for soliciting broad public support. The question next arose of what to do about the Ispolkom. The consensus was that since it was a private body it should arrange for its own evacuation.* On October 5, government experts reported that the evacuation of the executive

---

*Revoliutsiia, V, 23. According to Kerensky, these discussions were secret, but they immediately leaked to the press: *Ibid.*, V, 81.

offices to Moscow would require two weeks. Plans were drawn up for the relocation inland of Petrograd industries.[136]

These precautions made good military and political sense: it was what the French had done in September 1914 as the Germans approached Paris and what the Bolsheviks would do in March 1918 under similar circumstances. But the socialist intelligentsia saw in them only a ploy of the "bourgeoisie" to turn over to the enemy "Red Petrograd," the main bastion of "revolutionary democracy." As soon as the press made public the government's evacuation plans (October 6) the Bureau of the Ispolkom announced that no evacuation could take place without its approval. Trotsky addressed the Soldiers' Section of the Soviet and persuaded it to adopt a resolution condemning the government for wanting to abandon the "capital of the Revolution": if unable to defend Petrograd, his resolution said, it should either make peace or yield to another government.[137] The Provisional Government at once capitulated. That same day it declared that in view of objections it would delay the evacuation for a month. Eventually it gave up the idea altogether.[138]

On October 9, the government ordered additional units of the garrison to the front to help stem the anticipated German assault. As could have been expected from past experience, the garrison resisted.[139] The dispute was turned over to the Ispolkom for adjudication.

At its meeting later that day, Mark Broido, a worker affiliated with the Mensheviks, moved a resolution calling on the Petrograd garrison to prepare to defend the city and for the Soviet to form (or, rather, reconstitute) a "Committee of Revolutionary Defense" to "work out a plan" to this end.[140] Caught by surprise, the Bolsheviks and Left SRs opposed Broido's resolution on the grounds that it would strengthen the Provisional Government. It passed but with the barest majority (13–12). Following the vote, the Bolsheviks realized they had made a mistake. They had a Military Organization which they were grooming for armed insurrection: it was subordinated to the Bolshevik Central Committee and independent of the Soviet. This status was a mixed blessing: for while the Military Organization could be depended on faithfully to execute the orders of the Bolshevik high command, as the organ of one political party it could not act on behalf of the Soviet in whose name Bolsheviks intended to carry out their power seizure. A few years later, Trotsky would recall that the Bolsheviks, aware of this handicap, had decided already in September 1917 to avail themselves of any opportunity to create what he calls a "non-party 'soviet' organ to lead the uprising."[141] This is confirmed by K. A. Mekhonoshin, a member of the Military Organization, who says that the Bolsheviks felt it necessary "to transfer the center linking [them] with units of the garrison from the Military Organization of the party to the Soviet so as to be able, at the moment of action, to step forward in the name of the Soviet."[142] The organization proposed by the Mensheviks was ideally suited for this purpose.

That evening (October 9) when the Menshevik proposal came up for a vote at the Plenum of the Soviet, the Bolshevik deputies reversed their stand:

they now agreed to the Soviet's forming an organization to defend Petrograd from the Germans as long as it would defend it also from the "domestic" enemy. By the latter they meant the Provisional Government, which, in the words of one Bolshevik speaker, was conniving to surrender the "main bastion of the Revolution to the Kaiser, who, in turn, according to the Bolshevik resolution, was supported in his advance on Petrograd by the Allied Imperialists."[143] To this end, the Bolsheviks proposed that the "Military Defense Committee" should assume full charge of the city's security against threats from the German "imperialists" as well as from Russian "counterrevolutionaries."

Surprised by the way the Bolsheviks reformulated Broido's proposal and knowing why they did so, the Mensheviks resolutely opposed the amendment. Defense of the city was the responsibility of the government and its Military Staff. But the Plenum preferred the Bolshevik version and voted for the formation of a "Revolutionary Committee of Defense"

> to gather in its hands all the forces participating in the defense of Petrograd and its approaches [as well as] to take all measures to arm the workers, in this manner ensuring both the revolutionary defense of Petrograd and the security of the people against the openly prepared assault of the military and civilian Kornilovites.[144]

This extraordinary resolution adroitly combined the newly formed committee's responsibility for meeting the real threat posed by the German armies with the imaginary one from the supporters of Kornilov, who were nowhere in sight. The Mensheviks and SRs now reaped the harvest of their demagoguery, their insistence on the "bourgeois" character of the Provisional Government and their obsessive concern with the counterrevolution.

The vote had decisive importance. Trotsky later claimed that it sealed the fate of the Provisional Government: it represented, in his words, a "silent" or "dry" revolution that gained the Bolsheviks "three-quarters if not nine-tenths" of the victory consummated on October 25–26.[145]

The matter was still not completely settled, however, because the decision of the Plenum required the approval of the Ispolkom and the entire Soviet. At a closed session of the Ispolkom on October 12, the two Menshevik representatives assailed the Bolshevik resolution, but they again suffered defeat, the body backing the Plenum's decision unanimously, against their two votes. The Ispolkom renamed the new organization the Military-Revolutionary Committee (Voenno-Revoliutsionnyi Komitet, or Milrevkom for short) and empowered it to take charge of the defenses of the city.[146]

The issue was formally sealed at the meeting of the Soviet on October 16. To deflect attention from themselves, the Bolsheviks nominated as drafter of the resolution establishing the Milrevkom an unknown young paramedic, the Left SR P. E. Lazimir. The SRs, who belatedly awoke to the significance of the Bolshevik maneuver, sought, without success, to obtain a delay in the vote, probably to assemble their absent delegates; when this motion failed, they abstained. Broido once again warned that the Milrevkom was a deception, its true mission being not to defend Petrograd but to carry out a seizure of power. Trotsky diverted the attention of the Soviet by citing passages from a newspaper interview with Rodzianko, which he chose to interpret to mean that the onetime chairman of the Duma (who in any event held no post in the government) would welcome a German occupation of Petrograd.[147] The Bolsheviks nominated Lazimir to chair the Milrevkom, with Podvoiskii as his deputy (on the eve of the October coup Podvoiskii would formally assume leadership of the organization).* The remaining members of the Milrevkom are difficult to ascertain: they seem to have been exclusively Bolsheviks and Left SRs.† But it did not much matter who was on the Milrevkom since it was only a flag of convenience for the true organizer of the coup, the Bolshevik Military Organization.

Trotsky now launched a war of nerves. When Dan requested the Bolsheviks to state clearly in the Soviet whether or not they were preparing an uprising, as rumored, Trotsky maliciously asked whether he wanted this information for the benefit of Kerensky and his counterintelligence. "We are told that we are organizing a staff for the seizure of power. We make no secret of this. . . ."[148] Two days later, however, he asserted that if an insurrection were to take place, the Petrograd Soviet would make the decision: "We still have not decided on an insurrection."[149]

The deliberate ambivalence of these statements notwithstanding, the Soviet had been put on notice. The socialists either did not hear what Trotsky was saying or resigned themselves to the inevitability of a Bolshevik "adventure." They feared Bolshevik actions much less than possible right-wing responses, which would sweep them along with Lenin's followers. On the eve of the Bolshevik coup (October 19), the Military Organization of the Socialist-Revolutionary Party in Petrograd adopted a "neutral" position on the anticipated uprising. A circular note sent to its members and sympathizers in the garrison urged them to stay away from demonstrations and to be "fully prepared for the merciless suppression . . . of possible assaults by the Black Hundreds, pogromists, and counterrevolutionaries."[150] This left no doubt where the SR leaders saw the main threat to democracy.

Trotsky kept Petrograd in a state of constant tension, promising, warning, threatening, cajoling, inspiring. Sukhanov describes a typical scene he witnessed during those days:

> The mood of the audience of over three thousand, filling the hall, was definitely one of excitement; their hush indicated expectation. The public, of course, consisted mainly of workers and soldiers, though it had not a few typical petty bourgeois figures, male and female.

---

*Lazimir later joined the Bolshevik Party. He died in 1920 of typhus.
†N. Podvoiskii in *KL*, No. 8 (1923), 16–17. Trotsky wrote in 1922 that even if his life were at stake he would not be able to recall the makeup of the Milrevkom: *PR*, No. 10 (1922), 54.

63. The Military-Revolutionary Committee (Milrevkom), which staged the Bolshevik coup in October 1917. In center, Chairman Podvoiskii. On his right, Nevskii. On the extreme right, Raskolnikov.

The ovation given Trotsky seemed to have been cut short out of curiosity and impatience: what was he going to say? Trotsky at once began to heat up the atmosphere with his skill and brilliance. I recall that he depicted for a long time and with extraordinary force the difficult . . . picture of suffering in the trenches. Through my mind flashed thoughts about the unavoidable contradictions between the parts of this rhetorical whole. But Trotsky knew what he was doing. The essential thing was the *mood*. The political conclusions had been familiar for a long time . . .

Soviet power [Trotsky said] was destined not only to put an end to the suffering in the trenches. It would provide land and stop internal disorder. Once again resounded the old recipes against hunger: how the soldiers, sailors, and working girls would requisition the bread from the propertied, and send it free of charge to the front. . . . But on this decisive "Day of the Petrograd Soviet" [October 22] Trotsky went further:

"The Soviet government will give everything the country has to the poor and to the soldiers at the front. You, bourgeois, own two coats? Give one to the soldier freezing in the trenches. You have warm boots? Stay at home. Your boots are needed by a worker . . ."

The mood around me verged on ecstasy. It seemed that the mob would at any moment, spontaneously and unasked, burst into some kind of religious hymn. Trotsky formulated a short general resolution or proclaimed some general formula, on the order of: "We will defend the cause of the workers and peasants to the last drop of blood."

Who is in favor? The crowd of thousands raised its hands like one man.

I saw the uplifted hands and burning eyes of men, women, adolescents, workers, soldiers, peasants, and typical petty bourgeois figures . . .

[They] agreed. [They] vowed . . . I watched this truly grandiose spectacle with an unusually *heavy* heart.[151]

By October 16, the Bolsheviks had at their disposal two organizations, each nominally subject to the Soviet: the Military-Revolutionary Committee to carry out the coup and the forthcoming Second Congress of Soviets to legitimize it. They had by now effectively superseded the authority of the Provisional Government in the Military Staff and that of the Ispolkom in the soviets. The Milrevkom and the Congress of Soviets were to carry out the Bolshevik decision, taken in deep secrecy on October 10, to seize power.

Sometime between October 3 and 10, Lenin slipped back into Petrograd: he did it so surreptitiously that Communist historians to this day have been unable to determine the time of his return. He lived in concealment until October 24 in the Vyborg District, surfacing only after the Bolshevik coup was already underway.

On October 10—one day after the Ispolkom and the Soviet Plenum had voted to constitute a Defense Committee and very likely in connection with that event—twelve members of the Bolshevik Central Committee gathered to decide on the question of an armed uprising. The meeting took place at night, surrounded with extreme precautions, in the apartment of Sukhanov. Lenin came in disguise, clean-shaven, wearing a wig and glasses. Our knowledge of what transpired on this occasion is imperfect, because of the two protocols taken only one has been published and even this one in a doctored version.[152] The fullest account comes from the recollections of Trotsky.[153]

Lenin arrived determined to secure an unequivocal commitment to a coup before October 25. When Trotsky countered, "We are convening a Congress of Soviets in which our majority is assured beforehand," Lenin answered that

the question of the Second Congress of Soviets . . . held for him no interest whatever: of what importance is it? will it even take place? and what can it accomplish even if it does meet? It is necessary to tear out [*vyrvat'*] power. One must not tie oneself to the Congress of Soviets, it is silly and absurd to forewarn the enemy about the date of the uprising. October 25 may serve at best as camouflage, but the uprising must be carried out earlier and independently of the Congress of Soviets. The party must seize power, arms in hand, and then we will talk of the Congress of Soviets.[154]

Trotsky thought that Lenin not only gave too much credit to the "enemy" but also underestimated the value of the soviets as a cover: the party could not seize power as Lenin wanted, independently of the soviets, because the workers and soldiers learned everything, including what they knew of the Bolshevik Party, through the medium of the soviets. Taking power outside the soviet structure would only sow confusion.

64. Grigorii Zinoviev.

The differences between Lenin and Trotsky centered on the timing and justification for the coup. But some members of the Central Committee questioned whether the party should even attempt to take power. Uritskii argued that the Bolsheviks were technically unprepared for an uprising and that the 40,000 guns at their disposal were inadequate. The most strenuous objections came again from Kamenev and Zinoviev, who explained their position in a confidential letter to Bolshevik organizations.[155] The time for a coup was not yet: "We are profoundly convinced that to rise now means to gamble not only with the destiny of our party but with that of the Russian Revolution as well as that of the international revolution." The party could expect to do well in the elections to the Constituent Assembly, capturing at a minimum one-third of the seats, thereby bolstering the authority of the soviets, in which its influence was on the ascendant. "The Constituent Assembly plus the soviets—this is the type of combined government institutions toward which we strive." They rejected Lenin's claim that the majority of Russians and international labor supported the Bolsheviks. Their pessimistic assessment led them to counsel a patient, defensive strategy in place of armed action.

To this argument Lenin responded that it would be "senseless to wait for the Constituent Assembly, which will not be with us, because this will complicate our task." In this, he had the support of the majority.

As the discussions drew to a close, the Central Committee divided into three factions: (1) a faction of one, consisting of Lenin, who alone favored an immediate seizure of power, without regard to the Congress of Soviets and the Constituent Assembly; (2) Zinoviev and Kamenev, supported by Nogin,

65. L. B. Kamenev.

Vladimir Miliutin, and Aleksei Rykov, who opposed a coup d'état for the time being; and (3) the rest of the participants, six in number, who agreed on a coup but followed Trotsky in preferring that it be carried out in conjunction with the Congress of Soviets and under its formal sponsorship—that is, in two weeks. A majority of ten voted in favor of an armed rising as "unavoidable and fully matured."[156] The timing was left open. Judging by ensuing events, it was to precede the Second Congress of Soviets by one or more days. Lenin had to acquiesce to this compromise, having gained his main point that the congress merely be asked to ratify the coup.

The formation of the Military-Revolutionary Committee and the convocation of the Congress of Northern Soviets which, in turn, initiated the Second Congress of Soviets, described previously, implemented the decision of the Central Committee on October 10.

Kamenev found this decision unacceptable. He resigned from the Central Committee and a week later explained his stand in an interview with *Novaia zhizn'*. He said that he and Zinoviev had sent a circular letter to party organizations in which they "firmly argued against the party assuming the initiative in any armed uprisings in the near future." Even though the party had not decided on such an uprising, he lied, he, Zinoviev, and some others believed that to "seize power by force of arms" on the eve of the Congress of Soviets and independently of it would have fatal consequences for the Revolution. An uprising was inevitable, but in good time.[157]

The Central Committee held three more meetings before the coup: October 20, 21, and 24.[158] The first of these had on its agenda the alleged breach of party discipline committed by Kamenev and Zinoviev in making public their opposition to an armed uprising.* Lenin wrote the committee two angry letters in which he demanded the expulsion of the "strikebreakers": "We cannot tell the capitalists the truth, namely that we have *decided* [to go] on strike [read: make an uprising] and to *conceal* from them the *choice of timing.*"[159] The committee failed to act on this demand.

The minutes of these three meetings appear so truncated as to render them virtually useless: if one were to take them at face value, one would gather that the coup, by then already in progress, was not even on the agenda.

The Central Committee's tactic called for provoking the government into retaliatory measures which would make it possible to launch the coup disguised as a defense of the Revolution. The tactic was no secret. As summarized by the SR organ, *Delo naroda*, weeks before the event, the Provisional Government would be accused of conspiring with Kornilov to suppress the Revolution and with the Kaiser to turn Petrograd over to the enemy, as well as of preparing to disperse both the Congress of Soviets and the Constituent Assembly.[160] Trotsky and Stalin confirmed after the event that such had been the party's plan. In Trotsky's words:

> In essence, our strategy was offensive. We prepared to assault the government, but our agitation rested on the claim that the enemy was getting ready to disperse the Congress of Soviets and it was necessary mercilessly to repulse him.[161]

And according to Stalin:

> The Revolution [read: the Bolshevik Party] disguised its offensive actions behind a smoke screen of defenses in order to make it easier to attract into its orbit uncertain, hesitating elements.[162]

Curzio Malaparte describes the bewilderment of the English novelist, Israel Zangwill, who happened to be visiting Italy as the Fascists were taking power. Struck by the absence of "barricades, street fighting and corpses on the pavement," Zangwill refused to believe that he was witnessing a revolution.[163] But, according to Malaparte, the characteristic quality of modern revolutions is precisely the bloodless, almost silent seizure of strategic points by small detachments of trained shock troops. The assault is carried out with such surgical precision that the public at large has no inkling of what is happening.

This description fits the October coup in Russia (which Malaparte had studied and used as one of his models). In October, the Bolsheviks gave up on massive armed demonstrations and street skirmishes, which they had employed, on Lenin's insistence, in April and July, because the crowds had

*Lenin mistakenly believed that Zinoviev had joined Kamenev in the interview with *Novaia zhizn': Protokoly TsK,* 108.

proven difficult to control and provoked a backlash. They relied instead on small, disciplined units of soldiers and workers under the command of their Military Organization, disguised as the Military-Revolutionary Committee, to occupy Petrograd's principal communication and transport centers, utilities and printing plants—the nerve centers of the modern metropolis. Merely by severing the telephone lines connecting the government with its Military Staff they made it impossible to organize a counterattack. The entire operation was carried out so smoothly and efficiently that even as it was in progress the cafés and restaurants along with the opera, theaters, and cinemas were open for business and thronged with crowds in search of amusement.

The Milrevkom, which its secretary, the Bolshevik Antonov-Ovseenko, later described as a "fine formal cover for the military work of the Party,"[164] held only two meetings, just enough to allow the Bolshevik Military Organization to claim for itself the "soviet" label.[165] Antonov-Ovseenko concedes that it operated directly under the Bolshevik Central Committee and was "in fact its organ": so much so that for a while consideration was given to transforming the Milrevkom into a branch of the Military Organization.[166] As he describes it, its headquarters located in rooms 10 and 17 of Smolnyi, were crowded all day long with young men coming and going, creating conditions which precluded serious work even if such had been intended.

In Communist accounts, the Milrevkom is given credit for mobilizing all or nearly all of the Petrograd garrison for the armed insurrection: thus, Trotsky claims that in October "the overwhelming majority of the garrison were standing openly on the side of the workers."[167] Contemporary evidence indicates, however, that Bolshevik influence on the garrison was much more modest. The mood of the Petrograd garrison was anything but revolutionary. Overwhelmingly, the 160,000 men billeted in the city and the 85,000 deployed in the environs[168] declared "neutrality" in the looming conflict. A count of the garrison units which on the eve of October inclined toward the Bolsheviks shows that they constituted a small minority: Sukhanov estimates that at best one-tenth of the garrison took part in the October coup, and "very likely many fewer."[169] The author's own calculations indicate that the actively pro-Bolshevik element in the garrison (exclusive of the Kronshtadt naval base) amounted to perhaps 10,000 men, or 4 percent. The pessimists on the Central Committee opposed an armed insurrection precisely on the grounds that even with their advocacy of an immediate armistice, on which Lenin counted to win over the troops, the Bolsheviks did not enjoy the garrison's support.

But the optimists proved right, because the Bolsheviks did not so much need to win the support of the garrison as to deny it to the government: if they had only 4 percent of the garrison on their side, the government had even less. The Bolsheviks' principal concern was to prevent the government from calling out the troops against them as it had been able to do in July. To this end, they needed to delegitimize the Military Staff. This they accomplished on October 21–22, when, claiming to act in the name of the Soviet and its Soldiers' Section, they had the Milrevkom assert exclusive authority over the garrison.

To begin with, the Milrevkom dispatched 200 "commissars" to military units in and near Petrograd: most were junior officers from the Bolshevik Military Organization who had taken part in the July putsch and had been recently freed from prison on parole.[170] Next, on October 21, it convened at Smolnyi a meeting of regimental committees. Addressing the troops, Trotsky stressed the danger of a "counterrevolution" and urged the garrison to rally around the Soviet and its organ, the Milrevkom. He introduced a motion so vaguely worded that it received ready approval:

> Welcoming the formation of the Military-Revolutionary Committee of the Petrograd Soviet of Workers' and Soldiers' Deputies, the Petrograd garrison pledges the committee full support in all its efforts to bring closer the front and rear in the interest of the Revolution.[171]

Who could possibly be against bringing the front and rear closer in the interest of the February Revolution? But the Bolsheviks meant to interpret the resolution as empowering the Milrevkom to assume the functions of the staff of the Petrograd Military District. According to Podvoiskii, who directed the Military Organization, these measures marked the onset of the armed insurrection.[172]

The following night (October 21–22), a deputation from the Milrevkom appeared at the headquarters of the Military Staff. Its spokesman, the Bolshevik Lieutenant Dashkevich, informed the commander of the Petrograd Military District, Colonel G. P. Polkovnikov, that by authority of the garrison meeting the staff's orders to the garrison would henceforth acquire force only if countersigned by the Milrevkom. The troops, of course, had made no such decision, and even if they had, it would have had no validity: the deputation actually acted on behalf of the Bolshevik Central Committee. Polkovnikov replied that his staff did not recognize the delegation. After he threatened to have them arrested, the Bolshevik delegates left and returned to Smolnyi.[173]

Having heard the delegation's report, the Milrevkom convened a second meeting of garrison delegates. Who came and on whose behalf cannot be determined. But it did not matter: by now, any casually assembled group could claim to represent the "Revolution." On the Milrevkom's motion, the meeting approved a fraudulent statement which claimed that although on October 21 the garrison had designated the Milrevkom as its "organ," the staff refused both to recognize and to cooperate with it. No mention was made of the fact that the delegation had asked not for "recognition" or "cooperation," but for authority to countermand the Staff's orders. The resolution went on:

> In this manner, the staff has broken with the revolutionary garrison and the Petrograd Soviet of Workers' and Soldiers' Deputies. Having broken with the

organized garrison of the capital, the staff has turned into a direct weapon of counterrevolutionary forces. . . . Soldiers of Petrograd! (1) The defense of the revolutionary order against counterrevolutionary attempts falls on you, under the leadership of the Military-Revolutionary Committee. (2) All orders concerning the garrison lacking the signature of the Military-Revolutionary Committee are invalid . . .[174]

The resolution achieved three objectives: it designated the Provisional Government, allegedly in the name of the Soviet, as "counterrevolutionary"; it divested it of authority over the garrison; and it provided the Milrevkom with an excuse to conceal its bid for power as a defense of the Revolution. It was a declaration of war.

On October 22, having learned of the Milrevkom's attempt to take over the garrison, the Military Staff gave the Soviet an ultimatum: either retract its orders or face "decisive measures."[175] Thinking it prudent to play for time, the Bolsheviks accepted the ultimatum "in principle" and offered to negotiate even as they were proceeding with the coup.[176] Later that day, the staff and the Milrevkom reached agreement on creating a "consultative body" of Soviet representatives to sit on the staff. On October 23, a delegation from the Milrevkom was sent to the staff, ostensibly for talks, but in fact to carry out "reconnaissance."[177] These actions produced the desired effect, which was to prevent the government from arresting the Milrevkom. During the night of October 23–24, the cabinet (which seems to have led a kind of shadowy existence since the Kornilov days) ordered the closing of the two leading Bolshevik dailies and, for the sake of balance, an equal number of right-wing papers, including *Zhivoe slovo,* which in July had published information on Lenin's contacts with the Germans. Troops were sent for to protect strategic points, including the Winter Palace. But when Kerensky asked for authority to have the Milrevkom arrested, he was dissuaded on the grounds that the staff was negotiating its differences with the Milrevkom.[178]

Kerensky greatly underestimated the threat posed by the Bolsheviks: he not only did not fear a Bolshevik coup, he actually hoped for one, confident that it would enable him to crush and be rid of them once and for all. In mid-October, military commanders kept reporting to him that the Bolsheviks were making unmistakable preparations for an armed uprising. At the same time they assured him that in view of the Petrograd garrison's "overwhelming" opposition to a coup, such an uprising would be promptly liquidated.[179] On the basis of these assessments, which misinterpreted opposition to Bolshevik plans to mean support for his government, Kerensky offered reassurances to colleagues and foreign ambassadors. Nabokov recalls him prepared to "offer prayers to produce this uprising" because he had ample forces to crush it.[180] To George Buchanan, Kerensky said more than once: "I only wish that [the Bolsheviks] would come out, and I will then put them down."[181]

But Kerensky's self-assurance in the face of a clear and present danger was inspired not only by overconfidence: now, as during the rest of 1917, fear of the "counterrevolution" provides a key to his behavior and that of the entire non-Bolshevik left. Once Kerensky had charged Kornilov and other generals with treason and asked the Soviet for help against them, in the eyes of professional officers he was no longer distinguishable from the Bolsheviks. After August 27, therefore, any military action against the Bolsheviks was certain to result in Kerensky's downfall. Aware of this, Kerensky hesitated far too long in rallying the military. General A. I. Verkhovskii, the Minister of War, told the British Ambassador after the event that "Kerensky had not wanted the Cossacks to suppress the [October] rising by themselves, as that would have meant the end of the revolution."[182] On the basis of shared fears, a fatal bond was thus forged between two mortal enemies, "February" and "October." The only hope that Kerensky and his associates still entertained was that at the last moment the Bolsheviks would lose their nerve and back out, as they had done in July. P. I. Palchinskii, who directed the defense of the Winter Palace on October 24–26, jotted down during the siege of the palace or immediately after its fall his impression of the government's attitude: "Helplessness of Polkovnikov and the lack of any plans. Hope that the senseless step will not be taken. Ignorance of what to do if, nevertheless, it is."[183]

No serious military preparations were made to stave off a blow which everyone knew was coming. Kerensky later claimed that on October 24 he had requested reinforcements from front-line commanders, but historical researches have shown that he had issued no such orders until nighttime (October 24–25), by which time it was too late, for by then the coup was already being completed.[184] General Alekseev estimated that there were in Petrograd 15,000 officers, one-third of them ready to fight the Bolsheviks: his offer to organize them was ignored, and as a result, as the city was being taken over they either sat on their hands or reveled in drunken orgies.[185] Most astonishing of all, the nerve center of the government's defense, the Military Staff, located in the Engineers' (Mikhailovskii) Palace, was left unguarded: any passerby was free to enter it without being asked for identification.[186]

The final phase of the Bolshevik coup got underway in the morning of Tuesday, October 24, after the Military Staff had carried out the halfhearted measures ordered by the government the preceding night.

In the early hours of October 24, *iunkers* took over guard duty at key points. Two or three detachments were sent to protect the Winter Palace, where they were joined by the so-called Women's Death Battalion consisting of 140 volunteers, some Cossacks, a bicycle unit, forty war invalids commanded by an officer with artificial legs, and several artillery pieces. Surprisingly, no machine guns were deployed. *Iunkers* shut down the printing plants of *Rabochii put'* (ex-*Pravda*) and *Soldat*. The telephone lines to Smolnyi were disconnected. Orders went out to raise the bridges over the Neva to prevent pro-Bolshevik workers and soldiers from penetrating the city's center. The staff forbade the garrison to take any instructions from the Milrevkom. It also ordered, without effect, the arrest of the Milrevkom's commissars.[187]

These preparations produced an atmosphere of crisis. That day most offices closed by 2:30 p.m. and the streets emptied as people rushed home.

This was the "counterrevolutionary" signal the Bolsheviks had been waiting for. They first moved to reopen their two newspapers: this they accomplished by 11 a.m. Next, the Milrevkom sent armed detachments to take over the Central Telegraph Office and the Russian Telegraphic Agency. The telephone lines from Smolnyi were reconnected. Thus, the earliest objectives of the coup were centers of information and lines of communication.

The only violence that day occurred in the afternoon as units of the Milrevkom forced the lowering of the bridges across the Neva.

While the uprising was already in its final and decisive phase, in the evening of October 24 the Milrevkom issued a statement that, rumors notwithstanding, it was not staging an uprising but solely acting to defend the "interests of the Petrograd garrison and democracy" from the counterrevolution.[188]

Possibly under the influence of this disinformation, Lenin, who must have been completely out of touch, wrote a despairing note to his colleagues urging them to do what they were in fact doing:

I am writing these lines in the evening of the 24th [of October], the situation is most extremely critical. It is clearer than clear that now, truly, to delay the uprising is death.

With all my strength I want to convince my comrades that now everything hangs on a hair, that we are confronting questions that are not resolved by consultations, not by congresses (even by congresses of soviets), but exclusively by the people, by the masses, by the struggle of the armed masses.

The bourgeois pressure of the Kornilovites, the dismissal of Verkhovskii indicate that one cannot wait. It is necessary, no matter what, this evening, this night, to arrest the government, to disarm the *iunkers* (vanquishing them if they resist), etc. . . .

Who should take power?

This is not important right now: let the Military-Revolutionary Committee take it or "some other institution" . . .

Power seizure is the task of the uprising: its political goal will become clear after power has been taken.

It would be perdition or a formality to await the uncertain voting of October 25. The people have the right and duty to solve such questions not by voting but by force . . .*

Later that night Lenin made his way to Smolnyi: he was heavily disguised, his bandaged face said to have made him look like a patient in a dentist's office. En route, he was almost arrested by a government patrol but he saved himself

*Lenin, *PSS*, XXXIV, 435–36. Verkhovskii had been dismissed from his post the day before (October 23) for delivering a defeatist speech: *Revoliutsiia*, V, 160; S. P. Melgunov, *Kak bol'sheviki zakhvatili vlast'* (Paris, 1953), 59. See A. I. Verkhovskii's *Rossiia na Golgofe* (Petrograd, 1918).

by pretending to be drunk. In Smolnyi he stayed out of sight, in one of the back rooms, accessible only to closest associates. Trotsky recalls that Lenin grew apprehensive when he heard about the ongoing negotiations with the Military Staff, but as soon as he was assured that these talks were a feint, he beamed with pleasure:

> "Oh, that is goo-oo-d," Lenin responded gaily in a singsong voice, and began to pace up and down the room, rubbing his hands in excitement. "That is verr-rr-ry good." Lenin liked military cunning: to deceive the enemy, to make a fool of him—what delightful work![189]

Lenin spent the night relaxing on the floor while Podvoiskii, Antonov-Ovseenko, and G. I. Chudnovskii, a friend of Trotsky's, under Trotsky's overall command, directed the operation.

That night (October 24–25), the Bolsheviks systematically took over all the objectives of strategic importance by the simple device of posting pickets: it was a model modern coup d'état as described by Malaparte. *Iunker* guards were told to go home: they either withdrew voluntarily or were disarmed. Thus, under cover of darkness, one by one, railroad stations, post offices, telephone centers, banks, and bridges fell under Bolshevik control. No resistance was encountered, no shots fired. The Bolsheviks took the Engineers' Palace in the most casual manner imaginable: "They entered and took their seats while those who were sitting there got up and left; thus the staff was taken."[190]

At the Central Telephone Exchange, the Bolsheviks disconnected the lines from the Winter Palace, but they missed two which were not registered. Using these lines, the ministers, gathered in the Malachite Room, maintained contact with the outside. Although in his public pronouncements he exuded confidence, to an eyewitness Kerensky appeared old and tired as he stared into the void, seeing no one, his half-closed eyes hiding "suffering and controlled fear."[191] At 9 p.m., a delegation from the Soviet, headed by Theodore Dan and Abraham Gots, turned up to tell the ministers that under the influence of the "reactionary" Military Staff they greatly overestimated the Bolshevik threat. Kerensky showed them the door.[192] That night, Kerensky at last contacted front-line commanders and asked for aid. In vain: none was available. At 9 a.m. on October 25 he slipped out of the Winter Palace disguised as a Serbian officer and in a car borrowed from a U.S. Embassy official, flying the American flag, drove off to the front in search of help.

By then, the Winter Palace was the only structure still left in government hands. Lenin insisted that before the Second Congress of Soviets officially opened and proclaimed the Provisional Government deposed, the ministers had to be under arrest. But the Bolshevik forces proved inadequate to the task. It turned out that, for all their claims, they had no men willing to brave fire: their alleged 45,000 Red Guards and tens of thousands of supporters among the garrison were nowhere to be seen. A halfhearted assault on the palace was

66. N. I. Podvoiskii.

launched at dawn, but at the first sound of shots the attackers beat a retreat.

Burning with impatience, fearful of intervention by troops from the front, Lenin decided to wait no longer. Between 8 and 9 a.m. he made his way to the Bolshevik operations room. At first no one knew him. Bonch-Bruevich burst with joy when he realized who he was: "Vladimir Ilich, our father," he shouted as he embraced him, "I did not recognize you, dear one!"[193] Lenin sat down and drafted, in the name of the Milrevkom, a declaration announcing that the Provisional Government was deposed. Released to the press at 10 a.m. (October 25), it read as follows:

TO THE CITIZENS OF RUSSIA!

The Provisional Government has been deposed. Government authority has passed into the hands of the organ of the Petrograd Soviet of Workers' and Soldiers' Deputies, the Military-Revolutionary Committee, which stands at the head of the Petrograd proletariat and garrison.

The task for which the people have been struggling—the immediate offer of a democratic peace, the abolition of landlord property in land, worker control over production, the creation of a Soviet Government—this task is assured.

Long Live the Revolution of Workers, Soldiers, and Peasants!
The Military-Revolutionary Committee of the
Petrograd Soviet of Workers' and Soldiers' Deputies.*

This document, which takes place of pride in the corpus of Bolshevik decrees, declared sovereign power over Russia to have been assumed by a body

---

*Dekrety, I, 1–2. Kerensky's wife was arrested and detained for forty-eight hours the following day for tearing down this declaration: A. L. Fraiman, *Forpost Sotsialisticheskoi Revoliutsii* (Leningrad, 1969), 157.

which no one outside the Bolshevik Central Committee had given authority to do so. The Petrograd Soviet had formed the Milrevkom to defend the city, not to topple the government. The Second Congress of Soviets, which was to legitimize the coup, had not even opened when the Bolsheviks had already acted in its name. This procedure, however, was consistent with Lenin's argument that it was of no consequence in whose name power was formally taken: "This is not important right now: let the Military-Revolutionary Committee take it or 'some other institution,' " he had written the night before. Because the coup was unauthorized and so quietly carried out, the population of Petrograd had no reason to take the claim seriously. According to eyewitnesses, on October 25 life in Petrograd returned to normal as offices and shops reopened, factory workers went to work, and places of entertainment filled again with crowds. No one except a handful of principals knew what had happened: that the capital city was in the iron grip of armed Bolsheviks and that nothing would ever be the same again. Lenin later said that starting the world revolution in Russia was as easy as "picking up a feather."[194]

In the meantime, Kerensky was speeding to Pskov, the headquarters of the Northern Front. By an exquisite twist of history, the only troops available to move against the Bolsheviks were Cossacks of the same Third Cavalry Corps whom two months earlier he had accused of participating in Kornilov's "treason." They so despised Kerensky for having slandered Kornilov and driven their commander, General Krymov, to suicide that they refused to heed his pleas. Kerensky eventually persuaded some of them to advance on the capital by way of Luga. Under the command of Ataman P. N. Krasnov, they scattered the troops sent by the Bolsheviks and occupied Gatchina. That evening, they reached Tsarskoe Selo, a two-hour ride to the capital. But disappointed that no other units joined them, they dismounted and refused to go farther.

In Petrograd, the situation seemed material for comedy. After the Bolsheviks had proclaimed them deposed, the ministers remained in the Malachite Room, on the Neva side of the Winter Palace, awaiting the arrival of Kerensky at the head of relief troops. Because of that, the Second Congress of Soviets, assembled at Smolnyi, had to be postponed from hour to hour. At 2 p.m., 5,000 sailors arrived from Kronshtadt: but this "pride and beauty of the Revolution," so adept at roughing up unarmed civilians, had no stomach for battle. When their attempt to assault the palace was met with fire, they too gave up.

Lenin did not dare to show himself in public until the cabinet (presumably including Kerensky, of whose escape he was unaware) fell into Bolshevik hands. He spent most of October 25 bandaged, wigged, and bespectacled. After Dan and Skobelev, passing by, saw through his disguise,[195] he retired to his hideaway, where he took catnaps on the floor, while Trotsky came and went to report the latest news.

Unwilling to open the Congress of Soviets as long as the Winter Palace held out, yet afraid of losing the delegates, Trotsky convened at 2:35 p.m. an

Extraordinary Session of the Petrograd Soviet. It cannot be determined who took part in these deliberations: since the SRs and Mensheviks had left Smolnyi the day before and there were hundreds of Bolshevik and pro-Bolshevik delegates from the provinces in the building, it is safe to assume that it was virtually a completely Bolshevik and Left SR affair.

Opening the meeting (with Lenin still absent), Trotsky announced: "In the name of the Military-Revolutionary Committee, I declare that the Provisional Government has ceased to exist." When a delegate, in response to one of Trotsky's announcements, shouted from the floor, "You are anticipating the will of the All-Russian Congress of Soviets!" Trotsky retorted:

> The will of the All-Russian Congress of Soviets has been predetermined [*predreshena*] by the enormous feat of the uprising of Petrograd workers and soldiers which occurred last night. Now we only have to expand our victory.[196]

What "uprising" of workers and soldiers? one might well have asked. But the intention of these words was to let the congress know that it had no choice but to acquiesce to the decisions which the Bolshevik Central Committee had "predetermined" in its name.

Lenin now made a brief appearance, welcoming the delegates and hailing "the worldwide socialist revolution,"[197] following which he again dropped out of sight. Trotsky recalls Lenin telling him: "The transition from the underground and the Pereverzev experience [*pereverzevshchina*] to power is too sudden." And he added in German, making a circular motion: *"Es schwindelt"* ("It's dizzying").[198]

At 6:30 p.m., the Military-Revolutionary Committee gave the Provisional Government an ultimatum to surrender or face fire from the cruiser *Aurora* and the Peter and Paul Fortress. The ministers, expecting assistance at any moment, did not respond: at this time rumors spread that Kerensky was approaching at the head of loyal troops.[199] They chatted listlessly, conversed with friends on the phone, and rested, stretched out on settees.

At 9 p.m. the cruiser *Aurora* opened fire. Because it had no live ammunition aboard, it shot a single blank salvo and fell silent—just enough to secure it a prominent place in the legends about October. Two hours later, the Peter and Paul Fortress opened a bombardment, this time with live shells, but its aim was so inaccurate that of the thirty to thirty-five rounds fired only two struck the palace, inflicting minor damage.[200] After months of organizational work in the factories and garrisons, the Bolsheviks turned out to have no forces willing to die for their cause. The thinly defended seat of the Provisional Government stood defiant, mocking those who had declared it deposed. During pauses in the shelling, detachments of Red Guards penetrated the palace through one of its several entrances; inside, however, when confronted by armed *iunkers,* they immediately surrendered.

As night fell, the defenders of the palace, dispirited from the lack of the promised support, began to withdraw. The first to go were the Cossacks; they

67. Cadets *(iunkers)* defending the Winter Palace: October 1917.

were followed by the *iunkers* manning the artillery. The Women's Death Battalion stayed on. By midnight, the defense was reduced to them and a handful of teenage cadets guarding the Malachite Room. When no more gunfire issued from the palace, the Red Guards and sailors cautiously drew near. The first to penetrate were sailors and troops of the Pavlovskii Regiment who clambered through open windows on the Hermitage side.[201] Others made their way through unlocked gates. The Winter Palace was not taken by assault: the image of a column of storming workers, soldiers, and sailors as depicted in Eisenstein's film *Days of October* is pure invention, an attempt to give Russia its own Fall of the Bastille. In reality, the Winter Palace was overrun by mobs after it had ceased to defend itself. The total casualties were five killed and several wounded, most of them victims of stray bullets.

After midnight, the palace filled with a mob which looted and vandalized its luxurious interiors. Some of the women defenders are said to have been raped. P. N. Maliantovich, the Minister of Justice, left a graphic picture of the last minutes of the Provisional Government:

> Suddenly a noise arose somewhere: it at once grew in intensity and scope, drawing nearer. In its sounds—distinct but fused into a single wave—there at once resounded something special, something different from the previous noises: something final. . . . It became instantly clear that the end was at hand . . .
> Those lying or sitting sprang to their feet and reached for their over- coats . . .

And the noise grew all the time, intensified, and swiftly, with a broad wave, rolled toward us . . . It penetrated and seized us with an unbearable fear, like the onslaught of poisoned air . . .

All this in a few minutes . . .

At the door to the antechamber of the room where we were holding watch one could hear sharp, excited shouts of a mass of voices, a few isolated shots, the stamping of feet, some pounding, movements, the commingled, mounting, integrated chaos of sounds and the ever-mounting fear.

It was obvious: we were under assault: we were being taken by assault . . . Defense was useless; victims would be sacrificed in vain . . .

The door flew open . . . A *iunker* rushed in. At full attention, saluting, his face excited but determined: "What does the Provisional Government command? Defend to the last man? We are ready if the Provisional Government so orders."

"No need for this! It would be useless! This is clear! No bloodshed! Surrender!" we shouted like one without prior agreement, only looking at one another to read the same feelings and resolution in everyone's eyes.

Kishkin stepped forward. "If they are here, this means that the palace is already taken."*

"Yes. All the entrances have been taken. Everyone has surrendered. Only these quarters are still guarded. What does the Provisional Government command?"

"Say that we want no bloodshed, that we yield to force, that we surrender," Kishkin said.

And there, by the door, fear mounted without letup, and we became anxious lest blood flow, lest we be too late to prevent it . . . And we shouted anxiously: "Hurry! Go and tell them! We want no blood! We surrender!"

The *iunker* left . . . The entire scene, I believe, took no more than a minute.[202]

Arrested by Antonov-Ovseenko at 2:10 a.m., the ministers were taken under guard to the Peter and Paul Fortress. On the way they barely escaped being lynched.

Three and a half hours earlier, unable to hold out any longer, the Bolsheviks had opened their congress in Smolnyi, in the large colonnaded Assembly Hall used before 1917 for theatrical performances and balls. Cleverly exploiting Theodore Dan's vanity, they invited the Menshevik Soviet leader to inaugurate the proceedings, which had the effect of giving them an aura of Soviet legitimacy. A new Presidium was elected, composed of fourteen Bolshevik, seven Left SRs, and three Mensheviks. Kamenev took the chair. Although the legitimate Ispolkom had prescribed for the congress a very narrow agenda (the current situation, the Constituent Assembly, reelections to the Ispolkom), Kamenev altered it to something entirely different: governmental authority, war and peace, and the Constituent Assembly.

*N. M. Kishkin, a Kadet and member of the last Provisional Government, was placed in charge after Kerensky had left the Winter Palace.

68. The Winter Palace, after being seized and looted
by the Bolsheviks.

69. The Assembly Hall in Smolnyi, locale of the Second
Congress of Soviets (the same hall shown on page 84).

The composition of the congress bore little relationship to the country's political alignment. Peasant organizations refused to participate, declaring the congress unauthorized and urging the nation's soviets to boycott it.[203] On the same grounds, the army committees refused to send delegates.[204] Trotsky must have known better than to describe the Second Congress as "the most democratic of all parliaments in the history of the world."[205] It was, in fact, a gathering of Bolshevik-dominated urban soviets and military councils especially created for the purpose. In a statement issued on October 25, the Ispolkom declared:

> The Central Executive Committee [Ispolkom] considers the Second Congress as not having taken place and regards it as a private gathering of Bolshevik delegates. The resolutions of this congress, lacking in legitimacy, are declared by the Central Executive Committee to have no binding force for local soviets and all army committees. The Central Executive Committee calls on the soviets and army organizations to rally around it to defend the Revolution. The Central Executive Committee will convene a new Congress of Soviets as soon as conditions make it possible to do so properly.[206]

The exact number of participants in this rump congress cannot be determined: the most reliable estimate indicates about 650 delegates, among them 338 Bolsheviks and 98 Left SRs. The two allied parties thus controlled two-thirds of the seats—a representation more than double what they were entitled to, judging by the elections to the Constituent Assembly three weeks later.[207] Leaving nothing to chance, for they could not be entirely certain of the Left SRs, the Bolsheviks allocated to themselves 54 percent of the seats. How skewed the representation was is illustrated by the fact that, according to information made available seventy years later, Latvians, who had a strong Bolshevik movement, accounted for over 10 percent of the delegates.[208]

The initial hours were spent on raucous debates. While awaiting word that the ministers were under arrest, the Bolsheviks gave the floor to their socialist opponents. Amid hooting and heckling, the Mensheviks and the Socialists-Revolutionaries presented similar declarations denouncing the Bolshevik coup and demanding immediate negotiations with the Provisional Government. The Menshevik statement declared that the

> military conspiracy was organized and carried out by the Bolshevik Party in the name of the soviets behind the backs of all the other parties and factions represented in the soviets . . . the seizure of power by the Petrograd Soviet on the eve of the Congress of Soviets constitutes a disorganization and disruption of the entire soviet organization.[209]

Trotsky described the opponents as "pitiful entities [*edinitsy*]" and "bankrupts" whose place was on the "garbage heap of history," whereupon Martov declared he was leaving.[210]

This happened around 1 a.m. on October 26. At 3:10 a.m. Kamenev announced that the Winter Palace had fallen and the ministers were in custody. At 6 a.m. he adjourned the congress until the evening.

Lenin now went to Bonch-Bruevich's apartment to draft key decrees for the congress's ratification. The two principal decrees on which he counted to win the support of soldiers and peasants for the coup, dealing with peace and land, were later in the day submitted to a caucus of the Bolshevik delegates, which approved them without debate.

The congress resumed at 10:40 p.m. Lenin, greeted with tumultuous applause, presented the decrees on peace and land. They sailed through on a voice vote.

The Decree on Peace[211] was misnamed since it was not a legislative act, but an appeal to all the belligerent powers to open immediate negotiations for a "democratic" peace without annexations and contributions, guaranteeing every nation "the right to self-determination." Secret diplomacy was to be abolished and secret treaties made public. Until peace negotiations could get underway, Russia proposed a three-month armistice.

The Decree on Land[212] was lifted bodily from the program of the Socialist-Revolutionary Party as supplemented with 242 instructions from peasant communities published two months earlier in *Izvestiia of the All-Russian Union of Peasants' Deputies.*[213] Instead of ordering the nationalization all the land—that is, the transfer of ownership to the state—as the Bolshevik program demanded, it called for its "socialization"—that is, withdrawal from commerce and transfer to peasant communes for use. All landed properties of landlords, the state, the church, and others not engaged in farming were to be confiscated without compensation and turned over to the *volost'* land committees until such time as the Constituent Assembly decided on their ultimate disposal. Private holdings of peasants, however, were exempt. This was an unabashed concession to peasant wishes which had little in common with the Bolshevik land program and was designed to win peasant support in the elections to the Constituent Assembly.

The third and final decree presented to the delegates set up a new government called the Council of People's Commissars (Sovet Narodnykh Komissarov, or Sovnarkom). It was to serve only until the convocation of the Constituent Assembly, scheduled for the following month: hence, like its predecessor, it was named "Provisional Government."[214] Lenin at first offered its chairmanship to Trotsky, but Trotsky refused. Lenin was none too eager to enter the cabinet, preferring to work from behind the scenes. "At first Lenin did not want to join the government," Lunacharskii recalled. " 'I will work in the Central Committee of the party,' he said. But we said no. We would not agree to that. We made him assume principal responsibility. Everyone prefers to be only a critic."[215] So Lenin took over the chairmanship of the Sovnarkom, while concurrently serving, in fact if not in name, as chairman of the Bolshevik Central Committee. The new cabinet had the same structure as the old, with the addition of one new post, that of chairman (rather than commissar) for Nationality Affairs. All the commissars were members of the

Bolshevik Party and subject to its discipline: the Left SRs were invited to join but refused, insisting on a cabinet representative of "all the forces of revolutionary democracy," including the Mensheviks and SRs.[216] The composition of the Sovnarkom was as follows:*

Chairman	Vladimir Ulianov (Lenin)
Internal Affairs	A. I. Rykov
Agriculture	V. P. Miliutin
Labor	A. G. Shliapnikov
War and Navy	V. A. Ovseenko (Antonov)
	N. V. Krylenko
	P. E. Dybenko
Trade and Industry	V. P. Nogin
Enlightenment	A. V. Lunacharskii
Finance	I. I. Skvortsov (Stepanov)
Foreign Affairs	L. D. Bronstein (Trotsky)
Justice	G. I. Oppokov (Lomov)
Supply	I. A. Teodorovich
Post and Telegraphs	N. P. Avilov (Glebov)
Chairman for Nationality Affairs	I. V. Dzhugashvili (Stalin)

The existing Ispolkom was declared deposed and replaced with a new one, composed of 101 members, of whom 62 were Bolsheviks and 29 Left SRs. Kamenev was named chairman. In the decree establishing the Sovnarkom, drafted by Lenin, the Sovnarkom was made accountable to the Ispolkom, which thereby became something of a parliament with authority to veto legislation and cabinet appointments.

The Bolshevik high command, exceedingly anxious at this uncertain time not to appear to be preempting power, insisted that the decrees passed by the congress were enacted on a provisional basis, subject to approval, emendation, or rejection by the Constituent Assembly. In the words of a Communist historian:

> In the days of October, the sovereignty of the Constituent Assembly was not denied . . . in all its resolutions [the Second Congress of Soviets] took the Constituent Assembly into account and adopted its basic decisions "until its convocation."[217]

While the Decree on Peace did not refer to the Constituent Assembly, in his report on it to the Second Congress, Lenin promised: "We will submit all the peace proposals to the Constituent Assembly for decision."[218] The provisions of the Land Decree were conditional as well: "Only the all-national Constituent Assembly can resolve the land question in all its dimensions."[219] As con-

---

*Dekrety, I, 20–21; W. Pietsch, Staat und Revolution (Köln, 1969), 50; Lenin, PSS, XXXV, 28–29. Trotsky was the only Jew in the Sovnarkom. The Bolsheviks seemed to have been afraid of accusations that they were a "Jewish" party, setting up a government to serve the interests of "international Jewry."

cerned the new cabinet, the Sovnarkom, a resolution which Lenin drafted and the congress approved stated: "To form for the administration of the country, until the convocation of the Constituent Assembly, a Provisional Workers' and Peasants' Government to be called Council of People's Commissars."[220] Hence, it was logical for the new government, on its first day in office (October 27), to affirm that the elections for the Constituent Assembly would proceed as scheduled on November 12.[221] Hence, too, by dispersing the Assembly on its first day, before it had had a chance to legislate, the Bolsheviks delegitimized themselves, even by their own definition.

The Bolsheviks made their initial concessions to legality only because they could not be certain what the future held in store. They had to allow for the possibility of Kerensky arriving momentarily in Petrograd with troops, in which case they would need the support of the entire Soviet. They ventured to violate legal norms openly only a week or so later, after it had become apparent that no punitive expeditions would materialize.

The one armed clash between pro-Bolshevik and pro-government troops for control of the capital occurred on October 30 at Pulkovo, a hilly suburb. Krasnov's Cossacks, discouraged by lack of support and confused by Bolshevik agitators, after wasting three precious days in Tsarskoe Selo were finally persuaded to advance. They opened operations along the Slavianka River: here, 600 Cossacks confronted a force of Red Guards, sailors, and soldiers at least ten times larger.[222] The Red Guards and soldiers quickly fled, but the 3,000 sailors stood their ground and carried the day. Having lost their field commander, the Cossacks retreated to Gatchina. This ended the possibility of any further military intervention on behalf of the Provisional Government.

In Moscow, things went awry for the Bolsheviks from the start: they could have ended in disaster had the government representatives displayed greater determination.

Moscow's Bolsheviks had not prepared themselves for a power seizure because they sided with Kamenev and Zinoviev rather than Lenin and Trotsky: Uritskii told the Central Committee on October 20 that the majority of the Moscow delegates opposed an uprising.[223]

Having learned of the events in Petrograd on October 25, the Bolsheviks had the Soviet pass a resolution setting up a Revolutionary Committee. But whereas in the capital city the equivalent organization was under Bolshevik control, in Moscow it was intended as a genuine interparty Soviet organ and the Mensheviks, SRs, and other socialists were invited to join. While the SRs declined, the Mensheviks accepted the invitation but posed several conditions; these were rejected, whereupon they withdrew.[224] Emulating the Petrograd Milrevkom, the Moscow Revolutionary Committee issued at 10 p.m. an appeal to the city's garrison to be ready for action and obey only orders issued by it or carrying its countersignature.[225]

The Moscow Revolutionary Committee made its first move in the morning of October 26 by sending two commissars to the Kremlin to take over the ancient fortress and distribute weapons in its arsenal to pro-Bolshevik Red Guards. Troops of the 56th Regiment guarding the Kremlin obeyed, confused by the fact that one of these commissars was its own officer. Even so, the Bolsheviks were unable to remove the weapons because the Kremlin was soon encircled by *iunkers,* who gave them an ultimatum to surrender. When it was rejected, the *iunkers* attacked: a few hours later (6 a.m. on October 28) the Kremlin was in their hands.

Its capture gave the pro-government forces control of the city's center. At this point, the officials charged with military and civilian authority could have crushed the Bolshevik uprising. But they hesitated, in part from overconfidence, in part from a desire to avoid further bloodshed. Fear of the "counterrevolution" also weighed on their minds. The Committee of Public Safety, headed by the city's mayor, V. V. Rudnev, and the military command under Colonel K. I. Riabtsev, instead of arresting the Revolutionary Committee, entered into negotiations with it. These negotiations, which went on for three days (October 28–30), gave the Bolsheviks time to recover and bring in reinforcements from the industrial suburbs and nearby towns. The Revolutionary Committee, which during the night of October 28–29 had viewed its situation as "critical,"[226] two days later felt confident enough to go on the offensive. Ultimately, the only inhabitants of Moscow willing to defend democracy turned out to be teenage youths from military academies, universities, and gymnasia who put their lives on the line without leadership or support from their elders.

The negotiations between the Committee of Public Safety and the Revolutionary Committee for a peaceful resolution of the conflict broke down at

70. Cadets defending the Moscow Kremlin: November 1917.

71. Fires burning in Moscow during battle between loyal
and Bolshevik forces: November 1917.

midnight, October 30–31, when the latter unilaterally terminated the armistice
and ordered its units to charge.[227] The forces on both sides seem to have been
roughly equal, 15,000 men each. During the ensuing night, Moscow became
the scene of fierce house-to-house fighting. Determined to recapture the Kremlin, the Bolsheviks attacked with artillery fire, which inflicted damage on its
ancient walls. Although the *iunkers* acquitted themselves well, they were
gradually squeezed and isolated by the Bolshevik forces converging from the
suburbs. In the morning of November 2, the Committee of Public Safety
ordered its forces to cease resistance. That evening it signed with the Revolutionary Committee an act of surrender by virtue of which it dissolved itself and
its forces laid down arms.[228]

In other parts of Russia, the situation followed a bewildering variety of
scenarios, the course and outcome of the conflict in each city depending on
the strength and determination of the contending parties. Although Communist ideologists have labeled the period immediately following the October
coup in Petrograd "the triumphal march of Soviet power," to the historian the
matter looks different: it was not "Soviet" but Bolshevik power that was
spreading, often against the wishes of the soviets, and it was not so much
"triumphantly marching" as conquering by military force.

Because they followed no discernible pattern, it is next to impossible to
describe the Bolshevik conquests outside the two capital cities.[229] In some
areas, the Bolsheviks joined hands with the SRs and Mensheviks to proclaim
"soviet" rule; in others, they ejected their rivals and took power for themselves.
Here and there, pro-government forces offered resistance, but in many locali-

ties they proclaimed "neutrality." In most provincial cities local Bolsheviks had to act on their own, without directives from Petrograd. By early November, they were in control of the heartland of the Empire, Great Russia, or at any rate of the cities of that region, which they transformed into bastions in the midst of a hostile or indifferent rural population, much as the Normans had done in Russia a thousand years earlier. The countryside was almost entirely outside their grasp and so were most of the borderlands, which separated themselves to form sovereign republics. These, as we shall see, the Bolsheviks had to reconquer in military campaigns.

The vast majority of Russia's inhabitants at the time had no inkling of what had happened. Nominally, the soviets, which since February had acted as co-regent, assumed full power. This hardly seemed a revolutionary event: it was rather a logical extension of the principle of "dual power" introduced during the first days of the February Revolution. Trotsky's deception which disguised the Bolshevik power seizure as the transfer of power to the soviets succeeded brilliantly: looking back at the events of October, he rightly took pride in the skillful exploitation for Bolshevik ends of practices which the democratic socialists had introduced in February and March. The result of the deception was that the total break in government went virtually unnoticed, appearing merely as a "legal" resolution of yet another governmental crisis:

> We term the uprising "legal" in the sense that it grew out of the "normal" conditions of dual power. When the appeasers [SRs and Mensheviks] were in charge of the Petrograd Soviet it happened more than once that the Soviet checked and corrected the government's decisions. This [practice], as it were, formed part of the constitution of the regime known to history as "Kerensky-ism." We Bolsheviks, having taken power in the Petrograd Soviet, merely expanded and deepened the methods of dual power. We took it upon ourselves to check the order concerning the dispatch of the garrison [to the front]. In this manner, we concealed behind the traditions and practices of dual power what was a de facto rising of the Petrograd garrison. Moreover, by formally timing in our agitation the question of power to coincide with the moment of the Second Congress of Soviets, we developed and deepened the established traditions of dual power, preparing the framework of Soviet legality for the Bolshevik uprising on an all-Russian scale.[230]

Part of the deception was to keep hidden the socialist objective of the October coup: no official document issued in the first week of the new regime, when it felt still very unsure of itself, used the word "socialism." That this was deliberate practice and not oversight may be seen from the fact that in the original draft of the October 25 announcement declaring the Provisional Government deposed, Lenin had written the slogan "Long Live Socialism!" but then thought better of it and crossed it out.[231] The earliest official use of "socialism" occurred in a document written by Lenin and dated November 2, which stated that "the Central Committee has complete faith in the triumph of the socialist revolution."[232]

All this had the effect of lulling the sense that something drastic had happened, allaying public apprehension and inhibiting active resistance. How prevalent was ignorance of the meaning of the October coup may be illustrated by the reaction of the Petrograd Stock Exchange. According to the contemporary press, the Stock Exchange was "entirely unimpressed" by the change of regimes or even the subsequent announcement that Russia had had a socialist revolution. Although in the days immediately following the coup there was little trading in securities, prices held firm. The only indication of nervousness was the sharp fall in the value of the ruble: between October 23 and November 4, the ruble lost one-half of its foreign exchange value, declining from 6.20 to 12–14 to the U.S. dollar.[233]

The fall of the Provisional Government caused few regrets: eyewitnesses report that the population reacted to it with complete indifference. This was true even in Moscow, where the Bolsheviks had to overcome stiff opposition: here the disappearance of the government is said to have gone unnoticed. The man on the street seemed to feel that it made no difference who was in charge since things could not possibly get any worse.[234]

Building the One-Party State

On October 26, 1917, the Bolsheviks did not so much seize power over Russia as stake a claim to it. On that day they won from a rump Congress of Soviets, which they had convened in an unlawful manner and packed with adherents, only limited and temporary authority: the authority to form yet another Provisional Government. That government was to be accountable to the Central Executive Committee of the Soviet Congress and retire in a month, upon the convocation of the Constituent Assembly. It took them three years of civil war to make good this claim. Notwithstanding their precarious position, they proceeded almost at once to lay the foundations of a type of regime unknown to history, a one-party dictatorship.

On October 26, the Bolsheviks had a choice of three options. They could have declared their party to be the government. They could have dissolved the party in the government. And they could have kept party and government as separate institutions, and either directed the state from the outside or else meshed with it on the executive level, through interlocking personnel.[1] For reasons that will be spelled out, Lenin rejected the first and second of these alternatives. He hesitated briefly between the two variants of option three. Initially, he leaned toward variant one: rather than head the state, he preferred to govern as head of the party, which he saw as the incipient government of the world proletariat. But, as we have seen, his associates thought he was trying to evade responsibility for the October coup, which many of them had opposed, and forced him to give it up as well.[2] As a result, in the political system that came into being within hours of the coup d'état, party and state retained distinctive identities, meshing not institutionally but personally on the executive levels, first of all in the cabinet (Council of People's Commissars or Sovnarkom) in which the leaders of the party took all the ministerial posts. Under this arrangement, the Bolsheviks, as party officials, made policy decisions and executed them as heads of the state departments, using for this purpose the bureaucracy and the security police.

Such was the origin of a type of government that was to breed numerous offspring in the form of left and right one-party dictatorships in Europe and the rest of the world, and emerge as the main enemy of and alternative to parliamentary democracy. Its distinguishing quality was the concentration of executive and legislative authority, as well as the power to make all legislative, executive, and judiciary appointments in the hands of a private association, the "ruling party." Given that the Bolsheviks quickly outlawed all the other parties, the name "party" hardly applied to their organization. A "party"—the term derives from the Latin *pars,* or part—by definition cannot be exclusive, since a part cannot be the whole: a "one-party state" is, therefore, a contradiction in terms.[3] The term that fits it somewhat better is "dual state," coined later to describe a similar regime established in Germany by Hitler.[4]

This type of government had only one precedent, an imperfect and only partially realized one, on which it was in some measure modeled, namely the Jacobin regime of Revolutionary France. The hundreds of Jacobin clubs scattered throughout France, were not, strictly speaking, a party, but they did acquire many of its characteristics even before the Jacobins came to power: membership in them was strictly controlled, requiring adherence to a program as well as bloc voting, and the Paris Jacobin Club acted as their national center. From the fall of 1793 until the Thermidorean coup a year later, the Jacobin clubs, without formally meshing with the administration, seized the reins of government by monopolizing all executive positions and arrogating to themselves the power to veto government policies.[5] Had the Jacobins stayed in power longer, they might well have produced a genuine one-party state. As it was, they provided a prototype which the Bolsheviks, leaning on Russia's autocratic traditions, brought to perfection.

The Bolsheviks had never given much thought to the state that would come into being after they made the revolution, because they took it for granted that their revolution would instantly ignite the entire world and sweep away national governments. They improvised the one-party state as they went along, and although they never managed to provide it with a theoretical foundation, it proved to be the most enduring and influential of their accomplishments.

While he never doubted he would exercise unlimited power, Lenin had to make allowance for the fact that he had taken power in the name of "Soviet democracy." The Bolsheviks, it will be recalled, had carried out the coup d'état not on their own behalf—their party's name did not appear on any of the proclamations of the Military-Revolutionary Committee—but on that of the soviets. Their slogan had been "All Power to the Soviets"; their authority was conditional and provisional. The fiction had to be maintained for a time because the country would not have tolerated any one party arrogating to itself a monopoly of power.

Even the delegates to the Second Congress of Soviets, which the Bolsheviks had packed with adherents and sympathizers, did not intend to invest the Bolshevik leadership with dictatorial prerogatives. The delegates to the gathering which the Bolsheviks have ever since claimed as the source of legitimacy, when polled on how the soviets which they represented wished to reconstruct political authority, responded as follows:[6]

All power to the soviets	505	(75%)
All power to democracy	86	(13%)
All power to democracy but without Kadets	21	(3%)
A coalition government	58	(8.6%)
No answer	3	(0.4%)

The responses said more or less the same thing: that if the pro-Bolshevik soviets did not know precisely what kind of government they wanted, none of them envisaged any single party enjoying a political monopoly. Indeed, many of Lenin's closest associates also opposed excluding other socialist parties from the Soviet Government, and would resign in protest because Lenin and a handful of his most devoted followers (Trotsky, Stalin, Feliks Dzerzhinskii) insisted on such a course. This was the political reality that Lenin had to face. It forced him to continue hiding behind the façade of "soviet power" even as he was putting in place a one-party dictatorship. The overwhelmingly democratic and socialist sentiment of the population, imprecisely articulated but intensely felt, compelled him to keep intact the structure of the state in the guise of its new nominal "sovereign," the soviets, while accumulating all the strands of power in his own hands.

But there are good reasons why, even if the mood of the country had not forced him to perpetuate the deception, Lenin would have preferred to govern through the the state and keep the party separate from it. One factor was the shortage of Bolshevik personnel. Administering Russia under normal conditions required hundreds of thousands of functionaries, public and private. To administer a country in which all forms of self-government were to be extinguished and the economy nationalized, required many times that number. The Bolshevik Party in 1917–18 was much too small to cope with this task; in any event, very few of its adherents, most of them lifelong professional revolutionaries, had expertise in administration. The Bolsheviks had no choice, therefore, but to rely on the old bureaucratic apparatus and other "bourgeois specialists," and rather than administer directly, control the administrators. Emulating the Jacobins, they insinuated Bolshevik personnel into commanding positions in all the institutions and organizations without exception—personnel who owed allegiance and obedience not to the state but to the party. The need for reliable party personnel was so acute that the party had to expand more rapidly than its leaders wished, enrolling careerists, pure and simple.

The third consideration in favor of keeping the party distinct from the state was that such a procedure protected it from domestic and foreign criticism. Since the Bolsheviks had no intention of yielding power even if the population overwhelmingly rejected them, they needed a scapegoat. This was to be the state bureaucracy, which could be blamed for failures while the party maintained the pretense of infallibility. In carrying abroad subversive activities, the Bolsheviks would dispose of foreign protests by claiming that these were the work of the Russian Communist Party, a "private organization" for which the Soviet Government could not be held responsible.

The establishment in Russia of a one-party state required a variety of measures, destructive as well as constructive. The process was substantially completed (in central Russia, which is all the Bolsheviks controlled at the time) by the autumn of 1918. Subsequently they transplanted these institutions and practices to the borderlands.

First and foremost, they had to uproot all that remained of the old regime, tsarist as well as "bourgeois" (democratic): the organs of self-government, the political parties and their press, the armed forces, the judiciary system, and the institution of private property. This purely destructive phase of the Revolution, carried out in fulfillment of Marx's injunction of 1871 not to take over but "smash" the old order, was formalized by decrees but it was accomplished mainly by spontaneous anarchism, which the February Revolution had unleashed and the Bolsheviks had done their utmost to inflame. Contemporaries saw in this destructive work only mindless nihilism, but for the new rulers it was clearing the ground before the construction of the new political and social order could get underway.

Construction was the difficult part because it required that the Bolsheviks restrain the anarchistic instincts of the people and reimpose discipline from which the people thought the Revolution had freed them once and for all. It called for structuring the new authority *(vlast')* in a manner that had the appearance of folkish, "soviet" democracy but actually restored Muscovite absolutism with all the refinements made possible by modern ideology and technology. The Bolshevik rulers saw it as their most urgent immediate task to free themselves from accountability to the soviets, their nominal sovereign. Next, they had to be rid of the Constituent Assembly, to the convocation of which they had committed themselves but which was certain to remove them from power. And finally, they had to transform the soviets into compliant tools of the party.

T hat the Bolshevik Party had to be de facto as well as de jure the engine driving the Soviet Government no Bolshevik ever questioned. Lenin merely uttered a truism when he said at the Tenth Party Congress in 1921: "Our party is the governmental party and the resolution which the Party Congress adopts will be obligatory for the entire republic."[7] A few years later Stalin defined even more explicitly the party's constitutional primacy when he stated that "in our country not a single important political or organizational question is decided by our soviet and other mass organizations without guiding directions from the party."[8]

And yet, for all its acknowledged public authority, the Bolshevik Party remained after 1917 what it had been before—namely, a private body. Neither the Soviet Constitution of 1918 nor that of 1924 made any reference to it. The party was first mentioned in a constitutional document in the so-called Stalin Constitution of 1936, Article 126 of which described it as "the vanguard of the toilers in their struggle for the strengthening and development of the socialist order" and the "leading core of all the organizations of toilers, social as well as governmental." To ignore in legislation the most essential was very much in the Russian tradition: after all, tsarist absolutism found its first and rather casual definition in Peter the Great's "Military Regulation" more than two centuries after it had become the country's central political reality, and serfdom, its basic social reality, never received legal acknowledgment. Until 1936, the party depicted itself as a transcendental force which guided the country by example and inspiration. Thus, the program, adopted in March 1919, defined its role as "organizing" and "leading" the proletariat, and "explaining" to it the nature of the class struggle, without once alluding to the fact that it also ruled the "proletariat" as it did all else. Anyone who drew his knowledge of Soviet Russia exclusively from official documents of the time would have no inkling of the party's involvement in the day-to-day life of the country, although that was what distinguished the Soviet Union from every other country in the world.*

Thus, after the power seizure the Bolshevik Party retained its private character even though it had in the meantime become the complete master of state and society. As a result, its statutes, procedures, decisions, and personnel were subject to no external supervision. Its 600,000 to 700,000 members, who, according to Kamenev's statement made in 1920, "governed" a Russia composed overwhelmingly of non-Bolsheviks,[9] resembled an elite cohort rather than a political party.† While nothing escaped its control, the party acknowl-

---

*This device was surprisingly successful with foreigners. In the 1920s Communist Russia was widely perceived by foreign socialists and liberals as a democratic government of a new, "soviet" type. Early visitors' accounts rarely mentioned the Communist Party and its dominant role, so effectively was it concealed.

†Hitler, who fashioned the Nationalist-Socialist Party closely on the Bolshevik and Fascist models, told Hermann Rauschning that the term "party" was really a misnomer for his organization. He preferred it to be called "an order": Rauschning, *Hitler Speaks* (London, 1939), 198, 243.

edged no control over itself: it was self-contained and self-accountable. This created an anomalous situation that Communist theorists have never been able to explain satisfactorily, since it can only be done—if it can be done at all—with reference to such metaphysical concepts as Rousseau's "general will," said by him to express everyone's will and yet to be somehow distinct from the "will of all."

The rolls of the party grew exponentially in the three years during which the Bolsheviks conquered Russia and placed their agents in charge of all the institutions. In February 1917 it had 23,600 members; in 1919, 250,000; in March 1921, 730,000 (including candidate members).[10] Most of the newcomers joined as the Bolsheviks appeared to be winning the Civil War in order to qualify for the benefits traditionally associated in Russia with state service. During those years of extreme privation, a party card assured the minimum of housing, food, and fuel, as well as immunity from the political police for all but the most egregious crimes. Party members alone were allowed to carry weapons. Lenin, of course, realized that most of the newcomers were careerists and that their bribe-taking, thieving, and bullying brought nothing but harm to the party's reputation; but his aspirations to total authority left him no choice but to enroll anyone with the proper social credentials and willingness to carry out orders without questions or inhibitions. At the same time, he made certain that key positions in the party and government were reserved for the "old guard," veterans of the underground: as late as 1930, 69 percent of the secretaries of the central committees of the national republics and the regional *(oblast'* and *krai)* committees had joined before the Revolution.[11]

Until mid-1919, the party retained the informal structure of underground years, but as its ranks expanded, undemocratic practices became institutionalized. The Central Committee remained the center of authority, but in practice, because its members dashed around the country on special assignments, decisions usually were made by the few members who happened to be on hand. Lenin, who was so afraid of assassination that he almost never traveled, served as permanent chairman. Although as the country's dictator he relied heavily on coercion and terror, within his own cohort he preferred persuasion. He never forced anyone out of the party because of disagreement: if he failed to obtain a majority on some important issue, he only had to threaten resignation to bring his followers into line. Once or twice he was on the verge of a humiliating defeat from which only Trotsky's intervention saved him. On a few occasions he had to acquiesce to policies of which he disapproved. By the end of 1918, however, his authority had grown to the point where no one would oppose him. Kamenev, who had often taken issue with Lenin in the past, spoke for many Bolsheviks when he told Sukhanov in the autumn of 1918:

I become ever more convinced that Lenin never makes a mistake. In the end, he is always right. How many times it seemed that he had blundered, in his prognosis or political line—and always, in the end, his prognosis and his line turned out to have been correct.[12]

Lenin had little patience for discussions, even in the circle of his most intimate associates: typically, during cabinet meetings, he would thumb through a book and rejoin the debate to lay down policy. From October 1917 until the spring of 1919 he made many decisions for the party as well as the government in collaboration with his indispensable assistant, Iakov Sverdlov. Possessed of a filing-cabinet sort of mind, Sverdlov could supply Lenin with names, facts, and such other kinds of information as was required. After he had fallen ill and died in March 1919, the Central Committee had to be restructured: at this time a Politburo was created to guide policy, an Orgburo to take care of administration, and a Secretariat to manage party personnel.

The cabinet, or Sovnarkom, was made up of high party officials serving in a double capacity. Lenin, who directed the Central Committee, served also as chairman of the Sovnarkom, the equivalent of a Prime Minister. As a rule, important decisions were first taken up in the Central Committee or Politburo and then submitted to the cabinet for discussion and implementation, often with the participation of non-Bolshevik experts.

In a country of over one hundred million inhabitants, it was, of course, impossible, relying exclusively on the party membership, to "smash" thoroughly a social, economic, and political order built over centuries. One had to harness the "masses": but since the multitude of workers and peasants knew nothing of socialism or the proletarian dictatorship, they had to be prodded into action with appeals to self-interest most narrowly defined.

In the *Satyricon* of Petronius, that unique picture of daily life in ancient Rome, there occurs a passage very relevant to the politics which the Bolsheviks pursued during the initial months in power:

> How would a confidence man or a pickpocket survive if he did not drop little boxes of clinking bags into the crowd to hook his victims? Dumb animals are snared with food and men can't be caught unless they are nibbling at something.

It was a principle that Lenin instinctively understood. On taking office he turned Russia over to the populace to divide its wealth under the slogan *"Grabi nagrablennoe"* ("Loot the loot"). While the people were busy "nibbling," he disposed of his political rivals.

The Russian language has a term, *duvan,* borrowed from Turkish by way of the Cossack dialect. It means a division of spoils, such as the Cossack bands in southern Russia used to carry out after raids on Turkish and Persian settlements. In the fall and winter of 1917–18, all of Russia became the object of *duvan.* The main commodity to be divided was agricultural land, which the Land Decree of October 26 had turned over to communal peasants. Distributing this loot among households, according to criteria which each commune set for itself, kept the peasants occupied well into the spring of 1918. During this period, they lost such little interest in politics as they had.

Similar processes also took place in industry and in the armed forces. The Bolsheviks initially turned over the running of industrial plants to Factory

72. Iakov Sverdlov.

Committees, whose workers and lower clerical personnel were under the influence of syndicalism. These committees removed the owners and directors and took over the management. But they also used the opportunity to appropriate the assets of the plants, distributing among themselves the profits as well as matériel and equipment. According to one contemporary, in practice "worker management" reduced itself to the "division of the proceeds of a given industrial enterprise among its workers."[13] Before they headed for home, front-line soldiers broke into arsenals and storehouses, taking whatever they could carry: the rest they sold to local civilians. A Bolshevik newspaper provided a description of this kind of military *duvan*. According to its reporter, a discussion of the Soldiers' Section of the Petrograd Soviet on February 1, 1918 (NS), revealed that in many units troops demanded the contents of regimental depots: it was common for them to take home the uniforms and weapons obtained in this manner.[14]

The notion of national or state property thus disappeared along with that of private property, and it did so with the encouragement of the new government. It was as if Lenin had studied the history of the peasant rebellion under Emelian Pugachev in the 1770s, who had succeeded in seizing vast areas of eastern Russia by appealing to the anarchist and anti-proprietary instincts of the peasantry. Pugachev had exhorted peasants to exterminate all landlords and to take their lands as well as Crown lands. He promised them no more taxes and military recruitment, and distributed among them the money and the grain taken from their owners. He further pledged to abolish the government and replace it with Cossack "liberties"—that is, communal anarchy. Pugachev might well have brought down the Russian state had he not been crushed by Catherine's armies.[15]

In the winter of 1917–18, the population of what had been the Russian Empire divided among itself not only material goods. It also tore apart the Russian state, the product of 600 years of historical development: sovereignty itself became the object of *duvan*. By the spring of 1918, the largest state in the world fell apart into innumerable overlapping entities, large and small, each claiming authority over its territory, none linked with the others by institutional ties or even a sense of common destiny. In a few months, Russia reverted politically to the early Middle Ages when she had been a collection of self-governing principalities.

The first to separate themselves were the non-Russian peoples of the borderlands. After the Bolshevik coup, one ethnic minority after another declared independence from Russia, partly to realize its national aspirations, partly to escape Bolshevism and the looming civil war. For justification they could refer to the "Declaration of the Rights of the Nations of Russia," which the Bolsheviks had issued on November 2, 1917, over the signatures of Lenin and Stalin. Made public without prior approval of any Soviet institution, it granted the peoples of Russia "free self-determination, including the right of separation and the formation of an independent state." Finland was the first to declare herself independent (December 6, 1917, NS); she was followed by Lithuania (December 11), Latvia (January 12, 1918), the Ukraine (January 22), Estonia (February 24), Transcaucasia (April 22), and Poland (November 3) (all dates are new style). These separations reduced the Communist domain to territories inhabited by Great Russians—that is, to the Russia of the mid-seventeenth century.

The process of dismemberment was not confined to the borderlands: centrifugal forces emerged also within Great Russia, as province after province went its own way, claiming independence from central authority. This process was facilitated by the official slogan "All Power to the Soviets," which allowed regional soviets at different levels—region *(oblast')*, province *(guberniia)*, district *(uezd)*, and even *volost'* and *selo*—to claim sovereignty. The result was chaos:

> There were city soviets, village soviets, *selo* soviets, and suburban soviets. These soviets acknowledged no one but themselves, and if they did acknowledge, it was only "up to the point" that happened to have been advantageous to them. Every soviet lived and struggled as the immediate surrounding conditions dictated, and as it could and wanted to. They had no, or virtually no . . . bureaucratic soviet structures.[16]

In an attempt to bring some order the Bolshevik Government created in the spring of 1918 territorial entities called *oblasti*. There were six of them, each composed of several provinces and enjoying quasi-sovereign status:* Moscow with nine adjoining provinces; the Urals, centered on Ekaterinburg; the "Toilers Commune of the North," embracing seven provinces with the capital in Petrograd; Northwest, centered on Smolensk; West Siberia, with the center in Omsk; and Central Siberia, based on Irkutsk. Each had its own administration, staffed by socialist intelligentsia, and convened Congresses of Soviets. Some even had their own Councils of People's Commissars. A conference of the soviets of the Central Siberian Region held in Irkutsk in February 1918 rejected the peace treaty with Germany which the Soviet Government was about to sign and, to demonstrate its independence, appointed its own Commissar of Foreign Affairs.[17]

Here and there *gubernii* proclaimed themselves "republics." This happened in Kazan, Kaluga, Riazan, Ufa, and Orenburg. Some of the non-Russian peoples living in the midst of Russians, such as the Bashkirs and Volga Tatars, also formed national republics. One count indicates that on the territory of the defunct Russian Empire there existed in June 1918 at least thirty-three "governments."[18] To have its decrees and laws implemented, the central government often had to request the assistance of these ephemeral entities.

The regions and provinces, in turn, broke up into subunits, of which the *volost'* was the most important. The vitality of the *volost'* derived from the fact that for the peasants it was the largest entity within which to distribute the appropriated land. As a rule, peasants of one *volost'* would refuse to share the looted properties with those of neighboring *volosti,* with the result that hundreds of these tiny territories became, in effect, self-governing enclaves. As Martov observed:

> We have always pointed out that the popularity of the slogan "All Power to the Soviets" among peasants and the backward segment of the working class can be in large measure explained by the fact that they invest this slogan with the primitive idea of the supremacy of local workers or local peasants over a given territory, much as they identify the slogan of worker control with the idea of seizure of a given factory and that of agrarian revolution with the idea of a given village appropriating a given estate.[19]

The Bolsheviks made some unsuccessful military forays into the separated borderlands to bring them back into the fold. But by and large, for the time being they did not interfere with the centrifugal forces inside Great Russia, because these furthered their immediate objective, which was the thorough destruction of the old political and economic system. These forces also prevented the emergence of a strong state apparatus able to stand up to the Communist Party before it had the time to consolidate its power.

In March 1918, the government approved a constitution for the Russian

*B. Eltsin in *VS,* No. 6/7 (May 1919), 9–10. The author claims that these institutions, created on orders of the Central Committee and the government, initiated the process of the "gathering of the Russian lands," a term traditionally applied to early modern Moscow.

Soviet Federated Socialist Republic (RSFSR). Lenin entrusted the drafting of this document to a commission of judicial experts, chaired by Sverdlov: its most active members were Left SRs, who wanted to replace the centralized state with a federation of soviets, on the model of the French communes of 1871. Lenin left them undisturbed although their intention ran entirely contrary to his own goal of a centralized state. He who paid scrupulous attention to the least details of administration, to the extent of deciding what soldiers guarded his office in Smolnyi, stayed out of the deliberations of the constitutional commission, and merely scanned the results of its work. It was indicative of his contempt for the written constitution: it suited his purposes to give the state structure a loose, quasi-anarchic façade to conceal the hidden steel of party control.[20]

The Constitution of 1918 met Napoleon's criterion: a good constitution, he said, was short and confused. The opening article proclaimed Russia "a republic of soviets of workers', soldiers' and peasants' deputies"; "all power in the center and in the localities" belonged to the soviets.[21] These statements raised more questions than they answered because the articles that followed failed to clarify the division of authority either between the center and the localities or among the soviets themselves. According to Article 56, "within the borders of its jurisdiction, the congress of soviets (of the region, province, district, and *volost'*) is the highest authority." Since, however, each region embraced several provinces, and each province numerous districts and *volosti,* the principle was meaningless. To further complicate matters, Article 61 contradicted the principle that congresses of soviets were the "highest authority" on their territory by requiring local soviets to confine themselves to local issues and to execute the orders of the "supreme organs of the Soviet Government."

The failure of the 1918 Constitution to specify the spheres of competence of the soviet authorities at their different territorial levels merely emphasized that the Bolsheviks did not view the matter as a serious inhibition. Even so, it strengthened centrifugal tendencies by giving them constitutional sanction.*

To gain full freedom of action, Lenin had to rid himself quickly of accountability to the Central Executive Committee (CEC).

On Bolshevik initiative, the Second Congress of Soviets dismissed the old Ispolkom and elected a new one, in which the Bolsheviks held 58 percent of the seats. This arrangement guaranteed that the Bolsheviks, who voted as a bloc, could carry or defeat any motion, but they still had to contend with a vociferous minority of Left SRs, SRs, and Mensheviks. The SRs and Mensheviks refused to acknowledge the legitimacy of the October coup and denied the Bolsheviks the right to form a government. The Left SRs accepted the October coup, but they retained all kinds of democratic illusions, one of which

---

*These tendencies were exacerbated by the government's refusal to fund provincial soviets. In February 1918, Petrograd responded to the requests from provincial soviets for money by telling them that they should obtain it by "mercilessly" taxing the propertied classes: *PR,* No. 3/38 (1925), 161–62. This order led local authorities to levy arbitrary "contributions" on the "bourgeoisie" in their area.

was a coalition government composed of all parties represented in the soviets.

The non-Bolshevik minority took seriously the principle, to which the Bolsheviks paid only lip service, that the CEC was a socialist legislature which had final say on the composition of the cabinet and its activities. These powers it enjoyed by virtue of a resolution of the Second Congress of Soviets which had been drafted by Lenin himself:

> The All-Russian Congress of Soviets of Workers', Soldiers', and Peasants' Deputies resolves: To constitute for the administration of the country prior to the convocation of the Constituent Assembly a Provisional Workers' and Peasants' Government to be known as the Council of People's Commissars. . . . Control over the activity of the People's Commissars and the right of replacing them is vested in the All-Russian Congress of Workers', Soldiers', and Peasants' Deputies and its Central Executive Committee.[22]

Nothing could be clearer. Nevertheless, Lenin was firmly determined to throw this principle overboard and make his cabinet independent of the CEC or any other external body. This he achieved within ten days after becoming head of state.

The historic confrontation between the Bolsheviks and the CEC occurred over the insistence of the latter that the Bolsheviks broaden the Sovnarkom to include representatives of the other socialist parties. All the parties opposed the Bolsheviks' monopolizing of the ministerial posts: after all, they had been chosen by the Congress of Soviets to represent the soviets, not themselves. This opposition surfaced and assumed dangerous forms three days after the Bolshevik coup, when the Union of Railroad Employees, the largest trade union in Russia, presented an ultimatum demanding a socialist coalition government. Anyone whose memories reached to October 1905 would have remembered the decisive role which the railroad strike played in the capitulation of tsarism.

The union, which had hundreds of thousands of members dispersed throughout the country, had the capacity to paralyze transport. In August 1917 it had supported Kerensky against Kornilov. In October, it initially favored the slogan "All Power to the Soviets," but as soon as its officers realized the uses which the Bolsheviks made of it, they turned against them, insisting that the Sovnarkom give way to a coalition cabinet.[23] On October 29, the union declared that unless the government was promptly broadened to include other socialist parties, it would order a strike. This was a serious threat, for the Bolsheviks, in preparation for Kerensky's counteroffensive, needed trains to move troops to the front.

The Bolsheviks convened the Central Committee. Lenin and Trotsky, busy organizing the defenses against Kerensky, could not attend. In their absence, the Central Committee, apparently in a state of panic, surrendered to the union's demands, conceding the necessity of "broadening the base of government through the inclusion of other socialist parties." It also reconfirmed that the Sovnarkom was a creation of the CEC and accountable to it. The committee delegated Kamenev and G. Ia. Sokolnikov to negotiate with the union and the other parties the formation of a new Soviet Provisional Government.[24] This resolution, in essence, meant a surrender of the powers won in the October coup.

Later that day (October 29), Kamenev and Sokolnikov attended a meeting, convened by the Union of Railroad Employees, of eight parties and several intraparty organizations. Following the resolution of the Bolshevik Central Committee, they agreed to have the SRs and Mensheviks enter the Sovnarkom on condition that they accept the resolutions of the Second Congress of Soviets. The meeting designated a committee to work out the terms for the restructuring of the Sovnarkom. Its ultimatum met, late that evening the union ordered its branches to call off the strike but to remain on the alert.[25]

Any sense of relief the Bolsheviks may have received from this agreement vanished the next day when they learned that the union, supported by the socialist parties, had raised its stakes and now demanded that the Bolsheviks remove themselves from the government altogether. The Bolshevik Central Committee, still minus Lenin and Trotsky, spent most of the day discussing this demand. It did so in a highly charged atmosphere, for the pro-Kerensky forces under Ataman Krasnov were expected to break into the city at any moment. Seeking to salvage something, Kamenev proposed a compromise: Lenin would resign the chairmanship of the Sovnarkom in favor of the SR leader Victor Chernov, and the Bolsheviks would accept secondary portfolios in a coalition government dominated by SRs and Mensheviks.[26]

It is difficult to tell what would have become of these concessions were it not that late that evening news arrived that Krasnov's forces had been beaten back.

The military threat lifted, Lenin and Trotsky now turned their attention to the catastrophic political situation created by the "capitulationist" policy of the Central Committee. When the committee reconvened on the evening of November 1, Lenin exploded with uncontrolled fury.[27] "Kamenev's policy," he demanded, "must be stopped at once." The committee should have carried out negotiations with the union as "diplomatic camouflage for military action"—that is, presumably not in good faith, but only to secure its assistance against Kerensky's troops. The majority of the Central Committee was unmoved: Rykov ventured the opinion that the Bolsheviks would not be able to keep power. A vote was taken: ten members favored continuing the talks with the other socialist parties about a coalition government, and only three sided with Lenin (Trotsky, Sokolnikov, and probably Dzerzhinskii). Even Sverdlov opposed Lenin.

Lenin faced a humiliating defeat: his comrades were prepared to throw away the fruits of the October victory, and instead of establishing a "proletarian dictatorship," would share power as minor partners with "petty bourgeois" parties. He was saved by Trotsky, who intervened with a clever compromise. Trotsky began with a tirade against concessions:

We are told we are incapable of constructive work. But if this is the case, then we should simply turn power over to those who had been right in fighting us. In fact, we have already accomplished a great deal. It is impossible, we are told, to sit on bayonets. But without bayonets one cannot manage either. . . . This whole petty bourgeois scum which now is unable to side with either this or that side, once it learns that our authority is strong, will come over to us, [the union] included. . . . The petty bourgeois mass is looking for a force to which to submit.[28]

As Alexandra liked to remind Nicholas: "Russia loves to feel the whip."

Trotsky proposed a formula to gain time: negotiations over a coalition cabinet should continue with the Left SRs, the only party that accepted the October coup, but they should cease with the other socialist parties if no agreement was reached after one more attempt. This did not seem to be an unreasonable way out of the impasse and the proposal carried.

Lenin, determined to put an end to defeatism in his ranks, returned to the fray the next day with the demand that the Central Committee condemn the "opposition." It was a strange demand, given that it was he who opposed the will of the majority. In the debates that ensued, he managed to split his rivals. A resolution condemning them won with a vote of 10–5. As a result, the five who stood up against Lenin to the end—Kamenev, Zinoviev, Rykov, Miliutin, and Nogin—resigned. On November 4, *Izvestiia* carried a letter in which they explained their action:

> On November 1, the Central Committee . . . adopted a resolution which, in effect, rejected agreement with [other] parties in the Soviet for the purpose of forming a socialist Soviet Government. . . . We regard the formation of such a government essential to the prevention of further bloodshed. . . . The dominant group in the Central Committee has undertaken a number of acts which demonstrate clearly its firm determination not to allow the formation of a government made up of soviet parties and insists on a purely Bolshevik Government, no matter what the consequences and how many victims the workers and soldiers will have to sacrifice. We cannot assume responsibility for this fatal policy of the Central Committee, pursued in opposition to the will of the vast part of the proletariat and the troops. . . . On these grounds, we resign from the Central Committee so as to have the right to defend our point of view openly before the mass of workers and soldiers and to appeal to them to support our slogan: "Long live the government of soviet parties!"[29]

Two days later, Kamenev resigned as chairman of the CEC; four People's Commissars (out of eleven) did likewise: Nogin (Trade and Industry), Rykov (Interior), Miliutin (Agriculture), and Teodorovich (Supply). Shliapnikov, the Commissar for Labor, signed the letter but stayed on the job. Several Bolshevik lower-level commissars resigned as well. "We take the position," the commissars' letter read:

> that it is necessary to form a socialist government of all the soviet parties. We believe that only the formation of such a government would make it possible

to consolidate the results of the heroic struggle of the working class and the revolutionary army in the days of October–November. We believe that there is only one alternative to this: the maintenance of an exclusively Bolshevik Government by means of political terror. This is the path taken by the Council of People's Commissars. We cannot and do not want to go this way. We see that this leads to the removal of mass proletarian organizations from the management of political life, to the establishment of an irresponsible regime, and to the destruction of the Revolution and the country. We cannot bear responsibility for this policy and therefore tender to the CEC our resignations as People's Commissars.[30]

Lenin lost no sleep over these protests and resignations, confident that the straying sheep would soon return to the fold, as indeed they did. Where else could they go? The socialist parties ostracized them; the liberals, should they take power, would put them in jail; while the politicians of the right would hang them. Their very physical survival depended on Lenin's success.

The decisions adopted by the Bolshevik Central Committee signified that the Bolsheviks would share power only with parties that were prepared to accept a role of junior partner and rubber-stamp Bolshevik resolutions. Except for four months (December 1917–March 1918) when the Bolsheviks allowed a few Left SRs into their cabinet, the so-called Soviet Government never reflected the composition of the soviets: it was and remained a Bolshevik Government in soviet disguise.

Lenin had now managed to beat off the claims for a share of power by rival socialist parties, but he still had to cope with the insistence of the CEC that it was the soviet parliament to which his commissars owed responsibility.

The CEC which the Bolsheviks had handpicked in October thought of itself as a socialist Duma empowered to monitor the government's actions, appoint the cabinet, and legislate.* The day after the coup, it proceeded to work out its statutes, providing for an elaborate structure of plenums, presidia, and commissions of all sorts. Lenin thought such parliamentary pretensions ridiculous. From the first day he ignored the CEC whether in appointing officials or in issuing decrees. This can be illustrated by the casual manner in which he elected the CEC's new chairman. He decided that Sverdlov would be the best man to replace Kamenev. He had no reason to doubt that the CEC would approve his choice, but since he could not be absolutely certain, he bypassed it. He summoned Sverdlov: "Iakov Mikhailovich," he said, "I would like you to become the chairman of the CEC: what do you say?" Apparently, Sverdlov said yes, for Lenin promised that after the Central Committee had approved the choice, he would be "carefully" voted in by the CEC's Bolshevik majority. Lenin instructed him to count heads and make certain that the entire Bolshevik faction turned up for the vote.[31] All went as planned, and on November 8, Sverdlov was "elected"

*W. Pietsch, *Revolution und Staat* (Köln, 1969), 63. The old CEC, disbanded by the Bolsheviks, continued to meet, sometimes in the open, sometimes clandestinely, until the end of December 1917: *Revoliutsiia,* III, 90–91.

by a vote of 19–14.* In this post, which he held until his death in March 1919, Sverdlov ensured that the CEC ratified all party decisions after perfunctory discussion.

Lenin similarly ignored the CEC in choosing replacements for the commissars who had resigned from the cabinet: these he handpicked on November 8–11 after casual consultation with associates but without asking the CEC's approval.

He still faced the critical issue of the legislative authority of the CEC, its right to approve or veto government decrees.

In the first two weeks of the new regime, Chairman Kamenev had managed to insulate the Sovnarkom from the CEC by convoking it on short notice and failing to provide it beforehand with an agenda. During this brief interlude, the Sovnarkom legislated without bothering to obtain the CEC's approval. Indeed, government procedures at the time were so lax that some Bolsheviks who were not even members of the cabinet issued decrees on their own initiative without informing the Sovnarkom, let alone the Soviet Executive. Two such decrees brought about a constitutional crisis. The first was the Decree on the Press, issued on October 27, the initial day of new government. It bore the signature of Lenin, although it had been drafted by Lunacharskii, almost certainly with Lenin's encouragement and approval.† This remarkable document asserted that the "counterrevolutionary press"—a term which it did not define, but which obviously applied to all papers that did not acknowledge the legitimacy of the October coup—was causing harm, for which reason "temporary and emergency measures had to be taken to stop the torrent of filth and slander." Newspapers that agitated against the new authority were to be closed. "As soon as the new order has been firmly established," the decree went on, "all administrative measures affecting the press will be lifted [and] the press will be granted full freedom . . ."

The country had grown accustomed since February 1917 to violence against newspapers and printing plants. First, the "reactionary" press was attacked and closed; later, in July, the same fate befell Bolshevik organs. Once in power, the Bolsheviks expanded and formalized such practices. On October 26, the Military-Revolutionary Committee carried out pogroms of the oppositional press. It closed the uncompromisingly anti-Bolshevik *Nashe obschee delo* and arrested Vladimir Burtsev, its editor. It also suppressed the Menshevik *Den'*, the Kadet *Rech'*, the right-wing *Novoe vremia*, and the right-of-center *Birzhevye vedomosti*. The printing plants of *Den'* and *Rech'* were confiscated and turned over to Bolshevik journalists.[32] Most of the suppressed dailies promptly reappeared under different names.

The Decree on the Press went much further: if enforced, it would have eliminated in Russia the independent press whose origins went back to the reign of Catherine II. The outrage was universal. In Moscow, the Bolshevik-

---

*The Left SRs on this occasion voted against him: *Revoliutsiia,* VI, 99.
†*Dekrety,* I, 24–25. Lunacharskii is credited with its authorship by Iurii Larin in *NKh,* No. 11 (1918), 16–17.

controlled Military-Revolutionary Committee went so far as to overrule it, declaring on November 21 that the emergency was over and the press once again could enjoy full freedom of expression.[33] In the CEC, the Bolshevik Iurii Larin denounced the decree and called for its revocation.[34] On November 26, 1917, the Union of Writers issued a one-time newspaper, *Gazeta-Protest,* in which some of Russia's leading writers expressed anger at this unprecedented attempt to stifle freedom of expression. Vladimir Korolenko wrote that as he read Lenin's *ukaz* "blood rushed to his face from shame and indignation":

> Who, by what right, has deprived me, as reader and member of the [Poltava] community, of the opportunity to learn what is happening in the capital city during these tragic moments? And who presumes to prevent me, as a writer, of the opportunity to express freely to my fellow citizens my views on these events without the censor's imprimatur?[35]

Anticipating that this and similar measures, especially those concerning the economy, would arouse strong opposition in the Congress of Soviets and the CEC, the Bolsheviks issued yet another law bearing on the question of relations between government and soviets. Called "Concerning the Procedure for the Ratification and Promulgation of Laws," the decree claimed for the Sovnarkom the right to act in a legislative capacity: the CEC's power was limited to ratifying or abrogating decrees after they had gone into effect. This document, which completely subverted the conditions under which the Congress of Soviets only a few days before had authorized the Bolsheviks to form a government, bore Lenin's signature. But it is claimed in the recollections of Iurii Larin, a Menshevik who in September had gone over to Lenin and become his most influential economic adviser, that it was he who had drafted and issued it on his own authority without Lenin's knowledge: Lenin is said to have learned of this law only when he read it in the official *Gazette.*[36]

The Larin-Lenin decree claimed to have validity only until the convocation of the Constituent Assembly. It declared that until then laws would be drafted and promulgated by the Provisional Government of Workers and Peasants (Sovnarkom). The Central Executive Committee retained the right to "suspend, change, or annul" such laws retroactively.* With this decree, the Bolsheviks claimed the right to legislate by the equivalent of Article 87 of the Fundamental Laws of 1906.

This simplified procedure, which rid the government of parliamentary "obstructionism," would have warmed the heart of Goremykin and any other conservative bureaucrat of the old regime, but it was not what the socialists had expected of the "Soviet" Government. The CEC followed these developments with growing alarm; it protested the Sovnarkom's infringement of its authority through uncontrolled "bossing" *(khoziaistvovanie)* and the promulgation of decrees in the CEC's name but without its approval.[37]

---

*Dekrety, I, 29–30. The date when the decree was issued cannot be established: it appeared in the Bolshevik press on October 31 and November 1, 1917.

The issue came to a head at a meeting of November 4 which decided the fate of "soviet democracy." Lenin and Trotsky were invited to explain themselves, much as before the Revolution Imperial ministers had been subject to Duma "interpellations" about the legality of their actions. The Left SRs wanted to know why the government was repeatedly violating the will of the Second Congress of Soviets, which had made the government responsible to the Central Executive Committee. They insisted that the government cease ruling by decree.[38]

Lenin regarded this as "bourgeois formalism." He had long believed that the Communist regime had to combine both legislative and executive powers.[39] As was his wont when confronted with questions he could not or would not answer, he immediately went on the offensive, filling the air with counter-charges. The Soviet Government could not be bound by "formalities." Kerensky's inactivity had proven fatal. Those who questioned his actions were "apologists of parliamentary obstructionism." Bolshevik power rested on the "confidence of the broad masses."[40] None of this explained why he was violating the terms under which he had assumed office a mere week before. Trotsky gave a slightly more substantive response. The Soviet parliament (meaning the Congress of Soviets and its Central Executive Committee), unlike the "bourgeois" one, had no antagonistic classes and therefore no need for the "conventional parliamentary machinery." The implication of the argument was that where there were no class differences there could be no differences of opinion: from which it followed that differences of opinion signified ipso facto "counter-revolution." The government and the "masses," Trotsky went on, were linked not by formal institutions and procedures but by a "vital and direct bond." Anticipating Mussolini, who would use analogous arguments to justify fascist practices, he said: "It may be true that our decrees are not smooth . . . but the right of vital creativity transcends formal perfection."[41]

Lenin's and Trotsky's irrelevancies and inconsistencies failed to persuade the majority of the CEC; even some Bolsheviks felt uneasy. The Left SRs responded sharply. V. A. Karelin said:

> I protest the abuse of the term "bourgeois." Accountability and strict order in detail are mandatory not only for a bourgeois government. Let us not play on words and cover up our mistakes and blunders with a separate, odious word. Proletarian government, which in its is essence popular, must also allow controls over itself. After all, the workers taking over an enterprise does not lead to the abolition of bookkeeping and accounting. This hasty cooking of decrees, which not only frequently abound in juridical omissions but are often illiterate, leads to still greater confusion of the situation, especially in the provinces, where they are accustomed to accepting a law in the form in which it is given from above.[42]

Another Left SR, P. P. Proshian, described the Bolshevik Press Decree as a "clear and determined expression of a system of political terror and incitement to civil war."[43]

The Bolsheviks readily won the vote on the Press Decree: a motion to abrogate the decree, introduced by Larin, went down 34–24, with one abstention.* Despite this endorsement, the Bolsheviks were unable to silence the press until August 1918, when they eliminated in one fell swoop all independent newspapers and periodicals. Until then, Soviet Russia had a surprising variety of newspapers and journals, including those of a liberal and even conservative orientation: heavily fined and harassed in other ways, they somehow managed to stay alive.

There still remained the critical issue of the Sovnarkom's responsibility to the CEC. On this matter, the Bolshevik Government, for the first and last time, submitted itself to a vote of confidence. It came on a motion of the Left SR V. B. Spiro: "The Central Executive Committee, having heard the explanations offered by the chairman of the Council of People's Commissars, finds them unsatisfactory." The Bolshevik M. S. Uritskii responded with a countermotion expressing confidence in Lenin's government:

> In regard to the interpellation, the Central Executive Committee determines:
>   1. The Soviet parliament of the working masses can have nothing in common in its procedures with the bourgeois parliament, in which are represented various classes with antagonistic interests and where the representatives of the ruling class transform rules and instructions into weapons of legislative obstruction;
>   2. The Soviet parliament cannot refuse the Council of People's Commissars the right to issue, without prior discussion by the Central Executive Committee, urgent decrees within the framework of the general program of the All-Russian Congress of Soviets;
>   3. The Central Executive Committee exercises general control over the activity of the Council of People's Commissars and is free to change the government or its individual members . . .[44]

Spiro's no-confidence motion was defeated 25 to 20: the low vote resulted from the withdrawal of the nine Bolsheviks, some of them commissars, who had announced their resignation at this meeting (see above, page 519). The negative victory was not enough for Lenin: he wanted it affirmed, formally and unequivocally, by a vote on Uritskii's motion, that his government had the power to legislate. But the prospect looked in doubt because Bolshevik ranks had suddenly shrunk: a preliminary count showed that a vote on Uritskii's motion would produce a tie (23–23). To prevent this, Lenin and Trotsky announced that they would take part in the voting—an action equivalent to ministers joining the legislature in voting on a law which they had submitted for its approval. If Russia's "parliamentarians" had had more experience, they would have refused to participate in the travesty. But they stayed and they voted. Uritskii's motion carried 25–23, the decisive two votes being cast by

---

*A. L. Fraiman, *Forpost sotsialisticheskoi revoliutsii* (Leningrad, 1969), 169–70. The Bolsheviks took the precaution of increasing their representation on the CEC with five reliable members (*Revoliutsiia*, VI, 72).

Lenin and Trotsky. By this simple procedure, the two Bolshevik leaders arrogated to themselves legislative authority and transformed the CEC and the Congress of Soviets, which it represented, from legislative into consultative bodies. It was a watershed in the history of the Soviet constitution.

Later that day, the Sovnarkom announced that its decrees acquired force of law when they appeared in the pages of the official *Gazette of the Provisional Workers' and Peasants' Government (Gazeta Vremennogo Rabochego i Krest'ianskogo Pravitel'stva).*

The Sovnarkom now became in theory what it had been in fact since its inception, an organ combining executive and legislative authority. The CEC was allowed for a while longer to enjoy the right to debate the actions of the government, a right which, even if it had no effect on policy, at least provided opportunities for criticism. But after June–July 1918, when non-Bolsheviks were ejected from it, the CEC turned into an echo chamber in which Bolshevik deputies routinely "ratified" the decisions of the Bolshevik Sovnarkom, which, in turn, implemented decisions of the Bolshevik Central Committee.*

This sudden and complete collapse of democratic forces and their subsequent inability to reclaim constitutional powers recalls the failure of the Supreme Privy Council in 1730 to impose constitutional restraints on the Russian monarchy: then, as now, a firm "no" from the autocrat proved sufficient.

From this day on, Russia was ruled by decree. Lenin assumed the prerogatives that the tsars had enjoyed before October 1905: his will was law. In the words of Trotsky: "From the moment the Provisional Government was declared deposed, Lenin acted in matters large and small as the government."† The "decrees" which the Sovnarkom issued, although bearing a name borrowed from revolutionary France and previously unknown to Russian constitutional law, corresponded fully to imperial *ukazy* in that like them they dealt indiscriminately with the most fundamental as well as most trivial matters, and went into effect the instant the autocrat affixed his signature to them. (According to Isaac Steinberg, "Lenin was ordinarily of the opinion that his signature had to suffice for any governmental act.")[45] Bonch-Bruevich, Lenin's executive secretary, writes that decrees acquired force of law only after being signed by Lenin, even if issued on the initiative of one of the commissars.[46]‡ These practices would have been entirely understandable to a Nicholas I or Alexander III. The system of government which the Bolsheviks set in place within two weeks of the October coup marked a reversion to the autocratic regime that had ruled Russia before 1905: they simply wiped out the twelve intervening years of constitutionalism.

---

*In December 1919, the few powers still nominally vested in the CEC were transferred to its chairman, who thereby became "head of state." CEC meetings, which originally had been intended to be continuous, took place ever less frequently: in 1921, the CEC met only three times. See E. H. Carr, *The Bolshevik Revolution,* I (New York, 1951), 220–30.

†*"kak pravitel'stvo":* L. Trotskii, *O Lenine* (Moscow, 1924), 102. The English translator distorted this passage to read that Lenin "acted as a government should": L. Trotsky, *Lenin* (New York, 1971), 121.

‡As we shall note below, there were exceptions to this rule.

The intelligenstia was the one group that did not participate in the nationwide *duvan* and would not allow itself to be diverted by "clinking bags." It had welcomed the February Revolution with boundless enthusiasm; it rejected the October coup. Even some Communist historians have come to concede that students, professors, writers, artists, and others who had led the opposition to tsarism, overwhelmingly opposed the Bolshevik takeover: one of them states that the intelligentsia "almost to a man" engaged in "sabotage."[47] It took the Bolsheviks months of coercion and cajolery to break this resistance. The intelligentsia began to cooperate with the Bolsheviks only after it had concluded that the regime was here to stay and boycotting it would only make matters worse.

The most dramatic manifestation of the refusal by Russia's educated class to accept the October coup was the general strike of white-collar personnel *(sluzhashchie)*. Although the Bolsheviks then and since have dismissed this action as "sabotage," it was, in fact, a grandiose, non-violent act of protest by the nation's civil servants and employees of private enterprises against the destruction of democracy.[48] The strike, intended to demonstrate to the Bolsheviks their unpopularity and, at the same time, make it impossible for them to govern, broke out spontaneously. It quickly acquired an organizational structure, first in the shape of strike committees in the ministries, banks, and other public institutions and then in a coordinating body called the Committee for the Salvation of the Fatherland and the Revolution (Komitet Spaseniia Rodiny i Revoliutsii). The committee originally consisted of Municipal Duma officials, members of the Central Executive Committee of Soviets dissolved by the Bolsheviks, representatives of the All-Russian Congress of Peasant Soviets, the Union of Unions of Government Employees, and several clerical unions, including that of postal workers. Gradually, representatives of Russian socialist parties, the Left SRs excepted, also joined. The committee appealed to the nation not to cooperate with the usurpers and to fight for the restoration of democracy.[49] On October 28 it called on the Bolsheviks to relinquish power.[50]

On October 29, the Union of Unions of Government Employees in Petrograd, in cooperation with the committee (which apparently financed the strike), asked its membership to stop work:

> The committee of the Union of Unions of Government Employees at Petrograd, having discussed with the delegates of the central committees of the All-Russian Union of Government Employees the question of the usurpation of power by the Bolshevik group in the Petrograd Soviet a month before the convocation of the Constituent Assembly, and considering that this criminal act threatens the destruction of Russia and all the conquests of the Revolution, in accord with the All-Russian Committee for the Salvation of the Fatherland and the Revolution . . . resolved that:

1. Work in all the administrative departments of the government shall cease immediately;

2. The questions of food supply for the army and the population, as well as the activity of the institutions concerned with the maintenance of public order, are to be decided by the Committee for the Salvation [of the Fatherland and the Revolution] in cooperation with the committees of the Union of Unions;

3. The action of the administrative departments which have already ceased their work is approved.[51]

The appeal was widely heeded: soon work in all the ministries in Petrograd ground to a halt. Except for porters and some secretarial staff, their personnel either failed to come to work or came and sat doing nothing. The freshly appointed Bolshevik commissars, having no place to go, hung around Lenin's headquarters in Smolnyi, issuing orders to which no one paid attention. Access to the ministries was barred to them:

When, after the first October days, the People's Commissars came to work in the former ministries, they found, along with mountains of papers and folders, only couriers, cleaning people, and doormen. All the officials, beginning with the directors and administrators and ending with typists and copiers, considered it their duty to refuse to recognize the commissars and to stay away from work.[52]

Trotsky had an embarrassing experience when on November 9—two weeks after receiving his appointment—he ventured to visit the Ministry of Foreign Affairs:

Yesterday, the new "minister," Trotsky, came to the Ministry of Foreign Affairs. After calling together all the officials, he said: "I am the new Minister of Foreign Affairs, Trotsky." He was greeted with ironic laughter. To this he paid no attention and told them to go back to their work. They went . . . but to their own homes, with the intention of not returning to [the] office as long as Trotsky remained head of the ministry.[53]

Shliapnikov, the Commissar of Labor, had a similar reception when he tried to take charge of his ministry.[54] The Bolshevik Government thus found itself in the absurd situation of being unable, weeks after it had assumed authority, to persuade the country's civil servants to work for it. It could hardly be said, therefore, to have functioned.

The strike spread to non-governmental institutions. Private banks had shut their doors as early as October 26–27. On November 1, the All-Russian Union of Postal and Telegraph Employees announced that unless the Bolshevik Government gave way to a coalition cabinet it would order its membership to stop work.[55] Soon telegraph and telephone workers walked out in Petrograd, Moscow, and some provincial towns. On November 2, Petrograd's pharmacists went on strike; on November 7, water transport workers followed suit as did schoolteachers. On November 8, the Union of Printers in Petrograd announced that if the Bolsheviks carried out their Press Decree they, too, would strike.

For the Bolsheviks, the most painful were work stoppages at the government's fiscal institutions, the State Bank and the State Treasury. They could manage for the time being, without the ministries of Foreign Affairs or of Labor, but they had to have money. The bank and the Treasury refused to honor the Sovnarkom's requests for funds, on the grounds that it was not a legitimate government: couriers sent by Smolnyi with drafts signed by People's Commissars came back empty-handed. The staffs of the bank and the treasury recognized the old Provisional Government and paid only its representatives; they also honored requests from legitimate public authorities and the military. On November 4, in response to Bolshevik charges that its actions were causing hardship to the population, the State Bank declared that during the preceding week it had paid out 610 million rubles for the needs of the population and the armed forces; 40 million of that sum went to representatives of the old Provisional Government.[56]

On October 30, the Sovnarkom ordered all state and private banks to open for business the next day. Refusal to honor checks and drafts from government institutions, it warned, would lead to the arrest of the directors.[57] Under this threat, some private banks reopened, but still none would cash checks issued by the Sovnarkom.

Desperate for money, the Bolsheviks resorted to harsher measures. On November 7, V. R. Menzhinskii, the new Commissar of Finance, appeared at the State Bank with armed sailors and a military band. He demanded 10 million rubles. The bank refused. He returned four days later with more troops and presented an ultimatum: unless money was forthcoming within twenty minutes, not only would the staff of the State Bank lose their jobs and pensions but those of military age would be drafted. The bank stood firm. The Sovnarkom dismissed some of the bank's officials, but it still had no money, more than two weeks after assuming governmental responsibilities.

On November 14, the clerical personnel of Petrograd banks met to decide what to do next. Employees of the State Bank voted overwhelmingly to deny recognition to the Sovnarkom and go on with the strike. Clerks of private banks reached the same conclusion. The staff of the State Treasury voted 142–14 to refuse the Bolsheviks access to government funds: they also rejected a Sovnarkom request for a "short-term advance" of 25 million rubles.[58]

In the face of this resistance, the Bolsheviks had recourse to force. On November 17, Menzhinskii reappeared at the State Bank: he found it deserted, save for some couriers and watchmen. Officers of the bank were brought in under armed guard. When they refused to hand over money, guards compelled them to open the vaults, from which Menzhinskii removed 5 million rubles. He carried it to Smolnyi in a velvet bag, which he triumphantly deposited on Lenin's desk.[59] The whole operation resembled a bank holdup.

The Bolsheviks now had access to Treasury funds, but strikes of bank personnel continued, despite arrests; nearly all banks remained closed. The State Bank, occupied by Bolshevik troops, was inoperative. It was to break the resistance of financial personnel that Lenin initially created, in December 1917, his security police, the Cheka.

A contemporary survey showed that in mid-December work was at a standstill at the ministries (now renamed commissariats) of Foreign Affairs, Enlightenment, Justice, and Supply, while the State Bank was in complete disarray.[60] White-collar strikes also broke out in the provincial towns: in mid-November the municipal workers of Moscow struck; their colleagues in Petrograd followed suit on December 3. These work stoppages had one common purpose: modeled on the General Strike of October 1905, they were to force the government to renounce claims to autocracy. It was this powerful demonstration that persuaded Kamenev, Zinoviev, Rykov, and some other associates of Lenin that they had to share power with other socialist parties or the government could not function.

Lenin, however, held his ground and in mid-November ordered a counter-offensive. The Bolsheviks now physically occupied, one by one, every public institution in Petrograd and compelled their employees, under threat of severe punishment, to work for them. The following incident, reported by a contemporary newspaper, was repeated in many places:

> On December 28 [OS], the Bolsheviks seized the Department of Customs. Directing the occupied Customs office is an official named Fadenev. On the eve of the Christmas holidays, following a general meeting of departmental employees, Fadenev had ordered everyone to return to work on December 28: those who failed to appear, he threatened, would lose their jobs and be liable to prosecution. On December 28, the department building was occupied by inspectors. The Bolsheviks allowed into the building only those employees who would sign a statement of full subordination to the "Council of People's Commissars."[61]

The directors of the Customs Department were subsequently dismissed and replaced with lower clerical staff. This pattern was repeated as the Bolsheviks conquered, in the literal sense of the word, the apparatus of the central government, often with the support of the junior staff whom they won over with promises of rapid promotion. They broke the strike of white collar employees only in January 1918, after they had dispersed the Constituent Assembly and ended all hope that they would voluntarily surrender or even share power.

During its initial three weeks, the Sovnarkom led a paper existence since it had neither a staff to execute its orders nor money to pay its own people. The Bolshevik commissars, barred from their offices, operated from Room 67 at Smolnyi, where Lenin had his headquarters. Lenin, ever fearful of attempts

73. Latvians guarding Lenin's office in Smolnyi: 1917.

on his life, ordered that no one except People's Commissars be allowed into his office: he rarely left Smolnyi, where he lived and officiated closely guarded by Latvians.*[62] As the Secretary of the Sovnarkom he picked the twenty-five-year-old N. P. Gorbunov. The new secretary, who had no administrative experience, confiscated a typewriter and a table and proceeded to peck out decrees with two fingers.[63] V. Bonch-Bruevich, a devoted Bolshevik and a student of religious dissenters, was appointed Lenin's private assistant. The two men hired clerical personnel. By the end of the year, the Sovnarkom had forty-eight clerical employees; in the next two months it acquired seventeen more. Judging by a group photograph taken in October 1918, a high proportion of these were clean-cut bourgeois young ladies.

　　Prior to November 15, 1917, the Sovnarkom held no regular sessions: according to Gorbunov one meeting took place on November 3, but its only order of business was to hear a report by Nogin on the fighting in Moscow. During this period such decrees and ordnances as came out were the work of Bolshevik functionaries, who acted independently, often without consulting Lenin. According to Larin, only two of the first fifteen decrees issued by the Soviet Government were discussed in the Sovnarkom: the Decree on the Press, drafted by Lunarcharskii, and the Decree on Elections to the Constituent Assembly, prepared by himself. Gorbunov says Lenin authorized him to cable directives to the provinces on his own, showing him only every tenth telegram.[64]

　　The first regular meeting of the Sovnarkom took place on November 15, with an agenda of twenty items. It was agreed that the commissars would move

_____

*According to Professor John Keep, in the first eighteen weeks in power—that is, until early March 1918 when he moved to Moscow—Lenin left Smolnyi only twenty-one times: Report presented at the Conference on the Russian Revolution, Hebrew University, Jerusalem, January 1988.

74. Lenin and secretarial staff of the Council of People's Commissars: October 1918.

out of Smolnyi as expeditiously as possible and take over their respective commissariats, which they did in the weeks that followed, with the help of armed detachments. From that day onward, the Sovnarkom met almost daily on the third floor of Smolnyi, usually in the evening: the meetings sometimes ran all night. Attendance was not much restricted, with many lower-level officials and non-Bolshevik technical experts brought in as the need arose. The commissars, lifelong revolutionaries, felt awkward. Simon Liberman, a Menshevik timber expert who occasionally attended Sovnarkom sessions, recalls the meetings as follows:

> A peculiar atmosphere prevailed at the conferences of the highest administrative councils of Soviet Russia, presided over by Lenin. Despite all the efforts of an officious secretary to impart to each session the solemn character of a cabinet meeting, we could not help feeling that here we were, attending another sitting of an underground revolutionary committee! For years we had belonged to various underground organizations. All of this seemed so familiar. Many of the commissars remained seated in their topcoats or greatcoats; most of them wore the forbidding leather jackets. In wintertime some wore felt boots and thick sweaters. They remained thus clothed throughout the meetings.
>
> One of the commissars, Alexander Tsuriupa, was nearly always ill; he attended these sessions in a semi-reclining position, his feet stretched out on a nearby chair. A number of Lenin's aides would not take their seats at the conference table but shoved their chairs around helter-skelter all over the room. Lenin alone invariably took his seat at the table as the presiding officer of the occasion. He did so in a neat, almost decorous way. Fotieva, as his personal secretary, sat beside him.[65]

Lenin, irritated by the unpunctuality and verbosity of his colleagues, worked out strict rules. To prevent chatter, he insisted on strict adherence to

75. One of the early meetings of the Council of People's
Commissars. Lenin in the center. Behind him, hand at
mouth, Stalin.

the agenda.* To ensure that his commissars showed up on time, he set fines
for lateness: five rubles for less than half an hour, ten for more.[66]

According to Liberman, the meetings of the Sovnarkom which he attended never decided on policy but dealt only with implementation:

> I never heard arguments over matters of principle; the discussion always re-
> volved around the problem of finding the best possible methods of carrying out
> a given measure. Matters of principle were decided elsewhere—in the Political
> Bureau of the Communist Party.... The two highest organs of the Government
> which I knew—the Council of People's Commissars and the Council of Labor
> and Defense—discussed practical ways to effect measures already decided upon
> by the inner sanctum of the party—its Political Bureau.†

*BK, No. 1 (1934), 107. Jay Lovestone, a founder of the American Communist Party, told the
author that once, when speaking with Lenin, he used three-by-five cards. Lenin wanted to know
their purpose. When Lovestone explained that, to save Lenin's time, he had written down on them
what he intended to say, Lenin said that Communism would come to Russia when she too learned
to use three-by-five cards.

†S. Liberman, *Building Lenin's Russia* (Chicago, 1945), 13. The minutes of the Sovnarkom,
which, next to the protocols of the Bolshevik Central Committee, constitute the most important
source on early Bolshevik policies, are preserved at the Central Party Archive (TsPA) of the
Marx-Lenin Institute in Moscow, under the shelf mark "Fond 19." They are made available only
to the most trusted Communist historians. Others must rely on secondhand references, such as those
contained (in very incomplete form) in the biographical chronicle of Lenin's life: Institut Marksizma-Leninizma pri TsK KPSS, *Vladimir Il'ich Lenin: Biograficheskaia Khronika, 1870–1924,*
V–XII (Moscow, 1974–82). See further E. B. Genkina, *Protokoly Sovnarkoma RSFSR* (Moscow,
1982).

To relieve the Sovnarkom of the many trivial issues that threatened to overburden its agenda, a Small Sovnarkom was created on December 18, 1917.

Government decisions became law when signed by Lenin and usually co-signed by one of the commissars, and then published in the official *Gazette,* the first issue of which appeared on October 28. It then acquired the status of a "decree" *(dekret).* Orders issued by the commissars on their own initiative were usually called "resolutions" *(postanovleniia).* Theory, however, was not always observed in practice. On certain occasions—this happened especially with laws sure to be unpopular—Lenin preferred that decrees be issued by the CEC and signed by its chairman, Sverdlov: this procedure had the effect of shifting the blame from the Bolsheviks onto the soviets. Some important laws were never published—such as the one creating the Cheka. Other measures—for instance, the introduction of the practice of taking hostages (September 1918)—came out in the name of the Commissar of Internal Affairs: it was published in *Izvestiia,* but is not included in the corpus of Soviet laws and decrees. Before long, the Bolsheviks reverted to the tsarist practice of legislating by means of secret circulars, which were not published at the time and many of which remain unpublished to this day: as under the old regime, the government resorted to this practice in matters involving state security.

In the first months of Bolshevik rule, decrees were issued not so much for their practical effect as for purposes of propaganda.[67] Without means to enforce his laws, and uncertain how long his regime would survive, Lenin thought of them as models from which future generations could learn how to make revolution. Since they were not expected to be implemented, the early decrees were exhortative in tone and careless in phrasing. Lenin gave this matter serious attention only three months after coming to power: on January 30, 1918, he ordered that legislative drafts be submitted for review to the Commissariat of Justice, which had trained jurists.[68] Laws issued from the spring of 1918 onward became so convoluted it is obvious they were not only reviewed but drafted by experienced bureaucrats of the old regime, who now entered Soviet service in large numbers.

It will be recalled (page 519, above) that to appease critics on the Central Committee, Lenin and Trotsky agreed to continue negotiating with the Left SRs on their entry into the government, and to make one more effort to come to terms with the Mensheviks and SRs. The latter objective they never seriously pursued; Lenin had no desire to admit his socialist rivals into partnership. But he did want to bring in the Left SRs. He knew them for what they were: a loosely knit band of revolutionary hotheads, drunk on words, incapable of concerted action because of their faith in mass "spontaneity." They were no threat, but they had their uses. Their presence in the cabinet would disarm the charge that the Bolsheviks monopolized the government: it would prove that any party prepared to "accept October"—the Bolshevik coup—was welcome. Still more valuable was the ability of the Left SRs to provide the Bolsheviks entry to the peasantry, with whose organizations they had no contact. Since it was absurd to pretend to the status of a government of "workers and peasants" without any peasant representatives, the Left SR access to the peasantry was a considerable asset. Lenin had great hopes (unrealistic, as events were to show) that the Left SRs would split the peasant vote for the Constituent Assembly and possibly give the Bolsheviks and their allies a majority.

The two parties negotiated in secret. On November 18, *Izvestiia* announced—prematurely, it turned out—that agreement had been reached with the Left SRs on their entry into the Sovnarkom. But the talks went on for three more weeks, in the course of which the two parties established a close working relationship. The Left SRs now joined forces with the Bolsheviks and helped them destroy the independent peasant movement dominated by the Socialists-Revolutionaries.

The Congress of Peasants' Deputies, which represented four-fifths of Russia's population, rejected the October coup. It sent no delegates to the Second Congress of Soviets, joining instead the Committee for the Salvation of the Fatherland and the Revolution. This opposition was awkward for the Bolsheviks; they had to win over the Peasants' Congress or, failing that, replace it with another body, friendly to them. Their strategy, which they subsequently repeated in regard to the Constituent Assembly and other democratic but anti-Bolshevik representative bodies, involved three steps. First, they sought to gain control of a given body's Mandate Commission, which determined who could attend: this enabled them to bring in more Bolshevik and pro-Bolshevik deputies than they would have obtained in free elections. If such a body, packed with their followers, nevertheless failed to pass Bolshevik resolutions, they disrupted it with noise and threats of violence. If that method also failed, then they declared the meeting unlawful, walked out, and set up a rival meeting of their own.

As the elections to the Constituent Assembly, held in the second half of November, would demonstrate, the Bolsheviks enjoyed no support in the rural areas. This bode ill for their prospects at the Congress of Peasants' Deputies, scheduled for the end of November, where the SRs were certain to pass resolutions denouncing the Bolshevik dictatorship. To prevent this, the Bolsheviks, helped by the Left SRs, tried to manipulate the Mandate Commission demanding that the delegates to the congress, ordinarily elected by provincial and district soviets, be augmented with representatives from military units. This demand had no justification, since the military already were represented in the Soldiers' Section of the Soviet. But the SRs on the Mandate Commission, eager to placate the Bolsheviks, agreed: as a result, instead of completely dominating the Peasants' Congress, they had to make do with a bare majority. The final tally of deputies to the Peasants' Congress showed 789 delegates, of whom 489 were bona fide peasant representatives, chosen by the rural soviets, and 294 were men in uniform handpicked by the Bolsheviks and Left SRs from the garrisons of Petrograd and vicinity. The party affiliation showed 307 SRs and 91 Bolsheviks; the affiliation of the remaining 391 was not stated, but judging by subsequent voting results, a high proportion of them were Left SRs.*

In yet another conciliatory gesture, the SR leadership agreed to giving the chairmanship of the congress to Maria Spiridonova, the leader of the Left SRs. Although the peasants indeed idolized her for her terrorist exploits before the Revolution, it was an ill-considered concession because the impulsive Spiridonova was completely manipulated by the Bolsheviks.

The Second Congress of Peasants' Deputies opened in Petrograd on November 26 in the Alexander Hall of the Municipal Duma. From the outset, Bolshevik deputies, cheered on by the Left SRs, engaged in disruptive tactics, hooting, screaming, and shouting down speakers from rival parties; for a while they physically occupied the rostrum. The disturbance forced Spiridonova on several occasions to declare a recess.

The critical session took place on December 2. On that day, several SR speakers protested the arrest and harassment of delegates to the Constituent Assembly, some of whom were also elected to the Peasants' Congress. During one of these speeches, Lenin appeared. An SR, pointing at him, shouted to the Bolsheviks: "You will bring Russia to the point where Nicholas will be replaced by Lenin. We need no autocratic authority. We need the rule of soviets!" Lenin asked to speak in his capacity as head of state, but he was told that since no one had elected him, he could only have the floor as head of the Bolshevik Party. His address denigrated the Constituent Assembly and dismissed complaints of Bolshevik harassment of its deputies. Lenin promised, however, that the Assembly would meet when a quorum of 400 deputies had gathered in Petrograd.

When he left, Chernov moved a resolution which rejected the Bolshevik claim that to acknowledge the authority of the Constituent Assembly was tantamount to rejecting the soviets:

> The congress believes that the soviets of workers', soldiers', and peasants' deputies, as the ideological and political guides of the masses, should be the strong combat points of the Revolution standing guard over the conquests of peasants and workers. With its legislative creativity, the Constituent Assembly must translate into life the aspirations of the masses, as expressed by the soviets. In consequence, the congress protests against the attempts of individual groups to pit the soviets and the Constituent Assembly against each other.†

The Bolsheviks and Left SRs introduced a counterresolution which called on the congress to approve the Bolshevik measures against the Kadets and

---

DN, No. 222 (December 2, 1917), 3. The protocols of this congress have not been published: the fullest description of the proceedings, on which the following account is based, appeared in the SR daily, *Delo naroda*, November 20–December 13, 1917.

†*DN*, No. 223 (December 3/16, 1917), 3. The Communist chronicle of the Revolution (*Revoliutsiia*, VI, 258) distorts the sense of this resolution when it claims that the SRs demanded that power be taken away from the soviets and turned over to the Constituent Assembly. The SRs, in fact, wanted the Assembly and the soviets to cooperate.

some other deputies to the Constituent Assembly on the grounds that the Assembly did not enjoy parliamentary immunity.[69]

Chernov's resolution carried, 360–321. The Bolsheviks persuaded Spiridonova to set this vote aside: on the following day she declared that it had not been a binding vote, but only the "basis" for one. Before this matter could be cleared up, Trotsky made an appearance and asked for the floor to report on the progress of the peace negotiations at Brest-Litovsk. The diversionary move was greeted with hoots, whereupon Trotsky departed, followed by the Bolshevik and Left SR delegates.

The following day, December 4, the Bolsheviks and the Left SRs returned to the Alexander Hall and renewed disruptive tactics. In the resulting bedlam no speaker could be heard, whereupon the SRs and their adherents, singing the "Marseillaise," walked out. They resumed deliberations at the Agricultural Museum on the Fontanka, the seat of the Central Executive Committee of the Congress of Peasants' Deputies. From this moment, the "right" and "left" wings of the congress met separately: attempts to reunite them failed due to the Bolshevik refusal to acknowledge the validity of the December 2 vote on the Constituent Assembly. On December 6, the Bolsheviks and Left SRs declared their sessions at the Municipal Duma to be the only legitimate spokesman for the peasant soviets, although in fact there were no representatives of peasant soviets present. They denied all authority to the Central Executive Committee of the Peasants' Congress, divested it of its technical apparatus and personnel, and stopped the per diems which the peasants' deputies were paid by the government. Finally, on December 8, the Bolshevik and Left SR rump Congress of Peasants' Deputies fused with the Bolshevik-controlled All-Russian Central Executive Committee.

Thus, the Bolsheviks took over the Peasants' Congress, first by introducing into it deputies whom they, not the peasants, had chosen, and then by declaring these deputies to be the sole legitimate representatives of the peasantry. They could not have accomplished this without the collaboration of the Left SRs. As a reward for this service, and in anticipation of further services, the Bolsheviks made major concessions to the Left SRs to bring them into the government as junior partners.

The two parties reached agreement on the night of December 9–10, immediately after liquidating jointly the Peasants' Congress.[70] Its terms have never been published and have to be reconstructed from subsequent events. The Left SRs posed several conditions: lifting the Press Decree, inclusion of other socialist parties in the government, abolition of the Cheka, prompt convocation of the Constituent Assembly. On the first demand, the Bolsheviks yielded in effect by allowing all sorts of hostile newspapers to appear, without formally repealing the Press Decree. On the second issue, Lenin proved conciliatory: he merely asked that the other socialist parties follow the example of the Left SRs and acknowledge the October Revolution. Since no party was inclined to do that, this particular concession cost him nothing. On the Cheka, the Bolsheviks stood firm: they would neither do away with it nor formally circumscribe its authority—the counterrevolution did not permit such luxury—but the Left SRs could have representatives in the Cheka Collegium to satisfy themselves there was no unnecessary terror. On the Constituent Assembly, the Bolsheviks reluctantly granted the Left SR demand. It is virtually certain that it is Left SR insistence that made the Bolsheviks give up the idea of annulling the elections and to allow it to meet, if only briefly. Trotsky recalls Lenin saying: "Of course, we must disperse the Constituent Assembly, but what is to be done about the Left SRs?"[71]

On the basis of these compromises, the Left SRs joined the Sovnarkom, where they were given five portfolios: Agriculture, Justice, Post and Telegraphs, Interior, and Local Self-Government. They were also admitted in subordinate capacities into other state institutions, including the Cheka, where the Left SR Petr Aleksandrovich Dmitrievskii (Aleksandrovich) took over as Dzerzhinskii's deputy. The Left SRs found this arrangement satisfactory: they liked the Bolsheviks and approved of their objectives, even if they thought them a bit hotheaded. The Left SR V. A. Karelin defined his party as "a regulator moderating the excessive zeal of the Bolsheviks."[72]

The disruption of the Second Peasants' Congress by the joint action of Bolsheviks and Left SRs spelled the demise of independent peasant organizations in Russia. In the middle of January 1918, the Bolshevik–Left SR Executive Committee of the self-styled Peasants' Congress convened a Third Congress of Peasants' Deputies, fully under their control. It was scheduled to meet concurrently with the Third Congress of Soviets of Workers' and Soldiers' Deputies: on this occasion, the two institutions, heretofore separate, "merged" and the Congress of Soviets of Workers' and Soldiers' Deputies added "Peasants' Deputies" to its designation. This event, according to one Bolshevik historian, "completed the process of creating a single supreme organ of Soviet authority" and "put an end to the Right SR policy of running the Peasants' Congress apart from the Congress of Workers' and Soldiers' Deputies."[73] It would be more accurate, however, to say that this shotgun marriage put an end to the peasantry's self-government and completed the process of its disenfranchisement.

To free themselves completely from democratic control, they had one more hurdle to overcome: the Constituent Assembly, which, according to one contemporary, "stuck like a bone" in their throat.[74]

By early December, the Bolsheviks had succeeded in (1) shunting aside the legitimate All-Russian Congress of Soviets and unseating its Executive Committee, (2) depriving the executive organ of the soviets of control over legislation and senior appointments, and (3) splitting the legitimate Peasants' Congress and replacing it with a handpicked body of soldiers and sailors. They could get away with such subversive acts because they involved manipulation of institutions in faraway Petrograd which the country at large could not easily either follow or understand. But the Constituent Assembly was another matter. This body, chosen by the entire nation, was to be the first truly representative gathering in Russian history. To prevent it from meeting or dispersing it would constitute the most audacious coup d'état of all, a direct challenge to the nation's will, the disenfranchisement of tens of millions. And yet, until and unless this was done, the Bolsheviks could not feel secure because their legitimacy, grounded in the resolutions of the Second Congress of Soviets, was conditional on the approval of the Assembly—approval which it was certain to deny them.

To make matters still worse, the Bolsheviks had on many occasions committed themselves to the convocation of the Assembly. Historically, the Constituent Assembly was identified with the Socialist-Revolutionary Party, which made it the centerpiece of its political program, confident that given its hold on the peasants it would enjoy in it an overwhelming majority: this the SRs intended to use to transform Russian into a republic of "toilers." Had they been politically more astute, the SRs would have pressed the Provisional Government to hold elections as soon as possible. But they procrastinated like everyone else, which handed the Bolsheviks the opportunity to pose as the Assembly's champions. From the late summer of 1917, the Bolsheviks accused the Provisional Government of deliberately delaying the elections in the hope that time would cool the people's revolutionary ardor. In launching the slogan "All Power to the Soviets," they argued that only the soviets could guarantee the Constituent Assembly. In September and October 1917 Bolshevik propaganda shouted loud and clear that the transfer of power to the soviets alone would save the Constituent Assembly.[75] As they prepared to seize power, they sometimes sounded as if their main objective was to defend the Assembly from the designs of the "bourgeoisie" and other "counterrevolutionaries." As late as October 27, *Pravda* told its readers that

> the new revolutionary authority will permit no hesitations: under conditions of social hegemony of the interests of the broad popular masses, it alone is capable of leading the country to a Constituent Assembly.[76]

There could be no question, therefore, that Lenin and his party were committed to holding elections, convening it and submitting to the Assembly's will. But since this Assembly was almost certain to sweep them from power, they had a problem on their hands. In the end, they gambled and won: and only after this triumph, on the ruins of the Constituent Assembly, could they feel confident of never again being challenged by democratic forces.

In assaulting the Constituent Assembly, they could find justification in Social-Democratic theory. The Social-Democratic program adopted in 1903 did call for the convocation of a Legislative Assembly, elected by the people on the basis of universal, equal, and direct voting; but neither the Bolsheviks nor the Mensheviks made a fetish of free elections. Long before the Revolution they were prepared to argue that the ballot box was not necessarily the best

76. Voting for the Constituent Assembly: November 1917.

indicator of the people's "true" interests. The founder of Russian Social-Democracy, Plekhanov, delivered at the Second Party Congress in 1903 some remarks on the subject, with which the Bolsheviks were later to taunt their opponents:

> Every given democratic principle must be viewed not abstractly, on its own merits, but in its relationship to that principle which may be called the basic principle of democracy: *salus populi suprema lex.* Translated into the language of a revolutionary, this means that the success of the revolution is the supreme law. And if, for the sake of the revolution, it should become necessary temporarily to restrict the action of one or another democratic principle, then it would be criminal not to do so. As a personal opinion I shall state that one must view even the principle of the universal vote from the point of view of the above-mentioned fundamental principle of democracy. Hypothetically, one can conceive of a situation where we Social Democrats would oppose the universal vote. . . . If in an outburst of revolutionary enthusiasm the people would elect a very good parliament . . . then we should try to transform it into a Long Parliament; and if the elections turned out unfavorably, then we should try to disperse it—not in two years, but, if possible, in two weeks.*

Lenin shared these sentiments and in 1918 would quote them with evident relish.[77]

The Provisional Government had scheduled the elections for November 12, 1917, which happened to be two weeks after it fell from power. The Bolsheviks hesitated at first whether to adhere to this date, but in the end decided to do so, and issued a decree to this effect.[78] But what to do next? While discussing the question among themselves, they interfered with the ability of their opponents to campaign. This was perhaps the principal intention behind

---

*Vtoroi S'ezd RSDSRP: Protokoly (Moscow, 1959), 181–82. Trotsky in 1903 said something similar: "All democratic principles must be subordinated exclusively to the interests of the party." (M. Vishniak, *Bolshevism and Democracy,* New York, 1914, 67.)

77. Electoral poster of the Constitutional-Democrats:
"Vote for the Party of National Freedom."

the Press Decree and an ordinance issued by the Military-Revolutionary Committee on November 1 placing Petrograd under a state of siege: one of its
provision forbade outdoor assemblies.[79]

In Petrograd, the voting for the Assembly began on November 12, and
went on for three days. Moscow voted on November 19–21; the rest of the
country, in the second half of November. Eligible, according to criteria set by
the Provisional Government, were male as well as female citizens twenty years
and over. Voting took place over the entire territory of what had been the
Russian Empire except for areas under enemy occupation—that is, Poland and
the provinces on Russia's western and northwestern frontiers. In Central Asia
the results were not tabulated; the same lapse occurred in a few remote regions.
Voters turned out in impressive numbers: in Petrograd and Moscow some 70
percent of those eligible went to the polls, and in some rural areas the turnout
reached 100 percent, the peasants often voting as one body for a single ticket,
usually the Socialist-Revolutionary. According to the most reliable count, 44.4
million cast ballots. Here and there, observers noted minor irregularities: the
garrison troops, who favored the Bolsheviks for their promises of a quick
peace, sometimes intimidated candidates of the other parties. But by and large,
especially if one considers the difficult conditions under which they were held,
the elections justified expectations. Lenin, who had no interest in praising
them, stated on December 1: "If one views the Constituent Assembly apart
from the conditions of the class struggle, which verges on civil war, then as
of now we know of no institution more perfect as a means of expressing the
people's will."[80]

Voting was very complicated, given that many splinter parties put up candidates, sometimes in blocs with other parties: the configuration differed from region to region, becoming especially complex in such borderland areas as the Ukraine, where, alongside Russian parties, there were parties representing the local minorities.

Of the socialists, the Bolsheviks alone campaigned without a formal platform. They apparently counted on winning votes with broad appeals to workers, soldiers, and peasants, centered on the slogans "All Power to the Soviets," and on promises of immediate peace and the confiscation of landlord properties. In electoral appeals they sought to broaden the class basis of their constituency, borrowing the SRs' un-Marxist term "the toiling masses." In evaluating the results of the elections, therefore, it must be borne in mind that many and perhaps even most of those who cast ballots for the Bolsheviks were expressing approval, not of the Bolshevik platform, of which they knew nothing because it did not even exist, let alone of the hidden Bolshevik agenda of a one-party dictatorship, never mentioned in Bolshevik pronouncements, but of the rule of soviets, an end to the war, and the abolition of private landholding in favor of communal redistribution, none of which figured among ultimate Bolshevik objectives.

Lenin, hoping against hope, for a while deluded himself that the Left SRs would tear the SR Party apart to such an extent as to give the Bolsheviks a victory.[81] The strong showing which the Left SRs made at the Petrograd City Conference in November gave some substance to this hope.[82] But in the end it proved unfounded: although the Bolsheviks made a strong showing, especially in the cities and among the military, they came in second place, trailing far behind the Socialists-Revolutionaries. This outcome sealed the fate of the Assembly.

The results of the elections cannot be precisely determined because in many localities the parties and their offshoots ran in coalitions, sometimes of a very complicated nature: in Petrograd alone, nineteen parties competed. The problem is exacerbated by the practice of the Communist authorities, who control the raw data, of lumping together under the categories "bourgeois" and "petty bourgeois" parties and groupings that ran on separate tickets. As best can be determined, the final results were (in thousands) as follows (see table on page 542).[83]

The results, although not entirely unexpected, disappointed Lenin. The peasants, whom he had hoped to attract by adopting the SR land program, not only did not vote Bolshevik: they did not even vote for the Left SRs. One of the arguments the Bolsheviks later used to challenge the validity of the elections was that the split in the SR party had occurred too late for the Left SRs to run on separate ballots. But there exist figures which demonstrate that this argument had no substance. In several electoral districts (Voronezh, Viatka, and Tobolsk) the Left SRs and the mainstream SRs did run on separate tickets. In none of them did the Left SRs win significant support: the tally showed 1,839,000 votes cast for the SR Party and a mere 26,000 for the Left

RUSSIAN SOCIALIST PARTIES: 68.9%

Socialists-Revolutionaries	17,943	(40.4%)
Bolsheviks	10,661	(24.0%)
Mensheviks	1,144	(2.6%)
Left SRs	451	(1.0%)
Others	401	(0.9%)

RUSSIAN LIBERAL AND OTHER
NON-SOCIALIST PARTIES: 7.5%

Constitutional-Democrats	2,088	(4.7%)
Others	1,261	(2.8%)

NATIONAL MINORITY PARTIES: 13.4%

Ukrainian SRs	3,433	(7.7%)
Georgian Mensheviks	662	(1.5%)
Mussavat (Azerbaijan)	616	(1.4%)
Dashnaktsutiun (Armenia)	560	(1.3%)
Alash Orda (Kazakhstan)	262	(0.6%)
Others	407	(0.9%)

UNACCOUNTED	4,543	(10.2%)

SRs.[84] The Bolsheviks gained 175 out of 715 seats in the Assembly; together with the SR deputies who identified themselves as Left, they had 30 percent of the delegates.*

The Bolsheviks were also unhappy over the strong showing of the Kadets, the opposition party they feared the most. Although the Kadets had gained less than 5 percent of the national vote, the Bolsheviks viewed them as the most formidable rival: they had the largest number of active supporters and the most newspapers; they were far better organized and financed than the SRs; and unlike the Bolsheviks' socialist rivals, they did not feel constrained by a sense of comradeship, dedication to a common social ideal, and fear of the "counterrevolution." As the only major non-socialist party still functioning in late 1917, the Kadets were likely to attract the entire right-of-center electorate, monarchists included. If one looks at the overall election results one may indeed conclude that the Kadets "had experienced not so much a walloping as a washout."[85] But this would be a superficial conclusion. The nationwide figures concealed the important political fact that the Kadets did very well in

---

*O. N. Znamenskii, *Vserossiiskoe Uchreditel'noe Sobranie* (Leningrad, 1976), 338. Much of the Left SR support came from Petrograd workers and radicalized sailors in the Baltic and Black Sea navies.

the urban centers which the Bolsheviks needed to control to offset their weakness in the countryside and viewed as the decisive battleground in the coming civil war. In Petrograd and Moscow, the Kadets ran a strong second to the Bolsheviks, winning 26.2 percent of the vote in the former and 34.2 percent in the latter. If one subtracted from the Bolshevik total in Moscow the vote of the military garrison, which was in the process of evanescing, the Kadets had 36.4 percent of the vote as against the Bolshevik 45.3 percent.[86] Furthermore, the Kadets bested the Bolsheviks in eleven out of thirty-eight provincial capitals and in many others ran a close second. They thus represented a much more formidable political force than one could conclude from the undifferentiated election returns.

These disappointments notwithstanding, the outcome held some consolation for the Bolsheviks. Lenin, who analyzed the figures with the detachment of a commander surveying the order of battle—he even referred to the various electoral blocs as "armies"[87]—could take comfort in the fact that his party did best in the center of the country: the large cities, the industrial areas, and the military garrisons.[88] The victorious SRs drew their strength from the black-earth zone and Siberia. As he was later to observe, this geographic distribution of votes foreshadowed the front lines in the civil war between the Red and White armies,[89] in which the Bolsheviks would control the heartland of Russia and their opponents the rimlands.

Another source of satisfaction for the Bolsheviks was the support of soldiers and sailors, especially units billeted in the cities. These troops had only one desire: to get home, the quicker the better, to share in the repartition of land. Since the Bolsheviks alone of all the parties promised to open immediate peace negotiations, they showed for them a strong preference. The Petrograd and Moscow garrisons cast, respectively, 71.3 and 74.3 percent of the vote for the Bolsheviks. The front-line troops in the northwest, near Petrograd, also gave them majorities. The Bolsheviks did not do as well at the more distant fronts, where their anti-war propaganda had less resonance, but even so, in the four field armies for which records are available, they won 56 percent of the vote.[90] Lenin had no illusions about the solidity of this support, which was bound to evaporate as the troops headed home. But for the time being the backing of the military was decisive: the pro-Bolshevik troops formed a power that even in small numbers could intimidate the democratic opposition. Analyzing the election results, Lenin noted with satisfaction that in the military the Bolsheviks possessed "a political striking force which assured them of an overwhelming preponderance of forces at the decisive point in the decisive moment."[91]

The Sovnarkom discussed the Constituent Assembly on November 20. Several important decisions were taken.[92] The opening of the Assembly was postponed indefinitely. The ostensible reason was the difficulty of gathering a quorum by November 28;[93] the true reason was to allow the Bolsheviks more time. Instructions went out to provincial soviets to report on all electoral "abuses"; they were to serve as a pretext for "reelections."[94] P. E. Dybenko, the Commissar of the Navy, received orders to assemble in Petrograd between 10,000 and 12,000 armed sailors.[95] And perhaps most significantly, it was decided to convene the Third Congress of Soviets on January 8: packed solidly with their supporters and Left SRs, it was to be a surrogate for the Assembly. These measures indicated Bolshevik intentions to abort the Constituent Assembly in one manner or another.

The government's announcement indefinitely postponing the opening of the Assembly evoked strong protests from the socialist parties and deputies to the Peasants' Congress. On November 22–23, a Union for the Defense of the Constituent Assembly came into being, composed of representatives of the Petrograd Soviet, trade unions, and all the socialist parties except the Bolsheviks and Left SRs.[96]

The Bolsheviks began their assault on the Assembly by harassing its Electoral Commission (*Vsevybor*). Under orders of the Sovnarkom, Stalin and Grigorii Petrovskii on November 23 ordered the commission to turn over its files: when it refused, the Cheka took its staff into custody. M. S. Uritskii, who later was to head the Petrograd Cheka, was appointed head of the Electoral Commission for the Assembly, which gave him wide discretion to determine who could attend.[97]

In response, the Union for the Defense of the Constituent Assembly decided to open the Assembly on schedule in disregard of Bolshevik orders.[98] On November 28, members of the Electoral Commission, just released from prison, began to deliberate in Taurida Palace. Uritskii appeared to inform them they could meet only in his presence, but he was ignored. Supporters of the Assembly gathered demonstratively in front of Taurida: students, workers, soldiers, and striking civil servants, carrying banners "All Power to the Constituent Assembly." One paper estimated the crowd at 200,000, but the figure seems considerably inflated: Communist sources speak of 10,000.[99] On Uritskii's orders, Latvian Riflemen, the most dependable pro-Bolshevik troops in Petrograd, surrounded Taurida but did not interfere: some told the demonstrators they had come to protect the Constituent Assembly. Inside, forty-five deputies, mostly from Petrograd and vicinity, elected a Presidium.

The next day, armed troops formed a solid ring around Taurida: the Latvian Riflemen were back, augmented by soldiers from the Lithuanian Reserve Regiment, detachments of sailors, and a machine gun company. They kept the crowds at a safe distance, allowing into the building only delegates and accredited journalists. Toward evening, sailors ordered the deputies to leave. The following day the troops barred the entrance to everybody. These events were a rehearsal for the real trial of strength on January 5/18.

Pressing their offensive, the Bolsheviks outlawed the Constitutional-Democratic Party. Already on the opening day of the elections in Petrograd, they had dispatched armed thugs to smash the editorial offices of the Kadet *Rech'*; it resumed publication as *Nash vek* two weeks later. On November 28, Lenin wrote an ordinance under the typically propagandistic title "Decree concerning the arrest of the leaders of the civil war against the Revolution."[100]

The Kadet leaders were declared "enemies of the people" and were ordered taken into custody. That night and the following day, Bolshevik detachments seized every prominent Kadet they could lay their hands on, among them several delegates to the Assembly (A. I. Shingarev, P. D. Dolgorukov, F. F. Kokoshkin, S. V. Panina, A. I. Rodichev, and others). All of them were subsequently released (Panina after a brief and rather comical trial) except for Shingarev and Kokoshkin, whom Bolshevik sailors murdered in the prison hospital. As "enemies of the people" the Kadets could not participate in the Constituent Assembly. They were the first political party outlawed by the Bolshevik Government. Neither the Mensheviks nor the Socialists-Revolutionaries seemed very upset by this action.

Harassment and intimidation did not solve for the Bolsheviks the nagging problem of what to do about the Assembly. Some wanted to resort to force: one week before the elections, V. Volodarskii, a member of the Central Committee, said that "the masses never suffer from parliamentary cretinism," least of all in Russia, and hinted that the Constituent Assembly might have to be dispersed.[101] Nikolai Bukharin thought he had a better idea. On November 29 he proposed to the Central Committee that the Kadets be ejected from the Assembly and then the Bolshevik and Left SR deputies proclaim themselves a Revolutionary Convention: a reference to the French Convention of 1792, which took the place of the Legislative Assembly. "If the others open [a rival body] we shall arrest them," he explained. Stalin made short shrift of this proposal on grounds of impracticability.[102]

Lenin had another solution: placate the Left SRs by letting the Assembly convene, then manipulate its membership so as to obtain a more compliant body. This would be done by resorting to "recall," "a basic, essential condition of genuine democracy."[103] By this device, voters in districts which had chosen undesirable delegates would be persuaded to have them recalled and replaced with Bolsheviks and Left SRs. But this was at best a slow procedure, and while it was being put into effect, the Assembly could pass all manner of hostile resolutions.

Lenin finally made up his mind on this matter on December 12, immediately after reaching an accord with the Left SRs: his decision was made public the next day in *Pravda* under the title "Theses on the Constituent Assembly."[104] It was a death sentence on the Assembly. The thrust of Lenin's argument was that changes in party alignments, notably the split in the SR Party, the shift in class structures, and the outbreak of the "counterrevolution," all of which had allegedly occurred since October 25–26, had rendered the elections invalid as an indicator of the popular will:

The march of events and the development of class war in the Revolution has produced a situation in which the slogan "All Power to the Constituent Assembly" . . . has, in effect, turned into a slogan of the Kadets, the followers of Kaledin, and their accomplices. It is becoming clear to the whole people that this slogan, in fact, means the struggle for the elimination of soviet authority and that the Constituent Assembly, if separated from soviet authority, would inevitably be condemned to political death. . . . Any attempt, direct or indirect, to view the question of the Constituent Assembly from a formal juridical point of view . . . signifies betrayal of the cause of the proletariat and a transition to the point of view of the bourgeoisie.

Nothing in this argument made sense. The elections to the Assembly had taken place, not before October 26, but in the second half of November—that is, only seventeen days earlier: in the interim nothing had happened to invalidate Lenin's verdict of December 1 that they were the "perfect" reflection of the people's will. The principal champions of the Assembly were not the Kadets and certainly not the followers of the Cossack general Aleksei Kaledin, the latter of whom wanted to topple the Bolshevik regime by force of arms, but the Socialists-Revolutionaries. By turning out in large numbers at the polling stations, the "whole people," on whose behalf Lenin claimed to speak, had shown, not that they regarded the Assembly as anti-Soviet, but looked to it with hope and expectation. And as for the claim that the Assembly was antithetical to the rule of the soviets, only people with very short memories could have forgotten that a mere seven weeks earlier, as they were reaching for power, the same Bolsheviks had insisted that soviet rule alone would guarantee the convocation of the Assembly. But here, as always, Lenin's arguments were not meant to persuade: the key phrase occurred toward the end of the article, that further support for the Assembly was tantamount to treason.

Lenin went on to say that the Assembly could meet only if the deputies were subject to "recall"—that is, if it consented to its composition being arbitrarily altered by the government—and if it further acknowledged, without qualifications, "Soviet authority"—that is, the Bolshevik dictatorship:

Outside these conditions, the crisis connected with the Constituent Assembly can be solved only in a revolutionary manner by means of the most energetic, rapid, firm, and decisive measures on the part of Soviet authority. . . . Any attempt to tie the hands of Soviet authority in this struggle would signify complicity with the counterrevolution.

On these terms, the Bolsheviks agreed to have the Assembly meet on January 5/18, 1918, provided that at least 400 deputies turned up. At the same time they issued instructions for the convocation three days later (January 8/21) of the Third Congress of Soviets.

The Bolsheviks now launched a noisy propaganda campaign, the theme of which Zinoviev stated in a speech to the CEC on December 22: "We know very well that behind the pretext of the convocation of the Constituent Assembly, under the celebrated slogan 'All Power to the Constituent Assembly,' lies concealed the cherished slogan 'Down with the Soviets.' "[105] This proposition the Bolsheviks made official by having it adopted by the CEC on January 3, 1918.[106]

The protagonists of the Assembly rallied their forces. They had been put on notice. But in seeking to counter Bolshevik threats, they suffered under a grievous, indeed fatal handicap. In their eyes, the Bolsheviks had subverted democracy and forfeited the right to govern: but their removal had to be accomplished by the pressure of popular opinion, never by force, because the only beneficiary of an internecine conflict among the socialist parties would be the "counterrevolution." By December, Petrograd knew that on the Don the generals were assembling troops: their purpose could be nothing else but subverting the Revolution and arresting and perhaps lynching all socialists. This was to them a far worse alternative than the Bolsheviks, who were genuine, if misguided, revolutionaries: admittedly too impetuous, too lustful for power, too brutal, but still "comrades" in the same endeavor. Nor could one ignore their mass following. The democratic left was convinced then and in the years that followed that the Bolsheviks would sooner or later come to realize they could not govern Russia alone. Once this happened and the socialists were invited to share power, Russia would resume her progress toward democracy. This political maturation would take time, but it was bound to occur. For this reason, resistance to the Bolsheviks had to be confined to peaceful propaganda and agitation. The possibility that the Bolsheviks were perhaps the real counterrevolutionaries occurred only to a few left-wing intellectuals, mainly from the older generation. Socialist-Revolutionary and Menshevik leaders never ceased to view the Bolsheviks as deviant comrades in arms: they confidently awaited the time when they would come around. In the meantime, whenever the Bolsheviks came under the assault of outside forces, they could be depended on to rally to their side.

The Union for the Defense of the Constituent Assembly now initiated its own propaganda campaign. It printed and distributed hundreds of thousands of newspapers and pamphlets[107] to explain why the Assembly was not anti-Soviet and why it alone had the right to give the country a constitution. It staged demonstrations in the capital and the provincial cities calling for "All Power to the Constituent Assembly." It sent agitators to barracks and factories to obtain the signatures of soldiers and workers, including those who had voted for the Bolsheviks, on appeals calling for upholding the Assembly. The SRs and Mensheviks who organized these activities along with trade unions and striking civil servants evidently hoped that evidence of massive support would inhibit the Bolsheviks from using force against the Assembly.

A few socialists thought this was not enough: they came from the SR underground, and felt that only the methods used against tsarism—terror and street violence—would restore democracy. Their leader was Fedor Mikhailovich Onipko, an SR delegate from Stavropol and a member of the Military Commission of the Union for the Defense of the Constituent Assembly. Assisted by experienced conspirators, Onipko penetrated Smolnyi, planting there

78. F. M. Onipko.

four operatives in the guise of officials and chauffeurs. Tracking Lenin's movements and discovering that he slipped out of Smolnyi frequently to visit his sister, they placed in her house an agent posing as a janitor. Onipko wanted to kill Lenin and then Trotsky. The action was planned for Christmas day. But the SR Central Committee, which he asked for approval, absolutely refused to condone such action: if the SRs murdered Lenin and Trotsky, he was told they would be lynched by workers and only the enemies of the Revolution would benefit. Onipko was ordered to dissolve his terrorist group immediately.[108] He obeyed, but some conspirators (among them Nekrasov, Kerensky's closest associate) not connected with the SR Party carried out a clumsy attempt on Lenin's life on January 1. They inflicted a slight wound on the Swiss radical Fritz Platten, who was riding with Lenin.[109] After this incident, whenever he ventured out of Smolnyi, Lenin carried a revolver.

Onipko next sought to organize armed resistance against the anticipated Bolshevik assault on the Constituent Assembly. His plan, worked out with the Union for the Defense of the Constituent Assembly, called for a massive armed demonstration in front of Taurida on January 5 to intimidate pro-Bolshevik troops and ensure that the Assembly would not be dispersed. He managed to secure impressive backing. At the Preobrazhenskii, Semenovskii, and Izmailovskii Guard Regiments some 10,000 men volunteered to march, arms in hand, and fight if fired upon. Possibly as many as 2,000 workers, mainly from the Obukhov plant and the State Printing Office, agreed to join.

Before setting its plans in motion, the Military Commission went back to the Central Committee of the SR Party for authorization. The Central Committee again refused. It justified its negative stand with vague explanations, all, in the ultimate analysis, grounded in fear. No one had defended the Provisional Government, it argued. Bolshevism was a disease of the masses which required time to overcome. This was no time for risky "adventures."[110]

The Central Committee reconfirmed its intention to hold on January 5 a peaceful demonstration: the troops would be welcome but they had to come without arms. The committee counted on the Bolsheviks not daring to open fire on the demonstrators out of fear of provoking another Bloody Sunday. When, however, Onipko and his aides returned to the barracks with the news and asked the soldiers to come unarmed, they met with derision:

"Are you making fun of us, comrades?" they responded in disbelief. "You are asking us to a demonstration but tell us to come without weapons. And the Bolsheviks? Are they little children? They will for sure fire at unarmed people. And we: are we supposed to open our mouths and give them our heads for targets, or will you order us to run, like rabbits?"[111]

The soldiers refused to confront Bolshevik rifles and machine guns with bare hands and decided to sit out January 5 in their barracks.

The Bolsheviks, who got wind of these activities, took no chances and prepared for the decisive day as they would for battle. Lenin took personal command.

The first task was to win over or at least neutralize the military garrison. Bolshevik agitators sent to the barracks did not dare attack directly the Constituent Assembly because of its popularity; instead they argued that "counterrevolutionaries" were trying to exploit the Assembly to liquidate the soviets. With this argument they persuaded the Finnish Infantry Regiment to pass a resolution rejecting the slogan "All Power to the Constituent Assembly" and agreeing to support the Assembly only if it cooperated closely with the soviets. The Volhynian and Lithuanian regiments passed similar resolutions.[112] This was the extent of Bolshevik success. It appears that no military unit of any size would condemn the Constituent Assembly as "counterrevolutionary." The Bolsheviks, therefore, had to rely on hastily organized units of Red Guards and sailors. But Lenin did not trust Russians and gave instructions for the Latvians to be brought in: "the *muzhik* may waver if anything happens," he said.[113] This marked still greater involvement of the Latvian Riflemen in the Revolution on the side of the Bolsheviks.

On January 4, Lenin appointed N. I. Podvoiskii, the ex-chairman of the Bolshevik Military Organization, which had carried out the October coup in Petrograd, to constitute an Extraordinary Military Staff.[114] Podvoiskii once again placed Petrograd under martial law and forbade public assemblies. Proclamations to this effect were posted throughout the city. Uritskii announced in *Pravda* on January 5 that gatherings in the vicinity of Taurida Palace would be dispersed by force if necessary.

The Bolsheviks also sent agitators to the industrial establishments. Here they ran into hostility and incomprehension. In the largest factories—Putilov, Obukhov, Baltic, the Nevskii shipyard, and Lessner—workers had signed petitions of the Union for the Defense of the Constituent Assembly and could not understand why the Bolsheviks, with which many of them sympathized, had now turned against the Assembly.*

---

*E. Ignatov, in *PR*, No. 5/76 (1928), 37. The author claims that these worker signatures were forged but furnishes no proof.

As the decisive day approached, the Bolshevik press kept up a steady drumbeat of warnings and threats. On January 3, it informed the population that on January 5 workers were expected to stay in their factories and soldiers in their barracks. The same day Uritskii announced that Petrograd was in danger of a counterrevolutionary coup organized by Kerensky and Savinkov, who had secretly returned to Petrograd for that purpose.*[115] *Pravda* carried a headline: TODAY THE HYENAS OF CAPITAL AND THEIR HIRELINGS WANT TO SEIZE POWER FROM SOVIET HANDS.

On Friday, January 5, Petrograd, and especially the area adjoining Taurida Palace, resembled an armed encampment. The SR Mark Vishniak, who walked to Taurida in a procession of deputies, describes the sight that greeted his eyes:

> We began to move at noon, a spread-out column of some two hundred people, walking in the middle of the street. The deputies were accompanied by a few journalists, friends, and wives, who had obtained entry tickets to Taurida Palace. The distance to the palace did not exceed one kilometer: the closer one approached, the fewer pedestrians were to be seen and the more soldiers, Red Army men and sailors. They were armed to the teeth: guns slung over the shoulder, bombs, grenades, and bullets, in front and on the side, everywhere, wherever they could be attached or inserted. Individual passersby on the sidewalk, upon encountering the unusual procession, rarely greeted it with shouts: more often they followed it sympathetically with their eyes and then hurried on. The armed men approached, wanting to know who goes and where, and then returned to their stations and bivouacs. . . .
>
> The entire square in front of Taurida Palace was filled with artillery, machine guns, field kitchens. Machine gun cartridge belts were piled up pell-mell. All the gates to the palace were shut, except for a wicket gate on the extreme left, through which people with passes were let in. The armed guards attentively studied one's face before permitting entry: they inspected one's rear, felt the backside. . . . After going through the left door more controls. . . . The guards directed the delegates across the vestibule and Catherine's Hall into the Assembly Hall. Everywhere there were armed men, mostly sailors and Latvians. They were armed, as those on the street, with guns, grenades, munition bags, and revolvers. The number of armed men and weapons, the sound of clanking, created the impression of an encampment getting ready either to defend itself or to attack.[116]

The Bolshevik delegation, headed by Lenin, arrived at Taurida at 1 p.m. Lenin wanted to be on hand to make quick decisions as the situation unfolded. Sitting in what during the Duma period had been the "government loge," he directed Bolshevik actions for the next nine hours. Bonch-Bruevich remem-

*Kerensky was, in fact, in Petrograd at this time, but there is no evidence that he tried to organize anti-Bolshevik forces.

bered him "excited and pale like a corpse. . . . In this extreme white paleness of his face and neck, his head appeared even larger, his eyes were distended and aflame, burning with a steady fire."[117] It was, indeed, a decisive moment in which the fate of the Bolshevik dictatorship hung in the balance.

The Assembly was to open at midday, but Lenin, through Uritskii, refused to allow it to begin proceedings until he knew what happened outside, on the streets of Petrograd, where, in defiance of Bolshevik orders, a massive demonstration had been gathering all morning. Although its organizers stressed in their appeals that they intended it to be "peaceful" and confrontations were to be avoided,[118] Lenin had no assurance that his forces would not fold at the first sign of mass resistance. He must have had a contingency plan in mind in the event the demonstrators overwhelmed his forces: the SR Sokolov believes that if that happened, Lenin intended to come to terms with the Assembly.[119]

The Union instructed the demonstrators to gather by 10 a.m. at nine points in various parts of the city and from there proceed to the central gathering place, the Champs de Mars. At noon, they were to move in a body, under banners calling for "All Power to the Constituent Assembly," along Panteleimon Street to Liteinyi Prospect, immediately turn right onto Kirochnaia Street, left on Potemkin Street, and right on Shpalernaia, which ran in front of Taurida Palace. After passing the palace, they were to turn right onto Taurida Street and proceed to Nevsky, where they were to disperse.

The crowd which gathered that morning throughout Petrograd was impressive (some counted as many as 50,000 participants), but neither as large nor as enthusiastic as the organizers had hoped: the troops stayed in the barracks, fewer workers than expected turned up, with the result that the participants were mainly students, civil servants, and other intellectuals, all somewhat dispirited. Bolshevik threats and displays of force had made an impression.[120]

Podvoiskii knew the route the procession was to take, since the organizers had widely advertised it, and deployed his men to bar its way. The forward detachment of his troops, with loaded guns and machine guns, deployed on the streets and rooftops at the point where Panteleimon Street run into Liteinyi. As the head of the procession approached this crossing, shouts went up—"Hurrah for the Constituent Assembly!"—whereupon the troops opened fire. Some demonstrators fell, others ran for cover. But they soon re-formed and continued on their way. Because more troops barred access to Kirochnaia Street, the demonstration proceeded along Liteinyi, running into volleys of gunfire as it was about to turn into Shpalernaia. Here it broke up in disorder. Bolshevik soldiers pursued the demonstrators and seized their banners, tearing them to shreds or tossing them on bonfires. A different procession in another part of the city, composed mostly of workers, also met with gunfire. The same fate befell several smaller demonstrations.[121]

Russian troops had not fired on unarmed demonstrators since the fateful day in February 1917 when they dispersed crowds defying prohibitions against public gatherings: violence then had sparked mutinies and riots that marked the onset of the Revolution. And before that was Bloody Sunday and 1905. Given these experiences, it was not unreasonable for the organizers of the demonstrations to assume that this massacre, too, would ignite nationwide protests. The victims—according to some accounts eight, according to others twenty-one[122]—received a solemn funeral on January 9, the anniversary of Bloody Sunday, and were buried at the Preobrazhenskii Cemetery, close by the casualties of that time. Worker delegations carried wreaths, one of which was inscribed: "To the victims of the arbitrariness of Smolnyi autocrats."[123] Gorky wrote an angry editorial in which he compared the violence to Bloody Sunday.*

As soon as news reached him that the demonstrators had been dispersed and the streets were under Bolshevik control—this happened around 4 p.m.— Lenin ordered the meeting to begin. On hand were 463 deputies, slightly more than one-half of those elected, among them 259 SRs, 136 Bolsheviks, and 40 Left SRs.† From the opening bell, the Bolshevik deputies and armed guards jeered and booed non-Bolshevik speakers. Many of the armed men who filled the corridors and the balcony did not have to force themselves to behave raucously, for they had helped themselves to the vodka generously dispensed at the buffet. The minutes of the Assembly open with the following scene:

A member of the Constituent Assembly, belonging to the SR faction, exclaims from his seat: "Comrades, it is now 4 p.m., we suggest that the oldest member open the meeting of the Constituent Assembly." (Loud noise on the left, applause in the center and on the right, whistles on the left. . . . Inaudible. . . . Loud noise and whistles continue on the left and applause on the right.) The oldest member of the Constituent Assembly, Mikhailov, ascends [the podium].
    Mikhailov rings. (Noise on the left. Voice: "Down with the usurper!" Continuing noise and whistles on the left, applause on the right.)
    Mikhailov: "I declare an intermission."[124]

The Bolsheviks pursued a simple strategy. They would confront the Assembly with a resolution that would, in effect, delegitimize it: in the almost certain event that it failed, they would walk out, and without formally disbanding it, make further work by the Assembly impossible. Following this plan, F. F. Raskolnikov, the Bolshevik ensign from Kronshtadt, moved a motion. Although called "Declaration of the Rights of the Toiling and Exploited Masses," unlike its 1789 prototype, it had more to say about duties than rights: it was here that the Bolsheviks introduced the universal labor obligation.

*NZh, No. 6/220 (January 9/22, 1918), 1. Afraid of a backlash, the Bolsheviks ordered an inquiry into the shooting. It revealed that troops from the Lithuanian Regiment had fired on the demonstrators in the belief that in so doing they were defending the Assembly from "saboteurs" (NZh, No. 15/229, February 3, 1918, 11). The Commission of Inquiry discontinued its work at the end of January without issuing a report.
    †Znamenskii, Uchreditel'noe Sobranie, 339. The exact number of the deputies present is not known: it could have been as low as 410: Ibid.

Russia was proclaimed a "republic of soviets" and a number of measures which the Bolsheviks had previously passed were reconfirmed, among them the Land Decree, worker control over production, and the nationalization of banks. The critical article asked the Assembly to renounce its authority to legislate—the very authority for the sake of which it had been elected. "The Constituent Assembly concedes," it read, "that its tasks are confined to working out in general the fundamental bases of reorganizing society on a socialist basis." The Assembly was to ratify all the decrees previously issued by the Sovnarkom and then adjourn.[125]

Raskolnikov's motion lost 237–136: the vote indicates that all the Bolshevik delegates, but only they, voted in favor; the Left SRs apparently abstained. At this point, the Bolshevik delegation declared the Assembly to be controlled by "counterrevolutionaries" and walked out. The Left SRs kept their seats for the time being.

Lenin stayed in his loge until 10 p.m., when he, too, departed: he had not addressed the Assembly, so as not to give it any semblance of legitimacy. The Bolshevik Central Committee now met in another part of the palace and adopted a resolution dissolving the Assembly. Out of deference to the Left SRs, however, Lenin instructed the Taurida Guard not to use violence: any deputy who wished to leave the building was to be let go, but no one was to be allowed back in.[126] At 2 a.m., satisfied that the situation was under control, he returned to Smolnyi.

After the Bolsheviks had departed, Taurida resounded with interminable speeches, frequently disrupted by the guards who had descended from the balcony and filled the seats vacated by the Bolsheviks: many of them were drunk. Some soldiers amused themselves by aiming guns at the speakers. At 2:30 a.m. the Left SRs walked out, at which point commissar P. E. Dybenko, who was in charge of security, ordered the commander of the guard, a sailor, the anarchist A. G. Zhelezniakov, to close the meeting. Shortly after 4 a.m., as the chairman, Victor Chernov, was proclaiming the abolition of property in land, Zhelezniakov mounted the tribune and touched him on the back.* The following scene ensued, as recorded in the minutes:

> Citizen Sailor: "I have been instructed to inform you that all those present should leave the Assembly Hall because the guard is tired."
> Chairman: "What instruction? From whom?"
> Citizen Sailor: "I am the commander of the Taurida Guard. I have an instruction from the commissar."
> Chairman: "The members of the Constituent Assembly are also tired, but no fatigue can disrupt our proclaiming a law awaited by all of Russia."
> (Loud noise. Voices: "Enough, enough!")
> Chairman: "The Constituent Assembly can disperse only under the threat of force."

*Zhelezniakov was a leader of the anarchists who had occupied Peter Durnovo's villa the previous year and whose arrest caused the Kronshtadt sailors in June 1917 to revolt: *Revoliutsiia,* III, 108.

79. Victor Chernov.

(Noise.)
Chairman: "You declare it."
(Voices: "Down with Chernov!")
   Citizen Sailor: "I request that the Assembly Hall be immediately
vacated."*

While this exchange was taking place more Bolshevik troops crowded
into the Assembly Hall, looking very menacing. Chernov managed to keep the
meeting going for another twenty minutes, and then adjourned it until 5 p.m.
that day (January 6). But the Assembly was not to reconvene, for in the
morning Sverdlov had the CEC ratify the Bolshevik resolution dissolving it.[127]
Pravda on that day appeared with banner headlines:

THE HIRELINGS OF BANKERS, CAPITALISTS, AND LANDLORDS, THE ALLIES OF
KALEDIN, DUTOV, THE SLAVES OF THE AMERICAN DOLLAR, THE BACKSTAB-
BERS—THE RIGHT SR'S—DEMAND IN THE CONSTITUENT ASSEMBLY ALL
POWER FOR THEMSELVES AND THEIR MASTERS—ENEMIES OF THE PEOPLE.

THEY PAY LIP SERVICE TO POPULAR DEMANDS FOR LAND, PEACE, AND
[WORKER] CONTROL, BUT IN REALITY THEY TRY TO FASTEN A NOOSE
AROUND THE NECK OF SOCIALIST AUTHORITY AND REVOLUTION.

   *I. S. Malchevskii, ed., *Vserossiiskoe Uchreditel'noe Sobranie* (Moscow-Leningrad, 1930), 110.
Zhelezniakov was killed the following year, fighting in the Red Army.

BUT THE WORKERS, PEASANTS, AND SOLDIERS WILL NOT FALL FOR THE BAIT
OF LIES OF THE MOST EVIL ENEMIES OF SOCIALISM. IN THE NAME OF THE
SOCIALIST REVOLUTION AND THE SOCIALIST SOVIET REPUBLIC THEY WILL
SWEEP AWAY ITS OPEN AND HIDDEN KILLERS.[128]

The Bolsheviks had previously linked Russian democratic forces with "capitalists," "landlords," and "counterrevolutionaries," but in this headline they for the first time connected them also with foreign capital.

Two days later (January 8) the Bolsheviks opened their counter-Assembly, labeled "Third Congress of Soviets." Here no one could obstruct them because they had reserved for themselves and the Left SRs 94 percent of the seats,[129] more than three times what they were entitled to, judging by the results of the elections to the Constituent Assembly. The little left over they allocated to the opposition socialists—just enough to have a target for abuse and ridicule. The congress duly passed all the measures submitted to it by government spokesmen, including the "Declaration of Rights." Russia became a "Federation of Soviet Republics," to be known as the "Russian Soviet Socialist Republic," which name she retained until 1924, when she was renamed "Union of Soviet Socialist Republics." The congress acknowledged the Sovnarkom as the country's legitimate government, removing from its name the adjective "provisional." It also approved the principle of universal labor obligation.

The dissolution of the Assembly met with surprising indifference: there was none of the fury which in 1789 had greeted rumors that Louis XVI intended to dissolve the National Assembly, precipitating the assault on the Bastille. After a year of anarchy, Russians were exhausted: they yearned for peace and order, no matter how purchased. The Bolsheviks had gambled on that mood and won. After January 5, no one could any longer believe that Lenin's men could be talked into abandoning power. And since there was no effective armed opposition to them in the central regions of Russia, and what there was the socialist intelligentsia refused to use, common sense dictated that the Bolshevik dictatorship was here to stay.

An immediate result was the collapse of the strike of white-collar personnel in the ministries and private enterprises, who drifted back to work after January 5, some driven by personal need, others in the belief that they would be better able to influence events from the inside. The psychology of the opposition now suffered a fatal break: it is as if brutality and the disregard of the nation's will legitimized the Bolshevik dictatorship. The country at large felt that after a year of chaos, it at last had a "real" government. This certainly held true of the peasant and worker masses but, paradoxically, also of the well-to-do and conservative elements, *Pravda*'s "hyenas of capital" and "enemies of the people," who despised the socialist intelligentsia and street mobs even more than they did the Bolsheviks.* In a sense the Bolsheviks may be said to have become the government of Russia not so much in October 1917 as in January 1918. In the words of one contemporary, "authentic, genuine Bolshevism, the Bolshevism of the broad masses, came only after January 5."[130]

Indeed, the dispersal of the Constituent Assembly was in many respects more important for the future of Russia than the October coup which had been carried out behind the smoke screen of "All Power to the Soviets." If the purpose of October remained concealed from nearly everyone, including rank-and-file Bolsheviks, there could be no doubt about Bolshevik intentions after January 5, when they had made it unmistakably clear they intended to pay no heed to popular opinion. They did not have to listen to the voice of the people because, in the literal sense of the word, they were the "people."* In the words of Lenin, "The dispersal of the Constituent Assembly by Soviet authority [was] the complete and open liquidation of formal democracy in the name of the revolutionary dictatorship."[131]

The response to this historic event on the part of the population at large and the intelligentsia augured ill for the country's future. Russia, events confirmed once again, lacked a sense of national cohesion capable of inspiring the population to give up immediate and personal interests for the sake of the common good. The "popular masses" demonstrated that they understood only private and regional interests, the heady joys of the *duvan,* which were satisfied, for the time being, by the soviets and factory committees. In accord with the Russian proverb "He who grabs the stick is corporal," they conceded power to the boldest and most ruthless claimant.

The evidence indicates that the industrial workers of Petrograd, even as they voted for the Bolshevik ticket, had expected the Assembly to meet and give shape to the country's new political and social system. This is confirmed by their signatures on the various petitions of the Union for the Defense of the Constituent Assembly, *Pravda*'s complaints about workers' support for it,[132] and the frenetic appeals combined with threats which the Bolsheviks directed at the workers on the eve of the Assembly's convocation. And yet, when confronted with the unflinching determination of the regime to liquidate the Assembly, backed with guns that did not hesitate to fire, the workers folded.

---

*In May 1918, Vladimir Purishkevich, one of the most reactionary pre-revolutionary politicians, published an open letter in which he said that after having spent half a year in Soviet prison he remained a monarchist and would offer no apologies for the Soviet Government which was transforming Russia into a German colony. However, he went on, "Soviet authority is firm authority—alas, not from that direction which I would prefer to have firm authority in Russia, whose pitiful and cowardly intelligentsia is one of the main culprits of our humiliation and of the inability of Russian society to produce a healthy, firm authority of governmental scope": letter dated May 1, 1918, in *VO,* No. 36 (May 3, 1918), 4.

*This attitude was pointed out by Martov in the spring of 1918 when Stalin accused him of slander and brought suit before a Revolutionary Tribunal. Noting that these tribunals had been set up to try exclusively "crimes against the people," Martov asked: "Can an insult to Stalin be considered a crime against the people?" And he answered: "Only if one considers Stalin to be the people": "Narod eto ia," *Vpered,* April 1/14, 1918, 1.

Was it because they were betrayed by the intelligentsia, which urged them not to resist? If that was the case, then the role of intellectuals in the revolution against tsarism stands out in bold relief: without their prodding, it seems, Russian workers would not stand up to the government.

As for the peasants, they could not care less what went on in the big city. SR agitators told them to vote, so they voted; and if some other group of "white hands" took over, what difference did it make? Their concerns did not extend beyond the boundaries of their *volosti.*

That left the socialist intelligentsia, which, having gained a solid electoral victory, could act in confidence that the country was behind it. It was doomed by the refusal under any circumstances to resort to force against the Bolsheviks. Trotsky later taunted socialist intellectuals that they had come to Taurida Palace with candles, in case the Bolsheviks cut off power, and with sandwiches, in case they were deprived of food.[133] But they would not carry guns. On the eve of the convocation of the Assembly, the SR Pitirim Sorokin (later professor of sociology at Harvard), discussing the possibility of its being dispersed by force, predicted: "If the opening session is met with 'machine guns,' we will issue an appeal to the country informing it of this, and place ourselves under the protection of the people."[134] But they lacked the courage even for such a gesture. When, following the dissolution of the Assembly, soldiers approached socialist deputies with the offer to restore it by force of arms, the horrified intellectuals begged them to do nothing of the kind: Tsereteli said that it would be better for the Constituent Assembly to die a quiet death than to provoke a civil war.[135] Such people no one could risk following: they talked endlessly of revolution and democracy, but would not defend their ideals with anything other than words and gestures. This contradictory behavior, this inertia disguised as submission to the forces of history, this unwillingness to fight and win, is not easy to explain. Perhaps its rationale has to be sought in the realm of psychology—namely, the traditional attitude of the old Russian intelligentsia so well depicted by Chekhov, with its dread of success and belief that inefficiency was "the cardinal virtue and defeat the only halo."[136]

The capitulation of the socialist intelligentsia on January 5 was the beginning of its demise. "The inability to defend the Constituent Assembly marked the most profound crisis of Russian democracy," observed a man who had tried and failed to organize armed resistance. "It was the turning point. After January 5 there was no place in history, in Russian history, for what had been the idealistically dedicated Russian intelligentsia. It was relegated to the past."[137]

Unlike their opponents, the Bolsheviks learned a great deal from these events. They understood that in areas under their control they need fear no organized armed resistance: their rivals, though supported by at least three-fourths of the population, were disunited, leaderless, and, above all, unwilling to fight. This experience accustomed the Bolsheviks to resort to violence as a matter of course whenever they ran into resistance, to "solve" their problems by physically annihilating those who caused them. The machine gun became for them the principal instrument of political persuasion. The unrestrained brutality with which they henceforth ruled Russia stemmed in large measure from the knowledge, gained on January 5, that they could use it with impunity.

And they had to resort to brutality more and more often, for only a few months after they had assumed power their base of support began to erode: had they relied on popular backing, they would have gone the way of the Provisional Government. The industrial workers, who in the fall, along with the garrison troops, had been their strongest supporters, grew disenchanted very quickly. The change of mood had diverse causes, but the principal one was the worsening food situation. The government, having forbidden all private trade in cereals and bread, paid the peasant such absurdly low prices that he either hoarded the grain or disposed of it on the black market. The government did not obtain enough foodstuffs to supply the urban population with anything but the barest minimum: in the winter of 1917–18, the bread ration in Petrograd fluctuated between four and six ounces a day. On the black market, a pound of bread fetched from three to five rubles, which placed it out of the reach of ordinary people. There was massive industrial unemployment as well, caused mainly by fuel shortages: in May 1918 only 12–13 percent of the Petrograd labor force still held jobs.[138]

To escape starvation and cold, thousands of city inhabitants fled to the countryside, where they had relatives and the food and fuel situation was better. Due to this exodus, by April 1918 the labor force in Petrograd declined to 57 percent of what it had been on the eve of the February Revolution.[139] Those who stayed behind, hungry, cold, often idle, seethed with discontent. They resented Bolshevik economic policies which had produced this state of affairs, but they also objected to the dissolution of the Constituent Assembly, the humiliating peace treaty with the Central Powers (signed in March 1918), the high-handed behavior of Bolshevik commissars, and the scandalous corruption of officials on all but the highest levels of government.

This development had dangerous implications for the Bolsheviks, the more so in that the armed forces on which they had previously relied were all but gone as spring approached. The soldiers who did not return home formed marauding bands that terrorized the population and sometimes assaulted soviet officials.

The growing mood of disenchantment and the feeling that they could not obtain redress from existing institutions, firmly in Bolshevik hands, prompted the Petrograd workers to create new institutions, independent of the Bolsheviks and the bodies (soviets, trade unions, Factory Committees) which they controlled. On January 5/18, 1918—the day the Constituent Assembly opened—representatives or "plenipotentiaries" of Petrograd factories met to discuss the current situation. Some speakers referred to a "break" in worker attitudes.[140] In February, these plenipotentiaries began to hold regular meetings. Incomplete evidence indicates one such meeting in March, four in April, three in May, and three in June. The March meeting of delegates representing fifty-six factories, for which records exist,[141] heard strong anti-Bolshevik language. It protested that the government, while claiming to rule on behalf of workers and peasants, exercised autocratic authority and refused to hold new elections to the soviets. It called for a rejection of the Brest-Litovsk Treaty, the dissolution of the Sovnarkom, and the immediate convocation of the Constituent Assembly.

On March 31 the Bolsheviks had the Cheka search the headquarters of the Council of Workers' Plenipotentiaries and impound the literature found there. Otherwise they did not interfere as yet, probably from fear of provoking worker unrest.

Aware that the urban workers were turning against them, the Bolsheviks delayed holding soviet elections. When some independent soviets did so anyway, producing non-Bolshevik majorities, they disbanded them by force. The inability to use the soviets compounded the workers' frustration. In early May, many concluded that they had to take matters into their own hands.

On May 8, massive worker assemblies were held at the Putilov and Obukhov plants to discuss the two most burning issues: food and politics. At Putilov, over 10,000 workers heard denunciations of the government. Bolshevik speakers were given a hostile reception and their resolutions went down in defeat. The meeting demanded the "immediate unification of all socialist and democratic forces," the lifting of restrictions on free trade in bread, fresh elections to the Constituent Assembly, and reelections to the Petrograd Soviet by secret ballot.[142] Obukhov workers passed, with a virtually unanimous vote, a similar resolution.[143]

The next day an event occurred at Kolpino, an industrial town south of Petrograd, which added fuel to growing worker discontent. Kolpino had been especially badly served by government supply agencies: and with only 300 of the city's work force of 10,000 employed, few had money to buy food on the black market. A further delay in food deliveries provoked the women to call a city-wide protest. The Bolshevik commissar lost his head and ordered troops to fire on the demonstrators. In the ensuing panic the impression spread that there were numerous dead, although, as transpired later, there was only one fatality and six injured.[144] By standards of the time, nothing extraordinary: but Petrograd workers needed little cause to give vent to pent-up anger.

Having heard from emissaries sent by Kolpino what had happened there, the major Petrograd factories suspended work. The Obukhov workers passed a resolution condemning the government and demanding an end to the "rule of commissars" *(komissaroderzhavie)*. Zinoviev, the boss of Petrograd (the government having in March moved to Moscow), put in an appearance at Putilov. "I have heard," he told the workers, "of alleged resolutions having been adopted here charging the Soviet Government with pursuing incorrect policies. But one can change the Soviet Government at any time!" At these words the audience broke into an uproar: "It's a lie!" A Putilov worker named Izmailov accused the Bolsheviks of pretending to speak for the Russian workers while humiliating them in the eyes of the whole civilized world.[145] A gathering at the Arsenal approved 1,500–2 with 11 abstentions a motion to reconvene the Constituent Assembly.[146]

The Bolsheviks still prudently kept in the background. But to prevent these inflammatory resolutions from spreading, they shut down, permanently or temporarily, a number of opposition newspapers, four of them in Moscow. The Kadet *Nash vek,* which reported extensively on these events, was suspended from May 10 to June 16.

Since they planned to hold the Fifth Congress of Soviets early in July (the Fourth Congress having been held in March to ratify the peace treaty with Germany), the Bolsheviks had to hold elections to the soviets. These took place in May and June. The outcome exceeded their worst expectations: had they any respect for the wishes of the working class, they would have given up power. In town after town, Bolshevik candidates were routed by Mensheviks and SRs: "In all provincial capitals of European Russia where elections were held on which there are data, the Mensheviks and SRs won the majorities in the city soviets in the spring of 1918."[147] In the voting for the Moscow Soviet the Bolsheviks emerged with a pseudo-majority only by means of outright manipulation of the franchise and other forms of electoral fraud. Observers predicted that in the forthcoming elections to the Petrograd Soviet the Bolsheviks would find themselves in a minority as well[148] and Zinoviev would lose its chairmanship. The Bolsheviks must have shared this pessimistic assessment, for they postponed the elections to the Petrograd Soviet to the last possible moment, the end of June.

These stunning developements meant not so much an endorsement of the Mensheviks and SRs as a rejection of the Bolsheviks. The electors who wanted to turn the ruling party out of power had no alternative but to vote for the socialist parties since they alone were permitted to put up opposition candidates. How they would have voted had they been given a full choice of parties cannot, of course, be determined.

The Bolsheviks now had an opportunity to practice the principle of "recall," which Lenin had not long before described as "an essential condition of democracy," by withdrawing their deputies from the soviets and replacing them with Mensheviks and SRs. But they chose to manipulate the results, by using the Mandate Commissions, to declare the elections unlawful.

To distract the workers, the authorities had resorted to class hatred, inciting them this time against the "rural bourgeoisie." On May 20, the Sovnarkom issued a decree ordering the formation of "food supply detachments" *(prodovol'stvennye otriady),* made up of armed workers, which were to march on the villages and extract food from "kulaks." By this measure (it will be described in greater detail in Chapter 16) the authorities hoped to deflect the workers' anger over food shortages from themselves to the peasants, and, at the same time, gain a foothold in the countryside, still solidly under SR control.

Petrograd workers were not taken in by this diversion. Their plenipotentiaries on May 24 rejected the idea of food supply detachments on the grounds that it would cause a "deep chasm" between workers and peasants. Some speakers demanded that workers who joined such detachments be "expelled" from the ranks of the proletariat.[149]

On May 28, the excitement among Petrograd workers rose to a still higher pitch when the workers of Putilov demanded an end to the state's grain monopoly, guarantees of free speech, the right to form independent trade unions, and fresh elections to the soviets. Protest meetings which passed similar resolutions took place in Moscow and many provincial towns, including Tula, Nizhnii Novgorod, Orel, and Tver.

Zinoviev tried to calm the storm with economic concessions. He apparently persuaded Moscow to allocate to Petrograd additional food shipments, for on May 30 he was able to announce that the daily bread ration of workers would be raised to eight ounces. Such gestures failed to achieve their purpose. On June 1, the meeting of plenipotentiaries resolved to call for a city-wide political strike:

> Having heard the report of the representatives of factories and plants of Petrograd concerning the mood and demands of the worker masses, the Council of Plenipotentiaries notes with gratification that the withdrawal of the mass of workers from the government that falsely calls itself a government of workers is proceeding apace. The Council of Plenipotentiaries welcomes the readiness of workers to follow its appeal for a political strike. The Council of Plenipotentiaries calls on the workers of Petrograd vigorously to prepare the worker masses for a political strike against the current regime, which, in the name of the worker class, executes workers, throws them into prison, strangles freedom of speech, of press, of trade unions, [and] of strikes, which has strangled the popular representative body. This strike will have as its slogan the transfer of authority to the Constituent Assembly, the restoration of the organs of local self-government, the struggle for the integrity and independence of the Russian Republic.[150]

This, of course, was what the Mensheviks had been waiting for: workers, disenchanted with Bolsheviks, striking for democracy. Initially they did not favor the plenipotentiary movement because its leaders, suspicious of politicians, wanted independence from political parties. But by April they were sufficiently impressed to throw support behind the movement: on May 16, the Menshevik Central Committee called for the convocation of a nationwide conference of workers' representatives.*[151] The SRs followed suit.

If the situation were reversed, with the socialists in power and the Bolsheviks in opposition, the Bolsheviks undoubtedly would have encouraged worker discontent and done all they could to topple the government. But the Mensheviks and their socialist allies had strong inhibitions against such behav-

---

*The idea of a Workers' Congress had been first advanced by Akselrod in 1906, at which time it was rejected by both Mensheviks and Bolsheviks: Leonard Schapiro, *The Communist Party of the Soviet Union* (London, 1963), 75–76.

ior. They rejected the Bolshevik dictatorship and yet felt beholden to it. The Menshevik *Novaia zhizn'*, while unsparing in its criticism, made its readers understand that they had a vital interest in the survival of Bolshevism. This thesis it had expressed the day after the Bolshevik power seizure:

> It is essential, above all, to take into account the tragic fact that any violent liquidation of the Bolshevik coup will, at the same time, result inevitably in the liquidation of all the conquests of the Russian Revolution.[152]

After the Bolsheviks had disposed of the Constituent Assembly, the Menshevik organ lamented:

> We did not belong and do not belong to the admirers of the Bolshevik regime, and have always predicted the bankruptcy of its foreign and domestic policies. But neither have we forgotten nor do we forget for an instant that the fate of our revolution is closely tied to that of the Bolshevik movement. The Bolshevik movement represents a perverted, degenerate revolutionary striving of the broad popular masses . . .[153]

Such an attitude not only paralyzed the Mensheviks' will to act but made them into allies of the Bolsheviks, in that instead of fanning the flames of popular discontent, they helped put them out.*

When the Council of Workers' Plenipotentiaries reassembled on June 3, the Menshevik and SR intellectuals opposed the idea of a political strike, on the familiar grounds that it would play into the hands of the class enemy. They persuaded the workers' representatives to reconsider their decision and, instead of striking, send a delegation to Moscow to explore the possibility of founding a similar organization there.

On June 7, a delegate from Petrograd addressed a gathering of Moscow factory representatives; he accused the Bolshevik Government of pursuing anti-labor and counterrevolutionary policies. Such talk had not been heard in Russia since October. The Cheka viewed the matter very seriously, for Moscow was now the country's capital and unrest there was more dangerous than in "Red Petrograd." Security agents seized the Petrograd delegate when he finished speaking, but were forced to release him under pressure from fellow workers. It transpired that Moscow labor, although sympathetic, was not yet ready to form its own Council of Workers' Plenipotentiaries.[154] This may be explainable by the fact that the labor force in Moscow and surrounding areas

---

*In fairness it must be noted that a small group of old Mensheviks, among whom were the founders of Russian Social-Democracy—Plekhanov, Akselrod, Potresov, and Vera Zasulich— thought differently. Thus, Akselrod wrote in August 1918 that the Bolshevik regime had degenerated into a "gruesome" counterrevolution. Even so, he and his old Genevan comrades also opposed active resistance to Lenin, on the grounds that it would assist reactionary elements to return to power. A. Ascher, *Pavel Axelrod and the Development of Menshevism* (Cambridge, Mass., 1972), 344–46. On Plekhanov's attitude: Samuel H. Baron, *Plekhanov* (Stanford, Calif., 1963), 352–61. Potresov criticized his Menshevik colleagues then and later (*V plenu u illiuzii,* Paris, 1927), but he, too, would not participate in active opposition.

had lower skills and weaker traditions of trade unionism than the workers in Petrograd.

The process of worker disengagement from the soviets, begun in Petrograd, spread to the rest of the country. In many cities (Moscow was soon among them) where the local soviets were prevented from holding elections or where the elections had been disqualified, workers formed "workers' councils," "workers' conferences," or "assemblies of workers' plenipotentiaries" free of government control and unaffiliated with any political party.

Faced with a rising tide of discontent, the Bolsheviks struck back. In Moscow on June 13, they took into custody fifty-six individuals affiliated with the plenipotentiary movement, all but six or seven of them workers.[155] On June 16, they announced the convocation in two weeks of the Fifth Congress of Soviets, and in this connection instructed all soviets to hold new elections once again. Since such elections would certainly have again yielded Menshevik and SR majorities and placed the government in the position of an embattled minority at the Congress, Moscow moved to disqualify its rivals by ordering the expulsion of SRs and Mensheviks from all the soviets as well as from the CEC.[156] At the caucus of the Bolshevik faction of the CEC, L. S. Sosnovskii justified the decree with the argument that the Mensheviks and SRs would overthrow the Bolsheviks just as the Bolsheviks had toppled the Provisional Government.* The only choice offered the voters, therefore, was among official Bolshevik candidates, Left SRs, and a broad category of candidates without party affiliation known as "Bolshevik sympathizers."

This step marked the end of independent political parties in Russia. The monarchist parties—Octobrists, Union of the Russian People, Nationalists— had dissolved in the course of 1917 and no longer existed as organized bodies. The outlawed Kadets either shifted their activities to the borderlands, where they were beyond the reach of the Cheka, but also out of touch with the Russian population, or else went underground, where they formed an anti-Bolshevik coalition called the National Center.[157] The June 16 decree did not explicitly outlaw the Mensheviks and SRs but it did render them politically impotent. Although, as a reward for their support against the White armies, the two socialist parties were later reinstated and allowed to rejoin the soviets in limited numbers, this was a temporary expedient. Essentially, Russia now became a one-party state in which organizations other than the Bolshevik Party were forbidden to engage in political activity.

On June 16, the day the Bolsheviks announced the Fifth Congress of Soviets, which neither the Mensheviks nor the SRs would attend, the Council of Workers' Plenipotentiaries called for the convocation of an All-Russian Conference of Workers.[158] This body was to discuss and solve the most urgent problems facing the nation: the food situation, unemployment, the breakdown of law, and workers' organizations.

*NZh, No. 115/330 (June 16, 1918), 3. According to NV, No. 96/120 (June 19, 1918), 3, the Bolshevik faction of the CEC refused to eject the Mensheviks and SRs from the soviets but consented to their expulsion from the CEC.

On June 20, the head of the Petrograd Cheka, V. Volodarskii, was assassinated. In its search for the killer, the Cheka detained some workers, which set off protest meetings in factories. The Bolsheviks occupied the Neva worker district with troops and imposed martial law. The workers of Obukhov, the most troublesome factory, were locked out.[159]

It was in this highly charged atmosphere that elections to the Soviet took place in Petrograd. During the electoral campaign, Zinoviev was booed and prevented from speaking at Putilov and Obukhov. In factory after factory, workers, ignoring the decree prohibiting the two parties from participating in the soviets, gave majorities to Mensheviks and SRs. Obukhov chose 5 SRs, 3 partyless, and 1 Bolshevik. At Semiannikov, the SRs won 64 percent of the vote, the Mensheviks 10 percent, and the Bolshevik–Left SR bloc 26 percent. Similar results were obtained in other establishments.[160]

The Bolsheviks refused to be bound by these results. They wanted majorities and obtained them, usually by tampering with the franchise: some Bolsheviks were given as many as five votes.* On July 2, the results of the "elections" were announced. Of the 650 newly chosen deputies to the Petrograd Soviet, 610 were to be Bolsheviks and Left SRs; 40 seats were allotted to the SRs and Mensheviks, whom the official organs denounced as "Judases."† This rump Petrograd Soviet voted to dissolve the Council of Workers' Plenipotentiaries: a delegate from the council who sought to address the gathering was prevented from speaking and physically assaulted.

The Council of Workers' Plenipotentiaries sat in almost daily session. On June 26, it voted unanimously to call for a one-day political strike on July 2, under the slogans "Down with the Death Penalty," "Down with Executions and the Civil War," "Long Live the Freedom to Strike."[161] SR and Menshevik intellectuals again came out against the strike.[162]

The Bolshevik authorities posted placards all over the city which described the organizers of the strike as hirelings of White Guardists and threatened to turn all strikers over to Revolutionary Tribunals.[163] For good measure they set up machine gun posts at key points in the city.

Sympathetic reporters described the workers as vacillating: the Kadet *Nash vek* wrote on June 22 that they were anti-Soviet but confused. The difficult domestic and international situation, food shortages, and the absence of clear solutions induced in them "an extreme imbalance, a depression of sorts, and even perplexity."

The events of July 2 confirmed this assessment. The first political strike in Russia since the fall of tsarism sputtered and went out. The workers, discouraged by socialist intellectuals, intimidated by the Bolshevik show of

*V. Stroev in *NZh,* No. 119/334 (June 21, 1918), 1. According to one newspaper (*Novyi luch,* cited in *NZh,* No. 121/336, June 23, 1918, 1–2), of the 130 delegates initially "elected" to the Petrograd Soviet, 77 were handpicked by the Bolshevik Party: 26 from Red Army units, 8 from supply detachments, and 43 from among Bolshevik functionaries.

†*NZh,* No. 127/342 (July 2, 1918), 1. Somewhat different figures are given in Lenin, *Sochineniia,* XXIII, 547, where the total number of deputies is placed at 582, of whom 405 were Bolsheviks, 75 Left SRs, 59 Mensheviks and SRs, and 43 partyless.

force, uncertain of their strength and purpose, lost heart. The organizers estimated that between 18,000 and 20,000 workers obeyed the call to strike, which was no more than one-seventh of Petrograd's actual labor force. Obkuhov, Maxwell, and Pahl struck, but most of the other plants, Putilov included, did not.

This result sealed the fate of independent workers' organizations in Russia. Before long, the Cheka closed down the Council of Workers' Plenipotentiaries in Petrograd along with its provincial branches, sending the most outspoken leaders to prison.

Thus ended the autonomy of the soviets, the right of workers to their own representation, and what was still left of the multiparty system. These measures, enacted in June and early July 1918, completed the formation in Russia of a one-party dictatorship.

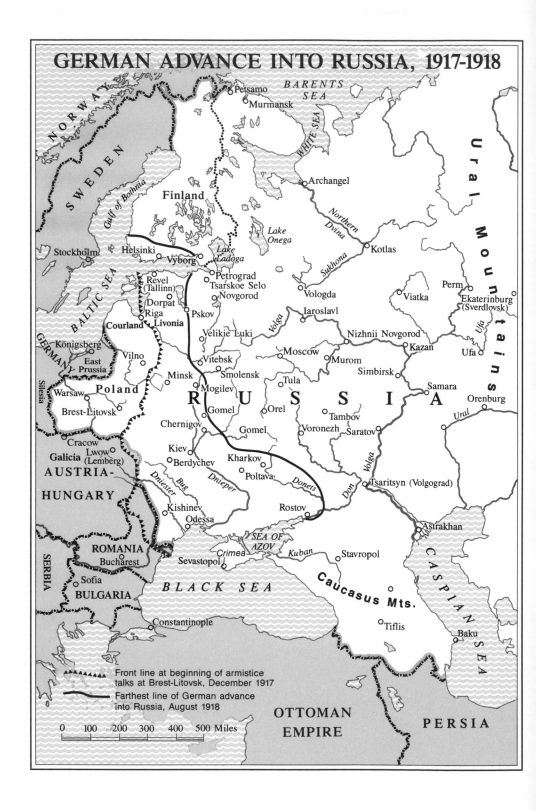

GERMAN ADVANCE INTO RUSSIA, 1917-1918

NORWAY

BARENTS SEA

Petsamo
Murmansk

SWEDEN

WHITE SEA

Finland

Archangel

Ural Mountains

Gulf of Bothnia

Lake Onega

Northern Dvina

Stockholm

Helsinki
Vyborg

Lake Ladoga

Petrograd
Tsarskoe Selo
Novgorod

Vologda

Kotlas

Sukhona

Volga

Viatka

Perm

Ekaterinburg (Sverdlovsk)

BALTIC SEA

Revel (Tallinn)
Dorpat
Riga
Livonia

Pskov

Iaroslavl

Nizhnii Novgorod

Kazan

Ufa

Ufa

Courland

Velikie Luki

GERMANY

Königsberg

Vilno

Vitebsk

Moscow

Murom

Simbirsk

East Prussia

Minsk

Smolensk

Tula

Samara

Orenburg

Silesia

Warsaw
Poland
Mogilev

RUSSIA

Orel

Tambov

Ural

Brest-Litovsk

Gomel

Voronezh

Saratov

Cracow

Chernigov

Gomel

Volga

Galicia
Lwow (Lemberg)

Kiev
Berdychev

Kharkov

Don

Tsaritsyn (Volgograd)

AUSTRIA-

Poltava

Donets

HUNGARY

Dniester

Bug

Dnieper

Kishinev
Odessa

Rostov

Astrakhan

ROMANIA
Bucharest

Crimea

SEA OF AZOV

Kuban

Stavropol

CASPIAN SEA

SERBIA

Sofia

Sevastopol

BLACK SEA

Caucasus Mts.

Baku

BULGARIA

Constantinople

Tiflis

▲▲▲▲▲ Front line at beginning of armistice talks at Brest-Litovsk, December 1917

—— Farthest line of German advance into Russia, August 1918

OTTOMAN
EMPIRE

PERSIA

0 100 200 300 400 500 Miles

Brest-Litovsk

The party's agitators must protest, time and again, against the foul slander, launched by capitalists, that our party allegedly favors a separate peace with Germany.

—*Lenin, April 21, 1917*[1]

The Bolsheviks' main concern after October was to solidify their power and to expand it nationwide. This difficult task they had to accomplish within the framework of an active foreign policy, at the center of which stood relations with Germany. In Lenin's judgment, unless Russia promptly signed an armistice with Germany, his chances of keeping power were close to nil; conversely, such an armistice and the peace that would follow opened for the Bolsheviks the doors to world conquest. In December 1917, when most of his followers rejected the German terms, he argued that the party had no choice but to do the Germans' bidding. The issue was starkly simple: unless the Bolsheviks made peace, "the peasant army, unbearably exhausted by the war, . . . will overthrow the socialist workers' government."[2] The Bolsheviks required a *peredyshka*, or breathing spell, to consolidate power, to organize the administration, and to build their own armed force.

Proceeding from this assumption, Lenin was prepared to make peace with the Central Powers on any terms as long as they left him a power base. The resistance which he encountered in party ranks grew out of the belief (which he shared) that the Bolshevik Government could survive only if a revolution broke out in Western Europe and the conviction (which he did not fully share) that this was bound to happen at any moment. To make peace with the "imperialist" Central Powers, especially on the humiliating terms which they offered, was to his opponents a betrayal of international socialism; in the long run, it spelled death for revolutionary Russia. In their view, Soviet Russia should not place her own short-term national interests above the interests of the international proletariat. Lenin disagreed:

> Our tactics ought to rest . . . [on the principle] how to ensure more reliably and hopefully for the socialist revolution the possibility of consolidating itself or even surviving *in one country* until such time as other countries joined in.[3]

On this issue the Bolshevik Party split in the winter of 1917–18 straight down the middle.

The history of Bolshevik Russia's relations with the Central Powers, notably Germany, during the twelve months that followed the October coup is of supreme interest because it is on this occasion that the Communists first formulated in theory and worked out in practice the strategy and tactics of their foreign policy.

Western diplomacy traces its origins to the Italian city-states of the fifteenth century. From there diplomatic practices spread to the rest of Europe and in the seventeenth century received codification in international law. Diplomacy was designed to regulate and peacefully resolve disputes among sovereign states; if it failed and arms were resorted to, its task was to keep the level of violence as low as possible and to bring hostilities to an early end. The success of international law rests on the acceptance by all parties of certain principles:

1. Sovereign states are acknowledged to have an unquestioned right to exist: whatever disagreements divide them, their existence itself can never be at issue. This principle underpinned the Treaty of Westphalia of 1648. It was violated at the end of the eighteenth century with the Third Partition of Poland, which led to that country's demise, but this was an exceptional case.

2. International relations are confined to contacts between governments: it is a violation of diplomatic norms for one government to go over the head of another with direct appeals to its population. In the practice of the nineteenth century, states normally communicated through the ministries of foreign affairs.

3. Relations among the foreign offices presume a certain level of integrity and goodwill, including respect for formal accords, since without them there can be no mutual trust, and without trust diplomacy becomes an exercise in futility.

These principles and practices, which evolved between the fifteenth and nineteenth centuries, assumed the existence of a Law of Nature as well as that of a supranational community of Christian states. The Stoic concept of the Law of Nature, which theorists of international law from Hugo Grotius onward applied to relations between states, posited eternal and universal standards of justice. The concept of a Christian community meant that, whatever divided them, the countries of Europe and their overseas offspring belonged to one family. Before the twentieth century, the precepts of international law were not meant to apply to peoples outside the European community—an attitude which justified colonial conquests.

Obviously, this whole complex of "bourgeois" ideas was repugnant to the Bolsheviks. As revolutionaries determined to overthrow the existing order, they could hardly have been expected to acknowledge the sanctity of the international state system. Appealing over the heads of governments to their populations was the very essence of revolutionary strategy. And as concerned honesty and goodwill in international relations, the Bolsheviks, in common with the rest of the Russian radicals, regarded moral standards to be obligatory only within the movement, in relations among comrades: relations with the class enemy were subject to the rules of warfare. In revolution, as in war, the only principle that mattered was *kto kogo*—who eats whom.

In the weeks that followed the October coup, most Bolsheviks expected their example to set off revolutions throughout Europe. Every report from abroad of an industrial strike or of a mutiny was hailed as the "beginning." In the winter of 1917–18, the Bolshevik *Krasnaia gazeta* and similar party organs reported in banner headlines, day after day, revolutionary explosions in Western Europe: one day in Germany, the next in Finland, then again in France. As long as this expectation remained alive, the Bolsheviks had no need to work out a foreign policy: all they had to do was repeat what they had always done—namely, fan the flames of revolution.

But these hopes waned somewhat in the spring of 1918. The Russian Revolution had as yet found no emulators. The mutinies and strikes in Western Europe were everywhere suppressed, and the "masses" continued to slaughter each other instead of attacking their "ruling classes." As this realization dawned, it became urgent to work out a revolutionary foreign policy. Here, the Bolsheviks lacked guidelines, since neither the writings of Marx nor the experience of the Paris Commune were of much help. The difficulty derived from the contradictory requirement of their interests as rulers of a sovereign state and as self-appointed leaders of world revolution. In the latter capacity they denied the right of other ("non-socialist") governments to exist and rejected the tradition of confining foreign relations to heads of state and their ministers. They wanted to destroy root and branch the entire structure of national, "bourgeois" states, and to do so they had to exhort the "masses" abroad to rebellion. Yet, inasmuch as they themselves now headed a sovereign state, they could not avoid relations with other governments—at least until these had been swept away by the global revolution—and this they had to do in accordance with traditional standards of "bourgeois" international law. They also needed the protection of these standards to ward off foreign intervention in their own internal affairs.

It is here that the dual nature of the Communist state, the formal separation of party and state, proved so useful. The Bolsheviks solved their problem

by constructing a two-level foreign policy, one traditional, the other revolutionary. For purposes of dealing with "bourgeois" governments, they established the Commissariat of Foreign Affairs, staffed exclusively with dependable Bolsheviks and subject to instructions from the Central Committee. This
institution functioned, at least on the surface, in accord with accepted norms
of diplomacy. Wherever permitted to do so by host countries, the heads of
Soviet foreign missions, no longer called "ambassadors" or "envoys," but
"political representatives" *(polpredy),* took over the old Russian Embassy
buildings, donned cutaways and top hats, and behaved much like their colleagues from "bourgeois" missions.* "Revolutionary diplomacy"—strictly
speaking, a contradiction in terms—became the province of the Bolshevik
Party acting either on its own or through the agency of special organs, such
as the Communist International. Its agents incited revolution and supported
subversive activities against the very foreign governments with which the
Commissariat of Foreign Affairs maintained correct relations.

This separation of functions, which reflected a similar duality inside
Soviet Russia between party and state, was described by Sverdlov at the
Seventh Congress of the Bolshevik Party in the course of discussions of the
Brest-Litovsk Treaty. Referring to the clauses of the treaty which forbade
the signatories to engage in hostile agitation and propaganda, he said:

> It follows inexorably from the treaty we have signed and which we must soon
> ratify at the Congress [of Soviets] that in our capacity as a government, as
> Soviet authority, we will not be able to conduct that broad international agita-
> tion which we have conducted until now. But this in no wise means that we
> have to cut back one iota on such agitation. Only from now on we shall have
> to conduct it almost always in the name, not of the Council of People's Com-
> missars, but of the Central Committee of the party . . .[4]

This tactic of treating the party as a private organization, for whose actions
the "Soviet" Government was not responsible, the Bolsheviks pursued with
rather comical determination. For example, when in September 1918 Berlin
protested against the anti-German propaganda in the Russian press (which by
then was entirely under Bolshevik control), the Commissariat of Foreign
Affairs archly replied:

> The Russian Government has no complaints that the German censorship and
> German police do not prosecute [their] press organs for . . . malicious agitation
> against the political institutions of Russia—that is, against the Soviet system.
> . . . Considering fully admissible the absence of any repressive measures on the
> part of the German Government against German press organs which freely
> express their political and social opposition to the Soviet system, it deems

*The earliest Soviet *polpredy* were stationed in neutral countries: V. V. Vorovskii in Stockholm, and Ia. A. Berzin in Berne. After the Brest Treaty had been ratified, A. A. Ioffe took over
the Berlin mission. The Bolsheviks tried to appoint first Litvinov and then Kamenev to the Court
of St. James's, but both were rejected. France also would not accept a Soviet representative until
after the Civil War.

equally admissible similar behavior in regard to the German system on the part of private persons and unofficial newspapers in Russia. . . . It is necessary to protest in the most decisive manner the frequent representations made by the German Consulate General that the Russian Government, by means of police measures, can direct the Russian revolutionary press in this or that direction and by bureaucratic influence instill in it such and such views.[5]

The Bolshevik Government reacted very differently when foreign powers interfered in internal Russian affairs. As early as November 1917, Trotsky, the Commissar of Foreign Affairs, protested Allied "interference" in Russian matters after Allied ambassadors, uncertain who the legitimate government of Russia was, had sent a diplomatic note to the Commander in Chief, General N. N. Dukhonin.[6] The Sovnarkom never let an occasion pass without voicing objections to foreign powers violating the principle of non-interference in the internal affairs of its country, even as it repeatedly violated this very same principle with its own conduct.

As stated, Lenin was prepared to accept any terms demanded by the Central Powers, but because of widespread suspicions that he was a German agent, he had to proceed with caution. Instead of entering immediately into negotiations with Germany and Austria, therefore, as he would have preferred, he issued appeals to all the belligerent powers to meet and make peace. Actually, general peace in Europe was the last thing he wanted: as we have seen, one reason for his urgency in seizing power in October was fear of just such an eventuality, which would foreclose the chances of unleashing a civil war in Europe. Apparently, he did not feel afraid to call for peace since previous appeals had fallen on deaf ears, including the proposals of President Wilson of December 1916, the peace resolution of the German Reichstag in July 1917, and the papal proposals of August 1917. Once the Allies rejected his offer, as he had every reason to expect they would, he would be free to make his own arrangements.

The curiously named "Decree on Peace," which Lenin had drafted and the Second Congress of Soviets adopted, proposed to the belligerent powers a three-month armistice. This proposal it coupled with an appeal to the workers of England, France, and Germany with their

> many-sided decisive and selflessly energetic activity [to] help us successfully complete the task of peace and, at the same time, the task of liberating the toiling and exploited masses of the population from all slavery and all exploitation.[7]

George Kennan has labeled this "decree" an act of "demonstrative diplomacy," intended "not to promote freely accepted and mutually profitable agreements between governments but rather to embarrass other governments and stir up opposition among their own people."* The Bolsheviks issued other proclamations in the same spirit, urging the citizens of the belligerent powers to rise in rebellion.[8] As head of state, Lenin could now advance the program of the Zimmerwald left.

The Bolsheviks transmitted their Peace Decree to the Allied envoys on November 9/22. The Allied governments rejected it out of hand, following which Trotsky informed the Central Powers of Russia's readiness to open negotiations for an armistice.

The policy of cultivating the Bolsheviks now paid generous dividends for the Germans. Russia's quest for a separate peace reminded some of them of the "miracle" of 1763, when the death of the pro-French Elizabeth and the accession of the pro-Prussian Peter III led to Russia's withdrawal from the Seven Years' War, which saved Frederick the Great from defeat and Prussia from destruction. Russia's defection from the alliance promised two benefits: the release of hundreds of thousands of troops for transfer to the west and a breach in the British naval blockade. The prospect made a German victory seem once again within grasp. On learning of the Bolshevik power seizure in Petrograd, Ludendorff drew up plans for a decisive offensive on the Western Front in the spring of 1918, with the help of divisions transferred from the Eastern Front. The Kaiser endorsed the plan.[9] At this stage, Ludendorff heartily approved of the policy of the Foreign Office, pursued by the architect of the pro-Bolshevik orientation, Richard von Kühlmann, to obtain a quick armistice with Russia followed by a dictated peace.

In the battle of wits between the Bolsheviks and the Central Powers, the latter appeared to enjoy all the advantages: stable governments with millions of disciplined troops, as compared with a regime of amateurs and usurpers whom few recognized, with a ragtag army in the process of dissolution. In reality, however, the balance of power was much less one-sided. By the end of 1917, the economic situation of the Central Powers had become so desperate that they were unlikely to stay in the war much longer. Austria-Hungary was in a particularly precarious condition: its Foreign Minister, Count Ottokar Czernin, told the Germans during the Brest negotiations that his country probably could not hold out until the next harvest.[10] The Germans were only marginally better off: some German politicians believed that the country would run out of grain by mid-April 1918.[11]

Germany and Austria also had problems with civilian morale, for the Bolshevik peace appeals aroused great hopes among their peoples. The German Chancellor advised the Kaiser that if talks with the Russians broke down, Austria-Hungary would probably drop out of the war and Germany would experience domestic unrest. The leader of the German Majority Socialists

---

*George Kennan, *Russia Leaves the War* (Princeton, N.J., 1956), 75–76. In early November, the Bolsheviks began to publish the secret treaties between Russia and the Allies from the files of the Ministry of Foreign Affairs. With their appeals, the Bolsheviks emulated the French revolutionaries who in November 1792 pledged "brotherhood and assistance" to any nation desirous of "regaining" its freedom.

(who supported the war), Philipp Scheidemann, predicted that the failure of peace negotiations with the Russians would "spell the demise of the German Empire."[12] For all these reasons—military, economic, and psychological—the Central Powers needed peace with Russia almost as much as Bolshevik Russia needed peace with them. These facts, of which the Russians could not have been fully aware, indicate that those Bolsheviks who opposed Lenin's capitulationist policy in favor of stringing the Germans and Austrians along were not as unrealistic as they are usually depicted. The enemy also negotiated with a gun to his head.

The Bolsheviks enjoyed a further advantage in that they had intimate knowledge of their opponent. Having spent years in the West, they were familiar with Germany's domestic problems, her political and business personalities, her party alignments. Nearly all of them spoke one or more Western languages. Because Germany was the main center of socialist theory and practice, they knew Germany at least as well as if not better than their own country, and if the occasion presented itself, the Sovnarkom would have gladly assumed power there. This knowledge enabled them to exploit discords inside the opponent's camp by pitting businessmen against the generals or left socialists against right socialists, and inciting German workers to revolution in readily understandable language. By contrast, the Germans knew next to nothing of those with whom they were about to enter into negotiations. The Bolsheviks, who had just emerged into the limelight, were to them a gaggle of unkempt, garrulous, and impractical intellectuals. The Germans consistently misinterpreted Bolshevik moves and underestimated their cunning. One day they saw them as revolutionary hotheads, whom they could manipulate at will, and the next as realists who did not believe their own slogans and were ready for businesslike deals. In their relations during 1917–18, the Bolsheviks repeatedly outwitted the Germans by assuming a protective coloring that disoriented the Germans and whetted their appetites.

To understand Germany's Soviet policy a few words need to be said about her so-called *Russlandpolitik.* For while her immediate interest in making peace with Russia derived from military considerations, Germany also had long-range geopolitical designs on that country. German political strategists had traditionally shown a keen interest in Russia: it was not by accident that before World War I no country had a tradition of Russian scholarship remotely approaching the German. Conservatives regarded it as axiomatic that their country's national security required a weak Russia. For one, only if the Russians were unable to threaten Germany with a second front could her forces confidently take on the French and the "Anglo-Saxons" in the struggle for global hegemony. Second, to be a serious contender in *Weltpolitik,* Germany required access to Russia's natural resources, including foodstuffs, which she could obtain on satisfactory terms only if Russia became her client. Having established a national state very late, Germany had missed out in the imperial scramble. Her only realistic chance of matching the economic prowess of her rivals lay in expanding eastward, into the vastness of Eurasia.

German bankers and industrialists looked on Russia as a potential colony, a kind of surrogate Africa. They drafted for their government memoranda in which they stressed how important it was for victorious Germany to import, free of tariffs, Russian high-grade iron ore and manganese, as well as to exploit Russian agriculture and mines.[13]

To transform Russia into a German client state, two things had to be done. The Russian Empire had to be broken up and reduced to territories populated by Great Russians. This entailed pushing Russia's frontiers eastward through the annexation by Germany of the Baltic provinces and the creation of a *cordon sanitaire* of nominally sovereign but in fact German-controlled protectorates: Poland, the Ukraine, and Georgia. This program, advocated before and during the war by the publicist Paul Rohrbach,[14] had a strong appeal, especially to the military. Hindenburg wrote the Kaiser in January 1918 that Germany's interests required Russia's borders to be shifted to the East, and her western provinces, rich in population and economic capacity, to be annexed.[15] Essentially this meant Russia's expulsion from continental Europe. In the words of Rohrbach, the issue was whether "*if our future is to be secure,* Russia is to be allowed to remain a European power in the sense that she had been until now, *or is she not to be allowed to be such?*"[16]

Second, Russia had to grant Germany all kinds of economic concessions and privileges that would leave her open to German penetration and, ultimately, hegemony. German businessmen during the war importuned their government to annex Russia's western provinces and subject Russia to economic exploitation.[17]

From this perspective, nothing suited Germany better than a Bolshevik Government in Russia. German internal communications from 1918 were replete with arguments that the Bolsheviks should be helped to stay in power as the only Russian party prepared to make far-reaching territorial and economic concessions and because their incompetence and unpopularity kept Russia in a state of permanent crisis. State Secretary Admiral Paul von Hintze expressed the consensus when in the fall of 1918 he stood up to those Germans who wanted to topple the Bolsheviks as unreliable and dangerous partners: eliminating the Bolsheviks "would subvert the whole work of our war leadership and our policy in the East, which strives for the military paralysis of Russia."[18] Paul Rohrbach argued in a similar vein:

> The Bolsheviks are ruining Great Russia, the source of any potential Russian future danger, root and branch. They have already lifted most of that anxiety which we might have felt about Great Russia, and we should do all we can to keep them as long as possible carrying on their work, so useful to us.[19]

If Berlin and Vienna agreed on the desirability of quickly coming to terms with Russia, in Petrograd opinions were sharply divided. Setting nuances aside, the division pitted those Bolsheviks who wanted peace at once, on almost any terms, against those who wanted to use the peace negotiations as a means for unleashing a European revolution.

Lenin, the leading advocate of the first course, found himself usually in a minority, sometimes a minority of one. He proceeded from a pessimistic estimate of the international "correlation of forces." While he, too, counted on revolutions in the West, he had a much higher opinion than his adversaries of the ability of "bourgeois" governments to crush them. At the same time, he was less sanguine than his colleagues about the staying power of the Bolsheviks: during one of the debates that accompanied the peace talks, he caustically observed that while there was as yet no civil war in Europe there was already one in Russia. From the perspective of time, Lenin can be faulted for underestimating the internal difficulties of the Central Powers and their need for a quick settlement: Russia's position in this respect was stronger than he realized. But his assessment of the internal situation in Russia was perfectly sound. He knew that by continuing in the war he risked being toppled from power either by his domestic opponents or by the Germans. He also knew that he desperately needed a respite to transform his claim to power into reality. This called for an organized political, economic, and military effort, possible only under conditions of peace, no matter how onerous and humiliating. True, this entailed sacrificing, for the time being, the interests of the Western "proletariat," but in his eyes, until the Revolution had fully succeeded in Russia, Russia's interests came first.

The position of the majority opposed to him, headed by Bukharin and joined by Trotsky, has been summarized as follows:

> The central powers would not permit Lenin so to use the respite: they would cut off Russia from the grain and coal of the Ukraine and the petrol of the Caucasus; they would bring under their control half the Russian population; they would sponsor and support counterrevolutionary movements and throttle the revolution. Nor would the Soviets be able to build up a new army during any respite. They had to create their armed strength in the very process of the fighting; and only so could they create it. True, the Soviets might be forced to evacuate Petrograd and even Moscow; but they had enough space into which to retreat and gather strength. Even if the people were to prove as unwilling to fight for the revolution as they were to fight for the old regime—and the leaders of the war faction refused to take this for granted—then every German advance, with all the accompanying terror and pillage, would shake the people from weariness and torpor, force them to resist, and finally generate a broad and truly popular enthusiasm for revolutionary war. On the tide of this enthusiasm a new and formidable army would rise. The revolution, unshamed by sordid surrender, would achieve its renaissance; it would stir the souls of the working classes abroad; and it would finally dispel the nightmare of imperialism.[20]

This division of opinion led in the early months of 1918 to the worst crisis in the history of the Bolshevik Party.

On November 15/28, 1917, the Bolsheviks again called on the belligerents to open negotiations. The appeal stated that since the "ruling classes" of Allied countries have failed to respond to the Peace Decree, Russia was prepared to open immediate talks on a cease-fire with the Germans and Austrians, who had responded positively. The Germans accepted the Bolshevik offer immediately. On November 18/December 1, a Russian delegation departed for Brest-Litovsk, the headquarters of the German High Command on the Eastern Front. It was headed by A. A. Ioffe, an ex-Menshevik and close friend of Trotsky's. It also included Kamenev and, as a symbolic gesture, representatives of the "toiling masses" in the persons of a soldier, sailor, worker, peasant, and one woman. Even as the train carrying the Russian delegation was en route to Brest, Petrograd called on German troops to mutiny.

The armistice talks opened on November 20/December 3, in what used to be a Russian officers' club. The German delegation was headed by Kühlmann, who regarded himself as something of an expert in Russian affairs and in 1917 had played a key role in making arrangements with Lenin. The parties agreed on a cease-fire to begin on November 23/December 6 and remain in force for eleven days. Before it expired, however, it was extended, by mutual agreement, to January 1/14, 1918. The ostensible purpose of this extension was to give the Allies an opportunity to reconsider and join the talks. Both sides knew, however, that there was no danger of the Allies complying: as Kühlmann advised his Chancellor, the German conditions for an armistice were so onerous the Allies could not possibly accept them.[21] The true purpose of the extension was to allow both sides to work out their positions for the coming peace talks. Even before these got underway, the Germans violated the terms of the cease-fire by transferring six divisions to the Western Front.*

How eager the Bolsheviks were for normal relations with Germany is seen from the fact that immediately after the cease-fire they welcomed to Petrograd a German delegation under Count Wilhelm von Mirbach. The delegation was to arrange for an exchange of civilian prisoners of war and the resumption of economic and cultural ties. Lenin received Mirbach on December 15/28. It is from this delegation that Berlin received the first eyewitness accounts of conditions in Soviet Russia.† The Germans first learned from Mirbach that the Bolsheviks were about to default on Russia's foreign debts. On receipt of this information, the German State Bank drafted memoranda indicating how this could be done with the least harm to German interests and the greatest to those

---

*J. Buchan, *A History of the Great War*, IV (Boston, 1922), 135. The Armistice Agreement forbade "major" transferals of troops from or to the Russian front while it was in force.

†According to the French general Henri A. Niessel, the Allies intercepted German cables from Petrograd to Brest and from them learned how desperately the Germans desired peace: General [Henri A.] Niessel, *Le Triomphe des Bolchéviks et la Paix de Brest-Litovsk: Souvenirs, 1917–1918* (Paris, 1940), 187–88.

80. The Russian delegation arrives at Brest-Litovsk. In
front, Kamenev. Speaking to German officer, A. Ioffe.

81. The signing of the Armistice at Brest (November
23–December 6, 1917). Sitting on the right, Kamenev and
behind him (concealed), Ioffe. On the German side sitting
fourth from left, General Hoffmann.

of the Allies. A proposal to this effect was outlined by V. V. Vorovskii, Lenin's old associate and now Soviet diplomatic representative in Stockholm, who proposed that the Russian Government annul only debts incurred after 1905: since most German loans to Russia had been made before 1905, the major burden of such a default would fall on the Allies.[22]*

The talks at Brest resumed on December 9/22. Kühlmann again headed the German delegation. The Austrian mission was chaired by Count Czernin, the Minister of Foreign Affairs; present were also the foreign ministers of Turkey and Bulgaria. The German peace proposals called for the separation from Russia of Poland as well as Courland and Lithuania, all of which at the time were under German military occupation. The Germans must have thought these terms reasonable, for they had come to Brest in a hopeful and conciliatory mood, expecting to reach agreement in principle by Christmas. They were quickly disappointed. Ioffe, under instructions to drag out the talks, made vague and unrealistic counterproposals (they had been drafted by Lenin) calling for peace "without annexations and indemnities" and "national self-determination" for the European nations as well as the colonies.[23] In effect, the Russian delegation, behaving as if Russia had won the war, asked the Central Powers to give up all their wartime conquests. This behavior raised among the Germans first doubts about Russian intentions.

The peace talks were carried out in an atmosphere of unreality:

> The scene in the Council Chamber at Brest-Litovsk was worthy of the art of some great historical painter. On one side sat the bland and alert representatives of the Central Powers, black-coated or much beribboned and bestarred, exquisitely polite. . . . Among them could be noted the narrow face and alert eyes of Kühlmann, whose courtesy in debate never failed; the handsome presence of Czernin, who was put up to fly the wilder sort of kite, because of his artless bonhomie; and the chubby Pickwickian countenance of General Hoffmann, who now and then grew scarlet and combative when he felt that some military pronouncement was called for. Behind the Teutonic delegates was an immense band of staff officers and civil servants and spectacled professorial experts. Each delegation used its own tongue, and the discussions were apt to be lengthy. Opposite the ranks of Teutondom sat the Russians, mostly dirty and ill-clad, who smoked their large pipes placidly through the debates. Much of the discussion seemed not to interest them, and they intervened in monosyllables, save when an incursion into the ethos of politics let loose a flood of confused metaphysics. The Conference had the air partly of an assembly of well-mannered employers trying to deal with a specially obtuse delegation of workmen, partly of urbane hosts presiding at a village school treat.[24]

On Christmas Day, carried away by the spirit of the occasion, Count Czernin, to the great irritation of the Germans, offered to surrender all the

*The Soviet Government's default on all state obligations, domestic as well as foreign, was announced on January 28, 1918. The sum of foreign debts annulled by this measure has been estimated at 13 billion rubles or $6.5 billion: G. G. Shvittau, *Revoliutsiia i Narodnoe Khoziaistvo v Rossii (1917–1921)* (Leipzig, 1922), 337.

territories Austria had conquered during the war if the Allies would join in the peace negotiations: he was under instructions to avoid at all costs a breakdown of the armistice and to be prepared, if necessary, to sign a separate treaty.[25] The Germans felt in a stronger position, since they were counting on the coming spring offensive in the West to bring them victory. In response to the Russian demand that the Central Powers give the inhabitants of Poland and other Russian areas occupied by them the right to self-determination, Kühlmann tartly responded that these areas had already exercised this right by separating themselves from Russia.

Having reached a stalemate, the talks were adjourned on December 15/28, but the less publicized negotiations between "expert" legal and economic commissions went on.

Assessing the results, some Germans began to wonder whether the Russians desired peace or were merely playing for time to unleash social unrest in Western Europe. Certain Russian actions lent support to the skeptics. German intelligence intercepted a letter from Trotsky to a Swedish collaborator in which the Commissar of Foreign Affairs wrote that "a separate peace involving Russia is inconceivable; all that matters is to prolong the negotiations so as to screen the mobilization of international Social-Democratic forces promoting general peace."[26] As if to demonstrate that such indeed was its intention, on December 26, in an action without precedent in international relations, the Soviet Government officially allocated 2 million rubles to foreign groups supporting the Zimmerwald-Kiental platform.* Nor were German suspicions assuaged by Ioffe's demand that the German Government emulate the Soviet example by publishing the stenographic records of the political talks at Brest, which were designed, on the Russian side, to carry Bolshevik propaganda to German workers.

At this point, the German military stepped in. In a letter to the Kaiser on January 7 (December 25), which was to exert on him a strong influence, Hindenburg complained that the "weak" and "conciliatory" tactics pursued by the German diplomats at Brest had given the Russians the impression that Germany needed peace as badly as they did. This had a detrimental effect on army morale. Without spelling out what he had in mind, Hindenburg was alluding to the alarming effects of the policy of "fraternization" of Russian and German troops, promoted by the Bolsheviks along the armistice front. It was time to act forcefully: if Germany did not show determination in the east, how could she expect to impose on the Western Allies the kind of peace that her world position required? Germany should redraw the borders in the east in a manner that would prevent wars in the future.[27]

The Kaiser, who was also losing patience with the diplomatic shilly-shallying at Brest, agreed. As a result, the German position appreciably hardened: the pretense of a negotiated peace was given up in favor of a dictated one.

---

*Text: J. Degras, ed., *Documents on Russian Foreign Policy,* I (London, 1951), 22. The money was placed at the disposal of Vorovskii.

82. Russian and German troops fraternizing:
Winter 1917–18.

The Brest talks resumed on December 27/January 9. This time Trotsky
headed the Russian delegation: he came with the intention of continuing to
play for time and broadcasting propaganda. Lenin agreed to this strategy only
reluctantly. Trotsky had to promise that if the Germans saw through it and
presented an ultimatum, the Russian delegation would capitulate.[28]

On his arrival, Trotsky had the unpleasant surprise of learning that
during the recess in the negotiations, the Germans had established separate
channels of communication with Ukrainian nationalists. On December 19/
January 1, a Ukrainian delegation, composed of young intellectuals, had arrived in Brest at the Germans' invitation to open separate talks.[29] The German
objective was to detach the Ukraine and make it into a protectorate. In
December 1917, the Ukrainian Council, or Rada, had proclaimed Ukrainian
independence. The Bolsheviks refused to recognize this act and, in violation
of the right of "national self-determination" which they had officially proclaimed, sent a military force to reconquer the region.[30] The Germans estimated that Russia received one-third of her food and 70 percent of her coal
and iron from the Ukraine: her separation would appreciably weaken the
Bolsheviks, making them even more dependent on Germany, and, at the same
time, go a long way toward meeting Germany's own pressing economic needs.
Assuming the role of a traditional diplomat, Trotsky declared that the German
action was interference in his country's internal affairs, but that was all he
could do. On December 30/January 12, the Central Powers recognized the
Ukrainian Rada as that country's legitimate government. This was a prelude
to a separate peace treaty with the Ukraine.

Then came the presentation of German territorial claims. Kühlmann advised Trotsky that his country found the Russian demand for a peace "without annexations and contributions" unacceptable and intended to detach territories under German occupation. As concerned Czernin's offer to give up all conquests, this lost its validity since it had been conditional on the Allies joining in the peace talks, which they had not done. On January 5/18, General Max Hoffmann unfolded a map which showed the disbelieving Russians the new border between the two countries.[31] It called for the separation of Poland and German annexation of extensive territories in western Russia, including Lithuania and southern Latvia. Trotsky responded that his government found such demands absolutely unacceptable. On January 5/18, which happened to have been the very day when the Bolsheviks were dispersing the Constituent Assembly, he had the temerity to say that the Soviet Government "adheres to the view that where the issue at stake is the destiny of a newly formed nation, a referendum is the best means of expressing the will of the people."[32]

Trotsky communicated the German terms to Lenin, following which he requested an adjournment of the political talks for twelve days. He departed for Petrograd the same day, leaving Ioffe behind. How nervous the Germans were about this postponement may be gathered from the fact that in informing Berlin, Kühlmann urged that the Bolshevik request for an adjournment not be treated as a rupture of negotiations.[33] The Germans had reason to fear that a collapse of the peace negotiations could set off civil disturbances in the industrial centers of Germany. On January 28, a wave of political strikes organized by the left wing of the socialist movement and involving more than one million workers did break out in various parts of Germany, including Berlin, Hamburg, Bremen, Kiel, Leipzig, Munich, and Essen. Here and there "workers' councils" sprang up. The strikers called for peace without annexations and contributions and self-determination for the nations of Eastern Europe—that is, for the acceptance of Russian peace terms.[34] While there exists no evidence of direct Bolshevik involvement, the influence of Bolshevik propaganda on the strikers was obvious. The German authorities responded with vigorous, occasionally brutal repression: by February 3 they had the situation under control. But the strikes were troublesome evidence that, whatever happened at the front, the situation at home could not be taken for granted. People longed for peace and the Russians seemed to hold the key to it.

The German demands split the Bolshevik leadership into three contending factions, which subsequently merged into two.

The Bukharin faction wanted to break off the talks and continue military operations, mainly by means of partisan warfare, while fanning the flames of revolution in Germany. This position enjoyed great popularity in Bolshevik ranks: both the Petrograd and Moscow bureaus of the party passed resolutions in this spirit.[35] Bukharin's biographer believes that his policy, later labeled "Left Communism," reflected the wishes of the majority of Bolsheviks.[36] Bukharin and his adherents saw Western Europe on the brink of social revolution: since such a revolution was acknowledged as essential to the survival of the Bolshevik regime, peace with "imperialist" Germany struck them as not only immoral but self-defeating.

Trotsky headed a second faction, which differed from the Left Communists only in tactical nuances. Like Bukharin, he wanted the German ultimatum rejected, but in the name of an unorthodox slogan of "neither war nor peace." The Russians would break off the Brest talks and unilaterally declare the war at an end. The Germans then would be free to do what they wanted and what the Russians could not prevent them from doing in any event—annex vast territories on their western and southwestern frontier—but they would have to act without Russian complicity. This procedure, Trotsky maintained, would free the Bolsheviks from the burden of carrying on an unpopular war, reveal the brutality of German imperialism, and encourage German workers to revolt.

Lenin, supported by Kamenev, Zinoviev, and Stalin, opposed Bukharin and Trotsky. His sense of urgency and his belief that Russia was in no position to bargain received reinforcement from a report submitted to the Sovnarkom on December 31/January 13 by Krylenko, the Commissar of War. On the basis of responses to questionnaires distributed to delegates at the All-Army Conference on Demobilization, Krylenko concluded that the Russian army, or what was left of it, retained no combat capability.[37] Without an army worthy of the name, Lenin reasoned, one could not stand up to a disciplined and well-equipped enemy.

Lenin formulated his views on January 7/20 in "Theses on the question of the immediate conclusion of a separate and annexationist peace."[38] Here he made the following points:

1. Before its ultimate triumph, the Soviet regime faced a period of anarchy and civil war: it needed time for "socialist reorganization."

2. Russia required at least several months, "in the course of which the regime must have a completely free hand to triumph over the bourgeoisie, to begin with, in its own country" and to organize its forces.

3. Soviet policy must be determined by domestic considerations because of the uncertainty whether a revolution would break out abroad.

4. In Germany, the "military party" had gained the upper hand: Russia will be presented with an ultimatum demanding territorial concessions and financial contributions. The government has done everything in its power to prolong the negotiations but this tactic has run its course.

5. The opponents of an immediate peace on German terms wrongly argue that such a peace would violate the spirit of "proletarian internationalism." If the government decided to continue fighting the Germans, as they wished, it would have no alternative but to seek help from the other "imperialist bloc," the Entente, which would turn it into an agent of France and England.

Continuing the war thus was not an "anti-imperialist" move, because it called for a choice between two "imperialist" camps. The task of the regime, however, was not to choose between "imperialisms," but to consolidate power.

6. Russia indeed must promote revolutions abroad, but this cannot be done without account of the "correlation of forces": at present Russian armies are powerless to stop a German advance. Furthermore, the majority of Russia's "peasant" army favored the "annexationist" peace demanded by Germany.

7. If Russia persisted in its refusal to accept current German peace terms, it would eventually have to accept even more onerous ones: but this would be done not by the Bolsheviks but by their successors, because in the meantime the Bolsheviks would have been toppled from power.

8. A respite will give the government the opportunity to organize the economy (nationalize the banks and heavy industry), which "will make socialism invincible in Russia and the entire world, creating, at the same time, a solid economic basis for a powerful worker-peasant Red Army."

Lenin had another reason in mind which he could not spell out because it would have revealed that, notwithstanding his protestations, he really desired the World War to continue. He felt certain that as soon as the "bourgeoisie" of the Central Powers and the Entente made peace, they would join forces and attack Soviet Russia. He hinted at this danger during the debates on the Brest Treaty: "Our revolution was born of the war: if there were no war, we would have witnessed the unification of the capitalists of the whole world, a unification on the basis of a struggle against us."[39] Projecting his own political militancy, he gave his "enemies" much too much credit for astuteness and decisiveness: in fact, no such "unification" would occur after the November 1918 Armistice. But believing in the danger, he had to prolong the war in order to gain time for building an armed force able to withstand the expected "capitalist" assault.

On January 8/21, 1918, the Bolsheviks convened a conference of party leaders from three strongholds: Petrograd, Moscow, and the Ural region. Lenin presented a resolution calling for the acceptance of the German ultimatum: it received a bare fifteen votes out of sixty-three. Trotsky's compromise resolution in favor of "neither peace nor war" won sixteen votes. The majority (thirty-two delegates) voted for the resolution of the Left Communists, demanding an uncompromising "revolutionary war."*

The discussion next shifted to the Central Committee. Here, Trotsky moved for an immediate, unilateral suspension of hostilities and the concurrent demobilization of the Russian army. The motion carried with the barest majority, 9–7. Lenin responded with an impassioned speech in favor of an

---

*Lenin, *PSS,* XXXV, 478; *LS,* XI, 41; Winfried Baumgart, *Deutsche Ostpolitik 1918* (Vienna-Munich, 1966), 22. Stalin, who supported Lenin, said that a revolution in the West was not in sight. The protocols of this conference are said to have disappeared. Isaac Steinberg says that the Left SRs liked the "neither war nor peace" formula and had a hand in its formulation: *Als ich Volkskommissar war* (Munich, 1929), 190–92.

immediate peace on German terms,[40] but he remained in the minority, which dwindled still further the next day when the Bolshevik Central Committee met in joint session with the Central Committee of the Left SRs, who strenuously opposed Lenin's peace proposals. Here again Trotsky's resolution carried the day.

With this mandate in hand, Trotsky returned to Brest. The talks resumed on January 15/28. Trotsky continued playing for time with irrelevant remarks and propagandistic speeches, which now began to irritate even the self-possessed Kühlmann.

While Russo-German negotiations bogged down in rhetoric, the Germans and Austrians settled with the Ukrainians. On February 9, the Central Powers signed a separate peace treaty with the Ukrainian Republic which made it a de facto German protectorate.[41] German and Austrian troops moved into the Ukraine, where they restored a certain degree of law and order. Their price for this welcome action was massive shipments westward of Ukrainian foodstuffs.

The deadlock in the Russo-German political talks was broken by a cable which the Kaiser, under the influence of his generals, sent to Brest on February 9. In it he ordered an ultimatum to be given to the Russians:

Today, the Bolshevik Government has addressed my troops *en clair* [*klerom*] by radio, and urged them to rise and openly disobey their military superiors. Neither I nor His Excellency Field Marshal von Hindenburg can accept and tolerate any longer such a state of affairs! This must be ended as soon as possible! Trotsky must sign by 8 p.m. tomorrow, the 10th [of February] . . . , *without procrastination, peace* on *our* terms. . . . In the event of refusal or attempts at procrastination and other pretexts, the negotiations are broken off at eight o'clock on the night of the 10th [and] the armistice terminated. In this event, the armies of the Eastern Front will move forward to the preassigned line.[42]

The next day, Kühlmann advised Trotsky of his government's ultimatum: he was to sign, without further discussions or other delays, the German text of the peace treaty. Trotsky refused to do so, saying that Soviet Russia was leaving the war and would proceed to demobilize her armies.[43] The economic and legal discussions, however, which had in the meantime moved to Petrograd, could continue, if so desired. Trotsky then boarded his train and left for Petrograd.

Trotsky's unorthodox move threw the German rank into complete confusion. By now, no one doubted any longer that the Russians were using the peace talks as a diversion. But this conceded, it was by no means obvious how Germany should respond. Continue the fruitless negotiations? Compel the Bolsheviks by military action to accept her ultimatum? Or remove them from power and put in their place a more acceptable regime?

German diplomats counseled patience. Kühlmann feared that German workers would fail to understand the resumption of hostilities on the Eastern Front and would cause trouble. He further worried that Austria-Hungary would be forced out of the war.[44]

But the military, who in the winter of 1917–18 dominated German politics, had different ideas. Massing forces in the west for the decisive campaign scheduled for mid-March, they had to have perfect certainty that the Eastern Front was secure or they could not continue shifting troops to the Western Front. They also needed access to Russian foodstuffs and raw materials. Military intelligence from Russia indicated that the Bolsheviks had the worst intentions toward Germany but also that they were in a most precarious position. Walther von Kaiserlingk, the Admiralty's Chief of Operations, who went to Petrograd with Mirbach's mission, sent back alarming reports.[45] Having observed the Bolshevik regime at close quarters, he concluded it was "insanity in power" *(regierender Wahnsinn)*. Run by Jews for Jews, it presented a mortal threat not only to Germany but to the entire civilized world. He urged that the German-Russian frontier be shifted far to the east, to shield Germany from this plague. Kaiserlingk further proposed the penetration of Russia by German business interests: for the second time in her history (an allusion to the Normans) Russia was ready to be colonized. Other firsthand reports depicted the Bolshevik regime as weak and despised. Lenin was said to be exceedingly unpopular and protected from assassins more assiduously than any tsar. Kühlmann's sources indicated that the Bolsheviks' only support came from the Latvian Riflemen: if they were bought off, the regime would collapse.[46] Such eyewitness accounts strongly impressed the Kaiser and inclined him toward the generals' point of view.

Combining the information he received on the instability of the Bolshevik regime with evidence of its systematic campaign to demoralize the German army, Ludendorff, with Hindenburg's backing, urged that the Brest negotiations be broken off, following which the army would march into Russia, remove the Bolsheviks, and install in Petrograd a more acceptable government.[47]

The recommendations of the Foreign Ministry and the General Staff clashed at a conference at Bad Homburg on February 13 which the Kaiser chaired.[48] Kühlmann pressed the conciliatory line. The sword, he argued, could not eliminate "the center of the revolutionary plague." Even if German forces occupied Petrograd, the problem would not disappear: the French Revolution demonstrated that foreign intervention only inflamed nationalist and revolutionary passions. The best solution would be an anti-Bolshevik coup carried out by Russians with German assistance: but whether he favored such policy, Kühlmann did not say. The Foreign Minister received support from the Vice-Chancellor, Friedrich von Payer, who spoke of the widespread desire for peace among the German people and the impossibility of overthrowing the Bolsheviks by military force.

Hindenburg disagreed. Unless decisive steps were taken in the east, the war on the Western Front could drag on for a long time. He wanted to "smash the Russians [and] topple their government."

The Kaiser sided with the generals. Trotsky had come to Brest not to make peace, he said, but to promote revolution, and he did so with Allied support. The British envoy in Russia should be told that the Bolsheviks are enemies: "England should fight the Bolsheviks alongside the Germans. The Bolsheviks are tigers, they must be exterminated in every way."[49] In any event, Germany had to act, otherwise Britain and the United States would take over Russia. The Bolsheviks, therefore, "had to go." "The Russian people have been turned over to the vengeance of Jews, who are connected with all the Jews in the world—that is, the Freemasons."*

The conference decided that the armistice would expire on February 17, following which German armies would resume offensive operations against Russia. Their mission was not clearly spelled out. The military plan to overthrow the Bolsheviks was soon given up, however, because of the objections of the civilian authorities.

In accord with these instructions, the German staff at Brest informed the Russians that Germany would recommence military operations on the Eastern Front at noon, February 17. The Mirbach mission in Petrograd was ordered home.

Despite their bravado, it is by no means clear that the Germans knew what they wanted: whether to compel the Bolsheviks to accept their peace terms or to remove them from power. Neither then nor later were they able to decide on their priorities: whether they were primarily interested in seizing more Russian territory or installing in Russia a more conventional government. In the end, territorial greed prevailed.

The German notification of impending military action reached Petrograd on the afternoon of February 17. At the meeting of the Central Committee, which convened immediately, Lenin renewed his plea to return to Brest and capitulate, but he again suffered a narrow defeat, 6–5.[50] The majority wanted to wait and see whether the Germans would carry out their threat: if they indeed marched into Russia and no revolution broke out in Germany and Austria, there would still be time to bow to the inevitable.

The Germans were true to their word. On February 17, their troops advanced and occupied Dvinsk without encountering resistance. General Hoffmann described the operation as follows:

This is the most comic war that I have ever experienced—it is waged almost exclusively in trains and automobiles. One puts on the train a few infantry with machine guns and one artillery piece, and proceeds to the next railroad station,

*Sovetsko-Germanskie Otnosheniia ot peregovorov v Brest-Litovske do podpisaniia Rapall'skogo dogovora, I (Moscow, 1968), 328. Although inspired by Kaiserlingk's dispatches from Petrograd, this anti-Semitic remark echoed the so-called *Protocols of the Elders of Zion,* which was soon to become favorite reading fare of the simpleminded in quest of an "explanation" for the World War and Communism.

seizes it, arrests the Bolsheviks, entrains another detachment, and moves on. The procedure has in any event the charm of novelty.[51]

For Lenin, this was the last straw. Though it was not entirely unexpected, he was appalled by the passivity of Russian troops. Given their unwillingness to fight, Russia lay wide open to the enemy's advance. Lenin seems to have been in possession of the most sensitive decisions of the German Government, possibly supplied by German sympathizers through Bolshevik agents in Switzerland or Sweden. On the basis of this information, he concluded that the Germans contemplated taking Petrograd and even Moscow. He was infuriated by the smugness of his associates. As he saw it, there was nothing to prevent the Germans from repeating their coup in the Ukraine—that is, replacing him with a right-wing puppet and then suppressing the Revolution.

But when the Central Committee reassembled on February 18, he once again failed to win a majority. His resolution in favor of capitulation to the German demands received six votes against seven cast for the motion jointly presented by Trotsky and Bukharin. The party leadership was hopelessly deadlocked. There was a danger that the division would split the party's rank and file, destroying the disciplined unity which was its main source of strength.

At this juncture, Trotsky came to Lenin's assistance: switching sides, instead of supporting his own resolution he voted for Lenin's. Trotsky's biographer believes that he did so partly in fulfillment of a promise to Lenin to give in if the Germans invaded Russia and partly to avert what could have been a disastrous cleavage in the party.[52] When another vote was taken, seven members voted in favor of Lenin's motion and six opposed it.[53] On the basis of this slenderest of majorities, Lenin drafted a cable informing the Germans that the Russian delegation was returning to Brest.[54] Several Left SRs were shown the text, and when they approved it, it was transmitted by wireless.

Then came the shock. The Germans and Austrians, instead of immediately suspending their offensive, kept on advancing into Russia's interior. In the north German units entered Livonia, while in the center they moved, still unopposed, on Minsk and Pskov. In the south the Austrians and Hungarians also went forward. On the face of it, these operations, carried out after the Russians had signaled their readiness to accept German terms, could have only one meaning: Berlin was determined to seize the Russian capitals and topple the Bolsheviks. This was where Lenin drew the line: according to Isaac Steinberg, he said on February 18 that he would fight only if the Germans demanded of his government to give up power.[55]

Days passed and there was still no response from the advancing Germans. At this point, panic seized the Bolshevik leaders: they passed emergency measures, one of which was to have especially grave consequences. On February 21–22, still without a word from the Germans, Lenin wrote and signed a decree entitled "The socialist fatherland in danger."[56] Its preamble stated that the actions of the Germans indicated they had decided to suppress the socialist government of Russia and restore the monarchy. To defend the "socialist fatherland" urgent measures were required. Two of these turned out to have lasting consequences. One called for the creation of battalions of forced labor made up of "all able-bodied members of the bourgeois class" to dig trenches. Resisters were to be shot. This initiated the practice of forced labor, which in time would affect millions of citizens. Another clause read: "Enemy agents, speculators, burglars, hooligans, counterrevolutionary agitators, German spies, are to be executed on the spot." The provision introduced irrevocable penalties for crimes which were neither defined nor on the statute books, since all laws had by then been annulled.[57] Nothing was said about trials or even hearings for the accused liable to capital punishment. In effect, the decree gave the Cheka the license to kill, of which it soon made full use. The two clauses marked the opening phase of Communist terror.

Lenin had warned his colleagues that if the Germans resumed military operations, the Bolsheviks would have to seek French and English help, which is what they now proceeded to do.

Although the Germans could not decide which to give precedence, they at least drew a distinction between their short-term interests in Russia, connected with the war, and Russia's long-term geopolitical importance to them. The Allies had only one interest in Russia, and that was to keep her in the war. Russia's collapse and the prospect of a separate peace were for the Allies calamities of the first order, likely to lead to a German victory, for with dozens of divisions transferred to the west, the Germans could crush the exhausted French and British forces before the Americans arrived in significant numbers. For the Allies, therefore, the uppermost priority in regard to Russia was reactivating the Eastern Front, with Bolshevik cooperation, if possible, and if not, then with any other force available: anti-Bolshevik Russians, Japanese, Czech prisoners of war interned in Russian camps, or, as a last resort, their own troops. Who the Bolsheviks were, what they stood for, was of no concern to them: they showed interest neither in the internal policy of the Bolshevik regime nor in its international objectives, which increasingly preoccupied the Germans. Bolshevik "fraternization" policies, their appeals to workers to strike and soldiers to mutiny, found as yet no response in Allied countries and hence gave no cause for alarm there. The Allied attitude was clear and simple: the Bolshevik regime was an enemy if it made peace with the Central Powers, but a friend and ally if it stayed in the fight. In the words of Arthur Balfour, Britain's Foreign Secretary, as long as the Russians fought the Germans their cause was "our cause."[58] The U.S. Ambassador to Russia, David Francis, expressed the same sentiments in a message of January 2, 1918, meant for transmittal to Lenin's government, although never sent:

> If the Russian armies now under the command of the people's commissaires commence and seriously conduct hostilities against the forces of Germany and

her allies, I will recommend to my Government the formal recognition of the de facto government of the people's commissaires.[59]

Because of their lack of interest in the subject, the Allies possessed very inadequate information on the internal conditions in Bolshevik Russia. They were not particularly well served by their diplomatic missions there. George Buchanan, the British Ambassador, was a competent but conventional foreign service officer, while Francis, a St. Louis banker, was, in the words of a British diplomat, "a charming old gentleman" but presumably no more than that. Neither seems to have been aware of the historic importance of the events in the midst of which they found themselves. The French envoy, Joseph Noulens, an ex-Minister of War and a socialist, was intellectually better prepared for his job, but his dislike of Russians and his brusque, authoritarian manner reduced his effectiveness. To make matters worse, in March 1918, the Allied missions lost direct contact with the Bolshevik leaders because they would not follow them to Moscow: from Petrograd they moved first to Vologda, and from there, in July, to Archangel.* This obliged them to rely on secondhand reports provided by their agents in Moscow.

The latter were young men who threw themselves body and soul into the Russian drama. Bruce Lockhart, a onetime British Consul in Moscow, served as a link between London and the Sovnarkom; Raymond Robins, head of the U.S. Red Cross mission to Russia, did the same for Washington; and Captain Jacques Sadoul, for Paris. The Bolsheviks did not take these intermediaries terribly seriously, but they realized their utility: they cultivated and flattered them, and treated them as confidants. In this manner they managed to persuade Lockhart, Robins, and Sadoul that if their countries offered Russia military and economic aid, the Bolsheviks would break with the Germans and perhaps even return to the war. Unaware that they were being used, the three agents adopted these views as their own and championed them vigorously with their governments.

Sadoul, a socialist, whose mother had taken part in the Paris Commune, felt the strongest ideological attraction for the Bolsheviks: in August 1918 he would defect to them, for which he would be condemned to death in absentia as a deserter and traitor.†

Robins was a devious individual who in his communications with Lenin and Trotsky expressed enthusiasm for their cause but on returning to the United States pretended to oppose Bolshevism. An affluent social worker and labor organizer with socialist leanings, the self-styled colonel, on the eve of his departure from Russia, sent Lenin a farewell note in which he wrote:

*Each of the three Allied ambassadors left memoirs: George Buchanan, *My Mission to Russia*, 2 vols. (London, 1923); David Francis, *Russia from the American Embassy* (New York, 1921); and Joseph Noulens, *Mon Ambassade en Russie Soviétique*, 2 vols. (Paris, 1933).

†The sentence was not carried out after Sadoul had returned home and joined the French Communist Party. His revolutionary experiences are recorded in an interesting book, first published in Moscow, in the form of letters to Albert Thoma: *Notes sur la Révolution Bolchevique* (Paris, 1920), supplemented by *Quarante Lettres de Jacques Sadoul* (Paris, 1922).

Your prophetic insight and genius of leadership have enabled the Soviet Power to become consolidated throughout Russia and I am confident that this new creative organ of the democratic life of mankind will inspire and advance the cause of liberty throughout the world.*

He further promised, on his return, to "continue efforts" in interpreting "the new democracy" to the American people. However, testifying soon afterward before a Senate committee on conditions in Soviet Russia, Robins urged economic assistance to Moscow on the disingenuous grounds that it was a way of "disorganizing Bolshevik power."†

Lockhart was ideologically the least committed of the three, but he, too, allowed himself to be turned into an instrument of Bolshevik policy.‡

Sadoul and Robins had met occasionally with Lenin, Trotsky, and the other Communist leaders after the Bolshevik coup. These contacts multiplied in the second half of February 1918, during the interval between the Bolshevik acceptance of the German ultimatum (February 17) and the ratification of the Brest-Litovsk Treaty (March 14). During these two weeks, the Bolsheviks, afraid that the Germans wanted to remove them from power, put out urgent appeals to the Allies for help. The Allies responded positively. The French were especially forthcoming. They abandoned now the anti-Bolshevik Volunteer Army being formed in the Don Region, which Noulens had supported financially because of its anti-German stand: on his recommendation the French Government had previously contributed 50 million rubles to General Alekseev to help organize a new Russian army. At the beginning of January 1918, General Henri Niessel, the new head of the French military mission in Russia, advised cutting off Alekseev on the grounds that he headed a "counterrevolutionary" force. The advice was adopted: assistance to Alekseev was terminated and Niessel received authority to open negotiations with the Bolsheviks.§ Lockhart similarly opposed support for the Volunteer Army, which he, too, depicted in dispatches to the Foreign Office as counterrevolutionary. In his judgment, the Bolsheviks were the most reliable anti-German force in Russia.[60]

*Letter dated April 25, 1918, in the Raymond Robins Collection, State Historical Society of Wisconsin, Madison, Wisconsin. In responding, Lenin expressed confidence that "proletarian democracy . . . will crush . . . the imperialist-capitalist system in the New and Old Worlds": Ministerstvo Inostrannykh Del SSSR, *Dokumenty vneshnei politiki SSSR,* I (Moscow, 1957), 276.

†George F. Kennan, *The Decision to Intervene* (Princeton, N.J., 1958), 237–38. In light of the above evidence it is difficult to agree with Kennan that Robins's "feelings with respect to the Soviet government did not rest on any partiality to socialism as a doctrine" or that he entertained no "predilection for communist ideology": *Ibid,* 240–41. Robins later eulogized Stalin and was received by him in 1933. See Anne Vincent Meiburger, *Efforts of Raymond Robins Toward the Recognition of Soviet Russia and the Outlawry of War, 1917–1933* (Washington, D.C., 1958), 193–99.

‡See his *Memoirs of a British Agent* (London, 1935) and *The Two Revolutions: An Eyewitness Account* (London, 1967).

§A. Hogenhuis-Seliverstoff, *Les Relations Franco-Soviétiques, 1917–1924* (Paris, 1981), 53. Niessel does not mention these facts in his memoirs, *Le Triomphe des Bolcheviks.*

During the hectic days that followed the resumption of German offensive operations, the Bolshevik high command decided to seek Allied help. On February 21, Trotsky communicated, through Sadoul, with Niessel to inquire whether France would be willing to help Soviet Russia stop the German offensive. Niessel contacted the French Ambassador, and received an affirmative response. That day Noulens cabled Trotsky from Vologda: "In your resistance to Germany you may count on the military and financial cooperation of France."[61] Niessel advised Trotsky on the measures Soviet Russia should take to impede the Germans and promised military advisers.

The French response was discussed by the Central Committee late in the evening of February 22. By this time Trotsky was in possession of a memorandum from Niessel outlining the measures which France was prepared to take to help the Russians.[62] The document, said to be lost, contained concrete proposals of French monetary and military aid. Trotsky urged acceptance and moved a resolution to this effect. Lenin, who could not attend, voted in absentia with a laconic note: "Please add my vote in favor of taking 'tatoes and weapons from the bandits of Anglo-French imperialism."[63] The motion barely passed, with six votes for and five against, because of the opposition of Bukharin and the other advocates of "revolutionary war." After he was defeated, Bukharin offered to resign from the Central Committee and the editorship of *Pravda,* but did neither.

As soon as the Central Committee had ended its deliberations—it was during the night of February 22–23—the issue was put before the Sovnarkom. Here Trotsky's motion carried as well, over the objections of the Left SRs.

The following day, Trotsky informed Sadoul of his government's readiness to accept French help. He invited Niessel to Smolnyi to consult with Podvoiskii, General Bonch-Bruevich, and other Bolshevik military experts on anti-German operations. Niessel was of the opinion that Soviet Russia had to form a fresh military force with the assistance of former tsarist officers, secured by appeals to patriotism.[64]

The Bolsheviks now positioned themselves to switch sides in the event the Germans tried to topple them. They knew that the Allies paid little attention to their policies at home and abroad and would give them generous help in return for a reactivation of the Eastern Front. There can be little doubt that if the Germans had followed through on the recommendations of Ludendorff and Hindenburg, the Bolsheviks, in order to stay in power, would have made common cause with the Allies and allowed them the use of Russian territory for military operations against the Central Powers.

It is indicative of how far along Russo-Allied cooperation had progressed that late in February Lenin dispatched Kamenev to Paris as Soviet "diplomatic representative." Kamenev traveled by way of London, arriving already after his government had ratified the Brest Treaty. He had a chilly reception. France refused him entry, following which he headed back home. En route to Russia he was intercepted by the Germans, who detained him for four months.[65]

Whether the Germans had gotten wind of Bolshevik negotiations with France or by mere coincidence, it so happened that their impatiently awaited response arrived on the very morning the Central Committee and the Sovnarkom had voted to seek Allied help.[66] It confirmed Lenin's worst fears. Berlin now demanded not only the territories that its troops had seized in the course of the war but also those they had occupied in the week following the breakdown of the Brest negotiations. The Russians were to evacuate the Ukraine and Finland, as well as demobilize; they were to pay a contribution and make a variety of economic concessions. The note was phrased as an ultimatum requiring an answer within forty-eight hours, following which a maximum of seventy-two hours was allowed for the treaty to be signed.

The next two days, the Bolshevik leadership sat in virtually continuous session. Lenin found himself time and again in a minority. He eventually prevailed only by threatening to resign from all posts in the party and government.

As soon as he had read the German note, Lenin convened the Central Committee. Fifteen members turned up.[67] The German ultimatum had to be accepted unconditionally, he said: "The politics of revolutionary phrasemongering have come to an end." The main thing was that the German demands, humiliating as they were, "did not affect Soviet authority"—that is, they allowed the Bolsheviks to stay in power. If his colleagues persisted in their unrealistic course of action, they would have to do so on their own, because he, Lenin, would leave both the government and the Central Committee.

He then presented three cleverly worded resolutions: (1) that the latest German ultimatum be accepted, (2) that Russia make immediate preparations to unleash a revolutionary war, and (3) that the soviets in Moscow, Petrograd, and the other cities be polled on their views of the matter.

Lenin's threat to resign worked: everyone realized that without him there would be neither a Bolshevik Party nor a Soviet state. On the first and critical resolution, he failed to win a majority, but because four members abstained, the motion carried 7–4. The second and third resolutions presented no problem. The tally over, Bukharin and three other Left Communists once again went through the motions of resigning from all "responsible posts" in the party and government so as to be free to agitate against the treaty inside and outside party circles.

Although the decision to accept the German ultimatum still required approval from the Central Executive Committee, Lenin felt sufficiently confident of the outcome to instruct the operators of the wireless transmitter at Tsarskoe Selo to keep one channel open for a message to the Germans.

That night Lenin gave the CEC a report on the situation.[68] In the voting that followed he won a technical victory for his resolution to accept the German ultimatum, but only because the Bolshevik members who opposed it had walked out and a number of the other opponents abstained. The final count was 116 for Lenin's resolution, 85 opposed, and 26 abstaining. On the basis of this far from satisfactory, but formally binding outcome, Lenin drafted in the early hours of the morning, in the name of the Central Executive Committee, an unconditional acceptance of the German ultimatum. It was at once communicated by wireless to the Germans.

In the morning of February 24, the Central Committee met to choose a delegation to go to Brest.[69] Now numerous resignations from state and party posts were handed in. Trotsky, who had already quit as Commissar of Foreign Affairs, now gave up his other posts as well. He favored a closer relationship with the French and British on the grounds that they were anxious to collaborate with Soviet Russia and had no designs on her territory. Several Left Communists followed the example of Bukharin and turned in their resignations. They spelled out their motives in an open letter. Capitulation to German demands, they wrote, dealt a heavy blow to the revolutionary forces abroad and isolated the Russian Revolution. Furthermore, the concessions which the Russians were required to make to German capitalism would have a catastrophic effect on socialism in Russia: "Surrender of the proletariat's position externally inevitably paves the way for an internal surrender." The Bolsheviks should neither capitulate to the Central Powers nor collaborate with the Allies, but "initiate a civil war on an international scale."[70]

Lenin, who had gotten what he wanted, pleaded with Trotsky and the Left Communists not to act on their resignations until after the Soviet delegation had returned from Brest. Throughout these trying days he displayed brilliant leadership, alternately cajoling and persuading his followers, never losing either patience or determination. It was probably the hardest political struggle of his life.

Who would go to Brest to sign the shameful *Diktat?* No one wanted his name associated with the most humiliating treaty in Russian history. Ioffe flatly refused, while Trotsky, having resigned, removed himself from the picture. G. Ia. Sokolnikov, an old Bolshevik and onetime editor of *Pravda,* nominated Zinoviev, whereupon Zinoviev reciprocated by nominating Sokolnikov.[71] Sokolnikov responded that if appointed he would quit the Central Committee. Eventually, however, he let himself be talked into accepting the chairmanship of the Russian peace delegation, which included L. M. Petrovskii, G. V. Chicherin, and L. M. Karakhan. The delegation departed for Brest on February 24.

How intense the opposition to the decision to capitulate to the Germans was even in Lenin's own ranks is indicated by the fact that on February 24 the Moscow Regional Bureau of the Bolshevik Party rejected the Brest Treaty and unanimously passed a vote of no confidence in the Central Committee.[72]

Notwithstanding the Russian capitulation, the German armies continued to move forward, toward a demarcation line drawn up by their command and intended as the permanent border between the two countries. On February 24 they occupied Dorpat (Iurev) and Pskov and positioned themselves some 250 kilometers from the Russian capital. The following day they took Revel and Borisov. They kept on advancing even after the Russian delegation had arrived in Brest: on February 28, the Austrians seized Berdichev, and on March 1, the Germans occupied Gomel, following which they went on to take Chernigov and Mogilev. On March 2, German planes dropped bombs on Petrograd.

Lenin took no chances—"there was not a shadow of doubt" that the Germans intended to occupy Petrograd, he said on March 7[73]—and ordered the evacuation of the government to Moscow. According to General Niessel, the removal of matériel from Petrograd was done with the help of specialists provided by the French military mission.[74] Without an official decree to this effect being issued, at the beginning of March the commissariats began to transfer to the ancient capital. An article titled "Flight" in *Novaia zhizn'* of March 9 depicted Petrograd in the grip of panic, its inhabitants jamming railway stations and, if unable to get on a train, escaping by cart or on foot. The city soon came to a standstill: there was no electric power, no fuel, no medical service; schools and city transport ceased functioning. Shootings and lynchings were a daily occurrence.[75]

Given the exposed position of Petrograd and the uncertainty regarding the intentions of the Germans, the decision to transfer the capital of the Communist state to Moscow made good sense. But one cannot quite forget that when the Provisional Government, for the same reasons, contemplated evacuating Petrograd half a year earlier, no one accused it of treason more vehemently than the same Bolsheviks.

The transfer was carried out under heavy security precautions. Top party and state officials were the first to go, including members of the Central Committee, Bolshevik trade union officials, and editors of Communist newspapers. In Moscow they moved into requisitioned private properties.

Lenin sneaked out of Petrograd at night on March 10–11, accompanied by his wife and his secretary, Bonch-Bruevich.[76] The journey was organized in the deepest secrecy. The party traveled by special train, guarded by Latvians. In the early hours of the morning, having run into a trainload of deserters whose intentions were not clear, it stopped while Bonch-Bruevich arranged to have them disarmed. The train then went on, arriving in Moscow late in the evening. No one had been told of the trip, and the self-styled leader of the world's proletariat slunk into the capital as no tsar had ever done, welcomed only by a sister.

Lenin established his residence as well as his office in the Kremlin. Here, behind the stone walls and heavy gates of the fortress constructed in the fifteenth century by Italian architects, was the new seat of the Bolshevik Government. The People's Commissars with their families also sought safety behind the Kremlin walls. The security of this fortress was entrusted to the Latvians, who expelled from the Kremlin many residents, including a group of monks.

Although it was taken out of considerations of security, Lenin's decision to transfer Russia's capital to Moscow and install himself in the Kremlin had deep significance. It symbolized, as it were, the rejection of the pro-Western course initiated by Peter I in favor of the older Muscovite tradition. Though declared "temporary," it became permanent. It also reflected the new leaders' morbid fear for their personal safety. To appreciate the significance of these actions one must imagine a British Prime Minister moving out of Downing Street and transferring his residence and office as well as those of his ministers to the Tower of London to govern from there under the protection of Sikhs.

The Russians reached Brest on March 1 and two days later, without further discussion, signed the German treaty.

The terms were exceedingly onerous. They give an idea of the kind of peace treaty that awaited the Allies had they lost the war, and demonstrate how baseless were German complaints about the Versailles *Diktat,* which was in every respect milder than the treaty that they had forced on helpless Russia.

Russia was required to make major territorial concessions which cost her most of the conquests made since the middle of the seventeenth century: in the west, northwest, and southwest her borders now shrank to those of the Muscovite state. She had to give up Poland and Finland, Estonia, Latvia, and Lithuania, as well as Transcaucasia, all of which either became sovereign states under a German protectorate or were incorporated into Germany. Moscow also had to recognize the Ukraine as an independent republic.* These provisions called for the surrender of 750,000 square kilometers, an area nearly twice that of the German Empire: by virtue of Brest, Germany tripled in size.[77]

The ceded territories, which Russia had conquered from Sweden and Poland, contained her richest and most populous lands. Here lived 26 percent of her inhabitants, including more than one-third of the urban population. By contemporary estimates,[78] these areas accounted for 37 percent of Russia's agricultural harvest. Here were located 28 percent of her industrial enterprises, 26 percent of her railway tracks, and three-quarters of her coal and iron deposits.

But even more galling to most Russians were the economic clauses spelled out in the appendices which granted Germans exceptional status in Soviet Russia.[79] Many Russians believed that the Germans intended to avail themselves of these rights not only to gain economic benefits but to strangle Russian socialism. In theory, these rights were reciprocal, but Russia was in no position to claim her share.

---

*In fulfillment of the peace terms, in mid-April Moscow proposed to the Ukrainian Government the opening of negotiations leading to mutual recognition. For various reasons having to do with internal Ukrainian politics, these negotiations got underway only on May 23. On June 14, 1918, the governments of Soviet Russia and the Ukrainian Republic signed a provisional peace treaty, which was to be followed by final peace negotiations, but these never took place: *The New York Times,* June 16, 1918, 3.

Citizens and corporations of the Central Powers received de facto exemption from the nationalization decrees which the Bolshevik authorities had passed since coming to power, being allowed to hold in Soviet Russia movable and immovable property as well as to pursue on her territory commercial, industrial, and professional activities. They could repatriate assets from Soviet Russia without paying punitive taxes. The ruling was retroactive: the real estate and the rights to exploit land and mines requisitioned from citizens of the signatory powers during the war were to be restored to their owners; if nationalized, the owners were to be adequately compensated. The same rule applied to the holders of securities of the nationalized enterprises. Provisions were made for the free transit of commercial goods from one country to the other, each of which also granted the other most favored nation status. Setting aside the January 1918 decree which repudiated Russian public and private debts, the Soviet Government acknowledged the obligation to honor such debts in regard to the Central Powers and to resume payments of interest on them, the terms to be determined by separate accords.

These provisions gave the Central Powers—in effect, Germany—unprecedented extraterritorial privileges in Soviet Russia, exempting them from her economic regime and allowing them to engage in private enterprise in what was increasingly becoming a socialized economy. The Germans, in effect, became co-proprietors of Russia; they were in a position to take over the private sector, while the Russian Government was left to manage the nationalized sector. Under the terms of the treaty it was possible for owners of Russian industrial enterprises, banks, and securities to sell their holdings to Germans, in this manner removing them from Communist control. As we shall see, to foreclose this possibility, in June 1918 the Bolsheviks nationalized all large Soviet industries.

Elsewhere in the treaty the Russians committed themselves to demobilize their army and navy—in other words, to remain defenseless; to desist from agitation and propaganda against the governments, public institutions, and armed forces of the other signatories; and to respect the sovereignty of Afghanistan and Persia.

When the Soviet Government made the terms of the Brest Treaty known to its citizens—and it did that with some delay, so fearful was it of the public reaction—there was outrage from the entire political spectrum, from the extreme left to the extreme right. According to John Wheeler-Bennett, Lenin became the most vilified man in Europe.[80] Count Mirbach, the first German Ambassador to Soviet Russia, cabled the Foreign Office in May that the Russians to a man rejected the treaty, finding it even more repugnant than the Bolshevik dictatorship:

> Although Bolshevik domination afflicts Russia with hunger, crimes, and silent executions in a horror for which there is no name, no Russian would even pretend to be willing to purchase German help against the Bolsheviks with the acceptance of the Brest Treaty.[81]

No Russian government had ever surrendered so much land or allowed a foreign power such privileges. Russia had not only "sold out the international proletariat": it had gone a long way toward turning herself into a German colony. It was widely expected—with glee in conservative circles and with rage in radical ones—that the Germans would use the rights given them in the treaty to restore free enterprise in Russia. Thus, in mid-March rumors circulated in Petrograd that the Germans were demanding the return to their owners of three nationalized banks and that before long all banks would be denationalized.

The constitutional law of the new state called for the treaty to be ratified by the Congress of Soviets in two weeks. The congress which was to do this was scheduled to convene in Moscow on March 14.

Although he had met all their conditions, Lenin still did not trust the Germans. He was well informed about the divisions within the German Government and knew that the generals insisted on his removal. He felt it prudent, therefore, to maintain contact with the Allies and to hold out the promise of a radical shift in his government's foreign policy in their favor.

After the Brest Treaty had been signed but before it was ratified, Trotsky handed Robins a note for transmittal to the U.S. Government:

In case (a) the All-Russian Congress of the Soviets will refuse to ratify the peace treaty with Germany, or (b) if the German Government, breaking the peace treaty, will renew the offensive in order to continue its robbers' raid, or (c) if the Soviet Government will be forced by the actions of Germany to renounce the peace treaty—before or after its ratification—and to renew hostilities—

In all these cases, it is very important for the military and political plans of the Soviet power for replies to be given to the following questions:

1. Can the Soviet Government rely on the support of the United States of North America, Great Britain, and France in its struggle against Germany?

2. What kind of support could be furnished in the nearest future, and on what conditions—military equipment, transportation supplies, living necessities?

3. What kind of support would be furnished particularly and especially by the United States?

Should Japan—in consequence of an open or tacit understanding with Germany or without such an understanding—attempt to seize Vladivostok and the Eastern Siberian Railway, which would threaten to cut off Russia from the Pacific Ocean and would greatly impede the concentration of Soviet troops toward the east about the Urals—in such case what steps would be taken by the other allies, particularly and especially by the United States, to prevent a Japanese landing on our Far East and to insure uninterrupted communications with Russia through the Siberian route?

In the opinion of the Government of the United States, to what extent—under the above-mentioned circumstances—would aid be assured from Great

Britain through Murmansk and Archangel? What steps could the Government
of Great Britain undertake in order to assure this aid and thereby to undermine
the foundation of the rumors of the hostile plans against Russia on the part of
Great Britain in the nearest future?

All these questions are conditioned with the self-understood assumption
that the internal and foreign policies of the Soviet Government will continue
to be directed in accord with the principles of international socialism and that
the Soviet Government retains its complete independence of all non-socialist
governments.[82]

The last paragraph of the note meant that the Bolsheviks reserved the right
to work for the overthrow of the very governments from which they were
soliciting help.

On the day when he handed the above note to Robins, Trotsky talked with
Bruce Lockhart.[83] He told the British agent that the forthcoming Congress of
Soviets would probably refuse to ratify the Brest Treaty and would declare war
on Germany. But for this to happen, the Allies had to offer Soviet Russia
support. Then, alluding to proposals circulating in Allied capitals of massive
landings of Japanese expeditionary forces in Siberia to engage the Germans,
Trotsky said that such a violation of Russian sovereignty would destroy any
possibility of a rapprochement with the Allies. Informing London of Trotsky's
remarks, Lockhart said that these proposals offered the best opportunity of
reactivating the Eastern Front. U.S. Ambassador Francis concurred: he cabled
Washington that if the Allies could prevail on the Japanese to give up their
plans for landings in Siberia, the Congress of Soviets would probably turn
down the Brest Treaty.[84]

There was, of course, not the remotest possibility that the Congress of
Soviets, packed with the customary Bolshevik majority, would dare to deprive
Lenin of his hard-won victory. The Bolsheviks used the bait to prevent something they genuinely feared—namely, occupation of Siberia by the Japanese
and their intervention in Russian affairs on the side of the anti-Bolshevik
forces. According to Noulens, the Bolsheviks had such confidence in Lockhart
that they permitted him to communicate with London in code, which even
official foreign missions were prohibited from doing.[85]

The first concrete result of the rapprochement with the Allies was the
landing on March 9 of a small Allied contingent at Murmansk. Since 1916,
nearly 600,000 tons of war matériel sent to the Russian armies, much of it
unpaid for, had accumulated here from lack of transport to move it inland.
The Allies feared that this matériel might fall into German hands as a result
of Brest-Litovsk or the capture of Murmansk by German-Finnish forces. They
also worried about the Germans seizing nearby Pechenga (Petsamo) and
constructing a submarine base there.

The initial request for Allied protection came from the Murmansk Soviet,
which on March 5 cabled Petrograd that "Finnish White Guards," apparently
assisted by German forces, were making preparations to attack Murmansk.
The soviet contacted a British naval force and at the same time requested

Petrograd for authorization to invite Allied intervention. Trotsky informed the Murmansk Soviet that it was free to accept Allied military assistance.[86] Thus, the first Western involvement on Russian soil occurred at the request of the Murmansk Soviet and with the approval of the Soviet Government. In a speech which he delivered on May 14, 1918, Lenin explained that the British and French had landed "to defend the Murmansk coast."[87]

The Allied party which disembarked at Murmansk consisted of 150 British sailors and a few Frenchmen as well as several hundred Czechs.[88] In the weeks that followed, Britain was in constant communication with Moscow on the subject of Murmansk: unfortunately, the contents of these communications have not been revealed. The two parties cooperated to prevent the Germans and Finns from seizing this important port. Later, under German pressure, Moscow issued protests against the Allied presence on Russian soil, but Sadoul, who was in close contact with Trotsky, advised his government not to take them to heart:

> Lenin, Trotsky, Chicherin accept, under the present circumstances, that is, in the hope of an entente with the Allies, the Anglo-French landings at Murmansk and Archangel, it being understood that in order to prevent giving the Germans an excuse for protesting this certain violation of the peace treaty, they themselves will address a purely formal protest to the Allies. They marvelously understand that it is necessary to protect the northern ports and the railroads leading there from German-Finnish ventures.[89]

On the eve of the Fourth Congress of Soviets, the Bolsheviks held the Seventh (Extraordinary) Congress of their party (March 6–8). The agenda of this hastily convened meeting of forty-six delegates centered on Brest-Litovsk. The discussions in the intimate circle of the initiated, especially Lenin's defense of his unpopular position, provide a rare insight into Communist attitudes toward international law and relations with other countries.

Lenin vigorously defended himself against the Left Communists.[90] He surveyed the recent past, reminding his audience how easy it had been to seize power in Russia and how difficult to organize it. One could not simply transfer the methods which had proven so effective in the capture of power to the arduous task of administration. He acknowledged that there could be no lasting peace with the "capitalist" countries and that it was essential to spread the revolution abroad. But one had to be realistic: not every industrial strike in the West spelled revolution. In a very un-Marxist aside, he conceded that it was far more difficult to make revolution in democratic and capitalist countries than in backward Russia.

All this was familiar. Novel were some of Lenin's candid reflections on the subject of war and peace. To an audience that feared that he had made perpetual peace with a leading "imperialist" power he gave reassurances. First, the Soviet Government had every intention of violating the provisions of the Brest Treaty: in fact, it had already done so "thirty or forty times" (in a mere three days!). Nor did peace with the Central Powers signify abandonment of the class struggle. Peace was by its nature transitory, an "opportunity to gather strength": "History teaches that peace is a breathing space for war." In other words, war is the normal condition, peace a respite: there could be no lasting peace with non-Communist countries but only a temporary suspension of hostilities, a truce. Even while the peace treaty was in force, Lenin went on, the Soviet Government—in disregard of its provisions—would organize a new and effective military force. Thus, Lenin comforted his followers, the peace treaty they were asked to approve was merely a detour on the road to global revolution.

The Left Communists restated their objections,[91] but failed to muster enough votes. The motion, approving the treaty, passed 28–9 with one abstention. Lenin then asked the Party Congress to pass a secret resolution, not subject to publication for an indefinite period, giving the Central Committee "the authority at any time to annul all peace treaties with imperialist and bourgeois governments and, in like manner, to declare war on them."[92] Readily approved and never formally rescinded, this resolution empowered the handful of men in the Bolshevik Central Committee, at their own discretion, to break all international agreements entered into by their government and to declare war on any and all foreign countries.

There still remained the formality of ratification. Notwithstanding the sham apprehensions Trotsky had confided to the Allied representatives, the issue was never in doubt. The congress was not a democratically elected body but an assembly of initiates: of the 1,100 to 1,200 delegates who gathered on March 14, two-thirds were Bolsheviks. Lenin delivered his standard defense of the treaty in two long-winded and rambling speeches—they were those of a thoroughly exhausted man—in which he pleaded for realism.

He was impatiently awaiting a response to his requests to the United States and British governments for economic and military assistance: he knew full well that as soon as the treaty had been ratified the chances of procuring it were nil.

In the early years of Bolshevik power, knowledge of Russia and interest in Russia's affairs were in direct proportion to a country's geographic proximity to her. The Germans, who lived closest, despised and feared the Bolsheviks even as they were dealing with them. France and England were not terribly concerned about the actions and intentions of the Bolsheviks, as long as they stayed in the war. The United States, an ocean away, seemed positively to welcome the Bolshevik regime, and in the months that followed the October coup, lured by fantastic visions of large-scale business opportunities, sought to ingratiate herself with its leaders.

Woodrow Wilson seems to have believed that the Bolsheviks truly spoke for the Russian people,[93] and formed a detachment of that grand international army that he imagined advancing toward universal democracy and eternal peace. Their appeals to the "peoples" of the world, he felt, required an answer. This he provided in the speech of January 8, 1918, in which he presented the celebrated Fourteen Points. He went out of his way to praise Bolshevik behavior at Brest:

> There is . . . a voice calling for these definitions of principle and of purpose which is, it seems to me, more thrilling and more compelling than any of the many moving voices with which the troubled air of the world is filled. It is the voice of the Russian people. They are prostrate and all but helpless, it would seem, before the grim power of Germany, which has hitherto known no relenting and no pity. Their power, apparently, is shattered. And yet their soul is not subservient. They will not yield either in principle or in action. Their conception of what is right, of what it is humane and honorable for them to accept, has been stated with a frankness, a largeness of view, a generosity of spirit, and a universal human sympathy which must challenge the admiration of every friend of mankind; and they have refused to compound their ideas or desert others that they themselves may be safe. They call to us to say what it is that we desire, in what, if in anything, our purposes and our spirit differ from theirs; and I believe that the people of the United States would wish me to respond, with utter simplicity and frankness. Whether their present leaders believe it or not, it is our heartfelt desire and hope that some way may be opened whereby we may be privileged to assist the people of Russia to attain their utmost hope of liberty and ordered peace.[94]

There existed one potentially serious obstacle to Bolshevik-Allied cooperation, and that was the issue of Russian debts. As noted, in January the Bolshevik Government defaulted on all Russian state obligations to both domestic and foreign lenders.[95] The Bolsheviks took this step with considerable trepidation: they feared that such a violation of international law, involving billions of dollars, could spark a "capitalist crusade." But the widespread expectation of an imminent revolution in the West overcame caution and the deed was done.

There was no revolution in the West and no anti-Bolshevik crusade. The Western powers took this fresh assault on international law surprisingly calmly. Indeed, the Americans went out of their way to assure the Bolsheviks they had nothing to fear from them. Iurii Larin, Lenin's closest economic adviser, had a visit from the American Consul in Petrograd, who told him that while the United States could not accept "in principle" the annulment of international loans, it was ready

> to accept it de facto, not to demand payment, and to open relations with Russia as if it were a state that had just made its appearance in the world. In particular, the United States could offer us [Soviet Russia] large-scale commercial credit, on the account of which Russia could draw from America machines and raw materials of all kinds with delivery to Murmansk, Archangel, or Vladivostok.

To ensure repayment, the U.S. Consul suggested, Soviet Russia might consider depositing some gold in neutral Sweden and granting the United States concessions in Kamchatka.[96]

What more proof was needed that one could do business with the "imperialist robbers" even while inciting their citizens to revolution? And why not play the business community of one country against that of another? Or pit capitalist industrialists and bankers against the military? The possibilities of such *divide et impera* policies were endless. And, indeed, the Bolsheviks would exploit to the fullest these opportunities to compensate for their appalling weakness, luring foreign powers with prospects of industrial imports in exchange for food and raw materials which they did not have, even as their own population was starving and freezing.

Every message which the U.S. Government transmitted to the Bolshevik authorities in the early months of 1918 conveyed the sense that Washington took at face value the Bolsheviks' professions of democratic and peaceful intentions and ignored their calls for world revolution. Hence Lenin and Trotsky had good reason to expect a positive response to their appeal to Washington for help.

The impatiently awaited American response to the inquiry of March 5 arrived on the opening day of the Fourth Congress of Soviets (March 14). Robins handed it to Lenin, who had it immediately published in *Pravda*. It was a noncommittal note, addressed not to the Soviet Government but to the Congress of Soviets, presumably on the assumption that this body was the equivalent of the U.S. legislature. It refused for the present to grant Soviet Russia aid, but accorded the regime something close to informal recognition. The American President wrote:

> May I now take advantage of the meeting of the Congress of the Soviets to express the sincere sympathy which the people of the United States feel for the Russian people at this moment when the German power has been thrust in to interrupt and turn back the whole struggle for freedom and substitute the wishes of Germany for the purpose of the people of Russia?
>
> Although the government of the United States is, unhappily, not now in a position to render the direct and effective aid it would wish to render, I beg to assure the people of Russia through the congress that it will avail itself of every opportunity to secure for Russia once more complete sovereignty and independence in her own affairs, and full restoration to her great role in the life of Europe and the modern world.
>
> The whole heart of the people of the United States is with the people of Russia in the attempt to free themselves forever from autocratic government and become the masters of their own life.
>
> Woodrow Wilson
>
> Washington, March 11, 1918[97]

The British Government reacted in a like spirit.[98]

This was not what the Bolsheviks had expected: they had overestimated their ability to play one "imperialist" camp against the other. Hoping that perhaps Wilson's cable was only the first installment, with more to come, Lenin kept on badgering Robins for a follow-up message. When it became obvious that no more would be forthcoming, Lenin drafted an insulting reply to the American "people" (rather than their President) in which he promised that the revolution in their country would not be long in coming:

> The congress expresses its gratitude to the American people, above all to the laboring and exploited classes of the United States, for the sympathy expressed to the Russian people by President Wilson through the Congress of Soviets in the days of severe trials.
>
> The Russian Socialistic Federative Republic of Soviets takes advantage of President Wilson's communication to express to all peoples perishing and suffering from the horrors of imperialistic war its warm sympathy and firm belief that the happy time is not far distant when the laboring masses of all countries will throw off the yoke of capitalism and will establish a socialistic state of society, which alone is capable of securing just and lasting peace, as well as the culture and well-being of all laboring people.[99]

Amid peals of laughter, the Congress of Soviets unanimously approved the resolution (with two minor changes), which Zinoviev described as a "resounding slap" in the face of American capitalism.[100]

The congress duly ratified the Brest Treaty. The motion to this effect received 724 votes, 10 percent less than there were Bolsheviks present, but more than a two-thirds majority; 276 delegates, or one-quarter, nearly all of them Left SRs, with the addition perhaps of some Left Communists, voted against; 118 delegates abstained. After the results had been announced, the Left SRs declared that they were withdrawing from the Sovnarkom. This ended the fiction of a "coalition government," although for the time being the Left SRs continued to work in lower-level Soviet institutions, including the Cheka.

In a secret vote, the congress approved the resolution of the Bolshevik Central Committee authorizing the government to renounce the Brest Treaty and declare war at its discretion.

Lenin has been widely credited by the Bolsheviks with prophetic vision in accepting a humiliating treaty that gave him the time he needed and then collapsed of its own weight. When the Bolsheviks renounced the Brest Treaty on November 13, 1918, following Germany's capitulation to the Western Allies, his stock in the Bolshevik movement rose to unprecedented heights. Nothing he had done contributed more to his reputation for infallibility: he never again had to threaten resignation to have his way.

And yet there is nothing to indicate that in pressuring his colleagues to accede to German demands Lenin had expected an imminent collapse of the Central Powers. In none of his speeches and writings between December 1917 and March 1918, private and public, when he used every conceivable argument to bring the opposition around, did he claim that time was running out for Germany and that Soviet Russia would soon regain all that she had to give up. Quite the contrary. In the spring and summer of 1918 Lenin seemed to have shared the optimism of the German High Command that they were about to deal the Allies a crushing defeat. Leonid Krasin certainly was not speaking only for himself when on his return from Germany early in September 1918 he assured the readers of *Izvestiia* that, thanks to her superb organization and discipline, Germany would have no difficulty staying in the war yet another, fifth, year.[101] The Bolshevik faith in Germany's victory is evidenced by the elaborate accords that Moscow concluded with Berlin in August 1918, accords viewed by both countries as a prelude to a formal alliance.[102] How inconceivable Germany's defeat appeared to Moscow is attested to by the fact that as late as September 30, 1918, when Imperial Germany lay in her death throes, Lenin authorized the transfer to Berlin of assets valued at 312.5 million deutsche marks, as provided for by the August 27 supplementary accord to the Brest Treaty, although he could have delayed this payment with impunity and then canceled it. One week before Germany sued for an armistice, the Soviet Government reconfirmed that German citizens could withdraw deposits from Soviet banks and take them out of the country.[103] The inescapable conclusion from this evidence is that Lenin bowed to the German *Diktat,* not because he believed that Germany would be unable to enforce it for very long, but, on the contrary, because he expected Germany to win and wanted to be on the winning side.

The circumstances surrounding the Brest-Litovsk Treaty furnish the classic model of what was to become Soviet foreign policy. Its principles may be summarized as follows:

1. The highest priority at all times is to be assigned to the retention of political power—that is, sovereign authority and the control of the state apparatus over some part of one's national territory. This is the irreducible minimum. No price is too high to secure it; for its sake anything and everything can be sacrificed: human lives, land and resources, national honor.

2. Ever since Russia had undergone the October Revolution and turned into the center ("oasis") of world socialism, its security and interests take precedence over the security and interests of every other country, cause, or party, including those of the "international proletariat." Soviet Russia is the embodiment of the international socialist movement and the base from which the socialist cause is promoted.

3. To purchase temporary advantages, it is permissible to make peace with "imperialist" countries, but such peace must be treated as an armed truce, to be broken when the situation changes in one's favor. As long as there is capitalism, Lenin said in May 1918, international agreements are "scraps of paper."[104] Even in periods of nominal peace, hostilities should be pursued by unconventional means with a view to undermining the governments with which one has signed accords.

4. Politics being warfare, foreign policy, as much as domestic policy, must always be conducted unemotionally, with the closest attention being paid to the "correlation of forces":

> We have great revolutionary experience, and from that experience we have learned that it is necessary to follow the tactics of relentless advance whenever objective conditions allow it. . . . But we have to adopt the tactic of procrastination, the slow gathering of forces when the objective conditions do not offer the possibility of making an appeal to the general relentless advance.[105]

Yet another fundamental principle of Bolshevik foreign policy was to be revealed after the enactment of the Brest Treaty: the principle that Communist interests abroad had to be promoted by the application of *divide et impera,* or, in Lenin's words, by the

> most circumspect, careful, cautious, skillful exploitation of every, even the smallest "crack" among one's enemies, of every conflict of interest among the bourgeoisie of the various countries, among the various groups or various species of the bourgeoisie within individual countries . . .[106]

14

The Revolution Internationalized

To obtain an armistice now means to *conquer the whole world.*
—*Lenin, September 1917*[1]

Although in time the Russian Revolution would exert an even greater influence on world history than the French, initially it attracted much less attention. This can be explained by two factors: the greater prominence of France and the different timing of the two events.

In the late eighteenth century, France was politically and culturally the leading power in Europe: the Bourbons were the premier dynasty on the Continent, the embodiment of royal absolutism, and French was the language of cultured society. At first, the great powers were delighted with the way the Revolution destabilized France, but they soon came to realize that it posed a threat also to their own stability. The arrest of the King, the September 1792 massacres, and the appeals of the Girondins to foreign nations to overthrow their tyrants left no doubt that the Revolution was more than a mere change of government. There followed a cycle of wars which lasted for nearly a quarter of a century, ending in a Bourbon restoration. The concern of European monarchs for the fate of the imprisoned French king is understandable given that their authority rested on the principle of legitimacy and that once this principle was abandoned in favor of popular sovereignty none of them could feel safe. True, the American colonies had proclaimed democracy earlier, but the United States was an overseas territory, not the leading continental power.

Since Russia lay on its periphery, half in Asia, and was overwhelmingly agrarian, Europe never considered her internal developments relevant to its own concerns. The turmoil of 1917 was generally interpreted to mark Russia's belated entry into the modern age rather than a threat to the established order.

This indifference was enhanced by the fact that the Russian Revolution, having occurred in the midst of the greatest, most destructive war in history, struck contemporaries as an episode in that war rather than as an event in its own right. Such excitement as the Russian Revolution generated in the West had to do almost exclusively with its potential effect on military operations. The Allies and the Central Powers both welcomed the February Revolution, although for different reasons: the former hoped that the removal of an unpopular tsar would make it possible to reinvigorate Russia's war effort, while the latter hoped it would take Russia out of the war. The October coup was, of course, jubilantly welcomed in Germany. Among the Allies it had a mixed reception, but it certainly caused no alarm. Lenin and his party were unknown quantities whose utopian plans and declarations no one took seriously. The tendency, especially after Brest-Litovsk, was to view Bolshevism as a creation of Germany which would vanish from the scene with the termination of hostilities. All European cabinets without exception vastly underestimated both the viability of the Bolshevik regime and the threat it posed to the European order.

For these reasons, neither in the closing year of World War I nor following the Armistice, were attempts made to rid Russia of the Bolsheviks. Until November 1918 the great powers were too busy fighting each other to worry about developments in remote Russia. Here and there, voices were raised that Bolshevism represented a mortal threat to Western civilization: these were especially loud in the German army, which had the most direct experience with Bolshevik propaganda and agitation. But even the Germans in the end subordinated concern with the possible long-term threat to considerations of immediate interest. Lenin was absolutely convinced that after making peace the belligerents would join forces and launch an international crusade against his regime. His fears proved groundless. Only the British intervened actively on the side of the anti-Bolshevik forces, and they did so in a halfhearted manner, largely at the initiative of one man, Winston Churchill. The effort was never seriously pursued, because the forces of accommodation in the West were stronger than those calling for intervention, and by the early 1920s the European powers made their peace with Communist Russia.

But even if the West was not much interested in Bolshevism, the Bolsheviks had a vital interest in the West. The Russian Revolution would not remain confined to the country of origin: from the instant the Bolsheviks seized power, it acquired an international dimension. Its geopolitical position alone ensured that Russia could not isolate herself from the World War. Much of Russia was under German occupation. Soon the British, French, Japanese, and Americans landed token contingents on Russian soil in a vain attempt to reactivate the Eastern Front. More important still was the conviction of the Bolsheviks that their revolution should not and could not be confined to

Russia, that unless it spread to the industrial countries of the West it was doomed. On the very first day of their rule in Petrograd, the Bolsheviks issued their Peace Decree, which exhorted workers abroad to rise and help the Soviet Government "bring to a successful resolution . . . the task of liberating the laboring and exploited masses from all slavery and all exploitation."[2]

Although couched in the novel language of class conflict, this was a declaration of war on all the existing governments, an intervention in the internal affairs of sovereign countries that would be often repeated then and later. Lenin did not deny that such was his intent: "We have thrown down a challenge to the imperialist plunderers of all countries."[3] Every Bolshevik attempt to promote civil war abroad—with appeals, subsidies, subversion, and military assistance—internationalized the Russian Revolution.

Such incitement of their citizens to rebellion and civil war by a foreign government gave the "imperialist plunderers" every right to retaliate in kind. The Bolshevik Government could not promote revolution outside its borders in disregard of international law and appeal to the same international law to keep foreign powers from intervening in its own internal affairs. In fact, however, for reasons stated, the great powers did not avail themselves of this right: no Western government, either during World War I or after it, appealed to the people of Russia to overthrow its Communist regime. Such limited intervention as occurred in the first year of Bolshevism was motivated exclusively by the desire to have Russia serve their particular military interests.

On March 23, 1918, the Germans launched their long-awaited offensive on the Western Front. Since the armistice with Russia, Ludendorff had transferred half a million men from the East to the West: he was prepared to sacrifice twice that many lives to gain victory. The Germans employed a variety of tactical innovations, such as attacking without preparatory artillery barrages and throwing into critical engagements specially trained "shock troops." They concentrated the brunt of the attack on the British sector, which came under immense pressure. Pessimists in the Allied command, among them General John J. Pershing, feared that the front would not withstand the force of the assault.

The German offensive worried the Bolsheviks as well. Although in official statements they pronounced plague on both "imperialist blocs" and demanded an immediate suspension of hostilities, in fact they wanted the war to go on. As long as the great powers were busy fighting one another, the Bolsheviks could consolidate their gains and build up the armed force they needed to meet the anticipated imperialist crusade, as well as to crush domestic opposition.

Even after they had signed a peace treaty with the Central Powers, the Bolsheviks wanted to maintain good relations with the Allies because they had no certainty that the "war party" would not ultimately prevail in Berlin, causing the Germans to march into Russia and remove them from power. The

German occupation in March of the Ukraine and the Crimea increased such apprehensions.

We have noted previously Trotsky's requests to the Allies for economic aid. In mid-March 1918, the Bolsheviks made urgent appeals for assistance in forming a Red Army and possibly intervening in Russia to stop a potential German invasion. Lenin entrusted the task of dealing with the Allies to Trotsky, the newly appointed Commissar of War, while he concentrated on Soviet-German relations. All of Trotsky's initiatives, of course, were sanctioned by the Bolshevik Central Committee.

The Bolsheviks decided early in March to proceed in earnest with the formation of an armed force. But like all Russian socialists, they saw the professional army as a breeding ground of counterrevolution. To create a standing army staffed with officers of the *ancien régime* meant courting self-destruction. Their preferred solution was a "nation in arms," or a people's militia.

Even after taking power, the Bolsheviks continued to dismantle what was left of the old army, depriving the officers of the little authority they still retained. Initially, they ordered that officers be elected, and then abolished military ranks, vesting the power to make command appointments in soldiers' soviets.[4] Under the incitement of Bolshevik agitators, soldiers and sailors lynched many officers: in the Black Sea Fleet such lynchings turned into wholesale massacres.

At the same time, Lenin and his lieutenants turned their attention to creating their own armed force. As his first Commissar of War, Lenin chose N. V. Krylenko, a thirty-two-year-old Bolshevik lawyer, who had served in the Imperial Army as a lieutenant in the reserves. In November, Krylenko went to Army Headquarters at Mogilev to replace the Commander in Chief, General N. N. Dukhonin, who had refused to negotiate with the Germans and was barbarously murdered by his troops. He appointed as the new Commander in Chief General M. D. Bonch-Bruevich, a brother of Lenin's secretary.

Professional officers actually proved to be much more willing to cooperate with the Bolsheviks than the intelligentsia. Brought up in a tradition of strict apoliticism and obedience to those in power, most of them dutifully carried out orders of the new government.[5] Even though the Soviet authorities have long been reluctant to make known their names, those who promptly recognized Bolshevik authority included some of the highest officers of the Imperial General Staff: A. A. Svechin, V. N. Egorev, S. I. Odintsov, A. A. Samoilo, P. P. Sytin, D. P. Parskii, A. E. Gutov, A. A. Neznamov, A. A. Baltiiskii, P. P. Lebedev, A. M. Zaionchkovskii, and S. S. Kamenev.[6] Later on, two tsarist ministers of war, Aleksis Polivanov and Dmitrii Shuvaev, also donned uniforms of the Red Army. At the end of November 1917, Lenin's military adviser, N. I. Podvoiskii, requested the General Staff's opinion whether elements of the old army could serve as the nucleus of a new armed force. The generals recommended that healthy units of the old army be used in this manner and that the army be reduced to its traditional peacetime strength of

1.3 million men. The Bolsheviks rejected this proposal in favor of an entirely new, revolutionary force, modeled on that fielded by France in 1791—that is, a *levée en masse,* but composed entirely of urban inhabitants, without peasants.[7]

Events, however, would not wait: the front continued to crumble and now it was Lenin's front—as he liked to say, after October the Bolsheviks had become "defensists." There was talk of creating an armed force of 300,000 to serve as the foundation of the new Bolshevik army.[8] Lenin demanded that this force be assembled and made combat-ready in a month and a half to meet the expected German assault. This order was reconfirmed on January 16 in the so-called Declaration of Rights, which provided for the creation of a Red Army to "ensure the full power of the toiling masses and prevent the restoration of exploiters."[9] The new Worker-Peasant Red Army (Raboche-Krest'ianskaia Krasnaia Armiia) was to be an all-volunteer force, made up of "tried revolutionaries," who were to be paid fifty rubles a month and be bound by "mutual guarantees" *(krugovaia poruka)* by virtue of which every soldier would be personally responsible for the loyalty of his comrades. To command this projected army, the Sovnarkom created on February 3 an All-Russian Collegium of the Red Army, chaired by Krylenko and Podvoiskii.[10]

Official government announcements justified the creation of a new, socialist army with the need of Soviet Russia to repulse the assault of the "international bourgeoisie." But this was only one of its stated missions, and not necessarily the most important. Like the Imperial Army, the Red Army had a dual function: to fight foreign enemies and to preserve internal security. In an address to the Soldiers' Section of the Third Congress of Soviets in January 1918, Krylenko declared that the foremost task of the Red Army was to wage "internal war" and ensure "the defense of Soviet authority."[11] In other words, it was primarily to serve the purpose of civil war, which Lenin was determined to unleash.

The Bolsheviks also charged their armies with the mission of spreading civil wars abroad. Lenin believed that the final triumph of socialism required a series of major wars between "socialist" and "bourgeois" countries. In a moment of uncharacteristic candor he said:

> The existence of the Soviet Republic alongside the imperialist states over the long run is unthinkable. In the end, either the one or the other will triumph. And until that end will have arrived, a series of the most terrible conflicts between the Soviet Republic and the bourgeois governments is unavoidable. This means that the ruling class, the proletariat, if it only wishes to rule and is to rule, must demonstrate this also with its military organization.[12]

When the organization of the Red Army was announced, an editorial in *Izvestiia* welcomed it as follows:

> The workers' revolution can triumph only on a global scale and for its enduring triumph requires the workers of various countries to offer each other mutual assistance.

And the socialists of that country where power has first passed into the hands of the proletariat may face the task of assisting, arms in hand, their brothers struggling against the bourgeoisie across the border.

The complete and final triumph of the proletariat is unthinkable without the triumphant conclusion of a series of wars on the external as well as domestic fronts. For this reason, the Revolution cannot manage without its own, socialist army.

"War is father of everything," said Heraclitus. *Through war lies also the road to socialism.* *

There are many other statements, some explicit, others veiled, to the effect that the Red Army's mission involved intervention abroad, or, as the decree of January 28, 1918, put it, "providing support to the coming socialist revolutions in Europe."[13]

All this lay in the future. For the time being, the Bolsheviks had only one reliable military force, the Latvian Rifles, whom we have encountered in connection with the dispersal of the Constituent Assembly and the security of the Kremlin. The Russian army formed the first separate Latvian units in the summer of 1915. In 1915–16, the Latvian Rifles were an all-volunteer force of 8,000 men, strongly nationalistic and with a sizable Social-Democratic contingent.[14] Reinforced with Latvian nationals from the regular Russian units, by the end of 1916 they had eight regiments totaling 30,000 to 35,000 men. This force resembled the Czech Legion, concurrently formed in Russia of prisoners of war, although their destinies were to be quite different.

In the spring of 1917, the Latvian troops reacted favorably to Bolshevik anti-war propaganda, hoping that peace and the principle of "natural self-determination" would allow them to return to their homeland, then under German occupation. Although still more driven by nationalism than socialism, they developed close ties with Bolshevik organizations, adopting their slogans against the Provisional Government. In August 1917, Latvian units distinguished themselves in the defense of Riga.

The Bolsheviks treated the Latvians differently from all the other units of the Russian army, keeping them intact and entrusting to them vital security operations. They gradually turned it into a combination of the French Foreign Legion and the Nazi SS, a force to protect the regime from internal as well as foreign enemies, partly an army, partly a security police. Lenin trusted them much more than Russians.

Early plans to create a Worker-Peasant Red Army came to naught. Those who enlisted did so mainly for the pay, which was soon raised from 50 to 150 rubles a month, and the opportunity to loot. Much of the army was riffraff made up of demobilized soldiers, whom Trotsky would later describe as "hooligans" and a Soviet decree would call "disorganizers, troublemakers, and self-seekers."[15] Contemporary newspapers are filled with stories of violent

---

*_Izvestiia,_ No. 22/286 (January 28, 1918), 1, emphasis added. Heraclitus actually said something slightly different: "Strife [not war] is the father and the king of all; some he has made slaves, and some free."

"expropriations" carried out by the early troops of the Red Army: hungry and ill paid, they sold uniforms and military equipment, and sometimes fought each other. In May 1918, having occupied Smolensk, they demanded that Jews be expelled from Soviet institutions in the name of the slogan "Beat Jews and Save Russia."[16] The situation was so bad that the Soviet authorities occasionally had to request German troops to intervene against mutinous Red Army units.[17]

Things could not go on like this and Lenin reluctantly began to reconcile himself to the idea of a professional army urged on him by the old General Staff and the French military mission. In February and early March 1918 discussions were held in the party between proponents of a "pure" revolutionary army, composed of workers and democratically structured, and those who favored a more conventional military force. The debate paralleled the one that went on concurrently between advocates of worker control of industry and advocates of professional management. In both instances, considerations of efficiency overruled revolutionary dogma.

On March 9, 1918, the Sovnarkom appointed a commission to provide in a week a "plan for the establishment of a military center for the reorganization of the army and the creation of a mighty armed force on the basis of a socialist militia and the universal arming of workers and peasants."[18] Krylenko, who had led the opposition to a professional armed force, resigned as Commissar of War and took over the Commissariat of Justice. He was replaced by Trotsky, who had had no military experience, since, like nearly all the Bolshevik leaders, he had dodged the draft. His assignment was to employ as much professional help, foreign and domestic, as required to create an efficient, combat-ready army that would pose no threat to the Bolshevik dictatorship either by defecting to the enemy or by meddling in politics. Concurrently, the government created a Supreme Military Council (Vysshyi Voennyi Soviet), chaired by Trotsky. The council's staff consisted of officials (the commissars of War and the Navy) and military professionals from the Imperial Army.[19] To ensure the complete political reliability of the armed force, the Bolsheviks adopted the institution of "commissars" to supervise military commanders.[20]

Trotsky continued military negotiations with the Allies. On March 21, he sent General Lavergne of the French military mission the following note:

> After a conversation with Captain Sadoul, I have the honor to request, in the name of the Council of People's Commissars, the technical collaboration of the French military mission in the task of reorganizing the army which the government of soviets is undertaking.

There followed a list of thirty-three French specialists in all branches of the military, including aviation, navy, and intelligence, whom the Russians wanted detailed to them.[21] Lavergne assigned three officers from his mission as advisers to the Commissar of War: Trotsky allotted them space near his office. The collaboration was handled very discreetly and is not much talked about in Soviet military histories. Later on, according to Joseph Noulens, Trotsky asked for five hundred French army and several hundred British naval officers; he also discussed military assistance with the U.S. and Italian missions.[22]

Organizing a Red Army from scratch, however, was a slow procedure. In the meantime the Germans were advancing southeast into the Ukraine and adjacent areas. In these circumstances, the Bolsheviks undertook to explore whether the Allies would be prepared to help stop the German advance with their own troops. On March 26, the new Commissar of Foreign Affairs, George Chicherin, handed the French Consul General, Fernand Grenard, a note requesting a statement of Allied intentions in the event Russia turned to Japan to help repel German aggression, or to Germany against Japan.[23]

The Allied ambassadors, established in Vologda, reacted skeptically to the Bolshevik approaches, which were made through Sadoul. They doubted whether the Bolsheviks really intended to deploy the Red Army against the Germans: as Noulens put it, its more likely use was to serve as a "Praetorian Guard" to solidify their hold on Russia. One can imagine their thoughts as they listened to Sadoul's impassioned plea on Moscow's behalf:

> The Bolsheviks will form an army, well or badly, but they cannot do it seriously without our assistance. And, inevitably, someday this army will stand up to Imperial Germany, the worst enemy of Russian democracy. On the other hand, because the new army will be disciplined, staffed by professionals and permeated with the military spirit, it will not be an army suited for a civil war. If we direct its formation, as Trotsky has proposed to us, it will become a factor of internal stability and an instrument of national defense at the Allies' disposal. The de-Bolshevization which we will thus accomplish in the army will have reverberations in the general policies of Russia. Do we not see already the beginnings of this evolution? One must be blinded by prejudice not to see, through the unavoidable brutalities, the rapid adaptation of the Bolsheviks to a realistic policy.[24]

This plea must be one of the very earliest claims on record that the Bolsheviks were "evolving" toward realism.

For all their suspicions, the Allied ambassadors did not want to reject the Soviet request out of hand. Communicating frequently with their governments as well as with Trotsky, they reached on April 3 an understanding among themselves on the following principles: (1) the Allies (without the United States, which refused to go along) will assist the organization of the Red Army, with the proviso that Moscow reintroduces military discipline, including the death penalty; (2) the Soviet Government will consent to Japanese landings on Russian soil: the Japanese forces, meshed with Allied units sent from Europe, will form a multinational force to fight the Germans; (3) Allied contingents will occupy Murmansk and Archangel; (4) the Allies will refrain from interfering in the internal affairs of Russia.*

While these talks were in progress, on April 4 the Japanese landed a small expeditionary force in Vladivostok. Its ostensible mission was to protect Japanese citizens, two of whom had recently been murdered there. But it was widely and correctly believed that the true objective of the Japanese was to seize and annex Russia's maritime provinces. Russian military experts pointed out that the collapse of transport and the breakdown of civic authority in Siberia precluded the movement of hundreds of thousands of Japanese troops, with the vast logistic support they required, to European Russia. But the Allies persisted in this plan, promising to dilute the Japanese expeditionary force with French, English, and Czechoslovak units.

At the beginning of June, the English landed 1,200 additional troops at Murmansk and 100 at Archangel.

Lenin did not give up hope of American economic aid to supplement the military help promised by France. The United States continued to profess amity for Russia even after the Brest Treaty had been ratified. The Department of State notified the Japanese that the United States continued to regard Russia and her people as "friends and allies against a common enemy" although she did not recognize her government.[25] On another occasion Washington declared that in spite of "all the unhappiness and misery" which the Russian Revolution had caused, it felt for it "the greatest sympathy."[26] Curious to know what these friendly professions meant concretely, Lenin on April 3 again asked Robins to sound out his government on the possibility of economic "cooperation."[27] In mid-May, he gave him a note for Washington which stated that the United States could replace Germany as the principal supplier of industrial equipment.[28] Unlike German business circles, the Americans showed little interest.

It is impossible to determine how far Bolshevik collaboration with the Allies might have gone, or even how seriously it was intended. The Bolsheviks, aware that the Germans knew of their every step, may well have made these overtures to force Germany to observe the terms of the Brest Treaty or risk pushing Russia into Allied arms. Be that as it may, the Germans came around and assured the Bolsheviks that they had no hostile intentions. In April the two countries exchanged diplomatic missions and made ready for talks on a commercial agreement. In mid-May, Berlin, abandoning the hard line advocated by the generals, advised Moscow it would occupy no more Russian territory. Lenin publicly confirmed these assurances in a talk he gave on May 14.[29] They paved the way for a Russo-German rapprochement. "When it emerged in the course of German-Russian relations that Germany did not intend to overthrow [the Bolsheviks], Trotsky gave up" the idea of Allied

---

*Joseph Noulens, *Mon Ambassade en Russie Soviétique,* II (Paris, 1933), 57–58; A. Hogenhuis-Seliverstoff, *Les Relations Franco-Soviétiques, 1917–1924* (Paris, 1981), 59. Noulens wanted to add a further condition that Allied citizens be granted in Russia "the same advantages, privileges, and compensations" that German nationals had received in the Brest Treaty, but he had to drop this demand: Hogenhuis-Seliverstoff, *Les Relations,* 59.

83. Kurt Riezler.

assistance.* From now on, relations between the Bolsheviks and the Allies rapidly deteriorated, as Moscow moved into the orbit of Imperial Germany, which seemed about to win the war.

Rebuffed by Moscow, the Allied missions in Russia had to confine themselves to desultory talks with pro-Allied opposition groups. Noulens, who was the most active in this regard, viewed Russians much like his German counterpart, Mirbach, as inept and passive, waiting on foreigners to liberate them. The Russian "bourgeoisie" impressed him as utterly devoid of initiative.[30]

In the second half of April 1918, Russia and Germany exchanged embassies: Ioffe went to Berlin, and Mirbach came to Moscow. The Germans were the first foreign mission accredited to Bolshevik Russia. To their surprise, the train in which they traveled was guarded by Latvians. One of the German diplomats wrote that the reception given them by the Muscovites was surprisingly warm: he thought that no victor had ever been so welcomed.[31]

The head of the mission, Count Mirbach, was a forty-seven-year-old career diplomat with considerable experience in Russian affairs. In 1908–11 he had served as counselor in the German Embassy in St. Petersburg and in December 1917 headed the mission to Petrograd. He came from a wealthy and aristocratic family of Prussian Catholics.† A diplomat of the old school, he was dismissed by some colleagues as a "rococo count," ill suited to deal with

---

*Winfried Baumgart, *Deutsche Ostpolitik 1918* (Vienna-Munich, 1966), 49. There is no basis whatever for Hogenhuis-Seliverstoff's claim (*Les Relations,* 60) that it was Noulens who deliberately "ruptured" a looming accord between the Allies and Moscow by giving, at the end of April, an admittedly tactless newspaper interview in which he justified Japanese landings in Vladivostok. The Bolsheviks were not that easily insulted.

†On him, see Wilhelm Joost, *Botschafter bei den roten Zaren* (Vienna, 1967), 17–63, which is not entirely reliable.

revolutionaries, but his tact and self-control earned him the confidence of the Foreign Office.

His right-hand man, Kurt Riezler, a thirty-six-year-old philosopher, also had much experience in Russian affairs.* In 1915, he played a part in Parvus's unsuccessful attempt to secure Lenin's cooperation. Posted to Stockholm in 1917, he served as the principal intermediary between the German Government and Lenin's agents, whom he paid subsidies from the so-called Riezler Fund for transfer to Russia. He is said to have assisted the Bolsheviks in carrying out the October coup, although his exact role in it is not clear. Like many of his compatriots, he welcomed the coup as a "miracle" that could save Germany. At Brest he advocated a conciliatory policy. Temperamentally, however, he was a pessimist who thought Europe was doomed no matter who won the war.

The third prominent member of the German mission was the military attaché, Karl von Bothmer, who reflected the views of Ludendorff and Hindenburg. He despised the Bolsheviks and believed Germany should be rid of them.[32]

None of the three German diplomats knew Russian. All the Russian leaders with whom they came into contact spoke fluent German.

The Foreign Office instructed Mirbach to support the Bolshevik Government and under no conditions to enter into communication with the Russian opposition. He was to inform himself of the true situation in Soviet Russia and of the activities there of Allied agents, as well as to lay the groundwork for the commercial negotiations between the countries stipulated by the Brest Treaty. The German mission, twenty diplomats and an equal number of clerical staff, took over a luxurious private residence on Denezhnyi Pereulok, off Arbat, the property of a German sugar magnate who wanted to keep it out of Communist hands.

Mirbach had been to Petrograd several months earlier and must have known what to expect: even so, he was appalled by what he saw. "The streets are very lively," he reported to Berlin a few days after his arrival,

> but they seem populated exclusively by proletarians; better-dressed people are rarely to be seen—it is as if the previous ruling class and the bourgeoisie had vanished from the face of the earth. . . . The priests, who previously had made up a goodly part of the public, have similarly disappeared from the streets. In the shops one can find mainly dusty remains of previous splendors, offered at fantastic prices. Pervasive avoidance of work and mindless idling are the characteristics of this overall picture. Since the factories are at a standstill and the soil remains largely uncultivated—at any rate, that was the impression we gained from our trip—Russia appears headed for a still greater catastrophe than the one inflicted on her by the [Bolshevik] coup.

*His papers were edited by Karl Dietrich Erdmann: *Kurt Riezler: Tagebücher, Aufsätze, Dokumente* (Göttingen, 1972). This edition has come under criticism from some German scholars for liberties alleged to have been taken with the texts. See further K. H. Jarausch in *SR*, XXXI, No. 2 (1972), 381–98.

Public security leaves something to be desired. Nevertheless, one can move about freely and alone in the daytime. In the evening, however, it is no longer advisable to leave one's house: one hears the frequent sounds of shooting and there seem to be continuous smaller and larger clashes . . .

Bolshevik mastery over Moscow is maintained, first and foremost, by the *Latvian* battalions. It depends furthermore on the numerous automobiles which the government has requisitioned: these constantly race across the city, delivering the troops, as they are needed, to endangered spots.

Where these conditions will lead cannot be determined as yet, but one cannot deny them for the moment the prospects of a certain stability.[33]

Riezler was equally depressed by Bolshevik-ruled Moscow: he was struck most by the pervasive corruption of Communist officials and their loose habits, especially their insatiable demand for women.[34]

In mid-May, Mirbach met with Lenin, whose self-confidence surprised him:

Lenin, in general, believes with rocklike firmness in his star and professes, over and over again, in an almost insistent manner, to a boundless optimism. At the same time, he also concedes that even though his regime still remains intact, the number of its enemies has grown and the situation calls for "more intense attention than even one month ago." He bases his self-confidence above all on the fact that the ruling party alone disposes of organized power, whereas all the other [parties] agree only in rejecting the existing regime; in other respects, however, they fly apart in all directions and have no power to match that of the Bolsheviks.*[35]

After one month in the Soviet capital, Mirbach began to experience misgivings about the viability of the Bolshevik regime and the wisdom of his government's basing its entire Russian policy on it. He continued to believe that the Bolsheviks were likely to survive: on May 24, he warned the Foreign Office against Bothmer and the other military men who predicted the imminent collapse of the Soviet regime.[36] But aware of the activities of Allied diplomatic and military personnel in Russia and their contacts with the opposition groups, he worried that should Lenin fall from power, the Germans would be left without any source of support in Russia. He favored, therefore, a more flexible policy combining reliance on the Bolsheviks with political insurance in the form of openings to the anti-Bolshevik opposition.

On May 20, Mirbach sent home the first pessimistic report on the situation in Soviet Russia and the dangers confronting German policy there. Popular support for the regime, he wrote, had greatly eroded in recent weeks: Trotsky was said to have referred to the Bolshevik Party as a "living corpse."

---

*It deserves note that neither then nor later in private conversation did Lenin claim popular support as a source of strength: he rather saw it in the disunity of his opponents. In 1920 he told Bertrand Russell that two years earlier he and his associates had doubted they could survive the hostility which surrounded them. "He attributes their survival to the jealousies and divergent interests of the different capitalist nations, also to the power of Bolshevik propaganda": Bertrand Russell, *Bolshevism* (New York, 1920), 40.

The Allies were fishing in these muddied waters, generously distributing funds to the SRs and Mensheviks-Internationalists, Serbian prisoners of war, and Baltic sailors. "Never was corruptible Russia more corrupt than now." Thanks to Trotsky's sympathies for them, the Allies had increased their influence over the Bolsheviks. To prevent the situation from getting out of hand, he required money to renew the subsidies to the Bolsheviks which the German Government had terminated in January.[37] Funds were needed to prevent both a shift of the Bolsheviks toward the Allies and a Bolshevik collapse followed by a power seizure by the pro-Allied SRs.[38]

This report, followed by others couched in progressively gloomier tones, did not go unheeded in Berlin. Early in June, Kühlmann reversed himself and authorized Mirbach to initiate talks with the Russian opposition.[39] He also allocated to him discretionary funds. On June 3, Mirbach cabled to Berlin that to keep the Bolsheviks in power he needed 3 million marks a month, which the Foreign Ministry interpreted to mean a total of 40 million marks.[40] Kühlmann, who concurred that preventing the Bolsheviks from switching to the Allies "would cost money, probably a great deal of money," approved the transfer of this sum to the Moscow embassy for secret Russian work.[41] It cannot be established exactly how this money was spent. Only about 9 million was actually allocated: it appears that about one-half of that sum went to the Bolshevik Government and the rest to their opponents, mainly the anti-Bolshevik Provisional Government of Siberia, centered in Omsk, and the Kaiser's favorite anti-Bolshevik, the Don Cossack ataman, P. N. Krasnov.*

The stumbling block confronting the Germans in their effort to reach the anti-Bolshevik opposition was Brest. No political group other than the Bolsheviks would accept this treaty, and even the Bolsheviks were divided. As Mirbach had observed, atrocious as conditions were in Soviet Russia, no non-Bolshevik Russian would purchase German help against the Bolsheviks if the price was acceptance of the Brest Treaty. In other words, to gain support from anti-Bolsheviks, Germany had to agree to substantial treaty revisions. In Mirbach's opinion, the opposition might acquiesce to the loss of Poland, Lithuania, and Courland, but not to the surrender of the Ukraine, Estonia, and probably Livonia.[42]

Mirbach entrusted to Riezler the delicate task of dealing with Russian opposition groups under the noses of the Cheka and Allied agents. Riezler dealt mainly with the so-called Right Center, a small conservative circle formed in mid-June by respected political figures and generals who had concluded that Bolshevism posed a greater threat to Russia's national interests than Germany and were prepared to come to terms with Berlin to be rid of it. Although they claimed solid contacts with financial, industrial, and military circles, they really had no significant following, because the overwhelming majority of politically active Russians regarded the Bolsheviks as a creation

---

*The Bolshevik Government received from the Germans monthly subsidies of 3 million marks in June, July, and August: Z. A. B. Zeman, ed., *Germany and the Revolution in Russia, 1915–1918* (London-New York, 1958), 130.

of Germany. The leading personality of the Right Center was Alexander Krivoshein, Stolypin's director of agriculture, a decent and patriotic man who might have made an acceptable figurehead in a Russian Government installed by the Germans, but who, being a typical bureaucrat of the *ancien régime,* was more used to obeying orders than giving them. Involved also was General Aleksei Brusilov, the hero of the 1916 offensive. Through intermediaries, Krivoshein informed Riezler that his group was prepared to overthrow the Bolsheviks and had the military means to do so but in order to act required Germany's active support.[43] For such collaboration to materialize, the Germans had to consent to changes in the Brest Treaty.

The Germans had little respect for the Russian opposition, even as they negotiated with it. Mirbach thought the monarchists "lazy," while Riezler spoke scornfully of the "moans and whines of the [Russian] bourgeoisie for German aid and order."[44]

Ioffe arrived in Berlin with his mission on April 19. German generals, correctly anticipating that Russian diplomats would engage mainly in espionage and subversion, wanted the Soviet Embassy located at Brest-Litovsk or some other city away from Germany, but the Foreign Office overruled them. Ioffe took over the old Imperial embassy at Unter den Linden 7, which the Germans had maintained in immaculate condition throughout the war. Over it he unfurled the red flag emblazoned with hammer and sickle. Subsequently, Moscow opened consulates in Berlin and Hamburg.

Initially, Ioffe's staff consisted of 30 persons, but it kept on expanding, and in November, when the two countries broke relations, numbered 180. In addition, Ioffe gave employment to German radicals to translate Soviet propaganda materials and carry out subversive missions. He maintained constant cable communications with Moscow: the Germans intercepted and decoded some of this traffic, but the bulk of it remains unpublished.*

The Soviet diplomatic representation in Berlin was no ordinary embassy: rather it was a revolutionary outpost deep in enemy territory, whose main function was to promote revolution. As an American journalist later put it, Ioffe acted in Berlin in "perfect bad faith."[45] Judging by his activities, he had three missions. One was to neutralize the German generals, who wanted the Bolshevik Government removed. This he accomplished by appealing to the interests of the business and banking community and negotiating a commercial treaty that gave Germany unique economic privileges in Russia. His second task was to assist revolutionary forces in Germany. The third was to collect intelligence on domestic conditions.

Ioffe carried out revolutionary activities with remarkable brazenness. He

---

*A selection of Ioffe's dispatches to Lenin appears in *ISSSR,* No. 4 (1958), 3–26, edited by I. K. Kobliakov.

84. A. Ioffe.

counted on German politicians and businessmen developing such an overriding interest in subjugating Russia to their economic exploitation that they would persuade the government to overlook his violations of diplomatic norms. In the spring and summer of 1918, he engaged mainly in propaganda, working closely with the Independent Socialist Party's extreme left wing, the Spartacist League. Later, as Germany began to disintegrate, he supplied money and weapons to stoke the fires of social revolution. The Independent Socialists, having turned into an affiliate of the Russian Communist Party, coordinated their activities with the Soviet Embassy: on one occasion, Moscow sent an official delegation to Germany to address that party's convention.[46] For this work, Ioffe was allocated by Moscow 14 million German marks, which he deposited with the German bank of Mendelssohn and withdrew as the need arose.*

Ioffe opened branches of the Soviet Berlin Information Bureau in a number of German provincial cities as well as in neutral Holland, from where propaganda was fed to Allied media.[47]

In 1919, Ioffe recounted, with evident pride, his accomplishments as Soviet representative in Berlin:

The [Soviet Embassy] directed and subsidized more than ten left-socialist newspapers . . . Quite naturally, even in its informational work, the plenipotentiary representation could not confine itself only to "legal opportunities." The informational material was far from limited to that which appeared in print. All that the censors struck out, and all that was not presented to them, because it was assumed beforehand that they would not pass it, was nevertheless illegally printed and illegally distributed. Very frequently it was necessary to

*Baumgart, *Ostpolitik,* 352n. Ioffe says that although he maintained contacts with all German parties, from extreme right to extreme left, he studiously avoided relations with the Social-Democrats, the party of "social traitors": *VZh,* No. 5 (1919), 37–38. This policy, pursued on Lenin's instructions, anticipated Stalin's policies fifteen years later, which, by forbidding the German Communists to cooperate with the Social-Democrats against the Nazis, has been widely blamed for making possible Hitler's rise to power.

utilize the parliamentary tribune: the material was passed on to members of the Reichstag from the Independent faction [of the Social-Democratic Party], who used it in their speeches; in this way it got into the papers anyway. In this work one could not confine oneself to Russian materials. The [Soviet mission], which had superb connections in all strata of German society and its agents in various German ministries, was much better informed even about German affairs than the German comrades. The information which it received it eventually passed on to the latter, and in this manner many machinations of the military party became in good time public knowledge.

Of course, in its revolutionary activity the Russian Embassy could not confine itself to information. In Germany there existed revolutionary groups which throughout the war had conducted underground revolutionary work. Russian revolutionaries, who had more experience in this kind of conspiratorial activity as well as greater opportunities, had to work, and indeed did work, in concert with these groups. All of Germany was covered with a network of illegal revolutionary organizations: hundreds of thousands of revolutionary pamphlets and proclamations were printed and distributed every week in the rear and at the front. The German Government once accused the Russians of importing into Germany agitational literature and, with an energy worthy of better application, searched for this contraband in the baggage of couriers, but it never entered its mind that that which the Russian Embassy brought into Germany from Russia represented only a drop in the sea compared to what was printed with the help of the Russian Embassy inside Germany.

In sum, according to Ioffe, the Russian Embassy in Berlin "worked constantly in close contact with German socialists in preparing the German revolution."[48]

It further served as a channel for distributing revolutionary literature and subversive funds to other European countries: through it passed a steady stream of couriers (between 100 and 200 was the German estimate) carrying diplomatic pouches for dispatch to Austria, Switzerland, Scandinavia, and the Netherlands. Some of these "couriers," after arriving in Berlin, vanished from sight.[49]

The German Foreign Office received frequent protests from military and civil authorities concerning these subversive actions,[50] but it refused to act, tolerating them for the sake of what it perceived to be higher German interests in Russia. When once in a while it ventured to object to some especially outrageous behavior on the part of the Soviet mission, Ioffe had an answer ready. As he explains:

The Brest Treaty itself furnished the opportunity for its circumvention. Since the contracting parties were governments, the prohibition on revolutionary action could be interpreted to apply to governments and their organs. It was thus interpreted by the Russian side, and every revolutionary action which Germany protested against was at once explained as the action of the Russian Communist Party and not of the government.[51]

Ioffe's operations in Germany made the timid attempts of Mirbach and Riezler in Moscow to communicate with the opposition look like a harmless flirtation.

From the point of view of Moscow's immediate interests, no less important than promoting revolution in Germany was gaining the support of German business circles so they would act jointly to block the anti-Bolshevik forces there.

Big business interests in Germany could hardly wait to lay their hands on Russia: and because they knew that only the Bolsheviks would allow them to do so, they turned into the most enthusiastic supporters of the Bolshevik regime. In the spring of 1918, following the signing of the peace treaty, numerous German Chamber of Commerce organizations petitioned their government to reopen commercial relations with Soviet Russia. On May 16, Krupp hosted in Düsseldorf a conference of prominent German industrialists, among them August Thyssen and Hugo Stinnes, to discuss this subject. The conference concluded that it was imperative to stop the penetration of "English and American capital" into Russia and to take steps that would enable German interests to establish there a dominant influence. Another business conference, held the same month under the auspices of the Foreign Office, stressed the desirability of Germany's taking control of Russian transport, a goal facilitated by Moscow's request for German help in reorganizing its railroads.[52] In July, German businessmen sent a trade delegation to Moscow. The bankers lionized Ioffe on his arrival in Berlin. "The director of the Deutsche Bank frequently visits us," Ioffe boasted to Moscow, "Mendelssohn has long sought a meeting with me, and Solomonssohn has already come three times under various pretexts."[53]

Such commercial zeal enabled Moscow to transform influential circles of German industry and finance into a friendly lobby. Here, the Bolsheviks reaped the advantages of superior knowledge. They were intimately familiar with the internal situation of Germany and with the mentality of her elite. Independent Socialists supplied them with sensitive information with which to exploit conflicts in German circles. The Germans with whom they dealt knew next to nothing about the Bolsheviks and did not take them or their ideology seriously. They adapted themselves to this situation with consummate skill, taking on a protective coloring that gave them a non-threatening appearance: it was a very sophisticated example of political mimicry. The tactic which Ioffe and his associates pursued was to pose as "realists" who spouted revolutionary slogans but in reality desired nothing better than a deal with Germany. This tactic had an irresistible attraction for hardheaded German businessmen because it confirmed their conviction that no person in his right mind could take Bolshevik revolutionary rhetoric seriously.

How this deception worked is illustrated by the meetings Ioffe held in the summer of 1918 with Gustav Stresemann, a right-wing German politician, and other public figures of a liberal and conservative orientation. He was assisted by Leonid Krasin, who before and during the war had held high executive positions with Siemens and Schuckert and enjoyed excellent connections in Germany. At an informal talk on July 5, the two Russians assured the Germans that not only Lenin but also the pro-Allied Trotsky desired German "backing." Given the anti-German mood in Russia, a formal treaty of alliance between the two countries would be premature, but that mood could change if Germany pursued correct policies. One step in this direction would be for the Germans to share some of the grain which they were shipping from the Ukraine. It would also be helpful if the Germans gave Moscow guarantees that they did not intend to resume military operations on the Eastern Front: this would enable Moscow to concentrate its armed forces on expelling the British from Murmansk and crushing the uprising of the Czech Legion, which had recently erupted in Siberia. Germany stood to reap great benefits from good relations with Russia, since the Russians could provide her with all the raw materials she needed, including cotton, petroleum, and manganese. The Germans had no reason to worry about Moscow's revolutionary propaganda: "under the existing circumstances the Maximalist [Bolshevik] Government was prepared to give up its utopian goals and pursue a pragmatic socialist policy."[54]

Ioffe and Krasin put on a brilliant show. If the Germans had been better informed, less arrogant, and less captivated by geopolitical fantasies, they would have seen through it. For the Russians were offering them commodities available only in areas outside their control—Central Asia, Baku, and Georgia—and minimizing the radicalism of their government, which, far from giving up "its utopian goals," was at this very time entering its most radical phase. But the deception worked. Stresemann thus summarized his impressions:

> It seems to me . . . that we have every inducement to establish a far-reaching economic and political understanding with the present government [of Russia], which, at all events, is not imperialistic and can never come to terms with the Entente, if only because by defaulting on Allied loans it erected an insurmountable barrier between itself and the Entente. If this opportunity is missed and the present Russian government falls, then any successor will, in any event, be more favorable to the Entente than the present rulers and the danger of a new Eastern Front . . . will draw palpably nearer. . . . If our opponents see that we and Russia are drawing together they will also give up the hope of defeating us economically—they have long ago given up the hope of military victory—and we will be in a position to withstand any assault. By cleverly exploiting this factor, we will also be able to raise the spirit of the country to the victorious heights of the past. I would, therefore, greatly welcome it if these efforts were to gain also the support of the Supreme Military Command.[55]

The German Foreign Office shared these sentiments. An internal memorandum prepared by a member of its staff in May described the Soviet leaders as "Jewish businessmen" with whom Germany should be able to come to terms.[56]

In this friendly atmosphere, the two countries initiated in early July talks on a commercial agreement. Signed on August 27—immediately after the "Black Day" of the German armies on the Western Front which convinced even Ludendorff the war was lost—this so-called Supplementary Treaty established between the two countries a relationship that fell just short of a formal alliance.

As if the situation in Russia were not complicated enough, in the spring a further complication arose in the shape of a revolt of Czechoslovak former prisoners of war that deprived the Bolsheviks of control of vast regions in the Urals and Siberia.

During their successful campaign against the Austro-Hungarians in 1914, Russian armies had captured hundreds of thousands of prisoners, including 50,000 to 60,000 Czechs and Slovaks. In December 1914, the Imperial Government offered these prisoners, many of them passionately anti-German and anti-Magyar, an opportunity to form their own legion and return to the front to fight alongside Russian troops. Few Czechs took advantage of this offer; most were afraid that the Central Powers would treat members of this legion (called *Druzhina*) as traitors and, in the event of capture, put them to death. Even so, in 1916 there were two Czechoslovak regiments in existence: the nucleus of the future army of independent Czechoslovakia. Thomas Masaryk, the head of the Czechoslovak National Council in Paris, conceived the idea of forming the prisoners of war as well as civilians domiciled in Russia and elsewhere into a regular national army to fight on the Western Front. He initiated negotiations with the Imperial Government for the evacuation of the Czech POWs to France, but Petrograd proved uncooperative.

He resubmitted the proposal to the Provisional Government, which reacted favorably. The formation of Czech military units proceeded apace, and in the spring of 1917, 24,000 Czechs and Slovaks, organized in a corps, fought on the Eastern Front, distinguishing themselves in the June 1917 offensive. It was planned to transport these units and the remaining POWs in Russian camps to the Western Front, but the Bolshevik coup intervened.

In December 1917, the Allies recognized the Czechoslovak Corps in Russia as a separate army serving under the Supreme Allied Council. The following month, Masaryk returned to Russia to negotiate once again, this time with the Bolsheviks, the troops' evacuation to France. By now, the matter had acquired considerable urgency because the conclusion of a treaty between the Central Powers and the Ukraine made it likely that the Germans would occupy the Ukraine, where most of the Czechoslovaks were interned. The Bolsheviks delayed their decision until after the signing of the Brest Treaty: finally, in mid-March, when relations with the Allies were at their warmest, they gave their consent.[57]

Masaryk and the Allied command had originally intended to evacuate the Czechoslovaks through Archangel and Murmansk. But because the railroad lines to the northern ports were threatened by Finnish partisans and there was the additional danger of German submarines, it was decided to embark them at Vladivostok. Masaryk instructed the commanders of what became known as the Czech Legion to adopt a policy of "armed neutrality"[58] and under no circumstances to interfere in domestic Russian affairs. Because the territory which the Czechoslovaks had to traverse en route to Vladivostok was in a state of anarchy, Masaryk arranged with the Bolshevik authorities that his men would carry enough weapons to defend themselves.

The Czechoslovaks were well organized and eager to leave. As soon as the Bolsheviks gave them permission, they formed battalion-sized units, 1,000 men strong, each to fill a special train or, as it was known in Russia, *echelon*. When the first *echelon* reached Penza, it received a telegram from Stalin, dated March 26, 1918, which listed the conditions under which the evacuation was to proceed. The Czechoslovaks were to travel not as "combat units" but as "free citizens" carrying such arms as were required for their protection from "counterrevolutionaries." They were to be accompanied by commissars provided by the Penza Soviet.[59] The Czechoslovaks were unhappy over this order, behind which they suspected German pressure, because they had no confidence in the ill-trained and radicalized pro-Bolshevik forces, prominent among whom were fanatical Communists recruited from Hungarian and Czech POWs. Before leaving Penza, they reluctantly surrendered some weapons, kept a few openly, and concealed the rest. The evacuation then resumed.

Although they were strongly nationalistic and, therefore, unhappy with the Bolsheviks for signing a separate peace treaty with the Central Powers, in their political views the Czechoslovaks stood solidly to the left of center: one historian estimates that three-quarters of them were socialists.[60] Following Masaryk's orders, they ignored the approaches of both the Volunteer Army

85. Armored train of Czech Legion in Siberia: June 1918.

and the Bolsheviks, the latter using Czech Communists as intermediaries.[61] They had a single purpose in mind: to get out of Russia. Even so, they could not entirely avoid becoming entangled in Russian politics because they were traversing a territory in the grip of a civil war. As they passed towns along the Trans-Siberian Railroad, they established contact with local cooperatives, which provided them with food and other necessities: these happened to be largely in the hands of SRs, Siberia's dominant party. At the same time, they had occasional altercations with the urban soviets and their "international" military units, composed mostly of Magyar POWs, who wanted the Czechoslovaks to join the Revolution.

The involvement of the Czech Legion in Russian affairs at the end of May 1918 was not a deliberate reversal of the policy of neutrality. It began when the Germans, displeased at the prospect of tens of thousands of fresh and highly motivated Czechoslovaks reinforcing Allied troops on the Western Front, asked Moscow to halt their evacuation. Moscow issued an order to this effect, but it had no way of enforcing it and the legion continued on its way.[62] Next, the Allies became involved. Following the understanding reached in early April about the formation of an Allied force on Russian territory, they concluded there was no point in transporting the Czech Legion halfway around the world to France when it could remain in Russia and join this force, for which the Japanese were to furnish the bulk of the manpower. On May 2, the Allies, largely on British insistence, decided that the units of the legion located west of Omsk would not continue to Vladivostok but would proceed north, to Murmansk and Archangel, and there await further orders.[63] Moscow did not object, but the decision caused great unhappiness among the Czechoslovaks.

And now an unexpected event upset everyone's plans. On May 14, at the western Siberian town of Cheliabinsk, an altercation occurred between Czech soldiers and Hungarian POWs who were being repatriated. As best as can be reconstructed, a Hungarian threw an iron bar or some other metal object at Czechs standing on the railway platform, seriously injuring one of them. A fight broke out. When the Cheliabinsk Soviet detained some Czechoslovaks involved in the disturbance, others seized the local arsenal and demanded the immediate release of their comrades. Bowing to superior force, the soviet yielded.[64]

Up to this point, the Czechoslovaks had no intention of taking up arms against the Bolshevik Government. In fact, the whole trend of Czechoslovak politics had been one of friendly neutrality. Masaryk was so sympathetic that he urged the Allies to grant the Soviet Government de facto recognition. As for the troops of the legion, the Communist Sadoul wrote that their "loyalty to the Russian Revolution was incontestable."[65]

All this would now change because of one mindless act of Trotsky's. As the newly appointed Commissar of War, Trotsky wanted to act the part, although he had virtually no troops under his command. This ambition in no time transformed a body of well-disposed Czechoslovaks into a "counterrevolutionary" army which in the summer of 1918 presented the Bolsheviks with the most serious military threat since they had taken power.

As soon as Trotsky learned what had transpired at Cheliabinsk and that the Czechs had convened a "Congress of the Czechoslovak Revolutionary Army," he ordered that the representatives of the Czechoslovak National Council in Moscow be placed under arrest. The frightened Czech politicians agreed to all of Trotsky's demands, including complete disarmament of the legion. On May 21, Trotsky ordered that all further movement of the legion eastward must cease: its men were to join the Red Army or be pressed into "labor battalions"—that is, become part of the Bolshevik compulsory labor force. Those who disobeyed were to be confined to concentration camps.* On May 25, Trotsky followed with another order:

> All soviets along the railroad are instructed, under heavy responsibility, to disarm the Czechs. Any Czech along the railroad line found in possession of weapons is to be executed on the spot. Any military train [*echelon*] containing a *single* armed Czech is to be unloaded and [its personnel] placed in a prisoner-of-war camp.[66]

It was a singularly inept command, not only because it was unnecessarily provocative but because Trotsky had no means of enforcing it: the Czech Legion was far and away the strongest military force in Siberia. At the time, it was widely believed that Trotsky acted under German pressure, but it has been established since that the Germans bore no responsibility for these May orders.[67] It was Trotsky's very un-Bolshevik disregard of the "correlation of forces" that sparked the Czechoslovak rebellion.

The Czechoslovaks on May 22 rejected Trotsky's order to disarm:

> The Congress of the Czechoslovak Revolutionary Army, assembled at Cheliabinsk, declares . . . its feelings of sympathy with the Russian revolutionary people in their difficult struggle for the consolidation of the Revolution. However, the Congress, convinced that the Soviet Government is powerless to guarantee our troops free and safe passage to Vladivostok, has unanimously decided not to surrender its arms until it receives assurance that the Corps will be allowed to depart and receive protection from counterrevolutionary trains.[68]

In communicating this decision to Moscow, the Czechoslovak Congress said that it had "unanimously decided not to surrender arms before reaching Vladivostok, considering them a guarantee of safe travel." It expressed the hope that no attempts would be made to impede the departing Czechoslovak troops, since "every conflict would only prejudice the position of the local soviet organs in Siberia."[69] The Allied instructions for units of the legion to be rerouted to Murmansk and Archangel were simply ignored.

When Trotsky's instructions became known, 14,000 Czechoslovaks had already reached Vladivostok, but 20,500 were still strung out along the length

---

*This seems to be the earliest mention of concentration camps in Soviet pronouncements.

86. General Gajda, Commander of the Czech Legion.

of the Trans-Siberian and railroads in central Russia.* Convinced that the Bolsheviks intended to turn them over to the Germans and threatened by the local soviets, they seized control of the Trans-Siberian. But even while so doing, they reaffirmed that they would have no dealings with anyone fighting the Soviet Government.[70]

Once the Czechoslovak troops took over the railroads Bolshevik authority in the cities along them crumbled; and as soon as that happened, the Russian rivals of the Bolsheviks moved in to fill the vacuum. On May 25, the Czechoslovaks occupied the railroad junctions at Mariinsk and Novonikola-evsk, which had the effect of cutting Moscow off from rail and telegraph communications with much of Siberia. Two days later, they took over Cheliabinsk. On May 28 they seized Penza, on June 4 Tomsk, on June 7 Omsk, and on June 8 Samara, the latter of which was defended by the Latvians. As their military operations expanded, the Czechoslovaks centralized the command, choosing as their chief the self-styled "General" Rudolf Gajda, an ambitious adventurer, whose considerable military talents were not matched by political sense. His men had unbounded confidence in him.†

A lthough not directed against it, the Czechoslovak rebellion presented the Bolshevik Government with its first serious military challenge since the

---

*M. Klante, *Von der Wolga zum Amur* (Berlin, 1931), 157. Sadoul, who may have received his information from Trotsky, distributed the legion at the end of May differently: 5,000 in Vladivostok, 20,000 between Vladivostok and Omsk, and another 20,000 west of Omsk, in European Russia: J. Sadoul, *Notes sur la Révolution Bolchevique* (Paris, 1920), 366.

†A medical assistant in the Austro-Hungarian army, he had been promoted to the rank of captain in the Czechoslovak Corps. In 1919, he fought in the armies of Admiral Kolchak. After Czechoslovakia gained independence, he served as chief of staff, until his arrest on charges of betraying military secrets, of which the courts acquitted him. Later still, he collaborated with the Nazis.

Brest-Litovsk Treaty. Despite months of talk, the Red Army existed largely on paper. Bolshevik effectives in Siberia consisted of a few thousand "Red Guards" and a like number of pro-Communist German, Austrian, and Hungarian POWs. This motley force, without central command, was no match for the Czechoslovaks. Desperate, the Soviet Government asked Berlin at the end of June for permission to arm German prisoners of war in Russia for use against them.[71]

It was the Czechoslovak rebellion that finally forced the Bolsheviks to tackle the formation of an army in earnest. The ex-tsarist generals on the Supreme Military Council had been urging them all along to give up the idea of an all-volunteer force composed exclusively of "proletarian" elements and go over to general conscription. Given Russia's population structure, in a conscript army peasants would constitute the overwhelming majority. Lacking any realistic alternatives, Lenin and Trotsky now overcame their aversion to a regular army with a professional officer corps and a mass of peasant conscripts. On April 22 the government ordered all male citizens aged eighteen to forty to undergo an eight-week course of military training. The ruling applied to workers, students, and peasants not engaged in "exploitation"—i.e., not employing hired labor.[72] This was the first step. On May 29 Moscow ordered general mobilization to be carried out in phases. First to be called to colors would be workers from Moscow, Don, and Kuban, born in 1896 and 1897; they were to be followed by workers from Petrograd; then the turn would come for railroad workers and white-collar employees. They were to serve six months. Peasants were as yet unaffected. In June, soldiers' pay was raised from 150 to 250 rubles a month, and the first attempt was made to outfit them with standard uniforms.[73] At the same time, the government began the voluntary registration of ex-officers of the Imperial Army and opened a General Staff Academy.[74] Finally, on July 29, Moscow issued two further decrees, which laid the foundations of the Red Army, as it has been known since. One introduced compulsory military service for all males aged eighteen to forty.[75] Under the provisions of this decree, over half a million men were to be conscripted.[76] The second ordered the registration of all officers of the old army (born in the years 1892 to 1897 inclusive) in designated areas, under threat of punishment by Revolutionary Tribunals.[77]

Such was the origin of the Red Army. Organized with the assistance of professional officers, and soon commanded almost exclusively by them, in structure and discipline it not unnaturally modeled itself on the Imperial Army.[78] Its only innovation was the introduction of political "commissars," posts entrusted to dependable Bolshevik *apparatchiki,* who were to be responsible for the loyalty of the command at all levels. Addressing the Central Executive Committee on July 29, Trotsky, with the bluster that made him so unpopular, assured those worried about the reliability of the former tsarist officers, now called "military specialists," that any who contemplated betraying Soviet Russia would be shot out of hand. "Next to every specialist," he said, "there should stand a commissar, one on the right and another to the left, revolver in hand."[79]

The Red Army quickly became the pampered child of the new regime. As early as May 1918, soldiers were receiving higher pay and bread rations than industrial workers, who loudly protested.[80] Trotsky reintroduced spit and polish along with traditional military discipline. The first parade of the Red Army, held on May 1 at Moscow's Khodynka Field, was a dispirited affair, dominated by Latvians. But in 1919 and the years that followed, Trotsky staged on Red Square meticulously organized and ever more elaborate parades that brought tears to the eyes of the old generals.

The Czechoslovak revolt presented the Bolsheviks with not only a military challenge but also a political one. The cities of the Volga-Ural region and Siberia were crowded with liberal and socialist intellectuals who lacked the courage to stand up to the Bolsheviks but were prepared to exploit any opportunity provided by others. They concentrated in Samara and the Siberian city of Omsk. After the dissolution of the Constituent Assembly some seventy SR deputies traveled to Samara to proclaim themselves Russia's rightful government. Omsk was the headquarters of more centrist elements, led by the Kadets: the politicians here were content to isolate Siberia from Bolshevism and the Civil War. As soon as the Czech Legion had cleared the Bolsheviks out of the principal towns along the central Volga and in Siberia, these intellectuals began to stir.

After the legion had taken Samara (June 8), the deputies of the Constituent Assembly, who under the Bolsheviks had led a conspiratorial existence, emerged into the open and formed a Committee of the Constituent Assembly (Komitet Uchreditel'nogo Sobrania, or Komuch), headed by a five-person directorate. Its program called for "All Power to the Constituent Assembly" and the abrogation of the Brest-Litovsk Treaty. In the weeks that followed, Komuch issued edicts that conformed to the program of Russian democratic socialism, including the abolition of limitations on individual liberty and the dissolution of Revolutionary Tribunals. Komuch reinstated, as organs of general self-government, the old *zemstva* and Municipal Councils, but it also retained the soviets, ordering them to hold new elections. It denationalized the banks and expressed a readiness to honor Russian state debts. The Bolshevik Land Decree, copied from the SR agrarian program, was kept in force.[81]

While Komuch saw itself as a replacement of the Bolshevik regime, the Siberian politicians in Omsk had more modest regional objectives. They organized in areas which the Czechoslovaks had cleared of Bolsheviks, and on June 1, 1918, proclaimed themselves the Government of Western Siberia.

The Czechoslovaks at first showed no sympathy for the Russian opponents of the Bolsheviks.[82] When the SRs approached them for support, they refused, on the grounds that their sole mission was to ensure safe and prompt transit to Vladivostok. Wish it or not, however, they could not avoid becoming involved in Russian politics because to realize their objective they had to deal with the local authorities, which meant increased relations with Komuch and the Siberian Government.[83]

When the Czechoslovaks rebelled, Moscow believed that they were acting under instructions from Allied governments. Communist historians have adhered to this version, although there is no evidence to support it. On the French side, we have the word of a historian who had seen all the pertinent archival materials that "nothing indicates the French were the instigators of the [Czechoslovak] uprising."[84] This confirms the view of Sadoul, who tried at the time, without much success, to convince his friend Trotsky that the French Government bore no responsibility for the Czechoslovak armies.[85] In fact, initially at least, the Czechoslovak rising was a disagreeable surprise for the French because it upset their plans to bring the legion to the Western Front.[86] Nor is there evidence of British involvement. Communist historians later tried to pin the blame on Masaryk, who actually was the unhappiest of all, because the Czechoslovak entanglement in Russian affairs interfered with his plan to assemble in France a national Czech army.*

But whatever the historical truth, in the heat of events it was as natural for Moscow to see the Allied hand behind General Gajda as it was for the Czech Legion to see German pressure in the orders to have it disarmed. The Czechoslovak affair destroyed such chance as existed of Bolshevik economic and military cooperation with the Allies and pushed Moscow—not entirely unwillingly—into German arms.

Until June 1918, the generals were the only influential party in Germany that demanded a break with the Bolsheviks. They were overruled by the industrialists and bankers who worked hand in glove with the Foreign Office. But now the generals found an unexpected ally. After the Czechoslovak uprising, Mirbach and Riezler lost all faith in the viability of Lenin's regime and urged Berlin still more strongly to seek an alternate base of support in Russia. Riezler's recommendations were based not only on impressions; he had firsthand knowledge that the forces on which the Bolsheviks counted to stop the Czechoslovaks were about to desert them. On June 25, he advised Berlin that although the Moscow Embassy was doing all it could to help the Bolsheviks against the Czech Legion and domestic opponents, the effort seemed futile.[87] What he had in mind became known only years later. To persuade Lieutenant Colonel M. A. Muraviev, the commander of the Red Army on the Eastern Front in the civil war to fight the Czechs, Riezler had to bribe him.† Even more

---

*"One is reduced to the conclusion that external instigation or encouragement, either from the Allies or from the central headquarters of the underground Whites, played no significant part in the decision of the Czechs to take arms against the Soviet power. The outbreak of these hostilities was a spontaneous occurrence . . . desired by none of the parties concerned": G. F. Kennan, *The Decision to Intervene* (Princeton, N.J., 1958), 164.

†Baumgart, *Ostpolitik*, 227; Erdmann, *Riezler*, 474; Alfons Paquet in Winfried Baumgart, ed., *Von Brest-Litovsk zur deutschen Novemberrevolution* (Göttingen, 1971), 76. Muraviev defected anyway in early July and died at the hands of his troops.

troubling was the growing reluctance of the Latvians to continue fighting for the Bolsheviks. Sensing that the fortunes of their Bolshevik patrons were on the decline and afraid of being isolated, they contemplated switching sides. It took more of Riezler's money to persuade them to help suppress Savinkov's uprising in Iaroslavl in July.[88]

Meanwhile, the Czechs were capturing one city after another. On June 29 they seized Vladivostok and on July 6 Ufa. In Irkutsk, they ran into Bolshevik resistance, but they overcame it and on July 11 occupied the town. By this time, the entire length of the Trans-Siberian with its feeder lines in eastern Russia, from Penza to the Pacific, was in their hands.

The unimpeded Czechoslovak advance and the threat of defections from Bolshevik ranks filled Mirbach and Riezler with the gloomiest forebodings. Their fear was that the Allies would take advantage of the crisis to engineer an SR coup which would bring Russia back into the Allied fold. To prevent the catastrophe, Riezler urged Berlin to make approaches to the liberal and conservative Russians, represented by the Right Center, the Kadet Party, the Omsk Government, and the Don Cossacks.*

The alarming reports from the Moscow Embassy, added to the complaints of the military, moved the German Government to put the "Russian question" once again on the agenda. The question it faced can be formulated as follows: whether to stick with the Bolsheviks through thick and thin because (1) they devastated Russia so thoroughly as to remove her as a threat for a long time to come and (2) by acquiescing to the Brest-Litovsk Treaty they placed at Germany's disposal the richest regions of Russia; or else to drop them in favor of a more conventional but also more viable regime that would keep Russia within the German orbit, even if this meant giving up some of the territories acquired at Brest-Litovsk. Advocates of these respective positions disagreed over the means. Their objectives were identical—namely, so to weaken Russia that she would never again help France and England "encircle" Germany and, at the same time, lay her wide open to economic penetration. But whereas the anti-Bolshevik party wanted to attain these objectives by carving Russia up into dependent political entities, the Foreign Office preferred to do so by using the Bolsheviks to drain the country from within. Settling this matter one way or another was a matter of some urgency in view of the unanimous opinion of the Moscow Embassy that the Bolsheviks were about to fall.

No one in the German Government desired the Bolsheviks to stay in power for long: the dispute was over the short term, the duration of the war. The difficulty of resolving the dispute was compounded by the volatility of the Kaiser, who one day fulminated against the "Jewish" Bolsheviks and wanted an international crusade against them and the next spoke of the same Bolsheviks as Germany's best partners.

Ludendorff pressed to have the Bolsheviks liquidated. They were treach-

---

*Erdmann, *Riezler*, 711–12. Riezler included the Kadets among Germany's potential allies because their leader, Miliukov, then living in the Ukraine, had come out in favor of a pro-German orientation. Other Kadets remained true to the Allies.

erous: "we can expect nothing from this Soviet Government even though it lives at our mercy." He was especially worried by the "infection" of German soldiers with Bolshevik propaganda, which, following the transfer of hundreds of thousands of troops from the east, spread to the Western Front. He wanted to weaken Russia and "claim it [for Germany] by force."[89]

The Moscow Embassy sided with the military, but it recommended revisions in the Brest Treaty as a price of winning support from respectable Russian political groupings.

The contrary point of view was advanced by Kühlmann and the foreign service (except for the Moscow Embassy) with the backing of many politicians and most of the German business community. A Foreign Office memorandum, drafted in May, formulated an argument for continued collaboration with the Bolsheviks:

> The pleas for German help which issue from diverse sources in Russia—mainly from reactionary circles—can best be explained by the fear of the propertied classes of the Bolshevik threat to their possessions and assets. Germany is to play the role of the bailiff who chases the Bolsheviks out of the Russian house and restores the reactionaries, who will then pursue against Germany the very same policy which the tsarist regime pursued in the last decades. . . . In regard to Great Russia, we have only one overriding interest: to promote the forces of decomposition and to keep the country weak for a long time to come, exactly as Prince Bismarck had done in regard to France after 1871. . . .
>
> It is in our interest soon genuinely to normalize relations with Russia in order to seize the country's economy. The more we mix in this country's internal affairs, the wider will grow the chasm that already separates us from Russia. . . . It must not be overlooked that the Brest-Litovsk Treaty was ratified only by the Bolsheviks, and not even by all of them. . . . It is, therefore, in our interest to have the Bolsheviks remain at the helm for the time being. In order to stay in power, they will, for now, do all they can to maintain toward us the appearance of loyalty and to keep the peace. On the other hand, their leaders, being Jewish businessmen, will before long give up their theories in favor of profitable commercial and transport practices. Here we must proceed slowly but purposefully. Russia's transport, industry, and entire national economy must fall into our hands.[90]

With such thoughts in mind, Kühlmann advocated a strict hands-off policy in Russia. In response to what apparently was a Bolshevik inquiry, he wanted to assure Moscow that neither the Germans nor the Finns had any designs on Petrograd: such assurances would make it possible to shift Latvian troops from west to east, where they were desperately needed to fight the Czech Legion.[91]

For those who believe that some days are more "historic" than others, June 28, 1918, should loom as one of the most historic of modern times, for it was on that day that the Kaiser, with one impulsive decision, saved the Bolshevik regime from the sentence of death which it was in his power to pass. The occasion was a report on the Russian question forwarded to him at his headquarters. He had before him two memoranda, one from the Foreign

Office, signed by Chancellor Georg von Hertling, the other from Hindenburg. The rapporteur, Baron Kurt von Grünau, represented the Foreign Office on the Kaiser's staff. Anyone with experience in such matters is aware of the power which a rapporteur wields on such occasions. When he presents to the chief executive policy options which require the latter to make a choice on the basis of very imperfect knowledge of the facts, he can, by subtle manipulation, push the decision-maker in the direction he favors. Grünau made full use of this opportunity to advance the interests of the Foreign Office. To a large extent, the Kaiser made his critical decision as a result of the manner in which Grünau presented the policy options to him:

> It was an essential trait of the impulsive nature of the Kaiser, who was ruled by momentary moods and sudden flashes, to identify himself with the first arguments which an adviser presented to him, to the extent that they appeared to him to be conclusive [*schlüssig*]. So it happened on this occasion, too. Counselor Grünau succeeded in informing the Kaiser of the telegram from Hertling [with Kühlmann's recommendations] just before placing in front of him Hindenburg's preference. The Kaiser immediately declared himself in agreement with the Chancellor and stated in particular that the Germans were to undertake no military operations in Russia, that the Soviet Government be informed that it could safely withdraw troops from Petrograd and deploy them against the Czechs, and finally, "without foreclosing future opportunities," that support be extended to the Soviet Government as the only party that accepted the Brest Treaty.[92]

The immediate effect of the Kaiser's decision was to enable Trotsky to transfer Latvian regiments from the western border to the Volga-Ural front. Since they were the only pro-Bolshevik military units capable of combat, this action saved the Bolshevik regime in the east from total collapse. At the end of July, the 5th Latvian Regiment and elements of the 4th engaged the Czechoslovaks near Kazan, the 6th attacked them at Ekaterinburg, and the 7th suppressed an anti-Bolshevik uprising of armed workers at Izhevsk-Botkin. These operations turned the tide of battle in the Bolsheviks' favor. In a telegram to Ioffe which German intelligence intercepted, Chicherin stressed how helpful it was for Soviet Russia to be able to withdraw troops from the German front and throw them against the Czechoslovaks.[93]

The long-term effect of the Kaiser's verdict was to enable the Bolsheviks to weather the most critical period in their history. It would have cost the Germans no effort to seize Petrograd and only a bit more to occupy Moscow, both cities being virtually undefended. Then they could have repeated their Ukrainian operation and placed a puppet government over Russia. No one doubted their ability to do so. In April, when the Bolsheviks had been in a stronger position, Trotsky told Sadoul that they could be removed by a party backed by the Germans.[94] The Kaiser's decision at the end of June ended this possibility permanently: six weeks later, when their offensive in the west ground to a halt, the Germans were no longer in a position to intervene decisively in internal Russian affairs. The knowledge that the Germans continued to back the Bolsheviks also disheartened the Russian opposition. Relaying the Kaiser's wishes to Moscow, Kühlmann instructed the embassy at the end of June to continue collaborating with Lenin. On July 1, Riezler broke off talks with the Right Center.[95]

With the approach of summer 1918, the Left SRs grew restless. Romantic revolutionaries, they craved perpetual excitement: the ecstasy of October, the intoxication of February 1918, when the nation rose to repel the German invasion, unforgettable days celebrated by their poet, Alexander Blok, in the two most famous poems of the Revolution, "The Twelve" and "Scythians." But this was all in the past, and now they found themselves partners of a regime of calculating politicians, who made deals with the Germans and the Allies, and invited the "bourgeoisie" back to run factories and lead the armed forces. What happened to the Revolution? Nothing the Bolsheviks did after February 1918 pleased them. They despised the Brest Treaty, which in their eyes made Germany the master of Russia and Lenin a lackey of Mirbach's: instead of consorting with the Germans, they wanted to arouse the masses against these imperialists, with bare hands if need be, and carry the Revolution into the heart of Europe. When the Bolsheviks, disregarding their protests, signed and ratified Brest, the Left SRs quit from the Sovnarkom. They opposed no less vehemently the policy adopted by the Bolsheviks in May 1918 of sending armed detachments of workers to the villages to extract grain, since it caused bad blood between peasants and workers. They objected to the reintroduction of capital punishment and saved many lives by having their members veto every death sentence passed on political prisoners by the Collegium of the Cheka. Inexorably, they came to regard the Bolsheviks as traitors to the Revolution. As their leader, Maria Spiridonova, put it: "It is painful now . . . to realize that the Bolsheviks, with whom until now I have worked side by side, alongside whom I have fought on the same barricade, and with whom I have hoped to fight the glorious battle to the end, . . . have taken over the policies of the Kerensky government."[96]

In the spring of 1918, the Left SRs assumed toward the Bolsheviks the same attitude that the Bolsheviks had adopted in 1917 toward the Provisional Government and the democratic socialists. They posed as the conscience of the Revolution, the incorruptible alternative to a regime of opportunists and compromisers. As the Bolshevik influence among industrial workers waned, the Left SRs became a dangerous rival, for they appealed to the same anarchic and destructive instincts of the Russian masses which the Bolsheviks themselves had exploited on the road to power but once in power did all they could to quell. They enjoyed support among some of the rowdiest urban elements, including radical Petrograd workers and the sailors of what had been the Baltic and Black Sea fleets. Essentially, they appealed to the very groups which had helped bring the Bolsheviks to power in October and now felt betrayed.

On April 17–25, the Left SRs held a congress in Moscow. It claimed to represent over 60,000 members. Most delegates wanted a clean break with the Bolsheviks and their *"komissaroderzhavie"* ("rule of the commissars").[97] Two months later (June 24), at a secret meeting, the Central Committee of the Left SR Party decided to raise the banner of rebellion.[98] The "breathing spell" purchased by Brest was to be brought to an end. They would introduce at the forthcoming Fifth Congress of Soviets, scheduled for July 4, a motion calling for the abrogation of the Brest-Litovsk Treaty and a declaration of war on Germany. If it failed to pass, the Left SRs would initiate terroristic provocations to bring about a breach between Russia and Germany. The resolution adopted by that meeting read as follows:

> The Central Committee of the Left SR Party, having examined the present political situation of the Republic, resolves that in the interest of the Russian as well as the International Revolution, an immediate end must be put to the so-called breathing spell created by the Treaty of Brest-Litovsk.
>
> The Central Committee believes it to be both practical and possible to organize a series of terrorist acts against the leading representatives of German imperialism. In order to realize this, the forces of the party must be organized and all necessary precautions taken so that the peasantry and the working class will join this movement and actively help the party. Therefore, at the instant of the terrorist act all papers should make known our participation in the events in the Ukraine, in the agitation among the peasants, and in the blowing up of arsenals. This must be done after Moscow gives a signal. Such a signal may be an act of terrorism or it can take another form. In order to distribute the forces of the party, a committee of three (Spiridonova, Maiorov, and Golubovskii) has been appointed.
>
> In view of the fact that, contrary to the wishes of the party, this may involve a collision with the Bolsheviks, the Central Committee makes the following declaration: We regard our policy as an attack on the current policy of the Council of the People's Commissars, but definitely not as a fight against the Bolsheviks themselves. As it is possible that the Bolsheviks may take aggressive counteraction against our party, we are determined, if necessary, to defend our position with force of arms. In order to prevent the party from being exploited by counterrevolutionary elements, it is resolved that our new policy be stated clearly and openly, so that an international socialist-revolutionary policy may subsequently be inaugurated in Soviet Russia.[99]

As this resolution indicates, the Left SRs intended in many ways but one to emulate Bolshevik actions in October 1917: the one crucial difference being that they did not aspire to power. That was to be left in Bolshevik hands. The Left SRs wanted only to compel the Bolsheviks to abandon their "opportunistic" policies by provoking Germany to attack Soviet Russia in reaction to anti-German terrorism. The plan was entirely unrealistic: it gambled on the expectation that the Germans would impulsively give up the immense benefits they had gained at Brest, and altogether ignored the common interest linking Berlin and Moscow.

Spiridonova, the most powerful personality on the three-person Left SR

87. Maria Spiridonova, second from left.

committee, was possessed of a courage that in earlier centuries characterized religious martyrs, but nothing remotely resembling common sense. Foreigners who observed her during these days left very uncomplimentary accounts. For Riezler she was a "dried-up skirt." Alfons Paquet, a German journalist, saw her as

> a tireless hysteric with a pince-nez, the caricature of Athena, who, while speaking, always seemed to be reaching out for an invisible harp, and who, when the hall would burst into applause and rage, would impatiently stamp her feet, lifting the fallen shoulder straps of her dress.[100]

Immediately after the decision, the Left SRs went to work. They sent agitators to the military garrisons in Moscow and its suburbs: some of these they won to their side, the rest they succeeded in neutralizing. Left SRs working in the Cheka assembled a military force to fight in the event the Bolsheviks counterattacked. Preparations were made to carry out a terrorist act against the German Ambassador: his assassination was to serve as the signal for a nationwide rising. Emulating Bolshevik tactics on the eve of October, the Left SRs did not conceal their plans. On June 29, their organ *Znamia truda* carried on its front page an appeal to all able-bodied Left SRs to report no later than July 2 to their party's regional offices; regional committees of the party were instructed to give them military training.[101] The next day, Spiridonova declared publicly that only an armed uprising could save the Revolution.[102] It remains an inexplicable mystery how Dzerzhinskii and his Latvian associates in the Cheka could have ignored these warnings and let themselves be caught by surprise on July 6.

A partial, but only partial, answer to this question is provided by the fact that several of the conspirators worked in the directing organs of the Cheka. Dzerzhinskii had chosen as his deputy a Left SR, Petr Aleksandrovich Dmi-

trievskii, popularly known as Aleksandrovich, in whom he had complete faith
and entrusted with broad authority. Other Left SRs employed by the Cheka
and involved in the conspiracy included Iakov Bliumkin, whose responsibility
was counterespionage and penetration of the German Embassy, the photogra-
pher Nicholas Andreev, and D. I. Popov, the commander of a Cheka cavalry
detachment. These individuals hatched a conspiracy within the headquarters
of the secret police. Popov assembled several hundred armed men, mostly
pro-Left SR sailors. Bliumkin and Andreev assumed responsibility for assassinating Mirbach. The two familiarized themselves with the building of the
German mission and took photographs of the escape route they were to take
after killing the ambassador.

The *troika* which supervised these preparations planned to stage the
uprising on either the second or the third day of the Fifth Congress of Soviets,
scheduled for the evening of July 4. Spiridonova was to introduce a motion
calling for the abrogation of the Brest-Litovsk Treaty and a declaration of war
on Germany. Since the Mandate Committee, which determined the representation at the congress, had generously allotted them 40 percent of the seats,
and it was known that many Bolsheviks opposed Brest, the Left SR leaders
thought they stood a good chance of winning a majority. If, however, they
failed, they would raise the banner of rebellion with a terrorist act against the
German Ambassador. July 6 was a favorable day for action because it happened to fall on St. John's Day *(Ivanov den')*, a Latvian national holiday which
the Latvian Rifles were to celebrate with an outing at Khodynka Field on
the outskirts of Moscow, leaving behind only a skeleton staff to protect the
Kremlin.*

As subsequent events were to show, the situation in Moscow was so
tenuous that had the Left SRs wanted to seize power they could have done
so with even greater ease than the Bolsheviks in October. But they emphatically did not want the responsibility of governing. Their rebellion was not so
much a coup d'état as a coup de théâtre, a grand political demonstration
intended to galvanize the "masses" and revive their flagging revolutionary
spirit. They committed the very error that Lenin was forever warning his
followers against, that of "playing" at revolution.

When the Congress of Soviets opened at the Bolshoi Theater, the Left
SRs and Bolsheviks at once flew at each other's throats. Left SR speakers
accused the Bolsheviks of betraying the Revolution and instigating a war
between city and village, while the Bolsheviks charged the Left SRs with trying
to provoke a war between Russia and Germany. The Left SRs introduced a
motion calling for an expression of no confidence in the Bolshevik Govern-

*According to their commander, I. I. Vatsetis, by that time most of the Latvian units had
been dispatched to the Volga-Ural Front: *Pamiat'*, No. 2 (1979), 16.

ment, the abrogation of the Brest-Litovsk Treaty, and a declaration of war on Germany. The Bolshevik majority defeated the motion, whereupon the Left SRs walked out.[103]

According to Bliumkin, in the evening of July 4 Spiridonova requested him to come see her.[104] She said that the party wanted him to assassinate Mirbach. Bliumkin asked for twenty-four hours to make the necessary preparations. These included procuring for himself and Andreev a document bearing a forged signature of Dzerzhinskii requesting for the two men an audience with the German Ambassador, two revolvers, two bombs, and a car belonging to the Cheka chauffeured by Popov.

Around 2:15–2:30 p.m. on July 6 two representatives of the Cheka presented themselves at the German Embassy on Denezhnyi Pereulok. One identified himself as Iakov Bliumkin, an official of the Cheka counterintelligence service, the other as Nicholas Andreev, a representative of the Revolutionary Tribunal. They showed credentials signed by Dzerzhinskii and a secretary of the Cheka authorizing them to discuss "a matter of direct concern to the ambassador."[105] This turned out to be the case of a Lieutenant Robert Mirbach, believed to be a relative of the ambassador, whom the Cheka had detained on suspicion of espionage. The visitors were received by Riezler and an interpreter, Lieutenant L. G. Miller. Riezler told them that he had the authority to speak on Count Mirbach's behalf, but the Russians refused to deal with him, insisting that Dzerzhinskii had instructed them to speak personally with the ambassador.

The German Embassy had for some time been receiving warnings of possible violence. There were anonymous letters and suspicious incidents, such as visits by electricians to inspect lighting fixtures that were in perfect working order and strangers taking photographs of the embassy building. Mirbach was reluctant to meet with the visitors, but since they produced credentials from the head of the Cheka he came down to see them. The Russians said he might be interested in the case of Lieutenant Mirbach. The ambassador replied that he would prefer that the information be provided in writing. At this point, Bliumkin and Andreev reached into their briefcases and pulled out revolvers, which they fired at Mirbach and Riezler. All their shots missed. Riezler and Miller dropped to the floor. Mirbach rose and tried to escape through the main living room to the upstairs quarters. Andreev ran after him and fired at the back of the head. Bliumkin threw a bomb into the middle of the room. The two assassins jumped out of the open windows. Bliumkin injured himself, but he managed to follow Andreev and climb a two-and-a-half-meter-high iron fence surrounding the embassy building to reach the automobile which waited outside with its engine running. Mirbach, who never regained consciousness, died at 3:15 p.m.[106]

The embassy staff feared that the assault on its ambassador signaled a general attack. The military personnel assumed responsibility for security. Attempts to communicate with the Soviet authorities proved of no avail because the telephone lines had been cut. Bothmer, the military attaché, rushed to the Metropole Hotel, the seat of the Commissariat of Foreign Affairs. There he told Karakhan, Chicherin's deputy, what had happened. Karakhan contacted the Kremlin. Lenin received the news around 3:30 p.m. and immediately notified Dzerzhinskii and Sverdlov.[107]

Later that afternoon, a procession of Bolshevik notables visited the German Embassy. The first to arrive was Radek, with a sidearm which Bothmer describes as the size of a small siege gun. He was followed by Chicherin, Karakhan, and Dzerzhinskii. A squad of Latvian Rifles accompanied the Bolshevik notables. Lenin remained in the Kremlin, but Riezler, who assumed charge of the embassy, insisted that he appear in person with an explanation and apology. It was a most unusual demand for a foreign diplomat to make of a head of state, but such was the influence of the Germans at the time that Lenin had to obey. He came to the embassy, accompanied by Sverdlov, around 5 p.m. According to German witnesses, he displayed a purely technical interest in the tragedy, asking to be shown the place where the murder had been committed, the exact arrangement of the furniture, and the damage caused by the bomb. He declined to view the body of the deceased. He offered an apology which, in the words of one German, was as "cold as a dog's snout" and promised that the guilty would be punished.[108] Bothmer thought that the Russians looked very frightened.

When they fled, the assassins left their papers behind, including the document which had gained them admission to the embassy. From this material and information supplied by Riezler, Dzerzhinskii learned that the gunmen had presented themselves as representatives of the Cheka. Thoroughly alarmed, he set off for the Pokrovskii Barracks, which housed the Cheka Combat Detachment on Bol'shoi Trekhsviatitel'skii Pereulok 1. The barracks were under Popov's control. Dzerzhinskii demanded that Bliumkin and Andreev be turned over to him, under the threat of having the entire Central Committee of the Left SR Party shot. Instead of complying, Popov's sailors arrested Dzerzhinskii. He was to serve as a hostage to guarantee the safety of Spiridonova, who had gone to the Congress of Soviets to announce that Russia had been "liberated from Mirbach."[109]

These events took place in a torrential rain, accompanied by thunder, which soon enveloped Moscow in a thick fog.

On his return to the Kremlin, Lenin was horrified to learn that Dzerzhinskii was a prisoner of the Cheka: according to Bonch-Bruevich, when he heard this news "Lenin did not turn pale—he turned white."[110] Suspecting that the Cheka had betrayed him, Lenin, through Trotsky, ordered it dissolved. M. Ia. Latsis was to organize a fresh security police.[111] Latsis raced to the Cheka headquarters at Bolshaia Lubianka to find that this building, too, was under Popov's control. The Left SR sailors who escorted him to Popov's headquarters wanted to shoot Latsis on the spot: he was saved by the intercession of the Left SR Aleksandrovich.[112] It was a comradely gesture that Latsis would not reciprocate a few days later when the roles were reversed and Aleksandrovich fell into the hands of the Cheka.

That evening, the sailors and soldiers affiliated with the Left SRs went into the streets to take hostages: they stopped automobiles from which they removed twenty-seven Bolshevik functionaries.

At the disposal of the Left SRs were 2,000 armed sailors and cavalry, eight artillery guns, sixty-four machine guns, and four to six armored cars.[113] It was a formidable force, given that the bulk of Moscow's Latvian contingent was relaxing in the suburbs and that soldiers of the Russian garrisons either sided with the rebels or professed neutrality. Lenin now found himself in the same humiliating predicament as Kerensky the previous October, a head of state without an armed force to defend his government. At this point, had the Left SRs so desired, there was nothing to prevent them from seizing the Kremlin and arresting the entire Bolshevik leadership. They did not even have to use force, for the members of their Central Committee carried passes giving them access to the Kremlin, including the offices and private apartments of Lenin.[114]

But the Left SRs had no such intentions and it was their aversion to power that saved the Bolsheviks. Their aim was to provoke the Germans and arouse the Russian "masses." As one of the Left SR leaders told the captive Dzerzhinskii:

> You stand before a fait accompli. The Brest Treaty is annulled; a war with Germany is unavoidable. We do not want power: let it be here as in the Ukraine. We will go underground. You can keep power, but you must stop being lackeys of Mirbach. Let Germany occupy Russia up to the Volga.[115]

So instead of marching on the Kremlin and overthrowing the Soviet Government, a detachment of Left SRs, headed by P. P. Proshian, went to the Central Post and Telegraph Office, which it occupied without resistance and from where it sent out appeals to Russian workers, peasants, and soldiers as well as the "whole world."* These appeals were confused and contradictory. The Left SRs took responsibility for the murder of Mirbach and denounced the Bolsheviks as "agents of German imperialism." They declared themselves in favor of the "soviet system" but rejected all other socialist parties as "counter-revolutionary." In one telegram, they declared themselves to be "in power." In the words of Vatsetis, the Left SRs acted "indecisively."[116]

Spiridonova arrived at the Bolshoi Theater at 7 p.m. and delivered a long and rambling speech to the congress. Other Left SR speakers followed. There was total confusion. At 8 p.m. the delegates learned that armed Latvians had surrounded the building and sealed off the entrances, whereupon the Bol-

---

*V. Vladimirova in *PR*, No. 4/63 (1927), 122–23; Lenin, *Sochineniia*, XXIII, 554–56; *Krasnaia Kniga VChK*, II (Moscow, 1920), 148–55. Proshian had served as Commissar of Post and Telegraphs earlier in the year.

sheviks left. Spiridonova asked her followers to adjourn to the second floor. There she jumped on a table and screamed: "Hey, you, land, listen! Hey, you, land, listen!"[117] The Bolshevik delegates, assembled in a wing of the Bolshoi, could not decide whether they were attacking or under attack. As Bukharin later told Isaac Steinberg: "We were sitting in our room waiting for you to come and arrest us. . . . As you did not do it, we decided to arrest you instead."[118]

It was high time for the Bolsheviks to act; but hours went by and nothing happened. The government was in the grip of panic, for it had no serious force on which to rely. According to its own estimates, of the 24,000 armed men stationed in Moscow, one-third were pro-Bolshevik, one-fifth unreliable (i.e., anti-Bolshevik), and the rest uncertain.[119] But even the pro-Bolshevik units could not be moved. The Bolshevik leadership was in such desperate straits it considered evacuating the Kremlin.[120]

At 5 p.m., I. I. Vatsetis, the commander of the Latvian Rifles, was summoned by N. I. Muralov, the commander of the Moscow Military District, to his headquarters. Also awaiting him there was Podvoiskii. The two briefed Vatsetis on the situation and asked him to prepare a plan of operations. At the same time, they told the shocked Latvian that another officer would be put in charge of the operation. This lack of confidence was almost certainly due to the Kremlin's knowledge of Vatsetis's dealings with the German Embassy. After attempts to find another Latvian to take command had failed, Vatsetis offered his services, guaranteeing success "with his head." This was communicated to the Kremlin.*

Around 11:30 p.m. Lenin called to his office the Latvian political commissars attached to Vatsetis's headquarters and asked whether they could vouch for the commander's loyalty.[121] When they responded affirmatively, Lenin consented to having Vatsetis put in charge of the operation against the Left SRs, but as an added precaution had four political commissars attached to his staff, instead of the usual two.

At midnight, Vatsetis received a call to meet with Lenin. This is how he describes the encounter:

> The Kremlin was dark and empty. We were led into the meeting hall of the Council of People's Commissars and asked to wait. . . . The fairly spacious premises in which I now found myself for the first time were illuminated by a single electric bulb, suspended from under the ceiling somewhere in the corner. The window curtains were drawn. The atmosphere reminded me of the front in the theater of military operations. . . . A few minutes later the door at the opposite end of the room opened and Comrade Lenin entered. He approached me with quick steps and asked in a low voice: "Comrade, will we hold out till the morning?" Having asked the question, Lenin kept on staring at me. I had become accustomed that day to the unexpected, but Comrade Lenin's question took me aback with its sharp formulation. . . . Why was it important to hold out until the morning? Won't we hold out to the end? Was

---

*It is known from Riezler's recollections (Erdmann, *Riezler,* 474) that the German Embassy had to bribe the Latvians to move against the Left SRs.

88. Colonel I. Vatsetis, commander of Latvian Rifles, as an
officer in the Imperial Army.

our situation perhaps so precarious that my commissars had concealed from
me its true nature?[122]

Before answering Lenin's question, Vatsetis requested time to survey the
situation.[123] The city had fallen into the hands of the rebels, except for the
Kremlin, which stood out like a fortress under siege. When he arrived at
the headquarters of the Latvian Division, his chief of staff told Vatsetis that
the "entire Moscow garrison" had turned against the Bolsheviks. The so-called
People's Army (Narodnaia Armiia), the largest contingent of the Moscow
garrison, which was undergoing training to fight the Germans alongside
French and British troops, had decided to remain neutral. Another regiment
had declared itself in favor of the Left SRs. The Latvians were all that was
left: one battalion of the 1st Regiment, one battalion of the 2nd, and the 9th
Regiment. There was also the 3rd Latvian Regiment, but its loyalty was in
doubt. Vatsetis could also count on a Latvian artillery battery and a few
smaller units, including a company of pro-Communist Hungarian POWs,
commanded by Béla Kun.

With this information in hand, Vatsetis decided to delay the counterattack until the early hours of the morning, when the Latvian units would have
returned from Khodynka. He dispatched two companies of the 9th Latvian
Regiment to retake the Central Post and Telegraph Office, but they either
proved inept or else defected, for the Left SRs managed to disarm them.

At 2 a.m. Vatsetis returned to the Kremlin:

Comrade Lenin entered by the same door and approached me with the same
quick steps. I took several paces toward him and reported: "No later than

twelve noon on July 7, we shall triumph all along the line." Lenin took my right hand into both of his and, pressing it very hard, said, "Thank you, comrade. You have made me very happy."[124]

When he launched his counterattack at 5 a.m. in humid and foggy weather, Vatsetis had under his command 3,300 men, of whom fewer than 500 were Russians. The Left SRs fought back ferociously, and it took the Latvians nearly seven hours to reduce the rebel centers and release, unharmed, Dzerzhinskii, Latsis, and the remaining hostages. Vatsetis received from Trotsky a bonus of 10,000 rubles for a job well done.[125]

On July 7 and 8 the Bolsheviks arrested and questioned the rebels, including Spiridonova and other Left SR delegates to the Congress of Soviets. Riezler demanded that the government execute all those responsible for the murder of his ambassador, including the Central Committee of the Left SR Party. The government appointed two commissions, one to investigate the Left SR uprising, the other to look into the disloyal behavior of the garrison. Six hundred and fifty Left SRs were taken into custody in Moscow, Petrograd, and the provincial cities. A few days later it was announced that 200 of them had been shot.[126] Ioffe told the Germans in Berlin that among those executed was Spiridonova. This greatly pleased them, and the German press played up the executions. The information was false: but when Chicherin issued a denial, the German Foreign Office used its influence to keep it out of the newspapers.[127]

In reality, the Bolsheviks treated the Left SRs with most unusual forbearance. Instead of carrying out a mass execution of those who had fought them arms in hand, as they would do a few days later in Iaroslavl, they briefly interrogated the prisoners and then had most of them released. They executed twelve sailors from Popov's detachments as well as Aleksandrovich, whom they had caught at a railroad station trying to escape. Spiridonova and one of her associates were taken to the Kremlin and placed in a makeshift prison under Latvian guard. Two days later she was moved to a two-room apartment in the Kremlin, where she lived in relative comfort until her trial in November 1918. The Bolsheviks did not outlaw the Left SR Party and allowed it to bring out its newspaper. *Pravda,* referring to the Left SRs as "prodigal sons," expressed the hope that they would soon return to the fold.[128] Zinoviev lavished praise on Spiridonova as a "wonderful woman" with a "heart of gold" whose imprisonment kept him awake at night.[129]

Neither before nor after did the Bolsheviks show such leniency to their enemies. Indeed, this unusual behavior has led some historians to suspect that the murder of Mirbach and the Left SR uprising had been staged by the Bolsheviks, although it is difficult to find a motive for such elaborate deception or an explanation of how it could have been concealed from the participants.[130] The explanation, however, does not require any resort to conspiratorial theories. In July the Bolsheviks found themselves in what seemed a hopeless situation, under attack by the Czechs, facing armed rebellion in Iaroslavl and

Murom, abandoned by Russian workers and soldiers, unsure even of the loyalty of the Latvians. They were not about to antagonize the followers of the Left SR Party. But above all, they feared for their lives. Radek surely did not speak only for himself when he confided to a German friend that the Bolsheviks treated the Left SRs so leniently from fear of their revenge.[131] The ranks of that party were indeed filled with fanatics who thought little of sacrificing themselves for their cause: fanatics like Spiridonova herself, who in a letter to the Bolshevik leaders from prison came close to expressing regret that she had not been executed since her death might have brought them to their "senses."[132] Mirbach's successor, Karl Helfferich, also was of the opinion that the Bolsheviks were afraid to liquidate the Left SRs.[133]

In November 1918, the Revolutionary Tribunal tried the Left SR Central Committee, most of whose members had fled or gone underground. Spiridonova and Iu. V. Sablin, who did stand trial, received one-year terms. Spiridonova did not serve out her sentence; she was sprung from the Kremlin prison by the Left SRs in April 1919.* She spent the rest of her life in and out of prison. In 1937, she was condemned to twenty-five years for "counterrevolutionary activity": in 1941, as the German armies approached Orel, where she was imprisoned, she was taken out and shot.[134] Neither of Mirbach's assassins lived to a ripe old age. Andreev died of typhus in the Ukraine the following year. Bliumkin led an underground existence until May 1919, when he turned himself in. Having repented, he was not only forgiven but admitted into the Communist Party and appointed to Trotsky's staff. In late 1930 he had the bad judgment to carry messages to his followers in Russia. He was arrested and executed.[135]

In the wake of the July uprising the Left SRs split into two factions, one of which approved of it, the other of which disowned it. In time, both factions dissolved in the Communist Party, except for a minuscule group which went underground.[136]

Dzerzhinskii was suspended from his job. Officially, he resigned as chairman and member of the Cheka to serve as a witness in the forthcoming trial of Mirbach's assassins,[137] but since the Bolsheviks did not normally observe such legal niceties and no such trial took place, this was merely a face-saving formula. His suspension was almost certainly due to Lenin's suspicion that he had been implicated in the Left SR conspiracy. Latsis directed the secret police until August 22, when Dzerzhinskii was reinstated.

The Left SRs failed dismally not only because they had no clear objective and rebelled without being willing to assume responsibility for the political consequences, but also because they had completely miscalculated Bolshevik and German reactions. As it turned out, the two had much too much at stake to allow themselves to be provoked by the murder of an ambassador (which

---

*Before her escape, Spiridonova addressed a long letter to the Bolshevik Central Committee. It was published the following year by her followers under the title *Otkrytoe pis'mo M. Spiridonovoi Tsentral'nomu Komitetu partii bol'shevikov* (Moscow, 1920). The Hoover Institution Library has a copy.

was followed by the assassination of Field Marshal Hermann von Eichhorn by Left SRs in the Ukraine). The German Government virtually ignored the killing of Mirbach, and the German press, under its instructions, played it down. Indeed, in the fall of 1918, the two countries moved closer than ever.

The Bolsheviks were very fortunate in their choice of opponents.

By a remarkable coincidence another anti-Bolshevik rebellion broke out on the very same day, the morning of July 6, in three northeastern cities, Iaroslavl, Murom, and Rybinsk. It was the work of Boris Savinkov, the best organized and most enterprising of the anti-Bolshevik conspirators.

Born in Kharkov in 1879, Savinkov received his secondary education in Warsaw, following which he enrolled at the University of St. Petersburg.[138] There he became embroiled in student disorders, including the university strike of 1899. He joined the SRs and quickly rose to a leading position in its Combat Organization, in which capacity he carried out major terrorist missions, including the assassinations of Plehve and Grand Duke Sergei Aleksandrovich. In 1906 his terrorist activities came to a halt when the police agent Evno Azef betrayed him to the Okhrana. Sentenced to death, Savinkov managed to flee abroad, where he remained until the outbreak of the February Revolution, writing novels about the revolutionary underground. The war awakened in him patriotic impulses. He served in the French army until February 1917, when he returned to Russia. The Provisional Government appointed him a front-line commissar. Savinkov grew increasingly nationalistic and conservative, and, as we have seen, in the summer of 1917, while serving as acting director of the Ministry of War under Kerensky, he worked with Kornilov to restore discipline in the armed forces. Surrounded by an aura of romantic adventure, articulate and persuasive, he made a strong impression on whomever he cared to impress, including Winston Churchill.

In December 1917, Savinkov made his way to the Don, where he participated in the formation of the Volunteer Army. At Alekseev's request, he returned to Bolshevik Russia to make contact with prominent public figures.[139] His mission was to enlist those officers and politicians who, regardless of party affiliation, wanted to continue fighting the Germans and their Bolshevik minions. By virtue of his radical past and more recent patriotic record, Savinkov was ideally suited for this task. He spoke with Plekhanov, N. V. Chaikovskii, and other socialist luminaries known to follow a "defensist" line, but he had little success in enlisting them because, with a few exceptions, they preferred to wait for the Bolsheviks to collapse on their own rather than collaborate with nationalistic officers. Plekhanov refused even to receive him, saying: "I have given forty years of my life to the proletariat and it is not I who will shoot at workers even if they take the false path."[140] He had better success with demobilized officers, especially those who had served in the elite Guard and Grenadier Regiments.

His main problem was shortage of money: he was too poor even to afford a streetcar ticket. To build up a military force he had to pay allowances to his officers, most of whom were equally destitute, since no one dared to give them employment. To obtain funds, Savinkov turned to the representatives of the Allies. His private plans called for assassinating Lenin and Trotsky as a prelude to a coup against the Bolshevik regime. But he realized that the Allies did not much care who governed Russia, as long as she fought the Central Powers. Indeed, at this very time (March–April 1918) the French were assisting Trotsky organize the Red Army. Savinkov, therefore, concealed from the Allied representatives his true political objectives and presented himself as a patriotic Russian whose sole purpose was to restore Russia's military capabilities and resume the war against Germany.

The first to help was Thomas Masaryk. The Czech leader's motives in assisting Savinkov are obscure because in early 1918 he was negotiating with the Bolsheviks for the evacuation of his men from Russia and he could have had no conceivable interest in becoming involved in anti-Bolshevik activity. In his memoirs he writes that he had agreed to meet with Savinkov out of curiosity and was very disappointed to see a man seemingly unable to grasp the distinction between a "revolution" and a "terrorist act," whose moral standards did not rise above the "primitive level of a blood vendetta."[141] But this could well have been hindsight. What is certain is that in April 1918 Masaryk gave Savinkov his first money, 200,000 rubles.[142] A likely explanation for this transaction is that Savinkov, an expert at dissimulation, persuaded Masaryk that the money would be used to help Alekseev's Volunteer Army build up an anti-German force in central Russia.

Savinkov also contacted Lockhart and Noulens. Lockhart reacted skeptically to Savinkov's proposal to build an anti-German army under the very noses of the Bolsheviks, but he too came under Savinkov's spell, and might have helped him were it not that he received categorical instructions from Foreign Secretary Arthur Balfour "to have nothing whatever to do with Savinkov's plans, and avoid inquiring further into them."[143]

Noulens, a leading advocate of the idea of forming on Russian territory a multinational anti-German army, proved more helpful. He found Savinkov most impressive:

> He had a curious expression of impassivity, with a fixed gaze that shone from under his barely open Mongol eyelids, with permanently sealed lips, as if meant to conceal all his secret thoughts. By contrast, his profile and complexion were Western. It appeared that in him combined all the energy of one race and all the cunning and mystery of the other.[144]

At the beginning of May, Noulens gave Savinkov 500,000 rubles, which he followed with additional subsidies, for a total of up to 2,500,000.[145] As best as can be ascertained, these funds were to be used for military purposes, mainly the expenses of the Volunteer Army but also for some work behind German

89. Boris Savinkov.

lines on behalf of Allied military intelligence.[146] There exists no reliable evidence that Noulens conspired with Savinkov to overthrow the Bolshevik regime or that he was even acquainted with Savinkov's revolutionary plot.* Noulens extracted from Savinkov a promise that he would coordinate his action with the other Russian parties, presumably the pro-Allied National Center, but Savinkov broke this promise because he did not trust the latter to keep his plans secret. Grenard wrote in his memoirs that when Savinkov raised the banner of rebellion in July 1918, he "acted on his own in violation of the promises he had given to undertake nothing except in concert with the other Russian parties."[147]

With the help of Czech and French money, Savinkov expanded recruiting activities and by April 1918 enrolled in his organization, the Union for the Defense of the Fatherland and Freedom (Soiuz Zashchity Rodiny i Svobody), over 5,000 members, 2,000 of them in Moscow, the remainder in thirty-four provincial towns.† Most were officers, for Savinkov planned armed action and had little use for intellectuals and their endless chatter *(boltovnia)*. As his deputy he chose a forty-two-year-old professional artillery officer and graduate of the Imperial General Staff School, Lieutenant Colonel A. P. Perkhurov, a man with a distinguished war record and of legendary courage.

Savinkov had a program, or rather several programs, but he attached to

*On May 24, the French Consul General in Moscow, Grenard, who served as intermediary between the French Ambassador and Savinkov, advised Noulens that Savinkov was planning to stage an anti-Bolshevik uprising in the middle of June in the Volga area. That Noulens needed this information, not quite correct in any event, confirms his claim that he had not been involved in Savinkov's plot: Noulens, *Mon Ambassade,* II, 109–10. The Grenard dispatch is in the Archive of the French Foreign Ministry, Guerre, Vol. 671, Noulens No. 318, May 24, 1918.

†Boris Savinkov, *Bor'ba s Bol'shevikami* (Warsaw, 1923), 26. A. I. Denikin, *Ocherki Russkoi Smuty,* III (Berlin, 1924), 79, claims that the actual figure was 2,000–3,000.

them little importance because political discussions tended to divide and divert his followers from the task at hand. His stress was on patriotism. One program of the Union was divided into immediate and long-term objectives.* The immediate objective was to replace the Bolsheviks with a reliable national authority and create a disciplined army to fight the Central Powers. The long-term objective was vague. Savinkov spoke of holding fresh elections to the Constituent Assembly, presumably after the war, to give Russia a democratic regime. In recollections, published in Warsaw in 1923, he stressed that his organization enrolled representatives of all the parties, from monarchists to Socialists-Revolutionaries.[148] Savinkov could be all things to all men and it would be futile to expect from him a specific, formal plan for the future: it is certain only that he stood for firm national authority and the pursuit of the war, much as did Kornilov. To be admitted to Savinkov's Union, one only had to be committed to fighting the Germans and the Bolsheviks.

Savinkov structured his organization on a military model, drawing on his terrorist experience to conceal it from the Cheka. Under his command were several dozen skeletal "regiments" in Moscow and the provincial cities, staffed by professional officers. These units were isolated from one another and known only to their immediate superiors, so that in the event of arrest or betrayal the Cheka could not capture the entire organization.[149] This arrangement passed its test in mid-May, when a woman who had been jilted by one of the Union's members denounced it to the police. Following her lead, the Cheka discovered the Union's headquarters in Moscow, disguised as a medical clinic. It seized over 100 members (they were executed in July), but even though this discovery forced the Union to suspend its activities for two weeks, the Cheka failed to capture Savinkov or to liquidate his organization.[150]

Perkhurov had under him 150–200 officers, working in an elaborate command structure: there were departments responsible for recruitment, intelligence and counterintelligence, relations with the Allies, and the principal branches of the armed forces (infantry, cavalry, artillery, and engineering).[151] The Cheka later complimented Savinkov and Perkhurov on running their organization with "clocklike precision."[152]

Savinkov built up an organization but he had no concrete strategic plan. By June, he came under mounting pressure to act. Because the Czechs and the French had suspended their subsidies, his money was running out, and the nerves of his followers were becoming frayed from the constant danger of betrayal. According to his testimony, he initially contemplated striking at Moscow, but he gave up this idea out of fear that the Germans would respond by occupying the capital.[153] In view of persistent rumors, confirmed to him by French representatives, that the Allies would make additional landings at Archangel and Murmansk in early July, he decided to stage his uprisings in the region of the middle or upper Volga, from where he could establish contact

*Krasnaia Kniga VChK, I (Moscow, 1920), 1–42. At his trial in 1924 (*Boris Savinkov pered Voennoi Kollegiei Verkhovnogo Suda SSSR*, Moscow, 1924, 46–47), Savinkov denied having had a formal program.

with both the Czechoslovak armies and the Allied forces at Murmansk. His plan called for cutting the Bolsheviks off from the northern ports as well as Kazan and areas to the east.

In 1924, when he stood trial before a Soviet court, Savinkov claimed he had received from the French a firm commitment that if his men managed to hold out for four days, they would be relieved by an Allied force from Archangel, following which the combined Franco-Anglo-Russian army would advance on Moscow. Without such a promise, he said, his uprising made no sense.[154] He further claimed that Consul Grenard gave him a cable from Noulens that the Allied landings would take place between July 3 and 8 and that it was essential for him to move during that time.[155] According to the testimony he gave at his trial, he coordinated all activities with the French mission.

Unfortunately, one can never take Savinkov's statements at face value, not only because as an experienced conspirator he rarely told the full truth but also because he was quite capable of telling outright lies. Thus, at one time he claimed credit for Fannie Kaplan's attempt on Lenin's life (see below, pages 806–11), with which he is known to have had no connection; he also stated that in July 1918 he had acted on orders of the Moscow National Center, which happens to be untrue as well.[156] The Bolsheviks liked to link all resistance to them with foreign conspiracies to incite native xenophobia. It is almost certain that after his arrest in Soviet Russia in 1924, Savinkov struck a deal with the Bolshevik prosecutor to place the blame for his abortive coup of 1918 on the French, for now that the Allied archives for the period have been made available to scholars, no evidence has come to light to support this allegation. If the French mission indeed had not only authorized him to stage an anti-Bolshevik rebellion but demanded it, as he alleged, and further promised to help him capture Moscow, such an enterprise would certainly have left documentary evidence. Since none exists, one must conclude that Savinkov lied, perhaps in the hope of saving his life. As we have noted, Savinkov's main liaison with the French, Grenard, attested that he acted "on his own."*

Savinkov chose as the principal locus of his uprising Iaroslavl, and this for two reasons. One was the city's strategic location, on the railroad linking Archangel with Moscow, which facilitated both offensive and defensive operations. The other had to do with the fact that Perkhurov, whom Savinkov had sent to reconnoiter, brought from Iaroslavl encouraging reports of popular support.[157]

The final operational plans were drawn up at the end of June, when the Czech uprising was at its height. Perkhurov, who was to command the Iaroslavl operation, had barely ten days to organize. Savinkov undertook personally to direct a secondary uprising in nearby Rybinsk; a third action was scheduled

---

*A recent study by Michael Carley, *Revolution and Intervention: The French Government and the Russian Civil War, 1917–1919* (Kingston-Montreal, 1983), 57–60, 67–70, places rather more direct responsibility on the French, but it confuses general assistance given Savinkov with involvement in his uprising.

at Murom, on the Moscow–Kazan railroad. Savinkov is said by Perkhurov to have told his officers that he had firm promises of Allied assistance from Archangel, and that if they managed to hold out for four days, they would be relieved.[158]

Savinkov scheduled the Iaroslavl rising for the night of July 5–6, which preceded only by hours the time at which the Left SRs staged their rebellion. The coincidence notwithstanding, there is nothing to indicate that the two events had been coordinated. The Left SRs and Savinkov pursued entirely different aims, the former intending to leave the Bolsheviks in power, while Savinkov intended to overthrow them. Furthermore, it is inconceivable that the Left SRs would have had any dealings with a representative of the "counterrevolutionary" generals. Had he known of their plans, Savinkov would surely have followed his first inclination and staged a coup in Moscow rather than in Iaroslavl. This lack of coordination, about which Lenin spoke to Mirbach, was typical of the anti-Bolshevik opposition and a major reason for its ultimate failure.

To confuse the enemy and force him to scatter his forces, Savinkov and Perkhurov scheduled their rebellions at staggered times, with the Rybinsk operations to commence during the night of July 7–8 and the one at Murom the following night.

Perkhurov, who despite having little time had prepared the Iaroslavl rebellion with great precision, caught the Bolshevik authorities completely by surprise.[159] The action began at 2 a.m. on July 6, when a detachment of officers seized key points in the city: the arsenal, militia headquarters, the bank, and the post office. Another detachment proceeded to arrest leading Bolshevik and soviet officials, some of whom it is said to have shot. Officers employed as instructors in a local Red Army school promptly sided with the rebels, bringing along several machine guns and an armored car. Perkhurov proclaimed himself commander of the Iaroslavl Branch of the Northern Volunteer Army. These initial operations met with almost no resistance, and by daybreak the center of the city was in rebel hands. Soon others went over to the rebels, among them members of the militia, students, workers, and peasants: a Communist historian estimates that of the 6,000 participants in the Iaroslavl uprising, only 1,000 or so were officers.[160] It was a genuine popular rebellion against the Bolshevik regime, in which the peasants from the nearby villages proved especially helpful. The rebels tried to enlist for their cause German POWs who happened to have been passing through Iaroslavl en route home, but they met with refusal, following which they interned the Germans in the city theater. On July 8 Perkhurov informed them that his forces considered themselves at war with the Central Powers.[161]

Whereas the Murom and Rybinsk uprisings, each involving 300–400 men, collapsed in a matter of hours, Perkhurov held out for sixteen days. The

90. Lieutenant-Colonel A. P. Perkhurov.

pro-Bolshevik forces, gathered in the suburbs, counterattacked the following
night, but failed to recapture the city. They then subjected it to intense artillery
bombardment, which destroyed the water supply, with disastrous consequences for the rebels because the Reds controlled access to the Volga River,
the only alternative source. After a week or so of inconclusive fighting, Trotsky
placed in charge of the Iaroslavl operation A. I. Gekker, an ex-captain of the
Imperial Army who had gone over to the Bolsheviks on the eve of the October
coup. Gekker attacked the city with infantry, artillery, and airplanes. In the
heavy shelling, most of the city, with its celebrated medieval churches and
monasteries, was gutted.[162] The rebels, so short of water they scooped it up
from gutters, finally had to give up. On July 20, their representatives approached the German Repatriation Commission and declared they wished to
surrender: since they were at war with Germany, they expected to be treated
as prisoners of war. The head of the German commission accepted these terms
and promised not to turn the rebels over to the Red Army. On July 21, the
rebels laid down their arms and for a few hours Iaroslavl was under the
occupation of German POWs. That evening, however, confronted with an
ultimatum from the Bolsheviks, the Germans broke their promise and turned
over to them the prisoners. The Red Guards sorted out some 350 officers,
ex-officials, affluent citizens, and students, marched them out of town and had
them shot.[163] It was the first mass execution by the Bolsheviks. One consequence of the Iaroslavl uprising was that Moscow ordered indiscriminate
arrests of former Imperial officers: many of them were shot without a trial even
as others were being inducted into the Red Army.
    Savinkov managed to escape from Rybinsk. He later joined Admiral
Alexander Kolchak's armies and organized raids behind Bolshevik lines. After
Kolchak's defeat, he fled to Western Europe, where he kept busy organizing

anti-Bolshevik movements and smuggling agents into the Soviet Union. In August 1924, under the illusion that he could play an important role in post-Leninist Soviet Russia, he allowed himself to be lured by the GPU (the successor to the Cheka) into illegally crossing the frontier. He was promptly arrested. At a public trial later that year, he confessed to all his crimes, stressing the alleged involvement of the Allies in his subversive activities and pleading for mercy. His death sentence was commuted to ten years' imprisonment. He died the following year in jail under highly suspicious circumstances: officially, he was said to have committed suicide, but it is more likely that he was killed by the GPU—according to some accounts, by being pushed from a window.[164]

Perkhurov also joined Kolchak's forces, where he was raised to the rank of general and earned the sobriquet Perkhurov-Iaroslavskii. Captured by the Bolsheviks, he managed to disguise his identity and obtain a commission in the Red Army. His true identity was discovered in 1922. Tried by a Military Collegium of the Supreme Tribunal he was sentenced to death: in prison, he was made to write his confessions, which were subsequently published.[165] Rather than kill him in its dungeons, the GPU sent him to Iaroslavl, where on the fourth anniversary of the uprising he was paraded through the streets, taunted by the crowds and pelted with rocks, following which he was executed.[166]

Riezler, who took charge of the German Embassy, was regarded by some of his colleagues as confused and absentminded.[167] He spent less time on routine diplomatic affairs and more on negotiations with Russian opposition groups, which Berlin had instructed him to terminate on July 1. He did so out of an unalterable conviction that the Bolsheviks would not last and Germany needed contacts with their potential successors. His first reaction to Mirbach's murder was to urge severance of relations with Moscow;[168] this advice was rejected, and he was instructed to continue helping the Bolsheviks. In September 1918 he would state, without elaborating, that the Germans had on three occasions used "political" means to help save the Bolsheviks.[169]

While carrying out his government's directives, Riezler bombarded the Foreign Office with cables that the Bolsheviks were a spent force. On July 19, he wired:

> The Bolsheviks are dead. Their corpse lives [sic!] because the gravediggers cannot agree on who should bury it. The struggle which we presently wage with the Entente on Russian soil is no longer over the favors of this corpse. It has already turned into a struggle over the succession, over the orientation of the Russia of the future.[170]

While he agreed that the Bolsheviks were rendering Russia harmless for Germany, by the same token they were rendering it useless.[171] He recommended that Germany take charge of the "counterrevolution" and assist bourgeois forces in Russia. He thought it would require minimum effort to be rid of the Bolsheviks.

Acting on his own, Riezler laid out the groundwork for an anti-Bolshevik coup. The first step was to station a battalion of uniformed Germans in Moscow. Their ostensible mission would be to protect the embassy from future terrorist acts and to assist the Bolsheviks in the event of another rebellion; their true purpose would be to occupy strategic points in the capital if Bolshevik authority collapsed or Berlin decided the time had come to remove them from power.[172]

Germany agreed to dispatch a battalion to Moscow but only if the Soviet Government gave its approval. It also authorized Riezler to initiate discreet talks with the Latvian Rifles to sound them out about their intentions. Riezler, who had established good contacts with the Latvians, asked if they were prepared to defect. He was told they were. Vatsetis, the Latvian commander, describes as follows his thinking in the summer of 1918:

> Strange as [it may sound], at the time it was believed that central Russia would turn into a theater of internecine warfare and that the Bolsheviks would hardly hold on to power, falling victim to the hunger and the general discontent in the country's interior. One could not exclude the possibility of a move on Moscow by the Germans, Don Cossacks, and White Czechs. This latter version was at the time especially widespread. The Bolsheviks had under their authority no military power capable of combat. The units, over whose formation M. D. Bonch-Bruevich, the Military Director of the Supreme Military Council, labored so intelligently and cleverly, owing to the hunger in the western zone of European Russia, scattered in search of food, turning into robber bands dangerous to Soviet authority. Such armies—if one can apply to them this honorable title—fled at the very sight of the German helmet. On the western border instances occurred of German forces being called upon to pacify mutinous Red units. . . . In connection with all these speculations and rumors, I was extremely troubled by the question of what would happen to the Latvian regiments should there be further German intervention and should the Cossacks and White armies make an appearance in the center of Russia. Such a possibility was then seriously contemplated: it could have led to the complete annihilation of the Latvian Rifles . . .[173]

From his talks, Riezler learned that the Latvians were anxious to return to their German-occupied homeland, and if guaranteed amnesty and repatriation, would at least stay neutral in the event the Germans intervened against the Bolsheviks.[174]

Riezler also resumed conversations with the Right Center. Its new representative, Prince Grigorii Trubetskoi, Imperial Russia's wartime Ambassador to Serbia, pleaded for prompt German assistance to rid Russia of Lenin. He posed several conditions for the cooperation of his group: the Germans should allow the Russians to assemble their own military force in the Ukraine, so that Moscow would be liberated by Russians, not Germans; a pledge to revise the Brest Treaty; no pressure on the government that would replace the Bolsheviks; and Russia's neutrality in the World War.[175] Trubetskoi claimed that his group had contact with 4,000 combat-ready officers, who only needed weapons. Time was of the essence: the Bolsheviks were engaged in a regular "manhunt" for officers, executing dozens every day.[176]

By the time Mirbach's successor, Karl Helfferich, arrived in Moscow (July 28), Riezler had a plan for a full-fledged coup d'état. Once the German battalion took over Moscow (the Latvian Rifles guarding the city having been previously neutralized with pledges of amnesty and repatriation), it would take little to bring about a collapse of the Bolshevik Government. This would be followed by the installation of a Russian Government completely dependent on Germany, on the model of Hetman Skoropadski's regime in the Ukraine.[177]

Riezler's plans came to naught. Their key provision, the installation of a German battalion in Moscow, was vetoed by Lenin and dropped by Berlin. Yielding to Hindenburg's pressure, Wilhelmstrasse sent a note to the Soviet Government, which Riezler handed to Chicherin in the evening of July 14. It assured the Soviet Government that in proposing to send a uniformed detachment to Moscow, Germany had no intention of infringing on Soviet sovereignty: its only purpose was to ensure the safety of its diplomatic personnel. Furthermore, the note went on, should there be another anti-Bolshevik uprising, this force could help the Soviet Government to quell it.[178] Chicherin communicated the German note to Lenin, who was resting out of town. Lenin immediately saw through the German ploy. He returned to Moscow that night and consulted with Chicherin. This was an issue on which he was not prepared to yield: he would give the Germans almost anything they wanted as long as they did not threaten his power. The following day he addressed the Central Executive Committee on the German note.[179] He hoped, he said, that Germany would not insist on its proposal because Russia would rather fight than allow foreign troops on her soil. He promised to provide all the personnel needed to ensure the security of the German Embassy. Then he held out the bait of extensive commercial relations as a means of inducing German business interests to exert pressure on his behalf: it materialized in the form of the Supplementary Treaty concluded the following month. It is doubtful that Lenin could have stood up to the Germans had they been truly determined: he was now even weaker than in February, when he had capitulated to their every demand. But he was not put to the test, because the Foreign Office, apprised of his reaction, quickly dropped Riezler's proposal. It instructed Riezler "to continue supporting the Bolsheviks and merely [maintain] 'contact' with the others."[180]

Nor did Riezler have better luck with his proposal to win the neutrality of the Latvians with promises of amnesty and repatriation. This plan was scuttled by, of all people, Ludendorff, who feared "contaminating" Latvia with Bolshevik propaganda. The new Minister of Foreign Affairs, Admiral Paul von Hintze, who succeeded Kühlmann and was even more committed to collaboration with Lenin, needed to hear no more: he instructed the Moscow Embassy to suspend talks with the Latvians.[181]

To be prepared in the event of a Bolshevik collapse, the Foreign Office worked out its own contingency plans. If pro-Allied SRs seized power in Russia, the German army would strike from Finland, seize Murmansk and Archangel, and occupy Petrograd as well as Vologda. In other words, if the pessimists proved correct, rather than deliver the Bolsheviks a coup de grace and replace them with other Russians, Germany would march in and presumably restore them to power.[182]

Helfferich arrived in Moscow determined to implement the pro-Bolshevik policy of his government. But he quickly discovered that the embassy staff opposed it almost to a man. The briefings which he received on the evening of his arrival and such limited personal observations as he was able to make caused him to change his mind. On the afternoon of July 31, on his only venture outside the heavily guarded embassy compound during his brief stay in Moscow, he paid a visit to Chicherin to protest the murder by Left SRs of Field Marshal Eichhorn in the Ukraine and the continuing Left SR threats to embassy personnel. At the same time he assured him that the German Government intended to continue its support. He later learned that a few hours after his conversation with Chicherin, a meeting took place in the Kremlin at which Lenin told his associates that their cause was "temporarily" lost and that it had become necessary to evacuate Moscow. While this meeting was in progress, Chicherin arrived to say that Helfferich had just assured him of German backing.*

The mood in the Kremlin was already desperate enough when on August 1 it received news that a British naval force had opened fire on Archangel. This shelling marked the beginning of large-scale Allied intervention in Russia. Moscow, which had much less reliable intelligence on Allied intentions than on those of Germany, was certain the Allies intended to advance on Moscow. It now completely lost its head and flung itself into German arms.

It will be recalled that in March 1918 the Allies had discussed with the Bolshevik Government the landing of troops on Russian soil in the north (Murmansk and Archangel) and the Far East (Vladivostok) to protect these ports from the Germans as well as to secure bases for the projected Allied force in Russia. In return, they were to help organize and train the Red Army. The Allies, however, were slow to act. They did land token detachments in the three port cities and they assigned a few officers to Trotsky's Commissariat of War, but they had no large forces to spare at a time when the full brunt of the German offensive was upon them. The United States alone had the necessary manpower, but Woodrow Wilson opposed involvement in Russia, and as long as this was the case, nothing could be done.

The prospect of reactivating the Eastern Front improved substantially at the beginning of June when Wilson, impressed by the Czechoslovak uprising, experienced a change of heart. Feeling that the United States had a moral

---

*Baumgart, Ostpolitik, 237–38. It seems that Lenin was planning to move the seat of government to Nizhnii Novgorod: Ibid., 237, note 38. In 1920, Lenin told Bertrand Russell that two years earlier neither he nor his colleagues had believed their regime stood a chance of surviving. Bertrand Russell, Bolshevism: Practice and Theory (New York, 1920), 40.

obligation to help the Czechs and Slovaks repatriate, he yielded to British entreaties and agreed to provide troops for the Murmansk-Archangel expedition as well as for Vladivostok. American forces assigned to the operation were under strict orders not to interfere in internal Russian affairs.[183]

When it learned of Washington's decision (June 3), the Supreme Allied Council at Versailles ordered the dispatch of an Allied expeditionary force to Archangel under the command of the British general F. C. Poole. Poole's instructions were to defend the port city, make contact with the Czech Legion and with its help take control of the railway south of Archangel, and organize a pro-Allied army. Nothing was said of fighting the Bolsheviks: Poole's troops were told, "We do not meddle in internal affairs."[184]

These Allied decisions have been subsequently criticized on the grounds that no serious German threat existed to the northern Russian ports and that in any event German forces in Finland capable of such action were withdrawn in early August and sent to the Western Front. The implication of these criticisms is that the true reason for the expeditions to northern Russia was to overthrow the Bolshevik regime.[185] The charge cannot be sustained. It is known from German archives that the German High Command was indeed considering operations against the ports, either with its own troops or jointly with Finnish and Bolshevik forces. Such an operation made very good sense because control of Murmansk and Archangel would have enabled Germany to deny the Allies access to Russia and thus frustrated plans to reactivate the Eastern Front. Berlin opened negotiations to this end in late May 1918 with Ioffe. These talks eventually broke down, partly because of the inability of the Bolsheviks and Finns to agree on the terms of collaboration and partly because the Germans insisted on occupying Petrograd as a base of operations, to which the Russians would not consent.[186] But the Allies could not have foreseen this, any more than they could have known in June that two months later the Germans would withdraw troops from Finland. There is no evidence to indicate that in sending troops to Russia in 1918 the Allies intended to overthrow the Bolshevik Government. The British, who played a key role in the operation, expressed, both publicly and privately, complete lack of concern about the nature of the government administering Russia. Prime Minister David Lloyd George put the matter bluntly at the meeting of the War Cabinet on July 22, 1918, when he declared that it was none of Britain's business what sort of a government the Russians set up: a republic, a Bolshevik state, or a monarchy.[187] The indications are that President Wilson shared this view.

The Allied expeditionary force, initially 8,500 troops, 4,800 of them Americans, landed at Archangel on August 1–2. On August 10, General Poole received instructions "to cooperate in restoring Russia with the object of resisting German influence and penetration" and to help the Russians "take the field side by side with their Allies" for the recovery of their country.[188] He was further instructed to establish communications with the Czech Legion, so as to jointly secure railroads leading to the east and organize an armed force to fight the Germans.[189] While the language of these instructions could be interpreted to mean broader, more ambitious objectives than those stated in the June 3 directive, they provide no basis for the claim that the "future of the North Russian expedition would be in fighting the Bolsheviks, not the Germans."[190] At the time, the Bolsheviks appeared as, and indeed in considerable measure were, partners of the Germans: they took money from them, and more than once told the Germans that only the state of Russian public opinion prevented them from signing with them a formal alliance. The British and French, through their agents in Moscow, were informed of the role which the German Embassy played in keeping the Bolsheviks afloat. To disassociate—let alone contrast—Allied actions in 1918 against the Bolsheviks from those against the Germans, therefore, is to misunderstand both the perceptions and the mood of the time. If Poole's mission were to fight the Bolsheviks, he certainly would have been given unequivocal instructions to this effect and he would have established communication with opposition groups in Moscow. Of this, there is no evidence. The evidence which does exist indicates, on the contrary, that the task of the Allied expeditionary force in the north was to open a new front against the Germans in cooperation with the Czechoslovaks, the Japanese, and such Russians as were willing to join. It was a military operation intimately connected with the final stages of the World War.

Following the occupation of Archangel, a second Allied force, commanded by British Major General C. C. M. Maynard, landed in Murmansk, which had had a small British contingent since June. Maynard's force in time grew to 15,000 men, of which 11,000 were Allied troops and the remainder Russians and others. According to Noulens, the Archangel-Murmansk expeditionary force (then 23,500 men strong) nearly sufficed to reactivate the Eastern Front, a task which in the opinion of the Western military mission required 30,000 men.[191]

Unfortunately for the Allies, by the time they had finally deployed sufficient troops in the north, and this happened only in September, the Czech Legion ceased to exist as a viable offensive force.

As we have seen, the Czechoslovaks originally resorted to arms to ensure unimpeded passage to Vladivostok. In June, however, their mission changed because the Allied command came to regard them as the vanguard of the projected Allied army on the reactivated Eastern Front.[192] In a message to the Czechoslovak troops on June 7, General Ček thus defined their mission:

> Let it be known to all our brothers that on the basis of the decision of the Congress of the [Czechoslovak] Corps, in agreement with our National Council and by arrangement with all the Allies, our corps is designated as the vanguard of the forces of the Entente, and that the instructions issued by the staff of the Army Corps have as their sole purpose creating an anti-German front in Russia jointly with the entire Russian nation and our allies.[193]

In accord with these plans, in early July, the Czechoslovak commanders assigned their troops missions for which they had neither the capability nor the motivation.

To establish a front against the Germans, the Czechoslovaks had to redeploy from a horizontal line, running from west to east, to a diagonal one, running from north to south, along the Volga and the Urals.[194] Accordingly, the Czechoslovak forces still in western Siberia, some 10,000–20,000 strong, launched offensive operations to the north and south of Samara. On July 5, they captured Ufa, on July 21, Simbirsk, and on August 6, Kazan. The assault on Kazan marked the high point of their operations in Russia. After they had compelled a severely depleted 5th Latvian Regiment of 400 men defending the city to retreat, the Czechs captured a gold hoard of 650 million rubles of the Imperial Russian Treasury, evacuated there by the Bolsheviks in February. It enabled them to conduct large-scale military campaigns without resorting to taxation or forced food extractions.

The Czechoslovaks fought with vigor and skill. But they were meant to be only the vanguard—the vanguard of what? The Allies did not stir to help, although they were generous enough with instructions and advice. Nor were anti-Bolshevik Russians more helpful. Prodded by the Allies, the Czechoslovaks tried to unite the Russian political groupings in the Volga region and Siberia, but this proved a hopeless undertaking. On July 15, representatives of Komuch and the Omsk government conferring in Cheliabinsk failed to reach agreement. Disagreements also racked a second Russian political conference held on August 23–25. The squabbling of the Russians exasperated the Czechs.

Komuch attempted to raise an army to fight alongside the Czechoslovaks and the other Allies, but it had only limited success. On July 8, it announced the formation of a volunteer People's Army (Narodnaia Armiia) under the overall command of General Čeček. But as the Bolsheviks had also found out, a Russian army could not be created on a voluntary basis. Especially galling was Komuch's experience with the peasants, who, although violently anti-Communist, refused to enlist on the grounds that the Revolution had freed them of all obligations to the state. After inducting 3,000 volunteers, Komuch went over to conscription and in the course of August recruited 50,000–60,000 men, of whom only 30,000 had weapons and only 10,000 were trained for combat.[195] The military historian General N. N. Golovin estimates that at the beginning of September the pro-Allied contingent in western Siberia consisted of 20,000 Czechoslovaks, 15,000 Ural and Orenburg Cossacks, 5,000 factory workers, and 15,000 troops of the People's Army.[196] This multinational force had no central command and no political leadership.

In the meantime, Trotsky was energetically building up forces in the east. The Kaiser's pledge of late June not to imperil Soviet Russia allowed him to shift Latvian regiments from the west to the Urals, where they were the first to engage the Czechoslovaks. He then proceeded to press into the Red Army thousands of former tsarist officers and hundreds of thousands of conscripts. He reintroduced and freely applied the death penalty for desertion. The Red Army's first successes against the Czechoslovaks were won by the Latvians, who on September 7 retook Kazan and five days later Simbirsk. The news of these victories brought jubilation to the Kremlin: for the Bolsheviks they marked a psychological turning of the tide.

But all this lay in the future. On August 1, when the Kremlin received news of Allied landings in Archangel, the situation looked hopeless. In the east, the Czechoslovaks were capturing city after city and had full control of the middle Volga region. In the south, Denikin's Volunteer Army, headed by the Don Cossacks under General Krasnov, was advancing on Tsaritsyn, capture of which would allow it to link up with the Czechoslovaks and create an uninterrupted anti-Bolshevik front from the middle Volga to the Don. And now a sizable Anglo-American force was assembling in the north, apparently to launch an offensive into the interior of Russia.

The Bolsheviks saw only one way out of their plight and that was German military intervention. This they decided to request on August 1, the day after Helfferich had given Chicherin undertakings of continued German support. The meeting at which this decision was made is described in Communist sources as a session of the Sovnarkom, but as there exists no record of a meeting of the cabinet on that day, it is virtually certain it was made personally by Lenin, probably in consultation with Chicherin. The Russians were to propose to the Germans joint military action against Allied and pro-Allied forces: the Red Army, composed at this time essentially of Latvian units, would take up positions to the northeast of Moscow to defend it from the anticipated Allied assault, while the German Army would advance from Finland against the Anglo-American expeditionary force and from the Ukraine against the Volunteer Army. This decision is known to us mainly from the memoirs of Helfferich, who late on August 1 received another unexpected visit from Chicherin. The Commissar of Foreign Affairs told him that he had come directly from a meeting of the cabinet to request, on its behalf, German military intervention.* According to Helfferich, Chicherin said:

> In view of the state of public opinion, an open military alliance with Germany is not possible; what is possible is actual parallel action. His government intended to concentrate its forces in Vologda to protect Moscow. It was a condition of parallel action that we not occupy Petrograd: it was preferable that we avoid Petropavlovsk as well. In effect, this approach meant that in order to enable it to defend Moscow, the Soviet Government had to request us to defend Petrograd.

The Bolshevik proposal meant that German forces, from the Baltic areas and/or from Finland, would enter Soviet Russia, establish lines of defense

---

*In his brief recollections of this episode—apparently its only mention in Soviet literature—Chicherin, while confirming Helfferich's account, indicates that the matter was settled by Lenin personally: "Lenin i vneshniaia politika," *Mirovaia politika v 1924 godu* (Moscow, 1925), 5. See also his article in *Izvestiia,* No. 24/2059 (January 30, 1924), 2–3.

around Petrograd, and advance on Murmansk and Archangel to expel the Allies. But this was not all.

> [Chicherin] was no less worried about the southeast. . . . Under my questioning, he finally spelled out the nature of the intervention that was requested of us: "An active assault against Alekseev, no further [German] support of Krasnov." Here, as in the case of the north and for the same reasons, what was possible was not an overt alliance but only de facto cooperation: but this was a necessity. With this step, the Bolshevik regime requested the armed intervention of Germany on the territory of Great Russia.[197]

Helfferich forwarded to Berlin the Bolshevik request, which he summarized as calling for "silent [Bolshevik] tolerance of our intervention and actual parallel action."[198] Along with it he sent a pessimistic assessment of the situation in Russia. The main source of Bolshevik authority, he wrote, was the widespread belief that it enjoyed the support of Germany. But such a perception did not constitute a sound basis on which to conduct policy. He recommended that Germany pursue talks with those anti-Bolshevik groups which were not pro-Entente, among them the Right Center, the Latvians, and the Siberian Government.[199] He was of the opinion that if Germany did nothing more than demonstratively withhold support from the Bolsheviks, their opponents would rise and topple them.

Once again the advice of the Moscow Embassy was overruled, this time by Hintze. The Bolsheviks were not friends, he conceded, but they "abundantly" took care of German interests by helping to paralyze Russia militarily.[200] He was so displeased with Helfferich's recommendations that on August 6 he had him recalled to Berlin; the ambassador never returned to his post, which he had held less than two weeks. Hintze then liquidated the troublesome German Embassy, ordering it to leave Moscow so that it could no longer interfere with German-Soviet relations. A few days after Helfferich's departure, the embassy packed up and left, first for Pskov and then for Revel, both of which were under German occupation. Without a German mission in Russia, the center of Soviet-German relations shifted to Berlin, where Ioffe served as his government's spokesman and principal negotiator of the commercial and military accords which the two countries concluded at the end of August.*

The abortive efforts of some Germans to topple the Bolsheviks had an epilogue. In early September, the German Consul General in Moscow, Herbert Hauschild, had a visit from Vatsetis. The Latvian officer, who had just been appointed Commander in Chief of the armed forces of Soviet Russia, told Hauschild that he was not a Bolshevik but a Latvian nationalist, and that if his men were promised amnesty and repatriation they would place themselves

---

*Kurt Riezler, who at this point fades from the picture, returned after the war to his professorship in Frankfurt. When Hitler took power, he emigrated to the United States, where until his death in 1955 he taught at the New School for Social Research in New York City.

at the disposal of the Germans. Hauschild informed Berlin, which ordered him to drop the matter.*

The Brest Treaty called for a supplementary accord to regulate Russo-German economic relations.

The Germans were very eager to resume trade with Russia, their major commercial partner before 1914, when Russia had purchased from them nearly one-half of her imports. They wanted foodstuffs, first and foremost, as well as other raw materials, and they wished to establish a near-monopoly on Russia's foreign trade. In June 1918, Moscow provided the Germans with a list of goods which it claimed to have available for export: it included grain, of which, in reality, it had none to spare. Krasin painted a dazzling picture of the vast markets that Soviet Russia could provide for German manufactured goods, and to prove it, negotiated with his old employer, Siemens, for imports of electrical equipment. None of the proposals had any basis in reality: they were bait to serve political ends. The Germans soon grew impatient with Soviet Russia's failure to provide the promised goods. In June Dr. Alfred List, who had come to Moscow on behalf of the Bleichröder Bank, told Chicherin that the delays in Russian deliveries brought disappointment to those German circles "among which Great Russia could find the most likely sympathy for her political strivings."[201] Lenin was well aware that he could use such "circles"—bankers and industrialists—to neutralize other Germans, mainly among the military, who wanted to be rid of him. He therefore closely monitored the negotiations for the Supplementary Treaty, to which he attached the highest political importance.

The talks opened in Berlin at the beginning of July. The Soviet delegation was headed by Ioffe, who had the assistance of Krasin and various specialists sent by Moscow. The Germans fielded a large delegation of diplomats, politicians, and businessmen. The key person on the German side seems to have been a Foreign Ministry official named Johannes Kriege, whom the historian Winfried Baumgart calls the "gray eminence" of Germany's policy toward Bolshevik Russia.[202] Ioffe was under instructions to be very accommodating to German demands, but if the Germans became unreasonable, he was to make them understand that there were limits to Russia's compliance. As Ioffe confirmed to Lenin from Berlin: "[our] whole policy must center on demonstrat-

---

*Baumgart, Ostpolitik, 315–16. Vatsetis served as Soviet CIC until the summer of 1919, when he was arrested on charges of participating in a "counterrevolutionary conspiracy." After being released, he taught at the Soviet Military Academy. In 1938, during a classroom break, he was rearrested and soon afterward executed: Pamiat', No. 2 (1979), 9–10.

At about the same time the Cheka, then directed by the Latvians M.I. Latsis and Ia. Kh. Peters, engaged in a classic Russian police provocation. It sent a Latvian officer to Lockhart to say that his men were ready to abandon the Bolsheviks. Lockhart turned them over to the British intelligence agent Sidney Reilly, who gave them a considerable sum of money. This ploy was later used to justify Lockhart's arrest. See IA, No. 4 (1962), 234–37, and Uldis Germanis, Oberst Vacietis (Stockholm, 1974), 35.

91. A German-Russian love affair: contemporary Russian cartoon.

ing to the Germans that if they push us too far we will have to fight and then they will get nothing."[203]

Considering the complexity of the issues involved, agreement was reached speedily. The Germans made harsh demands. Ioffe managed to wring some concessions from them, but even so the accord, known as the Supplementary Treaty, signed on August 27, gave Germany most of the advantages. At issue were territorial and financial matters.*

Concerning territorial questions, Germany pledged not to interfere with the relations between Russia and her border regions: this clause repudiated specifically the efforts of the German military to create, under the name "Southern Union," a protectorate over the Caucasus and the adjoining Cossack regions.[204] Russia acknowledged the independence of the Ukraine and Georgia, and further agreed to surrender Estonia and Livonia, neither of which she had conceded in the Brest Treaty. In return, Russia obtained transit rights to the Baltic ports which she had lost. The Germans had initially demanded Baku, the center of Russia's petroleum industry, but they eventu-

---

*The text of the treaty, minus one of the three secret clauses, is reproduced by J. Wheeler-Bennett in *Brest-Litovsk: The Forgotten Peace* (New York, 1956), 427–46.

ally consented to leave it in Russia's hands in exchange for a promise of one-quarter of Baku's annual production. Baku had been occupied by a British force sent from Persia in early August: the German willingness to leave the city to the Bolsheviks was contingent on the Bolsheviks' expulsion of the British.[205] The Russians also undertook to remove the Allied force from Murmansk, while the Germans agreed to evacuate the Crimea and make some minor territorial adjustments on Russia's western border.

In the financial settlement, Russia agreed to pay Germany and German nationals full compensation for the losses which they had suffered in consequence of measures taken by the tsarist and Soviet governments, as well as for the costs which Germany claimed to have incurred for the upkeep of the Russian prisoners of war. The Germans estimated this sum to be between 7 and 8 billion deutsche marks. After Russian counterclaims had been taken into account, it was reduced to 6 billion: of this, 1 billion was to be paid by Finland and the Ukraine. Russia undertook to repay, over eighteen months, half of the 5 billion deutsche marks it owed by transferring to Germany 24.5 tons of gold, an agreed-upon quantity of rubles, and 1 billion rubles' worth of merchandise. The other half Soviet Russia was to repay from the proceeds of a forty-five-year loan floated in Germany. These payments were to satisfy all German claims, governmental as well as private, against Russia. Moscow reconfirmed the provisions of Brest by virtue of which it was to return to their German owners all nationalized and municipalized properties, including confiscated cash and securities, and allow them to repatriate these assets to Germany.

Although upon coming to power the Bolsheviks had condemned secret diplomacy in the strongest terms and made many secret treaties of the "imperialist powers" public, where their own interests were involved they showed no aversion to such practices. There were three secret clauses attached to the Supplementary Treaty, signed by Ioffe for Russia and Hintze for Germany: these became public knowledge only years afterward and have not been published to this day in the Soviet Union. They formalized Germany's acceptance of Moscow's requests of August 1 for German military intervention.

One of these secret provisions elaborated Article 5 of the Supplementary Treaty, in which the Russians undertook to expel the Allies from Murmansk. The clause specified that if the Russians were unable to do so, the task would be accomplished by a combined Finno-German force.*

To work out the plan of this operation, the commander of the Petrograd Military District, Vladimir Antonov-Ovseenko, went at the end of August to Berlin at the head of a delegation of the Commissariat of War.[206] He agreed that the projected assault on Murmansk would be carried out by German troops; as previously proposed, the mission of the Russian forces would be to intercept the British in the event they advanced on Moscow from Archangel. The two sides clashed over Petrograd. Ludendorff insisted that the Germans had to occupy Petrograd as a base of operations against Murmansk, but

---

*This clause was first published in *Europäische Gespräche,* IV, No. 3 (1926), 149–53. It is reproduced in Wheeler-Bennett, *Forgotten Peace,* 436.

Moscow would have none of it. To minimize the bad impression that the movement of German troops across Russian territory would produce, Moscow suggested a variety of deceptive measures, one of which had the German troops serving under the "nominal" command of a Russian officer.[207] The actual commander, the Russians agreed, would be a German general: at one point the Soviet side suggested for the part Field Marshal August von Mackensen, the Adjutant General of the Kaiser, who had dealt Russian forces a crushing defeat in Galicia in 1915.[208] The operation was being mounted when Germany surrendered.[209]

The second secret clause, even more sensitive because it involved German action not against foreign forces but against Russians, confirmed German acceptance of the Bolshevik request to initiate operations against the Volunteer Army. The Germans committed themselves to such action in the following words:

> Germany expects Russia to apply all the available means to suppress immediately the insurrections of General Alekseev and the Czechoslovaks: Russia, on the other hand, recognizes [*nimmt Akt*] that Germany, too, will proceed with all available forces against General Alekseev.*

This commitment the Germans also took seriously. On August 13, Ioffe communicated to Moscow that after the Supplementary Treaty had been ratified, the Germans would take energetic measures to crush the Volunteer Army.[210]

Germany promised to intervene against the British and Denikin's army in response to Soviet requests. The third secret clause came at German insistence and was forced on the unwilling Russians. It obliged the Soviet Government to expel from Baku the British force that had been there since August 4. As in the case of the other two clauses, it stipulated that if Soviet forces proved unequal to the task, the Wehrmacht would assume responsibility.† This provision was also not implemented, because the Turks occupied Baku on September 16, before the German forces were ready to move.

The three secret clauses ensured that if Germany had not collapsed, she would have secured not only an economic but also a military stranglehold on Soviet Russia.

In his report on the Supplementary Treaty to the Reichstag (of course, omitting mention of the secret clauses), Hintze asserted that it laid the basis for Russo-German "coexistence" *(Nebeneinanderleben)*.[211] Chicherin used similar language to the Central Executive Committee on September 2, which unanimously ratified the treaty: despite the "profoundest difference between the Russian and German systems and the basic tendencies of the two governments," he stated,

---

Europäische Gespräche, IV, No. 3 (1926), 150. Ioffe's acceptance: *Europäische Gespräche,* 152. Cf. H. W. Gatzke in *VZ,* III, No. 1 (January 1955), 96–97.

†Baumgart, *Ostpolitik,* 203. This third secret clause became public knowledge only after World War II. It was first published by Baumgart in *Historisches Jahrbuch,* LXXXIX (1969), 146–48.

peaceful coexistence [*mirnoe sozhitel'stvo*] of the two nations, which is always
the object of the strivings of our worker and peasant government, is at present
also desirable for the ruling circles of Germany.[212]

This is one of the earliest recorded uses in an official statement of the term
"peaceful coexistence," which the Soviet Government would dust off after
Stalin's death.

The two governments now drew steadily closer: one week before Germany's collapse, they were in a state of de facto political, economic, and
military alliance. Hintze was fanatically committed to the support of the
Bolsheviks. In early September, when Moscow unleashed its Red Terror,
in which thousands of hostages were massacred, he prevented the German
press from publishing full accounts of these atrocities sent by correspondents in Russia, for fear of creating public revulsion injurious to further
collaboration.[213]

In September, at Moscow's request, Germany began to supply Soviet
Russia with fuel and weapons. In response to an urgent appeal for coal, the
Foreign Office arranged in the second half of October for twenty-five German
ships to sail for Petrograd with 70,000 tons of coal and coke. Only about
one-half or less managed to reach its destination before the shipments were
suspended because the two countries broke off relations. The fuel unloaded in
Petrograd went to plants manufacturing weapons for the Red Army.[214]

In September, Ioffe requested 200,000 rifles, 500 million bullets, and
20,000 machine guns. Under pressure from the Foreign Office, Ludendorff
gave his reluctant consent, after managing to remove machine guns from the
list. This deal did not materialize, due to the departure of Hintze and Chancellor Hertling: the new Chancellor, Prince Maximilian of Baden, was much less
enthusiastic about a pro-Bolshevik policy.[215]

Despite the looming defeat of the Central Powers, Moscow punctiliously
fulfilled the financial obligations of the Supplementary Treaty. On September
10, it shipped to Germany gold worth 250 million deutsche marks as the first
payment of compensation, and on September 30, a second installment of 312.5
million deutsche marks, partly in gold and partly in rubles. The third installment, due on October 31, it did not pay because by then Germany was on the
verge of surrendering.

The Bolsheviks believed in the victory of their German friends as late
as the end of September 1918. Then things happened which forced them to
change their mind. The resignation on September 30 of Chancellor Hertling,
followed by the dismissal a few days later of Hintze, removed their most loyal
supporters in Berlin. The new Chancellor, Prince Maximilian, requested President Wilson to use his good offices to arrange for an armistice. These were
unmistakable symptoms of a looming collapse. Lenin, who at this time was

recovering at a *dacha* near Moscow from wounds suffered in an attempt on his life (see below, page 811), at once stirred into action. He instructed Trotsky and Sverdlov to convene the Central Committee to discuss urgent questions of foreign policy. On October 3 he sent to the Central Executive Committee an analysis of the situation in Germany in which he spoke glowingly of the prospects for an imminent revolution there.[216] At his recommendation, the CEC on October 4 adopted a resolution in which it "declare[d] to the entire world that Soviet Russia will offer all its forces and resources to aid the German revolutionary government."[217]

The new German Chancellor found such brazen appeals to subversion intolerable. By now even the Foreign Office had its fill of the Bolsheviks. At an interagency meeting in October, the Foreign Office for the first time agreed to a break with Moscow. A memorandum drafted by its staff toward the end of that month justified the change in policy as follows:

> We who are in bad odor for having invented Bolshevism and for having let it loose against Russia should now, at the last moment, at least cease to extend any longer a protective hand over it, in order not to forfeit also all the sympathies of future Russia . . .[218]

Germany had ample justification for breaking with Moscow, inasmuch as Ioffe, who even in the spring and summer of 1918 had pursued subversive activities on its soil, now openly stoked the fires of revolution. As he later boasted, at this time his embassy's agitational-propagandistic work

> increasingly assumed the character of decisive revolutionary preparation for an armed uprising. Apart from the conspiratorial groups of Spartacists, in Germany, and specifically in Berlin, there existed since the January [1917] strike— of course, illegally—soviets of workers' deputies. . . . With these soviets the embassy maintained constant communication. . . . The [Berlin] Soviet assumed that an uprising would be opportune only when the entire Berlin proletariat was well armed. We had to fight this. We had to demonstrate that if one awaited such a moment then no uprising would ever occur, that it is sufficient to arm only the vanguard of the proletariat. . . . Nonetheless, the striving of the German proletariat to arm itself was entirely legitimate and sensible and the embassy assisted it in every way.[219]

This assistance took the form of money and weapons. When the Soviet Embassy departed, it inadvertently left behind a document showing that between September 21 and October 31, 1918, it had purchased, for 105,000 deutsche marks, 210 handguns and 27,000 bullets.[220]

The declaration of the supreme soviet legislative body that it intended to assist the triumph of a revolutionary government in Germany, and Ioffe's efforts to implement this intention, should have sufficed for a break of diplomatic relations. But the German Foreign Office wanted more incontrovertible grounds and to this end it provoked an incident. Aware that Soviet couriers had for months brought to the embassy agitational materials for distribution in Germany, it arranged for a diplomatic box from Russia to drop and break, as if by accident, while being unloaded at a Berlin railroad station. This was done on the evening of November 4. Out of the damaged crate flew a shower of propaganda material exhorting German workers and soldiers to rise and overthrow their government.[221] Ioffe was told he would have to leave Germany at once. Although he displayed appropriate indignation, before departing for Moscow he did not forget to leave Dr. Oskar Cohn, a member of the Independent Socialist Party and a virtual resident of the Soviet mission, 500,000 deutsche marks and 150,000 rubles, to supplement the sum of 10 million rubles previously allocated "for the needs of the German revolution."*

On November 13, two days after the armistice on the Western Front, Moscow unilaterally abrogated both the Brest-Litovsk Treaty and the Supplementary Treaty.[222] The Allies also had Germany renounce the Brest Treaty as part of the Versailles settlement.[223]

The Russian Revolution was never a national event confined to Russia: from the moment the February Revolution broke out, but especially after the Bolsheviks seized Petrograd, it became internationalized and this for two reasons.

Russia had been a major theater of war. Its unilateral withdrawal from the war affected the most vital interests of both belligerent blocs: for the Central Powers it raised the hope of victory, for the Allies the specter of defeat. As long as the war continued, therefore, neither party could be indifferent to what happened to Russia: geographic location alone prevented Russia from escaping the maelstrom of global conflict. The Bolsheviks contributed to their country's involvement in this conflict by playing off the two belligerent blocs against each other. In the spring of 1918, they discussed with the Allies the formation on their territory of an anti-German multinational army, they agreed to the occupation of Murmansk, and invited help in building the Red Army. In the fall, they requested German military intervention to free the northern ports from the Allies and to crush the Russian Volunteer Army. Time and again, the Germans had to intervene, with political support and money, to prevent the Bolshevik regime from collapsing. Helfferich, referring to the Soviet regime's crisis of July–August 1918, conceded in his memoirs that "the strongest supporter of the Bolshevik regime during this critical time, even if unconsciously and unintentionally, was the German Government."[224] In view of these facts, it cannot be seriously maintained that foreign powers "intervened" in Russia in 1917–18 for the purpose of toppling the Bolsheviks from power. They intervened, first and foremost, in order to tip the balance

---

*Ioffe in *VZh,* No. 5 (1919), 45. Because of his close association with Trotsky, Ioffe later fell into disgrace: he committed suicide in 1927. See Lev Trotskii, *Portrety revoliutsionerov* (Benson, Vt., 1988), 377–401.

of power on the Western Front in their favor, either by reactivating the front in Russia, in the case of the Allies, or by keeping it quiescent, in the case of the Central Powers. The Bolsheviks actively participated in this foreign involvement, and invited it now from this party, now from that, depending on what their momentary interests called for. German "intervention," which they welcomed and solicited, very likely saved them from suffering the fate of the Provisional Government.

Second, the Bolsheviks from the outset declared that national borders in the era of socialist revolution and global class war had become meaningless. They issued appeals to foreign nationals to rise and overthrow their governments; they allocated state funds for this purpose; and where they were in a position to do, which for the time being was mainly Germany, they actively promoted revolution. By challenging the legitimacy of all foreign governments, the Bolsheviks invited all foreign governments to challenge theirs. If in fact no power chose to avail itself of that right in 1917–18, it was because none of them had an interest in so doing. The Germans found the Bolsheviks serving their purposes and propped them whenever they ran into trouble; the Allies were busy fighting for their lives. The question posed by one historian— "How . . . did the Soviet government, bereft of significant military force in the midst of what was until then mankind's most destructive war, succeed in surviving the first year of the revolution?"[225]—answers itself: this most destructive war completely overshadowed Russian events. The Germans supported the Bolshevik regime; the Allies had other concerns.

Hence, it is misleading to see foreign involvement in Russia in 1917–18 in terms of hostile "intervention." The Bolshevik Government both invited such intervention and aggressively intervened on its own account. Although the great powers, yearning for a return to normalcy, were reluctant to acknowledge it, the Russian Revolution never was a purely internal affair of Russia, important only insofar as it affected the outcome of the war. Russia's new rulers made certain that it would reverberate around the globe. The November 1918 armistice offered them unprecedented opportunities to organize revolutions in Germany, Austria, Hungary, and wherever else they could do so. Although these efforts failed for the time being, they ensured that the world would know no respite and no return to pre-1914 life.

One further thing needs to be said about foreign involvement on Russian soil during 1918. In all the talk of what the Allies did *in* Russia, which really was not very much, it is usually forgotten what they did *for* Russia, which was a great deal. After Russia had reneged on her commitments and left them to fight the Central Powers on their own, the Allies suffered immense human and material losses. As a result of Russia's dropping out of the war, the Germans withdrew from the inactive Eastern Front enough divisions to increase their effectives in the west by nearly one-fourth (from 150 to 192 divisions).[226] These reinforcements allowed them to mount a ferocious offensive. In the great battles on the Western Front in the spring and summer of 1918—St.-Quentin, the Lys, the Aisne, the Matz, the Marne, and Château-Thierry—the British,

French, and Americans lost hundreds of thousands of men. This sacrifice finally brought Germany to her knees.* And the defeat of Germany, to which it had made no contribution, not only enabled the Soviet Government to annul the Brest-Litovsk Treaty and recover most of the lands which it had been forced to give up at Brest but also saved Soviet Russia from being converted into a colony, a kind of Eurasian Africa, which fate Germany had intended for her.

*This point is vigorously and persuasively argued by Brian Pearce in *How Haig Saved Lenin* (London, 1987).

"War Communism"

The term "War Communism" has acquired over the years in Communist and non-Communist literature a precise meaning. In the words of the *Soviet Historical Encyclopedia:*

> *War Communism:* The name given to the economic policy of the Soviet Government during the years of the civil war and foreign intervention in the U.S.S.R., 1918–20. The policy of War Communism was dictated by the exceptional difficulties caused by the civil war [and] economic devastation.[1]

The notion that War Communism was "dictated" by circumstances, however, does violence to the historical record, as shown by the etymology of the term. The earliest official use of "War Communism" dates to the spring of 1921—that is, to the time when the policies so labeled were being abandoned in favor of the more liberal New Economic Policy. It was then that the Communist authorities, in order to justify their sudden turnabout, sought to blame the disasters of the immediate past on circumstances beyond their control. Thus, Lenin in April 1921 wrote: " 'War Communism' was imposed by war and ruin. It was not and could not be a policy that corresponded to the economic tasks of the proletariat. It was a temporary measure."[2] But this was hindsight. While some of its measures were indeed taken to meet emergencies, War Communism as a whole was not a "temporary measure" but an ambitious and, as it turned out, premature attempt to introduce full-blown communism.[3]

That Bolshevik economic policies in the first years of the regime were neither improvisations nor reactions is confirmed by no less an authority than Trotsky. Allowing that War Communism entailed "systematic regimentation of consumption in a besieged fortress," he goes on to say that

> in its original conception it pursued broader aims. The Soviet Government hoped and strove to develop these methods of regimentation directly into a system of planned economy in distribution as well as production. In other words, from [War Communism] it hoped gradually, but without destroying the system, to arrive at genuine communism.[4]

This view is corroborated by another Communist authority. War Communism, he says,

> was not only a product of war conditions and of other, spontaneously acting forces. It was also the product of a definite ideology, the realization of a sociopolitical design to construct the country's economic life on entirely new principles.[*]

Nothing attests more convincingly to the long-range Communist goals of the policies which the Bolsheviks pursued during the Civil War than the systematic assault on the institution of private property. The laws and decrees to this end, passed at a time when the Bolshevik regime was fighting for its life and which contributed nothing to its survivability, were inspired by an ideological belief in the need to deprive the citizens of ownership of disposable assets because they were a source of political independence. The process of expropriation began with real estate. The so-called Land Decree of October 26, 1917, deprived non-peasant owners of landed property. This was followed by decrees concerning urban real estate, which was first (December 14, 1917) withdrawn from commerce and later (August 24, 1918) expropriated on behalf of the state.[5] In January 1918 all state debts were repudiated. A decree of April 20, 1918, forbade the purchase, sale, and leasing of commercial and industrial enterprises. Another decree on that day required securities and bonds in private possession to be registered.[6] A major step in the abolition of private property was taken on May 1, 1918, with a decree outlawing inheritance.[7] None of these fell into the category of "emergency measures": each was intended to deprive private persons and associations of title to productive wealth and other assets.

In its mature form, which it attained only in the winter of 1920–21, War

*L. N. Iurovskii, *Denezhnaia politika sovetskoi vlasti (1917–1927)* (Moscow, 1928), 51. Another contemporary expert who concurs is the Left Communist L. Kritsman (*Geroicheskii period Velikoi Russkoi Revoliutsii,* 2nd ed., Moscow-Leningrad, 1926): he calls "so-called War Communism the first grandiose attempt at a proletarian-natural economy, *the attempt [to take] the first steps of transition to socialism"* (p. 77).

Communism involved a number of sweeping measures designed to place the entire economy of Russia—its labor force as well as its productive capacity and distribution mechanism—under the exclusive management of the state, or, more precisely, the Communist Party. It was intended both to undercut the economic base of the opposition to the Communist regime and to enable that regime to reorganize the national economy in a thoroughly "rational" manner. These measures were:

1. The nationalization of (a) the means of production, with the important (albeit temporary) exception of agriculture, (b) transport, and (c) all but the smallest enterprises.

2. The liquidation of private commerce through the nationalization of the retail and wholesale trade, and its replacement by a government-controlled distribution system.

3. The elimination of money as a unit of exchange and accounting in favor of a system of state-regulated barter.

4. The imposition on the entire national economy of a single plan.

5. The introduction of compulsory labor for all able-bodied male adults, but on occasion also for women, children, and elders.

These unprecedented measures, pursued not because of but despite the Civil War, were designed to provide Soviet Russia with a coherent and rational economic system conducive to most efficient productivity as well as fairness in distribution.

War Communism had several sources of inspiration. State control (though not ownership) of production and distribution of commodities and labor had been introduced by Imperial Germany during World War I. These emergency policies, known as "War Socialism" *(Kriegssozialismus),* made a great impression on Lenin and his economic adviser, Iurii Larin. The replacement of the free market for commodities with a network of state-run distribution centers was patterned on the ideas of Louis Blanc and the *ateliers* introduced in France in 1848 under his influence. In spirit, however, War Communism resembled most the patrimonial regime *(tiagloe gosudarstvo)* of medieval Russia, under which the monarchy treated the entire country, with its inhabitants and resources, as its private domain.[8] For the mass of Russians, who had never really been touched by Western culture, state control of the economy was more natural than abstract property rights and the whole complex of phenomena labeled "capitalism."

If one were to take at face value the flood of Soviet economic decrees issued between 1918 and 1921, one would likely conclude that by the end of this period the country's economy was completely state-managed. In fact, Soviet decrees of that time often reflected only intentions: the discrepancy between law and life was never greater. There is ample evidence that alongside the ever-expanding state sector there flourished a private sector which withstood all attempts at its elimination. Money continued to circulate even in an allegedly "moneyless" economy, and bread was sold on the open market despite the regime's claim to a grain monopoly. The central economic plan was never put into practice. In other words, in 1921, when it had to be given up, War Communism was only very incompletely realized. Its failure was only in part due to the government's inability to enforce its laws. No lesser a role was played by the realization that strict enforcement, even if it were possible, would bring about economic catastrophe: Communist sources conceded that without the illicit trade in food, which supplied the urban population with two-thirds of its bread, the cities would have starved. War Communism, under a new name and with fresh slogans, became a reality only ten years later, when Stalin resumed economic regimentation at the point where Lenin had left off.

The goal of War Communism was socialism or even communism. Its proponents had always believed that the socialist state would abolish private property and the free market, replacing them with a centralized, state-run and planned economic system. The main difficulty which the Bolsheviks faced in implementing this program derived from the fact that Marxism envisioned the abolition of private property and the market as the end result of a lengthy process of capitalist development which would concentrate production and distribution to such an extent that they could be nationalized by legislative fiat. But in Russia, at the time of the Revolution, capitalism was still in its infancy. Her overwhelmingly "petty bourgeois" economy, dominated by tens of millions of self-employed communal peasants and artisans, was further exacerbated by the Bolshevik policy of breaking up large estates for distribution to peasants and giving workers control of industrial enterprises.

Lenin gave ample proof of being an extraordinarily astute politician, but when it came to economic matters he revealed himself to be remarkably naïve. His knowledge of economics derived entirely from literary sources, such as the writings of the German socialist Rudolf Hilferding. In his influential *Finance Capital* (1910), Hilferding maintained that as capitalism entered its most advanced stage, that of "finance capitalism," it concentrated all economic power in the hands of banks. Once it reached its logical conclusion, "this trend would produce a situation in which a bank or a group of banks would have at their disposal the entire monetary capital. Such a 'central bank' would thereby secure control over the entire social production."[9] Connected with the notion of "finance capitalism" was an exaggerated view of the role of syndicates and trusts. Lenin and his associates believed that in Russia syndicates and trusts virtually controlled industry and trade, leaving market forces a small and diminishing scope.

From these premises it followed that nationalizing banks and syndicates would be tantamount to nationalizing the country's economy, which, in turn, meant laying the foundations of socialism. In 1917, Lenin argued that the concentration of economic power in the hands of banking institutions and cartels in Russia had attained a level at which finance and commerce could be nationalized by decree.[10] On the eve of the October coup, he made the astonishing statement that the creation of a single state bank would provide, in and of itself, "nine-tenths of the *socialist* apparatus."[11] Trotsky confirms Lenin's optimism:

In Lenin's "Theses on the Peace," written in early 1918, it says that "the triumph of socialism in Russia [required] a certain interval of time, *no less than a few months.*" At present [1924] such words seem completely incomprehensible: was this not a slip of the pen, did he not mean to speak of a few years or decades? But no: this was not a slip of the pen. . . . I recall very clearly that in the first period, at Smolnyi, at meetings of the Council of People's Commissars, Lenin invariably repeated that we shall have socialism in half a year and become the mightiest state.[12]

During the first six months in power Lenin thought of introducing into Russia a system which he called "state socialism." It was to be modeled on German *Kriegssozialismus,* with this difference that it would embrace the entire economy, not only the sector directly relevant to the war effort, and work for the benefit not of "capitalists and Junkers" but of the "proletariat." In September 1917, on the eve of the coup, he thus described what he had in mind:

Besides the predominantly "oppressive" apparatus of the standing army, police, officialdom, there exists in the contemporary state an apparatus, especially closely connected with banks and syndicates, which carries out a great deal of work of accounting and registering, if one may put it this way. This apparatus cannot and should not be smashed. It must be removed from its subjection to the capitalists, it must be *cut off* . . . from the capitalists with their threads of influence, one must *subordinate* it to the proletarian soviets, one must make it more comprehensive, more all-embracing, more national. And this *can* be done, leaning on the achievements already accomplished by large-scale capitalism. . . . The "nationalization" of the mass of employees of banks, syndicates, commercial societies, etc., is fully realizable both technically (thanks to preparatory work done for us by capitalism and finance capitalism) and politically under the condition of *Soviet* control and supervision.[13]

In late November 1917, Lenin jotted down the outline of an economic program:

Questions of Economic Policy
1. Nationalization of banks
2. Compulsory syndication
3. State monopoly of foreign trade
4. Revolutionary methods to combat looting
5. Publicizing financial and bank looting
6. Finance industry
7. Unemployment
8. Demobilization—of army? industry?
9. Supply[14]

This draft made no mention of state monopoly of domestic trade, or of nationalization of industry or transport, or of moneyless economy, which were to become the hallmarks of War Communism. Lenin at this time believed that the nationalization of financial institutions and the syndication of industrial and commercial enterprises would suffice to set the socialist economy on its way.

On October 25, 1917—that is, before he had even obtained from the Second Congress of Soviets the authority to form a government—Lenin approached Iurii Larin, a Menshevik recently turned Bolshevik. In socialist circles, Larin was considered an expert on the German wartime economy. "You have occupied yourself with questions of the organization of the German economy," Lenin said to him, "syndicates, trusts, banks. Study this subject for us."[15]

Soon afterward, Larin published in *Izvestiia* an impressionistic sketch of the Bolshevik economic program. It centered on the compulsory syndication of all raw material production, consumer industries, transport, and banks, each subordinated to a comprehensive national plan. Private shares in enterprises would be exchanged for syndicate shares, which would be traded on the open market. In the provinces, organs of self-rule (presumably soviets) would either syndicate or municipalize retail trade and residential quarters. The peasants too would be "syndicated" for the distribution of foodstuffs and agricultural equipment.[16] Under this program, the government would control private enterprise, but not abolish it.

At Lenin's request, Larin and his associates initiated discussions with Alexis Meshcherskii, one of Russia's most powerful industrialists. A self-made man, Meshcherskii under the old regime had been a typical "progressive" businessman who despised the bureaucracy and wanted Russia to become a free, democratic country, capable of realizing her immense productive potential.[17] Although not personally wealthy, he had considerable managerial responsibilities as director of the giant Sormova-Kolomna Metal Works, owned by Russian and foreign, mainly German, capital, employing 60,000 workers. At Larin's invitation, Meshcherskii drew up a blueprint for a joint venture involving private enterprise and the Bolshevik Government. He envisioned the creation of a Soviet Metallurgical Trust with a capital of one billion rubles, half supplied by private investors, half by the state, and managed by a board, on which the former would have 60 percent of the seats. The trust, employing 300,000 workers, was to manage a network of industrial enterprises, as well as coal and iron mines, and devote itself, in the first instance, to providing rolling stock for Russia's ailing railroad system.[18] In March, the Communist authorities discussed a similar joint venture with the directors of the Stakheev Group, which controlled some 150 industrial, financial, and commercial enterprises in the Urals. Its management proposed a trust to exploit the mineral deposits of the Urals financed with funds supplied by the Soviet Government as well as Russian and American interests.[19]

These proposals, which would have pushed the Soviet economy toward a mixed model, were aborted by the opposition of Bolshevik "purists." Under their pressure, government negotiators demanded an ever-greater proportion of the shares in the proposed Metallurgical Trust, until nothing was left for private capital. Meshcherskii and his associates were so eager for a deal with the Bolshevik regime that they agreed to concede the government even 100 percent of the trust's shares as long as they were promised priority should the government ever decide to sell them. Even this modest proposal was rejected. According to a Communist account, on April 14, 1918, with what is cryptically described as a "near majority of votes," the Supreme Council of the National Economy voted to terminate discussions.*

Although they had no result, the mere fact of these negotiations taking place helps explain the puzzling equanimity of Russia's business community toward a regime which openly threatened it with economic ruin and even physical annihilation. Russia's bankers and industrialists treated Bolshevik pronouncements as revolutionary rhetoric. In their view, the Bolsheviks would either turn to them for help in restoring a collapsing economy or fall. So it happened that in the spring of 1918 the Petrograd Stock Exchange, formally closed since the outbreak of the war, suddenly came to life, as securities, especially bank shares, rose in over-the-counter trading.[20] The optimism of big business, reinforced by Bolshevik overtures and the knowledge that the government was negotiating with Germany a trade agreement that would open Russia to German capital, caused it to turn a deaf ear to the pleas of White generals for financial assistance. In the spring of 1918, the White movement appeared to businessmen a hopeless gamble compared with the prospects of collaboration with the Bolshevik Government.

As soon as the Brest-Litovsk Treaty had been ratified, the Bolshevik leaders turned their attention to the economy: now that power was theirs, they were no longer interested in squandering the country's wealth by turning it over to the peasants and workers to divide among themselves. The time had come to organize production and distribution in a rational, efficient, "capitalist" manner, through the restoration of labor discipline, the reintroduction of accountability, and the adoption of the most modern technology and management methods. Trotsky signaled the change of attitude in a speech on May 28, 1918, with a strangely "Fascist" title, "Work, Discipline, and Order Will Save the Soviet Socialist Republic."[21] He called on the workers to exercise "self-restraint" and accept the fact that the management of Soviet industry would have to be turned over to specialists, drawn from the ranks of previous "exploiters."

At the time, Lenin argued with great conviction but little success in favor of state capitalism, which would place the marvels of capitalist management and technology at the disposal of the new state. Only by adopting the best that capitalism had to offer could Russia build socialism:

> Let us . . . take the most concrete example of state capitalism. Everybody knows this example. It is Germany. Here we have the "last word" in modern large-

*Meshcherskii in *NS*, No. 33 (May 26, 1918), 7; M. Vindelbot in *NKh*, No. 6 (1919), 24–32. According to *NV*, No. 101/125 (June 26, 1918), 3, Meshcherskii was arrested in June. He later emigrated to the West.

scale capitalist engineering and planned organization, *subordinated to Junker-bourgeois imperialism.* Cross out the words in italics, and in place of the militarist, Junker, bourgeois, imperialist *state* put *also a state,* but of a different social type, of a different class content—a *Soviet* state, that is, a proletarian state, and you will have the *sum total* of the conditions necessary for socialism.

Socialism is inconceivable without large-scale capitalist technology based on the latest discoveries of modern science. It is inconceivable without planned state organization, which makes tens of millions of people strictly observe a unified standard in production and distribution of products.[22]

What is state capitalism under Soviet power? To achieve state capitalism at the present time means putting into practice the accounting and control carried out by the capitalist classes. We have an example of state capitalism in Germany. We know that Germany has proven superior to us. But if you reflect even slightly on what it would mean if the foundations of such state capitalism were established in Russia, Soviet Russia, everyone who has not taken leave of his senses and has not stuffed his head with bits and pieces of book learning would have to say that state capitalism would be our salvation.

I said that state capitalism would be our salvation; if we had it in Russia, the transition to full socialism would be easy, within our grasp, because state capitalism is something centralized, calculated, controlled and socialized, and that is exactly what we lack. . . .[23]

The economic program that Lenin favored was thus much more moderate than the one that the Bolsheviks would actually adopt. Had he had his way, the "capitalist" sector would have been left essentially intact and placed under state supervision. The resulting cooperation, which posited the inflow of foreign (mainly German and American) capital, was meant to bring the Bolshevik economy all the benefits of advanced "capitalism" without its political side effects. The proposal had many features in common with the New Economic Policy introduced three years later.

But this was not to be. Lenin and Trotsky ran into fanatical opposition from a number of groups, of which the Left Communists were the most vociferous. Led by Bukharin, and comprising an important segment of the party's elite, the Left Communists had suffered a humiliating defeat over Brest-Litovsk, but they continued to operate as a faction within the Bolshevik Party and to argue their case in the pages of their organ, *Kommunist.* The group, which included Alexandra Kollontai, V. V. Kuibyshev, L. Kritsman, Valerian Obolenskii (N. Osinskii), E. A. Preobrazhenskii, G. Piatakov, and Karl Radek, saw itself as the "conscience of the Revolution." It believed that, since October, Lenin and Trotsky were sliding toward opportunistic accommodation with "capitalism" and "imperialism." Lenin treated the Left Communists as utopians and fantasts, victims of a "childhood disease of socialism." But the faction enjoyed powerful support among workers and intellectuals, especially in the Moscow party organization, who felt threatened by Lenin and Trotsky's proposals to introduce "capitalist" methods. The proposed changes calling for the dismantling of Factory Committees and the abandonment of "workers' control" in favor of a return to responsible individual management inevitably reduced the power and privilege of party officials. Lenin could ill afford to alienate these intellectuals and their supporters among the workers at a time when the Bolsheviks were under fire for Brest and had lost majorities in all the soviets. He could hardly insist on a course which commonsense recommended to him when he heard a metalworker say about the negotiations with Meshcherskii: "Comrade Lenin, you are a great opportunist, if you allow for a breathing spell also in this field."*

The elements of the War Communist system that actually won out found reflection in an essay which Larin published in April 1918. Although he pretended merely to elaborate on the principles enunciated in his November 1917 article, Larin now presented a new and different economic program. All Russian banks were to be nationalized. So was industry, branch by branch: there was to be no collaboration between the state and private trusts. "Bourgeois" specialists could work for the economy only as technical personnel. Private trade was to be abolished and replaced by cooperatives working under state supervision. The economy would be subjected to a single national plan. Soviet institutions would keep accounts without reference to money. In time, state control would be extended to agriculture, beginning with the unused land of ex-landlords. The only concession to private capital would be to foreign interests which would be permitted to participate in Soviet Russia's economic development by providing technical personnel and granting loans for the importation of equipment.[24]

With this program, the Left Communists in April 1918 overruled Lenin, plunging Russia headlong into the utopia of instant socialism.

Bukharin remained the leader of the Left Communists, but after suffering defeat over the Brest Treaty, he yielded to others the opposition to Lenin's state capitalism. The principal theorist of Left Communism was Valerian Obolenskii, better known by his pen name, N. Osinskii.† Born in 1887 the son of a veterinarian with radical sympathies, he joined the Bolsheviks at the age of twenty. He spent one year in Germany studying political economy, which, in his mind, qualified him to write on economic subjects, notably Russian agriculture. Immediately after their coup, the Bolsheviks appointed him director of the State Bank, which post he held until March 1918, when he resigned in protest against the Brest Treaty.

His *Construction of Socialism*, written in the summer of 1918 and pub-

---

*Vechernaia zvezda, April 19, 1918, in Peter Scheibert, *Lenin an der Macht* (Weinheim, 1984), 219. The reference, of course, is to the unpopular "breathing spell" which the Bolsheviks claimed to have secured with the Brest-Litovsk Treaty.

†On him: *Granat*, XLI, Pt. 2, 89–98. He was given a mock trial (along with Bukharin) in 1938 and presumably shot soon afterward for an alleged plot to assassinate Lenin: Robert Conquest, *The Great Terror* (New York, 1968), 398–400.

lished that fall, provided the blueprint for War Communism.[25] The regime's economic tasks, as Osinskii defined them, involved three operations: seizing control of the "strategic points" of the capitalist economy, purging it of unproductive elements, and imposing on the country a comprehensive economic plan.

Following Hilferding, Osinskii placed at the top of his priorities the seizure of banks, the "brain of capitalism." They were to be transformed into clearing agencies of the socialist economy.

Next came the nationalization of private property in the means of industrial and agricultural production, both large-scale and small. This meant not only the legal transfer of property titles but a purge of the personnel, with the previous owners and managers being replaced by workers. These measures would strike at the very heart of capitalism and, at the same time, make it possible to rationalize production, through the appropriate allocation of resources.

The next step, the nationalization of commerce, was the most difficult. The government would take over all commercial syndicates and large trading companies. Exercising a monopoly on wholesale trade, it would set prices on commodities; in time, all commodities would be distributed by state organs, preferably free of charge. The elimination of the free market was an essential measure:

> The market is the nidus of infection from which constantly ooze germs of capitalism. Mastery of the mechanism of social exchange will eliminate speculation, the accumulation of fresh capital, the emergence of new proprietors. . . . A correctly realized monopoly on all products of agriculture, under which it will be forbidden *to sell* on the side a single pound of grain, a single bag of potatoes, will make it utterly senseless to carry on independent village agriculture.[26]

Liquidation of retail trade called for a fourth step: compulsory consumer communes enjoying a monopoly on articles of prime necessity. This institution would do away with speculation and "sabotage" and deprive capitalists of yet another source of profit.

Finally, it would be necessary to introduce compulsory labor. Its guiding principle would be simple: "No one has the right to refuse work assigned to him by the [labor] bureau." Compulsory labor was not necessary, for the time being, in the rural areas, which had an excess of hands, but it was indispensable in the cities. Under this system, the "labor obligation . . . becomes a means of compelling people to work, replacing the old 'economic' stimulus, which, in plain language, meant the fear of dying from hunger."

It was a basic premise of Osinskii's plan that for political as well as economic reasons the economy could not be organized on a part-capitalist, part-socialist basis: a clear choice had to be made. Even so, in deference to Lenin, he called his program, not "socialism" or "War Communism," but "state capitalism."

The economic program of the Left Communists drew strong support from party members and workers, beneficiaries of workers' control, who in no time formed a new interest group: they no more wanted to give up the factories they had taken over in 1917 than the peasants to surrender the seized land. The Left SRs also sympathized with these ideas. Lenin viewed them skeptically but he had to give in: it was the price of regaining the popularity lost at Brest. In June 1918, under conditions which will be detailed below, Lenin decreed the nationalization of Russian industries. This measure ended the possibility of "state capitalism" in the sense in which Lenin understood the term. It was a leap into the unknown.

The architects of War Communism, its theorists and executors—Osinskii, Bukharin, Larin, Rykov, and others—had only the most superficial acquaintance with the discipline of economics and no experience in business management. Their knowledge of economics derived largely from socialist literature. None of them had run an enterprise or earned a ruble from manufacture or trade. Except for Krasin, who did not take part in these experiments, the Bolshevik leaders were professional revolutionaries, who, save for brief stints at Russian or foreign universities (devoted mostly to political activity), had spent their entire adult lives in and out of jail or exile. They were guided by abstract formulae, gleaned from the writings of Marx, Engels, and their German disciples and from radical histories of European revolutions. What Sukhanov said of Larin applied to all of them: "a poor cavalryman who knew no obstacles to the leaps of his fantasy, a cruel experimenter, a specialist in all the branches of state administration, a dilettante in all his specialties."[27] That such rank amateurs would undertake to turn upside down the fifth-largest economy in the world, subjecting it to innovations never attempted anywhere even on a small scale, says something of the judgment of the people who in October 1917 seized power in Russia. Observing these people in action, one recalls Taine's picture of the French Jacobin:

His principle is an axiom of political geometry, which always carries its own proof along with it: for like the axioms of common geometry, it is formed out of the combination of a few simple ideas, and its evidence imposes itself at once. . . . Men as they really are do not concern him. He does not observe them; he does not require to observe them; with closed eyes he imposes a pattern of his own on the human substance manipulated by him; the idea never enters his head of forming any previous conception of this complex, multiform, swaying material—contemporary peasants, artisans, townspeople, curés and nobles, behind their plows, in their homes, in their shops, in their parsonages, in their mansions, with their inveterate beliefs, persistent inclinations, and powerful wills. Nothing of this enters into or lodges in his mind; all its avenues are stopped by the abstract principle which flourishes there and fills it completely.

Should actual experience through the eye and ear plant some unwelcome truth forcibly in his mind, it cannot subsist there; however obstreperous and telling it may be, the abstract principle drives it out . . .[28]

These qualities were nowhere more evident than in early Bolshevik fiscal experiments designed to introduce a moneyless economy.

Marx had written a great deal of sophisticated nonsense about the nature and function of money, in which he employed Feuerbach's concepts of "projections" and "fetishes." He defined money variously as the "alienated ability of mankind," something that "confounds" all the "natural human qualities," "crystallized labor," and a "monster" which separates itself from man and comes to dominate him. These ideas greatly appealed to intellectuals who neither had money nor knew how to earn it but longed for the influence and gratifications that money brings. Had they been more familiar with economic history, they would have realized that some unit of measurement, whether or not called "money," had existed in every society practicing the division of labor and the exchange of goods and services.

Under the spell of these ideas, the Bolsheviks both overrated and underestimated the role of money. They overrated it in respect to "capitalist" economies, which they viewed as totally controlled by financial institutions. They underestimated it in respect to "socialist" economies, which they believed could dispense with it: as Bukharin and Preobrazhenskii put it: "Communist society will know nothing about money."[29]

It followed from Hilferding's thesis that by seizing Russia's banks, it was possible, in one fell swoop, to seize control of the country's industry and trade.* This belief accounted for Lenin's optimism that Russia could quickly become socialist—that nationalization of banks would accomplish "nine-tenths of socialism." Osinskii likewise declared it the single most important measure.† Although the expectation of a quick and easy conquest of Russia's capitalist economy by such means proved entirely illusory, the Bolshevik Party stubbornly adhered to Hilferding's doctrine. Its new program, adopted in 1919, claimed that by nationalizing Russia's state and commercial banks, the Soviet Government had "transformed the bank from a center of domination of finance capital . . . into a weapon of workers' power and the lever of economic revolution."[30]

As concerned money, the Bolshevik theoreticians wanted to abolish it altogether by depreciating it into "colored paper" and replacing it with a comprehensive system of distribution of commodities by means of ration

---

*According to Hilferding, in 1910 six of the largest Berlin banks controlled most of German industry: S. Malle, *The Economic Organization of War Communism, 1918–21* (Cambridge, 1985), 154.
†Russian banks, like those of Germany, participated directly in industrial and commercial ventures, and owned sizable portfolios of securities and debentures issued by these enterprises, which lent these notions the semblance of credibility.

cards. In Soviet publications in 1918–20 many articles argued that the disappearance of money was inevitable; the following is a fair sample:

> Parallel with the strengthening of the socialized economy and the introduction of greater planning in distribution, the need for monetary tokens [i.e., money] should diminish. As it gradually disappears from circulation in the socialized economy, money turns into a property outside the direct influence of government on the private producer, which is why, despite their constantly growing quantity and the continued need for further [money] emissions, money begins to play in the overall movement of the national economy an ever-diminishing role. And this process of, as it were, objective depreciation of money will receive further impetus to the extent that the socialized economy is strengthened and developed and an ever-widening circle of small private producers is pulled within its orbit—until, finally, following the decisive triumph of state productivity over private productivity, there will emerge the possibility of a deliberate withdrawal of money from circulation through the transition to a moneyless distribution.[31]

In the jargon which Marxists favored, the author was saying that money could not be dispensed with as yet because the "small private producer" (read: peasant) still remained outside state control and had to be paid for his product. Money would become redundant only "with the decisive triumph of state productivity over private productivity"—in other words, after full collectivization of agriculture.

The standard reason the Bolsheviks gave at the time for their failure to decree money out of existence was that even after the passage of various nationalization decrees much of the economy, including nearly all of the food production, remained in private hands. According to Osinskii, the existence of a "dual economy"—part state-owned, part private—necessitated the retention of the monetary system for an "indeterminate period."[32]

In fact, however, the peasant was paid such ludicrously low prices for his product that this consideration was nowhere as serious as the official explanations claimed. In the summer of 1920, Larin conceded that the bulk of the money printed by the Treasury went, not to buy food, but to pay the salaries of workers and officials. He estimated that Soviet Russia had 10 million wage earners, who received on the average 40,000 rubles a month, for a total of 400 billion rubles. Compared with this figure, the money paid to the peasant for food was minuscule: Larin estimated that all the foodstuffs acquired at fixed prices (in 1918–20) had cost the government less than 20 billion.[33]

The Bolsheviks could not nationalize banks immediately after taking power in Petrograd because of the near-unanimous refusal of banking personnel to acknowledge them as the legitimate government. This opposition, as we have seen, was eventually broken. By the end of the winter 1917–18, all banks were nationalized. The State Bank was renamed the People's Bank (Narodnyi Bank) and placed in charge of other credit institutions. By 1920, all the banks were liquidated, except for the People's Bank and its branches, which served as clearing agencies. Safes were ordered opened and gold found in them, as well as large amounts of cash and securities, was confiscated. These measures hardly fulfilled Bolshevik expectations: their result was not so much to give the government control of Russia's business as to choke off credit. It was a bitter disappointment to the new regime.[34]

Financially, the Bolshevik Government lived for a long time in a state of disarray. The tax system had all but broken down after October, and revenues were reduced to a trickle. The government improvised as best it could: among the currencies it resorted to were coupons from Kerensky's "Liberty Loans." There was nothing faintly resembling a regular budget: in May 1918, the Commissariat of Finance estimated (sic!) that in the preceding six months the government spent between 20 and 25 billion and took in 5 billion.* The government was unable to meet the needs of its provincial administrations, so it not only permitted but commanded *guberniia* and district soviets to extort money from the local "bourgeoisie." Lenin thought this set a bad precedent by encouraging every local soviet to regard itself as an "independent republic," and in May 1918 he demanded fiscal centralization.[35] But one could not centralize finances if the center lacked money: in the end Moscow told the provincial soviets to stop importuning it for subsidies and manage on their own.

To raise funds for extraordinary expenses, and at the same time undermine the economic power of the "class enemy," the Bolsheviks occasionally resorted to discriminatory taxes in the form of "contributions." Thus, in October 1918, a special one-time "contribution" of 10 billion rubles was imposed on the country's propertied classes. This extraordinary tax followed the Chinese model, which the Mongols had introduced to medieval Russia, in that it set quotas for cities and provinces and left it to them to distribute the payments. Moscow and Petrograd were required to pay 3 and 2 billion rubles, respectively. Elsewhere the local soviets were asked to prepare lists of individuals liable for payment.† Similar "contributions" were imposed by local soviets on their own initiative, sometimes to raise money for current expenses, sometimes as punishment.

Lenin was rather conservative in fiscal matters, and if he had his way, Soviet Russia would have adopted from the outset traditional methods of taxation and budgeting. He worried about the budgetary chaos. In May 1918, with his usual tendency to exaggerate the importance of whatever business happened to be at hand, he warned:

> All our radical reforms are condemned to failure if we do not succeed in financial policy. On this task depends the success of the immense endeavor we have conceived of reorganizing society on the socialist model.[36]

*E. H. Carr, *The Bolshevik Revolution, 1917–1923*, II (New York, 1952), 145. Carr says that "it is difficult to regard any of these figures as anything but guesses." Indeed, the state budget approved by the Sovnarkom in July 1918 retroactively for the preceding six months fixed expenditures at 17.6 billion and revenues at 2.85 billion: *NV*, No. 117/141 (July 14, 1918), 1. Another contemporary estimate placed expenditures for the first six months of 1918 at 20.5 billion and revenues at 3.3 billion: Lenin, *Sochineniia*, XXIII, 537–38.

†*Piatyi Sozyv VTsIK: Stenograficheskii Otchët* (Moscow, 1919), 289–92. It appears, however, that only a fraction of the desired sums was actually collected.

But as he had little time to devote to this matter, he turned it over to associates with very different ideas. They wanted to abolish money and finance altogether, so as to create an economy based on state-controlled production and distribution. In the second half of 1918, Soviet economic publications carried many articles promoting the idea of such an economy, which had the support of such Bolshevik notables as Bukharin, Larin, Osinskii, Preobrazhenskii, and A. V. Chaianov.* Their idea was to make money worthless through the unrestrained emission of paper currency. The place of money was to be taken by "labor units," similar to those issued in 1832 by Robert Owen's "Labor Exchange Banks," which were tokens representing quantities of expended labor entitling the holder to a comparable amount of goods and services. Owen's experiment failed miserably (his bank closed after two weeks), as did Louis Blanc's *ateliers sociaux,* introduced in France during the 1848 Revolution. Undaunted, Russian radical intellectuals would retrace this path.

The Communist Party declared the abolition of money an objective in the new party program adopted in March 1919. Here it was stated that while the abolition of money was not yet feasible, the party was determined to achieve it: "To the extent that the economy is organized according to a plan, the bank will be abolished and turned into the central bookkeeping office of Communist society."[37] Accordingly, the Soviet Commissar of Finance declared his job redundant: "Finance should not exist in a socialistic community and I must, therefore, apologize for speaking on the subject."†

The result was an accelerating devaluation of Russian currency which ultimately transformed it into "colored paper." The inflation which occurred in Soviet Russia in 1918–22 nearly matched the much more familiar inflation that Weimar Germany would experience shortly afterward. It was deliberate and accomplished by flooding the country with as much paper money as the printing presses were able to turn out.

At the time the Bolsheviks took power in Petrograd, paper money circulating in Russia totaled 19.6 billion rubles.[38] The bulk of it consisted of Imperial rubles, popularly known as "Nikolaevki." There were also paper rubles issued by the Provisional Government, called either "Kerenki" or "Dumki." The latter were simple talons, printed on one side, without serial number, signature, or name of issuer, displaying only the ruble value and a warning of punishment for counterfeiting. In 1917 and early 1918, "Kerenkis" circulated at a slight discount to Imperial rubles. After taking over the State Bank and the Treasury, the Bolsheviks continued to issue "Kerenkis" without altering their appearance. During the next year and a half (until February 1919), the Bolshevik Government produced no currency of its own, which was a striking forfeiture of

---

*A survey of the theoretical foundations of the projected moneyless economy can be found in Iurovskii's *Denezhnaia politika,* 88–125. A dominant influence on Bolshevik thinking on this subject was the German sociologist Otto Neurath.

†S. S. Katzenellenbaum, *Russian Currency and Banking, 1914–24* (London, 1925), 98n. In view of this evidence it is not possible to agree with Carr (*Revolution,* II, 246–47, 261) that Bolshevik fiscal policies which led to the total depreciation of Russian currency were the result not of plan or policy but of responses to desperate needs.

the traditional right of a sovereign power to issue its own money, and can only be explained by the fear that the population, especially the peasants, would refuse to accept it. Since the tax system broke down completely after October 1917 and other revenues fell far short of the government's needs, the Bolsheviks had recourse to the printing presses. In the first half of 1918, the People's Bank issued between 2 and 3 billion rubles a month, without any backing whatever.* In October 1918, the Sovnarkom raised the limit on the emission of uncovered bank notes from the 16.5 billion previously authorized by the Provisional Government, and long since exceeded, to 33.5 billion.[39] In January 1919, Soviet Russia had in circulation 61.3 billion rubles, two-thirds of them "Kerenkis" issued by the Bolsheviks. The following month, the government produced the first Soviet money, called "accounting tokens."† This new currency circulated alongside "Nikolaevkis" and "Kerenkis," but at a deep discount to them.

In early 1919, inflation, though increasingly severe, had still not reached the grotesque dimensions that lay ahead. Compared with 1917, the price index had increased 15 times: with 1913 as 100, it grew to 755 in October 1917, to 10,200 in October 1918, and to 92,300 in October 1919.[40]

Then the dam burst. On May 15, 1919, the People's Bank was authorized to emit as much money as in its view the national economy required.[41] From then on, the printing of "colored paper" became the largest and perhaps the only growth industry in Soviet Russia. At the end of the year, the mint employed 13,616 workers.[42] The only constraints on emissions were shortages of paper and ink: on occasion the government had to allocate gold to purchase printing supplies abroad.[43] Even so, the presses could not keep up with the demand. According to Osinskii, in the second half of 1919, "treasury operations"—in other words, the printing of money—consumed between 45 and 60 percent of budgetary expenditures, which served him as an argument for the most rapid elimination of money as a means of balancing the budget![44] In the course of 1919, the amount of paper money in circulation nearly quadrupled (from 61.3 to 225 billion). In 1920 it nearly quintupled (to 1.2 trillion), and in the first six months of 1921 it doubled again (to 2.3 trillion).[45]

By then, Soviet money had become, for all practical purposes, worthless: a 50,000-ruble bank note had the purchasing power of a prewar kopeck coin.[46] The only paper currency that still retained value was the Imperial ruble; these notes, however, were hoarded and all but disappeared from circulation.[47] But since people could not carry on without some unit to measure value, they resorted to money substitutes, the most common of which were bread and salt.[48] Inflation reached astronomical proportions, as the following tables indicate:

---

*It is surprising how little note financial markets took of this irresponsible fiscal policy and, indeed, how readily they accommodated themselves to Bolshevism. According to contemporary newspapers (NV, No. 102/126, June 27, 1918, 3), in June 1918 one could buy U.S. currency in Russia at the rate of 12.80 rubles for one dollar, which was the same rate as in early November 1917.

†Reproductions of Russian currency for the revolutionary period can be found in N. D. Mets's *Nash rubl'* (Moscow, 1960). According to Katzenellenbaum, the earliest Soviet currency came out in mid-1918 in Penza (*Russian Currency*, 81).

REAL VALUE OF RUSSIAN MONEY IN CIRCULATION[49]
(in billions of rubles)

November 1, 1917	1,919
January 1, 1918	1,332
January 1, 1919	379
January 1, 1920	93
January 1, 1921	70
July 1, 1921	29

PRICES IN RUSSIA, 1913–1923[50] (as of October 1)

1913	1.0
1917	7.55
1918	102
1919	923
1920	9,620
1921	81,900
1922	7,340,000
1923	648,230,000

"From January 1, 1917, to January 1, 1923," in the words of one economic historian, "the quantity of money [in Russia] increased 200,000 times and the price of goods increased 10 million times."*[51]

The Left Communists exulted. At the Tenth Party Congress, held in March 1921, before inflation had attained its apogee, Preobrazhenskii boasted that whereas the assignats issued by French revolutionaries had depreciated, at their lowest, 500 times, the Soviet ruble had already fallen to 1/20,000th of its value: "This means that we have overtaken the French Revolution 40 to 1."[52] On a more serious note, Preobrazhenskii observed that the massive inflation caused by the government's policy of printing unlimited quantities of money helped to extract food and other products from the peasantry: it was a kind of indirect tax that for three years had played a crucial role in supporting the Bolshevik revolution.[53] At the Eleventh Party Congress, the speaker on financial policies, G. Ia. Sokolnikov, remarked with surprise that his was the first full-length report on the subject ever presented to a Party Congress. The policy until then, he stated, had been to regard money and fiscal policy as something to be done away with. The means to this end was deliberate inflation.[54]

Students of economic history had long warned that money was an indis-

*In fact, prices increased 100 million times.

pensable element of every economic activity, not only in its "capitalist" form. In the words of Max Weber:

> The assumption that some sort of accounting system will somehow be "found" if one resolutely tackles the problem of a moneyless economy, is of no help. This is the basic problem of every "full socialization." One cannot speak of a *rational* "planned economy" as long as one does not have in *this* most decisive point a means of rationally establishing a "plan."*

Closer to home, Peter Struve had demonstrated both before and after the Revolution that since economic activity meant striving for the greatest return at the least cost, it required an accounting unit or "money," whatever its name or physical form. Money could not be abolished: whenever a government tried to prevent money from performing its natural function, the result was a split market (part regulated, part free).[55]

The Bolsheviks now discovered the truth of these observations. The one difficulty the advocates of a moneyless economy had not foreseen and which ultimately doomed their undertaking was their failure to provide a method for the settling of accounts among the nationalized enterprises and other state institutions. A decree of August 30, 1918,[56] instructed Soviet agencies to deposit their monetary assets, except those required for current expenses, with the People's Bank. They were to consign their products to appropriate agencies *(glavki)* of the Supreme Council of the National Economy (of which later) and receive, in return, equipment and raw materials. These transactions were to be carried out by means of book entries, without reference to money. But this procedure apparently did not work, for additional decrees came out the following year specifying in tortuous detail how to carry on moneyless bookkeeping of transactions between nationalized enterprises as well as between such enterprises and state agencies.[57] Osinskii claimed that government officials from the outset opposed and circumvented decrees regulating financial relations between Soviet institutions and enterprises; he would not concede that the system was unworkable.[58]

He and his fellow-hotheads were not fazed. In February 1920, Larin and his associates drafted a resolution for the forthcoming Congress of Soviets formally abolishing money. Lenin agreed in principle but wanted to discuss the matter.[59] A year later (February 3, 1921) a decree was ready for release which, if implemented, would have for the first time in recorded history abolished taxes.[60] It never came out, however, because the following month, with the introduction of the New Economic Policy, the government, even while turning out money at an accelerating pace, took steps to return to fiscal responsibility.

*M. Weber, *Wirtschaft und Gesellschaft,* I (Tübingen, 1947), Pt. 1, Chap. 2, 12. These strictures were directed at Otto Neurath, who believed he had worked out a system of keeping accounts without reference to money.

As previously noted, after seizing power in Petrograd, Lenin had no intention of expropriating Russia's industrial wealth. Although he tended greatly to oversimplify the complexities of managing an industrial economy, he was realist enough to understand that a party of professional revolutionaries could not possibly run it by itself. While political pressures had compelled him to give up his pet idea of "state capitalism," he continued to believe that the national economy required the discipline of a central plan. In March 1918 he spoke of the government facing the following tasks:

> the organization of accounting, control of large enterprises, the transformation of the whole of the state economic mechanism into a single huge machine, into an economic organism that will work in such a way as to enable hundreds of millions of people to be guided by a single plan.[61]

Trotsky agreed:

> The socialist organization of the economy begins with the liquidation of the market, and that means the liquidation of its regulator—namely, the "free" play of the laws of supply and demand. The inevitable result—namely, the subordination of production to the needs of society—must be achieved by *the unity of the economic plan,* which, in principle, covers all the branches of productivity.[62]

At Lenin's request, Larin drafted a project for a central administrative and planning agency to direct the economy of Russia. After some revisions, it was issued as a decree on December 2, 1917, which established a Supreme Council of the National Economy (Vysshyi Sovet Narodnogo Khoziaistva, or VSNKh).[63] This institution, which in 1921 would be renamed the State Planning Commission (Gosplan), was to enjoy the same monopoly in regard to the country's economy (at least in theory) that the Communist Party enjoyed in the realm of politics. We say "in theory" because in view of the existence of the private agricultural sector and the large and expanding black market in goods, the VSNKh never came even close to controlling Soviet Russia's economy. Operating directly under the Sovnarkom, its formal task was to "organize the national economy and state finances." It was to prepare and implement a master plan, to which end it was authorized to nationalize and syndicate all the branches of production, distribution, and finance. According to Trotsky, it had originally been intended to make the commissariats of Supply, Agriculture, Transport, Finance, and Foreign Trade into branches of the Supreme Economic Council.[64] The council was further to take charge of the economic sections of provincial soviets, and where these were lacking, to install its own branches. In conception, the Supreme Economic Council sought to adapt to the conditions of a socialist economy Hilferding's notion of a "General Cartel."[65] In actuality, it turned into something much more modest.

Lenin entrusted the direction of the council to Aleksei Rykov, whom one acquaintance described as a "warm-hearted Russian intellectual," rather like the "kindly doctors from the old-time provinces." Others he reminded of a "provincial *zemstvo* agronomist or statistician."[66] Certainly, he had neither the personality nor the expertise of a man to reorganize the Russian economy from top to bottom.[67] Born into a peasant family, he had received a sketchy education and then dedicated himself to full-time revolutionary work for Lenin, to whom he was fanatically devoted. Shabbily dressed and usually unkempt, he spoke little and slowly, a habit which earned him a reputation for forcefulness: but, as it turned out, when required to make decisions, he was quite helpless. His lack of administrative talents rendered his task, difficult to begin with, quite impossible.

The true driving force behind the Supreme Economic Council—the "Saint-Just of Russian economics"—was Iurii Larin. Although little known even to specialists, this half-paralyzed invalid, always in pain, could take credit for a unique historic accomplishment: certainly no one has a better claim to having wrecked a great power's national economy in the incredibly short span of thirty months. He exerted a powerful influence on Lenin, who in the first two and a half years of his dictatorship listened to Larin more attentively than to any other economic adviser. Larin was always ready with quick and radical solutions to difficult problems, which earned him the reputation of an economic "magician." His office, in a suite at the Metropole Hotel, was the place of pilgrimage for Russians with the most fantastic economic schemes: none of them was rejected out of hand, many were seriously considered, some were adopted. It was only in early 1920 that Lenin grew disenchanted with his advice and had him expelled from the Presidium of the Supreme Economic Council, which until then he had dominated by the force of his ideas and personality.*

Born in 1882 in the Crimea as Michael Aleksandrovich Lure into a Jewish intelligentsia family, Larin spent his childhood in what he himself described as an "oppositional atmosphere."[68] He joined a radical organization at the age of eighteen, and from then on led the life of a typical Russian revolutionary, alternating between underground work, organizing illegal workers' unions, and serving stretches in prison and exile. Politically, he sided with the Mensheviks. He had no higher education: such knowledge of economics as he acquired came mostly from the reading of newspapers, fat journals, and radical pamphlets. During the war he turned to journalism and filed from Stockholm reports on internal developments in Germany for the liberal newspaper *Russkie vedomosti.* His widely read articles, brought out after the Revolution in book form, displayed fascination with German "War Socialism."[69] In the spring of 1917 he worked in the Petrograd Soviet and in September went over

---

*Lenin, *Khronika,* VIII, 243, 267. While most of the economic planners of this period fell afoul of Stalin and were shot, Larin, a victim of childhood polio, had the good fortune in 1932 to die a natural death.

92. Iurii Larin.

to the Bolsheviks.[70] In the first months of the Bolshevik dictatorship he drafted and on occasion issued a number of important decrees. It was largely owing to him that Soviet Russia established the Supreme Economic Council, initiated economic planning, defaulted on its foreign debts, nationalized its industries, and, for all practical purposes, abolished money.

The Supreme Economic Council attracted non-Bolshevik intellectuals, mainly Mensheviks and independent experts, because it offered work that required no political commitment and allowed opponents of the regime to feel they were serving the people. In no time at all it expanded into a bloated bureaucratic hydra centered in Moscow in a sprawling building on Miasnit-skaia Street that had once housed a second-class hotel, its many heads spread across the country. Ten months after its creation (September 1918) it employed 6,000 functionaries, whom it paid 200,000 rubles a day in salary.[71] This staff and this payroll would not have been excessive if the Supreme Economic Council did what it was designed to do—namely, direct the country's econ-omy. But in reality it occupied itself mainly with issuing orders to which no one paid attention and forming bureaucratic organs that no one needed.

The Supreme Economic Council never even partially realized its mandate of "organizing the national economy and state finances" if only because of the vast private sector that remained outside its control. It did not even manage the task of distributing food and other consumer goods because it had to concede this responsibility to the Commissariat of Supply. In effect, the Su-preme Economic Council became the principal agency that administered—or, more accurately, attempted to administer—Soviet Russia's nationalized indus-tries: in other words, a Commissariat of Industry under a different name.

The Bolsheviks began to nationalize industrial enterprises soon after

October. In most cases, they took over plants on the grounds that the owners and managers engaged in "sabotage"; these they turned over to Factory Committees. On occasion—this happened to the textile mills of the former Provisional Government minister A. I. Konovalov—the expropriation was motivated by political vendetta. The owners of the nationalized enterprises received no compensation. This spontaneous, unplanned phase of nationalization culminated in the expropriation in December 1917 of the Putilov Works. Most expropriations were ordered by the local authorities on their own initiative rather than on government instructions—at first by the soviets and then by the regional branches of the Supreme Economic Council. A survey conducted in August 1918 showed that of the 567 enterprises that had been nationalized and the 214 that had been requisitioned, only one in five had been taken over on direct orders of Moscow.[72]

The systematic nationalization of Russian industry got underway with the decree of June 28, 1918.[73] The impetus came from Larin. Having attended the commercial negotiations in Berlin, Larin concluded that German businessmen intended to seize control of Russia's major industries. In the Brest-Litovsk Treaty, the Bolsheviks had agreed to exempt citizens and business firms of the Central Powers from Soviet economic laws, allowing them to hold properties and to pursue business activities on Russian territory. Owners of the nationalized properties were to be adequately compensated: a provision that made it possible for Russians to sell their enterprises to Germans, who could either take control or claim compensation. Larin convinced Lenin that only a sweeping nationalization measure could prevent the Germans from becoming masters of Russia's industry.[74] If Lenin hesitated to act it was out of concern over the German reaction: we know from Larin that many Bolsheviks feared the measure could provoke the Germans to break diplomatic relations and launch an anti-Bolshevik "crusade." The fears proved groundless: while complaining that it was "disloyal," "[the Germans] nevertheless acquiesced to the nationalization of all [Soviet] industry and did not declare war over it."[75] The reason was that German interests were guaranteed full compensation for their nationalized assets, whereas Allied interests received none.

The decree of June 28 ordered the nationalization, without recompense, of all industrial enterprises and railroads with capital of one million rubles or more owned by corporations or partnerships. Cooperatives were exempt. The equipment and other assets of the nationalized businesses were taken over by the state. Managers were ordered to remain at their posts under the threat of severe penalties.

From then on the process of nationalization proceeded apace. By the fall of 1920, the Supreme Economic Council was nominally in charge of 37,226 enterprises with a total work force of 2 million; 13.9 percent of the nationalized enterprises had one employee and almost half lacked any mechanical equipment. In fact, however, the council managed but a small portion of these establishments (4,547, according to one authority), the remainder being state-owned in name only.[76] In November 1920, the government issued a supplementary decree nationalizing most small-scale industries.[77] On paper, at the beginning of 1921, the government owned and managed nearly all of Russia's manufacturing facilities, from one-man workshops to giant factories. In reality, it controlled only a fraction and managed even fewer.*

The Supreme Economic Council—that "trust of trusts," as it has been called[78]—developed a massive bureaucratic machinery, headed by a Presidium. It was subdivided into agencies organized vertically (functionally) and horizontally (territorially). The vertical organizations were "trusts" called either *glavki* or *tsentry.* These numbered forty-two in late 1920, each responsible for one branch of industrial production and directed by a board. They bore melodious acronyms, such as Glavlak, Glavsol, and Glavbum, for the paint, salt, and paper industries, respectively.[79] Larin, who played a major role in designing the council's structure and operations, admitted later that he had borrowed his ideas from abroad: "I took the German *Kriegsgesellschaften,* translated them into Russian, infused them with worker spirit, and gave them currency under the name *glavki.*"[80] In addition to *glavki,* the Supreme Economic Council had a network of provincial branches, of which there were nearly 1,400 in 1920.[81] The organizational chart of the council resembled a celestial map on which the Presidium represented the sun and the *glavki, tsentry,* and regional agencies the planets and their moons.[82]

Abroad, this gigantic enterprise of "socialist construction" made a great impression. Soviet propaganda in the West spoke glowingly of the "rationalization" of Russian industry under the benevolent eye of an all-seeing government, but it stressed intent rather than performance. The graphs and charts depicting how Russian industry was regulated aroused the admiration of many Westerners trying to cope with the chaos of the postwar world. But inside Russia, from the pages of newspapers and journals, as well as reports of Party Congresses, a very different picture emerged. The claims of economic planning proved to be a travesty: as late as 1921 Trotsky confirmed that no central economic plan existed and that, at best, "centralization" was carried out 5–10 percent.[83] An article in *Pravda* in late 1920 bluntly admitted: *"khoziastvennogo plana net"* ("there is no economic plan").[84] The council's *glavki* had but the vaguest notion of the condition of industries for which they were responsible:

Not a single *glavka* or *tsentr* disposes of adequate and exhaustive data which would enable it to proceed to a genuine regulation of the country's industry and production. Dozens of organizations conduct parallel and identical work of collecting similar information, as a result of which they gather totally dissimilar data. . . . The accounting is conducted inaccurately, and sometimes up to 80 and 90 percent of the inventoried items escape the control of the relevant organization. The items which are unaccounted for become the object of wild

---

*The organization of defense industries is not clear. In August 1918, the Supreme Economic Council set up a Commission for the Production of Articles of Military Ordnance under the direction of Krasin. This commission received and passed on to industrial enterprises orders from the military which were mandatory. In time, responsibility for supplying the armed forces came under the Council of Defense (Sovet Oborony).

and unrestrained speculation, passing from hand to hand dozens of times until finally reaching the consumer.[85]

As for the regional branches of the council, these were said to be in a state of constant friction with their Moscow headquarters.[86]

In sum, contemporary accounts depict the council as a monstrous bureaucratic jumble which meddled instead of administering and whose main function was to provide a living for thousands of intellectuals. At the beginning of 1920, the council's regional branches and the economic departments of provincial soviets gave employment to nearly 25,000 people,[87] overwhelmingly members of the intelligentsia. A crass example of bureaucratic bloating was the Benzene Trust (Glavanil), which had on its payroll 50 officials to supervise a single plant employing 150 workers.* One of the Supreme Economic Council's officials has left a colorful description of the types who attached themselves to it. It deserves citation since it depicts a situation not unknown to other agencies of the Communist Government:

> The lower posts were occupied mainly by hordes of young ladies and gents, previously bookkeepers, shop assistants, clerks, or university, gymnasium, or "external" students. This whole army of youths was attracted to the service by the relatively high salary and the low amount of work required. They spent entire days loitering in the many corridors of the vast structure; they flirted, ran out to buy halvah and nuts for the office pool, distributed among themselves the theater tickets or meat conserves which one of their number had managed to get hold of, and, as a sort of accompaniment to these business dealings, cursed the Bolsheviks. . . .
>
> The next, most numerous category [of employees] consisted of onetime officials of the tsarist ministries. In joining the Soviet service they were motivated either by material need or, no less often, by longing for the accustomed work, to which each had devoted more than a decade of his life. One had to see with what passion they threw themselves on the "outgoing" and "incoming" materials, on "memoranda," "reports," and the rest of secretarial archwisdom, to understand that they found it more difficult to live without this atmosphere of paperwork than to make do without bread and shoes. These people tried to serve conscientiously; they were the first to come and the last to leave, they stuck to their chairs as if chained. But perhaps precisely because of this conscientiousness nothing ever came of their work except unbelievable nonsense, because the disorder and impulsiveness of the higher authorities confounded all the "incoming" materials and "memoranda" that they spun out with such loving care. . . .
>
> Finally, the non-Communist majority of middle-level officials and a segment of higher ones consisted of *intelligenty* of various types. There were here, so to say, romantic natures for whom service in one of the enemy's citadels smacked of high adventure. There were people of no principle, entirely indifferent to everything in the world except their own well-being. There were ordinary shady characters who sought to attach themselves to the Bolshevik chaos so as to be able, under the cover of its darkness and confusion, to loot for all it was worth. There were people of another type as well: specialists who

*Litvinov in *Pravda,* No. 262 (November 21, 1920), 1. Professor Scheibert (*Lenin,* 210) mistakenly deciphers the acronym Glavanil to mean "Vanilla Trust."

hoped to salvage the work that they held dear, and those, like myself, who joined in order to "soften the regime."[88]

So much for Lenin's pet idea, "the transformation of the whole of the state economic mechanism into a single huge machine" operating on a "single plan."

The Bolsheviks had somewhat better success in overcoming the managerial anarchy that followed the spread of workers' control. The syndicalist policies of the regime just before and just after October 1917 were a device to lure workers away from the Mensheviks: it helped the Bolsheviks gain majorities in the Factory Committees. After the signing of Brest, it was decided to revert to traditional methods of individual industrial management with the employment of "bourgeois specialists." Trotsky spoke about this in March and Lenin in May 1918.[89] In fact, many of the previous owners and managers had never left their jobs, and by terms of the June 28, 1918, nationalization decree were forbidden to do so. The Supreme Economic Council was full of these people as well. In the fall of 1919, a visitor from Siberia noted that at the head of many of Moscow's *tsentry* and *glavki*

> sit former employers and responsible officials and managers of business, and the unprepared visitor . . . who is personally acquainted with the former commercial and industrial world would be surprised to see previous owners of big leather factories sitting in Glavkozh [the leather syndicate], big manufacturers in the central textile organization, etc.[90]

But Lenin's and Trotsky's insistence on the need to utilize the skills of "bourgeois specialists" in the service of the "socialist" cause ran into resistance from Left Communists, trade union officials, and Factory Committees. Resenting the power and privilege which the members of the old "capitalist" elite enjoyed in Soviet industries by virtue of their expertise, they harassed and intimidated them.[91]

Until the end of the Civil War, the government had great difficulty enforcing the principle of personal management. In 1919, only 10.8 percent of industrial establishments had individual managers. But in 1920–21, Moscow vigorously resumed the campaign, and at the close of 1921, 90.7 percent of Russian factories were run in this manner.[92] The argument in favor of "collegiate" management, however, did not die down, its proponents arguing that individual management alienated workers from the regime and allowed "capitalists" to retain control of expropriated plants in the guise of serving the state.[93] Before long, this argument would be raised at the national level by the so-called Workers' Opposition.

The narrowly economic objective of Soviet industrial policies under War Communism was, of course, to raise productivity. Statistical evidence, however, demonstrates that the effect of these policies was precisely the contrary. Under Communist management, industrial productivity did not merely decline: it plunged at a rate which suggested that, if the process continued, by the mid-1920s Soviet Russia would be left without any industry. There exist various indices of this phenomenon.

I. OVERALL LARGE-SCALE INDUSTRIAL PRODUCTION*

1913	100
1917	77
1919	26
1920	18

II. OUTPUT OF SELECTED INDUSTRIAL GOODS IN 1920[94] (1913 = 100)

Coal	27.0
Iron	2.4
Cotton yarn	5.1
Petroleum	42.7

III. PRODUCTIVITY (in constant rubles) OF THE RUSSIAN WORKER[95]

1913	100
1917	85
1918	44
1919	22
1920	26

IV. NUMBER OF EMPLOYED INDUSTRIAL WORKERS†

1918	100
1919	82
1920	77
1921	49

*Kritsman, *Geroicheskii period*, p. 162. Figures in *Narodnoe Khoziaistvo SSSR v 1958 godu* (Moscow, 1959), 52–53, show a 69 percent decline in overall industrial production in 1921 compared with 1913, and a 79 percent decline in heavy industrial production.
†A. Aluf, cited in S. Volin, *Deiatel'nost' menshevikov v profsoiuzakh pri sovetskoi vlasti,* Inter-University Project on the History of the Menshevik Movement, Paper No. 13 (New York, 1962), 87. By 1918, of course, which is here taken as the base year, the number of employed workers had declined considerably compared with 1913–14.

In sum, under War Communism, the Russian "proletariat" fell by one-half, industrial output by three-quarters, and industrial productivity by 70 percent. Surveying the wreckage, Lenin in 1921 exclaimed: "What is the proletariat? It is the class engaged in large-scale industry. And where is large-scale industry? What kind of a proletariat is it? Where is your [sic!] industry? Why is it idle?"[96] The answer to these rhetorical questions was that utopian programs, which Lenin had approved, had all but destroyed Russian industry and decimated Russia's working class. But during this time of deindustrialization, the expenses of maintaining the bureaucracy in charge of the economy grew by leaps and bounds: by 1921 they absorbed 75.1 percent of the budget. As for the personnel of the Supreme Economic Council, which managed Russia's industry, it grew during this period a hundredfold.*

The decline in agricultural production was less drastic, but because of the small margin of food surplus, its effect on the population was even more devastating.

The Bolshevik Government treated the peasant population as a class enemy and waged on it a regular war by means of Red Army units and detachments of armed thugs. The program of 1918—to choke off all private trade in agricultural produce—had to be modified in view of fierce peasant resistance. In 1919 and 1920, the government extracted food from the peasantry by a variety of means: forced deliveries, barter of food for manufactured goods, and purchases at somewhat more realistic prices. In 1919, it allowed limited quantities of food to be sold on the open market. Dairy products, meats, fruits, most vegetables, and all foodstuffs growing wild were initially exempt from state control but later regulated as well.

Through a combination of coercion and inducement, the government managed somehow to feed the cities and industrial centers, not to speak of the Red Army. But the prospects for the future looked bleak because the peasant, having no incentives to grow more than he needed for himself, kept on reducing the cultivated acreage. In the grain-growing provinces, between 1913 and 1920, the area under cultivation diminished by 12.5 percent.[97] The decline in sown acreage, however, does not fully reveal the fall in cereal production. First of all, since the peasants either consumed or set aside for seed three-quarters of the harvest, a decline of 12.5 percent in sown acreage meant that the arable land available to produce a grain surplus for the non-agrarian population dropped by one-half. Second, yields kept on declining at the same time that the sown area shrank, due largely to the shortage of draft horses, one-quarter of which had been requisitioned by the armed forces. The yields per acre in 1920 were only 70 percent what they had been before the war.[98] A 12.5 decline in acreage accompanied by a 30 percent decline in yields meant that the grain output was only 60 percent of the prewar figure.

*Buryshkin in *EV,* No. 2 (1923), 141. The figures for the Supreme Economic Council are 318 employees in March 1918 and 30,000 in 1921.

A Communist economist provides statistics which show that this, indeed, is what happened:

PRODUCTION OF CEREAL GRAINS IN CENTRAL RUSSIA[99] (in millions of tons)

1913	78.2
1917	69.1
1920	48.2

It required only a spell of bad weather for the harvest to fall to the level of starvation. Under Communist management, there was no surplus and hence no capacity to absorb the consequences of a poor harvest. That such a calamity was in the offing became a near-certainty in the fall of 1920, when Communist papers began to carry warnings of a new "enemy"—*zasukha,* or drought.[100]

True famine, Asiatic famine such as neither Russia nor the rest of Europe had ever experienced and in which millions were to perish, still lay in the future. For the time being, there was hunger, a permanent state of undernourishment that drained energy, the ability to work, the very will to live. A leading Bolshevik economist, analyzing in 1920 the decline in industrial productivity, ascribed it principally to food shortages. According to his calculations, between 1908 and 1916 the average Russian worker had consumed 3,820 calories a day, whereas by 1919 his intake was reduced to 2,680 calories, not enough for heavy manual labor.[101] This 30 percent drop in caloric intake, in his opinion, was the main cause of the 40 percent decline in worker productivity in the large cities. This, of course, was a great oversimplification, but it pointed to a very real problem. Another Communist expert estimated that using pre-revolutionary criteria, according to which an annual bread consumption of 180–200 kilograms meant hunger, the Soviet worker in the northern regions in 1919–20, with a consumption of 134 kilograms, was starving.[102] If Russian cities at this point did not collapse from hunger, it was due to the fortuitous coincidence that just as this was about to happen, the Bolsheviks won the Civil War and reconquered Siberia as well as the North Caucasus and the Ukraine, which under non-Communist rule had managed to accumulate rich stores of grain.

In the words of Trotsky, "the socialist organization of the economy begins with the liquidation of the market." Indeed, to the Marxist, the market, the arena for the exchange of commodities, is the heart of the capitalist economy, just as money is its lifeblood. Without it, capitalism cannot function. The choking off of the free exchange of products and services, therefore, constituted a central objective of Bolshevik economic policy. Nationalization of the market and centralization of distribution were not, as is often erroneously argued, responses to shortages caused by the Revolution and the Civil War, but positive initiatives directed against the capitalist enemy, which caused shortages.

The Bolsheviks went to extreme lengths to eliminate the free exchange of commodities. They spelled out their intention in the 1919 party program:

> In the realm of distribution, the task of Soviet authority at present consists in steadfastly pursuing the replacement of trade by a planned and nationally organized distribution of products. The objective is the organization of the entire population in a single network of consumer communes which will be capable, most speedily, in a planned manner, economically and with the least expenditure of labor, of distributing all the necessary products, strictly centralizing the entire mechanism of distribution.[103]

The Bolsheviks pursued this goal by a variety of means, including the confiscation of the means of production of goods other than food, forceful requisitions of foodstuffs and other commodities, a state monopoly on trade, and destruction of money as a medium of exchange. Goods were distributed to the population by means of ration cards, initially (1918–19) at nominal prices, later (1920) free of charge. Housing, utilities, transport, education, and entertainment were also withdrawn from the market and eventually made available at no cost.

While the production of industrial goods was turned over to the Supreme Economic Council, responsibility for the distribution of commodities was assigned to the Commissariat of Supply (Kommissariat po Prodovolstviiu), another bureaucratic empire with an array of its own *glavki* and a network of distribution agencies. Its head, Alexander Tsiurupa, had only limited business experience, having been employed before 1917 as manager of a landed estate. His commissariat was a very costly operation. Komprod, as it was popularly known, first and foremost received and distributed the foodstuffs which the government managed to collect through purchase, barter, or forceful requisitions. It was also supposed to receive for purposes of barter consumer goods from the nationalized industrial establishments and household industries. For distribution, it relied to some extent on its own network of state-run stores, but mainly on the consumer cooperatives which had developed before the Revolution and which the Bolsheviks, with some reluctance, retained after removing the SRs and Mensheviks from their directing staffs.[104] In the spring of 1919 these cooperatives were nationalized. A decree of March 16, 1919,[105] ordered the creation in all cities and rural centers of "consumer communes" *(potrebitel'skie kommuny),* which all the inhabitants of a given area, without exception, had to join. The communes were supposed to provide food and other basic necessities upon presentation of ration cards. Such cards came in several categories, the most generous ones being issued to workers in heavy industry: the "bourgeoisie" received at best one-quarter of a worker's ration, and often nothing.[106]* The system lent itself to terrible abuses: in Petrograd in 1918, for instance, one-third more ration cards were issued than there were inhabitants, and in 1920, the Commissariat of Supply distributed ration cards for 21.9 million urban residents whereas their actual count was only 12.3 million.[107]

In the words of Milton Friedman, the more significant an economic theory, "the more unrealistic the assumptions." The Soviet experiment in the nationalization of trade amply corroborated this statement. The measures enacted under War Communism, instead of eliminating the market, split it in two: in 1918–20 Russia had a state sector, which distributed goods by ration cards at fixed prices or free of charge, and, alongside it, an illicit private sector, which followed the laws of supply and demand. To the surprise of Bolshevik theoreticians, the more the nationalized sector expanded, the larger loomed what one Bolshevik economist called its "irremovable shadow," the free sector. Indeed, the private sector battened on the state sector, for the simple reason that a large part of the consumer goods which the workers bought at token prices or received gratis from state stores or "consumer communes" found their way to the black market.[108]

The government inaugurated free public services in October 1920 with a law exempting Soviet institutions from paying for telegraph, telephone, and postal services; the following year, these were offered free to all citizens. During this time government employees received all utilities gratis. In January 1921, residents of nationalized and municipalized houses were freed from the payment of rents.[109] In the winter of 1920–21, Komprod is estimated to have assumed responsibility for supplying, at virtually no cost, the basic needs of 38 million people.[110]

Obviously, such largesse was possible only temporarily, as long as the Bolshevik regime could spend capital inherited from tsarism. It was able to dispense with the collection of rents because it neither built housing nor paid for its maintenance: nearly the entire residential housing of urban Russia, consisting of about half a million structures, had been built before 1917. When War Communism was at its height, the government constructed and repaired only 2,601 buildings in the country.[111] The other factor which made the policy of free distribution possible was the food that was extracted from the peasants without compensation or with make-believe compensation in the form of worthless money. Clearly, neither situation could continue forever, as buildings decayed and the peasant refused to grow surplus food.

In the meantime, the private sector burgeoned. It traded every conceivable commodity, and above all, foodstuffs. The bulk of the food consumed by the non-agrarian population of Soviet Russia under War Communism came not from state outlets but from the free market. In September 1918 the regime was forced to permit peasants to bring into the cities and sell at market prices

*Possession of a card entitling one to the lowest ration (*paëk*) served the Cheka as a means of identifying members of the "bourgeoisie." The holders of such cards were natural victims of terror and extortion.

up to one and a half puds (25 kilograms) of cereals.[112] These *polutorapudniki,* or "one-and-a-half-puders," accounted for the lion's share of the bread and produce consumed by the cities. A Soviet statistical survey conducted in the winter of 1919–20 indicated that urban inhabitants obtained only 36 percent of their bread from state stores; the remainder came, as the survey evasively put it, "from other sources."[113] It has been established that of all the foodstuffs consumed in Russian cities in the winter of 1919–20 (cereals, vegetables, and fruits), as measured by their caloric value, the free market furnished from 66 to 80 percent. In the rural districts, the proportion of victuals supplied by the "consumer communes" amounted to a mere 11 percent.[114]

A foreign visitor to Russia in the spring of 1920 found nearly all the stores closed or boarded up. Here and there small shops stayed open to dispense clothing, soap, and other consumer goods. Outlets of Narkomprod (Commissariat of Supply) were also few and far between. But the illicit street trade was booming:

> Moscow lives. But it lives only in part from rationed goods and from earned money. In large measure, Moscow lives off the black market: actively and passively. It sells on the black market, it buys on the black market, it profiteers, profiteers, profiteers . . .
>
> In Moscow money is made on everything. Everything is traded on the black market: from a pin to a cow. Furniture, diamonds, white cake, bread, meat, everything is sold on the black market. The Sukharevka in Moscow is a black-market bazaar, a black-market warehouse. From time to time, the police carry out raids, but these do not suppress the black market. It is a proliferating hydra, it reappears with a thousand heads.
>
> Moscow has free markets, a number of them, officially tolerated markets, supplementary ones, delicatessen markets. For example, there is a supplementary market near Theater Square, dealing in cucumbers, fish, biscuits, eggs, vegetables of all sorts. It is a tumult on a long sidewalk. There are booths on the curbs, traders squat, traders whisper offers into the ears of buyers.
>
> A cucumber costs 200–250 rubles, an egg 125–150 rubles: other items fetch corresponding prices. This is not much when converted into Western European currency, especially dollars. During my stay in Moscow, currency speculators paid 1,000 Bolshevik rubles for one dollar. I was told that one American exchanged $3,000 for 9 million Bolshevik rubles. It is forbidden to speculate . . . But there is speculation in currency. Profits are made on everything, naturally also on money . . .
>
> This profiteering, this black marketeering, this hoarding hinders work. Profiteering sits in the soul of workers. They profiteer while they work, they profiteer while they should be working.[115]

Many of the peddlers were soldiers who were disposing of their uniforms, which explains why at this time so many Muscovites appeared on the streets in military garb.[116] Dignified ladies could be seen standing self-consciously on the sidewalks offering for sale personal belongings from happier days.

The "unconquerable stubbornness of small production in its insistence on

93. A common sight on the streets of Moscow and
Petrograd in 1918–21.

the methods of commodity economy," as one Soviet economist described the
vitality of the free market,[117] defeated all government efforts to monopolize
distribution. The government found itself in the absurd situation in which the
strict enforcement of its prohibitions on private trade would have caused the
entire urban population to starve to death. A Soviet economic publication in
early 1920 ruefully conceded that the private ("speculative") market was
flourishing at the expense and with the help of the state supply system. "One
of the most striking contradictions of our current economic reality," it wrote,

> is the contrast between the gaping emptiness of Soviet stores with their signs
> "Haberdashery Store of the Moscow Soviet," "Bookstore," . . . and so on, and
> the teeming activity of the market trade on Sukharevka, the Smolensk market,
> Okhotnyi Riad, and other centers of the speculative market. . . . [The merchan-
> dise for the latter] has its exclusive source in the warehouses of the Soviet
> Republic and reaches Sukharevka by criminal routes.[118]

So powerful did the private sector become that when in early 1921 the government finally faced reality and (temporarily) gave up the monopoly on trade
under the New Economic Policy (NEP), it was only acknowledging the status
quo. "In certain respects," writes E. H. Carr, "NEP did little more than
sanction methods of trade which had grown up spontaneously, in defiance of
Government decrees and in face of Government repressions, under War Communism."[119]

In October 1917, the Bolsheviks seized power in Petrograd in the name
of the "proletariat." The Soviet state was declared the embodiment of the will

of the working class and the "vanguard" of the socialist order. This being the case, one might have expected Bolshevik labor policies greatly to improve, if not necessarily the economic, then certainly the social and political status of industrial labor compared with what it had been under the "bourgeois" Imperial and Provisional governments. But in this respect, too, the effects were the very opposite of proclaimed intentions: the status of Russia's working class deteriorated significantly in every respect but the symbolic. In particular, it now lost its hard-won right to organize and to strike, the two indispensable weapons in labor's self-defense.

It can be argued, of course, and the argument has been made, that under conditions of revolution and civil war the Bolsheviks had no choice but to curb the rights of labor in order to keep the economy going: to save the "proletarian revolution" they had to suspend the rights of the "proletariat." In this interpretation, Bolshevik labor policies, like the rest of War Communism, were regrettable but unavoidable expedients.

The trouble with this interpretation is that the anti-labor measures introduced when the Bolshevik regime was indeed struggling to survive turned out to be not just temporary devices but expressions of a whole social philosophy which the situation made it possible to justify as emergency measures but which outlasted the emergency. The Bolsheviks regarded compulsory labor, the abolition of the right to strike, and the transformation of trade unions into agencies of the state as essential not only for victory in the Civil War but for the "construction of communism": which is why they retained their anti-labor policies after the Civil War had been won and their regime was no longer in danger.

The concept of compulsory labor was embedded in Marxism. Article 8 of the *Communist Manifesto* of 1848 called for the "equal liability of all to labor. Establishment of industrial armies, especially for agriculture." Obviously, in a regimented economy, without a free commodity market, it made no sense to maintain a free market in labor services. Trotsky, who often spoke on the subject, reinforced the economic argument with a psychological one— namely, that man is basically indolent and driven to work only by the fear of starvation: once the state assumed responsibility for feeding its citizens, this motive disappeared and it became necessary to resort to compulsion.* In effect, Trotsky presented forced labor as an inseparable feature of socialism. "One may say that man is rather a lazy creature," he said. "As a general rule, man strives to avoid work. . . . The only way to attract the labor power necessary for economic tasks is to introduce *compulsory labor service.*"[120] Lest some Soviet citizens delude themselves that compulsory labor was only a transitional measure, meant for the "duration" of the crisis, Trotsky put them on notice this was not so. In March 1920, at the Ninth Party Congress, convened after the Whites had been for all practical purposes defeated and the Civil War was virtually over, Trotsky minced no words:

*The notion that man works only to avoid starvation Trotsky took from Marx, who had found it in the writings of the Reverend J. Townsend on the Poor Laws: *Das Kapital,* I, Chap. 25, Sect. 4.

We are making the first attempt in world history to organize labor in the interests of that laboring majority. But this, of course, does not mean liquidating the element of compulsion. The element of compulsion does not disappear from historic accounts. No, compulsion plays and will play an important role for a significant period of history.[121]

Trotsky spoke especially bluntly on this subject at the Third Congress of Trade Unions in April 1920. Responding to a Menshevik motion calling for the abolition of compulsory labor on the grounds that it was less productive than free labor, Trotsky defended serfdom:

When the Mensheviks in their resolution say that compulsory labor always results in low productivity, then they are captives of bourgeois ideology and reject the very foundations of the socialist economy. . . . In the era of serfdom it was not so that gendarmes stood over every serf. There were certain economic forms to which the peasant had grown accustomed, which, at the time, he regarded as just, and he only rebelled from time to time. . . . It is said that compulsory labor is unproductive. This means that the whole socialist economy is doomed to be scrapped, because there is no other way of attaining socialism except through the command allocation of the entire labor force by the economic center, the allocation of that force in accord with the needs of a nationwide economic plan.[122]

In sum, forced labor was not only indispensable to socialism but actually beneficial: "Forced serf labor did not emerge because of the ill will of the feudal class: it was a progressive phenomenon."[123]

The notion that the worker must become a peon of the "socialist" state— that is, on the face of it, a slave of himself, since he was said to be "master" of that state—embedded in the Marxist theory of a centralized, organized economy and its misanthropic view of human nature, was further strengthened by the extremely low opinion which the Bolshevik leaders had of Russia's workers. Before the Revolution, they had idealized them, but contact with the worker in the flesh quickly put an end to illusions. While Trotsky extolled the virtues of serfdom, Lenin dismissed the Russian "proletariat." At the Eleventh Party Congress, in March 1922, he said:

Very often, when they say "workers" it is thought that this means the factory proletariat. But it means nothing of the kind. In our country, since the war, the people who went to work in factories and plants were not proletarian at all, but those who did so to hide from the war. And do we now have social and economic conditions which induce true proletarians to go to work in factories and plants? This is not the case. It is correct according to Marx, but Marx wrote not about Russia but about capitalism as a whole, beginning with the fifteenth century. For six hundred years this was correct, and for today's Russia it is not correct. Those who go into the factories are through and through not proletarians but all kinds of casual elements.[124]

The implications of this astonishing admission were not lost on some Bolsheviks: for Lenin was saying nothing less than that the October Revolution had not been made by or even for the "proletarians." Shliapnikov alone had the courage to point this out: "Vladimir Ilich said yesterday that the proletariat in the sense in which Marx perceived it does not exist. . . . Allow me to congratulate you on being the vanguard of a nonexistent class."[125]

With such a view of human nature in general and Russian labor in particular as Lenin and Trotsky entertained, they could hardly have tolerated free labor and independent trade unions even if other considerations had not spoken against them.

The official reasons for the introduction of compulsory labor were the requirements of economic planning: economic planning, it was argued, not inconsistently, could not be realized unless labor were subject to the same controls as all the other economic resources. The Bolsheviks spoke of the need for compulsory labor obligation as early as April 1917, before coming to power.[126] Lenin apparently saw no contradiction in saying that whereas the introduction of compulsory labor in capitalist Germany in wartime "inevitably meant military penal servitude [*katorga*] for the workers," under Soviet rule the same phenomenon represented "a giant *step toward* socialism."[127]

True to their word, the Bolsheviks declared the intention of introducing labor conscription on their first day in office. On October 25, 1917, almost in the same breath in which he announced the deposition of the Provisional Government, Trotsky told the Second Congress of Soviets: "The introduction of the universal labor obligation is one of the most immediate objectives of a genuine revolutionary government."[128] Probably most of the delegates thought this statement applied only to the "bourgeoisie." And, indeed, in the first months of his dictatorship, Lenin, driven by personal animosity, went out of his way to humiliate the "bourgeoisie," compelling people unaccustomed to manual labor to perform menial chores. In the draft of the decree nationalizing banks (December 1917), he wrote:

> Article 6: universal labor obligation. The first step—consumer-labor, budget-labor booklets for the rich, control over them. Their duty: to work as ordered, else—"enemies of the people."

And in the margin he added: "Dispatch to the front, compulsory labor, confiscation, arrests (execution by shooting)."[129] Later it was a common sight in Moscow and Petrograd to see well-dressed people performing menial duties under guard. The benefit of this forced labor was probably close to nil, but it was intended to serve "educational" purposes—namely, to incite class hatred.

As Lenin had indicated, this was only the first step. Before long, the principle of compulsory labor was extended to other social strata: it meant not only that every adult had to be productively employed but that he or she had to work where ordered. This obligation, which returned Russia to the practices of the seventeenth century, was decreed in January 1918 in the "Declaration of the Rights of the Toiling and Exploited Masses," which contained the following clause: "For the purpose of destroying the parasitic elements of the population and for the organization of the economy, there is introduced the universal labor obligation."[130] Inserted into the 1918 Constitution, this principle became the law of the land and has served ever since as the legal basis for treating anyone shirking state employment as a "parasite."

The principle of labor conscription was worked out in practical detail at the end of 1918. A decree of October 29, 1918, established a nationwide network of agencies to "distribute the labor force."[131] On December 10, 1918, Moscow issued a detailed "Labor Code" which provided for all male and female citizens between the ages of sixteen and fifty, with some exceptions, to render "labor service." Those who already held regular jobs were to stay at them. The others were to register with Departments for the Allocation of the Labor Force (Otdely Raspredeleniia Rabochei Sily, or ORRS). These organs had the authority to assign them to any work anywhere they saw fit.

Not only did the decrees on compulsory labor apply to minors (children sixteen to eighteen) but special ordinances permitted children employed in war industries or other enterprises of special importance to the state to be made to work overtime.[132]

By late 1918, it became common practice for the Bolshevik authorities to call up workers and specialists in various fields for state service exactly as they drafted recruits into the Red Army. The practice was for the government to announce that workers and technical specialists in a specified branch of the economy were "mobilized for military service" and subject to court-martial: those leaving jobs to which they had been assigned were treated as deserters. Persons with skills in critical fields, but not currently employed in jobs where they could use them, had to register and await a call-up. The first civilians to be "mobilized" were railroad workers (November 28, 1918). Other categories followed: persons with technical education and experience (December 19, 1918), medical personnel (December 20, 1918), employees of the river and ocean fleets (March 15, 1919), coal miners (April 7, 1919), postal, telephone, and telegraph employees (May 5, 1919), workers in the fuel industry (June 27, 1919, and November 8, 1919), wool industry workers (August 13, 1920), metalworkers (August 20, 1920), and electricians (October 8, 1920).[133] In this manner, industrial occupations became progressively "militarized" and the difference between soldiers and workers, military and civilian sectors, was blurred. Efforts to organize industrial labor on the military model could not have worked well in view of the plethora of decrees on this subject, setting up ever new punishments for "labor deserters," ranging from the publication of their names to confinement in concentration camps.[134]

Whatever its formal economic justification, the practice of forced labor meant a reversion to the Muscovite institution of *tiaglo,* by virtue of which all adult male and female peasants and other commoners could be called upon to perform chores on behalf of the state. Then, as now, its main forms were carting goods, cutting lumber, and construction work. The description of the duty imposed on peasants in 1920 to furnish fuel would have been quite comprehensible to Muscovite Russians:

The peasants were ordered . . . as a sort of labor service expected of them by the Government . . . to cut down so many cords of wood in designated forests. Every horse-owning peasant had to transport a certain quantity of wood. All this wood had to be delivered by the peasant to river jetties, cities, and other terminal points.[135]

The principal difference between compulsory labor, or *tiaglo,* in Muscovite Russia and that in Communist Russia was that in the Middle Ages it had been a sporadic duty, imposed to meet specific needs, whereas now it became a permanent obligation.

In the winter of 1919–20, Trotsky conceived an ambitious scheme of "militarizing labor" in which soldiers in uniform would perform productive economic work while civilian workers would be subjected to military discipline. This throwback to the infamous "military colonies" instituted a century earlier by Alexander I and Arakcheev met with skepticism and hostility. But Trotsky persisted and would not be dissuaded. Back from his triumph in the Civil War, full of his own importance and eager to gain fresh laurels, he insisted that Russia's economic problems could be resolved only by the same rough-and-ready methods which the Red Army had used to defeat the external enemy. On December 16, 1919, he drafted a set of "Theses" for the Central Committee.[136] He argued that economic problems had to be stormed with blindly disciplined armies of workers. Russia's labor force was to be regimented in military fashion: the shirking of duty (refusal to take on assigned work, absenteeism, drinking on the job, etc.) was to be treated as a crime and the culprits turned over to courts-martial. Trotsky further proposed that Red Army units no longer needed for combat duty, instead of being demobilized and sent home, be transformed into "Labor Armies" *(Trudarmii).* These "Theses" were not intended for publication, but Bukharin, the editor of *Pravda,* printed them anyway, either inadvertently (as he claimed) or to discredit Trotsky (as others believed). Published in *Pravda* on January 22, 1920, they unleashed a storm of protests, in which the epithet "Arakcheevshchina" was commonly heard.

Lenin was won over because of the desperate need to halt the further deterioration of the country's economy. On December 27, 1919, he agreed to the creation of a Commission on Labor Obligation, with Trotsky, who retained the post of Commissar of War, as president. Trotsky's program entailed two sets of measures:

1. Military units no longer required at the front would not be demobilized but would be transformed into peacetime Labor Armies and assigned to such tasks as repairing railroad beds, transporting fuel, and fixing agricultural machinery. The Third Army Corps, which had fought in the Urals, was the first to undergo this transformation. Later other units were converted. In March 1921, one-quarter of the Red Army was employed in construction and transport.

2. Concurrently, all workers and peasants were made subject to military

discipline. At the Ninth Party Congress in 1920, where this policy provoked intense controversy, Trotsky insisted that the government had to be free to use civilian labor wherever it was needed, without regard to the personal preferences of the workers, exactly as in the armed forces. "Mobilized" labor was to be assigned to enterprises requesting it through the Commissariat of Labor. In 1922, looking back at this experiment, an official of this commissariat stated: "We supplied labor according to plan and, consequently, without taking into account the individual peculiarities or wishes of the worker to engage in this or that kind of work."[137]

Neither the Labor Armies nor militarized labor fulfilled the expectations of their protagonists. Soldier workers produced only a fraction of the output of trained civilians; they also deserted in droves. The government faced insurmountable technical difficulties in attempting to administer, feed, and transport the militarized labor force. Hence, this prototype of Stalin's and Hitler's slave-labor organizations had to be abandoned: industrial mobilization was abolished on October 12, 1921, and the Labor Armies one month later.[138]

The experiment discredited Trotsky and weakened him in the struggle for the succession to Lenin not only because it had failed but because it made him vulnerable to charges of "Bonapartism." For indeed, if Russia's economy had been militarized, officers subordinate to him would have acquired a dominant role in the civilian sector. "Trotskyism" as a term of abuse gained currency in 1920 in connection with this scheme.[139]

In a regime based on compulsory labor there was, of course, no place for free trade unions. There were logical reasons why such unions could not be allowed, since in a "worker" state the workers by definition could not have interests separate from those of their employer. As Trotsky once put it, the Russian worker was "obligated to the Soviet state, under its orders in every direction, for it is *his* state"[140]—in obeying it, therefore, he was obeying himself, even if he happened to think otherwise. There were also practical reasons why independent trade unions could not be tolerated, inasmuch as they were incompatible with central planning. Hence, the Bolsheviks lost no time in depriving of independence the two main organizations of Russian labor— Factory Committees and trade unions.

It will be recalled that after the outbreak of the February Revolution, with Bolshevik encouragement, Factory Committees spread and gained influence in Russia as organs of workers' control. In conditions of spreading anarchy, they expanded at the expense of the trade unions, organized nationally by crafts, because the workers found more in common with others employed in the same plant than with fellow workers possessing the same skills but employed elsewhere. Inspired by syndicalist ideas, the Factory Committees gravitated leftward and in the fall of 1917 provided one of the main sources of Bolshevik strength.

But once in power, the Bolsheviks found little use for these committees. Pursuing their private interests and tending to treat industrial establishments as property, they interfered with production and obstructed economic planning. In the weeks that followed the October coup, while they were still insecurely in power, the Bolsheviks continued to curry favor with them. A decree of November 27, 1917, provided for the establishment of Workers' Committees in all enterprises employing five or more workers. They were to supervise production, determine the minimum output, set production costs, and enjoy access to the accounting books.[141] This was syndicalism, pure and simple. But Lenin no more intended workers to run Russia's industries than peasants to own Russia's agricultural land, soldiers to run their regiments, or national minorities to secede. All these were means to an end, the end being the conquest of power. Hence, he inserted into the decree on Factory Committees two provisions, little noted at the time, which gave the government the right to abrogate it. One stated that while the decisions of the workers or their representatives were binding on the owners of enterprises, they were subject to annulment by "trade unions and [their] congresses." Another clause stipulated that in enterprises designated as being of "state importance"—that is, either working for defense or producing articles "necessary for the existence" of the masses—the Workers' Committees were accountable to the state "for the maintenance of the strictest order and discipline." As one historian observes, these vague provisions soon rendered the decree on workers' control "not to be worth the paper it was written on."[142]

In time, the Factory Committees were emasculated by being subjected to bureaucratic oversight. The decree on workers' control required each committee to render accounts to the Regional Council of Workers' Control; these Regional Councils, in turn, were subordinated to the All-Russian Council of Workers' Control. Officials running these supervisory organs received their appointments from the Communist Party and were duty-bound to carry out its instructions.[143] These institutions prevented Factory Committees from forming their own national organization independent of the state. The decree establishing the Supreme Economic Council (December 1917) gave it authority over all existing economic bodies, including the All-Russian Council of Workers' Control.

The fate of the Russian labor movement, in its anarcho-syndicalist as well as trade union form, was largely settled at the First Congress of Trade Unions, held in Petrograd in January 1918.[144] Here, socialist intellectuals, Bolsheviks and Mensheviks alike, criticized the anarcho-syndicalist tendencies of industrial workers and rejected demands for workers' control as detrimental to productivity and inimical to socialism. Despite heated arguments in favor of workers' control, the congress, dominated by Bolsheviks, who on this issue had the backing of the Mensheviks and SRs, adopted a resolution shifting the means of exercising workers' control over production from Factory Committees to the trade unions. Factory Committees now lost many of the powers granted them in November, including that of interfering with financial matters. "Control over production," the resolution stated, "does *not* mean the transfer of the enterprise into the hands of workers."

When the congress turned its attention to trade unions, the Mensheviks parted ways with the Bolsheviks. Since they enjoyed strong support among some of the largest national unions, the Mensheviks favored independent trade unionism. The Bolsheviks maintained that trade unions should serve as instruments of the state, its agents in "organizing production" and "rehabilitating the country's shattered economic forces." Among their tasks was "enforcing the universal obligation to work." "The congress is convinced," the Bolshevik resolution read, "that trade unions will inevitably become transformed into organs of the socialist state":

> The entire process of the full fusion of the trade unions with the organs of state authority (the so-called process of *ogosudarstvlenie*) must occur as the completely inevitable result of their joint, closest, and harmonized activity and the training by trade unions of the broad worker masses for the task of administering the state apparatus and all the organs in charge of the economy.[145]

This was very much in line with a tradition of Russian history by virtue of which the state, sooner or later, coopted and subordinated to itself all institutions originally formed, sometimes on its own initiative, as independent, self-governing bodies.

Once it had been decreed that individual Factory Committees were subject to the All-Russian Council of Workers' Control, that this council, in turn, had to account to the trade unions and their congresses, and that the proper function of trade unions was to serve as "organs of the socialist state," the fate of Factory Committees was sealed. The history of workers' control institutions following the First Congress of Trade Unions is one of relentless decline: they shrank, wilted, and died, one by one. The abortive movement in the spring of 1918 to create a nationwide network of workers' plenipotentiaries was the last gasp of the movement. By 1919, they were only a memory.

As concerns trade unions, they increased their scope if not their authority as the Civil War neared its climax and the government came to rely on them to enforce labor discipline. The party increasingly assumed the right to appoint trade union officials, removing elected officials of whom it did not approve.[146] In 1919 and 1920, state and party resolutions still paid lip service to the principle that trade unions helped run the nation's economy. But in reality by then their main task was to serve as transmitters of government directives. This is how Trotsky defined the role of trade unions in April 1920:

> In the socialist state under construction, trade unions are needed not to struggle for better working conditions—this is the task of the social and political organization as a whole—but to organize the working class for the purpose of production: to educate, discipline, allocate, collect, attach individual categories and individual workers to their jobs for a set period: in a word, hand in hand with the government in an authoritative manner to bring workers into the framework of a single economic plan.[147]

The trade unions proved a harder nut to crack than the ephemeral Factory Committees: after the Civil War, in 1920–21, an explosion would occur in Bolshevik ranks over the practice of replacing elected union officials with appointed party bureaucrats. This issue would cause a great deal of internal friction and give Lenin the pretext for outlawing the formation of factions in the Communist Party.

Once it had been established that the function of trade unions was not to defend the interests of their members, but to serve the state, it was logical for membership in them to be made mandatory. Compulsory enrollment was not decreed but introduced gradually in one trade after another, until, at the end of 1918, three-quarters of the working force was subject to compulsory unionization.[148] The larger their membership, the more impotent the trade unions became.

The right to strike was considered fundamental to labor's interests and was reconfirmed as such at the trade unions' Third All-Russian Conference in June 1917.[149] The Communist Government neither then nor later issued a decree outlawing strikes: it was obvious, nevertheless, that the Bolsheviks would not tolerate work stoppages against state enterprises. They were inhibited from outlawing strikes by legislative fiat as long as the overwhelming majority of industrial enterprises were in private hands, but they were not prepared to confirm this right. At the Congress of Trade Unions in January 1918, the trade unionist G. Tsyperovich moved that the "professional worker movement continues, as before, to regard the strike as a means of defending its interests" with the understanding that under "the new conditions of workers' control of production, [strikes] can be more soundly implemented." The congress, dominated by Bolsheviks, ignored this resolution.[150] In practice, strikes were permitted against privately owned enterprises, as long as these existed, but not in state enterprises. The progressive nationalization of industry had the effect of making strikes unlawful. The implications of the de facto abolition of the right to strike in Soviet Russia are thus defined by one scholar:

> The first assumption [of the Soviet Government] was that collective bargaining and the strength of the unions did not rest on the right to call a work stoppage, but on its political relationship with the state and Party. In all cases, the burden of responsibility for avoiding and terminating strikes was now transferred to the trade unions, the very institutions for which the right to strike was vital. The trade unions were left in the impossible position of having to deny the one power that would give them strength and enable them to protect their membership.[151]

This spelled the death of trade unionism in Soviet Russia.

The policies subsequently christened War Communism were meant to raise economic performance to a peak never known: it was the most ambitious

attempt ever made until then to rationalize completely production and distribution through the elimination of market forces. Did it produce the desired
results? Clearly not. Even the most fanatical advocates of these policies had
to admit that after three years of experimentation the Soviet economy lay in
shambles. As rapidly as the regime nationalized everything in sight, the illicit
free market expanded, threatening to absorb what remained of Russia's
wealth. And there was not that much left to absorb. Russia's Gross National
Income in 1920 fluctuated between 33 and 40 percent of what it had been in
1913. The living standard of workers by then had declined to one-third of its
prewar level.[152]

The facts were indisputable, but their interpretations differed. The Left
Communists and other advocates of immediate socialization, standing in the
midst of the wreckage they had wrought, facing the prospect of imminent
famine, refused to concede failure. In a treatise published in 1920 Bukharin
spoke glowingly of the collapse of the Soviet economy. In his view, it was the
legacy of "capitalism" that was being destroyed: "such a grand debacle had
never happened before," he boasted. It was all "historically inevitable and
historically necessary." His book, filled with Marxist clichés, contained no
facts, statistical or other, on the actual condition of Soviet Russia's economy:
facts that would have demonstrated that the culprit was not "capitalism" but
Bolshevism.*

Other Communists found the cause of the economy's calamitous condition in the survival of the private sector. They had always insisted that socialism could not succeed under conditions of partial nationalization and now felt
vindicated: the trouble lay not in the government's pressing socialism too hard,
but in not pressing it hard enough. A typical defense of War Communism in
this spirit appeared in *Pravda* in early 1921, just as it was being abandoned. The
author, V. Frumkin, ascribed the shortcomings of Soviet Russia's economy to
the fact that its "entire apparatus lies in the hands of bourgeois and petty
bourgeois elements, our class enemies." This could be overcome only by the
formation of "sufficiently large cadres of Red commanders of the economic
front," a task which he perceived as lying in the "more or less distant future."[153]

More sober heads realized that, far from being responsible for the failure
of socialist experiments of 1918–20, "capitalism" had made such experiments
possible in the first place. Essentially, under War Communism the Bolsheviks
had been living off the human and material resources accumulated by bourgeois Russia. But there was a limit to those. An analysis published in the
summer of 1920 in the leading Soviet economic newspaper concluded: "We
have completely exhausted the supplies of the more important resources and
raw materials bequeathed to us by capitalist Russia. Henceforth, all economic
gains will have to be made from our own current production."[154]

*N. Bukharin, *Ekonomika perekhodnogo perioda*, Pt. 1 (Moscow, 1920), 5–6, 48. The second
part, which was to have provided empirical data (p. 6), never appeared.

This agenda would be adopted in the spring of 1921 under the New Economic Policy: a transitional period of indeterminate duration, modeled on Lenin's original concept of "state capitalism," during which the government would retain a monopoly on political power but allow private enterprise a limited role in restoring the country's productive forces. During this period, it would ready cadres of "Red commanders of the economic front." Once productivity had been sufficiently improved and the personnel stood available, a fresh offensive would be launched to exterminate the "bourgeois" and "petty bourgeois" class enemy for good and then to proceed in earnest with the construction of socialism.

War on the Village

By the spring of 1918, the communes had distributed to their members the properties they had seized since the February Revolution. There was little subsequent distribution: the demobilized soldiers and industrial workers who arrived late rarely managed to secure allotments. But the peasant who expected to be able to enjoy his loot in peace would soon be disabused. To the Bolsheviks, the "Grand Repartition" of 1917–18 was only a detour on the road to collectivization. They laid claim to the harvest of 1918 by virtue of edicts which appropriated for the state all the grain over and above what the peasant required for his consumption and seed. The free market in grain was abolished. The peasant, bewildered by the unexpected turn of events, fought back ferociously in defense of his property, rising in rebellion that in numbers and territory involved exceeded anything seen in tsarist Russia. It was to little avail. He was about to learn that "to rob" and "to be robbed" are merely different modes of the same verb.

Perhaps the greatest paradox of the October coup d'état was that it sought to establish the "dictatorship of the proletariat" in a country in which workers (including self-employed artisans) constituted at best 10 percent of those gainfully employed, while fully 80 percent were peasants. And, in the view of Social-Democrats, the peasants—except for the minority of landless agricultural laborers—formed part of the "bourgeoisie" and, as such, were a class enemy of the "proletariat."

This perception of the class nature of the self-employed (or "middle") peasant was at the heart of the disagreement between the Social-Democrats and Socialists-Revolutionaries, the latter of whom classified peasants along with industrial workers as "toilers." Marx, however, had defined the peasant as a class enemy of the worker and a "bulwark of the old society."[1] Karl Kautsky asserted that the objectives of the peasantry were contrary to those of socialism.[2] In a statement on the agrarian question which it submitted in 1896 to the Congress of the Socialist International, the Russian Social-Democratic delegation referred to peasants as a backward class, closed to socialist ideas and best left alone.[3]

Lenin shared this assessment. "The class of small producers and small cultivators . . . ," he wrote in 1902, "is a *reactionary* class."[4] However, in line with his general policy of drawing into the revolutionary process every group and class that for one reason or another had a quarrel with the status quo, he made allowance for the "petty bourgeois" peasantry helping the "proletarian" cause. In this respect—and it was a question of tactics only—he differed from the other Social-Democrats. Lenin assumed that rural Russia was still in the grip of predominantly "feudal" relations. To the extent that the peasantry struggled against this order, it performed a progressive function:

> We demand the complete and unconditional, not reformatory but revolutionary abolition and destruction of the survivals of serfdom; we acknowledge as the peasants' those lands which the gentry government had cut off from them and which to this day continue to keep them under de facto slavery. In this manner we become—by way of exception and by virtue of special historic circumstances—defenders of small property. But we defend it only in its struggle against that which has survived of the "old regime" . . .[5]

It was from such purely tactical considerations that in 1917 Lenin took over the SR land program and encouraged Russia's peasants to seize privately owned landed property.

But once the objective of this tactic—the collapse of the "old regime" and its "bourgeois" successor—had been attained, the peasant, in Lenin's eyes, reverted to his traditional role as a "petty bourgeois" counterrevolutionary. The danger of the "proletarian revolution" in Russia drowning in a sea of peasant reaction obsessed Russian Social-Democrats, conscious as they were of the role which the French peasantry had played in helping suppress urban radicalism, especially in 1871. Bolshevik insistence on spreading their revolution to the industrial countries of the West as rapidly as possible was in good measure inspired by the desire to avoid this fate. To leave the peasants in permanent possession of the land was tantamount to giving them a stranglehold on the food supply to the cities, the bastions of the Revolution. Lenin noted that European revolutions had failed because they had not dislodged the "rural bourgeoisie."[6] For some of Lenin's more fanatical followers, even the landless rural proletarian, whom Lenin, following Engels, was willing to see as an ally, could not be relied upon because he, too, was "after all, a peasant—that is, potentially a kulak."[7]

Lenin was determined not to let history repeat itself. Much as he counted on the outbreak of revolutions in the West, he would not allow the fate of the Russian Revolution to depend on developments abroad over which he had no control. In contemplating the peasant problem in Soviet Russia, he thought in terms of a two-phase solution. Over the long run, the only satisfactory outcome was collectivization—that is, the expropriation of all the land and its product by the state and the transformation of peasants into wage earners. This measure alone would resolve the contradiction between the objectives of communism and the social realities of the country in which it first came to power. Lenin regarded the 1917 Land Decree and the other agrarian measures which the Bolsheviks had introduced during and after October as temporary expedients. As soon as the situation permitted, the communes would be dispossessed and turned into state-run collectives.* No secret was made of this long-term objective. In 1918 and 1919 the Soviet authorities on numerous occasions confirmed that collectivization was inevitable: an article in *Pravda* in November 1918 predicted that the "middle peasantry" would be dragged into collective farming "screaming and kicking" *(vorcha i ogryzaias')* as soon as the regime was able to do so.[8]

Until then, in Lenin's view, it was necessary to (1) assert state control over the food supply by means of a strictly enforced monopoly on the grain trade and (2) introduce Communist power bases in the countryside. These objectives required nothing less than declaring civil war on the village. Such a war the Bolsheviks launched in the summer of 1918. The campaign against the peasantry, virtually ignored in Western historiography, constituted a critical phase in the Bolshevik conquest of Russia. Lenin himself believed that it prevented a rural counterrevolution and ensured that the Russian Revolution, unlike its Western precursors, would not stop halfway and then slide backward into "reaction."

To understand the successes as well as the failures of the Bolshevik assault on the village it is necessary to form an idea of the effects of the Revolution on Russia's rural economy. As previously noted, in October 1917

---

*For instance, on December 11, 1918, at a Congress of Committees of the Poor, Lenin moved a resolution calling for the collectivization of land at the earliest possible time: Lenin, *PSS,* XXXVII, 356, and Lenin, *Sochineniia,* XXIII, 587–88. The Law on the Socialization of Land, issued on January 27/February 9, 1918, committed the government to "developing collective agriculture as more convenient in terms of economizing labor and products, at the expense of individual farming, for the purpose of a transition to a socialist economy": *Dekrety,* I, 408.

the Bolsheviks had set aside their own agrarian program, centered on the nationalization of land, in favor of the SR land program, much more popular among the peasantry, which called for the expropriation, without compensation, and distribution among the communes of all privately held lands, except those belonging to small peasant proprietors.

There is no dispute that the peasants of central Russia welcomed the Land Decree, which realized their old dream of a "Black Repartition." Even peasants who stood to lose from it because their private holdings were likely to be taken away from them bowed to the inevitable.

But it is a different question altogether whether these essentially demagogic and tactical measures either significantly improved the economic status of the Russian peasant or benefited the country at large.

Land, being an immovable object, can, of course, be distributed only there where it happens to lie. In pre-revolutionary Russia, the bulk of private (non-communal) land subject to expropriation under the Land Decree had been located not in the central, Great Russian provinces, which the Bolsheviks controlled and which had the greatest incidence of rural overpopulation, but on the periphery of the Empire—the Baltic areas, the western provinces, the Ukraine, and the North Caucasus, all of which after October 1917 were outside Bolshevik control. As a consequence, the pool of land available for distribution in Bolshevik-held areas fell considerably short of peasant expectations.

But even in these areas it proved difficult to achieve an equitable land distribution because the peasant refused to share his loot with both outsiders *(inogorodnye)* and peasants from adjacent communes. Here is a contemporary description of land distribution as it worked in practice:

> The agrarian question is solved in a simple manner. The entire land of the landlord has become the property of the commune. Every rural community receives its land from its previous landlord, and does not yield one inch of it to any outsider, even if it has too much and the neighboring communities are short. . . . It prefers to leave the [surplus] land in the landlord's hands, as long as none of it falls into the hands of peasants from another community. The peasants say that as long as the landlord uses the land, they will still be able to earn something, and when it becomes necessary, they will take it away.[9]

It is not easy to determine how much arable land the Russian peasantry actually obtained in 1917–18: estimates vary widely from as little as 20 to as much as 150 million *desiatiny*.[10] A major obstacle lies in the imprecise use of the term "land" *(zemlia)*. As employed in the various statistical surveys conducted after the Revolution, it applies to very different things: arable land *(pashnia)*, its most valuable form, but also meadow, forest, and land of no economic use (desert, marsh, tundra). It is only by lumping these diverse objects under the meaningless rubric of "land" that one can arrive at the fantastic figure of 150 million *desiatiny*—first introduced by Stalin in 1936 and for long mandatory in Communist literature—allegedly acquired by Russian peasants in consequence of the Revolution.[11]

Reliable statistics indicate a much more modest result. Figures compiled by the Commissariat of Agriculture in 1919–20 showed that peasants received a total of 21.15 million *desiatiny* (23.27 million hectares).[12] This land was very unevenly distributed. Fifty-three percent of Russian communes gained no land from the Revolution.[13] This nearly corresponds to the number of villages (54 percent) that, according to the same source, said they felt "unhappy" over the results of land redistribution.[14] The remaining 47 percent of the villages acquired arable land in very unequal shares. Of the thirty-four provinces for which figures exist, the communes in six received less than one-tenth of one *desiatina* per member; those in twelve gained between one-tenth and one-quarter *desiatina;* in nine they obtained between one-quarter and one-half; peasants of four acquired from one-half to a full *desiatina;* and only in three provinces did the peasants secure between one and two *desiatiny.* [15] Nation-wide, the average communal allotment of arable land per peasant, which before the Revolution had been 1.87 *desiatiny,* rose to 2.26.[16] This would represent an increment of 0.4 *desiatina* of arable land per communal adult *(edok)* or 23.7 percent. This figure, first cited in 1921, has been confirmed by recent studies, the most authoritative of which somewhat vaguely says that the land which the average peasant received "did not exceed" 0.4 *desiatina,* or approximately one acre*—far below what the peasant had expected from the Black Repartition.

But even this modest figure overstates the economic benefits of the repartition, for a good part (two-thirds) of the land which the peasants seized in 1917–18 they had previously leased. The "socialization" of that land, therefore, did not so much increase the arable land available to them as absolve them from the payment of rent.[17] In addition to being freed from such rents, estimated at 700 million rubles a year, the peasants also benefited from the cancellation by the Communist regime of their debts to the Peasants' Land Bank, amounting to 1.4 billion rubles.[18]

The peasants viewed their title to the new land skeptically, for they heard that the new government intended someday to introduce collectives: the Decree on the Socialization of Land issued in April 1918 stated that the transfer of land to the communes was "provisional" or "temporary" *(vremennoe)*. They wondered for how long they would be allowed to keep it and decided to act as if it were only until the next harvest was over. Hence, rather than incorporate the acquired land into communal holdings, they kept it separate, so that if required to surrender the new land, they could still hold on to their old allotments.[19]† As a result, the much-lamented strip farming *(chere-*

---

*V. R. Gerasimiuk in *ISSSR,* No. 1 (1965), 100. V. P. Danilov, *Pereraspredelenie zemel'nogo fonda Rossii* (Moscow, 1979), 283–87 (cited in V. V. Kabanov, *Krest'ianskoe khoziaistvo v usloviiakh "Voennogo Kommunizma,"* Moscow, 1988, 49), says that as a result of the Revolution peasant holdings increased 29.8 percent, but from this figure one must deduct the land taken over by collective and other Soviet farms. Radical intellectuals in the late nineteenth century gathered from peasants that they had hoped the Black Repartition would bring them from 5 to 15 *desiatiny:* V. L. Debagorii-Mokrievich, *Vospominaniia* (St. Petersburg, 1906), 137, and G. I. Uspenskii, *Sobranie Sochinenii,* V (Moscow, 1956), 130.

†According to one intellectual who lived from October 1918 until November 1920 in a village in the Tambov province, the peasants doubted that the land they had acquired was really theirs

spolositsa) intensified. Many peasants had to travel fifteen, thirty, and even sixty kilometers to reach their new allotments: if the distance was too great, they simply abandoned them.[20]

So much for the economic benefits which the Russian peasant derived from the Revolution. They were by no means free. Historians usually ignore the costs of the agrarian revolution to the peasant, although they can be shown to have been considerable. These costs were of a twofold nature: the loss of savings due to inflation and the loss of land held by peasants in private (non-communal) ownership.

Before the Revolution, Russian peasants had accumulated considerable savings, some of which they kept at home and the rest of which they deposited in government savings banks *(sberegatel'nye kassy)*. These savings grew considerably during the prosperous war years and the first year of the Revolution when peasants benefited from rising food prices. It is impossible to calculate precisely the amount of peasant savings at the time of the October coup, but some idea may be obtained from official figures as supplemented by informed estimates. At the beginning of 1914, the government savings banks had on deposit 1.55 billion rubles.[21] Between July 1914 and October 1917, they are estimated to have taken in an additional 5 billion, of which 60–75 percent is believed to have come from rural depositors.[22] If the same ratio had held for pre-1914 depositors, the peasants may be estimated to have had on deposit in savings banks at the time of the October coup some 5 billion rubles, to which must be added the moneys they kept at home. The Bolsheviks exempted government savings banks from the decree nationalizing private banks, so that in theory peasants and other small depositors retained access to their money. But it was not long before inflation rendered these deposits as worthless as if they had been confiscated outright. As shown in the preceding chapter, the Bolsheviks proceeded deliberately and systematically to devalue money: during their first five years, the purchasing power of the ruble depreciated millions of times, which had the effect of turning it into colored paper. As a consequence Russian peasants, far from receiving the landlord's land free of charge, paid for it dearly. For the 21 million *desiatiny* which they had been allowed to appropriate, they lost in bank savings alone an estimated 5 billion rubles.* If one accepts the contemporary estimate that they kept in mattresses and buried in the ground an additional 7 to 8 billion, then it follows that for his average allotment of one acre of arable land (0.4 *desiatina*) the peasant paid 600 pre-1918 rubles. Before the Revolution, the average price for this land would have been 64.4 rubles.†

Peasants paid for their new allotments in still another way. When speak-

---

because it was not given them by the Tsar: A. L. Okninskii, *Dva goda sredi krest'ian* (Riga, [1936]), 27. It is the land they allotted to poor peasants, if forced to share the loot with them.

*With the prewar ruble worth 0.78 gram of gold, these savings would have purchased 3,900 tons of gold.

†Properties bought by the Land Bank from landlords between 1906 and 1915 cost, on the average, 161 rubles per *desiatina*: P. I. Liashchenko, *Istoriia narodnogo khoziaistva SSSR,* II, 3rd ed. (Leningrad, 1952), 270. The estimate of peasants' home savings comes from *NZh,* No. 56/271 (March 31, 1918), 2.

ing of privately owned land in Russia one tends to think of the properties of landlords *(pomeshchiki)*, the Crown, merchants, and clergy which the Land Decree specified as subject to confiscation and distribution. But a great deal—over one-third—of private agricultural land (arable, forest, and meadow) in Russia before the Revolution was the property of peasants, held individually or, more usually, in associations. In fact, on the eve of the Revolution peasants and Cossacks owned nearly as much land as "landlords." Of the 97.7 million *desiatiny* of land (arable, woodland, and pasture) in private ownership in European Russia in January 1915, 39 million, or 39.5 percent, was held by landlords (gentry, officials, and officers) and 34.4 million (34.8 percent) by peasants and Cossacks.[23]

Lenin's Land Decree exempted from expropriation the holdings of "ordinary peasants and ordinary Cossacks." But in many localities in central Russia communal peasants ignored this provision and proceeded to seize the land belonging to their fellow peasants along with that of the landlords, placing it in the communal pool for distribution. Included in these seizures were both *khutora* and *otruba*, including onetime communal land whose cultivators, taking advantage of the Stolypin legislation, had withdrawn from the commune.* As a result, in no time at all, the peasants wiped out much of the achievement of Stolypin's agrarian reform: the communal principle swept everything before it. Communal peasants treated the landed property which members of the commune had purchased outside the commune the same way: this land too was added to the communal reserve. Here and there, communes left peasants their properties on condition that they reduce them to the size of communal allotments: in January 1927, on the eve of collectivization, of the 233 million *desiatiny* of peasant land in the Russian Republic (RSFSR), 222 million, or 95.3 percent, were held communally and only 8 million, or 3.4 percent, as *otruba* or *khutora*—that is, in private property.[24]

In view of these facts, it is misleading to say that the Russian peasantry gained from the Revolution, free of charge, large quantities of agricultural land. Its gains were neither generous nor free. The Russian peasantry cannot be treated as homogeneous: the term "Russian peasantry" is an abstraction covering millions of individuals, some of whom had succeeded, by dint of industry, thrift, and business sense, to accumulate capital, which they held in cash or invested in land. All this cash and nearly all this land they now lost. Once such factors are taken into account, it is clear that the *muzhik* greatly overpaid for the properties which he had seized under the Communist-sponsored *duvan*.

The agrarian revolution made peasant holdings more equal. In the repartitions which took place across Russia in 1917–18, the communes reduced holdings that were larger than the norm, their principal criterion for redistributing allotments being the number of *edoki*, or "eaters," per household. This procedure resulted in the number of households with large allotments (four

---

*Otruba were land allotments intermingled with communal strips, while *khutora* formed separate farmsteads. Both were held in private property.

desiatiny or more) being reduced by almost one-third (from 30.9 to 21.2 percent of the total), while the number of those holdings less than four *desiatiny* significantly increased (from 57.6 to 72.2 percent).* These figures indicate that there occurred a sizable rise in the number of "middle peasants," whose ranks were swollen both by the decrease in the number of land-rich peasants and by the granting of allotments to some peasants who previously had had no land: the number of the latter was cut almost in half.[25] In consequence of this leveling, Russia became more than ever a country of small, self-sufficient farmers. One contemporary compared post-revolutionary Russia to a "honeycomb in which small commodity producers . . . have succeeded in equalizing control over the partitioned land, creating a network of parcels, approximately equal in size."[26] The "middle peasant" of Marxist jargon—one who neither hired labor nor sold his own—emerged as the greatest beneficiary of the agrarian revolution: a fact which it took some time for the Bolsheviks to acknowledge.

Not everyone, of course, profited from the Black Repartition: its main beneficiaries were those who already had held communal allotments in 1917 and dominated the communal assemblies. Many of the peasants who in 1917 and 1918 had streamed back to the village from the cities to claim allotments found themselves either excluded from the redistribution or forced to accept substandard lots. The same applied to that one-half of the landless peasants *(batraki)* who ended up empty-handed. Better-off peasants ignored the wishes of the Bolshevik authorities who in the Land Socialization Decree had instructed village soviets to show particular solicitude for the landless and land-poor peasants.[27] Russia simply lacked sufficient agrarian land to give his norm to everyone who demanded it in the name of "socialization." As a result, the landless and land-poor communal peasants received only small allotments at best.[28]

The Russian Revolution carried the rural commune to its historic apogee: paradoxically, it was the Bolsheviks who brought about its golden age, even though they despised it. "The commune that had been whittled back in the course of the preceding decade blossomed over virtually all of the agricultural land in the country."[29] This was a spontaneous process that the Bolsheviks did not immediately oppose because the commune for them performed the same functions that it had under tsarism—namely, guaranteeing fulfillment of obligations to the state.

The economic and social consequences of the Revolution thus aggravated the problem which the Bolsheviks had faced from the beginning: not

---

*Gerasimiuk in *ISSSR*, No. 1 (1965), 100; *O zemle: sbornik statei*, I (1921), 25, gives slightly different figures. The reduction in larger holdings was in some measure due to the acceleration of the breakup of joint families in favor of nuclear ones, which had already begun in the late nineteenth century but which the land policies of the Bolsheviks encouraged, because farmers wanted to share in the distribution of confiscated properties, which they could do best as heads of households.

e

only had they declared the "dictatorship of the proletariat" in a country that was already overwhelmingly "petty bourgeois" but their policies made it even more so. It is against this background that in the early summer of 1918 Moscow took the decision to storm the village. The exact circumstances under which this decision was taken are not known, but enough information is available to make it possible to provide a general account of its antecedents and intent.

As had been the case with the October coup, in launching the invasion of the countryside, the Bolsheviks acted in the name of spurious objectives. Their true purpose was to consummate the October coup by imposing control over the peasantry. But since this would not have been a popular slogan, they carried out the campaign against the peasantry for the ostensible purpose of extracting from the "kulaks" food for the hungry cities. Food shortages, of course, were a very real problem, but as will be shown below, there existed easier and more effective ways of drawing supplies from the countryside. In their internal communications, the authorities frankly admitted that food extraction was a subsidiary task. Thus, a secret Bolshevik report, referring to the decree ordering the creation in every village of Committees of the Poor, explained the measure as follows:

> The decree of July 11, concerning the organization of the village poor, defined the nature of the organization and assigned it supply functions. But its true purpose was *purely political:* to carry out a class stratification in the village, to arouse to active political life those strata that were capable of assimilating and realizing the tasks of the proletarian socialist revolution and even leading onto this path the middle toiling peasantry by freeing it from the economic and social influence of the kulaks and rich peasants who had seized control of the rural soviets and transformed them into organs of opposition to Soviet socialist construction.[30]

In other words, the extraction of foodstuffs ("supply functions") for the cities was camouflage for a political operation designed to bring Bolshevism to the village by inflaming social animosities.

In pre-revolutionary Russia, the bulk of the food reaching the market came either from large private estates or from farms of well-to-do peasants, both of which employed hired labor: middle and poor peasants consumed nearly all the food they produced. The confiscation and distribution to the communes of all the gentry land and much of the land held by peasants in private ownership, aggravated by the government's prohibition on the employment of hired labor (even though it was widely ignored), removed the main source of food supply for the non-agrarian population. With rural Russia reverting to the self-sufficiency of the pre-capitalist era, the non-agricultural population faced starvation. This fact alone contributed to the severe food shortages that occurred after the Bolshevik coup.*

*About one-third of what used to be privately owned agricultural land—3.2 percent of the acreage under cultivation—mainly large estates devoted to "technical" cultures, was taken over by state-run collective farms. In theory, they could have helped alleviate the food shortage in the cities.

Even under such adverse conditions the peasant might have been able to feed the townspeople if the Bolsheviks, for what appear to have been mainly political reasons, did not deprive him of incentives to part with the surplus.

One of the few measures passed by the Provisional Government that the Bolsheviks retained was the law of March 25, 1917, establishing a state monopoly on commerce in grain. The law provided that all the grain that the producer had left over after satisfying his personal needs and providing for seed belonged to the state and had to be sold to its agencies at fixed prices. Surplus grain that was not turned over was subject to being requisitioned at half price. The Provisional Government obtained in this manner 14.5 percent of the harvest,[31] but even so, as long as it was in power, the grain trade went on as before. The Bolsheviks, however, enforced this rule with increasing brutality, treating all sales of grain and its products to the consumer as "speculation" subject to severe penalties. In its first months the Cheka expended most of its energy pursuing peasant "bagmen" *(meshochniki)* and confiscating their merchandise: sometimes it sent peasant peddlers to jail and even executed them. Undeterred, the peasants kept on coming, feeding millions.

The Bolshevik Government insisted that the peasants sell the grain surplus to state agencies at prices that inflation made increasingly absurd: on August 8, 1918, the official tariff was set (depending on the region) at between 14 and 18 rubles per pud (16.3 kilograms) of rye grain, which on the free market was fetching in Moscow 290 and in Petrograd 420 rubles a pud.* There was a similar disparity between fixed and free market prices on other staples, such as meat and potatoes which became controlled in January 1919. The peasant responded to this pricing policy both by hoarding and by curtailing his acreage. The decline in the grain harvest followed inexorably.[32]

If one further allows that, as a result of the Brest Treaty, Russia lost the Ukraine, which previously had supplied the country with more than one-third of its cereals, and that in June 1918 the Czechoslovak rebellion cut off access to Siberia, the tragic situation confronting the urban inhabitants of central and northern Russia in mid-1918 becomes apparent. All the cities and industrial centers, and an increasing number of villages located in the less productive regions or with developed cottage industries, suffered hunger and faced the almost certain prospect of a devastating famine should the weather take a turn for the worse.

For the Bolsheviks this situation held dangers as well as opportunities. Hunger in the cities and industrial regions stimulated discontent and eroded their political base. In 1918, Russian cities were in constant turmoil from food shortages. The situation was especially explosive in Petrograd, where in late January 1918 the daily ration consisted of 4 ounces of bread adulterated with

---

But their inventory having been looted by local peasants, they were of little, if any, help: L. N. Kritsman, *Proletarskaia revoliutsiia i derevnia* (Moscow-Leningrad, 1929), 86–87.

*Kabanov, *Krest'ianskoe khoziaistvo,* 159. The peasant who received such unrealistic prices for his product had to buy manufactured goods (e.g., matches, nails, and kerosene), which were becoming scarcer each day, at free market prices.

milled straw.[33] Since this ration was not adequate to sustain life, the inhabitants had to resort to the open market, where prices were driven artificially high by the Cheka's harassment of food peddlers. Here, the price of bread fluctuated between 2 and 5 or more rubles a pound, which placed it out of the reach of workers, who, if fortunate enough to find employment, earned at best between 300 and 400 rubles a month.[34] During 1918, the food ration in Petrograd was adjusted every few days either upward or downward, depending on the ability of supply trains to run the gauntlet of armed deserters and peasants who lay in ambush: if they succeeded in overpowering the guards they stripped the train in no time, and it reached Petrograd empty. In March, the bread ration in Petrograd rose slightly to 6 ounces, only to drop toward the end of April to 2 ounces. The situation was no better in the provincial cities. In Kaluga, for instance, the daily bread allotment in early 1918 was set at 5 ounces.[35]

To escape the hunger, urban inhabitants fled the cities in droves: among the refugees were many peasants who had come during the war to work in the defense industries and demobilized garrison troops. Contemporary statistics indicate a drastic fall in the population of Petrograd: by April 1918, 60 percent of the industrial workers employed there in January 1917 (221,000 out of 365,000) had fled to the countryside.[36] An exodus of nearly equal proportions occurred in Moscow. During the Revolution and the Civil War, Moscow would lose one-half of its population and Petrograd two-thirds,[37] a process which dramatically reversed the urbanization of Russia and enhanced her rural character.* Russian statisticians estimate that between 1917 and 1920, 884,000 families, or some 5 million people, abandoned the cities for the countryside.[38] This nearly corresponds to the number of peasants who had moved into the urban areas during the war (6 million).

Those who stayed behind grumbled, demonstrated, and sometimes rioted over food shortages. Lower-class men and women, crazed by hunger, looted food warehouses and stores. Newspapers carried reports of housewives running in the streets screaming "Give us bread!" Peddlers who demanded exorbitant prices risked lynching. Many cities issued ordinances excluding outsiders. Petrograd was tightly sealed off: in February 1918 Lenin signed a decree forbidding nonresidents to enter the capital and certain areas in northern Russia. Other cities passed similar laws.[39]

In the atmosphere of hunger and lawlessness, urban crime soared. Police records indicate that in the third month of Bolshevik rule the inhabitants of Petrograd reported 15,600 burglaries, 9,370 incidents of store looting, 203,801 incidents of pickpocketing, and 125 murders.[40] How many crimes went unreported there is no way of knowing, but there must have been very many, since it was common at the time for ordinary criminals to rob under the pretext of carrying out "expropriations," which the victims were too terrorized to report.

*One well-informed visitor to Soviet Russia in 1920 reported even more staggering reductions. Petrograd's population is said to have declined from 3 million in 1917 to 500,000: Alexander Berkman, *The Bolshevik Myth (Diary 1920–1922)*, (London, 1925), 33.

The countryside was in the grip of similar lawlessness. In some provinces (such as Voronezh) food was abundant; in others (such as nearby Riazan) it was desperately short. It was not uncommon for one district to enjoy a comfortable surplus while its neighbors went starving. As a rule, those who had a surplus either disposed of it on the free market or hoarded it in expectation that the state grain monopoly would collapse. Charity was unknown: well-fed peasants refused to feed the hungry ones, and if they came begging, chased them away.[41]

The picture of rural life in the first half of 1918 provided by the contemporary press is one of unrelieved horror. An account published in *Riazanskaia zhizn'* in early March may not be quite representative, because Riazan suffered extreme food shortages, but it gives some idea how rapidly the Russian village deteriorated under Bolshevik rule, plunging into primeval anarchy. Having looted state liquor stores, the peasants of this province were in a state of perpetual drunkenness. They fought each other in wild orgies, assisted by old men and young girls. To keep them quiet, children were plied with vodka. Afraid of losing their savings through confiscation or inflation, peasants gambled frantically, usually at blackjack; it was not uncommon for an ordinary *muzhik* to lose one thousand rubles in an evening.

> The old men . . . buy pictures of the Last Judgment. Deep in their hearts the peasants believe that the "end of the world" is near. . . . And before hell comes, everything that exists on earth and that has been built so recently with such effort is being demolished. They so smash everything that the noise reverberates throughout the district.[42]

In areas where the food situation was especially desperate, the peasants staged "hunger rebellions," destroying everything in sight. After one such uprising in a district of Novgorod province, the local Communist authorities imposed on the 12,000 inhabitants a "contribution" of 4.5 million rubles, as if they were rebellious natives of a conquered colony.[43]

Hunger posed dangers, but from the Bolshevik point of view it also had a positive side. For one, the state monopoly on the food trade, even though detrimental to the supply of food, enabled the regime to maintain a rationing system that served to control the urban population and discriminate in favor of its supporters. Second, hunger depressed the spirit of the population, robbing it of the will to resist. The psychology of hunger is not well known, but Russian observers noted that it made people more willing to submit to authority. "Hunger is a poor companion of creativity," one Bolshevik observed, "it inspires blind destructiveness, dark fear, a desire to surrender, to hand over one's destiny to the will of someone who will take it and organize it."[44] Starving people, if capable of putting up a fight, dissipate their energies battling each other for food. Such political apathy, being self-induced, does more to promote submissiveness than even police repression.

That the Bolsheviks were aware of the political benefits of hunger is

attested to by their refusal to relieve it in the only feasible way, the one they
would adopt in 1921 when confident of their control over Russia: reinstating
the free market in grain. As soon as this was done, production soared and
before long attained prewar levels. That this would happen is known not only
by hindsight. In May 1918, a grain specialist, S. D. Rozenkrants, explained to
Zinoviev that the food shortages were due not to "speculation" but to the
absence of production incentives. Under the grain monopoly the peasant had
no inducement to grow grain beyond his own immediate needs. By planting
the surplus acreage with root vegetables (potatoes, carrots, beets) for sale on
the open market, as the authorities permitted him to do, he earned more
money than he knew what to do with: at the free market rate of 100 rubles for
a pud of such produce, one *desiatina* earned him 50,000–60,000 rubles. Why
should he bother with grain only to have the state confiscate it at its ridiculous
"fixed prices"? Rozenkrants expressed confidence that if the government
adopted a more businesslike approach it would resolve the food problem in two
months.[45]

Some Bolsheviks liked this solution. Rykov, the head of the State Planning Commission, advocated a combination of compulsory grain deliveries
and collaboration with rural cooperatives and private enterprise.[46] Others
suggested that the government purchase grain at close to market prices (60
rubles per pud minimum) and sell it to the population at a discount.[47] But all
these proposals were rejected for political reasons. As the Menshevik *Socialist
Courier* would explain,[48] the grain monopoly was essential to the survival of
the Communist dictatorship: with the immense rural labor force outside its
control, it had to resort to the control of the agrarian product. Indeed, according to this source, by early 1921 the Bolsheviks were discussing a proposal by
Osinskii to transform peasants into state employees who would be permitted
to cultivate the land only on condition of sowing an area predetermined by the
authorities and turning over all the surplus—a proposal that had to be shelved
with the outbreak of the Kronstadt rebellion and the adoption of the New
Economic Policy. If the food trade were set free, the peasant would soon
accumulate wealth and gain even greater economic independence, presenting
a serious "counterrevolutionary" threat. Such a risk could be taken only after
the regime was indisputably master of Russia. Lenin's government was prepared to subject the country to a famine claiming millions of lives if this was
required to ensure its hold on state power.

Such being the political realities, all the economic measures with which
the Bolsheviks sought to improve the food situation in the first half of 1918
proved of no avail. They kept on issuing decrees that either modified procedures for the collection and distribution of food or else threatened food "speculators," whom they persisted in treating as the cause of the shortages rather
than their consequence, with the most dire punishments. Among the most
irrelevant of such decrees was one drafted by Lenin at the end of December
1917. "The critical situation of the food supply, the threat of famine caused by
speculation," Lenin wrote, "the sabotage of capitalists and bureaucrats, as well

as the prevailing chaos, make it necessary to take extraordinary revolutionary measures to combat the evil." These "measures," however, turned out to have nothing to do with the food supply, but instead consisted of nationalizing Russia's banks and declaring a default on the domestic and foreign debts of the Russian Government.* According to Alexander Tsiurupa, the strike of the 1,300 employees of the Commissariat of Supply protesting the Bolshevik dictatorship aggravated the situation, because they were replaced with officials who had no idea what to do.[49]

Unwilling to give up the monopoly on grain, the Bolsheviks did nothing to forestall the famine predicted by the contemporary press. Like the tsarist regime when confronted with a domestic crisis, they resorted to bureaucratic reshufflings and procedural changes. Since this was not the manner which the Bolsheviks adopted when confronting problems that really concerned them, it is difficult to escape the conclusion that hunger was not in that category.

On February 13, Trotsky was appointed head of the Extraordinary Commission for Supply. His task as "Supply Dictator" was to organize the flow of foodstuffs to the cities with the help of "extraordinary revolutionary measures," "revolutionary" in this instance being a euphemism for military force.[50] But he had hardly assumed this responsibility when he was appointed Commissar of War: there is no record of his having accomplished anything. The regime kept on flooding the country with appeals to help starving Petrograd and Moscow,[51] appeals laced with invective against the domestic and foreign "bourgeoisie," which was blamed for the shortages. In February 1918, the government ordered the death penalty for "bagmen."[52] On March 25, Moscow tried to draw out food from the countryside with resort to barter. It allocated 1.16 billion rubles—the two-week output of Soviet printing presses—for the purchase of consumer goods to be exchanged for 2 million tons of grain.[53] But because the consumer goods on which the whole scheme depended could not be found, the project fell through. In April, having run out of ideas that had any semblance of realism, the government conceived the plan of building a new railroad to carry grain from the surplus areas.[54] Not one foot of track was ever laid down, nor would it have made any difference if it had.

By the beginning of May the Bolsheviks no longer could play at solving the food shortages, for the supply situation in the cities and industrial areas had reached alarming dimensions: telegrams poured into the Kremlin reporting that the workers, the recipients of the most generous rations, were going hungry.[55] In Petrograd, a pound loaf of bread on the open market, which in January had fetched 3 rubles, now cost between 6 and 12.[56] Something had to be done. Since opening the grain trade to the free play of the market forces, which the experts urged and the factory workers demanded, was unacceptable on political grounds, another solution had to be found. That solution was invading and conquering the village by force of arms.

Dekrety, I, 227–28. In the final, published version of this decree, Lenin's spurious rationale for these fiscal measures was omitted (p. 230): apparently its absurdity struck even Lenin.

Sverdlov announced the new policy on May 20, 1918:

> If we can say that revolutionary Soviet authority is sufficiently strong in the cities . . . then the same cannot be said in regard to the village. . . . For that reason we must most seriously confront the question of the differentiation of the village, the question of creating in the village two contrasting and hostile forces. . . . Only if we succeed in splitting the village into two irreconcilably hostile camps, if we are able to inflame there the same civil war that had occurred not so long ago in the cities . . . only then will we be in a position to say that we will do that in relation to the village that we were able to do for the city.[57]

This extraordinary pronouncement meant that the Bolsheviks had decided to incite one part of the rural population against another, unleashing a civil war among citizens who were living peacefully side by side, in order to gain in the village the power base which had so far eluded them. The assault troops designated for this campaign were to consist of urban workers as well as poor and landless peasants: the "enemy" were the rich peasants, or kulaks, the rural "bourgeoisie."

Lenin hated what he perceived to be the "bourgeoisie" with a destructive passion that fully equalled Hitler's hatred of the Jews: nothing short of its physical annihilation would satisfy him. The urban middle class—the professionals, financiers, merchants, industrialists, rentiers—gave him little trouble, for they submitted at once, corroborating the thesis of the founding manifesto of Russian Social-Democracy of 1898 that the further east one moved, the more supine the bourgeoisie. When told to shovel snow, they shoveled snow, and even posed for photographs, smiling wanly. When subjected to "contributions," they dutifully paid up. They studiously avoided contacts with anti-Bolshevik armies or underground organizations. Most of them hoped for some miracle, perhaps German intervention, or perhaps the evolution of Bolshevik policies toward greater "realism." In the meantime, their instincts told them to lie low. When in the spring of 1918 the Bolsheviks, in an effort to raise productivity, began to reemploy them in industrial enterprises, their hopes rose. As *Pravda* put it, from such a "bourgeoisie" there was nothing to fear.[58] The same applied to the socialist intelligentsia whom the Bolsheviks dubbed "petty bourgeois": they too, for their own reasons, refused to resist. They criticized the Bolsheviks, but whenever the opportunity presented itself to fight, they looked the other way.

The situation was different in the countryside. By Western standards, Russia, of course, had no "rural bourgeoisie," only a class of peasants who were marginally better off by virtue of a few hectares of additional land, an extra horse or cow, some cash, and the occasional services of a hired hand.

94. A typical peasant "bourgeois-capitalist."

But Lenin was obsessed with the image of "class differentiation" in the Russian village. As a young man, he had scrutinized *zemstvo* statistics, noting the slightest shifts in the economic condition of the various rural strata: anything that indicated a growing divergence between rich and poor peasants, no matter how minute, spelled to him a potential for social conflict which the revolutionaries could exploit.[59] To penetrate the village, he had to incite a civil war there, and to do that he required a class enemy. For this purpose he created the myth of a powerful, numerous, and counterrevolutionary class of kulaks bent on destroying the "proletariat."

The trouble was that whereas Hitler would be able to produce genealogical ("racial") criteria for determining who was a Jew, Lenin had no standards to define a kulak. This term never had a precise social or economic content: in fact, one observer, who spent the Revolution in the countryside, found that the peasants themselves did not use it.[60] It had entered the Russian vocabulary in the 1860s, at which time it referred not to an economic category but to a type of peasant who, by virtue of his personality, stood out from the mass of the communal peasantry: it was used to describe what in American slang would be called a "go-getter." Such peasants tended to dominate village assemblies and the *volost'* courts; sometimes they also acted as moneylenders, but this was not their defining quality. Radical publicists and novelists of the late nineteenth century, enamored of an ideal, perfectly egalitarian commune, gave kulaks a bad name as village exploiters, but there is no evidence that their fellow peasants regarded with hostility those to whom the term applied.[61] In fact, radical agitators who in the 1870s went "to the people" discovered that deep in his heart every peasant aspired to becoming a kulak. Not surprisingly, therefore, neither before nor after 1917 was it possible to distinguish a middle peasant from a kulak by any objective criteria—a fact that even Lenin, in a moment of candor, was forced to admit.[62]

How difficult it was to assign the term "kulak" a precise, operative meaning became apparent when the Bolsheviks attempted to unleash a class war in the countryside. To the commissars charged with organizing the "poor" peasants against the kulaks, this was a next-to-impossible task because they found nothing corresponding to these concepts in the communes with which they came in contact. In the province of Samara, one such official concluded that 40 percent of the peasants were kulaks,[63] while Bolshevik officials in the province of Voronezh informed Moscow that "it is impossible to wage the struggle against kulaks and the rich, because they constitute the majority of the population."[64]

But Lenin had to have a rural class enemy: as long as the village remained outside their political control and under SR influence, the Bolshevik bastions in the cities remained highly vulnerable. The refusal of the peasants to surrender food at fixed prices offered Lenin an opportunity to rally the urban population against the peasantry, ostensibly for the sake of extracting food but, in fact, as a device to bring it to heel.

It was Engels who had said that the poor and landless rural proletariat could, under certain conditions, become an ally of the industrial working class. Lenin adopted this point of view.[65] This premise he now put to use. In August 1918, he loosely bandied about statistics on the class structure of the Russian village which were to have deadly consequences. "Let us allow," he said,

> that we have in Russia some 15 million agricultural peasant families, taking into account previous Russia, before the robbers had detached from us the Ukraine, etc. Of this 15 million, certainly about 10 million are the poor, who live from the sale of their labor or enslave themselves to the rich, or who lack surplus grain and have been especially ruined by the burdens of the war. About 3 million must be counted as middle peasants, and hardly over 2 million are kulaks, rich men, bread speculators.[66]

These figures bore not the slightest relationship to reality: they merely repeated in rounded numbers the kind of calculations that Lenin used to make before the Revolution on the "class differentiation" of the Russian village. Thus, in 1899 he had calculated that the proportion of rich to middle to poor peasant households was 2 to 4 to 4. In 1907, he concluded that 80.8 percent of the peasant households were "poor," 7.7 percent "middle," and 11.5 percent well-to-do.[67] Lenin's most recent figures ignored the fact that, as a result of the agrarian revolution, the number of poor and rich peasants had declined. Half a year after declaring the "poor" to be two-thirds of the peasantry, he described the middle peasantry as the "most powerful force."[68] Clearly, his figures were not statistical data, but political slogans, drawn from Engels, who had laid it down in 1870, in regard to Germany, that "agricultural laborers form the most numerous class in the countryside."[69] Whatever validity this generalization may have had for late-nineteenth-century Germany, it had none for post-1917 Russia, where the "most numerous class in the countryside" consisted of self-employed middle peasants.

The vaunted "class differentiation" in the Russian village was also a figment of the imagination of urban intellectuals who drew their information from statistical abstracts. How did one define rural capitalism? According to Lenin, "the principal symptom and indicator of capitalism in agriculture is hired labor."[70] Now, according to the agrarian census of 1917, in the nineteen provinces for which information was available, only 103,000 rural households out of nearly 5 million employed hired labor, which would yield a proportion of rural "capitalists" equal to 2 percent. But even this figure loses significance when one takes into account that these 103,000 households employed a total of 129,000 laborers, or barely more than one per household.[71] Such laborers may have been hired because someone in the household had fallen ill or been drafted into the army. In any event, with a mere 2 percent of the households employing on the average one hired hand, it would stretch this concept to its most extreme limits to speak of the penetration of "capitalism" into the Russian village, let alone to claim that 2 million kulaks were exploiting 10 million "poor" peasants. Using another criterion—namely, lack of access to communal land—Communist statisticians have determined that less than 4 percent of the rural population qualified as "poor."[72]

Lenin ignored this empirical evidence: determined to unleash a "class war" between town and country, he drew a fantastic picture of socioeconomic conditions in the rural areas so as to have an excuse for invading them. His true criteria for determining who was "bourgeois" in the village were not economic but political: in his eyes, every anti-Bolshevik peasant qualified as a kulak.

The agrarian decrees which the Bolsheviks issued in May and June 1918 had a fourfold purpose: (1) to destroy the politically active peasants, almost to a man loyal to the SRs, by labeling them "kulaks"; (2) to undermine communal landholding and lay the groundwork for state-run collective farming; (3) to revamp the rural soviets by ejecting the SRs and replacing them with urban Bolsheviks or non-party Bolshevik sympathizers; and (4) to extract food for the cities and industrial centers. Food collection was given the greatest prominence in government propaganda, but in Bolshevik plans it was assigned the lowest priority. When the smoke cleared, the quantity of food extracted from the villagers turned out to be piddling: the political results were another matter.

The campaign against the village was conducted with the precision and brutality of a military operation. The main strategic decisions received approval at meetings of the Sovnarkom on May 8 and 9, presumably after having been previously voted on by the Bolshevik Central Committee. The Sovnarkom reconfirmed the state monopoly on the grain trade. The Commissar of Supply, Tsiurupa, received extraordinary powers to enforce the provisions of the decree of May 13,[73] which required every peasant to deliver his surplus grain to designated collection points in return for a payment at fixed prices. Peasants who failed to do so and hoarded their surplus or used it to make moonshine were declared "enemies of the people." The masses were exhorted by Lenin to wage a "merciless and terroristic war against the peasant bourgeoisie."[74] This campaign was designed as a two-pronged offensive against the "kulak": from within by means of a fifth column, composed of poor peasants organized into Committees of the Poor *(kombedy)*, and from without by means of "food detachments" *(prodovol'stvennye otriady)* of armed workers who were to march on the village and force the "kulaks" at gunpoint to disgorge their hoard.

The preamble of the May 13 decree accused the "village bourgeoisie" of having waxed rich on the war and refusing to sell food to the government so as to be able to dispose of it on the black market at speculative prices. The alleged aim of the rich peasants was to force the government to give up its monopoly on commerce in grain. Should the government succumb to this blackmail, the decree went on, ignoring the relationship between supply and demand, bread prices would skyrocket and place food entirely beyond the reach of workers. The "stubbornness" of village "kulaks" had to be broken: "Not a single pud of grain should remain in the hands of peasants except for that needed to sow the fields and feed their families until the next harvest." Detailed procedures were worked out concerning the manner in which food was to be extracted. Every peasant without exception was to deliver within one week of the decree all his surplus grain. Those who failed to do so were to be turned over to Revolutionary Tribunals, where they faced prison sentences of no less than ten years, confiscation of all property, and expulsion from the commune.*

Armed bands, sometimes formed into Red Guards, had been raiding villages in search of food since the preceding winter. They usually ran into fierce resistance from the peasants, reinforced by soldiers who had come home from the front with their weapons; they usually returned to town empty-handed.[75] Lenin had proposed in January 1918 the formation of "several thousand supply detachments," with ten to fifteen workers each, empowered to shoot recalcitrant peasants, but the idea failed to gain support.[76] It was only

*Tsiurupa defined as "surplus" all grain in excess of 12 puds of grain or flour (196 kilograms) per person and 1 pud (16.3 kilograms) of groats; he also established norms of feed for horses and livestock: *Izvestiia,* No. 185/440 (August 28, 1918), 5.

in the spring of 1918 that the Bolsheviks proceeded systematically to organize rural terror units. The earliest measure was an appeal to the workers of Petrograd, issued on May 21 over the signature of Lenin.[77] Other appeals and instructions followed. The notion of extracting food by force was clearly modeled on the *armée révolutionnaire* created, as one of its first acts, by the French Committee of Public Safety in June 1793, and accompanied by laws prohibiting the hoarding of produce.

Russian workers had no taste for such methods. They could be mobilized against the *burzhui* or the landlord, from whom they were separated by an unbridgeable cultural gulf, but not against the village, where many of them had been born and still had relatives. They felt none of the class animus against the peasant, even the relatively well-to-do peasant, which Lenin and his follow-ers attributed to them. The Left SRs, who enjoyed considerable support among Petrograd workers, protested against Bolshevik measures kindling class hatred between workers and peasants. The Left SR Central Committee actually for-bade its party members to enroll in the food detachments. Zinoviev ran into considerable difficulties when he tried to implement the May decrees, even though he offered the volunteers generous inducements. On May 24 he an-nounced that detachments would depart in search of food in two days, but hardly anyone turned up. Meetings at Petrograd factories, organized by work-ers' plenipotentiaries, passed resolutions opposing this measure.[78] Five days later, Zinoviev repeated the appeal, coupling it with a threat to the "bourgeoi-sie": "We shall give them 1/16th of a pound a day so they won't forget the smell of bread. But if we must go over to milled straw, then we shall put the bourgeoisie on it first of all."[79] The workers remained unmoved, preferring, with a common sense sorely lacking among the Bolshevik intelligentsia, to solve the food shortage by freeing the trade in cereals. In time, however, by a combination of threats and inducements, Zinoviev managed to form some food detachments, the first of which, a unit of 400 men, departed for the countryside on June 1.[80]

The food detachments proved disappointing. Since bona fide workers stayed away, the majority of those who joined up were urban riffraff that went to the village to loot. Lenin soon received complaints to this effect.[81] Shortly after the first supply detachments had made their appearance in the villages, he sent the following message to the workers of one industrial establishment:

> I very much hope that the comrade workers of Vyksa will carry out their admirable plan of launching a mass movement for bread with machine guns as genuine revolutionaries—that is, that they will staff the detachments with picked individuals, reliable men, not looters, who will work according to in-structions in full agreement with Tsiurupa for the common task of saving from hunger all those who go hungry and not only for themselves.[82]

Judging by peasant complaints, it was common practice for the armed bands from the cities to load up on stolen produce and get drunk on requisitioned moonshine.[83] Despite threats of severe punishment, such activities persisted and in the end the government had to allow members of food detachments to retain for their personal use up to 20 pounds of foodstuffs, including a maximum of 2 pounds of butter, 10 pounds of bread, and 5 pounds of meat.[84]

But neither threats of punishment nor concessions to self-interest worked and before long the regime had to turn to the newly formed Red Army. It was no coincidence that the decree introducing compulsory military service into Soviet Russia, issued on May 29, 1918, coincided with the establishment of food detachments. There was a revealing directive from Lenin's hand, drafted on May 26 and approved by the Central Committee the following day, which indicates that the earliest mission of the newly constituted Red Army was to wage war against the Russian peasant:

> 1. The Commissariat of War is to be transformed into a Military-Supply Commissariat—that is, nine-tenths of the work of the Commissariat of War is to concentrate on adapting the army for the war for bread and the conduct of such a war for three months: June–August.
> 2. During the same period, place the entire country under martial law.
> 3. Mobilize the army, separating its healthy units, and induct nineteen-year-olds, at least in some regions, for systematic operations to conquer the harvest and to gather food and fuel.
> 4. Introduce the death penalty for lack of discipline . . .
>
> .   .   .   .   .
>
> 9. Introduce collective responsibility for entire [supply] detachments, the threat of execution of every tenth for each incident of looting.[85]

Only the outbreak of the Czech rebellion prevented the entire Red Army from being assigned to fight the peasantry; even so, it played a considerable role in this campaign. As the Red Army was forming, Trotsky announced that its mission in the next two or three months would be "fighting hunger,"[86] which was a delicate way of saying "fighting the peasant." Although no medals were issued for this campaign, the war against the *muzhik* provided the Red Army with its first combat experience. Ultimately, 75,000 regular soldiers joined 50,000 armed civilians in battling the nation's food producers.[87]

The peasants responded to force with force. Contemporary newspapers are filled with accounts of pitched engagements between government units and peasants. The commanders of military and civilian units marching on the villages reported routinely on "kulak uprisings," but the evidence makes it clear that the resistance they encountered was spontaneous defense by the peasants of their property, involving not only the "rich" but the entire rural population. "When more carefully examined, the so-called kulak rebellions seem nearly always to have been general peasant uprisings, in which no class distinctions can be traced."[88] The peasants cared not a whit about the needs of the city and knew nothing of "class differentiation." All they saw was armed bands from the cities, often ex-peasants in leather jackets or army uniforms, come to rob them of their grain. They had never been made to surrender their harvest even under serfdom and they were not about to do so now.

The following contemporary newspaper account of incidents in the second half of 1918 in scattered rural areas is representative of the genre:

> When the supply detachment arrived in the Gorodishchenskaia *volost'* of Orel province, the women, instead of turning the produce over, dumped it into the water, and fished it out after the unexpected visitors had departed. In the Lavrov *volost'* of the same province, the peasants disarmed a "Red detachment." In Orel province requisitions are carried out on the broadest scale. Preparations are made as if for a regular war. "In some districts . . . during the requisitioning of bread, all private automobiles, saddle horses, and carriages have been mobilized." In the Nikolskaia *volost'* and its neighborhood regular battles take place: there are wounded and killed on both sides. The detachment requested by wire to have Orel send ammunition and machine guns. . . . It is reported from Saratov province . . . : "The village has become alerted and is ready for battle. In some villages of the Volskii district, the peasants met Red Army troops with pitchforks and compelled them to disperse." In Tver province, "the partisan detachments sent to the village in search of food meet everywhere with resistance; there are reports of encounters from various localities; to save the grain from requisition, the peasants hide it in the forests [and] bury it in the ground." At the bazaar in Korsun, in the province of Simbirsk, peasants came to blows with Red Army troops attempting to requisition grain; one Red Army soldier was killed, several were wounded.[89]

In January 1919, *Izvestiia* carried a report of a government investigation of a "White Guard kulak" uprising in a village in the province of Kostroma which illustrates what the assault on the village "bourgeoisie" really involved. The investigation revealed that the chairman of the village Executive Committee regularly beat peasant petitioners, sometimes with canes. Some of his victims were stripped of their shoes and forced to sit in the snow. So-called food requisitions were really ordinary robberies, in the course of which peasants were pummeled with Cossack *nagaiki.* As it approached a village, the food detachment would open machine gun fire to frighten the peasants. Then the beatings would begin. "The peasants had to put on five or more shirts to ward off the blows, but that did not do much good because the whips were laced with wire: after a beating the shirts stuck to the flesh and dried, so they had to be loosened by soaking in warm water." Members of the detachment urged the soldiers to beat the peasants with whatever they could lay their hands on, "so that they would remember Soviet authority."[90]

As the government pressed its campaign, the countryside rose in revolt. This was an event unprecedented in Russian history, for previous uprisings, such as Razin's or Pugachev's, had been regional affairs, usually confined to the eastern and southeastern borderlands. Nothing like it had ever occurred in the heartland of Russia. Rural resistance to the Bolsheviks that erupted in the summer of 1918 represented, in both extent and numbers involved, far and away the greatest peasant rebellion that the country had ever experienced.*

*One student of the subject makes the convincing case that in terms of numbers involved and the threat posed "the magnitude of the Bolshevik war with peasants on the internal front eclipsed by far the front-line civil war with the Whites": Vladimir Brovkin, "On the Internal Front: The

Its course, however, is still imperfectly known, because of the refusal of the authorities in charge of Soviet archives to release the relevant documents and the inexplicable lack of interest in the subject by Western historians.* The Cheka reported that in 1918 there occurred 245 rural "uprisings" *(vosstaniia)* which cost the lives of 875 Bolsheviks and 1,821 rebels. In addition, 2,431 rebels were executed.[91] This figure, however, can reflect only a fraction of the casualties, perhaps only those suffered by Cheka's own personnel. A recent work by a Communist historian states that, judging by incomplete data, between July and September 1918 alone, in twenty-two provinces, some 15,000 Soviet "supporters" *(storonniki)* had been killed, by which are meant Red Army troops, members of supply detachments, and Communist officials.[92] A history of the Communist Party in Cheliabinsk shows a photograph of a Red Army detachment of 300 men posing around a machine gun. According to the caption, the entire unit, save for a single survivor, perished in the course of a "kulak uprising."[93] Obviously, comparable casualties must have been incurred in other regions and provinces, on both sides.[94]

The anti-Communist peasant rising of 1918–19, whose course is not even approximately known, was ultimately suppressed. Although the peasant rebels exceeded government forces manifold, they were handicapped by lack of firepower and, above all, lack of organization: each rising was spontaneous and localized.[95] The SRs, despite their dominant role in the village, refused to organize the peasants, almost certainly out of fear of playing into the hands of the Whites.

Notwithstanding the brutality of the supply detachments, only negligible food supplies reached the cities: the little food that they managed to extract was appropriated by their members. On July 24, 1918, two months after the food detachments had been instituted, Lenin informed Stalin that as yet no food had reached either Petrograd or Moscow.[96] This fiasco of the most brutal policy conceivable drove Lenin into paroxysms of fury. As the time for the harvest approached and dispatches from the rural "front" indicated continued lack of success, he berated Bolshevik commanders for their irresolution and ordered ever more savage reprisals. On August 10, he cabled Tsiurupa:

> 1. It is an arch-scandal, an insane scandal, that Saratov has bread and we are unable to collect it. . . .
> 2. A decree project: in every bread-producing district, 25–30 *hostages* from among the *rich,* who answer with their *lives* for the collection and delivery of *all* the surplus.[97]

Bolsheviks and the Greens," paper delivered at the 20th National Convention of the American Association for the Advancement of Slavic Studies, November 1988, 1.

*Information on "disturbances," whether by workers or peasants, was censored and newspapers which published it were often fined and even suspended. By early 1919, all such information had to be cleared by military censors, who routinely removed it from the handful of non-Bolshevik papers still allowed to appear: *DN,* No. 2 (March 21, 1919), 1. The only scholarly monograph on the subject is Mikhail Frenkin's *Tragediia krest'ianskikh vosstanii v Rossii 1918–1921 gg.* (Jerusalem, 1988). The 1918–19 uprisings are treated here in Chap. 4, pp. 73–111.

When Tsiurupa responded: "One can take hostages when one has real power. Does it exist? This is doubtful." Lenin wrote back: "I propose not to *take* the 'hostages' but to *designate* them."[98] This was the earliest mention of the practice of hostage-taking, which four weeks later, under the "Red Terror," would be carried out on a mass scale. That Lenin was earnest about this barbarian policy is evident from an instruction that he sent to Penza province, where a peasant revolt was in progress:

> While suppressing the uprising in the five districts, apply all efforts and adopt all measures in order to remove all the grain surpluses from their owners, accomplishing this concurrently with the suppression of the uprising. For this purpose designate in every district (designate, do not seize) hostages, by name, from among kulaks, rich men, and exploiters, whom you are to charge with responsibility for the collection and delivery to assigned stations or grain-collecting points and for turning over to the authorities of all the surplus grain without exception.
>
> The hostages are answerable with their lives for the accurate and prompt payment of the contribution . . .[99]

On August 6, Lenin decreed an "intensification of the merciless mass terror" against the "counterrevolutionary" part of the "bourgeoisie" and the "merciless extermination of the traitors" who used hunger as a "weapon." All who resisted seizures of surplus grain, including "bagmen," were to be turned over to Revolutionary Tribunals, and if caught armed, to be shot on the spot.[100] In a spell of mindless wrath, Lenin ordered that the "kulaks" be deprived not only of their surplus grain but also of that required to sow the next crop.[101] His speeches and written instructions of this period indicate that his frustration at the peasantry's resistance robbed him of the ability to think rationally. This is evident from his appeal to industrial workers in August 1918, in which he exhorted them to "the last, decisive battle":

> The kulak insanely detests Soviet authority and is ready to suffocate, to carve up hundreds of thousands of workers. . . . Either the kulaks will cut up a boundless number of workers, or the workers will mercilessly crush the uprisings of the thievish minority of the people against the power of toilers. There can be no middle ground here. . . . The kulaks are the most beastly, the coarsest, the most savage exploiters. . . . These bloodsuckers have waxed rich during the war on the people's want, they have amassed thousands and hundreds of thousands. . . . These spiders have grown fat at the expense of peasants, impoverished by the war, of hungry workers. These leeches have drunk the blood of toilers, growing the richer the more the worker starved in the cities and factories. These vampires have gathered and continue to gather in their hands the lands of landlords, enslaving, time and again, the poor peasants. Merciless war against these kulaks! Death to them.*

*Lenin, *PSS*, XXXVII, 39–41. Cf. Robespierre: "If the rich farmers persist in sucking the people's blood, we will turn them over to the people themselves. If we find too many obstacles in dealing out justice to these traitors, the conspirators, the profiteers, then we will have the people deal with them." Ralph Korngold, *Robespierre and the Fourth Estate* (New York, 1941), 251.

As one historian has aptly observed, "this was probably the first occasion when the leader of a modern state incited the populace to the social equivalent of genocide."[102] It was characteristic of Lenin to disguise an offensive action as self-defense, in this case defense against a completely imaginary threat on the part of the "kulaks" physically to annihilate the working class. His fanaticism on the subject knew no limits: in December 1919 he said that "we"—a pronoun he did not further define but which was unlikely to include himself and his associates—"will sooner all perish" than allow free trade in grain.[103]

To overcome peasant resistance, the Sovnarkom on August 19 placed the Commissar of War, Trotsky, in charge of all units involved in this action, including the civilian supply detachments, which had until then been subordinate to the Commissariat of Supply.[104] The following day Tsiurupa issued instructions militarizing the food-requisitioning operation. Supply detachments came under the command of the provincial and military authorities and were subject to military discipline. Each detachment was to have a minimum of 75 men and two or three machine guns. They were to maintain links with nearby cavalry units and arrange for combining several detachments into one should the strength of peasant resistance require it. Assigned to each detachment, as to regular Red Army units, was a political commissar, whose responsibility it was to organize the Committees of the Poor.[105]

As previously noted, these Committees of the Poor were intended to function as a "fifth column" inside the enemy camp that would assist the Red Army and the supply detachments. By playing on the economic resentments of the most indigent rural elements, Lenin hoped to rally them against the richer ones and, in the ensuing clash, gain political entry into the village.

His expectation was disappointed for two reasons. The actual social structure of the Russian village bore no resemblance to the one that he took as his point of departure: Lenin's notion that three-quarters of the peasants were "poor" was sheer fantasy. The "landless proletariat," the core of the village poor, constituted in central Russia at most 4 percent of the rural population: the remaining 96 percent were "middle peasants" with a scattering of "rich." The Bolsheviks thus lacked a realistic social base from which to instigate a class war in the village.

To make matters worse, even that 4 percent would not cooperate. Much as the peasants bickered among themselves, when threatened from the outside, whether by the authorities or by peasants from other areas, they closed ranks. On such occasions, rich, middle, and poor became as one family. In the words of a Left SR: "When the food detachments show up in a village, they obtain no food, of course. What do they accomplish? They create a united front from the kulaks to your landless peasants who fight the virtual war which the city has declared on the village."[106] A peasant foolhardy enough to turn informer against his fellow villagers, in the hope of securing the rewards promised him by the regime, signed his social and even physical death warrant: the moment the supply detachment withdrew, he would be chased out of the commune, if not killed. Under these conditions, the whole concept of pitting the "poor" against the "rich" in a "merciless" class war proved utterly unrealistic.

Lenin either did not know these facts or chose to ignore them because of overriding political considerations. As Sverdlov had conceded in May, the Bolshevik Government was weak in the countryside and it could insinuate itself there only by "inflaming civil war." The soviets, which had originated in the cities, were not popular among the peasants because they duplicated the village assembly, the traditional rural form of self-government. In the summer of 1918, most rural localities had no soviets; where they existed, they functioned rather perfunctorily under the leadership of the more outspoken peasants or the village intelligentsia, adherents of the SR Party. This situation Lenin was determined to change.

The ostensible purpose of the Committees of the Poor was to help the supply detachments and Red Army units uncover hoards of grain. But their true mission was to serve as nuclei of new rural soviets directed by reliable urban Communists and acting in strict conformity with the directives of Moscow.

The Ispolkom discussed the creation of these committees, or *kombedy*, on May 20 and decreed their establishment throughout Russia on June 11.[107] When it came up for discussion at the Ispolkom, there was vigorous criticism from the Mensheviks and the Left SRs,[108] which the Bolshevik majority overruled. The regime issued a "Decree concerning the organization and provisioning" of the village poor, which provided for the establishment in every *volost'* and large village *(selo)*, alongside existing soviets and under their supervision, of Committees of the Poor made up of both local peasants and new settlers, with the exclusion of "notorious kulaks and rich men," heads of households disposing of a surplus of grain and other produce, those who owned commercial and industrial establishments, and those who employed hired labor. The task of the committees was to help Red Army units and supply detachments locate and confiscate food hoards. To secure their cooperation, members of *kombedy* were promised a share of the confiscated hoard, free of charge until June 15 and at a token cost after that date. To make membership in the *kombedy* still more attractive, the committees were also authorized to confiscate from the "village bourgeoisie" and divide among themselves its equipment and inventory. Thus, one part of the rural population was encouraged to denounce and despoil the other.

Although the consequences for those to whom it applied were certain to be immense, the provisions of the decree were vague. Who were the "notorious kulaks and rich men" and how were they to be distinguished from other peasants who had surplus grain? In what sense were the *kombedy* subordinated to the local soviets, which had charge of local government and responsibility for food distribution?

As it turned out, the poor peasants were as unwilling to enroll in the *kombedy* as the industrial workers were to join the supply detachments. Despite immense pressure, as of September 1918, three months after they had been decreed, only one village in six was reported to have a Committee of the Poor. Many provinces, among them Moscow, Pskov, Samara, and Simbirsk— major agricultural regions—had none.[109] The government kept on allocating large sums of money for this purpose, without much success. Where rural soviets did not exist, the order was ignored. Where they did exist, they usually declared *kombedy* to be redundant, and instead created their own "supply commissions," which defeated the whole purpose of the undertaking.

Undaunted, the Bolsheviks pressed the campaign. Thousands of Bolsheviks and Bolshevik sympathizers were sent to the countryside to agitate, organize, and overcome the resistance of rural soviets. The following incident illustrates how such methods worked:

> From the protocols of the Saransk district conference of *volost'* and village soviets and the representatives of the Committees of the Poor held on July 26, 1918:
>> *Resolved:* that the functions of the Committees of the Poor are to be entrusted to the *volost'* and village soviets.
>
> After the vote had been taken, Comrade Kaplev [the deputy chairman] informed the conference in the name of the local committee of Communists-Bolsheviks that apparently the majority of those attending the conference had voted against the decision of the central authority due to a misunderstanding. For this reason, on the basis of the decree and instructions concerning the matter, the party will send to the localities its representatives, who will explain to the population the significance of the Committees of the Poor and proceed to organize them, in accordance with the [government's] decree.[110]

In this fashion, party officials invalidated the vote of the peasants rejecting the creation of Committees of the Poor. Using such strong-arm methods, by December 1918 the Bolsheviks organized 123,000 *kombedy,* or slightly more than one per two villages.[111] Whether these organizations actually functioned or even existed it is impossible to tell: one suspects that in many cases they existed only on paper. In the majority of cases, the chairmen of the *kombedy* either belonged to the Communist Party or declared themselves "sympathizers."[112] In the latter case they were under the thumb of outsiders, mainly urban *apparatchiki,* for at this time there were almost no peasants in the Communist Party: a statistical survey of twelve provinces of central Russia indicated in 1919 only 1,585 Communists in the rural areas.[113]

Moscow saw the *kombedy* as a transitional institution: it was Lenin's intention to have them transformed into soviets. In November 1918 he declared: "We shall fuse the *kombedy* with the soviets, we will arrange it so that the *kombedy* will become soviets."[114] The next day, Zinoviev addressed the Congress of Soviets on this subject. He declared that it was the task of the *kombedy* to reshape rural soviets so that they would resemble urban ones, that is, become organs of "socialist construction." This required nationwide "reelections" to the rural soviets on the basis of rules which the Central Executive Committee would lay down.[115] These rules were announced on December 2.[116] Here it was stated that because the rural soviets had been elected before the "socialist revolution" reached the countryside, they continued to be dominated by "kulaks." It had now become necessary to bring rural soviets into "full harmony" with the urban ones. Nationwide reelections to soviets on the village and *volost'* level were to take place under the supervision of the *kombedy*. To ensure that the new rural soviets acquired a proper "class" character, the executives of the provincial city soviets would supervise the elections and where necessary, remove from them undesirable elements.* Kulaks and other speculators and exploiters were to be disenfranchised. Ignoring the provisions of the 1918 Constitution that all power in the country belonged to the soviets, the decree defined the "main task" of the freshly elected rural soviets to be the "realization of all the decisions of the corresponding higher organs of the Soviet authority"—that is, the central government. Their own authority—closely modeled on that of the *zemstva* of tsarist Russia—was to be confined to raising the "cultural and economic standards" of their area by such means as gathering statistical data, promoting local industry, and helping the government to appropriate grain. In other words, they were to be transformed primarily into conveyors of bureaucratic decisions and secondarily into institutions charged with improving the living conditions of the population. Once they had accomplished their mission, *kombedy* were to be dissolved.†

The reelections to the *volost'* and village soviets, which took place in the winter of 1918–19, followed closely the pattern previously established by the Bolsheviks in the cities.[117] All executive posts were preassigned to members of the Communist Party as well as to "sympathizers" or "partyless." Since the peasants stubbornly elected and reelected their own candidates, Moscow devised methods that ensured the results it wanted. In most localities, the voting was done in the open,[118] which had an intimidating effect, since a peasant who did not vote as directed risked being labeled a "kulak." No party other than the Communist was allowed to participate: this was ensured by a provision that only those parties and factions could put up candidates which "stood on the platform of Soviet authority." Protests that the 1918 Constitution made no mention of parties taking part in soviet elections were brushed aside.[119] In many localities, Communist Party cells insisted on approving every candidate who stood for the election. If, these precautions notwithstanding, "kulaks" or other undesirables still managed to win executive positions, as seems frequently to have happened, the Communists resorted to their favorite technique

---

*This resembled the authority vested in the 1880s in tsarist governors, by virtue of which they were empowered to remove elected *zemstvo* officials unable to satisfy the monarchy's criteria of "reliability."

†E. H. Carr, (*The Bolshevik Revolution*, II, London, 1952, 159) errs, therefore, when he says that the dissolution order proved the failure of *kombedy*, inasmuch as they had been intended from the outset as transitional institutions.

of declaring the election invalid and ordering it repeated. This could be done as often as necessary until the desired results were obtained. One Soviet historian says that it was not uncommon for three or four or more "elections" to be held in succession.[120] And still, the peasants kept on electing "kulaks"— that is, non-Bolsheviks and anti-Bolsheviks. Thus, in Samara province in 1919 no fewer than 40 percent of the members of the new *volost'* soviets turned out to be "kulaks."[121] To put an end to such insubordination, the party issued on December 27, 1919, a directive instructing party organizations in the Petrograd region to submit to the rural soviets a single list of "approved" candidates.[122] This practice, in time extended to other areas, put an end to the rural soviets as organs of self-government.

If one were to assess the results of the Bolshevik campaign against the village in the military terms in which it was conceived, one would have to declare the village the winner. While the Bolsheviks did gain some of their political objectives, they failed both to divide the peasantry against itself and to extract from it significant quantities of food. Even its political gains were soon erased: for as the Red Army units were recalled in 1919 to meet the threat from the White armies, the village reverted to its old ways.

The extraction of foodstuffs also gave the regime little cause for satisfaction. Communist sources are uncharacteristically reticent about the quantities of food obtained by means of forceful seizures, but such evidence as they do provide suggests they were minuscule. It is said that during the 1918 harvest (lasting from mid-August to early November) the supply detachments, assisted by the Red Army, and the Committees of the Poor extracted from the twelve provinces with surpluses 35 million puds, or 570,000 tons, of grain.* Since the 1918 harvest yielded 3 billion puds, or 49 million tons,[123] it appears that all that effort and all that brutality—troops firing machine guns, pitched battles, hostages with death sentences hanging over their heads—brought in only one-hundredth of the harvest. The authorities acknowledged the failure of the policy of raiding the countryside when they introduced on January 11, 1919, taxation in kind *(prodovol'stvennaia razvërstka* or *prodrazvërstka)*, which replaced confiscations of all surplus with strict norms specifying the quantities the peasant had to turn over. These were established on the basis of the state's needs, without regard to the producers' ability to deliver. To ensure delivery, the government reverted to the Chinese-Mongol system of imposing quotas on districts and subdistricts, which then distributed the load among their villages and communes. The latter were bound, as in earlier tsarist days, by collective responsibility *(krugovaia poruka)* for meeting their obligations. This system, which at least introduced some order, originally covered grain and feed, but

*LS, XVIII, 158n. But Lenin, (PSS, XXXVII, 419) claimed that the regime obtained 67 million puds.

was later extended to include virtually all foodstuffs. For the goods which he was compelled to turn over the peasant received money which bought nothing: in 1920 Lenin described to the visiting Bertrand Russell with a chuckle how his government forced the *muzhik* to take worthless paper for his grain.*[124] And even so, barely two years later, in the spring of 1921, yielding to stubborn reality, Lenin, who had said that he would rather have everyone die of hunger than allow free trade in grain, had to back down and give up the grain monopoly.

The regime also failed to unleash a class war in the village. The small minority of "rich" peasants and the equally small minority of "poor" ones drowned in the sea of "middle" peasants, all three of whom refused to wage fratricidal war. In the words of one historian, "the kulak stood for the village and the village for the kulak."[125]

In two months, the Bolsheviks realized their mistake. On August 17, 1918, Lenin and Tsiurupa issued a special directive ordering a drive to win over the middle peasantry and unite it with the poor against the rich.[126] Lenin repeatedly asserted afterward that his regime was not an enemy of the middle peasant.[127] But such verbal concessions meant little, given that the middle peasant had the food and hence was the main victim of Bolshevik food-extraction policies.

Peasants were utterly confounded by Bolshevik agrarian policies. They had understood the "Revolution" to mean *volia,* or anarchy, which to them meant relief from all obligations to the state. Peasants were heard to complain: "They promised to turn over all the land, not to collect taxes, not to take into the army, and now what . . . ?"[128] Indeed, their obligations to the Communist state were much heavier than under tsarism: by calculations of Communist scholars at the very least twice as heavy, since they now consisted not only of taxes but also of forced labor and other obligations, of which the duty to cut and cart lumber was the most onerous.[129] The vocabulary of *sutsilism,* as they called it, which urban agitators tried to foist on them, struck the peasants as gibberish, and they reacted as they had always done under similar circumstances, retranslating foreign words into language familiar to them. They began to suspect they had been had, but they were determined to hold out, believing themselves to be indispensable and, therefore, invincible. In the meantime, common sense told them that as long as they could not dispose of it on the open market, there was no profit in producing a surplus. This led to a steady decline of food production that in 1921 would contribute greatly to the famine.

The Bolsheviks could claim to their credit that they had at last penetrated the village by inserting there a network of soviets under their control. But this was to some extent an illusion. Studies carried out in the early 1920s revealed

---

*"When I put a question to [Lenin] about socialism in agriculture, he explained with glee how he had incited the poorer peasants against the richer ones, 'and they soon hanged them from the nearest tree—ha! ha! ha!' His guffaw at the thought of those massacred made my blood run cold." Bertrand Russell, *Unpopular Essays* (New York, 1950), 171.

that the villages ignored the Communist soviets, set up at such cost and effort. Authority by then had reverted to communal organizations, run by heads of households, just as if there had been no Revolution. The village soviets had to obtain approval of their resolutions from the commune; many did not even have their own budget.[130]

In the light of these facts, it is astonishing to have Lenin claim that the campaign against the village had not only been a complete success but transcended in historic importance the October coup. In December 1918 he boasted that during the past year the regime had solved problems that "in previous revolutions had been the greatest impediment to the work of socialism." In the initial stage of the Revolution, he said, the Bolsheviks had joined with the poor, middle, and rich peasants in the fight against the landlords. This alliance left the rural "bourgeoisie" intact. If that situation were allowed to become permanent, the Revolution would have stopped halfway and then inevitably receded. Such a danger was now averted because the "proletariat" had awakened the rural poor and together with them attacked the village bourgeoisie. The Russian Revolution thus had already progressed beyond the Western European bourgeois-democratic revolutions, creating the basis for a merger of the urban and rural proletariats and laying the groundwork for the introduction in Russia of collective farming. "Such is the significance," Lenin exulted,

> of the revolution which occurred during the current summer and fall in the most out-of-the-way corners of rural Russia. It was not noisy, it was not clearly visible, and it did not strike everyone's eyes as much as did the October Revolution of last year, but it had an *incomparably deeper and greater significance.* [131]

Of course, this was wild exaggeration. The Bolshevization of the village of which Lenin boasted would be accomplished only ten years later by Stalin. But, as in so many other respects, Stalin's course had been charted by Lenin.

Murder of the Imperial Family

On the night of July 16–17, 1918, at approximately 2:30 a.m. in the Ural city of Ekaterinburg, a squad of Chekists murdered, in the basement of a private home, the ex-Emperor, Nicholas II, his wife, their son and four daughters, the family physician, and three servants. This much is known with certainty. The steps that led to this tragedy, however, remain obscure, despite the immense literature, and will remain such until all the pertinent archives are thrown open to scholars.*

Two other European monarchs had lost their lives in consequence of revolutionary upheavals: Charles I in 1649 and Louis XVI in 1793. Yet, as is

---

*The basic account remains that of Nicholas A. Sokolov, the chairman of a special commission appointed by Admiral Kolchak to investigate the crime: *Ubiistvo tsarskoi sem'i* (Paris, 1925) (available in French and German translations). Of the secondary sources, the best are by Paul Bulygin, *The Murder of the Romanovs* (London, 1935) and S. P. Melgunov, *Sud'ba Imperatora Nikolaia II posle otrecheniia* (Paris, 1957). For the fate of the other Romanovs, the main source is Serge Smirnoff, *Autour de l'Assasinat des Grands-Ducs* (Paris, 1928). P. M. Bykov's Bolshevik account in its original version: "Poslednie dni poslednego tsaria," in N. I. Nikolaev, ed., *Rabochaia revoliutsiia na Urale* (Ekaterinburg, 1921), 3–26, is helpful. The dossiers of Sokolov's commission deposited at the Houghton Library of Harvard University are indispensable: a scholarly selection has been edited by Nicholas Ross, *Gibel' tsarskoi sem'i* (Frankfurt, 1987).

In 1989, the Soviet press began to publish important new materials. The most valuable are the recollections of Ia. M. Iurovskii, the commandant of the murder squad, published by Edvard Radzinskii in *Ogonëk*, No. 21 (1989), 4–5, 30–32. The film producer Gelii Riabov, who claims to have discovered the remains of the Imperial family, brought out in *Rodina* (No. 4 and No. 5, for 1989) some interesting additional information; unfortunately it is edited in a very slipshod manner.

the case with so much that concerns the Russian Revolution, while the super-ficial features of events are familiar, all else is unique. Charles I was tried by a specially constituted High Court of Justice, which lodged formal charges and gave him an opportunity to defend himself. The trial was held in the open and its records were published while it was still in progress; the execution took place in public view. The same held true of Louis XVI. He was tried before the Convention, which sentenced him to death by a majority vote after a long debate, in the course of which a lawyer defended the king. The trial records, too, were published. The execution was carried out in broad daylight in the center of Paris.

Nicholas II was neither charged nor tried. The Soviet Government, which had condemned him to death, has never published the relevant documents: such facts as are known of the event are mainly the result of the efforts of one dedicated investigator. In the Russian case, the victims were not only the deposed monarch but also his wife, children, and staff. The deed, perpetrated in the dead of night, resembled more a gangster-type massacre than a formal execution.

The Bolshevik seizure of power at first brought no significant change to the ex-Tsar's family and its retainers living in Tobolsk, where they had been exiled by Kerensky. In the winter of 1917–18, life in the Governor's House and its annexes went on much as before. The family was allowed to take walks, to attend religious services in a nearby church, to receive newspapers and correspond with friends. In February 1918, their state subvention was cut off and their allowance reduced to 600 rubles a month, but even so they lived in reasonable comfort. The Bolsheviks, who had their hands full with more urgent matters, gave little thought to the Romanovs, all of whom had with-drawn from public affairs. They discussed what to do with the ex-Tsar as early as November 1917 but took no decision.[1]

The situation began to change in March, in connection with the signing of the Brest-Litovsk Treaty. The treaty brought terrible odium to the Bol-shevik regime. In this atmosphere attempts at restoration could not have been precluded, the more so that the Bolsheviks were aware of pro-monarchist sentiments among German generals. To avoid trouble, precautions were taken to remove the Romanovs from the scene. On March 9, Lenin signed a decree ordering into exile Grand Duke Michael, the putative heir to the Russian throne. Michael had shown no interest in politics since rejecting the crown offered him by Nicholas in March 1917. He lived quietly on his estate at Gatchina, near Petrograd, shunning politics and keeping out of the public eye.[2] How unconcerned he was with political events may be gathered from the fact that a few days after turning down the throne, he appeared before the aston-ished officials of the Petrograd Soviet with a request for permission to hunt on his estate.[3] In the summer of 1917 he asked the British Ambassador for a visa to England, but was turned down with the explanation that "His Majesty's Government do not wish members of the Imperial Family to come to England during the war."[*4] At the end of 1917, Michael's petition to Lenin for permission to change his royal name to that of his wife's, Countess Brasova, received no response.[5]

Michael was now placed under arrest, first at Smolnyi and then at the Cheka headquarters. On March 12, following the departure of Lenin and the rest of the government for Moscow, he was sent under guard to Perm, not far from Tobolsk. Because the Bolsheviks feared that the Germans might occupy Petrograd and get hold of members of the Imperial family, they decided to remove them from this exposed area. On March 16, Uritskii, the head of the Petrograd Cheka, ordered all members of the family in Petrograd and vicinity to register.[6] Later that month, he issued a further order that all these individuals were to be deported to the provinces of Perm, Vologda, or Viatka, at their choice. Once there, they were to report to the local soviet and receive from it residential permits.[7] As it turned out, all the Romanovs, except those who were in prison or lived outside Bolshevik control, ended up in Perm. This region had the largest concentration of Bolshevik Party members after Petrograd and Moscow who could be relied upon to keep a sharp eye on the Imperial clan.

These were precautionary measures, for the Bolshevik leadership had not as yet decided what to do with the ex-Tsar and his relatives. In 1911 Lenin had written that "it was necessary to behead at least one hundred Romanovs."[8] Such mass execution, however, would be dangerous, because of the strong monarchist sentiments of the village. One possibility was to try Nicholas before a Revolutionary Tribunal. Isaac Steinberg, who as Commissar of Justice at the time was in a position to know, writes that such a trial was under consideration in February 1918 to prevent a restoration of the monarchy—tacit admission that one year after his universally welcomed abdication, the unpopular Nicholas appealed to enough Russians to worry the Bolsheviks. According to Steinberg, at a meeting of the Central Executive Committee, Spiridonova opposed a trial on the grounds that Nicholas would be lynched en route from Tobolsk. Lenin decided that it was still too early for legal proceedings against the ex-Tsar but ordered that materials for them be gathered.[†]

In the middle of April, the Russian press carried reports of an impending trial of "Nicholas Romanov." This, it was said, would be the first of a series of trials of prominent figures of the old regime which Krylenko was readying

---

*Michael's friend, O. Poutianine, therefore is incorrect in claiming that Michael refused to seek asylum in England in the belief that the Russian people would do him no harm: *Revue des Deux Mondes,* XVIII (November 15, 1923), 297–98.

†I. Steinberg, *Spiridonova, Revolutionary Terrorist* (London, 1935), 195. On January 12/25, 1918, *Vechernii chas* carried an interview with Steinberg in which he expressed confidence that a trial would take place: "As is known, it was originally proposed that the ex-Tsar be tried by the Constituent Assembly, but it now appears that his fate will be decided by the Council of People's Commissars." It has been confirmed since that the Council of People's Commissars passed on January 29, 1918, a resolution to turn Nicholas II over to a court: G. Ioffe in *Sovetskaia Rossiia,* No. 161/9,412 (July 12, 1987), 4.

as head of the Supreme Investigatory Commission. The ex-Tsar would be charged with only those "crimes" which he had committed as constitutional ruler—that is, after October 17, 1905. Among them would be the so-called coup d'état of June 3, 1907, which had violated the Fundamental Laws by arbitrarily changing the electoral law; the improper expenditure of national resources through the "reserved" part of the budget; and other abuses of authority.[9] But on April 22 the press reported a denial by Krylenko that Nicholas would be tried. According to Krylenko, the rumors were due to a misunderstanding: the government really meant to try an agent provocateur by the name of Romanov.[10]

The fact that Tobolsk had no railroad saved it from being immediately caught up in the revolutionary turmoil, for at this time the "Revolution" was spread mainly by gangs of armed men traveling by train. This explains why as late as February 1918 Tobolsk had no Communist Party cell and its soviet remained under the control of SRs and Mensheviks.

Tobolsk's isolation ended in March when the Bolsheviks of nearby Ekaterinburg and Omsk evinced an interest in its royal residents. In February, Ekaterinburg held a Congress of Soviets of the Ural Region at which it elected a five-man Presidium controlled by the Bolsheviks. Its chairman, the twenty-six-year-old Alexander Beloborodov, a locksmith or electrician by profession, had been Bolshevik deputy to the Constituent Assembly.* But the most influential member of the Presidium, by virtue of his intimate friendship with Sverdlov, was Isai Goloshchekin, the Military Commissar of the Ural Region. Born in Vitebsk in 1876 in a Jewish family, Goloshchekin had joined Lenin in 1903 and became a member of the Central Committee in 1912. Goloshchekin also served as member of the Ekaterinburg Cheka. He and Beloborodov were to play critical roles in the destiny of the Imperial family.

Our knowledge of the political situation in Ekaterinburg in the spring and summer of 1918 derives almost entirely from a single Communist source, the accounts of P. M. Bykov, which also provide the earliest Soviet version of the Ekaterinburg tragedy.† The Ekaterinburg Bolsheviks were annoyed by the comforts the ex-Tsar was enjoying in Tobolsk and alarmed by the degree of freedom allowed him and his entourage. They feared that with the coming of the spring thaws the Imperial family would flee.[11] At the time persistent

*On him see, *Granat*, XLI, Pt. 1, 26–29. Anti-Semitic monarchists, determined to blame the murder of the Imperial family on Jews, have decided that Beloborodov's real name was "Weissbart," for which there exists no evidence whatever.

†Bykov first published under the title "Poslednie dni poslednego tsaria" in N. I. Nikolaev, ed., *Rabochaia revoliutsiia na Urale* (Ekaterinburg, 1921), 3–26; this text was reprinted in *ARR*, XVII (1926), 302–16. He was subsequently given access to some unpublished materials, on the basis of which he drew up the official story: *Poslednie dni Romanovykh* (Sverdlovsk, 1926). The latter book has been translated into English, German, and French. For all its obvious tendentiousness it has value because it makes reference to documents locked up in Communist archives. Bykov was chairman of the Ekaterinburg Soviet after the October coup.

rumors circulated in the Urals that all sorts of suspicious individuals were assembling in and around Tobolsk.* Some of the Ekaterinburg Communists were extremists who hated Nicholas II—"Nicholas the Bloody"—with genuine passion because of the persecutions they had suffered at the hands of his police. But all of them were afraid of a restoration of the monarchy: not so much out of any abstract political considerations as from fear for their lives. They reasoned as did Robespierre when he pleaded in 1793 before the Convention for a sentence of death to be passed on Louis XVI: "If the king is not guilty, then those who have dethroned him are."[12] They wished the Romanovs out of the way as quickly and expeditiously as possible: and to make certain the ex-Tsar would not get away, they wanted him under their own control, in Ekaterinburg. To this end, in March–April 1918 they contacted Sverdlov.

Omsk had similar ideas, but it lacked connections in Moscow and in the end lost out.

The Ural Regional Soviet in Ekaterinburg discussed the Imperial family as early as February 1918, at which time some deputies expressed fears that by May, when the ice melted on the rivers, the Romanovs would either escape or be abducted. In early March the Ekaterinburg Bolsheviks requested from Sverdlov permission to remove the Imperial family.[13] A similar request came from Omsk.

To leave nothing to chance, Ekaterinburg dispatched on March 16 to Tobolsk a secret mission to investigate conditions there. After the mission had returned and delivered its report, Ekaterinburg sent an armed detachment to Tobolsk to lay the groundwork for the transfer of the Romanov family. It also posted patrols along possible routes of escape. Upon reaching Tobolsk on March 28, this detachment discovered that it had been preceded by a group of armed Communists sent by Omsk for the same purpose. The Omsk group, which had arrived two days earlier, had dispersed the city Duma and evicted the SRs and Mensheviks from the local soviet. The two groups disputed who was in charge. Being the weaker, the Ekaterinburg detachment had to retreat, but it returned on April 13 with reinforcements led by the Bolshevik S. S. Zaslavskii and took charge. Zaslavskii demanded that the Imperial family be incarcerated.[14] To this end, cells were readied in the local prison.[15]

These events disrupted the calm which the Imperial family had been enjoying until then. Alexandra noted in her diary on March 28/April 10 that she "sewed up" jewels with the help of the children.† Although no evidence has come to light that the Imperial family made plans to escape, and all alleged plots toward this end by sympathizers turned out to be empty talk, an oppres-

---

*Report of the Chekist F. Drugov, who says he heard it at the time (fall 1918) from a fellow Chekist, Tarasov-Rodionov: *IR*, No. 10/303 (February 28, 1931), 10. Drugov's account, however, loses some of its credibility because he reports having met and talked to Tarasov-Rodionov while traveling on a nonexistent railroad from Tobolsk to Ekaterinburg.

†The diaries of the ex-Empress, written in her idiosyncratic English, have never been published in entirety. The American journalist Isaac Don Levine brought out a photographic copy and published extensive excerpts in the Chicago *Daily News,* June 22–26 and 28, 1920, and in *Eyewitness to History* (New York, 1963).

sive sense that they were captives rather than exiles overcame the Imperial household. Any possibility, however remote and unreal, of escaping from the Bolsheviks now vanished.[16]

At the end of March, Goloshchekin left for Moscow. He reported to Sverdlov on the situation in Tobolsk, warning of the need for urgent measures to prevent the Imperial family's escape. Approximately at the same time—the first week of April—the Presidium of the CEC in Moscow also heard a report on the situation in Tobolsk from a representative of the local guard. According to an account given to the CEC by Sverdlov on May 9, this information persuaded the government to authorize the transfer of the ex-Tsar to Ekaterinburg. This explanation, however, is a post facto attempt to justify events which unfolded contrary to the government's intentions. For it is known that on April 1 the Presidium resolved "if possible" to bring the Romanovs to Moscow.[17]

On April 22, there appeared in Tobolsk Vasilii Vasilevich Iakovlev, an emissary from Moscow. Long a mysterious figure, suspected even of being an English agent, he has recently been identified as an old Bolshevik whose real name was Konstantin Miachin. Born in 1886 near Orenburg, he had joined the Social-Democratic Party in 1905 and taken part in many Bolshevik armed robberies ("expropriations"). In 1911 he emigrated under false identity (Iakovlev) and worked in Belgium as an electrician. He returned to Russia after the February Revolution. In October 1917 he served on the Military-Revolutionary Committee and was a delegate to the Second Congress of Soviets. In December 1917 he was appointed to the Collegium of the Cheka. He participated in the dispersal of the Constituent Assembly.[18] In other words, he was a tried and trusted Bolshevik.

Iakovlev-Miachin was silent about the ultimate purpose of his mission, and Communist sources have been similarly reticent. But it can be established with certainty that his task was to bring Nicholas, and, if feasible, the rest of his family, to Moscow, where the ex-Tsar was to stand trial. This can be established from circumstantial evidence: common sense dictates that the government would not have sent an emissary from Moscow to Tobolsk, nearly 2,000 kilometers away, to escort the Imperial family to nearby Ekaterinburg, especially since the Ekaterinburg Bolsheviks were most eager to have them in their custody. But there exists also direct evidence to this effect, supplied by N. Nemtsov, a Bolshevik commissar from Tiumen and chairman of the Perm Guberniia Central Executive Committee. Nemtsov recounts that in April he had a visit from Iakovlev, who appeared with a "Moscow detachment" of forty-two men:

> [Iakovlev] presented me with a mandate for the "removal" of Nicholas Romanov from Tobolsk and his delivery to Moscow. The mandate was

signed by the chairman of the Council of People's Commissars, Vladimir Ilich Lenin.*

This testimony, which somehow slipped by the exceedingly tight Soviet censorship on all information concerning the fate of the Romanovs, should put an end to speculation that Iakovlev either was under orders to bring the Romanovs to Ekaterinburg or that he was a secret White agent sent to abduct them and bring them to safety.

En route to Tobolsk, Iakovlev stopped in Ufa to meet with Goloshchekin. He showed his mandate and asked for additional men. From there he proceeded to Tobolsk, going not by the direct route through Ekaterinburg, but by a roundabout way through Cheliabinsk and Omsk.[19] He did so apparently out of fear that the Ekaterinburg hotheads, eager to lay their hands on Nicholas, would abort his mission, for the success of which he had assumed personal responsibility. Indeed, while he was en route to Tobolsk, Ekaterinburg attempted to anticipate him by sending a company of soldiers to bring back the ex-Tsar "dead or alive." Iakovlev almost caught up with this detachment, arriving in Tobolsk a couple of days later.[20] He had a guard of 150 cavalry, 60 of them provided by Goloshchekin. The party was armed with machine guns.

Iakovlev spent two days in Tobolsk acquainting himself with the situation. He met with the local garrison and won its favor by distributing its overdue pay. He also familiarized himself with conditions inside the Governor's House. He learned that Alexis was severely ill. The Tsarevich, who had suffered no hemophiliac attacks since the fall of 1912, had bruised himself on April 12 and since then was confined to bed. He was in great pain, with both legs swollen and paralyzed. Iakovlev twice visited the Imperial household and convinced himself that the Tsarevich indeed was in no condition to undertake the hazardous journey to Moscow. ("Intelligent, highly nervous workman, engineer" was Alexandra's impression of him.) April was the worst possible time for traveling in the Urals because by that time the snow had melted sufficiently to impede the movement of sleds and carts but not enough to free the rivers for navigation. On April 24, Iakovlev communicated with Moscow by wire: he was instructed to bring Nicholas alone and for the time being leave the family behind.[21]†

Up to this time, Iakovlev had been extremely polite, almost deferential, to the Imperial family, which aroused the suspicions of the soldiers of his entourage and of the Tobolsk garrison. They thought it highly suspect that a Bolshevik would so demean himself as to shake hands with "Nicholas the Bloody."[22] After receiving fresh instructions, Iakovlev retained his good man-

---

*Krasnaia niva, No. 27 (1928), 17. Avdeev in KN, No. 5 (1928), 190, confirms that Iakovlev carried a mandate from Lenin. According to I. Koganitskii (PR, No. 4, 1922, 13) Iakovlev had orders to bring Nicholas to Moscow, which suspicious local Bolsheviks authenticated by communicating with the capital.

†For purposes of security, the communications between Iakovlev and the Kremlin referred to the ex-Tsar and his family as "merchandise." The official in Moscow told Iakovlev to "bring only the main part of the baggage": Iakovlev in Ural, No. 7 (1988), 160.

ners but turned official. On the morning of April 25, he told E. S. Kobylinskii, the commandant of the Governor's House, that he had to remove the ex-Tsar; where to he would not say, although he apparently let it slip that the destination was Moscow. He requested an "audience," which was set for two o'clock that afternoon. On arriving in the Governor's House, Iakovlev was annoyed to find Nicholas in the company of Alexandra and Kobylinskii. He requested them to leave, but Alexandra made such a scene that he agreed to them staying. He told Nicholas that he had instructions from the Central Executive Committee to depart with him early the next day. His original orders had called for him to take along the entire family, but in view of Alexis's condition, he was now instructed to bring only Nicholas. The response of the ex-Tsar to Iakovlev's news is recorded in two versions. According to an interview which Iakovlev gave to *Izvestiia* the following month, Nicholas merely asked: "Where shall they take me?" Kobylinskii, however, recalls Nicholas saying: "I shan't go anywhere," which seems rather out of character. According to Kobylinskii, Iakovlev responded:

> Please, don't do that. I must carry out my orders. If you refuse to go, I will either have to use force or resign my mission. In that case, they may replace me with someone who will be less humane. You may rest easy. I answer with my head for your life. If you do not wish to travel alone, you may take with you whomever you wish. We depart at four tomorrow morning.[23]

Iakovlev's order threw the Imperial couple, especially Alexandra, into a state of extreme agitation. According to him, Alexandra cried out: "This is too cruel. I do not believe you will do that . . . !"[24] He would not say where he was to take Nicholas, and later, writing for a White newspaper, claimed that he did not know. This, of course, is untrue, and was probably intended to give credence to rumors, favorable to him at the time, after he had gone over to the Whites, that he really had meant to bring Nicholas into areas controlled by them.*

After Iakovlev left, Nicholas, Alexandra, and Kobylinskii discussed the situation. Nicholas agreed with Kobylinskii that he was to be brought to Moscow to sign the Brest Treaty. If so, the mission was in vain: "I will rather have my hand cut off than do this."[25] That Nicholas could believe the Bolsheviks needed his signature to formalize the Brest Treaty shows how little he understood of what had happened in Russia since his abdication and how irrelevant he had become. Alexandra, who also believed that this was the purpose of Iakovlev's mission, was far less confident of her husband's steadfastness: she had never forgiven him for agreeing to abdicate and felt certain that had she been in Pskov on that fateful day, she would have stopped him. She suspected that unbearable pressure would be brought on Nicholas in Moscow, mainly by threats against his family, to sign the disgraceful treaty and that unless she

---

*In October 1918, Iakovlev defected to the Whites and gave an interview to the newspaper *Ural'skaia zhizn'*; it is reprinted in the monarchist journal *RL*, No. 1 (1921), 150–53.

stood by his side he would cave in. Kobylinskii overheard her saying to a close friend, Prince Ilia Tatishchev: "I fear that if he is alone he will do something stupid there."[26] She was beside herself, torn between love for her sick child and what she felt to be her duty to Russia. And in the end the woman who for years had been accused of betraying her adopted country chose Russia.

The Tsarevich's Swiss tutor, P. Gilliard, who met with her at 4 p.m., describes the scene thus:

> The Czarina . . . confirmed that I had heard that Iakovlev has been sent from Moscow to take the Czar away and that he is to leave tonight.
>
> "The commissar says that no harm will come to the Czar, and that if anyone wishes to accompany him, there will be no objection. I cannot let the Czar go alone. They want to separate him from the family as they did before . . .
>
> "They're going to try to force his hand by making him anxious about his family . . . The Czar is necessary to them; they feel that he alone represents Russia . . . Together we shall be in a better position to resist them, and I ought to be at his side in the time of trial . . . But the boy is so ill . . . Suppose some complication sets in . . . Oh, God, what ghastly torture! . . . For the first time in my life I don't know what I ought to do; I've always felt inspired whenever I've had to take a decision, and now I can't think . . . But God won't allow the Czar's departure; it can't, it must not be. I'm sure the thaw will begin tonight . . ."
>
> Tatiana Nikolaevna here intervened:
>
> "But, Mother, if Father has to go, whatever we say, something must be decided . . ."
>
> I took up the cudgels on Tatiana Nikolaevna's behalf, remarking that Alexis Nikolaevich was better, and that we should take great care of him . . .
>
> Her Majesty was obviously tortured by indecision; she paced up and down the room, and went on talking, rather to herself than to us. At last she came up to me and said:
>
> "Yes, that will be best; I'll go with the Czar; I shall trust Alexis to you . . ."
>
> A moment later the Czar came in. The Czarina walked towards him, saying:
>
> "It's settled; I'll go with you, and Marie will come too."
>
> The Czar replied: "Very well, if you wish it." . . .
>
> The family have spent the whole afternoon at the bedside of Alexis Nikolaevich.
>
> This evening at half past ten we went up to take tea. The Czarina was seated on the divan with two of her daughters beside her. Their faces were swollen with crying. We all did our best to hide our grief and to maintain outward calm. We felt that for one to give way would cause all to break down. The Czar and Czarina were calm and collected. It is apparent that they are prepared for any sacrifices, even of their lives, if God in his inscrutable wisdom should require it for the country's welfare. They have never shown greater kindness and solicitude.
>
> This splendid serenity of theirs, this wonderful faith proved infectious.
>
> At half past eleven the servants were assembled in the large hall. Their

Majesties and Marie Nikolaevna took leave of them. The Czar embraced every man, the Czarina every woman. Almost all were in tears. Their Majesties withdrew; we all went down to my room.

At half past three the conveyances drew up in the courtyard. They were the horrible *tarantass*. Only one was covered. We found a little straw in the backyard and spread it on the floor of the carriages. We put a mattress in the one to be used by the Czarina.

At four o'clock we went up to see Their Majesties and found them just leaving Alexis Nikolaevich's room. The Czar and Czarina and Marie Nikolaevna took leave of us. The Czarina and the Grand-Duchesses were in tears. The Czar seemed calm and had a word of encouragement for each of us; he embraced us. The Czarina, when saying good-bye, begged me to stay upstairs with Alexis Nikolaevich. I went to the boy's room and found him in bed crying.

A few minutes later we heard the rumbling of wheels. The Grand-Duchesses passed their brother's door on their way to their rooms, and I could hear them sobbing . . .[27]

Iakovlev was in a desperate hurry. Any moment the thaw could set in and make the roads impassable. He also knew of lurking dangers. His orders were to safeguard the life of the ex-Tsar and deliver him safely to Moscow. But everything he had learned on his mission convinced him that the Bolsheviks of Ekaterinburg had different plans. The Bolshevik conference of the Ural Region at this very time voted in favor of a prompt execution of Nicholas to prevent his flight and a restoration of the monarchy.[28] Iakovlev had information that Zaslavskii, one of the Bolshevik commissars in Tobolsk, had fled to Ekaterinburg on the day of his arrival; there were rumors that he had set up an ambush at Ievlevo, where the road leading to the railroad junction of Tiumen crossed the Tobol River, with the intention of capturing and, if necessary, killing Nicholas.[29]

The party left as scheduled, traveling in *tarantassy* (or, as they are known in Siberia, *koshevy*), long, springless carts pulled by two or three horses. They were accompanied by a bodyguard of thirty-five. In front rode two men armed with rifles, followed by a cart with two machine guns and two more riflemen. Next came the *tarantass* carrying Nicholas and Iakovlev, who had insisted on sitting by the ex-Tsar. Behind were two more riflemen, the *tarantass* with Alexandra and Maria, followed by more riflemen, machine guns, and carts. Included in the party were Dr. Evgenii Botkin, the family's physician, Prince Alexander Dolgorukii, the Court Marshal, and three domestics. Alexandra put her favorite daughter, Tatiana, in charge of the boy and the two sisters. Iakovlev promised that as soon as the rivers became ice-free, which was expected to occur in two weeks, the children would rejoin their parents. He remained secretive about the ultimate destination: the Imperial couple knew only they were being taken to Tiumen, the nearest railroad junction, 230 kilometers away.

The road to Tiumen was in an atrocious condition, badly rutted after the winter and in parts dissolved in mud. Four hours from Tobolsk, they forded the Irtysh River, with the horses wading deep into the icy waters. Halfway, at Ievlevo, they ran into the Tobol River: here the water had flooded the ice and they crossed it walking on wooden planks. Just before Tiumen, they traversed the Tura River, partly on foot, partly by ferry. Iakovlev had organized along the way relays of horses, which reduced stops to a minimum. At one point, Dr. Botkin became ill and the party halted for two hours to allow him to recover. In the evening of the first day, after sixteen hours of travel, they arrived at Bochalino, where arrangements had been made to spend the night. Alexandra jotted down in her diary before retiring:

> Marie in a tarantass. Nicholas with Commissar Yakovlev. Cold, gray and windy, crossed the Irtish after changing horses at 8, and at 12 stopped in a village and took tea with our cold provisions. Road perfectly atrocious, frozen ground, mud, snow, water up to the horses' stomachs, fearfully shaken, pains all over. After the 4th change the poles, on which the body of the tarantass rests, slipped, and we had to climb over into another carriage-box. Changed 5 times horses . . . At 8 got to Yevlevo where we spent the night in house where was the village shop before. We slept 3 in one room, we on our beds, Marie on the floor on her mattress . . . One does not tell us where we are going from Tiumen, some imagine Moscow, the little ones are to follow us soon as river free and Baby well.[30]

En route Iakovlev permitted Alexandra to post letters and telegrams to the children. At one of the stops a peasant approached to ask where Nicholas was being taken. When told he was going to Moscow, the peasant responded: "Glory be to the Lord . . . to Moscow. That means we will now have order here in Russia again."[31]

The guards accompanying the party grew ever more suspicious of Iakovlev because of the deferential manner with which he continued to treat the ex-Tsar. They could not understand why Nicholas seemed so cheerful and began to wonder whether Iakovlev did not intend to spirit him away to eastern Siberia or even Japan. Through patrols which had been posted along the way, they communicated their misgivings to Ekaterinburg.

At 4 a.m. on April 27, after a night passed without incident—the expected ambush had not materialized—the journey resumed. At noon, the party stopped at Pokrovskoe. This village, one of thousands scattered across Siberia, had been the home of Rasputin. Alexandra noted: "stood long before our Friend's house, saw His family and friends looking out of the window."

According to Iakovlev, Nicholas seemed to flourish from the exercise and fresh air, while Alexandra "was silent, talked to no one, and acted proud and unapproachable,"[32] but both greatly impressed him: "I was struck by the humbleness of these people," he later told a journalist, "They never complained of anything."[33]

As far as one can determine from the confusing evidence, Iakovlev intended to get to Ekaterinburg as quickly as possible and, leaving it fast behind, proceed to Moscow. But he grew anxious about the prospects of getting his charges safely through that city. He would have been even more alarmed had he known that on April 27, while his party was on the second leg of its journey, a commissar from the Ekaterinburg Soviet appeared at the residence of the engineer Nicholas Ipatev, on the corner of Voznesenskii Prospekt and Voznesenskii Street, to inform him that his house was requisitioned for the needs of the Soviet and he was to vacate it within forty-eight hours.[34] Ekaterinburg had its own plans for the Romanovs.

Iakovlev's party arrived at Tiumen at 9 p.m. on April 27. There it was at once surrounded by a troop of cavalrymen, who escorted it to the railroad station, where stood a locomotive and four passenger cars. Iakovlev supervised the transfer of the Imperial family, its staff, and their belongings. Then Nemtsov appeared and, as the Romanovs retired to sleep, the two commissars went to the telegraph office. Using the Hughes apparatus, Iakovlev communicated to Sverdlov his misgivings about the intentions of the local Bolsheviks and requested authorization to remove the Imperial family to a safe place in Ufa province. In the course of a five-hour conversation, Sverdlov rejected this proposal. He agreed, however, to Iakovlev's proceeding to Moscow not directly, through Ekaterinburg, but by the same roundabout route he had taken earlier that month on his way to Tobolsk—that is, through Omsk, Cheliabinsk, and Samara. To conceal his plan, Iakovlev instructed the station master to send the train in the direction of Ekaterinburg, then, at the next station, attach a new engine, reverse directions and have it proceed at full speed through Tiumen toward Omsk.[35] At 4:30 a.m. on Sunday, April 28, the train bearing the Imperial family left for Ekaterinburg and then turned around. By way of explanation, Iakovlev told Avdeev, an associate of Zaslavskii's, he had information that Ekaterinburg intended to blow up the train.[36]

When he awoke in the morning, Nicholas noted with surprise that his train was traveling eastward. He wondered in his diary: "Where are they going to take us after Omsk? To Moscow or Vladivostok?"* Iakovlev would not say. Maria struck up a conversation with the guards, but even her beauty and charm failed to draw them out. Very likely they, too, were ignorant.

Ekaterinburg was advised in the early hours of the morning that the train with the Imperial family was on its way. It only learned of Iakovlev's ruse later in the day from a telegram sent by Avdeev. The Presidium declared Iakovlev "a traitor to the Revolution" and placed him "outside the law." Wires to this effect were dispatched in all directions.[37]

On receipt of this information, Omsk sent a military detachment to intercept Iakovlev's train before it reached the Kulomzino junction, where it could turn west and, bypassing Omsk, head for Cheliabinsk. When Iakovlev learned that he was accused of attempting to abduct his charges, he stopped the train at the Liubinskaia station. Leaving three passenger cars under guard, he detached the locomotive and proceeded in the fourth to Omsk, to communicate with Moscow. This happened during the night of April 28–29.

---

*Nicholas's diaries for 1918 are in *KA*, No. 1/26 (1928), 110–37.

The substance of Iakovlev's conversation with Sverdlov is known only from a most suspect secondhand account by Bykov:

> [Iakovlev] called Sverdlov to the telegraph and explained the circumstances which had caused him to change the itinerary. From Moscow came the proposition [*predlozhenie*] that he take the Romanovs to Ekaterinburg and there turn them over to the Ural Regional Soviet.*[38]

This version is almost certainly false, for three reasons. For one, Iakovlev did not "change the itinerary" but proceeded exactly as Sverdlov had instructed him during their previous conversation. Second, the powerful chairman of the All-Russian Central Executive Committee and Lenin's close confidant would not "propose" to a minor functionary, but would order him. Third, if Sverdlov indeed wanted Iakovlev to turn over the Imperial family to the Ekaterinburg Soviet, there would not have occurred the next day a three-hour altercation in Ekaterinburg between Iakovlev and the local Bolshevik Party. The most plausible explanation—though it is only conjecture—is that Sverdlov told Iakovlev to avoid getting into an argument with the Ekaterinburg Soviet, which mistrusted him, and to proceed to Moscow by way of Ekaterinburg so as to put to rest suspicions that he intended to abduct the ex-Tsar.

After talking to Sverdlov, Iakovlev ordered the engineer to reverse direction. All this transpired during the night, while Nicholas and family were asleep. On awakening in the morning of April 29, Nicholas noted that the train was now traveling westward, which confirmed his earlier belief that he was being taken to Moscow. Alexandra noted in her diary, most likely from information supplied by Iakovlev: "Omsk soviet would not let us pass Omsk and feared one wished to take us to Japan." Nicholas wrote on that day: "We are all in good spirits." Thus, the prospect of being delivered out of the hands of their tormentors to foreigners did not please them, but it raised their spirits to be taken to Russia's ancient capital, now the main citadel of Bolshevism.

They traveled all that day and the night that followed, with occasional stops, to cover the 850 kilometers between Omsk and Ekaterinburg. The voyage was uneventful. Iakovlev recalled that the ex-Tsarina was so painfully shy that she would wait for hours to go to the lavatory, until the car was clear of strangers, and remain there until she was sure there was no one in the corridor.[39]

The train pulled into the main Ekaterinburg station on April 30 at 8:40 a.m. Here a large hostile crowd had gathered, apparently assembled by the local Bolsheviks to pressure Iakovlev into turning over his charges. The events of the next three hours, during which the train stood in place, its passengers forbidden to leave, are shrouded in confusion. It seems that Iakovlev refused

---

*According to a recent account by a historian with access to the archives, Iakovlev talked with Sverdlov, who then communicated with Ekaterinburg, requesting "guarantees," presumably of the safety of the Imperial family. Ekaterinburg is said to have given these guarantees on condition that it be allowed to take charge of the prisoners: Ioffe in *Sovetskaia Rossiia*, No. 161/9,412 (July 12, 1987), 4.

to surrender Nicholas and Alexandra because they would not be safe in Ekaterinburg. According to Nicholas's diary: "We waited three hours at the station. A strong conflict [literally: fermentation] occurred between the local commissars and ours. In the end, the former won out." Nicholas, in his simplicity, believed that the argument was over which station to detrain, because shortly after noon they were shunted to a secondary, commercial depot, Ekaterinburg II. Alexandra knew better: "Yakovlev had to give us over to the Ural regional soviet," she wrote in her diary. The dispute between Iakovlev and the local commissars was indeed over the question whether the party would proceed to Moscow. Iakovlev lost the argument, possibly after the intervention of Moscow, which did not wish to antagonize the Ekaterinburg Bolsheviks and was not quite certain what to do with the Romanovs in any event. Leaving them in Ekaterinburg in safe hands, until some future trial of the ex-Tsar, may well have appeared to Lenin and Sverdlov as not a bad compromise.

Once the train pulled into Ekaterinburg II, Iakovlev turned over the prisoners to Beloborodov, obtaining from him a handwritten receipt which absolved him of further responsibility in the matter.[40] He demanded guards, presumably to protect the Imperial family from mob violence.[41] Before being allowed to depart for Moscow he had to explain his actions to the Ekaterinburg Soviet, which he apparently did to its satisfaction.[42] That he had done nothing wrong in the eyes of his superiors in Moscow is indicated by the fact that a month later he was appointed chief of staff of the Red Army forces in Samara and, subsequently, commander of the Second Red Army on the Eastern (Ural) Front.*

At 3 p.m. Nicholas, Alexandra, and Maria, accompanied by Beloborodov and Avdeev, were taken in two open cars to the center of town, followed by a truck which Alexandra described as filled with soldiers "armed to their teeth." According to Avdeev,[43] Beloborodov told Nicholas that the Central Executive Committee in Moscow had ordered him and his family detained until his forthcoming trial. The cars stopped at Ipatev's large, whitewashed house, which the owner had vacated the day before and which the Bolsheviks now called the "House of Special Designation." The Imperial family would not leave it alive.

Nicholas Ipatev, a retired army engineer, was a well-to-do businessman. He had acquired the house only a few months earlier, and used it partly as

---

*A. P. Nenarokov, *Vostochnyi front, 1918* (Moscow, 1969), 54, 72, 101. After defecting to the Whites later that year, Iakovlev was arrested by Czech counterintelligence. He fled to China, returned to the Soviet Union, and was arrested. After spending some time in a concentration camp at the Solovetskii Monastery, he was freed, and appointed commandant of an NKVD camp. Sometime later he was rearrested and executed. I owe this information to the Soviet writer, Mr. Vladimir Kashits.

95. Ipatev's house—the "House of Special Designation":
The murder occurred in the basement room with the
arched-frame window on the lower left.

residence, partly as business office. It was a two-story stone building, constructed in the late nineteenth century in the ornate style favored by Muscovite
boyars which returned to fashion at that time, with unusual luxuries such as
hot running water and electric lights. He had furnished only the upper story,
which consisted of three bedrooms, dining room, salon, reception room,
kitchen, bathroom, and lavatory. The lower story, a semi-basement, was
empty. The building had a small garden and several attached structures, one
of which was used to store the belongings of the Imperial family. While the
train was shuttling between Ekaterinburg and Omsk, workers had constructed
a crude palisade to conceal the house from the street and block the inmates'
view. On June 5, another, taller palisade was added.

The house was converted into a high-security prison. The palisades prevented any communication with the outside world; and as if this were not
enough, on May 15 the sealed windows were covered with white paint, except
for a narrow strip at the top. The prisoners were allowed to send and receive
a limited amount of correspondence, mainly with the children, which had to
pass through censorship by the Cheka and the soviet, but this privilege was
soon withdrawn. Once in a while outsiders were allowed in—priests and
charwomen—but conversation with them was forbidden. The guards too had
instructions not to speak with the prisoners. For a time newspapers were
delivered but that ceased on June 5. Food brought from town—at first from
the canteen of the soviet, later from a nearby convent—underwent inspection
by the guards. The prisoners' isolation was complete.

The guard of seventy-five men, all Russians except for two Poles,[44] recruited from among local factory workers, was divided into internal and

96. Ipatev's house surrounded by a palisade. Photograph
taken in the Fall of 1918 by an American soldier.

external detachments. They were well paid, receiving 400 rubles a month in
addition to food and clothing. The smaller internal detachments lived in
Ipatev's house; the external guard was initially billeted on the lower floor but
later moved into a private residence across the street. While on duty, the
guards carried revolvers and grenades. Two or three of them manned posts on
the upper floor, keeping the prisoners under constant surveillance. Four machine guns defended the house: on the second floor, on the terrace, on the
lower floor, and in the attic. Guards were posted outside, protecting the
entrances and ensuring that no unauthorized persons came near. Avdeev had
overall command. He set up his office and sleeping quarters in the reception
room on the upper floor.

Nicholas and Alexandra fretted about the children, but their worries
came to an end in the morning of May 23 when the three girls and Alexis
suddenly appeared. They had traveled by steamer on the Tobolsk River as far
as Tiumen, and from there by train. The girls had concealed in their special
corsets a total of 8 kilograms of precious stones. On arrival, the guards forbade
servants to help them with the luggage.

The Cheka arrested four retainers: Prince Ilia Tatishchev, Nicholas's
adjutant; A. A. Volkov, the Empress's valet; Princess Anastasia Gendrikova,
her maid of honor; and Catherine Schneider, the Court Lectrice. They were
taken to the local prison, to join Prince Dolgorukii, who had accompanied
Nicholas and Alexandra from Tobolsk. With a solitary exception, they were
all to perish. Most of the remaining members of the Imperial suite were told
to leave Perm province. Alexis's personal attendant, K. G. Nagornyi, and the
valet Ivan Sednev moved into Ipatev's residence. Dr. Vladimir Derevenko,
Alexis's physician, received permission to stay in Ekaterinburg as a private

citizen. He visited the Tsarevich twice a week, always in the company of Avdeev.

The Tobolsk party had brought a great deal of luggage, which was stored in the garden shed: members of the Imperial family frequently went there to fetch things, accompanied by guards. The guards helped themselves to the contents. When Nagornyi and Sednev protested the thefts, they were arrested (May 28) and sent to prison, where four days later the Cheka killed them. These pilferings caused Nicholas and Alexandra a great deal of anxiety because the baggage included two boxes with their personal correspondence and Nicholas's diaries.

At the end of May 1918, Ipatev's residence housed eleven inmates. Nicholas and Alexandra occupied the corner room. Alexis at first shared the bedroom of his sisters, but on June 26, for reasons which will be spelled out, moved in with his parents. The princesses had the middle room, where they slept on folding cots. A. S. Demidova, the lady-in-waiting, was the only prisoner to have a room to herself, next to the terrace. Dr. Botkin occupied the salon. In the kitchen lived the three servants: the cook, Ivan Kharitonov, and his apprentice, a boy named Leonid Sednev (a nephew of the arrested valet), and the valet of the princesses, Aleksei Trup.

The family settled into a monotonous routine. They rose at nine o'clock, took tea at ten. Lunch was served at one, dinner between four and five, tea at seven, supper at nine. They went to sleep at eleven o'clock.[45] Except for the meals, the prisoners were confined to their rooms. Life grew so dull that Nicholas began to skip entries in his journal. Much time was spent reading aloud from the Bible and from Russian classics, sometimes by candlelight because of the frequent power failures: Nicholas had his first opportunity to read *War and Peace*. The family prayed a great deal. They were allowed short

97. Alexis and Olga on board the ship *Rus* on their last journey from Tobolsk to Ekaterinburg: May 1918.

walks in the garden, fifteen minutes at most, but no physical exercise, which
was very hard on Nicholas. In good weather, Nicholas carried his disabled son
into the yard. They played bezique and Russian backgammon, called trick-
track. They were not allowed to attend church, but on Sundays and holidays
a priest would hold services in an improvised chapel in the salon, under the
watchful eye of the guards.

There exist many lurid stories about the abuse of the Imperial family at
the hands of the guards. It is said that the latter entered the rooms occupied
by the princesses any time of day or night, helped themselves to the food which
the family, at Nicholas's insistence, shared with their servants at a common
table, and even jostled the ex-Tsar. These stories, while not baseless, tend to
be exaggerated: the behavior of the commandant and his guards was undoubtedly rude, but no evidence exists of actual maltreatment. Even so, the conditions which the Imperial family endured were exceedingly painful. The guards
posted on the second floor amused themselves by accompanying the princesses
to the lavatory, demanding to know why they were going there and standing
outside until they came out.[46] It was not uncommon for obscene drawings and
inscriptions to be found in the lavatory and bathroom. A proletarian lad
named Faika Safonov amused friends with renditions of obscene ditties under
the windows of the Imperial prisoners.

The Romanovs bore their confinement, discomforts, and indignities with
remarkable serenity. Avdeev thought that Nicholas did not behave like a
prisoner at all, displaying "natural gaiety." Bykov, the Communist historian
of these events, speaks with irritation of Nicholas's "idiotic indifference to the
events occurring around him."[47] The behavior of the ex-Tsar and his family,
however, was due not to indifference but to a sense of decorum and a fatalism
rooted in religious faith. We shall, of course, never know what went on in the
minds of the prisoners, behind the façade of Nicholas's "natural gaiety,"
Alexandra's hauteur, and the children's irrepressible spirits, for they confided
in no one: Nicholas's and Alexandra's diaries for the period are logs rather
than intimate journals. But an unexpected insight into their inner feelings is
provided by the discovery among their belongings of a poem called "Prayer."
It was written by S. S. Bekhteev, a brother of Zinaida Tolstoy, a close friend
of Alexandra's, in October 1917 and sent to Tobolsk with a dedication to Olga
and Tatiana. In the papers of the Imperial family, two copies of this poem were
found, one in the hand of Alexandra, the other in that of Olga. It read:

> Give patience, Lord, to us Thy children
> In these dark, stormy days to bear
> The persecution of our people,
> The tortures falling to our share.
>   Give strength, Just God, to us who need it,
>   The persecutors to forgive,
>   Our heavy, painful cross to carry
>   And Thy great meekness to achieve.

> When we are plundered and insulted,
> In days of mutinous unrest,
> We turn for help to Thee, Christ-Savior,
> That we may stand the bitter test.
>> Lord of the world, God of Creation,
>> Give us Thy blessing through our prayer,
>> Give peace of heart to us, O Master,
>> This hour of deadly dread to bear.
> And on the threshold of the grave
> Breathe power divine into our clay
> That we, Thy children, may find strength
> In meekness for our foes to pray.[48]

In the spring of 1918, when they had confined Nicholas and his family in Ekaterinburg and the rest of the Romanov clan in other towns of Perm province, the Bolsheviks were placing them in what appeared to be a safe area: far away from the German front and the White Army, in the midst of a Bolshevik stronghold. But the situation in this territory changed dramatically with the outbreak of the Czech rebellion. By the middle of June, the Czechs controlled Omsk, Cheliabinsk, and Samara. Their military operations endangered the province of Perm, located directly north of these cities, and placed the Romanovs close to a battlefront where the Bolsheviks were in retreat.

What was to be done with them? In June, Trotsky still favored a spectacular trial:

> During one of my brief visits to Moscow—I believe it was a few weeks before the execution of the Romanovs—I remarked in passing to the Politburo that, considering the bad situation in the Urals, one should speed up the Tsar's trial. I proposed an open court that would unfold a picture of the entire reign (peasant policy, labor, nationalities, culture, the two wars, etc.). The proceedings of the trial would be broadcast nationwide by radio; in the *volosti,* accounts of the proceedings would be read and commented upon daily. Lenin replied to the effect that this would be very good if it were feasible. But . . . there might not be time enough. . . . No debate took place, since I did not insist on my proposal, being absorbed in different work. And in the Politburo there were only three or four of us: Lenin, myself, Sverdlov . . . Kamenev, as I recall, was not present. At that time Lenin was rather gloomy and had no confidence that we would succeed in building an army . . .[49]

By June 1918 the idea of a trial had ceased to be realistic. There exists convincing evidence that shortly after the outbreak of the Czech uprising, Lenin authorized the Cheka to make preparations for the execution of all the Romanovs in Perm province, using for pretext the device of contrived "escapes." On his instructions, the Cheka arranged for elaborate provocations in the three towns where members of the Romanov family were then either confined or living under surveillance: Perm, Ekaterinburg, and Alapaevsk. In Perm and Alapaevsk the plan succeeded; in Ekaterinburg it was abandoned.

A rehearsal for the massacre of Nicholas and his family was staged in Perm, the place of exile of Grand Duke Michael.[50] On his arrival in Perm in March, in the company of his secretary, the Englishman Nicholas Johnson, Michael was placed in jail. He was soon released, however, and allowed to take up residence, along with Johnson, a servant, and a chauffeur, in a hotel, where he lived in relative comfort and freedom. Although under Cheka surveillance, had he wished to escape he could have done so without difficulty, for he was permitted to move freely about town. But like the other Romanovs he displayed utter passivity. His wife visited him during the Easter holidays, but at his request returned to Petrograd, from where she eventually escaped and made her way to England.

On the night of June 12–13, five armed men drove up in a troika at Michael's hotel.[51] They awoke the Grand Duke and told him to dress and follow them. Michael asked for their credentials. When they could not produce any, he demanded to see the head of the local Cheka. At this point (as Michael's valet later told a fellow prisoner before being himself executed), the visitors lost patience and threatened to resort to force. One of them whispered something in the ear of either Michael or Johnson which seems to overcome their doubts. It is almost certain that they posed as monarchists on a rescue mission. Michael dressed and, accompanied by Johnson, entered the visitors' vehicle parked in front of the hotel.

The troika sped away in the direction of the industrial settlement of Motovilikha. Out of town, it turned into the woods and stopped. The two passengers were told to step out, and as they did so, they were cut down by bullets, probably shot in the back, as was the Cheka's custom at the time. Their bodies were burned in a nearby smelting furnace.

Immediately after the murder, the Bolshevik authorities in Perm informed Petrograd and cities in the area that Michael had escaped and a search was underway. Simultaneously, they spread rumors that the Grand Duke had been abducted by monarchists.[52]

The local newspaper, *Permskie Izvestiia,* carried the following report of the incident:

> During the night of May 31 [June 12] an organized band of White Guardists with forged mandates appeared at the hotel inhabited by Michael Romanov and his secretary, Johnson, abducted them, and took them to an unknown destination. A search party sent out that night found no trace. The searches continue.[53]

This was a tissue of lies. Michael and Johnson in fact had been abducted not by "White Guardists" but by the Cheka, headed by G. I. Miasnikov, an ex-locksmith and professional revolutionary, chairman of the Motivilikha Soviet. His four accomplices were pro-Bolshevik workers from the same town.

Since the myth of a "White Guard" plot could not be sustained once the remains of Michael and Johnson had been located by the Sokolov commission the next year, the subsequent official Communist version has claimed that Miasnikov and his accomplices had acted on their own, without authorization either from Moscow or from the local soviet—a version which must strain the credulity of even the most credulous.*

On June 17, newspapers in Moscow and Petrograd carried reports of Michael's "disappearance."† Concurrently rumors spread that Nicholas had been killed by a Red Army soldier who had broken into Ipatev's house.[54] These rumors could have originated spontaneously, but it is much more likely that they were intentionally floated by the Bolsheviks to test the reaction of both the Russian public and foreign governments to the killing of Nicholas, preparations for which were underway. What gives credence to this hypothesis is the extraordinary behavior of Lenin. On June 18, he gave an interview to the daily *Nashe slovo* in which he said that while he could confirm reports of Michael's escape, his government was unable to determine whether the ex-Tsar was dead or alive.[55] It was most unusual for Lenin to give an interview to *Nashe slovo,* a liberal newspaper and as critical of the Bolshevik regime as the conditions permitted, with which the Bolsheviks normally had no dealings. Equally curious was his pleading ignorance about the fate of the ex-Tsar, since the government could readily establish the facts of the case: as late as June 22, the Press Bureau of the Sovnarkom stated that it still did not know the fate of Nicholas, although it admitted to maintaining daily communication with Ekaterinburg.[56] This behavior of the government lends strong support to the hypothesis that Moscow spread these rumors to test the public reactions to the projected murder of the ex-Tsar.‡

Apart from aristocratic and monarchist circles, the Russian population, intelligentsia and "masses" alike, gave no indication of caring one way or another what happened to Nicholas. Nor was foreign opinion upset. A dispatch filed by the Petrograd correspondent of *The Times* of London on June 23 and published on July 3 carried an ominous hint:

> Every time this kind of public prominence is given to the Romanoff family people think that something serious is on foot. Bolshevists are getting impatient of these frequent surprises about the deposed dynasty, and the question is again

*Bykov, *Poslednie dni,* 121. Miasnikov later became one of the leaders of the Workers' Opposition, for which he was expelled from the party in 1921 and arrested in 1923. In 1924 or 1925 he turned up in Paris, where he peddled a manuscript describing Michael's murder. He is said to have published it in Moscow in 1924 (*Za svobodu!,* April 1925).

†E.g., *NVCh,* No. 91 (June 17, 1918), 1. A month later the Press Bureau of the Sovnarkom issued a communiqué that Michael had fled to Omsk and was probably in London: *NV,* No. 124/148 (July 23, 1918), 3.

‡P. B.[ulygin] in *Segodnia* (Riga), No. 174 (July 1, 1928), 2–3. Only on June 28 did the Soviet authorities confirm that Nicholas and his family were safe, having allegedly received a wire from Ekaterinburg from the commander in chief of the Northern Urals front, that he had inspected the Ipatev house on June 21 and found its residents alive: *NV,* No. 104/128 (June 29, 1918), 3. Cf. M. K. Diterikhs, *Ubiistvo tsarskoi sem'i i chlenov doma Romanovykh na Urale,* I (Vladivostok, 1922), 46–48. The delay of one week in reporting this information is inexplicable except in the context of deliberate dissimulation.

raised as to the advisability of settling the fate of the Romanoffs, so as to be done with them once for all.

"Settling the fate of the Romanovs" could, of course, only mean killing them. This rather crude feeler fell on deaf ears.

The indifference to these rumors inside Russia and abroad seems to have sealed the fate of the Imperial family.

On June 17, the family heard the welcome news that the nuns of the Novotikhvinskii Convent, whose previous requests of this nature had been rejected, would be allowed to deliver eggs, milk, and cream to them. As became subsequently known, this was done not out of concern for their well-being but as part of a Cheka plot.

On June 19 or 20, the Imperial prisoners received from the nuns a container of cream, the cork of which had concealed a piece of paper with the following message, carefully penned or more likely copied by someone with poor knowledge of French:

> Les amis ne dorment plus et espèrent que l'heure si longtemps attendue est arrivée. La revolte des tschekoslovaques menace les bolcheviks de plus en plus serieusement. Samara, Tschelabinsk et toute la Sibirie orientale et occidentale est au pouvoir de gouvernement national provisoir. L'armée des amis slaves est à quatre-vingt kilometres d'Ekaterinbourg, les soldats de l'armée rouge ne resistent pas efficassement. Soyez attentifs au tout mouvement de dehors, attendez et espérez. Mais en même temps, je vous supplie, soyez prudents, parce que les bolcheviks avant d'être *vaincus represent pour vous le peril réel et sérieux.* Soyez prêts toutes les heures, la journée et la nuit. Faite le croquis des *vos deux chambres,* les places, des meubles, des lits. Ecrivez bien l'heure quand vous allez couchir vous tous. L'un de vous ne doit dormir de 2 à 3 heure toutes les nuits qui suivent. Repondez par quelques mots mais donnez, je vous en prie, tous les renseignements utiles pour vos amis de dehors. C'est au même soldat qui vous transmet cette note qu'il faut donner votre reponse *par ecrit mais dites pas un seul mot.*
>
> Un qui est prêt a mourir pour vous
L'officieu [sic] de l'armée Russe.*

*"The friends sleep no longer and hope that the hour so long awaited has arrived. The revolt of the Czechoslovaks menaces the Bolsheviks ever more seriously. Samara, Cheliabinsk and all of eastern and western Siberia are under the control of the national provisional government. The army of the Slavic friends is eighty kilometers from Ekaterinburg, the soldiers of the Red Army are not resisting effectively. Be attentive to all outside movement, wait and be of good hope. But at the same time, I implore you, be prudent because the Bolsheviks, prior to being *defeated, represent for you a real and serious danger.* Be ready at all hours, day and night. Make a sketch of *your two rooms,* the places, the furniture, the beds. Write clearly the hour when all of you go to bed. One of you ought not to sleep between 2 and 3 every night from now on. Answer in a few words, but give, I beg you, all the useful information for your friends outside. Give your reply to the same soldier who transmits to you this note *in writing but say not one word.*

One who is prepared to die for you
An officer of the Russian army."

The response was supplied on the same sheet of crumpled notebook paper. Next to the inquiry about the hour when the family retired, is written "à 11½"; the query about "two rooms" is corrected to "three rooms." Underneath is written in a firm, legible hand:

du coin jusqu'au balcon. 5 fenêtres donnent sur la rue, 2 sur la place. Toutes les fenêtres sont fermées, collées et peintes en blanc. Le petit est encore malade et au lit, et ne peut pas marcher du tout—chaque secousse lui cause des douleurs. Il y a une semaine, qu'a cause des anarchist[es] on pensait a nous faire partir à Moscou la nuit. Il ne faut rien risquer sans être *absolument sûr* du résultat. Sommes presque tout le temps sous observation attentive.*

This secret message from alleged rescuers has some puzzling features. To begin with, its language. The letter is not written in a form which a monarchist officer would adopt toward his sovereign: it is hard to conceive that he would address him as "vous" instead of "Votre Majesté." Altogether, the vocabulary and style of this letter are so unusual that one investigator of the Ekaterinburg tragedy believed it to be an outright forgery.[57] Then there is the question of how the letter reached the prisoners. Its author refers to a soldier, presumably a guard. But Avdeev, the commandant of the Ipatev guards, writes that the secret letter was discovered in the cork of a bottle with cream brought by the nuns, and turned over to the Chekist Goloshchekin, who had it copied before delivering it to the prisoners. According to Avdeev,[58] the Cheka pursued the matter and found the author to be a Serbian officer by the name of "Magich," whom it arrested. There was, indeed, in the area a Serbian officer and member of the Serbian military mission to Russia, Major Jarko Konstantinovich Mičič (Michich), who had aroused suspicion by requesting to see Nicholas.[59] It is also known that Mičič traveled to the Urals to locate and rescue the Serbian Princess Helen Petrovna, the wife of Grand Duke Ivan Konstantinovich, interned at Alapaevsk. But it can be established from the recollections of Mičič's traveling companion, Serge Smirnov, that the two men had arrived in Ekaterinburg only on July 4, which meant that Mičič could not have written from there on June 19–20.[60]

Another possible bearer of the initial note was Alexis's physician, Dr.

*"from the corner up to the balcony. 5 windows face the street, 2 the square. All the windows are closed, sealed and painted white. The little one is still sick and in bed, and cannot walk at all—every concussion causes him pain. A week ago, because of the anarchists, thought was given to having us moved to Moscow at night. One must risk nothing without being *absolutely sure* of the result. We are almost all the time under careful observation."

The four letters smuggled to the Imperial family in late June and early July 1918, with their replies, were first published in Russian in the Moscow daily *Vechernye Izvestiia,* No. 208 (April 2, 1919), 1–2, and No. 209 (April 3, 1919), 1–2. In November 1919, the Communist historian Michael Pokrovskii provided photographic copies of the originals to Isaac Don Levine, who published them in English translation in the Chicago *Daily News,* December 18, 1919, and again in his autobiography, *Eyewitness to History* (New York, 1973), 138–41. Levine adopted the dating and sequence suggested to him by Soviet archivists, which, as can be established from internal evidence, cannot be correct. Letter #2 in his version should be Letter #3, and vice versa; Letter #4, which he dates June 26, had to have been written after July 4. Mrs. Levine kindly allowed me to make copies of her late husband's materials, and the correspondence appears here in the original French for the first time.

Derevenko. It is known, however, from Derevenko's deposition, given the Soviet authorities in 1931, that he was forbidden during his visits to have any communication with the prisoners.[61] It can be further established from Alexandra's diaries that he paid his last visit to Ipatev's house on June 21, which makes it theoretically possible for him to have carried the first secret message, but even this was not likely since, confirming Derevenko, Alexandra wrote that he never appeared "without Avdeev, so impossible to say one word to him."

It thus seems reasonable to suppose that the letter was fabricated by the Cheka and delivered to the prisoners by a guard involved in the provocation.*

According to Avdeev, Nicholas replied to the first letter two or three days after he had received it,[62] which would date it between June 21 and 23. The response was, of course, intercepted, setting in motion the Cheka's scheme.

On June 22, apparently in reaction to Nicholas's response, workers inspected the windows in the Imperial couple's bedroom. The next day, to the latter's delight, one of the double windows was removed and a ventilation pane opened, letting fresh air into the stuffy and hot upper floor. The prisoners were forbidden to lean out: when one of the girls stuck her head out too far, a guard fired.

On June 25, a second secret message arrived; a third followed on June 26. Incontrovertible evidence that these letters reached the Imperial family comes from the diary of Nicholas, who under the date June 14 [27] incautiously wrote: "We have recently received two letters, one after the other, which advised us to be ready to be spirited away by some devoted people!"

The second letter urged the recipients not to worry: their rescue carried no risks whatsoever. It was an astonishing assurance, even if one makes allowance for the desire of the alleged conspirators to allay the fears of the captives, given that they were surrounded by dozens of armed guards. It certainly casts the deepest doubts on its authenticity. It was "absolutely necessary," the letter went on, that one of the windows be unglued—which indeed had been arranged, two days earlier, by the obliging commandant. Alexis's inability to walk "complicated matters," but it was "not too great an inconvenience."

To this letter Nicholas responded at some length on June 25. He informed the correspondents that two days earlier one of their windows had indeed been opened. It was imperative to save not only them but also Dr. Botkin and the servants: "It would be ignoble for us, even if they do not want to burden us, to leave them behind after their following us into exile voluntarily." Nicholas then expressed concern over the fate of two boxes stored in the shed, a smaller one, labeled AF No. 9 (i.e., Alexandra Fedorovna No. 9), and a larger one, designated "No. 13 N.A." (Nicholas Alexandrovich), which contained "old letters and diaries."

*It has been recently revealed that this and the subsequent letters from alleged monarchist rescuers were drafted by one P. Voikov, a member of the Ural Ispolkom and a graduate of Geneva University, and copied by another Bolshevik with neater handwriting: E. Radzinskii in *Ogonëk*, No.2 (1990), 27.

The third letter from the stranger requested additional information. Regrettably, it might not be possible to rescue everyone, he wrote. He promised to provide a "detailed plan of operations" by June 30, and instructed the family to be on the alert for a signal (which he did not describe): as soon as they heard it, they were to barricade the door leading to the hall and descend from the open window by means of a rope which they were somehow to procure.

That night (June 26–27), in anticipation of the promised rescue attempt, Alexis was moved to his parents' room. The family did not go to sleep. "We spent an anxious night and kept vigil, dressed," Nicholas noted. But the signal never came. "The waiting and uncertainty were most excruciating."

What happened to have caused the Cheka to cancel its plan cannot be determined.

On the following night, Nicholas or Alexandra overheard a conversation that made them give up the thought of escape. "We heard in the night," Alexandra wrote on June 28, "sentry under our rooms, being told quite particularly to watch every movement at our window—they have become again most suspicious since our window is opened." This seems to have persuaded Nicholas to communicate to his correspondent a tortured note to the effect that he was not prepared to escape although he was not averse to being abducted:

Nous ne voulons et ne pouvons pas *FUIRE.* Nous pouvons seulement *être enlevés* par force, comme c'est la force qui nous a emmenés de Tobolsk. Ainsi, ne comptez sur *aucune aide active* de notre part. Le commandant a beaucoup d'aides, les changent souvent et sont devenu *soucieux.* Ils gardent notre emprisonnement ainsi nos vies consciencensement et son bien avec nous. Nous ne voulons pas qu'ils souffrent à cause de nous, ni vous pour nous. Surtout au nom de Dieu évitez l'effusion de sang. Renseignez vous sur eux vous même. Une descente de la fenêtre sans escalier est completement impossible. Même descendu on est encore en grand danger à cause de la fenêtre ouverte de la chambre des commandants et la mitrailleuse de l'étage en bas, où l'on pénètre de la cour intérieure. [Crossed out: Renoncez donc à l'idée de nous enlever.] Si vous veillez sur nous, vous pouvez toujours venir nous sauver *en cas* de danger imminent et réel. Nous ignorons completement ce qui si passe a l'extérieur, ne recevant ni journaux, ni lettres. Depuis qu'on a permi d'ouvrir la fenêtre, la surveillance a augmenté et on défend même de sortir la tête, au risque de recevoir un balle dans la figure.*

*"We do not want to and cannot *FLEE.* We can only be abducted by force, as it was force that carried us from Tobolsk. Thus, do not count on *any active assistance* from us. The commandant has many assistants, they are frequently changed and have become *anxious.* They attentively guard our prison as well as our lives, and are good to us. We do not want them to suffer because of us, nor you for us. Above all, for God's sake, avoid spilling blood. Obtain information about them yourselves. It is utterly impossible to descend from the window without a ladder. Even after the descent there still exists great danger because of the open window from the room of the commandants and the machine gun on the lower floor which one enters from the inside court. [Crossed out: "Therefore give up the idea of abducting us."] If you are watching over us, you can always come to save us *in case* of imminent and real danger. We are completely ignorant of what goes on outside, receiving neither newspapers nor letters. After permission has been given to open the window, the surveillance has intensified and it is prohibited even to put one's head out of the window, at the risk of getting a bullet in the face."

At this stage the spurious rescue operation was aborted. The Imperial family received yet another, fourth and final, secret communication, which had to have been written after July 4 because it requested information about the new commandant of Ipatev's, who replaced Avdeev on that day. It was a crude fabrication of the Cheka, which assured the Imperial family that its friends "D and T"—obviously, Dolgorukii and Tatishchev—had already been "saved," whereas in fact both had been executed the previous month.

After these experiences, the appearance of Nicholas and the children changed: Sokolov's witnesses told him they looked "exhausted."[63]

Although it has been the undeviating practice of Communist authorities then and since to lay responsibility for the decision to execute the Imperial family on the Ural Regional Soviet, this version, made up to exonerate Lenin, is certainly misleading. It can be established that the final decision to "liquidate" the Romanovs was taken personally by Lenin, most likely at the beginning of July. One could have inferred this fact much from the knowledge that no provincial soviet would have dared to act on a matter of such importance without explicit authorization from the center. Sokolov was convinced of Lenin's responsibility in 1925, when he published the results of his investigation. But there exists incontrovertible positive evidence to this effect from no less an authority than Trotsky. In 1935, Trotsky read in an émigré newspaper an account of the death of the Imperial family. This prodded his memory and he wrote in his diary:

> My next visit to Moscow took place after Ekaterinburg had already fallen [i.e., after July 25]. Speaking with Sverdlov, I asked in passing, "Oh yes, and where is the Tsar?" "Finished," he replied. "He has been shot." "And where is the family?" "The family along with him." "All?" I asked, apparently with a trace of surprise. "All," Sverdlov replied. "Why?" He awaited my reaction. I made no reply. "And who decided the matter?" I inquired. "We decided it here. Ilich thought that we should not leave the Whites a live banner, especially under the present difficult circumstances . . ." I asked no more questions and considered the matter closed.[64]

Sverdlov's offhand remark undercuts once and for all the official version that Nicholas and his family had been executed on the initiative of the Ekaterinburg authorities to prevent them from either escaping or being captured by the Czechs. The decision fell not in Ekaterinburg but in Moscow, at a time when the Bolshevik regime felt the ground giving way and feared a restoration of the monarchy—a prospect that only a year earlier would have appeared too fantastic to contemplate.*

*The Ekaterinburg massacre, once the details became known from the investigations of commissions set up by Admiral Kolchak, led to a revolting outpouring of anti-Semitic literature by some Russian publicists and historians, which found repercussions in the West. Much of this

At the end of June, Goloshchekin, the most powerful Bolshevik in the Urals and a friend of Sverdlov's, left Ekaterinburg for Moscow. His mission, according to Bykov, was to discuss the fate of the Romanovs with the Central Committee of the Communist Party and the Central Executive Committee of the Soviets.[65] That the Ekaterinburg Bolsheviks and Goloshchekin in particular wanted the Romanovs out of the way is well established: hence it can reasonably be deduced that he sought from Moscow authorization to proceed with the execution. Lenin approved this request.

The determination to execute the ex-Tsar, and possibly the rest of his immediate family, seems to have been taken in the first days of July, very likely at the meeting of the Sovnarkom in the evening of July 2. Two facts speak in favor of this hypothesis.

One of the items on the agenda of this Sovnarkom session was the nationalization of the properties of the Romanov family. A commission was appointed to draft a decree to this effect.[66] This could hardly have been considered an urgent matter in those critical days, given that all the Romanovs living under Communist rule were either in jail or in exile and their properties had long been taken over by the state or distributed to peasants. It seems likely, therefore, to have been raised in connection with the decision to execute Nicholas. A decree formally nationalizing the properties of the Romanov family was signed into law on July 13, three days before the murder, but in an unusual departure from practice not published until six days later—that is, on the day the news of the murder was made public.[67]

The other fact which speaks in favor of this conjecture is that immediately afterward, on July 4, the responsibility for guarding the Imperial family was shifted from the Ekaterinburg Soviet to the Cheka. On July 4, Beloborodov wired to the Kremlin:

> Moscow. Chairman Central Executive Committee Sverdlov for Goloshchekin. Syromolotov just departed to organize affairs in accord with center's instructions fears groundless stop Avdeev replaced his assistant Koshkin [Moshkin] arrested instead Avdeev Iurovskii internal guard all changed replaced by others stop Beloborodov*

Iakov Mikhailovich Iurovskii, the head of the Ekaterinburg Cheka, was the grandson of a Jewish convict sentenced for an ordinary crime and exiled to Siberia long before the Revolution. After a sketchy education he was ap-

---

literature blamed the Ekaterinburg massacre on Jews and interpreted it as part of a worldwide "Jewish conspiracy." In the account of the Englishman Robert Wilton, a London *Times* correspondent, and even more in that of his Russian friend, General Diterikhs, the Judeophobia assumed pathological dimensions. Probably nothing that happened at the time contributed more to the spread of anti-Semitism and the popularization of the spurious *Protocols of the Elders of Zion*. So determined were these writers to blame the tragedy on Jews, they conveniently forgot that the death sentence was passed by the Russian Lenin.

*Sokolov, *Ubiistvo*, Photograph No. 129, between pp. 248 and 249. A. M. Moshkin, Avdeev's assistant, was arrested on charges of stealing from the Imperial family.

98. The murderer of Nicholas II, Iurovskii (upper right), with his family.

prenticed to a watchmaker in Tomsk. During the 1905 Revolution he joined the Bolsheviks. Later he spent some time in Berlin, where he converted to Lutheranism. On returning to Russia, he was exiled to Ekaterinburg, where he opened a photographic studio said to have served as a secret meeting place for Bolsheviks. During the war, he underwent paramedical training. On the outbreak of the February Revolution, he deserted and returned to Ekaterinburg, where he agitated among soldiers against the war. In October 1917, the Ural Regional Soviet appointed him "Commissar of Justice," following which he joined the Cheka. He was by all accounts a sinister person, full of resentment and frustration, a type that gravitated to the Bolsheviks in those days and provided prime recruits for the secret police. From interrogations of his wife and family, Sokolov obtained the portrait of a self-important, willful man, with a domineering, cruel disposition.[68] Alexandra took an instant dislike to him, calling him "vulgar and unpleasant." He had several virtues which made him valuable to the Cheka: scrupulous honesty in dealing with state property, unrestrained brutality, and considerable psychological insight.

The first thing Iurovskii did upon taking charge of Ipatev's house was to put a stop to the stealing: this indeed presented a danger from the point of view of security, because thieving guards could be bribed to carry messages to and from the prisoners outside Cheka channels and even help them escape. On his first day, he had the Imperial family produce all the valuables in its possession (minus those which, unknown to him, the women had sewn into their undergarments). After making an inventory, he placed the jewelry in a sealed box, which he allowed the family to keep but inspected daily. Iurovskii also put a lock on the shed where the family's luggage was stored. Nicholas, always ready to think the best of others, believed that these measures were taken for his family's benefit:

> [Iurovskii and his assistant] explained that an *unpleasant* incident had occurred in our house; they mentioned the loss of our belongings. . . . I feel sorry for

Avdeev that he is guilty of not having prevented his men from stealing out of the trunks in the shed. . . . Iurovskii and his assistant begin to understand *what sort of people had surrounded and guarded us, stealing from us.**

Alexandra's diary confirms that on July 4 the internal guards were replaced by a fresh crew. Nicholas thought they were Latvians, and so did the captain of the guard when interrogated by Sokolov. But at the time the term "Latvians" was applied loosely to all kinds of pro-Communist foreigners. Sokolov learned that Iurovskii spoke with five of the ten new arrivals in German.[69] There can be little doubt that they were Hungarian prisoners of war, some of them Magyars, some Magyarized Germans.† They had moved from the Cheka headquarters, housed at the American Hotel.[70]

This was the execution squad. Iurovskii assigned them to the lower floor. He himself did not move into Ipatev's house, preferring to stay with his wife, mother, and two children. Into the commandant's room moved his assistant, Grigorii Petrovich Nikulin.

On July 7, Lenin instructed Ekaterinburg to grant the chairman of the Ural Regional Soviet, Beloborodov, direct wire access to the Kremlin. He acted in response to Beloborodov's request of June 28 for such access "in view of the extraordinary importance of events."[71] Until July 25, when Ekaterinburg fell to the Czechs, all communications between the Kremlin and that city on military matters and the fate of the Romanovs were conducted by means of this channel, often in cipher.

Goloshchekin returned from Moscow on July 12 carrying the death warrant. On the same day, he reported to the Executive Committee of the Soviet on "the attitude of central authority toward the execution of the Romanovs." He said that Moscow had originally intended to try the ex-Tsar, but in view of the proximity of the front, this ceased to be feasible: the Romanovs were to be executed.[72] The Committee rubber-stamped Moscow's decision.[73] Now, as afterward, Ekaterinburg assumed responsibility for the execution, pretending that it was an emergency measure to prevent the Imperial family from falling into Czech hands.‡

The following day, July 15, Iurovskii was seen in the woods north of Ekaterinburg. He was looking for a place to dispose of the bodies.

The Imperial family suspected nothing because Iurovskii maintained a strict routine at Ipatev's and with his solicitous manner even gained its trust. On June 25/July 8, Nicholas wrote: "Our life has not changed in any respect under Iurovskii." Indeed, in some respects it improved, for the family now received all the provisions brought by the nuns, whereas Avdeev's guards used

---

*According to Alexandra's diary, on July 6 Iurovskii returned to Nicholas a stolen watch.

†Sokolov found on a wall in Ipatev's house an inscription in Hungarian: "Verhás András 1918 VII/15e—Örsegen" (Andras Verhas July 15, 1918—Guard). Houghton Archive, Harvard University, Sokolov File, Box 3.

‡In memoirs written in 1920 but published only in 1989, Iurovskii said that the coded order for the "extermination" *(istreblenie)* of the Romanovs was received on July 16 from Perm. Perm was the provincial capital used by Moscow as a communications center for the Urals region. According to him, the final execution order was signed by Goloshchekin at 6 p.m. the same day. *Ogonëk*, No. 21 (1989), 30.

to steal them. On July 11, workmen installed iron railings on the single open window, but this too did not strike them as unusual: "Always fright of our climbing out no doubt or getting into contact with the sentry," Alexandra noted. Now that the Cheka had given up its plan of a spurious escape, Iurovskii wanted to take no chances on a genuine escape. On Sunday, July 14, he permitted a priest to come and say mass. As he was leaving, the priest thought he had heard one of the princesses whisper: "Thank you."[74] On July 15, Iurovskii, who had some medical knowledge, spent time with the bed-ridden Alexis, discussing his health. The next day he brought him some eggs. On July 16, two charwomen came to clean. They told Sokolov that the family seemed in fine spirits and that the princesses laughed as they helped them make the beds.

All this time, the Imperial family was still hoping to hear from their rescuers. The last entry in Nicholas's diary, dated June 30/July 13, reads: "We have no news from the outside."

Until recently, the bloody events which transpired at Ipatev's house on the night of July 16–17 were known almost entirely from the evidence gathered by Sokolov's commission. The Bolsheviks abandoned Ekaterinburg to the Czechs on July 25. Russians who entered the city with the Czechs rushed to Ipatev's house: they found it empty and in disarray. On July 30 an inquiry opened to determine the fate of the Imperial family, but the investigators allowed precious months to pass without any serious effort. In January 1919, Admiral Kolchak, recently proclaimed Supreme Ruler, appointed General M. K. Diterikhs to direct the work, but Diterikhs lacked the necessary qualifications and in February was replaced by the Siberian lawyer Nicholas Sokolov. For the next two years Sokolov pursued with unflagging determination every eyewitness and every material clue. When forced to flee Russia in 1920, he carried with him the records of his investigation. These materials and the monograph he wrote on the basis of them provide the principal evidence on the Ekaterinburg tragedy.* The recent publication of the recollections of Iurovskii supplements and amplifies the depositions of P. Medvedev, the captain of the guard, and additional witnesses whom Sokolov had questioned.[75]

The Imperial family spent July 16 in its customary manner. Judging by the final entry in Alexandra's diary, made at 11 p.m. as the family retired for

---

*A carbon copy of the Sokolov Commission's inquiry, in seven typewritten folders, is on deposit at Harvard's Houghton Library: it originally belonged to Robert Wilton, the Russian correspondent of *The Times* of London who accompanied Sokolov. The fate of the manuscripts, of which there were three, is discussed by Ross in *Gibel'*, 13–17. There is some additional evidence on the Ekaterinburg events in Diterikhs, *Ubiistvo tsarskoi sem'i*.

the night, they had no premonition that anything unusual was about to happen.

Iurovskii had been busy all that day. Having selected the place where the bodies were to be cremated and interred—an abandoned mineshaft near the village of Koptiaki—he arranged for a Fiat truck to park inside the palisade by the main entrance to Ipatev's house. At the approach of evening, he asked Medvedev to relieve the guards of their revolvers. Medvedev collected twelve revolvers of the Nagan type, standard issue for Russian officers, each capable of firing seven bullets, and took them to the commandant's room. At 6 p.m. Iurovskii fetched from the kitchen Leonid Sednev, the cook's apprentice, and sent him away: he told the worried Romanovs that the boy was to meet his uncle, the valet Ivan Sednev. He was lying, because the elder Sednev had been shot by the Cheka weeks before, but even so it was his only humane act during these days, for it saved the child's life. Around 10 p.m., he told Medvedev to inform the guards that the Romanovs would be executed that night and not to be alarmed when they heard shots. The truck, which was due at midnight, arrived one and half hours late, which delayed the execution.

Iurovskii awakened Dr. Botkin at 1:30 a.m. and asked him to arouse the others. He explained that there was unrest in the city and for their safety they were to be moved to the lower floor. This explanation must have sounded convincing, for residents of Ipatev's house had often heard sounds of shooting from the streets: the preceding day Alexandra noted hearing during the night an artillery shot and several revolver shots.* It took the eleven prisoners half an hour to wash and dress. Around 2 a.m. they descended the stairs. Iurovskii led the way. Next came Nicholas with Alexis in his arms: both wore military shirts and caps. Then followed the Empress and her daughters, Anastasia with her pet King Charles spaniel, Jemmy, and Dr. Botkin. Demidova carried two pillows, concealed in one of which was a box with jewelry. Behind her came the valet, Trup, and the cook, Kharitonov. Unknown to the family, the execution squad of ten, six of them Hungarians, the rest Russians, was in an adjoining room. According to Medvedev, the family "appeared calm as if expecting no danger."

At the bottom of the inner staircase, the procession stepped into the courtyard and turned left to descend to the lower floor. They were taken to the opposite end of the house, to a room previously occupied by the guards, five meters wide and six meters long, from which all furniture had been removed. It had one window, half-moon in shape, high on the outer wall, barred with a grille, and only one open door. There was a second door at the opposite end, leading to a storage space, but it was locked. The room was a cul-de-sac.

Alexandra wondered why there were no chairs. Iurovskii, as always

---

*Some accounts state that the Imperial family was told they would be taken to a safe place away from Ipatev's house, but this version is contradicted by the fact that they left their rooms without any of the items they would have been likely to take with them, including an ikon from which Alexandra never separated when traveling: Diterikhs, *Ubiistvo,* I, 25.

obliging, ordered two chairs to be brought in, on one of which Nicholas placed his son; Alexandra took the other. The rest were told to line up. A few minutes later, Iurovskii reentered the room in the company of ten armed men. He thus describes the scene that ensued:

> When the party entered, [I] told the Romanovs that in view of the fact that their relatives continued their offensive against Soviet Russia, the Executive Committee of the Urals Soviet had decided to shoot them. Nicholas turned his back to the detachment and faced his family. Then, as if collecting himself, he turned around, asking "What? What?" [I] rapidly repeated what I had said and ordered the detachment to prepare. Its members had been previously told whom to shoot and to aim directly at the heart to avoid much blood and to end more quickly. Nicholas said no more. He turned again toward his family. The others shouted some incoherent exclamations. All this lasted a few seconds. Then commenced the shooting which went on for two or three minutes. [I] killed Nicholas on the spot.[77]

It is known from eyewitnesses that the Empress and one of her daughters barely had time to cross themselves: they too died instantly. There was wild shooting as the guards emptied their revolvers: according to Iurovskii, the bullets, ricocheting from the walls and floor, flew around the room like hail. The girls screamed. Struck by bullets, Alexis fell off the chair. Kharitonov "sat down and died."

It was hard work. Iurovskii had assigned each executioner one victim and they were to aim straight at the heart. Still six of the victims—Alexis, three of the girls, Demidova, and Botkin—were alive when the salvos stopped. Alexis lay in a pool of blood, moaning: Iurovskii finished him off with two shots in the head. Demidova offered furious defense with her pillows, one of which had a metal box, but then she too went down, bayoneted to death. "When one of the girls was stabbed, the bayonet would not go through the corset," Iurovskii complained. The whole "procedure," as he calls it, took twenty minutes. Medvedev recalled the scene: "They had several gun wounds on various parts of their bodies; their faces were covered with blood, their clothes too were blood-soaked."[78]

The shots were heard on the street even though the truck engine was running to muffle them. One of the witnesses who testified for Sokolov, a resident of Popov's house across the street, where the external guard was billeted, recalled:

> I can reconstruct well the night from the 16th to the 17th in my memory because that night I couldn't get a wink of sleep. I recall that around midnight I went into the yard and approached the shed. I felt unwell and stopped. A while later I heard distant volleys. There were some fifteen of them, followed by separate shots: there were three or four of those, but they did not come from rifles. It was after 2 a.m. The shots came from Ipatev's house; they sounded muffled as if coming from a basement. After this, I quickly returned to my room, for I was afraid that the guards of the house where the ex-Emperor was held prisoner

could see me from above. When I returned, my next-door neighbor asked: "Did you hear?" I answered: "I heard shots." "Get it?" "Yes, I get it," I said, and we fell silent.[79]

The executioners brought sheets from the upstairs rooms, and after stripping the corpses of valuables, which they pocketed, carried them, dripping with blood, on improvised stretchers across the lower floor to the truck waiting at the main gate. They spread a sheet of rough military cloth on the floor of the vehicle, piled the bodies on top of one another, and covered them with a sheet of similar cloth. Iurovskii demanded under threat of death the return of the stolen valuables: he confiscated a gold watch, a diamond cigarette case, and some other items. Then he left with the truck.

Iurovskii charged Medvedev with supervising the cleaning-up. Guards brought mops, pails of water, and sand with which to remove the bloodstains. One of them described the scene as follows:

> The room was filled with something like a mist of gun-powder and smelled of gun-powder. . . . There were bullet holes on the walls and the floor. There were especially many bullets (not the bullets themselves but holes made by them) on one wall. . . . There were no bayonet marks anywhere on the walls. Where there were bullet holes on the walls and floor, around them was blood: on the walls there were splashes and stains, and on the floor, small puddles. There were also drops and pools of blood in all the other rooms which one had to cross to reach the courtyard of Ipatev's house from the room with the bullet holes. There were similar bloodstains on the stones in the courtyard leading to the gate.[80]

A guard who entered Ipatev's house the next day found it in complete disarray: clothing, books, and ikons lay scattered pell-mell on tables and floors, after they had been ransacked for hidden money and jewelry. The atmosphere was gloomy, the guards uncommunicative. He was told that the Chekists had refused to spend the rest of the night in their quarters on the lower floor and moved upstairs. The only living reminder of the previous residents was the Tsarevich's spaniel, Joy, who somehow had been overlooked: he stood outside the door to the princesses' bedroom, waiting to be let in. "I well remember," one of the guards testified, "thinking to myself: you are waiting for nothing."

For the time being, the external guards remained at their posts, creating the impression that nothing had changed at Ipatev's. The purpose of the deception was to stage a mock escape attempt during an "evacuation" in the course of which the Imperial family would be said to have been killed. On July 19, the most important belongings of the Tsar and Alexandra, including their private papers, were loaded on a train and taken by Goloshchekin to Moscow.[81]

Aware that the Russian people assigned miraculous powers to the remains of martyrs, and anxious to prevent a cult of the Romanovs, the Ekaterinburg Bolsheviks went to great pains to destroy all trace of their bodies. The place that Iurovskii and his associate, Ermakov, had selected for the purpose were woods near the village Kiptiaki, 15 kilometers north of Ekaterinburg, an area full of swamps, peat bogs and abandoned mineshafts.

A few miles out of town, the truck carrying the bodies ran into a party of twenty-five mounted men with carts:

> They were workers (members of the soviet, its executive committee and so on) assembled by Ermakov. They shouted: "Why did you bring them dead?" They thought they were to be entrusted with the execution of the Romanovs. They started to transfer the bodies to carts. . . . Right away they began to clean out [the victims'] pockets. Here too I had to threaten death by shooting and to post guards. It turned out that Tatiana, Olga, and Anastasia wore some kind of special corsets. It was decided to strip the bodies naked—not here, though, but where they were to be buried.

It was 6–7 a.m. when the party reached an abandoned gold mine nearly three meters deep. Iurovskii ordered the corpses undressed and burned.

> When they began to undress one of the girls, they saw a corset partly torn by bullets: in the gash showed diamonds. The eyes of the fellows really lit up. [I] had to dismiss the whole band. . . . The detachment proceeded to strip and burn the bodies. Alexandra Fedorovna turned out to wear a pearl belt made of several necklaces sewn into linen. (Each girl carried on her neck an amulet with Rasputin's picture and the text of his prayer.) The diamonds were collected; they weighed about half a pud [8 kilograms]. . . . Having placed all the valuables in satchels, other items found on the bodies were burned and the corpses themselves were lowered into the mine.[82]

What indignities were perpetrated on the bodies of the six women must be left to the reader's imagination: suffice it to say that one of the guards who took part in this work later boasted that he could "die in peace because he had squeezed the Empress's ———."[83]

It is this place, known to local peasants as "Four Brothers" for four large pines that once had grown here from a single stem, that Sokolov excavated for several months to unearth the Romanov remains. He located much material evidence—ikons, pendants, belt buckles, spectacles, and corset fastenings—all of which were identified as belonging to members of the Imperial family. A severed finger was also found, believed to be the Empress's, probably hacked off to remove a tight ring.* A set of false teeth was identified as belonging to Dr. Botkin. The executioners had not bothered to cremate the dog, Jemmy, whose decomposed corpse was found in the shaft. They either missed or accidentally dropped a ten-carat diamond belonging to the Empress, a present from her husband, and the ex-tsar's Ulm Cross, both left in the grass.

---

*It could have been Nicholas's, however: on July 4, Alexandra, referring to Iurovskii's demand that they turn over to him all jewelry, noted that her husband's engagement ring would not come off.

The remains of the victims, however, were nowhere to be found and this led for many years to conjectures that some or even most members of the Imperial family had survived the massacre. The mystery was cleared up only with the publication of Iurovskii's memoir, from which it transpires that the bodies were buried at Four Brothers only temporarily.

Iurovskii thought the Four Brothers' mine too shallow to conceal the grave. He returned to town to make inquiries, from which he learned of the existence of deeper mines on the road to Moscow. He soon returned with a quantity of kerosene and sulphuric acid. In the night of July 18, having closed neighboring roads, Iurovskii's men, helped by a detachment of the Cheka, dug up the corpses and placed them on a truck. They proceeded to the Moscow road but on the way the truck got stuck in mud. The burial took place in a shallow grave nearby. Sulphuric acid was poured on the faces and bodies of the victims and the graveside covered with earth and brushwood. The place of burial remained secret until 1989.

While the murderers were concealing traces of their crime, another act of the Romanov tragedy was played out at Alapaevsk, 140 kilometers northeast of Ekaterinburg. Here, the Bolsheviks had kept in confinement since May 1918 several members of the Imperial clan: Grand Duke Sergei Mikhailovich, Grand Duchess Elizaveta Fedorovna (the widow of Grand Duke Sergei Aleksandrovich, murdered by terrorists in 1905, and sister of the ex-Empress, now a nun), Prince Vladimir Pavlovich Palei (Paley), and three sons of Grand Duke Constantine—Igor, Constantine, and Ivan. Attended by aides and domestics, they lived under house arrest, in a school building outside Alapaevsk guarded by Russians and Austrians.

On June 21—the very time when the prisoners in Ipatev's house received the first communication from their alleged rescuers—the status of the Alapaevsk detainees changed. They were now put on a strict prison regime. Except for two retainers—a secretary named F. S. Remez and a nun—their companions were removed, valuables confiscated, and freedom of movement severely restricted. This was done on orders of Beloborodov, issued from Ekaterinburg, allegedly to prevent a repetition of the "escape" of Michael from Perm the week before.

On July 17, the day the Imperial family was murdered, the Alapaevsk prisoners were told they would be moved to a safer place. That evening the authorities staged a mock attack on the school building where the Romanovs were held by an armed band disguised as "White Guardists." The prisoners were said to have taken advantage of the ensuing melee to escape. In reality, they were taken to a place called Verkhniaia Siniachikha, marched into the woods, severely beaten, and killed.

At 3:15 a.m., July 18, the Alapaevsk Soviet wired Ekaterinburg, which had staged the whole charade, that the Romanov prisoners had fled. Later that day

Beloborodov cabled to Sverdlov in Moscow and Zinoviev and Uritskii in Petrograd:

> Alapaevsk Executive Committee informed attack morning 18th unknown band on building where kept onetime Grand Dukes Igor Konstantinovich Konstantin Konstantinovich Ivan Konstantinovich Sergei Mikhailovich and Poley [Paley] stop despite guard resistance princes were abducted stop victims on both sides searches underway stop.[84]

Autopsies performed by the Whites revealed that all the victims, save for Grand Duke Sergei, who apparently resisted and was shot, were still alive when thrown into the mineshaft where they were found. The five victims and the nun companion of Grand Duchess Elizaveta perished from lack of air and water, possibly only days afterward. The postmortem revealed traces of earth in the mouth and stomach of Grand Duke Constantine.[85]

Even if there did not exist incontrovertible evidence that the murder of the Romanovs had been ordered in Moscow, one would have strongly suspected this to have been the case from the fact that the official news of the "execution" of Nicholas was issued not in Ekaterinburg, where the decision had allegedly been made, but in the capital. Indeed, the Ural Regional Soviet was not permitted to make a public announcement of the event until five days after it had happened, by which time it had already been publicized abroad.

Although the evidence is inconclusive, it appears that Moscow ordered Ekaterinburg to withhold the announcement because of the very sensitive issue of the fate of the Empress and children.

The problem was the Germans, whom the Bolsheviks at this time went to extreme lengths to cultivate. The Kaiser was a cousin of Nicholas and a godfather of the Tsarevich. Had he been so inclined, he could have demanded that the ex-Tsar and his family be turned over to Germany as part of the Brest-Litovsk peace settlement, a demand that the Bolsheviks would have been in no position to refuse. But he did nothing. When in early March the King of Denmark asked him to intercede on their behalf, the Kaiser responded that he could not offer asylum to the Imperial family because the Russians would interpret it as an attempt at a restoration of the monarchy.[86] He also rejected the request of the Swedish King to help ease the plight of the Romanovs.[87] The most likely explanation of this behavior was provided by Bothmer, who thought it was due to fear of the German left-wing parties.*

For all its indifference to the fate of Nicholas, Berlin displayed some

---

*K. von Bothmer, *Mit Graf Mirbach in Moskau* (Tübingen, 1922), 104. A German scholar, defending the behavior of his country, cites the statement of Alexandra as recorded by the Tsarevich's tutor, Gilliard, that she would rather "die a violent death in Russia than be saved by the Germans": Jagow in *BM*, No. 5 (1935), 371. This may be true, but, of course, the German Government had no way of knowing at the time that she felt this way.

concern for the safety of the Tsarina, who was of German origin, her daughters, and the several other German ladies at the Russian court, among them Elizaveta Fedorovna, Alexandra's sister, whom they referred to collectively as the "German princesses." Mirbach raised the issue with Karakhan and Radek on May 10, and reported as follows to Berlin:

> Of course, without venturing to act as an advocate for the overthrown regime, I have nevertheless expressed to the commissars the expectation that the *German* princesses will be treated with all possible consideration and, in particular, that there will be no small chicaneries, let alone threats to their lives. Karakhan and Radek, who represented the indisposed Chicherin, received my remarks in a very forthcoming and understanding manner.[88]

On the morning of July 17, an official of the soviet in Ekaterinburg—almost certainly its chairman, Beloborodov—appears to have sent a cable to the Kremlin with a report on the events of the preceding night. The extremely detailed chronicle of Lenin's life, which traces his public activities hour by hour, notes cryptically in an entry under that date: "Lenin receives (at 12 noon) a letter from Ekaterinburg and writes on the envelope: 'Received. Lenin.' "[89] Since at this time Ekaterinburg did not communicate with the Kremlin by post but by direct wire, it can be taken for granted that the document in question was not a letter but a telegram. Second, the chronicle in question normally provides the gist of those messages to Lenin which it lists. The omission in this case suggests that it concerned the murder of the Imperial family, a subject which Communist literature invariably disassociates from Lenin. Apparently the message was not specific enough about the fate of Nicholas's wife and children, because the Kremlin telegraphed Ekaterinburg for clarification. Later that same day Beloborodov sent to Moscow a coded message which sounds as if it were a response to a query. Sokolov found a copy of this cable at the Ekaterinburg telegraph office. He was unable to break the code. This was accomplished only two years later in Paris by a Russian cryptographer. The document settled the question of the final fate of the Imperial family:

> MOSCOW Kremlin Secretary of Council of People's Commissars Gorbunov with return verification. Inform Sverdlov whole family suffered same fate as head officially family will perish during evacuation. Beloborodov.[90]

Beloborodov's message reached Moscow that night. The following day, Sverdlov announced the news to the Presidium of the All-Russian Central Executive Committee, carefully omitting to mention the death of Nicholas's family. He spoke of the grave danger of the ex-Tsar falling into Czech hands and obtained from the Presidium formal approval of the actions of the Ural Regional Soviet.[91] He did not bother to explain why the Imperial family had not been moved to Moscow in June or early July, when there had been ample time to do so.

Late that day, Sverdlov dropped in on a meeting of the Council of People's Commissars which was in progress in the Kremlin. An eyewitness describes the scene:

> During the discussion of a project concerning public health, reported on by Comrade Semashko, Sverdlov entered and took his seat, a chair behind Ilich. Semashko finished. Sverdlov approached, bent over Ilich, and said something.
> "Comrade Sverdlov asks for the floor to make an announcement."
> "I have to say," Sverdlov began in his customary steady voice, "that we have received information that in Ekaterinburg, by decision of the Regional Soviet, Nicholas has been shot. Alexandra Fedorovna and her son are in reliable hands. Nicholas wanted to escape. The Czechs were drawing near. The Presidium of the Executive Committee has given its approval."
> General silence.
> "We shall now proceed to read the project, article by article," Ilich suggested.
> The reading, article by article, got underway, followed by a discussion of the project on statistics.[92]

It is difficult to know what to make of this charade, for surely the members of the Bolshevik cabinet knew the truth.* Such procedures seemed to satisfy the Bolshevik need for formal "correctness" with which to justify arbitrary actions.

Sverdlov next drafted an official statement which he gave to *Izvestiia* and *Pravda* for publication the following day, July 19. As translated by *The Times* of London, where it appeared on July 22, it read as follows:

> At the first session of the Central Executive Committee elected by the Fifth Congress of the Councils a message was made public, received by direct wire from the Ural Regional Council, concerning the shooting of the ex-Tsar, Nicholas Romanoff.
> Recently Ekaterinburg, the capital of the Red Ural, was seriously threatened by the approach of the Czecho-Slovak bands. At the same time a counter-revolutionary conspiracy was discovered, having for its object the wresting of the tyrant from the hands of the Council's authority by armed force.
> In view of this fact the Presidium of the Ural Regional Council decided to shoot the ex-Tsar, Nicholas Romanoff. This decision was carried out on July 16.
> The wife and son of Romanoff have been sent to a place of security. Documents concerning the conspiracy which were discovered have been forwarded to Moscow by a special messenger.
> It had been recently decided to bring the ex-Tsar before a tribunal, to be tried for his crimes against the people, and only later occurrences led to delay in adopting this course. The Presidency of the Central Executive Committee, after having discussed the circumstances which compelled the Ural Regional

---

*Bruce Lockhart claims that Karakhan had told him already in the evening of July 17 that the entire Imperial family had perished: *Memoirs of a British Agent* (London, 1935), 303–4. One wonders why it did not occur to anyone to ask in whose "hands" were Nicholas's four daughters.

Council to take the decision to shoot Nicholas Romanoff, decided as follows: The Russian Central Executive Committee, in the persons of the Presidium, accept the decision of the Ural Regional Council as being regular.

The Central Executive Committee has now at its disposal extremely important material and documents concerning the Nicholas Romanoff affair: his own diaries, which he kept almost to the last days; the diaries of his wife and children; his correspondence, amongst which are letters by Gregory Rasputin to Romanoff and his family. All these materials will be examined and published in the near future.

Thus the official legend was born: that Nicholas—and he alone—was executed because he had attempted to escape and that the decision was made by the Ural Regional Soviet rather than the Bolshevik Central Committee in Moscow.

On and immediately following July 19, when *Pravda* and *Izvestiia* carried the first announcements of the alleged decisions of the Ekaterinburg Soviet— along with the decree nationalizing Romanov properties signed into law on July 13—the Ekaterinburg Soviet still maintained a stony silence.

The world press reported the story according to the official Bolshevik version. *The New York Times* broke the news on the front page of its Sunday edition, July 21, under the heading "Ex-Czar of Russia Killed by Order of the Ural Soviet. Nicholas Shot on July 16 When it was Feared that Czechoslovaks Might Seize Him. Wife and Heir in Security." The accompanying obituary patronizingly described the executed monarch as "amiable but weak." As Moscow had correctly anticipated from the indifference that had met rumors of Nicholas's death the preceding month, the world took the execution in stride.

On the day when the Soviet press broke the news, Riezler met with Radek and Vorovskii. He perfunctorily protested the execution of Nicholas, which he said world opinion was certain to condemn, but stressed again his government's concern for the "German princesses." Radek must have exercised supreme self-control when he responded that if the German Government was truly concerned about the ex-Empress and her daughters, they could be allowed to leave Russia for "humanitarian considerations."[93] On July 23, Riezler again raised the matter of the "German princesses" with Chicherin. Chicherin did not respond immediately, but the next day told Riezler that "as far as he knew" the Empress had been evacuated to Perm. Riezler had the impression that Chicherin was lying. By this time (July 22) Bothmer knew the "horrible details" of the Ekaterinburg events, and had no doubt that the entire family had been murdered on orders of Moscow, the Ekaterinburg Soviet having been given a free hand to determine the time and manner of the execution.[94] And yet as late as August 29, Radek proposed to the German Government to exchange Alexandra and her children for the arrested Spartacist, Leon Jogiches. Bolshevik officials repeated this offer on September 10 to the German Consul, but became evasive when pressed for details, claiming that the family of the ex-Tsar was cut off by military operations.[95]

On July 20, the Ural Soviet drafted an announcement and asked Moscow for permission to publish.[96] The announcement read:

> EXTRA EDITION. By Order of the Executive Committee of the Soviet of Workers', Peasants', and Soldiers' Deputies of the Urals and the Revolutionary Staff, the ex-Tsar and autocrat, Nicholas Romanov, has been shot along with his family on July 17. The bodies have been buried. Chairman of the Executive Committee, Beloborodov. Ekaterinburg, July 20, 1918, 10 a.m.*

Moscow forbade the release of this announcement because it referred to the death of Nicholas's family. In the only known copy of this document, the words "along with his family" and "the bodies have been buried" have been crossed out by someone with an illegible signature, who scribbled: "Forbidden to publish."

On July 20, Sverdlov wired to Ekaterinburg the text of the approved announcement which he had drafted and published in the Moscow press.[97] On July 21, Goloshchekin broke the news to the Ural Regional Soviet: A week before, apparently unknown to itself, it had decided to shoot the ex-Tsar. This decision had now been duly carried out. The population of Ekaterinburg was informed of this in broadsheets that were posted on July 22 and reproduced the following day in *The Ural Worker (Rabochii Urala)*. This newspaper ran the story under a headline: "White Guardists attempted to abduct the ex-Tsar and his family. Their plot was discovered. The Regional Soviet of Workers and Peasants of the Urals anticipated their criminal design and executed the all-Russian murderer. This is the first warning. The enemies of the people will no more achieve a restoration of autocracy than they succeeded in laying hands on the crowned executioner."[98]

On July 22, the guards protecting Ipatev's house were withdrawn: Iurovskii gave them 8,000 rubles to divide among themselves and informed them they would be sent to the front. That day Ipatev received a telegram from his sister-in-law: "Resident departed."[99]

Eyewitnesses agree that the population—at any rate, the inhabitants of the cities—showed no emotion when told of the ex-Tsar's execution. Services were held in some Moscow churches in memory of the deceased, but otherwise

---

*The text of this document has become available in the West under rather suspicious circumstances. In the spring of 1956 there appeared at the editorial offices of the West German mass-circulation weekly *7 Tage* an individual who identified himself as Hans Meier. He claimed to have been directly involved, as an Austrian POW, in the Ekaterinburg decision in 1918 to execute the Imperial family, and produced documents bearing on the matter which he said he had concealed for eighteen years while living in eastern Germany. His version of the events was full of fantastic details: its main purpose seems to have been to remove any doubt that Anastasia, stories of whose alleged survival began to circulate once again in the West, had perished along with the rest of the family. Meier's documents seem partly authentic, partly fabricated: the most probable explanation is that he acted on behalf of the Soviet security police. His account is in *7 Tage,* Nos. 27–35 (July 14–August 25, 1956). The above draft announcement, which appears authentic, was reproduced in *7 Tage* on August 25, 1956. On Meier's "evidence," see P. Paganutstsi in *Vremia i my,* No. 92 (1986), 220–21. The author states that a German court which inspected Meier's documents in connection with a suit brought by the so-called Anastasia declared them a forgery.

the reaction was muted. Lockhart notes that "the population of Moscow received the news with amazing indifference."[100] Bothmer had the same impression:

> The population accepted the murder of the Tsar with apathetic indifference. Even decent and cool-headed circles are too accustomed to horrors, too immersed in their own worries and wants, to feel something special.[101]

Ex-Prime Minister Kokovtsov even discerned signs of positive satisfaction while riding a Petrograd streetcar on July 20:

> Nowhere did I observe the slightest ray of pity or commiseration. The dispatch was read aloud, with smirks, jeers, mockeries, and with the most heartless comments. . . . One heard the most disgusting expressions, "It should have been done long ago" . . . "Eh, brother Romanov, your jig is up."[102]

The peasants kept their thoughts to themselves. But we have a glimpse of their reaction, expressed with their peculiar logic, in the thoughts which an elderly peasant confided in 1920 to an intellectual:

> Now, we know for sure that the landlords' land was given to us by Tsar Nicholas Alexandrovich. For this them ministers, Kerensky and Lenin and Trotsky and the others, first sent the Tsar off to Siberia, and then they killed him, and the Tsarevich too, so that we would have no tsar and they could rule the people forever themselves. They didn't want to give us the land, but our boys stopped them when they came to Moscow and Petrograd from the front. And now them ministers, because they had to give us the land, choke us. But they ain't gonna strangle us. We are strong and we will hold out. And later on, us oldsters, or our sons, or our grandchildren, it don't make no difference, we will take care of all them Bolsheviks and their ministers. Never you mind. Our time will come.[103]

During the next nine years, the Soviet Government stubbornly adhered to the official lie that Alexandra Fedorovna and her children were safe: Chicherin claimed as late as 1922 that Nicholas's daughters were in the United States.[104] The lie found favor with Russian monarchists who could not reconcile themselves to the thought that the entire Imperial family had been wiped out. On reaching the West, Sokolov was cold-shouldered by monarchist circles: Nicholas's mother, Empress Dowager Marie, and Grand Duke Nikolai Nikolaevich, the most prominent surviving Romanov, refused even to see him.[105] He died, ignored and impoverished, a few years later.

A Soviet participant, P. M. Bykov, in an early account of these events, published in Ekaterinburg in 1921, had told the truth about the fate of the family, but this work was promptly withdrawn from circulation.[106] Only in

1926, after the appearance of Sokolov's book in Paris had made the old version untenable, was Bykov authorized to write an official Communist account of the Ekaterinburg tragedy. This book, which Moscow had translated into the principal European languages, finally admitted that Alexandra and the children had perished along with the ex-Tsar. Bykov wrote:

> Much has been said about the absence of corpses. But . . . the remains of the corpses, after being burned, were taken quite far away from the mines and buried in mud, in an area where the volunteers and investigators did not excavate. There the corpses remained and by now have duly rotted.*

Iurovskii, having escaped from Ekaterinburg ahead of the Czechs, subsequently returned but later moved to Moscow, where he worked for the government. As reward for his services he was honored with an appointment to the Collegium of the Cheka: in May 1921, he was warmly received by Lenin.† The revolver with which he killed Nicholas was placed in the special depository of the Museum of the Revolution in Moscow. He died a natural death in August 1938 in the Kremlin hospital.[107] As a Chekist and "comrade-in-arms of Dzerzhinskii" he has earned himself a niche in the pantheon of minor Bolshevik heroes: he is the subject of a novel and of a biography, which depicts him as a "typical" Chekist: "closed, severe but with a soft heart."[108] The other principals in the Ekaterinburg tragedy fared less well. Beloborodov at first made a rapid career, being admitted in March 1919 to membership in the Central Committee and the Orgbiuro, and eventually attaining the rank of Commissar of the Interior (1923–27). But he was undone by his friendship with Trotsky: arrested in 1936, he was shot two years later. Goloshchekin was also a victim of Stalin's purges and perished in 1941. Both were subsequently "rehabilitated."

Ipatev's house served for many years as a club and a museum. But the authorities grew anxious over the number of visitors who came to Ekaterinburg (now renamed Sverdlovsk) to see the building, some of them seemingly on a religious pilgrimage. In the fall of 1977, they ordered it torn down.‡

---

*Bykov, *Poslednie dni,* 126. It is said that the first admission of the death of the family was made in P. Iurenev's "Novye materialy o rasstrele Romanovykh," *Krasnaia gazeta,* December 28, 1925 (Smirnoff, *Autour,* 25).

†*Leninskaia Gvardiia Urala* (Sverdlovsk, 1967), 509–14. An English officer, interested in the fate of the Imperial family, visited him in Ekaterinburg in 1919: Francis McCullagh in *Nineteenth Century and After,* No. 123 (September 1920), 377–427. Iurovskii kept a journal while commandant of Ipatev's house: it remains unpublished except for brief fragments in Riabov's article in *Rodina,* No. 4 (April 1989), 90–91.

‡The Ekaterinburg tragedy had a bizarre sequel. In September 1919, the Executive Committee of the Perm Soviet tried twenty-eight persons for the murder of the late Tsar, his family, and retainers. Although none is known to have had any connection with the event, the Left SR M. Iakhontov "confessed" to having ordered and personally participated in the murder of the Imperial family. He and four other defendants were sentenced to death for the alleged crime. The background and purpose of this mock trial cannot be determined: Robert Wilton, *The Last Days of the Romanovs* (London, 1920) 102–3, citing *Rossiia* (Paris), No. 1, December 17, 1919, with reference to *Pravda;* see also *New York Times,* December 7, 1919, p. 20.

In view of the tens of thousands of lives which the Cheka would claim in the years that followed the Ekaterinburg tragedy, and the millions killed by its successors, the death at its hands of eleven prisoners hardly qualifies as an event of extraordinary magnitude. And yet, there is a deep symbolic meaning to the massacre of the ex-Tsar, his family, and staff. Just as liberty has its great historic days—the battles of Lexington and Concord, the storming of the Bastille—so does totalitarianism. The manner in which the massacre was prepared and carried out, at first denied and then justified, has something uniquely odious about it, something that radically distinguishes it from previous acts of regicide and brands it as a prelude to twentieth-century mass murder.

To begin with, it was unnecessary. The Romanovs had willingly, indeed happily, withdrawn from active politics and submitted to every demand of their Bolshevik captors. True, they were not averse to being abducted and brought to freedom, but hope of escape from imprisonment, especially imprisonment imposed without charges or trial, hardly qualifies as the "criminal design" that it was designated by the Ekaterinburg Bolsheviks to justify the execution. In any event, if the Bolshevik Government indeed feared their fleeing and turning into a "live banner" for the opposition, it had ample time to bring them to Moscow: Goloshchekin had no difficulty leaving Ekaterinburg by train for the capital with the Imperial family's belongings three days later. There they would have been beyond the reach of Czechs, Whites, and other opponents of the Bolshevik regime.

If this was not done, the reason must be sought not in such spurious excuses as lack of time, the danger of flight, or of capture by the Czechs, but in the political needs of the Bolshevik Government. In July 1918 it was sinking to the nadir of its fortunes, under attack from all sides and abandoned by many of its supporters. To cement its deserting following it needed blood. This much was conceded by Trotsky when, reflecting on these events in exile, he concurred with Lenin's decision seventeen years earlier to dispatch the wife and children of the ex-Tsar—an act for which he bore no personal responsibility and therefore had no need to justify:

> The decision was not only expedient but necessary. The severity of this punishment showed everyone that we would continue to fight on mercilessly, stopping at nothing. The execution of the Tsar's family was needed not only to frighten, horrify, and instill a sense of hopelessness in the enemy but also to shake up our own ranks, to show that there was no retreating, that ahead lay either total victory or total doom.[109]

On one level, Trotsky's justification is without merit. Had the Bolsheviks indeed killed the ex-Tsar's wife and children in order to instill terror in their enemies and loyalty in their followers, they would have proclaimed the deed loud and clear, whereas in fact they denied it then and for years to come. But Trotsky's terrible confession is correct in a deeper moral and psychological sense. Like the protagonists in Dostoevsky's *Possessed,* the Bolsheviks had to spill blood to bind their wavering adherents with a bond of collective guilt. The more innocent victims the Bolshevik Party had on its conscience, the more the Bolshevik rank and file had to realize that there was no retreating, no faltering, no compromising, that they were inextricably bound to their leaders, and could only either march with them to "total victory," regardless of the cost, or go down with them in "total doom." The Ekaterinburg massacre marked the beginning of the "Red Terror," formally inaugurated six weeks later, many of whose victims would consist of hostages executed, not because they had committed crimes, but because, in Trotsky's words, their death "was needed."

When a government arrogates to itself the power to kill people, not because of what they had done or even might do, but because their death is "needed," we are entering an entirely new moral realm. Here lies the symbolic significance of the events that occurred in Ekaterinburg in the night of July 16–17. The massacre, by secret order of the government, of a family that for all its Imperial background was remarkably commonplace, guilty of nothing, desiring only to be allowed to live in peace, carried mankind for the first time across the threshold of deliberate genocide. The same reasoning that had led the Bolsheviks to condemn them to death would later be applied in Russia and elsewhere to millions of nameless beings who happened to stand in the way of one or another design for a new world order.

The Red Terror

Terror is for the most part useless cruelties
committed by frightened people to reassure
themselves.

—*F. Engels to K. Marx*[1]

Systematic state terror is hardly a Bolshevik invention: its antecedents go back to the Jacobins. Even so, the differences between Jacobin and Bolshevik practices in this respect are so profound that one can credit the Bolsheviks with having invented terror. Suffice it to say that the French Revolution culminated in terror, whereas the Russian one began with it. The former has been called a "brief parenthesis," a "countercurrent":[2] the Red Terror constituted from the outset an essential element of the regime, which now intensified, now abated, but never disappeared, hanging like a permanent dark cloud over Soviet Russia.

As in the case of War Communism, the Civil War, and other unsavory aspects of Bolshevism, Bolshevik spokesmen and apologists like to place the blame for terror on their opponents. It is said to have been a regrettable, but unavoidable reaction to the counterrevolution: in other words, a practice they would have shunned if given the chance. Typical is the verdict of Lenin's friend Angelica Balabanoff:

> Unfortunate though it might be, the terror and repression which had been inaugurated by the Bolsheviks had been forced upon them by foreign intervention and by Russian reactionaries determined to defend their privileges and reestablish the old regime.[3]

Such apologias can be dismissed on several grounds.

If terror had indeed been "forced" on the Bolsheviks by "foreign interventionists" and "Russian reactionaries," then they would have abandoned it as soon as they had decisively defeated these enemies—that is, in 1920. They did nothing of the kind. Although with the termination of the Civil War they did put an end to the indiscriminate massacres of 1918–19, they made certain to leave intact the laws and institutions which had made them possible. Once Stalin became undisputed master of Soviet Russia all the instruments which he required to resume the terror on an incomparably vaster scale lay at hand. This fact alone demonstrates that for the Bolsheviks terror was not a defensive weapon but an instrument of governance.

This interpretation is confirmed by the fact that the principal institution of Bolshevik terror, the Cheka, was founded in early December 1917, before any organized opposition to the Bolsheviks had had a chance to emerge and when the "foreign interventionists" were still assiduously courting them. We have it on the authority of one of the most sadistic functionaries of the Cheka, the Latvian Ia. Kh. Peters, that in the first half of 1918, when the Cheka began to experiment with terror, "counterrevolutionary organizations . . . as such were not observed."*

The evidence shows that Lenin, its most determined instigator, regarded terror as an indispensable instrument of revolutionary government. He was quite prepared to resort to it preventively—that is, in the absence of active opposition to his rule. His commitment to it was rooted in a deep-seated belief in the rightness of his cause and in an inability to perceive politics in hues other than pure white and pure black. It was essentially the same outlook that had driven Robespierre, to whom Trotsky had compared Lenin as early as 1904.[4] Like the French Jacobin, Lenin sought to build a world inhabited exclusively by "good citizens." This objective led him, like Robespierre, morally to justify the physical elimination of "bad" citizens.

From the time he formed the Bolshevik organization, for which he was proud to claim the title "Jacobin," Lenin spoke of the need for revolutionary terror. In a 1908 essay, "Lessons of the Commune," he made revealing observations on this subject. Having listed the achievements and failures of this first "proletarian revolution," he indicated its cardinal weakness: the proletariat's "excessive generosity—it should have *exterminated its enemies,*" instead of trying "to exert moral influence on them."[5] This remark must be one of the earliest instances in political literature in which the term "extermination," normally used for vermin, is applied to human beings. As we have seen, Lenin habitually described those whom he chose to designate as his regime's "class enemies" in terms borrowed from the vocabulary of pest control, calling kulaks "bloodsuckers," "spiders," and "leeches." As early as January 1918 he used inflammatory language to incite the population to carry out pogroms:

> The communes, small cells in the village and city, must themselves work out and test thousands of forms and methods of practical accounting and control

PR, No. 10/33 (1924), 10. Peters served as deputy director, and, in July–August 1918, as acting director of the Cheka.

over the rich, swindlers, and parasites. Variety here is a guarantee of vitality, of success and the attainment of the single objective: the *cleansing of Russia's soil of all harmful insects, of scoundrel fleas, bedbugs—the rich,* and so on.[6]

Hitler would follow this example in regard to the leaders of German Social Democracy, whom he thought of as mainly Jews, calling them in *Mein Kampf* "*Ungeziefer,*" or "vermin," fit only for extermination.[7]

Nothing illustrates better how deeply the passion for terror was embedded in Lenin's psyche than an incident which occurred on his first day as head of state. As the Bolsheviks were taking power, Kamenev asked the Second Congress of Soviets to abolish the death penalty for front-line deserters, which Kerensky had reintroduced in mid-1917. The congress adopted this proposal and abolished capital punishment at the front.[8] Lenin, busy elsewhere, missed this event. According to Trotsky, when he learned of it, he became "utterly indignant." "Nonsense," he said,

> how can you make a revolution without executions? Do you expect to dispose of your enemies by disarming yourself? What other means of repression are there? Prisons? Who attaches significance to that during a civil war, when each side hopes to win? . . . It is a mistake, he repeated, impermissible weakness, pacifist illusion, and so on.[9]

This was said at a time when the Bolshevik dictatorship was barely in the saddle, when no organized opposition had formed because no one believed the Bolsheviks would last, when there was as yet nothing remotely resembling a "civil war." On Lenin's insistence, the Bolsheviks ignored the congress's action in regard to the death penalty and reintroduced it more or less formally the following June.

Although Lenin preferred to direct the terror from behind the scenes, he occasionally let it be known he had no patience with complaints about "innocent" victims of the Cheka. "I judge soberly and categorically," he replied in 1919 to a Menshevik worker who criticized arrests of innocent citizens, "what is better—to put in prison a few dozen or a few hundred inciters, *guilty or not,* conscious or not, or to lose thousands of Red Army soldiers and workers? The former is better."[10] This kind of reasoning served to justify indiscriminate persecution.*

Trotsky fell in step. On December 2, 1917, addressing the new, Bolshevik Ispolkom, he said:

> There is nothing immoral in the proletariat finishing off the dying class. This is its right. You are indignant . . . at the petty terror which we direct against

---

*Compare this with Heinrich Himmler's exhortation to the SS in a 1943 speech in Poznan: "Whether during the construction of a tank trap 10,000 Russian women die of exhaustion or not interests me only insofar as the tank trap for Germany has been constructed. . . . When someone comes to me and says: 'I cannot build tank traps with women and children, that is inhuman, they will die,' I shall say to him: 'You are the murderer of your own blood, because if the tank trap is not built, German soldiers shall die.' "

our class opponents. But be put on notice that in one month at most this terror will assume more frightful forms, on the model of the great revolutionaries of France. Our enemies will face not prison but the guillotine.[11]

He defined the guillotine on this occasion (plagiarizing from the French revolutionary Jacques Hébert) as a device which "shortens a man by the length of a head."

In light of this evidence it is absurd to talk of Red Terror as an "unfortunate" policy "forced" upon the Bolsheviks by foreign and domestic opponents. As it had been for the Jacobins, terror served the Bolsheviks not as a weapon of last resort, but as a surrogate for the popular support which eluded them. The more their popularity eroded, the more they resorted to terror, until in the fall and winter of 1918–19 they raised it to a level of indiscriminate slaughter never before seen.*

For these reasons, the Red Terror cannot be compared either with the so-called White Terror of the anti-Bolshevik armies in Russia, to which the Bolsheviks habitually referred for self-justification, or with the Jacobin Terror of France, which they liked to claim as a model.

The White armies did, indeed, execute many Bolsheviks and Bolshevik sympathizers, usually in summary fashion, sometimes in a barbarous manner. But they never elevated terror to the status of a policy and never created a formal institution like the Cheka to carry it out. Their executions were as a rule ordered by field officers, acting on their own initiative, often in an emotional reaction to the sights which greeted their eyes when they entered areas evacuated by the Red Army. Odious as it was, the terror of the White armies was never systematic, as was the case with the Red Terror.

The Jacobin Terror of 1793–94, for all its psychological and philosophical similarities with the Red Terror, also differed from it in several fundamental ways. For one, it had its origin in pressures from below, from the streets, from mobs outraged by shortages of food and in search of scapegoats. The Bolshevik terror, by contrast, was imposed from above on a population that had had its fill of bloodshed. As we shall see, Moscow had to threaten provincial soviets with severe punishments for failing to implement its terroristic directives. Although there was a great deal of spontaneous violence in 1917–18, there exists no evidence of mobs calling for the blood of entire social classes.

Second, the two terrors were of a very different duration. The Jacobin Terror took up less than one year of a revolution that by the narrowest definition lasted a decade: hence it could properly be described as an episode, "a brief parenthesis." Immediately after the 9th of Thermidor, when the Jacobin leaders were arrested and guillotined, the French terror came to a sudden and permanent halt. But in Soviet Russia, the terror never ceased,

---

*By 1919–20, Lenin had many socialists in jail. When Fritz Platten, his Swiss friend, protested that surely they were not counterrevolutionaries, Lenin responded: "Of course not. . . . But that's exactly why they are dangerous—just because they are honest revolutionists. What can one do?": Isaac Steinberg, *In the Workshop of the Revolution* (London, 1955), 177.

going on intermittently, although at varying levels of intensity. While the death penalty was once again abolished at the end of the Civil War, executions went on as before, with minimum respect for judiciary procedures.

The difference between the Jacobin and Bolshevik terrors is perhaps best symbolized by the fact that in Paris no monuments have been raised to Robespierre and no streets named after him, whereas in the capital of Soviet Russia a giant statue of Feliks Dzerzhinskii, the founder of the Cheka, stands in the heart of the city, dominating a square named in his honor.

Bolshevik terror involved much more than mass executions: in the opinion of some contemporaries, these executions, terrible as they were, had a less oppressive effect than the pervasive atmosphere of repression. Isaac Steinberg, who was in a unique position to evaluate the phenomenon by virtue of his legal training and his experience as Lenin's Commissar of Justice, noted in 1920 that even though the Civil War was over, the terror continued, having become an intrinsic feature of the regime. Summary executions of prisoners and hostages were to him only "the most glittering object in the somberly flickering firmament of terror that dominates the revolutionary earth," "its bloody pinnacle, its apotheosis":

> Terror is not an individual act, not an isolated, fortuitous—even if recurrent—expression of the government's fury. Terror is a *system* . . . a legalized plan of the regime for the purpose of mass intimidation, mass compulsion, mass extermination. Terror is a calculated register of punishments, reprisals, and threats by means of which the government intimidates, entices, and compels the fulfillment of its imperative will. Terror is a heavy, suffocating cloak thrown from above over the entire population of the country, a cloak woven of mistrust, lurking vigilance, and lust for revenge. Who holds this cloak in his hands, who presses through it on the *entire* population, without exception? . . . Under terror, force rests in the hands of a minority, the notorious minority, which senses its isolation and fears it. Terror exists precisely because the minority, ruling on its own, regards an ever-growing number of persons, groups, and strata as its enemy. . . . This "enemy of the Revolution" . . . expands until he dominates the entire expanse of the Revolution. . . . The concept keeps on enlarging until, by degrees, it comes to embrace the entire land, the entire population, and, in the end, "all with the exception of the government" and its collaborators.*

Steinberg included among the manifestations of the Red Terror the dissolution of free trade unions, the suppression of free speech, the ubiquity of police agents and informers, the disregard for human rights, and the all-pervasive hunger and want. In his view, this "atmosphere of terror," its ever-present threat, poisoned Soviet life even more than the executions.

At the root of the terror lay Lenin's Jacobin conviction that if the Bolsheviks were to stay and expand their power, the embodiment of "evil" ideas

---

*I. Steinberg, *Gewalt und Terror in der Revolution* (Berlin, 1974), 22–25. The book, written between 1920 and 1923 (first published in 1931), describes Leninist, not Stalinist, Russia.

99. Isaac Steinberg.

and interests, labeled "bourgeoisie," had to be physically exterminated. The term "bourgeoisie" the Bolsheviks applied loosely to two groups: those who by virtue of their background or position in the economy functioned as "exploiters," be they a millionaire industrialist or a peasant with an extra acre of land, and those who, regardless of their economic or social status, opposed Bolshevik policies. One could thus qualify as a "bourgeois," objectively as well as subjectively, by virtue of one's opinions. There exists telling testimony of Lenin's genocidal fury in Steinberg's recollections of his days in the Sovnarkom. On February 21, 1918, Lenin submitted to the cabinet the draft of a decree called "The Socialist Fatherland in Danger!"[12] The inspiration was the German advance into Russia following the Bolshevik failure to sign the Brest Treaty. The document appealed to the people to rise in defense of the country and the Revolution. In it, Lenin inserted a clause that provided for the execution "on the spot"—that is, without trial—of a broad and undefined category of villains labeled "enemy agents, speculators, burglars, hooligans, counterrevolutionary agitators, [and] German spies." Lenin included summary justice for ordinary criminals ("speculators, burglars, hooligans") in order to gain support for the decree from the population, which was sick of crime, but his true target was his political opponents, called "counterrevolutionary agitators."

The Left SRs criticized this measure, being opposed in principle to the death penalty for political opponents. "I objected," Steinberg writes:

> that this cruel threat killed the whole pathos of the manifesto. Lenin replied with derision, "On the contrary, herein lies true revolutionary pathos. Do you really believe that we can be victorious without the very cruelest revolutionary terror?"

It was difficult to argue with Lenin on this score, and we soon reached an impasse. We were discussing a harsh police measure with far-reaching terroristic potentialities. Lenin resented my opposition to it in the name of revolutionary justice. So I called out in exasperation, "Then why do we bother with a Commissariat of Justice? Let's call it frankly the *Commissariat for Social Extermination* and be done with it!" Lenin's face suddenly brightened and he replied, "Well put . . . that's exactly what it should be . . . but we can't say that."*

Although Lenin all along provided the main driving force for the Red Terror and often had to cajole his more humane colleagues, he went to extraordinary lengths to disassociate his name from the terror. He who insisted on affixing his signature to all laws and decrees omitted to do so whenever acts of state violence were involved: in these cases, he preferred to give credit to the chairman of the Central Committee, the Commissar of the Interior, or some other authority, such as the Ural Regional Soviet, which he made falsely assume responsibility for the massacre of the Imperial family. He desperately wanted to avoid having his name historically linked with the inhumanities which he instigated. "He took care," writes one of his biographers,

> to speak of the terror only in the abstract, disassociating himself from individual acts of terrorism, the murders in the basement of the Lubianka and in all the other basements. . . . Lenin kept himself so remote from the terror that the legend has grown up that he took no active part in it, leaving all decisions to Dzerzhinskii. It is an unlikely legend, for he was a man constitutionally incapable of deputing authority on important matters.[13]

In fact, all decisions bearing on this matter, whether they concerned general procedures or the execution of important prisoners, required the approval of the Bolshevik Central Committee (later the Politburo), of which Lenin was the permanent de facto chairman.[14] The Red Terror was Lenin's child, even if he desperately tried to deny parenthood.

The guardian of this unacknowledged progeny was Dzerzhinskii (Dzierzyński), the Cheka's founder and director. Almost forty at the outbreak of the Revolution, he was born near Vilno into a patriotic Polish gentry family. He broke with his family's religious and nationalist heritage and joined the Lithuanian Social-Democratic Party, turning into a full-time revolutionary organizer and agitator. He spent eleven years in tsarist prisons and on hard labor. These were harsh years, which left indelible scars on his psyche, developing in him an indomitable will as well as an unquenchable thirst for revenge. He was capable of perpetrating the worst imaginable cruelties without pleasure, as an idealistic duty. Lean and ascetic, he carried out Lenin's instructions with a religious dedication, sending "bourgeois" and "counterrevolutionaries" before firing squads with the same joyless compulsion with which centuries earlier he might have ordered heretics burned at the stake.

*Steinberg, *In the Workshop,* 145. Steinberg mistakenly attributes the authorship of this decree to Trotsky.

100. Feliks Dzerzhinskii.

The first step in the introduction of mass terror to Soviet Russia was the elimination of all legal restraint—indeed, of law itself—and its replacement by something labeled "revolutionary conscience." Nothing like this had ever happened anywhere: Soviet Russia was the first state in history formally to outlaw law. This measure freed the authorities to dispose of anyone they disliked and legitimized pogroms against their opponents.

Lenin had planned it this way long before he took power. He believed that one of the cardinal mistakes of the Paris Commune had been its failure to abolish France's legal system. This mistake he meant to avoid. In late 1918, he defined the dictatorship of the proletariat as "rule unrestricted by any law."[15] He viewed law and courts in the Marxist fashion as tools by means of which the ruling class advanced its interests: in "bourgeois" society, under the guise of enforcing impartial justice, law served to safeguard private property. This point of view was articulated in early 1918 by N. V. Krylenko, who would later serve as Commissar of Justice:

It is one of the most widespread sophistries of bourgeois science to maintain that the court . . . is an institution whose task it is to realize some sort of special "justice" that stands above classes, that is independent in its essence of society's class structure, the class interests of the struggling groups, and the class ideology of the ruling classes . . . "Let justice prevail in courts"—one can hardly conceive more bitter mockery of reality than this. . . . Alongside, one can quote many such sophistries: that the court is a guardian of "law," which, like "governmental authority," pursues the higher task of assuring the harmonious development of "personality" . . . Bourgeois "law," bourgeois "justice," the interests of the "harmonious development" of bourgeois "personality" . . . Translated into the simple language of living reality this meant, above all, the preservation of private property . . .[16]

101. N. V. Krylenko.

From this premise, Krylenko concluded that the disappearance of private property would automatically lead to the disappearance of law: socialism would thus "destroy in embryo" the "psychological emotions" that made for crime. In this view, law did not prevent but caused crime.

Of course, some judiciary institutions would have to remain during the transition to full socialism, but these would serve the purposes not of hypocritical "justice" but of class war. "We need the state, we need compulsion," Lenin wrote in March 1918. "The organs of the proletarian state in realizing this compulsion are to be Soviet courts."[17]

True to his word, shortly after taking office, Lenin, with a stroke of the pen, liquidated Russia's entire legal system as it had developed since the reform of 1864. This he accomplished with the decree of November 22, 1917, released after prolonged discussion in the Sovnarkom.[18] The decree in the first instance dissolved nearly all existing courts, up to and including the Senate, the highest court of appeals. It further abolished the professions associated with the judiciary system, including the office of the Procurator (the Russian equivalent of the Attorney General), the legal profession, and most justices of the peace. It left intact only the "local courts" *(mestnye sudy)* which dealt with minor offenses.

The decree did not explicitly invalidate the laws on the statute books— this was to come one year later. But it produced the same effect by instructing judges of the local courts to be "guided in making decisions and passing sentences by the laws of the overthrown government only to the extent that these have not been annulled by the Revolution and do not contradict the revolutionary conscience and the revolutionary sense of legality." An amendment clarifying this vague provision specified that those laws were annulled which ran contrary to Soviet decrees as well as to the "programs-minimum of the Social-Democratic Labor Party and the Party of the Socialists-Revolutionaries." Essentially, in offenses still subject to judiciary procedures, guilt was determined by the impression gained by the judge or judges.

In March 1918, the regime replaced the local courts with People's Courts *(narodnye sudy)*. These were to deal with every category of crime of citizen against citizen: murder, bodily injury, theft, etc. The elected judges of these courts were not bound by any formalities concerning evidence.[19] A ruling issued in November 1918 forbade judges of People's Courts to refer to laws enacted before October 1917; it also absolved them further from having to observe any "formal" rules of evidence. In rendering verdicts, they were to be guided by the decrees of the Soviet Government and, when these were lacking, by the "socialist sense of justice" *(sotsialisticheskoe pravosoznanie).* [20]

In line with the traditional Russian practice of treating crimes against the state and its representatives differently from crimes against private persons, the Bolsheviks concurrently (November 22, 1917) introduced a new type of court, modeled on a similar institution of the French Revolution, called Revolutionary Tribunals. These were to try persons charged with "counterrevolutionary crimes," a category which embraced economic crimes and "sabotage."[21] To give them guidance, the Commissariat of Justice, then headed by Steinberg, issued on December 21, 1917, a supplementary instruction, which specified that "in setting the penalty, the Revolutionary Tribunal shall be guided by the circumstances of the case and the dictates of revolutionary conscience."[22] How the "circumstances of the case" were to be determined and what exactly constituted "revolutionary conscience" was left unsaid.* In effect, therefore, the Revolutionary Tribunals, from their foundation, operated as kangaroo courts, which sentenced defendants on the basis of a commonsensical impression of guilt. Initially, the Revolutionary Tribunals had no authority to mete out capital punishment. This situation was reversed with the surreptitious introduction of the death penalty. On June 16, 1918, *Izvestiia* published a "Resolution" signed by the new Commissar of Justice, P. I. Stuchka, which stated: "Revolutionary Tribunals are not bound by any rules in the choice of measures against the counterrevolution except in cases where the law defines the measure in terms of 'no lower than' such punishment." This convoluted language meant that Revolutionary Tribunals were free to sentence offenders to death as they saw fit, but were required to do so when the government mandated such punishment. The first victim of this new ruling was the Soviet commander of the Baltic Fleet, Admiral A. M. Shchastnyi, whom Trotsky accused of plotting to surrender his ships to the Germans: his example was to

---

*Even pre-revolutionary Russian law operated with such subjective concepts as "goodwill" and "conscience." The statutes that defined the procedures for conciliation courts, for example, instructed judges to mete out sentences "in accord with [their] conscience," a formula used also in some criminal proceedings. This Slavophile legacy in Imperial statutes had been criticized by one of Russia's leading legal theorists, Leon Petrazhitskii. See Andrzej Walicki, *Legal Philosophies of Russian Liberalism* (Oxford, 1987), 233.

serve as a lesson to the other officers. Shchastnyi was tried and sentenced on June 21 by a Special Revolutionary Tribunal of the Central Executive Committee, set up on Lenin's orders to try cases of high treason.[23] When the Left SRs objected to this revival of the odious practice of the death penalty, Krylenko replied that the admiral "had been condemned not 'to death' but 'to be shot.' "[24]

With the expulsion of other parties from Soviet institutions, first the Mensheviks and SRs and then the Left SRs, the Revolutionary Tribunals turned into tribunals of the Bolshevik Party thinly disguised as public courts. In 1918, 90 percent of their staff were members of the Bolshevik Party.[25] To be appointed a judge on a Revolutionary Tribunal one needed no formal qualifications other than the ability to read and write. According to contemporary statistics, 60 percent of the judges on these tribunals had less than secondary schooling.[26] Steinberg writes, however, that some of the worst offenders were not such semi-educated proletarians but intellectuals who used the tribunals to pursue personal vendettas and who were not above taking bribes from families of the accused.[27]

Those living under Bolshevik rule found themselves in a situation for which there was no historic precedent. There were courts for ordinary crimes and for crimes against the state, but no laws to guide them; citizens were sentenced by judges lacking in professional qualifications for crimes which were nowhere defined. The principles *nullum crimen sine lege* and *nulla poena sine lege*—no crime without a law and no punishment without a law—which had traditionally guided Western jurisprudence (and Russia's since 1864), went overboard as so much useless ballast. The situation struck contemporaries as unusual in the extreme. One observer noted in April 1918 that in the preceding five months no one had been sentenced for looting, robbery, or murder, except by execution squads and lynching mobs. He wondered where all the criminals had disappeared to, given that the old courts had had to work around the clock.[28] The answer, of course, was that Russia had been turned into a lawless society. In April 1918, the novelist Leonid Andreev described what this meant for the average citizen:

> We live in unusual conditions, still comprehensible to a biologist who studies the life of molds and fungi, but inadmissible for the psycho-sociologist. There is no law, there is no authority, the entire social order is defenseless. . . . Who protects us? Why are we still alive, unrobbed, not evicted from our homes? The old authority is gone; a band of unknown Red Guards occupies the neighborhood railroad station, learns how to shoot . . . carries out searches for food and weapons, and issues "permits" for travel to the city. There is no telephone and no telegraph. Who protects us? What remains of reason? Chance that no one has noticed us. . . . Finally, some general human cultural experiences, sometimes simple, unconscious habits: walking on the right side of the road, saying "good day" on meeting someone, tipping one's own hat, not the other person's. The music has long stopped, and we, like dancers, continue rhythmically to shuffle our feet and sway to the inaudible melody of law.[29]

To Lenin's disappointment, the Revolutionary Tribunals did not turn into instruments of terror. The judges worked lackadaisically and passed mild sentences. One newspaper noted in April 1918 that they had done little more than shut down a few newspapers and sentence a few "bourgeois."[30] Even after being empowered to do so, they were reluctant to pass sentences of death. In the course of 1918, a year which included the official Red Terror, the Revolutionary Tribunals tried 4,483 defendants, one-third of whom it sentenced to hard labor, another third to the payment of fines, and only fourteen to death.[31]

This is not what Lenin intended. The judges, who in time were almost exclusively members of the Bolshevik Party, were urged to pass extreme sentences and given ever wider discretion to do so. In March 1920, the tribunals

> received the authority to refuse to call and interrogate witnesses if their testimony during the preliminary inquest was clear, as well as the authority to stop at any moment the judiciary proceeding if [they] determined that the circumstances of the case had been adequately clarified. Tribunals had the authority to refuse the plaintiff and the defendant the right to appear and plead.[32]

These measures returned Russian judiciary procedures to the practices of the seventeenth century.

But even thus streamlined, the Revolutionary Tribunals proved too slow and too cumbersome to satisfy Lenin's quest for rule "unrestricted by any laws." Hence, he increasingly came to rely on the Cheka, which he endowed with the license to kill without having to follow even the most perfunctory procedures.

The Cheka was born in virtual secrecy. The decision to create a security force—essentially, a revived tsarist Department of Police and Okhrana—was adopted by the Sovnarkom on December 7, 1917, on the basis of Dzerzhinskii's report on fighting "sabotage," by which was meant the strike of white-collar employees.* The Sovnarkom's resolution was not made public at the time. It first appeared in print in 1924 in a falsified and incomplete version, then again in 1926 in a fuller but still falsified version, and in its full and authentic version only in 1958.[33] In 1917, there was published in the Bolshevik press only a terse, two-sentence announcement that the Sovnarkom had established an "Extraordinary Commission to Fight the Counterrevolution and Sabotage" *(Chrezvychainaia kommissia po bor'be s kontrrevoliutsiei i sabotazhem),* the office of which would be located in Petrograd at Gorokhovaia 2.[34] Before the Revolution this building had served as the bureau of the city's governor as well as

---

*Iz istorii Vserossiiskoi Chrezvychainoi Kommissii, 1917–1921 gg. (Moscow, 1958), 78–79. Under pressure of the Peasants' Congress, which on November 14 passed a resolution to this effect, the Bolsheviks dissolved the Military-Revolutionary Committee *(Revoliutsiia,* VI, 144). The Cheka was its successor.

of the local branch of the Department of Police. Neither the powers nor the responsibilities of the Cheka were spelled out.

The failure of the Bolshevik Government to make public, at the time of its founding, the functions and powers of the Cheka had dire consequences, because it enabled the Cheka to claim authority which it had not been intended to have. The Cheka's original mandate, it is now known, modeled on the tsarist security police, charged it with investigating and preventing crimes against the state. It was to have no judiciary powers: the Sovnarkom intended for the Cheka to turn over political suspects to Revolutionary Tribunals for prosecution and sentencing. The pertinent clause of the secret resolution setting up the Cheka read as follows:

> The tasks of the [Extraordinary] Commission: (1) to suppress [*presek(at')*] and liquidate all attempts and acts of counterrevolution and sabotage throughout Russia, from every quarter; (2) to turn over all saboteurs and counterrevolutionaries to the court of the Revolutionary Tribunal and to work out the means of combating them; (3) the Commission conducts only a preliminary investigation to the extent that this is necessary to bar [counterrevolution and sabotage].[35]

In the first published versions of this resolution (1924, 1926) one critical word was changed. As is now known, in the manuscript of the resolution the word "to suppress"—"*presekat'* "—appeared in an abbreviated form as "*presek[at']*." In the earliest published versions, this word was altered to read "*presledovat',*" which means "to prosecute."[36] The transposition and substitution of a few letters had the effect of giving the Cheka judiciary powers. This forgery, revealed only after Stalin's death, allowed the Cheka and its successors (GPU, OGPU, and NKVD) to sentence political prisoners, by summary procedures conducted in camera, to a full range of punishments, including death. The Soviet security police was deprived of this right, which had claimed the lives of millions, only in 1956.

The Bolsheviks, who were normally punctilious about bureaucratic proprieties, made a significant exception in the case of the secret police. This institution, which was subsequently credited with saving the regime, had for a long time no legal standing.[37] Ignored in the Collection of Laws and Ordinances *(Sobranie Uzakonenii i Rasporiazhenii)* for 1917–18, it lacked a formal identity. This was deliberate policy. In early 1918, the Cheka forbade any information to be published on it except with its approval.[38] The injunction was not strictly observed, but it gives an idea of the Cheka's conception of itself and its role in society. In this, the Bolsheviks followed the precedent set by Peter the Great, who had established Russia's first political police, the Preobrazhenskii Prikaz, without a formal *ukaz.* *

*"The institution was introduced so surreptitiously that historians to this day have not been able to locate the decree authorizing its establishment or even to determine the approximate date when it might have been issued": Richard Pipes, *Russia under the Old Regime* (London, 1974), 130.

The Cheka began with a small staff of officials and some military units. In March it moved with the rest of the government to Moscow, where it took over the spacious quarters of the Iakor Insurance Company on Bolshaia Lubianka II. At the time it claimed to have only 120 employees, although some scholars estimate the true figure to have been closer to 600.[39] The Chekist Peters conceded that the Cheka had difficulty recruiting personnel because Russians, with the tsarist police fresh in mind, reacted "sentimentally," and unable to distinguish persecution by the old regime from that of the new, refused to join.[40]* As a consequence, a high proportion of Cheka functionaries were non-Russians. Dzerzhinskii was a Pole, and many of his closest associates were Latvians, Armenians, and Jews. The guards the Cheka used to protect Communist officials and important prisoners were recruited exclusively from the Latvian Rifles because Latvians were considered more brutal and less susceptible to bribery. Lenin strongly favored this reliance on foreigners. Steinberg recalls his "fear" of the Russian national character. He thought that Russians lacked firmness: " *'Soft, too soft is the Russian,'* he would say, 'He is incapable of applying the harsh measures of revolutionary terror.' "[41]

Employing foreigners had the additional advantage that they were less likely to be bound to their potential victims by ties of kinship or inhibited by opprobrium of the Russian community. Dzerzhinskii, for one, had grown up in an atmosphere of intense Polish nationalism: as a youth he wanted to "exterminate all Muscovites" for the suffering they had inflicted on his people.† The Latvians looked on Russians with contempt. During his brief internment by the Cheka in September 1918, Bruce Lockhart heard from his Latvian guards that Russians were "lazy and dirty" and in battle always "let them down."[42] Lenin's reliance on foreign elements to terrorize the Russian population recalled the practice of Ivan the Terrible, who had also filled his terror apparatus, the Oprichnina, with foreigners, mostly Germans.

To remove some of the odium which attached to the political police in a socialist country, the Bolsheviks combined the Cheka's primary mission, which was political, with the task of fighting ordinary crime. Soviet Russia was in the grip of murders, lootings, and robberies, which the citizens desperately wanted to stop. To make the new political police more acceptable, the regime also assigned the Cheka responsibility for eradicating ordinary crimes, including banditry and "speculation." In an interview with a Menshevik daily in June 1918, Dzerzhinskii laid stress on the Cheka's twin missions:

[The task of the Cheka] is to fight the enemies of Soviet authority and of the new way of life. Such enemies are both our political opponents and all bandits, thieves, speculators, and other criminals who undermine the foundations of the socialist order.[43]

*Their confusion may have been partly due to the fact, reported on by many contemporaries, that many Cheka employees, including jailers, had served in the same capacities under tsarism.
†*PR*, No. 9 (1926), 55. Later on, Lenin would charge him and the Georgian Stalin with Russian chauvinism.

Bridling at the limitations which its mandate imposed, the Cheka sought unrestricted freedom to deal with political undesirables. This led to a conflict with the Commissariat of Justice.

From the day of its foundation, the Cheka arrested on its own authority persons suspected of engaging in "counterrevolution" and "speculation." The prisoners were delivered under guard to Smolnyi. This procedure did not suit Commissar of Justice Steinberg, a twenty-nine-year-old Jewish lawyer who had received his degree in Germany with a dissertation on the Talmudic concept of justice. On December 15 he issued a resolution forbidding further delivery of arrested citizens either to Smolnyi or to the Revolutionary Tribunal without prior approval of the Commissariat of Justice. Prisoners in the Cheka's custody were to be released.[44]

Apparently confident of Lenin's backing, Dzerzhinskii ignored these instructions. On December 19, he arrested the members of the Union for the Defense of the Constituent Assembly. As soon as he learned of Dzerzhinskii's action, Steinberg countermanded it, ordering the prisoners set free. The dispute was placed on the Sovnarkom's agenda for that evening. The cabinet sided with Dzerzhinskii and reprimanded Steinberg for releasing Cheka prisoners.[45] But Steinberg, undeterred by this defeat, asked the Sovnarkom to regularize relations between the Commissariat of Justice and the Cheka, and presented the Sovnarkom with a draft project, "On the Competence of the Commissariat of Justice."[46] The document forbade the Cheka to carry out political arrests without prior sanction from the Commissariat of Justice. Lenin and the rest of the cabinet approved Steinberg's proposal, for the Bolsheviks did not want at this time to quarrel with the Left SRs. The resolution adopted required that all orders for arrests "with prominent political significance" carry the countersignature of the Commissar of Justice. Presumably the Cheka could carry out ordinary arrests on its own authority.

But even this limited concession was almost immediately withdrawn. Two days later, probably responding to Dzerzhinskii's complaints, the Sovnarkom approved a very different resolution. While confirming that the Cheka was an investigatory body, it enjoined the Commissariat of Justice and all other bodies from interfering with its power to arrest important political figures. The Cheka had merely to inform the commissariats of Justice and of the Interior of its actions after the fact. Lenin added a stipulation that persons already under arrest be either turned over to the courts or released.[47] The next day, the Cheka arrested the center which directed the strike of white-collar employees in Petrograd.[48]

As part of the agreement with the Bolsheviks, concluded in December 1917, the Left SRs received the right to have representatives on the Cheka governing board, known as the Collegium. This concession ran contrary to the Bolshevik intention to keep the Cheka 100 percent Bolshevik, but Lenin agreed to it over Dzerzhinskii's objections. The Sovnarkom appointed a Left SR deputy director of the Cheka and added several members of this party to the Collegium.[49] The Left SRs further secured acceptance of the principle that the Cheka would carry out no executions except with the unanimous consent of the Collegium, which gave them a veto over death sentences. On January 31, 1918, the Sovnarkom confirmed, in an unpublished resolution, that the Cheka had exclusively investigatory responsibilities:

> The Cheka concentrates in its hands the entire work of intelligence, suppression [*presechenie*] and prevention of crimes, but the entire subsequent conduct of the investigation and the presentation of the case to the court is entrusted to the Investigatory Commission of the [Revolutionary] Tribunal.[50]

This restriction was abandoned a month later in the decree "The Socialist Fatherland in Danger!"[51] The document did not spell out who would "shoot on the spot" counterrevolutionaries and other enemies of the new state, but there could be no doubt that this responsibility devolved on the Cheka. The next day the Cheka confirmed that this was indeed the case by warning the population that "counterrevolutionaries" would be "mercilessly liquidated on the spot."[52] That day, February 23, Dzerzhinskii advised provincial soviets by wire that in view of the prevalence of anti-regime "plots" they should proceed at once to set up their own Chekas, arrest "counterrevolutionaries," and execute them wherever apprehended.[53] The decree thus transformed the Cheka, formally and permanently, from an investigating agency into a full-fledged machine of terror. The transformation was made with Lenin's concurrence.

In Moscow and Petrograd the Cheka was prevented from executing political offenders by agreements with the Left SRs. As long as the Left SRs worked in the Cheka—that is, until July 6, 1918—no formal political executions took place in either of those cities. The first victim of the February 22 decree was an ordinary criminal who under the alias "Prince Eboli" had impersonated a Chekist.[54] In the provinces, however, the organs of the Cheka were not bound by such restrictions and routinely executed citizens for political offenses. The Menshevik Grigorii Aronson recalled, for example, that in the spring of 1918 the Vitebsk Cheka arrested and executed two workers charged with distributing posters of the Council of Workers' Plenipotentiaries.* How many fell victim of such arbitrary executions will probably never be known.

Emulating the Corps of Gendarmes of the tsarist security system, the Cheka acquired an armed force. The first military unit to come under its control was a small Finnish detachment. Other units were added, and at the end of April 1918 the Cheka had a *Boevoi Otriad* (Combat Detachment) of six

---

*Grigorii Aronson, *Na zare krasnogo terrora* (Berlin, 1929), 32. G. Leggett, therefore, is not correct when, following Latsis, he says that until July 6, 1918, the Cheka "executed only criminals and spared political adversaries": *The Cheka: Lenin's Political Police* (Oxford, 1986), 58.

companies of infantry, fifty cavalrymen, eighty bicyclists, sixty machine gunners, forty artillerymen, and three armored cars.[55] It was these detachments which in April 1918 carried out perhaps the only popular action ever undertaken by the Cheka, the disarming in Moscow of the "Black Guards," bands of anarchists who had occupied residential buildings and terrorized the civilian population. Acquiring a rudimentary military force was only the first step in the expansion of the political police into a virtual state within the state. In June 1918, at a conference of Chekists, voices were heard demanding the creation of a regular Cheka armed force and entrusting the Cheka with the security of the railways as well as borders.[56]

Much of the efforts of the Cheka in the first months of its existence went to fighting ordinary commercial activities. Since the most routine retail trade transactions, such as selling a bag of flour, were now classified as "speculation," and the Cheka's mandate included fighting speculation, its agents spent much time chasing peasant "bagmen," inspecting luggage of railway passengers, and raiding black markets. This preoccupation with "economic crimes" prevented it from keeping an eye on far more dangerous anti-government plots that were beginning to take shape in the spring of 1918. In the first half of 1918, its only success in this field was uncovering the Moscow headquarters of Savinkov's organization. This, however, was due to a fortuitous accident and, in any event, did not enable the Cheka to penetrate the center of Savinkov's Union for the Defense of the Fatherland and Freedom, with the result that the Iaroslavl uprising in July caught it completely by surprise. Even more astonishing was the Cheka's ignorance of Left SR plans for a rebellion, given that the Left SR leaders had all but advertised their intentions. To make matters worse, the Left SR plot was hatched inside the Cheka headquarters and was supported by its armed detachments. This resounding fiasco forced Dzerzhinskii on July 8 to relinquish his office, which was temporarily entrusted to Peters. He was reinstated on August 22, just in time to suffer another humiliating embarrassment, the failure to forestall a nearly successful terrorist attempt on the life of Lenin.

No tsar, even at the height of radical terrorism, was as afraid for his life and as well protected as Lenin. The tsars traveled in Russia and abroad; they entertained and appeared frequently at public functions. Lenin cowered behind the brick walls of the Kremlin, guarded around the clock by Latvian Riflemen. When from time to time he went to the city, it was usually without prior notice. Between his move to Moscow in March 1918 and his death in January 1924, he revisited Petrograd, the scene of his revolutionary triumph, only twice, and he never traveled to see the country or mingle with the population. The farthest he ventured was to travel in his Rolls-Royce for occasional rests at Gorki, a village near Moscow, where an estate had been requisitioned for his use.

Trotsky showed greater daring, traveling incessantly to the front to talk to the commanders and inspect the troops. He frequently changed schedules and itineraries to throw off potential assassins.

No serious assassination attempts against the lives of Lenin and Trotsky took place before September 1918 because the Central Committee of the SR Party, the terrorist party par excellence, opposed active resistance to the Bolsheviks. Its unwillingness to resort to methods used against the tsars and their officials stemmed from two considerations. One was the belief of the SR leadership that time was on its side and that all it had to do was to sit tight and await the resurgence of democracy in Russia. The murder of the Bolshevik leaders was certain, in its view, to ensure the victory of the counterrevolution. The second consideration was fear of Bolshevik reprisals and pogroms.

Not all SRs shared this outlook. Some party members were prepared to take up arms against the Bolsheviks, with or without the approval of the Central Committee. One such group began to form in Moscow in the summer of 1918, under the very noses of the Cheka.

It was the custom of Bolshevik leaders, Lenin included, every Friday afternoon or evening to address workers and party members in various parts of Moscow. Lenin's appearances were usually not announced beforehand. On Friday, August 30, he was scheduled to attend two rallies: one in the Basmannyi District, in the building of the Grain Commodity Exchange, another at the Mikhelson factory in the southern part of the city. Earlier that day news had arrived that the chief of the Petrograd Cheka, M. S. Uritskii, had been shot. The assassin was a Jewish youth, L. A. Kannegisser, a member of the moderate Popular Socialist Party. It later transpired that he had acted on his own, to avenge the execution of a friend. But this was not known at the time and fears arose that perhaps a terrorist campaign was underway. Worried family members urged Lenin to cancel his appearances, but he quite uncharacteristically chose to face danger and went to town in a car, driven by his trusted chauffeur, S. K. Gil. He first appeared at the Grain Commodity Exchange, from where he proceeded to Mikhelson's. Although the audience half expected Lenin, there was no certainty he would appear until his car pulled into the courtyard. Lenin delivered his customary canned speech attacking Western "imperialists." He concluded with the words: "We shall die or triumph!" As Gil later told the Cheka, while Lenin was speaking, a woman dressed in work clothes came up and asked whether Lenin was inside. He gave an evasive reply.

As Lenin was making his way to the exit through a dense crowd, someone close behind him slipped and fell, barring the crowd. Lenin went into the courtyard followed by a few people. As he was about to enter his car, a woman approached to complain that bread was being confiscated at railroad stations. Lenin said that instructions had been issued to stop this practice. He had a foot on the running board when three shots rang out. Gil swung around. He recognized the person firing from several paces away as the woman who had inquired about Lenin. Lenin fell to the ground. Panic-stricken onlookers fled in all directions. Drawing his revolver, Gil raced in pursuit of the assassin, but she had vanished. Children who remained in the courtyard indicated the direction in which she had fled. A few people followed her. She kept on running, but then abruptly stopped and faced her pursuers. She was arrested and taken to Cheka headquarters in the Lubianka.

Lenin was carried unconscious into his car and driven at top speed to the Kremlin. A physician was called for. By then he was barely able to move. His pulse grew faint and he bled profusely. It seemed he was breathing his last. A medical examination revealed two wounds: one, relatively harmless, lodged in the arm; the other, potentially fatal, at the juncture of the jaw and neck. (The third bullet, it was learned later, struck the woman who had been conversing with Lenin when he was shot.)

In the next several hours, the terrorist underwent five interrogations by Cheka personnel.* She was very uncommunicative. Her name was Fannie Efimovna Kaplan, born Feiga Roidman or Roitblat. Her father was a teacher in the Ukraine. It was later learned that as a young girl she had joined the anarchists. She was sixteen when a bomb which anarchists were assembling in her room to kill the governor-general of Kiev exploded. A field court-martial condemned her to death, then commuted the sentence to lifelong hard labor, which she served in Siberia. There she met Spiridonova and other convicted terrorists, under whose influence she became a Socialist-Revolutionary. Early in 1917, benefiting from the political amnesty, she returned to central Russia, settling first in the Ukraine and then in the Crimea. By then, her family had emigrated to the United States.

According to her deposition, she had decided in February 1918 to assassinate Lenin to avenge the dissolution of the Constituent Assembly and the imminent signing of the Brest Treaty. But her objections to Lenin ran deeper: "I shot Lenin because I believe him to be a traitor," she told the Cheka. "By living long, he postpones the idea of socialism for decades to come." She further said that although she belonged to no political party, she sympathized with the Committee of the Constituent Assembly in Samara, liked Chernov, and favored an alliance with England and France against Germany. She steadfastly denied having any accomplices and refused to say who had given her the gun.†

After her interrogation, Kaplan was briefly detained in the same cell at the Lubianka where the Cheka confined Bruce Lockhart, whom it had arrested in the middle of the night on suspicion of complicity: "At six in the morning [of August 31]," he writes,

a woman was brought into the room. She was dressed in black. Her hair was black, and her eyes, set in a fixed stare, had great black rings under them. Her

*The protocols of these interrogations were published in *PR*, No. 6–7 (1923), 282–85. According to Peters, the principal interrogator, the existing dossier on the case is "very incomplete," whatever this may mean: *Izvestiia*, No. 194/1,931 (August 30, 1923), 1.

†That gun, a Browning, disappeared from the scene of the crime: on September 1, 1918, *Izvestiia* (No. 188/452, 3) carried a Cheka announcement requesting information on its whereabouts.

face was colorless. Her features, strongly Jewish, were unattractive. She might have been any age between twenty and thirty-five. We guessed it was Kaplan. Doubtless, the Bolsheviks hoped that she would give us some sign of recognition. Her composure was unnatural. She went to the window and, leaning her chin upon her hand, looked out into the daylight. And there she remained, motionless, speechless, apparently resigned to her fate, until presently the sentries came and took her away.[57]

She was moved from the Lubianka to one of the basement cells in the Kremlin where the most prominent political prisoners were held and from which few emerged alive.

In the meantime, a team of physicians attended Lenin, who was hovering between life and death, but retained enough presence of mind to make certain his doctors were Bolsheviks. The patient's prospects were not hopeless, even though blood had entered one of his lungs. Bonch-Bruevich, Lenin's devoted secretary, watching him, had a religious vision: the sight "suddenly reminded me of a famous European painting of the deposition of Christ from the cross, crucified by priests, pontiffs, and the rich. . . ."* Such religious associations soon became an inseparable element of the Lenin cult which had its beginning with tales of his miraculous survival. It was evident in the reverential description in *Pravda* on September 1, by its editor, Bukharin: Lenin was "the genius of the world revolution, the heart and the brain of the great worldwide movement of the proletariat," "the unique leader in the world," a man whose analytic skills gave him an "almost prophetic ability to predict." He went on to give a fantastic account of what had happened immediately after the attempt by Kaplan, whom he ridiculed as a latter-day Charlotte Corday, the assassin of Marat:

> Lenin, shot through twice, with pierced lungs, spilling blood, refuses help and goes on his own. The next morning, still threatened by death, he reads papers, listens, learns, observes to see that the engine of the locomotive that carries us toward global revolution has not stopped working.

Such images were calculated to appeal to the Russian masses' belief in the holiness of those who escape certain death.

The official announcement, published on the front page of *Izvestiia* on August 31, signed by Sverdlov, was decidedly unchristian in tone. It asserted, without providing any proof, that the authorities had "no doubt that here too will be discovered the fingerprints of the Right SRs . . . of the hirelings of the English and French." These accusations were made in a document dated 10:40 p.m. on August 30, which was an hour or so before Kaplan underwent her first interrogation. "We call on all comrades," it went on,

> to maintain complete calm and to intensify their work in combating counter-revolutionary elements. The working class will respond to attempts against its

---

*V. Bonch-Bruevich, *Tri Pokusheniia na V. I. Lenina* (Moscow, 1924), 14. This passage was removed from subsequent editions of Bonch-Bruevich's memoirs. Klara Zetkin, in 1920, saw in Lenin's face a resemblance to Grünewald's Christ: *Reminiscences of Lenin* (London, 1929), 22.

leaders with even greater consolidation of its forces, with merciless mass terror against all the enemies of the Revolution.

In the days and weeks that followed, the Bolshevik press (the non-Bolshevik press having been eliminated by then) was filled with similar exhortations and threats, but it provided surprisingly little information either about the murder attempt or about the actual condition of Lenin's health, apart from regular medical bulletins of which laymen could not make much sense. The impression one gains from reading this material is that the Bolsheviks deliberately underplayed the event to convince the public that whatever happened to Lenin, they were firmly in control.

On September 3, the commandant of the Kremlin, an ex-sailor named P. Malkov, was called to the Cheka and told that it had condemned Fannie Kaplan to death. He was to carry out the sentence at once. As Malkov describes it, he recoiled: "Shooting a person, especially a woman, is no easy task." He asked about the disposal of the body. He was told to consult Sverdlov. Sverdlov said that Kaplan was not to be interred: "Her remains are to be destroyed without trace." As the place of execution Malkov chose a narrow courtyard adjoining the Kremlin's Large Palace and used as a parking lot for military vehicles.

> I ordered the commander of the Automobile Combat Detachment to move some trucks from the enclosures and to start the engines. I also gave orders to send a passenger car to the blind alley, turning it to face the gate. Having posted at the gate two Latvians with orders to allow no one in, I went to fetch Kaplan. A few minutes later I was leading her to the courtyard. . . . "Into the car!" I snapped a sharp command. I pointed to the automobile that stood at the end of the cul-de-sac. Convulsively twisting her shoulders, Fannie Kaplan took one step, then another . . . I raised the pistol . . .*

Thus perished a young woman ridiculed as the Russian Charlotte Corday: without the semblance of a trial, shot in the back while the truck engines roared to drown out her screams, her corpse disposed of like so much garbage.

The details of the terrorist plot that led to the attempt on the life of Lenin, and, as it turned out, also on the lives of Trotsky and other Soviet leaders, became known to the Cheka only three years later. The main source of this information was a veteran SR terrorist, G. Semenov (Vasilev). Semenov emigrated abroad but changed his mind and in 1921 returned to Russia, where he turned renegade and denounced his past associates. His testimony, no doubt doctored to some extent, was subsequently used by the Bolshevik prosecutor in the trial of the Socialists-Revolutionaries in 1922.[58]

*P. Malkov, *Zapiski komendanta Moskovskogo Kremlia* (Moscow, 1959), 159–61. In the second edition, published in 1961, this passage is omitted. Here, Malkov is merely made to say: "We ordered Kaplan to go into the car, which had been previously prepared" (p. 162). A brief announcement of her execution appeared in *Izvestiia* on September 4 (No. 190/454, 1).

As best as can be determined, the SR Combat Organization was reactivated in Petrograd at the beginning of 1918, The group, which numbered fourteen people, some of them intellectuals, some workers, for a while shadowed Zinoviev and Volodarskii. In June 1918, one of its members, the worker Sergeev, assassinated Volodarskii. This terrorist underground acted on its own without sanction of the SR Central Committee. In the spring of 1918, after the Bolshevik Government had moved to Moscow, some members of the Combat Organization followed it. They chose Trotsky as their first victim in the belief that his death would have the greatest effect on the Bolshevik cause since he directed the war effort. Lenin was to follow. Adopting methods perfected against tsarist officials, members of the group stalked their victims to determine the pattern of their movements. They learned that Trotsky traveled constantly and unpredictably between Moscow and the front, and hence, "for technical reasons," as Semenov would later explain, it was decided to dispose of Lenin first.

Before carrying out their mission, the terrorists requested the approval of the SR Central Committee. By this time most SR leaders had moved to Samara, but a branch of the committee remained in Moscow, headed by Abraham Gots. Gots and one other committee member, D. Donskoi, refused to sanction the attempt on Lenin's life, but said they would not object to it as long as it was done as an "individual" act, without implicating the party. They also promised that the party would not repudiate Lenin's murder.

While laying his plans, Semenov learned that Fannie Kaplan and two associates were working independently toward the same end. Kaplan impressed him as a resolute "revolutionary terrorist"—in other words, a suicidal type. He invited her to join his group.

To track Lenin's appearances at worker meetings, Semenov divided Moscow into four districts, to each of which he assigned two members of his organization: one to act as observer *(dezhurnyi),* the other as "executor" *(ispolnitel').* The former was to mix with the crowds to learn when and where Lenin would speak. As soon as he had the information, he was to contact the "executor," who would wait at a central location within the zone. These preparations took place in August 1918, at the time when the SRs in Samara, taking advantage of the military victories of the Czechs, were laying claim to authority over Russia.

Lenin addressed a gathering of the Moscow Committee of the Party on Friday, August 16, but due to some mishap Semenov's observer failed to appear. The following Friday, Lenin spoke again, this time at the Polytechnic Museum. Word got around of his appearance and a large crowd turned up. This time everything went according to plan, but the "executor" lost his nerve, for which Semenov expelled him from the Combat Organization. Semenov had intelligence that the following Friday, August 30, Lenin would make one or more appearances in the southern zone. To make certain that nothing would go wrong this time, he assigned to this area his two most trusted agents: an experienced terrorist, the worker Novikov, to act as observer, and Kaplan as executor. In the tradition of SR terrorists, Kaplan was prepared to give up her own life for the one she took: she told Novikov that after shooting Lenin she would surrender. Just in case she changed her mind, however, he hired a hack to stand by.

In the afternoon of August 30, Kaplan took up her post at Serpukhovskii Square. In her purse she carried a loaded Browning; three bullets had crosslike incisions, into which had been rubbed a deadly Indian poison, curare.*

Novikov learned that Lenin would speak at the Mikhelson factory. To make certain that the information was correct, Kaplan questioned Lenin's chauffeur, after which she entered the building, placing herself near the exit. (Other sources have her waiting in the courtyard.) It was Novikov who staged the accident on the steps leading to the exit, purposely falling to hold back the crowd so as to give Kaplan undisturbed access to her victim. After firing her revolver, Kaplan seems to have forgotten her promise to surrender and instinctively ran away, but then stopped and gave herself up.

On September 6, *Pravda* carried a brief statement from the Central Committee of the SR Party, disclaiming, on its behalf and that of its affiliates, any connection with the attempt on Lenin's life. This violated the agreement which Semenov had made with Gots and Donskoi, and considerably dampened the terrorists' spirits. They made an attempt on the life of Trotsky, as he was departing for the front, but Trotsky eluded them by switching trains at the last moment. To keep the organization going, they carried out several "expropriations" of Soviet institutions, but their morale kept on sinking, especially after the Bolsheviks had regained the initiative against the Whites. Sometime toward the end of 1918, the Combat Organization dissolved.

Lenin recovered remarkably quickly. This attested to his strong constitution and will to live, but to his associates it implied supernatural qualities; it was as if God Himself intended Lenin to live and his cause to triumph. As soon as he regained some strength, he resumed work, but he overexerted himself and suffered a relapse. On September 25, on his physicians' insistence, he and Krupskaia left for Gorki. Lenin spent three weeks there convalescing; although he kept in touch with events and did some writing, he left the day-to-day conduct of affairs of state to others. One of the few visitors allowed to see him was Angelica Balabanoff, an old comrade and a Zimmerwald participant. As she recalls it, when she raised the matter of Fannie Kaplan's execution, Krupskaia became "very upset"; later, when the two women were alone, she shed bitter tears over it. Lenin, Balabanoff felt, preferred not to discuss it.[59] At this time, the Bolsheviks still felt embarrassment about executing fellow socialists.

Lenin returned to Moscow on October 14. On October 16, he attended a meeting of the Central Committee and the following day a session of the

---

*This was confirmed in April 1922 when physicians removed the bullet from Lenin's neck and found on it an incision shaped like a cross: P. Posvianskii, ed., *Pokushenie na Lenina 30 avgusta 1918 g.*, 2nd ed. (Moscow, 1925), 64. The poison, however, seems to have lost its effectiveness, since it was not mentioned in the medical bulletins.

Sovnarkom. To assure the populace that he had fully recovered, motion-picture cameras were brought to the Kremlin courtyard and filmed him in conversation with Bonch-Bruevich. On October 22, Lenin made his first public appearance, after which he returned to full-time work.

The most immediate effect of Kaplan's attempt was the unleashing of a wave of terror which in its lack of discrimination and number of victims had no historic precedent. The Bolsheviks were thoroughly frightened, and acted exactly as Engels had said frightened people did: to reassure themselves they perpetrated useless cruelties.

The assassination attempt and Lenin's recovery had another consequence as well, in the long run perhaps no less important: it inaugurated a deliberate policy of deifying Lenin which after his death would turn into a veritable state-sponsored Oriental cult. Lenin's rapid recovery from a near-fatal injury seems to have stirred among his lieutenants, prone to venerating him even before, a superstitious faith. Bonch-Bruevich cites with approval the remark of one of Lenin's physicians that "only those marked by destiny can escape death from such a wound."[60] Although Lenin's "immortality" was later exploited for very mundane political ends, to play on the superstitions of the masses, there is no reason to doubt that many Bolsheviks genuinely came to regard their leader as a supernatural being, a latter-day Christ sent to save humanity.*

Until Fannie Kaplan's attempt on his life, the Bolsheviks had been rather reticent about Lenin. In personal contact, they treated him with a deference in excess of that normally shown political leaders. Sukhanov was struck that in 1917, even before Lenin had taken power, his followers displayed "quite exceptional piety" toward him, like the "knights of the Holy Grail."[61] Lenin's stature rose with each of his successes. As early as January 1918, Lunacharskii, one of the better-educated and more levelheaded of the Bolshevik luminaries, reminded Lenin that he no longer belonged to himself but to "mankind."[62] There were other early inklings of an incipient cult, and if the process of deification did not unfold as yet, it was because Lenin discouraged it. Thus, he stopped Soviet officials who wanted to enforce on his behalf tsarist laws savagely punishing the defacement of the ruler's portrait.[63] His peculiar vanity dissolved tracelessly in the "movement": it received complete gratification from its successes without requiring a "personality cult."

Lenin was exceedingly modest in his personal wants: his living quarters, his food, his clothing were strictly utilitarian. He carried to an extreme the notorious indifference of the Russian intelligentsia for the finer things, leading even at the height of his power an austere, almost ascetic, style of life. He

> always wore the same dark-colored suit, with pipelike trousers that seemed a trifle too short for his legs, with a similarly abbreviated, single-breasted coat, a soft white collar, and an old tie. The necktie, in my opinion, was for years the same: black, with little white flowers, one particular spot showing wear.[64]

*The evolution of the Lenin cult is the subject of Nina Tumarkin's *Lenin Lives!* (Cambridge, Mass., 1983).

Such simplicity, emulated by many later dictators, did not, however, preclude—and, indeed, perhaps even encouraged—the rise of a personality cult. Lenin was the first of the modern "demotic" leaders who, even while dominating the masses, in appearance and ostensible lifestyle remained one of them. This has been noted as a characteristic of contemporary dictatorships:

> In modern absolutisms the leader is not distinguished, as many former tyrants were, by the *difference* between himself and his subjects, but is, on the contrary, like the embodied essence of what they all have in common. The 20th-century tyrant is a "popular star" and his personal character is obscured . . .[65]

Russian literature on Lenin published in 1917 and the first eight months of 1918 is surprisingly sparse.[66] In 1917 most of what was written about him came from the pen of his opponents, and although the Bolshevik censorship soon put a stop to such hostile literature, the Bolsheviks themselves wrote little on their leader, who was hardly known outside the narrow circles of the radical intelligentsia. It was Fannie Kaplan's shots that opened the floodgates of Leninist hagiography. As early as September 3–4, 1918, a paean to Lenin by Trotsky and Kamenev came out in an edition of one million copies.[67] Zinoviev's eulogy, around the same time, had a printing of 200,000, and a brief popular biography came out in 300,000 copies. According to Bonch-Bruevich, Lenin terminated this outpouring as soon as he recovered,[68] although he allowed it to resume on a more modest scale in 1920, in connection with his fiftieth birthday and the end of the Civil War. By 1923, however, when Lenin's health forced him to withdraw from active politics, Leninist hagiography turned into an industry, employing thousands, much as did the painting of religious ikons before the Revolution.

On the present-day reader this literature makes an odd impression: its sentimental, mawkish, worshipful tone contrasts sharply with the brutal language which the Bolsheviks liked to affect in other walks of life. The image of the Christ-like savior of mankind, descended from the cross and then resurrected, is difficult to reconcile with the theme of a "merciless struggle" against his enemies. Thus Zinoviev, who had mocked the "bourgeoisie" as fit to eat straw, could describe Lenin as the "apostle of world communism" and "leader by the grace of God," much as Mark Antony in his funeral oration for Caesar had extolled him as a "god in the sky."[69] Other Communists exceeded even this hyperbole, one poet calling Lenin "the invincible messenger of peace, crowned with the thorns of slander." Such allusions to the new Christ were common in Soviet publications in late 1918, which the authorities distributed in massive editions while massacring hostages by the thousands.[70]

There was, of course, no formal deification of the Soviet leader, but the qualities attributed to him in official publications and pronouncements—omniscience, infallibility, and virtual immortality—amounted to nothing less. The "cult of genius" went further in Soviet Russia in regard to Lenin (not to speak of Stalin later on) than the subsequent adoration of Mussolini and Hitler, for which it provided the model.

Why this quasi-religious cult of a politician by a regime espousing materialism and atheism? To this question there are two answers, one having to do with the internal needs of the Communist Party, the other with the relationship of that party to the people whom it ruled.

Although they claimed to be a political party, the Bolsheviks were really nothing of the kind. They resembled rather an order or cohort gathered around a chosen leader. What held them together was not a program or a platform—these could change from one day to the next in conformity with the leader's wishes—but the person of the leader. It was his intuition and his will that guided the Communists, not objective principles. Lenin was the first political figure of modern times to be addressed as "leader" *(vozhd')*. He was indispensable, for without his guidance the one-party regime had nothing to hold it together. Communism repersonalized politics, throwing it back to the times when human will rather than law directed state and society. This required its leader to be immortal, if not literally then figuratively: he had to lead in person, and after he was gone, his followers had to be able to rule in his name and claim to receive direct inspiration from him. The slogan "Lenin Lives!" launched after Lenin's death was, therefore, no mere propagandistic catchphrase, but an essential ingredient of the Communist system of government.

This accounts in good measure for the need to deify Lenin, to raise him above the vagaries of ordinary human existence, to make him immortal. His cult began the instant he was believed to stand on the threshold of death and became institutionalized five years later when he actually died. Lenin's inspiration was essential to maintain the vitality and indestructibility of the party and the state which he had founded.

The other consideration had to do with the regime's lack of legitimacy. This had not been a problem in the first months of the Bolshevik regime when it had acted as a catalyst of world revolution. But once it became clear that there would be no world revolution anytime soon and that the Bolshevik regime would have to assume responsibility for administering a large, multinational empire, the requirements changed. At this point, the loyalty of Soviet Russia's seventy-odd million inhabitants under its control became a matter of grave concern. This loyalty the Bolsheviks could not secure by ordinary electoral procedures: at the height of their popularity, in November 1917, they won less than one-quarter of the vote, and they certainly would have gained only a fraction of that later on, after disenchantment had set in. In their hearts, the Bolsheviks knew that their authority rested on physical force embodied in a thin layer of workers and soldiers of questionable commitment and staying power. It could not escape them that in July 1918, when their regime came under assault from the Left SRs, the workers and soldiers in the capital city declared "neutrality" and refused to help.

Under these conditions, the deification of the founding father served the Bolsheviks as the next-best thing to true legitimacy and a surrogate for the missing popular mandate. Historians of antiquity have noted that in the Middle East, institutionalized cults of rulers began on a large scale only after

Alexander of Macedon had conquered diverse non-Greek peoples over whom he could not claim legitimate authority, and who, furthermore, were bound neither to the Macedonians nor to each other by bonds of ethnic identity. Alexander, and even more so his successors, as well as the Roman emperors, had recourse to self-deification as a device for securing with appeals to celestial authority that which terrestrial authority refused to grant them:

> The successors of Alexander were Greek Macedonians who occupied, by right of conquest and force of arms, thrones usurped from autochthonous sovereigns. In these countries of ancient and refined civilization, the power of the sword was not everything and the law of the stronger might not have provided adequate legitimation. For sovereigns, in general, love to legitimize themselves, because this often means reinforcing their position. Was it not wise on their part to present themselves as the titled heirs of these powers based on divine right, the heritage of which they had captured? To identify themselves as gods—was this not a way, presumed clever, to reap the veneration of their subjects, to unite their disparate populations under the same banner, and, in the ultimate analysis, to consolidate their dynastic position?[71]

> To a dynasty . . . deification meant legitimacy, the regularizing of right acquired by the sword. It meant, further, the elevation of the royal family above the ambition of men who had recently been their peers, the strengthening of the rights of sovereigns by fusing them in a single whole with the prerogatives of their divine predecessors, the presentation to subjects everywhere of a symbol round which they might, perchance, rally through religious sentiment since they could not do so through their national sentiment.[72]

How conscious the Bolsheviks were of these precedents and how aware of the conflict between their pretense at being "scientific" and their appeals to the most primitive craving for idol worship, it is difficult to tell. The chances are that they acted instinctively. If so, their instincts served them well, for these appeals proved much more successful in winning them mass support than all the talk of "socialism," "class struggle," and the "dictatorship of the proletariat." To the people of Russia "dictatorship" and "proletariat" were meaningless foreign words that most of them could not even pronounce. But the tales of the miraculous rise from the dead of the country's ruler evoked an instant emotional response and created something of a bond between the government and its subjects. This is why the cult of Lenin would never be abandoned, even if, for a time, it would be eclipsed by the state-fostered cult of another deity, Stalin.*

---

*For all the attention paid to Lenin by Soviet propaganda after August 30, 1918, apparently not everyone knew who he was. Angelica Balabanoff recalls an incident which occurred in early 1919, when Lenin went to visit Krupskaia in a sanatorium outside Moscow. The car in which he and his sister were riding was stopped by two men. "One pointed a gun and said: 'Your money or your life!' Lenin took out his identification card and said: 'I am Ulianov Lenin.' The aggressors did not even look at the card and repeated: 'Your money or your life!' Lenin had no money. He took off his coat, got out of the car, and without letting go of the bottle of milk for his wife, proceeded on foot.": *Impressions of Lenin* (Ann Arbor, Mich., 1964), 65.

The Bolsheviks had practiced terror from the day they seized power, intensifying it as their power grew and their popularity declined. The arrest of the Kadets in November 1917, followed by the unpunished murder of the Kadet leaders Kokoshkin and Shingarev had been acts of terror, as was the closing of the Constituent Assembly and the shooting of the demonstrators marching in its support. The Red Army troops and Red Guards who in the spring of 1918 dispersed and manhandled, in one city after another, the soviets that had voted the Bolsheviks out of power, perpetrated acts of terror. The executions, mainly carried out by provincial and district Chekas under the mandate given them by Lenin's decree of February 22, 1918, pushed terror to a still higher level of intensity: the historian S. Melgunov, then residing in Moscow, compiled from the press evidence of 882 executions in the first six months of 1918.[73]

Early Bolshevik terror, however, was unsystematic, rather like the terror of the Whites later on in the Civil War, and many of its victims were ordinary criminals as well as "speculators." It began to assume a more systematic political character only in the summer of 1918, when Bolshevik fortunes sank to their lowest. Following the suppression of the Left SR uprising on July 6, the Cheka carried out its first mass executions, the victims of which were members of Savinkov's secret organization, arrested the previous month, and some participants in the Left SR uprising. The expulsion of the Left SRs from the Cheka Collegium in Moscow removed the last restraints on the political police. In the middle of July, many officers who had taken part in the Iaroslavl uprising were shot. Frightened of military conspiracies, the Cheka now began to hunt down officers of the old army and execute them without trial. According to Melgunov's records, in the month of July 1918 alone, the Bolshevik authorities, mainly the Cheka, carried out 1,115 executions.[74]

The murder of the Imperial family and their relatives represented a further escalation of terror. Cheka agents now arrogated to themselves the right to shoot prisoners and suspects at will, although judging by subsequent complaints from Moscow, the provincial authorities did not always make use of their powers.

Notwithstanding this intensification of government terror, Lenin was still dissatisfied. He wanted to involve the "masses" in such action, presumably because pogroms which involved both agents of the government and the people helped bring the two closer together. He kept on badgering Communist officials and the citizenry to act more resolutely and rid themselves of all inhibitions against killings. How else could "class war" turn into reality? As early as January 1918, he complained that the Soviet regime was "too gentle": he wanted "iron power," whereas it was "inordinately soft, at every step more like jelly than iron."[75] When told in June 1918 that party officials in Petrograd had restrained workers from carrying out a pogrom to avenge the assassination of Volodarskii, he fired off an indignant letter to his viceroy there. "Comrade Zinoviev!" he wrote:

> The Central Committee has learned only today that in Petrograd *workers* wanted to react to the murder of Volodarskii with mass terror and that you (not you personally but the Petrograd Central Committee or Regional Committee) held them back. I protest decisively! We compromise ourselves: even in Soviet resolutions we threaten mass terror, and when it comes to action, we *impede* the *entirely* correct revolutionary initiative of the masses. This is imper-mis-si-ble![76]

Two months later, Lenin instructed the authorities in Nizhnii Novgorod to "introduce *at once* mass terror, *execute* and *deport hundreds* of prostitutes, drunken soldiers, ex-officers, etc."[77] These terribly imprecise three letters—"etc."—gave agents of the regime a free hand in selecting their victims: it was to be carnage for the sake of carnage as an expression of the indomitable "revolutionary will" of the regime, which was fast losing ground under its feet.

Terror spread to the countryside in connection with the government's declaration of war on the village. We have cited Lenin's exhortations to the workers to kill "kulaks." It is impossible to form even an approximate notion of the number of peasants who perished in the summer and fall of 1918 trying to save their grain from food detachments: given that the victims on the government side ran into the thousands, they were unlikely to have been smaller.

Lenin's associates now vied with each other in using language of explicit brutality to incite the population to murder and to make murder committed for the cause of the Revolution appear noble and uplifting. Trotsky, for instance, on one occasion warned that if any of the ex-tsarist officers whom he drafted into the Red Army behaved treasonably, "nothing will remain of them but a wet spot."[78] The Chekist Latsis declared that the "law of the Civil War [was] to slaughter all the wounded" fighting against the Soviet regime: "It is a life-and-death struggle. If you do not kill, you will be killed. Therefore kill that you may not be killed."[79]

No such exhortation to mass murder was heard either in the French Revolution or on the White side. The Bolsheviks deliberately sought to brutalize their citizens, to make them look on some of their fellow citizens just as frontline soldiers look on those wearing enemy uniforms: as abstractions rather than human beings.

This murderous psychosis had already attained a high pitch of intensity by the time bullets struck down Uritskii and Lenin. These two terrorist acts—as it turned out, unrelated, but at the time seen as part of an organized plot—unleashed the Red Terror in its formal sense. The majority of its victims were hostages chosen at random, mainly because of their social background, wealth, or connections with the old regime. The Bolsheviks considered these massacres necessary not only to suppress concrete threats to their regime but also to intimidate the citizens and force them into psychic submission.

The Red Terror was formally inaugurated with two decrees, issued on September 4 and 5, over the signatures of the commissars of the Interior and of Justice.

The first instituted the practice of taking hostages.* It was a barbarian measure, a reversion to the darkest of ages, which international tribunals after World War II would declare a war crime. The Cheka hostages were to be executed in reprisal for future attacks on Bolshevik leaders or any other active opposition to Bolshevik rule. In fact, they were lined up before firing squads around the clock. The official sanction for these massacres was given in the "Order Concerning Hostages" signed by Grigorii Petrovskii, the Commissar of the Interior, on September 4, 1918, one day before the Red Terror decree, and cabled to all provincial soviets:

> The killing of Volodarskii, the killing of Uritskii, the attempt to kill and the wounding of the chairman of the Council of People's Commissars, Vladimir Ilich LENIN, the mass executions of tens of thousands of our comrades in Finland, in the Ukraine, on the Don, and in [areas controlled by] the Czechoslovaks, the continuous discovery of conspiracies in the rear of our armies, the open admission by Right SRs and other counterrevolutionary scum [of their involvement] in these conspiracies, and, at the same time, the exceedingly insignificant number of serious repressions and mass executions of White Guardists and bourgeois by the soviets, show that, notwithstanding the constant talk of mass terror against the SRs, White Guardists, and bourgeoisie, the terror, in fact, does not exist.
>
> This situation must be decisively ended. An immediate stop must be put to slackness and pampering. All Right SRs known to local soviets must be immediately arrested. It is necessary to take from among the bourgeoisie and officers numerous hostages. In the event of the least attempts at resistance or the least stir in White Guard circles, resort must be had at once to mass executions. Executive Committees of local provincial soviets ought to display in this regard particular initiative.
>
> Administrative offices, using the militia and Chekas, must take all measures to identify and arrest all those who hide behind false names. All persons involved in White Guard work are subject to mandatory execution.
>
> All indicated measures are to be carried out immediately.
>
> All indecisive action in this regard by one or another organ of local soviets must be instantly communicated . . . to the People's Commissariat of the Interior.
>
> The rear of our armies must be finally completely rid of all White Guardists and all vile conspirators against the authority of the working class and the poorer peasantry. Not the slightest hesitation, not the slightest indecisiveness, in the application of mass terror.

*The earliest mention of hostages was in a speech by Trotsky on November 11, 1917, in which he said that military cadets taken prisoner would be held hostage: "if our men fall into the hands of the enemy . . . for every worker and for every soldier we shall demand five cadets": *Izvestiia*, No. 211 (November 12, 1917), 2.

Confirm acceptance of the aforesaid telegram.
Pass on to *uezd* soviets.

Commissar of the Interior, Petrovskii.[80]

This extraordinary document not only permitted but required indiscriminate terror under the threat of punishment for what it termed displays of "slackness and pampering"—in other words, humaneness—toward its designated victims. Soviet officials were required to perpetrate mass murder or else risk being charged with complicity in the "counterrevolution."

The second decree instituted the Red Terror with the adoption on September 5, 1918, of a "Resolution" approved by the Sovnarkom and signed by the Commissar of Justice, D. Kurskii.[81] It stated that the Sovnarkom, having heard a report from the director of the Cheka, decided that it was imperative to intensify the policy of terror. "Class enemies" of the regime were to be isolated in concentration camps and all persons with links to "White Guard organizations, conspiracies, and seditious actions [*miatezh*]" were subject to immediate execution.

Communist documentary and historical literature passes over in silence the origins of these orders: they are not to be found in collections of Soviet decrees. Lenin's name has been scrupulously disassociated from them, although he is known to have insisted on hostage-taking as essential to class war.[82] Who, then, was the author of these decrees? On the face of it, Lenin was at the time too weak from the loss of blood to take part in affairs of state. Yet it is difficult to believe that measures of such importance could have been taken by two commissars without his explicit approval. The suspicion that Lenin authorized the two decrees that launched the Red Terror receives support from the fact that on September 5 he managed to affix his signature to a very minor decree dealing with Russo-German relations.[83] If its existence does not conclusively prove Lenin's personal involvement, then at least it removes physical disability as a counterargument.

On August 31, even before official instructions to this effect had been issued, the Cheka at Nizhnii Novgorod rounded up 41 hostages identified as from the "enemy camp" and had them shot. The list of victims indicated that they consisted mainly of ex-officers, "capitalists," and priests.[84] In Petrograd, Zinoviev, as if wishing to make up for the "softness" for which Lenin had reprimanded him, ordered the summary execution of 512 hostages. This group included many individuals associated with the *ancien régime* who had spent months in jail and therefore could have had no connection with the terrorist assaults on the Bolshevik leaders.[85] In Moscow, Dzerzhinskii ordered the execution of several high officials of the tsarist government held in prison since 1917: among them, one minister of justice (I. G. Shcheglovitov), three ministers of the interior (A. N. Khvostov, N. A. Maklakov, and A. D. Protopopov), one director of the Police Department (S. P. Beletskii), and a bishop. All were has-beens of no threat whatever to the regime. One cannot, therefore, escape the impression that their murder was Dzerzhinskii's personal revenge for the many harsh years he had spent in prison while these men had been in charge of justice and the police.*

Cheka agents now were told they could deal with enemies of the regime as they saw fit. According to Cheka Circular No. 47, signed by Peters: "In its activity, the Cheka is entirely independent, conducting searches, arrests, and executions, accounts of which it renders subsequently to the Sovnarkom and Central Executive Committee."[86] With this power, and spurred by Moscow's threats, provincial and district Chekas all over Soviet Russia now energetically went to work. During September, the Communist press published a running account from the provinces on the progress of the Red Terror, column after column of reports of executions. Sometimes only the number of those executed was given, sometimes also their last names and occupations, the latter of which often included the designation *"kr,"* or "counterrevolutionary." At the end of September, the Cheka came out with a house organ, the *Cheka Weekly (Ezhenedel'nik VChK),* to assist the brotherhood of Chekists in their work through the exchange of information and experience. It regularly carried summaries of executions, neatly arranged by provinces, as if they were the results of regional football matches.

It is difficult to convey the vehemence with which Communist leaders at this time called for the spilling of blood. It was as if they vied to prove themselves less "soft," less "bourgeois" than the next man. The Stalinist and Nazi holocausts were carried out with much greater decorum. Stalin's "kulaks" and political undesirables, sentenced to die from hunger and exhaustion, would be sent to "correction camps," while Hitler's Jews, en route to gas chambers, would be "evacuated" or "relocated." The early Bolshevik terror, by contrast, was carried out in the open. Here there was no flinching, no resort to euphemisms, for this nationwide Grand Guignol was meant to serve "educational" purposes by having everyone—rulers as well as ruled—bear responsibility and hence develop an equal interest in the regime's survival.

Here is Zinoviev addressing a gathering of Communists two weeks after the launching of the Red Terror: "We must carry along with us 90 million out of the 100 million of Soviet Russia's inhabitants. As for the rest, we have nothing to say to them. They must be annihilated."[87] These words, by one of the highest Soviet officials, was a sentence of death on 10 million human beings. And here is the organ of the Red Army inciting the populace to pogroms:

> Without mercy, without sparing, we will kill our enemies by the scores of hundreds, let them be thousands, let them drown themselves in their own blood. For the blood of Lenin and Uritskii . . . let there be floods of blood of the bourgeoisie—more blood, as much as possible.[88]

---

*A similar phenomenon would be observed in Germany fifteen years later. When the Nazis came to power, members of the SA would often select for beating and torture personal enemies, including judges who had tried them under the Weimar Republic: Andrzej Kaminski, *Konzentrationslager 1896 bis heute: eine Analyse* (Stuttgart, 1982), 87–88.

Karl Radek applauded these massacres, referring to the guiltless victims of the terror as persons who did "not participate directly in the White movement." He spoke of their punishment as self-evident: "It is understood that for every Soviet worker, for every leader of the worker revolution who falls at the hands of agents of the counterrevolution, the latter will pay with tens of heads." His only complaint was that the public was still insufficiently involved:

> Five hostages taken from the bourgeoisie, executed on the basis of a public sentence announced by the plenum of the local soviet of workers, peasants, and Red Army deputies, in the presence of thousands of workers who approve of this act, is a more powerful act of mass terror than the execution of 500 persons by decision of the Cheka without the participation of the working masses.[89]

Such was the moral climate of the time that, according to one prisoner of the Cheka, Radek's article calling for "participatory terror" was hailed by prison inmates, many of them hostages, as a humanitarian gesture.[90]

Not one of the leaders of the Bolshevik Party and Government, including those later eulogized as the "conscience of the Revolution," objected publicly to these atrocities, let alone resigned in protest. Indeed, they gave them support: thus, on the Friday following the shooting of Lenin, the top Bolshevik leaders fanned out over Moscow to defend the government's policies. Such expressions of concern and disgust at the carnage and such attempts to save human lives as were made came from Bolsheviks of the second rank, among them M. S. Olminskii, D. B. Riazanov, and E. M. Iaroslavskii, who had little influence on the course of events.*

A curious aspect of the Red Terror in this early phase was that it did not strike at that political party which the Bolsheviks from the outset had identified as the main culprit of the anti-regime violence: the Socialists-Revolutionaries. Whether Moscow did not proceed against them because of their popularity with the peasantry, or because it needed their support in the struggle against the Whites, or because it feared the SRs unleashing a wave of terror against Bolshevik leaders, it never carried out the threat to arrest and shoot masses of SR hostages. During these so-called Lenin Days of the Red Terror, only one SR was executed in Moscow.[91] The great majority of the Cheka's victims were men of the *ancien régime* and ordinary well-to-do citizens, many of whom approved of the harsh repressions of the Bolsheviks. There is evidence of conservative bureaucrats and tsarist officers applauding, while in jail, Bolshevik repression, in the belief that such draconian measures would bring Russia out of chaos and restore her as a great power.[92] We have noted the conciliatory tone adopted in the spring of 1918 toward the Communist regime by the monarchist Vladimir Purishkevich, who praised it for being much

---

*In November 1918 the venerable anarchist theoretician Peter Kropotkin met with Lenin to protest the terror: Lenin, *Khronika*, VI, 195. In 1920 he wrote an impassioned plea against the "medieval" practice of taking hostages: G. Woodcock and I. Avakumovic, *The Anarchist Prince* (London-New York, 1950), 426–27.

"firmer" than the Provisional Government.[93] The fact that the Cheka selected its victims mainly from these groups—politically harmless and in some ways even supportive—confirms that the purpose of the Red Terror was not so much to destroy a specific opposition as to create an atmosphere of general intimidation, for which purpose the attitudes and activities of the terror's victims were a secondary consideration. In a sense the more irrational the terror, the more effective it was, because it made the very process of rational calculation irrelevant, reducing people to the status of a cowed herd. As Krylenko put it: "We must execute not only the guilty. Execution of the innocent will impress the masses even more."[94]

In recent years, the Soviet political police seems to have felt a strong urge to glorify its prototype, the Cheka. In the literature which it lavishly subsidizes, Chekists are depicted as heroes of the Revolution who carried out harsh and unpleasant duties without sacrificing their moral integrity. The typical Chekist is portrayed as uncompromisingly severe in his actions and yet sentimentally tender in his feelings, a spiritual giant with the rare courage and discipline to stifle in himself an inborn humanitarianism in order to accomplish a vital mission on humanity's behalf. Few deserved to join its ranks. As one reads this literature, one cannot help recall a speech by Himmler in 1943 to SS officers in which he hailed them as a superior breed because while massacring thousands of Jews they managed to retain their "decency." The effect of such remarks is to make terror seem harder on the perpetrators than on its victims.*

What it was really like and what kind of people the Cheka attracted can be reconstructed from the testimony of Chekists who either defected to the Whites or fell into their hands.

The procedures followed in taking and executing hostages was described by an ex-Chekist named F. Drugov.[95] According to his testimony, the Cheka initially had no method: it seized hostages for such diverse reasons as occupying important positions under tsarism (especially in the Corps of Gendarmes), holding high rank in the armed forces, owning property or criticizing the new regime. If something happened that in the opinion of the local Cheka office called for the "application of mass terror," an arbitrarily set number of such hostages were taken out of their prison cells and shot. There is evidence to support Drugov's account from one provincial city. In October 1918, in response to the killing of several Soviet officials in Piatigorsk, a North Caucasian city in which many notables of the old regime had taken refuge, the Cheka

---

*An example of such self-pity can be found in the following 1919 statement of a group of Chekists: "Working under . . . incredibly difficult conditions which demand unyielding will and great inner strength, those employees [of the Cheka] who, despite false slander and the swill which is maliciously poured on their heads, continue their work without blemish," etc.: V. P. Antonov-Saratovskii, *Sovety v epokhu voennogo kommunizma*, I (Moscow, 1928), 430–31.

executed fifty-nine hostages. The published list of the victims (which provided neither first names nor patronymics) included General N. V. Ruzskii, who had played an important role in the abdication of Nicholas II, S. V. Rukhlov, the wartime Minister of Transport, and six titled aristocrats. The remainder were mainly generals and colonels of the Imperial Army, with a smattering of others, including a woman identified only as "the daughter of a colonel."[96]

A more systematic approach in dealing with hostages was adopted in the summer of 1919 in connection with Denikin's advance toward Moscow and the need to evacuate prisoners and hostages to prevent their falling into White hands. At this time, according to Drugov, Soviet Russian jails held 12,000 hostages. Dzerzhinskii instructed his staff to work out priorities to establish the order in which hostages would be shot as the need arose. With the help of a certain Dr. Kedrov, Latsis and his fellow Chekists divided the hostages into seven categories, the principal criterion being the victim's personal wealth. The richest hostages, to whom were added ex-officials of the tsarist police, were placed in Category 7; they were to be executed first.

Unlike the mass murder of Jews by the Nazis, every aspect of which is known in sickening detail, even the general course of the Communist holocaust of 1918–20 remains concealed. The executions were often made public, but they were invariably carried out in secret. Of the few available accounts, some of the best are by German journalists in Russia, especially those published in the Berlin *Lokalanzeiger* in defiance of pressure from the Ministry of Foreign Affairs to suppress such information. The following description comes from the *Lokalanzeiger* by way of *The Times* of London:

> Details of these wholesale nocturnal executions are kept secret. It is said that on [Petrovskii] Square, brilliantly lighted with arc lamps, a squad of Soviet soldiers are kept always in readiness to receive victims from the great prison. No time is wasted and no pity expended. Anyone who does not place himself willingly on the place of execution and range himself according to order in the ranks of those about to be executed is simply dragged there.

These practices recall authenticated accounts from Nazi extermination camps. As for the executioners, the correspondent had this to say:

> It is related of some sailors who participated in the executions almost every night that they contracted the execution habit, executions having become necessary to them, just as morphia is to morphia maniacs. They volunteer for the service and cannot sleep unless they have shot some one dead.

Families were not notified of pending or completed executions.*
The worst bestialities were committed by some of the provincial Chekas—

The Times, September 28, 1918, p. 5a. Petrovskii Park, which served as a major slaughter area, subsequently became the locale of the Dynamo football stadium. It was close to Butyrki Prison, where most of the Moscow Cheka's prisoners—usually around 2,500—were incarcerated. Another execution field was located on the opposite, eastern end of Moscow, at Semenovskaia Zastava.

which operated at a distance from the eyes of central organs and had no fear
of being reported on by foreign diplomats or journalists. There exists a detailed
description of the operations of the Kiev Cheka in 1919 by one of its staff,
M. I. Belerosov, a former law student and tsarist officer, which he gave to
General Denikin's investigators.[97]

According to Belerosov, at first (fall and winter of 1918–19) the Kiev
Cheka went on a "continuous spree" of looting, extortion, and rape. Three-
quarters of the staff were Jews, many of them riffraff incapable of any other
work, cut off from the Jewish community although careful to spare fellow
Jews.* This "cottage industry" phase in the Kiev Cheka's Red Terror, as
Belerosov calls it, later gave way to "factorylike" procedures dictated from
Moscow. At its height, in the summer of 1919, before the city fell to the Whites,
the Kiev Cheka had 300 civilian employees and up to 500 armed men.

Death sentences were meted out arbitrarily: people were shot for no
apparent reason and equally capriciously released. While in Cheka prisons
they never knew their fate until that dreaded moment at night when they were
called out for "questioning":

> If a prisoner kept in the Lukianov jail was suddenly summoned to the
> "Cheka," then there could be no doubt as to the reason for the haste. Offi-
> cially, the inmate learned of his fate only when—usually at 1 a.m., the time
> of executions—the cell resounded with a shouted roster of those wanted "for
> questioning." He was taken to the prison department, the chancery, where he
> signed in the appropriate place a registration card, usually without reading
> what was on it. Usually, after the doomed person had signed, it was added:
> so-and-so has been informed of his sentence. In fact, this was something of a
> lie because after the prisoners had left their cells they were not treated "ten-
> derly" and told with relish what fate awaited them. Here the inmate was
> ordered to undress and then was led out for the sentence to be executed.
> . . . For executions there was set up a special garden by the house at 40
> Institute Street . . . where the Provincial Cheka had moved . . . [T]he execu-
> tioner—the commandant, or his deputy, sometimes one of his assistants, and
> occasionally a Cheka "amateur"—led the naked victim into this garden and
> ordered him to lie flat on the ground. Then with a shot in the nape of the
> neck he dispatched him. The executions were carried out with revolvers, usu-
> ally Colts. Because the shot was fired at such close range, the skull of the
> victim usually burst into pieces. The next victim was brought in a like man-
> ner, laid by the side of the previous one, who was usually in a state of agony.
> When the number of victims became too large for the garden to hold, fresh
> victims were placed on top of the previous ones or else shot at the garden's
> entrance . . . The victims usually went to the execution without resisting.
> What they went through cannot be imagined even approximately . . . Most of

*The Cheka, on Dzerzhinskii's instructions, took few Jewish hostages. This was not out of
preference to Jews. One of the purposes in taking hostages was to restrain the Whites from executing
captured Communists. Since the Whites were not expected to care about Jewish lives, taking Jews
hostage, according to Dzerzhinskii, would serve no useful purpose: M. V. Latsis, *Chrezvychainye
Kommissii po bor'be s kontr-revoliutsiei* (Moscow, 1921), 54. According to Belerosov (p. 137) this
policy was reversed in May 1919, when the Kiev Cheka received orders to "shoot some Jews" "for
agitational purposes" and keep them from top positions.

the victims usually requested a chance to say goodbye; and because there was no one else, they embraced and kissed their executioners.*

It is one of the striking features of the Red Terror that its victims almost never resisted or even attempted to flee: they bowed to it as to the inevitable. They seemed to have been under the illusion that by obeying and cooperating they would save their lives, apparently quite unable to realize—for the idea, indeed, defies reason—that they were being victimized not for what they did but for what they were, mere objects whose function it was to teach a lesson to the rest of the population. But there was at work here also a certain ethnic characteristic. Charles de Gaulle, serving in Poland during the Russo-Polish war of 1920, observed that the greater the danger, the more apathetic Slavs tend to become.[98]

As the Red Terror entered its second month, a revulsion made itself felt in middle-level Bolshevik ranks. It intensified during the winter of 1918–19, forcing the government to issue in February 1919 a set of regulations that restricted the Cheka's powers. These restraints, however, remained largely on paper. In the summer of 1919, as the Red armies were falling back before Denikin's offensive and the capture of Moscow seemed imminent, the frightened Bolshevik leadership restored to the Cheka the full freedom to terrorize the population.

Criticism of the Cheka inside the Communist apparatus was inspired less by humanitarian impulses than by annoyance at its independence and fear that unless it was brought under control it would soon threaten loyal Communists. The carte blanche that the Red Terror gave the Cheka endowed it with powers which, by implication, extended over the very leadership of the party. One can imagine the feelings of ordinary party members on hearing Chekists boast that if "they felt like it" they could arrest the Sovnarkom, even Lenin himself, because their only loyalty was to the Cheka.[99]

The first official to say what was on the minds of many rank-and-file Bolsheviks was Olminskii, a member of the *Pravda* editorial staff. In early October 1918 he accused the Cheka of considering itself to be above the party and the soviets.[100] Officials of the Commissariat of the Interior, who were supposed to supervise the provincial administration, expressed displeasure that provincial and *uezd* Chekas ignored the local soviets. In October 1918, the

---

*NChS, No. 9 (1925), 131–32. The Pictorial Archive at the Hoover Institution has a collection of slides, apparently taken by the Whites after capturing Kiev, which shows the local Cheka headquarters and in its garden shallow mass graves containing decomposed naked corpses. In December 1918, the Whites appointed a commission to study Bolshevik crimes in the Ukraine. Its materials were deposited in the Russian Archive in Prague, which the Czech Government, after World War II, turned over to Moscow. There it has been inaccessible to foreign scholars. Some of this commission's published reports can be found in the Melgunov Archive at the Hoover Institution, Box II, and in the Bakhmeteff Archive, Columbia University, Denikin Papers, Box 24.

commissariat sent out an inquiry to the provincial and *uezd* soviets asking how they envisioned their relationship with the local Chekas. Of the 147 soviets that responded, only 20 were content to have the local Cheka acting independently; the remaining 127 (85 percent) wanted them to operate under their supervision.[101] No less annoyed was the Commissariat of Justice, which saw itself eliminated from the process of trying and sentencing political offenders. Its head, N. V. Krylenko, was an enthusiastic proponent of terror, an advocate of executing even innocents, and later a leading prosecutor at Stalin's show trials. But he quite naturally wanted his commissariat to have a hand in the killings. In December 1918 he presented the party's Central Committee with a project which called for the Cheka to confine itself to its original function—namely, investigation—and leave to the Commissariat of Justice the task of trying and sentencing.[102] For the time being, the Central Committee shelved this proposal.

Criticism of the Cheka continued in the winter of 1918–19. There was widespread revulsion at the publication in the *Cheka Weekly,* without editorial comment, of a letter from a group of provincial Bolshevik officials expressing anger that Bruce Lockhart, whom the authorities had accused of complicity in the attempt on Lenin's life, had been released instead of being subjected to the "most refined tortures."[103] Olminskii returned to the fray in February 1919. One of the few prominent Bolsheviks to protest the executions of innocents, he wrote: "One can hold different opinions of the Red Terror. But what now goes on in the provinces is not Red Terror at all, but crime, from beginning to end."[104] Moscow gossip had it that the motto of the Cheka was: "Better execute ten innocent people than spare one who is guilty."[105]

The Cheka fought back. The task fell to Dzerzhinskii's Latvian deputies, Latsis and Peters, for early in October Dzerzhinskii left for a one-month vacation in Switzerland. He had been back on the job for six weeks, supervising the Lenin Days of the Red Terror, when something happened to him. He shaved off his beard and quietly slipped out of Moscow. Traveling by way of Germany to Switzerland, he joined his wife and children, whom he had settled in the Soviet mission in Berne. There exists a photograph of him, taken in October 1918, at the height of the Red Terror, posing in elegant mufti with family on the shores of Lake Lugano.[106] His apparent inability to stand the carnage is the best thing known of this grand master of terror: he would never again display such un-Bolshevik weakness.

In responding to the criticism, Cheka spokesmen defended their organization but also counterattacked. They called the critics "armchair" politicians who had no practical experience in combating the counterrevolution and failed to understand the necessity of conceding the Cheka unrestrained freedom of action. Peters charged that behind the anti-Cheka campaign stood "sinister" elements, "hostile to the proletariat and the Revolution," a hint that criticizing the Cheka could bring charges of treason.[107] To those who claimed that by acting independently of the soviets the Cheka violated the Soviet Constitution, the editorial board of the *Cheka Weekly* responded that the constitution could take effect only "after the bourgeoisie and counterrevolution have been totally crushed."*

But the Cheka apologists did not confine themselves to defending their institution: they glorified it as essential to the triumph of "proletarian dictatorship." Developing Lenin's theme of "class war" as a conflict that knew no frontiers, they depicted themselves as a counterpart of the Red Army, the sole difference between the two being that whereas the Red Army fought the class enemy outside Soviet boundaries, the Cheka and its armed forces combated him on the "domestic front." The notion of the Civil War as "war on two fronts" became one of the favorite themes of the Cheka and its supporters: those who served in the Red Army and those who served in the Cheka were said to be comrades-in-arms, fighting, each in his own way, the "international bourgeoisie."[108] This analogy allowed the Cheka to claim that its license to kill within Soviet territory paralleled the right, indeed the duty, of army personnel to kill on sight enemy soldiers at the front. War was not a court of justice: in the words of Dzerzhinskii (as reported by Radek), innocents died on the home front just as innocents died on the field of battle.[109] It was a position deduced from the premise that politics was warfare. Latsis pushed the analogy to its logical conclusion:

> The Extraordinary Commission [Cheka] is not an investigatory commission, nor is it a court or a tribunal. It is an organ of combat, active on the internal front of the Civil War. It does not judge the enemy: it smites him. It does not pardon those on the other side of the barricade but incinerates them.[110]

This analogy between police terror and military combat ignored, of course, the critical difference between the two—namely, that a soldier fights other armed men at the risk of his life, whereas Cheka personnel killed defenseless men and women at no risk to themselves. The "courage" which the Chekist had to display was not physical or moral courage, but the willingness to stifle his conscience: his "toughness" lay in the ability not to bear suffering but to inflict it. Nevertheless, the Cheka grew very fond of this spurious analogy, with which it sought to rebut criticism and overcome the loathing with which Russians regarded it.

Lenin had to step into the fray. He liked the Cheka and approved of its brutality, but agreed that some of its most egregious abuses had to be curbed, if only to improve its public image. Appalled by the item in the *Cheka Weekly* demanding the application of torture, he ordered this organ of Latsis's closed even as he called Latsis an outstanding Communist.† On November 6, 1918,

---

Pravda, No. 229 (October 23, 1918), 1. Much material on the Cheka controversy of this period is filed in the Melgunov Archive, Box 2, Folder 6, Hoover Institution. See further Leggett, *Cheka,* 121–57.

†On November 7, 1918, addressing a "meeting-concert" of Chekists, Lenin defended the Cheka from its critics. He spoke of its "difficult work" and dismissed complaints about it as "wailing" *(vopli).* Among the qualities of the Cheka he singled out decisiveness, speed, and, above all, "loyalty" *(vernost')* (Lenin, *PSS,* XXXVII, 173). It will be recalled that the device of Hitler's SS was: *"Unsere Ehre heisst Treue"* ("Our honor is called loyalty").

the Cheka was instructed to release all prisoners who had not been charged or against whom charges could not be brought within two weeks. Hostages were also to be let go, except "where needed."* The measure was hailed by Communist organs as an "amnesty" although it was nothing of the kind, since it applied to individuals who not only had not been tried and sentenced but had not even been charged. These rules remained a dead letter: in 1919 Cheka jails continued to overflow with prisoners incarcerated for no stated reason, many of them hostages.

Toward the end of October 1918, the government moved halfheartedly to limit the Cheka's independence by bringing it into a closer relationship with other state institutions. The Moscow headquarters of the Cheka was ordered to admit representatives of the commissariats of Justice and of the Interior; provincial soviets were authorized to appoint and dismiss local Cheka officials.[111] The only meaningful curtailment of police abuses, however, was the dissolution, on January 7, 1919, of the Chekas in the *uezdy*, the smallest administrative entities, which had acquired notoriety for committing the worst atrocities and engaging in large-scale extortion.[112]

The authorities were finally shaken from their complacency by signs of disaffection in the Moscow Committee of the Party, whose meeting on January 23, 1919, heard strong protests against the uncontrolled operations of the Cheka. A motion was introduced to abolish the Cheka: it was defeated as "bourgeois," but a point had been made.[113] A week later, the same committee, the country's most important, voted with a plurality of 4 to 1 to deprive the Cheka of the right to act as tribunal and to limit it to its original function of an investigatory body.[114]

Responding to this dissatisfaction, the Central Committee on February 4 reviewed Krylenko's December 1918 proposal. Dzerzhinskii and Stalin were asked to prepare a report. In recommendations presented a few days later, they proposed that the Cheka retain the double power of investigating sedition and suppressing armed rebellion, but that the sentencing for crimes against the state be reserved for Revolutionary Tribunals. An exception to this rule was to be made for areas under martial law, which happened to encompass large stretches of the country: here the Cheka should be allowed to operate as before and retain the right to mete out capital punishment.[115] The Central Committee approved this recommendation and forwarded it to the Central Executive Committee (CEC) for endorsement.

At the CEC session of February 17, 1919, Dzerzhinskii delivered the principal report.† During the first fifteen months of its existence, he said, the Soviet regime had had to wage a "pitiless" struggle against organized resistance from all quarters. Now, however, in good measure thanks to the work of the Cheka, "our internal enemies, ex-officers, the bourgeoisie and tsarist bureaucracy, are defeated, dispersed." Henceforth, the principal threat would

---

Dekrety, III, 529–30. This was a response to the request of the Presidium of the Moscow Soviet in early October that the Cheka do something about the numerous prisoners whom it was holding without charges: *Severnaia Kommuna*, No. 122 (October 18, 1918), 3.

†It was first published thirty-nine years later in *IA*, No. 1 (1958), 6–11.

102. Dzerzhinskii and Stalin in a jovial moment.

come from counterrevolutionaries who had infiltrated the Soviet apparatus in order to carry out "sabotage" from inside. This called for different methods of struggle. The Cheka no longer needed to wage mass terror: henceforth it would furnish the evidence to the Revolutionary Tribunals, which would try and sentence the offenders.

On the face of it, this marked the end of an era: some contemporaries hailed the reform, which the CEC routinely approved on February 17, as proof that the "proletariat," having crushed the enemy, no longer needed the weapon of terror.[116] But this was no Russian Thermidor: Soviet Russia did not dispense with terror either then or afterward. In 1919, 1920, and the years that followed, the Cheka and its successor, GPU, continued to arrest as well as try, sentence, and execute prisoners and hostages, without reference to the Revolutionary Tribunals. Indeed, as Krylenko explained, this did not matter since "qualitatively" there should have been no difference between the courts and the police.[117] His comment was correct in view of the fact, noted above, that as of 1920 judges could sentence defendants without the customary judiciary procedures if their guilt appeared "obvious," which is exactly what the Cheka did. In October 1919, the Cheka established its own "Special Revolutionary Tribunal."[118] The abortive efforts at reform, nevertheless, deserve to be remembered if only because they show that at least some Bolsheviks had a premonition as early as 1918–19 that the security police threatened not only the enemies of the regime, but also them, its friends.

By 1920, Soviet Russia had become a police state in the sense that the security police, virtually a state within the state, spread its tentacles to all Soviet institutions, including those that managed the economy. In a remarkably short time, the Cheka had transformed itself from an organ responsible for investigating and rendering harmless political dissent into a super-government which not only decided who lived and who died but supervised the day-to-day activities of the entire state apparatus. The development was inevitable. Having laid claim to running the country entirely on its own, the Communist regime had no choice but to engage hundreds of thousands of professionals—"bourgeois specialists" who, by its own definition, were a "class enemy." As such, they required close supervision. This had to be the responsibility of the Cheka, since it alone had the requisite apparatus—a responsibility that enabled the Cheka to insinuate itself into every facet of Soviet life. In his report of February 1919 to the CEC on the new functions of the Cheka Dzerzhinskii said:

> There is no longer any need to make short shrift of mass groupings. Now our enemies have changed the method of combat. Now they are endeavoring to worm themselves into Soviet institutions, so as to sabotage work from within our ranks, until the moment when our external enemies have broken us, and then, seizing the organs and machinery of power, turn them against us. . . . This struggle, if you will, is more individualistic [*edinichnaia*], more subtle. Here one must search; here it is not enough to stay put. . . . We know that in almost all our institutions there sit our enemies, but we cannot destroy our institutions: we must find the threads and catch them. And in this sense the methods of combat now must be entirely different.[119]

The Cheka used this excuse to penetrate all Soviet organizations. And because it retained unlimited power over human lives, its administrative supervision became yet another form of terror, which no Soviet wage earner, Communist or not, could escape. It was natural, therefore, that in March 1919 Dzerzhinskii, while retaining the directorship of the Cheka, was appointed Commissar of the Interior.

In line with its expanded mandate, in mid-1919 high Cheka officials acquired the authority preventively to arrest any citizen and to inspect any and all institutions. What these powers meant in practice can be gathered from the credentials issued to members of the Cheka Collegium. These empowered the bearers to: (1) detain any citizen whom they knew to be guilty or suspected of being guilty of counterrevolutionary activity, speculation, or other crimes, and turn him over to the Cheka; and (2) to have free entry into all state and public offices, industrial and commercial enterprises, schools, hospitals, communal apartments, theaters, as well as railroad and steamship terminals.[120]

The Cheka gradually took over the management and supervision of a broad variety of activities which would not normally be regarded as affecting state security. To enforce ordinances against "speculation"—that is, private trade—in the second half of 1918 the Cheka assumed control over railroads, waterways, highways, and the other means of transport. To carry out these responsibilities efficiently, Dzerzhinskii was appointed, in April 1921, Commissar of Communications.[121] The Cheka supervised and enforced all forms of compulsory labor and enjoyed wide discretionary powers to punish those who evaded this obligation or performed it unsatisfactorily. Execution by shooting was a common method used to this end. We have a valuable insight into the methods the Cheka employed to enhance economic performance from an eyewitness, a Menshevik timber specialist in Soviet employ who happened to be present when Lenin and Dzerzhinskii decided on the means to increase the production of lumber:

> A Soviet decree was then made public, obliging every peasant living near a government forest to prepare and transport a dozen cords of wood. But this raised the question of what to do with the foresters—what to demand of them. In the eyes of the Soviet authorities, these foresters were part and parcel of that sabotaging intelligentsia to whom the new government gave short shrift.
>
> The meeting of the Council of Labor and Defense, discussing this particular problem, was attended by Felix Dzerzhinsky, among other commissars. . . . After listening a while, he said: "In the interests of justice and equality I move: That the foresters be made personally responsible for the fulfilment of the peasants' quota. That, in addition, each forester is himself to fulfil the same quota—a dozen cords of wood."
>
> A few members of the council objected. They pointed out that foresters were intellectuals not used to heavy manual labor. Dzerzhinsky replied that it was high time to liquidate the age-old inequality between the peasants and the foresters.
>
> "Moreover," the Cheka head declared in conclusion, "should the peasants fail to deliver their quota of wood, the foresters responsible for them are to be shot. When a dozen or two of them are shot, the rest will tackle the job in earnest."
>
> It was generally known that the majority of these foresters were anti-Communist. Still, one could feel an embarrassed hush in the room. Suddenly I heard a brusque voice: "Who's against this motion?"
>
> This was Lenin, closing the discussion in his inimitable way. Naturally, no one dared to vote against Lenin and Dzerzhinsky. As an afterthought, Lenin suggested that the point about shooting the foresters, although adopted, be omitted from the official minutes of the session. This, too, was done as he willed.
>
> I felt ill during the meeting. For more than a year, of course, I had known that executions were decimating Russia—but here I myself was present while a five-minute discussion doomed scores of totally innocent men. I was shaken to my innermost being. A cough was choking me, but it was more than the cough of one of my winter colds.
>
> It was plain to me that, when within a week or two the executions of those foresters took place, their deaths would not have moved things forward one single iota. I knew that this terrible decision stemmed from a feeling of resentment and revenge on the part of those who invoked such senseless measures.[122]

There must have been many such decisions which left no trace in the documentation.

The Cheka steadily expanded its military force. In the summer of 1918 its Combat Detachments were formed into an organization separate from the Red

Army, designated as Korpus Voisk VChK (Corps of Armies of the All-Russian Cheka).[123] This security force, modeled on the tsarist Corps of Gendarmes, grew into a regular army for the "home front." In May 1919, on the initiative of Dzerzhinskii in his new capacity as Commissar of the Interior, the government combined all these units into Armies of the Internal Security of the Republic (Voiska Vnutrennei Okhrany Respubliki), placing them under the supervision not of the Commissar of War but of the Commissar of the Interior.[124] At this time, this internal army consisted of 120,000–125,000 men. By the middle of 1920, it doubled, totaling nearly a quarter of a million men who protected industrial establishments and transport facilities, helped the Commissariat of Supply obtain food, and guarded forced labor and concentration camps.[125]

Last but not least, the Cheka formed a bureau of counterintelligence for the armed forces, known as the Osobyi Otdel (Special Department).

By virtue of these functions and the powers which they carried, the Cheka became by 1920 the most powerful institution in Soviet Russia. The foundations of the police state thus were laid while Lenin was in charge and on his initiative.

Among the Cheka's most important responsibilities was organizing and operating "concentration camps," an institution which the Bolsheviks did not quite invent but which they gave a novel and most sinister meaning. In its fully developed form, the concentration camp, along with the one-party state and the omnipotent political police, was Bolshevism's major contribution to the political practices of the twentieth century.

The term "concentration camp" originated at the end of the nineteenth century in connection with colonial wars.* The Spaniards first instituted such camps during the campaign against the Cuban insurrection. Their camps are estimated to have held up to 400,000 inmates. The United States emulated the Spaniards while fighting the Philippine insurrection of 1898; so did Britain during the Boer War. But apart from the name, these early prototypes had little in common with the concentration camps introduced by the Bolsheviks in 1919 and later copied by the Nazis and other totalitarian regimes. The Spanish, American, and British concentration camps were emergency measures adopted during campaigns against colonial guerrillas: their purpose was not punitive but military—namely, the isolation of armed irregulars from the civilian population. Conditions in these early camps admittedly were harsh—as many as 20,000 Boers are said to have perished in British internment. But here there was no deliberate mistreatment: the suffering and deaths were due to the haste with which these camps had been set up, which resulted in

*The best history of this institution is Kaminski's *Konzentrationslager*. The subject has been surprisingly neglected by historians.

inadequate housing, provisioning, and medical care. The inmates of these camps were not made to perform forced labor. In all three cases, the camps were dismantled and the inmates released on the termination of hostilities.

Soviet concentration and forced labor camps *(kontsentratsionnye lageri* and *lageri prinuditel'nykh rabot)* were from the outset different in organization, operation, and purpose:

1. They were permanent: introduced during the Civil War, they did not disappear with the end of hostilities in 1920, but remained in place under various designations, swelling to fantastic proportions in the 1930s, when Soviet Russia was at peace and ostensibly "constructing socialism."

2. They did not hold foreigners suspected of assisting guerrillas, but Russians and other Soviet citizens suspected of political opposition: their primary mission was not to help subdue militarily a colonial people, but to suppress dissent among the country's own citizens.

3. Soviet concentration camps performed an important economic function: their inmates had to work where ordered, which meant that they were not only isolated but also exploited as slave labor.

Talk of concentration camps was first heard in Soviet Russia in the spring of 1918 in connection with the Czech uprising and the induction of former Imperial officers.* At the end of May, Trotsky threatened Czechs who refused to surrender arms with confinement to concentration camps.† On August 8, he ordered that, for the protection of the railroad line from Moscow to Kazan, concentration camps be constructed at several nearby localities to isolate such "sinister agitators, counterrevolutionary officers, saboteurs, parasites and speculators" as were not executed "on the spot" or given other penalties.[126] Thus, the concentration camp was conceived of as a place of detention for citizens who could not be specifically charged but whom, for one reason or another, the authorities preferred not to execute. Lenin used the term in this sense in a cable to Penza of August 9, in which he ordered that mutinous "kulaks" be subjected to "merciless mass terror"—that is, executions—but "dubious ones incarcerated in concentration camps outside the cities."‡ These threats acquired legal and administrative sanction on September 5, 1918, in the "Resolution on Red Terror," which provided for the "safeguarding of the Soviet Republic from class enemies by means of isolating them in concentration camps."

It seems, however, that few concentration camps were built in 1918 and that those which were owed their existence to the initiative of the provincial Chekas or of the military command. The construction of concentration camps

---

*The most comprehensive account of Soviet concentration camps is Mikhail Geller's *Kontsentratsionnyi mir i sovetskaia literatura* (London, 1974), of which there exist German, French, and Polish translations, but not an English one.

†L. D. Trotskii, *Kak vooruzhalas' revoliutsiia,* I (Moscow, 1923), 214, 216. According to Geller *(Kontsentratsionnyi mir,* 73), this is the earliest use of the term in Soviet sources.

‡Lenin, *PSS,* L, 143–44. Peters, in his capacity as deputy director of the Cheka, said that all those caught with arms would be "shot on the spot" and those who agitated against the government confined to concentration camps: *Izvestiia,* No. 188/452 (September 1, 1918), 3.

began in earnest in the spring of 1919 on the initiative of Dzerzhinskii. Lenin did not want his name linked with these camps, and the decrees establishing them and detailing their structure and operations came out in the name not of the Council of People's Commissars but of the Central Executive Committee of the Soviets and its chairman, Sverdlov. They implemented recommendations contained in the report by Dzerzhinskii of February 17, 1919, on the reorganization of the Cheka. Dzerzhinskii argued that the existing judiciary measures to combat sedition were not sufficient:

> Along with sentencing by courts it is necessary to retain administrative sentencing—namely, the concentration camp. Even today the labor of those under arrest is far from being utilized in public works, and so I recommend that we retain these concentration camps for the exploitation of labor of persons under arrest: gentlemen who live without any occupation [and] those who are incapable of doing work without some compulsion; or, in regard to Soviet institutions, such a measure of punishment ought to be applied for unconscientious attitude toward work, for negligence, for lateness, etc. With this measure we should be able to pull up even our very own workers.[127]

Dzerzhinskii, Kamenev, and Stalin (the co-drafters of this decree) conceived of the camps as a combination "school of work" and pool of labor. In accord with their recommendation, the CEC adopted the following resolution:

> The All-Russian Extraordinary Commission [Cheka] is empowered to confine to concentration camps, under the guidance of precise instructions concerning the rules of imprisonment in a concentration camp approved by the All-Russian Central Executive Committee.[128]

For reasons that are not clear, in 1922 and subsequently, the term "concentration camps" was replaced by "camps of forced labor" *(lageri prinuditel'nykh rabot)*.

On April 11, 1919, the CEC issued a "Decision" concerning the organization of such camps. It provided for the establishment of a network of forced labor camps under the authority of the Commissariat of the Interior—now headed by Dzerzhinskii:

> Subject to internment in the camps of forced labor are individuals or categories of individuals concerning whom decisions had been taken by organs of the administration, Chekas, Revolutionary Tribunals, People's Courts, and other Soviet organs authorized to do so by decrees and instructions.[129]   .

Several features of this landmark decree call for comment. Soviet concentration camps, as instituted in 1919, were meant to be a place of confinement for all kinds of undesirables, whether sentenced by courts or by administrative organs. Liable to confinement in them were not only individuals but also "categories of individuals"—that is, entire classes: Dzerzhinskii at one point proposed that special concentration camps be erected for the "bourgeoisie." Living in forced isolation, the inmates formed a pool of slave labor on which Soviet administrative and economic institutions could draw at no cost. The network of camps was run by the Commissariat of the Interior, first through the Central Administration of Camps and later through the Main Camp Administration (Glavnoe Upravlenie Lageriami), popularly known as Gulag. One can perceive here, not only in principle but also in practical detail, Stalin's concentration camp empire: it differed from Lenin's only in size.

The CEC resolutions approving the creation of concentration camps called for detailed instructions to guide their operations. A decree issued on May 12, 1919,[130] spelled out in meticulous bureaucratic language the constitution of the camps: how they were to be organized, what were the duties and putative rights of the inmates. The decree ordered every provincial capital city to construct a forced labor camp capable of holding 300 or more inmates. Since Soviet Russia had (depending on the shifting fortunes of the Civil War) about thirty-eight provinces, this provision called for facilities for a minimum of 11,400 prisoners. But this figure could be greatly expanded, for the decree authorized also district capital cities to construct concentration camps, and these numbered in the hundreds. Responsibility for organizing the camps was given to the Cheka; after they were in place, authority over them was to pass to the local soviets. This provision, one of many in Bolshevik legislation meant to keep alive the myth that the soviets were "sovereign" organs, was rendered inoperative by the assignment of responsibility for the "general administration" of the camps in Soviet Russia to a newly formed Department of Forced Labor (Otdel Prinuditel'nykh Rabot) of the Commissariat of the Interior, which, as noted, happened to have been headed by the same individual who directed the Cheka.

Russian governments had an old tradition of exploiting convict labor: "In no other country has the utilization of forced labor in the economy of the state itself played as significant a role as in the history of Russia."[131] The Bolsheviks revived this tradition. Inmates of Soviet concentration camps, from their birth in 1919, had at all times to perform physical labor either inside or outside the place of confinement. "Immediately upon their arrival in the camp," the instruction read, "all inmates are to be assigned to work and they are to occupy themselves with physical labor throughout their stay." To encourage camp authorities to exploit prison labor to the fullest, as well as to save the government money, it was stipulated that the camps had to be fully self-supporting:

> The costs of running the camp and the administration, when there is a full complement of inmates, must be covered by the inmates' labor. The responsibility for deficits will be borne by the administration and the inmates in accord with rules stipulated in a separate instruction.*

*It is incorrect, therefore, to argue, as is done by some authorities, that initially the Soviet concentration camps served to terrorize the population, acquiring economic significance only in 1927 under Stalin. In fact, the practice of having penal labor pay for itself and even bring the state income

Attempts to escape from the camps were subject to severe punishments: for a first attempt, a recaptured prisoner could have his sentence prolonged as much as ten times; for a second, he was to be turned over to a Revolutionary Tribunal, which could sentence him to death. To further discourage escapes, the camp authorities were empowered to institute "collective responsibility" *(krugovaia poruka),* which made fellow inmates accountable for each other. In theory, an inmate had the right to complain of mistreatment in a book kept for the purpose.

Thus, the modern concentration camp was born—an enclave within which human beings lost all rights and became slaves of the state. In this connection, the question may arise as to the difference between the status of an inmate in a concentration camp and that of an ordinary Soviet citizen. After all, no one in Soviet Russia enjoyed personal rights or had recourse to law, and everyone could be ordered, under decrees providing for compulsory labor, to work wherever the state wanted. The line separating freedom from imprisonment in the Soviet Russia of that time was indeed blurred. For example, in May 1919, Lenin decreed the mobilization of labor for military construction on the southern front.[132] He stipulated that the mobilized work force was to consist "primarily of prisoners as well as citizens confined to concentration camps and sentenced to hard labor." But if these were insufficient, the decree called for pulling "into the labor obligation also local inhabitants." Here, camp inmates were distinguished from ordinary, "free" citizens only by being the first to be drafted for forced labor. Even so, significant differences separated the two categories. Citizens not confined to camps normally lived with their families and had access to the free market to supplement their rations, whereas camp inmates could have only occasional visits from relatives and were forbidden to receive food packages. Ordinary citizens did not live, day in and day out, under the watchful eyes of the commandant and his assistants (often Communist trustees), who were held responsible for squeezing enough labor from their charges to cover their own salaries as well as the costs of running the camp. Also, they were not quite so liable to be punished, under the practice of "collective responsibility," for the actions of others.

At the end of 1920, Soviet Russia had eighty-four concentration camps with approximately 50,000 prisoners; three years later (October 1923), the number had increased to 315 camps with 70,000 inmates.[133]

Information on conditions in the early Soviet concentration camps is sparse and few scholars have shown an interest in the subject.[134] The occasional testimonies smuggled out by inmates or provided by survivors paint a picture that to the smallest detail resembles descriptions of Nazi camps: so much so that were it not that they had been published two decades earlier, one might suspect them to be recent forgeries. In 1922, Socialist-Revolutionary émigrés

---

went back to tsarist days; thus, in 1886 the Ministry of the Interior instructed the administration of hard labor installations to make certain that convict labor showed a profit: Pipes, *Russia under the Old Regime,* 310.

brought out in Germany, under the editorship of Victor Chernov, a volume of reports by survivors of Soviet prisons and camps. Included was a description of life in a concentration camp at Kholmogory, near Archangel, written in early 1921 by an anonymous female prisoner. The camp had four compounds holding 1,200 inmates. The prisoners were housed in an expropriated cloister whose accommodations were relatively comfortable and well heated. The author describes it nevertheless as a "death camp." Hunger was endemic: food packages, some sent by American relief organizations, were immediately confiscated. The commandant, who bore a Latvian name, had prisoners shot for the most trifling offenses: if a prisoner, while working in the fields, dared to eat a vegetable that he had dug up, he was killed on the spot and then reported as having tried to escape. The flight of a prisoner automatically led to the execution of nine others, bound to him by "collective responsibility," as provided for by law; a recaptured escapee was killed as well, sometimes by being buried alive. The administration regarded the inmates as ciphers, whose survival or death was a matter of no consequence.[135]

Thus came into existence a central institution of the totalitarian regime:

> Trotsky and Lenin were the inventors and the creators of the new form of the concentration camp. [This means not only] that they created establishments called "concentration camps." . . . The leaders of Soviet communism also created a specific method of legal reasoning, a network of concepts that implicitly incorporated a gigantic system of concentration camps, which Stalin merely organized technically and developed. Compared with the concentration camps of Trotsky and Lenin, the Stalinist ones represented merely a gigantic form of implementation [*Ausführungsbestimmung*]. And, of course, the Nazis found in the former as well as the latter ready-made models, which they merely had to develop. The German counterparts promptly seized upon these models. On March 13, 1921, the then hardly known Adolf Hitler wrote in the *Völkischer Beobachter:* "One prevents the Jewish corruption of our people, if necessary, by confining its instigators to concentration camps." On December 8 of that year, in a speech to the National Club in Berlin, Hitler expressed his intention of creating concentration camps upon taking power.[136]

The Red Terror had many aspects, but the historian's first and foremost concern must be with its victims. Their number cannot be determined, and it is unlikely that it ever will be, for it is almost certain that Lenin ordered the Cheka archives destroyed.[137] The closest to an official Soviet figure for the number executed between 1918 and 1920, furnished by Latsis, is 12,733. This figure, however, has been challenged as a vast underestimation on the grounds that, according to Latsis's own admission, in the twenty provinces of central Russia in a single year (1918) there were 6,300 executions, 4,520 of whose victims had been shot for counterrevolutionary activity.[138] Latsis's figures are entirely disproportionate to the statistics available for some of the major cities.

Thus, William Henry Chamberlin had seen at the Prague Russian Archive (now in Moscow) a report of the Ukrainian Cheka for the year 1920—by which time the death penalty had been formally abolished—listing 3,879 executions, 1,418 of them in Odessa and 538 in Kiev.[139] Inquiries into Bolshevik atrocities in Tsaritsyn came up with an estimate of 3,000 to 5,000 victims.[140] According to *Izvestiia,* between May 22 and June 22, 1920, the Revolutionary Tribunals alone—that is, without Cheka victims being taken into account—condemned to death 600 citizens, including 35 for "counterrevolution," 6 for spying, and 33 for dereliction of duty.* Using such figures, Chamberlin estimates a total of 50,000 victims of the Red Terror, and Leggett, 140,000.[141] All one can say with any assurance is that if the victims of Jacobin terror numbered in the thousands, Lenin's terror claimed tens if not hundreds of thousands of lives. Victims of the next wave of terror, launched by Stalin and Hitler, would be counted in the millions.

To what purpose this carnage?

Dzerzhinskii, supported by Lenin, was given to boasting that terror and its instrument, the Cheka, had saved the Revolution. This appraisal is proba- bly correct, as long as "the Revolution" is identified with the Bolshevik dicta- torship. There exists solid evidence that by the summer of 1918, when the Bolsheviks launched the terror, they were rejected by all strata of the popula- tion except for their own apparatus. Under these circumstances, "merciless terror" was indeed the only way of preserving the regime.

This terror had to be not only "merciless" (can one even conceive of "merciful" terror?) but also indiscriminate. If the opponents of the Bolshevik dictatorship had been an identifiable minority, then one could have targeted them for surgical removal. But in Soviet Russia it was the regime and its supporters that were a minority. To stay in power, the dictatorship had first to atomize society and then destroy in it the very will to act. The Red Terror gave the population to understand that under a regime that felt no hesitation in executing innocents, innocence was no guarantee of survival. The best hope of surviving lay in making oneself as inconspicuous as possible, which meant abandoning any thought of independent public activity, indeed any concern with public affairs, and withdrawing into one's private world. Once society disintegrated into an agglomeration of human atoms, each fearful of being noticed and concerned exclusively with physical survival, then it ceased to matter what society thought, for the government had the entire sphere of public activity to itself. Only under these conditions could a small minority subjugate millions.

But the price of such a regime was not cheap, either for its victims or for its practitioners. To stay in power against the wishes of the overwhelming majority, the Bolsheviks had to distort that power beyond all recognition. Terror may have saved communism, but it corroded its very soul.

Isaac Steinberg noted with a keen eye the devastating impact of the Red

---

*Izvestiia, No. 155/1,002 (July 16, 1920), 2. The largest number of victims (273) were executed for desertion and self-inflicted wounds to avoid military service.

Terror on both the citizens and the authorities. Traveling in a streetcar in 1920, he was struck by an analogy between that packed vehicle and the country at large:

> Does not our land resemble today's streetcars, which drag themselves along Moscow's dreary streets, worn out and creaking from old age, weighed down with people hanging on to it? How tightly these people are squeezed, how difficult it is to breathe here, as if after an exhausting fight. How hungry is the look in their eyes! See how shamelessly they steal seats from one another, how this mass of humanity, accidentally chained together, seems to lack all sense of mutual sympathy and understanding, how everyone sees in his fellow man only a rival! . . . Mindless hatred for the streetcar conductor—this expresses the feeling of this casual mass toward the government, the state, the organization. Indifference and irony toward those who crowd at the car's entrance hoping to get in—this is their attitude toward the community, toward solidarity. When one observes them more intently one realizes that at bottom they are close to one another: the same thought, the same spark shines fraternally in their hostile eyes; the same pain weeps in them all. But now, here, they are pitiless enemies.[142]

But he also notes the effect of terror on its perpetrators:

> When the terror strikes the class enemy, the bourgeois, when it tramples *his* self-esteem and the feeling of love, when it separates him from his family or confines him to his family, when it torments his spirit and causes it to wilt— whom does this terror strike? Only the class nature of the enemy, unique only to him and destined to disappear along with him? Or does it also, at the same time, strike something general, something that concerns all mankind, namely man's human nature? The feelings of pity and suffering, the longing for the spirit and for freedom, the attachment to the family, and the yearning for the far away—all that which makes "men" out of men—these things, after all, are known and common to *both* camps. And when the terror stamps out, banishes, and exposes to ridicule feelings common to mankind in one group, then it does the same everywhere, in all souls. . . . The sense of dignity violated in the camp of the enemy, the suppressed feelings of pity for the enemy, the pain inflicted on some enemy, rebound, through a psychological reflex, back to the camp of the victors. . . . Slavery produces the same effect in the soul of the victor as in that of the vanquished.[143]

The outside world heard muffled reverberations of the Bolshevik terror from newspaper accounts, reports of visitors, and Russian refugees. Some reacted with revulsion, a few with sympathy: but the prevalent response was one of indifference. Europe preferred not to know. It had just emerged from a war that had claimed millions of lives. It desperately wanted to return to normalcy; it felt incapable of absorbing still more stories of mass death. So it lent a willing ear to those who assured it, sometimes sincerely, sometimes deceptively, that things in Red Russia were not as bad as depicted, that the terror was over, and that, in any event, it had no bearing on its own destiny. It was, after all, the exotic, cruel Russia of Ivan the Terrible, Dostoevsky's "underground men," and Rasputin.

It was easy to be misled. The Soviet disinformation machine minimized the casualties of the terror and magnified its alleged provocations. It was especially effective with well-meaning foreign visitors, such as the rich American dilettante William Bullitt, who breezed through Soviet Russia in February 1919 on a mission for President Wilson. On his return, he informed the U.S. Congress that the tales of bloody terror had been wildly exaggerated. "The red terror is over," he assured his listeners, stating that the Cheka had executed in all of Russia "only" 5,000 people. "Executions are extremely rare."* Lincoln Steffens reported on his visit to Soviet Russia that "the Bolshevik leaders regret and are ashamed of their red terror."[144]

Although Bullitt and Steffens minimized the terror, at least they admitted it. But what is one to make of a "witness" like Pierre Pascal, a young French ex-officer posted in Russia turned Communist, later a professor at the Sorbonne, who denied it and mocked its victims? "The terror is finished," he wrote in February 1920:

> To tell the truth, it never existed. This word "terror," which for a Frenchman corresponds to a precise idea, has always made me laugh here, on seeing the moderation, the sweetness, the good nature of this terrible Extraordinary Commission [Cheka] charged with its enforcement.[145]

Others yet found consolation in the thought that if one kind of terror ravaged Soviet Russia, then another kind, said to be no less dreadful, afflicted Western Europe and the United States. In 1925, a group calling itself the International Committee for Political Prisoners published a collection of smuggled testimonies from prisoners in Soviet jails and camps. No one questioned their authenticity. Yet when the editor, Isaac Don Levine, asked some of the world's leading intellectuals what they thought of this appalling evidence, the responses ranged from mildly shocked to snide and cynical. Few saw the significance of this material, as did Albert Einstein, in the "tragedy of human history in which one murders for fear of being murdered." Romain Rolland, the author of *Jean Christophe,* made light of the evidence on the grounds that "almost identical things [were] going on in the prisons of California where they [were] martyring the workingmen of the I.W.W." Upton Sinclair seconded him by professing sham surprise that the treatment of Soviet prisoners was "about the same as the conditions of prisoners in the state of California." Bertrand Russell went one better: he "sincerely hoped" that the publication of these documents would contribute toward "the promotion of friendly relations" between Soviet and Western governments on the grounds that both engaged in similar practices.[146]

The Bullitt Mission to Russia (New York, 1919), 58, 50. Bullitt at the time favored U.S. recognition of the U.S.S.R. In 1933 he became America's first ambassador to that country. Later in his life he turned passionately anti-Communist.

Afterword

In November 1918, when the Great War came to an end, the Bolsheviks controlled twenty-seven provinces of European Russia, inhabited by some 70 million people, or one-half of the Empire's pre-war population. The borderlands—Poland, Finland, the Baltic area, the Ukraine, Transcaucasia, Central Asia, and Siberia—had either separated themselves and formed sovereign states or were controlled by anti-Bolshevik Whites. The Communist realm encompassed the defunct Empire's heartland, populated almost exclusively by Great Russians. Ahead lay a civil war in the course of which Moscow would reconquer by force of arms most but not all of its borderland areas and try to spread its regime to Europe, the Middle East, and East Asia. The Revolution now would enter another phase, that of expansion.

The first year of Bolshevik rule left Russians not only cowed by the unprecedented application of largely random terror but thoroughly bewildered. Those who had lived through it were exposed to a complete reevaluation of all values: whatever had been good and rewarded was now evil and punished. The traditional virtues of faith in God, charity, tolerance, patriotism, and thrift were denounced by the new regime as unacceptable legacies of a doomed civilization. Killing and robbing, slander and lying were good, if committed for the sake of a proper cause as defined by the new regime. Nothing made sense. The perplexity of contemporaries is reflected in the ruminations published in the summer of 1918 in one of the few relatively independent dailies still allowed to appear:[1]

There was a time when a man lived somewhere beyond the Narva Gate, in the morning drunk tea from a samovar placed in front of him. For dinner, he emptied half a bottle of vodka and read *The Petrograd Rag*. When once a year someone was murdered, he felt indignant for a whole week, at the very least. And now . . .

About murders, dear sir, they have stopped writing: on the contrary, they inform us that the day before only thirty people have been bumped off and another hundred robbed. . . . This means that everything is in order. And whatever happens, it is better not even to look out of the window. Today they parade with red flags, tomorrow with banners, then again with red ones, and then again with banners. Today Kornilov has been killed, tomorrow he is resurrected. The day after Kornilov is not Kornilov but Dutov, and Dutov is Kornilov, and they are, all of them, neither officers nor Cossacks nor even Russians but Czechs. And where these Czechs came from, no one knows. . . . We fight them, they fight us. Nicholas Romanov has been killed, he has not been killed. Who killed whom, who fled where, why the Volga is no longer the Volga and the Ukraine no longer Russia. Why the Germans promise to return to us the Crimea, where did the Hetman come from, what Hetman, why does he have a boil under his nose. . . . Why aren't we in an insane asylum?

So unnatural were the new conditions, they so outraged common sense and decency, that the vast majority of the population viewed the regime responsible for them as some terrible and inexplicable cataclysm which could not be resisted but had to be endured until it disappeared as suddenly as it had come. As time would show, however, these expectations were mistaken. Russians and the people under their rule would know no respite: those who experienced and survived the Revolution would never see the return of normalcy. The Revolution was only the beginning of their sorrows.

GLOSSARY

NOTE: The accent over a Russian letter indicates the stress.
The letter "ё" is pronounced "yo" and stressed.

apparátchik/i	Communist bureaucratic "operator/s"
artél'	worker or peasant cooperative
batrák/i	poor peasant/s; farmhand/s
bol'shák	head of peasant household
bunt	rebellion; mutiny
burzhúi	bourgeois
Cheká	Soviet secret police (1917–21)
cherespolósitsa	strip farming
chin	official rank
chinóvnik/i	official/s; bureaucrat/s
derévnia/i	village/s
desiatína/y	land measure equal to 2.7 acres
Dúma	lower house of Russian parliament
duván	division of loot
dvoevlástie	dyarchy
dvor	household; court
dvoriáne	gentry
dvorianín	a member of the gentry
dvoriánstvo	the gentry estate
eshelón (echelon)	military train
Fabzavkóm/y	Factory Committee/s (1917–20)
glásnost'	open government
glávka/i	subdivision/s of VSNKh
gosudár'	sovereign
gosudárstvo	state; government
gubérniia/i	province/s
Gubispolkóm/y	Provincial Soviet Executive Committee/s
Gulág	Administration of concentration camps
inogoródnyi	settler from other towns

intelligént/y	member/s of the intelligentsia
Ispolkóm	Executive Committee
isprávnik	tsarist police official
iúnker	student at military academy
izbá	peasant hut
kátorga	hard labor
khoziáin	same as *bol'shak*
khútor	farm; farmstead
kombédy	Committees of the [Village] Poor (1918)
Kompród	Commissariat of Supply
Komúch	Committee of the Constituent Assembly
kramóla	sedition
krest'iáne	peasants
krestiánstvo	peasantry
kulák	prominent peasant; rural exploiter
kustár'	craftsman; artisan
meshcháne	burghers
meshóchnik	illegal food peddler (1918–20)
miatézh	mutiny; revolt
Milrevkóm	Military-Revolutionary Committee
mir	peasant commune
muzhík/í	peasant/s
nadél/y	communal land allotment/s
nagáika	Cossack whip
naród	the people
Naródnaia Vólia	People's Will
Narodovól'tsy	members of People's Will
óblast'/i	region/s
obshchína	same as *mir*
Okhrána	Imperial security police
otrézok	small land allotment
ótrub	land in the commune privately owned
paëk	ration
páshnia	arable land
peredél	repartition of communal land
peredýshka	breathing spell; respite
pogróm	beating and looting, usually of Jews
polpréd	Soviet diplomatic representative
poméshchik/i	non-peasant landowner/s
pomést'e/ia	fief/s; landed estate/s
pop	Orthodox priest
pravítel'stvo	government
Pravoslávie	Greek Orthodox religion
prodrazvërstka	requisition of farm produce
prómysly	cottage industries

pud	weight measure equal to 16.38 kilograms
Ráda	Ukrainian for "Soviet"
raskól'niki	pejorative for religious dissenters
razgróm	assaults on property
samoderzhávie	autocracy
samoderzhávnyi	autocratic
seló/á	large village/s
sél'skii skhod	village assembly
soiúz	union; association
soslóvie/ia	legal estate/s
sovét/y	council/s
Sovnarkóm	Council of People's Commissars
ssýlka	penal exile
staroobriádtsy	Old Believers (lit. "Old Ritualists")
starósta	elected village official
tiáglo	in Muscovy, obligatory state labor
Trudármiia	Labor Army (introduced in 1920)
Trudovík	member of peasant party in Duma
tsentr/y	same as *glavka/i*
uézd	lowest administrative entity
ukáz	Imperial decree
vlast'	authority; government
vólia	freedom; license
vólost'	smallest rural administrative unit
vótchina	allodium; patrimony
vozhd'	leader
VSNKh	Supreme Council of the National Economy
zakónnost'	legality
Zemgór	Union of Municipal Councils and Zemstva
zemliá	land
zémstvo/a	organ/s of provincial self-government
zhid/ý	pejorative term for Jew/s

CHRONOLOGY

The chronology lists the principal events dealt with in this book. Unless otherwise indicated, dates prior to February 1918 are given according to the Julian calendar ("Old Style"), which was twelve days behind the Western calendar in the nineteenth century and thirteen days behind in the twentieth. From February 1918 on dates are given in the "New Style," which corresponds to dates in the Western calendar.

1899

February–March: Strike of Russian university students.
July 29: "Temporary Rules" authorizing induction into the armed forces of unruly
    students.

1900

Government restricts taxation powers of *zemstva*.
November: Disturbances in Kiev and at other universities.

1901

January II: Induction into the army of 183 Kievan students.
February: Assassination of Minister of Education Bogolepov. First police-sponsored
    (Zubatov) trade unions formed.

1902

Winter 1901–2: Formation of Russian Socialist-Revolutionary Party (PSR).
June: Liberals publish in Germany, under the editorship of Struve, fortnightly
    Osvobozhdenie (Liberation).
March: Lenin's *What Is to Be Done?*
April 2: Assassination of Interior Minister Sipiagin; he is succeeded by Plehve.

1903

April 4: Kishinev pogrom.
July–August: Second (founding) Congress of Russian Social-Democratic Party: split
    into Menshevik and Bolshevik factions.
July 20–22: Union of Liberation founded in Switzerland.

1904

January 3–5: Union of Liberation organized in St. Petersburg.
February 4: Plehve authorizes Gapon's Assembly.
February 8: Japanese attack Port Arthur; beginning of Russo-Japanese War.
July 15: Assassination of Plehve.
August: Russians defeated at Liaoyang.
August 25: Sviatopolk-Mirskii Minister of the Interior.
October 20: Second Congress of Union of Liberation.
November 6–9: Zemstvo Congress in St. Petersburg.
November–December: Union of Liberation organizes nationwide campaign of banquets.
December 7: Nicholas and high officials discuss reform proposals; idea of introducing elected representatives into State Council rejected.
December 12: Publication of edict promising reforms.
December 20: Port Arthur surrenders to the Japanese.

1905

January 7–8: Major industrial strike in St. Petersburg organized by Father Gapon.
January 9: Bloody Sunday.
January 18: Sviatopolk-Mirskii dismissed; replaced by Bulygin.
January 10 ff.: Wave of industrial strikes throughout Russia.
January 18: Government promises convocation of Duma and invites population to submit petitions stating grievances.
February: Government-sponsored elections in St. Petersburg factories.
February: Russians abandon Mukden.
March 18: All institutions of higher learning closed for remainder of academic year.
April: Second Zemstvo Congress calls for Constituent Assembly.
Spring: 60,000 peasant petitions submitted.
May 8: Union of Unions formed under chairmanship of Miliukov.
May 14: Russian fleet destroyed in battle of Tsushima Strait; D. F. Trepov appointed Deputy Minister of the Interior.
June: Riots and massacres in Odessa; mutiny on the battleship *Potemkin.*
August 6: Bulygin (consultative) Duma announced.
August 27: Government announces liberal university regulations.
September 5 (NS): Russo-Japanese peace treaty signed at Portsmouth, New Hampshire.
September: Students open university facilities to workers; mass agitation.
September 19: Strike activity resumes.
October 9–10: Witte urges Nicholas to make major political concessions.
October 12–18: Constitutional-Democratic (Kadet) Party formed.
October 13: Central strike committee formed in St. Petersburg, soon renamed St. Petersburg Soviet.
October 14: Capital paralyzed by strikes.
October 15: Witte submits draft of what became October Manifesto.
October 17: Nicholas signs October Manifesto.
October 18 ff.: Anti-Jewish and anti-student pogroms; rural violence begins.
October–November: As Chairman of Council of Ministers, Witte initiates discussions with public figures to have them join cabinet.
November 21: Moscow Soviet formed.

November 24: Preliminary censorship of periodicals abolished.
December 6: St. Petersburg Soviet orders general strike.
December 8: Armed uprising in Moscow suppressed by force.

1906

March 4: Laws issued guaranteeing the rights of assembly and association.
April 16: Witte resigns as Chairman of Council of Ministers, replaced by Goremykin.
April 26: New Fundamental Laws (constitution) made public; Stolypin Minister of the Interior.
April 27: Duma opens.
July 8: Duma dissolved; Stolypin appointed Chairman of Council of Ministers.
August 12: Attempt by Socialist-Revolutionary Maximalists on Stolypin's life.
August 12 and 27: Stolypin's first agrarian reforms.
August 19: Courts-martial for civilians introduced.
November 9: Stolypin's reform concerning communal landholding.

1907

February 20: Second Duma opens.
March: Stolypin announces reform program.
June 2: Second Duma dissolved; new electoral law.
November 7: Third Duma opens; in session until 1912.

1911

January–March: Western *zemstvo* crisis.
September 1: Stolypin shot; dies four days later; replaced by Kokovtsov.

1912

November 15: Fourth (and last) Duma opens.
Conclusive split between Bolsheviks and Mensheviks.

1914

January 20: Goremykin Chairman of Council of Ministers.
July 15/28: Nicholas orders partial mobilization.
July 17/30: Full Russian mobilization.
July 18/31: German ultimatum to Russia.
July 19/August 1: Germany declares war on Russia.
July 27: Russia suspends convertibility of ruble.
August: Russian armies invade East Prussia and Austrian Galicia.
Late August: Russian armies crushed in East Prussia.
September 3: Russians capture Lemberg (Lwow), capital of Austrian Galicia.

1915

April 15/28: Germans launch offensive operations in Poland.
June 11: Sukhomlinov dismissed as Minister of War; replaced by Polivanov.
June: Further cabinet changes.

June–July: Formation of Progressive Bloc.
July: Special Council of Defense of the Country created; other councils and committees follow to help with war effort, including Military-Industrial Committees.
July 9/22: Russians begin withdrawal from Poland.
July 19: Duma reconvened for six weeks; Russian troops evacuate Warsaw.
August 21: Most ministers request Nicholas to let Duma form cabinet.
August 22: Nicholas assumes personal command of Russian armed forces, departs for headquarters at Mogilev.
August 25: Progressive Bloc makes public nine-point program.
August: Government authorizes creation of national *zemstvo* and Municipal Council organizations.
September 3: Duma prorogued.
September: Zimmerwald Conference of anti-war socialists.
November: Central Workers' Group formed.
November: Zemgor created.

1916

January 20: Goremykin replaced as Chairman of Council of Ministers by Stürmer (Shtiurmer).
March 13: Polivanov dismissed as Minister of War; replaced by Shuvaev.
April: Kiental conference of anti-war socialists.
May 22/June 4: Brusilov offensive opens.
September 18: Protopopov Acting Minister of the Interior; promoted to Minister of the Interior in December.
October 22–24: Conference of Kadet Party decides on strategy of confrontation at forthcoming Duma session.
November 1: Duma reconvenes; Miliukov address implies treason in high places.
November 8–10: Dismissal of Stürmer.
November 19: A. F. Trepov, appointed Chairman of Council of Ministers, appeals to Duma for cooperation.
December 17: Murder of Rasputin.
December 18: Nicholas leaves Mogilev for Tsarskoe Selo.
December 27: Trepov dismissed, replaced by Golitsyn.

1917

January 27: Protopopov arrests Workers' Group.
February 14: Duma reconvened.
February 22: Nicholas departs for Mogilev.
February 23: Demonstrations in Petrograd in connection with International Women's Day.
February 24: More demonstrations in Petrograd.
February 25: Demonstrations turn violent; Nicholas orders them suppressed by force.
February 26: Petrograd under military occupation; unit of Volynskii Regiment fires on crowd, killing forty; company of Pavlovskii Regiment mutinies in protest.
Night of February 26–27: Pavlovskii Regiment troops hold all-night meeting, vote to disobey orders to fire on civilians.
February 27: Most of Petrograd in the hands of mutinous garrison; burning of government buildings; Nicholas orders General Ivanov to proceed to Petrograd

with special troops to quell disorders; Mensheviks call for elections to Soviet; in the evening, organizing meeting of Petrograd Soviet.

February 28: Early morning, Nicholas departs for Tsarskoe Selo; Duma Council of Elders meets, forms Provisional Committee; throughout Petrograd, factory and garrison units elect representatives to the Soviet; first plenary session of Soviet. Disturbances spread to Moscow.

Night of February 28–March 1: Imperial train stopped, diverted to Pskov.

March 1: Ispolkom drafts nine-point program to serve as basis of agreement with Duma Provisional Committee; issues Order No. 1. In the evening, Nicholas arrives in Pskov, agrees on urging of General Alekseev to formation of Duma ministry and orders General Ivanov to abort his mission. Formation of Moscow Soviet.

Night of March 1–2: Duma and Soviet representatives reach agreement on basis of eight-point program. In Mogilev, General Ruzskii has telegraphic conversation with Duma chairman, Rodzianko.

March 2: Provisional Government formed under chairmanship of G. E. Lvov; Alekseev communicates with front commanders; Nicholas agrees to abdicate in favor of son; Shulgin and Guchkov depart for Pskov; Nicholas talks with Court physician about Tsarevich, tells Shulgin and Guchkov he has decided to abdicate in favor of brother Michael, signs abdication manifesto. Ukrainian Rada (Soviet) formed in Kiev.

March 3: Provisional Government meets with Michael, persuades him to reject crown.

March 4: Nicholas's abdication manifesto and Michael's renunciation of throne made public. Provisional Government abolishes Police Department.

March 5: Provisional Government dismisses all governors and their deputies.

March 7: Ispolkom forms "Contact Commission" to oversee Provisional Government.

March 8: Nicholas bids farewell to army officers, departs for Tsarskoe Selo under arrest.

March 9: United States recognizes Provisional Government.

March 18: Ispolkom rules that every socialist party is entitled to three representatives.

March 22: Miliukov defines Russia's war aims.

March 25: Provisional Government introduces state monopoly on grain trade.

Late March: Britain withdraws offer to grant Imperial family asylum.

April 3: Lenin arrives in Petrograd.

April 4: Lenin's "April Theses."

April 21: First Bolshevik demonstrations in Petrograd and Moscow.

April 26: Provisional Government concedes its inability to maintain order.

April 28: Bolsheviks organize Red Guard.

Early April: All-Russian Consultation of Soviets convenes in Petrograd, constitutes All-Russian Central Executive Committee of Soviets (VTsIK or CEC).

May 1: CEC allows members to join Provisional Government.

Night of May 4–5: Formation of Coalition government under Lvov, with Kerensky Minister of War; six socialists enter cabinet.

May: Trotsky returns to Russia from New York.

June 3: First All-Russian Congress of Soviets opens.

June 10: Under CEC pressure, Bolsheviks give up idea of putsch.

June 16: Beginning of Russian offensive against Austria.

June 29: Lenin flees to Finland, where he remains until morning of July 4.

July 1: Provisional Government orders arrest of leading Bolsheviks.

July 2–3: Mutiny of 1st Machine Gun Regiment in Petrograd.

July 4: Bolshevik putsch quelled by release of information about Lenin's dealings with the Germans.

July 5: Lenin and Zinoviev go into hiding, first in Petrograd, then (July 9) in the countryside near the capital, and finally (September) Lenin goes to Finland.

July 11: Kerensky Prime Minister.

July 18: Kornilov appointed Commander in Chief.

End of July: Sixth Congress of Bolshevik Party in Petrograd.

July 31: Nicholas and family depart for Tobolsk.

August 9: Provisional Government schedules elections to Constituent Assembly for November 12 and its convocation for November 28.

August 14: Moscow State Conference opens: Kornilov accorded tumultuous reception.

August 20–21: Russians abandon Riga to the Germans.

August 22: V. N. Lvov meets with Kerensky.

August 22–24: Savinkov in Mogilev, transmits to Kornilov Kerensky's instructions.

August 24–25: Lvov sees Kornilov.

August 26: Lvov conveys to Kerensky Kornilov's alleged "ultimatum"; Kerensky's wire conversation with Kornilov; Lvov placed under arrest.

Night of August 26–27: Kerensky secures dictatorial powers from cabinet, dismisses Kornilov.

August 27: Kornilov pronounced traitor; Kornilov mutinies, calls on armed forces to follow him.

August 30: Provisional Government orders release of Bolsheviks still in prison for the July putsch.

September 10: Opening of Bolshevik-sponsored Third Regional Congress of Soviets in Finland.

September 12 and 14: Lenin writes Central Committee that time is ripe for a power seizure.

September 25: Bolsheviks win majority in Workers' Section of Petrograd Soviet; Trotsky elected chairman of Soviet.

September 26: CEC, under Bolshevik pressure, agrees to convene Second All-Russian Congress of Soviets on October 20.

September 28–October 8: Germans occupy islands in the Gulf of Riga, threatening Petrograd.

September 29: Lenin's third letter to Central Committee on power seizure.

October 4: Provisional Government discusses evacuation of Petrograd.

October 9: CEC, on Menshevik motion, votes to form military organization to defend capital (soon renamed Military-Revolutionary Committee).

October 10: Critical nighttime meeting of Bolshevik Central Committee in Petrograd, with Lenin present, votes in favor of armed power seizure.

October 11: Opening of Bolshevik-sponsored Congress of Soviets of the Northern Region in Petrograd; forms "Northern Regional Committee," which issues invitations to Second Congress of Soviets.

October 16: Soviet approves creation of Military-Revolutionary Committee (Milrevkom).

October 17: CEC postpones Second Congress of Soviets to October 25.

October 20: Milrevkom dispatches "commissars" to military units in and near Petrograd.

October 21: Milrevkom convenes meeting of regimental committees, has it pass innocuous resolution, which it presents to Military Staff as calling for its countersignature on any orders issued to troops. Demand is rejected.

October 22: Milrevkom declares Military Staff to be "counterrevolutionary."

October 23–24: Milrevkom carries on deceptive negotiations with Military Staff.

October 24: Units loyal to the government occupy key points in Petrograd, shut down Bolshevik newspapers; Bolsheviks react, take over much of Petrograd.

Night of October 24–25: Kerensky requests help from the front; Lenin, in disguise, makes his way to Smolnyi, where Bolshevik-sponsored Second Congress of Soviets is about to meet; Bolsheviks, using Milrevkom, complete occupation of the capital.

Morning of October 25: Kerensky escapes from Winter Palace to front in quest of military support; Lenin, in name of Milrevkom, declares the Provisional Government deposed, passage of power to soviets.

October 25: Unsuccessful attempts by Bolsheviks to capture Winter Palace, where government ministers await relief by loyal troops; in the afternoon, Trotsky opens Extraordinary Session of Petrograd Soviet; Lenin makes first public appearance since July 4; in Moscow, on Bolshevik motion, Soviet forms Military-Revolutionary Committee.

October 26: Troops of Moscow Milrevkom seize the Kremlin.

Night of October 25–26: Winter Palace falls, ministers arrested; Bolsheviks open Second Congress of Soviets.

Evening of October 26: Congress of Soviets passes Lenin's decrees on Land and on Peace; authorizes formation of new Provisional Government: Council of People's Commissars (Sovnarkom) with Lenin as chairman (Prime Minister); new, Bolshevik-dominated CEC appointed.

October 27: Second Congress of Soviets adjourns; opposition press outlawed (Press Decree).

October 28: Pro-government troops recapture Moscow Kremlin.

October 29: Union of Railroad Employees gives Bolsheviks ultimatum to broaden party composition of government; Kamenev agrees. Government announces it will issue laws without prior approval of Soviet Central Executive Committee. Union of Government Employees declares strike.

October 30: Clash between Cossacks and pro-Bolshevik sailors and Red Guards near Pulkovo; Cossacks withdraw. Union of Railroad Employees demands Bolsheviks quit government.

October 31–November 2: Fighting in Moscow, which ends with surrender of pro-government troops.

November 1–2: Bolshevik Central Committee rejects Union of Railroad Employees' demands; Kamenev and four other commissars resign to protest Lenin's refusal to compromise on broadening cabinet.

November 4: Critical encounter between Lenin and Trotsky and Central Executive Committee of Soviets: by manipulating vote, Sovnarkom obtains formal authority to legislate by decree.

November 9: Bolsheviks transmit their Peace Decree to Allied representatives, whose governments reject the call for an immediate armistice.

November 12: Elections to Constituent Assembly begin in Petrograd; they continue throughout unoccupied Russia until the end of the month. Socialists-Revolutionaries gain largest number of votes.

November 14: Bank employees refuse Sovnarkom's requests for money.

November 15: First regular meeting of Bolshevik Sovnarkom.

November 17: Bolshevik troops break into State Bank, remove 5 million rubles.

November 20/December 3: Armistice negotiations begin at Brest-Litovsk; Soviet delegation headed by Ioffe.

November 22: Decree dissolving most courts and the legal profession; creation of Revolutionary Tribunals.

November 22–23: Establishment of Union for the Defense of the Constituent Assembly.

November 23/December 6: Russians and Central Powers agree on armistice.

November 26: Peasants' Congress convenes in Petrograd.

November 28: Rump meeting of Constituent Assembly.

December: Supreme Council of the National Economy (VSNKh) created.

December 4: Bolsheviks and Left SRs break up Peasants' Congress.

December 7: Cheka established.

December 9–10: Bolsheviks reach accord with Left SRs; Left SRs enter Sovnarkom and Cheka.

December 15/28: Brest talks adjourn.

December 27/January 9: Brest talks resume; Trotsky heads Russian delegation.

December 30/January 12: Central Powers recognize Rada as government of the Ukraine.

Late December: Generals Alekseev and Kornilov found Volunteer Army.

1918

January 1: Attempt on Lenin's life.

January 5/18: One-day session of Constituent Assembly; demonstration in its support fired upon and dispersed. Workers' "plenipotentiaries" hold first meeting; Trotsky returns from Brest to Petrograd.

January 6: Constituent Assembly closed.

January 8: Opening of Bolshevik-sponsored Third Congress of Soviets; it passes "Declaration of the Rights of the Toiling and Exploited Masses" and proclaims Soviet Russian Republic.

January 15/28: Trotsky returns to Brest, talks resume.

January 21: Soviet Russia repudiates foreign and domestic debts.

January 28: Rada proclaims Ukrainian independence.

February 9: Central Powers sign separate peace with Ukraine; Kaiser orders German delegation at Brest to give Russians ultimatum.

February 17–18: Disputes among Bolsheviks about German peace demands; Lenin secures barest majority for their acceptance.

February 18: German and Austrian troops resume offensive against Russia.

February 21: Trotsky requests French military help.

February 21–22: Lenin's decree "The Socialist Fatherland in Danger!" authorizes summary execution of opponents.

February 23: German ultimatum arrives with fresh territorial demands.

February 24–25: Germans occupy Dorpat, Revel, and Borisov.

March 1: Russian delegation returns to Brest; two days later signs German text of the peace treaty.

Early March: Bolshevik government transfers to Moscow.

March 5: Murmansk Soviet requests and receives from Moscow authorization to have Allies land troops to protect it.

March 6–8: Seventh Congress of Bolshevik Party.

March: People's Courts introduced.

March 9: First Allied contingent lands in Murmansk.

March 14: Soviet Congress ratifies Brest Treaty; Left SRs leave Sovnarkom.

Night of March 10–11: Lenin moves to Moscow.

March 16: Grand dukes ordered to register with Cheka; subsequently exiled to the Urals.

April 4: First Japanese landings in Vladivostok.

April 13: Kornilov killed by stray shell; General Denikin assumes command of Volunteer Army.

April: Soviet Russia and Germany exchange diplomatic missions.

April 20: Decree outlawing purchase and leasing of industrial and commercial enterprises; all securities and bonds to be registered with government.

April 22: Transcaucasian Federation proclaims independence.

April 26: Nicholas, wife, and one daughter depart under guard from Tobolsk for Ekaterinburg; they arrive there April 30 and are imprisoned.

May 1: Inheritance abolished.

May 8–9: Sovnarkom decides to launch assault on the rural areas.

May 9: Bolsheviks fire on worker demonstrators at Kolpino.

May 13: Declaration of war on "peasant bourgeoisie" in decree giving Commissar of Supply extraordinary powers.

May 14: Altercation between Czech Legion and Magyar POWs in Cheliabinsk.

May 20: Decree creating "food supply detachments."

May 22: Czech Legion refuses to surrender arms; Trotsky orders it disarmed by force. Czech rebellion begins.

May 26: Transcaucasian Federation falls apart into independent republics of Georgia, Armenia, and Azerbaijan.

May–June: Elections to urban soviets in Russia; Bolsheviks lose majorities in all cities, reimpose them by force.

Early June: British landings at Archangel.

June 8: Czechs occupy Samara, following which Committee of the Constituent Assembly (Komuch) formed.

June 11: Decree ordering formation in the villages of Committees of the Poor *(kombedy)*.

Night of June 12–13: Grand Duke Michael and companion murdered near Perm.

June 16: Introduction of capital punishment.

June 26: Council of Workers' Plenipotentiaries calls for one-day political strike on July 2.

June 28: Kaiser Wilhelm II decides to continue support of Bolsheviks; Soviet Government orders large industrial enterprises nationalized.

Summer: Civil war in the countryside as peasants resist Bolshevik expropriations of grain.

July 1: Government of Western Siberia proclaimed in Omsk.

July 2: Unsuccessful anti-Bolshevik strike in Petrograd; probable date when Bolshevik leaders decide to execute ex-Tsar.

July 4: Fifth Congress of Soviets opens in Moscow; approves Soviet Constitution.

Night of July 5–6: Savinkov's uprising at Iaroslavl, followed by risings at Murom and Rybinsk.

July 6: Murder of Mirbach followed by Left SR uprising in Moscow.

July 7: Latvian troops suppress Left SR rebellion.

Night of July 16–17: Murder of Nicholas II, family, and servants in Ekaterinburg.

July 17: Massacre at Alapaevsk of several grand dukes and their companions.

July 21: Savinkov's forces surrender at Iaroslavl; massacre of 350 officers and civilians.

July 29: Compulsory military training introduced; officers of Imperial Army ordered
to register.

August 1–2: Additional Allied forces land at Archangel and Murmansk; Bolsheviks
request German help against Allies and the White (Volunteer) forces in the
south.

August 6: Berlin recalls German Ambassador from Moscow, follows by closing
embassy there.

August: Lenin calls on workers to exterminate "kulaks."

August 24: Urban real estate nationalized.

August 27: Supplementary Russo-German Treaty signed, with secret clauses.

August 30: Early in the day, M. S. Uritskii, head of Petrograd Cheka, assassinated;
in the evening, Fannie Kaplan shoots Lenin.

September 4: Instruction ordering the taking of hostages.

September 5: Red Terror officially launched; massacres of prisoners and hostages
throughout Bolshevik-controlled Russia.

October 21: All able-bodied Soviet citizens required to register with government
employment agencies.

October 30: 10-billion-ruble contribution imposed on the urban and village "bourgeoisie."

Early November: Soviet Embassy expelled from Berlin.

November 13: Soviet Government renounces Treaty of Brest-Litovsk and Supplementary Treaty.

December 2: Committees of the Poor dissolved.

December 10: "Labor Code" issued.

1919

January: Tax in kind *(prodrazvërstka)* introduced for peasants.

January 7: *Uezd* Chekas abolished.

February 17: Dzerzhinskii announces changes in operations of the Cheka: calls for
creation of concentration camps.

March: New party program adopted; party renamed Russian Communist Party;
creation of Politburo, Orgburo, and Secretariat.

March 16: Consumer communes introduced.

April 11: Regulations concerning concentration camps.

May 15: Government authorizes People's Bank to issue as many bank notes as
required.

December 27: Commission on Labor Obligation created under Trotsky: beginning
of "militarization of labor."

NOTES

Chapter 1

1. Somerset Maugham, *Ashenden* (New York, 1941), vii–viii.
2. Otto Hoetzsch, *Russland* (Göttingen, 1915), 309–11.
3. *NV*, No. 8, 240 (February 4, 1899), 3.
4. On these events, see Samuel Kassow, *The Russian University in Crisis: 1899–1911*, Ph.D. Dissertation, Princeton University, 1976, 130–47; *Byloe*, No. 16 (1921), 125–28, and M. Mogilianskii, *Byloe*, No. 24 (1924), 117–25.
5. *Byloe*, No. 16, 127; N. Cherevanin in *OD*, I, 267.
6. Kassow, *The Russian University*, 135.
7. *Ibid.*, 141–43.
8. *Byloe*, No. 16, 127–28.
9. *Ibid.*, 128.
10. Kassow, *The Russian University*, 155–56.
11. S. Iu. Vitte, *Vospominaniia*, II (Moscow, 1960), 199.
12. Ludwig Bazylow, *Polityka wewnetrzna caratu* (Warsaw, 1966), 197; E. N. Trubetskoi in Josef Melnik, *Russen über Russland* (Frankfurt, 1906), 17–18.
13. Cited in Edward H. Judge, *Plehve* (Syracuse, N.Y., 1983), 19.
14. Melnik, *Russen*, 18, 48.
15. See below, Chap. 3.
16. Judge, *Plehve*, 12–37.
17. Vitte, *Vospominaniia*, II, 34.
18. Judge, *Plehve*, 59.
19. On this, see below, Chap. 9.
20. *Rabochee delo*, No. 1 (1899), 24–34.
21. On him: Jeremiah Schneiderman, *Sergei Zubatov and Revolutionary Marxism* (Ithaca, N.Y., 1976).
22. V. I. Gurko, *Features and Figures of the Past* (Stanford, Calif., 1939), 116.
23. Dietrich Geyer, *Der russische Imperialismus* (Göttingen, 1977), 151; Abraham Ascher, *The Revolution of 1905* (Stanford, Calif., 1988), 44.
24. Andrew Malozemoff, *Russian Far Eastern Policy, 1881–1904* (Berkeley, Calif., 1958), 201–2.
25. *Ibid.*, 221.
26. *Osvobozhdenie*, III, No. 52 (July 19/August 1, 1904), 33.
27. [A. V. Bogdanovich], *Tri poslednikh samoderzhtsa* (Moscow-Leningrad, 1924), 335.
28. *IZ*, No. 77 (1965), 241.
29. *Ibid.*, 241–42; also Vitte, *Vospominaniia*, II, 324.
30. Dmitrii N. Shipov, *Vospominaniia i dumy o perezhitom* (Moscow, 1918), 240.
31. Shipov, *Vospominaniia*, 241; see also Richard Pipes, *Struve: Liberal on the Left* (Cambridge, Mass., 1970), 361–62.
32. S. E. Kryzhanovskii, *Vospominaniia* (Berlin, [1938]), 17–18.
33. E.g., [Bogdanovich], *Tri*, 299.

34. The protocols have been published under the title *Chastnoe soveshchanie zemskikh deiatelei prosikhodivshee 6, 7, 8 i 9 noiabria 1904 g. v S.-Petersburge* (Moscow, 1905). See further Shipov, *Vospominaniia*, 258–78; Shmuel Galai, *The Liberation Movement in Russia, 1900–1905* (Cambridge, 1973), 214–21; and Pipes, *Struve: Liberal on the Left*, 368–70.
35. Shipov, *Vospominaniia*, 269.
36. Ascher, *Revolution*, 66–68.
37. On the banquet campaign, see I. P. Belokonskii, *Zemskoe dvizhenie* (Moscow, 1914), 238–57, and Terence Emmons in *California Slavic Studies*, No. 10 (1977), 45–86.
38. Emmons, *loc. cit.*, 57.
39. New York Public Library: Russia, MVD, Department Politsii, *Sbornik sekretnykh tsirkuliarov*, December 10, 1904, shelf mark *QGF/+.
40. Shipov, *Vospominaniia*, 278–81; E. D. Chermenskii, *Burzhuaziia i tsarizm v pervoi russkoi revoliutsii* (Moscow, 1970), 37.
41. This document, which remains unpublished, is summarized in Andrew M. Verner, *Nicholas II and the Role of the Autocrat during the First Russian Revolution, 1904–1907*, Ph.D. Dissertation, Columbia University, 1986, 192–98.
42. *Ibid.*, 193–94.
43. Cited in Chermenskii, *Burzhuaziia*, 41.
44. Vitte, *Vospominaniia*, II, 331–32; Chermenskii, *Burzhuaziia*, 42–43.
45. Vitte, *Vospominaniia*, II, 335.
46. Text in G. G. Savich, ed., *Novyi gosudarstvennyi stroi Rossii* (St. Petersburg, 1907), 6–8.
47. Bazylow, *Polityka wewnetrzna*, 333.
48. *Osvobozhdenie*, No. 63 (January 7/20, 1905), 221.
49. On him, see his memoirs: George Gapon, *The Story of My Life* (New York, 1906); also D. Venediktov, *Georgii Gapon*, 2nd ed. (Moscow-Leningrad, 1931), and Walter Sablinsky, *The Road to Bloody Sunday* (Princeton, N.J., 1976).
50. Bazylow, *Polityka wewnetrzna*, 347.
51. Sablinsky, *The Road*, 117.
52. *Ibid.*, 130–31.
53. L. Ia. Gurevich in *Byloe*, No. 1 (1906), 197–98.
54. Ascher, *Revolution*, 82–83; Verner, *Nicholas II*, 226–27.
55. The fullest text of the petition: N. S. Trusova, ed., *Nachalo pervoi russkoi revoliutsii: ianvar'-mart 1905 goda* (Moscow, 1955), 28–30. An English translation is in Sablinsky, *The Road*, 344–49.
56. Diary of Sviatopolk-Mirskaia, *IZ*, No. 77 (1965), 273; A. N. Pankratova *et al.*, eds., *Revoliutsiia 1905–1907 gg. v Rossii: Dokumenty i materialy*, IV, Pt. 1 (Moscow, 1961), 35.
57. Vitte, *Vospominaniia*, II, 340.
58. Trusova, *Nachalo*, 52.
59. Verner, *Nicholas II*, 259; Sviatopolk-Mirskaia in *IZ*, No. 77 (1965), 247.
60. Ascher, *Revolution*, 94, 138, 151.
61. *Ibid.*, 157–60.
62. *Ibid.*, 172.
63. Kazimierz Niedzielski, *Z burzliwych dni, 1904–1905* (Warsaw, 1916), 240–41.
64. Ascher, *Revolution*, 120.
65. Salomon M. Schwarz, *The Russian Revolution of 1905* (Chicago, 1967), 123.
66. Sviatopolk-Mirskaia in *IZ*, No. 77 (1965), 247.
67. S. Iu. Vitte, *Vospominaniia*, (Moscow, 1960), III, 143–44.
68. *KA*, No. 1/8 (1925), 51–69.
69. *Ibid.*, 65.
70. Savich, *Novyi gosudarstvennyi stroi*, 11–14.
71. Ascher, *Revolution*, 114.
72. Chermenskii, *Burzhuaziia*, 57.
73. V. A. Maklakov, *Iz vospominanii* (New York, 1954), 324–25. The fullest account of this organization is Jonathan E. Sanders's *The Union of Unions*, Ph.D. Dissertation, Columbia University, 1985.

74. Galai, *Liberation Movement*, 245–48.
75. Shmuel Galai in *Jahrbücher*, No. 24 (1976), 522–23.
76. Vitte, *Vospominaniia*, II, 388.
77. *Ibid.*, II, 305.
78. *Ibid.*, 397.
79. Chermenskii, *Burzhuaziia*, 68.
80. *Ibid.*, 69.
81. Text of Trubetskoi's address is in *Pravitel'stvennyi vestnik*, June 8, 1905, p. 1. English translation: Martha Bohachevsky-Chomiak, *Sergei N. Trubetskoi* (Belmont, Mass., 1976), 150–54.
82. *Osvobozhdenie*, No. 75 (1905), 432.
83. *SZ*, No. 65 (1937), 226.
84. *Petergofskoe soveshchanie o proekte Gosudarstvennoi Dumy* (Berlin, n.d.).
85. Text in Savich, *Novyi gosudarstvennyi stroi*, 21–23. Chermenskii, *Burzhuaziia*, 105–8; Ascher, *Revolution*, 177–81. Its antecedents are dealt with in Gilbert S. Doktorow, *The Introduction of Parliamentary Institutions in Russia during the Revolution of 1905–1907*, Ph.D. Dissertation, Columbia University, 1975.
86. Ascher, *Revolution*, 179.
87. Vitte, *Vospominaniia*, II, 482.
88. Verner, *Nicholas II*, 353.
89. Vitte, *Vospominaniia*, II, 488.
90. Chermenskii, *Burzhuaziia*, 91–92.
91. Vitte, *Vospominaniia*, II, 551.
92. Galai, *Liberation Movement*, 259; Sanders, *Union of Unions*, 1030–46.
93. *RV*, No. 232 (August 27, 1905), 1.
94. J. D. Morison in F.-X. Coquin and C. Gervais-Francelle, eds., *1905: La Première Révolution Russe* (Paris, 1986), 68–69; Ascher, *Revolution*, 201.
95. Ascher, *Revolution*, 198.
96. *Iskra*, No. 107 (July 29, 1905), 1; emphasis supplied.
97. Trubetskoi in Melnik, *Russen*, 16–17.
98. Kassow, *The Russian University*, 381–83; Morison in Coquin and Gervais-Francelle, *1905*, 68–69; V. Voitinskii, *Gody pobed i porazhenii*, I (Berlin, 1923), 57–63.
99. Vitte, *Vospominaniia*, II, 544, 626–27.
100. Ascher, *Revolution*, 211; Oskar Anweiler, *The Soviets* (New York, 1974), 43; *IZ*, No. 11 (1941), 3–5.
101. Kassow, *The Russian University*, 386.
102. *KA*, No. 11–12 (1925), 55–56.
103. N. D. Obolenskii in Vitte, *Vospominaniia*, III, 26.
104. A. L. Sidorov, ed., *Vysshyi pod''ëm revoliutsii 1905–1907 gg.: vooruzhonnoe vosstanie, noiabr'–dekabr' 1905 goda*, I (Moscow, 1955), 47.
105. N. I. Sidorov, ed., *1905 god v Peterburge*, II (Leningrad, 1925), 101–2.
106. *KA*, No. 3/22 (1927), 173.
107. P. N. Miliukov, *Vospominaniia, 1859–1917*, II (New York, 1955), 342–43.
108. Schwarz, *Russian Revolution*, 333; L. Geller and N. Rovenskaia, eds., *Peterburgskii i Moskovskii Sovety Rabochikh Deputatov 1905 g. (v dokumentakh)* (Moscow-Leningrad, 1926), 9.
109. Anweiler, *Soviets*, 45.
110. *Ibid.*, 45.
111. Sidorov, *1905 god*, II, 102.
112. Voitinskii, *Gody pobed*, I, 93–94; *IZ*, No. 11 (1941), 7.
113. Geller and Rovenskaia, *Peterburgskii i Moskovskii Sovety*, 11.
114. Ascher, *Revolution*, 223.
115. See below, Chap. 8.
116. Sidorov, *1905 god*, II, 5.
117. Vitte, *Vospominaniia*, III, 14–15.
118. *Ibid.*
119. A. S. Alekseev in *Iuridicheskii vestnik*, XI/III (1915), 39.

120. *Byloe,* No. 14 (1919), 109.
121. *Ibid.,* 110–11.
122. Vitte, *Vospominaniia,* III, 17, 41–42.
123. Savich, *Novyi gosudarstvennyi stroi,* 25–27.
124. Geller and Rovenskaia, *Peterburgskii i Moskovskii Sovety,* 29–31.
125. M. Szeftel, *The Russian Constitution of April 23, 1906* (Brussels, 1976), 33–35.
126. *KA,* No.3/22 (1927), 168.
127. Ascher, *Revolution,* 229.
128. Verner, *Nicholas II,* 434.
129. Vitte, *Vospominaniia,* III, 68–69.
130. Verner, *Nicholas II,* 438.
131. Vitte, *Vospominaniia,* III, 68, 110.
132. Verner, *Nicholas II,* 438–40.
133. *KA,* No. 3/22 (1927), 187.
134. Ascher, *Revolution,* 253–62. On this, see further A. Linden, ed., *Die Judenpogrome in Russland* (Köln-Leipzig, 1910).
135. Vitte, *Vospominaniia,* III, 85–88.
136. *KA,* No. 3/22 (1927), 169.
137. See *Agrarnoe dvizhenie v Rossii v 1905–1906 gg.,* 2 vols. (St. Petersburg, 1908), *passim.*
138. Roberta T. Manning, *The Crisis of the Old Order in Russia: Gentry and Government* (Princeton, N.J., 1982), 155–57.
139. *Agrarnoe dvizhenie,* II, 30.
140. Manning, *Crisis,* 142.
141. *KA,* No. 3/22 (1927), 173–74.
142. Anweiler, *Soviets,* 59–60.
143. On him, see below, Chap. 9.
144. Anweiler, *Soviets,* 60; Ascher, *Revolution,* 301.
145. Ascher, *Revolution,* 108.
146. Vitte, *Vospominaniia,* III, 218–51.

Chapter 2

1. Jules Legras, *Au Pays Russe* (Paris, 1895), 356.
2. A. D. Gradovskii, *Sobranie sochinenii,* 2nd ed., VII (St. Petersburg, 1907), 1–2.
3. See V. O. Kliuchevskii, *Skazaniia inostrantsev o Moskovskom gosudarstve* (Moscow, 1918), and Karl H. Ruffman, *Das Russlandbild im England Shakespeares* (Göttingen, 1952).
4. A. Leroy-Beaulieu, *The Empire of the Tsars and the Russians,* II (New York-London, 1898), 10.
5. *Dnevnik Gosudarstvennogo Sekretariia A. A. Polovtsova,* II (Moscow, 1966), 70.
6. S. Iu. Vitte, *Samoderzhavie i zemstvo,* 2nd ed. (Stuttgart, 1903), 206, citing Mackenzie Wallace.
7. S. S. Oldenburg, *Tsarstvovanie Imperatora Nikolaia II,* I (Belgrade, 1939), 41.
8. See above, p. 27.
9. *Dnevnik V. N. Lamzdorfa (1886–1890)* (Moscow-Leningrad, 1926), 140.
10. *Ibid.,* 249–51.
11. S. Iu. Vitte, *Vospominaniia,* I (Moscow, 1960), 434–35; Andrew M. Verner, *Nicholas II and the Role of the Autocrat during the First Russian Revolution, 1904–1907,* Ph.D. Dissertation, Columbia University, 1986, 103.
12. *KA,* No.3/46 (1931), 10.
13. Vitte, *Vospominaniia,* II, 585–86.
14. V. Burtsev, *Za sto let,* I (London, 1897), 264.
15. Vitte, *Vospominaniia,* II, 266–67.
16. Cited by V. Kantorovich in *Byloe,* No. 22 (1923), 208–9.
17. *Ibid.,* 206.
18. Vitte, *Vospominaniia,* II, 328.
19. *Ibid.,* 474.

20. Kantorovich in *Byloe,* No. 22 (1923), 228.
21. Hans-Joachim Torke in *Forschungen,* XIII (1967), 227, 257.
22. N. M. Korkunov, *Russkoe gosudarstvennoe pravo,* 2nd ed., II (St. Petersburg, 1897), 552; *Brogkauz & Efron,* XXX, 441–42.
23. T. Taranovsky in *Canadian Slavonic Papers,* XXVI, No. 2–3 (1984), 213–14.
24. *Ibid.,* 212–13.
25. Theodore Taranovsky, *The Politics of Counter-Reform: Autocracy and Bureaucracy in the Reign of Alexander III, 1881–1894,* Ph.D. Dissertation, Harvard University, 1976.
26. Leroy-Beaulieu, *Empire of the Tsars,* II, 93–94.
27. V. A. Evreinov, *Grazhdanskoe sudoproizvodstvo v Rossii* (St. Petersburg, 1887), 39–41, 54; Torke in *Forschungen,* 14, 56.
28. P. A. Zaionchkovskii, *Pravitel'stvennyi apparat samoderzhavnoi Rossii v XIX v.* (Moscow, 1978), 90.
29. *Ibid.,* 95–96.
30. N. A. Maklakov in *Padenie,* V, 207.
31. Leroy-Beaulieu, *Empire of the Tsars,* II, 82–83.
32. *Ibid.,* 79.
33. *MG,* No. 10 (1908), 29–30.
34. M. N. Nikonov cited in *Dnevnik Lamzdorfa,* 135.
35. Pierre Dolgoroukov [Dolgorukov], *La Vérité sur la Russie* (Paris, 1860), 16.
36. Bernard Pares, *Russia and Reform* (London, 1907), 154.
37. See S. Frederick Starr, *Decentralization and Self-Government in Russia, 1830–1870* (Princeton, N.J., 1972).
38. Richard Pipes, *Russia under the Old Regime* (London-New York, 1974), 281.
39. Robert E. Jones, *The Emancipation of the Russian Nobility, 1762–1785* (Princeton, N.J., 1973), 182.
40. N. A. Rubakin cited in Neil B. Weissman, *Reform in Tsarist Russia* (New Brunswick, N.J., 1981), 11.
41. S. E. Kryzhanovskii, *Vospominaniia,* (Berlin, [1938]), 98–99.
42. Walter M. Pintner in *SR,* XXIX, No. 3 (1970), 432.
43. F. I. Dan, *Proiskhozhdenie Bol'shevizma* (New York, 1946), 443–44.
44. Taranovsky, *Politics of Counter-Reform,* 227.
45. *Zapiski Aleksandra Ivanovicha Kosheleva (1812–1883 gody)* (Berlin, 1884), 31–32.
46. Ministerstvo Vnutrennykh Del, *Istoricheskii ocherk* (St. Petersburg, 1901), 48–49.
47. *KA,* No. 3/22 (1927), 169.
48. Hans Rogger in *SR,* No. 4 (1966), 626.
49. *Dnevnik P. A. Valueva,* I (Moscow, 1961), 100, entry dated April 14, 1861.
50. Taranovsky, *Politics of Counter-Reform,* 234.
51. Cited in Zaionchkovskii, *Rossiiskoe samoderzhavie,* 237.
52. They are described in Pipes, *Russia,* 305–7.
53. Memorandum of October 30, 1885, cited in Zaionchkovskii, *Rossiiskoe samoderzhavie,* 236–39.
54. It is the subject of Daniel T. Orlovsky's *The Limits of Reform: The Ministry of Internal Affairs in Imperial Russia, 1802–1881* (Cambridge, Mass., 1981).
55. P. A. Zaionchkovskii, *Krizis samoderzhaviia na rubezhe 1870–1880kh godov* (Moscow, 1964), 395–96.
56. Weissman, *Reform,* 48.
57. *Ibid.,* 62.
58. P. P. Zavarzin, *Rabota tainoi politsii* (Paris, 1924), 11–13.
59. *Brogkauz & Efron,* XXXVII, 357.
60. Geoffrey Drage, *Russian Affairs* (London, 1904), 243.
61. Theodore H. Von Laue, *Sergei Witte and the Industrialization of Russia* (London-New York, 1963), 34–35.
62. *Ibid.,* 180.
63. Leo Pasvolsky and Harold G. Moulton, *Russian Debts and Russian Reconstruction* (New York, 1924), 16.

64. *Ibid.*, 1; John P. McKay, *Pioneers for Profit* (Chicago, 1970), 380.
65. McKay, *Pioneers*, 37.
66. P. B. Ol, *Inostrannye kapitaly v Rossii* (Petrograd, 1922), 8–9.
67. Von Laue, *Sergei Witte*, 274–75.
68. Edward C. Kirkland, *A History of American Economic Life*, 3rd ed. (New York, 1951), 541.
69. Rolf Wagenführ in *Vierteljahreshefte zur Konjunkturforschung*, Sonderheft 31 (Berlin, 1933), 18.
70. P. A. Khromov, *Ekonomicheskoe razvitie Rossii v XIX–XX vekakh* (Moscow, 1950), 452–54, 459, 462.
71. Vitte, *Vospominaniia*, II, 380.
72. P. A. Zaionchkovskii, *Samoderzhavie i russkaia armiia na rubezhe XIX–XX stoletii* (Moscow, 1973), 31.
73. Hans-Peter Stein in *Forschungen*, XIII (1967), 468. The text of the military oath is in *Polnoe Sobranie Zakonov*, 3rd ed., XIV (St. Petersburg, 1894), No. 11,014.
74. Zaionchkovskii, *Samoderzhavie i russkaia armiia*, 119, 197–99.
75. A. I. Denikin, *Staraia armiia* (Paris, 1929), 7.
76. Zaionchkovskii, *Samoderzhavie i russkaia armiia*, 212.
77. *Ibid.*, 221–23.
78. Matitiahu Mayzel in *Cahiers du Monde Russe et Soviétique*, XVI, No. 3/4 (1975), 297–321.
79. Denikin, *Staraia armiia*, 13.
80. A. I. Denikin, *Put' russkogo ofitsera* (New York, 1953), 121–22.
81. Stein in *Forschungen*, 474–79.
82. On this group see Pipes, *Russia*, Chap. 7.
83. *Ibid.*, 178–79.
84. Rostislav Fadeev, *Russkoe obshchestvo v nastoiaschem i budushchem (chem nam byt'?)* (St. Petersburg, 1874); A. D. Pazukhin in *RV*, No. 175 (January, 1885), 5–58; A. I. Elishev (A. I. Bukeevskii), *Dvorianskoe delo* (Moscow, 1898).
85. Roberta T. Manning, *The Crisis of the Old Order in Russia: Gentry and Government* (Princeton, N.J., 1982), *passim*.
86. Vitte, *Samoderzhavie i zemstvo*, 168.
87. *Petergofskoe soveshchanie o proekte Gosudartvennoi Dumy* (Berlin, n.d.), 149–50.
88. Manning, *Crisis*, 32–33.
89. Seymour Becker, *Nobility and Privilege in Late Imperial Russia* (De Kalb, Ill., 1985), 28.
90. Ivan Ozerov in Josef Melnik, *Russen über Russland* (Frankfurt, 1906), 214.
91. A. M. Anfimov and I. F. Makarov in *ISSSR*, No. 1 (1974), 85.
92. Leroy-Beaulieu, *Empire of the Tsars*, III, 512–13.
93. *Ibid.*, 182–83.
94. On this subject, see John S. Curtiss, *Church and State in Russia* (New York, 1972), Chap. 3.
95. *Ibid.*, 130.
96. *Ibid.*, 182–83.
97. *Ibid.*, 339–40.
98. Leroy-Beaulieu, *Empire of the Tsars*, II, 91.

Chapter 3

1. Theodore Shanin, *The Awkward Class* (Oxford, 1972), 64–68, 90–91. Cf. Stepniak [S. M. Kravchinskii], *The Russian Peasantry* (New York, 1888), 169.
2. N. A. Troinitskii, ed., *Pervaia Vseobshchaia Perepis' Naseleniia Rossiiskoi Imperii 1897 g.: Obshchii Svod*, I (St. Petersburg, 1905), 16.
3. Stepniak, *Russian Peasantry*, 79, 81.
4. Jack Goody et al., eds., *Family and Inheritance* (Cambridge, 1976), 1.
5. Tadashi Fukutake, *Asian Rural Society: China, India, Japan* (Seattle-London, 1967), 4, 24.
6. P. N. Pershin, *Zemel'noe ustroistvo dorevoliutsionnoi derevni*, I (Moscow-Voronezh, 1928), 148–49.
7. *Brogkauz & Efron*, XXIX, 384.

8. S. M. Dubrovskii, *Stolypinskaia zemel'naia reforma* (Moscow, 1963), 189, 191.
9. V. A. Aleksandrov, *Sel'skaia obshchina v Rossii* (Moscow, 1976), 178–86, 314–15.
10. N. P. Oganovskii and A. V. Chaianov, eds., *Statisticheskii spravochnik po agrarnomu voprosu*, Vyp. I (Moscow, 1917), Table III, 10–11.
11. *Brogkauz & Efron*, XXIX, 382–83.
12. N. Rosnitskii, *Litso derevni* (Moscow-Leningrad, 1926), 16–18.
13. A. S. Ermolov, *Nash zemel'nyi vopros* (St. Petersburg, 1906), 66.
14. *Ibid.*, 72–75.
15. S. I. Bruk and V. M. Kabuzan in *ISSSR*, No. 3 (1980), 83–84.
16. Stepniak, *Russian Peasantry*, 147–48.
17. P. A. Khromov, *Ekonomicheskoe razvitie Rossii v XIX–XX vekakh* (Moscow, 1950), 439; P. I. Liashchenko, *Istoriia narodnogo khoziaistva SSSR*, II (Moscow, 1952), 163.
18. A. M. Anfimov, *Zemel'naia arenda v Rossii v nachale XX veka* (Moscow, 1961), 15.
19. A. G. Rashin, *Naselenie Rossii za 100 let (1811–1913 gg.)* (Moscow, 1956), 125, 129.
20. Joseph Bradley in *Russian History*, VI, Pt. 1 (1979), 22.
21. Rashin, *Naselenie Rossii*, 135–36.
22. Harold Frederic, *The New Exodus* (New York-London, 1892), 50.
23. James Y. Simms, Jr., in *SR*, XXXVI, No. 3 (1977), 377–98.
24. *Ibid.*, 385.
25. See above, note 13.
26. Rashin, *Naselenie Rossii*, 208.
27. G. von Schulze-Gävernitz, *Volkswirtschaftliche Studien aus Russland* (Leipzig, 1899), 146–65.
28. *Ibid.*, 131.
29. See my *Social-Democracy and the St. Petersburg Labor Movement* (Cambridge, Mass., 1963).
30. A notable exception is an article by C. Zajtzeff [K. Zaitsev] in *Jahrbücher für Kultur und Geschichte der Slaven*, Neue Folge, X, No. 3/4 (1934), 421–53.
31. The most important literary depictions of the Russian peasant are: A. N. Engelgardt, *Iz derevni;* Chekhov's short stories; Ivan Bunin, *The Village (Derevnia);* and Maxim Gorky's *O russkom krest'ianstve*.
32. Notably S. V. Pakhman's, *Obychnoe grazhdanskoe pravo v Rossii*, 2 vols. (St. Petersburg, 1877–79), and Alexandra Efimenko's *Issledovaniia narodnoi zhizni*, I: *Obychnoe pravo* (Moscow, 1884).
33. M. Ia. Fenomenov, *Sovremennaia derevnia*, II (Leningrad-Moscow, 1925), 95.
34. "Christianity and Patriotism" in *Complete Works*, Leo Wiener, tr., XX (Boston, 1905), 419–20.
35. A. I. Denikin, *Staraia armiia* (Paris, 1929), 50.
36. *Ibid.*, 50–51.
37. *KA*, No. 1/8 (1925), 53.
38. Stepniak, *Russian Peasantry*, 229–30.
39. Cited by Jeffrey Brooks in Wm. M. Todd III, ed., *Literature and Society in Imperial Russia* (Stanford, Calif., 1978), 124.
40. Iwan Oserov [Ozerov] in Josef Melnik, *Russen über Russland* (Frankfurt, 1906), 215; John S. Curtiss, *Church and State in Russia* (New York, 1972), 182–83.
41. Jeffrey Brooks in T. Emmons and W. S. Vucinich, eds., *Zemstvo in Russia* (Cambridge, 1982), 243–44; Ben Eklof in *Journal of Social History*, XIV, No. 3 (1981), 366.
42. Dietrich Geyer, *Der Russische Imperialismus* (Göttingen, 1977), 53–54.
43. Stepniak, *Russian Peasantry*, 144.
44. A. Leroy-Beaulieu, *The Empire of the Tsars and the Russians*, II (New York-London, 1898), 7.
45. K. Zaitsev, *I. A. Bunin* (Berlin, [1933]), 101–2.
46. "Vlast' zemli," in Gleb Uspenskii, *Polnoe sobranie sochinenii*, VIII (Moscow, 1949), 25.
47. E.g., Efimenko, *Issledovaniia*, I, 136–38.
48. Bohdan Kistiakovskii in *Vekhi* (Moscow, 1909), 143.
49. Efimenko, *Issledovaniia*, I, 174–75.
50. Stepniak, *Russian Peasantry*, 86.

51. A. N. Engelgardt, *Iz derevni* (Moscow, 1987), 430–31.
52. G. B. Sliozberg, *Dela minuvshikh dnei,* II (Paris, 1933), 248–49.
53. Zajtseff in *Jahrbücher für Kultur,* 444–45.
54. Stepniak, *Russian Peasantry,* 6. The identical point is made by A. Vasilchikov in *Zemlevladenie i zemledelie v Rossii i drugikh evropeiskikh gosudarstvakh,* I (St. Petersburg, 1876), 297–98.
55. Efimenko, *Issledovaniia,* I, 143–45.
56. Zajtseff in *Jahrbücher für Kultur,* 440–41; Fenomenov, *Sovremennaia derevniia,* 93.
57. K. V. Chistov, *Russkie narodnye sotsial'no-utopicheskie legendy* (Moscow, 1967).
58. Engelgardt, *Iz derevni,* 540–41.
59. *Ibid.,* 534; cf. Efimenko, *Issledovaniia,* I, 141.
60. Efimenko, *Issledovaniia,* 141–42.
61. Lev Tolstoi, "Zapisnaia knizhka" (1865), in his *Polnoe Sobranie Sochinenii,* XLVIII (Moscow, 1952), 85.
62. Zajtseff in *Jahrbücher für Kultur,* 422.
63. Engelgardt, *Iz derevni,* 540, 542.
64. Cited in Leroy-Beaulieu, *Empire of the Tsars,* II, 115.
65. Zajtseff in *Jahrbücher für Kultur,* 436–37.
66. Jeffrey Brooks in Todd, *Literature and Society,* 97–150.
67. *Ibid.,* 149–50.
68. J. C. Carothers in *Psychiatry,* XXI (1959), 317–18.
69. Eklof in *Journal of Social History,* 376.
70. *Rus',* No. 191 (August 17/30, 1905), 2.

Chapter 4

1. Jacques Ellul, *Autopsie de la Révolution* (Paris, 1969), 56. Albert Camus draws a similar distinction in *The Rebel.*
2. *Capitalism, Socialism and Democracy,* 3rd ed. (New York, 1950), 145.
3. Ferdinand Tönnies, *Community and Society* (East Lansing, Mich., 1957), 42–43.
4. Vilfredo Pareto, *The Mind and Society* (New York, 1935), No. 2,034 and No. 2,044n.
5. Etienne Gilson and Thomas Langan, *Modern Philosophy* (New York, 1963), 43.
6. On this see Ernst Cassirer, *Das Erkenntnisproblem in der Philosophie und Wissenschaft der neueren Zeit,* 2nd ed., 2 vols. (Berlin, 1911).
7. Albert Keim, *Helvétius, Sa Vie et Son Oeuvre* (Paris, 1907), 316n., 336; also Ian Cumming, *Helvétius* (London, 1955), 17.
8. Cited in Keim, *Helvétius,* 246.
9. *Ibid.,* 268.
10. C. A. Helvétius, *De l'Esprit, or Essays on the Mind* (London, 1810), 184, Essay II, Chap. 25.
11. *Ibid.,* 187.
12. *Ibid.,* 489, Essay IV, Chap. 17; cf. Mordecai Grossman, *The Philosophy of Helvétius* (New York, 1926), 74.
13. Elie Halévy, *La Jeunesse de Bentham* (Paris, 1901), cited in Grossman, *Helvétius,* 168.
14. Alfred Cobban and Robert A. Smith, eds., *The Correspondence of Edmund Burke,* VI (Cambridge, 1967), 47.
15. Elie Halévy, *The Growth of Philosophic Radicalism* (Boston, 1960), 20.
16. *The Old Regime and the French Revolution,* Pt. 3, Chap. 1.
17. A. Cochin, *Les Sociétés de Pensée et la Démocratie* (Paris, 1921), 5–6.
18. *Ibid.,* 9–10, 15.
19. Maia Kaganskaia in *22* (Jerusalem), No. 59 (1988), 118; Christian Saves, *La Signification de la Surenchère Linguistique dans la Phraséologie Bolchevique,* Thèse pour le Doctorat, Université des Sciences Sociales, Toulouse I, 1986.
20. Karl Griewank, *Der neuzeitliche Revolutsionsbegriff* (Weimar, 1955), 14, 22, 24, 30.
21. Augustin Cochin, *La Crise de l'Histoire Révolutionnaire* (Paris, 1909), 3.
22. A. Aulard, *The French Revolution,* III (New York, 1910), 86.
23. Cited in F. Furet, *Penser la Révolution Française* (Paris, 1983), 211n.

24. See the complaints of Bertrand de Jouvenel, Raymond Aron, and Karl Mannheim in George B. de Huszar, *The Intellectuals* (Glencoe, Ill., 1960), 3.
25. Schumpeter, *Capitalism,* 148–49.
26. Raymond Aron, *The Opium of the Intellectuals* (Garden City, N.Y., 1957), 203–4.
27. Cited in Huszar, *Intellectuals,* 367.
28. M. Bakunin "Gosudarstvennost' i anarkhiia," in Artur Lehning, ed., *Archives Bakounine,* III (Leiden, 1967), 150.
29. Karl Marx and Friedrich Engels, *The Holy Family* (Moscow, 1956), 174–76.
30. Leszek Kolakowski, *Main Currents of Marxism, I* (Oxford, 1978), 143–44.
31. Anatole Leroy-Beaulieu, *Les Doctrines de Haine* (Paris, [1902]), 8–9, 34–35.
32. L. Trotskii, *Literatura i revoliutsiia,* 2nd ed. (Moscow, 1924), 192–94.
33. Anatole Leroy-Beaulieu, *The Empire of the Tsars and the Russians,* II (New York-London, 1898), 67.
34. On this group, see N. M. Pirumova, *Zemskaia intelligentsiia i eë rol' v obshchestvennoi bor'be* (Moscow, 1986).
35. Richard Pipes, *Struve: Liberal on the Right* (Cambridge, Mass., 1980), 79.
36. Jules Legras, *Au Pays Russe* (Paris, 1895), 356–57.
37. O. V. Aptekman, *Obshchestvo "Zemlia i Volia" 70-kh godov* (Petrograd, 1924), 145.
38. Lev Tikhomirov, *Pochemu ia perestal byt' revoliutsionerom* (Moscow, 1895), 34–35.
39. Program of the People's Will (1879), in S. S. Volk, ed., *Revoliutsionnoe narodnichestvo 70-kh godov XIX veka,* II (Moscow-Leningrad, 1965), 173.
40. *K. Marks, F. Engel's i revoliutsionnaia Rossiia* (Moscow, 1967), 78–79.
41. Richard Pipes, *Struve: Liberal on the Left* (Cambridge, Mass., 1970), 50–51.
42. For its history, see Manfred Hildermeier, *Die Sozialrevolutionäre Partei Russlands* (Cologne-Vienna, 1978).
43. *Ibid.,* 61–62.
44. *Ibid.,* 65.
45. *Protokoly pervogo s"ezda Partii Sotsialistov-Revoliutsionerov* (Moscow, 1906), 360.
46. A. N. Spiridovich, *Revoliutsionnoe dvizhenie v Rossii,* II (Petrograd, 1916), 311–12; Hildermeier, *Sozialrevolutionäre Partei,* 136.
47. Cited in Hildermeier, *Sozialrevolutionäre Partei,* 112.
48. *Ibid.,* 117.
49. On the SRs: Maureen Perrie in *SS,* XXIV, No. 2 (1972), 223–50; on the SDs: David Lane, *The Roots of Russian Communism* (Assen, 1969).
50. Hildermeier, *Sozialrevolutionäre Partei,* 252.
51. Perrie in *SS,* 249–50; Lane, *Roots,* 50.
52. In *OD,* III, Book 5 (St. Petersburg, 1914), 99–100.
53. *RZ,* XIII (1939), 124.
54. Charles E. Timberlake, ed., *Essays on Russian Liberalism* (Columbia, Mo., 1972), 11.
55. Terence Emmons in *SR,* No. 3 (1973), 461–90.
56. Shmuel Galai, *The Liberation Movement in Russia, 1900–1905* (Cambridge, 1973).
57. V. V. Shelokhaev, *Kadety* (Moscow, 1983), 67–68, 84.

Chapter 5

1. S. Iu. Vitte, *Vospominaniia,* III (Moscow, 1960), 296; cf. M. Szeftel, *The Russian Constitution of April 23, 1906* (Brussels, 1976), 33–35.
2. Cited in G. A. Hosking, *The Russian Constitutional Experiment* (Cambridge, 1973), 92.
3. *Padenie,* V, 418.
4. P. A. Tverskoi in *VE,* XLVII, No. 4 (April 1912), 188; V. I. Startsev, *Russkaia burzhuaziia i samoderzhavie v 1905–17 gg.* (Leningrad, 1977), 121.
5. V. N. Kokovtsov, *Iz moego proshlogo,* I (Paris, 1933), 306.
6. M. Baring, *A Year in Russia* (London, 1907), 213; S. S. Oldenburg, *Tsarstvovanie Imperatora Nikolaia II,* II (Munich, 1949), 5.
7. On these groups, see V. Levitskii in *OD,* III, Book 5 (St. Petersburg, 1914), 347–469; and Hans

Rogger in *California Slavic Studies*, III (1964) 66–94, and in *Journal of Modern History*, XXXVI, No. 4 (1964), 398–415.

8. Testimony in *Padenie*, V, 378.
9. *Briefe Wilhelms II an den Zaren, 1894–1914* (Berlin, [1920?]), 376.
10. Introduction to *La Chute du Régime Tsariste: Interrogatoires* (Paris, 1927), 36.
11. S. E. Kryzhanovskii, *Vospominaniia* (Berlin, [1938]), 123.
12. *RM*, No. 1 (January 1907), Pt. 2, 131.
13. The best study of the Fundamental Laws of 1906 is Szeftel's *Russian Constitution*.
14. Guchkov in *PN*, No. 5,616 (August 9, 1936), 2.
15. N. P. Eroshkin, ed., *Ocherki istorii gosudarstvennykh uchrezhdenii dorevoliutsionnoi Rossii* (Moscow, 1960), 334.
16. The fullest collection of these laws is G. G. Savich, ed., *Novyi gosudarstvennyi stroi Rossii* (St. Petersburg, 1907).
17. On this subject, see V. M. Gessen, *Iskliuchetel'noe polozhenie* (St. Petersburg, 1908), and N. N. Polianskii, *Tsarskie voennye sudy v bor'be s revoliutsei 1905–1907 gg.* (Moscow, 1958), 8–42.
18. The Fundamental Laws of 1906 are translated, with commentaries, in Szeftel's *Russian Constitution*.
19. Maklakov, *Interrogatoires*, 35.
20. Startsev, *Russkaia burzhuaziia*, 11–13; Hosking, *Constitutional Experiment*, 16–17.
21. Guchkov in *PN*, No. 5,616 (August 9, 1936), 2.
22. Kryzhanovskii, *Vospominaniia*, 81–82, 84–86.
23. V. A. Maklakov, *Pervaia Gosudarstvennaia Duma* (Paris, 1939), 59–117.
24. P. G. Kurlov, *Gibel' Imperatorskoi Rossii* (Berlin, 1923), 66.
25. Manfred Hildermeier, *Die Sozialrevolutionäre Partei Russlands* (Köln-Wien, 1978), *passim*.
26. *Sbornik rechei Petra Arkadevicha Stolypina* (St. Petersburg, 1911), 9.
27. Gosudarstvennaia Duma, *Stenograficheskie Otchëty: 1907*, Sessiia II, Zasedanie 40-oe, II (St. Petersburg, 1907), 696.
28. Anna Geifman in *Jahrbücher*, XXXVI, No. 2 (1988), 250.
29. *Ibid.*, 250–51.
30. Maklakov, *Interrogatoires*, 40.
31. H. Nicolson, *Sir Arthur Nicolson, Bart.* (London, 1930), 225.
32. "Witte und Stolypin" in P. R. Rohden and G. Ostrogorsky, eds., *Menschen die Geschichte machten*, III (Vienna, 1931), 268.
33. Tverskoi in *VE*, XLVII, No. 4 (April 1912), 186.
34. *KA*, No. 4/17 (1926), 81–90.
35. A. Izgoev, *P. A. Stolypin: Ocherk zhizni i deiatel'nosti* (Moscow, 1912), 14.
36. Report of 1904 in *KA*, No. 4/17 (1926), 84.
37. Struve in *RM*, No. 10 (October 1911), Pt. 2, 139–40; cf. Kokovtsov, *Iz moego proshlogo*, I, 205, and Izgoev, *Stolypin*, 67.
38. Kryzhanovskii, *Vospominaniia*, 127–39.
39. A. V. Zenkovskii, *Pravda o Stolypine* (New York, 1956), 73–113.
40. *Byloe*, No. 5/6 (1917), 212–27.
41. N. Savickij in *Le Monde Slave*, IV, No. 12 (1934), 381; *Sbornik rechei Petra Arkadevicha Stolypina*, 28.
42. Izgoev, *Stolypin*, 42, and Richard Pipes, *Russia under the Old Regime* (London, 1974), 305–6.
43. Text in A. K. Drezen, ed., *Tsarizm v bor'be s revoliutsiei, 1905–07* (Moscow, 1936), 80–86.
44. Ludwig Bazylow, *Ostatnie lata Rosji Carskiej: Rzady Stolypina* (Warsaw, 1972), 172.
45. A. Ventin in *Sovremennyi mir*, No. 4 ([1910]), Pt. 2, 69.
46. *NoV*, No. 10,939 (August 27, 1906), 2.
47. Text in Savich, *Novyi gosudarstvennyi stroi*, 170–74.
48. *Ibid.*, 193–200.
49. Stolypin's Duma speech of March 6, 1907, in Gosudarstvennaia Duma, *Stenograficheskie Otchëty, 1907 god*, I, Sessiia Vtoraia, Zasedanie 5-oe (St. Petersburg, 1907), 115.
50. S. M. Dubrovskii, *Stolypinskaia zemel'naia reforma* (Moscow, 1963), 391.
51. Gosudarstvennaia Duma, *Stenograficheskie Otchëty, 1907 god*, II, Sessiia Vtoraia, Zasedanie 36-oe (St. Petersburg, 1907), 436–37.

52. See above, p. 120.
53. On this, David A. J. Macey, *Government and Peasant in Russia, 1861–1906* (De Kalb, Ill., 1987).
54. Roberta T. Manning, *The Crisis of the Old Order in Russia: Gentry and Government* (Princeton, N.J., 1982), 55.
55. Kryzhanovskii, *Vospominaniia,* 215–16.
56. Dubrovskii, *Stolypinskaia zemel'naia reforma,* 189.
57. Savich, *Novyi gosudarstvennyi stroi,* 232–38.
58. A. A. Kofod, *Russkoe zemleustroistvo,* 2nd ed. (St. Petersburg, 1914), 30.
59. See, e.g., A. V. Shestakov, *Kapitalizatsiia sel'skogo khoziaistva Rossii (1861–1914)* (Moscow, 1924).
60. Based on Dubrovskii, *Stolypinskaia zemel'naia reforma, passim.*
61. *Ibid.,* 199.
62. *Ibid.,* 206.
63. *Ibid.,* 305.
64. E. G. Vasilevskii, *Ideinaia bor'ba vokrug Stolypinskoi agrarnoi reformy* (Moscow, 1960), 67–84.
65. Based on Dubrovskii, *Stolypinskaia zemel'naia reforma,* 419.
66. L. Pasvolsky and H. G. Moulton, *Russian Debts and Russian Reconstruction* (New York, 1924), 91.
67. Bazylow, *Ostatnie lata,* 205; Kryzhanovskii, *Vospominaniia,* 93–94; Hosking, *Constitutional Experiment,* 150.
68. This exchange, which took place in July–August 1906, is reproduced in *KA,* No. 4 (1923), 132–35.
69. *KA,* No. 5 (1924), 105–7; Kokovtsov, *Iz moego proshlogo,* I, 236–38, and Szeftel, *Russian Constitution,* 296n–297n.
70. Kurlov, *Gibel',* 73–74; Kryzhanovskii in *Padenie,* V, 403, 415.
71. Startsev, *Russkaia burzhuaziia,* 111–16.
72. *Ibid.,* 82.
73. Richard Pipes, *Struve: Liberal on the Right* (Cambridge, Mass., 1980), 55–56.
74. P. P. Maslov in *OD,* III, Book 5, 117.
75. *Chetvërtyi (Ob"edinitel'nyi) S"ezd RSDRP; Protokoly,* (Moscow, 1959), 525–26.
76. Golovin in *Padenie,* V, 367, 373.
77. *KA,* No. 4 (1923), 132.
78. Kokovtsov in *Padenie,* VII, 88, 97.
79. Tverskoi in *VE,* XLVII, No. 4 (April 1912), 193.
80. Kryzhanovskii in *Vospominaniia,* 90, and *Padenie,* V, 401; and Kryzhanovskii's letter to V. N. Kokovtsov, dated June 20, 1929, in Kryzhanovskii Archive, Box 1, Bakhmeteff Archive, Columbia University.
81. Kurlov, *Gibel',* 94; Kryzhanovskii in *Padenie,* V, 421.
82. Kryzhanovskii, *Vospominaniia,* 114.
83. Kryzhanovskii in *Padenie,* V, 418; Szeftel, *Russian Constitution,* 259.
84. Hosking, *Constitutional Experiment,* 50.
85. Alexander Kerensky in *SZ,* LX (1936), 460.
86. Guchkov in *PN,* No. 5,619 (August 12, 1936), 2.
87. Kryzhanovskii in *Padenie,* V, 406, 411, 415.
88. [Konstitutsionno-Demokraticheskaia Partiia], *Tret'ia Gosudarstvennaia Duma: Materialy dlia otsenki eë deiatel'nosti* (St. Petersburg, 1912), vii.
89. Guchkov in *Padenie,* VI, 252–53.
90. Hosking, *Constitutional Experiment,* 136.
91. Kokovtsov, *Iz moego proshlogo,* II, 8.
92. Struve in *RM,* No. 10 (October 1911), Pt. 2, 140.
93. *Tret'ia Gosudarstvennaia Duma,* 286–90.
94. On this subject, see Hosking, *Constitutional Experiment,* 116–46.
95. Kryzhanovskii, *Vospominaniia,* 128–30.
96. Kryzhanovskii, *Vospominaniia,* 218; Guchkov in *PN,* No. 5,637 (August 30, 1936), 2.

97. The text of the bill as enacted on March 14, 1911, is in Zenkovskii, *Pravda o Stolypine*, 285–302.
98. A. Ia. Avrekh, *Stolypin i Tret'ia Duma* (Moscow, 1968), 334–35.
99. *Ibid.*, 331.
100. *Ibid.*, 337.
101. *Ibid.*, 337–38.
102. Guchkov in *PN*, No. 5,637 (August 30, 1936), 2.
103. Kokovtsov, *Iz moego proshlogo*, I, 457.
104. V. I. Gurko, *Features and Figures of the Past* (Stanford, Calif., 1939), 515.
105. Kokovtsov, *Iz moego proshlogo*, I, 463.
106. *Ibid.*, I, 460–61.
107. Kurlov, *Gibel'*, 128; Zenkovskii, *Pravda*, 234.
108. A. F. Girs cited in A. Serebrennikov *Ubiistvo Stolypina: svidetel'stva i dokumenty* (New York, 1986), 191.
109. Police documents on Bogrov, with his depositions, have been published by B. Strumillo in *KL*, No. 9 (1923), 177–89, and No. 1/10 (1924), 226–40. There exists a short apologetic biography of the assassin by his brother Vladimir: *Dmitrii Bogrov i ubiistvo Stolypina* (Berlin, 1931).
110. G. E. Rein, citing General Spiridovich in Serebrennikov, *Ubiistvo*, 197.
111. The theory that Stolypin had fallen victim of the Okhrana has been recently revived by Avrekh in his *Stolypin*, 367–406.
112. Kurlov, *Gibel'*, 75–76.
113. *Padenie*, VI, 252.
114. *KA*, No. 4/35 (1929), 210.
115. Kokovtsov, *Iz moego proshlogo*, II, 8.
116. P. A. Khromov, *Ekonomicheskoe razvitie Rossii v XIX–XX vekakh* (Moscow, 1950), 454–55.
117. Edmond Théry, *La Transformation Economique de la Russie* (Paris, 1914), xvii.
118. Pasvolsky and Moulton, *Russian Debts*, 177.
119. *Ibid.*, 50.
120. Leopold Haimson in *SR*, XXIII, No. 4 (December 1964), 634–36.
121. The proposition is argued by Haimson, *loc. cit.*, 619–42, and XXIV, No. 1 (March 1965), 1–22.
122. Calculated on the basis of figures in J. I. Griffin, *Strikes* (New York, 1939), 43.
123. K. G. J. C. Knowles, *Strikes: A Study in Industrial Conflict* (Oxford, 1952), 310.
124. Haimson in *SR*, XXIV, No. 1 (1965), 4–8.
125. On this, see Bernice Rosenthal, ed., *Nietzsche in Russia* (Princeton, N.J., 1986).
126. "Stikhiia i kultura" (1908) in his *Sobranie Sochinenii v vos'mi tomakh*, V (Moscow-Leningrad, 1962), 351, 359.

Chapter 6

1. Fritz Fischer, *War of Illusions* (London, 1975) and *Germany's Aims in the First World War* (New York, 1961).
2. V. N. Lamzdorf, *Dnevnik, 1891–92* (Moscow-Leningrad, 1934), 299.
3. V. A. Emets, *Ocherki vneshnei politiki Rossii: 1914–17* (Moscow, 1977), 52–53.
4. A. M. Zaionchkovskii, *Mirovaia voina 1914–18 gg.*, I (Moscow, 1938), 39–40.
5. N. N. Golovin, *Voennye usiliia Rossii v mirovoi voine*, II (Paris, 1939), 127; Emets, *Ocherki*, 46.
6. See J. K. Tanenbaum, in E. R. May, ed., *Knowing One's Enemies* (Princeton, N.J., 1984), 150–71.
7. Golovin, *Voennye usiliia*, II, 129–30; G. Frantz, ed., *Russland auf dem Wege zur Katastrofe* (Berlin, 1926), 68–69.
8. Norman Stone, *The Eastern Front, 1914–1917* (New York, 1975), 42.
9. Fischer, *War of Illusions*, 388.
10. A. Knox, *With the Russian Army, 1914–1917*, I (London, 1921), xix.
11. On Russia's entry into the war: D. C. B. Lieven, *Russia and the Origins of the First World War* (London, 1984).

12. W. A. Suchomlinow [Sukhomlinov], *Erinnerungen* (Berlin, 1924), 363–64.
13. Calculated from data in N. A. Troinitskii, ed., *Obshchii svod . . . pervoi vseobshchei perepisi naseleniia*, I (St. Petersburg, 1905), 56.
14. L. G. Beskrovnyi, *Armiia i flot Rossii v nachale XX veka* (Moscow, 1986), 15–16.
15. Emets, *Ocherki*, 33; Knox, *With the Russian Army*, II, 544.
16. Golovin, *Voennye usiliia*, I, 97–105.
17. A. Kersnovskii, *Istoriia Russkoi Armii*, Pt. 3 (Belgrade, 1935), 507; Knox, *With the Russian Army*, I, xxv–xxvi.
18. Kersnovskii, *Istoriia*, III, 613.
19. Golovin, *Voennye usiliia*, II, 121.
20. Knox, *With the Russian Army*, I, 31–32.
21. *Ibid.*, 222n.
22. *Ibid.*, 27.
23. Emets, *Ocherki*, 95.
24. Golovin, *Voennye usiliia*, II, 8.
25. *Ibid.*, 7.
26. A. L. Sidorov, *Ekonomicheskoe polozhenie Rossii v gody pervoi mirovoi voiny* (Moscow, 1973), 109–10.
27. Beskrovnyi, *Armiia i flot*, 105.
28. Knox, *With the Russian Army*, II, 525.
29. Zaionchkovskii, *Mirovaia voina*, I, 365.
30. Golovin, *Voennye usiliia*, I, 62.
31. Kersnovskii, *Istoriia*, IV, 877.
32. Bernard Pares, *The Fall of the Russian Monarchy* (London, 1929), 254–55.
33. *Padenie*, VII, 119.
34. P. B. Struve, "Ekonomicheskaia problema 'Velikoi Rossii,'" in *Velikaia Rossiia, Sbornik Statei*, Book 2 (Moscow, 1911), 151–52.
35. Guchkov in *PN*, No. 5,630 (August 23, 1936), 2.
36. Gen. B. Borisov in *Voennyi sbornik*, II (Belgrade, 1922), 21.
37. A. N. Iakhontov, August 4, 1915, in *ARR*, XVIII (1926), 36.
38. Cited in Sidorov, *Ekonomicheskoe polozhenie*, 56.
39. B. V. Mikhailovskii, *Russkaia literatura XX v.* (Moscow, 1939), 411–18.
40. Ludwig Bazylow, *Obalenie caratu* (Warsaw, 1976), 297–98; George Katkov in Richard Pipes, ed., *Revolutionary Russia* (Cambridge, Mass., 1968), 64–66.
41. S. Sazonov, *Fateful Years* (London, 1928), 32.
42. *KN*, No. 6/10 (1922), 182–99. English translation in F. A. Golder, *Documents of Russian History* (New York, 1927), 3–23.
43. S. Dobrovolskii in *Voennyi sbornik*, II (Belgrade, 1922), 63–64; Emets, *Ocherki*, 46.
44. N. Maklakov in *Padenie*, III, 103; Suchomlinow, *Erinnerungen*, 368–69.
45. Emets, *Ocherki*, 68, citing Gen. Iu. N. Danilov.
46. *Ibid.*, 50.
47. Knox, *With the Russian Army*, I, 60–61.
48. *Ibid.*, 90, 86.
49. H. von Moltke, *Erinnerungen, Briefe, Dokumente, 1877–1916* (Stuttgart, 1922), 434–35; *Mémoirs du Maréchal Joffre, 1910–17*, I (Paris, 1932), 353, 369.
50. Emets, *Ocherki*, 95.
51. J. Buchan, *A History of the Great War*, I (Boston, 1922), 526–27.
52. Knox, *With the Russian Army*, I, 268–69; Beskrovnyi, *Armiia i flot*, 15.
53. Moltke, *Erinnerungen*, 385.
54. *Ibid.*, 406, 414.
55. Kersnovskii, *Istoriia russkoi armii*, III, 729.
56. E. von Falkenhayn, *Die Oberste Heeresleitung, 1914–1916* (Berlin, 1920), 26.
57. Knox, *With the Russian Army*, I, 349.
58. A. G. Shliapnikov *et al.*, eds., *Kto dolzhnik?* (Moscow, 1926), 125.
59. *Ibid.*

60. Gen. Sérigny cited in Golovin, *Voennye usiliia*, II, 143.
61. Emets, *Ocherki*, 175; Sidorov, *Ekonomicheskoe polozhenie*, 95.
62. V. S. Diakin, *Russkaia burzhuaziia i tsarizm v gody pervoi mirovoi voiny (1914–17)* (Leningrad, 1967), 78, citing K. F. Shatsillo.
63. Stone, *Eastern Front*, 131–32, 147.
64. Reproduced in Suchomlinow, *Erinnerungen*, 414.
65. His memoirs: Suchomlinow, *Erinnerungen;* Russian translation: *Vospominaniia Sukhomlinova* (Moscow-Leningrad, 1926).
66. Diakin, *Russkaia burzhuaziia*, 79. On him, see further Sidorov, *Ekonomicheskoe polozhenie*, 77–79.
67. Bernard Pares, *The Fall of the Russian Monarchy* (London, 1939), 327.
68. B. Pares, ed., *Letters of the Tsaritsa to the Tsar, 1914–1916* (London, 1923), 108.
69. S. P. Beletskii, *Grigorii Rasputin* (Petrograd, 1923), 33–35.
70. Pares, *Letters*, 110.
71. Rodzianko in *Padenie*, VII, 153; Diakin, *Russkaia burzhuaziia*, 89.
72. B. B. Grave, ed., *Burzhuaziia nakanune fevral'skoi revoliutsii* (Moscow-Leningrad, 1927), 39.
73. Emets, *Ocherki*, 175.
74. Iakhontov in *ARR*, XVIII (1926), 15.
75. Pares, *The Fall*, 256.
76. Diakin, *Russkaia burzhuaziia*, 89–90.
77. On him, see Richard Abraham, *Alexander Kerensky: The First Love of the Revolution* (New York, 1987).
78. Tsentral'nyi Komitet Trudovoi Gruppy, *Aleksandr Fëdorovich Kerenskii (Po Materialam Departamenta Politsii)* (Petrograd, 1917).
79. E. H. Wilcox, *Russia's Ruin* (London, 1919), 193.
80. Abraham, *Kerensky*, 96.
81. Beletskii, *Rasputin*, 13.
82. Bazylow, *Obalenie caratu*, 65; Maurice Paléologue, *La Russie des Tsars pendant la Grande Guerre*, II (Paris, 1922), 54–55.
83. Diakin, *Russkaia burzhuaziia*, 113.
84. Iakhontov in *ARR*, XVIII, 53–56.
85. *Padenie*, VII, 68–69, 131; V. P. Semennikov, *Politika Romanovykh nakanune revoliutsii* (Moscow-Leningrad, 1926), 82–83.
86. Text: Iakhontov in *ARR*, XVIII, 98.
87. Pares, *The Fall*, 269.
88. Diakin, *Russkaia burzhuaziia*, 103.
89. The full English text in Pares, *The Fall*, 271–73.
90. Grave, *Burzhuaziia*, 27–29; *KA*, No. 1–2/50–51, (1932) 133–36; *ARR*, XVIII, 109–10.
91. See examples in Diakin, *Russkaia burzhuaziia*, 114.
92. Pares, *The Fall*, 275–76.
93. Grave, *Burzhuaziia*, 39.
94. *NoV*, No. 7,258 (May 14/26, 1896), 2.
95. Iakhontov in *ARR*, XVIII, 62.
96. *Ibid.*, 128.
97. *Ibid.*
98. Diakin, *Russkaia burzhuaziia*, 126–27.
99. *RV*, No. 221 (September 27, 1915), 2.
100. Pares, *The Fall*, 285.
101. *Ibid.*, 242–243.
102. Gosudarstvennaia Duma, *Stenograficheskie otchëty*, IV Sozyv, Sessiia IV, Zasedanie 4 (Petrograd, 1915), 303–5.
103. Beskrovnyi, *Armiia i flot*, 71.
104. Sidorov, *Ekonomicheskoe polozhenie*, 102–3.
105. *Padenie*, VII, 140.
106. A. P. Pogrebinskii in *IZ*, XI (1941), 164.

107. A. Shliapnikov, *Kanun semnadtsatogo goda*, 3rd ed., I (Moscow, n.d.), 95–121; Bazylow, *Obalenie caratu*, 100.
108. On it: Pogrebinskii in *IZ*, XI (1941), 189–99.
109. Sidorov, *Ekonomicheskoe polozhenie*, 200.
110. As does Stone, *Eastern Front*, 201.
111. Knox, *With the Russian Army*, I, 355–56.
112. Cited in Sidorov, *Ekonomicheskoe polozhenie*, 93.
113. On the Zemstvo Union, see S. Kotliarevskii in *RM*, No. 3 (March 1916), Pt. 2, 137–41, and T. I. Polner, *Russian Local Government during the War and the Union of Zemstvos* (New Haven, Conn., 1930).
114. On them: Bazylow, *Obalenie caratu*, 103–5.
115. E.g., Goremykin and Rukhlov in Sidorov, *Ekonomicheskoe polozhenie*, 97.
116. Grave, *Burzhuaziia*, 66.

Chapter 7

1. V. V. Shulgin, *Dni* (Belgrade, 1925), 156.
2. A. P. Pogrebinskii, *Gosudarstvennye finansy tsarskoi Rossii v epokhu imperializma* (Moscow, 1968), 64.
3. L. N. Yurovsky, *Currency Problems of the Soviet Union* (London, 1925), 12; Rudolf Claus, *Die Kriegswirtschaft Russlands* (Bonn-Leipzig, 1922), 21.
4. Estimates by S. N. Prokopovich in A. L. Sidorov, *Finansovoe polozhenie Rossii v gody pervoi mirovoi voiny, 1914–1917 gg.* (Moscow, 1960), 131–32.
5. Calculated on the basis of figures in Sidorov, *Finansovoe polozhenie*, 117.
6. Claus, *Kriegswirtschaft*, 25.
7. Sidorov, *Finansovoe polozhenie*, 146.
8. Claus, *Kriegswirtschaft*, 4.
9. *Ibid.*, 4–5.
10. N. P. Oganovskii and A. V. Chaianov, eds., *Statisticheskii spravochnik po agrarnomu voprosu*, I (Moscow, 1917), 10–11; *Predvaritel'nye itogi vserossisskoi sel'sko-khoziaistvennoi perepisi 1916 g.* (Petrograd, 1916), xv.
11. V. P. Bystrenin in *RM*, November 1916, 1; see also A. S. Izgoev, *RM*, October 1916, 2.
12. B. B. Grave, ed., *Burzhuaziia nakanune fevral'skoi revoliutsii* (Moscow-Leningrad, 1927), 137.
13. L. Bazylow, *Obalenie caratu* (Warsaw, 1976), 160.
14. M. Florinsky, *The End of the Russian Empire* (New Haven, Conn., 1931), 121.
15. Grave, *Burzhuaziia*, 131.
16. A. Knox, *With the Russian Army, 1914–1917*, II (London, 1921), 388; cf. A. M. Anfimov, *Rossiiskaia derevnia v gody pervoi mirovoi voiny, 1914–1917 gg.* (Moscow, 1962), 306–9.
17. V. S. Diakin, *Russkaia burzhuaziia i tsarizm v gody pervoi mirovoi voiny (1914–1917)* (Leningrad, 1967), 132–33.
18. Knox, *With the Russian Army*, II, 422.
19. A. A. Manikovskii, *Boevoe snabzhenie russkoi armii v mirovoiu voinu*, 2nd ed., I (Moscow-Leningrad, 1930), 398, 165.
20. Norman Stone, *The Eastern Front, 1914–1917* (London, 1976), 238.
21. Maurice Paléologue, *La Russie des Tsars pendant la Grande Guerre*, III (Paris, 1922), 92–93.
22. Bernard Pares, ed., *Letters of the Tsaritsa to the Tsar, 1914–1916* (London, 1923), xxix, and *The Fall of the Russian Monarchy* (London, 1939), 401, citing Iusupov.
23. Testimony of Stürmer in *Padenie*, I, 222.
24. *Ibid.*, VII, 205.
25. Knox, *With the Russian Army*, II, 413.
26. Gen. B. Gurko, *Memories and Impressions of War and Revolution in Russia, 1914–1917* (London, 1918), 188.
27. Knox, *With the Russian Army*, II, 416.
28. Diakin, *Russkaia burzhuaziia*, 274–75. Cf. Alexander Blok, "Poslednie dni imperatorskoi

vlasti," in *Sobranie sochinenii v vos'mi tomakh,* VI (Moscow-Leningrad, 1962), 193; also *RZ,* November 1916, 243.

29. *Rech',* January 3, 1917, cited in Diakin, *Russkaia burzhuaziia,* 275.
30. A. I. Spiridovich, *Velikaia voina i fevral'skaia revoliutsiia, 1914–1917 gg.,* III (New York, 1962), 13.
31. Knox, *With the Russian Army,* II, 424–25.
32. *KA,* No. 4/17 (1926), 24.
33. Grave, *Burzhuaziia,* 127.
34. *Ibid.,* 136.
35. Knox, *With the Russian Army,* II, 552; Pares, *Letters,* xxxviii.
36. Knox, *With the Russian Army,* II, 542.
37. Grave, *Burzhuaziia,* 134.
38. Knox, *With the Russian Army,* II, 515; Grave, *Burzhuaziia,* 133–34.
39. Izgoev in *RM,* October 1916, Pt. 3, 1–5.
40. A. Petrishchev in *RZ,* October 1916, 233–39.
41. A. L. Sidorov, *Ekonomicheskoe polozhenie Rossii v gody pervoi mirovoi voiny* (Moscow, 1973), 492, 496; P. I. Liashchenko, *Istoriia narodnogo khoziaistva SSSR,* 3rd ed., II (Moscow, 1952), 641.
42. Sidorov, *Ekonomicheskoe polozhenie,* 496.
43. Richard Pipes, *Struve: Liberal on the Right* (Cambridge, Mass., 1980), 230.
44. Bazylow, *Obalenie caratu,* 303–4.
45. On this, see S. P. Melgunov, *Legenda o separatnom mire* (Paris, 1957).
46. Grave, *Burzhuaziia,* 138.
47. *Ibid.,* 140–41, 147–48.
48. Pares, *The Fall,* 378–79.
49. Grave, *Burzhuaziia,* 141.
50. Pares, *Letters,* 395.
51. Pares, *The Fall,* 380.
52. E. D. Chermenskii, *IV Gosusdarstvennaia Duma i sverzhenie tsarizma v Rossii* (Moscow, 1976), 201.
53. Pares, *The Fall,* 380.
54. Gurko, *Memories and Impressions,* 184.
55. Guchkov, as reported in Pares, *The Fall,* 381.
56. Chermenskii, *IV Duma,* 196, note 4.
57. *Padenie,* I/2, 1–64.
58. Chermenskii, *IV Duma,* 198.
59. Diakin, *Russkaia burzhuaziia,* 268–69.
60. *Padenie,* IV, 29; George Katkov, *Russia 1917: The February Revolution* (New York, 1967), 213.
61. Pares, *The Fall,* 383.
62. Chermenskii, *IV Duma,* 204.
63. Grave, *Burzhuaziia,* 145–48; Diakin, *Russkaia burzhuaziia,* 236–37.
64. Grave, *Burzhuaziia,* 146–47.
65. *Ibid.,* 147.
66. Diakin, *Russkaia burzhuaziia,* 241.
67. V. P. Semennikov, *Monarkhiia pered krusheniem, 1914–1917* (Moscow, 1927), 130–31.
68. T. Hasegawa, *The February Revolution: Petrograd 1917* (Seattle-London, 1981), 55.
69. *KA,* No. 4 (1923), 196.
70. Chermenskii, *IV Duma,* 206.
71. *Ibid.*
72. *Ibid.,* 207.
73. *Ibid.*
74. Gosudarstvennaia Duma, *Stenograficheskii otchët,* IV Sozyv, Sessiia V, Zasedanie I (n.p., n.d.), 11–13.
75. *Ibid.,* 29–33.

76. A. S. Rezanov, *Shturmovoi signal P. N. Miliukova* (Paris, 1924), 43–61.

77. P. N. Miliukov, *Vospominaniia, 1859–1917*, II (New York, 1955), 276–77.

78. Miliukov to Petrunkevich in 1919, in Diakin, *Russkaia burzhuaziia*, 243.

79. Bazylow, *Obalenie caratu*, 204.

80. S. S. Oldenburg, *Tsarstvovanie Imperatora Nikolaia II*, II (Munich, 1949), 218–20.

81. Among contemporaries, this opinion was held by the Tsar's aide V. N. Voeikov (*S tsarem i bez tsariia*, Helsingfors, 1936, 166) and the liberal publicist Ariadna Tyrkova-Williams: *From Liberty to Brest Litovsk* (London, 1919), 3; among historians, by Chermenskii (*IV Duma*, 212–13), Diakin (*Russkaia burzhuaziia*, 275–76), and George Katkov, *Russia, 1917* (New York, 1967), 194–97.

82. Gosudarstvennaia Duma, *Stenograficheskii otchët*, IV Sozyv, Sessiia V, 68.

83. Voeikov, *S tsarem*, 185.

84. Bobrinskoi in *VE*, No. 12 (1916), 379.

85. Diakin, *Russkaia burzhuaziia*, 244.

86. *Lettres des Grands-Ducs à Nicolas II* (Paris, 1926), 258–59.

87. *Perepiska Nikolaia i Aleksandry Romanovykh, 1916–1917*, V (Moscow-Leningrad, 1927), 128–29, 131.

88. Diakin, *Russkaia burzhuaziia*, 244–45.

89. Spiridovich, *Velikaia voina*, II, 189, and *VE*, No. 2 (1917), 324.

90. Paléologue, *La Russie des Tsars*, III, 90.

91. *Ibid.*, 91.

92. *Ibid.*, 105.

93. *Rech'*, November 11–14, 1916, cited in *RZ*, November 1916, 238–39.

94. Diakin, *Russkaia burzhuaziia*, 248; Spiridovich, *Velikaia voina*, II, 175–76; *VE*, November 1916, 342–43.

95. Grand Duke Dmitrii in F. Iusupov, *Konets Rasputina* (Paris, 1927), 134.

96. Gosudarstvennaia Duma, *Stenograficheskie otchëty*, IV Sozyv, V Sessiia, Zasedanie 6 (November 19, 1916), 253–54.

97. *Ibid.*, Zasedanie 18 (December 16, 1916), 1225–26; Bazylow, *Obalenie caratu*, 248–49.

98. *KA*, No. 4 (1923), 187.

99. A. I. Spiridovich, *Raspoutine* (Paris, 1935), 335–38.

100. Pares, *Letters*, 221.

101. See his last will and testament in Aron Simanovitch, *Raspoutine* (Paris, 1930), 256; V. P. Semennikov, *Politika Romanovykh nakanune Revoliutsii* (Moscow-Leningrad, 1926), 92.

102. *Padenie*, IV, 14.

103. Kokovtsov, *Iz moego proshlogo*, II, 41.

104. Spiridovich, *Raspoutine*, 94.

105. Diakin, *Russkaia burzhuaziia*, 261.

106. *Perepiska Romanovykh*, V, 153; retranslated from the Russian.

107. Spiridovich, *Velikaia voina*, II, 177. Cf. Pares, *The Fall*, 382.

108. Protopopov in *Padenie*, IV, 15–16.

109. *Ibid.*, 31.

110. *Padenie*, IV, 5; Spiridovich, *Velikaia voina*, II, 176–77; A. A. Mossolov, *At the Court of the Last Tsar* (London, 1935), 170–73.

111. Katkov, *Russia, 1917*, 197.

112. Maklakov in *SZ*, XXXIV, 265.

113. Pares, *The Fall*, 396.

114. *Ibid.*, 396–97, 402.

115. Pares, *The Fall*, 403.

116. Spiridovich, *Raspoutine*, 369–70; Shulgin, *Dni*, 119.

117. Spiridovich, *Raspoutine*, 374.

118. Paléologue, *La Russie des Tsars*, III, 141.

119. Pares, *The Fall*, 406.

120. V. M. Purishkevich, *Ubiistvo Rasputina* (Paris, [1923]), 81.

121. Pares, *The Fall*, 462; *KA*, No. 4 (1923), 425.

122. Spiridovich, *Raspoutine,* 396.
123. Spiridovich, *Velikaia voina,* II, 207.
124. *Ibid.,* 216–17; Pares, *The Fall,* 410.
125. Voeikov, *S tsarem,* 178.
126. Iusupov, *Konets Rasputina,* 204.
127. *KA,* No. 1/20 (1927), 124.
128. Spiridovich, *Velikaia voina,* II, 203, 211.
129. *Ibid.,* II, 217.
130. Text in Voeikov, *S tsarem,* 182–83.
131. Spiridovich, *Velikaia voina,* II, 214–15.
132. *Ibid.,* III, 29.
133. *Ibid.,* II, 184; Diakin, *Russkaia burzhuaziia,* 287.
134. Pares, *The Fall,* 414.
135. Voeikov, *S tsarem,* 191.
136. Bazylow, *Obalenie caratu,* 338–39.
137. Spiridovich, *Velikaia voina,* III, 17.
138. *KA,* No. 1/20 (1927), 126.
139. Spiridovich, *Velikaia voina,* II, 19.
140. M. V. Rodzianko, *The Reign of Rasputin* (London, 1928), 253–54.
141. *SZ.* XXIV (1928), 279.
142. M. V. Rodzianko, *The Reign of Rasputin* (London, 1927), 253–54.
143. Maklakov in *SZ,* No. 34 (1928), 279.
144. Guchkov in *PN,* No. 5,647 (September 9, 1936), 2, and No. 5,651 (September 13, 1936), 2; see
     further Pares, *The Fall,* 427–48; *Padenie,* VI, 278; Diakin, *Russkaia burzhuaziia,* 301–2;
     Spiridovich, *Velikaia voina,* II, 166, and III, 46; Hasegawa, *February Revolution,* 187.
145. On this, see Pares, *The Fall,* 428–29; Diakin, *Russkaia burzhuaziia,* 300; Spiridovich, *Velikaia
     voina,* III, 14–17; Guchkov in *PN,* No. 5,651 (September 13, 1936), 2.
146. Police report of January 5, 1917, in Blok, "Poslednie dni," 203.
147. Blok, "Poslednie dni," 205; Bazylow, *Obalenie caratu,* 287.
148. Spiridovich, *Velikaia voina,* III, 42.
149. *Ibid.,* II, 188, and III, 41.
150. Diakin, *Russkaia burzhuaziia,* 273–74.
151. Spiridovich, *Velikaia voina,* III, 47; Katkov, *Russia, 1917,* 240.
152. *PR,* No. 13 (1923), 269–70.
153. Blok, "Poslednie dni," 207; Bazylow, *Obalenie caratu,* 344–45.
154. Spiridovich, *Velikaia voina,* III, 47, and Protopopov in *GM* XV, No. 2 (1926), 189–91.
155. Blok, "Poslednie dni," 220–21; Bazylow, *Obalenie caratu,* 344–45.
156. Diakin, *Russkaia burzhuaziia,* 274–75.
157. Spiridovich, *Velikaia voina,* III, 40.
158. P. E. Shchegolev, *Okhranniki i avantiuristy* (Moscow, 1930), 140–41.

Chapter 8

1. Tsentral'noe Statisticheskoe Upravlenie, *Trudy,* VII, Vyp. 1 (Moscow, 1921), 252.
2. *Padenie,* IV, 21.
3. E. I. Martynov, *Tsarskaia armiia v fevral'skom perevorote* (Leningrad, 1927), 118; A. P. Balk,
   "Poslednie piat' dnei tsarskogo Petrograda," Bakhmeteff Archive, Columbia University.
4. *PR,* No. 13 (1923), 290; J. L. H. Keep, *The Russian Revolution* (London, 1976), 58.
5. A. I. Spiridovich, *Velikaia voina i fevral'skaia revoliutsiia, 1914–1917 gg.,* III (New York, 1962),
   56–57; V. N. Voeikov, *S tsarem i bez tsariia* (Helsingfors, 1936), 193.
6. Martynov, *Tsarskaia armiia,* 60–61, 207.
7. Balk, "Poslednie piat' dnei."
8. T. Hasegawa, *The February Revolution: Petrograd 1917* (Seattle-London, 1981), 215–17, 222.
9. *Byloe,* No. 1/29 (1918), 161.
10. Hasegawa, *February Revolution,* 133–34.

11. Eyewitness account in M. Paléologue, *La Russie des Tsars pendant la Grand Guerre*, III (Paris, 1922), 215.
12. Spiridovich, *Velikaia voina*, III, 86–87; Paléologue, *La Russie des Tsars*, III, 215.
13. Description in Hasegawa, *February Revolution*, 232–46.
14. *KA*, No. 4 (1923), 208–10; retranslated from the Russian.
15. *Izvestiia*, No. 155 (August 27, 1917), 6.
16. E. R. Levitas, ed., *V ogne revoliutsionnykh boev (Raiony Petrograda v dvukh revoliutsiiakh 1917 g.)* (Moscow, 1967), 84.
17. Vasilev in P. E. Shchegolev, *Okhranniki i avantiuristy* (Moscow, 1930), 141–42.
18. *KA*, No. 2/21 (1927), 4–5.
19. D. N. Dubenskii in *RL*, No. 3 (Paris, 1922), 28–30.
20. *Padenie*, I, 190.
21. *Ibid.*
22. Martynov, *Tsarskaia armiia*, 82; *Revoliutsiia*, I, 35.
23. N. Sukhanov, *Zapiski o revoliutsii*, I (Berlin-Petersburg-Moscow, 1922), 53.
24. *KA*, No. 4 (1923), 209–10, letter of February 25.
25. Sukhanov, *Zapiski*, I, 53, 59.
26. Paléologue, *La Russie des Tsars*, III, 214, 218, citing the memoirs of Gabriel Senac de Meilhan.
27. Martynov, *Tsarskaia armiia*, 206.
28. On their condition and mood, see *ibid.*, 58–59.
29. Rodzianko to Ruzskii in *RL*, No. 3 (1922), 147.
30. Martynov, *Tsarskaia armiia*, 207.
31. Sukhanov, *Zapiski*, I, 54.
32. *Byloe*, No. 1/29 (1918), 173–74.
33. Martynov, *Tsarskaia armiia*, 208.
34. Incident described in *ibid.*, 85–88, and I. Lukash, *Pavlovtsy* (Petrograd, 1917).
35. *Vospominaniia Generala A. S. Lukomskogo*, I (Berlin, 1922), 124.
36. S. P. Melgunov, *Martovskie dni* (Paris, 1961), 84.
37. Alekseev in *RL*, No. 3 (1922), 118; Khabalov in *Padenie*, I, 203.
38. Khabalov in *Padenie*, I, 196; Martynov, *Tsarskaia armiia*, 88–89.
39. L. Trotsky, *The History of the Russian Revolution*, I (New York, 1937), 121–22.
40. *Revoliutsiia*, I, 37.
41. *Ibid.*, 38.
42. *Ibid.;* Fredericks in *Padenie*, V, 38.
43. *KA*, No. 2/21 (1927), 8; Melgunov, *Martovskie dni*, 157.
44. A. Blok, "Poslednie dni imperatorskoi vlasti," in *Sobranie sochinenii v vos'mi tomakh*, VI (Moscow-Leningrad, 1962), 243.
45. Martynov, *Tsarskaia armiia*, 104.
46. Voeikov in *Padenie*, III, 71. Text: *RL*, No. 3 (1922), 114.
47. P. K. Benckendorff, *Last Days at Tsarskoe Selo* (London, 1927), 2–3.
48. *Revoliutsiia*, I, 40.
49. Dubenskii in *RL*, No. 3 (1922), 38.
50. His orders in Martynov, *Tsarskaia armiia*, 114–15; *RL*, No. 3 (1922), 117.
51. *RL*, No. 3 (1922), 115.
52. *KA*, No. 2/21 (1927), 10–11.
53. N. de Basily, *Diplomat of Imperial Russia, 1903–1917: Memoirs* (Stanford, Calif., 1973), 109.
54. A. Shliapnikov, *Semnadtsatyi god*, 2nd ed., I (Moscow, n.d.), 155.
55. Benckendorff, *Last Days*, 10; Basily, *Diplomat*, 113–14; Dubenskii in *RL*, No. 3 (1922), 38.
56. *Padenie*, III, 74.
57. Dubenskii in *RL*, No. 3 (1922), 46–47.
58. Hasegawa, *February Revolution*, 492.
59. V. V. Shulgin, *Dni* (Belgrade, 1925), 214; Melgunov, *Martovskie dni*, 53–55; Martynov, *Tsarskaia armiia*, 140.
60. Hasegawa, *February Revolution*, 348.
61. Shulgin, *Dni*, 157–58. The protocols of this meeting, taken by an unidentified participant and

first published in *Volia Rossii* (Prague), No. 153 (March 15, 1921), 4, are translated in Alexander Kerensky and Robert Browder, *The Russian Provisional Government, 1917,* I (Stanford, Calif., 1961), 45–47: see also I. Vardin, *KN,* No. 2/12 (1923), 267–93.

62. Zinaida Gippius, *Siniaia kniga* (Belgrade, 1929), 89: diary entry of February 28, 1917; Shulgin (*Dni,* 241) corroborates her intuition.

63. Leonard Schapiro in Richard Pipes, ed., *Revolutionary Russia* (Cambridge, Mass., 1968), 128–30; Alexander Kerensky, *The Catastrophe* (New York-London, 1927), 12.

64. Melgunov, *Martovskie dni,* 27–28.

65. *Ibid.,* 28.

66. *Ibid.,* 80.

67. *Ibid.;* Martynov, *Tsarskaia armiia,* 134.

68. Shulgin, *Dni,* 233–34, 239.

69. Martynov, *Tsarskaia armiia,* 112.

70. *Ibid.,* 110; *Revoliutsiia,* I, 41–42.

71. Hasegawa, *February Revolution,* 330–31. Text in M. Smilg-Benario, *Der Zusammenbruch der Zarenmonarchie* (Vienna, 1928), Table 13; cf. Marc Ferro, *Des Soviets au Communisme Bureaucratique* (Paris, 1980), 30–31.

72. Iu. S. Tokarev, *Petrogradskii Sovet Rabochikh i Soldatskikh Deputatov v marte–aprele 1917 g.* (Leningrad, 1976), 33–34.

73. *Revoliutsiia,* I, 40–41.

74. Hasegawa, *February Revolution,* 380.

75. A. Shliapnikov, *Semnadtsatyi god,* III (Moscow-Leningrad, 1927), 167–70.

76. Sukhanov, *Zapiski,* I, 190.

77. Shliapnikov, *Semnadtsatyi god,* III, 173.

78. Ferro, *Des Soviets,* 37. Cf. Oskar Anweiler, *The Soviets* (New York, 1974), 104–6.

79. V. B. Stankevich, *Vospominaniia, 1914–1919 g.* (Berlin, 1920), 80–82.

80. Melgunov, *Martovskie dni,* 12–13.

81. P. N. Miliukov, *Istoriia Vtoroi Russkoi Revoliutsii,* I, Pt. 1 (Sofia, 1921), 51.

82. *Revoliutsiia,* I, 49–50; Sukhanov, *Zapiski,* I, 256–60.

83. *Revoliutsiia,* I, 49; Miliukov, *Istoriia,* I, Pt. 1, 46, P. N. Miliukov, *Vospominaniia, 1859–1917,* II (New York, 1955), 307.

84. Full text in Martynov, *Tsarskaia armiia,* 177–78.

85. *Revoliutsiia,* I, 53.

86. Miliukov, *Istoriia,* I, Pt. 1, 47.

87. S. E. Kryzhanovskii, *Vospominaniia* (Berlin, [1938]), 124.

88. Tokarev, *Petrogradskii Sovet,* 94.

89. Miliukov, *Istoriia,* I, Pt. 1, 45; Hasegawa, *February Revolution,* 525.

90. A. I. Denikin, *Ocherki russkoi smuty,* I, Pt. 1 (Paris, 1921), 75.

91. Miliukov, *Istoriia,* I, Pt. 1, 67.

92. Kerensky, *Catastrophe,* 120.

93. *V. D. Nabokov and the Russian Provisional Government* (New Haven, Conn.-London, 1976), 84.

94. T. I. Polner, *Zhiznennyi put' G. E. L'vova* (Paris, 1932), 151.

95. See above, p. 224.

96. D. F. Sverchkov, *Kerenskii,* 2nd ed. (Leningrad, 1927), 21. Melgunov, *Martovskie dni,* 112–13.

97. Gippius, *Siniaia kniga,* 95.

98. Shliapnikov, *Semnadtsatyi god,* 2nd ed., I, 173–74; cf. Tokarev, *Petrogradskii Sovet,* 61–62.

99. Martynov, *Tsarskaia armiia,* 212.

100. Gippius, *Siniaia kniga,* 97.

101. Text in *Revoliutsiia,* I, 176–77.

102. B. Ia. Nalivaiskii, ed., *Petrogradskii Sovet Rabochikh i Soldatskikh Deputatov: Protokoly Zasedanii Ispolnitel'nogo Komiteta i Biuro Ispolnitel'nogo Komiteta* (Moscow-Leningrad, 1925), 17.

103. Text in *Revoliutsiia,* I, 180–81.

104. A. Shliapnikov, *Semnadtsatyi god,* II (Moscow-Leningrad, 1925), 236.

105. E. N. Burdzhalov, *Vtoraia russkaia revoliutsiia: Vosstanie v Petrograde* (Moscow, 1967), 352; Shulgin, *Dni,* 150.
106. Melgunov, *Martovskie dni,* 135; Guchkov cited in Burdzhalov, *Vtoraia russkaia revoliutsiia,* 352.
107. *KA,* No. 4 (1923), 215; retranslated from the Russian.
108. *RL,* No. 3 (1922), 119.
109. *KA,* No. 2/21 (1927), 19.
110. Text in Martynov, *Tsarskaia armiia,* 144–45.
111. Basily, *Diplomat,* 116–17.
112. S. N. Vilchkovskii in *RL,* No. 3 (1922), 169–70.
113. *RL,* No. 3 (1922), 133, 176; P. E. Shchegolev, ed., *Otrechenie Nikolaia II* (Leningrad, 1927), 153.
114. Text of tape in Shchegolev, *Otrechenie,* 197–201.
115. *RL,* No. 3 (1922), 133–34.
116. Shchegolev, *Otrechenie,* 149; *RL,* No. 3 (1922), 133–34, 172.
117. Text: Shchegolev, *Otrechenie,* 202–3.
118. *RL,* No. 3 (1922), 177–78.
119. Shchegolev, *Otrechenie,* 154.
120. *Ibid.,* 154–55.
121. The texts of these cables in *ibid.,* 203–5; cf. 155; *KA,* No. 2/21 (1927), 72–73. Gen. Savvich published his recollections of these events in *Otechestvo* (Archangel), Nos. 5–7/102–104 (January 10–12, 1919), the manuscript of which is in the Kryzhanovskii Archive, Box No. 3, Bakhmeteff Archive, Columbia University.
122. Handwritten facsimile in Martynov, *Tsarskaia armiia,* 159.
123. Text in *RL,* No. 3 (1922), 140.
124. Story of the drafting and the text, with corrections, in Basily, *Diplomat,* 122–25. Also Martynov, *Tsarskaia armiia,* 159; *KA,* No. 3/22 (1927), 7.
125. See above, p. 227.
126. *RL,* No. 3 (1922), 179.
127. Fedorov's note to Martynov in Martynov, *Tsarskaia armiia,* 160; Benckendorff, *Last Days,* 46–47.
128. A. D. Gradovskii, *Sobranie sochinenii,* VII (St. Petersburg, 1901), 158–62.
129. Nabokov, *Provisional Government,* 49.
130. Accounts by Guchkov in *Padenie,* VI, 263–66, and Basily, *Diplomat,* 127–31; Shulgin, *Dni,* 265–83. See also Shchegolev, *Otrechenie,* 163–71.
131. Ruzskii in Shchegolev, *Otrechenie,* 138.
132. Shchegolev, *Otrechenie,* 169–71; Martynov, *Tsarskaia armiia,* 167–70.
133. Basily, *Diplomat,* 128; Martynov, *Tsarskaia armiia,* 169.
134. Guchkov to Basily, in Basily, *Diplomat,* 128.
135. Smilg-Benario, *Zusammenbruch,* Table 36. Text also in Martynov, *Tsarskaia armiia,* 173–74.
136. Basily, *Diplomat,* 129–30.
137. Both documents in Martynov, *Tsarskaia armiia,* 174.
138. Benckendorff, *Last Days,* 17.
139. Martynov, *Tsarskaia armiia,* 174–75; Shchegolev, *Otrechenie,* 158–60.
140. Miliukov's recollections of the meeting with Michael can be found in his *Istoriia Vtoroi Russkoi Revoliutsii* I, Pt. 1 (Sofia, 1921), 54–55, and Guchkov's in Basily, *Diplomat,* 143–45. Shulgin's recollections are in *Dni,* 295–306.
141. Melgunov, *Martovskie dni,* 226.
142. *Ibid.,* 227.
143. Basily, *Diplomat,* 144.
144. *ARR,* VI (1922), 62.
145. Martynov, *Tsarskaia armiia,* 181; Shulgin, *Dni,* 302–3.
146. Melgunov, *Martovskie dni,* 233–34; facsimile of original: Smilg-Benario, *Zusammenbruch,* Table 37.
147. A copy can be found at Houghton Library, Harvard, under the shelf mark +56−909.

148. Kerensky in *SZ*, No. 50 (1932), 409.
149. *Ibid.*
150. Above, p. 298.
151. *Revoliutsiia*, I, 73.
152. Nabokov, *Provisional Government*, 61–62.
153. J. Godechot, *Les Institutions de la France sous la Révolution et l'Empire* (Paris, 1951), 89–91; G. Lefebvre, *La Révolution* (Paris, 1957), 165–67.
154. Nabokov, *Provisional Government*, 83.
155. *Revoliutsiia*, I, 82.
156. Nabokov, *Provisional Government*, 135.
157. M. N. Tsapenko, ed., *Vserossiiskoe Soveshchanie Sovetov Rabochikh i Soldatskikh Deputatov: Stenograficheskii Otchët* (Moscow-Leningrad, 1927), 38.
158. I. G. Tsereteli, *Vospominaniia o Fevral'skoi Revoliutsii,* I (Paris-The Hague, 1963), 97.
159. *Ibid.*, 107–08.
160. *Revoliutsiia*, I, 114.
161. Nalivaiskii, *Petrogradskii Sovet*, 9.
162. *Ibid.*, 10.
163. *Revoliutsiia*, I, 64.
164. *Ibid.*, 72.
165. *Ibid.*, 80.
166. *Ibid.*, 71–72.
167. Miliukov, *Istoriia*, I, Pt. 1, 74.
168. Nalivaiskii, *Petrogradskii Sovet*, 118.
169. *Ibid.*, 61–62.
170. Tokarev, *Petrogradskii Sovet*, 145–46.
171. Protocols of the Consultation in Tsapenko, *Vserossiiskoe Soveshchanie;* cf. *Revoliutsiia*, I, 162–63.
172. Tokarev, *Petrogradskii Sovet*, 148–52.
173. Its legislative output is assembled in the three-volume collection edited by Alexander Kerensky and Robert Browder, *The Russian Provisional Government* (Stanford, Cal., 1961).
174. R. Wojna, *Walka o ziemie w Rosji w 1917 roku* (Wroclaw, 1977), 79.
175. *Revoliutsiia*, I, 96.
176. K. G. Kotelnikov and V. L. Meller, eds., *Krest'ianskoe dvizhenie v 1917 godu* (Moscow-Leningrad, 1927).
177. John L. H. Keep, *The Russian Revolution* (London, 1976), 162–63.
178. *Revoliutsiia*, I, 84–85.
179. Tsentral'noe Statisticheskoe Upravlenie, Otdel Voennoi Statistiki, *Rossiia v Mirovoi Voine 1914–1918 goda (v tsifrakh)* (Moscow, 1925), 26.
180. Nabokov, *Provisional Government*, 135.
181. M. V. Vishniak, *Vserossiiskoe Uchreditel'noe Sobranie* (Paris, 1932), 73.
182. Sukhanov, *Zapiski,* II, 140.
183. Tsereteli, *Vospominaniia,* I, 40.
184. Marc Ferro in Pipes, *Revolutionary Russia,* 143–57, esp. 151.
185. Tokarev, *Petrogradskii Sovet*, 145.
186. *KA*, No. 3/22 (1927), 57.
187. L. Bazylow, *Obalenie caratu* (Warsaw, 1976), 376n.
188. *Izvestiia*, No. 15 (March 15/28, 1917), 1.
189. V. S. Vasiukov, *Vneshniaia politika Vremennogo Pravitel'stva* (Moscow, 1966), 87–88.
190. Text in *Revoliutsiia*, I, 195–96.
191. Miliukov, *Vospominaniia,* II, 345–46.
192. *Revoliutsiia*, I, 30–52, *passim.*
193. W. H. Chamberlin, *The Russian Revolution, 1917–1921,* I (New York, 1935), 85.
194. This development, the subject of my *Formation of the Soviet Union: Communism and Nationalism, 1917–23,* 2nd ed. (Cambridge, Mass., 1964), will be treated at length in my forthcoming *Russia under the New Regime.*

195. V. V. Rozanov, *Apokalipsis nashego vremeni* (Berlin-Paris, 1917), 5. Written in 1917–18.
196. Denikin, *Ocherki,* I, Pt. 1, 54. This document remains unpublished.
197. *KA,* No. 3/22 (1927), 54; Martynov, *Tsarskaia armiia,* 187–89.
198. G. Buchanan, *My Mission to Russia,* II (Boston, 1923), 104.
199. Public Record Office, London, FO 371–3008, p. 1, Reel 22, Doc. 196482.
200. *Revoliutsiia,* I, 73–74, 76; Nalivaiskii, *Petrogradskii Sovet,* 29–30.
201. *RL,* No. 3 (1922), 96–97.
202. *Ibid.,* 97–98.
203. *KA,* No. 20 (1927), 138. Description in Dembovskii, *RL,* No. 3 (1922), 87–88: here the event is mistakenly dated March 6.
204. Martynov, *Tsarskaia armiia,* 194.
205. Benckendorff, *Last Days,* 30–31.
206. *KA,* No. 3/22 (1927), 67.
207. Martynov, *Tsarskaia armiia,* 196–97.
208. *Ibid.,* 197.
209. Reproduced in *ibid.,* 200–1.
210. Kerensky, *Catastrophe,* 264–69; *KA,* No. 20 (1927), 140.
211. See, e.g., articles by Miliukov and "Dioneo" in *PN,* No. 4099 (June 12, 1932), 2.
212. Kenneth Rose, *King George V* (London, 1983), 211–14.
213. Public Record Office, London, FO 800–383, p. 32, April 7, 1917 (March 25 OS).
214. S. P. Melgunov, *Sud'ba Imperatora Nikolaia II posle otrecheniia* (Paris, 1951), 175.
215. Kerensky, *Catastrophe,* 111.
216. Rozanov, *Apokalipsis,* 6.
217. Tsereteli, *Vospominaniia,* I, 124; *Revoliutsiia,* II, 74.

Chapter 9

1. Institut Marksizma-Leninizma, *Khronologicheskii ukazatel' proizvedenii V. I. Lenina,* I (Moscow, 1959), 1–8.
2. Institut MELS, *Vospominaniia rodnykh o V. I. Lenine* (Moscow, 1955), 85.
3. On this, see Nikolai Valentinov, *The Early Years of Lenin* (Ann Arbor, Mich., 1969), 111–12.
4. A. I. Ulianova-Elizarova in Institut Marksizma-Leninizma, *Vospominaniia o Vladimire Il'iche Lenine* I (Moscow, 1956) 13.
5. *Molodaia gvardiia,* No. 1 (1924), 89.
6. A. I. Ulianova-Elizarova in *Aleksandr Il'ich Ulianov i delo 1 marta 1887 g.* (Moscow-Leningrad, 1927), 97, and V. Alekseev and A. Shver in *Sem'ia Ulianovykh v Simbirske, 1896–1897* (Leningrad, 1925), 48–51.
7. V. Vodovozov in *NChS,* XII (1925), 175.
8. Valentinov, *Early Years,* 111–38 and 189–215, based on conversations with Lenin.
9. *SR,* XII, No. 36 (1934), 592–93.
10. K. Marx and F. Engels, *Werke,* XXXIV (Berlin, 1966), 477.
11. This subject is treated at length in my *Struve: Liberal on the Left, 1870–1905* (Cambridge, Mass., 1970), 28–51.
12. Richard Pipes in Pipes, ed., *Revolutionary Russia* (Cambridge, Mass., 1968), 32.
13. Ulianova-Elizarova in *Vospominaniia rodnykh,* 29.
14. Marx and Engels, *Werke,* XXII, 509–27.
15. On this usage, see my article in *SR,* XXIII, No. 3 (1964), 441–58.
16. Lenin, *PSS,* I, 105; *LS,* XXXIII, 16.
17. Lenin, *PSS,* I, 312.
18. Karl Radek in *Rabochaia Moskva,* No. 92/656 (April 22, 1924).
19. A. N. Potresov, *Posmertnyi sbornik proizvedenii* (Paris, 1937), 294; R. H. B. Lockhart, *Memoirs of a British Agent* (London, 1935), 237; Angelica Balabanoff, *Impressions of Lenin* (Ann Arbor, Mich., 1964), 123.
20. Potresov, *Posmertnyi sbornik,* 301.
21. Robert Michels, *Political Parties* (Glencoe, Ill., 1949), 227n.

22. Potresov, *Posmertnyi sbornik*, 300.
23. L. Trotskii, *O Lenine* (Moscow, 1924), 6–7.
24. Lenin, *PSS*, XXXVI, 23.
25. N. [L.] Trotskii, *Nashi politicheskie zadachi* (Geneva, 1904), 96.
26. Nina Tumarkin, *Lenin Lives!* (Cambridge, Mass., 1983), 77.
27. M. Gorkii, *Vladimir Il'ich Lenin* (Leningrad, 1924), 9; *NZh*, No. 177 (November 10, 1917), cited in H. Ermolaev, ed., Maxim Gorky, *Untimely Thoughts* (New York, 1968), 89.
28. V. Vodovozov in *NChS*, XII, 176–77.
29. Gorkii, *Lenin*, 10; M. Gorki, *Lenine et le Paysan Russe* (Paris, 1924), 96.
30. *La Grande Revue*, XXVII, No. 8 (August 1923), 206.
31. B. D. Wolfe, *Three Who Made a Revolution* (New York, 1948), 219–20.
32. Potresov, *Posmertnyi sbornik*, 296–97.
33. *SR*, XII, No. 36 (1934), 593.
34. Gorki, *Lenine et le Paysan Russe*, 64.
35. *Ibid.*, 83–84.
36. Lenin, *PSS*, XXXVI, 346.
37. *La Grande Revue*, XXVII, No. 9 (September 1923), 459.
38. Gorki, *Lenine et le Paysan Russe*, 16–17.
39. K. Marx, *Critique of Hegel's Philosophy of Right*, J. O'Malley, ed. (Cambridge, 1970), 133.
40. Lenin, *PSS*, XV, 296–97.
41. N. K. Takhtarev in *Byloe*, No. 24 (1924), 22.
42. Lenin's first St. Petersburg period (1893–97) is recounted in my *Social-Democracy and the St. Petersburg Labor Movement* (Cambridge, Mass., 1963).
43. *Perepiska G. V. Plekhanova i P. B. Aksel'roda*, I (Moscow, 1925), 271.
44. Lenin, *PSS*, I, 279–80, and II, 433–70.
45. *Ibid.*, II, 84.
46. Karl Radek in *Rabochaia Moskva*, No. 92/656 (April 22, 1924).
47. Lenin, *PSS*, II, 104; emphasis supplied.
48. *Ibid.*, 84, 101–2; emphasis supplied.
49. Pipes, *Struve: Liberal on the Left*, 223–26.
50. *Ibid.*, 227–32.
51. Lenin, *PSS*, IV, 193–94.
52. *Ibid.*, 373.
53. The background of these negotiations is described in my *Struve: Liberal on the Left*, 260–70.
54. *Ibid.*, 276.
55. Lenin, *PSS*, XXXIV, 40.
56. On this, see V. A. Tvardovskaia in *IZ*, No. 67 (1960), 103–44; S. S. Volk, *Narodnaia volia* (Moscow-Leningrad, 1966), 250–77; and F. Venturi, *Roots of Revolution* (New York, 1960), 650–53.
57. Volk, *Narodnaia volia*, 254–55.
58. Lenin, *PSS*, VIII, 384–85.
59. Volk, *Narodnaia volia*, 203–12.
60. Leonard Schapiro, *The Communist Party of the Soviet Union* (New York, 1960), 49.
61. *Ibid.*, 58–59.
62. *Ibid.*, 61.
63. Trotskii, *Nashi politicheskie zadachi*, 93.
64. Lenin, *PSS*, VIII, 370.
65. Letter to Karl Kautsky, June 1904, cited in A. Ascher, *Pavel Axelrod and the Development of Menshevism* (Cambridge, Mass., 1972), 211.
66. L. Martov, *Spasiteli ili uprazdniteli?* (Paris, 1911), 3.
67. Z. A. B. Zeman and W. B. Scharlau, *The Merchant of Revolution: The Life of Alexander Israel Helphand (Parvus)* (London, 1965), 76.
68. *LS*, V (1926), 456–59.
69. On this, see Oskar Anweiler, *The Soviets* (New York, 1974), 76–86.
70. N. Mendeleev in *NZh*, No. 6 (November 2, 1905), 5.

71. Anweiler, *Soviets,* 84–85.
72. N. K. Krupskaia, *Vospominaniia o Lenine,* I (Moscow-Leningrad, 1930), 120.
73. Schapiro, *Communist Party,* 86, 105.
74. The information which follows is drawn largely from D. Lane's *The Roots of Russian Communism* (Assen, Holland, 1969).
75. Schapiro, *Communist Party,* 101.
76. Lane, *Roots,* 21.
77. *Ibid.,* 44–45.
78. *Ibid.,* 210.
79. On the early manifestations of this attitude, see my *Social-Democracy and the St. Petersburg Labor Movement, passim.*
80. L. M[art]ov in *OD,* III, Book 5, 572.
81. Anweiler, *Soviets,* 278n.
82. M[art]ov, *OD,* III, Book 5, 570.
83. *Ibid.,* 571.
84. Schapiro, *Communist Party,* 76.
85. See below, p. 719.
86. Krupskaia, *Vospominaniia o Lenine,* I, 107–9.
87. John L. H. Keep, *The Rise of Social Democracy in Russia* (Oxford, 1963), 194–95.
88. Lenin, *PSS,* XVII, 31–32.
89. Richard Pipes, *The Formation of the Soviet Union: Communism and Nationalism, 1917–23* (Cambridge, Mass., 1954), 31–33.
90. Lenin, *PSS,* II, 452.
91. Pipes, *Formation,* 35–49.
92. Wolfe, *Three,* 261; Schapiro, *Communist Party,* 88.
93. Keep, *Social Democracy,* 181–82, 205.
94. M. N. Liadov [M. N. Mandelshtam] and S. M. Pozner, eds., *Leonid Borisovich Krasin ("Nikitich"): Gody podpol'ia* (Moscow-Leningrad, 1928), 142.
95. Martov, *Spasiteli ili uprazdniteli?,* 22–23; B. Bibineishvili, *Kamo* (Moscow, 1934), 142n.–143n.
96. David Shub, *Lenin* (Garden City, N.Y., 1948), 101–2; *Pis'ma Akselroda i Martova* (Berlin, 1924), 184.
97. Martov, *Spasiteli, passim.*
98. *Ibid.,* 18.
99. On him, see Liadov and Pozner, *Krasin,* and M. Glenny in *SS,* No. 22 (1970), 192–221.
100. Liadov and Pozner, *Krasin,* 236–39 and *passim.*
101. Shub, *Lenin,* 104–5.
102. Wolfe, *Three,* 379; T. Aleksinskii in *La Grande Revue,* XXVII, No. 9 (September 1923), 456–57.
103. On this, see S. Shesternin in *SB,* No. 5/8 (1933), 155–56; N. K. Krupskaia, *Vospominaniia o Lenine* (Moscow, 1932), 141–42, and Dietrich Geyer, *Kautskys Russisches Dossier* (Frankfurt-New York, 1981), 18–25.
104. Geyer, *Kautskys Russisches Dossier,* 24.
105. *La Grande Revue,* XXVII, No. 9 (September 1923), 448.
106. *Padenie,* I, 315. On him, see R. C. Elwood, *Roman Malinovsky* (Newtonville, Mass., 1977).
107. Lenin, *PSS,* XLVIII, 140 and 133.
108. Shub, *Lenin,* 117.
109. M. A. Tsiavlovskii, *Bol'sheviki: Dokumenty po istorii bol'shevizma s 1903 po 1916 god byvsh. Moskovskogo Okhrannogo Otdeleniia* (Moscow, 1918), xiii.
110. V. Burtsev in *Struggling Russia,* I, No. 9–10 (1919), 139.
111. A. I. Spiridovich, *Istoriia Bol'shevizma v Rossii* (Paris, 1922), 260.
112. Burtsev, *Struggling Russia,* 139.
113. Tsiavlovskii, *Bol'sheviki,* xiv. See, for example, his speech of December 7, 1912, in Gosudarstvennaia Duma, *Stenograficheskie Otchëty,* Sozyv IV, Sessiia I, Zasedanie 8 (St. Petersburg, 1913), 313–27.
114. *Padenie,* III, 281, 286; Spiridovich, *Istoriia Bol'shevizma,* 258; Burtsev in *Padenie,* I, 316. A

police instruction to this effect from the winter of 1916–17: B. Ia. Nalivaiskii, ed., *Petrogradskii Sovet Rabochikh i Soldatskikh Deputatov: Protokoly Zasedanii Ispolnitel'nogo Komiteta i Biuro Ispolnitel'nogo Komiteta* (Moscow-Leningrad, 1925), 312–13.

115. Spiridovich, *Istoriia Bol'shevizma,* 231.
116. On this organization and its activities, see Zeman and Scharlau, *Merchant,* 132–36.
117. T. Hornykiewicz, ed., *Ereignisse in der Ukraine, 1914–1922,* I (Philadelphia, 1966), 183.
118. Unpublished document in the Central Party Archive, summarized in Lenin, *Khronika,* III, 269.
119. *LS,* II (1924), 180.
120. Unpublished document in the Central Party Archive, summarized in Lenin, *Khronika,* III, 273. On these events, see Ganetskii in *LS,* II (1924), 173–87, and Krupskaia, *Vospominaniia,* 212–16.
121. O. G. Gankin, *The Bolsheviks and the World War* (Stanford, Calif., 1940), 54–55.
122. *Ibid.,* 59.
123. Lenin, *PSS,* XLVIII, 155.
124. *Ibid.,* XXVI, 1–7.
125. *Ibid.,* XLIX, 15.
126. Dispatch of January 1915, in Z. A. B. Zeman, ed., *Germany and the Revolution in Russia, 1915–1918* (London, 1958), 1–2.
127. On Parvus's encounter with Lenin, see Zeman and Scharlau, *Merchant,* 157–59.
128. *Ibid.,* 158–59.
129. Zeman, *Germany,* 11–13; A. Shliapnikov, *Kanun semnadtsatogo goda,* 3rd ed., Pt. 1 (Moscow, n.d.), 154.
130. As asserted by J. Braunthal, *History of the International,* II (New York-Washington, 1967), 47.
131. Gankin, *The Bolsheviks,* 329–33.
132. *Ibid.,* 333–37, 347–49.
133. *Ibid.,* 422; emphasis in the original.
134. *Ibid.,* 426–27; emphasis in the original.
135. *Ibid.,* 461.
136. On his Swiss period, see Shub, *Lenin,* 143–53.
137. G. A. Solomon, *Lenin i ego sem'ia* (Paris, 1931), 78.
138. Bertram D. Wolfe, *Strange Communists Whom I Have Known* (New York, 1965), 138–64; Angelica Balabanoff, *Impressions of Lenin* (Ann Arbor, Mich., 1964), 14.
139. A. Shliapnikov, *Kanun semnadtsatogo goda,* 3rd ed., Pt. 2, (Moscow, [1923?]), 37–44.
140. Lenin, *PSS,* XXX, 328.

Chapter 10

1. M. Bronskii in *PR,* No. 4/27 (1924), 30–39.
2. *Neue Zürcher Zeitung,* No. 458 (March 15, 1917), 2; Lenin, *PSS,* XLIX, 398–99.
3. *Ibid.,* 399.
4. *Ibid.,* XXXI, 491.
5. W. Hahlweg, *Lenins Rückkehr nach Russland, 1917* (Leiden, 1957), 15–16; Lenin, *PSS,* XLIX, 406; G. E. Zinoviev, *God revoliutsii,* II (Leningrad, 1926), 503.
6. Lenin, *PSS,* XXXI, 7.
7. A. Shliapnikov, *Semnadtsatyi god,* 2nd ed., I (Moscow, n.d.), 99; E. N. Burdzhalov in *VI,* No. 4 (1956), 39n.
8. A. Shliapnikov, *Kanun semnadtsatogo goda,* 3rd ed. Pt. 2 (Moscow, [1923?]), 35–42.
9. Burdzhalov in *VI,* No. 4 (1956), 40; N. F. Kudelli, *Pervyi legal'nyi Petersburskii Komitet Bol'shevikov v 1917 g.* (Moscow-Leningrad, 1927).
10. Burdzhalov in *VI,* No. 4 (1956), 41–42; *Izvestiia,* No. 7 (March 6, 1917), 6.
11. Kamenev, *Pravda,* No. 9 (March 15, 1917), 1; Stalin, *Pravda,* No. 10 (March 16, 1917), 2 (reprinted in I. V. Stalin, *Sochineniia,* III, Moscow, 1946, 4–8).
12. Shliapnikov, *Semnadtsatyi god,* II (Moscow-Leningrad, 1925), 185–86.

13. Kudelli, *Pervyi,* 50.
14. *Revoliutsiia,* I, 147.
15. Lenin, *PSS,* XXXI, 11–33.
16. *Pravda,* No. 14 (March 21, 1917), 2–3, and continued in No. 15 (March 22, 1917), 2; Burdzhalov in *VI,* No. 4 (1956), 49.
17. Hahlweg, *Lenins Rückkehr,* 10.
18. General M. Hoffmann, *Der Krieg der versäumten Gelegenheiten* (Munich, 1923), 174.
19. B. Nikitin, *Rokovye gody* (Paris, 1937), 108.
20. Z. A. B. Zeman and W. B. Scharlau, *The Merchant of Revolution: The Life of Alexander Israel Helphand (Parvus)* (London, 1965), 207–8.
21. P. Scheidemann, *Memoiren eines Sozialdemokraten* (Dresden, 1930), 427–28.
22. Hahlweg, *Lenins Rückkehr,* 47. Memorandum dated April 2 [March 20], 1917.
23. *Ibid.,* 49–50. Cable of April 3 [March 21], probably referring to Lenin's first "Letter from Afar" published in *Pravda* on that day. See further *ibid.,* 51–54.
24. *Ibid.,* 10.
25. *LS,* II (1924), 389–90. Lenin, *PSS,* XXXI, 498.
26. Hahlweg, *Lenins Rückkehr,* 28.
27. Z. A. B. Zeman, ed., *Germany and the Revolution in Russia, 1915–1918* (London, 1958), 24; *LS,* II (1924), 390.
28. Richard M. Watt, *Dare Call It Treason* (New York, 1963), 138.
29. Fritz Platten, *Die Reise Lenins durch Deutschland* (Berlin, 1924), 56; *Izvestiia,* No. 32 (April 5, 1917), 2; Zinoviev, *God revoliutsii,* II, 503.
30. K. Radek, *Living Age,* No. 4,051 (February 25, 1922), 451.
31. Hahlweg, *Lenins Rückkehr,* 99–100; J. Görgen in *Weltspiel* (Berlin), No. 12,632 (April 12, 1987); Lenin, *Khronika,* IV, 45–46.
32. Zeman and Scharlau, *Merchant,* 217–19.
33. *V. D. Nabokov and the Russian Provisional Government, 1917* (New Haven, Conn.-London, 1976), 119.
34. *Izvestiia,* No. 32 (April 5, 1917), 1.
35. N. Sukhanov, *Zapiski o revoliutsii,* III (Berlin-Petersburg-Moscow, 1922), 26–27.
36. Lenin, *PSS,* XXXI, 72–78; Lenin, *Sochineniia,* XX, 640.
37. *Pravda,* No. 25 (April 6, 1917), 1.
38. Burdzhalov in *VI,* No. 4 (1956), 51.
39. Kudelli, *Pervyi,* 88.
40. Burdzhalov in *VI,* No. 4 (1956), 52.
41. Zeman, *Germany,* 51.
42. C. Malaparte, *Coup d'Etat: The Technique of Revolution* (New York, 1932), 220.
43. I. G. Tsereteli, *Vospominaniia o Fevral'skoi Revoliutsii,* II (Paris-The Hague, 1963), 302.
44. Letter to Dr. Kugelmann of 1871 cited in Lenin, *PSS,* XXXIII, 37.
45. April 8, 1917 (NS), in Lenin, *PSS,* XXXI, 91–92.
46. Cf. H. Delbrück, *Geschichte der Kriegskunst,* IV (Berlin, 1920), 492–94; G. Lefebvre, *Napoléon,* I (New York, 1969), 230–31.
47. Lenin, *PSS,* XLV, 381.
48. G. Le Bon, *The Crowd* (London, 1952), 73.
49. E. Canetti, *Crowds and Power* (Middlesex, Eng.-New York, 1973), 24–25.
50. P. Lepeshinskii, *Zhiznennyi put' Lenina,* 2nd ed. (Moscow, 1925), 44.
51. Nikitin, *Rokovye gody,* 78–79; George Katkov, *The Kornilov Affair* (London-New York, 1980), 54.
52. V. S. Vasiukov, *Vneshniaia politika Vremennogo pravitel'stva* (Moscow, 1966), 124.
53. Alexander Kerensky, *The Catastrophe* (New York-London, 1927), 135.
54. Text in *Revoliutsiia,* II, 247–48.
55. Vasiukov, *Vneshniaia politika,* 128.
56. See his statement in *NZh,* No. 5 (April 23, 1917), 6.
57. Account of his death by P. N. Krasnov in *ARR,* I (1921), 105–12.
58. *Revoliutsiia,* II, 50.

59. Kerensky, *Catastrophe,* 136.
60. Burdzhalov in *VI,* No. 4 (1956), 51.
61. Lenin, *Sochineniia,* XX, 648. Text in *ibid.,* 608–9, from *Pravda,* No. 37 (April 21, 1917), 1; Lenin, *PSS,* XXXI, 291–92.
62. Kudelli, *Pervyi,* 92–94.
63. Lenin, *PSS,* XXXI, 309–11.
64. Lenin, *Khronika,* IV, 107.
65. The figure is from G. N. Golikov and Iu. S. Tokarev in *IZ,* No. 57 (1956), 51.
66. *KL,* No. 7 (1923), 91; F. F. Raskolnikov, *Na boevykh postakh revoliutsionnykh boev* (Moscow, 1964), 69.
67. Lenin, *Khronika,* IV, 106–10.
68. P. Miliukov, *Istoriia Vtoroi Russkoi Revoliutsii,* I, Pt. 1 (Sofia, 1921), 98–99.
69. *Revoliutsiia,* II, 57.
70. Lenin, *PSS,* XXXI, 361.
71. *Ibid.,* XXXIV, 216.
72. Sukhanov, *Zapiski,* III, 299.
73. *Revoliutsiia,* II, 74.
74. *Ibid.,* 82.
75. *PN,* No. 5,668 (September 30, 1936), 2.
76. Tsereteli, *Vospominaniia,* I, 135–36.
77. *Revoliutsiia,* II, 95.
78. *Ibid.,* 98–99; *Ibid.,* III, 13–14.
79. Crane Brinton, *Anatomy of Revolution* (New York, 1938), 163–71.
80. Marc Ferro in R. C. Elwood, *Considerations of the Russian Revolution* (Ann Arbor, Mich., 1976), 100–32.
81. John L. H. Keep, *The Russian Revolution* (London, 1976), 79.
82. Resolution in *Oktriabr'skaia revoliutsiia i Fabzavkomy,* I (Moscow, 1927), 22–24.
83. *Ibid.,* 6.
84. Paul Avrich in *Jahrbücher,* XI, No. 2 (1963), 166–68; *Revoliutsiia,* II, 231–33.
85. V. Malakhovskii in *PR,* No. 10/93 (1929), 29–31.
86. *Revoliutsiia,* II, 82–84.
87. Malakhovskii in *PR,* No. 10/93 (1929), 31.
88. D. A. Chugaev, ed., *Revoliutsionnoe dvizhenie v Rossii v mae–iune 1917 goda: Iunskaia demonstratsiia,* (Moscow, 1959), 488.
89. Sukhanov, *Zapiski,* IV, 289–90.
90. *Shestoi s"ezd RSDRP (bol'shevikov): Protokoly* (Moscow, 1958), 147–50; *PR,* No. 5/17 (1923), 287–88; V. P. Budnikov, *Bol'shevistskaia partiinaia pechat' v 1917 g.* (Kharkov, 1959), *passim.*
91. *Soldatskaia Pravda,* No. 1 (April 15, 1917), 1.
92. Zeman, *Germany,* 94.
93. *Vorwärts,* January 14, 1921, 1.
94. Alexander Kerensky, *The Crucifixion of Liberty* (New York, 1934), 325–26; Nikitin, *Rokovye gody,* 116–17.
95. Nikitin, *Rokovye gody,* 117.
96. Kerensky, *Crucifixion,* 326.
97. Nikitin, *Rokovye gody,* 112–14, where also other examples. Cf. Lenin, *Sochineniia,* XXI, 570.
98. Nikitin, *Rokovye gody,* 107.
99. Lenin, *PSS,* XLIX, 437, 438.
100. Nikitin, *Rokovye gody,* 109–10.
101. Kerensky, *Catastrophe,* 209.
102. Vasiukov, *Vneshnaia politika,* 191.
103. E. H. Wilcox, *Russia's Ruin* (New York, 1919), 196.
104. *Ibid.,* 197, citing V. I. Nemirovich-Danchenko.
105. Alexander Kerensky, *Russia and History's Turning Point* (New York, 1965), 277.
106. W. H. Chamberlin, *The Russian Revolution,* I (New York, 1935), 152.
107. Chugaev, *Revoliutsionnoe dvizhenie v Rossii v mae-iiunie 1917 g.,* 486.
108. Sukhanov, *Zapiski,* IV, 317–18.

109. Chugaev, *Revoliutsionnoe dvizhenie,* 485–87.

110. *Soldatskaia Pravda,* June 10, 1917, cited in A. Rabinowitch, *Prelude to Revolution* (Bloomington, Ind., 1968), 69.

111. Sukhanov, *Zapiski,* IV, 307–10; Tsereteli, *Vospominaniia,* II, 228.

112. *Pravda,* No. 80 (June 13, 1917), 1; emphasis supplied.

113. Tsereteli, *Vospominaniia,* II, 52–54.

114. C. R. M. F. Cruttwell, *A History of the Great War, 1914–1918* (Oxford, 1936), 630–32; Tsentral'noe Statisticheskoe Upravlenie, Otdel Voennoi Statistiki, *Rossiia v Mirovoi Voine 1914–1918 goda (v tsifrakh)* (Moscow, 1925), 4n.

115. *Rossiia v Mirovoi Voine,* 4; Iu. A. Poliakov, *Sovetskaia strana posle okonchaniia grazhdanskoi voiny* (Moscow, 1986), 99.

116. L. G. Beskrovnyi, *Armiia i flot Rossii v nachale XX v.* (Moscow, 1986), 17.

117. Calculated on the basis of figures in the sources cited in notes 114, 115, and 116 above.

118. Shliapnikov in *PR,* No. 4/51 (1926), 59.

119. P. Stulov in *KL,* No. 3/36 (1930), 65–66; Tsereteli, *Vospominaniia,* II, 270.

120. Stulov, *loc. cit.,* 70.

121. *PR,* No. 5/17 (1923), 6.

122. *PR,* No. 4/51 (1926), 56.

123. *PR,* No. 5/17 (1923), 7.

124. *Revoliutsiia,* III, 110.

125. F. F. Raskolnikov in *Pravda,* No. 159 (July 16, 1927), 3, and No. 168 (July 27, 1927), 3; see also his *Kronshtadt i Piter v 1917 godu* (Moscow-Leningrad, 1925).

126. *Revoliutsiia,* III, 84, 105, 108.

127. Stulov in *KL,* No. 3/36 (1930), 93.

128. Lenin, *Khronika,* IV, 266; V. D. Bonch-Bruevich, *Na boevykh postakh* (Moscow, 1930), 58.

129. Nikitin, *Rokovye gody,* 111.

130. *Ibid.,* 115–16.

131. *Ibid.,* 120, 122–23.

132. Bonch-Bruevich, *Na boevykh postakh,* 87–90; Nikitin, *Rokovye gody,* 123–25.

133. Nikitin, *Rokovye gody,* 115–16.

134. *Pravda,* No. 98 (July 4, 1917), cited in O. N. Znamenskii, *Iul'skii krizis 1917 goda* (Moscow-Leningrad, 1964), 47.

135. *Pravda,* July 2, 1917, cited in Rabinowitch, *Prelude,* 139; *Revoliutsiia,* III, 305–6; Vladimirova in *PR,* No. 5/17 (1923), 9.

136. *Revoliutsiia,* III, 305; Znamenskii, *Iul'skii krizis,* 47.

137. Stulov in *KL,* No. 3/36 (1930), 96.

138. G. Veinberg in *Petrogradskaia Pravda,* No. 149 (July 17, 1921), 3.

139. Leon Trotsky, *The History of the Russian Revolution,* II (New York, 1937), 13.

140. Stulov in *KL,* No. 3/36 (1930), 97–98.

141. D. A. Chugaev, ed., *Revoliutsionnoe dvizhenie v Rossii v iiule 1917 g.* (Moscow, 1959); B. I. Kochakov in *Uchënye Zapiski Leningradskogo Gosudarstvennogo Universiteta,* No. 205 (1956), 65–66.

142. Stulov in *KL,* No. 3/36 (1930), 101; Miliukov, *Istoriia,* I, Pt. 1, 243.

143. *Shestoi Kongress RKP (b): Protokoly* (Moscow, 1958), 17; also Vladimirova in *PR,* No. 5/17 (1923), 11.

144. Trotsky, *History,* II, 20.

145. *Revoliutsiia,* III, 132.

146. Chugaev, *Revoliutsionnoe dvizhenie v iiule,* 90–91. Cf. Raskolnikov in *PR,* No. 5/17 (1923), 53–58.

147. Chugaev, *Revoliutsionne dvizhenie v iiule,* 91; Raskolnikov, *loc. cit.,* 55.

148. Vladimirova in *PR,* No. 5/17 (1923), 20–21.

149. *V. D. Nabokov and the Russian Provisional Government,* 146.

150. A Sobolev in *Rech',* No. 155/3,897 (July 5, 1917), 1.

151. Flerovskii in *PR,* No. 7/54 (1926), 73–75; N. Arskii in *Sbornik Perezhitoe,* I (Moscow, 1918), 36.

152. Raskolnikov in *PR,* No. 5/17 (1923), 59; B. Elov in *KL,* No. 7 (1923), 101.

153. Vladimirova in *PR*, No. 5/17 (1923), 13.
154. Testimony of V. I. Nevskii in *Revoliutsiia*, III, 135; also Vladimirova in *PR*, No. 5/17 (1923), 17.
155. Rabinowitch, *Prelude*, 281.
156. Chugaev, *Revoliutsionnoe dvizhenie v iiule*, 19.
157. Rabinowitch, *Prelude*, 174-75.
158. Lenin, *PSS*, XXXII, 408-9.
159. Rabinowitch, *Prelude*, 180.
160. *Revoliutsiia*, III, 140.
161. Chugaev, *Revoliutsionnoe dvizhenie v iiule*, 39-40.
162. Raskolnikov in *PR*, No. 5/17 (1923), 61-62. The figure is from Nikitin, *Rokovye gody*, 131.
163. Chugaev, *Revoliutionnoe dvizhenie v iiule*, 96. Cf. Lenin, *PSS*, XXXIV, 23-24; Flerovskii in *PR*, No. 7/54 (1926), 77.
164. *Pravda*, July 5, 1917, in Vladimirova in *PR*, No. 5/17 (1923), 36.
165. Raskolnikov in *PR*, No. 5/17 (1923), 71; *PR*, No. 8-9/67-68 (1927), 62.
166. Chugaev, *Revoliutsionnoe dvizhenie v iiule*, 49.
167. *NV*, No. 118/142 (July 16, 1918), 1.
168. Rabinowitch, *Prelude*, 195-96.
169. *Revoliutsiia*, III, 151.
170. Zinoviev in *PR*, 8-9/67-68 (1927), 62.
171. F. F. Raskolnikov in *Pravda*, No. 160/3,692 (July 17, 1927), 3.
172. *NoV*, No. 14,822 (July 9, 1917), 4.
173. *NZh*, No. 68 (July 7, 1917), 3.
174. Chugaev, *Revoliutsionnoe dvizhenie v iiule*, 290.
175. Nikitin, *Rokovye gody*, 153-54.
176. Bonch-Bruevich, *Na boevykh postakh*, 87-90.
177. *Zhivoe slovo*, No. 51/404 (July 5, 1917), 2. Text also in Lenin, *Sochineniia*, XXI, 509-10.
178. Tsereteli, *Vospominaniia*, I, 91.
179. Sukhanov, *Zapiski*, IV, 440-43.
180. Raskolnikov, *PR*, No. 5/17 (1923), 72. Cf. Nikitin, *Rokovye gody*, 149.
181. L. Trotskii, *O Lenine* (Moscow, 1924), 58.
182. *NoV*, No. 14,821 (July 8, 1917), 2.
183. Lenin, *Khronika*, IV, 281-82; Nikitin, *Rokovye gody*, 151.
184. P. A. Polovstoff, *Glory and Downfall* (London, 1935), 256-58; *Revoliutsiia*, III, 167; *Zhivoe slovo*, No. 52/406 (July 6, 1917), 1.
185. Lenin, *Sochineniia*, XXI, 470.
186. *NV*, No. 118/142 (July 16, 1918), 1.
187. *NZh*, No. 70 (July 9, 1917), 1.
188. Stroev in *NZh*, No. 68 (July 7, 1917), 1.
189. Vladimirova in *PR*, No. 5/17 (1923), 44.
190. Raskolnikov in *PR*, No. 5/17 (1923), 78.
191. Shliapnikov in *PR*, No. 5/52 (1926), 24.
192. *NZh*, No. 71 (July 11, 1917), 3; Lenin, *PSS*, XXXII, 414-18, 424-26; XXXIV, 22-23.
193. Lenin, *PSS*, XXXII, 433-34; XXXIV, 8-9, 459-60.
194. Zinoviev in *PR*, No. 8-9/67-68 (1927), 68.
195. Lenin, *Khronika*, IV, 277.
196. Sukhanov, *Zapiski*, IV, 480-81.
197. Kerensky, *Catastrophe*, 240.
198. Richard Abraham, *Alexander Kerensky: The First Love of the Revolution* (New York, 1987), 244.
199. *Revoliutsiia*, III, 178.
200. S. P. Melgunov, *Sud'ba Imperatora Nikolaia II posle otrecheniia* (Paris, 1951), 180.
201. *Ibid.*, 192-201.
202. *Ibid.*, 179.
203. Trotskii, *O Lenine*, 59.

Chapter 11

1. Alexander Kerensky, *The Catastrophe* (New York-London, 1927), 318.
2. Alexander Kerensky, *The Prelude to Bolshevism* (New York, 1919), xiii; D. A. Chugaev, ed., *Revoliutsionnoe dvizhenie v Rossii v avguste 1917 g.: Razgrom Kornilovskogo miatezha* (Moscow, 1959), 429.
3. Zinaida Gippius, *Siniaia kniga* (Belgrade, 1929), 152.
4. E. I. Martynov, *Kornilov* (Leningrad, 1927), 33–34.
5. A. Kerenskii, *Delo Kornilova* (Ekaterinoslav, 1918), 20–21.
6. Martynov, *Kornilov*, 36.
7. *Ibid.*, 34.
8. Boris Savinkov, *K delu Kornilova* (Paris, 1919), 13–14.
9. *Ibid.*, 15; P. N. Miliukov, *Istoriia Vtoroi Russkoi Revoliutsii*, I, Pt. 2 (Sofia, 1921), 105.
10. Kerenskii, *Delo*, 23; Savinkov, *K delu*, 15–16; Miliukov, *Istoriia*, I, Pt. 2, 99.
11. *Revoliutsiia*, IV, 69–70.
12. *Ibid.*, 54.
13. Savinkov, *K delu*, 15.
14. Kerenskii, *Delo*, 56–57; Kerensky, *Catastrophe*, 318.
15. Savinkov, *K delu*, 12–13; George Katkov, *The Kornilov Affair* (London-New York, 1980), 54.
16. A. S. Lukomskii, *Vospominaniia*, I (Berlin, 1922), 227.
17. Katkov, *Kornilov*, 170.
18. Lukomskii, *Vospominaniia*, I, 228, 232.
19. Chugaev, *Revoliutsionnoe dvizhenie v avguste*, 429.
20. *Ibid.*, 429–30.
21. *Revoliutsiia*, IV, 37–38; Lukomskii, *Vospominaniia* I, 224–25.
22. Miliukov, *Istoriia*, I, Pt. 2, 107–8; Trubetskoi in *Obshchee delo*, No. 8 (October 4, 1917), cited in Martynov, *Kornilov*, 53.
23. Kerenskii, *Delo*, 81; Gippius, *Siniaia kniga*, 164–65.
24. Kerenskii, *Delo*, 56–57.
25. Cited in *DN*, No. 135 (August 24, 1917), 1.
26. *NZh*, No. 110 (August 25, 1917), 1.
27. N. N. Golovin, *Rossiiskaia kontr-revoliutsiia v 1917–1918 gg.*, I, Pt. 2 (Tallinn, 1937), 15.
28. Kerenskii, *Delo*, 62.
29. From the deposition of Savinkov in *Revoliutsiia*, IV, 85.
30. Miliukov, *Istoriia*, I, Pt. 2, 158.
31. The protocols of the meeting, taken down by Savinkov, are reproduced in Chugaev, *Revoliutsionnoe dvizhenie v avguste*, 421–23. Another protocol, signed by Kornilov and two generals, is in Katkov, *Kornilov*, 176–78. Savinkov's recollections: *K delu Kornilova*, 20–23.
32. Miliukov, *Istoriia*, I, Pt. 2, 175; Chugaev, *Revoliutsionnoe dvizhenie v avguste*, 422.
33. Savinkov in *RS*, No. 207 (September 10, 1917), 3.
34. Miliukov, *Istoriia*, I, Pt. 2, 178.
35. Cited from the testimony of Kornilov by Miliukov in his *Istoriia*, I, Pt. 2, 202; cf. *Revoliutsiia*, IV, 91.
36. Martynov, *Kornilov*, 94; cf. Miliukov, *Istoriia*, I, Pt. 2, 202.
37. Lukomskii, *Vospominaniia*, I, 238.
38. *Ibid.*, 237–38.
39. *Ibid.*, 232.
40. I. G. Tsereteli, *Vospominaniia o Fevral'skoi Revoliutsii*, I (Paris, 1963), 108–9; V. D. Nabokov *and the Russian Provisional Government, 1917* (New Haven, Conn.-London, 1976), 90; Katkov, *Kornilov*, 85.
41. Kerenskii, *Delo*, 85.
42. Chugaev, *Revoliutsionnoe dvizhenie v avguste*, 427.
43. Katkov, *Kornilov*, 179; Lukomskii, *Vospominaniia*, I, 238–39.
44. Lukomskii, *Vospominaniia*, I, 238–39.
45. Savinkov in *RS*, No. 207 (September 10, 1917), 3.

46. Katkov, *Kornilov,* 179–80.
47. Lukomskii, *Vospominaniia,* I, 239.
48. *Ibid.,* 241; Chugaev, *Revoliutsionnoe dvizhenie v avguste,* 432.
49. Chugaev, *Revoliutsionnoe dvizhenie v avguste,* 442.
50. Kerenskii, *Delo,* 88.
51. Katkov, *Kornilov,* 90–91; emphasis supplied. The original Russian text is in Chugaev, *Revoliutsionnoe dvizhenie v avguste,* 443.
52. Kerenskii, *Delo,* 91.
53. Miliukov, *Istoriia,* I, Pt. 2, 200; Lukomskii, *Vospominaniia,* I, 241.
54. Accounts of this meeting: N. V. Nekrasov in *RS,* No. 199 (August 31, 1917), 2, and Martynov, *Kornilov,* 101.
55. *NZh,* No. 120/126 (September 13, 1917), 3.
56. *Revoliutsiia,* IV, 98.
57. Gippius, *Siniaia kniga,* 180–81.
58. *Revoliutsiia,* IV, 99; Lukomskii, *Vospominaniia,* I, 242; Kerenskii, *Delo,* 113–14; Golovin, *Kontr-revoliutsiia,* I, Pt. 2, 33–34.
59. Lukomskii, *Vospominaniia,* 242; *Revoliutsiia,* IV, 100.
60. Lukomskii, *Vospominaniia,* 242–43.
61. Full text in Chugaev, *Revoliutsionnoe dvizhenie v avguste,* 448–52.
62. *NZh,* No. 114 (August 29, 1917), 3.
63. *Revoliutsiia,* IV, 111.
64. Gippius, *Siniaia kniga,* 187.
65. Kerenskii, *Delo,* 104–5.
66. Savinkov, *K delu,* 26; Golovin, *Kontr-revoliutsiia,* I, Pt. 2, 35.
67. Boris Savinkov in *Mercure de France,* No. 503/133 (June 1, 1919), 438.
68. Richard Abraham, *Alexander Kerensky: The First Love of the Revolution* (New York, 1987), 277.
69. Chugaev, *Revoliutsionnoe dvizhenie v avguste,* 445–46; *Revoliutsiia,* IV, 101–2.
70. Chugaev, *Revoliutsionnoe dvizhenie v avguste,* 446.
71. Golovin, *Kontr-revoliutsiia,* I, Pt. 2, 37.
72. *Revoliutsiia,* IV, 109.
73. *Ibid.,* 115.
74. Miliukov, *Istoriia,* I, Pt. 2, 162n.; Kerenskii, *Delo,* 80.
75. *Revoliutsiia,* IV, 109.
76. Lukomskii, *Vospominaniia,* I, 245.
77. *Revoliutsiia,* IV, 125.
78. Golovin, *Kontr-revoliutsiia,* I, Pt. 2, 71, 101.
79. Khan Khadzhiev, *Velikii boiar* (Belgrade, 1929), 123–30.
80. Golovin, *Kontr-revoliutsiia,* I, Pt. 2, 71. The tapes of the conversations between Alekseev and Kornilov and Kornilov and Kerensky on August 30–September 1, 1917, are in the Denikin Archive, Box 24, Bakhmeteff Archive, Columbia University.
81. *NZh,* No. 107/322 (June 4, 1918), 3; *NV,* No. 96/120 (June 19, 1918), 3.
82. Chugaev, *Revoliutsionnoe dvizhenie v avguste,* 431.
83. E. H. Wilcox, *Russia's Ruin* (New York, 1919), 276.
84. Kerenskii, *Delo,* 65.
85. Miliukov, *Istoriia,* I, Pt. 2, 15n., citing *Echo de Paris,* 1920, *Otechestvo,* No. 1, and *Poslednie Izvestiia* (Revel), April 1921.
86. *Revoliutsiia,* IV, 299–300, 70.
87. *NZh,* No. 108 (August 23, 1917), 1–2, and No. 109 (August 24, 1917), 4; W. G. Rosenberg in *SS.* No. 2 (1969), 160–61.
88. *Revoliutsiia,* III, 122; Rosenberg, *loc. cit.*
89. Golovin, *Kontr-revoliutsiia,* I, Pt. 2, 53–54.
90. Sokolnikov in *Revoliutsiia,* IV, 104.
91. *Ibid.,* V, 269.
92. S. P. Melgunov, *Kak bol'sheviki zakhvatili vlast'* (Paris, 1953), 13.

93. *NZh,* No. 116 (August 31, 1917), 2.
94. *NZh,* No. 149/143 (October 10, 1917), 3.
95. *NZh,* No. 125/119 (September 12, 1917), 3.
96. *NZh,* No. 123/117 (September 9, 1917), 4.
97. *PR,* No. 8–9/67–68 (1927), 67–72.
98. Cited by Lenin, *PSS,* XXXIII, 37.
99. *Ibid.,* 116.
100. *Ibid.,* 90.
101. Lenin, "The Looming Catastrophe and How to Fight It," *ibid.,* XXXIV, 151–99, and "Will the Bolsheviks Hold On to State Power?," *ibid.,* 287–339.
102. *Ibid.,* 2–5; emphasis supplied.
103. Lenin, *Sochineniia,* XXI, 512, note 18.
104. *Revoliutsiia,* III, 383–84.
105. Leningradskii Istpart, *Vtoraia i tret'ia Petrogradskie Obshchegorodskie Konferentsii Bol'-shevikov* (Moscow-Leningrad, 1927), 77.
106. *Izvestiia,* No. 164 (September 5, 1917).
107. *Izvestiia,* No. 195 (October 12, 1917), 1.
108. *Ibid.,* No. 200 (October 18, 1917), 1.
109. Lenin, *PSS,* XXXIV, 239–41.
110. *Ibid.,* 245.
111. L. Trotsky, *The History of the Russian Revolution,* III (New York, 1937), 355.
112. *Protokoly Tsentral'nogo Komiteta RSDRP (b)* (Moscow, 1958), 74.
113. *SD,* No. 169 (September 28, 1917), 1.
114. Lenin, *PSS,* XXXIV, 403, 405.
115. *Izvestiia,* No. 186 (October 1, 1917), 8.
116. *Revoliutsiia,* V, 53; *Izvestiia,* No. 197 (October 14, 1917), 5.
117. *NZh,* No. 138, September 27, 1917, 3.
118. Leonard Schapiro, *The Communist Party of the Soviet Union* (London, 1960), 164.
119. *Revoliutsiia,* IV, 197, 214.
120. *Ibid.,* 256.
121. *Protokoly TsK,* 73, 76.
122. *Revoliutsiia,* V, 65.
123. *Protokoly TsK,* 264; *Revoliutsiia,* V, 63.
124. Alexander Rabinowitch, *The Bolsheviks Come to Power* (New York, 1976), 209–11.
125. *Revoliutsiia,* V, 71–72.
126. *Ibid.,* 65.
127. *NZh,* No. 138/132 (September 27, 1917), 3.
128. *Revoliutsiia,* V, 78.
129. *Ibid.,* 246, 254.
130. See the government's declaration of September 25–27 in *Revoliutsiia,* IV, 403–6.
131. *Izvestiia,* No. 201 (October 19, 1917), 7.
132. *Ibid.,* No. 200 (October 18, 1917), 1.
133. *Ibid.,* No. 203 (October 21, 1917), 5.
134. *Revoliutsiia,* V, 109; *NZh,* No. 156/150 (October 18, 1917), 3.
135. The operation is described in M. Schwarte *et al., Der Grosse Krieg, 1914–1918: Der deutsche Landkrieg* (Leipzig, 1925), Pt. 3, 323–27.
136. *Revoliutsiia,* V, 30–31.
137. *Izvestiia,* No. 191 (October 7, 1917), 4; *Revoliutsiia,* V, 37.
138. *Revoliutsiia,* V, 38, 67.
139. *Ibid.,* 52.
140. *Ibid.,* 52, 237–38.
141. *PR,* No. 10 (1922), 53–54.
142. *Ibid.,* 86.
143. I. I. Mints, ed., *Dokumenty velikoi proletarskoi revoliutsii,* I (Moscow, 1938), 22.
144. *Rabochii put',* No. 33 (1917), cited in *Revoliutsiia,* V, 238.

145. Trotsky, *History,* III, 353.
146. *Rabochii put',* No. 35 (1917), cited in *Revoliutsiia,* V, 70–71; *Izvestiia,* No. 197 (October 14, 1917), 5.
147. *Utro Rossii,* cited in Melgunov, *Kak bol'sheviki,* 34n.
148. *Izvestiia,* No. 199 (October 17, 1917), 8; *Revoliutsiia,* V, 101.
149. *Izvestiia,* No. 201 (October 19, 1917), 5.
150. *Revoliutsiia,* V, 132.
151. N. Sukhanov, *Zapiski o revoliutsii,* VII (Berlin-Petersburg-Moscow, 1923), 90–92.
152. *Protokoly TsK,* 83–86.
153. L. Trotskii, *O Lenine* (Moscow, 1924), 70–73.
154. *Ibid.,* 70–71.
155. *Protokoly TsK,* 87–92.
156. *Ibid.,* 86; Trotskii, *O Lenine,* 72.
157. Iu. Kamenev in *NZh,* No. 156/150 (October 18, 1917), 3.
158. Truncated minutes in *Protokoly TsK,* 106–21.
159. *Ibid.,* 113.
160. *DN,* No. 154 (September 11, 1917), 3, and No. 169 (October 1, 1917), 1.
161. Trotskii, *O Lenine,* 69.
162. Mints, *Dokumenty,* I, 3.
163. C. Malaparte, *Coup d'Etat: The Technique of Revolution* (New York, 1932), 180.
164. V. A. Antonov-Ovseenko, *V semnadtsatom godu* (Moscow, 1933), 276.
165. Robert V. Daniels, *Red October* (New York, 1967), 118.
166. See *Kritika,* IV, No. 3 (Spring 1968), 21–32; N. I. Podvoiskii, *God 1917* (Moscow, 1958), 104.
167. Trotsky, *History,* III, 290–91.
168. G. L. Sobolev in *IZ,* No. 88 (1971), 77.
169. Sukhanov, *Zapiski,* VII, 161.
170. O. Dzenis in *Living Age,* No. 4,049 (February 11, 1922), 328.
171. *Izvestiia,* No. 204 (October 22, 1917), 3; *Revoliutsiia,* V, 144–45.
172. Podvoiskii, *God 1917,* 106–8.
173. Melgunov, *Kak bol'sheviki,* 68–69; Antonov-Ovseenko, *V semnadtsatom godu,* 283; *NZh,* No. 161/155 (October 24, 1917), 3.
174. D. A. Chugaev, ed., *Petrogradskii Voenno-Revoliutsionnyi Komitet: Dokumenty i materialy,* I (Moscow, 1966), 63. This declaration first appeared on October 24 in the Bolshevik daily *Rabochii put'.*
175. *NZh,* No. 161/155 (October 24, 1917), 3.
176. *Protokoly TsK,* 119, 269; *Revoliutsiia,* V, 160.
177. A. Sadovskii in *PR,* No. 10 (1922), 76–77; *Revoliutsiia,* V, 151; Melgunov, *Kak bol'sheviki,* 69.
178. *Revoliutsiia,* V, 163–64; Melgunov, *Kak bol'sheviki,* 69.
179. *Revoliutsiia,* V, 111–12.
180. *Nabokov and the Provisional Government,* 78.
181. G. Buchanan, *My Mission to Russia* (Boston, 1923), II, 201; Cf. J. Noulens, *Mon Ambassade en Russie Soviétique, 1917–1919,* I (Paris, 1933), 116.
182. Buchanan, *Mission,* II, 214.
183. *KA,* 1/56 (1933), 137.
184. Melgunov, *Kak bol'sheviki,* 93–94.
185. *Ibid.,* 88–89.
186. P. N. Maliantovich in *Byloe,* No. 12 (1918), 113.
187. *Revoliutsiia,* V, 164, 263–64.
188. *SD,* No. 193 (October 26, 1917), 1.
189. Trotskii, *O Lenine,* 74.
190. Maliantovich in *Byloe,* No. 12 (1918), 114.
191. *Ibid.,* 115.
192. Melgunov, *Kak bol'sheviki,* 84–85; Alexander Kerensky, *Russia and History's Turning Point* (New York, 1965), 435–36.
193. S. Uralov in *PR,* No. 10/33 (1924), 277.
194. Lenin, *PSS,* XXXVI, 15–16.

195. Trotsky, *History*, III, 305–6.
196. K. G. Kotelnikov, ed., *Vtoroi Vserossiiskii S"ezd Sovetov R. i S.D.* (Moscow-Leningrad, 1928), 164, 166.
197. *Ibid.,* 165–66.
198. Trotskii, *O Lenine,* 77.
199. *Rech',* No. 252 (October 26, 1917), in *Revoliutsiia,* V, 182.
200. *Revoliutsiia,* V, 189.
201. Dzenis in *Living Age,* No. 4,049 (February 11, 1922), 331.
202. Maliantovich in *Byloe,* No. 12 (1918), 129–30.
203. Decision of the Ispolkom of the All-Russian Soviet of Peasants' Deputies on October 24, in A. V. Shestakov, ed., *Sovety krest'ianskikh deputatov i drugie krest'ianskie organizatsii,* I, Pt. 1 (Moscow, 1929), 288.
204. *Revoliutsiia,* V, 182.
205. L. Trotskii, *Istoriia russkoi revoliutsii,* II, Pt. 2 (Berlin, 1933), 327.
206. *Revoliutsiia,* V, 284.
207. Oskar Anweiler, *The Soviets* (New York, 1974), 260–61.
208. G. Rauzans in *Cina* (Riga), November 7, 1987. I owe this reference to Professor Andrew Ezergailis.
209. Kotelnikov, *S"ezd Sovetov,* 37–38, 41–42.
210. Sukhanov, *Zapiski,* VII, 203.
211. *Dekrety,* I, 12–16.
212. *Ibid.,* 17–20.
213. *Ibid.,* 17–18.
214. *Ibid.,* 20–21.
215. Sukhanov, *Zapiski,* VII, 266. Lenin's offer to Trotsky: Isaac Deutscher, *The Prophet Armed: Trotsky, 1879–1921* (New York-London, 1954), 325.
216. *Revoliutsiia,* VI, 1.
217. E. Ignatov in *PR,* No. 4/75 (1928), 31.
218. Lenin, *PSS,* XXXV, 20.
219. *Dekrety,* I, 18.
220. *Ibid.,* 20.
221. *Ibid.,* 25–26.
222. Melgunov, *Kak bol'sheviki,* 209–10.
223. *Protokoly TsK,* 106–7.
224. *Revoliutsiia,* V, 193–94; *Revoliutsiia,* VI, 4–5; D. A. Chugaev, ed., *Triumfal'noe shestvie sovetskoi vlasti* (Moscow, 1963), 500.
225. V. A. Kondratev, ed., *Moskovskii Voenno-Revoliutsionnyi Komitet: Oktiabr'–Noiabr' 1917 goda* (Moscow, 1968), 22.
226. *Ibid.,* 78.
227. *Ibid.,* 103–4.
228. *Ibid.,* 161.
229. Among those who have are V. Leikina in *PR,* No. 2/49 (1926), 185–233, No. 11/58 (1926), 234–55, and No. 12/59 (1926), 238–54, and John L. H. Keep in Richard Pipes, ed., *Revolutionary Russia* (Cambridge, Mass., 1968), 180–216.
230. L. Trotskii, *Sochineniia,* III, Pt. 1 (Moscow, n.d.), L.
231. *Dekrety,* I, 2.
232. W. Pietsch, *Revolution und Staat* (Köln, 1969), 68; Lenin, *PSS,* XXXV, 46.
233. *NZh,* No. 173/167 (November 5, 1917), 1.
234. *NZh,* No. 171/165 (November 3, 1917), 3. The French Consul, F. Grenard, reports a similar reaction in Petrograd: *La Révolution Russe* (Paris, 1933), 285. For the provinces, see Keep in Pipes, *Revolutionary Russia,* 211.

Chapter 12

1. W. Pietsch, *Revolution und Staat* (Köln, 1969), 140.
2. N. Sukhanov, *Zapiski o revoliutsii,* VII (Berlin-Petersburg-Moscow, 1923), 266.

3. R. M. MacIver, *The Web of Government* (New York, 1947), 123.

4. E. Frankel, *The Dual State* (London-New York, 1941).

5. C. C. Brinton, *The Jacobins* (New York, 1961).

6. K. G. Kotelnikov, ed., *Vtoroi Vserossiiskii S''ezd Sovetov R. i S.D.* (Moscow-Leningrad, 1928), 107.

7. *Desiatyi S''ezd RKP (b), Mart 1921 goda: Stenograficheskii otchët* (Moscow, 1963), 407.

8. I. Stalin, *Voprosy Leninizma,* 11th ed. (Moscow, 1952), 126.

9. *Deviatyi S''ezd RKP (b): Protokoly* (Moscow, 1960), 307.

10. Leonard Schapiro, *The Communist Party of the Soviet Union* (London, 1960), 231; *BSE,* XI, 531.

11. Merle Fainsod, *How Russia Is Ruled* (Cambridge, Mass., 1963), 177.

12. Sukhanov, *Zapiski,* II, 244.

13. B. Avilov in *NZh,* No. 18/232 (January 25/February 7, 1918), 1.

14. *Krasnaia gazeta,* No. 7 (February 2, 1918), 4.

15. See *Dokumenty stavki E. I. Pugacheva, povstancheskikh vlastei i uchrezhdenii, 1773–1774* (Moscow, 1975), 48, and R. V. Ovchinnikov, *Manifesty i ukazy E. I. Pugacheva* (Moscow, 1980), 122–32.

16. V. Tikhomirnov in *VS,* No. 27 (1918), 12.

17. Pietsch, *Revolution,* 77.

18. J. Bunyan and H. H. Fisher, *The Bolshevik Revolution, 1917–18: Documents and Materials* (Stanford, Calif., 1934), 277.

19. L. M[artov] in *Novyi luch,* No. 10/34 (January 18, 1918), 1.

20. Pietsch, *Revolution,* 80.

21. S. Studenikin, ed., *Istoriia sovetskoi konstitutsii v dekretakh i postanovleniiakh sovetskogo pravitel'stva 1917–1936* (Moscow, 1936), 66.

22. *Dekrety,* I, 20.

23. A. Taniaev, *Ocherki po istorii dvizheniia zheleznodorozhnikov v revoliutsii 1917 goda (Fevral'–Oktiabr')* (Moscow-Leningrad, 1925), 137–39.

24. *Protokoly Tsentral'nogo Komiteta RSDRP (b): Avgust 1917–Fevral' 1918* (Moscow, 1958), 271; and *Revoliutsiia,* VI, 21.

25. *Revoliutsiia,* VI, 22–23. P. Vompe's *Dni oktiabr'skoi revoliutsii i zheleznodorozhniki* (Moscow, 1924), which is said to contain minutes of the meetings of the Union of Railroad Employees and Workers, was not available to me.

26. *Protokoly TsK,* 271–72. According to L. Schapiro, *The Origin of the Communist Autocracy,* 2nd ed. (Cambridge, Mass., 1977), 74, the minutes of this meeting have been removed from the published protocols of the Central Committee. They can be found in L. Trotskii's *Stalinskaia shkola fal'sifikatsii* (Berlin, 1932), 116–31. See also *Oktiabr'skoe vooruzhonnoe vosstanie,* II (Leningrad, 1967), 405–10.

27. *Protokoly TsK,* 126–27.

28. Trotskii, *Stalinskaia shkola fal'sifikatsii,* 124.

29. *Izvestiia,* November 4/17, 1917, cited in *Protokoly TsK,* 135.

30. *Revoliutsiia,* VI, 423–24.

31. V. D. Bonch-Bruevich, *Vospominaniia o Lenine* (Moscow, 1969), 143.

32. A. L. Fraiman, *Forpost sotsialisticheskoi revoliutsii* (Leningrad, 1969), 166–67.

33. *Revoliutsiia,* VI, 91.

34. Fraiman, *Forpost,* 169.

35. Korolenko, "Protest," in *Gazeta-Protest Soiuza Russkikh Pisatelei,* November 26, 1917. A copy of this paper is available at the Hoover Institution.

36. Iu. Larin in *NKh,* No. 11 (1918), 16–17.

37. M. P. Iroshnikov, *Sozdanie sovetskogo tsentral'nogo gosudarstvennogo apparata,* 2nd. ed. (Leningrad, 1967), 115; John L. H. Keep, ed., *The Debate on Soviet Power* (Oxford, 1979), 78–79.

38. *Protokoly zasedanii Vserossiiskogo Tsentral'nogo Ispolnitel'nogo Komiteta Rabochikh, Soldatskikh, Krest'ianskikh i Kazach'ikh Deputatov II Sozyva* (Moscow, 1918), 28.

39. Lenin, *PSS,* XXXIV, 304–5.

40. *Ibid.,* XXXV, 58.
41. *Protokoly zasedanii,* 31.
42. *Ibid.,* 32.
43. *Revoliutsiia,* VI, 73.
44. *Protokoly zasedanii,* 31–32.
45. I. Steinberg, *Als ich Volkskommissar war* (Munich, 1929), 148.
46. S. Piontkovskii in *BK,* No. 1 (1934), 112.
47. S. A. Fediukin, *Velikii Oktiabr' i intelligentsiia* (Moscow, 1972); E. Ignatov in *PR,* No. 4/75 (Moscow, 1928), 34.
48. The story of these events is very inadequately covered. See D. Antoshkin, *Professional'noe dvizhenie sluzhashchikh, 1917–1924 gg.* (Moscow, 1927), and Z. A. Miretskii in A. Anskii, ed., *Professional'noe dvizhenie v Petrograde v 1917 g.: Ocherki i materialy* (Leningrad, 1928), 231–42.
49. *DN,* Nos. 191 and 192 (Oct. 28, 1917); *NZh,* No. 164/158 (October 27, 1917), 3.
50. *Revoliutsiia,* VI, 14.
51. *Volia naroda,* No. 156 (October 29, 1917), cited in Bunyan and Fisher, *Bolshevik Revolution,* 225.
52. *VS,* No. 11 (1919), 5.
53. *DN,* No. 191 (November 10, 1917), 3, cited in Bunyan and Fisher, *Bolshevik Revolution,* 226.
54. *Protokoly II'go Vserossiskogo S"ezda Kommissarov Truda* (1918), 9 and 17, cited in M. Dewar, *Labour Policy in the USSR* (London, 1956), 17–18.
55. *Revoliutsiia,* VI, 50.
56. *NZh,* No. 178/172 (November 11/24, 1917), 3; B. M. Morozov, *Sozdanie i ukreplenie sovetskogo gosudarstvennogo apparata* (Moscow, 1957), 52.
57. *Dekrety,* I, 27–28.
58. *NZh,* No. 182/176 (November 16/29, 1917).
59. N. Osinskii in *EZh,* No. 1 (November 6, 1918), 2–3. See also A. M. Gindin, *Kak bol'sheviki ovladeli Gosudarstvennym Bankom* (Moscow, 1961).
60. *NV,* No. 6 (December 6/18, 1917), 3.
61. *Ibid.,* No. 25 (December 30, 1917), 3.
62. *LS,* XXXV, 7.
63. N. Gorbunov in *Pravda,* No. 255/3,787 (November 6/7, 1927), 9.
64. *Ibid.;* Larin in *NKh,* No. 11 (1918), 16–17.
65. S. Liberman, *Building Lenin's Russia* (Chicago, 1945), 13.
66. D. A. Chugaev, ed., *Triumfal'noe shestvie sovetskoi vlasti,* Pt. 1 (Moscow, 1963), 140.
67. L. Trotskii, *Moia zhizn',* II (Berlin, 1930), 65; Lenin, *PSS,* XXXVIII, 198; Liberman, *Building,* 8.
68. *SUiR,* I, No. 309, 296–97.
69. *Izvestiia,* No. 244 (December 6, 1917), 6–7.
70. *Ibid.,* No. 249 (December 12, 1917), 6.
71. *Pravda,* No. 91 (April 20, 1924), 3.
72. *NZh,* No. 206/200 (December 20, 1917/January 2, 1918), cited in *Revoliutsiia,* VI, 377.
73. Kh. A. Eritsian, *Sovety krest'ianskikh deputatov v oktiabr'skoi revoliutsii* (Moscow, 1960), 143.
74. Steinberg, *Als ich Volkskommissar war,* 42.
75. See, for example, Trotsky's speech in the Petrograd Soviet as reported in *NZh,* No. 138/132 (September 27, 1917), 3.
76. *Pravda,* No. 170/101 (October 27, 1917), 1.
77. N. Krupskaia, *Vospominaniia o Lenine* (Moscow, 1957), 74; Lenin, *PSS,* XXXV, 185.
78. *Dekrety,* I, 25–26.
79. *Izvestiia,* No. 213 (November 1, 1917), 2.
80. Lenin, *PSS,* XXXV, 135.
81. *Ibid.,* XXXIV, 266.
82. Peter Scheibert, *Lenin an der Macht* (Weinheim, 1984), 418.
83. Based on L. M. Spirin, *Klassy i partii v grazhdanskoi voine v Rossii (1917–20 gg.)* (Moscow, 1968), 416–25, and L. M. Spirin, *Krushenie pomeshchich'ikh i burzhuaznykh partii v Rossii* (Moscow, 1977), 300–41.

84. *DN,* No. 2/247 (January 4, 1918), 1.
85. Oliver Radkey, *The Election to the Russian Constituent Assembly of 1917* (Cambridge, Mass., 1950), 15.
86. O. N. Znamenskii, *Vserossiiskoe Uchreditel'noe Sobranie* (Leningrad, 1976), Tables 1 and 2.
87. Lenin, *PSS,* XL, 7.
88. Radkey, *Election,* 38.
89. Lenin, *PSS,* XL, 16–18.
90. Znamenskii, *Uchreditel'noe Sobranie,* 275, 358.
91. Lenin, *PSS,* XL, 10.
92. Fraiman, *Forpost,* 163.
93. *Dekrety,* I, 159.
94. *Revoliutsiia,* VI, 187.
95. Fraiman, *Forpost,* 163.
96. *Revoliutsiia,* VI, 192.
97. *Ibid.,* 199.
98. *NV,* No. 1 (November 30, 1917), 1–2, and No. 2 (December 1, 1917), 2; *Pravda,* No. 91 (April 20, 1924), 3; and Znamenskii, *Uchreditel'noe Sobranie,* 309–10.
99. *NV,* No. 1 (November 30, 1917), 2; *Revoliutsiia,* VI, 225.
100. *Dekrety,* I, 162.
101. Znamenskii, *Uchreditel'noe Sobranie,* 231.
102. *Protokoly TsK,* 149–150.
103. Lenin, *PSS,* XXXV, 106.
104. *Ibid.,* 164–65, 166.
105. *Protokoly TsK,* 175.
106. *Znamia truda,* No. 111 (January 5/18, 1918), 3.
107. N. Rubinshtein, *Bol'sheviki i Uchreditel'noe Sobranie* (Moscow, 1938), 76.
108. B. F. Sokolov in *ARR,* XIII (Berlin, 1924), 48; Fraiman, *Forpost,* 201.
109. V. D. Bonch-Bruevich, *Tri pokusheniia na V. I. Lenina* (Moscow, 1930), 3–77.
110. Sokolov in *ARR,* XIII, 50, 60–61.
111. *Ibid.,* 61.
112. *Pravda,* No. 3/230 (January 5/18, 1918), 4.
113. Trotsky in *ibid.,* No. 91 (April 20, 1924), 3.
114. Znamenskii, *Uchreditel'noe Sobranie,* 334–35; Fraiman, *Forpost,* 204.
115. *Pravda,* No. 2/229 (January 4/17, 1918), 1, 3.
116. M. V. Vishniak, *Vserossiiskoe Uchreditel'noe Sobranie* (Paris, 1932), 99–100.
117. V. D. Bonch-Bruevich, *Na boevykh postakh fevral'skoi i oktiabr'skoi revoliutsii* (Moscow, 1930), 256.
118. *DN,* No. 2/247 (January 4, 1918), 2.
119. Sokolov in *ARR,* XIII, 66.
120. A. S. Izgoev in *ARR,* X, 24–25; Znamenskii, *Uchreditel'noe Sobranie,* 340.
121. Descriptions in *DN,* No. 4 (January 7, 1918), 2; *Griaduiushchyi den',* No. 30 (January 6, 1918), 4; *Pravda,* No. 5 (January 6/19, 1918), 2.
122. *NZh,* No. 7/23 (January 11/24, 1918), 2, and Scheibert, *Lenin,* 19.
123. *NZh,* No. 7/23 (January 11/24, 1918), 2.
124. I. S. Malchevskii, ed., *Vserossiiskoe Uchreditel'noe Sobranie* (Moscow-Leningrad, 1930), 3.
125. *Dekrety,* I, 321–23.
126. Lenin, *Khronika,* V, 180–81; Malchevskii, *Uchreditel'noe Sobranie,* 217.
127. Bunyan and Fisher, *Bolshevik Revolution,* 384–86.
128. *Pravda,* No. 4/231 (January 6/19, 1918), 1.
129. *NV,* No. 7 (January 12/25, 1918), 3, in Bunyan and Fisher, *Bolshevik Revolution,* 389.
130. Sokolov in *ARR,* XIII, 54.
131. Trotsky in *Pravda,* No. 91 (April 20, 1924), 3.
132. E. Ignatov in *PR,* No. 5/76 (1928), 28–29.
133. Trotsky in *Pravda,* No. 91 (April 20, 1924), 3.
134. Znamenskii, *Uchreditel'noe Sobranie,* 323.

135. V. I. Ignatev, *Nekotorye fakty i itogi chetyrëkh let grazhdanskoi voiny* (Moscow, 1922), 8.
136. D. S. Mirsky, *Modern Russian Literature* (London, 1925), 89.
137. Sokolov in *ARR*, XIII, 6.
138. Dewar, *Labour Policy*, 37.
139. A. S. Izgoev in *NV*, No. 94/118 (June 16, 1918), 1.
140. G. Aronson, "Na perelome," Manuscript, Hoover Institution, Nikolaevskii Archive, DK 265.89/L2A76, is the best account of these events.
141. *Kontinent*, No. 2 (1975), 385–419.
142. *NV*, No. 91/115 (May 9, 1918), 3.
143. *NV*, No. 92/116 (May 10, 1918), 3.
144. *NS*, No. 23 (May 15, 1918), 3.
145. *NV*, No. 92/116 (May 10, 1918), 3.
146. *Ibid.*
147. Vladimir Brovkin in *RR*, January 1983, 47. Aronson, "Na perelome," 23–24, confirms this assessment.
148. B. Avilov in *NZh*, No. 96/311 (May 22, 1918), 1.
149. *Ibid.*, No. 99/314 (May 25, 1918), 4.
150. *Utro*, June 3, 1918, cited in Aronson, "Na perelome," 15–16.
151. Aronson, "Na perelome," 7–8.
152. *NZh*, No. 164/158 (October 27, 1917), 1.
153. *NZh*, No. 20/234 (January 27, 1918), 1.
154. *NZh*, No. 111/326 (June 8, 1918), 3.
155. Aronson, "Na perelome," 21.
156. *Dekrety*, II, 30–31; Lenin, *PSS*, XXXVII, 599.
157. W. G. Rosenberg, *Liberals in the Russian Revolution* (Princeton, N.J., 1974), 263–300.
158. *NZh*, No. 115/330 (June 16, 1918), 3.
159. W. G. Rosenberg in *SR*, XLIV, No. 3 (July 1985), 235.
160. *NZh*, No. 122/337 (June 26, 1918), 3.
161. See, e.g., Stroev in *NZh*, No. 127/342 (July 2, 1918), 1.
162. *NV*, No. 106/130 (July 2, 1918), 3.
163. *NV*, No. 107/131 (July 3, 1918), 3, and No. 108/132 (July 4, 1918), 4; *NZh*, No. 128/343 (July 3, 1918), 1.

Chapter 13

1. Lenin, *PSS*, XXXI, 310.
2. *Ibid.*, XXXV, 250.
3. *Ibid.*, 247; emphasis supplied.
4. *Sed'moi Ekstrennyi S"ezd RKP (b)* (Moscow, 1962), 171.
5. *Sovetsko-Germanskie Otnosheniia ot peregovorov v Brest-Litovske do podpisaniia Rapall'skogo dogovora*, I (Moscow, 1968), 647–49.
6. C. K. Cumming and W. W. Pettit, eds., *Russian-American Relations March 1917–March 1920* (New York, 1920), 53–54.
7. *Dekrety*, I, 16.
8. E.g. *Revoliutsiia*, V, 285–86.
9. Fritz Fischer, *Germany's Aims in the First World War* (New York, 1967), 477.
10. *Sovetsko-Germanskie Otnosheniia*, I, 278.
11. *Ibid.*, 108.
12. *Ibid.*, 184.
13. One example in *ibid.*, 68–75. See also Fischer, *Germany's Aims*, 483–84.
14. See, e.g., Paul Rohrbach's *Russland und wir* (Stuttgart, 1915).
15. *Sovetsko-Germanskie Otnosheniia*, I, 194–96.
16. Rohrbach, *Russland und wir*, 3.
17. Fritz Fischer, *Griff nach der Weltmacht* (Düsseldorf, 1967), *passim*.
18. Winfried Baumgart, *Deutsche Ostpolitik 1918* (Vienna-Munich, 1966), 245–46.

19. *Deutsche Politik,* No. 26 (June 28, 1918), 805–6.
20. Isaac Deutscher, *The Prophet Armed: Trotsky, 1879–1921* (New York-London, 1954), 387.
21. *Sovetsko-Germanskie Otnosheniia,* I, 153–54.
22. *Ibid.,* I, 66–67.
23. *Ibid.,* 59–60; Fischer, *Germany's Aims,* 488, has a six-point program.
24. J. Buchan, *A History of the Great War,* IV (Boston, 1922), 137.
25. *Sovetsko-Germanskie Otnosheniia,* I, 148–50; Fischer, *Germany's Aims,* 487–90.
26. Gerald Freund, *Unholy Alliance* (New York, 1957), 4.
27. *Sovetsko-Germanskie Otnosheniia,* I, 194–97, 208.
28. Lenin, *PSS,* XXXVI, 30.
29. *Sovetsko-Germanskie Otnosheniia,* I, 183, 190; Fischer, *Germany's Aims,* 487.
30. See my *Formation of the Soviet Union: Communism and Nationalism, 1917–23* (Cambridge, Mass., 1954), 114–26.
31. *Sovetsko-Germanskie Otnosheniia,* I, 229; J. Wheeler-Bennett, *Brest-Litovsk: The Forgotten Peace* (London-New York, 1956), 173–74.
32. W. Hahlweg, *Der Diktatfrieden von Brest-Litowsk* (Münster, 1960), 375.
33. *Sovetsko-Germanskie Otnosheniia,* I, 229–30.
34. On the January 1918 strikes: G. Rosenfeld, *Sowjet-Russland und Deutschland 1917–1922* (Köln, 1984), 46–55; Wheeler-Bennett, *Forgotten Peace,* 196.
35. Lenin, *Sochineniia,* XXII, 599.
36. Stephen Cohen, *Bukharin and the Bolshevik Revolution* (London, 1974), 65.
37. Lenin, *Sochineniia,* XXII, 599; John Erickson in Richard Pipes, ed., *Revolutionary Russia* (Cambridge, Mass., 1968), 232–33; E. N. Gorodetskii, *Rozhdenie Sovetskogo Gosudarstva* (Moscow, 1965), 406–7.
38. Lenin, *PSS,* XXXV, 243–52.
39. *Ibid.,* 324; cf. Hahlweg, *Diktatfrieden,* 48.
40. Lenin, *PSS,* XXXV, 255–58.
41. Russian text in *Sovetsko-Germanskie Otnosheniia,* I, 298–308; English translation in Wheeler-Bennett, *Forgotten Peace,* 392–402.
42. *Sovetsko-Germanskie Otnosheniia,* I, 311–12.
43. Soviet declaration in Lenin, *Sochineniia,* XXII, 555–58.
44. *Sovetsko-Germanskie Otnosheniia,* I, 314–15.
45. They are reproduced in *VZ,* XV, No. 1 (January 1967), 87–104.
46. *Sovetsko-Germanskie Otnosheniia,* I, 278.
47. *Ibid.,* 289–90, 318–19.
48. Protocols in *Sovetsko-Germanskie Otnosheniia,* I, 322–29; see also Baumgart, *Ostpolitik,* 23–26.
49. *Sovetsko-Germanskie Otnosheniia,* I, 326–27; in German: Baumgart, *Ostpolitik,* 25.
50. Lenin, *Sochineniia,* XXII, 677.
51. K. F. Nowak, ed., *Die Aufzeichnungen des General Majors Max Hoffmann,* I (Berlin, 1929), 187.
52. Deutscher, *Prophet Armed,* 383, 390.
53. Lenin, *Sochineniia,* XXII, 677, and *PSS,* XXXV, 486–87.
54. *Dekrety,* I, 487–88; Lenin, *PSS,* XXXV, 339.
55. I. Steinberg, *Als ich Volkskommissar war* (Munich, 1929), 206–7.
56. *Dekrety,* I, 490–91.
57. See below, Chap. 18.
58. R. Ullman, *Intervention and the War* (Princeton, N.J., 1961), 74.
59. Cumming and Pettit, *Russian-American Relations,* 65.
60. Ullman, *Intervention,* 137–38.
61. Lenin, *Sochineniia,* XXII, 607; Gen. [Henri A.] Niessel, *Le Triomphe des Bolcheviks et la Paix de Brest-Litovsk: Souvenirs, 1917–1918* (Paris, 1940), 277–78.
62. J. Sadoul, *Notes sur la Révolution Bolchevique* (Paris, 1920), 244–45.
63. Lenin, *PSS,* XXXV, 489.
64. Niessel, *Triomphe,* 279–80.

65. Wheeler-Bennett, *Forgotten Peace*, 284–85; Sadoul, *Notes*, 262–63; Ullman, *Intervention*, 81.
66. *Sovetsko-Germanskie Otnosheniia*, I, 341–43.
67. *Protokoly Tsentral'nogo Komiteta RSDRP (b)* (Moscow, 1958), 211–18.
68. Lenin, *PSS*, XXXV, 376–80.
69. *Protokoly TsK*, 219–28.
70. Lenin, *Sochineniia*, XXII, 558.
71. Lenin, *PSS*, XXXV, 385–86.
72. *Ibid.*, 399.
73. *Ibid.*, XXXVI, 24.
74. Niessel, *Triomphe*, 299.
75. Ia. Piletskii in *NZh*, No. 38/253 (March 9, 1918), 2; see also V. Stroev, *NZh*, No. 40/255 (March 12, 1918), 1.
76. See V. D. Bonch-Bruevich, *Pereezd V. I. Lenina v Moskvu* (Moscow, 1926).
77. Hahlweg, *Diktatfrieden*, 51.
78. Piletskii in *NZh*, No. 41/256 (March 14, 1918), 1.
79. These are documented in *Sovetsko-Germanskie Otnosheniia*, I, 370–430, and analyzed in Wheeler-Bennett, *Forgotten Peace*, 269–75.
80. Wheeler-Bennett, *Forgotten Peace*, 275.
81. W. Baumgart in *VZ*, XVI, No. 2 (January 1968), 84.
82. J. Degras, *Documents of Russian Foreign Policy*, I (London, 1951), 56–57. Document dated March 5, 1918.
83. Cumming and Pettit, *Russian-American Relations*, 82–84.
84. *Ibid.*, 85–86.
85. J. Noulens, *Mon Ambassade en Russie Soviétique*, II (Paris, 1933), 116; cf. Cumming and Pettit, *Russian-American Relations*, 161–62.
86. *NZh*, No. 54/269 (March 16/29, 1918), 4; D. Francis, *Russia from the American Embassy* (New York, 1922), 264–65. Brian Pearce, *How Haig Saved Lenin* (London, 1988), 15–16.
87. *NS*, No. 23 (May 15, 1918), 2.
88. *NZh*, No. 54/269 (March 16/29, 1918), 4.
89. Letter dated April 12, 1918, in Sadoul, *Notes*, 305. On German pressure: Lenin in *NS*, No. 23 (May 15, 1918), 2.
90. Lenin, *PSS*, XXXVI, 3–26.
91. Lenin, *Sochineniia*, XXII, 559–61, 613.
92. *KPSS v rezoliutsiiakh i resheniiakh s"ezdov, konferentsii i plenumov TsK, 1898–1953*, 7th ed., I (Moscow, 1953), 405; cf. Lenin, *PSS*, XXXVI, 37–38, 40.
93. George Kennan, *Russia Leaves the War* (Princeton, N.J., 1956), 255.
94. Cumming and Pettit, *Russian-American Relations*, 70.
95. *Dekrety*, I, 386–87; on this, see below, Chap. 15.
96. *NKh*, No. 11 (1918), 19–20.
97. Cumming and Pettit, *Russian-American Relations*, 87–88.
98. *Ibid.*, 91–92.
99. *Ibid.*, 89; Russian original in Lenin, *PSS*, XXXVI, 91.
100. Noulens, *Mon Ambassade*, II, 34–35.
101. *Izvestiia*, No. 190/454 (September 4, 1918), 3.
102. See below, Chap. 14.
103. *Izvestiia*, No. 242/506 (November 5, 1918), 4.
104. Lenin, *PSS*, XXXVI, 331.
105. *Ibid.*, 340.
106. *Ibid.*, XLI, 55.

Chapter 14

1. Lenin, *PSS*, XXXIV, 245.
2. *Dekrety*, I, 16.
3. Lenin, *PSS*, XXXVII, 79.

4. E. N. Gorodetskii, *Rozhdenie sovetskogo gosudarstva* (Moscow, 1965), 402–3; John Erickson in Richard Pipes, ed., *Revolutionary Russia* (Cambridge, Mass., 1968), 230–31.

5. M. Mayzel, *An Army in Transition: The Russian High Command, October 1917–May 1918* (Tel Aviv University, 1976), in *Slavic and Soviet Series*, I, No. 5 (September 1976).

6. A. G. Kavtaradze, *Voennye spetsialisty na sluzhbe Respubliki Sovetov, 1917–1920 gg.* (Moscow, 1988), *passim.*

7. Gorodetskii, *Rozhdenie*, 399–401; Erickson in Pipes, *Revolutionary Russia*, 232.

8. Gorodetskii, *Rozhdenie*, 416.

9. *Dekrety*, I, 342, 356–57.

10. *Dekrety*, I, 588; *Izvestiia*, No. 17/281 (January 23, 1918), 3.

11. *NZh*, No. 23/237 (February 13, 1918), 1; cf. Leon Trotsky, *Revolution Betrayed* (New York, 1972), 210–11.

12. Lenin, *PSS*, XXXVIII, 139.

13. *Dekrety*, I, 356.

14. Ia. Kaimin, *Latyshskie strelki v bor'be za pobedu Oktriabr'skoi revoliutsii* (Riga, 1961), 27–37.

15. *NZh*, No. 112/327 (June 9, 1918), 3; *Dekrety*, II, 440.

16. *NZh*, No. 101/316 (May 28, 1918), 4.

17. I. I. Vatsetis in *Pamiat'*, No. 2 (Paris, 1979), 44.

18. *Dekrety*, I, 577.

19. *Ibid.*, 522–23; II, 63–70, 569–70; Lenin, *Khronika*, V, 291; Kavtaradze, *Voennye spetsialisty*, 72–88.

20. *Dekrety*, II, 63–70.

21. Gen. [Henri A.] Niessel, *Le Triomphe des Bolcheviks et la Paix de Brest-Litovsk: Souvenirs, 1917–1918* (Paris, 1940), 329–30.

22. J. Noulens, *Mon Ambassade en Russie Soviétique*, II (Paris, 1933), 27; cf. J. Sadoul, *Notes sur la Révolution Bolchevique* (Paris, 1920), 274, 277; Niessel, *Triomphe*, 331.

23. Noulens, *Mon Ambassade*, II, 70–71.

24. Sadoul, *Notes*, 290–91. Letter dated April 6, 1918.

25. C. K. Cumming and W. W. Pettit, eds., *Russian-American Relations March 1917–March 1920* (New York, 1920), 98.

26. *Ibid.*, 100.

27. Lenin, *Khronika*, V, 356; *Russian-American Relations*, 130–31.

28. Lenin, *Khronika*, V, 452–53; G. Kennan, *The Decision to Intervene* (Princeton, N.J., 1958), 217–18; Winfried Baumgart, *Deutsche Ostpolitik 1918* (Vienna-Munich, 1966), 265–66; Lenin, *PSS*, L, 74–75.

29. *NS*, No. 23 (May 15, 1918), 2.

30. Noulens, *Mon Ambassade*, II, 53.

31. K. D. Erdmann, ed., *Kurt Riezler: Tagebücher, Aufsätze, Dokumente* (Göttingen, 1972), 462.

32. See his *Mit Graf Mirbach in Moskau* (Tübingen, 1922). Bothmer kept a diary, which has not been published: W. Baumgart in *VZ*, XVI, No. 1 (1968), 73n.

33. Report of April 30, 1918, in *VZ*, XVI, No. 1 (1968), 77–78. English translation in Z. A. B. Zeman, ed., *Germany and the Revolution in Russia, 1915–1918* (London, 1958), 120–21.

34. Erdmann, *Riezler*, 463.

35. Baumgart in *VZ*, XVI, No. 1 (1968), 80. Report dated May 16. Cf. Zeman, *Germany*, 126–27.

36. Archives of German Ministry of Foreign Affairs, Deutschland, No. 131, Geheime Akten, Russland No. 134.

37. Baumgart in *VZ*, XVI, No. 1 (1968), 81–83.

38. *Ibid.*, 83.

39. Erdmann, *Riezler*, 466n.

40. Zeman, *Germany*, 130, 133.

41. Baumgart, *Ostpolitik*, 213.

42. Baumgart in *VZ*, XVI, No. 1 (1968), 88.

43. *Ibid.*, 89–90, 92–93; Erdmann, *Riezler*, 466–67.

44. Zeman, *Germany*, 138, 131.

45. Louis Fischer, *The Soviets in World Affairs*, I (London, 1930), 75.

46. Lenin, *Khronika*, VI, 146; J. Wheeler-Bennett, *Brest-Litovsk: The Forgotten Peace* (London-New York, 1956), 355.
47. *VZh*, No. 5 (1919), 35.
48. *Ibid.*, 36–37.
49. H. Tiedemann, *Sowjetrussland und die Revolutionierung Deutschlands, 1917–1919* (Berlin, 1936), 74; Baumgart, *Ostpolitik*, 349n.
50. Baumgart, *Ostpolitik*, 338–41.
51. *VZh*, No. 5 (1919), 35.
52. Baumgart, *Ostpolitik*, 262–64.
53. I. K. Kobliakov in *ISSSR*, No. 4 (1958), 12.
54. Text: H. W. Gatzke in *VZ*, III, No. 1 (1955), 79; cf. Baumgart, *Ostpolitik*, 283–84.
55. Gatzke in *VZ*, III, No. 1 (1955), 94. Letter dated August 8, 1918.
56. See below, p. 633.
57. Lenin, *Khronika*, V, 318–19; R. Ullman, *Intervention and the War* (Princeton, N.J., 1961), 152.
58. T. G. Masaryk, *Die Weltrevolution* (Berlin, 1925), 197–99, 209.
59. M. Klante, *Von der Wolga zum Amur* (Berlin, 1931), 137.
60. S. P. Melgunov, *Tragediia Admirala Kolchaka*, I (Belgrade, 1930), 133.
61. N. N. Golovin, *Rossiiskaia kontr-revoliutsiia v 1917–1918 gg.*, Pt. 3, Book 7 (Tallinn-Paris, 1937), 67; Klante, *Von der Wolga*, 134–36.
62. Klante, *Von der Wolga*, 100.
63. Ullman, *Intervention*, 154–55; Baumgart, *Ostpolitik*, 53.
64. Sadoul, *Notes*, 368; Kennan, *Decision*, 150.
65. Sadoul, *Notes*, 366; Golovin, *Kontr-revoliutsiia*, Pt. 3, Book 7, 71n.
66. V. Maksakov and A. Turunov, *Khronika grazhdanskoi voiny v Sibiri, 1917–1918* (Moscow-Leningrad, 1926), 168.
67. Baumgart, *Ostpolitik*, 56–57.
68. J. Bunyan, *Intervention, Civil War, and Communism in Russia* (Baltimore, 1936), 89.
69. *Ibid.*, 90.
70. Melgunov, *Tragediia Admirala Kolchaka*, I, 43.
71. Baumgart, *Ostpolitik*, 345; Bothmer, *Mit Graf Mirbach*, 63.
72. *Dekrety*, II, 151–53.
73. *Ibid.*, 334–35.
74. *NZh*, No. 110/325 (June 7, 1918), 3.
75. *Dekrety*, III, 108–9.
76. Erickson in Pipes, *Revolutionary Russia*, 248.
77. *Dekrety*, III, 111–13.
78. Erickson in Pipes, *Revolutionary Russia*, 257–58.
79. *Protokoly zasedanii Vserossiiskogo Tsentral'nogo Ispolnitel'nogo Komiteta 5-go Sozyva: Stenograficheskii Otchët* (Moscow, 1919), 80.
80. *NZh*, No. 93/308 (May 18, 1918), 3.
81. G. Lelevich [L. Mogilevskii], *V dni samarskoi uchreditilki* (Moscow, 1921), 9–10 and *passim;* also Lenin, *Sochineniia*, XXIII, 644; G. Stewart, *The White Armies of Russia* (New York, 1933), 145.
82. Klante, *Von der Wolga, passim.*
83. Golovin, *Kontr-revoliutsiia*, Pt. 3, Book 7, 72.
84. A. Hogenhuis-Seliverstoff, *Les Relations Franco-Soviétiques, 1917–1924* (Paris, 1981), 65.
85. Sadoul, *Notes*, 369–71.
86. Klante, *Von der Wolga*, 178.
87. Erdmann, *Riezler*, 711.
88. *Ibid.*, 474.
89. *Ibid.*, 81, 269–70, 279–80.
90. *Ibid.*, 385–87.
91. *Ibid.*, 74–75.
92. Baumgart, *Ostpolitik*, 84.
93. *Ibid.*, 110, note 78.

94. French Foreign Ministry Archives, April 26, 1918, Lavergne, Z 391.9.
95. Baumgart, *Ostpolitik,* 84; Erdmann, *Riezler,* 467.
96. *Izvestiia,* No. 138 (July 5, 1918), 5.
97. V. Vladimirova in *PR,* No. 4/63 (1927), 110–11.
98. On the meeting: *Krasnaia Kniga VChK,* II (Moscow, 1920), 129–30; K. Gusev, *Krakh partii levykh eserov* (Moscow, 1963), 193–94.
99. *Krasnaia Kniga VChK,* II, 129–30.
100. Erdmann, *Riezler,* 467; A. Paquet, *Im Kommunistischen Russland: Briefe aus Moskau* (Jena, 1919), 26.
101. *Znamia truda,* No. 238 (June 29, 1918), 1; repeated on June 30 and July 2.
102. Bunyan, *Intervention,* 197–98.
103. *Ibid.,* 198–204.
104. Deposition dated May 8, 1919, in *Krasnaia Kniga VChK,* II, 224–33.
105. Text in *Boris Savinkov pered Voennoi Kollegiei Verkhovnogo Suda SSSR* (Moscow, 1924), 225–26; Erdmann, *Riezler,* 713–15.
106. This description follows the deposition made by Riezler in 1952: Erdmann, *Riezler,* 713–14.
107. Lenin, *Khronika,* V, 606.
108. Erdmann, *Riezler,* 715; Baumgart, *Ostpolitik,* 228, note 71.
109. L. M. Spirin, *Krakh odnoi avantiury* (Moscow, 1971), 35
110. *Ibid.,* 38.
111. *Krasnaia Kniga VChK,* II, 194.
112. Vladimirova in *PR,* No. 4/63 (1927), 121.
113. Vatsetis in *Pamiat',* No. 2, 19.
114. *Piatyi Vserossiiskii S"ezd Sovetov: Stenograficheskii Otchët* (Moscow, 1918), July 9, 1918, 3rd session, 109.
115. F. Z. Dzerzhinskii in *Pravda,* No. 139 (July 8, 1918); reproduced in his *Izbrannye Proizvedeniia,* I (Moscow, 1967), 265.
116. Vatsetis in *Pamiat',* No. 2, 19.
117. *NV,* No. 113/137 (July 10, 1918), 3.
118. J. [Isaac] Steinberg, "The Events of July 1918," Manuscript, Hoover Institution Archive, DK 265. S818, p. 20.
119. Spirin, *Krakh,* 42.
120. Steinberg, "The Events," 122.
121. Lenin, *Khronika,* V, 610.
122. Vatsetis in *Pamiat',* No. 2, 26–27.
123. *Ibid.,* 27.
124. *Ibid.,* 28.
125. *Ibid.,* 40–41.
126. Erdmann, *Riezler,* 715.
127. K. Helfferich, *Der Weltkrieg,* III (Berlin, 1919), 654.
128. *Pravda,* No. 156 (July 27, 1918), 1.
129. *Petrogradskaia Pravda,* No. 233/459 (October 24, 1918), 1.
130. George Katkov in David Footman, ed., *St. Antony's Papers, No. 12: Soviet Affairs,* No. 3 (London, 1962), 53–93.
131. Winfried Baumgart, ed., *Von Brest-Litovsk zur deutschen Novemberrevolution* (Göttingen [1971]), 65.
132. Spirin, *Krakh,* 80.
133. Helfferich, *Der Weltkrieg,* III, 654
134. I. Steinberg, *Spiridonova* (New York, 1935), 247; *Pamiat',* No. 2, 80.
135. Spirin, *Krakh,* 85. I. Deutscher, *The Prophet Armed: Trotsky, 1879–1921* (New York-London, 1954), 403; Lev Trotskii, *Portrety revoliutsionerov* (Benson, Vt., 1988), 268–78.
136. Lenin, *Sochineniia,* XXIII, 561, 581–84.
137. *Pravda,* No. 139 (July 8, 1918), 1.
138. A biographical sketch of him by S. P. Melgunov can be found in *Na puti k "tretei" Rossii* (Warsaw, 1920).

139. A. I. Denikin, *Ocherki russkoi smuty,* III (Berlin, 1924), 79.
140. *PN,* No. 1342 (September 10, 1924), 2.
141. Masaryk, *Die Weltrevolution,* 209.
142. Boris Savinkov, *Bor'ba s Bol'shevikami* (Warsaw, 1923), 26; *Boris Savinkov pered Voennoi Kollegiei Verkhovnogo Suda SSSR* (Moscow, 1924), 64; Denikin, *Ocherki,* III, 79.
143. Ullman, *Intervention,* 190.
144. Noulens, *Mon Ambassade,* II, 108–9.
145. French Foreign Ministry Archives, No. 223, May 5, 1918; *Savinkov pered Voennoi Kollegiei,* 58.
146. Perkhurov in S. and M. Broide, *Iaroslavskii miatezh: po zapiskam Generala Perkhurova* (Moscow, 1930), 16.
147. F. Grenard, *La Révolution Russe* (Paris, 1933), 322; cf. Kennan, *Decision,* 436, McLaren to Poole.
148. Savinkov, *Bor'ba,* 24.
149. Organization described in *Savinkov pered Voennoi Kollegiei,* 48–49, 51.
150. Broide, *Iaroslavskii miatezh,* 17–18; Savinkov, *Bor'ba,* 29–30.
151. Broide, *Iaroslavskii miatezh,* 14–15.
152. *Golos minuvshego na chuzoi storone,* No. 6/19 (1928), 117.
153. Savinkov, *Bor'ba,* 28.
154. *Savinkov pered Voennoi Kollegiei,* 56–57; Perkhurov in Broide, *Iaroslavskii miatezh,* 25.
155. *Savinkov pered Voennoi Kollegiei,* 60.
156. Savinkov, *Bor'ba,* 28.
157. Perkhurov in Broide, *Iaroslavskii miatezh,* 19.
158. Perkhurov in *ibid.,* 25.
159. *Krasnaia Kniga VChK,* II (Moscow, 1920), 101.
160. Spirin, *Krakh,* 11.
161. Testimony of the head of the German Repatriation Commission, Lt. Balk, in Bothmer, *Mit Graf Mirbach,* 150–54.
162. *Krasnaia Kniga VChK,* II, 106; Bothmer, *Mit Graf Mirbach,* 150–54.
163. *Pravda,* No. 155 (July 26, 1918), 3; Bothmer, *Mit Graf Mirbach,* 110.
164. The record of his trial: *Savinkov pered Voennoi Kollegiei* and *Delo Borisa Savinkova* (Moscow, 1924).
165. In Broide, *Iaroslavskii miatezh.*
166. N. G. Palgunov and O. I. Rozanova, eds., *Shesnadtsat' dnei: materialy po istorii iaroslavskogo belogvardeiskogo miatezha* (Iaroslavl, 1924), 135–41.
167. A. Pacquet in Baumgart, *Von Brest-Litovsk,* 66–67.
168. Baumgart, *Ostpolitik,* 230.
169. Erdmann, *Riezler,* 474.
170. *Ibid.,* 719.
171. *Ibid.,* 474–75.
172. Riezler in Baumgart, *Ostpolitik,* 230–31.
173. *Pamiat',* No. 2, 43–44.
174. Erdmann, *Riezler,* 112–13; Helfferich, *Der Weltkrieg,* III, 652.
175. Denikin archive in Bakhmeteff Archive, Columbia University, "Iz dnevnika kniaziia Grigoriia Trubetskogo," 8.
176. Erdmann, *Riezler,* 722.
177. Riezler's cable of July 28, in Erdmann, *Riezler,* 732.
178. Baumgart, *Ostpolitik,* 231; Lenin, *PSS,* XXXVI, 523.
179. Lenin, *PSS,* XXXVI, 523–26.
180. Erdmann, *Riezler,* 467.
181. Baumgart, *Ostpolitik,* 244.
182. Draft of policy paper dated July 11, as summarized in Baumgart, *Ostpolitik,* 225–26.
183. Kennan, *Decision,* 391–404; Ullman, *Intervention,* 192, 195–96.
184. Ullman, *Intervention,* 240–42.
185. *Ibid.*

186. Baumgart, *Ostpolitik,* 102–4.
187. Martin Gilbert, *Winston S. Churchill,* IV (London, 1975), 224.
188. Ullman, *Intervention,* 240.
189. *Ibid.*
190. *Ibid.*
191. Noulens, *Mon Ambassade,* II, 176.
192. Klante, *Von der Wolga,* 180–81.
193. J. Skačel, *Československa Armada v Rusku a Kolčak* (Prague, 1926), 36.
194. Klante, *Von der Wolga,* 195.
195. Melgunov, *Tragediia,* I, 100–1.
196. Golovin, *Kontr-revoliutsiia,* Pt. 3, Book 7, 119.
197. Helfferich, *Der Weltkrieg,* III, 653. Further: Lenin, *PSS,* L, 134–35; G. Rosenfeld, *Sowjet-Russland und Deutschland, 1917–1922* (Köln, 1984), 119; Baumgart, *Ostpolitik,* 108–10.
198. Erdmann, *Riezler,* 472n.
199. Baumgart, *Ostpolitik,* 239–40. Cf. Rosenfeld, *Sowjet-Russland,* 119, where first publication of a similar analysis made by Helfferich on August 19.
200. Baumgart, *Ostpolitik,* 245–46.
201. Rosenfeld, *Sowjet-Russland,* 106.
202. Baumgart, *Ostpolitik,* 275.
203. *ISSSR,* No. 4 (1958), 13–14.
204. Baumgart, *Ostpolitik,* 186, 280.
205. Lenin, *Khronika,* VI, 83.
206. Baumgart, *Ostpolitik,* 114.
207. Intercepted message from Ioffe to Moscow in H. W. Gatzke, *VZ,* III, No. 1 (1955), 96–97, dated August 13.
208. Baumgart, *Ostpolitik,* 115.
209. *Europäische Gespräche,* IV, No. 3 (1926), 148.
210. Gatzke in *VZ,* III, No. 1 (1955), 96–97.
211. Baumgart, *Ostpolitik,* 302–3.
212. *Protokoly VTsIK, 5-go Sozyva,* 95.
213. Baumgart, *Ostpolitik,* 317–18.
214. Kobliakov in *ISSSR,* No. 4 (1958), 15; Baumgart, *Ostpolitik,* 319–21.
215. Baumgart, *Ostpolitik,* 321–22; General Ludendorff, *My War Memories,* II (London, n.d.), 659.
216. Lenin, *PSS,* XXXVII, 97–100.
217. Bunyan, *Intervention,* 151; *Protokoly VTsIK, 5-go Sozyva,* 251–53.
218. Baumgart, *Ostpolitik,* 357.
219. Ioffe in *VZh,* No. 5 (1919), 38.
220. Tiedemann, *Sowjetrussland,* 74; Baumgart, *Ostpolitik,* 365n.
221. Baumgart, *Ostpolitik,* 358. Soviet account of this episode in *Dokumenty vneshnei politiki SSSR,* I (Moscow, 1957), 560–64.
222. *SUiR,* 1917–18, No. 947, 2, 207–8.
223. Wheeler-Bennett, *Forgotten Peace,* 370–71, 451–53.
224. Helfferich, *Der Weltkrieg,* III, 656.
225. Richard K. Debo, *Revolution and Survival* (Liverpool, 1979), xiii.
226. Bryan Pearce, *How Haig Saved Lenin* (London, 1987), 7.

Chapter 15

1. *Sovetskaia Istoricheskaia Entsiklopediia,* III (Moscow, 1963), 600.
2. Lenin, *PSS,* XLIII, 220.
3. Concerning this controversy, see Paul Craig Roberts in *Alienation and the Soviet Economy* (University of New Mexico Press, 1971), 20–47, and S. Malle, *The Economic Organization of War Communism, 1918–1921* (Cambridge, 1985), 1–23.
4. L. Trotskii, *Chto takoe SSSR i kuda on idët?* (Paris, n.d.), 16.
5. *SUiR,* No. 154, 152; No. 674, 743–46.

6. *Ibid.,* No. 425, 397–98 and No. 420, 394–96.

7. *Ibid.,* No. 456, 428–30.

8. On this, see my *Russia under the Old Regime* (New York, 1974), especially Chap. 4.

9. Cited in R. Lorenz, *Anfänge der Bolschewistischen Industriepolitik* (Köln, 1965), 85. See further Leszek Kolakowski, *Main Currents of Marxism,* II (Oxford, 1978), 297–304.

10. F. Pollock, *Die Planwirtschaftlichen Versuche in der Sowjetunion, 1917–1927* (Leipzig, 1929), 33.

11. Lenin, *PSS,* XXXIV, 307.

12. L. Trotskii, *O Lenine* (Moscow, 1924), 112.

13. Lenin, *PSS,* XXXIV, 307–8.

14. *Ibid.,* XXXV, 123.

15. Iu. Larin in *NKh,* No. 11 (1918), 16.

16. *Izvestiia,* No. 229 (November 18, 1917), 3.

17. On him: Simon Liberman, *Building Lenin's Russia* (Chicago, 1945), 55; *NKh,* No. 6 (1919), 27–32; Lorenz, *Anfänge,* 137–40; G. Tsyperovich, *Sindikaty i tresty v dorevoliutsionnoi Rossii i v SSSR* (Leningrad, 1927), 387–92.

18. See Meshcherskii's account in *NS,* No. 33 (May 26, 1918), 3; Lorenz, *Anfänge,* 138.

19. Lorenz, *Anfänge,* 140; Tsyperovich, *Sindikaty i tresty,* 386–87.

20. *NZh,* No. 79/294 (April 28, 1918), 3.

21. Published in Germany as *Arbeit, Disziplin und Ordnung werden die Sozialistische Sowjet-Republik Retten* (Berlin, 1919).

22. Lenin, *PSS,* XXXVI, 300.

23. *Ibid.,* 255; emphasis supplied.

24. *Izvestiia,* No. 76/340 (April 17, 1918), 2.

25. N. Osinskii, *Stroitel'stvo sotsializma* (Moscow, 1918).

26. *Ibid.,* 46.

27. N. N. Sukhanov, *Zapiski o revoliutsii,* II (Berlin-Petersburg-Moscow, 1922), 239.

28. H. Taine, *The French Revolution,* II (New York, 1892), 13–14.

29. Cited in Malle, *War Communism,* 165.

30. *Vosmoi S"ezd RKP (b): mart 1919 g., Protokoly* (Moscow, 1959), 407–8.

31. S. Chutskaev in *EZh,* No. 225 (November 13, 1920), 2.

32. *NKh,* No. 1–2 (1920), 9.

33. *EZh,* No. 167 (July 31, 1920), 1.

34. E. H. Carr, *The Bolshevik Revolution, 1917–23,* II (New York, 1952), 246.

35. Lenin, *PSS,* XXXVI, 351.

36. Lenin, *Sochineniia,* XXIII, 18; Lenin, *PSS,* XXXVI, 351, omits first sentence in this citation.

37. *Vosmoi S"ezd RKP (b),* 407–8.

38. L. N. Iurovskii, *Denezhnaia politika sovetskoi vlasti (1917–27)* (Moscow, 1928), 43.

39. *Dekrety,* III, 454.

40. S. S. Katzenellenbaum, *Russian Currency and Banking, 1914–24* (London, 1925), 74–75.

41. *Dekrety,* V, 189–90.

42. Iurovskii, *Denezhnaia politika,* 75.

43. Z. V. Atlas, *Ocherki po istorii denezhnogo obrashcheniia v SSSR (1917–25)* (Moscow, 1940), 58–59.

44. *NKh,* No. 1–2 (1920), 10.

45. Iurovskii, *Denezhnaia politika,* 71.

46. *Ibid.,* 75.

47. Malle, *War Communism,* 164.

48. Peter Scheibert, *Lenin an der Macht* (Weinheim, 1984), 250.

49. Iurovskii, *Denezhnaia politika,* 73.

50. Katzenellenbaum, *Russian Currency,* 74–75.

51. *Ibid.,* 77.

52. *Deviatyi S"ezd RKP (b): Protokoly* (Moscow, 1960), 426.

53. *Ibid.,* 425.

54. *Odinadtsatyi S"ezd RKP (b): Stenograficheskii Otchët* (Moscow, 1961), 296.

55. Richard Pipes, *Struve: Liberal on the Right, 1905–1944* (Cambridge, Mass., 1980), 140–41.

56. J. Bunyan, *Intervention, Civil War, and Communism in Russia 1918* (Baltimore, 1936), 406–7.
57. *Dekrety*, IV, 314–16, 457–61; V, 217–31.
58. *NKh*, No. 1–2 (1920), 8–9.
59. Lenin, *Khronika*, VIII, 291; cf. *LS*, XXIV, 95.
60. L. N. Yurovsky, *Currency Problems and Policy of the Soviet Union* (London, 1925), 22.
61. Lenin, *PSS*, XXXVI, 7.
62. *EZh*, No. 261 (November 9, 1920), 1.
63. *Dekrety*, I, 172–74. Its history can be found in V. Z. Drobizhev, *Glavnyi shtab sotsialisticheskoi promyshlennosti* (Moscow, 1966), and Tsyperovich, *Sindikaty i tresty*, 373–511.
64. *EZh*, No. 261 (November 9, 1920), 1.
65. Pollock, *Planwirtschaftlichen Versuche*, 80.
66. Liberman, *Building*, 67; A. Gurovich in *ARR*, VI (1922), 319.
67. Gurovich, *loc. cit.*
68. On him, see his autobiographical sketch in *Granat*, XLI, Pt. 1, 272–82, and recollections in *NKh*, No. 11 (1918), 16–23. Also Liberman, *Building*, 20–23.
69. Iu. Larin [M. Lure], *Pis'ma o Germanii* (Petrograd, n.d.).
70. See his letter in *Revoliutsiia*, IV, 383–84.
71. Rykov in *NKh*, No. 10 (1918), 31–32.
72. V. Miliutin, *La Nationalisation de l'Industrie* (Moscow, 1919), 8–9.
73. *Dekrety*, II, 498–503.
74. Larin in *NKh*, No. 11 (1918), 20; Liberman, *Building*, 24–26.
75. Larin, *loc. cit.*
76. L. N. Kritsman, *Geroicheskii period Velikoi Russkoi Revoliutsii* (Moscow-Leningrad, 1926), 64, 131–32.
77. *Ibid.*, 62.
78. G. G. Shvittau, *Revoliutsiia i narodnoe khoziaistvo v Rossii (1917–21)* (Leipzig, 1922), 74.
79. A full list is in Kritsman, *Geroicheskii period*, 103–4.
80. Larin in *NKh*, No. 9–10 (1922), 40.
81. On these, see A. Vainshtein in *NKh*, No. 5–6 (1920), 54–56.
82. V. P. Miliutin, *Narodnoe Khoziaistvo Sovetskoi Rossii* (Moscow, 1920), Appendix.
83. *Deviatyi S"ezd RKP (b)*, 104.
84. Litvinov in *Pravda*, No. 262 (November 21, 1920), 1.
85. R. Arskii in *EZh*, No. 14 (November 23, 1918), 1.
86. A. Kaktyn in *NKh*, No. 4 (1919), 16–19.
87. Vainshtein in *NKh*, No. 5–6 (1920), 54–55.
88. Gurovich in *ARR*, VI (1922), 315–16.
89. Trotsky, *Arbeit*, 11–13; Lenin, *PSS*, XXXVI, 380–81.
90. G. K. Guins, *Sibir', Soiuzniki i Kolchak*, II (Peking, 1921), 429.
91. Examples in Carr, *Bolshevik Revolution*, II, 186.
92. Drobizhev, *Glavnyi shtab*, 121.
93. E.g., G. Krumin in *EZh*, No. 230 (October 15, 1919), 1.
94. Kritsman, *Geroicheskii period*, 163–64.
95. *Ibid.*, 190.
96. Lenin, *PSS*, XLIV, 326.
97. Kritsman, *Geroicheskii period*, 153–54.
98. *Ibid.*, 154–55.
99. *Ibid.*, 155.
100. *EZh*, No. 215 (September 28, 1920), 1, and No. 219 (October 2, 1920), 1.
101. S. Strumilin, in *EZh*, No. 225 (October 9, 1920), 2.
102. Kritsman, *Geroicheskii period*, 184–85.
103. *Vosmoi S"ezd RKP (b)*, 407.
104. On them, Scheibert, *Lenin*, 254–62.
105. *Dekrety*, IV, 491–508.
106. Kritsman, *Geroicheskii period*, 113.
107. *Ibid.*, 220.
108. *Ibid.*, 141.

109. *Dekrety,* XII, 10–12; *Dekrety,* XI, 43–45; *SUiR,* 1921, No. 6, art. 47, cited in Carr, *Bolshevik Revolution,* II, 260; Malle, *War Communism,* 181–82.
110. Pollock, *Plantwirtschaftlichen Versuche,* 70–71.
111. E. Gan in *Izvestiia,* No. 243 (October 30, 1920), 1. Cf. Kritsman, *Geroicheskii period,* 133.
112. Kritsman, *Geroicheskii period,* 140.
113. A. Lositskii in *EZh,* No. 111 (May 25, 1920), 1.
114. Kritsman, *Geroicheskii period,* 139.
115. A. Goldschmidt, *Moskau 1920* (Berlin, 1920), 30, 87–88.
116. V. Beliaev, *Ispoved' komissara* (New York, 1921), 8–10.
117. Kritsman, *Geroicheskii period,* 140.
118. *EZh,* No. 36 (February 18, 1920), 1.
119. Carr, *Bolshevik Revolution,* II, 244.
120. L. Trotskii, *Sochineniia,* XII (Moscow, n.d.), 128–29.
121. *Deviatyi S"ezd RKP (b),* 91.
122. *Tretii Vserossiiskii S"ezd Professional'nykh Soiuzov: Stenograficheskiie Otchët,* Pt. 1 (Moscow, 1921), 87–88.
123. *Ibid.,* 89.
124. *Odinadtsatyi S"ezd RKP (b),* 37–38.
125. *Ibid.,* 103–4.
126. *Kommunisticheskaia Partiia Sovetskogo Soiuza v Rezoliutsiakh i Resheniiakh S"ezdov, Konferentsii, Plenumov TsK,* 7th ed., I (Moscow, 1953), 351.
127. Lenin, *PSS,* XXXIV, 193.
128. *Vtoroi Vserossiiskii S"ezd Sovetov Rabochikh i Soldatskikh Deputatov* (Moscow-Leningrad, 1928), 165.
129. *Dekrety,* I, 226.
130. *Ibid.,* 322; based on Lenin's draft, *ibid.,* 316.
131. *Ibid.,* III, 461–63.
132. *Izvestiia,* No. 279/126 (December 11, 1920), 2.
133. M. Dewar, *Labour Policy in the USSR, 1917–1928* (New York, 1956), 174–99.
134. Trotskii, *Sochineniia,* XV (Moscow-Leningrad, 1927), 126.
135. Liberman, *Building,* 19.
136. L. Trotskii, *Kak vooruzhalas' revoliutsiia,* II, Pt. 2 (Moscow, 1924), 33–36.
137. Cited in Carr, *Bolshevik Revolution,* II, 210.
138. Dewar, *Labour Policy,* 213.
139. Liberman, *Building,* 73.
140. Trotskii, *Sochineniia,* XII, 160.
141. *Dekrety,* I, 77–85; Malle, *War Communism,* 93.
142. M. Brinton, *The Bolsheviks and Worker's Control: 1917 to 1921* (London, 1970), 16.
143. *Ibid.,* 18.
144. *Pervyi Vserossiiskii S"ezd Professional'nykh Soiuzov 7–17 Ianvariia 1918 g.* (Moscow, 1918).
145. *Vtoroi Vserossiiskii S"ezd Professional'nykh Soiuzov* Pt. I (Moscow, 1921), 97.
146. *Ibid.*
147. Trotskii, *Kak vooruzhalas',* II, Pt. 2, 78.
148. P. A. Garvi, *Professional'nye soiuzy v Rossii v pervye gody revoliutsii* (New York, 1958), 46.
149. Iu. Milonov, *Putevoditel' po rezoliutsiiam Vserossiiskikh S"ezdov i Konferentsii Professional'nykh Soiuzov* (Moscow, 1924), 61.
150. *Pervyi Vserossiiskii S"ezd Professional'nykh Soiuzov,* 367.
151. J. Sorenson, *The Life and Death of Soviet Trade Unionism: 1917–28* (New York, 1969), 37–38.
152. Kritsman, *Geroicheskii period,* 165, 186.
153. *Pravda,* No. 30 (February 11, 1921), 1. Also Larin in *EZh,* No. 173 (August 7, 1920), 1.
154. G. Krumin in *EZh,* No. 118 (June 3, 1920), 1.

Chapter 16

1. *Das Kapital,* I, Chap. 15, Sec. 10. On this subject, see D. Mitrany, *Marx Against the Peasant* (Chapel Hill, N.C., 1951).

2. H. Willets in L. Schapiro and P. Reddaway, eds., *Lenin: The Man, the Theorist, the Leader* (London, 1967), 212.
3. "Agrarnyi vopros i sotsial'naia demokratiia v Rossii," in *Doklad delegatsii Russkikh Sotsial-Demokratov na mezhdunarodnom sotsialisticheskom kongresse v Londone v 1896 godu* (Geneva, 1896). Written by P. B. Struve.
4. Lenin, *PSS,* VI, 310.
5. *Ibid.,* 347–48.
6. E.g., *ibid.,* XXXVII, 352–64.
7. N. Orlov cited by V. V. Kabanov in *IZ,* No. 82 (1968), 28.
8. *Pravda,* No. 240 (November 5, 1918), 2. Further on this subject: V. V. Kabanov, *Krest'ianskoe khoziaistvo v usloviiakh "Voennogo Kommunizma,"* (Moscow, 1988), 22–32.
9. A.T. in *Svoboda Rossii,* No. 26 (May 16, 1918), 6.
10. Iu. A. Poliakov in *Istoriia sovetskogo krest'ianstva i kolkhoznogo stroitel'stva v SSSR* (Moscow, 1963), 16.
11. *Ibid.,* 16; Dorothy Atkinson, *The End of the Russian Land Commune, 1905–1930* (Stanford, Calif., 1983), 178–80.
12. V. P. Danilov, *Pereraspredelenie zemel'nogo fonda Rossii* (Moscow, 1979), 283–87, cited in Kabanov, *Krest'ianskoe khoziaistvo,* 49.
13. Ia. Bliakher in *Vestnik statistiki,* XIII, No. 1–3 (1923), 138.
14. *Ibid.,* 146–47.
15. V. R. Gerasimiuk in *ISSSR,* No. 1 (1965), 100.
16. *O zemle: sbornik statei,* I (1921), 9.
17. Ia. Piletskii in *NZh,* No. 18/232 (January 25/February 7, 1918), 1.
18. A. M. Anfimov, in *VI,* No. 1 (1955), 111–12.
19. Kabanov, *Krest'ianskoe khoziaistvo,* 50–51.
20. *Ibid.,* 52–53.
21. *BSE,* L, 359.
22. I. V. Nazarov in *NZh,* No. 50/265 (March 24, 1918), 1.
23. A. M. Anfimov and I. F. Makarov in *ISSSR,* No. 1 (1974), 85.
24. D. Thorniley, *The Rise and Fall of the Soviet Rural Communist Party, 1927–1939* (Birmingham, 1988), 10.
25. Gerasimiuk in *ISSSR,* No. 1 (1965), 100.
26. *Ibid.,* 102.
27. *Dekrety,* I, 410.
28. Gerasimiuk in *ISSSR,* No. 1 (1965), 100.
29. Atkinson, *Russian Commune,* 185.
30. V. R. Gerasimiuk, *Nachalo sotsialisticheskoi revoliutsii v derevne* (Moscow, 1958), 73; emphasis supplied.
31. Kabanov, *Krest'ianskoe khoziaistvo,* 182.
32. See above, pp. 697–98.
33. *NZh,* No. 12/226 (January 18/31, 1918), 1.
34. *Ibid.*
35. *NZh,* No. 25/239 (February 15, 1918), 4.
36. *NZh,* No. 100/315 (May 26, 1918), 1.
37. B. Brutzkus in *Quellen und Studien,* N.F., No. 2 (Berlin, 1925), 160, cited in Friedrich Pollock, *Die Planwirtschaftlichen Versuche in der Sowjetunion, 1917–1927* (Leipzig, 1929), 71.
38. Poliakov in *Istoriia sovetskogo krest'ianstva,* 38.
39. *Dekrety,* I, 406; *NZh,* No. 82/297 (May 3, 1918), 4.
40. *ND,* No. 1 (February 1/14, 1918), 1.
41. E.g., *NZh,* No. 41/256 (March 14, 1918), 4.
42. Reprinted in *NZh,* No. 39/254 (March 10, 1918), 4.
43. *NZh,* No. 79/294 (April 28, 1918), 4.
44. N. Orlov, *Deviat' mesiatsev prodovol'stvennoi raboty sovetskoi vlasti* (Moscow, 1918), 44–45. I owe this reference to Mr. Leonid Heretz.
45. *NZh,* No. 98/313 (May 24, 1918), 3.
46. *LS,* XVIII, 81.

47. Orlov, *Deviat' mesiatsev,* 82.
48. *SV,* No. 4 (March 18, 1921), 4.
49. Tsiurupa in *Piatyi Vserossiiskii S"ezd Sovetov: Stenograficheskii Otchët* (Moscow, 1918), 140–41.
50. *Dekrety,* I, 459–60; cf. *LS,* XVIII, 78–79.
51. E.g., *Dekrety,* I, 502.
52. *NZh,* No. 29/243 (February 20, 1918), 1.
53. Lenin, *Sochineniia,* XXIII, 542.
54. *Dekrety,* II, 48–50.
55. *LS,* XVIII, 92.
56. *NZh,* No. 99/314 (May 25, 1918), 1.
57. *Protokoly zasedanii Vserossiiskogo Tsentral'nogo Ispolnitel'nogo Komiteta 4-go Sozyva* (Moscow, 1920), 294.
58. Cited in *NZh,* No. 71/286 (April 19, 1918), 1.
59. Richard Pipes, *Struve: Liberal on the Left, 1870–1905* (Cambridge, Mass., 1970), 129–30.
60. A. L. Okninskii, *Dva goda sredi krest'ian* (Riga, [1936]), 93.
61. On this subject, see C. Frierson, *From Narod to Kulak: Peasant Images in Russia, 1870 to 1885,* Ph.D. Dissertation, 1985, Harvard University.
62. Lenin, *PSS,* XXXVIII, 197.
63. V. P. Antonov-Saratovskii, ed., *Sovety v epokhu voennogo kommunizma, 1918–21,* I (Moscow, 1928), 131.
64. *NZh,* No. 117/332 (June 19, 1918), 3.
65. E.g., Lenin, *PSS,* XXXVII, 354–55.
66. Lenin, *PSS,* XXXVII, 40.
67. *Ibid.,* III, 62, and XVI, 205.
68. *Ibid.,* XXXVIII, 255.
69. F. Engels, "Prefatory Note to *The Peasant War in Germany,*" in K. Marx and F. Engels *Selected Works,* I (Moscow, 1962), 647.
70. Lenin, *PSS,* XXVII, 226.
71. V. P. Miliutin, *Agrarnaia politika SSSR* (Moscow-Leningrad, 1929), 106.
72. *Ibid.*
73. *Dekrety,* II, 264–66; *LS,* XVIII, 82–88.
74. *LS,* XVIII, 82.
75. E.g., *NZh,* No. 71/286 (April 19, 1918), 4.
76. John L. H. Keep, *The Russian Revolution* (London, 1976), 424.
77. *Dekrety,* II, 298–301.
78. *NZh,* No. 99 (May 25, 1918), 4, and No. 102/317 (May 29, 1918), 3.
79. *Ibid.,* No. 104/319 (May 31, 1918), 1.
80. *NZh,* No. 105/320 (June 1, 1918), 1.
81. Lenin, *Khronika,* VI, 313, 369, 507, 542. See *EZh,* No. 17 (November 27, 1918), 1–2, for a description of the type of person who enrolled in these detachments.
82. *Dekrety,* II, 387.
83. See, e.g., speech by Tsiurupa in *Piatyi S"ezd Sovetov,* 144.
84. *Dekrety,* III, 178–80.
85. *LS,* XVIII, 93–94.
86. *NZh,* No. 112/327 (June 9, 1918), 3.
87. Atkinson, *Russian Commune,* 191–93.
88. Teodor Shanin, *The Awkward Class* (Oxford, 1972), 147.
89. *NV,* No. 97/121 (June 20, 1918), 4.
90. V. Kerzhentsev in *Izvestiia,* No. 15/567 (January 22, 1919), 1.
91. M. Ia. Latsis, *Dva goda bor'by na vnutrennem fronte* (Moscow, 1920), 75.
92. L. M. Spirin, *Klassy i partii v grazhdanskoi voine v Rossii, 1917–1920 gg.* (Moscow, 1968), 185.
93. *Ocherki istorii Cheliabinskoi Oblastnoi partiinoi organizatsii* (Cheliabinsk, 1967), 94.
94. Additional information: Okninskii, *Dva goda,* 128–51; *NZh,* No. 71/286 (April 19, 1918), 4; Gerasimiuk, *Nachalo,* 84–85; L. G. Sytov, ed., *Penzenskaia organizatsiia KPSS v gody grazhdanskoi voiny* (Penza, 1960), 87–99; *LS,* XVIII, 202–5; Antonov-Saratovskii, *Sovety,* I, 151.
95. M. Frenkin, *Tragediia krest'ianskikh vosstanii* ([Jerusalem, 1987]), 79, 85–88.

96. Lenin, *PSS,* L, 126–27.
97. *LS,* XVIII, 145.
98. *Ibid.,* 146.
99. *Ibid.,* 203.
100. *Dekrety,* III, 178–80.
101. *LS,* XVIII, 146.
102. Keep, *Russian Revolution,* 462.
103. Lenin, *PSS,* XXXIX, 407.
104. *Dekrety,* III, 224–26.
105. Antonov-Saratovskii, *Sovety,* I, 54–56.
106. Kamkov in *Piatyi S"ezd Sovetov,* 75.
107. *Dekrety,* II, 295, 416–20.
108. *Protokoly . . . VTsIK 4-ogo Sozyva,* 398–419.
109. V. R. Gerasimiuk in *ISSSR,* No. 4 (1960), 122, 125.
110. V. N. Averev, ed., *Komitety bednoty: sbornik materialov,* I (Moscow-Leningrad, 1933), 120.
111. Gerasimiuk in *ISSSR,* No. 4 (1960), 122.
112. Averev, *Komitety bednoty,* I, 183.
113. E. G. Gimpel'son, *Sovety v gody interventsii i grazhdanskoi voiny* (Moscow, 1968), 68.
114. Lenin, *PSS,* XXXVII, 181.
115. *Dekrety,* III, 540–41.
116. *Ibid.,* IV, 112–19.
117. Cf. Gimpel'son, *Sovety, passim.*
118. *Ibid.,* 49.
119. Antonov-Saratovskii, *Sovety,* I, 264, 405.
120. Gimpel'son, *Sovety,* 54.
121. Antonov-Saratovskii, *Sovety,* I, 129.
122. *Ibid.,* 439; also 264, 435.
123. L. N. Kritsman, *Geroicheskii period Velikoi Russkoi Revoliutsii* (Moscow-Leningrad, 1926), 155.
124. Bertrand Russell, *Bolshevism: Practice and Theory* (New York, 1920), 37.
125. J. M. Meijer in Richard Pipes, ed., *Revolutionary Russia* (Cambridge, Mass., 1968), 268.
126. *LS,* XVIII, 143–44.
127. E.g., speech of December 11, 1918, in Lenin, *PSS,* XXXVII, 361.
128. *RM,* No. 9/12 (1923–24), 200.
129. Kabanov, *Krest'ianskoe khoziaistvo,* 202.
130. Shanin, *Awkward Class,* 164–69.
131. Lenin, *PSS,* XXXVII, 354; emphasis supplied.

Chapter 17

1. Sverdlov addressing the Central Executive Committee (CEC) on May 9, 1918, in *Protokoly zasedanii Vserossiiskogo Tsentral'nogo Ispolnitelnogo Komiteta 4-go Sozyva* (Moscow, 1920), 240.
2. *NV,* No. 63/87 (April 2, 1918), 3.
3. Simon Liberman, *Building Lenin's Russia* (Chicago, 1945), 56–57.
4. George Buchanan to A. Balfour, September 8, 1917, Public Record Office (London), F.O. 371/3015.
5. Lenin, *Khronika,* V, 165–66.
6. *NZh,* No. 43/258 (March 16, 1918), 1.
7. *NZh,* No. 51/266 (March 26, 1918), 3; *NV,* No. 73/97 (April 4, 1918), 3.
8. Lenin, *PSS,* XXI, 17.
9. *NS,* No. 1 (April 13, 1918), 2; *NV,* No. 73/97 (April 14, 1918), 3.
10. *NVCh,* No. 65 (April 22, 1918), 1.
11. A. D. Avdeev in *KN,* No. 5 (1928), 187.
12. G. Lefebvre, *The French Revolution* (New York, 1962), 270.

13. P. M. Bykov, "Poslednie dni poslednego tsaria," in N. I. Nikolaev, ed., *Rabochaia revoliutsiia na Urale* (Ekaterinburg, 1921), 7.

14. P. M. Bykov, *Poslednie dni Romanovykh* (Sverdlovsk, 1926), 89, 307–8; P. Bulygin, *The Murder of the Romanovs* (London, 1935), 203–5; N. A. Sokolov, *Ubiistvo tsarskoi sem'i* (Paris, 1925), 42–43; S. P. Melgunov, *Sud'ba Imperatora Nikolaia II posle otrecheniia* (Paris, 1951), 276–79.

15. I. Koretskii in *PR*, No. 4 (1922), 13.

16. P. Gilliard, *Thirteen Years at the Russian Court* (New York, 1921), 257–58; Melgunov, *Sud'ba*, 250–58.

17. *Protokoly VTsIK 4-go sozyva* (Moscow, 1920), 240–41; cf. Bykov, *Poslednie dni*, 89, and G. Ioffe in *Sovetskaia Rossiia*, No. 161/9, 412 (July 12, 1987), 4.

18. G. Z. Ioffe, *Krakh rossiiskoi monarkhicheskoi kontrrevoliutsii* (Moscow, 1977), 148–57; also *Ural*, No. 7 (1988), 147–50.

19. Bykov, *Poslednie dni*, 90.

20. *Ibid.*, 91.

21. Sokolov, *Ubiistvo*, 44.

22. Avdeev in *KN*, No. 5 (1928), 191.

23. Sokolov, *Ubiistvo*, 45.

24. Iakovlev in *Izvestiia*, No. 96/360 (May 16, 1918), 2.

25. Kobylinskii in Robert Wilton, *The Last Days of the Romanovs* (London, 1920), 206.

26. Iakovlev in *Izvestiia*, No. 96/360 (May 16, 1918), 2.

27. Gilliard, *Thirteen Years*, 260–63.

28. Bykov, *Poslednie dni*, 99.

29. Avdeev in *KN*, No. 5 (1928), 190, 193; Bykov, "Poslednie dni," 10.

30. Isaac Don Levine, *Eyewitness to History* (New York, 1963), 130.

31. M. K. Kasvinov, *Dvadsat' tri stupeni v niz* (Moscow, 1978), 454–55.

32. Iakovlev in *RL*, No. 1 (1921), 152.

33. *Ibid.*

34. Sokolov Archive, Houghton Library, Harvard University, Box 67, pp. 212–13.

35. Bykov, *Poslednie dni*, 97; this is confirmed by the tapes of the conversation between Iakovlev and Sverdlov as summarized by Ioffe in *Sovetskaia Rossiia*, No. 161/9,412 (July 12, 1987), 4; Iakovlev in *Ural*, No. 7 (1988), 162.

36. Avdeev in *KN*, No. 5 (1928), 195–96.

37. Bykov, *Poslednie dni*, 98.

38. *Ibid.*, 100.

39. Iakovlev in *Izvestiia*, No. 96/360 (May 16, 1918), 2.

40. Bykov, *Poslednie dni*, 64–65; Sokolov, *Ubiistvo*, 52.

41. Bykov, "Poslednie dni," 12.

42. Avdeev in *KN*, No. 5 (1928), 199–200.

43. *Ibid*, 197.

44. Sokolov, *Ubiistvo*, 124.

45. Avdeev in *KN*, No. 5 (1928), 203.

46. Sokolov, *Ubiistvo*, 129, 131.

47. Avdeev in *KN*, No. 5 (1928), 203; Bykov, "Poslednie dni," 15.

48. S. S. Bekhteev, *Pesni russkoi skorbi i slëz*, I, (Munich, 1923), 18; Sokolov, *Ubiistvo*, 282. The above translation is from Bulygin, *Murder*, 25–26, with one minor change.

49. Trotsky's Diary, entry for April 9, 1935, in Trotsky Archive, Houghton Library, Harvard University, bMS/Russ 13, T-3731, p. 110.

50. On Grand Duke Michael: O. Poutianine, in *Revue des Deux Mondes*, XVIII (November 1, 1923), 56–78, and XVIII (November 15, 1923), 290–310; G.B. in *Rul'*, No. 2472 (January 13, 1929), 5.

51. Poutianine in *Revue*, 309–10, based on an account of Michael's valet as told to a Swiss acquaintance; see also Sokolov, *Ubiistvo*, 265–66.

52. Bykov, *Poslednie dni*, 121; Sokolov, *Ubiistvo*, 266.

53. Melgunov, *Sud'ba*, 388.

54. *NZh,* No. 120/335 (June 22, 1918), 3; *NV,* No. 96/120 (June 19, 1918), 2; *NVCh,* No. 93 (June 19, 1918), 1. For reports abroad, see *New York Times,* July 1, 1918, 5, and *The Times,* July 3, 1918, 6.

55. *NS,* No. 48 (June 19, 1918) (not available to me), as reported in *NV,* No. 97/121 (June 29, 1918), 3; cf. Lenin, *Khronika,* V, 552.

56. *NV,* No. 100/124 (June 23, 1918), 2.

57. M. K. Diterikhs, *Ubiistvo tsarskoi sem'i i chlenov doma Romanovykh na Urale,* I (Vladivostok, 1922), 61.

58. Avdeev in *KN,* No. 5 (1928), 202. Avdeev mistakenly identifies him as an Austrian.

59. Bykov, "Poslednie dni," 17–18.

60. Serge Smirnoff, *Autour de l' Assassinat des Grand-Ducs* (Paris, 1928), 14–15, 114n., 92–93, 104, 143. Bykov ("Poslednie dni," 18) confirms that Smirnoff was arrested with Mičič (whom he mistakenly calls "Migich").

61. *Rodina,* No. 4 (1989), 95.

62. Avdeev in *KN,* No. 5 (1928), 202.

63. Sokolov, *Ubiistvo,* 147.

64. Trotsky's Diary, *loc. cit.,* p. 111, entry dated April 9, 1935.

65. Bykov, *Poslednie dni,* 106.

66. *Dekrety,* III, 22.

67. *Ibid.,* 21–22; *SUiR,* No. 583, 611–12.

68. Sokolov Archive, Houghton Library, Harvard University, Box 7.

69. Sokolov, *Ubiistvo,* 138.

70. *Ibid.;* Wilton, *The Last Days,* 82.

71. Lenin, *Khronika,* V, 580, 616.

72. Kasvinov, *Dvadsat' tri stupeni,* 489; Bykov, *Poslednie dni,* 114.

73. Bykov, "Poslednie dni," 20.

74. F. McCullagh in *Nineteenth Century and After,* No. 123 (September 1920), 417.

75. Sokolov, *Ubiistvo,* 230–38; *Ogonëk,* No. 21 (1989), 30–32.

76. Sokolov, *Ubiistvo,* 224–29.

77. *Ogonëk,* No. 21 (1989), 30.

78. Sokolov, *Ubiistvo,* 232.

79. *Ibid.,* 219.

80. *Ibid.,* 222–23.

81. *Ibid.,* 254.

82. *Ogonëk,* No. 21 (1989), 30–31.

83. Deposition of P. V. Kukhtenko in Sokolov Dossier I, dated September 8, 1918; omission in the original.

84. Sokolov, *Ubiistvo,* 261.

85. Bulygin, *Murder,* 256.

86. K. Jagow in *BM,* No. 5 (May 1935), 932.

87. Winfried Baumgart, *Deutsche Ostpolitik 1918* (Vienna-Munich, 1966), 337, note 13.

88. Jagow in *BM,* 393.

89. Lenin, *Khronika,* V, 642.

90. Sokolov, *Ubiistvo,* 247–49.

91. *Dekrety,* III, 57–58.

92. V. Miliutin in *Prozhektor,* No. 4 (1924), 10.

93. Jagow in *BM,* 398.

94. *Ibid.,* 399; Karl von Bothmer, *Mit Graf Mirbach in Moskau* (Tübingen, 1922), 103.

95. Jagow in *BM,* 400.

96. Bulygin, *Murder,* 244.

97. Sokolov, *Ubiistvo,* 246, 252–53.

98. Bykov, *Poslednie dni,* 113.

99. Sokolov Archive, Houghton Library, Harvard University, Box 1, No. 67, 212–13.

100. R. H. B. Lockhart, *Memoirs of a British Agent* (London, 1935), 304.

101. Bothmer, *Mit Graf Mirbach,* 98.

102. Cited in Levine, *Eyewitness,* 137.
103. A. L. Okninskii, *Dva goda sredi krest'ian* (Riga, n.d.), 292–93.
104. Smirnoff, *Autour,* 142.
105. P. Paganutstsi, *Pravda ob ubiistve tsarskoi sem'i* (Jordanville, N.J., 1981), 29–30.
106. Bykov, "Poslednie dni," 3–26.
107. *Pravda,* No. 212/7,537 (August 3, 1938), 5; G. Riabov in *Rodina,* No. 5 (1989), 2, 12.
108. *Leninskaia Gvardiia Urala* (Sverdlovsk, 1967), 508; Kasvinov, *Dvadsat' tri stupeni,* 560, note 11.
109. Trotsky's Diary, entry for April 9, 1935, in Trotsky Archive, Houghton Library, Harvard University, bMS/Russ 13, T-3731, p. 111.

Chapter 18

1. *Marx-Engels Briefwechsel,* IV (1913), 329; letter dated September 4, 1870.
2. F. Furet and D. Richet, *La Révolution Française* (Paris, 1973), 10, 203.
3. A. Balabanoff, *My Life as a Rebel* (Bloomington, Ind., 1973), 183–84.
4. See above, p. 349.
5. Lenin, *PSS,* XVI, 452; emphasis supplied.
6. Lenin, *PSS,* XXXV, 204; first published in 1929; emphasis supplied.
7. Andrzej Kaminski, *Konzentrationslager 1896 bis heute: eine Analyse* (Stuttgart, 1982), 86.
8. K. G. Kotelnikov, ed., *Vtoroi Vserossiiskii S"ezd R. i S.D.* (Moscow-Leningrad, 1928), 94.
9. L. Trotskii, *O Lenine* (Moscow, 1924), 101.
10. Lenin, *PSS,* XXXVIII, 295. Emphasis supplied.
11. *DN,* No. 223 (December 3, 1917), 4.
12. *Dekrety,* I, 490–91.
13. Robert Payne, *The Life and Death of Lenin* (New York, 1964), 517.
14. Simon Liberman, *Building Lenin's Russia* (Chicago, 1945), 13–15.
15. Lenin, *PSS,* XXXVII, 245.
16. "Revoliutsionnye Tribunaly," *VZh,* No. 1 (1918), 81.
17. Lenin, *PSS,* XXXVI, 163.
18. *Dekrety,* I, 124–26.
19. *Ibid.,* 469.
20. *Ibid.,* IV, 101.
21. *Ibid.,* I, 125–26.
22. *SUiR,* I, No. 12 (1917–18), 179–81.
23. *Dekrety,* II, 335–39.
24. *Izvestiia,* No. 128/392 (June 23, 1918), 3.
25. M. V. Kozhevnikov, *Istoriia sovetskogo suda, 1917–56 gg.* (Moscow, 1957), 40.
26. *Ibid.*
27. I. Steinberg, *Als ich Volkskommissar war* (Munich, 1929), 123–28.
28. S. Varshavskii in *NS,* No. 4 (April 17, 1918), 1.
29. *SiM,* No. 6 (1985), 65.
30. *NS,* No. 4 (April 17, 1918), 1.
31. Ia. Berman in *PRiP,* No. 1/11 (1919), 70.
32. Kozhevnikov, *Istoriia,* 83.
33. *PR,* No. 10/33 (1924), 5–6; *PR,* No. 9/56 (1926), 82–83; *V. I. Lenin i VChK: Sbornik Dokumentov* (Moscow, 1975), 36–38.
34. *Izvestiia,* No. 248 (December 10/23, 1917), 3.
35. *Lenin i VChK,* 36–37.
36. *PR,* No. 10/33 (1924), 5; M. Pokrovskii in *Pravda,* No. 290/3,822 (December 18, 1927), 2.
37. N. V. Krylenko, *Sudoproizvodstvo RFSSR* (Moscow, 1924), 100, cited in G. Leggett, *The Cheka: Lenin's Political Police* (Oxford, 1986), 18.
38. *NZh,* No. 71/286 (April 19, 1918), 3.
39. P. G. Sofinov, *Ocherki istorii Vserossiiskoi Chrezvychainoi Komissii (1917–22 gg.)* (Moscow, 1960), 21. The higher figure is from Leggett, *Cheka,* 34.

40. Ia. Kh. Peters in *PR*, No. 10/33 (1924), 10–11.
41. I. Steinberg, *In the Workshop of the Revolution* (London, 1955), 145.
42. R. H. B. Lockhart, *Memoirs of a British Agent* (London, 1935), 333.
43. *NZh*, No. 112/327 (June 9, 1918), 4.
44. L. Gerson, *The Secret Police in Lenin's Russia* (Philadelphia, 1976), 27; Leggett, *Cheka*, 47–48.
45. *LS*, XXI, 111–12.
46. *Ibid.*, 112–13.
47. *Ibid.*, 113–14.
48. Gerson, *Secret Police*, 30.
49. Sofinov, *Ocherki*, 23.
50. D. L. Golinkov, *Krushenie antisovetskogo podpol'ia v SSSR*, I (Moscow, 1980), 62.
51. *Dekrety*, I, 490–91.
52. *Izvestiia*, No. 32/296 (February 10/23, 1918), 1.
53. *Iz istorii Vserossiiskoi Chrezvychainoi Komissii, 1917–1921 gg.* (Moscow, 1958), 96–98.
54. Leggett, *Cheka*, 58; details in *IR*, No. 7/300 (February 7, 1931), 6–9.
55. Sofinov, *Ocherki*, 39.
56. *Iz istorii VChK*, 138. Other important resolutions in Leggett, *Cheka*, 38–39.
57. Lockhart, *Memoirs*, 320.
58. G. Semenov [Vasilev], *Voennaia i boevaia rabota Partii Sotsialistov-Revoliutsionerov za 1917–18 gg.* (Berlin, 1922).
59. Balabanoff, *Life as a Rebel*, 187–88.
60. V. Bonch-Bruevich, *Tri pokusheniia na V. I. Lenina* (Moscow, 1930), 98.
61. N. N. Sukhanov, *Zapiski o revoliutsii*, III (Berlin-Petersburg-Moscow, 1922), 23, 26.
62. *LN*, LXXX (1971), 52.
63. Richard Pipes, *Russia under the Old Regime* (New York, 1974), 309; *Iz istorii VChK*, 263–64.
64. Liberman, *Building*, 9.
65. J. Monnerot, *Sociology and Psychology of Communism* (Boston, 1953), 223.
66. See L. V. Bulgakova, *Materialy dlia bibliografii Lenina, 1917–23* (Leningrad, 1924).
67. Cf. *Izvestiia*, No. 190/454 (September 4, 1918), 6–7.
68. V. Bonch–Bruevich, *Tri pokusheniia na V. I. Lenina* (Moscow, 1930), 103.
69. G. Zinoviev cited in Nina Tumarkin, *Lenin Lives!* (Cambridge, Mass., 1983), 82; L. Cerfaux and J. Tondriau, *Le Culte des Souverains dans la Civilisation Greco-Romaine* (Tournai, 1957), 291.
70. For examples, see Tumarkin, *Lenin*, 83–86.
71. Cerfaux and Tondriau, *Le Culte*, 427.
72. W. S. Ferguson in *The Cambridge Ancient History*, VII (Cambridge, 1928), 21.
73. Melgunov Archive, Hoover Institution, Box 4, Folder 26.
74. *Ibid.*
75. Lenin, *PSS*, XXXVI, 196.
76. *Ibid.*, L, 106.
77. *Ibid.*, 142.
78. *Izvestiia*, No. 134/398 (June 30, 1918), 3.
79. *Ibid.*, No. 181/445 (August 23, 1918), 2.
80. *Ibid.*, No. 190/454 (September 4, 1918), 5.
81. *Dekrety*, III, 291–92.
82. See, for instance, Chap. 16 above.
83. SUiR, I (1917–18), 777.
84. *Izvestiia*, No. 189/453 (September 3, 1918), 4.
85. *Ibid.*
86. *Ezhenedel'nik VChK*, No. 2 (September 29, 1918), 11.
87. *Severnaia kommuna*, No. 109 (September 19, 1918), 2, cited in Leggett, *Cheka*, 114.
88. *Krasnaia gazeta*, September 1, 1918, cited in Leggett, *Cheka*, 108.
89. Karl Radek in *Izvestiia*, No. 192/456 (September 6, 1918), 1.
90. Grigorii Aronson, *Na zare krasnogo terrora* (Berlin, 1929), 56.
91. *Cheka i materialy po deiatel'nosti Chrezvychainykh Komissii* (Berlin, 1922), 80.
92. Steinberg, *In the Workshop*, 163; Aronson, *Na zare*, 27.

93. See above, Chap. 12.
94. Steinberg, *In the Workshop,* 227.
95. *IR,* No. 9/302 (February 21, 1931), 8–9.
96. Melgunov Archive, Hoover Institution, Box 4, Folder 26, pp. 9–10.
97. *NChS* (Berlin-Prague), No. 9 (1925), 111–41.
98. D. Venner, *Histoire de l'Armée Rouge* (Paris, 1981), 141.
99. Zinoviev in *Ezhenedel'nik VChK,* No. 6 (October 27, 1918), 21; K. Alinin in *Cheka* (Odessa, 1919), 3. Further on fears of the Cheka in Bolshevik ranks: Alfons Paquet, *Im kommunistischen Russland* (Jena, 1919), 124–25.
100. *Pravda,* No. 216 (October 8, 1918), 1.
101. *Petrogradskaia Pravda,* No. 237/463 (October 29, 1918), 1.
102. Golinkov, *Krushenie,* I, 232.
103. *Ezhenedel'nik VChK,* No. 3 (October 6, 1918), 7–8.
104. *Vechernye Izvestiia,* No. 161 (February 3, 1919).
105. N. Moskovskii in *Petrogradskaia Pravda,* No. 237/463 (October 29, 1918), 1.
106. N. Zubov, *F. E. Dzerzhinskii: Biografiia,* 3rd ed. (Moscow, 1971), 80–81.
107. Cited by Krylenko in *Izvestiia,* No. 25/577 (February 4, 1919), 1.
108. E.g., G. Moroz in *VS,* No. 11 (1919), 4–6, and Zinoviev in *Ezhenedel'nik VChK,* No. 6 (October 27, 1918), 10.
109. Leggett, *Cheka,* 69.
110. *Kievskie Izvestiia,* No. 44 (May 17, 1919).
111. *Dekrety,* III, 458–59.
112. Golinkov, *Krushenie,* I, 232.
113. *Izvestiia,* No. 17/569 (January 25, 1919), 3.
114. *Vechernye Izvestiia,* No. 159 (January 31, 1919); cf. Krylenko in *Izvestiia,* No. 25/577 (February 4, 1919), 1.
115. *Lenin i VChK,* 144–45.
116. E.g., N. Norov in *Vechernye Izvestiia,* No. 172 (February 15, 1919).
117. N. V. Krylenko, *Sud i pravo v SSSR,* cited in Melgunov Archive, Hoover Institution, Box 4, Folder 25.
118. Leggett, *Cheka,* 216.
119. *IA,* No. 1 (1958), 8–9.
120. I. Polikarenko, ed., *Osoboe zadanie* (Moscow, 1977), illustration between pp. 296 and 297.
121. Leggett, *Cheka,* 208–9, 238.
122. Liberman, *Building,* 14–15.
123. Leggett, *Cheka,* 93.
124. *Ibid.,* 210.
125. *Ibid.,* 212–13.
126. L. Trotskii in *Izvestiia,* No. 171 (August 11, 1918), 1.
127. *IA,* No. 1 (1958), 10.
128. *Dekrety,* IV, 400–2.
129. *Ibid.,* V, 69–70.
130. *Ibid.,* 174–81.
131. D. J. Dallin and B. I. Nicolaevsky, *Forced Labor in Soviet Russia* (New Haven, Conn., 1947), 299.
132. *Dekrety,* V, 511–12.
133. Kaminski, *Konzentrationslager,* 87.
134. A. Solzhenitsyn cited in Kaminski, *Konzentrationslager,* 87. See further James Bunyan, *The Origin of Forced Labor in the Soviet State: 1917–1921* (Baltimore, 1967).
135. *Cheka i materialy,* 242–47.
136. Kaminski, *Konzentrationslager,* 82–83.
137. Boris Nikolaevskii in *SV,* No. 8–9/732–733 (1959), 167–72; G. H. Leggett in *Survey,* No. 2/107 (1979), 193–99.
138. Leggett, *Cheka,* 464; M. Ia. Latsis, *Dva goda bor'by na vnutrennem fronte* (Moscow, 1920), 75.
139. *Otchët Tsentral'nogo Upravleniia Chrezvychainykh Komissii pri Sovnarkome Ukrainy za 1929*

god (Kharkov, 1921), in W. H. Chamberlin, *The Russian Revolution, 1917–21,* II (New York, 1935), 75.

140. Lower figure in K. Alinin, *Tche-Ka* (London, n.d.), 65, higher in Leggett, *Cheka,* 464.
141. Chamberlin, *Revolution,* II, 75; Leggett, *Cheka,* 359.
142. I. Steinberg, *Gewalt und Terror in der Revolution* (Berlin, 1974), 16.
143. *Ibid.,* 138–39.
144. *The Bullitt Mission to Russia* (New York, 1919), 115.
145. Pierre Pascal, *En Russie Rouge* (Petrograd, 1920), 6.
146. International Committee for Political Prisoners, *Letters from Russian Prisons* (New York, 1925), 2, 15, 13.

Afterword

1. A. Ksiunin in *VO,* No. 55 (June 22, 1918), 1.

ONE HUNDRED WORKS ON THE
RUSSIAN REVOLUTION

The following selection of literature on the Russian Revolution is admittedly subjective: I have chosen books from which I have learned the most. Unfortunately, although the serious literature in Western languages increases each year, the bulk of the material is still in Russian. Additional references will be found in the footnotes and endnotes.

Part I

The best general surveys of the final years of the monarchy are by Bernard Pares, who was both an eyewitness and a historian: *Russia and Reform* (London, 1907) and *The Fall of the Russian Monarchy* (London, 1929). There exists a sympathetic history of Nicholas II by S. S. Oldenburg, *Tsarstvovanie Imperatora Nikolaia II* [*The Reign of Emperor Nicholas II*], 2 vols. (Belgrade-Munich, 1939–49). It has been translated as *Last Tsar: Nicholas II, His Reign and His Russia*, 4 vols. (Gulf Breeze, Fla., 1975–78). Anatole Leroy-Beaulieu's three-volume *The Empire of the Tsars and the Russians* (New York-London, 1898) is a comprehensive survey of Imperial Russia in the 1880s. The reader may also wish to consult my *Russia under the Old Regime* (London-New York, 1974), which interprets the course of Russia's political and social history.

There exists a unique source of testimonies by high officials on the last years of the old regime taken by a commission of the Provisional Government and published under the editorship of P. E. Shcheglovitov: *Padenie tsarskogo rezhima* [*The Fall of the Tsarist Regime*], 7 vols. (Leningrad, 1924–27). Selections from it have been published in French: *La Chute du Régime Tsariste: Interrogatoires* (Paris, 1927). A six-volume "chronicle" of the year 1917 edited by N. Avdeev *et al., Revoliutsiia 1917: khronika sobytii* [*The Revolution of 1917: A Chronicle of Events*] (Moscow, 1923–30), delivers much more than its title promises, for it contains a wealth of information from rare and unpublished contemporary sources.

Of the memoir literature on late Imperial Russia, the most outstanding are the recollections of Sergei Witte, *Vospominaniia* [*Memoirs*], 3 vols. (Moscow, 1960). The one-volume English condensation by Abraham Yarmolinsky, *Memoirs of Count Witte* (London-Garden City, N.Y., 1921), is a pale shadow of the original. Very informative on the mentality of the high Imperial bureaucracy are the recollections of State Secretary S. E. Kryzhanovskii, *Vospominaniia* [*Memoirs*] (Berlin, [1938]). The recollections of the liberal leader Paul Miliukov appeared posthumously: *Vospominaniia* [*Memoirs*] (New York, 1955) (in English: *Political Memoirs, 1905–1917*, Ann Arbor, Mich., 1967). Dmitrii Shipov, a leading liberal-conservative, wrote

Vospominaniia i dumy o perezhitom [*Recollections and Reflections on the Past*] (Moscow, 1918).

The best study of the late Imperial bureaucracy unfortunately remains unpublished: Theodore Taranovsky, *The Politics of Counter-Reform: Autocracy and Bureaucracy in the Reign of Alexander III, 1881–1894*, Ph.D. Dissertation, 1976, Harvard University.

On the peasants, outstanding are the personal observations of A. N. Engelgardt, *Iz derevni* [*From the Village*] (Moscow, 1987), and Stepniak [S. M. Kravchinskii], *The Russian Peasantry* (New York, 1888). Theodore Shanin's *The Awkward Class* (Oxford, 1972) is a study of Russian peasants under tsarist and Communist rule.

On the phenomenon of the intelligentsia, there is an informative collection of essays edited by George B. de Huszar, *The Intellectuals* (London and Glencoe, Ill., 1960). There exists no satisfactory history of the Russian intelligentsia in the twentieth century. On the Socialists-Revolutionaries, there is Manfred Hildermeier's *Die Sozialrevolutionäre Partei Russlands* [*The Russian Socialist-Revolutionary Party*] (Köln-Vienna, 1978). On the Social-Democrats, the reader may consult Leonard Schapiro's *The Communist Party of the Soviet Union* (New York, 1960) and John L. H. Keep's *The Rise of Social Democracy in Russia* (Oxford, 1963). On the early liberals, Shmuel Galai has written *The Liberation Movement in Russia, 1900–1905* (Cambridge, 1973). The four-volume *Obshchestvennoe dvizhenie v Rossii v nachale XX-go veka* [*Public Currents in Russia at the Beginning of the Twentieth Century*] (St. Petersburg, 1910–14), edited by Martov and other Mensheviks, provides an intelligent if partisan survey. Revolutionary terrorism is recounted in A. Spiridovich's *Histoire du Terrorisme Russe, 1886–1917* (Paris, 1930). My two-volume biography, *Struve: Liberal on the Left (1870–1905)* (Cambridge, Mass., 1970) and *Struve: Liberal on the Right (1905–1944)* (Cambridge, Mass., 1980), deals with an outstanding Russian intellectual of the age who evolved from Marxism to liberalism and ended up as a monarchist.

The first Russian Revolution is the subject of Abraham Ascher's *The Revolution of 1905* (Stanford, Calif., 1988); a sequel, dealing with 1906, is in progress. Andrew M. Verner's *Nicholas II and the Role of the Autocrat during the First Russian Revolution, 1904–1907*, Ph.D. Dissertation, Columbia University, 1986, supplies much archival information on tsarist policies.

The 1906 Fundamental Laws are translated and analyzed in M. Szeftel's *The Russian Constitution of April 23, 1906* (Brussels, 1976).

The Duma period is discussed in G. A. Hosking, *The Russian Constitutional Experiment* (Cambridge, 1973). The best history of Stolypin's administration, alas, is available only in Polish: Ludwig Bazylow, *Ostatnie lata Rosji Carskiej: Rzady Stolypina* [*The Final Years of Tsarism: The Rule of Stolypin*], (Warsaw, 1972). Stolypin's peasant policies are the subject of S. M. Dubrovskii's *Stolypinskaia zemel'naia reforma* [*Stolypin's Agrarian Reform*] (Moscow, 1963). Materials on his assassination have been collected by A. Serebrennikov, *Ubiistvo Stolypina: svidetel'stva i dokumenty* [*The Murder of Stolypin: Testimonies and Documents*] (New York, 1986).

Russia at war is treated by Norman Stone, *The Eastern Front, 1914–1917* (London and New York, 1975). A. Knox's *With the Russian Army*, 2 vols. (London, 1921), is an informative account by the British military attaché. V. A. Emets in *Ocherki vneshnei politiki Rossii, 1914–17* [*Outlines of Russia's Foreign Policy, 1914–17*] (Moscow, 1977) and V. S. Diakin's *Russkaia burzhuaziia i tsarizm v gody pervoi mirovoi voiny (1914–1917)* [*The Russian Bourgeoisie and Tsarism during the World War (1914–1917)*] (Leningrad, 1967) provide analyses of the political situation in Russia during World War I, relatively free of customary Soviet distortions. The same holds true of the book by the Polish historian Ludwig Bazylow, *Obalenie caratu* [*The Overthrow of Tsarism*] (Warsaw, 1976). There is much to be learned from A. I. Spiridovich's *Velikaia voina i fevral'skaia revoliutsiia, 1914–1918 gg.* [*The Great War and the February Revolution*], 3 vols. (New York, 1962). The economic antecedents of the Revolution are treated by A. L. Sidorov's *Ekonomicheskoe polozhenie Rossii v gody pervoi mirovoi voiny* [*The Economic Situation of Russia during World War I*] (Moscow, 1973).

The letters of Alexandra Fedorovna to Nicholas II during the war have been edited by Bernard Pares: *Letters of the Tsaritsa to the Tsar, 1914–1916* (London, 1923). Nicholas's letters to his wife during this period are available only in a Russian translation in *KA*, No. 4 (1923). Immensely valuable are the minutes of the cabinet meetings in 1915–16, prepared by A. N. Iakhontov in *Arkhiv russkoi revoliutsii*, XVIII (1926); they have been translated by Michael Cherniavsky as *Prelude to Revolution* (Englewood Cliffs, N.J., 1967).

The best treatment of Rasputin is by high officials of the security services: S. P. Beletskii, *Grigorii Rasputin* (Petrograd, 1923), and A. I. Spiridovich, *Raspoutine* (Paris, 1935).

The situation in Russia on the eve of the February Revolution is reflected in the remarkably objective and well-informed confidential reports by the Corps of Gendarmes, published by B. B. Grave under the misleading title *Burzhuaziia nakanune fevral'skoi revoliutsii* [*The Bourgeoisie on the Eve of the February Revolution*] (Moscow-Leningrad, 1927). E. D. Chermenskii's *IV Gosudarstvennaia Duma i sverzhenie tsarizma v Rossii* (Moscow, 1976) is a conventional Communist account that has its uses because of the author's access to archival sources.

The standard history of February 1917 is T. Hasegawa's *The February Revolution: Petrograd, 1917* (Seattle-London, 1981). Very informative is E. I. Martynov's *Tsarskaia armiia v fevral'skom perevorote* [*The Tsarist Army in the February Revolution*] (Leningrad, 1927), which deals with much besides the armed forces and provides solid documentation. S. P. Melgunov's *Martovskie dni* [*The March Days*] (Paris, 1961), as everything by this author, is well informed but contentious and disorganized. Of the memoir literature on 1917, pride of place belongs to the recollections of Nicholas Sukhanov, *Zapiski o revoliutsii* [*Notes on the Revolution*], 7 vols. (Berlin-Petersburg-Moscow, 1922–23), a Menshevik who was directly involved in the events and who had, in addition, uncommon literary gifts. A good part of this work has been translated and edited by Joel Carmichael: N. N. Sukhanov, *The Russian Revolution: A Personal Record* (Oxford, 1955). Paul Miliukov's *Istoriia Vtoroi Russkoi Revoliutsii* [*The History of the Second Russian Revolution*], 2 pts. (Sofia, 1921), is part history, part memoirs. In English: Paul Miliukov, *The Russian Revolution*, 3 vols. (Gulf Breeze, Fla., 1978). A. Shliapnikov's *Semnadtsatyi god* [*The Year 1917*], 3 vols. (Moscow-Leningrad, various dates in the 1920s), are the memoirs of an important Bolshevik. I. G. Tsereteli's *Vospominaniia o Fevral'skoi Revoliutsii*, [*Memoirs of the February Revolution*], 2 vols. (Paris-The Hague, 1963), are an overly long but important account by the Menshevik leader of the Petrograd Soviet. Maxim Gorky's *Untimely Thoughts* (New York, 1968), translated by H. Ermolaev, is a collection of his forceful comments in 1917–18 on the pages of the daily *Novaia zhizn'*.

The basic texts on the abdication of Nicholas II are in P. E. Shchegolev, ed., *Otrechenie Nikolaia II* [*The Abdication of Nicholas II*] (Leningrad, 1927).

Part II

A very good account of Russia in 1917–18 is Volume I of William Henry Chamberlin's *Russian Revolution* (London and New York, 1935). Leon Trotsky's

The Russian Revolution, 3 vols. (New York, 1937), is partly political tract, partly literature. Peter Scheibert's *Lenin an der Macht [Lenin in Power]* (Weinheim, 1984) is a storehouse of little-known information about Russia under Lenin's rule.

On Lenin, several biographies can be recommended. David Shub, a Menshevik with a keen sense for the milieu in which Lenin worked, is the author of *Lenin* (New York, 1948; London, 1966). Adam Ulam's *The Bolsheviks* (New York, 1965; London, 1966) also focuses on the Communist leader. There are insights into his personality in Leon Trotsky's *O Lenine [About Lenin]* (Moscow, 1924) and Maxim Gorky's *Vladimir Il'ich Lenin* (Leningrad, 1924). N. Valentinov's *The Early Years of Lenin* (Ann Arbor, Mich., 1969) is based on personal conversations.

Lenin's return to Russia by way of Germany is discussed and documented in W. Hahlweg's *Lenins Rückkehr nach Russland, 1917 [Lenin's Return to Russia, 1917]* (Leiden, 1957). Essential documents on Lenin's relations with the Germans from the archives of the German Foreign Office have been published by Z. A. B. Zeman, *Germany and the Revolution in Russia, 1915–1918* (London, 1958).

Kerensky edited in collaboration with Robert Browder a three-volume collection of documents under the title *The Russian Provisional Government, 1917* (Stanford, Calif., 1961). His recollections of 1917 are available in several versions, of which the best are *The Catastrophe* (New York-London, 1927) and *Crucifixion of Liberty* (London and New York, 1934). There is an admiring biography by Richard Abraham, *Alexander Kerensky: The First Love of the Revolution* (New York, 1987).

The Provisional Government is viewed from the inside in *V. D. Nabokov and the Russian Provisional Government, 1917* (New Haven-London, 1976), which contains his memoirs as State Secretary. The best account of the rival organization is by Oskar Anweiler, *The Soviets* (New York, 1974).

The July Bolshevik putsch has not yet found an authoritative historian. Many key documents have been published under the editorship of D. A. Chugaev, *Revoliutsionnoe dvizhenie v Rossii v iiule 1917 g. [The Revolutionary Movement in Russia in July 1917]* (Moscow, 1959). There is a great deal of information on this event as well as on other Bolshevik activities during 1917 in the recollections of the head of Kerensky's counterintelligence, Colonel B. Nikitin, *Rokovye gody* (Paris, 1937) (in English: *The Fateful Years,* London, 1938).

John L. H. Keep's *The Russian Revolution* (London, 1976) analyzes the social changes in Russia in 1917–18.

D. A. Chugaev edited a collection of documents on the Kornilov Affair under the title *Revoliutsionnoe dvizhenie v Rossii v avguste 1917 g.: Razgrom Kornilovskogo miatezha [The Revolutionary Movement in Russia in August 1917: The Crushing of Kornilov's Mutiny]* (Moscow, 1959). Of the secondary accounts, the best are by E. I. Martynov, *Kornilov* (Leningrad, 1927) (hostile to Kornilov), and George Katkov, *The Kornilov Affair* (London-New York, 1980) (friendly).

The October coup is imperfectly reflected in the heavily doctored minutes of the Central Committee: *Protokoly Tsentral'nogo Komiteta RSDRP (b): avgust 1917–fevral' 1918 [Protocols of the Central Committee of the Russian Social-Democratic Labor Party (Bolsheviks): August 1917–February 1918]* (Moscow, 1958). Of the histories, outstanding are S. P. Melgunov's, *Kak bol'sheviki zakhvatili vlast' [How the Bolsheviks Seized Power]* (Paris, 1953) (an English condensation: *The Bolshevik Seizure of Power,* Santa Barbara, Calif., 1972) and Robert V. Daniels's *Red October* (New York, 1967; London, 1968).

For the Communist dictatorship, an indispensable source is the decrees (not entirely complete) published as *Dekrety sovetskoi vlasti* (Moscow, 1957), of which at the time of writing 13 volumes have appeared. Leonard Schapiro's *The Origin of the*

Communist Autocracy, 2nd ed. (London and Cambridge, Mass., 1977), traces the rise of the one-party dictatorship into the early 1920s. There is a reasonably good Communist account of the same process, seen from a very different perspective, by M. P. Iroshnikov, *Sozdanie sovetskogo tsentral'nogo gosudarstvennogo apparata* [*The Creation of the Soviet Central State Apparatus*], 2nd ed. (Leningrad, 1967). Trotsky's *Stalinskaia shkola fal'sifikatsii* [*The Stalin School of Falsification*] (Berlin, 1932) has important documentation not available elsewhere.

On the Constituent Assembly, there are the memoirs of its Secretary, M. V. Vishniak, *Vserossiiskoe Uchreditel'noe Sobranie* [*The All-Russian Constituent Assembly*] (Paris, 1932), and an identically titled monograph by the Soviet historian O. N. Znamenskii, published in Leningrad in 1976.

The story of the Brest-Litovsk Treaty by J. Wheeler-Bennett, *Brest-Litovsk: The Forgotten Peace* (London-New York, 1956), although first published over half a century ago, has still not been superseded. There are important documents on German-Soviet relations in Vol. I of *Sovetsko-Germanskie Otnosheniia* [*Soviet-German Relations*] (Moscow, 1968). The tangled story of German-Russian relations in 1918 is told authoritatively by Winfried Baumgart in *Deutsche Ostpolitik 1918* [*Germany's Ostpolitik in 1918*] (Vienna-Munich, 1966).

The Czech uprising is recounted by M. Klante, *Von der Wolga zum Amur* [*From the Volga to the Amur*] (Berlin-Königsberg, 1931).

There are no satisfactory treatments of either the Left SR uprising or Savinkov's rising in Iaroslavl.

In many ways the best book on War Communism is by a participant, L. N. Kritsman, *Geroicheskii period Velikoi Russkoi Revoliutsii* [*The Heroic Period of the Great Russian Revolution*] (Moscow-Leningrad, 1926). Much data can be found in S. Malle, *The Economic Organization of War Communism, 1918–1921* (Cambridge, 1985). Communist treatment of labor is the subject of M. Dewar's *Labour Policy in the USSR, 1917–1928* (New York, 1979). Simon Liberman's *Building Lenin's Russia* (Chicago, 1945), illuminates the human side of Soviet economic experimentation.

No comprehensive study has been written on the peasantry in the first years of Communist rule. Among the most informative are D. Atkinson's *The End of the Russian Land Commune, 1905–1930* (Stanford, Calif., 1983) and V. V. Kabanov's *Krest'ianskoe khoziaistvo v usloviiakh "Voennogo Kommunizma"* [*The Peasant Economy under Conditions of "War Communism"*] (Moscow, 1988). Mikhail Frenkin's *Tragediia krest'ianskikh vosstanii v Rossii, 1918–1921 gg.* [*The Tragedy of Peasant Uprisings in Russia, 1918–1921*] (Jerusalem, 1988) describes peasant resistance to Communist agrarian policies.

On the Imperial family in 1917–18 there is S. P. Melgunov's *Sud'ba Imperatora Nikolaia II posle otrecheniia* [*The Fate of Emperor Nicholas II after Abdication*] (Paris, 1951). N. A. Sokolov's *Ubiistvo tsarskoi sem'i* [*The Murder of the Imperial Family*] (Paris, 1925) summarizes the findings of the investigatory commission which the author chaired (in French: *Enquête Judiciaire sur l'Assassinat de la Famille Impériale Russe,* Paris, 1924). The fate of the other Romanovs in Soviet hands is the subject of Serge Smirnoff's *Autour de l'Assassinat des Grands-Ducs* [*About the Assassination of the Grand Dukes*] (Paris, 1928).

The most important work on the Red Terror in all its dimensions is G. Leggett's *The Cheka: Lenin's Political Police* (Oxford, 1986). On early Soviet concentration camps, there is James Bunyan's *The Origin of Forced Labor in the Soviet State, 1917–1921* (Baltimore, Md., 1967).

INDEX

In the text of the book, many Russian names have been Anglicized. Here, save for a few (e.g., Tolstoy and Trotsky) that have entered the English vocabulary, they are given in their original spelling. Since Russian stressing practices follow no obvious rules, proper names frequently referred to in the book are provided with a stress: thus, "Kérensky" should be accented on the first syllable. The letter "ë" is pronounced "yo" and stressed.

Page numbers in italics indicate illustrations.

TEXTUAL ACKNOWLEDGMENTS

Grateful acknowledgment is made to the following for permission
to reprint previously published material:

Gerald Duckworth & Company Ltd.: Excerpt from *Letters of Tsarita to the Tsar 1914–1916* edited
by Sir Bernard Pares, Duckworth & Co., 1923. Reprinted by permission of Gerald Duckworth
& Company Ltd.

Europe Printing Establishment and *Mouton de Gruyter*: Translation by Richard Pipes of excerpts
from Kantorovich in *Byloe*, No. 22 (1923); Maliantovich in *Byloe*, No. 12 (1918); Gorovich in
ARR, VI (1922); and *NChS*, No. 9 (1925). Reprinted by permission of Europe Printing Establishment and Mouton de Gruyter, a division of Walter de Gruyter & Co.

Karin Kramer Verlag: Translation by Richard Pipes of excerpts from *Gewalt und Terror in der
Revolution* by Isaak Steinberg (1974). Reprinted by permission of Karin Kramer Verlag, Berlin.

Peters Fraser & Dunlop Group Ltd.: Excerpt from *The Kornilov Affair: Kerensky and the Break-up
of the Russian Army* by George Katkov, Longman Group Ltd., London. Copyright © 1980
by George Katkov. Reprinted by permission of the Peters Fraser & Dunlop Group Ltd.

Royal Institute of International Affairs: Excerpt from *Soviet Documents on Foreign Policy*, Vol. I,
1917–1924, selected and edited by Jane Degras. Published by Oxford University Press for the
Royal Institute of International Affairs, London, 1951. Reprinted by permission.

Times Newspapers Limited: "Ex-Tsar Shot: Official Approval of Crime" from *The Times*, July 22,
1918. Copyright by Times Newspapers Limited. Reprinted by permission.

The University of Chicago Press: Excerpt from *Building Lenin's Russia* by Simon Liberman. Copyright 1945 by the University of Chicago. Reprinted by permission of The University of Chicago
Press.

Excerpt from *The Catastrophe: Kerensky's Own Story of the Russian Revolution* by Alexander F.
Kerensky, 1927, published by Penguin USA for D. Appleton and Company.

Excerpt from *The Murder of the Romanovs* by Captain Paul Bulygin, 1935, published by Random
Century Group, London, for Hutchinson & Co. Ltd.

A Note About the Author

Richard Pipes has been a professor of History at Harvard
University since 1958. He was the Director of East Euro-
pean and Soviet Affairs for the National Security Council
in 1981–82 and he is a two-time recipient of a Guggenheim
fellowship. His previous books include *Survival Is Not
Enough, U.S.–Soviet Relations in the Era of Detente,
Russia under the Old Regime, Europe Since 1815,* and *The
Formation of the Soviet Union.*

A Note on the Type

The text of this book was set in a typeface called Times
Roman, designed by Stanley Morison (1889–1967) for *The
Times* (London) and first introduced by that newspaper
in 1932.

Among typographers and designers of the twentieth
century, Stanley Morison was a strong forming influence—as a typographical advisor to The Monotype Corporation, as a director of two distinguished English publishing houses, and as a writer of sensibility, erudition, and
keen practical sense.

Composed by ComCom, Allentown, Pennsylvania,
a division of The Haddon Craftsmen, Inc.
Printed and bound by Halliday Lithographers,
West Hanover, Massachusetts.
Designed by Anthea Lingeman